THE DEVELOPING LABOR LAW

THE DEVELOPING LABOR LAW

The Board, the Courts, and the National Labor Relations Act

EDITOR IN CHIEF

Charles J. Morris
Professor of Law
Southern Methodist University

CO-EDITORS

George E. Bodle
Attorney at Law
Los Angeles, Calif.

Jay S. Siegel
Attorney at Law
Hartford, Conn.

Section of Labor Relations Law
American Bar Association

BNA
BOOK

The Bureau of National Affairs, Inc. • Washington, D.C.

1971

197059

Printed in the United States of America
Library of Congress Catalog Card Number: 74–106074
Standard Book Number: 87179–051–3

8

CONTRIBUTING ATTORNEYS

Cosimo Abato
Granville M. Alley, Jr.
Jerry D. Anker
Vincent J. Apruzzese
David S. Barr
William Barton
Florian J. Bartosic
Hugh Beins
Cecil Branstetter
Sheldon M. Charone
Sam Houston Clinton, Jr.
James J. Cronin
Milton Denbo
James E. Fagan
Joseph J. Halbach
Winthrop A. Johns
Jerome B. Kauff
Robert H. Kleeb

Scott Kneese
Robert LeProhn
Robert Lewis
Stuart Linnick
Walter P. Loomis, Jr.
Marcus Manoff
Kenneth C. McGuiness
Robert G. Mebus
Albert S. C. Millar, Jr.
Daniel F. Minahan
Thomas L. Morrissey
Patrick C. O'Donoghue
Lester G. Ostrov
Julius Reich
David R. Richards
Suzanne Richards

Melvin L. Rosenbloom
William J. Rosenthal
Loren R. Rothschild
Arnold Schlossberg
Frederick T. Shea
Edward Silver
Gerard C. Smetana
Evan J. Spelfogel
Julius Topol
David L. Trezise
Ruth Weyand
Frank L. Wiegand, Jr.
John W. Wilcox, Jr.
William H. Willcox
James E. Youngdahl
James R. Zazzali
Norman Zolot

STUDENT CONTRIBUTORS*

Gene R. Beaty
Laura Davidson
David M. Ellis
John B. Esch

Alfred J. Harper II
Ruth L. Kovnat
James K. Murphey III

Beverly Neblett
John Rinehart
L. Chapman Smith

---

*Southern Methodist University School of Law

FOREWORD

I once thought I would write a Labor Law treatise; then I thought I might write a hornbook; with relief, I settle for a Foreword. If I may be forgiven another brief personal note, I would like to tell of my critical contribution to the realization of THE DEVELOPING LABOR LAW. I remember well a telephone call from the then-chairman of the American Bar Association's Section of Labor Relations Law. He reported, with some embarrassment, that he had just invited Professor Morris to serve as chairman of a committee to write a book on the National Labor Relations Act, and that Professor Morris had indicated his willingness but had suggested that I be asked first because of my recent service as co-chairman of the Section's Committee on the Development of Law under the National Labor Relations Act. By this time in my life, I was cured of the treatise fantasy and convalescing nicely from the hornbook notion. I deferred with warm thanks to Professor Morris. Had I accepted, I find it impossible to believe that I would have surmounted all the obstacles to completion, as he has. The fragile project would be lying somewhere in shards. Thus, I can say, quite literally, that but for me this book would never have been written. Though I have not pressed that claim, Professor Morris and the Section's Council did me the considerable honor of asking me to write this Foreword.

I accepted in awe of the accomplishment. The writing of THE DEVELOPING LABOR LAW required scholarly insight, editorial acuity, and a large measure of delicate mediation and sensitive leadership. THE DEVELOPING LABOR LAW is probably the only reference work that had not only to be written but to be negotiated as well with counsel for management and labor. That a highly useful volume has emerged is remarkable. That it is not an anthology but an integrated whole, stamped with the same style throughout, is little short of a miracle. The result is a tribute both to the many talents of Professor Morris and his co-workers and to the great capacity for cooperation that our profession can bring to a task when it is stimulated to do so.

THE DEVELOPING LABOR LAW bears only one birth scar. Professor Morris admits it freely in his preface. He says:

> "If the text draws value judgments or enunciates policies, these are the judgments and policies of the Congress, the Board, and the courts. At least this has been our intention, for we have tried to present objectively whatever the law was and whatever it now is."

Good lawyer that he is, Professor Morris has converted a necessity into a virtue. To get a thundering herd of committeemen to agree on what the law *is* must have been hard, but it was at least possible; to get them to agree on what the law *should be* would have been out of the question.

Nonetheless, as I read the manuscript, I missed the occasional impatience with foolish doctrine, the vigorous urging of reform that a lone author is free to attempt. I missed it all the more because I know how perceptively critical Professor Morris and his colleagues can be. If Professor Morris is ever rash enough to attempt a second edition, I hope he will bargain for the right to insert an occasional editor's comment, clearly labeled as such if need be.

Of far greater interest to most readers will be the book's response to its most serious challenge—the problem of volatility. Many a potential author has been deterred from trying to write a Labor Law book by the risk of being out of date before the ink is dry. I agree with Professor Morris' assertion that "[t]here is more stability in many labor law doctrines than some popular critics may be willing to concede." Compared to, say, 15 years ago, Labor Law has become almost stodgy in the degree to which it has settled down. But settled doctrine has a way of coming unglued. *San Diego Building Trades Council* v. *Garmon,* for example, has seemed a cornerstone of federal labor policy for almost 12 years—a long time in Labor Law. While sizeable pieces have been chipped out of it, its central core has seemed impregnable. Yet the skirmishing during the Supreme Court's 1969-70 term in *ILA, Local 1416* v. *Ariadne Shipping Co.* and *Taggart* v. *Weinacker's, Inc.,* strongly suggests that the justices are taking a fresh look at preemption. The result may well be substantial erosion of *Garmon.* And, as the personnel of the Board and of the Supreme Court change with changes in the Presidency, no one really expects Labor Law to be unaffected by those comings and goings.

Professor Morris and the Section have promised us annual supplements to be prepared by the Section's Committee on the Development of Law under the National Labor Relations Act. In my judgment, Professor Morris and his colleagues have done even better than that. Time and again they have analyzed a rule, a principle, or a trend so thoroughly that all of the relevant considerations and possible solutions are readily apparent. To be sure, the reader needs to be told, and the book does, of course, tell him, which solution is the current choice. If and when reversal comes, the change of a few words will be all that is necessary to make such discussions fully current.

Professor Morris and his fellow committeemen have done their work surpassingly well. They have, as they hoped to do, set forth clearly, succinctly and fairly "whatever the law was and whatever it now is." The practitioner will find in THE DEVELOPING LABOR LAW a useful, practical guide to the law he needs to know. The student will find a helpful crutch. Fortunately, Labor Law is so rich in mysteries and so overflowing with potential insights into legal processes that those of us who work behind the lectern need not fear being rendered redundant by any work of scholarship. Law professors will in fact find THE DEVELOPING LABOR LAW a useful adjunct to their teaching. Even our jewel of the curriculum has an occasional dull facet. I am, for example, bored to death whenever I teach the materials covered in this book under the heading "Representation Proceedings and Elections." I shall skip the topic from now on; a reference to this book will be enough.

Professor Morris, his committee, and the Section of Labor Relations Law have rendered us all a large service. We are in their debt.

MICHAEL I. SOVERN*

December 1970

---

* Dean, School of Law, Columbia University

INTRODUCTION

In 1945, the Section of Labor Relations Law was established by the American Bar Association. The basic purpose of the Section as set forth in the resolution adopted by the House of Delegates was "to study the law of labor relations . . . and to promote its fair and just administration. . . ."

From its inception, the Section's annual meetings and committee activities have provided a forum for the exchange of views on the highly controversial issues in the field of labor relations. From this have come valuable recommendations for the modification of existing laws and administrative rules and regulations. The Section has been influential in securing the adoption of many of these recommendations by the National Labor Relations Board and other governmental agencies. In addition, the House of Delegates of the American Bar Association has adopted a number of proposals of the Section as the official policy of the American Bar Association and has urged their adoption and implementation by the Congress.

The role of the Section in this regard has been of unusual importance because of the bifurcated nature of the Section's membership: Lawyers representing either management or labor organizations comprise the bulk of the Section membership. The Section has provided a meeting place where the conflicting views of the two groups could be reconciled and a consensus reached. This dichotomy has resulted also in the adoption of the practice of giving management lawyers and labor organization lawyers equal representation on the Council and among the officers of the Section. The success of the Section's activities is attested by the rapid growth in membership of the Section, from 130 members in 1946 to over 4,000 in 1970.

The Secretary of the Section is, each year, a noted scholar. Various secretaries in the past have included Professors Alexander Frey, Paul H. Saunders, Archibald Cox (former U.S. Solicitor General), Paul Hays (now Judge of the Second Circuit Court of

Appeals), Donald H. Wollett, Clyde W. Summers, Robert Koretz, Frank J. Dugan, Charles H. Livengood, Jr., Merton C. Bernstein, and Sanford H. Kadish (a member of President Johnson's Crime Commission). This year Reverend Dexter Hanley, S.J., President of Scranton University, the present Secretary, and Professor Theodore St. Antoine of Michigan Law School, the Secretary-Elect, continue in the fine tradition of this office. The Secretary at the annual meeting of the Section reviews the labor law decisions of the United States Supreme Court of the previous term. These papers have been much quoted and cited both by lawyers and by the courts.

The Section functions primarily through its Council and its 21 standing committees, to which several hundred members of the Section are appointed annually. The reports of the various committees, together with the proceedings of the annual meeting of the Section, are published annually. These reports are an important source of continuing information on different phases of the law of labor relations. None of these committee reports has been of more practical value than that of the committee on the Development of Law under the National Labor Relations Act. It was from the annual reports of that committee that the concept of this volume on THE DEVELOPING LABOR LAW evolved; and in 1966 under the chairmanship of the late Marion Plant, the project was initiated.

THE DEVELOPING LABOR LAW meets a long-felt need in the labor relations field. It is the first book to chronicle the development of the law under the National Labor Relations Act and to state the present decisional law not only with exactness but also in relation to its historical background. Kept current by annual supplements, to be prepared by the Section's Committee on the Development of Law under the National Labor Relations Act, this volume will be an invaluable aid, not only to every lawyer who specializes in the labor relations field, but also to the general practitioner who needs a comprehensive source of reference.

It is with great satisfaction and pride that the Section of Labor Relations Law presents THE DEVELOPING LABOR LAW to the profession. It is the result of the intellectual and physical efforts of some 60 prominent specialists in the labor relations field, all members of this Section, who have participated in the writing of the book under the guidance and direction of the Editor in Chief, Charles J. Morris, Professor of Law at Southern Methodist University. The two Co-Editors, George E. Bodle, a union attorney of Los Angeles, Calif., and Jay S. Siegel, a management attorney of Hartford, Conn., were responsible for extensive editorial work. They served as the principal liaison between the Section and the editors. Eight distinguished labor law professors served as associate editors. All of those who helped in the preparation of this book did so without compensation, motivated solely by their desire to make the book a significant contribution on the part of the Section to the field of Labor Relations Law.

The plan of organization of the book is the work of Professor Morris, the Editor in Chief. Many of the chapters were wholly rewritten by him, and the final editing was largely his responsibility. For the balanced objectivity, the high standard of scholarship, and the fine expository, yet analytical, style of the book, Professor Morris must be given primary credit. The Council and the Section are greatly indebted to him for the thousands of hours of work which he expended upon the book.

To the Editor in Chief, the Co-Editors, the Associate Editors and the other contributors, we render our thanks for their efforts and the resulting contribution to their profession, this Section, and the American Bar Association. We are indebted to Southern Methodist University for making its facilities available and for furnishing stenographic, proofreading, and other services, including invaluable help from many law students and administrative personnel.

Finally, we wish to express our appreciation to the officers of the American Bar Association for their support during the four years that this momentous project has been in progress.

> Chairmen of the Section of Labor Relations Law of the American Bar Association:
>
> Thurlow Smoot (1966-67)
> Frank A. Constangy (1967-68)
> C. Paul Barker (1968-69)
> Harry S. Benjamin, Jr. (1969-70)
> Plato E. Papps (1970-71)

December 1970

PREFACE

The Developing Labor Law is a book about the National Labor Relations Act, *i.e.,* the Wagner Act of 1935, as amended by the Taft-Hartley Act of 1947 and the Landrum-Griffin Act of 1959. It is about a statute whose contours have directly shaped labor relations for the greater part of the private sector in the United States and have indirectly influenced the newly forming patterns in labor relations for the public sector. This volume was written in an effort to fill a need for a comprehensive and analytical treatise on this important subject.

In 1966, when the American Bar Association Section of Labor Relations Law, of which Ted Smoot was then Chairman, graciously invited me to serve as general editor of the project from which this worked emerged, none of us involved in the early planning could foresee the complexity of the task which we were about to undertake.

During the first year of the project it became apparent that fulfillment of our ambitious goal would require much more than writing and editing a collection of essays on various aspects of the statute; so we decided to commence an intensive study of the thousands of decisions and rules which had been unfolding since 1935 in the National Labor Relations Board and in the courts. Here was a magnificent opportunity to chronicle the legislative and common-law development of this body of jurisprudence that had become deeply woven into the institutional fabric of our society in a relatively short period of time.

The opportunity was within our reach because we could and did draw from a rich reservoir of legal talent that was uniquely available in the Labor Relations Law Section. At the final counting, a total of 72 persons have contributed to the research, writing, and editing of this volume—nine professors of labor law, 53 practicing labor lawyers, and 10 senior law students. This group of lawyers and scholars proceeded in its task of uncovering and recording the evolutionary movements in the pertinent case law and the more abrupt changes wrought by congressional action. Our intent was to produce a volume which would provide, in historical perspective, a clear view of the ever-changing landscape covered by this statute. We attempted to make visible—generally as to the entire Act and its amendments, but specifically as to each rule of law for which the statute is a primary or significant source— all important changes in the law and also the interplay between the NLRB and the courts that provided the principal medium for these changes.

The book was designed, however, to be more than a history of past events; we also intended that it would be a practical compendium of the current state of the law under and concerning the National Labor Relations Act. In this regard, we have tried to be concise and objective. If the text draws value judgments or enunciates policies, these are the judgments and policies of the Congress, the Board, and the courts. At least this has been our intention, for we have tried to present objectively whatever the law was and whatever it now is.

Of course we write on shifting sands. The title of the book is a testament to the transitory quality of the subject matter. Yet there is more stability in many labor law doctrines than some popular critics may be willing to concede, and this volume demonstrates that teaching. But as to large areas where the law is undergoing change, we are again fortunate in being able to rely on the considerable talent found in the Labor Relations Law Section of the ABA, for that Section's Committee on Development of Law under the National Labor Relations Act will key its future reports to the organization of this volume, and those reports will be published as annual supplements.

This book is organized along functional lines. It is divided into seven parts, the first being devoted to historical materials and the last to administration of the statute. The parts in between follow a rough chronology coinciding with the development of prototypical labor relations: Part II, employee rights (including treatment of organizational and preelection activity and discrimination in employment); Part III, the representation process and union recognition; Part IV, the collective bargaining process; Part V, economic activity; and Part VI, relations between the employee and the union. We trust that this organizational structure will help the reader to find some order from the seeming chaos of thousands of labor law decisions and hundreds of law review articles which have been written about subjects under this Act. The reader must judge for himself the extent to which we have succeeded in achieving our objectives.

I wish to express profound indebtedness to the many persons who made this book possible—first and foremost to my academic and professional colleagues and to my students who contributed so generously of their time and talent in valuable research and writing. I also want to thank scores of other unnamed but not unappreciated lawyers and law students who assisted in myriad tasks associated with our effort to achieve accuracy in citation and reporting. I also acknowledge the generosity of Texas Instruments, Inc., in making unlimited Xerox facilities available for the project. And special thanks are due to Hibernia Turbeville, Law Librarian of Southern Methodist University, for her ready assistance in securing research materials, and to Lois Blackburn, my secretary, for typing reams of manuscript and helping in many ways. Thanks are extended also to Ogden W. Fields, Executive Secretary of the National Labor Relations Board, for providing full texts of all NLRB decisions promptly upon issuance; and to Donald F. Farwell, Howard J. Anderson, and other members of the BNA staff for their editorial assistance and infinite patience.

For my wife and children—who managed to put up with me during the four years of the project—there are no words adequate to express my appreciation for their vital contributions. I am very grateful to them.

Though this book is a cooperative venture, I alone am responsible for weaknesses in its organizational structure and any errors in reporting. Nothing herein should be deemed to represent the view or action of the American Bar Association or its Section of Labor Relations Law, unless and until adopted by the Association or Section pursuant to their bylaws.

CHARLES J. MORRIS

December 1970

SUMMARY TABLE OF CONTENTS

PART I

HISTORY OF THE
NATIONAL LABOR RELATIONS ACT

PART II

EMPLOYEE RIGHTS

PART III

THE REPRESENTATION PROCESS AND UNION RECOGNITION

PART IV

THE COLLECTIVE BARGAINING PROCESS

Part V

ECONOMIC ACTIVITY

DETAILED TABLE OF CONTENTS

Page

Part II

EMPLOYEE RIGHTS

PART III

THE REPRESENTATION PROCESS
AND UNION RECOGNITION

Page

Page

Part IV

THE COLLECTIVE BARGAINING PROCESS

Page

Page

Page

Page

PART V

ECONOMIC ACTIVITY

Page

Page

Page

Part VI

RELATIONS BETWEEN THE EMPLOYEE
AND THE UNION

PART VII

ADMINISTRATION OF THE ACT

Page

Page

PART I

HISTORY OF THE
NATIONAL LABOR RELATIONS ACT

CHAPTER 1

HISTORICAL BACKGROUND OF THE WAGNER ACT

By the early 1930s organized labor had been a part of the American scene for over a century.[1] In the resulting lush progression of crises and governmental countermeasures, it is fairly easy to pick out, with a comfortable perspective of four decades, three major themes:

1. The case law affords a cumulative demonstration that the courts were not institutionally capable of formulating or implementing a workable labor policy.

2. The course of legislative and judicial action reveals increasing awareness that the role of organized labor presented a question of national proportions that no state was capable of answering definitively.

3. There was the development of two mutually incompatible national policies towards organized labor, one regarding it as creating market restraints inimical to the national economy and the other regarding it as necessary to a regime of industrial peace based upon a balanced bargaining relationship between employees wielding the combined power of incorporated capital wealth and unions wielding the power or organized labor.

I. THE INADEQUACIES OF JUDICIAL REGULATION

The inability of the courts to provide viable solutions to the problems presented by the labor movement was twofold. First,

---

1 The "first" American labor case, known as the Philadelphia Cordwainers' case, was decided in 1806. *See* Gregory, LABOR AND THE LAW 22 (2d rev. ed., 1961) (hereinafter cited as Gregory). For a detailed account of the trial see Lieberman, UNIONS BEFORE THE BAR 1-15 (rev. ed., 1960).

the process of case-by-case adjudication was an inadequate instrument for the formulation of a cohesive policy or rational substantive norms of conduct. The industrial revolution, and the combinations of capital and of labor that it called to life, presented problems that called for broad legislative solutions. The courts were unable to develop any workable standards for governing concerted employee conduct; they did not even try to establish any standards to regulate the behavior of employers towards labor organizations. Second, court procedures proved too cumbersome, and judicial remedies too inflexible, to effectuate whatever substantive standards the courts announced.

American courts engaged in an early flirtation with the proposition that any concerted employee action, even to raise wages, was indictable as criminal conspiracy, even though the motivating purpose and the means utilized would be legal if similar action were taken by individuals. During the first 40 years of the nineteenth century, numerous convictions were upheld ostensibly upon the conspiracy theory, although many of the decisions in fact involved violence or coercion, or contained language suggesting that the crime in question required either a motivating purpose or resort to means that would be illegal under some established category of common law.[2] Chief Justice Shaw of Massachusetts drew these threads together in his 1842 opinion in *Commonwealth v. Hunt*,[3] in which the conspiracy doctrine was narrowed and rationalized as requiring either an illegal purpose or resort to illegal means.

The *Hunt* decision also provided a bridge between declining use of the conspiracy doctrine, whose criminal sanctions produced overwhelmingly adverse public reaction,[4] and judicial use of civil remedies to regulate union activity. Since *Hunt*, "American legal history is a steady accumulation of instances where the line has been drawn between purposes and acts permitted, and purposes and acts forbidden."[5] But after *Hunt*, the evolution of these standards occurred primarily in the context of civil proceedings for damages or injunction, rather than in criminal prosecutions.

---

[2] The Philadelphia Cordwainers' case; *see* Frankfurter & Greene, THE LABOR INJUNCTION 2-3 (1930) (hereinafter cited as Frankfurter & Greene).
[3] 4 Met. 111 (1842).
[4] Gregory 27.
[5] Frankfurter & Greene 4-5.

Even this basic analytical division into purposes and means was not without its difficulties. In many instances, it merely provided alternative avenues for judicial condemnation of union activity. Inducing a strike against *A* to discourage *A* from doing business with *B* may be condemned upon the theory that its secondary purpose is illegal or, quite as easily, upon the theory that the secondary boycott is an illegal means.[6] Similarly, federal courts were inclined to make the legality of an organizational strike depend upon the manner in which it was conducted, while "in Massachusetts, the rationale for decision shifts almost completely to an emphasis upon the issue of justifiable ends." [7]

Aside from the ambiguity inherent in the easy interchangeability of the two tests of "ends" and "means," in the administration of each test serious problems were encountered. Even when the means test was utilized to condemn such clearly reprehensible conduct as threatening physical injury to person or property, there was a tendency toward judicial subjectivity. As late as 1900, for example, the Supreme Court of Massachusetts suggested that a threat to strike was illegal because it necessarily implied accompanying violence and injury, "however mild the language or suave the manner in which the threat to strike is made." [8]

It was in judging the legality of purposes of labor activity that the gravest difficulties were encountered. Although a few courts briefly entertained contentions to the contrary,[9] the view quickly and overwhelmingly prevailed that intentional infliction of economic harm, even by means that were not illegal, was actionable unless justified by some legitimate purpose creating a defense of privilege.[10] The difficulty was that judges were unable to agree as to what purposes were sufficient to justify the infliction of harm. Some adopted the position that any economic self-interest was an adequate justification. Their thesis was that competition was worth more to society than it cost, or at any rate that this was a

---

[6] The "objectives" test was adopted in Massachusetts under the persuasive aegis of Holmes, C. J., in *Plant* v. *Woods,* 176 Mass 492 (1900) (although Holmes himself dissented in this case) ; the "means" test found favor in certain federal courts, *e.g., Atchison, Topeka & Santa Fe Ry. Co.* v. *Gee,* 139 F 582 (SD Iowa, 1905) (peaceful picketing compared with chaste vulgarity) ; Frankfurter and Greene 24-46.

[7] Frankfurter & Greene 27.

[8] Plant v. Woods, 176 Mass 492, 497 (1900).

[9] Gregory 76-82, in which this minority view is called the "civil rights" view.

[10] Vegelahn v. Guntner, 167 Mass 92, 105 (1896) (Holmes, J., dissenting) ; *see* Restatement, Torts §775 (1939).

basic value judgment of the common law, the alteration of which was the proper business of legislators but not of judges.[11] Other judges undertook to assess the importance of the union's asserted interest and to weigh it against competing interests of other segments of society, and frequently found organized labor on the light side of the scales.[12]

Needless to say, the economic sophistication and bias of an individual judge were often pivotal when such balancing was undertaken. Between the pure bargaining strike by employees against their own employer, which came to be quite generally accepted,[13] and the many forms of secondary boycott, which were condemned with equal generality on a wide variety of rationales,[14] there was a diversity of judicial opinion as to the legitimacy of almost all peaceful forms of concerted employee conduct.[15] Thus one judge might conclude that a concerted refusal to work for the purpose of expanding union membership was not justified by any legitimate purpose. Another judge, attributing greater weight to the importance to the union of a strong bargaining position, might find that the same strike was for the ultimate purpose of raising wages, and therefore privileged.[16]

On the remedial side, other institutional shortcomings of judicial regulation become evident. Broad use of criminal sanctions imposed for peaceful labor activity quickly proved unacceptable to the public at large, and was abandoned. Money damages, the standard remedy in actions at law, imposed an inordinately heavy sanction for peaceful conduct condemned upon such unreliable criteria as those just discussed, especially since a business enterprise's capacity for economic injury so far exceeds the usual employee's ability to pay damages.[17] Because of the uncertain legality of much proposed union action under the substantive law, the deterrent effect of either criminal penalties or damages was too undiscriminating; in close cases, deterrence operated with equal

---

11 Vegelahn v. Guntner, *supra,* at 106 (Holmes, J., dissenting); Duplex Printing Press Co. v. Deering, 254 US 443, 488 (1921) (Brandeis, J., dissenting).

12 Vegelahn v. Guntner, *supra* note 10; Plant v. Woods, *supra* note 8.

13 Gregory 60.

14 Frankfurter & Greene 43.

15 *Id.* at 26-27.

16 *Compare* the majority opinion by Hammond, J., in Plant v. Woods, *supra,* note 6, *with* the dissent by Chief Justice Holmes in the same case, *id.* at 504.

17 *E.g.,* in Loewe v. Lawlor, 298 US 274 (1908), plaintiffs were seeking $80,000 in damages from union members.

effect whether the proposed concerted action would ultimately be determined to have been permissible or not. The only traditionally judicial remedy that transcended these limitations was the equitable remedy of injunction, and American courts turned increasingly to its use during the last two decades of the nineteenth century.[18]

The injunction was used in the labor field almost exclusively at the behest of employers to prevent injury by restraining concerted labor activity.[19] It easily lent itself to this role, since it provided prompt provisional restraint of the activity complained of, unlike criminal and common-law sanctions. But where the substantive law was uncertain, the availability of temporary injunctive relief became more important as a practical matter than the substantive law ultimately applied, since the momentum of a temporarily enjoined strike could not normally be regained even if the injunction ultimately was vacated.[20] There were other objectionable features of labor injunctions. They were frequently so vaguely worded as to be unintelligible. Contempt sanctions enabled courts to punish violations by criminal penalties, without the intercession of a jury or even of a judge, other than the author of the prohibition. And all this coercive machinery could be set in motion by an ex parte application for provisional relief supported only by affidavits of interested parties.[21] The resulting "government by injunction" became a national political issue as early as 1896.[22]

By the 1930s, it had been clear for some time that the courts could not be expected to provide answers to the problems presented by the labor movement. They were not the appropriate institution to formulate a rational basis for discriminating between tolerable and intolerable concerted employee activity, with the single exception of nonpeaceful conduct. Although they had extrapolated from precedent in an attempt to regulate union activity, it would probably have been preferable had they not done so, and certainly no one had ever expected them to make

---

18 In re Debs, 158 US 564 (1895); Frankfurter & Greene 17-18, 23.
19 On rare occasion a union successfully obtained injunctive relief; *see* Frankfurter & Greene 108.
20 *See* In re Debs, *supra,* note 18; Frankfurter & Greene 17.
21 Cox & Bok, LABOR LAW CASES AND MATERIALS 100-101 (6th ed., 1965) (hereinafter cited as Cox & Bok); Frankfurter & Greene 53-60.
22 Frankfurter & Greene 1.

a similar effort in order to formulate norms for employer conduct. Thus by the time a controversy reached the courts, industrial strife usually already had occurred, and the remedies available limited the range of judicial decision to the question whether the union activity in question should be punished or suppressed, and, if so, by what sanction.

II. THE RISE OF FEDERAL REGULATION

Federal courts played two roles in regulating labor disputes before the Wagner Act. In exercising their diversity-of-citizenship jurisdiction, they were major participants in the unsuccessful attempt to make common-law precedents answer the challenge of organized labor. In exercising federal-question jurisdiction under several federal statutes, for a time they imported much of this unfortunate common-law precedent into national policy, and they marked out—in what proved to be a tentative fashion—the permissible limits of federal governmental action to regulate labor disputes.

Under the doctrine of *Swift v. Tyson*,[23] federal courts deciding questions of state common law were not bound to follow decisions of state courts as precedents. Federal judges, enjoying tenure for life as a practical matter,[24] were on the whole far less sensitive to the demands of organized labor than their brothers on the state bench, whose tenure frequently was less secure. Thus in many instances an employer might expect a more favorable result in federal than in state court. And employers, as plaintiffs, were able to manipulate the matter of citizenship with considerable success to enable themselves to maintain suit in federal court. Thus there grew a large body of federal "common law" applicable to labor disputes. Further, federal equity practice, which had always been independent of state law, provided fertile soil for the development of labor injunctions.[25]

As late as 1930, it appears, a majority of the labor cases in federal court got there because of diversity jurisdiction.[26] But beginning before 1900, an increasing number of cases—many of them extremely influential—were brought into federal court by

---

[23] 41 US 1 (1842).
[24] U.S. Const. Art. III, §1.
[25] Frankfurter & Greene 5-17.
[26] *Id.* at 210.

virtue of federal legislation. In 1895, in the landmark case of *In re Debs*,[27] the Supreme Court upheld the jurisdiction of a federal court to enjoin labor violence in a railroad strike, at the instance of the United States, on the basis of statutes prohibiting obstruction of the mails and regulating interstate commerce. The latter of these, the Interstate Commerce Act,[28] was used as the basis of federal intervention in a number of labor cases, marked by uncertainty as to the applicability of the common law tests of illegal means and illegal ends.[29]

This problem never had to be resolved; even before the *Debs* case, lower federal courts had commenced to use another statute as a basis for federal-question jurisdiction to intervene in labor disputes.[30] This was the Sherman Act,[31] enacted in 1890. Section 1 of the Act rendered illegal "every contract, combination in the form of trust or otherwise, or conspiracy, in restraint of trade or commerce among the several states." The Act created a cause of action for treble damages for persons injured by violations, authorized injunctions and criminal prosecution of violations, at the instance of the United States, and created federal jurisdiction over all such proceedings.

The Supreme Court avoided the question of the Sherman Act's role in labor cases in the *Debs* litigation, but ultimately faced it in a series of decisions beginning in 1908 with *Loewe v. Lawlor*,[32] the celebrated *Danbury Hatters'* case. A threshold question in this respect, which has been extensively and acrimoniously debated, was whether the Sherman Act was applicable to labor unions at all.[33] The Act was intended primarily "as a safeguard against the social and economic consequences of massed capital," [34] but its substantive provisions are broad enough to encompass violations by labor organizations, and a proposed amendment to exempt them specifically was advanced in the Senate but never incorporated into the statute. In any event the question was resolved in favor of applicability in the *Danbury Hatters'* decision.

---

27 158 US 564 (1895).
28 24 Stat 379 (1887), 49 USC §§1-22 (1964).
29 Toledo, A.A. & N.M. Ry. Co. v. Pennsylvania Co., 54 F 730 (ND Ohio, 1893); Knudson v. Benn, 123 F 636 (D Minn, 1903).
30 United States v. Debs, 64 F 724 (ND Ill., 1894).
31 26 Stat 209 (1890), 15 USC §§1-7 (1964).
32 208 US 274 (1908).
33 *See* Millis & Brown, FROM THE WAGNER ACT TO TAFT-HARTLEY 9 (1949).
34 Frankfurter & Greene 8.

Without more, the Supreme Court's decision that labor organizations were not excluded from the category of potential violators of the Sherman Act meant merely that it would be possible for an employer to state a claim for treble damages against a union and its adherents "arising under" the Act and thus within the jurisdiction of federal courts, and that there similarly would be judicial cognizance of government proceedings to impose injunctive or penal sanctions. But deciding this does not decide what ingredients are essential to a violation of the statute in a labor dispute.

As muddy as the common law was in its application to labor activity, it seems clear that Congress intended the Court to turn to the common law to determine the scope of the Sherman Act's prohibitions.[35] It seems odd that the Court did not accept this invitation to indulge its own economic and social ideas in determining what purposes and means of concerted action should or should not render it prohibited under the Act. Several decisions and further action by Congress were required for the Court to reach something approximating this result. In its first application of the Sherman Act to organized labor in the *Danbury Hatters'* case, the Court indicated that it would be enough to establish a violation if the employees' concerted action obstructed the flow of the employer's product in interstate commerce.[36] The activity actually before the Court in the case could for the most part have been condemned on narrower grounds; in an attempt to insulate its gains from price competition by nonunion products, the union was utilizing primary and secondary consumer boycotts to organize a nonunion manufacturer. All this pressure might have been condemned under the means and objectives tests at common law; but the rule adopted by the Court was much broader.

A degree of flexibility was added to the rule in two decisions in 1921 and 1922, with the result that federal regulation of union activity under the Sherman Act conformed somewhat more closely with the results reached at common law. The first of these involved the Clayton Act,[37] which, as a result of lobbying in response to the *Danbury Hatters'* decision, contained two provisions that were widely thought to relieve the strictures that case had im-

---

35 Gregory 205.
36 Loewe v. Lawlor, *supra* note 32, at 292-93.
37 38 Stat 730 (1914), 15 USC §§12-27 (1964). *See* notes 39 and 40 *infra* for cases.

posed upon union activity. These provisions, Sections 6 and 20 of the Clayton Act, are discussed subsequently.[38] It is enough here to say that they were very narrowly construed by the Supreme Court in *Duplex Printing Press Co. v. Deering*[39] and held to exempt only concerted activity already regarded as lawful at common law, and then only when engaged in by employees in an effort to settle a labor dispute with their own employer. With this exception, any concerted action was a violation of the Sherman Act if it produced a disruption in the flow of goods in interstate commerce. The activity involved in *Duplex* was a secondary labor boycott; again it seems that the Court might have condemned it on the narrower ground that it would have been illegal under the means or objectives tests at common law. As it was, the *Duplex* decision imported into the Sherman Act a line of distinction—between pressure upon one's employer and pressure exerted upon others—closely akin to the distinction utilized by common law to condemn secondary boycotts.

A closer conformity between the Sherman Act and the common law was achieved one year later in *United Mine Workers v. Coronado Coal Co.*[40] As in the two boycott cases, the union ultimately was concerned with elimination of price competition from nonunion-produced commodities. The concerted action took the form of a strike accompanied by violence and property destruction, the effect of which was to halt the mining of coal, and thereby, of course, to disrupt the flow of the employer's product in interstate commerce. The Court chose to differentiate between this kind of disruption, caused by interference with manufacturing or mining the product, and the disruptions caused by boycotts which inhibited demand for the product. The former was characterized as an "indirect" obstruction to interstate commerce, and the Court took the view that such an indirect restraint would violate the Sherman Act only if used to further an intention to create a market restraint or monopoly in interstate commerce.[41] This, of course, was the ultimate purpose in the two boycott cases as well as in the *Coronado* case. But in the latter, since the obstruction to interstate commerce was "indirect," proving the purpose became crucial. This meant that, given ade-

---

[38] *See* Chapter 29 *infra*.
[39] 254 US 443 (1921).
[40] 259 US 344 (1922).
[41] *Id.* at 410-11.

quate proof of this subjective purpose, the federal courts had a means of condemning organizational strikes while leaving purely bargaining strikes uncondemned by the Sherman Act.[42]

Thus the Supreme Court ultimately conformed its applications of the Sherman Act to organized labor to a pattern not greatly different from that reached by many courts at common law. The major differences, aside from the requirement of a disruption of interstate commerce, were (1) that the Sherman Act, as amended by the Clayton Act, gave to employers the remedy of treble damages as well as the injunction and (2) that the United States was empowered to sue for injunctions and to institute criminal prosecutions for violations of the Sherman Act.

At best, all this amounted to in terms of substantive law was a step backward. Partially counterbalancing this, however, is the consideration that some degree of federal power to regulate labor disputes under the commerce clause was thoroughly established. Indeed, even an "indirect" obstruction caused by a cessation of mining or manufacturing had been recognized as a sufficient link to validate regulation by Congress. From this it was only a step—albeit not an easy one—to recognition of Congress' power to regulate labor policies of employers engaged in interstate commerce, as well as organized employee activities.

III.   AN AFFIRMATIVE NATIONAL LABOR POLICY: THE ANCESTRY OF THE WAGNER ACT

While the federal courts were pursuing their unsuccessful quest for an answer to the challenge posed by the labor movement, the two other branches of the federal government became increasingly sensitive to the same challenge and slowly began to articulate a policy of their own toward organized labor. The judicial policy in essence was one of selective suppression of organized labor's activities whenever they trenched too heavily upon the interests of any other segment of society. Commercial interests must not be injured by disruption of the interstate flow of goods; consumers and unorganized laborers must not be injured by wage standardization; employers and the public at large must not be injured by expansion of labor disputes through secondary boycotts. Save for the bargaining strike and accompanying picketing,

---

[42] Coronado Coal Co. v. United Mine Workers, 268 US 295 (1925). The "fink" had been discovered. *See* Gregory 216.

very little indulgence was given to the claims of organized labor to an institutional role in the nation's economy.

The rival policy that was developed by the executive and legislative branches of government assigned an important function to organized labor in the operation of the national economy, and sought to protect this function in two ways: by eliminating judicial interference with the operation of labor organizations, and by affording some of these operations affirmative legal protection.

A. The Erdman Act

The history of this governmental second labor front begins with the 1894 Pullman strike, which gave rise to the *Debs* case. The United States Strike Commission, appointed by President Cleveland to inquire into the matter, filed a report adopting ideas that are now a part of our national labor policy. The commission concluded that the judicial approach to labor organization was inappropriate in the light of "the rapid concentration of power and wealth, under stimulating legislative conditions, in persons, corporations, and monopolies." [43] It was suggested that organization of employees was beneficial to the employment relationship because it tended to reduce failures of communication and promote rational and responsible settlement of labor disputes by peaceful means. At least some of the courts were nonetheless "still poring over the law reports of antiquity in order to construe conspiracy out of labor unions." [44]

The commission's central conclusion was that employers should recognize and deal with labor organizations: If employers "take labor into consultation at proper times, much of the severity of strikes can be tempered and their number reduced." [45] "Yellow dog" contracts obligating employees to abstain from union membership should be made illegal. In response to the railway strike that had occasioned its inquiry, the commission recommended a permanent federal commission to investigate, conciliate, and if necessary decide railway labor disputes, with judicial enforcement power. The parties to each dispute—employees through their unions if they so chose—should be entitled to representation in

---

[43] United States Strike Commission, REPORT ON THE CHICAGO STRIKE OF JUNE-JULY 1894 XLVII (1894).
[44] *Ibid.*
[45] *Id.* at LIV.

the hearing body. While proceedings were pending, and for six months thereafter, a moratorium should be imposed upon concerted union activity against the employer and upon employer discrimination against adherents of the union. More broadly, the presidential commission's report recommended that the states establish agencies to mediate and conciliate labor disputes and to encourage and facilitate arbitration, and that the states give labor organizations "standing before the law." [46]

This report became the basis of the Erdman Act, enacted by Congress in 1898.[47] Though limited to employees engaged in the operation of interstate trains, the Act suggested what was to become the basis for future legislation relating to organized labor. It imposed criminal penalties for the discharge or threatened discharge of employees for union membership, and, utilizing unions as representatives of employees, provided facilities for mediation and conciliation of railway labor disputes. The mediators were directed to encourage submission of unsettled disputes to arbitration.

The mediation provisions of the Erdman Act operated with moderate success until World War I, when the government took over the railroads.[48] The prohibition in Section 10 of the Act against anti-union discrimination, however, was held unconstitutional by the Supreme Court in *Adair v. United States*,[49] decided one week before the *Danbury Hatters'*[50] case in early 1908. Against the background of *In re Debs*[51] and *Danbury Hatters'*, the *Adair* opinion is difficult to understand. The Court concluded that Section 10 of the Act deprived the railroads and their agents, as well as railroad employees, of liberty of contract without due process of law, in violation of the Fifth Amendment, and, further, that the commerce power did not authorize Congress to make this regulation of contractual relations. A railroad employee's membership in a labor organization, the Court said,

> cannot have, *in itself* and in the eye of the law, any bearing upon the commerce with which the employé is connected by his labor and services.
> * * * One who engages in the service of an interstate carrier will, it

---

46 *Ibid.*
47 30 Stat 424 (1898).
48 Cox & Bok 70.
49 208 US 161 (1908).
50 Loewe v. Lawlor, 208 US 274 (1908).
51 158 US 564 (1895).

must be assumed, faithfully perform his duty, whether he be a member or not a member of a labor organizations.[52]

Thus, in *Adair* the Court disagreed with the factual conclusions reached by President Cleveland's commission, and by Congress as well, that disruptions in interstate transportation were traceable directly to the railroads' refusal to deal with labor organizations. A majority of the Justices could conceive of only one national policy towards organized labor, which they attributed to Congress a week later in the *Danbury Hatters'* case. Symptomatic relief of commercial disruptions was deemed a legitimate exercise of federal power, but Congress could not root out the cause by regulating the employment relationships out of which commercial disruptions arose. State legislation implementing the recommendations of the commission's report met a similar fate by application of the due-process clause of the Fourteenth Amendment.[53]

B. The Clayton Act

Sections 6 and 20 of the Clayton Act,[54] which deal expressly with organized labor, may best be regarded historically as a response to the Supreme Court's *Adair* and *Danbury Hatters'* decisions. In those two cases, the Court had told Congress: first, that it had no power to protect interstate commerce against labor disruptions by regulating employers' hiring and firing practices to promote the growth of unions; and second, that Congress had, in the Sherman Act, adopted a contrary policy of suppressing the activities of organized labor when they interfered with the flow of goods in interstate commerce. On the first of these points, Congress recognized that the Supreme Court has the final say because of its power to determine the constitutionality of federal legislation. On the second, however, Congress recognized that it had the power to alter the policy attributed to it by the Court's interpretation of the Sherman Act in the *Danbury Hatters'* decision. In the labor provisions of the Clayton Act, this is what Congress sought to do. Accepting the Court's admonition that affirmative promotion of unionism by regulation of employer conduct was beyond its constitutional power, Congress sought to advance the same policy in a negative fashion by limiting very narrowly the

---

[52] Adair v. United States, 208 US 161, 178 (1908).
[53] Coppage v. Kansas, 236 US 1 (1915).
[54] 38 Stat 731 (1914), 15 USC §17 (1964); 38 Stat 738 (1914), 29 USC §52 (1964). For general discussion of the applicability of the antitrust laws to labor union activity, *see* Chapter 29 *infra*.

circumstances in which the courts might intervene to assist an employer in resisting the organizational efforts of labor unions.

There appears to have been some fear after the *Danbury Hatters'* decision that the Supreme Court might resurrect ancient law under the Sherman Act to conclude that *all* organized labor activity interfering with the flow of goods in interstate commerce was in violation of the Act, since the basic principle of labor organization is combination to control the supply, and thereby the price, of labor in a given market.[55] Section 6 of the Clayton Act was designed to eliminate this possibility by providing that labor itself is not "an article of commerce," and that the antitrust laws do not prohibit the existence of labor organizations or their "lawfully carrying out" their "legitimate objectives."

The full meaning of Section 6 standing alone is quite nebulous; in order to determine what concerted employee activity is exempted from the antitrust laws, it is necessary to give some content to the phrase "lawfully carrying out . . . legitimate objectives." The operative words "lawfully" and "legitimate" suggest, of course, the two-part formulation of the common law: the concerted activity must not itself be an illegal means, and it must be justified by a legitimate purpose. But the content that the common law gave to these two tests was itself amorphous. Further light is cast upon the scope of the Section 6 exemption by Section 20.

Section 20 of the Clayton Act consists of two paragraphs. The first of these sought to eliminate the broad-scale use of labor injunctions by revitalizing the classical requirement of equity jurisdiction that there must be actual or threatened injury and no adequate remedy at law before an injunction will issue—a requirement that had somehow fallen by the wayside with the growth of labor-injunction practice prior to the turn of the century.[56] In this paragraph Congress referred to the cases it was dealing with as those "between an employer and employees, or between persons employed and persons seeking employment, involving, or growing out of, a dispute concerning terms or conditions of employment."

The second paragraph of Section 20 limits labor injunctions by

---

[55] Gregory 205, 208.
[56] *Id.* at 98-99; Frankfurter & Greene 23, 60, 200-01.

a different technique. It describes several basic categories of concerted labor activity, and provides that none of these activities shall "be considered or held to be violations of any law of the United States," and that even if there is injury and no adequate remedy at law, so that an injunction might issue under the first paragraph of Section 20, "no such . . . injunction shall prohibit" any of the described activities. Needless to say, Congress did not intend to legitimate violent acts, physical injuring of persons or property, threats of such conduct, or similar illegal means. The categories of activity legalized by the second paragraph of Section 20 reflect this at several points. Persuading others to strike must be "by peaceful means"; proselytizing for a union is limited to "any place where any such person or persons may lawfully be," and the persuasion must be exercised "peacefully." One may persuade others to cease to patronize "by peaceful and lawful means." Groups may "peaceably" assemble, "in a peaceful manner, and for lawful purposes." With the sole exception of the last-quoted phrase, Section 20 makes no reference to legality of purpose. To the contrary, the final category of activity legitimated by the section indicates that Congress intended to extend immunity without regard to the objective of the activity, so long as the activity did not fall within any established, nonlabor-oriented category of illegality at common law: no one, singly or in concert, is to be restrained "from doing any act or thing which might lawfully be done in the absence of such [labor] dispute by any party thereto." The section thus appeared to remove all limitations upon the permissible purposes of concerted labor activity. Not even economic self-interest was required. The Act appeared to adopt a "civil rights" labor philosophy that had found only temporary acceptance in even the most liberal state courts.[57]

The Clayton Act also amended the Sherman Act by authorizing private injunction suits to restrain violations.[58] It was such a suit that brought Sections 6 and 20 of the Clayton Act before the Supreme Court in *Duplex Printing Press Co. v. Deering*.[59] The defendants had imposed a secondary labor boycott in an effort to complete the organization of the newspaper-press-

57 Gregory 76-82.
58 38 Stat 737 (1914), 15 USC §26 (1964).
59 254 US 443 (1921).

manufacturing industry and thereby protect union gains already made in that industry against price competition from Duplex's nonunion-made presses. The boycott successfully halted the movement of Duplex presses in interstate commerce, and so violated Section 1 of the Sherman Act as interpreted in the *Danbury Hatters'* case, unless the Clayton Act had changed the law.

The Supreme Court concluded that if the Clayton Act had changed the law, it had done so only to a very slight extent. The Court read the first paragraph of Section 20, requiring the absence of an adequate remedy at law, as an approval of existing practice rather than an attempt to resurrect a fallen barrier to the issuance of injunctions in labor cases. The only significance attributed to the paragraph was the restriction it was found to impose upon the second paragraph. The first paragraph's reference to cases "between an employer and employees" was read to mean between an employer and *his* employees. The second paragraph was read as legalizing the described categories of concerted activity only in such cases, since it afforded protection against injunctions issued subject to the requirements of the first paragraph. This restrictive reading was reinforced, the Court found, by the emphasis in the second paragraph "on the words 'lawful' and 'lawfully,' 'peaceful' and 'peacefully,' " in describing the activities to be afforded protection. The Court found in this emphasis legislative approval and adoption of the common law's unmanageable tests for the legality of concerted employee action, rather than a legislative command not to interfere with such action in the absence of violence or similar misconduct. Since secondary boycotts were illegal at common law, the second paragraph of Section 20 did not mean to legalize them, and this reinforced the conclusion that Section 20 applied only to cases between an employer and his own employees.[60]

Two incompatible policies toward organized labor thus were fairly well crystallized by the Clayton Act and the *Duplex* decision. The polarity of these policies should not be obscured by the fact that the Supreme Court managed to read one policy into legislation designed to promulgate the other,[61] a distortion facilitated by the remarkable turgidity of Congress' language in Sections 6 and 20. It remained for Congress to design and enact

---

60 *Id.* at 470-74.
61 *Id.* at 484-86 (Brandeis, J., dissenting).

legislation that would effectuate its policy of fostering collective bargaining in the face of opposition not only from employers, but from the Supreme Court as well.

C. The Railway Labor Act

In *Adair v. United States*,[62] the Supreme Court had invalidated only Section 10 of the Erdman Act, and the statutory machinery for settlement of railway labor disputes remained intact. The report of President Cleveland's United States Strike Commission was joined by others in 1902 and 1915 making similar recommendations for the fostering of labor relations based upon collective bargaining between employers and labor organizations.[63] The Wilson Administration, under which Congress had enacted the Clayton Act provisions that Samuel Gompers had hopefully dubbed "labor's charter of freedom," extended more effective protection to the labor movement when, in 1917, government intervention to prevent labor disputes became necessary to maintain the production of war materials. President Wilson established the War Labor Conference Board in early 1918, and upon its recommendations established the National War Labor Board.

The fundamental policy adopted by the new Board was as follows:

> The right of workers to organize in trade unions and to bargain collectively, through chosen representatives, is recognized and affirmed. This right shall not be denied, abridged, or interfered with by the employers in any manner whatsoever. [64]

Employers who persisted, in defiance of orders of the Board, in tactics designed to discourage organization of their employees—such as discharge for union activities, espionage, and interrogation of employees—in several cases found their businesses seized and operated by the government.[65]

Although business and government repudiated the collective bargaining policy as a general proposition when the crisis of war was past, the Railway Shopmen's strike in 1922 ultimately pro-

---

62 208 US 161 (1908).
63 *Anthracite Coal Strike Comm. Rep.*, S. Doc. 6. 58th Cong., Spec. Sess., 63 (1902); United States Comm. on Industrial Relations *Report*, published in 1915, is carefully analyzed in Adams, AGE OF INDUSTRIAL VIOLENCE 1910-15 (1966).
64 National War Labor Board, PRINCIPLES AND RULES OF PROCEDURE 4 (1919); Cox & Bok 81.
65 Cox & Bok 81.

duced, in 1926, a statute that successfully established the collective bargaining policy on the railroads, the Railway Labor Act.[66] In addition to machinery for settlement of minor disputes, the Act established a presidentially appointed board with authority to mediate contract-negotiation disputes, implementing a statutory duty imposed upon both sides to make "every reasonable effort to make and maintain agreements concerning rates of pay, rules, and working conditions." Should mediation fail and the parties be unwilling to submit to arbitration, the Board was to notify the President if the dispute threatened a disruption of interstate commerce sufficient to deprive any section of the country of essential transportation services. The President might then appoint another board with power to investigate and report upon the dispute. During this process, the statute imposed a moratorium for up to 60 days upon any change in the status quo by either party to the dispute.

The provisions of the Railway Labor Act had been largely negotiated in advance by the railroads and the railroad brotherhoods.[67] The 60-day embargo had been conceded by labor in exchange for provisions protecting union organizational efforts. The Act provided that "collective action, without interference, influence or coercion exercised by either party over the self-organization or designation of representatives by the other," was to be the manner in which representatives of parties to labor disputes under the Act should be selected.

The Railway Labor Act was challenged in *Texas & New Orleans RR. Co. v. Brotherhood of Railway & S.S. Clerks,*[68] which reached the Supreme Court in 1930. The railroad had sought to establish a company-dominated union and in so doing had engaged in a campaign of discharges for union activity and other forms of coercion. Since the Act did not provide any means of enforcement of the employees' right to select their representatives without "interference, influence or coercion" by the employer, the union brought suit in federal court to enjoin the employer's anti-union activities. The Supreme Court upheld the suit, and in doing so removed major obstacles to further legislative implementation of the policy fostering collective bargaining.

---

[66] 44 Stat 577 (1926), 45 USC §§161-163 (1964).
[67] Cox & Bok 113.
[68] 281 US 548 (1930).

Specifically, the Court recognized that Congress, in exercising its power to regulate commerce,

> may facilitate the amicable settlements of disputes which threaten the service of the necessary agencies of interstate transportation. In shaping its legislation to this end, Congress was entitled to take cognizance of actual conditions and to address itself to practicable measures. The legality of collective action on the part of employees in order to safeguard their proper interests is not to be disputed. . . . Congress was not required to ignore this right of the employees but could safeguard it and seek to make their appropriate collective action an instrument of peace rather than of strife.[69]

Adair v. United States [70] was distinguished upon the unconvincing basis that, unlike the Erdman Act, the Railway Labor Act "does not interfere with the normal exercise of the right of the carrier to select its employees or to discharge them," but is aimed rather "at the interference with the right of employees to have representatives of their own choosing." [71] Freedom to engage in such interference was not a right protected by the Constitution.

D. The Norris-LaGuardia Act

The last piece of major labor legislation enacted before the advent of the New Deal was the Norris-LaGuardia Act.[72] The Supreme Court's decisions upholding the constitutionality of the Railway Labor Act as an exercise of the national power to regulate interstate commerce had not overturned the Court's established view that this power did not extend to local businesses such as manufacturing and mining, and this limited vision of the commerce power was a major factor in the shaping of the new legislation. It sought not to regulate labor relations under the commerce power, but to further the policy of collective bargaining by preventing judicial interference with labor activities in an exercise of Congress' power under Article I, Section 8 of the Constitution to regulate the jurisdiction of the lower federal courts under Article III.

Two important sections of the statute—Sections 4 [73] and 7 [74]—

---

69 *Id.* at 570.
70 208 US 161 (1908).
71 Texas & N.O.R.R. Co. v. Brotherhood of Railway & S.S. Clerks, *supra* note 68, at 571.
72 47 Stat 70 (1932), 29 USC §§101-15 (1964).
73 47 Stat 70 (1932), 29 USC §104 (1964).
74 47 Stat 71 (1932), 29 USC §107 (1964).

are reminiscent of Section 20 of the Clayton Act, with these exceptions:

(1) they are phrased as denials of jurisdiction, rather than as prohibitions against the issuance of injunctions;

(2) Section 7 imposes more rigid restrictions upon the issuance of labor injunctions than the mere absence of an adequate remedy at law;

(3) there is no provision giving substantive legitimacy to the activities that are thus exempted from injunction; and

(4) primarily by a broad definition of "labor dispute" in Section 13 (c), the provisions of Sections 4 and 7 are made applicable "whether or not the disputants stand in the proximate relation of employer and employee," thus avoiding possible judicial emasculation such as that suffered by the Clayton Act provisions in the *Duplex* case.

Because the Norris-LaGuardia Act operated solely to restrict federal judicial intervention in labor disputes, it has been said that the point of the Act "is not what it does for organized labor but what it permits organized labor to do for itself without judicial interference." [75] It would be inaccurate, however, to attribute to Congress a neutral attitude toward labor disputes in enacting the statute. Through the medium of eliminating judicial interference, the statute was designed to promote employer recognition of unions and thus foster the practice of collective bargaining as an institution in the conduct of labor relations. It was primarily because of limitations upon its power to regulate employer conduct under the commerce clause as then construed by the Supreme Court that Congress limited itself to this method of effectuating its policy. Section 2 of the Act contains a statement of the national policy the Act was designed to advance:

> Whereas under prevailing economic conditions, developed with the aid of governmental authority for owners of property to organize in the corporate and other forms of ownership association, the individual unorganized worker is commonly helpless to exercise actual liberty of contract and to protect his freedom of labor, and thereby to obtain acceptable terms and conditions of employment, wherefore, though he should be free to decline to associate with his fellows, it is necessary that he have full freedom of association,

---

[75] Gregory 186. For a discussion of judicial adaptation of the Norris-LaGuardia Act to enforcement of collective bargaining agreements, *see* Chapter 17 *infra.*

self-organization, and designation of representatives of his own choosing, to negotiate the terms and conditions of his employment, and that he shall be free from the interference, restraint, or coercion of employers of labor, or their agents, in the designation of such representatives or in self-organization or in other concerted activities for the purpose of collective bargaining or other mutual aid or protection. . . .[76]

Additional provisions of the Act, in furtherance of this policy, render unenforceable in federal courts the "yellow-dog" contract, by which employees obligated themselves to refrain from union membership; limit the imposition of vicarious liability upon union officials and members for acts of other agents of the union; deny injunctive relief to any party who has not attempted to settle the dispute by negotiation or resort to available governmental machinery for mediation or voluntary arbitration; and impose procedural safeguards for litigants against whom contempt sanctions are sought.

The length to which Congress went to promote union organization in the Norris-LaGuardia Act is perhaps most vividly evident in the scope given the Act by the definitional provisions in Section 13.[77] The Act was made applicable to any case involving or growing out of a labor dispute. Such a case was defined as one involving "persons who are engaged in the same industry, trade, craft, or occupation; or have direct or indirect interests therein," and labor dispute was defined to include "any controversy concerning terms or conditions of employment, or concerning the association or representation of persons in negotiating, fixing, maintaining, changing, or seeking to arrange terms or conditions of employment, regardless of whether or not the disputants stand in the proximate relation of employer and employee." The "allowable area of economic conflict" [78] had been enlarged, for purposes of federal injunction practice, as much as organized labor had any reason to wish.

This is it, as the saying goes. In this definition of labor disputes and of cases arising out of labor disputes, Congress gave complete recognition to certain theretofore proscribed stranger activities of unions in fulfillment of their heartfelt need to organize entire in-

---

[76] 47 Stat 70 (1932), 29 USC §102 (1964).

[77] 47 Stat 73 (1932), 29 USC §113 (1964).

[78] Frankfurter & Greene, Chap. I.

dustries so that, by standardizing employment conditions throughout such industries, they could eliminate the competitive hazard to already established standards in existing unionized units of such industries, presented by the undercutting effects of nonunion wage and labor standard differentials.[79]

---

[79] Gregory 190. For an account of American labor history during the era preceding the New Deal, *see* I. Bernstein, THE LEAN YEARS—A HISTORY OF THE AMERICAN WORKER 1920-1933 (1960).

CHAPTER 2

THE WAGNER ACT PERIOD

I. THE POLITICAL CLIMATE

The Great Depression and the advent of the New Deal spawned a political climate that was favorable to—or at least tolerant of—the major federal legislation thought necessary at the time to promote the growth of organized labor. This growth was considered by many to be essential if employees in American industry were to acquire sufficient economic leverage to bargain effectively with management. It was hoped that the end result of these concurrent developments would be an equitable division between labor and management of the spoils of private enterprise and, coincidentally, an important impetus to the revitalization of the economy. The economic conditions prevailing during the early 1930s focused attention on the plight of the working man, and economists were quick to point out that low spending power among the employees of American business would prolong the Depression. The infallibility of industry management was disproved by post-1929 events, and the political influence that management could marshal against pro-union legislation was considerably diminished by the abrupt change from a boom to a bust economy.

The Norris-LaGuardia Act[1] had given organized labor a shield against judicial interference with the tools of union self-help. But by itself the Act was, in fact, of little value in promoting the growth of organized labor and the development of collective bargaining in American industry. Similarly, Section 7 (a) of the National Industrial Recovery Act,[2] passed by Congress in 1933, had attempted to persuade industry to recognize employee rights

---

[1] 47 Stat 70 (1932), 29 USC 101-115 (1964). *See* Chapter 1 *supra*.
[2] 48 Stat 198 (1933).

to organize and to bargain collectively, but the absence of any power to enforce these "rights" rendered them virtually useless in the face of management's understandable hesitancy to aid the growth of organized labor. Most employers rebuffed union efforts and refused recognition and collective bargaining; in the alternative, employers created company unions and agreed to bargain with these unions, but with no others.[3] In this way an employer was able to go through the motions of recognizing and cooperating with organized labor, but was able to avoid the danger inherent in the recognition of a union that had a mind of its own. Also, while employees had a "right" to organize into labor unions, employers had a commensurate "right" to inflict serious injury— in particular, discharge—upon any employee brash enough to exercise his organizational "right." [4]

II. THE ROLE OF SENATOR WAGNER

These, then, were the conditions prevailing in 1934, when Senator Robert Wagner introduced a far-reaching bill that he felt would give the needed federal support to employee organization and to collective bargaining.[5] In particular, Senator Wagner stressed the failure of mere persuasion under Section 7(a) of the NIRA and proposed in his bill the creation of a quasi-judicial tribunal with defined legal authority and the power to have its orders enforced by court decree. In the face of well-organized industry opposition, Wagner's bill had little chance of success; however, on June 19, 1934, Congress did enact a compromise measure, Resolution 44, authorizing the President's appointment of a board with the power to order and conduct elections, and the power to investigate labor controversies "arising under" Section 7 (a) of the NIRA or burdening the "free flow of interstate commerce."[6] But neither Senator Wagner nor others of the same view were placated by this compromise measure, and in 1935 Wagner introduced another bill, similar to his 1934 bill.

---

[3] A. Link & W. Catton, AMERICAN EPOCH 416 (1963).

[4] For a general discussion of the failure of §7 (a) of the NIRA, see I. Bernstein, TURBULENT YEARS 172-85 (1970).

[5] See H. Millis & E. Brown, FROM THE WAGNER ACT TO TAFT-HARTLEY 24 (1950).

[6] 48 Stat 1183 (1934). For a more complete discussion of Resolution 44 and its place in the legislative developments of the early 1930s, see Madden, The Origin and Early History of the National Labor Relations Board, 29 GEO. WASH L. REV. 234, 237-238 (1960).

As in 1934, Senator Wagner's bill met with vigorous opposition from industry, but in 1935 this opposition did not create in Congress a climate incompatible with the bill's passage. Another potential obstacle arose as the Administration refused to support the Wagner bill when it was first introduced.[7] Although President Roosevelt eventually joined the Wagner camp, he delayed until after the bill had been passed by the Senate and passage by the House was a certainty. In short, the bill's passage was dependent, to a large extent, upon the ability of Senator Wagner, in particular his talent for coordinating the support of his colleagues, and upon the sentiment of the times. Unlike other major New Deal legislation, the Wagner Act was the product of a single man's efforts; and, although the political climate of 1935 may have been favorable to these efforts, it required Wagner's energy and expertise as a legislative midwife to bring forth the origin of modern labor law—the Wagner Act.[8]

III. ONE-SIDED LEGISLATION

From the outset, Wagner considered his legislation to be more than a weapon against the disruption of industry by labor-management disputes. This was, of course, an important function of the Wagner Act, but in the Senator's eyes its reach was far broader.[9] As was implicit in his recurrent statements on the Senate floor in support of the bill, he envisioned the proposed legislation as an "affirmative vehicle"[10] for economic and social progress:

Caught in the labyrinth of modern industrialism and dwarfed by the size of corporate enterprise, [the employee] can attain freedom and dignity only by cooperation with others of his group.[11]

[7] In addition to Administration neutrality, there seems to have been active opposition to the Wagner Bill among several high-ranking members of the Roosevelt Administration. See Keyserling, The Wagner Act: Its Origin and Current Significance, 29 GEO. WASH. L. REV. 199, 203-204 (1960).
[8] See Address by Judge J. Warren Madden, Section on Labor Relations Law of the ABA, Luncheon Meeting, Aug. 9, 1966, in 1966 SECTION OF LABOR RELATIONS LAW PROCEEDINGS, MONTREAL, CANADA 24 (1967).
[9] The broad reach desired by Senator Wagner was, in fact, embodied in the final version of his bill as enacted. Despite the language of §1, which described the purpose of the Act almost exclusively in terms of "industrial strife" and "burdening or obstructing commerce," the provisions of the Act created the substantive rights and federal machinery that Senator Wagner believed would produce economic and social progress. The actual language of §1 seems to have been designed primarily to give the Act a jurisdictional basis under the Commerce Clause and did not indicate a failure by Senator Wagner to achieve the broad reach that he sought.
[10] Keyserling, The Wagner Act: Its Origin and Current Significance, 29 GEO. WASH. L. REV. 199, 218 (1960).
[11] 79 CONG. REC. 7565 (1935) (remarks of Senator Wagner).

To accomplish this broad purpose, the Act created a right for employees to organize and, unlike the earlier provisions of the NIRA, made this right legally enforceable.[12] The Act also gave meaning to this organizational right by requiring employers to bargain collectively with employees[13] through representatives chosen by the employees.[14] The cornerstone of the Act was Section 7, which originally provided:

> Employees shall have the right to self-organization, to form, join or assist labor organizations, to bargain collectively through representatives of their own choosing, and to engage in concerted activities for the purpose of collective bargaining or other mutual aid or protection.

This troika of rights— (1) the right to organize, (2) the right to bargain collectively, and (3) the right to engage in strikes, picketing and other concerted activities—was considered essential to establish a balance of bargaining power between employer and employee and thereby to avoid the pitfalls and inadequacies which had characterized earlier labor legislation.

To enforce the substantive rights given employees by Section 7 and the specific provisions implementing those rights—particularly the provisions of Section 8 defining employer unfair labor practices—the Wagner Act established the type of administrative agency which had become a hallmark for much of the New Deal legislation. Sections 3 through 6 created the National Labor Relations Board (NLRB) and set out various details of its operation. Section 9, in addition to introducing into labor relations the principle of majority rule, gave the NLRB exclusive jurisdiction over questions of representation. Section 10 accorded the Board exclusive jurisdiction over the unfair labor practices defined by Section 8 and also set forth the broad outlines for NLRB procedure,[15] including provisions for judicial review and court enforcement of Board orders.[16]

The most conspicuous characteristic of the Wagner Act, when set in the context of the shield given employee activities by the Norris-LaGuardia Act, was its one-sided nature. The prime function of the Act was to protect employees against employer tactics

---

12 *See* Chapter 31 *infra.*
13 *See* Part IV, Chapters 11-18 *infra.*
14 *See* Part III, Chapters 8-10 *infra.*
15 *See* Chapter 30 *infra.*
16 *See* Chapters 31 and 32 *infra.*

designed either to obstruct organizational efforts or to withhold the fruits of those efforts. Management was given no corresponding protection against union actions, and little attention was paid to the protection of employee interests from union abuse.[17] The main function of the Act was focused on the creation of a meaningful—*i.e.*, enforceable—right to organize and to bargain collectively; and, in fulfilling this primary function, Senator Wagner and Congress had looked no further than the needs of the employee who was bent on organizing. But Congress' tunnel vision could not have been fairly criticized at the time, for in 1935 it was generally believed that the shortcomings of federal labor law arose primarily from the inability of employees to join together into units having sufficient economic leverage to bargain with their employers. Management could and did frustrate attempts at organization with its arsenal of self-help devices; the threat of discharge, for example, was a formidable weapon during the depression, when jobs were few and far between. And in 1935 the one-sided nature of the Wagner Act did not seem to be a conspicuous deficiency, for labor unions then were a force of less than awesome proportions.[18] Furthermore, one-sided legislation may have been deliberately chosen by Senator Wagner and Congress as the best means to ensure that organizational rights were, in fact, respected and enforced. If the Wagner Act had included express restrictions on union activities, the attainment of its principal goal—protecting organizational efforts—might have been jeopardized.

Today, when critics of the Wagner Act have before them evidence of 35 years of operation and two major enactments that have emphasized the fallibilities of the Act,[19] it may be easy to criticize Congress' action in 1935. But whatever stigma may attach retroactively, it is certain that the Act was the starting point for modern labor law. Whatever the justification, the Wagner Act, as set against the Norris-LaGuardia backdrop, was the statute that gave labor unions the power to become an important force in American industry.

---

17 The §9 provision for majority rule afforded some protection to the employee—at least in the initial stage when employees chose their bargaining representative. And a proviso in §9 (a) seemed to guard against union inaction by extending to each employee the "right" to present grievances to his employer.

18 *See* I. Bernstein, note 4 *supra* at 318-51, for a colorful description of the passage of the Act. For a discussion of union membership trends during the 1930s, *see* H. Millis & R. Montgomery, ORGANIZED LABOR 192-201 (1945).

19 The Taft-Hartley amendments, discussed in Chapter 3 *infra,* and the Landrum-Griffin amendments, discussed in Chapter 4 *infra.*

IV. CRITICISM OF THE ACT

Critics of the Wagner Act set to work immediately following its passage by Congress in 1935. The first step was to urge the unconstitutionality of the Act in the hope that the judiciary would be less receptive to Senator Wagner's efforts than Congress had been. In 1935, a group of 58 prominent lawyers and public figures published the "Report on the Constitutionality of the National Labor Relations Act," which was essentially a brief *pro bono publico* setting forth the opinion that the Wagner Act was unconstitutional. This Liberty League Brief, as it was called, marshaled forces along two fronts: the Due Process Clause and the Commerce Clause. It argued that Section 9(a) and its provision for majority rule deprived minority groups and individual employees of their right to negotiate with their employers, thereby infringing the constitutional requirement of due process. More basically, the brief claimed that Congress was without jurisdiction to impose the Wagner Act's provisions upon employers and employees; the Commerce Clause, it was urged, did not give Congress the carte blanche which it had used to pass this legislation. The Supreme Court, apparently by coincidence, lent considerable support to the arguments offered by the brief when *United States v. Butler*[20] and *Carter v. Carter Coal Co.*[21] were handed down in 1936.

The NLRB was not oblivious to the constitutional threat posed by the Liberty League Brief and by the precedents of the Supreme Court; thus it was very careful not to allow the constitutional issue to be presented to the Court in an unfavorable posture. Considerable effort was made to have insignificant cases settled or terminated before court action,[22] and the Board was successful in delaying adjudication of the constitutional issues until 1937, when five cases presenting these issues in what the agency believed was a satisfactory context were brought to the Court. On April 12, 1937, the Court rejected the suggestions made

---

[20] 297 US 1 (1936) (holding the Agriculture Adjustment Act, 1933, unconstitutional).
[21] 298 US 238 (1936) (holding the Bituminous Coal Conservation Act of 1935 unconstitutional).
[22] *See* Madden, note 8 *supra*.

by critics of the Wagner Act, and in *Jones & Laughlin Steel Corp.*[23] held the Act to be constitutional. Concluding that the Commerce Clause issue was pivotal, the Court adopted a more liberal definition of the commerce power than that which it had accepted in its earlier opinions—for example, in *Carter Coal Co.* The constitutional criterion, the Court said, was not the locus of the actions and conditions which Congress sought to regulate; rather, it was whether or not those actions and conditions were the *source* of burdens and obstructions to the free flow of commerce. In this light, the Wagner Act's purpose and effect clearly fell within the scope of congressional powers.

With the Court's settlement of the constitutional issue, the critics of the Act changed their tack and concentrated upon particular revisions of the statutory scheme which they considered desirable. Although some continued to press for outright repeal of the Act, most believed that any chance for its complete demise was lost when the Supreme Court handed down its decision in *Jones & Laughlin.* Numerous bills were introduced in Congress to amend the regulatory scheme created by the Norris-LaGuardia and Wagner Acts. In 1940, and again in 1941, Representative Howard W. Smith of Virginia introduced bills to amend the Wagner Act, and in each instance the bill was passed by the House but then failed to be reported out of committee in the Senate.[24]

Critics took the view that the Act was slanted heavily in favor of organized labor and therefore a number of "equalizing" amendments were needed. The primary spokesmen of the campaign to equalize the Act were the U. S. Chamber of Commerce and the National Association of Manufacturers. The AFL was also in favor of limited amendments during this period.[25] It was disturbed over certain Board decisions which it felt showed favoritism toward the emerging CIO unions.[26]

The drive for amendment faltered as the nation busied itself with the problems of World War II. However, a series of work

---

23 NLRB v. Jones & Laughlin Steel Corp., 301 US 1 (1937). *See* further discussion of the Act's constitutionality in Chapter 28 *infra.*
24 *See* Reilly, *The Legislative History of the Taft-Hartley Act,* 29 GEO. WASH. L. REV. 285, 287 (1960).
25 H. Millis & E. Brown, FROM THE WAGNER ACT TO TAFT-HARTLEY 284 (1950).
26 *See, e.g.,* the *American Can* case, 13 NLRB 1252, 4 LRRM 392 (1939).

stoppages in the coal industry in 1943 focused public attention on the problem of labor relations. These stoppages were especially unpopular since unions were operating under a no-strike pledge for the duration of the war. The displeasure of Congress over the strikes was reflected in the passage of the Smith-Connally War Labor Disputes Act [27] over the veto of President Roosevelt.

When World War II ended, a renewed campaign to amend the Wagner Act gained momentum from certain well-publicized activities of some labor unions. The wartime strikes of the United Mine Workers had aroused public feeling that unions were becoming irresponsible. Both employers and the general public were disturbed over friction and division within the labor movement. These controversies often resulted in "raiding" practices between unions competing to represent certain units, and in jurisdictional disputes which caught the employer in the middle. A union tactic that had considerable news-media coverage was mass picketing during strikes. In addition, certain types of secondary boycotts came under close scrutiny, as, for example, the practice of picketing or boycotting small retail outlets rather than directly organizing the workers.[28] Finally, there were isolated instances of glaring abuses in the conduct of the internal affairs of some unions, including exorbitant dues under closed-shop situations and cases of racketeering. It was charged that some unions practiced discrimination in choosing their membership and expelled members under vague and undemocratic circumstances.[29]

In 1946 both Houses passed the Case Bill, aimed at curbing abuse of union power under the existent statutory scheme, but the bill was vetoed, and the House was unable to muster the necessary two-thirds vote to override the veto.[30]

The publicizing of union misconduct, however random, coupled with the effective campaign still being waged by the Chamber of

---

[27] The Smith-Connally Act gave the President authority to seize and operate struck plants, made instigating a strike subject to criminal penalties, and required 30 days' notice of any labor dispute that might interrupt production. On the thirtieth day the NLRB was required to conduct a secret strike vote. Act of June 25, 1943, ch. 144, §§1-11, 57 Stat 163, appendix, 50 USC §§1501-11 (1964). §8 of the War Labor Disputes Act, 57 Stat 167, §1508 of appendix, 50 USC, dealing with the function of the NLRB to take secret ballots of employees on the question of an interruption of war production, was abolished by 5 USC §133y-16, Reorg. Plan of 1946, No. 3, Part VII, 701 (1964).

[28] Millis & Brown, *supra* note 25, at 279.

[29] *Id.* at 280.

[30] H.R. 4908, 79th Cong., 2d Sess. (1946).

Commerce and the NAM, led to continued legislative activity. Indeed, prior to 1947, most of the major provisions of Taft-Hartley had been introduced in Congress in one or more forms. Professors Millis and Brown point out that 230 major bills dealing with amendment of the Wagner Act were introduced from 1936 to the passage of Taft-Hartley, excluding the Taft-Hartley proposals.[31] They divide these bills into several distinct categories, which reflect the major criticisms of the Wagner Act in the 12-year period.

(1) *NLRB organization and procedures:* [32] One of the most common complaints was that the NLRB combined the functions of investigation, prosecution, and adjudication. Other dissatisfactions with the Board stemmed from its handling of evidence, its treatment of employers' rights of speech in organizational campaigns, and its use of subpoena powers. Another complaint was that there was inadequate court review provided for the Board's decisions. Proposed bills in this area ranged from changing the size of the Board to removing its unfair labor practice jurisdiction.

(2) *Representation problems:* There was much criticism of the Board's determination of the appropriate bargaining unit, and various proposals to amend the majority-rule concept of Section 9(a). Much of this controversy was directly attributable to the craft-unit question arising out of the disputes between the AFL and the CIO.

(3) *The scope and procedures of collective bargaining:* Of particular concern was the growing union practice of bargaining for the closed shop. Some of the proposals would have placed unions under the antitrust laws.

(4) *Union or employee unfair labor practices.*

(5) *Stricter controls of unions and disputes:* Other proposals were offered to place restrictions on certain types of concerted activities, to place stricter legal obligations and responsibilities on unions and employers, and to provide better methods of dispute settlement.

The large number of bills introduced in Congress in the first 12 years of the Wagner Act reflected the increasing pressure to amend

---

31 Millis & Brown, *supra* note 25, at 333.
32 For a more detailed treatment of this point, see D. Wollett, LABOR RELATIONS AND FEDERAL LAW 3027 (1949).

the law.[33] Although no proposal was ultimately successful, except the extraordinary Smith-Connally Act, the problem areas were explored and the foundation was laid for legislative action in 1947.

[33] Developments on the state level also reflected a growing mood of disillusionment with major portions of the Wagner Act. Although a few states had passed legislation after 1937 modeled after the Wagner Act, an overall trend of restrictive legislation was established in the late forties.

By 1947, only three states still had legislation modeled after the Wagner Act. See Millis & Brown, *supra* note 2, at 316-32.

Chapter 3

THE TAFT-HARTLEY CHANGES

I. INDUSTRIAL UNREST AND CONGRESSIONAL RESPONSE

A. Union Growth

While pre-1947 attempts to revise the Wagner Act had not met with tangible success, such efforts did make an important contribution to the political atmosphere of 1947. When the Eightieth Congress convened in January it was apparent that the status quo was not immune. Between 1935 and 1947 unions had flourished in the climate provided by the Norris-LaGuardia Act [1] and the Wagner Act.[2] Union membership had expanded from three to 15 million.[3] In some industries, such as coal mining, construction, railroading, and trucking, four fifths of the employees were working under collective bargaining agreements.[4] Under governmental policy prevailing during World War II, union leaders had assumed important and prestigious positions and were often consulted by the Administration in an obvious attempt to maintain internal industrial peace. This growing image of union power led one commentator to conclude in 1947 that the labor movement in the United States was the "largest, the most powerful, and the most aggressive that the world has ever seen; and the strongest unions . . . are the most powerful private economic organizations in the country." [5] Moreover, organized labor was not at all hesitant to exercise this burgeoning power to obtain the benefits it wanted.

---

1 47 Stat 70 (1932), 29 USC §101-115 (1964).
2 *See* Chapter 2 *supra*.
3 A. Cox & D. Bok, Labor Law, Cases and Materials 130 (6th ed., 1965).
4 *Ibid.*
5 S. Slichter, The Challenge of Industrial Relations 154 (1947).

Perhaps the most notorious example of the exercise of this power occurred during the Second World War when John L. Lewis conducted two prolonged and crippling strikes of coal miners, who returned to work only after the government had made substantial concessions.[6] And following the war, in 1946, a wave of strikes developed, shutting down steel mills, seaports, automobile assembly plants, and many other industries which played vital roles in the American economy.[7]

B.   A Republican Congress

1. Response to President Truman's Proposals. The disorderly state of industrial relations and resulting public indignation toward union strike activity created important issues for the mid-term political campaign of 1946, when the elections established Republican majorities in both houses of Congress for the first time since 1930. On the first day of the new congressional session, 17 bills [8] dealing with labor relations were introduced,[9] and by the end of the first week no fewer than 200 bills on the subject had been offered. Additional labor bills continued to pour in during the next few weeks, with added momentum provided by President Truman's State of the Union Message, in which he proposed a limited revision of the nation's labor laws. His proposals included: (1) prevention of jurisdictional disputes, (2) prohibition of certain secondary boycotts, (3) establishment of machinery to help solve disputes arising under existing collective bargaining agreements, and (4) creation of a temporary commission to investigate the entire field of labor-management relations.[10]

When the hearings opened in the House and Senate, however, it soon became obvious that Congress had stronger legislation in mind than the President had proposed. The Senate and House committee hearings on the numerous bills did much to marshal support for statutory revision. The emphasis in the House hearings was an investigation of abuse by labor of its power; the em-

---

6 Cox & Bok 130.

7 See Reilly, *The Legislative History of the Taft-Hartley Act*, 29 GEO. WASH. L. REV. 285, 288 (1960).

8 Perhaps the most outspoken advocate of change was Senator Joseph Ball of Minnesota, who had presented four bills, including Senate Bill 360, which was to become the skeleton for Title I of the Taft-Hartley Act, the title which amended the basic Wagner Act. See Reilly, note 7 *supra*, at 289-291.

9 See H. Millis & E. Brown, FROM THE WAGNER ACT TO TAFT-HARTLEY 363 (1950).

10 *Id.* at 364.

phasis in the Senate hearings was on the accumulation of testimony from all sides on the merits and demerits of the proposed reforms. Although major labor legislation was by no means a foregone conclusion in January, as the session progressed it became increasingly clear that such legislation was likely.

2. Problem Areas. Attention focused upon several problem areas that had come to prominence during the war and in the immediate postwar period. These were spotlighted by the hearings: (1) the secondary boycott, which had proved to be a potent tool in the hands of some unions, injuring third parties as well as the immediate parties to the labor dispute, (2) closed- and union-shop agreements, which in many instances had led to abuse and certainly contributed to labor's political and economical strength, (3) strikes and picketing, which had often turned into violence when unions were unable to achieve their goals by peaceful means, (4) corruption, which had appeared in some unions, although it was not as conspicuous during the 1940s as it later became during the 1957 McClellan Committee investigation, and (5) frequent jurisdictional disputes between unions in the construction industry, which halted large projects for long periods as unions bickered about the rights of different employees to various job assignments.[11]

The committee hearings were extensive. Opinions differed as to their objectivity, although it was generally conceded that the Senate hearings were conducted fairly.[12] Senator Taft noted that no bill with which he had ever been concerned had ever "been considered in more detail and more thoroughly studied." [13] But as to the House proceedings, Professors Millis and Brown concluded that they "did not do credit to that body in terms of adequate and relevant analysis of the important issues presented," [14] and even

---

[11] *See* H. REP. No. 245 on H.R. 3020, 80th Cong., 1st Sess. (1947), 1 LEGISLATIVE HISTORY OF THE LMRA 292-354; S. REP. No. 105 on S. 1126, 80th Cong., 1st Sess. (1947), 1 LEGISLATIVE HISTORY OF THE LMRA 407-462.

[12] Senator Morse, who opposed the majority bill, stated that "the bill represents a fine example of committee work in which men devoted to the public welfare did their best to resolve their differences on a basis of fair compromise." 93 Cong. Rec. 3786 (April 17, 1947); *see also* 1 LEGISLATIVE HISTORY OF THE LMRA 1000.

[13] 93 CONG. REC. 3786-3787 (April 17, 1947); *see also* 1 LEGISLATIVE HISTORY OF THE LMRA 1001.

[14] Millis & Brown 374. The authors commented on the minority charge that the bill was "one-sided" and that the "wishes of employers expressed during the hearings had been given full satisfaction while labor appeals were ignored" by noting that labor representatives had failed to propose any suggested legislation of their own and would not admit that there were any abuses which would stand legislative treatment. *Id.* at 372.

the Senate debate, in their view, "did not match the difficulty of the subject or the needs of the times." [15]

3. Differences Between Senate and House Bills. The Senate and House each passed a version of a labor reform bill, with the House bill being broader in scope and more restrictive on unions. The Conference Committee was faced with the following provisions in the House bill which differed substantially from the Senate version:

a. The NLRB was abolished and a new board to hear cases and an agency to prosecute cases were created.

b. A long and detailed list of concerted activities by unions were declared unlawful, and unions were placed under the anti-trust laws.

c. Employers were permitted to seek injunctions against unions' unlawful concerted activities.

d. Economic strikes were permitted only after an employee vote of approval and after notice and a "cooling-off" period.

e. Mass picketing was made unlawful.

f. Employer payments to joint health and welfare funds were outlawed.

g. Industry-wide bargaining was severely limited.

h. Detailed regulation of internal union activity was provided.

i. Strikes by government employees were banned.

j. Political contributions or expenditures in national elections were banned.[16]

On the following points, the two bills were similar though not identical:

a. Certain union unfair labor practices were specified.

b. "Free speech" rights were extended to employers.

c. The closed shop was outlawed.

d. Involuntary checkoff was prohibited.

---

15 *Id.* at 381.
16 *Id.* at 383.

e. Supervisors were removed from coverage of the NLRA.

f. Bargaining rights were denied to unions with Communist officers.

g. The government was empowered to seek injunctions in "national emergency" disputes.

h. An independent agency for mediation and conciliation was established outside the Department of Labor.

i. Provision was made for damage suits in federal district courts for violation of collective bargaining agreements and for certain unlawful concerted activities.[17]

C. Presidential Veto

When the Conference Committee had completed its work, the resulting bill reflected the fact that the Senate Taft bill had served as the model for the final draft.[18] The conference report was passed by the House 320 to 79 and by the Senate 54 to 17. President Truman vetoed the bill, however, stating that, in his view:

> The bill taken as a whole would reverse the basic direction of our national labor policy, inject the Government into private economic affairs on an unprecedented scale, and conflict with important principles of our democratic society. Its provisions would cause more strikes, not fewer. It would contribute neither to industrial peace nor to economic stability and progress. It would be a dangerous stride in the direction of a totally managed economy. It contains seeds of discord which would plague this Nation for years to come.[19]

Congress was willing to risk the test of history.[20] The veto was overridden by a vote of 68 to 25 in the Senate and 331 to 83 in the House, and the bill became law on August 22, 1947.

---

[17] *Ibid.*

[18] S. 1126, 80th Cong., 1st Sess. (1947). The only two major provisions on which the Senate yielded were the sections dealing with strikes by government employees and political contributions by unions.

[19] President's Message on Veto of Taft-Hartley Bill (June 20, 1947), 20 LRRM 22 (1947).

[20] According to Gerard Reilly, who served as special counsel to the Senate Labor Committee and assisted in the drafting of the bill, President Truman, in his veto message, "relied upon a staff memorandum of the N.L.R.B. attacking the conference bill in the same extreme and irrational terms that characterized the C.I.O. literature on the subject. . . . Senator Taft . . . on the networks that same evening was able to make an effective rebuttal." Reilly, note 7 *supra*, at 300. *But see* Millis & Brown 389-390, regarding the President's study of the legislation and the preparation of the veto message.

II. THE NEW AMENDMENTS

The new statute, named the Labor Management Relations Act of 1947, shifted the emphasis of federal labor law. From an attitude of federal protection for the rights of employees to organize into unions and to engage in concerted economic activity and collective bargaining, the emphasis shifted to a more balanced [21] statutory scheme that added restrictions on unions and also guaranteed certain freedoms of speech and conduct to employers and individual employees.[22]

A. Employee Rights

The change was reflected in the amended Section 1 "Findings and Policy" and in the amended Section 7 "Rights of Employees." Whereas Section 1 in the Wagner Act spoke of "denial by some employers of the right of employees to organize . . ." and "inequality of bargaining power between employees . . . and employers . . .," the amended Section 1 was directed equally at labor organizations:

> . . . certain practices by some labor organizations . . . have the intent or the necessary effect of burdening or obstructing commerce . . . through strikes . . . or concerted activities. . . . The elimination of such practices is a necessary condition to the assurance of the rights herein guaranteed.

Section 7 was amended to give employees the right to *refrain* from engaging in activities protected in the original Section 7: [23]

> [Employees] . . . shall also have the right to refrain from any or all such activities except to the extent that such right may be affected by an agreement requiring membership in a labor organization as a condition of employment as authorized in section 8 (a) (3).

B. Structural Changes in Board Administration

One of the earlier criticisms of the Wagner Act had been directed at the NLRB procedure and structure itself.[24] Section

---

21 Organized labor contended that the new statute was overbalanced in favor of employers and dubbed the legislation a "slave labor" law. Millis & Brown 389. *See* notes 47-48 and accompanying text *infra*.

22 The entire Labor Management Relations Act contains five titles, but only Title I is treated here because the scope of this book is limited to the National Labor Relations Act, which Title I amended.

23 *See* Chapter 5 *infra* for a detailed comparison of the old §7 and the amended version.

24 *See* Chapter 2 *supra*.

3(a) increased the size of the Board from three to five members. Section 3(d) met the primary criticism by separating the office of General Counsel from the Board proper. The General Counsel was given supervision over the attorneys employed by the Board and over the officers and employees in the regional offices. He was also given final authority over investigating charges, issuing complaints, and prosecuting them before the Board. The function of adjudication was thus separated from investigation and prosecution.[25]

C. Union Unfair Labor Practices

Section 8(b), which creates six union unfair labor practices, was added in its entirety. Section 8(b)(1) forbids restraint or coercion of employees "in the exercise of the rights guaranteed in Section 7." [26] Section 8(b)(2) makes it an unfair labor practice for a union "to cause . . . an employer to discriminate against an employee in violation of subsection (a)(3) . . ." [27] Section 8(b)(3) places an affirmative duty on employee representatives to bargain collectively with their employer.[28] Section 8(b)(4)(A), (B), and (C) outlaw various secondary boycotts.[29]

Section 8(b)(4)(D) makes it an unfair labor practice for a union to force or require assignment of work in a jurisdictional dispute.[30]

Section 8(b)(5) forbids a union to charge excessive or discriminatory initiation fees.[31] Section 8(b)(6) is directed at the practice of "featherbedding," i.e., causing or attempting to cause an employer to pay for services not performed.[32]

D. "Free Speech" Proviso

Section 8(c), the "free speech" proviso, was added as a guarantee for both employers and unions:

The expressing of any views, argument, or opinion, or the dissemination thereof, whether in written, graphic, or visual form, shall not

---

[25] *See* Chapter 30 *infra.*
[26] *See* Chapter 5 *infra.*
[27] *See* Chapter 6 *infra.* The "closed shop" was made unlawful, but a "union shop" was allowed in those states where it was lawful under state law. *See* §8 (a) (3) *proviso* and §14 (b) and Chapter 26 *infra.*
[28] *See* Chapters 11-18 *infra.*
[29] *See* Chapter 23 *infra.*
[30] *See* Chapter 25 *infra.*
[31] *See* Chapter 26 *infra.*
[32] *See* Chapter 25 *infra.*

constitute or be evidence of an unfair labor practice under any of the provisions of this Act, if such expression contains no threat of reprisal or force or promise of benefit.

E.   Collective Bargaining Duties

Section 8(d) sets out the duties of the parties in collective bargaining:

> To bargain collectively is the performance of the mutual obligation of the employer and the representative of the employees to meet at reasonable times and confer in good faith with respect to wages, hours, and other terms and conditions of employment . . . [but] . . . such obligation does not compel either party to agree to a proposal or require the making of a concession.[33]

Section 8(d) also provides that either party to a collective bargaining contract desiring termination or modification of the contract must (1) serve a 60-day written notice prior to the expiration date of the contract, (2) offer to meet and confer, (3) notify the Federal Mediation and Conciliation Service (and any comparable state mediation agency) within 30 days, and (4) continue all the terms of the agreement in full force and effect,

> without resorting to strike or lockout . . . for a period of sixty days after such notice is given or until the expiration date of such contract, whichever occurs later. . . . Any employee who engages in a strike within the sixty-day period specified in this subsection shall lose his status as an employee . . . for the purposes of sections 8, 9, and 10. . . .[34]

F.   Representation Under Section 9

Section 9 also made important changes. Section 9(a) gives individual employees the right to present grievances to their employer "and to have such grievances adjusted, without the intervention of the bargaining representative, as long as the adjustment is not inconsistent with the . . . collective bargaining contract" and if the "bargaining representative has been given an opportunity to be present. . . ."[35]

Section 9(b) provides that the Board shall not: (1) combine professional and nonprofessional employees in the same unit unless a majority of the professional employees vote for inclusion; (2)

---

[33] See Chapter 11 *infra.*
[34] See Chapters 11 and 19 *infra.*
[35] See Chapter 27 *infra.*

decide that any craft unit is inappropriate on the ground that a different unit has been established by a prior Board determination, unless a majority in the proposed craft unit vote against separate representation; or (3) include plant guards in a unit with other employees.[36]

Section 9(c) made changes in the area of representation questions. It gives the employer the right to file a representation petition and employees the right to file a petition to decertify a union. It forbids the Board to treat unaffiliated unions in a manner different from affiliated unions. Section 9(c)(3) was also added:

> No election shall be directed in any bargaining unit . . . within which, in the preceding twelve-month period, a valid election shall have been held. Employees on strike . . . not entitled to reinstatement shall not be eligible to vote. . . . In any election where none of the choices . . . receives a majority, a run-off shall be conducted . . . between the two choices receiving the largest and second largest number of valid votes. . . .[37]

Section 9(e) established a procedure whereby 30 percent of the employees in a bargaining unit could request an election to rescind a union security agreement.[38]

G. Regulation of Internal Union Affairs

Section 9(f) was directed at regulating internal affairs of unions and required any union that desired coverage or protection under the Act to file with the Secretary of Labor copies of its constitution and bylaws and a report showing:

(1) The name of the organization and its principal place of business.

(2) The name and title of, and compensation paid to, any officer or agent who was paid more than $5,000 in the preceding year.

(3) The manner in which these officers were selected.

(4) Initiation fees for new members.

(5) Dues of regular members.

(6) A detailed statement of the procedure followed with respect to qualifications for membership, election of officers and

---

[36] *See* Chapter 9 *infra.*
[37] *See* Chapter 8 *infra.*
[38] *See* Chapter 26 *infra.*

stewards, calling of meetings, levying of assessments, imposition of fines, authorization of bargaining demands, ratification of contract terms, authorization for strikes, authorization for disbursement of union funds, audit of union financial transactions, participation in insurance or other benefit plans, and grounds for expulsion of members.

Also required was a report showing union receipts and their sources, total union assets and liabilities, and a list of disbursements made and their purposes.

Section 9(g) provided that any union failing to meet the foregoing filing requirements would not be certified under the Act and no complaint would be issued on a charge filed by it. Section 9(h) provided for the filing of non-Communist affidavits. No benefits of the Act would be accorded to any labor organization whose officers had not submitted affidavits within the preceding 12 months showing that they were free from Communist Party affiliation or belief.[39]

H. Procedural Changes

Section 10(a) gives the Board authority to cede jurisdiction to state agencies in certain cases, even though the dispute might affect commerce, where the applicable state law is consistent with the NLRA.[40] Section 10(b) provides that no complaint may issue where the unfair labor practice occurred more than six months prior to the filing of the charge.[41]

Section 10(e) provides that "findings of the Board with respect to questions of fact if supported by substantial evidence on the record considered as a whole shall be conclusive." [42]

I. Injunctions

Section 10(j), the "discretionary injunction" section, was added. It provides that when the Board had issued a complaint charging that any person has engaged or is engaged in an unfair labor practice, it may petition a district court for appropriate temporary relief or restraining order as the court deems "just and proper." [43]

---

[39] §§9 (f) , (g) , and (h) were repealed by the Landrum-Griffin Act in 1959. See Chapter 4 infra.
[40] See Chapters 28 and 29 infra.
[41] See Chapter 30 infra.
[42] See Chapters 31 and 32 infra.
[43] Ibid.

Section 10(k) relates to Section 8(b)(4)(D). It requires the Board to hear and determine cases involving jurisdictional strikes unless the parties are able to show within 10 days that they have settled the dispute themselves.[44] Section 10(l), the "mandatory injunction" section, requires the Board to give priority over all other cases to any charge of an unfair labor practice under 8(b)(4)(A), (B), and (C)—the secondary boycott provisions. If there are reasonable grounds for believing the charge to be true, the Board officer or regional attorney is required to petition a district court for injunctive relief pending Board determination.[45]

J. "Right to Work" Laws

Finally, Section 14(b) was added to give state "right to work" laws precedence over the new union-shop proviso in Section 8(a)(3):

> Nothing in this Act shall be construed as authorizing the execution or application of agreements requiring membership in a labor organization as a condition of employment in any State or Territory where such . . . is prohibited. . . .[46]

III. THE REACTION

A. Labor Response

American labor policy had undergone its second sweeping revision in 12 years. The initial response of organized labor to passage of the Taft-Hartley Act was to publicize its opposition to what it called the "slave labor law." It was the objective of labor leaders of all unions to work steadfastly for repeal.[47] This response was not surprising; it was consistent with the position that organized labor had taken throughout the legislative proceedings. In the face of some recognized shortcomings within the labor movement, and even in the light of President Truman's limited call for labor legislation, the unions decided to oppose any and all revision of the Wagner Act. In adopting this intransigent position, labor virtually destroyed any chance that it might have had of exerting significant influence on the final outcome of Taft-Hartley. The result was a statute on which union views had no

---

44 See Chapter 25 infra.
45 See Chapters 31 and 32 infra.
46 See Chapter 26 infra.
47 A. McAdams, POWER AND POLITICS IN LABOR LEGISLATION 29 (1964).

measurable impact. Indeed, labor's critics were able to exert the most influential pressures on the 1947 legislation. As Professors Archibald Cox and Derek Bok explain,

> the Taft-Hartley Act was the product of diverse forces—the off-spring, a critic might say, of an unhappy union between the opponents of all collective bargaining and the critics of the unions' abuses of power. The former group was probably the more influential of the two in writing the Taft-Hartley amendments, for organized labor's unfortunate decision to oppose all legislation left its sympathetic critics in a dilemma.[48]

Union leadership continued to hold to this "all or nothing at all" attitude in the period immediately following passage of the Act. Its aim was not to amend but to repeal. The first manifestation of this approach was seen in 1948, when union leaders—erroneously assessing the upset victory of President Truman—thought the time had come to wipe Taft-Hartley off the books. In the words of one commentator, labor viewed the election as a "popular mandate" to "return to the good old days of the Wagner Act." [49] Leaders of both the AFL and the CIO publicly urged Congress to follow a "two-package approach" toward labor legislation: it should immediately repeal Taft-Hartley and restore the status quo of the Wagner Act; only then should it consider the Administration's proposed amendments.[50]

B. Congressional Response

The House response was to pass a bill which substantially re-enacted Taft-Hartley. In the Senate, a substitute bill sponsored by Senator Taft was passed in place of an Administration bill. At this point, the Administration chose to drop the fight, and Taft-Hartley was left on the books unchanged. The tactics of organized labor had been proved unrealistic:

> Their "all or nothing" demands seemed arrogant and unreasonable, especially when contrasted with the deceptively conciliatory proposals of Taft to discuss and, if need be, amend or eliminate any provision of the existing law that was demonstrably unworkable or prejudicial to labor's legitimate interests. Whatever slight hope there might have been for popular support of substantial revision of Taft-Hartley was shattered by the unions' intransigent position.[51]

---

48 Cox & Bok 133.
49 Aaron, *Amending the Taft-Hartley Act: A Decade of Frustration*, 11 INDUS. AND LABOR RELATIONS REV. 327, 329 (1958).
50 *Ibid.*
51 *Id.* at 330.

C. Stalemate Years

The years 1949 to 1952 were marked by a general stalemate in attempts to revise Taft-Hartley. This was a period of intense internal rivalry within the labor movement. Individual unions had embarked on a program of pursuing their individual interests, opposing any suggestions from rival unions which might threaten their own positions.[52]

In the early 1950s both management and labor began developing programs of proposed legislation to amend the National Labor Relations Act. Management groups had two primary goals: to close "loopholes" in Section 8(b)(4), which still permitted certain types of secondary activities (such as "hot cargo" agreements and "roving picketing") and to establish strict regulations for organizational picketing. As they had done in 1937, management interests set up an informal organization, known as the Secondary Boycott Committee, to further these goals. Its first move was to undertake a broad program aimed at educating the business community, the public, and Congress. Two subcommittees were formed, one concentrating on drafting legislation and presenting it to Congress, and the other providing materials aimed at the general public.[53] In contrast to labor, management was able to put aside other differences and present a generally united front on matters pertaining to labor legislation.[54]

Certain labor unions did develop specific proposals that they wished to see enacted. For example, the building and construction trades desired a provision allowing "prehire" agreements. Since the employers in the building industry depend heavily on transient labor, each union wanted to be allowed to negotiate a contract with a contractor before the union's status as a representative had been certified by the time-consuming process of an NLRB election or even before the workers were hired for the job. Such an arrangement was an unfair labor practice under Taft-Hartley.

Although both management and labor groups had definite amendments to the NLRA in mind during the early 1950s, neither

---

52 McAdams, note 47 *supra*, at 32.
53 *Id.* at 68-69.
54 *Id.* at 71.

side was able to generate much support for its proposals. It was not until 1957 that the issue of labor legislation again came to the forefront.

CHAPTER 4

THE LANDRUM-GRIFFIN CHANGES

I. THE IMPETUS OF LEGISLATIVE INVESTIGATION

The attention of the nation was focused once again on labor problems in 1957 when the Senate Committee on Improper Activities in Labor-Management Relations, chaired by Senator McClellan (D., Ark.), opened hearings to investigate alleged wrongdoings in the labor-management field.[1] As the hearings progressed, they gradually began to center on corruption in several strong unions. Testimony indicated that certain high officials within these unions were engaged in misconduct "ranging from embezzlement to illicit secret profits."[2] Because so much public feeling was aroused by the disclosures, one commentator concluded that the activity of the committee "was clearly the motivating force in bringing about the passage of legislation in 1959."[3]

The public clamor and legislative interest in corrective labor legislation were directed primarily at achieving internal union democracy, a subject not theretofore effectively covered by the national labor laws.[4] At the same time, the labor unions attempted to turn congressional attention to amending the Taft-Hartley Act.

---

[1] See A. McAdams, POWER AND POLITICS IN LABOR LEGISLATION 36-40 (1964) (hereinafter cited as McAdams) for a discussion of the political make-up of the McClellan Committee. See also THE LABOR REFORM LAW (Washington: BNA Books, 1959).
[2] A. Cox, LAW AND THE NATIONAL LABOR POLICY 18 (1960).
[3] McAdams 39.
[4] As Benjamin Aaron points out, "the Labor Management Relations (Taft-Hartley) Act of 1947 included only a few provisions purporting to regulate the conduct of union government." Aaron, *The Labor-Management Reporting and Disclosure Act of 1959*, 73 HARV. L. REV. 851 (1960). During passage of Taft-Hartley a campaign had begun to strengthen, through federal legislation, internal union democracy. It was "formally launched by the American Civil Liberties Union, which submitted a Trade Union Democracy bill to the Congress during the 1947 hearings on new labor legislation." *Ibid.* See Chapter 3 *supra.* See also Aaron & Komaroff, *Statutory Regulation of Internal Union Affairs—II*, 44 ILL. L. REV. 631, 636-672 (1949).

In 1958 Congress made its first unsuccessful response to the McClellan Committee disclosures. The Senate passed the bipartisan Kennedy-Ives bill [5] by a vote of 88 to one. This bill had five titles directed at abuses that had been spotlighted by the McClellan Committee and a sixth title containing limited amendments to the Labor Management Relations Act of 1947. The sixth title had been added as a "sweetener" for certain unions in return for their support of the bill.[6] The union strategy was to oppose any labor legislation that did not also include several desired amendments to the 1947 Act.

Despite its overwhelming passage in the Senate, the bill had received only lukewarm backing of most of the senators, and it was doomed to failure in the House. The sweeteners had not succeeded in stimulating enthusiastic labor support for the bill. The AFL-CIO ostensibly supported it, but George Meany's comment, "God save us from our friends," [7] reflected labor's true attitude.

II. THE POLITICAL CLIMATE

The national elections in the fall of 1958 had a misleading effect on efforts to pass labor legislation in 1959. The Republican party, attempting to capitalize on the public resentment raised by the McClellan disclosures, chose to make "right to work" laws a major issue in a number of states.[8] Fearing widespread enactment of new right-to-work legislation, organized labor threw all the opposition it could muster into these campaigns. As a result, all the right-to-work laws but one were defeated and 70 percent of the AFL-CIO-supported candidates for Congress won.[9] The Republican response bordered on despair, and "union bosses" were generally credited with the Democratic sweep.[10] Conversely, the Democrats were elated; however, the Democratic leadership was convinced that it was necessary to pass a labor reform bill, plus certain amendments to the Taft-Hartley Act, in order to demonstrate the "responsibility" of the Democratic party in the area of union regulation.[11] A combination of factors—McClellan

---

5 S. 3974, 85th Cong., 2d Sess. (1958).
6 McAdams 45.
7 Id. at 46.
8 Id. at 2.
9 Id. at 48.
10 N. Y. Times, Dec. 1958, at p. 1, col. 1.
11 McAdams 9.

Committee publicity, confidence given labor by the success of the 1958 elections, Democratic determination to pass a bill, and public endorsement of legislation by President Eisenhower—resulted in passage of the Landrum-Griffin Act, a statute which many have considered to be less favorable to labor than the political climate of 1958 would have indicated.[12]

III. SENATE ACTION

Early in the 1959 session, Senator John F. Kennedy (D., Mass.) found himself in an uncomfortable position in relation to organized labor. The Democratic leadership had concluded that the Kennedy-Ives bill failed in the House in 1958 because of the Title VI sweeteners added to garner union support. The Democratic leadership therefore wanted to pursue a two-package approach by splitting the reform measures and the amendments to the 1947 Act into separate bills. They would first secure passage of a reform measure, then proceed with the amendments.[13] Influential labor leaders, however, made it known to Kennedy that they would not support any reform bill that did not also contain the sweeteners. Labor's refusal to compromise proved a major tactical error. The labor demand for Taft-Hartley amendments had opened Pandora's box, and now labor was unable to control the cumulative response of a national demand for more restrictive Taft-Hartley amendments.

Acceding to union wishes, Senator Kennedy introduced the Kennedy-Ervin bill.[14] It was closely modeled upon the 1958 bill and, like its predecessor, contained the sweeteners.[15] Other bills, including the McClellan bill [16] and the Administration bill,[17] also were introduced.

---

12 For treatment of the legislative background of the Landrum-Griffin Act, see THE LABOR REFORM LAW (Washington: BNA Books, 1959); LEGISLATIVE HISTORY OF THE LABOR-MANAGEMENT REPORTING AND DISCLOSURE ACT OF 1959 (GPO, 1959).
13 McAdams 49.
14 S. 505, 86th Cong., 1st Sess. (1959) (drafted in major part by Archibald Cox and Arthur Goldberg).
15 The sweeteners were found in S. 505, Title VI, which amended the 1947 Act. They included §603 (a) (authorizing prehire agreements in the building and construction industry), §604 (amending §9 (c) (3) to permit voting by economic strikers), and §605 (restricting the definition of "supervisor" in §2 (11)).
16 S. 1137, 86th Cong., 1st Sess. (1959) (containing no Taft-Hartley amendments).
17 S. 748, 86th Cong., 1st Sess. (1959) (sponsored by Senator Goldwater and containing revisions to Taft-Hartley desired by both labor and management).

When the Labor Subcommittee, chaired by Senator Kennedy, began its hearings, it became apparent that management would not support a bill that included sweeteners only for labor and not for management.[18] Organized employers thus demanded further statutory restrictions on union activities, especially picketing and boycotts.[19] Nevertheless, the Administration bill, which contained the desired management sweeteners, was defeated in subcommittee. And the Kennedy-Ervin bill, after referral to the full committee, was reported out with no management sweeteners.[20]

Senators McClellan and Ervin asked Senator Kennedy to drop the Title VI sweeteners in return for full support of the reform measures and aid in defeating any amendments offered from the floor that were unfavorable to labor. The labor leadership, again misreading the temper of Congress, refused to support the bill without the Title VI provisions.[21] As a result, Senator McClellan introduced a floor amendment which became known as the Mc-Clellan "Bill of Rights of Members of Labor Organizations." [22] This amendment provided for more extensive regulation of internal union affairs than did the Kennedy bill. Following an impassioned speech by Senator McClellan, the amendment passed by the slim margin of 47 to 46.[23]

After passage of the McClellan amendment, several other amendments, previously expected to meet with rejection, also were passed, further changing the complexion of the original bill. Added were provisions dealing with economic strikers, "hot cargo" agreements, the "no man's land" jurisdictional question, and organizational picketing. After some modification of the Bill of Rights section, the bill (now with seven titles)[24] was passed and sent to the House.

IV. STRUGGLE IN THE HOUSE

During the interim before House consideration of the Senate bill, the AFL-CIO developed a strategy that it would follow in

---

18 Senate Subcommittee on Labor, *Hearings*, 86th Cong., 1st Sess. 145-148 (1959).
19 *See* Aaron, *The Labor-Management Reporting and Disclosure Act of 1959*, 73 HARV. L. REV. 851, 1088 (1960).
20 S. 1555, 86th Cong., 1st Sess. (1959).
21 McAdams 87-88.
22 105 CONG. REC. 5810 (daily ed., Apr. 22, 1959).
23 *Id.* at 5827.
24 McClellan's Bill of Rights amendment became Title I of the seven titles of S. 1555.

the House. It was decided that no further support would be given to the Kennedy bill because of distaste for the Title I Bill of Rights section and the Title VII provisions dealing with hot-cargo agreements and organizational picketing.[25] However, at the same time labor intended to continue to press for the desirable Title VII provisions amending Taft-Hartley.

When hearings began in the House Labor Committee, the AFL-CIO felt it had enough votes to bottle up the Kennedy bill in committee. Again, labor had miscalculated its strength. The House was under the same pressure to pass a bill as the Senate had been. When it finally became obvious that a bill was, indeed, emerging from committee, union leaders adopted the strategy of supporting a straight reform bill without any amendments to the LMRA.[26] But this concession had come too late. The Administration and many influential congressmen were now pressing for the restrictive amendments dealing with hot-cargo agreements, secondary boycotts, and organizational picketing. Title VII remained intact. After several weeks of "wrangling," the committee reported out the Elliott bill,[27] which was, nevertheless, "more favorable to labor than had been the Senate bill." [28]

Once the Elliott bill had been reported out of committee, other bills were introduced. The most important of these were the Shelley [29] and the Landrum-Griffin bills.[30] The Shelley bill was substantially the same as the Elliott bill except that it deleted the Title VII provisions offensive to labor. The Landrum-Griffin proposals were also substantially identical to the Elliott bill but included stringent provisions in Title VII relating to hot-cargo agreements, secondary boycotts, and recognitional and organizational picketing. The AFL-CIO supported the Shelley bill, although it obviously stood no chance of passing.[31]

Once the Landrum-Griffin bill was unveiled, management groups throughout the country launched a massive campaign of support for it. The campaign reached its peak when President

---

25 McAdams 123.
26 *Id.* at 148. This was the approach originally suggested by the Democratic leadership.
27 H.R. 8342, 86th Cong., 1st Sess. (1959).
28 Levitan, *Union Lobbyists' Contributions to Tough Labor Legislation*, 10 LAB. L.J. 675, 678 (1959).
29 H.R. 8490, 86th Cong., 1st Sess. (1959).
30 H.R. 8400, 8401, 86th Cong., 1st Sess. (1959).
31 *See* Levitan, note 28 *supra*, at 678.

Eisenhower went on nationwide television and radio to plead for public support for the measure.[32] After his address, Congress was deluged with mail supporting the bill. Backers of the moderate Elliott bill, primarily the House Democratic leadership, were left in a precarious position: Labor supported the Shelley bill, but widespread public support was growing for the Landrum-Griffin bill. When debate began in the House, the Landrum-Griffin bill was substituted for the committee's Elliott bill.[33] The Landrum-Griffin bill passed by a vote of 303 to 125,[34] and the House then requested that a House-Senate conference committee be appointed to resolve the differences between it and the Senate bill.

V. RECONCILING TITLE VII

The conference committee had little trouble reconciling the first six titles of the Senate and House bills and came to agreement on these provisions in a little more than three days.[35] The real struggle was to come over the Title VII provisions.

An examination of the pertinent Title VII provisions of the two bills illustrates the major differences that had to be resolved by the committee.

A. A Jurisdictional Problem: No Man's Land

The first major discrepancy in the two bills concerned the "no-man's-land" question. The Senate bill provided that state agencies but *not* courts could assert jurisdiction over cases that

---

[32] McAdams 193-198.

[33] In commenting on the procedures employed in the House in adopting the LMRDA, Goldberg and Meiklejohn concluded:

"It is, of course, unusual for either body of Congress to adopt a bill on the floor without prior consideration by the appropriate committee. This is true of nearly all legislation, let alone legislation of the importance and far-reaching effect of that here involved.

"Yet, the Landrum-Griffin Bill was adopted by the House in precisely this unorthodox manner. The House Education and Labor Committee . . . reported out the Elliott Bill. Although the Landrum-Griffin Bill was substantially different from the Elliott Bill in major respects, it was substituted for this bill directly on the House floor and adopted without referral to the Labor Committee for study and calm consideration." Goldberg and Meiklejohn, *Title VII: Taft-Hartley Amendments, with Emphasis on the Legislative History*, 54 Nw. U. L. REV. 747, 780 (1960).

[34] 105 CONG. REC. 14540-14541 (daily ed., Aug. 14, 1959).

[35] McAdams 249-251.

the NLRB had declined to accept.[36] The Senate version further provided that when the state agencies took such jurisdiction, they had to apply federal law and that enforcement and appeal would be through federal courts. The Landrum-Griffin bill provided that state agencies *and* courts could take jurisdiction over cases that the NLRB had declined to handle. The Board was empowered to decline jurisdiction "over any labor dispute involving any class or category of employers, where, in the opinion of the Board, the effect of such labor dispute on commerce is not sufficiently substantial to warrant the exercise of its jurisdiction." [37] The House bill made no mention of which law was to be applied in such cases.

When the conference committee met, a modified version of the Landrum-Griffin "no-man's-land" provision was accepted. The Board was forbidden to decline jurisdiction of those disputes that were within its jurisdictional standards on August 1, 1959.[38]

B. The Hot-Cargo Provision

A second amendment to Taft-Hartley dealt with hot-cargo agreements. The Senate bill made it an unfair labor practice to make a hot-cargo agreement with a *common carrier*. The House bill made it an unfair labor practice to make a hot-cargo agreement with *any employer*. The House bill also made it an unfair labor practice for a union to induce individuals employed by any person to refuse to handle goods in order to force any person to cease doing business with another person. The House bill further

---

36 This provision, Section 701 of Title VII, was originally a product of the Mc-Clellan Committee. This committee had recommended that states assume jurisdiction over those labor disputes that the Board refused to hear. SENATE SELECT COMM. ON IMPROPER ACTIVITIES IN THE LABOR AND MANAGEMENT FIELD, INTERIM REPORT, S. DOC. No. 1417, 85th Cong., 2d Sess. 453 (1958) (41 LRRM 54). During the First Session of the 86th Congress, the Senate Labor Committee had included in the Kennedy-Ervin bill a proposal that the Board be required to assert jurisdiction over all disputes arising under the National Labor Relations Act. Goldberg and Meiklejohn, *Title VII: Taft-Hartley Amendments, with Emphasis on the Legislative History*, 54 Nw. U. L. REV. 747 (1960). This proposal was rejected by the Senate, and thus the Senate bill provided that state agencies but not courts could assert jurisdiction over such cases. See discussion of *Guss* v. *Utah L.R.B.*, 353 US 1, 39 LRRM 2567 (1957), and the jurisdictional "no man's land" which precipitated this legislative drive, Chapters 28 and 29 *infra*.
37 S. 1555, as passed by the House of Representatives Aug. 14, 1959, 86th Cong., 1st Sess., §701.
38 The House version of §701 was also modified to provide for a procedural change amending §3 (b) of the Act and empowering the Board to refer representation cases to its regional directors for a final determination, subject to the Board's review. See Goldberg and Meiklejohn, *Title VII: Taft-Hartley Amendments, with Emphasis on the Legislative History*, 54 Nw. U. L. REV. 747, 750 (1960).

made it unlawful for a union to "threaten" any person to force any person to cease doing business with another.

C. Restrictions on Organizational and Recognitional Picketing

There were differences in the two bills concerning organizational and recognitional picketing.[39] The Senate bill provided that organizational picketing was an unfair labor practice if the employer had recognized another union, or if a valid representation election had been held in the preceding nine months without the picketing union being certified as the bargaining representative. The Senate version also provided that an employer unfair labor practice was a defense to a charge of unlawful picketing.

The House version provided that such picketing was an unfair labor practice if:

(1) another union had been recognized by the employer or,

(2) a valid election had been held in the preceding 12 months without the picketing union being certified or,

(3) the union could not show "sufficient interest" on the part of the employees or,

(4) the picketing had continued for 30 days without the filing of an election petition.

The House bill had no provision making an employer unfair labor practice a defense to the charge of unlawful picketing.

D. Prehire Agreements

The Senate bill permitted prehire agreements in the construction industry requiring union membership after seven days' employment. Landrum-Griffin allowed such agreements only where there had been a prior history of collective bargaining and left the time limit for union membership at 30 days.

---

[39] These provisions were to be the most bitterly opposed provisions in the Act. Organized labor asserted such provisions were designed to undermine legitimate labor activities rather than smoke out "racketeers." Business and management groups argued that the provisions were necessary to cope with the corrupt and improper activities within the unions. *Id.* at 762.

E. Voting Rights for Economic Strikers

The Senate bill provided that economic strikers could vote subject to regulations prescribed by the NLRB. The House bill contained no provisions at all on this subject.

VI. THE COMPLETED VERSION

A. The Changes

The final bill hammered out by the conference committee made several important changes in the NLRA:

1. Recognitional and Organizational Picketing. Section 8(b)(7) was added to deal with the issue of recognitional or organizational picketing.[40] Such picketing was made unlawful if:

(a) another union had been recognized and a question of representation could not be raised or,

(b) a valid election had been held within the preceding 12 months or,

(c) the picketing continued without the filing of an election petition within a reasonable time, not to exceed 30 days.

Expedited investigations are required under this provision, and when a petition is filed under (c) an election must be directed forthwith without regard to the 30-percent showing of interest. A proviso to (c) permits truthful "publicity" picketing not having the effect of inducing individuals employed by other persons "not to pick up, deliver or transport any goods or not to perform any services."

2. Secondary-Boycott Changes. Section 8(b)(4) was amended to tighten up "loopholes" in the secondary-boycott provisions of Taft-Hartley.[41] Taft-Hartley had made it an unfair labor practice for a union to "engage in, or to induce or encourage the employees of any employer to engage in, a strike or a concerted refusal in the course of their employment" for the proscribed objects enumerated in 8(b)(4). This provision had been interpreted not to extend to direct pressure on neutral employers.[42] The section was

---

40 *See* Chapter 21 *infra.*
41 *See* Chapter 23 *infra.*
42 *See* discussion of the 1959 amendments in Chapter 23 *infra* and discussion of "person" in Chapter 28 *infra.*

amended to read that "threatening, coercing or restraining any person" for the proscribed objects constitutes an unfair labor practice.

A proviso to Section 8(b)(4) exempts from the secondary-boycott ban the publication of a labor dispute (other than by picketing) for the purpose of truthfully advising the public that a primary dispute exists with an employer and that the employer's products are being distributed by another employer. The proviso further states, however, that such publicity shall not result in inducing any individual employed by any person other than the primary employer to refuse to pick up, deliver, or transport any goods or to fail to perform any services at the establishment of the employer engaged in such distribution.

3. "Employer" and "Employee" Redefined. The definitions of "employer" and "employee" were amended to include "any individual employed by any person." [43] Under the old definitions agricultural laborers, family employees, employees covered by the Railway Labor Act, government employees, supervisors, and independent contractors had not been included.[44] Taft-Hartley had banned the inducement or encouragement of employees engaged in a *concerted* refusal to perform a service. To prohibit appeals to individual employees or neutral employers, the Landrum-Griffin amendment deleted the word "concerted."

4. Hot-Cargo Restrictions. Section 8(e), dealing with the hot-cargo issue,[45] was added in full. This amendment made it an unfair labor practice "for any labor organization and any employer to enter into any contract or agreement, express or implied, whereby such employer ceases or refrains . . . from handling . . . any of the products of any other employer. . . ." Thus, if any such agreement is made, it is unenforceable. Exempted from this provision are such agreements in the construction industry (if the work is to be performed at the site) and in the apparel and clothing industry.

5. Prehire Agreements. Section 8(f) was added to permit the execution of prehire agreements in the building and construction industry.[46]

---

[43] §8 (b) (4) (i).
[44] *See* Chapter 28 *infra.*
[45] *See* Chapter 24 *infra.*
[46] *See* Chapters 11 and 26 *infra.*

6. Voting Rights for Economic Strikers. Taft-Hartley had provided in Section 9(c)(3) that "[e]mployees on strike who are not entitled to reinstatement shall not be eligible to vote." [47] This provision was interpreted to mean that a replaced economic striker was ineligible to vote. It was amended to read as follows:

> Employees engaged in an economic strike who are not entitled to reinstatement shall be eligible to vote under such regulations as the Board shall find are consistent with the purposes and provisions of this Act in any election conducted within twelve months after the commencement of the strike.

7. Delegation of Board Authority Authorized. Section 3(b) was amended to change certain internal operations of the Board. The Board was empowered to delegate to regional directors its Section 9 powers of determining the appropriate bargaining unit, of investigating and providing for hearings, and of determining whether questions of representation exist.[48]

8. Taft-Hartley Provision Repealed. Finally, Section 9(f), (g), and (h) of the Taft-Hartley Act were repealed by 201(d) of the LMRDA.[49]

B. Enactment

The bill containing the Title VII amendments to the NLRA was signed into law by President Eisenhower on September 14, 1959. The national labor policy had undergone another important and, in this case, unexpected change. The change was the culmination of campaigns launched by both labor and management groups in 1947 to amend the Taft-Hartley Act. As long as the political strength of these two groups remained balanced, no effort to amend that Act was successful. The equilibrium was upset in 1959 by two factors: (1) the McClellan Committee and its attendant publicity and (2) labor's unwillingness to support any legislation unless its demands for Taft-Hartley changes were met.[50] Once the drive for Taft-Hartley amendments had been launched, labor was unable to control its course. The outcome for organized labor was a bitter lesson in political expediency.

---

47 *See* Chapter 8 *infra*.
48 *See* Chapter 30 *infra*.
49 *See* note 4 *supra*. Titles I through VI of the LMRDA pertain to internal union affairs and are outside the scope of the present work.
50 *See* Aaron, *The Labor-Management Reporting and Disclosure Act of 1959*, 73 HARV. L. REV. 851 (1960), and Levitan, *Union Lobbyists' Contributions to Tough Labor Legislation*, 10 LAB. L.J. 675 (1959).

PART II

EMPLOYEE RIGHTS

CHAPTER 5

INTERFERENCE WITH PROTECTED RIGHTS AND RESTRICTIONS ON PREELECTION ACTIVITY

I. OVERVIEW

A. Introduction

In the area of organizational activities, the NLRB is faced with the problem of balancing the rights of the employees against those of the employer and, to a lesser extent, those of the union.[1] The background of the various sections of the Act and the Board's preelection rules will be examined, and their application and interrelation will be discussed in the context of particular kinds of conduct.

B. Section 7—Rights of Employees

1. To Form, Join, or Assist Labor Organizations. Since its inception in 1935, the NLRA has had as its primary concern the rights of employees, both individually and collectively.

> It is hereby declared to be the policy of the United States . . . [to protect] the exercise by workers of full freedom of association, self-

---

1 *See* Bok, *The Regulation of Campaign Tactics in Representation Elections Under the National Labor Relations Act,* 78 HARV. L. REV. 38 (1964); Christensen, *Free Speech, Propaganda and the National Labor Relations Act,* 38 NYU L. REV. 243 (1963); Aaron, *Employer Free Speech: The Search for Policy,* in PUBLIC POLICY AND COLLECTIVE BARGAINING 28 (Shister, Aaron & Summers, eds., 1962); Pokempner, *Employer Free Speech Under the National Labor Relations Act,* 25 MD. L. REV. 111 (1965); Koretz, *Employer Interference With Union Organization Versus Employer Free Speech,* 29 GEO. WASH. L. REV. 399 (1960); Fairweather, *What Can Employers Do in Election Campaigns,* NYU SEVENTEENTH ANNUAL CONFERENCE ON LABOR 183 (Washington: BNA Books, 1964); Brown, *Free Speech in NLRB Representation Proceedings,* 50 LRRM 72 (1962); Fields, *Free Speech Under the Taft-Hartley Act,* 14 LAB. L.J. 967 (1963); Platt, *Rules on Free Speech Under Taft-Hartley Act,* 55 LRRM 105 (1964).

organization, and designation of representatives of their own choosing, for the purpose of negotiating the terms and conditions of their employment or other mutual aid or protection.[2]

Section 7 was fashioned to implement this policy. The 1935 statute provided that the rights of employees shall include the right to "self-organization, to form, join, or assist labor organizations" . . . and to engage in "other concerted activities for the purpose of collective bargaining or other mutual aid or protection." The Act made it an unfair labor practice for an employer "to interfere with, restrain or coerce employees" in the exercise of these guaranteed rights.

2. To Refrain From Such Activities. In 1947, the protection of Section 7 was expanded by the Taft-Hartley Act. In Section 8(b)(1)(A), employees were guaranteed the right "to refrain from any or all of such activities," and, to protect this right, further amendments made it an unfair labor practice for a union to restrain or coerce employees in the exercise of their Section 7 rights. The amendments were rooted in the statute's amended declaration of policy "to protect the rights of individual employees in their relations with labor organizations. . . ."[3]

The outer limit of protected concerted rights thus far reached by any tribunal is probably to be found in *United Packinghouse Workers (Farmers' Cooperative),*[4] in which Judge Skelly Wright, writing for the D. C. Circuit, held that racial discrimination by an employer violates Section 8(a)(1) where it interferes with or restrains employees in the exercise of their right to act concertedly

---

[2] §1.
[3] §1(b), Short Title and Declaration of Policy, Labor-Management Relations Act of 1947, Public Law No. 101, 80th Cong., Ch. 120, 1st Sess.
[4] 416 F 2d 1126, 70 LRRM 2489 (CA DC, 1969). The Board will have an opportunity to write on the point, for the case was remanded to the Board for a factual determination as to whether the employer maintained a racially discriminatory policy. The court was of the opinion that "an employer's invidious discrimination on account of race or national origin has . . . [a twofold effect]: (1) racial discrimination sets up an unjustified clash of interests between groups of workers which tends to reduce the likelihood and the effectiveness of their working in concert to achieve their legitimate goals under the Act; and (2) racial discrimination creates in its victims an apathy or docility which inhibits them from asserting their rights against the perpetrator of the discrimination." In the court's view, *"the confluence of these two factors sufficiently deters the exercise of Section 7 rights as to violate Section 8(a)(1)."* 70 LRRM at 2495. The Board has held that racial discrimination by a union violates the duty of fair representation, hence §8(b)(1)(A); *see* Chapter 27 *infra.*

for their own aid or protection. The Board has not so held, however.

3. Other Concerted Activities. The protection extended to employees by Section 7 is not limited to the right to join or assist labor organizations, or to refrain from such activities, but also includes activity for "other mutual aid or protection" and has been invoked to protect concerted employee activity unrelated to union organization.[5] Interference, restraint, or coercion in the exercise of these additional rights is an unfair labor practice under Section 8(a)(1); discrimination against engaging in such concerted activities may also result in a violation of Section 8(a)(3).[6]

The ambit of Section 7, while not unlimited, is nonetheless broad. Employee activity to be protected must be of a "concerted" nature, but a conversation may constitute concerted activity, "although it involves only a speaker and a listener," if it has some relation to group action in the interests of employees.[7] Activity for "mutual aid and protection" has been construed to embrace expressions of "common cause" with workers employed elsewhere, perhaps in the hope of reciprocal support at future times.[8] However, the protective umbrella of Section 7 will be removed from concerted activity that is violent, unlawful, in breach of contract, or "indefensibly disloyal." [9]

C. Employer Interference With Section 7 Rights: Section 8(a)(1)

The mandate of Section 8(a)(1) is the broadest of the subdivisions of Section 8(a). Violations of Section 8(a)(1) are regarded as either derivative or independent.

---

5 Wall's Mfg. Co. v. NLRB, 321 F 2d 753, 53 LRRM 2428 (CA DC, 1963), *cert. denied,* 375 US 923, 54 LRRM 2576 (1963) (writing a letter complaining of sanitary conditions on behalf of fellow employees); Red Wing Carriers, Inc., 137 NLRB 1545, 50 LRRM 1440 (1962), *affirmed,* Teamsters Local 79 v. NLRB, 325 F 2d 1011, 54 LRRM 2707 (CA DC, 1963), *cert. denied,* 377 US 905, 55 LRRM 3023 (1964) (refusing, in the course of employment, to cross a picket line located at another employer's place of business); Salt River Valley Water Users' Ass'n v. NLRB, 206 F 2d 325, 32 LRRM 2598 (CA 9, 1953) (circulating a petition to authorize an individual to collect wages allegedly due under the Fair Labor Standards Act).

6 *See* Chapter 6 *infra.*

7 *Cf.* Mushroom Transp. Co. v. NLRB, 330 F 2d 683, 685, 56 LRRM 2034 (CA 3, 1964).

8 NLRB v. Peter Cailler Kohler Swiss Chocolate Co., 130 F 2d 503, 10 LRRM 852 (CA 2, 1942); *see* General Electric Co., 169 NLRB n. 155, 67 LRRM 1326 (1968).

9 NLRB v. Washington Aluminum Co., 370 US 9, 50 LRRM 2235 (1962); *see* Chapter 6 *infra.*

1. Derivative Violations. The Board has noted since its earliest days that "a violation by an employer of any of the four subdivisions of Section 8, other than subdivision one, is also a violation of subdivision one." [10]

2. Independent Violations. Some acts infringe upon Section 8(a)(1) only and are not incidental to the violation of any other subdivision of Section 8. Acts constituting general interference with Section 7 rights, but not specifically prohibited by other subdivisions of Section 8(a), fall within this category.

3. Motive as an Element of a Section 8(a)(1) Violation. Motive, in the NLRB's view, is not the critical element of a Section 8(a)(1) violation. The Board's "well settled" test has been that

> interference, restraint, and coercion under Section 8(a)(1) of the Act does not turn on the employer's motive or on whether the coercion succeeded or failed. The test is whether the employer engaged in conduct which, it may reasonably be said, tends to interfere with the free exercise of employee rights under the Act.[11]

The view of the Supreme Court has not been nearly so clear.[12] In *Burnup & Sims* [13] the Court seemingly upheld the Board's position in the context of a good-faith discharge of employees engaged in protected activity. The employer's good-faith but mistaken belief as to the employee's conduct was held not to be a defense to the resultant interference with the employees' Section 7 rights. Justice Harlan wrote in a separate opinion, however, that only in a "rare situation" might the Board ignore motive. In contrast, Justice Harlan asserted in his opinion for the Court in the *Darlington case* [14] that " a violation of Section 8(a)(1) alone . . . presupposes an act which is unlawful even absent a discriminatory

---

[10] 3 NLRB ANN. REP. 52 (1939).

[11] Cooper Thermometer Co., 154 NLRB 502, 503, n. 2, 59 LRRM 1767 (1965); American Freightways Co., 124 NLRB 146, 147, 44 LRRM 1302 (1959); *see also* NLRB v. Illinois Tool Works, 153 F 2d 811, 17 LRRM 841 (CA 7, 1946).

[12] For a detailed analysis of this problem, see Christensen and Svanoe, *Motive and Intent in the Commission of Unfair Labor Practices: The Supreme Court and the Fictive Formality*, 77 YALE L.J. 1269 (1968), and Oberer, *The Scienter Factor in Sections 8(a)(1) and (3) of the Labor Act: Of Balancing Hostile Motive, Dogs and Tails*, 52 CORNELL L.Q. 491 (1967).

[13] NLRB v. Burnup and Sims, Inc., 379 US 21, 57 LRRM 2385 (1964).

[14] Textile Workers v. Darlington Mfg. Co., 380 US 263, 58 LRRM 2657 (1965).

motive." [15]   Justice Harlan's citations of *Republic Aviation Corp.*[16] and *Nutone* [17] in this connection bolster the conclusion that motive is not an essential element. But this seemingly clear picture was blurred by succeeding cases.

In the later context of lockout cases, the Court in the *Brown* [18] and *American Shipbulding* [19] cases placed great emphasis upon motive in finding no violation of Section 8(a)(1). The Court referred to the distinction it drew in *Erie Resistor* [20] between acts that are so "inherently discriminatory" or "destructive" of employee rights that the employer may be held to have foreseen the unlawful consequences, and those that are not inherently discriminatory or destructive. Since the Court viewed the employer's acts as neither "inherently discriminatory" nor *per se* unlawful, the lack of a hostile motive appeared to be determinative.[21]

A clear evaluation still remained elusive after the Court's divided 1967 decisions in *Fleetwood Trailer* [22] and *Great Dane.*[23] Those cases involved rights of striking employees and were decided in the context of Section 8(a)(3) violations. Presence or absence of unlawful motivation was not relied upon by the Court in upholding the finding of a Section 8(a)(3) violation. This view of Section 8(a)(3) may portend an additional dimension in assessing Section 8(a)(1) violations.

Reconciling the positions taken by the Court in these cases, while difficult, may involve an examination of the terms on which the Court chose to decide the cases. Despite the Board's finding of Section 8(a)(1) and (3) violations in *Burnup & Sims,* for ex-

---

15 *Id.* at 269.
16 Republic Aviation Corp. v. NLRB, 324 US 793, 16 LRRM 620 (1945).
17 NLRB v. Steelworkers (Nutone, Inc.), 357 US 357, 42 LRRM 2324 (1958).
18 NLRB v. Brown, 380 US 278, 58 LRRM 2663 (1965).
19 American Ship Bldg. Co. v. NLRB, 380 US 300, 58 LRRM 2672 (1965). *See* Chapter 20 *infra.*
20 NLRB v. Erie Resistor Corp., 373 US 221, 53 LRRM 2121, 2124 (1963).
21 These decisions appeared to manifest the Court's renewed emphasis upon motive when viewed in the light of its earlier opinion in *NLRB* v. *Exchange Parts,* 375 US 405, 55 LRRM 2098 (1964). In that case a basic Section 8(a)(1) violation stemming from preelection wage increases was made dependent upon unlawful motive. Earlier, in *ILGWU* v. *NLRB,* 366 US 731, 739, the Court stated that "[w]e find nothing in the statutory language prescribing scienter as an element of the unfair labor practices [8(a)(1) and (2)] here involved."
22 NLRB v. Fleetwood Trailer Co., 389 US 375, 66 LRRM 2737 (1967).
23 NLRB v. Great Dane Trailers, Inc., 388 US 26, 65 LRRM 2465 (1967).

ample, the Court rested its decision solely on Section 8(a)(1). Conversely, the Court's decision in *Darlington* was grounded solely upon Section 8(a)(3), whereas the Board had also found a violation of Section 8(a)(1). The extent to which a Section 8(a)(1) violation overlaps an 8(a)(3) violation may also be relevant. One commentator [24] has suggested that in overlapping situations it may make sense to engraft a hostile-motive requirement, but that this should not normally be done in the case of independent Section 8(a)(1) violations. He further suggests a rough "rule of thumb" that motive should be "presumptively irrelevant" in cases of independent Section 8(a)(1) violations and "presumptively relevant" in Section 8(a)(3) violations.[25]

D. Union Restraint and Coercion—Section 8(b)(1)(A)

Section 8(b)(1)(A) is concerned with the rights of individual employees in their relations with labor organizations. The section makes it an unfair labor practice for a union to "restrain or coerce employees in the exercise of the rights guaranteed in Section 7: Provided, that this paragraph shall not impair the right of a labor organization to prescribe its own rules with respect to the acquisition or retention of membership therein. . . ."

1. Not a Derivative Counterpart of Section 8(a)(1). Although Section 8(b)(1)(A) may be thought of generally as a counterpart of Section 8(a)(1), the Board from the outset has taken the position that "Congress did not intend that Section 8(b)(1)(A) be given the broad application accorded Section 8(a)(1)." [26] Thus, in its earliest decision under the section, *National Maritime Union*,[27] the Board concluded that violations of other sections of Section 8(b) did not give rise to derivative violations of Section 8(b)(1)(A).

> Nothing in this legislative history indicates that a union which refuses to bargain is to be considered as having per se "restrained" or "coerced" employees in the exercise of their rights guaranteed in Section 7. . . . Nor is there any suggestion in the legislative history of Section 8(b)(1)(A) that "coercion" and "restraint" may be found to flow automatically from a union's violation of Section 8(b)(2). . . .[28]

---

24 *See* Oberer, note 12 *supra*, at 516.
25 *Ibid. See* Chapter 6 *infra* for a discussion of discrimination under §8 (a) (3) .
26 14 NLRB ANN REP. 81 (1950) .
27 National Maritime Union, 78 NLRB 971, 22 LRRM 1289 (1948) , *enforced*, NLRB v. National Maritime Union, 175 F 2d 686, 24 LRRM 2268 (CA 2, 1949) .
28 78 NLRB at 985.

This relatively narrow construction of Section 8(b)(1)(A) was given specific approval by the Supreme Court in *Curtis Bros.*[29] The Court cited with approval the Board's decision in *National Maritime Union,* noting that:

> Section 8(b)(1)(A) is a grant of power to the Board limited to authority to proceed against union tactics involving violence, intimidation, and reprisal or threats thereof—conduct involving more than the general pressures upon persons employed by the affected employers implicit in economic strikes.[30]

2. Nature of the Violation. Violence or threats thereof constitute coercion and restraint within the meaning of Section 8(b)(1)(A). Thus, threatening an employee with bodily harm may constitute an unfair labor practice.[31] Restraint and coercion are also found in cases where nonviolent physical force is used to prevent employees from exercising their Section 7 rights, *e.g.,* mass picketing by the union preventing employees from gaining entrance to the employer's premises.[32]

Although the Act literally proscribes only restraint and coercion of "employees" in Section 8(b)(1)(A), violent conduct directed at nonemployees has been held violative of the section when it is substantially certain that employees will hear about it [33] or when the violence is committed in their presence.[34]

Resort to the Board is not the exclusive remedy for such conduct. States, under their criminal laws, may punish violence that constitutes an unfair labor practice,[35] or enjoin it.[36] State courts may also grant compensatory and punitive damages in common-law tort actions involving intimidation or violence.[37]

---

[29] NLRB v. Drivers Local 639, 362 US 274, 45 LRRM 2975 (1960).

[30] *Id.* at 290. *See* Chapter 27 *infra* for treatment of §8(b)(1)(A) conduct which constitutes a breach of a union's duty of fair representation.

[31] *E.g.,* Mid-States Metal Prods., Inc., 156 NLRB 872, 61 LRRM 1159 (1966).

[32] Longshoremen's and Warehousemen's Local 6 (Sunset Line and Twine Co.), 79 NLRB 1487, 23 LRRM 1001 (1948).

[33] Brooklyn Spring Corp., 113 NLRB 815, 36 LRRM 1372 (1955), *enforced,* 233 F 2d 539, 38 LRRM 2134 (CA 2, 1956).

[34] Retail, Wholesale & Dep't Store Union (I. Posner, Inc.), 133 NLRB 1555, 49 LRRM 1066 (1961); Retail, Wholesale & Dep't Store Union (B. Brown Associates, Inc.), 57 NLRB 615, 61 LRRM 1382 (1966), *enforced,* 375 F 2d 745, 64 LRRM 2750 (CA 2, 1967).

[35] UAW (Kohler Co.) v. Wisc. Employment Relations Board, 351 US 266, 38 LRRM 2165 (1956).

[36] *Ibid.*

[37] *See* United Constr. Workers v. Laburnam Constr. Corp., 347 US 656, 34 LRRM 2229 (1954). *See also* UAW v. Russell, 356 US 634, 42 LRRM 2142 (1958). *See* Chapter 29 for a discussion of federal preemption and its exceptions.

Threats of loss of employment as a means of inducing employees to obtain union membership violate Section 8(b)(1)(A).[38] Threats regarding employment-related matters, such as seniority [39] or availability of promotions,[40] also are violative of Section 8(b)(1)(A). General pressures implicit in peaceful economic strikes do not constitute restraint or coercion,[41] but a violation may nevertheless be found where an object of the strike is to compel an employer to discriminate against an employee in reprisal for his exercise of Section 7 rights.[42]

The proviso to Section 8(b)(1)(A) states that unions may prescribe their own rules "with respect to the acquisition or retention of membership therein." This proviso has been interpreted very broadly by both the Board and the courts in cases where union membership only is at stake. Thus, expulsion alone is not restraint or coercion under Section 8(b)(1)(A),[43] even where such expulsion is for failure to engage in conduct unlawful under the Act.[44] Similarly, unions may suspend membership [45] and impose fines for breach of internal union rules without restraining or coercing employees within the meaning of the Act. The Supreme Court held in *NLRB* v. *Allis-Chalmers Mfg. Co.*[46] that a union may seek enforcement in state court of such fines in cases where the employee enjoys "full membership" in the union. "Full membership" is to be distinguished from the mere tender of periodic dues and initiation fees for the purpose of compliance with a union security clause. The court expressly left open the question of whether employees enjoying less than full membership could, consistent with Section 8(b)(1)(A), be subjected to such disciplinary measures.[47] In 1969 the Supreme Court decided *Scofield* v.

---

[38] Seamprufe, Inc., 82 NLRB 892, 23 LRRM 1647 (1949), *enforced,* 186 F 2d 671, 27 LRRM 2216, *cert. denied,* 342 US 813, 28 LRRM 2625 (1951).

[39] Red Ball Motor Freight, Inc., 157 NLRB 1237, 61 LRRM 1522 (1966), *enforced,* 379 F 2d 137, 65 LRRM 2309 (CA DC, 1967).

[40] Hughes Aircraft Co., 159 NLRB 1080, 62 LRRM 1312 (1966).

[41] NLRB v. Drivers' Local 639, 362 US 274, 45 LRRM 2975 (1960).

[42] Wyandotte Chems. Corp., 108 NLRB 1406, 34 LRRM 1220 (1954).

[43] American Newspaper Publishers' Ass'n v. NLRB, 193 F 2d 782, 29 LRRM 2230 (CA 7, 1951). *But see* Chapter 26 *infra* on union security and Chapter 27 *infra* on duty of fair representation.

[44] 193 F 2d 782.

[45] Administrative Ruling of NLRB General Counsel, 44 LRRM 1113 (1959).

[46] NLRB v. Allis-Chalmers Mfg. Co., 388 US 175, 65 LRRM 2449 (1967); Scofield v. NLRB (Wisconsin Motor Corp.), 394 US 423, 70 LRRM 3105 (1969). *See* Chapters 26 and 27 *infra.*

[47] 388 US 175, 197, 65 LRRM 2449 (1967). For a discussion of some of the implications of this distinction, see Hanley, *Labor Law Decisions of the Supreme Court, 1966-67 Term,* LABOR RELATIONS YEARBOOK—1967, 140.

NLRB [48] and substantially clarified the status of union fines under the Act. The union in question had a rule designed to discourage piecework operators from exceeding a stipulated production ceiling. The rule imposed a fine upon members who demanded full payment when they exceeded the production ceiling; the employer voluntarily retained the excess payments to be paid out to the employees for days on which the production ceiling had not been reached because of machine breakdown or other reason. Several members who had been fined filed charges with the NLRB. The Board found no violation of Section 8(b)(1)(A) and the Seventh Circuit affirmed. The Supreme Court agreed, and listed four requirements for lawful imposition of union fines under the Act:

> §8(b)(1)(A) leaves a union free to enforce a [1] properly adopted rule which [2] reflects a legitimate union interest, [3] impairs no policy which Congress has imbedded in the labor laws, and is [4] reasonably enforced against union members who are free to leave the union and escape the rule.[49]

Illustrative of union action deemed an impairment of Congressional labor policy are cases in which the Board has found Section 8(b)(1)(A) violations because a union member was fined, suspended, or expelled from membership for exercising his right to make use of the Board [50] or for encouraging others to do so.[51] This line of decisions is designed to keep the Board effectively accessible to all. But this policy has not been extended to members expelled for filing a decertification petition, for in such a case the union's existence as an "institution" is considered threatened.[52]

The proviso does not, however, authorize a union to extend its membership rules to cover the right of a member to his job [53] or

---

48 Scofield v. NLRB, note 46 *supra*. *Compare:* Machinists Lodge 405 (The Boeing Co.), 185 NLRB No. 23, 75 LRRM 1004 (1970); Machinists Lodge 504 (Arrow Devel. Co.), 185 NLRB No. 22, 75 LRRM 1008 (1970).
49 394 US at 430.
50 NLRB v. Marine & Shipbuilding Wkrs., 391 US 418, 68 LRRM 2257 (1968); Cannery Workers' Union, 159 NLRB 843, 62 LRRM 1298 (1966); Local 138, Operating Engineers, 148 NLRB 679, 57 LRRM 1009 (1964); H. B. Roberts (Wellman-Lord Eng'r, Inc.), 148 NLRB 674, 57 LRRM 1012 (1964).
51 Philadelphia Moving Picture Mach. Operators' Local 307, 159 NLRB 1614, 62 LRRM 1315 (1966).
52 Tawas Tube Prods., Inc., 151 NLRB 46, 58 LRRM 1330 (1965). However, in *Molders and Allied Wkrs., Local 125* (Blackhawk Tanning Co., Inc.), 178 NLRB No. 25, 72 LRRM 1049 (1969), the Board found a violation where a member was *fined* for filing a decertification petition.
53 H. M. Newman, 85 NLRB 725, 24 LRRM 1463 (1949); NLRB v. Philadelphia Iron Works, Inc., 211 F 2d 937, 33 LRRM 2799 (CA 3, 1954), *enforcing* 103 NLRB 596, 31 LRRM 1539 (1953); Great Atl. & Pac. Tea Co., 110 NLRB 918, 35 LRRM 1159 (1954).

to such related matters as union determination of seniority,[54] eligibility for unemployment compensation,[55] or the right to have grievances fairly processed.[56]

3. Motive as Critical Element in Section 8(b)(1)(A) Case. The NLRB does not require evidence of unlawful intent to support a finding of violation of 8(b)(1)(A).[57] As in the case of Section 8(a)(1), however, there is uncertainty on this point in the courts.

E. "Freedom of Speech"—Section 8(c)

Section 8(c) of the Taft-Hartley amendments was the result of a line of early Board decisions severely limiting an employer's freedom of speech.[58] The Board insisted that the employer maintain strict impartiality in matters pertaining to unions and held that statements concerning unionism constituted interference with Section 7 rights of employees.[59] However, the Supreme Court in *NLRB* v. *Virginia Elec. & Power Co.*[60] held that employers had a constitutional right to express opinions that were noncoercive in nature. The Board then developed a somewhat less restrictive approach toward employer speeches, but continued otherwise to limit the right of free speech.[61] There was some indication prior to the passage of Taft-Hartley that the NLRB had changed its position and was according more latitude to employer speeches.[62] The shift, however, came too late to prevent passage of Section 8(c). As stated in the Senate Report: [63] "The committee

---

[54] Teamsters Local 41, 94 NLRB 1494, 28 LRRM 1224 (1951), *enforcement denied,* NLRB v. Teamsters Local 41, 196 F 2d 1, 30 LRRM 2039 (1952), *reversed sub nom.,* Radio Officers v. NLRB, 347 US 17, 33 LRRM 2417 (1954).

[55] Carpenters Local 1400, 115 NLRB 126, 37 LRRM 1255 (1956).

[56] Peerless Tool & Eng'r Co., 111 NLRB 853, 35 LRRM 1598 (1955). See Chapter 27 *infra.*

[57] Ladies' Garment Workers' (Bernard-Altman Texas Corp.) v. NLRB, 366 US 731, 48 LRRM 2251 (1961).

[58] *See* commentary, note 1 *supra.*

[59] *E.g.,* Schult Trailers, Inc., 28 NLRB 975, 7 LRRM 162 (1941); Ford Motor Co., 23 NLRB 342, 6 LRRM 310 (1940); Southern Colorado Power Co., 13 NLRB 699, 4 LRRM 341 (1939).

[60] NLRB v. Virginia Elec & Power Co., 314 US 469, 9 LRRM 405 (1941). *See also* NLRB v. American Tube Bending Co., 134 F 2d 993, 12 LRRM 615 (CA 2, 1943), *cert. denied,* 320 US 768, 13 LRRM 850 (1943).

[61] *See, e.g.,* Monumental Life Ins., 69 NLRB 247, 18 LRRM 1206 (1946) (holding speech coercive where coupled with other unfair labor practices); Clark Bros. Co., 70 NLRB 802, 18 LRRM 1360 (1946) (speech during working time on plant premises held to be unfair labor practice).

[62] *See* Herzog, *Words and Acts: Free Speech and the NLRB,* 18 LRRM 147 (1946).

[63] S. Rep. No. 105 on S. 1126, 1 LEGISLATIVE HISTORY OF THE LABOR MANAGEMENT RELATIONS ACT 1947, 429-430 (1948).

believes these decisions to be too restrictive and . . . provides that if, under all the circumstances, there is neither an express or [sic] implied threat of reprisal, force, or offer of benefit, the Board shall not predicate any finding of unfair labor practice upon the statement." The House version was more restrictive: "[A] statement may not be used against the person making it unless it, standing alone, is unfair within the express terms of Section 7 and 8 of the amended act." [64] The final version of 8(c) as passed by Congress was the House version with only minor changes:

> It is provided that expressing any views, argument, or opinion or the dissemination thereof . . . is not to constitute or be evidence of an unfair labor practice if such expression contains no threat of force or reprisal or promise of benefit.[65]

Following passage of Section 8(c), the Board engaged in a continuing effort to balance the right of free speech and the prohibition upon interference, restraint, or coercion of employees in their exercise of Section 7 rights.[66] The character of threats or promises found unlawful over the years spans the range of human expression. A sampling of one year's decisions discloses Board condemnation of

> threatened loss of employment, threatened closing of plant or going out of business, threatened moving of plant to new location, threatened unfavorable reply concerning credit rating, threatened loss or reduction in pay or overtime, threatened loss of promotion, and threatened violence.[67]

During the same year the Board found unlawful promises

> to "take care" of employees who voted against the union, to give paid holidays, to assist in securing Air Force approval for additional benefit, to grant raises if the pay scale rose in the area, or to "get a raise next week" for the employee who affirmed he was on the employer's side.[68]

1. Threat or Prophecy? The most troublesome element in employer-speech cases has been that of distinguishing between illegal threats and legitimate prophecies. The Board has held that a "prophecy that unionization might ultimately lead to loss of employment is not coercive where there is no threat that the em-

---

[64] H. R. Rep. No. 345 on H. R. 3020, 1 LEGISLATIVE HISTORY OF THE LABOR MANAGEMENT RELATIONS ACT 1947, 299, 324.
[65] H. R. Rep. No. 510, 80th Cong., 1st Sess. 45 (1947).
[66] See Koretz, supra note 58, and Bok, supra note 1.
[67] 27 NLRB ANN. REP. 89 (1963).
[68] Ibid.

ployer will use its economic power to make its prophecy come true."[69] The courts continue to give substance to this distinction. Despite the clarity of phrasing, in practice the line of demarcation has, predictably, been less than rigid.

The Sixth Circuit, in a detailed attempt at clarification, held that no violation would have occurred had an employer's remarks "been limited to a prediction of economic problems if the union came in." But a violation resulted when the employer went on to advert "to the probability that if the company did not choose to meet the excessive union demands and a strike resulted, the company might decide to move the operation elsewhere or to shut it down." The court held that such a statement went further than

> predicting the economic result which would necessarily follow from the advent of the union, over which the employer had no control, in that it involved possible action on the part of the company to close down the plant rather than meet the union's demands.[70]

Similarly, the District of Columbia Circuit found unprotected by Section 8(c) an employer's remark that he could not say "whether the plant would move or not, but he would say two of [its] biggest customers . . . wouldn't do business with a union company [and also] that possibly [the plant] would be cut down to three or four days in operation a week . . . ."[71] The same court, however, differed with the Board's finding that the following "serious harm" notice violated section 8(a)(1):

> Our sincere belief is that if the Union were to get in here it would not work to your benefit but would in the long run itself operate to your serious harm. It is our intention to oppose the Union and by every proper means to prevent it from coming into this operation.

Although the Board had found this statement to be a veiled threat of reprisal, the court concluded that absent supporting evidence

---

[69] Chicopee Mfg. Co., 107 NLRB 106, 107, 33 LRRM 1064 (1953).

[70] Surprenant Mfg. Co. v. NLRB, 341 F 2d 756, 58 LRRM 2484 (CA 6, 1965). *Surprenant* was cited in *Sinclair* for the proposition that predictions must be in terms of demonstrable economic consequences. The First Circuit noted that the prediction that unionization "will or may result" in plant closure "is not a statement of fact, unless, which is most improbable, the eventuality of closing is capable of proof." Sinclair Co., 164 NLRB No. 49, 65 LRRM 1087 (1967), *enforced*, 397 F 2d 157, 68 LRRM 2720 (CA 1, 1968).

[71] IUE (NECO Elec. Prod. Corp.) v. NLRB, 289 F 2d 757, 46 LRRM 2534 (CA DC, 1960).

in the surrounding circumstances the statement alone was not violative of the Act.[72]

In distinguishing between threat and prophecy, the Board and the courts long have been concerned with the effect to be given circumstances surrounding employer speech. *Virginia Electric*,[73] a pre-Section 8(c) case, suggested that the "totality of conduct" be considered so the Board might "look at what the Company has said, as well as what it has done." [74] Decisions during the Eisenhower administration after the passage of Section 8(c) "tended to view each contested statement in isolation from other comments or conduct of the employer." [75] During the 1960s, the Board began placing greater emphasis upon surrounding conduct so that the existence of a violation turned not upon the express words used but upon their meaning in the context in which they were uttered.[76]

2. The Outer Limit of Employer Speech. The outer limit of employer speech has been viewed in two ways: speech that is coercive under Section 8(a)(1) is not protected by Section 8(c); or speech that is protected under Section 8(c) is not violative of Section 8(a)(1). The outer limit may vary depending upon which starting point is emphasized. A Ninth Circuit case in 1967 illustrates, in part, the difference in approach. In *NLRB* v. *TRW-Semiconducters, Inc.*,[77] the Board found that a series of electioneering communications amounted to a violation of Section 8(a)(1). It did not specifically refer to Section 8(c). In a strongly worded opinion the court held that the "broad language of Section 8(a)(1) is not the test of whether election propaganda violates the Act." Rather, it "must first be found that it contains a threat of force or reprisal or promise of benefit." Finding none, the court declared that Section 8(c) determined the outer limit. The trial examiner had considered the surrounding circumstances in which

---

[72] Clothing Workers (Hamburg Shirt Corp.) v. NLRB, 365 F 2d 898, 63 LRRM 2581, (CA DC, 1966). For similar results, *see* Wellington Mill Division v. NLRB, 330 F 2d 579, 55 LRRM 2914 (CA 4, 1964).

[73] 314 US 469, 9 LRRM 405 (1941).

[74] *Id.* at 478; *see* NLRB v. Eastern Oil Co., 340 F 2d 607, 58 LRRM 2255 (CA 1, 1965), *cert. denied,* 381 US 951, 59 LRRM 2432 (1965).

[75] Christensen, note 1 *supra,* at 258.

[76] Lord Baltimore Press, 142 NLRB 328, 53 LRRM 1019 (1963); Lake Catherine Footwear, Inc., 133 NLRB 433, 48 LRRM 1683 (1961); *see also* Dal-Tex Optical Co., 137 NLRB 1782, 50 LRRM 1489 (1962).

[77] 385 F 2d 753, 66 LRRM 2707 (CA 9, 1967), *denying enforcement of* 159 NLRB 415, 62 LRRM 1469 (1966).

the statements were made and their impact upon the employees, relying on the Supreme Court's decision in *Exchange Parts*.[78] The Ninth Circuit indicated that whatever the impact and intent of the propaganda, it did not deprive the employer of the protection of Section 8(c).[79]

In direct contrast to the approach taken by the Ninth Circuit was that of the First Circuit in the 1968 *Sinclair* case.[80] There it was contended that, since each of a series of statements was lawful in itself, the statements in combination could not be considered illegal.[81] Moreover, the Board's order in the case was challenged on the ground that it failed to specify the conduct it purported to proscribe. In upholding the order, the First Circuit stated that in considering coercive effect the test must include the totality of the circumstances; whether language is coercive in its effect is for the Board to resolve on the basis of its specialized experience. The Supreme Court affirmed the approach taken by the Board and the First Circuit in *Sinclair*,[82] holding that any assessment of the precise scope of employer expression must be made in the context of its setting and should thus "take into account the economic dependence of the employees on their employers, and the necessary tendency of the former, because of that relationship, to pick up

---

[78] NLRB v. Exchange Parts, 375 US 405, 55 LRRM 2098 (1964). *See* note 217 *infra* and accompanying text.

[79] Unless *Exchange Parts* can be considered simply as a clear promise-of-benefit case, it may be difficult to link the importance of impact and intent since they formed the basis of the Supreme Court's decision. The essence of the Court's opinion seems to lie in its dramatic comparison of the preelection increase to "the fist inside the velvet glove." The opinion was cast in terms of § (a) (1), so it may be that the court was not ignoring §8(c) but simply was looking inside the "velvet glove." The underlying question may perhaps turn on the degree to which §8(c) will be read literally. The Supreme Court's 1969 *Gissel* opinion, note 200 *infra*, provides some clarification.

[80] Sinclair Co., 164 NLRB No. 49, 65 LRRM 1087 (1967), *enforced*, 397 F 2d 157, 68 LRRM 2720 (CA 1, 1968), *aff'd sub nom.*, NLRB v. Gissel Packing Co., 395 US 575, 71 LRRM 2481 (1969). *See* Chapter 10 *infra* for the *Gissel* holding concerning union recognition without an election; *see also* note 200 *infra*, this chapter.

[81] *Ibid. But cf.* American Greetings Corp., 146 NLRB 1440, 56 LRRM 1064 (1964), in which a similar pattern with similar content was held not to interfere with free choice in the election. *Compare* the split opinions of the Seventh Circuit in Wausau Steel Corp. v. NLRB, 377 F 2d 369, 65 LRRM 2001 (CA 7, 1967), and the Second Circuit in NLRB v. Golub Corp., 388 F 2d 921, 66 LRRM 2769 (CA 2, 1967). The *Golub* case is especially noteworthy because of the exhaustive majority opinion and its indication that while conduct may be "intertwined" with words, the case before it was stripped of the intertwining. The dissent points out the difficulty in judicial attempts to identify threatening language.

[82] Note 80 *supra*.

intended implications of the latter that might be more readily dismissed by a more disinterested ear." [83]

The Seventh Circuit has provided a rule of caution, stating that "one who engages in 'brinksmanship' may easily overstep and tumble into the brink." [84]

F. Preelection Rules of Conduct

Both before and after the enactment of Taft-Hartley, the Board imposed restrictions upon preelection activities of the parties. These have included such mechanical devices as rules prohibiting electioneering activities at the polling place,[85] prohibiting speech-making to captive audiences within 24 hours preceding the election,[86] and requiring management to provide names and addresses of all employees qualified to vote in the election.[87] These and other prospective rules, made pursuant to the Board's power to conduct elections for certification of a bargaining agent, are mandatory rules for the conduct of elections, and their violation furnishes ground for setting aside the election without reference to whether the conduct constituted an unfair labor practice.

1. "Laboratory Conditions": The General Shoe Doctrine. The protection of Section 8(c) literally applies only to unfair labor practice cases. The Board has made extensive use of this distinction in regulating elections. In its 1948 *General Shoe Corp.*[88] decision the Board held:

> [T]he criteria applied . . . in a representation proceeding . . . need not necessarily be identical to those employed in testing whether an

---

83 71 LRRM at 2497. *See* further discussion under "Threats and Loss of Benefits," *infra,* this chapter.
84 Wausau Steel Corp. v. NLRB, 377 F 2d 369, 65 LRRM 2001 (CA 7, 1967).
85 Alliance Ware, Inc., 92 NLRB 55, 27 LRRM 1040 (1950); Detroit Creamery Co., 60 NLRB 178, 15 LRRM 221 (1945); Kilgore Mfg. Co., 45 NLRB 468, 11 LRRM 139 (1942); *cf.* J. I. Case Co., 85 NLRB 576, 24 LRRM 1431 (1949); Higgins, Inc., 106 NLRB 845, 32 LRRM 1566 (1953).
86 Peerless Plywood Co., 107 NLRB 427, 33 LRRM 1151 (1953). In *Honeywell, Inc.,* 162 NLRB 323, 64 LRRM 1007 (1966), the prohibition on speechmaking within 24 hours preceding the election was extended to include informal "question and answer" sessions; however, the *Peerless Plywood* rules have been held inapplicable to sound-car broadcasting so long as the broadcasts consisted not of speeches, but merely of appeals interspersed with music. Southland Cork Co., 146 NLRB 906, 55 LRRM 1426 (1964), *enforced in part,* 342 F 2d 702, 58 LRRM 2555 (CA 4, 1965). *But see* U. S. Gypsum Co., 115 NLRB 734, 37 LRRM 1374 (1956). *See* note 156 *infra.*
87 Excelsior Underwear, Inc., 156 NLRB 1236, 61 LRRM 1217 (1966). *See* note 165 *infra.*
88 77 NLRB 124, 21 LRRM 1337 (1948).

unfair labor practice was committed. . . . In election proceedings, it is the Board's function to provide a laboratory in which an experiment may be conducted, under conditions as nearly ideal as possible, to determine the uninhibited desires of the employees . . .[89]

Under this doctrine fault is not an issue. When conduct affecting the election drops below acceptable standards, the requisite "laboratory conditions" are not present and the experiment must be conducted again.

During the period of the Eisenhower Board the *General Shoe* doctrine was eclipsed in favor of Section 8(c) as an outer limit in election cases.[90] In some instances Section 8(c) was applied more restrictively in employer unfair labor practice cases than were the Board's rules for employer conduct during an election campaign.[91]

2. *Dal-Tex Optical*: Resurgence of *General Shoe*. With the advent of a new Board in 1961 the criteria applied to employer speeches were changed radically. In *Dal-Tex Optical Co.*[92] the Board stated:

> Conduct violative of Section 8(a)(1) is, a *fortiori*, conduct which interferes with the exercise of a free and untrammeled choice in an election. This is so because the test of conduct which may interfere with the "laboratory conditions" for an election is considerably more restrictive than the test of conduct which amounts to interference, restraint, or coercion which violates Section 8(a)(1).

Thus, conduct that is an unfair labor practice under the Act is also viewed as violative of the Board's election rules. Other conduct that destroys the "laboratory conditions" established by the Board, even though not constituting an unfair labor practice, may also violate the Board's election rules.

3. Timing of "Laboratory Period." In contrast to the six-month "statute of limitations" established for unfair labor practices,[93] in postelection objection proceedings the Board bases its findings only upon conduct that occurred between an established cutoff date and the election, whatever the period of time involved.

---

[89] *Id.* at 127. As to how realistic this objective is, see Bok, *supra* note 1, at 45-47.
[90] *See* National Furniture Co., 119 NLRB 1, 40 LRRM 1442 (1957); Lux Clock Mfg. Co., 113 NLRB 1194, 36 LRRM 1432 (1955); Esquire, Inc., 107 NLRB 1238, 33 LRRM 1367 (1954); American Laundry Mach. Co., 107 NLRB 511, 33 LRRM 1181 (1953).
[91] Wirtz, *The New National Labor Relations Board; Herein of "Employer Persuasion,"* 49 Nw. U. L. Rev. 594 (1954).
[92] 137 NLRB 1782, 50 LRRM 1489 (1962).
[93] §10(b).

The establishment of an optimum cutoff date represents an attempt to balance the advantage of "eliminating from postelection consideration conduct too remote to have prevented free choice" [94] with the disadvantage of intentional delays for the purpose of strategic interference. In the *A&P* case [95] in 1952 the Board established the cutoff date as either (1) the execution date of a consent-election agreement, or (2) in contested cases, the issuance of a notice of hearing. In *Woolworth*,[96] two years later, the Board moved the cutoff date in contested cases closer to the election, namely, to the date of issuance of the Board's direction of election.

In 1961 the Board reconsidered its view in the light of experience with its delegation of decisional authority in representation cases to its regional directors.[97] Since this delegation resulted in a decrease in the elapsed time between the filing of a petition and an election, former considerations of remoteness were no longer as compelling. Thus, *Woolworth* was overruled in the *Ideal Electric* case,[98] and the cutoff date was established as of filing of the petition rather than the direction of election.

Left unchanged by *Ideal Electric* was the cutoff date in uncontested elections. Uniformity in cutoff dates was prescribed the following year in *Goodyear Tire*.[99] Thereafter, the filing of the petition marked the commencement of the "laboratory period" for purposes of the representation case.

There is no assurance that the "laboratory" standard will remain continuously in effect during the entire time between the filing of the petition and the election. If, for example, the petition is withdrawn and shortly thereafter refiled, employer conduct in the interval that otherwise might merit Board remedial action may be countenanced.[100] On the other hand, a promise of benefit issued immediately after an election is not immunized because it did not affect the election, but may fall within the proscription

---

[94] Ideal Elec. & Mfg. Co., 134 NLRB 1275, 1277, 49 LRRM 1316 (1961). Objectionable conduct occurring on the *day* the petition was filed but before the actual filing will still be considered as ground for setting aside the election. W. Texas Equip. Co., 142 NLRB 1358, 53 LRRM 1249 (1963).
[95] Great Atl. and Pac. Tea Co., 101 NLRB 1118, 31 LRRM 1189 (1952).
[96] F. W. Woolworth Co., 109 NLRB 1446, 34 LRRM 1584 (1954).
[97] Ideal Elec. & Mfg. Co., 134 NLRB 1275, 49 LRRM 1316 (1961).
[98] *Ibid.*
[99] Goodyear Tire and Rubber Co., 138 NLRB 453, 51 LRRM 1070 (1962).
[100] *See* Sigo Corp., 146 NLRB 1484, 56 LRRM 1078 (1964).

of Section 8(a)(1) because of its effect on a possible second election.[101]

4. Procedural Considerations. The procedural posture in which an election campaign case arises should be underscored since it may materially affect the criteria used in judging the lawfulness of employer communications. If preelection conduct is being ruled upon in a representation case, the criteria for judgment will be compliance with "laboratory conditions," whereas the same conduct will be judged by the less stringent standard of Section 8(c) if it is the subject of an unfair labor practice charge.[102] However, electioneering conduct resists ready categorization into separate unfair labor practice and representation compartments, so that these dual criteria may arise in the same case with respect to the same conduct. This is especially so in *Bernel Foam* [103] cases where a union may be seeking concurrently to set aside an election and to obtain a bargaining order. It is thus seeking remedial action in both a representation case and an unfair labor practice case.[104] Where the matters are consolidated,[105] the trial examiner would presumably have two standards for guidance in judging identical conduct. The possibility of having these standards become entangled as a case moves from the trial examiner to the Board and perhaps to the courts is not difficult to visualize.[106] An

---

[101] *See* Ralph Printing and Lith. Co., 158 NLRB 1353, 1354, n. 3., 62 LRRM 1233 (1966).

[102] Dal-Tex Optical Co., 137 NLRB 1782, 1785, 50 LRRM 1489 (1962); *see also* Eagle-Picher Indus., Inc., 171 NLRB No. 44, n. 1, 68 LRRM 1570 (1968).

[103] Bernel Foam Prods. Co., 146 NLRB 1277, 56 LRRM 103 (1964). *See* discussion of the *Bernel Foam* doctrine in Chapter 10 *infra*.

[104] Prior to *Bernel Foam* a union which proceeded to a representation election and lost could not then assert its majority by filing a Section 8(a)(5) unfair labor practice charge. Under the Board's previous *Aiello* rule in 1954, this dual procedure was considered inconsistent. Aiello Dairy Farms, 110 NLRB 1365, 35 LRRM 1235 (1954). *Bernel* expressly overruled *Aiello* in 1964, and this dual representation-unfair labor practice procedure has been widely utilized since then. *See* Chapter 10 *infra*.

[105] Ordinarily, both the objections to the election and the unfair labor practice complaint will be consolidated for hearing before the trial examiner. NLRB Field Manual 11420.1. *See* discussion of this procedure in *Freeport Marble & Tile Co.*, 153 NLRB 810, 813, 814, 59 LRRM 1561 (1965), *enforced in part*, 367 F 2d 371, 63 LRRM 2289 (CA 1, 1966). In *Bernel* the proceedings were not consolidated. However, there is no prohibition upon a union's initially seeking a determination from the regional director on the objections in the representation case and thereafter filing unfair labor practice charges—so long as it stays within the six-month statute of limitations prescribed in §10(b).

[106] *See* Eagle-Picher Indus., Inc., 171 NLRB No. 44, 68 LRRM 1570 (1968).

illustration of disentangling the standards appears in *Sinclair Co.*,[107] where, in the course of recommending a bargaining order, the trial examiner, citing Dal-Tex Optical,[108] found employer communications to have violated Section 8(a)(1) and also to have interfered with the free choice in the election. The examiner recommended that, "assuming *arguendo*" that the employer's conduct was not held to be violative of Section 8(a)(1), the election nevertheless be set aside because of impairment of "laboratory conditions" for a free choice. Although the Board and First Circuit affirmed the bargaining order, thus not reaching the alternative conclusion, the trial examiner's analysis is of interest.

Prior to *Bernel Foam* the possibility of dual criteria in the same case normally did not arise, since the union would have to choose the remedial procedure under which it sought to have the employer's conduct tested. However, *NLRB v. Realist, Inc.*[109] provides an illustration of a dual-standards problem. The first election was set aside because of an employer preelection speech that was found to interfere with "laboratory conditions." After the union won the second election, the employer refused to bargain in order to contest the setting aside of the first election. In the context of an unfair labor practice case resulting from the refusal to bargain, a majority of the Seventh Circuit upheld the Board's application of laboratory conditions, while the dissent held that employee rights should have been tested under Section 8(c).[110]

---

107 164 NLRB No. 49, 65 LRRM 1087 (1967), *enforced*, 397 F 2d 157, 68 LRRM 2720 (CA 1, 1968), *aff'd sub nom.* NLRB v. Gissel, 395 US 575, 71 LRRM 2481 (1969). *See* note 200 *infra*.

108 137 NLRB 1782, 50 LRRM 1489 (1962).

109 328 F 2d 840, 55 LRRM 2523 (CA 7, 1964).

110 *See also* Mallory Plastics Co., 149 NLRB 58, LRRM 1014 (1964), *enforcement denied*, 355 F 2d 509, 61 LRRM 2139 (CA 7, 1966), where the Board found statements by the employer sufficient to justify setting aside an election, and to be violative of Section 8(a)(1). The Seventh Circuit denied enforcement of the Section 8(a)(1) order but did not have occasion to pass on the objections in the representation case. The Board was then confronted with a question of whether to proceed to a second election, since under its *General Shoe* doctrine conduct may be deemed to invalidate an election notwithstanding its failure to constitute an unfair labor practice. Since the Board itself had already found a violation of Section 8(a)(1), under *Dal-Tex Optical* the conduct, *a fortiori*, interfered with the election. Nonetheless, the Board did not proceed to a second election and certified the results of the first election. It sought to deal with this apparent inconsistency by a footnote disclaimer of any rejection of the principle established in the *General Shoe* case. Mallory Plastics Co., 158 NLRB 954, 956, n. 4, 62 LRRM 1146 (1966).

II. CONDUCT AFFECTING ORGANIZING AND ELECTIONS

The primary objective of organizing is to obtain bargaining rights. While the procedural preelection issues noted above may be useful analytically, an organizing campaign is not normally intiated with the ultimate administrative or judicial forum clearly in view. Thus, conduct will be discussed here in terms of an organizational campaign leading to an election, rather than in terms of what may result in a representation proceeding or an unfair labor practice case.

A. Restrictions on Union Activity on Employer Property

The access or nonaccess to employees is plainly a threshhold concern in an organizing campaign. Understandably, the Board and the courts have long been engaged in "working out an adjustment between the undisputed right of self-organization assured to employees . . . and the equally undisputed right of employers to maintain discipline in their establishments." [111] It is apparent that "reasonable men can and do differ in striking this adjustment . . .," [112] so that strong reliance has been placed upon presumptions to facilitate the decision-making process.

1. Basic Presumptions. In its early landmark decision in *Republic Aviation*,[113] the Supreme Court adopted the presumption that the enforcement and promulgation of a rule prohibiting union solicitation by employees outside working time, although on company property, "is an unreasonable impediment to self organization and therefore discriminatory in the absence of evidence that special circumstances make the rule necessary" for maintaining "production and discipline." [114] The genesis of this presumption was the Board's 1943 decision in *Peyton Packing Company*.[115] In that case the Board had formulated the corollary presumption that the promulgation and enforcement of a nosolicitation rule for working hours "must be presumed to be valid in the absence of evidence that it was adopted for a discriminatory

---

111 Republic Aviation Corp. v. NLRB, 324 US 793, 16 LRRM 620 (1945).
112 Stoddard-Quirk Mfg. Co., 138 NLRB 615, 616 n. 2, 51 LRRM 1110 (1962).
113 324 US 793, 16 LRRM 620 (1945).
114 *Id.* at 803 n. 10, *citing* Peyton Packing Co., 49 NLRB 828, 843-844, 12 LRRM 183 (1943), *enforced*, 142 F 2d 1009, 14 LRRM 792 (CA 5, 1944), *cert. denied*, 323 US 730, 15 LRRM 973 (1944).
115 *Supra* note 114.

purpose." The Board's rationale was that "working time is for work" but that the time outside working hours "is an employee's time to use as he wishes without unreasonable restraint although the employee is on company property." [116]

2. Rights of employees and nonemployees. There is a distinction between rules of law applicable to employees and those applicable to nonemployees, *i.e.*, union organizers, and "the distinction is one of substance." [117] Consequently, the Supreme Court in *Babcock and Wilcox* [118] held that an employer may prohibit the distribution of union literature by nonemployee union organizers if: (1) "reasonable efforts . . . through other available channels of communication will enable it to reach the employees," and (2) the employer does not discriminate against the union by allowing distribution by other nonemployees.[119]

The Court also took cognizance of the plant location and that of employees' residences, noting that if employees were beyond the reach of reasonable union efforts to locate them, the employer's property must be made available.[120] Special problems of communications obviously exist in company towns and lumber camps.[121] The 1968 decision of the Board in *Solo Cup Company* [122] concerning industrial parks, however, suggests that this special problem of nonaccessibility may not be confined to lumber camps and company towns. Rather, the analogy was drawn to the privately owned shopping center as discussed by the Supreme Court in *Logan Valley Plaza* [123] earlier in 1968. These forms of business were viewed as the functional equivalent of a "normal municipal business district" to which the public had unrestricted access. In the circumstances of that case the Board found the

---

116 *Ibid.*

117 NLRB v. Babcock & Wilcox, 351 US 105, 113, 38 LRRM 2001 (1956).

118 *Ibid.*

119 For an example of the distinction between rules applicable to employees and union organizers, see G. C. Murphy Co., 171 NLRB No. 45, 68 LRRM 1108 (1968).

120 NLRB v. Babcock & Wilcox, 351 US 105, 113, 38 LRRM 2001 (1956).

121 *See* NLRB v. Lake Superior Lumber Corp., 167 F 2d 147, 150, 21 LRRM 2707 (1948), and NLRB v. Stowe Spinning Co., 336 US 226, 23 LRRM 2371 (1949).

122 172 NLRB No. 110, 68 LRRM 1385 (1968); *reversed and modified*, 422 F 2d 1149, 73 LRRM 2789 (CA 7, 1970). *See* Chapter 19 *infra* at note 18.

123 Amalgamated Food Employees Local 590 v. Logan Valley Plaza, Inc., 391 US 308, 68 LRRM 2209 (1968). *See* Chapter 19 *infra*.

barring of organizers from private property to be a violation; the Seventh Circuit, however, reversed the decision.[124]

Shortly before *Logan Valley*, the Board, with approval of the Second Circuit, had ordered a resort hotel to permit union organizers on its premises for purposes of solicitation. In that case many of the employees had their living, eating, and recreational facilities on the hotel premises so that they could not be reached by "any means practically available to union organizers." [125]

3. Solicitation and Distribution. A different adjustment has been struck for oral solicitation from that of distribution of literature. Distribution has been regarded as posing different problems, such as littering, and different techniques, such as the setting and opportunity for effectively communicating a message.[126] In striking a balance, the "development of the law regarding oral solicitation has been attended with less travail than that regarding the distribution of literature." [127]

Republic Aviation spoke specifically to the problem of solicitation. The Board has maintained the position that oral solicitation by employees may be prohibited only during working time.[128] But distribution by employees may be prohibited both during working time and in working areas.[129] The Board, with approval of the Second Circuit, has invalidated a prohibition of distribution which extends beyond working areas and into nonworking areas,[130] but this position has not been accepted in two other circuits.[131]

Solicitation of authorization cards falls within the category of oral solicitation.[132]

---

[124] NLRB v. Solo Cup Co., 422 F 2d 1149, 73 LRRM 2789 (1969). The Board had found that almost 99 percent of the employees drove into work from dispersed outlying areas, and distribution immediately outside the park was prohibitive in terms of safety. Also, the employer had refused to furnish a list of employee names and addresses. *See* Chapter 19 *infra* at note 18.

[125] NLRB v. S. & H. Grossinger's, Inc., 372 F 2d 26, 30, 64 LRRM 2295 (CA 2, 1967), *enforcing in part*, 156 NLRB 233, 61 LRRM 1025 (1965). *See* note 161 *infra*.

[126] *See* Bok, *supra* note 1, at 93.

[127] Stoddard-Quirk Mfg. Co., 138 NLRB 615, 51 LRRM 1110 (1962).

[128] *Ibid.*

[129] *Ibid.*

[130] United Aircraft Corp., 139 NLRB 39, 51 LRRM 1259 (1952), *enforced*, 324 F 2d 128, 54 LRRM 2492 (CA 2, 1963), *cert. denied*, 376 US 951, 55 LRRM 2769 (1964).

[131] Republic Aluminum Co. v. NLRB, 374 F 2d 183, 64 LRRM 2447 (CA 5, 1967); NLRB v. Rockwell Mfg. Co., 271 F 2d 109, 44 LRRM 3004 (CA 3, 1959). *See* Chapter 17 *infra* at notes 133-135 for treatment of no-solicitation clauses in collective bargaining contracts.

[132] Stoddard-Quirk Mfg. Co., 138 NLRB 615, 619, n. 5, 51 LRRM 1119 (1962); *see also* Rose Co., 154 NLRB 228, 229, n. 1, 59 LRRM 1738 (1965).

4. Presumptions of Validity. It is only those rules which prohibit union solicitation during the employees' working time that are presumed to be valid. However, the language used to frame no-solicitation rules has been far from uniform. But even a rule tailored to be clothed with the presumption of validity may be violative if promulgated or enforced in a discriminatory manner.

a. Face Validity of Rule. No-solicitation rules drawn so broadly as to encompass nonworking time are presumptively unlawful.[133] An exception to this presumption is made for retail department stores, which may prohibit employee solicitation on the selling floor even during nonworking time because of the nature of the business.[134] While these guidelines are clear, cases have arisen in which the no-solicitation rule was susceptible of a number of interpretations. For example, a rule in a retail establishment prohibiting solicitation "on store premises during working hours by any persons . . ." has been held invalid because it could be read as prohibiting employee activity in nonselling areas during employees' nonworking time.[135] The Board's position regarding ambiguous rules is aptly summed up in the Second Circuit's declaration that "the risk of ambiguity must be held against the promulgator of the rule rather than the employees who are supposed to abide by it." [136]

b. Unlawful Promulgation or Enforcement. A rule presumptively valid on its face is also presumptively valid as to its promulgation and enforcement. But these presumptions can be rebutted by evidence establishing a discriminatory purpose in the adoption or application of the rule.[137] A significant development in Board law has involved the nature of the evidence that would serve to rebut the presumption of validity and establish the

---

133 For an exhaustive collection of such cases, see Gould, *The Question of Union Activity on Company Property,* 18 VAND. L. R. 73, 75-76, n. 10 (1964).
134 Meier & Frank Co., 89 NLRB 1016, 26 LRRM 1081 (1950); Goldblatt Bros., 77 NLRB 1262, 22 LRRM 1153 (1948); Marshall Field & Co., 34 NLRB 1, 8 LRRM 325 (1941); *see also* Maxam Buffalo, Inc., 139 NLRB 1040, 51 LRRM 1459 (1962).
135 G. C. Murphy, 171 NLRB No. 45, 68 LRRM 1108 (1968). *But see* Ward Mfg., Inc., 152 NLRB 1270, 59 LRRM 1325 (1965), where prohibition "during working hours" was held to be valid on its face, and Pepsi Cola Bottlers of Miami, Inc., 155 NLRB 527, 60 LRRM 1356 (1965), where prohibition against solicitation "on the job" was held to be valid on its face.
136 NLRB v. Miller Charles & Co., 341 F 2d 870, 58 LRRM 2507 (CA 2, 1965); G. C. Murphy Co., 171 NLRB No. 45, 68 LRRM 1108 (1968); Fashion Fair, Inc., 163 NLRB No. 22, 64 LRRM 1318 (1967).
137 Walton Mfg. Co., 126 NLRB 697, 45 LRRM 1370 (1960), *enforced,* 289 F 2d 177, 47 LRRM 2794 (CA 5, 1961).

illegality of a rule valid on its face. In *Star-Brite Industries* [138] a rule presumptively valid because it referred only to "working time" was challenged on the ground that it was promulgated shortly after a union organizing campaign began and applied only to union activities. The Board found that the limitation and timing of the rule did not establish a discriminatory purpose because it would be "an anomaly" to permit an employer to adopt a rule but "hold that he may not do so when the occasion for its use arises." [139] As to the actual enforcement of the rule by interrogation and warning of two employees, the Board found no evidence that the rule had been unfairly applied.

In 1964 the overruling of *Star-Brite* signalled a change in the "nature of evidence required to establish a discriminatory motive in adopting and/or enforcing a no-solicitation rule." [140] Since then, careful consideration has been given to the extent to which the promulgation of a rule coincided with the ebb and flow of union activity.[141]

A *prima facie* case rebutting the presumption of validity has been established by the following: [142] (1) promulgation at the time of "intensive union activity" [143] and application in the first instance to a known union adherent; (2) the permission of solicitations of other kinds during working time; (3) a pattern of conduct hostile to organizational efforts and found violative of Sections 8(a)(1) and (3).

5. Union Buttons or Insignias. The right of employees to wear union buttons while at work was upheld in the *Republic Aviation* [144] case as a protected activity. This general rule also encom-

---

138 127 NLRB 1008, 1010, 46 LRRM 1139 (1960).
139 *Id.* at 1011.
140 Wm. H. Block Co., 150 NLRB 341, 343, n. 6, 57 LRRM 1531 (1964), the Board specifically stating that it would have found a violation on the *Star-Brite* facts.
141 *See* Ward Mfg., Inc., 152 NLRB 1270, 59 LRRM 1325 (1965), where the rule was promulgated one day after the first union meeting; *see also* Pepsi Cola Bottlers of Miami, Inc., 155 NLRB 527, 60 LRRM 1357 (1965). The timing of the notice was not controlling; *see* F. P. Adams Co., 166 NLRB No. 112, 65 LRRM 1695 (1967), where the Board emphasized that the "surrounding circumstances were devoid of unlawful activity." Nonetheless, it remains an important consideration. State Chemical Co., 166 NLRB 455, 65 LRRM 1612 (1967); Sardis Luggage Co., 170 NLRB No. 187, 70 LRRM 1230 (1968).
142 State Chemical Co., 166 NLRB 455, 65 LRRM 1612 (1967).
143 *Compare* Rose Co., 154 NLRB 228, 59 LRRM 1738 (1965), *with* Serv-Air, Inc., 161 NLRB 382, 63 LRRM 1270 (1966), *reversed on that point*, 395 F 2d 557, 67 LRRM 2337 (CA 10, 1968).
144 324 US 793, 16 LRRM 620 (1945).

passes the right to wear other emblems demonstrating union support, such as badges and T-shirts.[145] Again, this right must be balanced against the right of the employer to manage his business in an orderly fashion. The resulting adjustment permits the promulgation of a rule prohibiting the wearing of union emblems only where it is necessary because of "special circumstances" [146] for the maintenance of production and discipline. Where friction and animosity exist between groups of employees in the context of a strike, the prohibition of union insignias may be a legitimate precaution against discord and violence.[147]

Buttons that are not provocative and do not serve to alienate customers, particularly when worn by employees not in contact with the public, may not be prohibited.[148] But in order to be beyond the reach of reasonable employer rules, emblems must be sufficiently identified with employee sympathies. The mere wearing of flowers, unaccompanied by any legend, by some of the 5,000 employees in a large department store was judged not to have this effect.[149]

Employer-supplied campaign badges may be ground for the setting aside of an election. Such badges, the Board has said, place employees in the position of declaring themselves as if they had been interrogated.[150]

6. "Captive Audience" Speeches. Added complexity results when the employer makes a "captive audience speech" while using a no-solicitation/distribution rule to deny a union an oppor-

---

145 De Vilbiss Co., 102 NLRB 1317, 31 LRRM 1374 (1953).

146 Standard Fittings Co., 133 NLRB 928, 48 LRRM 1808 (1961); Floridan Hotel of Tampa, Inc., 137 NLRB 1484, 50 LRRM 1433 (1962), *enforced as modified*, 318 F 2d 545, 53 LRRM 2420 (CA 5, 1963). *See also* May Dep't. Stores Co., 174 NLRB No. 109, 70 LRRM 1307 (1969).

147 United Aircraft Corp., 134 NLRB 1632, 49 LRRM 1384 (1961), where pins were worn by employees who had not crossed the picket line during a bitter strike; Caterpillar Tractor Co. v. NLRB, 230 F 2d 357, 37 LRRM 2619 (CA 7, 1956), involving "scab buttons"; Boeing Airplane Co. v. NLRB, 217 F 2d 369, 34 LRRM 2821 (CA 9, 1954), involving rival unions in a violent strike. The Board's citation of all three cases for the same proposition in *Floridan Hotel of Tampa, Inc.*, 137 NLRB 1484, 1486, n. 6, 50 LRRM 1433 (1962), *enforced as modified*, 318 F 2d 545, 53 LRRM 2420 (CA 6, 1963), may indicate an adoption of the Seventh and Ninth Circuit decisions as consistent with *United Aircraft*.

148 Floridan Hotel of Tampa, Inc., *supra* note 147. This was the form in which the court enforced the Board's order. Whether the corollary would be true is uncertain since the Board did not accept the Fifth Circuit's original remand invitation to explore the wider ramifications. NLRB v. Floridan Hotel of Tampa, Inc., 300 F 2d 204, 49 LRRM 2780 (CA 5, 1962).

149 Gimbel Bros., 147 NLRB 500, 505, 56 LRRM 1287 (1964).

150 Chas. V. Weise Co., 133 NLRB 765, 48 LRRM 1709 (1961).

tunity to reply under similar conditions. Prior to the advent of Section 8(c), the Board adopted a rule of absolute prohibition of captive-audience speeches.[151] In 1948 this rule was repudiated as inconsistent with Section 8(c).[152] The Board, nonetheless, attempted to control captive-audience speeches to some degree by formulating its *Bonwit-Teller* [153] doctrine of equal opportunity. That doctrine held that captive-audience speeches by the employer coupled with a no-solicitation rule constituted a discriminatory application of the rule. The Board sought to avoid conflict with Section 8(c) by emphasizing the refusal to permit a reply under similar conditions rather than the delivery of a noncoercive speech. Two years later, in 1953, a reconstituted Board panel rejected the equal-opportunity doctrine. In *Livingston Shirt Corp.* the Board held that "an employer does not commit an unfair labor practice if he makes a preelection speech on company time and premises to his employees and denies the union's request for an opportunity to reply." [154] The Supreme Court in the *NuTone* and *Avondale* cases seemingly affirmed this rule, at least where the union has other means to carry its message to the employees.[155]

Decided with *Livingston Shirt*, interestingly, was *Peerless Plywood*,[156] which formulated the still-current "24-hour rule" prohibiting both unions and employers from delivering captive-audience speeches within 24 hours of an election. Conflict with Section 8(c) is avoided because an infringement of the rule is not an unfair labor practice but merely is ground for setting aside the election.

In 1962, another reconstituted Board, in *May Dept. Stores*,[157] distinguished *Livingston Shirt* on the ground that the *Livingston* no-solicitation rule was presumptively valid and inapplicable to nonworking hours. But use of a broad, privileged no-solicitation rule coupled with anti-union speeches created "a glaring 'imbalance in opportunities for organizational communication' " within

---

[151] Clark Bros., 70 NLRB 802, 18 LRRM 1360 (1946). For a general discussion of captive-audience speeches, see Note, *NLRB Regulation of Employer's Pre-Election Captive Audience Speeches*, 65 MICH. L. REV. 1236 (1967).
[152] Babcock & Wilcox Co., 77 NLRB 577, 578, 22 LRRM 1057 (1948).
[153] Bonwit-Teller, Inc., 96 NLRB 608, 28 LRRM 1547 (1951).
[154] Livingston Shirt Corp., 107 NLRB 400, 409, 33 LRRM 1156 (1953).
[155] NLRB v. United Steelworkers (Nutone, Inc.), 357 US 357, 364, 42 LRRM 2324 (1958).
[156] Peerless Plywood Co., 107 NLRB 427, 33 LRRM 1151 (1953). *See* note 86 *supra.*
[157] May Dep't Stores Co., 136 NLRB 797, 49 LRRM 1862 (1962).

the *NuTone* doctrine, thus violating Section 8(a)(1). The Sixth Circuit refused enforcement on the ground that the Board had failed to give adequate consideration to the various other means of communication available to the union.[158] But the Board adhered to its position and in *Montgomery Ward & Co.*[159] found a violation where an unlawful no-solicitation rule (banning union solicitation in nonworking areas during nonworking time) prevented a response to anti-union speeches to massed employees during working time. The Board found the speeches coercive and unprotected by Section 8(c), and when coupled with a no-solicitation rule they created a "glaring imbalance" in organizational communication. The Sixth Circuit granted enforcement of the Board's order, distinguishing the *May* decision on the ground that the *May* no-solicitation rule was valid and the speeches noncoercive.[160]

In *S and H Grossinger's, Inc.*,[161] the Board conditioned an employer's continued anti-union speeches during working time upon the granting of a similar opportunity to the union. Since many of the employees lived on the premises of the resort hotel involved, meaningful outside communication was blocked. The Second Circuit held that an equal-opportunity requirement may be imposed only when the employer is enforcing the no-solicitation rule. Since it upheld the Board's invalidation of a rule excluding union organizers from the employer's property,[162] the court found that there was no necessity to order the employer to provide the union with an equal opportunity to address the employees.[163]

In the face of court refusal to follow the Board's position in *May* and *Bonwit-Teller*, the Board itself has declined to establish the *Bonwit-Teller* doctrine as a preelection rule of conduct. Such an extension would theoretically not conflict with decisions such as *Babcock & Wilcox* since there would be no Section 8(a)(1) finding. In *General Elec. Co.*[164] the employer made speeches on company time to massed employees, who were informed, however, that attendance was not mandatory. The union was denied equal

---

158 May Dep't Stores Co. v. NLRB, 316 F 2d 797, 53 LRRM 2172 (CA 6, 1963).
159 Montgomery Ward & Co., 145 NLRB 846, 55 LRRM 1063 (1964).
160 Montgomery Ward & Co. v. NLRB, 339 F 2d 889, 58 LRRM 2115 (CA 6, 1965).
161 156 NLRB 233, 61 LRRM 1025 (1965). *See* note 125 *supra.*
162 NLRB v. S. & H. Grossinger's, Inc., 372 F 2d 26, 64 LRRM 2295 (CA 2, 1967).
163 *Ibid. See also* NLRB v. H. W. Elson Bottling Co., 379 F 2d 223, 65 LRRM 2673 (CA 6, 1967).
164 156 NLRB 1247, 61 LRRM 1222 (1966).

time. In a petition to set aside the election, the union urged the Board to overrule *Livingston Shirt* and reactivate and extend *Bonwit-Teller* as a substantive rule of preelection conduct. The Board declined, preferring to postpone any reconsideration of current board doctrine in the area of plant access until after it had the benefit of experience with the rule adopted in *Excelsior Underwear, Inc.*[165] *Excelsior* holds that parties to a pending election may have access to a list of the names and addresses of all employees eligible to vote.

The Board has shown concern over a practice of incumbent unions and employers of providing for no-solicitation, no-distribution rules in collective agreements which prohibit solicitation by outside unions. It has found such contractually promulgated rules to be invalid insofar as they place restrictions upon nonworking areas and nonworking time.[166] The Sixth and Seventh Circuits rejected this position on the ground that the provisions were the fruits of free collective bargaining and not unilaterally imposed.[167] However, the Board stuck to its guns and has since been supported by the District of Columbia, Fifth, and Eighth Circuits.[168]

B. Prohibited Conduct

A wide assortment of traditional and imaginative techniques have been employed either to frustrate or to further union organizational efforts. Usually these have been utilized during election campaigns and have been evaluated by the Board in terms of election interference. In some instances, however, they have been employed at other stages of employer-employee relationships and have been evaluated in the broader context of interference with

---

[165] 156 NLRB 1236, 61 LRRM 1217 (1966). The *Excelsior* rule, though not the means of its promulgation, was approved by the Supreme Court in *NLRB* v. *Wyman-Gordon Co.*, 394 US 759, 70 LRRM 3345 (1969). *See* Chapters 8 and 30 *infra. See also* Bok, note 1 *supra.*
[166] Gale Prod. Div., 142 NLRB 1246, 53 LRRM 1242 (1963); Armco Steel Corp., 148 NLRB 1179, 57 LRRM 1132 (1964); General Motors Corp., 147 NLRB 509, 56 LRRM 1241 (1964).
[167] Armco Steel Corp. v. NLRB, 344 F 2d 621, 59 LRRM 2077 (CA 6, 1964), *setting aside* 148 NLRB 1179, 57 LRRM 1132 (1964); General Motors Corp. v. NLRB, 345 F 2d 516, 59 LRRM 2080 (CA 6, 1964), *setting aside* 147 NLRB 509, 56 LRRM 1241 (1964). NLRB v. Gale Prod. Div., 337 F 2d 390, 57 LRRM 2164 (CA 7, 1964).
[168] Steelworkers (Armco Steel Corp.) v. NLRB, 377 F 2d 140, 64 LRRM 2009 (CA DC. 1966); NLRB v. Mid-States Metal Prod., Inc., 403 F 2d 702, 69 LRRM 2656 (CA 5, 1968); Machinists, Dist. 9 v. NLRB (McDonnell Douglas Corp.), 415 F 2d 113, 72 LRRM 2206 (1969). *See also* General Motors Corp., 158 NLRB 1723, 62 LRRM 1210 (1966); H. & F. Binch Co., 168 NLRB No. 128, 67 LRRM 1129 (1967).

Section 7 rights. In the discussion that follows, the various techniques are considered in terms of their legality or illegality, regardless of setting.

1. Campaign Propaganda and Misrepresentation. The Board has long been reluctant to undertake the censorship of election propaganda,[169] explicitly stating that "exaggeration, inaccuracies, half-truths, and name calling, though not condoned, will not be grounds for setting aside an election."[170] In the Board's view, "absolute precision of statement and complete honesty are not always attainable in an election campaign, nor are they expected by the employees."[171] Consequently, the Board's preference has been to leave misstatements for the opposing parties to correct and for the employees to evaluate.[172] Nevertheless, this preference is limited by the need to "balance the right of employees to an untrammeled choice, and the right of the parties to wage a free and vigorous campaign with all the normal legitimate tools of electioneering."[173]

a. The Hollywood Ceramics *rule.* The formula for striking the desired balance had been phrased in many ways. Usually emphasized have been (1) the materiality of the misstatement, (2) the special knowledge of the speaker, (3) lack of opportunity for rebuttal, and (4) lack of independent knowledge on the part of employees as a basis for proper evaluation.[174] In *Hollywood Ceramics*[175] the Board preserved these criteria[176] while restating the rule as follows:

> [A]n election should be set aside only where there has been a misrepresentation or other similar campaign trickery, which involves a substantial departure from the truth, at a time which prevents the other party or parties from making an effective reply, so that the misrepresentation, whether deliberate or not, may reasonably be expected to have a significant impact on the election.[177]

---

[169] Cleveland Trencher Co., 130 NLRB 600, 603, 47 LRRM 1371 (1961); Merck & Co., 104 NLRB 891, 32 LRRM 1160 (1953); Gummed Prod. Co., 112 NLRB 1092, 36 LRRM 1156 (1955).
[170] Hollywood Ceramics Co., 140 NLRB 221, 224, n. 6, 51 LRRM 1600 (1962).
[171] *Id.* at 223.
[172] United States Gypsum Co., 130 NLRB 901, 904, 47 LRRM 1436 (1961).
[173] Hollywood Ceramics Co., 140 NLRB 221, 224, 51 LRRM 1600 (1962). *Cf.* Linn v. United Plant Guard Wkrs., Local 114, 383 US 53, 61 LRRM 2345 (1966), discussed in Chapter 29 *infra* at note 88.
[174] U.S. Gypsum Co., 130 NLRB 901, 47 LRRM 1436 (1961).
[175] 140 NLRB 221, 51 LRRM 1600 (1962).
[176] *Id.* at 224 n. 6-10.
[177] *Id.* at 224. The restatement made it clear that the misrepresentation need not be deliberate and expressly overruled any decisions to the contrary.

The phrasing of the rule is in the conjunctive so that even a substantial misrepresentation may not upset an election if it concerned an unimportant matter and had only a *de minimis* effect. Similarly, the misrepresentation may be "so extreme so as to put employees on notice of its lack of truth," or the employees themselves may have independent knowledge permitting them to evaluate the statements.[178]

If there is a fair opportunity for rebuttal, even at a late moment, an election will not be set aside.[179] But opportunity for rebuttal of a particular last-minute statement may not be controlling if the issue itself was injected in the campaign sufficiently in advance of the election to provide a basis for evaluation by the employees and exploration by the parties.[180]

b. Misleading Wage and Fringe-Benefit Data. Wages and fringe benefits prevailing, or contractually obtained, elsewhere in comparable companies may be presented in a way that is quite misleading yet literally true. An assertion just before an election that a contract elsewhere "provides for" a stated increase without disclosing that the increase has been spread over three years may be misleading but literally true, absent the representation that the increases are effective immediately.[181] Some assertions may be so misleading as to leave little or no room for literal truth or varied interpretations.[182] Since different estimates may be made as to the monetary value of fringe benefits contained in an "economic package," the Board has tolerated some "puffing."[183]

---

178 *Ibid.*

179 *Ibid.; see also* General Electric Co., 162 NLRB 912, 64 LRRM 1104 (1967).

180 Elmcrest Convalescent Hosp. Management Corp., 173 NLRB No. 7, 69 LRRM 1196 (1968). *Cf.* United States Gypsum, 130 NLRB 901, 47 LRRM 1436 (1961), where an election was set aside because the earlier interjection of the issue did not assume the dominant role as did the later telegram.

181 Russell-Newman Mfg. Co., 158 NLRB 1260, 62 LRRM 1195 (1966); *but see* S. S. Kresge Co., K-Mart Div., 173 NLRB No. 84, 69 LRRM 1382 (1968), *on remand from* Gallenkamp Stores Co., 402 F 2d 525, 69 LRRM 2024 (CA 9, 1968), *denying enforcement of* 162 NLRB No. 41, 64 LRRM 1045 (1966).

182 Grede Foundries, Inc., 153 NLRB 984, 59 LRRM 1552 (1965), where union handbills distributed the day before an election claimed that the "average" take-home pay under one of its contracts was $140 per week when, in fact, only two of the 350 employees received that "average."

183 Southern Foods, Inc., 171 NLRB No. 131, 68 LRRM 1230 (1968). In *Hollywood Ceramics* the Board stated that messages that are "inartistically or vaguely worded and subject to different interpretations will not suffice to . . . set the election aside." 140 NLRB 221, 224, 51 LRRM 1600 (1962).

The circuit courts have, in many instances, taken a more restrictive view of last-minute misstatements about wage rates and fringe benefits than has the Board.[184]

c. Special Knowledge of the Speaker. Special knowledge of the assertions made has occasionally been controlling. An employer's estimation as to the likelihood of a rise in union dues, based upon hearsay, will not invalidate an election.[185] The First Circuit's view of *Hollywood Ceramics* is that the test implied is not "whether the speaker in fact had special knowledge, but whether listeners would believe that he had." [186] This view was applied by the Board in a subsequent case where a union misquoted an employer's speech in such a manner as to represent the employer's position falsely as one of support for the union. In overturning the election the Board found that the union's message "lent itself to the belief that" the employer had confided privately to the union official "what he could not express publicly." [187]

Issues of misrepresentation and campaign trickery take many forms. The use of literature that conceals the true identity of the sponsor may be ground for setting aside an election.[188] Thus, employer issuance of anti-union materials over the signature of popular employees,[189] or distribution by one union of alleged reports from rival union organizers describing employees in insulting terms, is improper.[190] On the other hand, the use of pay stubs to dramatize an employer's union-dues argument is not necessarily improper. The validity of the technique will depend upon the accuracy of the deduction, the timing, the manner of distribution, and the accompanying description—*e.g.*, whether dues checkoff is represented as being mandatory.[191] The portrayal of unionization as inevitably giving rise to violence through such devices as the film "And Women Must Weep" has caused the Board to set aside

---

184 *See* NLRB v. Bonnie Enterprises, Inc., 341 F 2d 712, 58 LRRM 2395 (1965); NLRB v. Allis-Chalmers Mfg. Co., 261 F 2d 613, 43 LRRM 2246 (CA 7, 1958); *see also* 3 ALR 3rd 889 for a comprehensive collection of cases.
185 York Furniture Corp., 170 NLRB No. 169, 67 LRRM 1606 (1968).
186 NLRB v. A. G. Pollard Co., 393 F 2d 239, 67 LRRM 2997 (CA 1, 1968).
187 Cranbar Corp., 173 NLRB No. 200, 69 LRRM 1581 (1968).
188 Kelsey-Hayes Co., 126 NLRB 151, 45 LRRM 1290 (1960).
189 Timken-Detroit Axle Co., 98 NLRB 790, 792, 29 LRRM 1401 (1952), *petition to restrain enforcement dismissed*, 197 F 2d 512, 30 LRRM 2328 (CA 6, 1952).
190 Sylvania Electric Prods., Inc., 119 NLRB 824, 828, 41 LRRM 1188 (1954).
191 Fontaine Truck Equipment Co., Inc., 166 NLRB No. 50, 65 LRRM 1552 (1967); TRW, Inc., 173 NLRB No. 223, 70 LRRM 1017 (1968); Crown Laundry & Dry Cleaners, Inc., 160 NLRB 746, 63 LRRM 1035 (1966); Trane Co., 137 NLRB 1506, 50 LRRM 1434 (1962); Mosler Safe Co., 129 NLRB 747, 47 LRRM 1058 (1960).

an election. While misrepresentation as to the particular union may be involved, the grounds for objection to the film have usually been broader.[192]

2. Threats and Loss of Benefits. In contrast to a selling approach of propaganda and promises, election campaigns, and anti-union activity generally, have sometimes been marked by loss of benefits and threats, both express and implied. The discontinuance of benefits such as coffee breaks and discount privileges on employee purchases [193] is an example of objectionable reprisal. Exclusion of unionized employees from an employee stock plan has also been found to violate Section 8(a)(1).[194] Direct threats to close a plant [195] or to discharge union adherents,[196] as a method of combating an organizational drive, constitute interference. More troublesome are implied threats.

Certain campaign themes have become familiar in the election arena. Employers seeking to inform employees of unfavorable consequences of unionization may develop the themes in a number of written and oral messages. The trend of Board decisions has been to evaluate the messages, not in isolation from each other, but in their "total context." [197] Under this approach the tolerance for ambiguity is not as broad as it is for misrepresentations. If the overall effect of the messages is to create an atmosphere of fear by portraying the selection of a bargaining agent as "futile" and the "economic hazards" as "inevitable," a free choice

---

[192] Plochman & Harrison—Cherry Lane Foods, Inc., 140 NLRB 130, 51 LRRM 1558 (1962). *But see* Southwire Co. v. NLRB, 383 F 2d 235, 65 LRRM 3042 (CA 5, 1967), in which the Fifth Circuit reversed the holding of the Board that the showing of "And Women Must Weep" constituted an unfair labor practice under §8(a)(1), as distinguished from the Board's action in *Plochman & Harrison*, where only the election was set aside. The court in *Southwire* found the showing of the film protected by §8(c). *Accord*, NLRB v. Hawthorn Co., 404 F 2d 1205, 70 LRRM 2193 (CA 8, 1969).

[193] Davis Wholesale Co., 165 NLRB 271, 65 LRRM 1494 (1967); Buddy Schoellkopf Prods., Inc., 164 NLRB No. 82, 65 LRRM 1231 (1967).

[194] Bendix-Westinghouse Automatic Air Brake Co., 185 NLRB 29, 75 LRRM 1079 (1970). *But see* Goodyear Tire and Rubber Co. v. NLRB, 413 F 2d 158, 71 LRRM 2977 (CA 6, 1969).

[195] *Cf.* Textile Workers Union v. Darlington Mfg. Co., 380 US 263, 274, n. 20, 58 LRRM 2657 (1965), where the Court distinguished a termination of a business from the unjustifiable threat to do so. *See* Chapter 6 *infra*.

[196] NLRB v. Neuhoff Bros., Packers, 375 F 2d 372, 64 LRRM 2673 (CA 5, 1967), where a flagrant election campaign is discussed in lively fashion by Judge Brown.

[197] Arch Beverage Corp., 140 NLRB 1385, 52 LRRM 1251; *see* notes 77-83 *supra* and accompanying text; *see also* Kleeb, *Taft-Hartley Rules During Union Organizing Campaigns*, 55 LRRM 114, 117 (1964), *and* Bok, note 1 *supra*.

may be rendered impossible.[198] The conveyance of a "clear message" to employees "that it was futile for them to select [the union] as their bargaining representative for the purpose of improving their conditions of employment, and that selection . . . could only bring strikes, violence and loss of jobs" has caused the invalidation of an election.[199]

Reviewing the First Circuit's *Sinclair* decision, as part of the opinion in the *Gissel* case, the Supreme Court established the following guidelines to test preelection predictions:

[A]n employer is free to communicate to his employees any of his general views about unionism or any of his specific views about a particular union, so long as the communications do not contain a "threat of reprisal or force or promise of benefit." He may even make a prediction as to the precise effects he believes unionization will have on his company. In such a case, however, the prediction must be carefully phrased on the basis of objective fact to convey an employer's belief as to demonstrably probable consequences beyond his control or to convey a management decision already arrived at to close the plant in case of unionization. . . . If there is any implication that an employer may or may not take action solely on his own initiative for reasons unrelated to economic necessities and known only to him, the statement is no longer a reasonable prediction based on available facts but a threat of retaliation based on misrepresentation and coercion, and as such without the protection of the First Amendment. We therefore agree with the court below that "conveyance of the employer's belief, even though sincere, that unionization will or may result in the closing of the plant is not a statement of fact unless, which is most improbable, the eventuality of closing is capable of proof." . . . [A]n employer is free only to tell "what he reasonably believes will be the likely economic consequences of unionization that are outside his control," and not "threats of economic reprisal to be taken solely on his own volition."[200]

a. Futility. That it would be futile to select a bargaining agent has been conveyed by an explanation that the employer's wage policies would continue to be determined unilaterally, "union or no union."[201] A sense of futility was imparted in blunter terms where an employer indicated that it would abide by its present

---

[198] Oak Mfg. Co., 141 NLRB 1323, 52 LRRM 1502 (1963), Storkline Corp., 142 NLRB 875, 53 LRRM 1160 (1963).
[199] General Industries Electronics Co., 146 NLRB 1139, 1141, 56 LRRM 1015 (1964).
[200] NLRB v. Gissel Packing Co., 395 US 575, 618-619, 71 LRRM 2481. *See* note 107 *supra*. The Court cited Textile Workers v. Darlington Mfg. Co., 380 US 263, 274, n. 20, 58 LRRM 2657 (1965) and NLRB v. River Togs, Inc., 382 F 2d 198, 202, 65 LRRM 2987 (CA 2, 1967).
[201] Trane Co., 137 NLRB 1506, 50 LRRM 1434 (1962).

policies "even if Jesus Christ were representing" the employees.[202] But conveyance of a sense of futility may, perhaps, not be sufficient to set aside an election unless the employer has stated "either expressly, or by clear implication that it would not bargain in good faith with a union even if it were selected by the employees." [203] An employer's warning that "he could make negotiations last a year and therefore another election would be necessary" was ground for setting aside an election.[204] But not all promises of future litigation will be treated in the same manner, particularly if the surrounding circumstances are devoid of coercive conduct.[205]

b. *Inevitability.* Depicting strikes, violence, and loss of jobs as the inevitable consequence of unionization, has been ground for setting aside an election.[206] In *Storkline Corporation* [207] the employer's warning that economic injury would be likely to befall employees, intensified by the showing of the film "And Women Must Weep," was held to have created an "unreasoning fear" that impaired a free choice. However, stressing the likelihood of strikes is not necessarily improper if it is germane to the strike record and claims of job security of the union in issue, and is not simply raised as a "straw man" to create unwarranted fear.[208] Similarly, predictions of loss of customer patronage, resulting in loss of employment, may be treated differently, depending upon whether the loss is portrayed as an inevitable or a possible result.[209] Unions are also susceptible to having election victories invalidated where loss of employment has been stressed as a consequence of not supporting it,[210] or of voting for a rival union.[211]

---

202 Metropolitan Life Ins. Co., 53 LRRM 1187 (1963).
203 American Greetings Corp., 146 NLRB 1440, 1445, n. 4, 56 LRRM 1064 (1964). *See also* Dal-Tex Optical Co., 137 NLRB 1782, 1783, 50 LRRM 1489 (1962), in which the Board held persuasive the employer's statement that the election process "would not mean a thing if the union wins" because the employer would take a "couple of years" to litigate it.
204 Wall Colmonoy Corp., 173 NLRB No. 8, 69 LRRM 1205 (1968).
205 W. T. Grant Co., 147 NLRB 420, 56 LRRM 1231 (1964).
206 Storkline Corp., 142 NLRB 875, 53 LRRM 1160 (1963).
207 *Ibid. Cf.* note 192 *supra.*
208 American Greetings Corp., 146 NLRB 1440, 56 LRRM 1064 (1964); Coors Porcelain Co., 158 NLRB 1108 (1966); Universal Elec. Co., 156 NLRB 1101, 61 LRRM 1189 (1966).
209 *Compare* Haynes Stellite Co., 136 NLRB 95, 49 LRRM 1711 (1962), *enforcement denied sub nom.*, Union Carbide Corp. v. NLRB 310 F 2d 844, 52 LRRM 2001 (CA 6, 1962) and R. D. Cole Mfg. Co., 133 NLRB 1455, 49 LRRM 1033 (1961), *with* Freeman Mfg. Co., 148 NLRB 577, 57 LRRM 1047 (1964).
210 Aire Flo Corp., 167 NLRB No. 145, 66 LRRM 1214 (1967).
211 Vicker's Inc., 152 NLRB 793, 59 LRRM 1196 (1965).

c. Assessing Campaign Phrases. The Board's attempt to assess employer statements in the context of its pattern of conduct is illustrated in its treatment of recurrent phrases used in election campaigns—"bargaining from scratch," for example. The implication might be that existing benefits may be diminished or discontinued if the employer is forced to negotiate with the union.[212] On the other hand, the phrase might simply be a reminder that the selection of a union will not automatically produce any increases.[213] Whether or not the phrase is legally objectionable will depend upon the reading of the statement as a whole and "evidence of accompanying unfair labor practices which might reasonably color an employee's view of the statement." [214]

Assessments are difficult, and unanimity not always attainable, as the Board has conceded in a divided opinion:

> Realizing full well that in all cases such as this one, where one must attempt to fathom the meaning of another's words and assess the impress of such words on employees, reasonable men may differ, we differ with our colleague.[215]

3. Promise or Grant of Benefits. Organizational campaigns have been waged with promises of benefits as well as threats. But "interference is no less interference because it is accomplished through allurement rather than coercion." [216] The promise or grant of benefits to stifle, or in some circumstances to further, an organizational campaign may be unlawful interference even though no strings are explicitly attached. The infringement may stem from the timing and the impact. Said the Supreme Court:

> The danger inherent in well-timed increases and benefits is the suggestion of a fist inside a velvet glove. The employees are not likely to miss the inference that the source of benefits now conferred is also the source from which future benefits must flow and which may dry up if it is not obliged.[217]

The fact that the benefits are not conditioned upon voting against the union is not controlling if the purpose is that of "impinging

---

212 Cargill, Inc., Nutrena Mills Div., 172 NLRB No. 24, 69 LRRM 1293 (1968).
213 Wagner Industrial Prods. Co., 170 NLRB No. 157, 67 LRRM 1581 (1968).
214 *Ibid.* Compare Trent Tube Co., 147 NLRB 538, 56 LRRM 1251 (1964), *with* Marsh Supermarkets, Inc., 140 NLRB 899, 52 LRRM 1134 (1963), *enforced,* 327 F 2d 109, 55 LRRM 2017 (CA 7, 1963), *and* Astronautics Corp., 164 NLRB 623, n. 2, 65 LRRM 1161 (1967).
215 Allied/Egry Business Systems, Inc., 169 NLRB No. 60, 67 LRRM 1195 (1968).
216 NLRB v. Crown Can Co., 138 F 2d 263, 267, 13 LRRM 568 (CA 8, 1943), *citing* Western Cartridge Co. v. NLRB, 134 F 2d 240, 244, 12 LRRM 541 (1943).
217 NLRB v. Exchange Parts Co., 375 US 405, 409, 55 LRRM 2098 (1964). For a critique of this analysis, see Bok, *supra* note 1, at 113.

upon . . . freedom of choice for or against unionization, and is reasonably calculated to have that effect." [218]

a. Employer Inducements. Not every promise or grant of benefit subsequent to the advent of a union campaign will result in setting aside an election. The Board does not insist that all "existing terms of employment . . . remain static until a union campaign, no matter how extended in duration, comes to an end." [219] Mechanical or *per se* approaches have not been favored by the Board,[220] so if a valid reason unrelated to union activity can be established for a change in benefits, no interference will be found.[221] However, the burden of rebutting the unfavorable inference is upon the employer.[222]

In some cases the result is predictable. An offer of money accompanied by an urging to vote a particular way will be considered interference.[223] A bribe to work against the union will have the same result.[224] In cases not so clearly drawn, the Board has condemned increases where they (1) were given in the context of repeated references to the union; [225] (2) were made effective just before an election; [226] (3) conformed to an earlier union campaign promise; [227] and (4) were announced before an election when they could reasonably have been delayed until afterward.[228]

Making effective improvements decided upon prior to the advent of a union may present a dilemma for an employer, since failure to proceed may appear to be a reprisal. A factor that will weigh heavily with the Board is whether the employer had previously told the employees of its decision to make the improve-

---

[218] 375 US at 409. In an early case, the Supreme Court said: "There could be no more obvious way of interfering with these rights of employees than by grants of wage increases upon the understanding that they would leave the union in return. The action of employees with respect to the choice of their bargaining agents may be induced by favors bestowed by the employer as well as by his threats or domination." Medo Photo Supply Corp. v. NLRB, 321 US 678, 686, 14 LRRM 581 (1944).

[219] Drug Fair-Community Drug Co., 162 NLRB No. 72, 64 LRRM 1079 (1967).

[220] Champion Pneumatic Mach. Co., 152 NLRB 300, 306, 59 LRRM 1089 (1965); International Shoe Co., 123 NLRB 682, 43 LRRM 1520 (1959).

[221] *Ibid.*

[222] International Shoe Co., *supra* note 220.

[223] Coca Cola Bottling Co., 132 NLRB 481, 48 LRRM 1370 (1961).

[224] Heck's Inc., 166 NLRB No. 38, 65 LRRM 1639 (1967).

[225] Allegheny Mining Corp., 167 NLRB No. 15, 65 LRRM 1751 (1967).

[226] NLRB v. Exchange Parts Co., 375 US 405, 55 LRRM 2098 (1964).

[227] Seneca Plastics, Inc., 149 NLRB 320, 57 LRRM 1314 (1964).

[228] International Shoe, 123 NLRB 682, 43 LRRM 1520 (1959).

ments.[229] Promising a benefit only for the purpose of withholding its actual grant, assertedly to avoid the commission of an unfair labor practice, has been characterized as the "carrot on the stick" and held to be interference.[230]

b. Union Inducements. Union promises have customarily been considered part of the give-and-take of campaign propaganda and not legally objectionable.[231] However, the promise of life insurance coverage to prospective voters has been considered comparable to an employer's grant of a wage increase in anticipation of an election and therefore ground for setting aside an election. Such a gift is different from a waiver of initiation fees because it results in the "enhancement of the employees' economic position" and not "merely an avoidance of possible future liability." [232]

Preelection promises by a union to waive initiation fees have troubled the Board and the courts. For many years the Board has regarded an offer to waive initiation fees as a legitimate recruiting and campaign technique.[233] But in its 1954 *Lobue* [234] decision the Board held that the offer of free membership after election and certification was improper because it was contingent upon the outcome of the election. In no subsequent published decision during the ensuing 13 years did the Board apply the *Lobue* rule to invalidate an election.[235] Finally, in its 1967 *DIT-MCO* decision,[236] the Board overruled *Lobue* and returned to its former position that a waiver of fees does not justify setting aside an election even if contingent upon the outcome of the election.

The circuit courts have, in other contexts, treated the waiver of initiation fees differently. In *NLRB* v. *Gilmore Industries, Inc.,*[237] the Sixth Circuit disagreed with the Board and held that the "economic inducement . . . was material and impeded a

---

[229] *Cf.* Crown Tar & Chem. Works, Inc. v. NLRB, 365 F 2d 588, 63 LRRM 2067 (CA 10, 1966). *See also* Louisiana Plastics, Inc. 173 NLRB No. 218, 70 LRRM 1019 (1968). In *Exchange Parts,* note 226 *supra,* the employer vainly asserted that the "policy" behind the announcement of benefits had been established earlier.

[230] Goodyear Tire & Rubber Co., 170 NLRB No. 79, 67 LRRM 1555 (1968); Cadillac Overall Supply Co., 148 NLRB 1133, 1136, 57 LRRM 1136 (1964); Interstate Smelting & Ref. Co., 148 NLRB 219, 221, 56 LRRM 1489 (1964).

[231] Shirlington Supermarket, Inc., 106 NLRB 666, 32 LRRM 1519 (1953).

[232] Wagner Electric Corp., 167 NLRB 532, 66 LRRM 1073 (1967); *but see* Primco Casting Corp., 174 NLRB No. 44, 70 LRRM 1128 (1969).

[233] *See* DIT-MCO, Inc., 163 NLRB 1019, 64 LRRM 1476 (1967).

[234] Lobue Bros., 109 NLRB 1182, 34 LRRM 1528 (1954).

[235] DIT-MCO, Inc., *supra* note 233.

[236] *Ibid.*

[237] 341 F 2d 240, 242, 58 LRRM 2419 (CA 6, 1965).

reasoned choice." However, an issue of misrepresentation was also present in the case. In waiving the initiation fee the union did nothing to debunk a widespread rumor that the fee was $300.00 when in fact it was only a $6.00 fee that was being waived.

The First Circuit has also regarded the waiver of an initiation fee as possibly interfering with free choice.[238] Again, an issue of misrepresentation was also present, *i.e.*, there was an ostensible waiver of an alleged "regular initiation fee" whereas in fact there was "in no real sense a regular initiation fee" to pay.

In a different context, the Second Circuit has upheld the validity of authorization cards challenged on the ground that they were secured by the offer to waive initiation fees.[239]

4. Interrogation and Polling. With the advent of a union campaign, employers may be tempted to learn about the campaign by questioning individual employees.[240] Interrogation as to union sympathy and affiliation has been held violative "because of its natural tendency to instill in the minds of employees fear of discrimination on the basis of the information the employer has obtained." [241] Employers "cannot discriminate against union adherents without first ascertaining who they are." [242] Questioning employees as to their union sympathies is not looked on as an expression of views or opinion within the meaning of Section 8(c) because the "purpose of an inquiry is not to express views but to ascertain those of the person questioned." [243]

Originally the Board viewed all interrogation by an employer as unlawful per se.[244] In response to judicial disapproval, the *per se*

---

238 NLRB v. Gorbea, Perez & Morrell, 328 F 2d 679, 55 LRRM 2586 (CA 1, 1964).
239 Amalgamated Clothing Workers v. NLRB, 345 F 2d 264, 59 LRRM 2228 (CA 2, 1965).
240 *See* Kleeb, *Taft-Hartley Rules During Union Organizing Campaigns,* 55 LRRM 114, 115 (1964), where an employer's temptation has been pictured as follows:

"When an employer learns that an organizational campaign is going on among his employees, human nature being what it is, he's just bursting with curiosity to know whether any of his employees have joined, if there have been union meetings, who has attended them, and what was said? How better can he find out than to ask his employees? There would be no problem for the employer or the Board if it could be established that such interrogation was purely motivated. Unfortunately for this point of view, experience has shown that in many cases such questioning is followed by reprisals against union adherents."

241 NLRB v. West Coast Gasket Co., 205 F 2d 902, 904, 32 LRRM 2353 (CA 9, 1953).
242 Cannon Elec. Co., 151 NLRB 1465, 58 LRRM 1629 (1965).
243 Struksnes Const. Co., 165 NLRB 1062, 65 LRRM 1385 (1967); NLRB v. Lorben Corp., 345 F 2d 346, 59 LRRM 2184 (CA 2, 1965).
244 Standard-Coosa-Thatcher Co., 85 NLRB 1358, 24 LRRM 1575 (1949).

test was abandoned and a more permissive test formulated.[245] In 1954, the Board held in *Blue Flash* [246] that it would find interrogation unlawful only when it was coercive in the light of surrounding circumstances, adding that "the time, place, personnel involved, information sought, and . . . the employer's known preference must be considered." [247]

a. Polling. Blue Flash involved the validity of a poll conducted by the employer to determine the extent of the employees' support for the union. The Board found the poll to be lawful on the basis of its application of these guides: (1) the employer's sole purpose was to ascertain whether the union demanding recognition actually represented a majority of the employees, (2) the employees were so informed, (3) assurances against reprisal were given, and (4) the questioning occurred in a background free from employer hostility to union organization.[248]

In applying the *Blue Flash* rule the Board encountered reversals because of disagreement by the circuit courts as to the proper weight to be given the circumstances surrounding the interrogation.[249] The Second Circuit, for example, held that interrogation which is not threatening in itself will not be an unfair labor practice unless it "meets certain fairly severe standards." [250] In setting aside the Board finding of unlawful polling,[251] the Second Circuit based its holding on five criteria: background of employer hostility, the identity of the interrogator, *i.e.*, how high he is in the employer hierarchy, the place of the interrogation, the method used, and the truthfulness of the employee's response.

The result of the use of differing criteria by the circuits and the Board in applying the *Blue Flash* rule was "considerable uncertainty in this area of labor-management relations." [252] Moreover, the Board finally concluded that the rule did not operate to discourage intimidation of employees by employer polls.[253] Pursuant to a suggestion upon remand by the District of Columbia

---

245 Struksnes Const. Co., *supra* note 243. *See* discussion in NLRB v. Lorben Corp., 345 F 2d 346, 59 LRRM 2184 (CA 2, 1965).

246 Blue Flash Express, Inc., 109 NLRB 591, 34 LRRM 1384 (1954).

247 Struksnes Const. Co., *supra* note 243.

248 *Ibid.*

249 *Id.* at n. 10.

250 Bourne v. NLRB, 332 F 2d 47, 56 LRRM 2241 (CA 2, 1964).

251 Bourne Co., 144 NLRB 805, 54 LRRM 1158 (1963).

252 Struksnes Const. Co., *supra* note 243.

253 *Ibid.*

Circuit that it "come to grips with this constantly recurring problem," [254] the Board ultimately revised the *Blue Flash* criteria in *Struksnes Construction Co., Inc.*[255]

> Absent unusual circumstances, the polling of employees by an employer will be violative of Section 8(a)(1) of the Act unless the following safeguards are observed: (1) the purpose of the poll is to determine the truth of a union's claim of majority, (2) this purpose is communicated to the employees, (3) assurances against reprisal are given, (4) the employees are polled by secret ballot, and (5) the employer has not engaged in unfair labor practices or otherwise created a coercive atmosphere.

The new element in the revision is the requirement that polls be conducted by secret ballot. The Board cautioned against the use of polls while a petition for a Board election is pending because it would not "serve any legitimate interest of the employer that would not be better served by the forthcoming Board election." [256] In *Struksnes* no specific ground rules were prescribed for actually conducting the secret ballot.[257]

    b. Individual or Isolated Questioning. The *Struksnes* case is concerned specifically with systematic polling.[258] The criteria to be applied in determining the validity of interrogation by means other than polling are not altogether clear.[259] Where interrogation is sufficiently isolated, an election will not be set aside,[260] nor will a remedial order issue in an unfair labor practice case.[261] Generally, the Board seems to use the approach it adopted in *Blue Flash* of evaluating interrogation in the light of all the surrounding circumstances, including the time, place, personnel involved, and known position of the employer.[262] Where the employer seeks

---

254 Operating Engineers Local 49 v. NLRB, 353 F 2d 852, 856, 60 LRRM 2353 (CA DC, 1965).
255 Struksnes Const. Co., *supra* note 243. 165 NLRB at 1063. *See also* Tom Woods Pontiac, Inc., 179 NLRB No. 98, 72 LRRM 1494 (1969); Wm. Walters, Inc., a/k/a Computronics, Inc., 179 NLRB No. 123, 72 LRRM 1504 (1969).
256 *Ibid. See also* Leonard Fontana, 169 NLRB No. 56, 67 LRRM 1210 (1968).
257 *See* Oleson's Food Stores, 167 NLRB 543, 66 LRRM 1108 (1967), where the ballots were privately counted by the employer in the absence of any observers.
258 *See* R.M.E., Inc., 171 NLRB No. 32, n. 1, 68 LRRM 1459 (1968).
259 *See* Bok, *supra* note 1, at 107, and *compare* West Texas Equip. Co., 142 NLRB 1358, 53 LRRM 1249 (1963), *with* Zayre Corp., 154 NLRB 1372, 60 LRRM 1222 (1965), where the examiner noted that tests applicable to systematic polling do not necessarily apply to other types of interrogation, but considered the Second Circuit's test as an outer limit in finding a violation. *See also* Charlotte Union Bus Station, Inc., 135 NLRB 228, 49 LRRM 1461 (1962); Gruber's Food Center, Inc., 159 NLRB 629, 62 LRRM 1271 (1966).
260 West Texas Equipment Co., *supra* note 259.
261 Dieckbroder Express, Inc., 168 NLRB No. 113, 67 LRRM 1081 (1967).
262 *See* Bok, *supra* note 1, at 107; Gruber's Food Center, Inc., *supra* note 259.

to force an employee to disclose his union sentiments [263] without communicating a valid purpose and an assurance against reprisal, questioning will normally be held coercive. Questioning which places an employee in the position of acting as an informer regarding the union activities of his fellow employees will likewise be unlawful.[264] On the other hand, where the inquiry is innocuous,[265] or is part of a normal response to a conversation initiated by an employee, it will not rise to the level of coercion.[266]

c. Interviewing. Conducting individual interviews with employees in the employer's office, or at the employees' homes, may be ground for setting aside an election.[267] The Board seeks to prevent interviewing at places that may be construed as the "locus" of managerial authority.[268] Thus, individual interviews conducted in a storeroom in which the manager's desk is located may upset an election.[269] It is not necessary to the setting aside of an election that a majority of the employees be interviewed, particularly where there exists a strong likelihood that other employees will learn of the questioning.[270]

d. Preparation of Defense for Trial of Unfair Labor Practice Case. Despite the "inherent danger of coercion," [271] an employer may exercise a limited privilege of interrogating employees in the "investigation of facts concerning issues raised in a complaint," [272] where this is necessary to the preparation of his defense for the pending trial.[273] To minimize the coercive impact and to strike

---

[263] Charlotte Union Bus Station, Inc., *supra* note 259.
[264] Abex Corp., 162 NLRB 328, 64 LRRM 1004 (1966).
[265] Sandy's Stores, Inc., 163 NLRB 728, 65 LRRM 1034 (1967), *enforcement denied on other grounds,* 398 F 2d 268, 68 LRRM 2800 (CA 1, 1968).
[266] Phillips-Van Heusen Corp., 165 NLRB 1, 65 LRRM 1355 (1967). For extensive discussion of the factual setting in which interrogations are evaluated, see the trial examiner's decision in Campbell Soup Co., 170 NLRB No. 167, 68 LRRM 1036 (1968).
[267] Peoria Plastic Co., 117 NLRB 545, 39 LRRM 1281 (1957); The Hurley Co., 130 NLRB 282, 47 LRRM 1293 (1961).
[268] Peoples Drug Stores, Inc., 119 NLRB 634, 41 LRRM 1141 (1957).
[269] National Caterers, Inc., 125 NLRB 110, 45 LRRM 1070 (1959).
[270] The Great Atl. & Pac. Tea Co., 140 NLRB 133, 51 LRRM 1570 (1962).
[271] Johnnie's Poultry Co., 146 NLRB 770, 774, 55 LRRM 1403 (1964), *enforcement denied,* 344 F 2d 617, 59 LRRM 2117 (CA 8, 1965).
[272] *Ibid.*
[273] *Ibid.* The Eighth Circuit's denial of enforcement did not express disagreement with the standards but held that the factual determinations were "not supported by substantial evidence." 344 F 2d at 619. The Board's standards and application were upheld in other circuits. *See* UAW v. NLRB, 392 F 2d 801, 66 LRRM 2548 (CA DC, 1967); NLRB v. Neuhoff Bros. Packers, 375 F 2d 372, 64 LRRM 2673 (CA 5, 1968); Montgomery Ward & Co. v. NLRB, 377 F 2d 452, 65 LRRM 2285 (CA 6, 1967).

a balance between conflicting interests, a number of safeguards have been established by the Board. These are as follows:

(1) The purpose of the questioning must be communicated to the employee.

(2) An assurance of no reprisal must be given.

(3) The employee's participation must be obtained on a voluntary basis.

(4) The questioning must take place in an atmosphere free from anti-union animus.

(5) The questioning itself must not be coercive in nature.

(6) The questions must be relevant to the issues involved in the complaint.

(7) The employee's subjective state of mind must not be probed.

(8) The questions must not "otherwise interfere with the statutory rights of employees." [274]

5. Surveillance. Since the earliest days of the Act, surveillance of employees by an employer, whether with supervisors, rank-and-file employees, or outsiders, has consistently been held to violate Section 8(a)(1).[275] The Board has successfully maintained that surveillance violates 8(a)(1) regardless of whether the employees know of the surveillance.[276] The law is equally clear that the employer violates Section 8(a)(1) of the Act if he creates the impression among employees that he is engaged in surveillance,[277] for by highlighting his "anxiety" concerning union activities the employer tends to inhibit an employee's future union activities.[278] Moreover, the Board has found an 8(a)(1) violation for surveillance

---

[274] Johnnie's Poultry Co., *supra* note 271.

[275] Consolidated Edison Co. v. NLRB, 305 US 197, 3 LRRM 646 (1938). In *Elder-Beerman Stores Corp.* v. *NLRB*, 415 F 2d 1375, 72 LRRM 2510 (CA 6, 1969), an employer violated §8(a)(1) by instructing a supervisor to engage in surveillance of employees' union activity and by discharging him for failure to comply. The conduct was deemed unlawful regardless of whether the employees had knowledge of the instruction or the reason for the discharge.

[276] NLRB v. Grower-Shipper Vegetable Ass'n, 122 F 2d 368, 8 LRRM 891 (CA 9, 1941); Bethlehem Steel Co. v. NLRB, 120 F 2d 641, 8 LRRM 962 (CA DC, 1941).

[277] Because of the unusually broad, and perhaps vague, conduct forbidden by a cease-and-desist order directed against creating the "impression" of surveillance, the First Circuit added a limitation to the order. It enforced an order which it interpreted as meaning "willful conduct and a justifiable impression." NLRB v. Simplex Time Recorder Co., 401 F 2d 547, 69 LRRM 2465 (CA 1, 1968). *See also* NLRB v. Rybold Heater Co. 408 F 2d 888, 70 LRRM 3159 (CA 6, 1969).

[278] Hendrix Mfg. Co. v. NLRB, 321 F 2d 100, 53 LRRM 2831 (CA 5, 1963); NLRB v. Prince Macaroni Mfg. Co., 329 F 2d 803, 55 LRRM 2852 (CA 1, 1964).

of union activities by supervisors who were motivated solely by
their own curiosity and who were subsequently forbidden by the
employer to continue such surveillance.[279] Similarly, an employer
violates the Act if he encourages employees to engage in surveillance of union activities.[280]

6. Third-Party Conduct. In several cases outsiders such as townspeople of the community in which the plant was located have
joined in the campaign against the union, on the premise that
unionization would cause the plant to shut down or move. This
has presented special problems where the employer did not agree
with, participate in, condone, or otherwise support the campaign.
In fact, the employer might have been unable to prevent it. Nonetheless, in a representation case the right to a free and untrammeled
choice of bargaining representative is not diminished by the fact
that the campaign against the union is conducted by, or in the
name of, townspeople rather than the employer.[281] The reaction
of the employer to the third-party campaign may be determinative.
Adequate disavowal of objectionable community campaigning
may dissipate the impact of the objectionable features and obviate
the need to set the election aside.[282]

In *Falmouth Co.*,[283] a citizens group actively campaigned to defeat the union, emphasizing and utilizing rumors of plant closure.[284] The employer disclaimed the rumors, but the Board
held the disclaimer to be insufficient and ordered a new election,
despite its failure to find the employer at fault in the preelection
campaign. In *Utica-Herband Tool Division* [285] the employer took
positive advantage of objectionable campaigning against union-

---

279 Intertype Co. v. NLRB, 371 F 2d 787, 64 LRRM 2257 (CA 4, 1967).
280 Saginaw Furniture Shops, Inc. v. NLRB, 343 F 2d 515, 58 LRRM 2417 CA 7,
1965); NLRB v. Saxe-Glassman Shoe Corp., 201 F 2d 238, 31 LRRM 2271 (CA 1,
1953).
281 P. D. Gwaltney Jr. & Co., 74 NLRB 371, 379, 20 LRRM 1172 (1947); Universal
Mfg. Corp., 156 NLRB 1459, 61 LRRM 1258 (1966). *See also* NLRB v. General
Metal Products Co., 410 F 2d 473, 70 LRRM 3327 (CA 6, 1969), *cert. denied,* 396
US 830, 72 LRRM 2432 (1969).
282 Falmouth Co., 114 NLRB 896, 37 LRRM 1057 (1955); Utica-Herband Tool
Div., 145 NLRB 1717, 55 LRRM 1223 (1964); Claymore Mfg. Co., 146 NLRB 1400,
56 LRRM 1080 (1964); Electra Mfg. Co., 148 NLRB 494, 57 LRRM 1054 (1964).
283 *Supra* note 282.
284 *See* General Metal Prods. Co., 164 NLRB 64, 65 LRRM 1002 (1967). *But see*
Raytheon Co., 179 NLRB No. 116, 72 LRRM 1454 (1969), where the Board found
no violation when the employer remained silent following a radio news broadcast
quoting "informed sources "as predicting the closing of the plant if the union won
the election.
285 *Supra* note 282.

ization, and the Board set aside the election. However, in *Claymore Manufacturing Co.*[286] an unequivocal disclaimer by the employer was sufficient to forestall remedial action by the Board. At the union's request the employer issued a letter to employees disavowing rumors created by the community campaign and stating it would continue operations whatever the result of the election.

Where the employer is charged with an unfair labor practice, rather than with objectionable preelection conduct only, considerations of agency are more significant. An election may be set aside without a showing of fault by a party,[287] but coercive conduct must be attributable to an employer before an unfair labor practice will be found.[288]

7. Violence. Although no longer a common subject of litigation, the Board is still confronted with the need to discourage violence and to mitigate its effects. Its decisions have gone beyond the prohibition of direct threats against employees.[289] It will set aside an election where there is an "atmosphere" of violence or threats of violence, since this may impair a free choice by employees. It is not "material that fear and disorder may have been created by individual employees or nonemployees and that their conduct cannot probatively be attributed either to the Employer or to the Union. The significant fact is that such conditions existed and that a free election was thereby rendered impossible." [290] Under this policy parties may have an incentive not only to refrain from violence but to discourage others from engaging in it.

The Board has also sought to discourage violence by withholding an otherwise meritorious bargaining order from an offending union.[291] The fact that a union's violence is directed at the em-

---

286 *Supra* note 282.
287 Al Long, Inc., 173 NLRB No. 76, 69 LRRM 1366 (1968) ; *see* Section I.F.2 *supra.*
288 Dean Industries, Inc., 162 NLRB No. 106, 64 LRRM 1193 (1967).
289 *E.g.,* Casino Operations, Inc., 169 NLRB No. 43, 67 LRRM 1177 (1968); Vera Ladies Belt & Novelty Corp., 156 NLRB 291, 61 LRRM 1066 (1965), involving picket-line violence. *See also* Steelworkers Local 586 (Inspiration Consol. Copper Co.,) 174 NLRB No. 34, 70 LRRM 1123 (1968) ; Mine Wkrs. (Weirton Construction Co.) , 174 NLRB No. 52 (1968) ; Teamsters Local 563 (Fox Valley Material Suppliers Assn.) , 176 NLRB No. 51, 71 LRRM 1231 (1969).
290 Al Long, Inc., *supra* note 287, involving anonymous telephone calls threatening bodily injury, rifle shots by unknown persons, bomb threats, and massed and unruly picketing. *See also* cases involving the showing of the film "And Women Must Weep," *supra* note 192, particularly insofar as it affects "laboratory conditions" as opposed to §8(a) (1) cases. As to the agency issue *see* Gabriel Co., 137 NLRB 1252, 50 LRRM 1369 (1962).
291 Laura Modes Co., 144 NLRB 1592, 54 LRRM 1299 (1963).

ployer and not the employees does not immunize it from illegality, since the violence has a coercive impact upon the employees.[292]

Employer violence also need not be aimed directly at employees to be unlawful. Physical assaults upon union organizers and condonation of assaults by employees through failure to discipline have been held unlawful.[293]

8. Racial Prejudice. The injection of racial prejudice into a preelection campaign will not necessarily be ground for setting aside an election where the subject is germane to the issues. Employees are free to allow their prejudices to affect their choice in union representation matters. But where pure racial prejudice, or fear inspired by racial conflict, is made the dominant theme of a campaign so as to reduce the election to a vote on race questions rather than on collective bargaining questions, this is ground for setting aside the election.[294]

The rules for determining whether an election should be set aside on this ground were enunciated in *Sewell Mfg. Co.*[295] The Board invalidated an election in two Georgia plants where the anti-union campaign was based on appeals to prejudice by excessive publicizing of an AFL-CIO donation of money to the Committee on Racial Equality to be used to support freedom-ride projects in Alabama and Mississippi. The publicizing included photographs of a white AFL-CIO official dancing with a Negro woman, which were not germane to the election.

In setting aside the election in *Sewell*, the Board announced its test for application to future cases: When a party injects racial subjects into an election, it must limit comment to truthful statements of the other party's position on racial matters and must not seek to overstress or exacerbate racial feelings by irrelevant and inflammatory appeals; the party who brings racial statements into the campaign has the burden of establishing that they were both truthful and germane to the election issues.[296]

---

[292] Retail, Wholesale & Dep't Store Union (I. Posner, Inc.), 133 NLRB 1555, 49 LRRM 1066 (1961).
[293] Browning Indus., 142 NLRB 1397, 53 LRRM 1266 (1963); Lipman Bros., 147 NLRB 1342, 56 LRRM 1420 (1964).
[294] For a thorough review of the race issue in election campaigns, see Pollit, *The National Labor Relations Board and Race Hate Propaganda in Union Organization Drives*, 17 STAN. L. REV. 373 (1965); *see also* Sovern, *The National Labor Relations Act and Racial Discrimination*, 62 COLUM. L. REV. 563 (1962).
[295] 138 NLRB 66, 50 LRRM 1532 (1962).
[296] *Ibid.*

This burden was successfully sustained in *Allen Morrison Sign Co.*[297] An employer wrote a truthful letter that dealt in part with race relations. The letter said that the international union seeking to represent employees had given financial, moral, and official backing to desegregation activities and that one local had been placed in trusteeship when its members voted to purchase bonds to finance segregated white schools in an attempt to combat public-school integregation. The employer did not have the support of widespread community campaigning in this matter, as he did in others, and the letter was not the sole or central theme of the employer's campaign. It presented factual argument which the employees could consider in the light of their racial prejudices instead of substituting appeals to racial prejudice for factual argument, as in *Sewell Mfg. Co.* The union's loss of the election was certified.[298]

In *P. D. Gwaltney, Jr. and Co., Inc.*[299] where 80 percent of the employees were Negroes, the employer, the local press, the sheriff, and other public officials made known their anti-union sympathies. The threat of Ku Klux Klan reactivation in the event of a union victory was prominently proclaimed; two black union members who had come to the city to speak at a union meeting were frightened away before the meeting began; and the sheriff and the chief of police stationed themselves at the polling place throughout the elections. "[I]n the experienced judgment of the Board" the freedom of choice guaranteed by the Act was made impossible.[300]

The Board, however, refused to set aside an election where the union and a ministerial alliance based a campaign on a racial appeal. The Board found that the literature used was not designed to inflame racial hatred but, rather, to encourage racial pride and concerted efforts for betterment. Moreover, the Board held that the racial question was germane to the key issue of the campaign—

---

[297] Allen-Morrison Sign Co., 138 NLRB 73, 50 LRRM 1535 (1962); *see also* Archer Laundry Co., 150 NLRB 1427, 58 LRRM 1212 (1965); Aristocrat Linen Supply Co., 150 NLRB 1448, 58 LRRM 1216 (1965).

[298] The result of the two cases may be that the Board "labored mightily in the *Sewell* and *Allen-Morrison* decisions only to bring forth a mouse." Pollit, *supra* note 294, at 400.

[299] 74 NLRB 371, 20 LRRM 1172 (1947).

[300] *Id.* at 373.

the advantages and disadvantages of the union.[301] Similarly, in *Baltimore Luggage Co.*[302] the Board upheld an election where the union had made racial appeals to black employees, holding that such appeals were for the purpose of inducing collective action by the disadvantaged and not for the purpose of inflaming racial prejudice. The Fourth Circuit, however, seemingly disagrees. In *NLRB* v. *Schapiro & Whitehouse, Inc.*[303] the court set aside an election where the union had made racial appeals to Negro employees.

9. Interference With Board's Election Process. Unlike the noncensoring view taken of normal campaign propaganda, the Board looks with disfavor "upon any attempt to misuse its processes to secure partisan advantage."[304] Reproduction of ballots and other Board documents by the parties, and electioneering while balloting is in process, exemplify such misuse.[305]

a. Reproduction of ballots and other Board documents. The distribution of a facsimile of an official ballot marked in a way that suggests "either directly or indirectly to the voters" that the Board "endorses a particular choice" will result in the setting aside of the election if it is the successful party that used this technique.[306] This rule is "not limited to exact reproductions, but is aimed at the reproduction of documents 'purporting' to be a copy of the Board's ballot." [307] Nor is the stricture limited to ballots. Reproduction of a complaint which seeks to invoke the support of the government by conveying the impression of actual findings of violations of federal law, as opposed to unproven allegations, also is cause for setting aside an election.[308] Duplication of part of the

---

[301] Archer Laundry Co., *supra* note 297; Aristocrat Linen Supply Co., *supra* note 297; Hobco Mfg. Co., 168 NLRB No. 71, 66 LRRM 1330 (1967); *see also* Chock Full O' Nuts, 120 NLRB 1296, 42 LRRM 1152 (1958), where a Negro vice-president told Negro employees that jealousy and antipathy toward him on the part of white employees because of his race was the reason for union activity.
[302] 162 NLRB No. 113, 64 LRRM 1145 (1967).
[303] 356 F 2d 675, 61 LRRM 2289 (CA 4, 1966).
[304] Allied Electric Prods., Inc., 109 NLRB 1270, 1271, 34 LRRM 1538 (1954).
[305] *See* Chapter 8 *infra* for discussion of election procedures.
[306] *See* Allied Electric Prods., Inc., *supra* note 304, where a facsimile ballot was marked "Sample" but with an "X" in the "Yes" box.
[307] Custom Molders of P.R., 121 NLRB 1007, 1009, 42 LRRM 1505 (1958), where deletion of the official headnote of the ballot did not prevent the Board from setting the election aside. *But see* Glidden Co., 121 NLRB 752, 42 LRRM 1428 (1958), and Paula Shoe Co., 121 NLRB 673, 42 LRRM 1419 (1958), where only portions of the ballot were reproduced as part of a handbill, in such a manner as to avoid the impression of governmental endorsement.
[308] Mallory Capacitor Co., 161 NLRB 1510, 63 LRRM 1473 (1966).

Board's election notice with a partisan supplement attached to it will have the same result.[309]

b. *Electioneering at the polls.* In the actual conduct of the election the Board is "especially zealous in preventing intrusions."[310] It has long been held that campaigning too close to the polls may be objectionable.[311] In 1968 the Board adopted the "strict" rule that, "regardless of the content of the remarks exchanged," prolonged conversation by representatives of any party with prospective voters in the polling area "constitutes conduct which, in itself," will invalidate an election.[312] The Board's zeal extends also to impressions conveyed to employees during the balloting. Keeping a list of employees who have voted, aside from the official eligibility list used to check off voters as they receive their ballots, has been found to interfere with an election.[313] Supervisory participation as an observer has had the same result.[314] Even the Board's own agents must avoid creating impressions that will impair the integrity and neutrality of its election procedures.[315]

---

[309] Rebmar, Inc., 173 NLRB No. 215, 70 LRRM 1018 (1969).

[310] Claussen Baking Co., 134 NLRB 111, 112, 49 LRRM 1092 (1961).

[311] *Ibid.*; Continental Can Co., 80 NLRB 785, 23 LRRM 1126 (1948).

[312] Michelm, Inc., 170 NLRB No. 46, 67 LRRM 1395 (1968), emphasizing the importance of ensuring that "[t]he final minutes before an employee casts his vote should be his own, as free from interference as possible." The *Michelm* rule apparently contemplates that the Board agent conducting the balloting will specify the "no electioneering" or polling area. Star Expansion Indus. Corp., 170 NLRB No. 47, 67 LRRM 1400 (1968). But the rule does not apply to "conversations with prospective voters unless the voters are . . . in the polling area or in line waiting to vote." Harold W. Moore & Son, 173 NLRB No. 191, 70 LRRM 1002 (1968).

[313] Piggly-Wiggly, 168 NLRB No. 101, 66 LRRM 1360 (1967), where the making of notations on a list as employees passed by to enter the employer's premises during the balloting caused the election to be set aside. Use of this technique may cause employees to infer that their names are being recorded. A. D. Juilliard & Co., 110 NLRB 2197, 2199, 35 LRRM 1401 (1954). *See also* International Stamping Co., 97 NLRB 921, 29 LRRM 1158 (1951); NLRB Form 722 instructing observers not to keep such lists; and Chapter 8 *infra.*

[314] Cooper Supply Co., 120 NLRB 1023, 42 LRRM 1094 (1958).

[315] Athbro Precision Eng'g Corp., 166 NLRB 966, 65 LRRM 1699 (1967). The Board's interest in protecting the integrity of the election process is also illustrated in its decision to set aside an election where the ballot box was left unsealed and unattended for only two to five minutes, without regard to what might have occurred. Austill Waxed Paper Co., 169 NLRB No. 169, 67 LRRM 1366 (1968).

CHAPTER 6

DISCRIMINATION IN EMPLOYMENT

I. STATUTORY PROVISIONS

Discrimination in employment for the purpose of discouraging or encouraging membership in a union is a frequent subject of NLRB decisions. For example, about two thirds of all charges filed against employers in 1966 alleged this unfair labor practice.[1] The reported cases since 1935 number in the thousands. This chapter deals with the general problem of employment discrimination. Discrimination that is specifically related to strikes, lockouts, union security, and the union's duty of fair representation will be treated in detail in later chapters.[2]

A. Discrimination as an Unfair Labor Practice

Section 8 (a) (3) of the National Labor Relations Act declares that it is an unfair labor practice for an employer "by discrimination in regard to hire or tenure of employment or any term or condition of employment to encourage or discourage membership in any labor organization." This language has remained unchanged since its original enactment in 1935. A proviso to the section permits an employer and a union to enter into a union-shop agreement under certain conditions.[2] Under a second proviso, however, a union-shop agreement is no justification for dis-

---

[1] 31 NLRB ANN. REP. 8 (1966).

[2] See Chapters 19, 20, 26, and 27 respectively. For scholarly comment on the subject of discrimination under the Act, see the following: Christensen & Svanoe, Motive and Intent in the Commission of Unfair Labor Practices: The Supreme Court and the Fictive Formality, 77 YALE L.J. 1269 (1968); Cox, The Right to Engage in Concerted Activities, 26 IND. L.J. 319 (1951); Getman, Section 8(a)(3) of the NLRA and the Effort to Insulate Free Employee Choice, 32 U. CHI L. REV. 735 (1965); Getman, The Protection of Economic Pressure by Section 7 of the National Labor Relations Act, 115 U. PA. L. REV. 1195 (1967); Janofsky, New Concepts in Interference and Discrimination under the NLRA: The Legacy of American Shipbuilding and Great Dane Trailers, 70 COLUM. L. REV. 81 (1970); Oberer, The Scienter Factor in Sections 8(a)(1) and (3) of the Labor Act: of Balancing, Hostile Motive, Dogs and Tails, 52 CORNELL L.Q. 491 (1967); Schatzki, Some Observations and Suggestions Concerning a Misnomer—"Protected Concerted Activities," 47 TEX. L. REV. 378 (1969).

criminating against a nonunion employee if the employer "has reasonable grounds for believing that . . . membership was not available to the employee on the same terms and conditions generally applicable to other members," or if he "has reasonable grounds for believing that membership was denied or terminated for reasons other than failure . . . to tender the periodic dues and the initiation fees uniformly required as a condition of acquiring or retaining membership." [3]

Section 8 (b) (2) corresponds to Section 8 (a) (3), but its prohibition is directed at unions. It is an unfair labor practice for a labor organization or its agents "to cause or attempt to cause an employer to discriminate against an employee in violation of subsection (a) (3) or to discriminate against an employee with respect to whom membership in such organization has been denied or terminated on some ground other than his failure to tender the periodic dues and the initiation fees uniformly required as a condition of acquiring or retaining membership." [4]

Under Section 8(a)(4), it is an unfair labor practice for an employer "to discharge or otherwise discriminate against an employee because he has filed charges or given testimony under this Act." [5]

B. Remedial Orders in Discrimination Cases

Remedial orders are authorized by Section 10 (c). On finding that unfair labor practices have been committed, the Board is instructed to issue cease and desist orders "and to take such affirmative action including reinstatement of employees with or without pay, as will effectuate the policies of this Act." The Taft-Hartley amendments to the Act added several provisions to Section 10(c) which affected remedies in discrimination cases. Where reinstatement is ordered, "back pay may be required of the employer or labor organization, as the case may be, responsible for the dis-

[3] Under §14 (b) an agreement requiring membership in a labor organization as a condition of employment may be prohibited by state or territorial law. The second proviso was incorporated into the Act in 1947, when the Labor-Management Relations Act was passed. The first proviso existed in the original Act in a simpler form, permitting the closed shop. *See* discussion of union security in Chapter 26 *infra*.

[4] This unfair labor practice was created by the Taft-Hartley Act of 1947. *See* Chapter 26 *infra*.

[5] This has been an unfair labor practice since the original Act. For the full meaning of §§8 (a) (3), 8 (b) (2), and 8 (a) (4), refer to definitions of certain words and phrases found in §2 of the Act. In particular, *see* definitions of "employer," "employee," "labor organization," "labor dispute," and "agent." §§2 (2), (3), (5), (9), (13). *See also* Chapter 28 *infra*.

crimination suffered." A respondent may be required "to make reports from time to time showing the extent to which it has complied with . . . [a remedial] order." And a limitation was imposed on remedial orders: "No order of the Board shall require the reinstatement of any individual as an employee who has been suspended or discharged, or the payment to him of any back pay, if such individual was suspended or discharged for cause." [6]

C. Judicial Review in Discrimination Cases

There was a time when a question existed as to whether the scope of judicial review in discrimination cases differed from the scope of review applicable to other unfair labor practices. As a general proposition, when a court of appeals reviews a Board decision, the "findings of the Board with respect to questions of fact if supported by substantial evidence on the record considered as a whole shall be conclusive." This language is found in Sections 10(e) and (f) and was written into the Act in 1947. It replaced a simpler statement that Board findings of fact were conclusive if supported "by evidence" and thus broadened the scope of review of Board findings and orders.

The authoritative exposition of the purpose and effect of the new language was set forth in *Universal Camera Corp. v. NLRB.*[7] Speaking for the Supreme Court, Justice Frankfurter described the extent to which a reviewing court should assume greater responsibility for the reasonableness and fairness of Board decisions:

> Whether or not it was ever permissible for courts to determine the substantiality of evidence supporting a Labor Board decision merely on the basis of evidence which in and of itself justified it, without taking into account contradictory evidence or evidence from which conflicting inferences could be drawn, the new legislation definitely precludes such a theory of review and bars its practice. The substantiality of evidence must take into account whatever in the record fairly detracts from its weight. . . .[8]

The Court cautioned that the new requirement for canvassing the whole record was not intended to negative the function of the

---

[6] See Chapter 31 *infra* for detailed treatment of remedies in cases under §§8 (a) (3), 8 (a) (4), and 8 (b) (2). See also Chapter 19 *infra* at notes 41-42.
[7] 340 US 474, 27 LRRM 2373 (1951). The Court was considering the effect of the "substantial evidence" language in both the Taft-Hartley Act and Section 10 (e) of the Administrative Procedure Act, 5 USC §1009 (e) (1965), on the duty of the courts of appeals when reviewing Board orders.
[8] 340 US at 487-488.

Board to deal with a specialized field of knowledge. And even as to matters not requiring expertise, a court may not displace the Board's choice "between two fairly conflicting views, even though the court would justifiably have made a different choice had the matter been before it *de novo*. Congress has merely made it clear that a reviewing court is not barred from setting aside a Board decision when it cannot conscientiously find that the evidence supporting that decision is substantial, when viewed in the light that the record in its entirety furnishes, including the body of evidence opposed to the Board's view." [9]

The test of substantiality of evidence on the whole record operates evenly on all types of findings of fact and orders, including those involving remedies in discrimination cases. In *NLRB v. Walton Manufacturing Co.*[10] the Supreme Court considered whether the test of substantiality is more onerous as to an order of reinstatement with back pay than as to a simple cease and desist order. The Fifth Circuit had refused to enforce an order of the former type where the accused employer denied that a discharge or refusal to reemploy was discriminatory and testified that he had a different reason for his action.[11] The court stated that the employer's oath could not be disregarded on suspicion of lying unless he was impeached, or there was substantial contradiction, or circumstances raising doubts were inconsistent with his sworn testimony.[12] The Supreme Court rejected the lower court's view, stating that "[t]here is no place in the statutory scheme for one test of substantiality of evidence in reinstatement cases and another test in other cases." [13] Thus the Board may reject testimony of an employer, and make findings of discrimination on the basis of other evidence, direct and circumstantial.

---

[9] *Id.* at 488. For treatment of judicial review generally, *see* Chapter 32 *infra*.

[10] 369 US 404, 49 LRRM 2962 (1962), *on remand,* 322 F2d 187, 54 LRRM 2118 (CA 5, 1963).

[11] 286 F2d 16, 47 LRRM 2367 (CA 5, 1961).

[12] The Fifth Circuit had repeatedly followed this special and more onerous rule for reinstatement cases since the rule was announced in NLRB v. Tex-O-Kan Flour Mills Co., 122 F2d 433, 8 LRRM 675 (CA 5, 1941). *See* NLRB v. Allure Shoe Corp., 277 F2d 231, 45 LRRM 3157 (CA 5, 1960); NLRB v. Williamson-Dickie Mfg. Co., 130 F2d 260, 10 LRRM 867 (CA 5, 1942).

[13] 369 US at 407.

II. SECTION 8(a)(3) CASES
ELEMENTS OF THE UNFAIR LABOR PRACTICE

A. Purpose of Discrimination

The unfair labor practice defined in Section 8 (a) (3) encompasses discrimination having as a purpose the encouragement or discouragement of membership in a union. In *Radio Officers' Union v. NLRB* [14] the Supreme Court explained:

> The language of §8 (a) (3) is not ambiguous. The unfair labor practice is for an employer to encourage or discourage membership by means of discrimination. Thus this section does not outlaw all encouragement or discouragement of membership in labor organizations; only such as is accomplished by discrimination is prohibited. Nor does this section outlaw discrimination in employment as such; only such discrimination as encourages or discourages membership in a labor organization is proscribed.[15]

The employer's purpose determines whether an unfair labor practice has occurred when he discriminates among his employees; however, specific anti-union purpose need not be proved in certain types of cases:

> But it is also clear that specific evidence of intent to encourage or discourage is not an indispensable element of proof of violation of 8 (a) (3) . . . . [A]n employer's protestation that he did not intend to encourage or discourage must be unavailing where a natural consequence of his action was such encouragement or discouragement. Concluding that encouragement or discouragement will result, it is presumed that he intended such consequence. In such circumstances intent to encourage is sufficiently established. . . .[16]

The Board has authority to draw reasonable inferences from the evidence presented; [17] thus discouragement may be inferred from facts proved for purposes of a Section 8 (a) (3) violation.

Invariably, where a violation of Section 8 (a) (3) is charged, the employer's action in changing his employees' tenure or terms or conditions of employment is not disputed. What is in contention is whether the employer intended to encourage or discourage membership in a union. If the employer has expressed himself in connection with his action, direct proof of his intent may be available.

---

14 347 US 17, 33 LRRM 2417 (1954). *See* note 90 *infra*.
15 *Id*. at 42-43.
16 *Id*. at 44-45. *Compare* NLRB v. Burnup & Sims, Inc., 379 US 21, 57 LRRM 2385 (1964), Chapter 5 *supra*.
17 Republic Aviation Corp. v. NLRB, 324 US 793, 16 LRRM 620 (1945). *See also* discussion of conduct which carries its own indicia of intent to discriminate, notes 77-85 *infra* and accompanying text.

But Section 8 (c) protects his right of free speech, and "[t]he expressing of any views, argument, or opinion, or the dissemination thereof, whether in written, printed, graphic, or visual form, shall not constitute or be evidence of an unfair labor practice under any of the provisions of this Act, if such expression contains no threat of reprisal or force or promise of benefit." Thus, anti-union statements not including threat of reprisal or force or promise of benefit are not admissible on this issue.[18]

The cases are legion in which threats or promises have constituted weighty evidence of an employer's intent to discriminate. The NLRB reports are full of cases in which an employer is accused of having fired an employee in order to discourage union membership, and the employer offers evidence that some other motive (reduction of force due to slackening production needs, neglect of work, absenteeism, fighting, refusal to follow orders, poor workmanship, etc.) was the true cause for the termination. It is the Board's task to weigh the evidence, both direct and circumstantial, to credit and discredit testimony, to draw inferences, and to make ultimate findings of fact as to whether a violation of Section 8 (a) (3) has occurred.

An employer has a right to take disciplinary action for good cause related to the maintenance of order and efficiency in his plant.[19] Section 10 (c) recognizes this right by prohibiting Board orders of reinstatement and back pay where an employee has been "suspended or discharged for cause." Implicit in the notion of "cause" is that it motivated (or was the main reason for) the disciplinary action. The employer's motivation may be challenged, and then the question becomes: What was the real reason for dis-

---

[18] Indiana Metal Prod. Corp. v. NLRB, 202 F2d 613, 31 LRRM 2490 (CA 7, 1953); Pittsburgh S. S. Co. v. NLRB, 180 F2d 731, 735, 25 LRRM 2428 (CA 6, 1950); affirmed, 340 US 498, 27 LRRM 2382 (1951). Such statements may be admissible to show background or anti-union animus, however. See Chapter 5 supra for discussion of §8 (c) in relation to independent §8 (a) (1) cases.

[19] Indeed, an employer may discharge for poor cause or no cause, and there is no violation of Section 8 (a) (3) unless the employer's purpose is to encourage or discourage union membership. Associated Press v. NLRB, 301 US 103, 132, 1 LRRM 732 (1937); NLRB v. McGahey, 233 F2d 406, 38 LRRM 2142 (CA 5, 1956); Indiana Metal Products v. NLRB, 202 F2d 613, 31 LRRM 2490 (CA 7, 1953); NLRB v. Montgomery Ward, 157 F2d 486, 19 LRRM 2008 (CA 8, 1946); NLRB v. Condenser Corp., 128 F2d 67, 10 LRRM 483 (CA 3, 1942).

charge? [20] The burden of proof on this issue is on the General Counsel of the Board.[21]

B. Discriminatory Acts

Section 8 (a) (3) speaks of "discrimination in regard to hire or tenure of employment or any term or condition of employment." Thus, an employer's discriminatory acts may be any of a great variety affecting his employees' work situation other than suspension from work or discharge. Among acts found to have been discriminatory are demotion, transfer from one department or location to another, assignment to disagreeable tasks, denial of preferred job assignments, denial of overtime work, subcontracting of work with consequent laying off of employees, making a plant physically less comfortable, denial of sick leave, and condoning of violence on the part of anti-union employees.[22]

Discrimination in regard to tenure of employment that encourages union membership is permissible to the extent that it follows upon, or is in performance of, a union-shop agreement that satisfies the requirements of the provisos to Section 8 (a) (3). Conversely, if an employer and a union enter into a union-shop or preferential-hiring agreement not authorized by the provisos, or enforce it contrary to the provisos, a clear case of violation of Section 8 (a) (3) is made out.[23] In situations where no valid union

---

[20] *E.g.*, Laidlaw Corp., 171 NLRB No. 175, 68 LRRM 1252 (1968); Wellington Mill Division v. NLRB, 330 F2d 579, 55 LRRM 2914 (CA 4, 1964), *cert. denied*, 379 US 882, 57 LRRM 2276 (1964), *denying enforcement of the Board's order in* 141 NLRB 819, 52 LRRM 1445 (1963); Edward G. Budd Mfg. Co. v. NLRB, 138 F2d 86, 13 LRRM 512 (CA 3, 1943).

[21] *See* discussion of unfair labor practice hearing in Chapter 30 *infra*.

[22] NLRB v. Murray Ohio Mfg. Co., 326 F2d 509, 55 LRRM 2181, 328 F2d 613, 55 LRRM 2663 (CA 6, 1964) (court rejected Board's finding that evaluation program was applied in discriminatory manner); NLRB v. Lowell Sun Publishing Co., 320 F2d 835, 53 LRRM 2480 (CA 1, 1963); Trumbull Asphalt Co. of Delaware v. NLRB, 314 F2d 382, 52 LRRM 2570 (CA 7, 1963), *cert. denied*, 374 US 808, 53 LRRM 2468 (1964) (disagreeable work, deprivation of overtime); NLRB v. Kelly & Picerne, Inc., 298 F2d 895, 49 LRRM 2663 (CA 1, 1962); Indianapolis Wirebound Box Co., 89 NLRB 617, 26 LRRM 1005 (1950); Harold W. Baker Co., 71 NLRB 44, 18 LRRM 1464 (1946); Caroline Mills, Inc., 64 NLRB 200, 17 LRRM 100 (1945) (heaters removed from plant); Taylor Colquitt Co., 47 NLRB 225, 12 LRRM 5 (1945).

[23] Carpenters Local 60 v. NLRB, 365 US 651, 47 LRRM 2900 (1961). In this case the Supreme Court refused to enforce that part of the Board's order requiring reimbursement to *all* employees of dues and fees collected under the illegal union security contract during the six months preceding the filing of unfair labor practice charges. This type of order was first issued in *United Association of Journeymen & Apprentices (Brown-Olds Plumbing & Heating Corporation)*, 115 NLRB 594, 37 LRRM 1360 (1956). The Court held that the order was punitive and not supported by proof that all the employees had joined the union or maintained their membership because of the illegal agreement. *See* Chapter 26 *infra*.

ˌsted, it has been held that an employer may
ˌployee's seniority standing for delinquency in
ˌnay not grant a retroactive wage increase to union
ˌ.[24] It seems equally clear that neither action could
a valid union-shop agreement were in force.

ˌnployees Covered by the Section

The protection of Section 8 (a) (3) extends to applicants for
work as well as to persons already employed. The landmark case
of *Phelps Dodge Corporation v. National Labor Relations Board* [25]
established that an unfair labor practice is committed if an employer discriminates against union members in hiring new employees. The Supreme Court had no difficulty in reading
"discrimination in regard to hire" as covering the situation. A
similar interpretation was given to the coverage of the remedial
authority granted to the NLRB by Section 10 (c). The Board is
granted authority "to take such affirmative action, including reinstatement of employees with or without back pay, as will effectuate
the policies of this Act." The Court refused to limit the remedy
of "reinstatement" in a job to persons who had been employees of
the respondent employer. "To attribute such a function to the
participial phrase introduced by 'including' is to shrivel a versa-
tile principle to an illustrative application." [26] The controlling
language was that the Board may "take such affirmative action . . .
as will effectuate the policies of this Act." Reference was also made
to the broad definition of "employee" found in Section 2 (3).[27]

D. The Lockout

The subject of lockouts is treated extensively in Chapter 20
infra; but inasmuch as Section 8(a)(3) questions are raised in many
types of lockouts, some of the illustrative and leading cases are
also discussed herein. Obviously, to lock out employees or shut
down the plant in order to discourage union membership violates

---

24 Radio Officers' Union v. NLRB, 347 US 17, 33 LRRM 2417 (1954).
25 313 US 177, 8 LRRM 439 (1941). *Accord,* Atlantic Maintenance Co. v. NLRB, 305
F2d 604, 50 LRRM 2494 (CA 3, 1962).
26 313 US at 189.
27 "The term 'employee' shall include any employee, and shall not be limited to
the employees of a particular employer. . . ."

Section 8(a)(3), and the Board will order back pay for all the employees for the period of the lockout.[28]

A different question is presented if an employer locks out while collective bargaining is going on or when an impasse is reached. In *American Ship Building Co. v. NLRB* [29] the employer and a group of unions reached a collective bargaining impasse on August 9, 1961. The employer was in the business of repairing ships at four different cities on the Great Lakes. The business was highly seasonal, being concentrated in the winter months. The employer was apprehensive that negotiations might be delayed into the winter when a strike (or threat thereof) would have great economic leverage. On August 11 the employer laid off practically all the employees at two ports and started a gradual layoff of employees at the other ports. Collective bargaining was resumed soon thereafter, and on October 27 a new contract was signed. The next day the laid-off employees were recalled to work.

The employer was charged with violating Section 8 (a) (3), among other sections. Rejecting the trial examiner's conclusion that the layoff was economically justified and motivated, the NLRB held that the employees had been coerced in the exercise of their bargaining rights and discriminated against within the meaning of Section 8 (a) (3).[30] The Court of Appeals for the District of Columbia enforced the Board's order.[31]

The Supreme Court, however, reversed the lower court's decision. A lockout, or threat of lockout, used to injure a labor organization or to *avoid* the duty to bargain collectively is an unfair labor practice. It was also generally regarded as unlawful, in the absence of special circumstances, if used to buttress an employer's bargaining position.[32] The Court noted, however, that special circumstances have been deemed to permit a lockout: if there is reasonable ground to believe that a strike is threatened or immi-

28 NLRB v. Somerset Shoe Co., 111 F2d 681, 6 LRRM 709 (CA 1, 1940); Republic Steel Corporation v. NLRB, 107 F2d 472, 5 LRRM 740 (CA 3, 1939); Mooresville Cotton Mills v. NLRB, 94 F2d 61, 1-A LRRM 601 (CA 4, 1938); 97 F2d 959, 2 LRRM 687 (1938); 110 F2d 179, 6 LRRM 780 (1940); Centre Brass Works, Inc., 10 NLRB 1060, 3 LRRM 497 (1939); Hopwood Retinning Co., Inc., 4 NLRB 922, 1-A LRRM 416 (1938); NLRB v. Savoy Laundry, Inc., 327 F2d 370, 55 LRRM 2285 (CA 2, 1964).
29 380 US 300, 58 LRRM 2672 (1965). *See* Chapter 20 *infra*.
30 142 NLRB 1362, 53 LRRM 1245 (1963).
31 331 F2d 839, 55 LRRM 2913 (1964).
32 Quaker State Oil Ref. Co., 121 NLRB 334, 337, 42 LRRM 1343 (1958).

nent and the lockout is a safeguard against business loss,[33] and where a multiemployer bargaining unit is threatened with a whip-saw strike against one of the employers.[34]

The Court then considered the question of "whether an employer commits an unfair labor practice . . . when he temporarily lays off or 'locks out' his employees during a labor dispute to bring economic pressure in support of his bargaining position." [35] The Court answered that he does not if an impasse has been reached and the temporary layoff is "for the sole purpose of bringing economic pressure to bear in support of his legitimate bargaining position." [36] It was observed that the employer's action in the instant case was not taken in order to frustrate collective bargaining. Nor was there any specific discrimination against union members. No tendency to destroy unionism was discerned. The unions' right to strike was not preempted, because they did not have the exclusive right to time the cessation of work activities.

The Court acknowledged that a finding of violation of Section 8(a)(3) "will normally turn on the employer's motivation." For example, when a union leader who breaks shop rules is discharged,

> the problem posed is to determine whether the employer has acted purely in disinterested defense of shop discipline or has sought to damage employee organization. It is likely that the discharge will naturally tend to discourage union membership in both cases, because of the loss of union leadership and the employees' suspicion of the employer's true intention. But we have consistently construed the section to leave unscathed a wide range of employer actions taken to serve legitimate business interests in some significant fashion, even though the act committed may tend to discourage union membership.[37]

In the present case, "[t]he purpose and effect of the lockout was only to bring pressure upon the union to modify its demands," and the "arguable possibility that someone . . . [might] feel him-

---

[33] Betts Cadillac-Olds, 96 NLRB 268, 28 LRRM 1509 (1951); Int'l Shoe Co., 93 NLRB 907, 27 LRRM 1504 (1951); Duluth Bottling Ass'n, 48 NLRB 1335, 12 LRRM 151 (1943); Link-Belt Co., 26 NLRB 227, 6 LRRM 565 (1940).

[34] NLRB v. Truck Drivers Local Union, 353 US 87, 39 LRRM 2603 (1957).

[35] 380 US at 301-302. See discussion of impasse as a factor in lawful lockouts, Chapter 20 infra.

[36] Id. at 318.

[37] Id. at 311.

self discouraged in his union membership" did not establish a violation of Section 8 (a) (3) in the absence of unlawful intent.[38]

E. Shutdown of Plant

Permanent shutting down of a business is to be distinguished from a lockout, in which an employer intends to resume operations when he has achieved his end. In *Textile Workers Union v. Darlington Manufacturing Co.*[39] the Supreme Court considered the right of an employer to shut down his plant because the employees had voted for union representation. The Court held that closing down an entire business is not an unfair labor practice even though motivated by vindictiveness toward a union. "A proposition that a single businessman cannot choose to go out of business if he wants to would represent such a startling innovation that it should not be entertained without the clearest manifestation of legislative intent or unequivocal judicial precedent so construing the Labor Act." [40] A discriminatory lockout "is a lever which has been used to discourage collective employee activities in the future. But a complete liquidation of a business yields no such future benefit for the employer if the termination is bona fide. It may be motivated more by animosity toward the union than by business reasons, but it is not the type of discrimination that is prohibited by the Act." [41]

Partial closing of a business for discriminatory reasons is a different matter. In the Court's words:

> [A] discriminatory partial closing may have repercussions on what remains of the business, affording employer leverage for discouraging the free exercise of §7 rights among remaining employees of much the same kind as that found to exist in the "runaway shop" and "temporary closing" cases. . . . Moreover, a possible remedy open to the Board in such a case, like the remedies available in the "runaway shop" and "temporary closing" cases, is to order reinstatement of the discharged employees in the other parts of the business. No such remedy is available when an entire business has been terminated. By analogy to those cases involving a continuing enterprise we are constrained to hold . . . that a partial closing is an unfair

---

[38] *Id.* at 312, 313. To the same effect, *see* NLRB v. Brown, dba Brown Food Store, 380 US 278, 58 LRRM 2663 (1965) , also discussed in Chapter 20 *infra*.
[39] 380 US 263, 58 LRRM 2657 (1965) .
[40] *Id.* at 270.
[41] *Id.* at 271, 272. *Accord,* NLRB v. New Madrid Mfg. Co., 215 F2d 908, 914, 34 LRRM 2844 (CA 8, 1954). For the consequences of a threat to close a business, *see* Chapter 5 *supra*.

labor practice under §8 (a) (3) if motivated by a purpose *to chill unionism* in any of the remaining plants of the single employer and if the employer may reasonably have foreseen that such closing will likely have that effect.[42]

F. The "Runaway Shop"

The problem of the "runaway shop" has confronted the Board in a number of cases. If the employer's purpose in moving his business is to discourage union membership or collective bargaining, he violates Section 8 (a) (3).[43] The Board's remedy is to order reinstatement to jobs with back pay and moving expenses (or reimbursement for increased costs in traveling to and from the new work location).[44] The difficult cases are those in which an employer is proved to have been anti-union in feeling but nevertheless had good economic reason for moving his business. If the preponderant motive for moving is economic necessity, anti-union animus does not make the move an unfair labor practice.[45]

Other types of business decisions prejudicial to employees have been held not violative of Section 8 (a) (3) where economic reasons were advanced, even though the employer manifested an anti-union attitude.[46]

III. DISCRIMINATION FOR
PARTICIPATION IN CONCERTED ACTIVITIES

Section 7 of the Act declares that employees "shall have the right . . . to engage in . . . concerted activities for the purpose of collec-

---

[42] 380 US at 274, 275 (emphasis added). In *A. C. Rochat Co.*, 163 NLRB 421 64 LRRM 1321 (1967), the Board held that an employer did not violate §8(a)(3) by shutting down part of his business, even though prompted by antiunion considerations, for his purpose was to chill unionism in other parts of the business. To the same effect, *see* Motor Repair, Inc., 168 NLRB No. 148, 67 LRRM 1051 (1968).
[43] Local 57, Int'l Ladies' Garment Workers' Union v. NLRB, 374 F2d 295, 64 LRRM 2159 (CA DC, 1967); NLRB v. Preston Feed Corp., 309 F2d 346, 51 LRRM 2362 (CA 4, 1962); NLRB v. New Madrid Mfg. Co., 215 F2d 908, 34 LRRM 2844 (CA 8, 1954); NLRB v. Industrial Fabricating, Inc., 272 F2d 184, 45 LRRM 2137 (CA 6, 1959); NLRB v. Wallick, 198 F2d 477, 30 LRRM 2529 (CA 3, 1952); NLRB v. Schieber Millinery Co., 116 F2d 281, 7 LRRM 658 (CA 8, 1940); Rome Product Co., 77 NLRB 1217, 22 LRRM 1138 (1948); Jacob H. Klotz, 13 NLRB 746, 4 LRRM 344 (1939).
[44] *See* discussion of the remedy in *Darlington* in notes 150-152 and accompanying text, Chapter 31 *infra.*
[45] NLRB v. Rapid Bindery, 293 F2d 170, 48 LRRM 2658 (CA 2, 1961); NLRB v. Adkins Transfer Co., 226 F2d 324, 36 LRRM 2709 (CA 6, 1955); Mount Hope Finishing Co. v. NLRB, 211 F2d 365, 33 LRRM 2742 (CA 4, 1954).
[46] NLRB v. Lansing, 284 F2d 781, 47 LRRM 2277 (CA 6, 1960), *cert. denied*, 366 US 909, 48 LRRM 2070 (1961); NLRB v. R. C. Mahon Co., 269 F2d 44, 44 LRRM 2479 (CA 6, 1959); NLRB v. Houston Chronicle Pub. Co., 211 F2d 848, 33 LRRM 2847 (CA 5, 1954).

tive bargaining or other mutual aid or protection." Interference, restraint, or coercion in the exercise of this right is an unfair labor practice under Section 8 (a) (1). Discrimination against employees for engaging in concerted activities is just a step removed from discrimination for the purpose of discouraging union membership. Since the early days of the Act, discrimination of this type has been held to be a violation of Section 8 (a) (3).[47]

A. Concerted Activities Before Demand on Employer

In *NLRB v. Washington Aluminum Co.*[48] the Supreme Court enforced a Board order reinstating with back pay seven employees whom the respondent employer had discharged for leaving their work without permission.[49] The employees had claimed that their shop was too cold to work in. The court of appeals had refused to enforce the Board's order because the workers (who were unorganized) had left their employment without affording the company an opportunity to avoid the work stoppage by granting a concession to a demand.[50] But the Supreme Court held that the "language of §7 is broad enough to protect concerted activities whether they take place before, after, or at the same time . . . a demand is made." [51] A plant rule forbidding employees to leave work without their foreman's consent did not make the discharges "for cause" where the employees engaged in an activity protected by Section 7.

B. Concerted Activities Without Union Participation

Concerted activities are protected by Section 7 even though no union leadership or membership is involved. A variety of such activities have been held protected, with the consequence that the imposition of disciplinary penalties is discriminatory and in viola-

---

47 "Under §8 (a) (3) , it is unlawful for an employer by discrimination in terms of employment to discourage 'membership in any labor organization,' which includes discouraging participation in concerted activities . . . such as a legitimate strike." NLRB v. Erie Resistor Corp., 373 US 221, 233, 53 LRRM 2121 (1963) , citing NLRB v. Wheeling Pipe Line, Inc., 229 F2d 391, 37 LRRM 2403 (CA 8, 1956) ; Republic Steel Corp. v. NLRB, 114 F2d 820, 7 LRRM 364 (CA 3, 1940) .
48 370 US 9, 50 LRRM 2235 (1962) .
49 128 NLRB 643, 46 LRRM 1385 (1960) .
50 291 F2d 869, 48 LRRM 2558 (CA 4, 1961) .
51 370 US at 14.

tion of Section 8 (a) (3).[52] Spontaneous work stoppages have been held protected.[53] A walkout because of abnormally dangerous working conditions is protected under Section 502 of the LMRA.[54]

C. Unprotected Concerted Activities

Some concerted activities are not protected by Section 7, and discharge or other discipline may be meted out to employees who engage in such activities. Serious trespass, destruction of property, and violence are cause for discharge,[55] as is a mutiny aboard ship in violation of a federal criminal statute.[56] A strike in violation of a collective bargaining contract is not protected by Section 7;[57] nor is a "wildcat" strike if in derogation of the authority of the recognized collective bargaining representative.[58]

---

[52] B & P Motor Express, Inc. v. NLRB, 413 F2d 1021, 71 LRRM 3176 (CA 7, 1969); NLRB v. R. C. Can Co., 328 F2d 974, 55 LRRM 2642 (CA 5, 1964); Western Contracting Corp. v. NLRB, 322 F2d 893, 54 LRRM 2216 (CA 10, 1963); NLRB v. Solo Cup Co., 237 F2d 521, 38 LRRM 2784 (CA 8, 1956); Salt River Valley Water Users' Assn. v. NLRB, 206 F2d 325, 32 LRRM 2598 (CA 9, 1953) (circulating petition for back wages); Modern Motors, Inc. v. NLRB, 198 F2d 925, 30 LRRM 2628 (CA 8, 1952); NLRB v. J. I. Case Co., Bettendorf Works, 198 F2d 919, 30 LRRM 2624 (CA 8, 1952); NLRB v. Kennametal, Inc., 182 F2d 817, 26 LRRM 2203 (CA 3, 1950); Ohio Oil Co., 92 NLRB 1597, 27 LRRM 1288 (1951); Root-Carlin, Inc., 92 NLRB 1313, 27 LRRM 1235 (1951). However, the activity must be for "mutual aid or protection and over a matter as to which the employer has some control. Joanna Cotton Mills v. NLRB, 176 F2d 749, 24 LRRM 2416 (1949); G & W Electric Specialty Co. v. NLRB 360 F2d 873, 62 LRRM 2085 (1966).

[53] See court of appeals cases in note 52 supra. But see AHI Machine Tool & Die, Inc. v. NLRB, 432 F2d 190, 75 LRRM 2353 (1970), reversing 172 NLRB No. 57, 72 LRRM 1442 (1969).

[54] NLRB v. Knight Morley Co., 251 F2d 753, 41 LRRM 2242 (CA 6, 1957), cert. denied, 357 US 927, 42 LRRM 2307 (1958), construing 61 Stat 136 (1947), 29 USC §143 (1965) (". . . nor shall the quitting of labor by an employee or employees in good faith because of abnormally dangerous conditions for work at the place of employment of such employee or employees be deemed a strike under this Act.").

[55] NLRB v. Fansteel Metallurgical Corp., 306 US 240, 4 LRRM 515 (1939) (sit-down strike); NLRB v. Clearfield Cheese Co., 213 F2d 70, 34 LRRM 2132 (CA 3, 1954); Stewart Die Casting Corp. v. NLRB, 114 F2d 849, 6 LRRM 907 (CA 7, 1940), cert. denied, 312 US 680, 7 LRRM 326 (1940); Republic Steel Corp. v. NLRB, 107 F2d 472, 5 LRRM 740 (CA 3, 1939); Berkshire Knitting Mills, 46 NLRB 955, 11 LRRM 248 (1943).

[56] Southern Steamship Co. v. NLRB, 316 US 31, 10 LRRM 544 (1942).

[57] NLRB v. Rockaway News Supply Co., 345 US 71, 31 LRRM 2432 (1953); NLRB v. Sands Mfg. Co., 306 US 332, 4 LRRM 530 (1939); United Elec. Workers v. NLRB, 223 F2d 338, 36 LRRM 2175 (CA DC, 1955); Joseph Dyson & Sons, Inc., 72 NLRB 445, 19 LRRM 1187 (1947); Scullin Steel Co., 65 NLRB 1294, 17 LRRM 286 (1946). But see Mastro Plastics Corp. v. NLRB, 350 US 270, 37 LRRM 2587 (1956), where an unfair labor practice strike during the life of a collective bargaining contract was held to be not a breach of contract and not a violation of §8(d) of the Act, and the Board's order to reinstate the strikers was upheld. (See discussion of Mastro Plastics in Chapters 17 and 19 infra.) But if a grievance procedure is readily available or if the unfair labor practice is not serious, breach of contract may be made out justifying discharge. Arlan's Dept. Store, 133 NLRB 802, 48 LRRM 1731 (1961); Mid-West Metallic Prod., Inc., 121 NLRB 1317, 42 LRRM 1552 (1958).

[58] NLRB v. Sunbeam Lighting Co., 318 F2d 661, 53 LRRM 2367 (CA 7, 1963);

Concerted activities must have lawful objectives and must be carried on in a lawful manner.[59] A strike to compel an employer to grant a wage increase in violation of a wartime wage stabilization statute is unprotected.[60] The same is true of a strike to compel the employer to commit an unfair labor practice.[61] One may assume that jurisdictional strikes and secondary boycotts, both prohibited by the Act, are unprotected and cause for discipline.[62]

Apart from violence, trespass, violation of statute, or breach of contract, concerted activities are sometimes carried on in conflict with an employer's right to operate his plant and direct his forces, or at a time and in a manner inappropriate to the situation. The employer may suffer disproportionate loss and inconvenience. It is a question of degree, and if employees go too far they lose the protection of Sections 7 and 8 (a) (3).[63] In *Elk Lumber Co.*[64] five carloaders were discharged because they slowed down when their pay was changed from a piecework rate to an hourly rate. There was no collective bargaining contract and no union. The NLRB said that the test of whether the employees were protected was "whether the particular activity involved is so indefensible as to warrant the employer in discharging the participating employees." [65] In effect, the carloaders had refused the terms of employment set by their employer and had continued work on

---

Confectionery & Tobacco Drivers & Warehousemen, Local 805 v. NLRB, 312 F2d 108, 52 LRRM 2163 (CA 2, 1963) ; Plasti-Line, Inc., Sign Fabricators v. NLRB, 278 F2d 482, 46 LRRM 2291 (CA 6, 1960) ; Harnischfeger Corp. v. NLRB, 207 F2d 575, 33 LRRM 2029 (CA 7, 1953) ; NLRB v. Draper Corp., 145 F2d 199, 15 LRRM 580 (CA 4, 1944) ; *but see* NLRB v. R. C. Can Co., 328 F2d 974, 55 LRRM 2642 (CA 5, 1964) *and* Tanner Motor Livery Ltd., 148 NLRB 1402, 57 LRRM 1170 (1964), *remanded*, 349 F2d 1, 59 LRRM 2784 (CA 9, 1965) , *affirmed*, 166 NLRB 551, 65 LRRM 1502 (1967). In *Tanner* the Board held that wildcat stoppages which coincide with the objectives of the bargaining representative are protected. *See* Gould, *Black Power in the Unions: The Impact Upon Collective Bargaining Relationships*, 79 YALE L.J. 46 (1969). *See* Gould, *The Status of Unauthorized and "Wildcat" Strikes Under the National Labor Relations Act*, 52 CORNELL L. Q. 672 (1967).
59 23 NLRB ANN. REP. 64 (1959).
60 NLRB v. Indiana Desk Co., 149 F2d 987, 16 LRRM 817 (CA 7, 1945) ; American News Co., 55 NLRB 1302, 14 LRRM 64 (1944).
61 Hoover Co. v. NLRB, 191 F2d 380, 28 LRRM 2353 (CA 6, 1951) ; Thompson Prod., Inc., 72 NLRB 886, 19 LRRM 1216 (1947).
62 *See* Local 1229, Electrical Workers v. NLRB, 202 F2d 186, 187, 31 LRRM 2093 (CA DC, 1952). *See also* Chapters 23 and 25 *infra*.
63 NLRB v. Jamestown Veneer & Plywood Corp., 194 F2d 192, 29 LRRM 2420 (CA 2, 1952) (stopping work before end of shift in protest of short notice of layoff) ; Terry Poultry Co., 109 NLRB 1097, 34 LRRM 1516 (1954) (leaving job to present grievance) .
64 91 NLRB 333, 26 LRRM 1493 (1950) .
65 *Id.* at 337.

their own terms. Thus, it was held that the employer did not violate Sections 7 and 8(a)(3).

A number of decisions have sustained the right of an employer to discharge employees who engaged in partial, intermittent, or "quickie" strikes; [66] dissatisfied employees cannot strike and maintain their pay status at the same time.

When employees of one employer refuse to cross a picket line maintained at a second employer's premises, they engage in a concerted activity which has a secondary-boycott aspect. Congress was careful to provide that the activity is not a union unfair labor practice if "the employees of . . . [the picketed] employer are engaged in a strike ratified or approved by a representative of such employees whom such employer is required to recognize under this Act." [67] Nevertheless, a refusal to cross a picket line may constitute a partial strike in breach of the contract with the first employer.[68] The refusal challenges the employer's right to direct his work force and to insist that employees perform all the duties for which they were hired. In these circumstances the employer has a right to suspend or discharge.[69]

The concept of "disloyalty" has been used to deny certain concerted activities the protection of Section 7. In *NLRB v. IBEW,*

---

[66] NLRB v. Blades Mfg. Corp., 344 F2d 998, 59 LRRM 2210 (CA 8, 1965); NLRB v. Montgomery Ward & Co., 157 F2d 486, 19 LRRM 2008 (CA 8, 1946) (refusal to process orders coming from another plant); C. G. Conn, Ltd. v. NLRB, 108 F2d 390, 5 LRRM 806 (CA 7, 1939) (refusal to work overtime); Raleigh Water Heater Mfg. Co., 136 NLRB 76, 49 LRRM 1708 (1962) (slowdown); Scott Lumber Co., Inc., 117 NLRB 1790, 1824, 40 LRRM 1086 (1957) (refusal to do certain assigned work); Honolulu Rapid Transit Co., 110 NLRB 1806, 35 LRRM 1305 (1954) (intermittent strikes); Valley City Furniture Co., 110 NLRB 1589, 35 LRRM 1265 (1954), *enforced*, 230 F2d 947, 37 LRRM 2740 (CA 6, 1956) (daily strikes for an hour); Pacific Tel & Tel. Co., 107 NLRB 1547, 33 LRRM 1433 (1954) (same); Phelps Dodge Copper Products Corp., 101 NLRB 360, 31 LRRM 1072 (1952); Elk Lbr. Co., 91 NLRB 333, 26 LRRM 1493 (1950).
[67] First proviso of §8(b)(4)(D).
[68] *See* text and cases cited at note 57 *supra.*
[69] NLRB v. Rockaway News Supply Co., 345 US 71, 31 LRRM 2432 (1953); NLRB v. L. G. Everist, Inc., 334 F2d 312, 56 LRRM 2866 (CA 8, 1964); Redwing Carriers, 137 NLRB 1545, 50 LRRM 1440 (1962), *enforced*, 325 F2d 1011, 54 LRRM 2707 (CA DC, 1963), *cert. denied*, 377 US 905, 55 LRRM 3023 (1964); Thurston Motor Lines, Inc., 166 NLRB No. 101, 65 LRRM 1674 (1967); Liberty Electronics Corp., 138 NLRB 1074, 51 LRRM 1194 (1962); Robinson Freight Lines, 114 NLRB 1093, 37 LRRM 1086 (1955); Auto Parts Co., 107 NLRB 242, 33 LRRM 1114 (1953). The NLRB has taken the view that an employee who refuses to cross a picket line can be replaced, but until he is permanently replaced his unconditional request for reinstatement must be granted. *See* Chapter 19 *infra* at pp. 535-38 for more detailed treatment of the rights of employees respecting picket lines.

Local 1229,[70] a technicians union had a collective bargaining dispute with a television station. While remaining on the job, some of the technicians distributed handbills during their off hours severely criticizing the quality of programming and suggesting that the city was being treated as "second class." The handbills made no reference to the union, collective bargaining, or the current labor dispute. It was held by the Supreme Court that the employer had cause for discharging the employees who distributed the handbills. While employees continue at work, they owe a duty not to disparage the product or services of their employer or to hamper his sales.[71] The duty may persist even during a strike, since the strikers have an intent to return to work and have certain rights to reinstatement.[72]

D. Protected Concerted Activity

The primary strike is protected whether called for economic reasons or to protest unfair labor practices. As a general rule, economic strikers have a right to reinstatement upon unconditional request until their jobs are filled by permanent replacements.[73] Unfair labor practice strikers are entitled to reinstatement whether or not their jobs have been filled, and if the work force has been reduced they must be put on a preferential-hiring list.[74] If unfair labor practices occur during and prolong an

---

70 346 US 464, 33 LRRM 2183 (1953).

71 Boeing Airplane Co. v. NLRB, 238 F2d 188, 38 LRRM 2276 (CA 9, 1956); Hoover Co. v. NLRB, 191 F2d 380, 28 LRRM 2353 (CA 6, 1951).

72 Patterson-Sargent Co., 115 NLRB 1627, 38 LRRM 1134 (1956). *See* Chapter 19 *infra*.

73 NLRB v. Mackay Radio & Tel. Co. 304 US 333, 2 LRRM 610 (1938); Texas Foundries v. NLRB, 211 F2d 791, 33 LRRM 2883 (CA 5, 1954); NLRB v. Jackson Press, Inc., 201 F2d 541, 546, 31 LRRM 2315 (CA 7, 1953); Hot Shoppes, Inc., 146 NLRB 802, 55 LRRM 1419 (1964); Kerrigan Iron Works, 108 NLRB 933, 34 LRRM 1118 (1954). Employees who refuse to cross a picket line established against their employer by other employees are treated as economic strikers. Morris Fishman & Sons, Inc., 122 NLRB 1436, 43 LRRM 1321 (1959); West Coast Casket Co., 97 NLRB 820, 29 LRRM 1147 (1951); Montag Brothers, 51 NLRB 366, 12 LRRM 270 (1943), *enforced*, 140 F2d 730, 13 LRRM 776 (CA 5, 1944); *cf.* Pacific Tel. & Tel. Co., 107 NLRB 1547, 33 LRRM 1433 (1954). The proviso to §8(b)(4)(B) of the NLRA states that "nothing contained in this clause (B) shall be construed to make unlawful, where not otherwise unlawful, any primary strike or primary picketing." *See* notes 86-89 *infra* and accompanying discussion for exceptions to the statement in the text. *See also* Chapter 19 *infra*.

74 NLRB v. My Stores, Inc., 345 F2d 494, 498, 58 LRRM 2775 (CA 7, 1963), *cert. denied*, 382 US 824, 60 LRRM 2424 (1965); NLRB v. Fotochrome, Inc., 343 F2d 631, 633, 58 LRRM 2844 (CA 2, 1965); NLRB v. Thayer Co., 213 F2d 748, 34 LRRM 2250 (CA 1, 1954); American Stores Packing Co., 158 NLRB 620, 62 LRRM 1093 (1966); Collins & Aikman Corp., 165 NLRB No. 76, 65 LRRM 1484 (1967); Remington Rand, Inc., 2 NLRB 626, 737, 1 LRRM 88 (1937), *enforced*, 94 F2d 862, 1-A LRRM 585 (CA 2, 1938); Brown Shoe Co., 1 NLRB 803, 1 LRRM 78 (1936).

economic strike, from that point on the strike is treated as an unfair labor practice strike.[75]

If there are insufficient jobs for economic strikers because permanent replacements have been hired, it is a violation of Section 8 (a) (3) if the employer, in rehiring, discriminates among the strikers on the basis of their union activities.[76] Even if he rehires without discrimination, specially imposed terms or conditions may violate Section 8 (a) (3). In *NLRB v. Erie Resistor Corp.*[77] a strike was called when collective bargaining on a new contract bogged down. After some weeks the employer notified the union that it would begin hiring replacements and that strikers would retain their jobs until replaced. Several weeks later, in order to assure the replacements that they would not be laid off at the end of the strike, the employer announced that 20 years' additional seniority would be awarded to replacements and strikers who returned to work by a certain date. An increasing number of strikers returned to work, and eventually the union capitulated and signed a contract with the employer. Thereafter the union charged that the granting of superseniority during the strike was an unfair labor practice.

The Supreme Court reversed the judgment below and affirmed the Board's decision that an unfair labor practice had been committed.[78] The Court contrasted cases in which there is specific evidence of subjective intent to discourage union membership, converting into unfair labor practices what would otherwise be innocent or ambiguous actions normally incident to the conduct of a business, and cases in which an employer's actions are inherently discriminatory or destructive of the right to join a union or to engage in concerted activities. In the latter type of case an employer properly offers evidence, as it did in the instant case, that its purpose was not to discriminate but to promote a legitimate business end. But it was a question for the Board "of weigh-

---

[75] NLRB v. Pecheur Lozenge Co., 209 F2d 393, 33 LRRM 2324 (1953), *cert. denied*, 347 US 953, 34 LRRM 2027 (1954); NLRB v. Waukesha Lime & Stone Co., 343 F2d 504, 508, 58 LRRM 2782 (CA 7, 1965); Hawaii Meat Co., 139 NLRB 966, 51 LRRM 1430 (1962), *set aside*, 321 F2d 397, 53 LRRM 2872 (CA 9, 1963).
[76] NLRB v. Mackay Radio & Telegraph Co., 304 US 333, 2 LRRM 610 (1938); Home Beneficial Life Inc. Co. v. NLRB, 159 F2d 280, 19 LRRM 2208 (CA 4, 1947); General Electric Co., 80 NLRB 174, 23 LRRM 1059 (1948).
[77] 373 US 221, 53 LRRM 2121 (1963).
[78] 132 NLRB 621, 48 LRRM 1379 (1961), *enforcement denied*, 303 F2d 359, 50 LRRM 2186 (CA 3, 1962), *reversed*, 373 US 221, 53 LRRM 2121 (1963).

ing the interests of employees in concerted activity against the interest of an employer in operating his business in a particular manner and of balancing in the light of the Act and its policy the intended consequences upon employee rights against the business ends to be served by the employer's conduct." [79]

The Board had noted the following characteristics of the award of superseniority: (1) the tenure of all strikers was affected, whereas permanent replacement affected only those strikers who were actually replaced; (2) superseniority operated to the detriment of participants in the strike; (3) in effect, individual benefits were offered to strikers who returned to work; (4) the offer of superseniority was a crippling blow to the strike effort; and (5) future collective bargaining was made difficult because the bargaining unit was divided between those who stayed with the union and those who returned to work before the strike ended. The Court was of the opinion that the Board could treat the employer's conduct as carrying its own indicia of intent to discriminate and could hold that overriding business purpose did not save it from illegality. The Board's decision was thus sustained "in view of the deference paid the strike weapon by the federal labor laws and the devastating consequences upon it which the Board found was and would be precipitated by respondent's inherently discriminatory superseniority plan." [80]

NLRB v. Great Dane Trailers, Inc.,[81] a landmark case, deals with another type of preferential action affecting economic strikers. The parties had a contract effective until March 31, 1963. Vacation benefits were payable under the contract on or about July 1 of each year to employees who met certain qualifications. The contract was temporarily extended beyond March 31, 1963, while collective bargaining continued. On May 16, after proper notice, a strike was called which lasted until December. The employer continued in operation, using nonstrikers, replacements, and strikers who had returned to work.

On July 12, 1963, a number of strikers demanded accrued vacation pay. The company rejected the demand, saying that all contractual obligations had been terminated by the strike. Shortly thereafter, however, the company announced that it would allow

[79] 373 US at 229.
[80] 373 US at 235.
[81] 388 US 26, 65 LRRM 2465 (1967).

vacation pay (computed in accordance with the expired contract) to employees who were at work on July 1. The company asserted that the allowance of vacation pay was pursuant to a new policy unilaterally adopted. Violations of Sections 8 (a) (1) and (3) were charged, and the Board held that the company's actions were discrimination discouraging union membership. It ordered the company to cease and desist and to pay vacation benefits to strikers.

The Supreme Court enforced the Board's order, reversing the court of appeals.[82] The Court had no doubt that discrimination had taken place discouraging concerted activities. "The act of paying accrued benefits to one group of employees while announcing the extinction of the same benefits for another group of employees who are distinguishable only by their participation in protected concerted activity surely may have a discouraging effect on either present or future concerted activity." [83] But the inquiry under Section 8 (a) (3) did not stop at this point because a "finding of a violation normally turns on whether the discriminatory conduct was motivated by an antiunion purpose." The Court then reviewed its opinions in the *American Ship Building, Erie Resistor Corp.,* and *Brown* cases.[84] "[S]everal principles of controlling importance" concerning motive, legitimacy of purpose, and burden of proof were stated:

First, if it can reasonably be concluded that the employer's discriminatory conduct was "inherently destructive" of important employee rights, no proof of an antiunion motivation is needed and the Board can find an unfair labor practice even if the employer introduces evidence that the conduct was motivated by business considerations. Second, if the adverse effect of the discriminatory conduct on employee rights is "comparatively slight," an antiunion motivation must be proved to sustain the charge *if* the employer has come forward with evidence of legitimate and substantial business justifications for the conduct. Thus, in either situation, once it has been proved that the employer engaged in discriminatory conduct which could have adversely affected employee rights to *some* extent, the burden is upon the employer to establish that it was motivated

---

[82] 150 NLRB 438, 58 LRRM 1097 (1964), *enforcement denied,* 363 F2d 130, 62 LRRM 2456 (CA 5, 1966).

[83] 388 US at 32.

[84] The first two cases are cited at notes 29 and 77 *supra.* NLRB v. Brown, 380 US 278, 58 LRRM 2663 (1965), dealt with an employer's right to lock out and hire temporary replacements during a whipsaw strike; it is cited at note 38 *supra. See also* Radio Officers' Union v. NLRB, 347 US 17, 33 LRRM 2417 (1954), notes 14 *supra* and 90 *infra.*

by legitimate objectives since proof of motivation is most accessible to him." [85]

Because the employer did not come forward with evidence of legitimate motives for its discriminatory action, the Board's conclusions were held amply supported.

An employer's duty toward replaced economic strikers has been expanded beyond the simple duty not to discriminate against them in favor of new hires when they apply for openings occurring at a later date. In *Laidlaw Corporation* [86] economic strikers applied unconditionally for reinstatement, and the employer was careful to reinstate some of them to jobs that had not been filled by permanent replacements on the application dates. However, when replacements quit their jobs at later dates, the company employed new men and did not seek out the economic strikers even though it knew the applications for reinstatement were still outstanding and active. The Board held, and the Seventh Circuit agreed, that by-passing of economic strikers in favor of inexperienced new hires was conduct inherently destructive of employee rights and a violation of Section 8(a)(3). The Board was of the opinion that this result followed directly from *Great Dane Trailers* [87] and *NLRB v. Fleetwood Trailer Co.* [88] Overruled were earlier decisions [89] limiting the right of reinstatement of economic strikers to those jobs that had not been permanently filled on the dates of the strikers' unconditional applications for reinstatement. Thus it now appears that economic strikers who unconditionally apply for reinstatement and make known their continued availability for work are entitled to reinstatement when permanent replacements leave their jobs, unless there is legitimate and substantial business justi-

---

85 388 US at 34. *See also* extended discussion of this issue in the lockout cases, Chapter 20 *infra*.

86 171 NLRB No. 175, 68 LRRM 1252 (1968), *aff'd*, 414 F2d 99, 71 LRRM 3054 (CA 7, 1969), *cert. denied*, 397 US 920, 73 LRRM 2537 (1970). *See also* discussion of *Laidlaw* in notes 47-49 and accompanying text, Chapter 19, and in note 68, Chapter 31 *infra*.

87 Discussed at note 81 *supra*.

88 389 US 375, 68 LRRM 2737 (1967). In this case jobs were not available to economic strikers on the date of their applications for reinstatement. Two months later, jobs became available when the employer resumed full production. The employer hired new employees instead of qualified strikers and was held to have violated §8(a)(3). The Supreme Court pointed out that the strikers remained "employees" under §2(3) until they obtained regular and substantially equivalent employment elsewhere. *See* Chapter 19 *infra* at note 46.

89 Brown & Root, Inc., 132 NLRB 486, 48 LRRM 1391 (1961), *enforced*, 311 F2d 447, 52 LRRM 2115 (CA 8, 1963); Atlas Storage Division, 112 NLRB 1175, 1180 n. 15, 36 LRRM 1171 (1955), *enforced*, 38 LRRM 2095 (CA 7, 1956); Bartlett-Collins Co., 110 NLRB 395, 397, 398, 35 LRRM 1006 (1954), *affirmed*, 230 F2d 212, 37 LRRM 2409 (CA DC, 1956), *cert. denied*, 351 US 988, 38 LRRM 2238 (1956).

fication (*e.g.*, change of operations, lack of required skills) for denying them the jobs. Absent genuine business justification in such cases, the failure to offer reinstatement to the strikers is an unfair labor practice without regard to specific anti-union animus on the employer's part.

IV. UNION INDUCEMENT OF EMPLOYER TO DISCRIMINATE

Section 8 (b) (2) makes it an unfair labor practice for a union "to cause or attempt to cause" an employer to discriminate in violation of Section 8 (a) (3). The quoted expression is broader than "restrain or coerce," found in Sections 8 (a) (1) and 8 (b) (1). Clearly, trespass and violence and threats thereof are covered. The cases range from coercion by strike and picketing and threats thereof to polite requests followed by compliance. The discriminatory action complained of is usually discharge, but it can take a variety of forms.[90] Obviously, causing an employer to discharge an employee pursuant to the terms of an illegal union security contract is a violation of Section 8 (b) (2).[91]

International Brotherhood of Teamsters, Local 357 v. NLRB[92] is a leading case in which a contract arrangement other than a union-shop contract was drawn into question under Sections 8 (a) (3) and 8 (b) (2). The employer (trucking associations) and the union entered into a hiring-hall agreement. Casual employees were to be dispatched from hiring halls, wherever maintained, on the basis of seniority in the trucking industry. Seniority began with a minimum of three months' service, "irrespective of whether such employee is or is not a member of the Union." The employer agreed not to hire out of line of seniority as long as the hiring hall had employees to dispatch. The union procured the discharge of a union member because he obtained employment without being dispatched by the union. The member brought charges of unfair

[90] Radio Officers' Union v. NLRB, 347 US 17, 33 LRRM 2417 (1954); United Nuclear Corp. v. NLRB, 340 F2d 133, 58 LRRM 2211 (CA 1, 1965); NLRB v. St. Joe Paper Co., 319 F2d 819, 53 LRRM 2633 (CA 2, 1963); NLRB v. Iron Workers Local 494, 295 F2d 808, 49 LRRM 2047 (CA 10, 1961); NLRB v. Longshoremen & Warehousemen Local 10, 283 F2d 558, 46 LRRM 3141 (CA 9, 1960); Local 9, Operating Engineers, 147 NLRB 393, 56 LRRM 1225 (1964). *See* Chapter 27 *infra* for discussion of fair representation cases involving §8(b)(2).
[91] Plasterers Protective & Benevolent Society of Chicago, Local 5 v. NLRB, 341 F2d 539, 58 LRRM 2449 (CA 7, 1965); NLRB v. Industrial Rayon Corp., 297 F2d 62, 49 LRRM 2265 (CA 6, 1961). *See* Chapter 26 *infra*.
[92] 365 US 667, 47 LRRM 2906 (1961). *See* Chapter 26 *infra* at notes 98-99.

labor practices against the union and the employer. The Board ruled that the hiring-hall agreement was unlawful and that the member's discharge was in violation of Sections 8 (a) (3) and 8 (b) (2).[93] The hiring-hall arrangement was made the subject of a cease and desist order, and the employer and union were made liable jointly and severally for back pay. The court of appeals upheld the Board's order,[94] but the Supreme Court reversed.[95]

The Board's decision was based on its earlier holding in *Mountain Pacific Chapter*,[96] wherein a hiring-hall agreement was held illegal despite the inclusion of a nondiscrimination clause. In the Board's view the agreement unduly enhanced the union's control over employment, made the employer appear subservient, and led to an inference that the union's control would be exercised to gain union memberships or other type of fealty.

The Supreme Court noted that hiring halls came into being to eliminate time-consuming and repetitive scouting for jobs by workmen and haphazard, uneconomical searches by employers. The hiring hall had not been expressly outlawed, and Senator Robert Taft had had some kind things to say for the institution in debates on the Act. The Court stated that discrimination could not be inferred from the face of an agreement which specifically prohibited discrimination against casual employees because of union membership or nonmembership.

The Court assumed that the existence of a hiring hall encourages union membership, particularly where provided for in a collective bargaining contract. This was compared to the negotiation of increased wages and improved working conditions, which encourages union membership but does not violate Section 8(a)(3) or 8 (b) (2). The Court conceded that hiring halls might need more regulation, but, as the law stood, it was a matter for Congress or for negotiation between the parties. The Board had "no power to compel directly or indirectly that the hiring hall be included or excluded in collective agreements." [97]

While a hiring-hall agreement may be nondiscriminatory on its face, its administration may be otherwise. In a number of cases

---

93 121 NLRB 1629, 43 LRRM 1029 (1958).
94 275 F2d 646, 45 LRRM 2752 (CA DC, 1960).
95 Note 92 *supra*.
96 119 NLRB 883, 41 LRRM 1460 (1958).
97 365 US at 676.

decided since the *Teamsters* case, discrimination in practice has
been proved and remedial orders have issued.[98]

V. DISCRIMINATION BECAUSE OF USE OF NLRB PROCEDURES

The number of complaints filed under Section 8 (a) (4) is
minuscule compared with the number filed under the other subsections describing employer unfair labor practices. While the
number is small, the cases exhibit a variety of kinds of discrimination.[99]

The narrow scope of the unfair labor practice is to be noted.
The reason for the discrimination must be that an employee "has
filed charges or given testimony under this Act." Planning to file
charges or to testify does not come within the language of Section
8 (a) (4).[100] Nor does filing charges or testifying under legislation
other than the NLRA.[101] But if an employer discriminates for
either of these reasons, he can be held guilty of interference with
concerted activities (Sections 7 and 8 (a) (1)) or discrimination on
their account (Section 8 (a) (3)).[102]

---

[98] NLRB v. Local 269, IBEW, 357 F2d 51, 61 LRRM 2371 (CA 3, 1966); Lummus
Co. v. NLRB, 339 F2d 728, 56 LRRM 2425 (CA DC, 1964); NLRB v. Houston
Maritime Assn., 337 F2d 333, 57 LRRM 2170 (CA 5, 1964); NLRB v. Southern
Stevedoring & Contr. Co., 332 F2d 1017, 56 LRRM 2507 (CA 5, 1964); Cargo
Handlers, 159 NLRB 321, 62 LRRM 1228 (1966); Local 742, Carpenters (J. L. Sim-
mons Co.), 157 NLRB 451, 61 LRRM 1370 (1966). *See also* Summers, *A Summary
Evaluation of the Taft-Hartley Act*, 11 IND. & LAB. REL. REV. 405, 409, 410 (1958).
[99] NLRB v. News Syndicate Co., Inc., 279 F2d 323, 334, 46 LRRM 2275, (CA 2,
1960), *affirmed*, 365 US 695, 47 LRRM 2916 (1961); Vogue Lingerie, Inc. v. NLRB,
280 F2d 224, 46 LRRM 2653 (CA 3, 1960); Electric Motors & Specialties, Inc., 149
NLRB 131, 57 LRRM 1258 (1964); Ritchie Mfg. Co., 147 NLRB 1257, 56 LRRM
1405 (1964), *modified*, 354 F2d 90, 61 LRRM 2013 (CA 8, 1965); East Tennessee
Undergarment Co., 139 NLRB 1129, 51 LRRM 1466 (1962), *enforced*, 53 LRRM
2461 (CA 6, 1963); Beiser Aviation Corp., 135 NLRB 399, 433, 450, 49 LRRM 1508,
1512, 1514 (1962); Thomas J. Aycock, Jr., 135 NLRB 1357, 49 LRRM 1723 (1962);
Esgro, Inc., 135 NLRB 285, 49 LRRM 1472 (1962); Brunswick-Balke-Collender Co.,
131 NLRB 156, 48 LRRM 1025 (1961), 135 NLRB 574, 49 LRRM 1531 (1962),
enforced, 318 F2d 419, 53 LRRM 2430 (CA 3, 1963); Central Rigging & Contracting
Corp., 129 NLRB 342, 46 LRRM 1548 (1960).
[100] Ogle Protection Service, Inc., 149 NLRB 545, 566, 57 LRRM 1337 (1964).
[101] *See* B & M Excavating, Inc., 155 NLRB 1152, 1160, 60 LRRM 1466 (1965).
[102] Salt River Valley Ass'n v. NLRB, 206 F2d 325, 32 LRRM 2598 (CA 9, 1953);
B & M Excavating, Inc., note 101 *supra;* Ogle Protection Service, Inc., 149 NLRB
545, 57 LRRM 1337 (1964); Montgomery Ward & Co., Inc., 154 NLRB 1197, 60
LRRM 1110 (1965); Gibbs Corporation, 131 NLRB 955, 48 LRRM 1167 (1961);
Duralite Co., Inc., 128 NLRB 648, 46 LRRM 1385 (1960); Spandsco Oil & Royalty
Co., 42 NLRB 942, 10 LRRM 208 (1942).

CHAPTER 7

EMPLOYER DOMINATION AND ASSISTANCE TO LABOR ORGANIZATIONS

I. INTRODUCTION

It is an unfair labor practice for an employer "to dominate or interfere with the formation or administration of any labor organization or contribute financial or other support to it. . . ."[1] This restriction was stated first in Section 8 (2) of the Wagner Act; it was retained without change as Section 8 (a) (2) of the Taft-Hartley Act.[2]

The purpose of this provision was to insure that an organization that purports to represent employees in collective bargaining will not be subject to control by an employer, or so dependent on his favor that it would be unable to give wholehearted effort to the employees it represents.[3]

The prohibition protects from employer influence only those employee groups that are in fact labor organizations. An employer is free to support employee recreation committees, credit unions, and other nonlabor organizations.[4] Once the existence of a labor organization is established, the Board and the courts have readily identified the unfair labor practice when such organization is

---

[1] National Labor Relations Act (Wagner Act) §8 (2), 29 USC §148, 48 Stat. 449 (1935). The additional language of the clause reads as follows: ". . . *Provided,* That subject to rules and regulations made and published by the Board pursuant to section 6, an employer shall not be prohibited from permitting employees to confer with him during working hours without loss of time or pay. . . ."

[2] The literature dealing with this provision includes the following: Crager, *Company Unions Under the National Labor Relations Act,* 40 MICH. L. REV. 831 (1942); Dusen, *What is Employer Domination and Support?,* 13 TEMP. L. Q. 63 (1938); Annot., 10 ALR. 3d 861 (1966); Annot., 100 ALR 2d 1280 (1965).

[3] Hot Point Div., G. E. Co., 128 NLRB 788, 46 LRRM 1421 (1960); Holland Mfg. Co., 129 NLRB 766, 47 LRRM 1067 (1960).

[4] Chicago Rawhide Mfg. Co. v. NLRB, 221 F 2d 165, 35 LRRM 2665 (CA 7, 1955).

dominated or controlled by the employer.[5] It is more difficult to resolve the questions posed by the statute when employer activity amounts only to aid that falls in the gray area between illegal assistance and legal cooperation.[6] When the Board has found an 8 (a) (2) violation by an employer, such finding may also support an 8 (b) (1) (A) charge against the union for having interferred with the employees' right to organize, as by entering into an illegal contract with the employer.[7]

II. LABOR ORGANIZATION

From the first there have been difficulties in determining whether certain employee committees or groups are labor organizations within the meaning of the Act.[8] Section 2 (5) defines a labor organization as:

> . . . any organization of any kind, or any agency or employee representation committee, or plan, in which employees participated and which exists for the purpose, in whole or in part, of dealing with employers, concerning grievances, labor disputes, wages, rates of pay, hours of employment, or conditions of work.

In *NLRB v. Cabot Carbon Co.*,[9] for example, the employer organized a committee to provide "a procedure for considering employees' ideas and problems of mutual interest to the employees and management." [10] The Supreme Court held that since the committee discussed seniority, job classifications, holidays, vacations, and various other conditions of employment, it existed *at least in part* for the purpose "of dealing with employers concerning grievances, labor disputes, wages, rates of pay, hours of employment, or conditions of work." A key issue in the case was whether Section 9 (a), a Taft-Hartley amendment, sanctioned such committees. According to the Court, the 9 (a) amendment merely provided "that any individual employee or group of employees shall have the right personally to present their own grievances to their employer"; it did not state that an employer may form or

---

5 The Carpenter Steel Co., 76 NLRB 670, 21 LRRM 1232 (1948); Matter of Pennsylvania Greyhound Lines, 1 NLRB 1, 1 LRRM 303 (1935), *enforced* 303 US 261, 2 LLRM 600 (1938).

6 NLRB v. Magic Slacks, Inc., 314 F 2d 844, 52 LRRM 2641 (CA 7, 1963); Coppus Engineering Corp. v. NLRB, 240 F 2d 564, 39 LRRM 2315 (CA 1, 1957).

7 NLRB v. Kaase Co., 346 F 2d 24, 59 LRRM 2290 (CA 8, 1965); Ellery Products Mfg. Co., 149 NLRB 1388, 57 LRRM 1478 (1964). *See* note 80 *infra* and accompanying text.

8 NLRB v. Cabot Carbon Co., 360 US 203, 44 LRRM 2204 (1959).

9 *Ibid.*

10 *Id.* at 205.

maintain an employee committee for the purpose of dealing with the employer concerning grievances, and therefore the amendment did not limit the traditional 8 (a) (2) proscription on employer-dominated labor organizations.[11]

Similarly, employer programs to aid in communicating with employees or motivating workers to accept employer goals, such as multiple management plans, junior boards of directors, or employee suggestion committees, have sometimes been treated as employer-dominated labor organizations.[12] They are deemed labor organizations when they have employee participation and their discussions include rates of pay, hours of employment, and working conditions.[13]

III. EMPLOYER DOMINATION

Once an employee group is identified as a labor organization, it must be insulated from employer *domination* or *control*. Prohibited control obtains when the labor organization is the creation of the employer rather than the employees.[14] Initially the prohibition was aimed at employers who had created subjugated unions to minimize the threat of organization by an outside union, for "company unions" were popular during the thirties.[15] The first case reported by the NLRB under the Wagner Act involved Pennsylvania Greyhound Lines, which had formed and controlled a union to handle employee grievances in an effort to avoid dealing with a more militant outside organization. The Board completely disestablished the organization, The Employees Association of Pennsylvania Greyhound Lines, and ordered the employer never to bargain with it again. But by the eve of the enactment of the Taft-Hartley amendments in 1947, Board Chairman Herzog was able to observe in the *Detroit Edison* case [16] that employer domination had ceased to be the problem which it had been in 1935. The prohibition was, nevertheless, kept intact in the new Act.

---

11 *Id.* at 217–18. *See* Chapters 11 and 27 *infra* for discussion of the proviso to §9(a).
12 NLRB v. Cabot Carbon Co., 360 US 203, 44 LRRM 2204 (1959) ; NLRB v. Jas. H. Matthews & Co., 156 F 2d 706, 18 LRRM 2265 (CA 3, 1946) .
13 *Ibid.*
14 Han Dee Spring & Mfg. Co., 132 NLRB 1542, 48 LRRM 1566 (1961) ; Wahlgren Magnetics, 132 NLRB 1613, 48 LRRM 1542 (1961) .
15 Pennsylvania Greyhound Lines, Inc., 1 NLRB 1, 1 LRRM 303 (1935), *enforced* 303 US 261, 2 LRRM 600 (1938) .
16 74 NLRB 267, 20 LRRM 1160 (1947) .

The Board has used certain characteristics to identify domination, although "the test . . . is not an objective one but rather subjective from the standpoint of the employee."[17] The Board found domination in *Wahlgren Magnetics*,[18] where the employer organized the functions, nature, and structure of the employee grievance committee, the supervisors conducted committee meetings, and committee members were paid for time spent conducting committee business. The Board also has found domination where an employer controlled an employee association by subsidizing it, donating to its treasury, controlling its charter and internal operation, giving automatic membership to all employees, and having supervisors attend and participate in meetings.[19]

These factors have been found to support a finding of domination in given situations, but since the test of control is subjective rather than objective,[20] the presence of one particular factor does not constitute a *per se* violation. Furthermore, the presence of a potential to dominate has been held not to be equivalent to domination, and an unfair labor practice finding by the Board without the presence of actual domination has been rejected on appeal.[21]

IV. EMPLOYER INTERFERENCE

Another unlawful means of counteracting legitimate employee organizational efforts is for the employer to *interfere* with the creation or operation of a labor organization. This type of activity goes beyond interfering with the rights of individual employees in violation of Section 8 (a) (1) ; it is aimed at the labor organization as an entity.[22] It differs from domination in that control is not so great that the organization is subjugated to the employer's will.

---

[17] Chicago Rawhide Mfg. Co. v. NLRB, 221 F 2d 165, 166, 35 LRRM 2665, 2666 (CA 7, 1955) ; NLRB v. Sharples Chemicals, 209 F 2d 645, 652, 33 LRRM 2438, 2444 (CA 6, 1954) ; NLRB v. Wemyss, 212 F 2d 465, 471, 34 LRRM 2124, 2129 (CA 9, 1954) .

[18] 132 NLRB 1613, 48 LRRM 1542 (1961) .

[19] Thompson Ramo Wooldridge, Inc., 132 NLRB 993, 48 LRRM 1470 (1961) .

[20] Chicago Rawhide Mfg. Co. v. NLRB, 221 F 2d 165, 166, 35 LRRM 2665 (CA 7, 1955) ; NLRB v. Sharples Chemicals, 209 F 2d 645, 652, 33 LRRM 2438 (CA 6, 1954) ; NLRB v. Wemyss, 212 F 2d 465, 471, 34 LRRM 2124 (CA 9, 1954) .

[21] Chicago Rawhide Mfg. Co. v. NLRB, 221 F 2d 165, 166, 35 LRRM 2665 (CA 7, 1955) ; Coppus Engineering Corp. v. NLRB, 240 F 2d 564, 39 LRRM 2315 (CA 1, 1957) .

[22] *See, e.g.,* Nassau and Suffolk Contractors Assn., 118 NLRB 174, 40 LRRM 1146 (1957) .

An employer may not form a labor organization for employees,[23] and neither may he interfere with organizational efforts by employees by engaging in a competitive organizational campaign.[24] However, an employer has been allowed to tell employees that he favors an inside union,[25] and he may even suggest they form one if he does not help them plan and organize it.[26]

Efforts to protect labor organizations from employer influence during the organizing period include preventing unions from enlisting the support of friendly supervisors.[27] "[A]n employer may properly be held responsible for interfering in the affairs of a union because of participation by his supervisors even though such participation was not expressly authorized or ratified."[28] The employer may, therefore, object to having a union placed on the ballot in a Board election if the authorization cards have been collected by the employer's supervisors.[29] Such objection at one time could be voiced at the representation hearing,[30] but now must be raised prior to the hearing. When such objection is made, the validity of the union showing of interest is determined in a separate administrative investigation in the same manner as allegations of fraud, misrepresentation, or coercion.[31] When an organization has obtained its showing of interest by supervisors having solicited authorization cards, no representation question is presented because the union is incapable of representing the employees.[32]

After a union has been recognized, the Board has found a violation when supervisors and company executives have retained union

---

[23] The Carpenter Steel Co., 76 NLRB 670, 21 LRRM 1232 (1948).
[24] Jack Smith Beverage Co., Inc., 94 NLRB 1401, 28 LRRM 1199 (1951). In *Oil Transport Co.*, 182 NLRB No. 148, 74 LRRM 1259 (1970), the Board found unlawful assistance to a union where the employer (1) threatened to go out of business or to refuse to negotiate if the employees selected a rival union, (2) attempted to dissuade union leaders from switching their allegiance to the rival union, and (3) recognized and signed a contract with the union on the same day.
[25] Chicago Rawhide Mfg. Co. v. NLRB, *supra* note 4.
[26] Coppus Engineering Corp. v. NLRB, 240 F 2d 564, 39 LRRM 2315 (CA 1, 1957).
[27] *See, e.g.,* Wolfe Metal Products, 119 NLRB 659, 41 LRRM 1164 (1957); Desilu Productions, 106 NLRB 179, 32 LRRM 1418 (1953); Alaska Salmon Industry, Inc., 78 NLRB 185, 22 LRRM 1190 (1948).
[28] Plumbers, Local 636 v. NLRB, 287 F 2d 354, 47 LRRM 2457 (CA DC, 1961); *See also* NLRB v. Park Edge Sheridan Meats, Inc., 323 F 2d 956, 54 LRRM 2411 (CA 2, 1963).
[29] American District Telephone Co. (Pittsburgh, Pa.), 89 NLRB 1635, 26 LRRM 1135 (1950); Wolfe Metal Products, 119 NLRB 659, 41 LRRM 1164 (1957).
[30] *Ibid.*
[31] Georgia Kraft Co., 120 NLRB 806, 42 LRRM 1066 (1958).
[32] Desilu Productions, 106 NLRB 179, 32 LRRM 1418 (1953); American District Telephone Co. (Pittsburgh, Pa.), 89 NLRB 1635, 26 LRRM 1135 (1950). *See* Chapter 8 infra at notes 74-75.

membership, obtained prior to their rise from the ranks of employees, and have voted in internal union elections.[33] A further violation occurs when supervisors who are also union members become members of the union bargaining committee, even though they constitute a minority of its membership.[34] But these restrictions imposed by the Act only preclude supervisors from voting in elections and participating in union administration or in bargaining; they do not bar a supervisor from remaining in a union in a passive role.[35] These restrictions apply only to supervisors within the definition of the Act, not to nonsupervisory employees such as lead men.[36] The Board has found it necessary, however, to make special allowances for men in the construction industry because of the frequent movement in that industry between supervisory and nonsupervisory positions.[37]

V. SUPPORT v. COOPERATION

While the Board and the courts have had little difficulty in dealing with employer domination, there has been considerable disagreement among the cases that have involved employer assistance or *support* to labor organizations.[38]

The Act specifically prohibits an employer from contributing "financial or other support" to a labor organization. Indirect employer support which has been invalidated has included allowing an organization to use company facilities,[39] time,[40] or concessions.[41] And NLRB suspicion has been aroused when an employer has allowed an inside union [42] or other favored organization [43] to use

---

[33] Nassau and Suffolk Contractors Assn., 118 NLRB 174, 40 LRRM 1146 (1957).
[34] *Ibid.*
[35] NLRB v. Valentine Sugars, Inc., 211 F 2d 317, 33 LRRM 2679 (CA 5, 1954).
[36] *See, e.g.,* Mason Au & Magenheimer Confectionery Mfg. Co., 137 NLRB 680, 50 LRRM 1235 (1962); NLRB v. Valentine Sugars, Inc., 211 F 2d 317, 33 LRRM 2679 (CA 5, 1954).
[37] *See* Plumbers, Local 636 v. NLRB, 287 F 2d 354, 47 LRRM 2457 (CA DC, 1961).
[38] *See, e.g.,* NLRB v. Magic Slacks, Inc., 314 F 2d 844, 52 LRRM 2641 (CA 7, 1963); NLRB v. Post Publishing Co., 311 F 2d 565, 52 LRRM 2106 (CA 7, 1962); NLRB v. Valentine Sugars, Inc., 211 F 2d 317, 33 LRRM 2679 (CA 5, 1954).
[39] Chicago Rawhide Mfg. Co. v. NLRB, *supra* note 4.
[40] Kimbrell v. NLRB, 290 F 2d 799, 48 LRRM 2310 (CA 4, 1961); NLRB v. Clinton Woolen Mfg. Co., 141 F 2d 753, 14 LRRM 632 (CA 6, 1944).
[41] Farrington Mfg. Co., 93 NLRB 1416, 27 LRRM 1598 (1951); NLRB v. Post Publishing Co., *enforcement denied,* 311 F 2d 565, 52 LRRM 2106 (CA 7, 1962).
[42] Chicago Rawhide Mfg. Co. v. NLRB, *supra* note 4.
[43] NLRB v. Corning Glass Works, 204 F 2d 422, 32 LRRM 2136 (CA 1, 1953); Novak Logging, 119 NLRB 1573, 41 LRRM 1346 (1958).

company bulletin boards,[44] company meeting rooms,[45] or company printing equipment to print notices.[46] Employers granting concessions to a favored organization, such as allowing the union officers to handle grievances and other organizational duties on company time [47] and employers paying overtime rates for performing such duties after business hours,[48] have been subjected to remedial orders. Allowing a favored organization to operate and retain the profits from employer concessions, such as lunch rooms or cigarette machines,[49] is another form of interdicted aid.

The Board initially treated assisting activities as *per se* violations of the Act, but after encountering enforcement difficulty [50] it adopted a less rigid policy.[51] Although the Board may still find an unfair labor practice as a result of the presence of such factors,[52] it will not find a violation if the assistance is minimal and does not endanger the independence of the labor organization.[53]

When reviewing violations based upon such assistance, the courts have attempted to differentiate support from cooperation.[54] A history of anti-union activity is deemed important; [55] if the employer does not have such a background, a determination may be made as to whether the employer took an active part in initiating the organization.[56] When the employer has had a history of clean hands, the courts have looked for evidence of prior complaints concerning the subject activity,[57] and then to the extent

44 Webb Mfg., Inc., 154 NLRB 827, 60 LRRM 1041 (1965); Farrington Mfg. Co., 93 NLRB 1416, 27 LRRM 1598 (1951).
45 Merrill Transport Co., 141 NLRB 1089, 52 LRRM 1452 (1963); Edmont, Inc., 139 NLRB 1528, 51 LRRM 1534 (1962).
46 NLRB v. Post Publishing Co., *supra* note 41.
47 Wean Mfg. Co., 147 NLRB 112, 56 LRRM 1177 (1964).
48 Coppus Engineering Corp. v. NLRB, *supra* note 26.
49 NLRB v. Post Publishing Co., *supra* note 41; Farrington Mfg. Co., *supra* note 41.
50 NLRB v. Magic Slacks, Inc., 314 F 2d 844, 52 LRRM 2641 (CA 7, 1963); NLRB v. Post Publishing Co., 311 F 2d 565, 52 LRRM 2106 (CA 7, 1962); Coppus Engineering Corp. v. NLRB, 240 F 2d 564, 39 LRRM 2315 (CA 1, 1957); NLRB v. Valentine Sugars, Inc., 211 F 2d 317, 33 LRRM 2679 (CA 5, 1954).
51 Coamo Knitting Mills, Inc., 150 NLRB 579, 58 LRRM 1116 (1964); Manuela Mfg. Co., 143 NLRB 379, 53 LRRM 1337 (1963) (Trial Examiner's Report).
52 Webb Mfg. Co., 154 NLRB 827, 60 LRRM 1041 (1965); Wean Mfg. Co., 147 NLRB 112, 56 LRRM 1177 (1964).
53 Coamo Knitting Mills, Inc., 150 NLRB 579, 58 LRRM 1116 (1964).
54 NLRB v. Post Publishing Co., 311 F 2d 565, 52 LRRM 2106 (CA 7, 1962); NLRB v. Magic Slacks, Inc., 314 F 2d 844, 52 LRRM 2641 (CA 7, 1963); Chicago Rawhide Mfg. Co. v. NLRB, 221 F 2d 165, 35 LRRM 2665 (CA 7, 1955).
55 Coppus Engineering Corp. v. NLRB, *supra* note 26.
56 NLRB v. Post Publishing Co., *supra* note 54.
57 Chicago Rawhide Mfg. Co. v. NLRB, *supra* note 4.

and nature of the aid and the presence or absence of employer interference in the administration of the organization. When it has been found that the organization is in fact independent of employer control and that the support given is of a trivial nature, courts have applied the *de minimis* doctrine and have avoided the literal language of the Act.[58] Courts have been unwilling to find unfair labor practices and to decertify labor organizations where merely a cooperative spirit, which advanced the industrial stability intended by the Act, was evidenced, particularly if the employees have not been deprived of Section 7 rights.[59] This judicial policy of encouraging union-employer cooperation was finally accepted by the Board in *Coamo Knitting Mills* [60] where the Board held that "the use of company time and property does not, *per se*, establish unlawful assistance."

VI. THE REQUIREMENT OF NEUTRALITY

Since Section 8 (a) (2) prohibits an employer from contributing "support" to a labor organization, an employer generally violates the Act if he aids one of two competing labor unions. The goal of the competing labor organizations is to become the collective bargaining representative of the employees in question, and the employer facilitates one organization's efforts to achieve this goal by recognizing it as the bargaining agent. ᐸThe Board took special cognizance of this problem two years before the Taft-Hartley amendments in *Midwest Piping Co., Inc.*[61] In this case the Steelworkers and the Steamfitters each petitioned the Board for an election; while the petitions were pending, the employer recognized and entered into a closed-shop contract [62] with the Steamfitters. The Board held that this contract violated employee rights under Section 7 and employer obligations under Section 8 (1). Although an 8 (1) violation was found, the substance of the offense involved 8 (2) because the employer had interfered with the employees by giving illegal "support" to the Steamfitters.[63] The Board thus established the *Midwest Piping* doctrine, declaring

---

58 Coppus Engineering Corp. v. NLRB, 240 F 2d 564, 570, 39 LRRM 2315 (CA 1, 1957) (concurring opinion).
59 Chicago Rawhide Mfg. Co. v. NLRB, 221 F 2d 165, 35 LRRM 2665 (CA 7, 1955); NLRB v. Magic Slacks, Inc., 314 F 2d 844, 52 LRRM 2641 (CA 7, 1963).
60 150 NLRB 579, 582, 58 LRRM 1116 (1964). *See also* Manuela Mfg. Co., Inc., 143 NLRB 379, 385, 53 LRRM 1337 (1963) (Trial Examiner's Report).
61 63 NLRB 1060, 17 LRRM 40 (1945).
62 The closed shop was not illegal under the original Wagner Act.
63 Midwest Piping Co., Inc., 63 NLRB 1060, 1071, 17 LRRM 40 (1945).

that it was an unfair labor practice for an employer to recognize one of two or more competing unions after a representation question had been submitted to the Board by the filing of a petition.

In 1951 the doctrine was narrowed by *William D. Gibson Co.*[64] In that case the Steelworkers Union contract, covering a unit of production and maintenance employees, had run out, and the union and the employer were in negotiations for a new agreement. The Machinists Union asserted that it represented 30 tool room employees, who had been included in the 500-man plant unit. When the employer refused the Machinists' demand for recognition, this outside organization petitioned the Board for an election. While the matter was pending before the Board, the employer entered into a new contract with the Steelworkers, with the tool room included in its coverage. The Machinists charged that this agreement violated *Midwest Piping*, but the Board held that application of the doctrine in this case would not aid the statutory goal of industrial stability. It held that the contract with an *incumbent* union, even though challenged by an outside union, justified the exception.

In 1958, in *Shea Chemical Corp.*,[65] the Board was again called upon to review *Midwest Piping*. The Chemical Workers Union had demanded that it be recognized by the company; but prior to receiving the demand, the company had entered into a recognition agreement with the United Mine Workers. After the Chemical Workers' demand was denied by the employer, the union petitioned for a Board election, whereupon the company and the Mine Workers entered into a collective bargaining agreement, although the Chemical Workers' petition was still pending before the Board. The Board overruled *Gibson*, holding that the employer violated the Act by entering into a collective bargaining agreement while the representation case was still pending, even though the contracting union had been recognized as the bargaining representative before the intervening union filed its petition. The Board stated its new version of the *Midwest Piping* doctrine as follows:

> Upon presentation of a rival or conflicting claim which raises a *real* question concerning representation an employer may not go so far as to bargain collectively with the incumbent (or any other) union

---

[64] 110 NLRB 660, 35 LRRM 1092 (1954).
[65] Shea Chemical Corp., 121 NLRB 1027, 42 LRRM 1486 (1958).

unless and until the question concerning representation has been settled by the board.[66]

But after announcing this policy, the Board added this exception:

The Midwest Piping Doctrine does not apply in situations when, because of contract bar or certification year or other established reason, the rival claim does not raise a real representation question.[67]

In an earlier case [68] the same year, the Board had held that an employer could not recognize one of two competing unions once "a real question concerning representation" had arisen. According to the Board, "a real question concerning representation" was presented when a competing union filed a petition and the Board indicated that it had administratively determined that there was a showing of interest by taking cognizance of the case.[69]

In 1961 the Third Circuit rejected this position and held that the Board must have more substantial evidence of a real question concerning representation before it may find that an employer has committed an unfair labor practice by signing a contract with an incumbent union. In this case there was no evidence to support the challenging union's claim of majority status except that the petition had been filed, and the Board had scheduled a hearing.[70] The court insisted that the Board must have substantial evidence to support its determination that a real question concerning representation existed, and that the mere filing of a petition coupled with the Board's scheduling of a hearing did not establish, in itself, that there was such a question. It appears, however, that the Board has refused to adopt the view of the Third Circuit, for it still applies the same test.[71]

The question of illegal support also arises when an employer purchases the plant of a second employer and attempts to impose the union representing the employees of his original plant on the employees of the new plant in lieu of their former bargaining representative. In *Illinois Malleable Iron* [72] the Board found an 8 (a) (2) violation in such a situation. The purchasing employer granted a check-off agreement covering the new plant to the union

---

66 *Id.* at 1028.

67 *Ibid.*

68 Novak Logging, 119 NLRB 1573, 41 LRRM 1436 (1958).

69 Swift & Co., 128 NLRB 732, 46 LRRM 1381 (1960).

70 NLRB v. Swift & Co., 294 F 2d 285, 48 LRRM 2699 (CA 3, 1961). *See also,* NLRB v. North Electric Co., 296 F 2d 137, 49 LRRM 2128 (CA 6, 1961).

71 Connie Jean, Inc., 162 NLRB 154, 64 LRRM 1243 (1966).

72 120 NLRB 451, 41 LRRM 1510 (1958). *See also* Wm. J. Burns Int'l. Detective Agency, Inc., 182 NLRB No. 50, 74 LRRM 1098 (1970), Chapter 13 *infra* at note 35.

with which it had been dealing, although it never had been determined that a company-wide bargaining unit was appropriate or that the purchased plant was an accretion to the existing bargaining unit. The Board has been particularly watchful in this area to insure that an employer does not enter into a contract which includes a union security clause or an exclusive bargaining agreement before the union actually represents a majority of the employees in the unit.[73] Contracts with union security clauses make it difficult for the employees to extract themselves from the union, for they must sacrifice the initiation fees and dues they are forced to pay to the incumbent if they decide to select a new representative.

Broad application of these principles was evident in the Supreme Court's holding in the *Bernhard-Altman* case,[74] that if an employer recognizes a union as a sole representative of its employees before the union has gained a majority, the employer's good faith will not constitute a defense. The contract in question, however, did not contain a union-shop provision. Recognition of a union which does not in fact represent a majority, even if there is no rival union in the picture, violates Section 8(a)(2). Nor was it a defense that the union achieved a majority between the time of recognition and the time of execution of a formal collective bargaining agreement.[75] The Board and the Court assumed that the support provided by premature recognition gives the union added status, thus interfering with the employees' freedom of choice.

The Supreme Court, however, has refused to approve the Board's theory that the six-month statute of limitations for filing an unfair labor practice charge is tolled when the union gains a majority as a result of its illegal status.[76] After the Board had found the employer guilty of an unfair labor practice in a case in which the charge was filed more than six months after the union had gained a majority, the Court held that Board action was barred by limitations under Section 10 (b).[77]

---

[73] *See, e.g.,* Ellery Products Mfg. Co., 149 NLRB 1388, 57 LRRM 1478 (1964); Kenrich Petrochemicals, Inc., 149 NLRB 910, 57 LRRM 1395 (1964); Sinko Mfg. & Tool Co., 149 NLRB 201, 57 LRRM 1281 (1964). *See* Chapter 26 *infra.*
[74] Int'l Ladies' Garment Workers' Union v. NLRB, 366 US 731, 48 LRRM 2251 (1961). The Act does not, the Court pointed out, make *scienter* the basis of an unfair labor practice. *See* discussion of motive as an element of a §8 (a)(1) violation, Chapter 5 *supra.*
[75] *Ibid.*
[76] Local Lodge No. 1424, IAM v. NLRB, 362 US 411, 45 LRRM 3212 (1960).
[77] *Ibid. Cf.* Retail Clerks Locals 128 & 633 v. Lion Dry Goods, Inc., 369 US 17, 49 LRRM 2670 (1962), discussed in Chapter 17 *infra.*

In noting the potential liability of an employer who makes a good-faith mistake and prematurely recognizes a bargaining representative, it should also be noted that an employer under certain circumstances may be liable under Section 8(a)(5) if he fails to bargain with a union that does in fact represent a majority of the employees.[78] This kind of dilemma was reached by the Board in 1953 when it held that an employer does not violate Section 8(a)(5) if he fails to bargain with a majority union because he incorrectly guesses that a rival has raised "a real question concerning representation." [79]

VII. THE UNION AS A PARTY TO THE EMPLOYER'S DOMINATION OR SUPPORT

If a minority union enters into a contract with an employer in which it is made the sole bargaining representative, the union will be guilty of an unfair labor practice under Section 8 (b) (1) (A) of the Act.[80] And it is unlawful for a union to coerce an employer into granting a contract which violates Section 8 (a) (2). In *Ellery Products Mfg. Co.*[81] a minority union refused to show signed representation cards of the employees and induced the employer to extend recognition by threatening to strike at a time of peak production. Both parties were found guilty of unfair labor practices.

A more subtle type of pressure was applied against the employer in *Kenrich Petrochemicals, Inc.,*[82] by the union's filing of a Section 8(a)(5) refusal-to-bargain charge. The employer had refused to bargain when the union failed to produce authorization cards, and although the company was still in doubt as to the union's status, it finally acceded to the union's demand rather than face the threat of Board action or an unfair labor practice strike. The employer and union then agreed on a contract with a union security clause. Both parties were charged successfully with unfair labor practices under Sections 8 (a) (2) and 8 (b) (1) (A), respec-

---

78 *See* Chapter 10 *infra.*
79 National Carbon Div., Union Carbide, 105 NLRB 441, 32 LRRM 1276 (1953).
80 Int'l Ladies' Garment Workers' Union v. NLRB, 366 US 731, 48 LRRM 2251 (1961), note 74 *supra;* Ellery Products Mfg. Co., 149 NLRB 1388, 57 LRRM 1478 (1964); Kenrich Petrochemicals, Inc., 149 NLRB 910, 57 LRRM 1395 (1964).
81 149 NLRB 1388, 57 LRRM 1478 (1964).
82 149 NLRB 910, 57 LRRM 1395 (1964).

tively, as the General Counsel was able to show that only three persons in the seven-man unit were union members.

Another joint offense was found when an employer and a union entered into an illegal hiring arrangement which required new employees to become union members.[83] This resulted in an 8 (a) (2) violation by the employer and an 8 (b) (1) (A) violation by the union. The parties had entered into a contract containing a union security clause; a violation was found, although the union represented a majority of the employees, because it was not an uncoerced majority.

VIII. REMEDYING THE EFFECT OF EMPLOYER DOMINATION OR SUPPORT

Wherever the Board has found employer control of an organization to be so extensive that it constitutes domination, the Board has disestablished the organization.[84] Prior to the Taft-Hartley amendments it was Board policy to disestablish a union whenever an 8 (a) (2) violation was found, provided the union was not affiliated with a national or international federation. The union could be certified again if selected by the employees at a later Board election if the affected union subsequently affiliated with such a national or international federation.[85] This policy was changed because Section 10 (c) of the Taft-Hartley Act dictated that remedies be applied against organizations involved in 8 (a) (2) violations without differentiation between independent unions and unions affiliated with national or international federations. The Board explained in *Carpenter Steel* that the policy prior to Taft-Hartley had been based on the belief that a national or international federation could not be permanently and completely subjugated to the employer's will; [86] thus complete disestablishment was not required to effectuate the performance of the statute.

Applying present statutory criteria, the Board in *Jack Smith Beverage Co.*[87] completely disestablished Teamsters Local 164 despite its international affiliation. Local 164 was found to be subject to the degree of control required for disestablishment. However, this remedy is rarely exercised against an affiliated

---

83 Shipwrecking, Inc., 136 NLRB 1518, 50 LRRM 1028 (1962).
84 The Carpenter Steel Co., 76 NLRB 670, 21 LRRM 1232 (1948).
85 *Id.* at 673.
86 *Id.* at 672.
87 94 NLRB 1401, 28 LRRM 1199 (1951).

union as there are few instances of a single employer dominating the affairs of a local with international affiliation.

In administering its remedial orders, the Board had established criteria prior to Taft-Hartley which have since guided it in determining whether the employer has complied with an order to disestablish a dominated union. It insisted that a line of cleavage be drawn between the employer and the dominated union.[88] This requires a public announcement of the company's intent to cease bargaining with the union [89] and of its intent to withdraw all support from it.[90] After this notice has been given, the employees may form a new organization, but the employer is not allowed to take any part in the reorganization,[91] and he is not allowed to reinstate his past support. When an employer has been ordered to cease giving prohibited support to a merely assisted organization, the criteria for determining compliance are self-evident, for the Board's remedy is a cease-and-desist order.

The Taft-Hartley amendments probably have had their greatest impact on unaffiliated unions which have been employer supported but not dominated. Prior to Taft-Hartley it had been the Board's practice to disestablish such unions,[92] but after the addition of Section 10 (c) the standard remedy has been to deny the union recognition until the employer support has been eliminated and the union has been certified following a Board election.[93]

In addition to disestablishing employer-dominated unions and ordering employers to stop bargaining with assisted unions until they have been cleared by Board certification, the Board, in its discretion, has ordered the employer to reimburse the employees for initiation fees and dues that have been checked off under a

---

[88] Dade Drydock Corp., 58 NLRB 833, 15 LRRM 67 (1944) ; Andrew Jergens Co., 43 NLRB 457, 11 LRRM 23 (1942).

[89] Kansas City Power & Light Co. v. NLRB, 111 F 2d 340, 6 LRRM 938 (CA 8, 1940) ; NLRB v. Tappan Stove Co., 174 F 2d 1007, 24 LRRM 2125 (CA 6, 1949) ; Remington Arms Co., 62 NLRB 611, 16 LRRM 199 (1945).

[90] American Smelting & Refining Co. v. NLRB, 126 F 2d 680, 10 LRRM 423 (1942).

[91] NLRB v. Continental Oil Co., 121 F 2d 20, 8 LRRM 907 (CA 10, 1941) ; Continental Oil Co. v. NLRB, 113 F 2d 473, 6 LRRM 1020 (CA 10, 1940).

[92] See The Carpenter Steel Co., 76 NLRB 670, 21 LRRM 1232 (1948) ; but see Detroit Edison Co., 74 NLRB 267, 20 LRRM 1160 (1947).

[93] The Carpenter Steel Co., supra note 84, where the Board declared its intent to apply the same remedy to both affiliated and unaffiliated labor organizations—this in response to the congressional mandate in §10(c).

tainted contract.[94] This reimbursement remedy has been used only in instances where the illegal contract forced the employees to pay dues and initiation fees. The typical situation in which reimbursement is required is where the employer and a union that does not represent an uncoerced majority of the employees have entered into a collective bargaining agreement that provides for exclusive representation, a union security clause, and dues check-off.[95] Under such circumstances, the union and the employer have been held jointly and severally liable for the cost of the agreement to the employees, including initiation fees, dues, and other obligations of union membership, plus an allowance for interest.[96]

Where there has been an illegal contract, but the employer has not enforced a check-off agreement, reimbursement has not been required.[97] Nor has reimbursement been required where union membership was not compulsory and the employees had consented to the check-off.[98] In other cases, where only certain employees were coerced to sign check-off authorizations, the employer has not been required to reimburse those who voluntarily signed. If there has been a check-off clause and a union security clause, but neither has been enforced, no reimbursement is ordered.[99] In line with this same policy, the Board does not require an employer to reimburse employees who have selected the union as their representative in a valid Board election, and this has also been true even with regard to dues paid prior to the election.[100] According to these holdings, the Board only requires reimbursement of money that has been paid against the employees' will to a labor organization that does not represent their interests, in keeping with the statutory requirement that the Board can only grant remedies, not impose penalties.[101]

---

[94] Virginia Electric & Power Co. v. NLRB, 319 US 533, 12 LRRM 739 (1943) ; Bernhardt Bros. Tugboat Serv., Inc. v. NLRB, 328 F 2d 757, 55 LRRM 2550 (CA 7, 1964) ; Supermarket Housewares, Inc., 133 NLRB 1273, 49 LRRM 1025 (1961).
[95] NLRB v. Downtown Bakery Corp., 330 F 2d 921, 56 LRRM 2097 (CA 6, 1964) ; Lunardi-Central Distributing Co., 161 NLRB 126, 63 LRRM 1457 (1966).
[96] NLRB v. Downtown Bakery Corp., 330 F 2d 921, 56 LRRM 2097 (CA 6, 1964).
[97] Lenscraft Optical Corp., 128 NLRB 836, 46 LRRM 1414 (1960) ; Bowman Transp., Inc., 112 NLRB 387, 36 LRRM 1021 (1955).
[98] Remington Arms Co. Inc., 62 NLRB 611, 16 LRRM 199 (1945) ; NLRB v. Shedd-Brown Mfg. Co., 213 F 2d 163, 34 LRRM 2278 (CA 7, 1954).
[99] NLRB v. Konner Chevrolet, Inc., 338 F 2d 972, 57 LRRM 2583 (CA 3, 1964).
[100] NLRB v. Englander Co., 237 F 2d 599, 38 LRRM 2765 (CA 7, 1956).
[101] See Chapter 31 infra for detailed treatment of Board remedies.

PART III

THE REPRESENTATION PROCESS

AND UNION RECOGNITION

CHAPTER 8

REPRESENTATION PROCEEDINGS AND ELECTIONS

I. QUESTIONS CONCERNING REPRESENTATION

Central to the administration of the National Labor Relations Act is the machinery that provides for determining union representation. The mandate which the Act creates is contained in a single sentence:

Representatives designated or selected for the purposes of collective bargaining by the majority of the employees in a unit appropriate for such purposes, shall be the exclusive representatives of all the employees in such unit for the purposes of collective bargaining in respect to rates of pay, wages, hours of employment or other conditions of employment. . . .[1]

The Act thus provides for union recognition and bargaining when the facts of *majority representation* and *appropriate unit* are present. Although the statute does not require the parties to use the formal processes of the NLRB to determine these questions,[2] it does provide administrative machinery under Section 9 to resolve questions concerning representation. A *question concerning representation* (often referred to as a QCR) exists when a labor organization (or individual) seeks recognition as bargaining agent and the employer declines to recognize it, thus requiring the Board to determine whether the union (or individual) represents a majority of the employees in an appropriate bargaining unit.

Employees and labor organizations (or employers) may file representation petitions to determine whether a labor organization or individual is entitled to recognition (or to continued recognition)

---

[1] §9 (a).
[2] *See* Chapters 10 and 11 *infra*.

for purposes of collective bargaining. The Board has charged its regional directors [3] with the investigation of these petitions to decide whether "a question of representation affecting commerce exists." [4] However, the employer and the labor organization may resolve by agreement between themselves that the labor organization is the choice of a majority of employees in the bargaining unit,[5] that certain employees constitute the unit,[6] and that the Act is applicable. But if the Board's processes are invoked by a representation petition, then the Board will decide whether a majority of employees has selected the organization, whether the bargaining unit is appropriate, and whether the Board's jurisdictional requirements are met.[7]

If, pursuant to a petition, the regional director holds a hearing and finds that a question concerning representation exists,[8] he directs an election and certifies the results. If two or more petitions are pending, they may be consolidated into one hearing because of common issues. An election may be held without a prior hearing when it appears to the Board, after investigation by the regional director, that an expedited election under Section 8(b)(7)(C) is warranted.[9] An election may also be held without a hearing on the basis of a consent-election agreement resolving certain issues preliminary to the election.[10]

After the hearing the regional director may transfer the record to the Board for a ruling on the petition. If, however, he rules on it initially, his decision is final subject to discretionary Board review upon timely request.[11] If, pursuant to his or the Board's direction, an election is held, ballots may be challenged and objections may be made to the election.[12] The postelection procedure to resolve such issues is similar in many respects to the preelection procedure; the most common pattern is investigation by

---

[3] For a discussion of the 1961 delegation of authority, see Chapter 30 *infra*, notes 26-28 and accompanying text.
[4] §9 (c) (2).
[5] *But see* Bernhard-Altmann Texas Corp., 122 NLRB 1289, 43 LRRM 1283 (1959), *enforced sub nom.*, 280 F 2d 616, 46 LRRM 2223 (CA DC, 1960), *affirmed*, 366 US 731, 48 LRRM 2251 (1961), discussed in Chapter 7 *supra*.
[6] *See* Chapter 9 *infra*.
[7] For discussion of the Board's administrative standards, see Chapter 28 *infra*.
[8] *See* Chapter 30 *infra*, notes 55-60 and accompanying text.
[9] *See* Chapter 21 *infra*.
[10] *See* Chapter 30 *infra*, notes 53-54 and accompanying text.
[11] *Id.* at notes 61-63 and accompanying text.
[12] *Id.* at notes 72-74 and accompanying text; *see also* Chapter 5 *supra*.

the regional director without a hearing, followed by his report and recommendations to the Board, with the Board making the determination. The conclusion of the process is marked by certification of the winning union (or individual) as exclusive bargaining representative, or by certification of the results if no union wins.

A. Petitions by Labor Organizations and Employees

1. Showing of Interest. A union (or individual) desiring to be certified as the collective bargaining representative files a petition, colloquially referred to as an "RC" petition, describing the bargaining unit alleged to be appropriate. Section 9(c)(1)(A) of the Act provides that the petition must be supported by a "substantial number of employees." The Board by rule defines "substantial" to mean at least 30 percent.[13] The evidence of support, which is usually in the form of signed and dated [14] authorization cards, must accompany the petition or be presented within 48 hours of its filing. The 30-percent showing is not necessarily required of a union seeking to intervene; its interest may be otherwise shown if it seeks the same unit as the petitioner.[15] A cross-petitioning union seeking a substantially different unit from that claimed to be appropriate by the initial petitioner must comply with the 30-percent showing.[16]

Investigation of the cards includes a check of them against a current payroll list of employees furnished by the employer to the regional director's agent. The agent's responsibility is to deter-

---

13 NLRB RULES AND REGULATIONS AND STATEMENTS OF PROCEDURE, SERIES 8, as amended, revised January 1, 1965, §101.18 (GPO, 1965) (hereinafter referred to as Rules and Regs. and Statements of Procedure).

14 Undated cards that are not current are not counted. Werman & Sons, Inc., 114 NLRB 629, 37 LRRM 1021 (1955). *See* Chapter 10 *infra* for discussion of card litigation in unfair labor practice cases.

15 23 NLRB ANN. REP. 14 (1959). *See* NLRB FIELD MANUAL, issued by General Counsel of the NLRB (8/1/68) (hereinafter referred to as NLRB Field Manual), 11022.3c and d: "A [*full* intervenor] union which seeks to intervene on the basis of a showing of designation by at least 10 percent of the employees . . . may 'block' any consent election in such unit; and it may participate fully in any hearing thereon. *Cf.* Corn Prods. Ref. Co., 87 NLRB 187, 25 LRRM 1085 (1949). . . . A [*participating* intervenor] union which seeks to intervene on a timely showing of less than 10 percent (it may be only one of two designations) in any unit may not 'block' a consent election in such unit. However, it should be accorded a place on the ballot under the terms agreed upon by the other parties. If a hearing is held it may participate fully. Union Carbide and Carbon Corp., 89 NLRB 460, 25 LRRM 1585 (1950)." *See* note 178 *infra*.

16 NLRB Field Manual, 11022.3b.

mine whether they are sufficient in number and current. The employer is not permitted to inspect the cards, and at the hearing no litigation will be permitted concerning fraud, forgery, or coercion in obtaining cards. The adequacy of petitioner's showing in general is by prehearing administrative determination of the Board, "not subject to direct or collateral attack at hearings." [17]

Decertification and deauthorization petitions: Employees who petition for a certification that an incumbent union no longer has the support of the unit (a decertification petition is colloquially referred to as an "RD") [18] or for rescission of the union's authority to make an existing union-shop agreement with the employer (a deauthorization petition is colloquially referred to as a "UD") [19] must make a 30-percent showing of interest.

No showing of interest is required for an expedited election under Section 8(b)(7)(C).

2. Employer Denial of Recognition. Section 9(c)(1)(A) contemplates an allegation that an employer "declines to recognize" the representative through which the employees wish to engage in collective bargaining. However, the failure of the union to demand recognition before filing the petition is not a basis for dismissing it,[20] provided the employer refuses at the hearing to recognize the union. Indeed, after a union has obtained recognition from an employer without certification, it may nonetheless seek and obtain an election by petition, in order to reap the statutory benefits conferred by the 1947 Taft-Hartley amendments upon unions that are certified as representatives within the meaning of Section 9.[21]

3. Joint Petitions. Joint petitions may be filed by two or more labor organizations that desire to act as a joint representative.[22] Authorizations may be in the individual name of any of the joint petitioners, and the cards may be silent as to the question of col-

17 O. D. Jennings & Co., 68 NLRB 516, 518, 18 LRRM 1133 (1946). *And see* Union Mfg. Co., 123 NLRB 1633, 44 LRRM 1188 (1959) (decertification proceedings, *semble*). Adequacy of showing of interest may be contested by submission of affidavits to the regional director.
18 §9 (c)(1)(A)(ii). Rules and Regs. §102.61; Statements of Procedure §101.18 The unit, for purposes of an "RD" election is coextensive with the contract unit. Arlan's Department Store, Inc., 131 NLRB 565, 567, n. 7, 48 LRRM 1115 (1961).
19 §9 (e)(1). Rules and Regs. Subpart E; Statements of Procedure Subpart E.
20 "M" Sys., Inc., 115 NLRB 1316, 38 LRRM 1055 (1956).
21 General Box Co., 82 NLRB 678, 23 LRRM 1589 (1949).
22 Mid-South Packers, Inc., 120 NLRB 495, 41 LRRM 1526 (1958).

lective representatives.[23] If the unions are successful, certification will issue in the joint names of the unions, and the employer may insist that they bargain jointly.

B. Petitions by Employers [24]

1. History Under the Wagner Act. Although the original statute declared that "whenever a question affecting commerce arises concerning the representation of employees, the Board may investigate such controversy," [25] it provided no mechanism for bringing the controversy to the attention of the Board. Drawing upon the experience of other government agencies, the Board adopted a procedure authorizing any *person* or *labor organization* desiring investigation of a controversy concerning representation to file a petition.[26] Thus there was no provision for employer petitions.[27]

This policy met with widespread opposition, especially as it affected an employer caught in the middle of a jurisdictional dispute. For example, one editorial advised: "Many of those connected with the NLRB admit in private that the employer is often at the mercy of two conflicting unions, neither of which will concede that the other has the right to bargain for the workers, though neither, until it is certain it has a majority, will ask for an election." [28] The American Bar Association's Committee on Labor Employment and Social Security called for amendment of the Act.[29]

The AFL also advocated amendment of the Act. It had charged that the Board, in acting upon union petitions, had exercised its discretion in favor of the CIO and against the AFL. To remedy this situation, it supported a bill [30] to amend Section 9(c) by making it mandatory upon the Board to investigate union petitions. At the same time, the bill would have amended Section 9(c) to provide for employer petitions.

---

23 The Stickless Corp., 115 NLRB 979, 37 LRRM 1466 (1956).
24 *See also* Lewis, *Employer Petitions-New York and Federal—A Comparison,* NYU FIFTH ANNUAL CONFERENCE ON LABOR 249 (1952).
25 §9(c).
26 NLRB RULES AND REGULATIONS, SERIES 1, Art. III, §1 (1935).
27 Nevertheless, it was not unusual for the regional director, at the instance of the employer, to induce the union to file a petition. Bowman, PUBLIC CONTROL OF LABOR RELATIONS 298 (1942) ; Rosenfarb, THE NATIONAL LABOR POLICY 303 (1940).
28 New York Times, Nov. 30, 1937, p. 22.
29 25 A.B.A.J. 119, 124 (1936).
30 S. 1000, 76th Cong., 1st Sess. (1939). For its legislative history, *see* H. Millis & E. Brown, FROM THE WAGNER ACT TO TAFT-HARTLEY 347-353 (1950).

The bill was not enacted into law. The Board was opposed to it, expressing its opposition thus:

> The reasons for not permitting employers an unlimited right of petition are first, that normally the employer has no legitimate interest in the question whether or when his employees wish to choose representatives or whom they wish to choose; and second, that if an employer is given the right to demand an election at will he can, by choosing a strategic time, effectively hinder or block self-organization among his employees. The right of employees to choose their representatives when and as they wish is normally no more the affair of the employer than the right of the stockholders to choose directors is the affair of the employees.[31]

However, in response to strong public pressure, the Board amended its rules in 1939 to grant employers a limited right to petition if the petition alleged that two or more unions were making conflicting claims of representative status.[32] This right was not altered under the statute or the rules until the Taft-Hartley amendments.

2. History Under the Taft-Hartley Act. The objection to employer petitions most frequently voiced in the debate on the 1947 amendments was that they could be used to force a premature test and thereby obtain a vote rejecting the union. A further objection was based upon another amendment disenfranchising permanently replaced economic strikers. The Presidential veto message stressed that employer petitions could be used to obtain elections during strikes and capitalize on the disenfranchisement.[33]

To meet these objections the measure, as enacted, conditioned the employer's right to petition for an election upon a prior claim for recognition by a union. Section 9(c)(1) reads as follows:

> Whenever a petition shall have been filed . . . by an employer, alleging that one or more individuals or labor organizations have presented to him a claim to be recognized as the representative defined in Section 9(a); the Board shall investigate such petition. . . .

Simply stated, this amendment was designed to grant an employer the right to petition in two situations previously unavailable to

---

31 Report of NLRB Before Sen. Comm. on Education and Labor, *Hearings on National Labor Relations Act and Proposed Amendments,* 76th Cong., 1st Sess., Part 3, pp. 467, 540-543 (1939).
32 NLRB Rules and Regulations, Series 2, Art. III, §§1-3 (1939).
33 H. R. Doc. No. 334, CONG. REC. 7486 (1947). For similar criticism, see statements of Senators Murray and Pepper, 93 CONG. REC. 4032, 6527 (1947).

him. The first involves a claim for recognition by one union only. Previously an employer's right to petition was contingent upon claims for recognition by two or more unions. The second concerns an employer desire to question the current majority standing of an incumbent union. Before 1947 the Board would not entertain an employer petition, now colloquially referred to as an "RM," in such a situation.[34]

a. Unrecognized Unions. Section 9(c)(1)(B) specifies that an employer petition must contain an allegation that a union (or individual) has "presented to [the employer] a claim to be recognized as the representative defined in Section 9(a)." The Board considers that absent such a claim it would be without jurisdiction to proceed with its investigation.[35] The phrase "representative defined in Section 9(a)" means a labor organization (or individual) chosen by a majority of employees in a unit appropriate for collective bargaining to be the exclusive representative of all employees therein for such purposes. Mere campaigning by a union and knowledge of such campaigning by the employer are not the equivalent of a claim by the union that it represents a majority of the employees, or of a request for exclusive bargaining rights under the Act.[36] It is not necessary, however, that a claim of majority representation be made in the exact terms of Section 9(a). It is sufficient to submit a proposed contract or to request one.[37]

b. Incumbent Unions. Section 9(c)(1)(B) is not restricted to situations where an unrecognized union claims recognition. A request by an incumbent union for renewal of its contract constitutes a "claim to be recognized" within the meaning of this section.[38] Therefore, when the employer questions a union's continuing support by a majority, he may file a petition for an election.

---

34 *E.g.*, Cincinnati Times-Star Co., 66 NLRB 414, 17 LRRM 340 (1946); Toledo Steel Products Co., 65 NLRB 56, 17 LRRM 211 (1945); Colonial Life Insurance Co. of America, 65 NLRB 58, 17 LRRM 195 (1945); Landis Machine Co., 65 NLRB 60, 17 LRRM 210 (1945).

35 Herman Loewenstein, Inc., 75 NLRB 377, 21 LRRM 1032 (1947).

36 Electro Metallurgical Co., 72 NLRB 1396, 19 LRRM 1291 (1947); The Baldwin Co., 81 NLRB 927, 23 LRRM 1438 (1949).

37 Johnson Bros. Furniture Co., 97 NLRB 246, 29 LRRM 1089 (1951); Kimel Shoe Co., 97 NLRB 127, 29 LRRM 1069 (1951); *see* Chapter 21 *infra* for a discussion of the nature of evidence used to show recognitional objectives.

38 Whitney's, 81 NLRB 75, 23 LRRM 1297 (1949).

Under former Board doctrine it was not necessary that the employer have a reasonable basis for his doubt, nor was he required to withdraw recognition.[39] The reasonable, or good-faith, basis for his doubt was only in issue in the event of subsequent unfair labor practice charges alleging a refusal to bargain.[40] In *United States Gypsum Co.*[41] the Board changed this rule, thenceforth dismissing an employer petition where no "reasonable basis" was shown for questioning the status of an incumbent union. The Board formulated a new "objective evidence" test, premising its rule in part upon its reading of the legislative history of Section 9(c)(1)(B), which it asserted contains a clear statement that the provision was designed to give relief to employers who had "reasonable grounds for believing" that the claiming union was not really the choice of the majority.

> There is no indication that Congress in enacting that Section contemplated the creation of a device by which an employer acting without a good-faith doubt of the union's status . . . could disrupt collective bargaining and frustrate the policy of the Act favoring stable relations.

> In light of the above, we are of the view that we should no longer adhere to the former interpretation of Section 9(c)(1)(B). We therefore now hold that in petitioning the Board for an election to question the continued majority of a previously certified incumbent union, an employer, in addition to showing the union's claim for continued recognition, must demonstrate by objective considerations that it has some reasonable grounds for believing that the union has lost its majority status since its certification.[42]

The Board subsequently decided that an employer's demonstration of the "objective considerations" was to be submitted confidentially to the regional director for administrative determination as to the *prima facie* showing. As an administrative determination, it would not be litigable at any stage of the representation proceeding.[43]

---

39 *Ibid.;* Continental Southern Corp., 83 NLRB 668, 24 LRRM 1127 (1949) ; J. C. Penney Co., 86 NLRB 920, 25 LRRM 1039 (1949) ; J. P. O'Neil Lumber Co., 94 NLRB 1299, 28 LRRM 1190 (1951) ; Philadelphia Elect. Co., 95 NLRB 71, 28 LRRM 1296 (1951) .

40 Celanese Corp. of America, 95 NLRB 664, 28 LRRM 1362 (1951) .

41 157 NLRB 652, 61 LRRM 1384 (1966) .

42 *Id.* at 656. For a detailed discussion of this history, see also Talent, *United States Gypsum Co.—More of the Same,* 17 LAB. L.J. 559 (1966) .

43 United States Gypsum Co., 161 NLRB 601, 63 LRRM 1308 (1966) ; J. C. Penney Co., 162 NLRB 144, 64 LRRM 1241 (1967) .

3. Disclaimer of Interest. The purpose of Section 9(c)(1)(B) is to permit the employer to file an election petition when a union is claiming to be the exclusive representative for collective bargaining. Apparently unforeseen by the drafters of this provision was the possibility that a union, having made such a claim, might withdraw it. When this situation was presented, the Board had to reconcile the union's disclaimer with the employer's statutory right to petition for an election.

The issue was first presented in *Ny-Lint Tool and Mfg. Co.*[44] The union had represented the employees for several years without benefit of Board certification. In August 1947, having given notice that it would not renew the current contract, it submitted to the employer a new contract covering the same employees. The employer thereupon expressed doubt that the union continued to represent a majority of the employees, refused to negotiate a new contract, and filed a petition. At the hearing, the union disavowed any claim to majority representation and asked that the employer's petition be dismissed. The Board did so, on the ground that since a question concerning representation no longer existed it was without jurisdiction to proceed. The Board continues to adhere to this policy, dismissing employer petitions whenever the union disclaims interest.[45]

Similarly, in the handling of a decertification petition, a disclaimer of interest by the union results in a dismissal of the petition. For example, in *Federal Shipbuilding and Drydock Co.*[46] the Board held that a union can disclaim interest even after the Board has directed that an election be held (but before the date of the election).

Neither the failure of a union to appear at the hearing[47] nor the failure of a union to intervene[48] constitutes a disclaimer of

---

[44] 77 NLRB 642, 22 LRRM 1061 (1948). Both majority and dissenting opinions observed that an incumbent contractual representative, as in this case, rather than an unrecognized union, presents the same issue and calls for the same construction of the statute.

[45] *E.g.,* Coeur D'Alene Grocers Ass'n, 88 NLRB 44, 25 LRRM 1301 (1950); Murray B. Marsh Co., 79 NLRB 76, 22 LRRM 1377 (1948); Brockton Wholesale Grocery Co., 78 NLRB 663, 22 LRRM 1264 (1948); Louella Balierino, 77 NLRB 738, 22 LRRM 1076 (1948); De De Johnson, 77 NLRB 730, 22 LRRM 1076 (1948); Josephine Furniture Co., Inc., 172 NLRB 22, 68 LRRM 1311 (1968).

[46] Federal Shipbuilding and Drydock Co., 77 NLRB 463, 22 LRRM 1034 (1948).

[47] Felton Oil Co., 78 NLRB 1033, 22 LRRM 1332 (1948).

[48] Penn Paper & Stock Co., 88 NLRB 17, 25 LRRM 1279 (1950).

interest. Nor is the union's filing of a refusal-to-bargain charge inconsistent with a disclaimer of interest.[49] In addition, a union may, in certain instances, disclaim interest but engage in picketing.[50] It was argued in *Hubach and Parkinson Motors* that the continued picketing demonstrated that the union's disclaimer was not made in good faith and that by virtue of such picketing the union was continuing to assert its claim to be the statutory representative of the employees. The Board disagreed, stating that,

> . . . to defeat an employer's petition or a petition for decertification, a union's disclaimer of status as exclusive bargaining representative must be clear and unequivocal. . . . in determining whether an expressed disclaimer is sufficient to defeat a petition, we should consider not only the words but also the other conduct of the union involved.[51]

The Board concluded that despite the resumption of picketing, the union's disclaimer had been clear and unequivocal.

Not all disclaimers of interest by unions result in the Board's dismissing the employer's petition. Where the disclaimer is not "clear and unequivocal," the Board will refuse to dismiss.[52] Nor will the Board dismiss the employer's petition where the union's picket signs may be interpreted as expressing a continued claim to majority representation, notwithstanding the disclaimer.[53]

II. TIMELINESS OF PETITIONS

A. One-Year Rule

1. The Statutory Bar. Representation elections may not be conducted more often than once a year in any given bargaining unit or subdivision thereof. This limitation was enacted in 1947 by the addition of Section 9(c)(3). In applying this rule the Board has stated that a representation petition filed within 60 days of

---

49 Franz Food Prods., Inc., 137 NLRB 340, 50 LRRM 1143 (1962).

50 Hubach & Parkinson Motors, 88 NLRB 1202, 25 LRRM 1466 (1950). To the same effect, *see* General Paint Corp., 95 NLRB 539, 28 LRRM 1345 (1951); Martino's Complete Home Furnishings, 145 NLRB 609, 55 LRRM 1003 (1963). *See also* Tribune Publishing Co., 147 NLRB 841, 56 LRRM 1273 (1964); Smith's Hardware Co., 93 NLRB 1009, 27 LRRM 1556 (1951); Hamilton's Ltd., 93 NLRB 1076, 27 LRRM 1538 (1951); Palace Knitwear & Co., 93 NLRB 872, 27 LRRM 1481 (1951); Bur-Bee Co., 90 NLRB 9, 26 LRRM 1153 (1950). *But see* Knitgoods Workers Union Local 155 (Boulevard Knitwear Corp.), 167 NLRB 109, 66 LRRM 1157 (1967) regarding picketing in violation of §8(b)(7) after disclaimer.

51 88 NLRB 1202, 1204, 25 LRRM 1466 (1950).

52 *E.g.,* Coca-Cola Bottling Co., 80 NLRB 1063, 23 LRRM 1160 (1948); Johnson Bros. Furniture Co., 97 NLRB 246, 29 LRRM 1089 (1951).

53 Kimel Shoe Co., 97 NLRB 127, 29 LRRM 1069 (1951).

the anniversary date of the earlier election will be processed, but the election itself will be scheduled for a date after the expiration of the one-year period. A petition filed more than 60 days before the anniversary date will be dismissed as untimely.[54] The prohibition, however, refers only to conclusive elections, and the Board is not precluded from directing a rerun or runoff election within the year, or from directing a second election within the year where the first election was set aside on the basis of valid timely filed objections.[55] A deauthorization election to revoke a union's authority to execute union security contracts is not barred by any form of election other than another deauthorization election within the one-year period.[56]

In the 1949 *National Container* case [57] the Board ruled that elections held by private or state agencies come within the 12-month bar of Section 9(c)(3). The Board reversed itself in 1950,[58] but has in more recent cases returned to the *National Container* rule. The Board's present position appears to be that elections conducted by responsible agencies which afford employees an opportunity to express their true desires, if they respect the fundamentals of due process, will bar National Labor Relations Board elections in the same unit within the year.[59]

Where no union is certified, the year begins to run from the date of the election.[60] The Board maintains this position even where there are postelection objections or challenges which are not resolved for several months.[61]

---

[54] Randolph Metal Works, Inc., 147 NLRB 973, 56 LRRM 1348 (1964).

[55] Napa New York Warehouse, Inc., 76 NLRB 840, 21 LRRM 1251 (1948); Cohn-Hall-Marx Co., 86 NLRB 101, 24 LRRM 1596 (1949).

[56] Monsanto Chem. Co., 147 NLRB 49, 56 LRRM 1136 (1964).

[57] National Container Corp., 87 NLRB 1065, 25 LRRM 1234 (1949).

[58] Punch Press Repair Corp., 89 NLRB 614, 26 LRRM 1012 (1950).

[59] Interboro Chevrolet Co., 111 NLRB 783, 35 LRRM 1567 (1955); T-H Prods. Co., 113 NLRB 1246, 36 LRRM 1471 (1955); Olin Mathieson Chem. Corp., 115 NLRB 1501, 38 LRRM 1099 (1956); West Indian Co., 129 NLRB 1203, 47 LRRM 1146 (1961). A Board majority failed to give effect to such an election in applying Section 8 (b)(7) in *Fowler-Hotel, Inc.,* 138 NLRB 1315, 51 LRRM 1180 (1962). And more recently the Board was chided for refusing to honor such an election in *NLRB v. Western Meat Packers,* 350 F 2d 804, 60 LRRM 2101 (CA 10, 1965). *Compare* Monroe Cooperative Oil Co., 86 NLRB 95, 24 LRRM 1591 (1949), *and* National Waste Material Corp., 93 NLRB 477, 27 LRRM 1413 (1951).

[60] Palmer Mfg. Co., 103 NLRB 336, 31 LRRM 1520 (1953); Mallinckrodt Chem. Works, 84 NLRB 291, 24 LRRM 1253 (1949). When balloting is conducted over a period of several weeks or months, the year begins at the end of the balloting period. Alaska Salmon Indus., 90 NLRB 168, 26 LRRM 1199 (1950).

[61] Bendix Corp., 179 NLRB No. 18, 72 LRRM 1264 (1969).

The one-year rule applies only to new elections in the same bargaining unit or in a subdivision of that unit. An election in a given unit will not preclude an election within a year in a broader, more inclusive unit.[62] Needless to say, a prior election in a larger unit will not preclude an election within a year in a smaller unit of employees where such employees were barred from voting in the first election.[63] On the other hand, the bar applies if the smaller unit is within the scope of the broader unit in which the prior election was held.[64]

2. The Certification Year. In order to permit collective bargaining to function and to stabilize industrial relations, the Board, with the approval of the Supreme Court, adopted a rule that in the absence of unusual circumstances a certified union's majority status must be honored for one year, and a petition filed during the one-year period will ordinarily be barred. This rule subsequently was incorporated by implication in the statute.[65] In *Brooks v. NLRB* the Supreme Court approved the Board's requirement that an employer must recognize a union for the entire "certification year" even if he has evidence of the union's loss of majority, except in "unusual circumstances." [66] Unusual circumstances, according to the Court, include (1) a schism within the certified union or its defunctness and (2) radical fluctuation in the size of the bargaining unit within a short period of time.

In *Mar-Jac Poultry Co.*[67] the Board modified its policy as approved by the Court in *Brooks*. This modification extends the certification period beyond one year when the employer's misconduct denies the union a year's fair opportunity to bargain. For

---

62 Robertson Bros. Dep't Store, Inc., 95 NLRB 271, 28 LRRM 1335 (1951).

63 Philadelphia Co., 84 NLRB 115, 24 LRRM 1251 (1949). *See also* Ideal Roller & Mfg. Co. v. Douds, 111 F Supp 156, 32 LRRM 2030 (SDNY, 1953).

64 Krambo Food Stores, Case No. 13-RC-57, Feb. 14, 1958; Allied Chem. & Dye Corp., Case No. 5-RC-1745, 1748, Aug. 19, 1955. (Not published in NLRB volumes.) Note that the prohibition on the holding of a representation election within a year of a previous election is not a defense to an employer's refusal to bargain with a union on the basis of authorization cards. Conren, Inc., 156 NLRB 592, 61 LRRM 1090 (1966), *enforced*, 368 F 2d 173, 63 LRRM 2273 (CA 7, 1966), *cert. denied*, 386 US 974, 64 LRRM 2640 (1967). *See* Chapter 10 *infra*.

65 §8(b)(7)(A), added in 1959.

66 Brooks v. NLRB, 348 US 96, 35 LRRM 2158 (1954), and cases cited therein; *and see* John Vilicich, 133 NLRB 238, 46 LRRM 1529 (1961), and Rocky Mountain Phosphates, 138 NLRB 292, 51 LRRM 1019 (1962). For discussion of schism and defunctness, see *infra* under *Contract Bar*.

67 136 NLRB 785, 49 LRRM 1854 (1962).

example, in *La Mar Hotel* [68] the Board gave the union an additional six months from the resumption of negotiations, since the union had, for six months of the certification year, been deprived of its right to an unimpeded opportunity to bargain. In the second stage of *Mar-Jac* [69] it appeared that the employer had indeed refused to bargain with the certified union, but subsequently he executed a settlement containing a promise to bargain. Under these circumstances the Board granted the union an additional period of an entire year for actual bargaining dating from the settlement agreement. The Board announced that it would do the same thing in future cases that revealed similar factors. The corollary of this Board theory would be a denial, as untimely, of a rival petition filed in the extended period.

B. Pendency of Unfair Practice Charge

Generally, unless the charging party requests the Board to proceed, the Board will decline to direct an election while unfair labor practice charges that affect the unit involved in the representation proceeding are pending. The rationale is that the charges, if true, would destroy the "laboratory conditions" necessary to permit employees to cast their ballots freely and without restraint or coercion. However, it is well established that this practice is not governed by statute, apart from the exceptional expedited election under Section 8(b)(7)(C), or by rules or regulations; rather, it lies within Board discretion as part of its responsibility to decide whether an election will effectuate the policies of the Act. [70]

Various exceptions have developed from the Board's frequent practice of directing elections forthwith as a means of effectuating the policies of the Act. Factors on which the Board has relied to proceed with a representation proceeding despite the pendency of charges include the following: (1) the length of time the proceeding has been pending, (2) the fact that employees in the unit have been without an election during that period, (3) the dismissal

---

[68] 137 NLRB 1271, 50 LRRM 1366 (1962); *see also* Cincinnati Gasket, Packing & Mfg. Co., 163 NLRB 104, 64 LRRM 1455 (1967); Mid-City Foundry Co., 167 NLRB 795, 66 LRRM 1154 (1967); Interstate Brick Co., 167 NLRB 831, 66 LRRM 1160 (1967).

[69] 136 NLRB 785, 49 LRRM 1854 (1962), overruling Daily Press, Inc., 112 NLRB 1434, 36 LRRM 1228 (1955), and similar inconsistent cases.

[70] American Metal Prods. Co., 139 NLRB 601, 51 LRRM 1338 (1962).

of earlier charges that were grounded upon the same basic pattern of conduct as the pending charges, (4) "eleventh hour" filing of the charges, (5) the existence of a strike, or (6) a past practice by the charging party of using the filing of charges as a tactic to delay representation proceedings.[71]

The Board has also directed an immediate election on a union's petition, notwithstanding the employer's pending Section 8(e) charge against that union resulting from its allegedly unlawful hot-cargo contract with an employer association.[72] The Board noted that, in contrast to Section 8(a) and (b) cases, a Section 8(e) charge, even if true, deals only with the terms of an agreement between an employer and labor organization, and that the agreement would not necessarily restrain or coerce employees or in any other way prevent a fair election. Thus, in the absence of any allegation that the union sought to influence the employees' choice of a bargaining representative, the Board will proceed with the election.

The Board has also directed an immediate election, despite pending charges, in order to hold the election within 12 months of the beginning of an economic strike so as not to disenfranchise economic strikers.[73]

C. Unlawful Employer Assistance

Even though no charge is pending, an election petition may be dismissed because of employer domination of, or assistance to, the petitioner. As seen above, whether the requisite showing of interest has been made is ordinarily not a matter of adversary dispute but rather one for administrative determination. However, when it can be shown that authorization cards have been obtained with the help of supervisors, allegations to that effect will be heard on collateral request to the regional director, accompanied by sup-

---

[71] Columbia Pictures Corp., 81 NLRB 1313, 23 LRRM 1504 (1949); Bercut Richards Packing Co., 70 NLRB 84, 18 LRRM 1336 (1946); West-Gate Sun Harbor Co., 93 NLRB 830, 27 LRRM 1474 (1951); Surprenant Mfg. Co., 144 NLRB 507, 54 LRRM 1097 (1963); Kingsport Press, 146 NLRB 260 and 1111, 56 LRRM 1006, 1007 (1964); NLRB v. Lawrence Typographical Union, 375 F 2d 643, 65 LRRM 2176 (CA 10, 1967).

[72] Holt Bros., 146 NLRB 383, 55 LRRM 1310 (1964). See note 98 infra.

[73] §9(c)(3) of the Act provides: employees "engaged in an economic strike who are not entitled to reinstatement shall be eligible to vote . . . in any election conducted within twelve months after the commencement of the strike." See American Metal Products Co., 139 NLRB 601, 51 LRRM 1338 (1962).

porting evidence. If it is thereafter administratively determined that the cards are tainted by reason of supervisory participation, the showing of interest may be found to be impaired and the petition dismissed.[74] The dismissal of a petition on these grounds does not affect subsequent proceedings on a new petition when there is a new showing of interest obtained without the assistance of supervisors.[75]

D. Fluctuating Workforce

A petition for an election among a fluctuating working force will be dismissed without prejudice to the filing of a petition at a more appropriate time if it appears that a representative employment complement has not yet been established, or where other substantial corporate changes are occurring. However, mere speculation as to the uncertainty of future operations will not render a petition untimely.[76]

In seasonal industries the Board usually directs that the election be held at or about the approximate seasonal peak. If the peak has already passed, the Board will usually fix the election date at or about the next seasonal peak.[77]

E. Contract-Bar Doctrine

In order to stabilize the employer-union relationship, the Board over the years has established a "contract bar" doctrine whereby a current and valid contract will ordinarily prevent the holding of an election for a certain period of time. This doctrine, although now recognized by implication in Section 8(b)(7), is self-imposed and discretionary. The establishment, application, and modification of the Board's contract-bar rules is considered to have been

---

74 Union Mfg. Co., 123 NLRB 1633, 44 LRRM 1188 (1959); Georgia Craft Co., 120 NLRB 806, 42 LRRM 1066 (1958). *See also* Modern Hard Chrome Serv. Co., 124 NLRB 1235, 44 LRRM 1624 (1959). Southeastern Newspapers, Inc., 129 NLRB 311, 46 LRRM 1541 (1960); Desilu Productions, Inc., 106 NLRB 179, 32 LRRM 1418 (1953); American Dist. Tel. Co., 89 NLRB 1635, 26 LRRM 1135 (1950); Alaska Salmon Indus., 78 NLRB 185, 22 LRRM 1190 (1948). *See* Chapter 7 *supra.*
75 Toledo Stamping & Mfg. Co., 56 NLRB 1291, 14 LRRM 192 (1944).
76 Meramec Mining Co., 134 NLRB 1675, 49 LRRM 1386 (1961); Douglas Motors Corp., 128 NLRB 307, 46 LRRM 1292 (1960); Gordon B. Irvine, 124 NLRB 217, 44 LRRM 1336 (1959). General Eng., 123 NLRB 586, 43 LRRM 1486 (1959); General Elec. Co., 106 NLRB 364, 32 LRRM 1465 (1953).
77 Cleveland Cliffs Iron Co., 117 NLRB 668, 39 LRRM 1319 (1957); Bordo Prods. Co., 117 NLRB 313, 39 LRRM 1220 (1957).

committed to its discretion without statutory restraint or judicial review.[78]

1. Requisites of the Contract: Duration. In order to bar an otherwise timely petition, a contract must be reduced to writing and executed by both parties. An oral agreement will not bar an election. Ratification by the union membership is not a prerequisite for upholding a contract as a bar, unless the contract itself requires ratification.[79]

The contract must have a *definite duration*.[80] It then serves to prevent a challenge to the incumbent union by the employer for its duration, and if the incumbent union is certified (and thus unable to benefit from the *General Box* [81] doctrine) it is likewise disabled from petitioning for the entire term of the contract, no matter how long.[82] Petitions on behalf of rival unions, however, are barred only for a reasonable part of the term of an agreement that has an unreasonably long duration.

At one time the Board looked to the "substantial part of the industry" test as a measure of the reasonable period during which a contract would bar a rival union petition. This test was abandoned in the *Pacific Coast* case as "administratively burdensome," [83] and two years was determined to be a reasonable period for all industries. In *General Cable Corp.*[84] the Board abandoned

---

78 Vincent v. Carpenters Local 1545, 286 F 2d 127, 47 LRRM 2304 (CA 2, 1960). *But see* Leedom v. IBEW Local 108, 278 F 2d 237, 44 LRRM 2754 (1960), *and* NLRB v. Wyman-Gordon Co., 394 US 759, 70 LRRM 3345 (1969). *See also* Chapter 32.

79 Appalachian Shale Prods. Co., 121 NLRB 1160, 42 LRRM 1506 (1958), overruling numerous earlier cases and eliminating exceptions. Thus, a provision for prior ratification contained in the union's constitution and bylaws, as distinguished from an express provision in the contract itself, will not remove the contract as a bar. 121 NLRB 1162.

80 Pacific Coast Ass'n of Pulp and Paper Mfrs., 121 NLRB 990, 42 LRRM 1477 (1958); Kroger Co., 173 NLRB No. 60, 69 LRRM 1333 (1968).

81 General Box Co., 82 NLRB 678, 23 LRRM 1589 (1949). In that case it was held that an uncertified union may file a petition during the term of the contract where it seeks the benefit of certification.

82 Absorbent Cotton Co., 137 NLRB 908, 50 LRRM 1258 (1962); Montgomery Ward and Co., 137 NLRB 346, 50 LRRM 1137 (1962).

83 Pacific Coast Ass'n of Pulp and Paper Mfrs., 121 NLRB 990, 992, 42 LRRM 1477 (1958). The Board's position at this point had evolved after experience with a variety of tests. Originally, a one-year contract was thought to be reasonable in conjunction with the test of "custom in the industry." Presumptions of reasonableness would vary in accordance with industry custom. For a discussion of this earlier development and application see Reed Roller Bit Co., 72 NLRB 927, 19 LRRM 1227 (1947); Puritan Ice Co., 74 NLRB 1311, 20 LRRM 1268 (1947); Cushman's Sons Inc., 88 NLRB 121, 25 LRRM 1296 (1950).

84 139 NLRB 1123, 51 LRRM 1444 (1962).

its uniform two-year rule in favor of the current *three-year rule.* Contracts of a definite duration for terms up to three years bar election petitions for the entire period, and contracts for longer fixed terms operate as a bar to rival petitions for the first three years.

If during the term of a contract the parties execute an amendment thereto, or execute a new contract which contains a terminal date later than that of the existing contract, the amendment or new contract will be considered "premature." A prematurely extended contract will not bar an election if the petition is otherwise timely,[85] i.e., filed at least 60 but not more than 90 days before the expiration of the first three years of the original contract. The premature-extension doctrine does not apply (1) to contracts executed during the 60-day insulated period preceding the terminal date of the old contract, (2) after the terminal date of the old contract, or (3) at a time when the existing contract would not have barred an election because of other contract-bar rules.[86]

2. Unlawful Clauses. The Board on several occasions has modified its contract-bar rules with respect to checkoff, union security, and other key contract provisions. As in most basic issues concerning contract-bar application, the Board attempts to strike a balance between the interests of industrial stability and the right to select bargaining representatives. The ebb and flow of these priorities is manifested in the effect given certain contractual provisions.

a. Union Security. In the 1958 *Keystone* case [87] the Board ruled that contracts containing union security and checkoff provisions would not bar elections unless on their face they conformed to the express terms of the Act. The effect of the rules of interpretation in *Keystone* was to "require a presumption of illegality with respect to any contract containing a union security clause which did not expressly reflect the precise language of the statute.[88] But in 1961 the Supreme Court cast serious doubt upon the exercise of administrative discretion when based on attaching presumptions of illegality to provisions in collective bargaining.[89] So in *Paragon*

---

85 *See infra* for discussion of rules for timeliness of petitions.
86 Deluxe Metal Furniture Co., 121 NLRB 995, 42 LRRM 1470 (1958). *See also* notes 128-143 *infra* and accompanying text.
87 Keystone Coat, Apron & Towel Supply Co., 121 NLRB 880, 42 LRRM 1456 (1958).
88 Paragon Prods. Corp., 134 NLRB 662, 664, 49 LRRM 1160 (1961).
89 NLRB v. News Syndicate Co., 365 US 695, 47 LRRM 2916 (1961).

Products Corp.[90] the Board, adverting to the "unsettling" of bargaining relationships engendered by the *Keystone* rules, reformulated its position, holding that:

> ...only those contracts containing a union-security provision which is clearly unlawful on its face, or which has been found to be unlawful in an unfair labor practice proceeding, may not bar a representation petition. A clearly unlawful union-security provision for this purpose is one which by its express terms clearly and unequivocally goes beyond the limited form of union security permitted by Section 8(a)(3) of the Act, and is therefore incapable of a lawful interpretation.[91]

Unlawful provisions under this rule would include a clause by which the employer agrees to give union members preference in hiring, layoff, or other terms of employment; or a clause specifically denying new employees, or incumbent nonunion employees, the statutory 30-day grace period; or a clause requiring the payment to the union of money other than "periodic dues and initiation fees uniformly required."

In further clarification the Board held that, absent express contractual saving features, the "mere existence of a clearly unlawful union security provision in a contract will render it no bar" regardless of intended enforcement.[92] But the Board also spelled out two ways of curing the defect—elimination of the unlawful clause by properly executed rescission or amendment, and inclusion of an express contractual provision clearly deferring the effectiveness of the unlawful clause.[93] These so-called deferral clauses were accorded this saving virtue in two 1961 Supreme Court cases.[94]

   b. Checkoff. The rule governing checkoff clauses has similarly been relaxed since *Keystone,* which was applicable to checkoff clauses in the same manner as to other union security provisions.[95] Currently, a checkoff clause does not affect the standing of a con-

---

90 134 NLRB 662, 49 LRRM 1160 (1961).

91 134 NLRB at 666.

92 *Id.* at 667.

93 *Ibid.* For a specific application see American Broadcasting Co., 134 NLRB 1458, 49 LRRM 1365 (1961); Columbia Broadcasting Sys., 134 NLRB 1466, 49 LRRM 1366 (1961). For general treatment of union security, *see* Chapter 26 *infra.*

94 NLRB v. News Syndicate Co., 365 U.S. 695, 47 LRRM 2916 (1961); International Typographical Union v. NLRB, 365 U.S. 705, 47 LRRM 2920 (1961).

95 The first modification was a response to certain Department of Justice interpretations. William Wolf Bakery, Inc., 122 NLRB 630, 43 LRRM 1147 (1958). Further relaxation came in the Boston Gas Co. cases, 129 NLRB 369, 46 LRRM 1546 (1960), and 130 NLRB 1230, 47 LRRM 1429 (1961).

tract as a bar to an election unless it is unlawful on its face, or has been held unlawful, either in an unfair labor practice proceeding or in court in a proceeding brought by the Attorney General.[96]

c. *Racial Discrimination.* Reflecting the upsurge of emphasis on civil rights, the Board has announced that a contract that discriminates by reason of race between groups of employees will not operate as a bar to an election.[97] Such discrimination is inherent in agreements that sanction groupings of employees along racial lines, and the Board concluded that to permit its rules to be used to shield such contracts from election petitions would in effect be to extend a governmental sanction to such discrimination.

d. *"Hot Cargo."* Although a clause may violate Section 8(e), the Board distinguishes between a hot-cargo provision and unlawful union security provisions, holding that the hot-cargo clause does not act as a restraint upon the employees' choice of a bargaining representative. Therefore, the presence of a clause that violates Section 8(e) does not remove a contract as a bar.[98]

3. Expanding Units. Current case law concerning expanding employee complements draws its essence from the Board's *General Extrusion*[99] doctrine. This is a contract-bar doctrine which establishes guidelines for determining whether an election should be directed in an expanding unit in the face of a valid contract. Formulated in 1958 along with many of the landmark contract-bar doctrines,[100] *General Extrusion* laid down a series of rules, as follows:

a. *Prehire Agreements.* A contract does not bar an election if executed before any employees have been hired, or prior to a

---

96 Gary Steel Supply Co., 144 NLRB 470, 54 LRRM 1082 (1963).

97 Pioneer Bus Co., 140 NLRB 54, 51 LRRM 1546 (1962). *See* Chapter 27 *infra.*

98 Food Haulers, Inc., 136 NLRB 394, 49 LRRM 1774 (1962), overruling Pilgrim Furniture Co., 128 NLRB 910, 46 LRRM 1427 (1960); American Feed Co., 129 NLRB 321, 46 LRRM 1541 (1960); and Calorator Mfg. Corp., 129 NLRB 704, 47 LRRM 1109 (1960). The same policy obtains when the §8(e) question takes the form of a blocking charge of unfair labor practice. *Holt Bros.,* note 72 *supra.* For general treatment of "hot cargo" clauses, *see* Chapter 24 *infra.*

99 General Extrusion Co., 121 NLRB 1165, 42 LRRM 1508 (1958).

100 *See* Deluxe Metal Furniture Co., 121 NLRB 995, 42 LRRM 1470 (1958); Appalachian Shale Prods. Co., 121 NLRB 1160, 42 LRRM 1506 (1958); Hershey Chocolate Corp., 121 NLRB 901, 42 LRRM 1460 (1958); Keystone Coat, Apron and Towel Supply Co., 121 NLRB 880, 42 LRRM 1456 (1958); Pacific Coast Ass'n of Pulp and Paper Mfrs., 121 NLRB 990, 42 LRRM 1477 (1958).

"substantial increase" in personnel. An agreement executed before a "substantial increase" will bar an election if (1) ". . . at least 30 percent of the complement employed at the time of the hearing had been employed at the time the contract was executed . . ." [101] *and* [102] (2) "50 percent of the job classifications in existence at the time of the hearing were in existence at the time the contract was executed." [103]

When a successor relationship is found, the objectionable "prehire" nature of the contract may be removed. Unlike an employer in a prehire situation, who is under an obligation *not* to bargain until a representative complement of employees has been hired, a successor employer is under an immediate obligation to bargain. In the successor situation the employees have already selected a bargaining representative, whereas in a prehire situation they have not.[104]

   b. Relocation and Consolidation. In *General Extrusion* the Board distinguished between a "relocation of operations" and a "consolidation of two or more operations." [105] It held that a contract would not be a bar if changes had occurred in the "nature as distinguished from the size of the operations between the execution of the contract and the filing of the petition, involving" (1) "a merger of two or more operations resulting in the creation

---

101 General Extrusion Co., 121 NLRB 1165, 1167, 42 LRRM 1508 (1958). But the actual date of signing may not, in all instances, be determinative. *See* H. L. Klion, 148 NLRB 652, 660, 57 LRRM 1073 (1964).

102 While the conjunctive "and" is used in *General Extrusion Co.*, note 101 *supra*, it was reemphasized in West Penn Hat and Cap Corp., 165 NLRB 77, n. 1, 65 LRRM 1417 (1967).

103 121 NLRB at 1167. A contract executed with a minority union pursuant to §8(f), although a legal contract, cannot function as a bar to a representation petition. However, if the union has attained majority status prior to the execution of the agreement, the ordinary rules of contract bar will apply. Mishara Construction Co., 171 NLRB No. 80, 68 LRRM 1120 (1968); Island Construction Co., 135 NLRB 13, 49 LRRM 1417 (1962). *See* Chapter 11 *infra* at note 436 and Chapter 26 *infra* at notes 58-61.

104 Western Freight Ass'n, 172 NLRB 46, 68 LRRM 1364 (1968); General Electric Co., 173 NLRB No. 83, 69 LRRM 1395 (1968). In *Davenport Insulation, Inc.*, 184 NLRB No. 114, 74 LRRM 1726 (1970), the Board distinguished *Ranch-Way, Inc.*, 183 NLRB No. 116, 74 LRRM 1389 (1970), note 112 *infra*, and reaffirmed that a successor employer was not obligated to bargain with a union that had executed a prehire §8(f) agreement with its predecessor, or to honor that agreement, in the absence of independent proof of the union's majority status. *See* Chapters 11 and 13 *infra*.

105 The Kroger Co., 155 NLRB 546, 548, 60 LRRM 1351 (1965). The Board in *General Extrusion* did not actually use the term "consolidation," but in *Kroger* it was given this interpretation.

of an entirely new operation with major personnel changes," [106] *or* (2) "resumption of operations at either the same or a new location, after an indefinite period of closing, with new employees." [107]

The Board distinguishes these patterns from a "mere relocation" involving a considerable transfer of employees to another plant without a change in the character of the jobs and the functions of the employees. In the latter situation the contract will not be removed as a bar.

Following a merger of two or more corporate entities covered by separate contracts with different unions, a resulting integration of operations may be found to be a new operation. In these circumstances the existing bargaining agreements may be deemed abrogated, and previously existing separate bargaining units may no longer be considered appropriate.[108]

---

[106] 121 NLRB at 1167. In *Kroger*, the contract bar was not upheld because of a merger of two or more operations. Plants A and B were closed and their operations transferred to plant C. Of the 69 employees at C, 42 were from A and 27 from B. This was held to create an entirely new operation with major personnel changes on the ground that plant C could not be regarded simply as a relocation of B, to the exclusion of A. *Accord:* General Electric Co., 170 NLRB 153, 67 LRRM 1561 (1968), where facilities A and B merged into C and the Board found C to be an "amalgam" of the two separate facilities" rather than a "relocation." Determinative factors were (1) the uncertainty of the proportion of employees transferring, (2) consolidation of different product lines, and (3) changes in supervisory personnel. *Contra:* Arrow Co., 147 NLRB 824, 56 LRRM 1303 (1964), where the Board found a "relocation" and upheld the bar where plants A and B closed and operations were transferred to C. Of 78 employees at C, 45 were from A and five tentatively from B. The ground for the holding was that "when the relocation . . . is complete" a "considerable portion" of the employees at A and B "will have been transferred" to C. On this basis, the decision is difficult to square with *General Extrusion* on timeliness and with *Kroger* and *General Electric* on the conclusion reached. Also puzzling was the Board's use of the term "consolidation" along with "relocation." The other ground for decision was that intervenor at C was the incumbent at both A and B. *See also* Bowman Dairy Co., 123 NLRB 707, 45 LRRM 1514 (1959), where a contract bar was upheld. *Bowman* was distinguished in *Kroger* on the ground it simply involved plant A merging into an existing plant B, without there being a newly constructed plant C, as in *Kroger*.

[107] For this precise fact situation see Slater Sys. Maryland, Inc., 134 NLRB 865, 49 LRRM 1294 (1961). *See also* Sheets and Mackey, 92 NLRB 179, 27 LRRM 1087 (1950).

[108] Hooker Electrochemical Co., 116 NLRB 1393, 38 LRRM 1482 (1965); Greyhound Garage, Inc., 95 NLRB 902, 28 LRRM 1388 (1951); L. B. Spear & Co., 106 NLRB 687, 32 LRRM 1535 (1953); Industrial Stamping & Mfg. Co., 111 NLRB 1038, 35 LRRM 1648 (1955); Pacific Isle Mining Co., 118 NLRB 740, 40 LRRM 1253 (1957). *See also* Panda Terminals, Inc., 161 NLRB 1215, 63 LRRM 1419 (1966), National Car-loading Corp., 167 NLRB 116, 66 LRRM 1166 (1967), General Electric Co., 170 NLRB 153, 67 LRRM 1561 (1968), where this issue was raised in an accretion context.

On the other hand, if, after merger, the previously independent companies continue as separate operating divisions of the newly created corporate entity (absent evidence of substantial integration and the factors of common operation discussed above), the pre-existing bargaining units, together with their collective bargaining relationships, will not be terminated.[109]

c. *Purchasers.* Under the *General Extrusion* rule, assumption of an operation by a good-faith purchaser who had not assumed the contract of the predecessor would remove the contract as a bar. This was an affirmance of the Board's earlier position.[110] However, in 1970 the Board substantially revised its successorship doctrines,[111] holding that

> . . . the normal presumption of union majority status which attaches during the term of a contract executed by the predecessor employer applies equally to its successor, and that the successor employer may not, during the life of the contract, assert a doubt as to its obligation to bargain with the incumbent union.[112]

The *General Extrusion* rule for contract-bar purposes thus would no longer apply.

4. Accretions. The acquisition or construction of an additional operation or facility by an employer after the execution of the contract frequently gives rise to a claim of accretion. One or both of the contracting parties may seek to have the additional facility "accreted." If the additional facility is found to be an accretion to the existing operation, the preexisting contract may be extended to cover employees in the new operation and thus bar an election there. The question of accretion can arise in myriad factual and

---

109 Illinois Malleable Iron Co., 120 NLRB 451, 41 LRRM 1510 (1958) ; Consolidated Edison Co., 132 NLRB 1518, 48 LRRM 1539 (1961) ; United Illuminating Co., Case No. 1-RC-6586 (1962—not published in NLRB volumes).
110 General Extrusion Co., 121 NLRB 1165, 1168, 42 LRRM 1508 (1958) ; Jolly Giant Lumber Co., 114 NLRB 413, 36 LRRM 1585 (1955).
111 Wm. J. Burns Int'l. Detective Agency, Inc., 182 NLRB No. 50, 74 LRRM 1098 (1970) ; Kota Div. of Dura Corp., 182 NLRB No. 51, 74 LRRM 1104 (1970) ; Travelodge Corp., 182 NLRB No. 52, 74 LRRM 1105 (1970) ; Hackney Iron & Steel Co., 182 NLRB No. 53, 74 LRRM 1102 (1970) ; Ranch-Way, Inc., 183 NLRB No. 116, 74 LRRM 1389 (1970). See Chapter 13 *infra.*
112 Ranch-Way, Inc., 183 NLRB No. 116, 74 LRRM 1389, 1392 (1970). For prior development of the applicability of the contract-bar doctrine in successorship cases, *see* Joseph Madruga & Duarte R. Madruga d/b/a M. V. Dominator, 162 NLRB 1514, 64 LRRM 1215 (1967). *Cf.* Glenn Goulding d/b/a Fed Mart, 165 NLRB 202, 65 LRRM 1303 (1967) ; Valleydale Packers, Inc., 162 NLRB 139, 64 LRRM 1212 (1967) ; Grainger Bros., 146 NLRB 609, 55 LRRM 1380 (1964) ; M. B. Farrin Lumber Co., 117 NLRB 575, 39 LRRM 1296 (1957).

procedural contexts,[113] but in most instances the Board utilizes established guidelines in making its determination.

The Board's guidelines encompass the presence or absence of a variety of factors such as (1) the degree of interchange among employees,[114] (2) geographic proximity,[115] (3) integration of operations, (4) integration of machinery and product lines,[116] (5) centralized administrative control,[117] (6) similarity of working conditions, skills, and functions,[118] (7) common control over labor relations,[119] (8) collective bargaining history, and (9) the size of and number of employees at the facility to be acquired as compared with the existing operation.[120] These factors determine the basic issue of whether the new facility is sufficiently integrated into the existing operation to justify the coverage and application of the contract as a bar. Applying these criteria, it is likely that a new facility will be treated as an independent operation and not an accretion where new employees are hired especially for the new facility, the facility is separately managed, there is no interchange of employees between the new and previous operations, and the facilities are geographically distant or the operation of the new facility is autonomous despite close geographical proximity.[121]

A conflict occasionally arises where the contracting parties have negotiated an "accretion clause" that clearly covers any new opera-

---

113 Procedurally, accretion may become an issue in a number of contexts in addition to the "contract bar" issue in representation proceedings: (1) unit clarification proceedings, *infra;* (2) as part of a defense to an unfair labor practice charge, Masters-Lake Success, Inc., 124 NLRB 580, 44 LRRM 1437 (1959); *enforced as modified,* 287 F 2d 35, 47 LRRM 2607 (CA 2, 1967); *see* The Great Atl. & Pac. Tea Co., 140 NLRB 1011, 52 LRRM 1155 (1963), containing an exhaustive discussion of the accretion doctrine by the trial examiner. Factually, accretion can involve a prototype situation such as the opening of a new store by a retail chain, Sunset House, 167 NLRB 870, 66 LRRM 1243 (1967), or a subdivision of store units, Parkview Drugs, Inc., 138 NLRB 194, 50 LRRM 1564 (1962), or categories of employees, The Horn & Hardart Co., 173 NLRB 164, 69 LRRM 1522 (1968). It can also involve extremely complex fact situations where two unions are each seeking to accrete the facility at which the other has a contract, Panda Terminals, Inc., 161 NLRB 1215, 63 LRRM 1419 (1966).
114 Dura Corp., 153 NLRB 592, 59 LRRM 1519 (1965), *enforced,* 375 F 2d 707, 64 LRRM 2828 (CA 6, 1967).
115 Sunset House, note 113 *supra.*
116 Beacon Photo Serv., Inc., 163 NLRB 98, 64 LRRM 1439 (1967); Coamo Knitting Mills, Inc., 150 NLRB 579, 593, 58 LRRM 1116 (1964).
117 Masters-Lake Success, Inc., note 113 *supra.*
118 Coamo Knitting Mills, Inc., 150 NLRB 579, 58 LRRM 1116 (1964).
119 Buy Low Supermarkets, Inc., 131 NLRB 23, 47 LRRM 1586 (1961).
120 Panda Terminals, note 113 *supra.* The Board refused to find an accretion where the new operation had four times as many employees as the old one.
121 Pay Less Drug Stores, 127 NLRB 161, 45 LRRM 1520 (1960).

tion the employer may subsequently own or operate. The Board is then confronted with the alternatives of (1) treating this issue as one of contract interpretation and (2) determining for itself, in accordance with its own guidelines, whether an accretion exists. Despite the holding of an arbitrator that a contract was intended to cover later-hired employees at new facilities, the Board refused to find the contract a bar to a petition without independent determination by it that the new facilities were an accretion to the contract unit.[122]

5. Schism and Defunctness. The Board has long held that a mere change in designation or affiliation of the contractual representative does not remove an otherwise valid and subsisting contract as a bar.[123] However, the Board does disregard the contract when the contracting union has become defunct. It also holds the contract to be no longer a bar if a schism arises and destroys the identity of the contractual bargaining representative.

a. Schism. Generally speaking, a schism occurs when some of the employees in the unit become dissatisfied with the representation. The crosscurrent must be so compelling that (1) there is a basic intra-union conflict over fundamental policy questions; and (2) employees take action that creates such confusion in the bargaining relationship that stability can be restored only by an election.

The conflict, described as a "schism" for this purpose, must pervade the local as well as the international level and be so disrupting as to warrant the conclusion that industrial stability would be served by affording the employees an opportunity to select a new bargaining representative. Up to now, the chief kinds of policy splits that have been considered schismatic by the Board have been on the issues of Communism and corruption.[124]

---

[122] Pullman Indus., Inc., 159 NLRB 580, 62 LRRM 1273 (1966); Beacon Photo Serv., note 116 *supra.* Anheuser-Busch, Inc., 170 NLRB 5, 67 LRRM 1376 (1968). *But compare* Horn & Hardart Co., note 113 *supra,* and Westinghouse Elec. Corp., 162 NLRB 81, 64 LRRM 1082 (1967), with Raley's, Inc., 143 NLRB 256, 53 LRRM 1347 (1963) and Insulation & Specialties, Inc., 144 NLRB 1540, 54 LRRM 1306 (1963), involving interpretations of contracts regarding preexisting facilities or employee categories. *See* Chapter 18 *infra.*

[123] Hershey Chocolate Corp., 121 NLRB 901, 910-911, 42 LRRM 1460 (1958).

[124] In addition to Hershey: The Great Atl. & Pac. Tea Co., 120 NLRB 656, 42 LRRM 1022 (1958); Lawrence Leather Co., 108 NLRB 546, 34 LRRM 1022 (1954). *See also* Swift & Co., 145 NLRB 756, 55 LRRM 1033 (1963); Clayton and Lambert Mfg. Co., 128 NLRB 209, 46 LRRM 1275 (1960); Arthur C. Harvey, 110 NLRB 338, 34 LRRM 1650 (1954); and American Seating Co., 106 NLRB 250, 32 LRRM 1439 (1953). *Compare* Prudential Ins. Co., 106 NLRB 237, 32 LRRM 1448 (1953).

b. Defunctness. A contract between an employer and a union that has become defunct will not operate as a bar. Generally, the Board holds a union to be defunct if it has ceased to exist as an effective labor organization and is no longer able and willing to fulfill its responsibilities in administering the contract. The Board will see whether the union has been processing grievances, holding meetings of the members, collecting dues, and electing officers. The absence of anyone remaining in the union to discharge the representative's responsibilities would show that the union was defunct. Procedural steps, such as surrender of the local charter and distribution or transfer of assets and records, taken to disaffiliate and sever all connection with the international, while significant, ordinarily are not sufficient to establish defunctness.[125]

Moreover, the Board has recognized that unions may be tempted to use the defunctness and schism exceptions to circumvent the contract-bar doctrine. Accordingly, the Board considers the good faith of various steps that might appear to lead to defunctness. Where it appears that the real purpose of the steps is to rid the local members of what they consider to be an unfavorable contract, the Board has refused to apply the exceptions on the ground that holding the contract to be a bar would be more likely to effectuate the policies of the Act.[126] The Board has also rejected arguments that an "old" union was defunct, finding rather that the "new" union was in fact the "alter ego" or "successor" to the old union.[127]

6. Expiration of the Contract Bar: Timeliness. Most of the rules concerning the contract-bar doctrine come sharply into focus as the period of the contract bar approaches its expiration date.

---

[125] In addition to *Hershey:* Swift & Co., 145 NLRB 756, 55 LRRM 1033 (1963); Francis L. Bennett, 139 NLRB 1422, 51 LRRM 1518 (1962); Polar Wear Co., 139 NLRB 1006, 51 LRRM 1452 (1962); Hebron Brick Co., 135 NLRB 245, 49 LRRM 1463 (1962); Pepsi Cola Bottling Co., 132 NLRB 1441, 48 LRRM 1514 (1961); Nicholson & Co., 119 NLRB 1412, 41 LRRM 1319 (1958); A. O. Smith Co., 107 NLRB 1415, 33 LRRM 1393 (1954); Aircraft Turbine Serv., Inc., 173 NLRB No. 110, 69 LRRM 1406 (1968).

[126] Schism: Allied Container Corp., 98 NLRB 580, 29 LRRM 1388 (1952); Saginaw Furniture Shops, Inc., 97 NLRB 1488, 29 LRRM 1281 (1952). Defunctness: News-Press Publishing Co., 145 NLRB 803, 55 LRRM 1045 (1964); Hebron Brick Co., 135 NLRB 245, 49 LRRM 1463 (1962).

[127] Charles Beck Mach. Corp., 107 NLRB 874, 33 LRRM 1248 (1954); Cleveland Decals, Inc., 99 NLRB 745, 30 LRRM 1129 (1952). *See also* Harbor Carriers v. NLRB, 306 F 2d 89, 49 LRRM 1869 (CA 2, 1962), *cert. denied,* 372 US 917, 52 LRRM 2471 (1963); NLRB v. Weyerhaeuser Co., 276 F 2d 865, 45 LRRM 3088 (CA 7, 1960); Carpinteria Lemon Ass'n v. NLRB, 240 F 2d 554, 35 LRRM 1724 (CA 9, 1957).

At this juncture three distinct procedural stages arise, and, in an attempt to reduce uncertainty,[128] the Board has developed rules of timeliness as to each stage.

a. The Open Period. In order to provide employees with an opportunity for a free choice of bargaining representative at reasonable intervals, the Board established an "open period" during which petitions could be filed. Formerly this "open period" extended from 150 days to 90 days prior to the terminal date,[129] *i.e.*, the expiration date of the contract or, if the contract exceeded three years, the last day of the third year. When the election process was speeded up upon delegation to the regional directors, the open period was changed to extend from 90 to 60 days prior to the terminal date.[130]

b. The Insulated Period. A petition will not be considered timely if filed during the 60-day period preceding the terminal date. This is the "insulated period" and immediately follows the "open period." It is in this period, the Board reasons, that the parties should be permitted to negotiate "free from the 'threat of overhanging rivalry and uncertainty'." [131]

In the borderline case, petitions filed on the sixtieth day preceding and including the terminal date will normally be considered untimely as falling within the insulated period. The Board has specifically held that where a contract provides that it is in effect "until" or "to" a specific date, the date following the words "until" or "to" will not be counted in the 60-day computation.[132]

---

128 Deluxe Metal Furniture Co., 121 NLRB 995, 42 LRRM 1470 (1958).

129 *Ibid.*

130 Leonard Wholesale Meats Co., 136 NLRB 1000, 41 LRRM 1901 (1962). A petition filed before the commencement of the "open" period, however, may be entertained as to seasonal operations. *See, e.g.,* Cooperative Azucevera Los Carros, 122 NLRB 817, 43 LRRM 1193 (1958).

131 Deluxe Metal Furniture Co., note 128 *supra;* Electric Boat Div., Gen. Dynamics Corp., 158 NLRB 956, 958, 62 LRRM 1132 (1966). In *Electric Boat* a petition filed during the insulated period was dismissed even though it was not processed until after the terminal date. However, the freedom to negotiate afforded the parties during the insulated period does not necessarily establish a "good faith" defense for the employer against unfair labor practice charges of assistance to the incumbent union stemming from the execution of the contract during the insulated period. *See* Chapter 7 *supra* for a discussion of the *Midwest Piping* doctrine, and *compare* Kenrich Petrochemicals, Inc., 149 NLRB 910, 57 LRRM 1395 (1964); Hart Motor Express, Inc., 164 NLRB 382, 65 LRRM 1218 (1967); *with* City Cab, Inc., 128 NLRB 493, 46 LRRM 1332 (1960).

132 Hemisphere Steel Prods., Inc., 131 NLRB 56, 47 LRRM 1595 (1961).

c. Post-terminal Date. If no contract is entered into during the 60-day insulated period, a petition may be entertained after the terminal date—subject to new tests of timeliness.[133] Previously, under the Board's *General Electric X-Ray* doctrine,[134] a union's bare claim to representation prevented another union's subsequent contract from being a bar if the claim was followed up within 10 days by a petition. The Board discarded this rule in the *Deluxe* case, stating that it had become a means of disrupting the stability of labor relations rather than a means of protecting employees' free choice of representative.[135]

In *Deluxe* the Board established the following rules:

(1) A contract executed after the expiration of a prior contract will not bar an election if a petition is filed with the Board (a) before the execution date of a contract effective immediately or retroactively, or (b) before the effective date if the contract goes into effect at some time after its execution.

(2) In the borderline case, a petition filed on the day the contract is executed is not timely unless the employer has "been informed at the time of the execution that a petition has been filed." [136]

(3) A petition filed the day before the contract's execution will always be timely.[137]

The Board seeks to avoid having its contract-bar rules circumvented by premature extensions of the expiration date of the contract. Yet there is no necessity for penalizing the parties by attaching more stringent rules than would otherwise have been applicable to the initial contract.

The primary purpose of the premature-extension rule is to protect petitioners in general from being faced with prematurely executed contracts at a time when the Petitioner would normally be permitted to file a petition. However, the Board's rule is not an absolute

---

133 For purposes of timeliness, at this stage there is no difference between petitions filed with respect to "old" contracts and petitions filed with respect to "first" contracts.

134 General Elec. X-Ray Corp., 67 NLRB 997, 18 LRRM 1047 (1946).

135 Deluxe Metal Furniture Co., note 128 *supra.*

136 As to what constitutes being "informed" in timely fashion, *see* Portland Associated Morticians, Inc., 163 NLRB 76, 64 LRRM 1402 (1967); Rappahannock Sportswear Co., 163 NLRB 66, 64 LRRM 1417 (1967).

137 The cutoff date in applying these rules is midnight, even though the contract eventually executed after midnight is the result of continuous bargaining. Deluxe Metal Furniture, note 128 *supra.*

ban on premature extensions, but only subjects such extensions to the condition that if a petition is filed during the open period calculated from the expiration date of the old contract, the premature extension will not be a bar.[138]

As suggested above, petitions filed during the insulated period of the old contract remain untimely.[139] Similarly, the premature-extension doctrine does not apply to a contract executed at a time when the existing contract would have been vulnerable because of other contract-bar rules, e.g., the contract containing a union security provision clearly unlawful on its face.[140]

Notice to modify the contract, or actual modification short of termination, will not remove the contract as a bar to an election, regardless of whether the contract contains a modification clause and regardless of the scope of any such clause.[141] This has not always been the case, however. The Board in *Deluxe Metal* overruled intervening decisions to the effect that the reopening destroyed the bar and returned to the earlier *Western Electric* rule.[142]

F. Clarification of Units

The Board's Rules and Regulations provide a means whereby either party to a bargaining unit, whether or not established by formal NLRB representation procedures, may obtain a clarification of the unit.[143] The rule provides that a petition for clarification of an existing bargaining unit or a petition for amendment of certification, in the absence of a question concerning representation, may be filed by a labor organization or by an employer.[144] In 1964 the Board held in the *Locomotive Firemen* case that such a petition may be filed even though the Board has never passed on the appropriateness of the bargaining unit and no certification

---

138 H. L. Klion, Inc., 148 NLRB 656, 660, 57 LRRM 1073 (1964).
139 Deluxe Metal Furniture, note 128 *supra.*
140 *Cf.* St. Louis Cordage Mills, 168 NLRB No. 135, 67 LRRM 1017 (1967).
141 *Ibid.*
142 Western Elec. Co., Inc., 94 NLRB 54, 28 LRRM 1002 (1951). *See also* Greenville Finishing Co., 71 NLRB 436, 19 LRRM 1023 (1946).
143 Rule 102.60(b)—"A petition for clarification of an existing bargaining unit or a petition for amendment of certification, in the absence of a question concerning representation, may be filed by a labor organization or by an employer. Where applicable the same procedures set forth in section 102.60(a) above shall be followed." *See also* Chapter 17 *infra* at note 109.
144 Rule 102.61(d) outlines the contents of a petition for clarification.

exists.[145] There the Board treated an employer's representation petition as a motion for clarification in view of (1) the parties' long bargaining history, (2) recognition of the union as the majority representative of the employees, and (3) a finding that the existing bargaining unit was not repugnant to the Act. The earlier *Bell Telephone* [146] decision had held that the Board, since it was not empowered to render declaratory judgments or advisory opinions, did not have authority to determine the status of employees with reference to an uncertified unit.

Locomotive Firemen is construed as holding only that the Board on proper motion will undertake to clarify an uncertified unit, not that any petition for election may be treated as one for clarification. The Board will not, without conducting an election, certify or recertify a union as an incident to clarifying the unit.[147] Whether certified or not, there must be a definite unit or the motion for clarification will be dismissed.[148] As stated in rule 102.60(b), there must be no question of representation. For example, clarification cannot be used as an alternative to a petition for election when the object is to add a classification of employees that had been deliberately omitted from the unit.[149] However, a petition for clarification will be entertained if there has been a proper accretion to the unit.[150] In *Western Cartridge Co.* the Board found a proper accretion because the employees in question were interchangeable with the existing unit, had a community of interest in employment conditions, performed the same duties, and were under common supervision.[151]

The Board has dismissed petitions for clarification where professionals were entitled to an election,[152] where the union sought to amend transfer certifications,[153] where the union wanted to sub-

---

145 Locomotive Firemen and Enginemen, 145 NLRB 1521, 55 LRRM 1177 (1964).
146 Bell Tel. Co., 118 NLRB 371, 40 LRRM 1179 (1957).
147 Crown Zellerbach Corp., 147 NLRB 1223, 56 LRRM 1438 (1964).
148 FWD Corp., 131 NLRB 404, 48 LRRM 1055 (1961).
149 Lufkin Foundry & Machine Co., 174 NLRB No. 90, 70 LRRM 1262 (1969); Dayton Power and Light Co., 137 NLRB 337, 50 LRRM 1147 (1962). *But compare:* Westinghouse Electric Co., 173 NLRB No. 43, 69 LRRM 1332 (1968); Libby-Owens-Ford Glass Co., 169 NLRB No. 2, 67 LRRM 1096 (1968).
150 Western Cartridge Co., 134 NLRB 67, 49 LRRM 1098 (1961). *See* discussion of accretions, this chapter, *supra.*
151 *Ibid.*
152 Lockheed Aircraft Corp., 155 NLRB 702, 60 LRRM 1390 (1965).
153 Monon Stone Co., 137 NLRB 761, 50 LRRM 1248 (1962).

stitute the name of another local for its own,[154] and where the union wanted to clarify by changing work assignments.[155] The clarification that is asked for must not have been precluded by a previous Board determination,[156] but to be conclusive the previous determination must have resolved the exact question upon which clarification is sought.[157]

III. ELECTION PROCEDURES

A. Direction of Election

A cardinal policy of the Act is to protect the exercise by workers of full freedom to express their desires on union representation. Such representatives become the sole representatives for purposes of collective bargaining if they are "designated or selected for the purposes of collective bargaining by the majority of the employees in a unit appropriate for such purposes." [158] The method for such designation is "an election by secret ballot" to be directed by the NLRB after a proper petition, hearing, and finding that a question of representation exists.[159]

Pursuant to Section 3(b) of the Act, the Board has delegated to the regional directors its above-mentioned powers under Section 9.[160] The election is conducted under the supervision of the regional director in whose region the representation case is pending; he is responsible for the proper conduct of the election.[161] The Board's "long established policy" lets the regional director, under ordinary circumstances, exercise his discretion concerning the conduct of elections.[162] However, he may transfer parts of the case to the Board for determination. He acts through an assigned Board agent, field attorney, or field examiner, any of whom may hold

---

154 Gulf Oil Corp., 135 NLRB 184, 49 LRRM 1465 (1962).
155 Ingersoll Prods., Div. of Borg-Warner, 150 NLRB 912, 58 LRRM 1168 (1965).
156 Security Guard Serv., Inc., 154 NLRB 33, 59 LRRM 1684 (1965).
157 Boston Gas Co., 136 NLRB 219, 49 LRRM 1742 (1962); West Virginia Pulp & Paper Co., 140 NLRB 1160, 52 LRRM 1196 (1963).
158 §9 (a).
159 §9(c)(1). Until the Taft-Hartley amendments, the Board had, though it did not use, "wide discretion" in determining how to insure free employee choice. Southern Steamship Co. v. NLRB, 316 US 31, 10 LRRM 544 (1942); NLRB v. A. J. Tower Co., 329 US 324, 19 LRRM 2128 (1946). See Chapters 3 supra and 10 infra.
160 Statements of Procedure §101.21 (a).
161 Rules and Regs. §102.69; NLRB Field Manual 11300.
162 V. La Rosa & Sons, 121 NLRB 671, 42 LRRM 1418 (1958); Independent Rice Mill, Inc., 111 NLRB 536, 35 LRRM 1509 (1955).

informal preelection conferences with interested parties to settle the details of the election.[163]

1. Types of Elections. The two consent types of elections[164] pursuant to which a regional office may conduct an election are: (1) Agreement for Consent Election [165] (colloquially referred to as a "pure consent"), providing for determination by the regional director of any dispute; and (2) Stipulation for Certification on Consent Election,[166] providing for a determination by the Board of any dispute. The agreement includes the details of the election (*i.e.*, time, place, etc.) and must be approved by the regional director, who also conducts the election. He rules on all requests or motions made after the execution of the agreement. His rulings (unless arbitrary or capricious) are final in connection with a "pure consent" election but reviewable by the Board in a Stipulation for Certification. Before approval by the regional director, any party may withdraw. After approval: (1) a petitioning union may withdraw prior to the election if no inconsistent action is taken (such as recognition picketing), subject to six months' prejudice in filing a new petition; (2) an intervening union may withdraw until administrative functions have begun (*i.e.*, the printing of ballots or notices); and (3) a petitioning employer may withdraw only if unusual and compelling reasons exist or the unions do not oppose the withdrawal.[167]

The preliminaries to an election in the usual case give way to an expedited election, without a showing of substantial interest if the petition is filed within 30 days of the commencement of picketing for certain objectives, such as recognition or organization.[168] Regional offices conduct these elections, but without the usual investigatory and hearing prerequisites.[169]

2. Details of the Election. *a. Date.* An election may not be held less than 10 days after the date the regional director schedules for

---

[163] NLRB Field Manual 11300; Statements of Procedure §101.19 (a)(1).

[164] §9 (a)(4).

[165] Rules and Regs. §102.62 (a).

[166] *Id.* at §102.62 (b).

[167] T. Kammholz & K. McGuiness, PRACTICE AND PROCEDURE BEFORE THE NATIONAL LABOR RELATIONS BOARD 19 (2d ed., 1966).

[168] §8 (b)(7)(C). *See* Chapter 21 *infra*.

[169] *Ibid. See* Rules and Regs. §102.67 (b), on the decision and direction of election by the regional director, and paragraph (j) on such orders by the Board. *See also* Woodco Corp., 129 NLRB 1188, 47 LRRM 1143 (1961), for a discussion of appropriate unit considerations in expedited elections.

receipt of the required list of eligible voters and their addresses.[170]
Unless a waiver of review of the direction of election is filed, the
regional director normally will not schedule an election until a
date more than 20 days but less than 30 days from the date of his
direction of election. This is to allow the Board to rule on any
request for review.[171] If the election is directed by the Board, the
election may be held any time within 30 days of the date of the
direction of election.[172] The exact day on which the election is
held will usually be one when it is likely that the greatest number
of eligible employees will be present and able to vote, *e.g.,* a payday
or a day in the middle of the workweek.

b. Time. The election may be held on company time with the
employer's permission; otherwise it is held on the employees' own
time. The actual time for voting will be set to give all eligible
employees adequate opportunity to vote, with minimum interference with the work day. In a multishift, multiplant, or multi-
employer situation the polls may be kept open just long enough to
give each employee sufficient chance to vote, then moved or reopened later so that another shift, plant, or unit may vote.

c. Place. The polls are situated for easy accessibility and convenience to the voters.[173] For this reason the election is usually
held on company property, if possible.

3. Voter List: Eligibility. After direction of election, or approval of the consent-election agreement, the employer will be
requested to prepare a list of eligible voters and their addresses and
file it with the regional director within seven days of such direction or approval. The regional director will then make the list
available to all parties.[174] In *Excelsior Underwear, Inc.,*[175] the
Board ruled that failure to furnish such list timely is ground for
setting aside the election on proper objection. The list is designed
to facilitate free and reasoned choice by employees and to avoid the
necessity of a challenge when an employee on the eligibility list,

---

[170] NLRB Field Manual 11302.1.
[171] Statements of Procedure §101.21 (d).
[172] McGuiness, SILVERBERG'S HOW TO TAKE A CASE BEFORE THE NATIONAL LABOR
RELATIONS BOARD (Washington: BNA Books, 1967).
[173] Manchester Knitted Fashions, Inc., 108 NLRB 1366, 34 LRRM 1214 (1954).
[174] NLRB Field Manual 11312.1; Blaise Parking Serv., Case No. 15-CA-3646, 65
LRRM 1707 (1967).
[175] 156 NLRB 1236, 61 LRRM 1217 (1966); NLRB Field Manual 11312.6. *But see*
Fuchs Baking Co., 12-RC-3087, 69 LRRM 1273 (1968). *See* Chapter 5 *supra,* at
note 165, and Chapter 30 *infra,* at notes 68 and 109-115.

but previously unknown to the union, appears to vote. The names and addresses should be listed systematically (*e.g.*, alphabetically, or by clock or card number, either as a whole or by department or unit). The list furnished by the employer will also serve as the basis for composing the voting list.[176] It should be checked and approved promptly by the parties (to allow maximum time for ironing out eligibility questions before the election) and should be kept up to date.[177] If the list is not received, or contains names but not addresses, the director will proceed to the election unless requested in writing not to do so by the petitioner or an intervenor with sufficient showing of interest.[178]

An early release of qualified voters' names and addresses is held necessary by the Board to an intelligent election, despite contentions that a subpoena for this purpose, directed to the employer, is beyond its investigatory powers.[179] The Supreme Court has directed enforcement of an *Excelsior* type of subpoena; but without concurrence of a majority of the justices in support of the reasons therefor,[180] and notwithstanding that a majority of them, though differing among themselves on the majority result in favor of enforcement, would hold applicable to such rules the formal procedures for rule making specified in the Administrative Procedure Act.[181]

Generally, all employees in the unit found appropriate who were employed during the payroll period immediately preceding the date of the direction of election are eligible to vote, provided

---

176 NLRB Field Manual 11312.3. Note that in "UD" elections, unlike other elections, the majority of employees eligible to vote is determinative, rather than a majority of employees actually voting. NLRB Field Manual 11512.

177 NLRB Field Manual 11312.4; Statements of Procedure §101.19 (a)(1).

178 NLRB Field Manual 11312.8. An intervenor with less than 30 percent cannot block the election, but may file objections, and the Board may set the election aside for failure to supply the list. A defective but bona fide list does not constitute grounds for setting the election aside. Valley Die Cast Corp., 160 NLRB 1881, 63 LRRM 1190 (1966). See note 15 *supra*.

179 NLRB v. Hanes Corp., 384 F 2d 188, 66 LRRM 2264 (CA 4, 1967), *cert. denied*, 390 US 950, 67 LRRM 2632; NLRB v. Rohlen, 385 F 2d 52, 66 LRRM 2481 (CA 7, 1967).

180 NLRB v. Wyman-Gordon Co., 394 US 759, 70 LRRM 3345 (1969).

181 5 USC §553. Chief Justice Warren and Justices Fortas, Stewart, and White were of this opinion, but favored enforcement of the subpoena anyway. Justices Douglas and Harlan in separate dissenting opinions argued that the *Excelsior* rules are invalid under the Administrative Procedure Act. Justices Black, Brennan, and Marshall argued that they are the by-product of the Board's adjudication, the "direct consequence of the proper exercise of its adjudicatory powers." See also Chapter 30 *infra* at notes 109-115.

they are still employed at the time of the election.[182] If the parties have a written agreement expressly providing that it shall be final and binding as to specified questions of eligibility, the Board will respect the agreement unless it is contrary to the Act or Board policy.[183]

Employees engaged in an economic strike who are "not entitled to reinstatement" (*i.e.*, have been permanently replaced) are eligible to vote, under Board regulations, in any election held within 12 months of the commencement of the strike.[184] The striker retains his right to vote absent some affirmative action other than replacement (such as the acceptance of permanent employment elsewhere, elimination of his job, discharge, or denial of reinstatement for conduct rendering him unsuitable for reemployment) indicating that his employment has ended.[185] Replacements employed on a permanent basis prior to the voting eligibility cutoff date also are eligible.[186] Employees who *are* entitled to reinstatement (unfair labor practice strikers) are entitled to vote regardless of the 12-month statutory limitation.[187] Replacements for such strikers are not.[188]

---

[182] Vultee Aircraft, Inc., 24 NLRB 1184, 6 LRRM 459 (1940); Columbia Pictures Corp., 61 NLRB 1030, 16 LRRM 128 (1945). *But see* Remington Rand Corp., 50 NLRB 819, 12 LRRM 219 (1943); Great Lakes Pipe Line Co., 64 NLRB 1296, 17 LRRM 169 (1945); Carl B. King Drilling Co., 164 NLRB 557, 65 LRRM 1096 (1967).

[183] Norris-Thermador Corp., 119 NLRB 1301, 41 LRRM 1283 (1958); Lake Huron Broadcasting Corp., 130 NLRB 908, 47 LRRM 1443 (1961); NLRB v. Joclin Mfgr. Co., 314 F 2d 627, 52 LRRM 2415 (CA 2, 1963); *but see* Shoreline Enterprises of America, Inc. v. NLRB, 262 F 2d 933, 43 LRRM 2407 (CA 5, 1959). Tidewater Oil Co. v. NLRB, 385 F 2d 363, 61 LRRM 2693 (CA 2, 1966) *denying enforcement of* 151 NLRB 1288, 58 LRRM 1639 (1965). For example, the Act §2(3) excludes supervisors, individuals employed by parent or spouse, etc. Uyeda v. Brooks, 348 F 2d 633, 59 LRRM 2850 (CA 6, 1965).

[184] §9(a)(3).

[185] W. Wilton Wood, Inc., 127 NLRB 1675, 46 LRRM 1240 (1969). *Cf.* Laidlaw Corp., 171 NLRB 175, 68 LRRM 1252 (1968), *enforced*, 414 F 2d 99, 71 LRRM 3054 (1969). *See* Chapter 19 *infra*.

[186] Pacific Tile & Porcelain Co., 137 NLRB 1358, 50 LRRM 1394 (1962). If the strike occurs after the direction of election, permanent replacements of economic strikers attain eligibility if they remain employees on election day. Tampa Sand & Material Co., 137 NLRB 1549, 50 LRRM 1438 (1962); Macy's Missouri-Kansas Div., 173 NLRB No. 232, 70 LRRM 1039 (1969) (strike began after direction of election and ended before election). But if the strike is called before the direction of election, replacements enjoy no exception to the general rule specifying eligibility both at the time of direction of election and on election day. Greenspan Engraving Corp., 137 NLRB 1308, 50 LRRM 1380 (1962).

[187] Kellburn Mfg. Co., 45 NLRB 322, 11 LRRM 142 (1942).

[188] Lock Joint Tube Co., 127 NLRB 1146, 46 LRRM 1170 (1960); Tampa Sand & Material Co., 137 NLRB 1549, 50 LRRM 1438 (1962).

Laid-off employees who have a "reasonable expectation of re-employment" in the foreseeable future are eligible to vote.[189] Employees who have quit or been discharged for cause before the election are ineligible,[190] but employees who have been discriminatorily discharged,[191] or have given notice of intent to quit but are still on the payroll at the time of the election,[192] are entitled to vote. Probationary employees are eligible to vote if their working conditions are substantially the same as those of regular employees and they have "reasonable expectation of permanent employment."[193] Employees on sick leave or leave of absence are eligible to vote if they are to be automatically restored to their duties when ready to resume work.[194] Generally, seasonal, casual, or temporary employees are not eligible to vote unless they have a reasonable expectation of reemployment and a substantial interest in working conditions at employer's place of business.[195] Regular part-time as distinguished from temporary or casual [196] employees may vote. Likewise, temporarily transferred employees may vote.[197] A dual-function employee who spends part of his time doing bargaining-

---

[189] NLRB v. Jesse Jones Sausage Co., 309 F 2d 664, 51 LRRM 2501 (CA 4, 1962); Marley Co., 131 NLRB 866, 48 LRRM 1168 (1961). See Chapter 9 infra for classification of employees on layoff status.

[190] Rish Equip. Co., 150 NLRB 1185, 58 LRRM 1274 (1965); Gemex Corp., 117 NLRB 656, 39 LRRM 1312 (1957); Dura Steel Prods. Co., 111 NLRB 590, 35 LRRM 1522 (1955); United States Rubber Co., 86 NLRB 338, 24 LRRM 1621 (1949).

[191] Sioux City Brewing Co., 85 NLRB 1164, 24 LRRM 1534 (1949); Tampa Sand & Material Co., 137 NLRB 1549, 50 LRRM 1438 (1962); see also Pacific Tile & Porcelain Co., 137 NLRB 1358, 50 LRRM 1394 (1962); (voting permitted even though pending grievance or arbitration procedure over discharged person had not been made subject of unfair labor practice charge).

[192] Reidbord Bros. Co., 99 NLRB 127, 30 LRRM 1047 (1952); NLRB v. General Tube Co., 331 F 2d 751, 56 LRRM 2161 (CA 6, 1964); Ely & Walker, 151 NLRB 636, 58 LRRM 1513 (1965).

[193] Beattie Mfg. Co., 77 NLRB 361, 22 LRRM 1015 (1948); Sheffield Corp., 123 NLRB 1454, 44 LRRM 1155 (1959); V.I.P. Radio, Inc., 128 NLRB 113, 46 LRRM 1278 (1960); Vogue Art Ware & China Co., 129 NLRB 1253, 47 LRRM 1169 (1961).

[194] NLRB v. Atkinson Dredging Co., 329 F 2d 158, 55 LRRM 2598 (CA 4, 1964), cert. denied, 377 US 965, 56 LRRM 2416 (1964); Helen Rose Co., 127 NLRB 1682, 46 LRRM 1242 (1960); Armour & Co., 83 NLRB 333, 24 LRRM 1062 (1949).

[195] William E. Locke, 137 NLRB 1610, 50 LRRM 1469 (1962); S. Martinelli & Co., 99 NLRB 43, 30 LRRM 1031 (1952). The Board frequently permits voting by employees who have worked a specified number of days within a stated period prior to election. Daniel Constr. Co., Inc., 133 NLRB 264, 48 LRRM 1636 (1961); Gurlick Drilling Co., 139 NLRB 1137, 51 LRRM 1461 (1962); Transfilm, Inc., 100 NLRB 78, 30 LRRM 1233 (1952). See discussion of special categories of employees in Chapter 9 infra.

[196] See Chapter 9 infra; see also Providence Pub. Market Co., 79 NLRB 1482, 23 LRRM 1011 (1948); Tol-Pac, Inc., 128 NLRB 1439, 46 LRRM 1485 (1960); Food Fair Stores, Inc., 120 NLRB 1669, 42 LRRM 1242 (1958).

[197] Huntley Van Buren Co., 122 NLRB 957, 43 LRRM 1228 (1959) (production employee temporarily assigned as night watchman).

unit work may have sufficient interest in conditions of employment in the unit to be eligible to vote without actually spending a majority of his time on unit work.[198]

4. Notice of Election. When a petition is filed, the parties receive a Board poster outlining their rights. The Board urges but does not require that this notice be posted. Prior to the date of election the holding of the election will be adequately publicized by the posting of official notices to inform eligible voters of the balloting details.[199] A standard Board form (NLRB 707), which reproduces a sample ballot and outlines such details as location of polls, time of voting, and eligibility rules, is used. The notices are posted by the employer in his place of business in conspicuous places, such as bulletin boards and timecard racks, whenever possible. Notices may also be posted in other places, or the publicizing of the election may be by the "use of other means considered appropriate and effective." [200]

5. Review of Direction of Election. The order of the regional director setting forth his findings, conclusions, and order or direction is final.[201] However, any party may, within 10 days of service of the direction, file a request for review with the Board. The request must be a self-contained document enabling the Board to rule on the basis of its contents without recourse to the record.[202] The Board will grant a request for review only where one or more of the following "compelling reasons" exist: (1) substantial question of law or policy is raised and there is an absence of or departure from officially reported Board precedent; (2) the regional director's decision on a substantial factual issue is both clearly erroneous on the record and prejudicial; (3) the conduct of the hearing resulted in prejudicial error; or (4) compelling reasons exist for reconsideration of an important Board rule or policy.[203] Any party, within seven days of the deadline for filing a request for review, may file a statement in opposition to the request.[204] If the request for review is granted, the Board will consider the

---

198 NLRB v. Joclin Mfg. Co., 314 F 2d 627, 52 LRRM 2415 (CA 2, 1963). Berea Publishing Co., 140 NLRB 516, 52 LRRM 1051 (1963). *See* Chapter 9 *infra* for discussion of dual-function employees.
199 Statements of Procedure §101.19 (a)(1) ; NLRB Field Manual 11314.
200 Statements of Procedure §101.19 (a)(1) ; NLRB Field Manual 11314.3.
201 Rules and Regs. §102.67 (b) .
202 *Id*. at §102.67 (d) .
203 Rules and Regs. §102.67 (c) .
204 *Id*. at §102.67 (e) .

entire record in the light of the grounds relied on for review. The parties may file briefs within seven days of the order granting review.[205]

The regional director, if it appears to him that the proceeding raises questions that should be decided by the Board, may transfer the case to the Board for decision. If the case is so transferred, the parties may file with the Board the briefs previously filed (or due to be filed) with the regional director.[206] The regional director must transmit the record to the Board immediately upon issuance of an order transferring the case or granting the request for review.[207]

Further briefs or reply briefs are permitted only by special leave of the Board. The Board then decides the issues referred to it (or reviews the regional director's decision) either on the record or after oral argument, submission of briefs, or further hearing. The Board then must direct an election, dismiss the petition, affirm or reverse the regional director's order, or dispose of the matter in such other way as it deems appropriate.[208]

Normally Board orders in election and certification proceedings under Section 9(c) are not directly reviewable by the courts. The Supreme Court in *Leedom v. Kyne* [209] held that a party might, by proceeding against the Board members in a district court, attack an order of election and unit determination if such an action is for the purpose of striking down a Board order made "in excess of its delegated powers and contrary to a specific prohibition in the Act." [210] However, the Court in subsequent cases has emphasized that the *Leedom* exception is a narrow one.[211] Such decisions are reviewable under the Act only where the dispute concerning the

---

[205] *Id.* at §102.67 (g) .
[206] *Id.* at §§102.67 (h) , 102.67 (i) .
[207] *Id.* at §102.68.
[208] *Id.* at §102.67 (j) .
[209] 388 US 184, 43 LRRM 2222 (1958) , *affirming* 249 F 2d 490, 40 LRRM 2600 (CA DC, 1957) , *affirming* 148 F Supp 597, 39 LRRM 2197 (D DC, 1956) .
[210] The Board had included both professional and nonprofessional employees in the same unit, without a vote of the professional employees, in contravention of §9 (b)(1) of the Act.
[211] Boire v. Greyhound Corp., 376 US 473, 55 LRRM 2694 (1964) . *See* Goldberg, *District Court Review of NLRB Representation Proceedings*, 42 IND. L.J. 455, 487, 489 (1967) . *Cf.* Railway Clerks v. Ass'n for Benefit of Non-Contract Employees, 380 US 650, 59 LRRM 2051 (1965) .

correctness of the certification eventuates in a finding by the Board that an unfair labor practice (*e.g.*, a refusal to bargain) has been committed.[212]

B. The Election Proper

1. Balloting. *a. The Ballot.* Ballots are in all cases furnished by the Board. The practice is that no one but the Board agent and the voter may handle a ballot. The color of the ballot for a particular group or unit will not be disclosed to the parties prior to the voting. The places on the ballot normally are agreed upon but, in the absence of agreement, are determined by chance. The regional director may permit a union to use a shortened name, regardless of whether the matter was raised in hearing, if he concludes that the voters will not be misled. The question on the ballot is determined by the consent agreement or direction of election.[213] The ballot gives the employee a choice whether to be represented or not, and, if two or more unions are competing, a choice of representative. In a severance election, however, the only question is by whom the employee wishes to be represented.

b. Voting. The actual polling is always conducted and supervised by Board agents.[214] Voting is by secret ballot and takes place in portable voting booths where it is necessary that the employees be furnished a place to vote in absolute secrecy. As the voter identifies himself his name is checked against the eligibility list, and the Board agent hands him a ballot. He marks only his choice on the ballot (any other mark may affect the validity of the ballot) and puts it directly into the ballot box provided by the Board.

c. Mail Ballots. The regional director may conduct the voting by mail, in whole or in part, when an election involves long distances or widely scattered voters.[215] Specific provision for voting by mail in the direction of election is not required.[216] Prospective

---

212 *See* §9(d), and the Administrative Procedure Act, 5 USC 554 (Supp 1966) in clause 6: "the certification of worker representatives." For detailed treatment of judicial review of representation orders, *see* Chapter 32 *infra.*
213 NLRB Field Manual 11306.
214 Statements of Procedure §101.19(a)(2). *See* discussion of craft severance in Chapter 9 *infra.*
215 NLRB Field Manual 11336; McGuiness, SILVERBERG'S HOW TO TAKE A CASE BEFORE THE NATIONAL LABOR RELATIONS BOARD, §9-20 (Washington: BNA Books, 1967).
216 Simplot Fertilizer Co., 107 NLRB 1211, 33 LRRM 1357 (1954).

voters are mailed notice of the election and a voting "kit" containing a ballot and return envelope. The parties are given notice at least 24 hours prior to dispatching the mail ballots. The returned envelopes are treated as voters for the purpose of identification and challenge, and the ballots are commingled with any regular ballots before counting.[217]

d. *Defective Ballots.* Unmarked [218] or improperly marked [219] ballots are void, as are write-in votes.[220] A ballot is invalid if identification of the voter is possible.[221] However, a defaced ballot is valid if the voter's intent is clearly indicated and the ballot has none of the above infirmities.[222]

2. Observers. Any party may be represented at the voting by observers of his own selection. In directed elections, this is a privilege extended by the Board; in consent elections, the consent agreement or stipulation form supplied by the Board provides for observers, making their use a matter of right. Each party may appoint an equal number of observers, the number to be determined by the Board agent from the circumstances of the election (such as number of voters, voting places, etc.). Parties may waive, expressly or by default, the opportunity to be represented by observers.[223]

The use of observers is also subject to such limitations as the regional director may prescribe to the end that they be "appropriate" representatives.[224] Board policy requires that observers be nonsupervisory employees [225] and not be "persons closely identi-

---

217 NLRB Field Manual 11336.2, 11336.3, 11336.5.
218 NLRB v. Vulcan Furniture Mfg. Corp., 214 F 2d 369, 34 LRRM 2449 (CA 5, 1954), *cert. denied*, 348 US 873, 35 LRRM 2058 (1954); Q-F Wholesalers, Inc., 87 NLRB 1085, 25 LRRM 1254 (1949).
219 Semi-Steel Casting Co. v. NLRB, 160 F 2d 388, 19 LRRM 2458 (CA 8, 1947), *cert. denied*, 332 US 758, 20 LRRM 2673 (1947).
220 Woodmark Indus., Inc., 80 NLRB 1105, 23 LRRM 1209 (1948).
221 Eagle Iron Works, 117 NLRB 1053, 39 LRRM 1379 (1957); George K. Garrett Co., 120 NLRB 484, 41 LRRM 1519 (1958); Burlington Mills Corp., 56 NLRB 365, 14 LRRM 148 (1944).
222 Belmont Smelting & Refining Works, Inc., 115 NLRB 1481, 38 LRRM 1104 (1956); American Cable & Radio Corp., 107 NLRB 1090, 33 LRRM 1324 (1954); General Motors Corp., 107 NLRB 1096, 33 LRRM 1318 (1954).
223 Rules and Regs. §102.69(a); NLRB Field Manual 11310.
224 Rules and Regs. §102.69(a); Statements of Procedure §101.19(a)(2).
225 NLRB Field Manual 11310; Worth Food Market Stores, Inc., 103 NLRB 259, 31 LRRM 1527 (1953). *But see* Soerens Motor Co., 106 NLRB 1388, 33 LRRM 1021 (1953) (presence of union secretary who was former employee of employer permitted, since (1) discharge was subject of unfair labor practice charges at time of election and (2) presence did not exert undue influence on voters).

fied" with the employer.[226] An employee who is eligible to vote may act as an election observer and still vote.[227] Neither nonparticipating unions nor "no-union" groups are permitted to select observers.[228]

A *preelection conference* of the parties and the Board agent is usually held at a designated time and place prior to the election. At this conference the voter eligibility list is checked, the authorized observers are designated, and other election details are handled.

Observers are given their instructions (Form NLRB 722) by the Board agent prior to the election. They check procedure at the balloting and counting of ballots, aid in identifying voters, and assist the Board agent. Their most important function is that of challenging voters. For this purpose they may keep a list of voters whose ballots they intend to challenge, but not a list to establish who voted in the election.[229]

3. Challenges. The Board agent or any party (through its authorized observers) has the privilege of challenging for good or reasonable cause the eligibility of any person to apply for a ballot and participate in the election. The ballots of such challenged persons are segregated and impounded.[230] This allows the Board to reserve ruling temporarily on questions of voter eligibility, and at the same time preserves the challenged votes in the event they are relevant. The Board agent must challenge anyone whose name is not on the official eligibility list, or any voter he knows or has reason to believe is ineligible. The reason for the challenge should be stated at the time the challenge is made.[231] Anyone in a job classification specifically excluded by the direction of election is denied a ballot, unless he presents plausible reasons for his voting

---

[226] International Stamping Co., 97 NLRB 921, 29 LRRM 1158 (1951) (son and sister-in-law of employer's president); Peabody Engineering Co., 95 NLRB 952, 28 LRRM 1391 (1951) (employer's attorney); Watkins Brick Co., 107 NLRB 500, 33 LRRM 1176 (1953) (employer's vice-president, treasurer, and office manager).

[227] Kroder-Reubel Co., 72 NLRB 240, 19 LRRM 1155 (1947).

[228] NLRB Field Manual 11310.

[229] Bear Creek Orchards, 90 NLRB 286, 26 LRRM 1204 (1950); Milwaukee Cheese Co., 112 NLRB 1383, 36 LRRM 1225 (1955) (use of duplicate of official voting list to check off employees voting held improper).

[230] Rules and Regs. §102.69(a); Statements of Procedure §101.19(a)(2).

[231] NLRB Field Manual 11338

despite the exclusion, or some question exists as to whether he is actually within the excluded group.[232]

In *NLRB v. Tower Co.*[233] the Supreme Court approved the requirement that challenges to the eligibility of voters be made "prior to the actual casting of ballots," thereby giving all uncontested votes absolute finality. The Court compared this rule with the rule in political elections that once a ballot has been cast without challenge and its identity lost, its validity cannot be challenged, adding that the political rule is "universally recognized as consistent with democratic process."[234] It follows from this rule that the Board will not permit challenges in the guise of objections after the election.[235] Each voter's ballot must be challenged individually when he appears at the polls; a party's statement at the opening of the polls that it challenges each and every voter is not a sufficient challenge.[236]

A challenged vote is cast as follows: The voter is given a ballot and an envelope identifying the voter, the reason for challenge, and the challenger. The voter then marks the ballot, puts it into the envelope, and casts the sealed envelope in the ballot box. At the time of the count the challenged ballots are segregated. If the number of challenged ballots is sufficient to affect the outcome of the election, the validity of the challenges must be determined. The director or Board need rule only on what is necessary to decide the election. If a ballot is ruled eligible, the challenge is waived unless objection is made within three days.[237]

C. Resolution of Challenges and Objections to the Election

1. Challenges. Prior to the count of the votes the parties may wish to dispose of some challenged ballots by consent (*i.e.*, by removing challenges, *not* by throwing the ballots out). The Board agent may encourage such action but should not urge it on re-

---

[232] NLRB Field Manual 11338.5.

[233] NLRB v. A. J. Tower Co., 329 US 324, 19 LRRM 2128 (1946); NLRB Field Manual 11360.

[234] 329 US at 332.

[235] Norris, Inc., 63 NLRB 502, 17 LRRM 4 (1945).

[236] William R. Whittaker Co., 94 NLRB 1151, 28 LRRM 1150 (1951); Cities Service Oil Co., 87 NLRB 324, 25 LRRM 1112 (1949); Westinghouse Electric Corp., 118 NLRB 1625, 40 LRRM 1440 (1957).

[237] Rules and Regs. §102.69 (g). If the number of challenged ballots is insufficient to affect the outcome, the challenges will not be resolved.

luctant parties.[238] If there remain a sufficient number of challenges to affect the results of the election,[239] and if the challenges were made before the challenged votes were cast,[240] the regional director investigates the challenges.[241] This investigation is nonadversary so far as the Board is concerned. The investigator is responsible for obtaining all available facts so that full consideration will be given to all matters elicited in the investigation, whether or not urged by, or known to, the parties.[242]

2. Objections to the Election.[243] Within five days after the parties are furnished with the tally of ballots (the parties usually receive the tally on the day of the election), any party may file with the regional director objections to the conduct of the election or to conduct affecting the result of the election.[244] The five-day limit is not tolled by unresolved challenges of voters sufficient to affect the election. The objections must contain a short statement of reasons and a recitation of service on the other parties (as well as their counsel) [245] within the five-day limit. The regional director must then conduct an investigation unless, upon request by the regional director, the party filing the objections is unable to furnish sufficient evidence to support a *prima facie* case.[246] The conduct of the investigation is similar to the investigation of challenges. If the "investigation reveals circumstances not alleged by the objector" but which were "reasonably within his knowledge," the regional director "should not sustain the objections on the basis of these circumstances." [247] If, however, the additional circumstances reveal a serious abuse or violation raising substantial and material issues, they will be included in the report.[248] The

---

238 NLRB Field Manual 11340.3.

239 Statements of Procedure §101.19 (a)(4) ; NLRB Field Manual 11360.

240 NLRB v. A. J. Tower Co., note 233 *supra*.

241 Rules and Regs. §102.69 (c) ; United States Rubber Co. v. NLRB, 373 F 2d 602, 64 LRRM 2393 (CA 5, 1967).

242 NLRB Field Manual 11362; J. Weingarten, Inc., 172 NLRB No. 228, 69 LRRM 1118 (1968).

243 *See* Chapters 5 *supra* and 10 *infra*.

244 The five-day limit means five *working days. See* NLRB Field Manual 11392.1 for procedure where the deadline is missed because of delays in the mail. *See also* Rio de Oro Uranium Mines, Inc., 119 NLRB 153, 41 LRRM 1057 (1957).

245 Rules and Regs. §102.69 (a). This rule is strictly enforced; failure to serve other parties within the allotted time will be fatal despite timely service upon the regional director. Brown Lumber Co., 143 NLRB 174, 53 LRRM 1283 (1963).

246 NLRB Field Manual 11392.5.

247 *Id.* at 11394. The Manual does not indicate whether the "circumstances" envisioned are those which are favorable or unfavorable to the objector.

248 *Ibid.*

time span of the investigation begins with the filing of the petition.[249]

The substantive grounds upon which an objection to conduct affecting the result of an election may be made are dealt with elsewhere.[250] In general, an objection to such conduct may be made where a party to the election engages in conduct that might destroy the "laboratory conditions" desired to allow employees an absolutely free choice in the election. Examples include a deliberate misstatement by a party of material facts within its special knowledge,[251] threats,[252] promises, and other misleading or inflammatory preelection propaganda.[253] An objection to the conduct of the election is appropriate when an occurrence during the election itself might have prejudiced a party's interest in the election (e.g., closing the polls prematurely, allowing a ballot to be marked in other than complete secrecy, or violating election procedures contained in the direction of election, the Board rules or regulations, or the Act). The Board may set aside an election without regard to whether the conduct would be deemed an unfair labor practice if such conduct constitutes substantial interference with the election.[254] However, an objection to the election cannot be based on the appropriateness of the bargaining unit or upon voter eligibility, for these questions must be raised in proper proceedings.[255]

3. Resolution of Challenges and Objections. If the election was held under a direction of election and it appears to the regional director that substantial and material factual issues exist which can be resolved only after a hearing, he must hold a hearing on

[249] Goodyear Tire & Rubber Co., 138 NLRB 453, 51 LRRM 1070 (1962). In F. W. Woolworth Co., 109 NLRB 1446, 34 LRRM 1584 (1954), it was established that conduct occurring before the Board's direction of election could not be the subject of objection to the election. Because of the success of regional directors in reducing delay after the delegation to them (see note 160 *supra*) this time was moved back from direction of election to the date of filing the petition in Ideal Electric & Mfg. Co., 134 NLRB 1446, 49 LRRM 1316 (1961), for contested cases; and in the *Goodyear* case the petition-filing date was taken instead of the direction-of-election date for all cases, whether of contested petitions, consent elections, or stipulated elections.
[250] *See* Chapter 5 *supra.*
[251] Hollywood Ceramics Co., 140 NLRB 221, 51 LRRM 1600 (1962).
[252] Dal-Tex Optical Co., 137 NLRB 1782, 50 LRRM 1489 (1962).
[253] McGuiness, SILVERBERG'S HOW TO TAKE A CASE BEFORE THE NATIONAL LABOR RELATIONS BOARD §9-9 (Washington: BNA Books, 1967).
[254] General Shoe Corp., 77 NLRB 124, 21 LRRM 1337 (1948). *See* discussion of "laboratory conditions" and the *General Shoe* doctrine in Chapter 5 *supra.*
[255] Representation hearing and challenges, respectively. On voter eligibility, *see* NLRB v. A. J. Tower Co., 329 US 324, 19 LRRM 2128 (1946).

such issues; otherwise the holding of a hearing is in the regional director's discretion.[256] Whether or not there is a hearing, in a directed election the regional director may: (1) issue a report on the objections and/or challenges, specifically recommend a disposition, and forward the report to the Board; or (2) issue a supplemental decision appropriately disposing of the objections and challenges himself. If he reports to the Board, the parties have a right to file exceptions to the report with the Board within 10 days. If he rules on the objections and challenges, parties may seek Board review. As in the case of orders directing elections, review is limited to four categories, namely: (1) departure from reported Board precedent involving a substantial question of law or policy, (2) clear and prejudicial error on the record on a substantial issue of fact, (3) prejudicial error in conduct of the hearing, and (4) compelling reasons to reconsider an important Board rule or policy.[257]

In a "pure consent" election it is otherwise: the director's decision is virtually final on all issues without even a discretionary appeal. In rare situations, however, the Board may consider a motion to set aside the director's decision as arbitrary or capricious.[258]

In a stipulated election the Board, rather than the regional director, makes final determinations of challenges and objections. The regional director, therefore, prepares a report on his investigation, serves it on the parties, and forwards it to the Board. He may omit making the report if he orders a hearing.[259]

When the director forwards a report to the Board, the parties have a right to file exceptions within 10 days. The exceptions may be accompanied by briefs and may be opposed by an answering brief from any other party within 17 days of the regional director's report. If no exceptions are filed, the Board may decide the case on the record or otherwise dispose of it.[260] If the election is pursuant to a stipulation agreement, and exceptions to the Board decision are filed which do not appear to raise substantial and material issues, the Board may decide and dispose of the case forth-

---

[256] Rules and Regs. §102.69 (c) ; Home Town Foods, Inc. v. NLRB, 379 F 2d 241, 65 LRRM 2681 (CA 5, 1967) (holding that the employer must be given an opportunity for a hearing to establish his charges if there are substantial and material factual issues).
[257] Rules and Regs. §§102.67 (c) , 102.69 (c) .
[258] Rules and Regs. §102.62 (a) .
[259] Rules and Regs. §102.69 (c) .
[260] Ibid.

with. However, if the exceptions do appear to raise such issues, the Board may order a further hearing and report. The parties again have the right to file (within 10 days) exceptions to the report, which the Board will then consider on their merits.[261]

If the objections to the election are overruled, a certification will be issued, provided there are no problems caused by unresolved challenges. If the objections are found to have merit, the election is set aside and a new election is conducted.[262] A decision of the Board sustaining objections, setting aside the election, and ordering a new vote is not directly reviewable in the courts.[263]

D. Runoff and Rerun Elections

A prerequisite to the holding of a runoff election is that none of the three or more choices that appeared on the ballot in the original election received a majority of the valid votes cast; e.g., in an election involving 18 eligible voters, union A received seven votes, "neither" received six votes, and union B received five votes. This would be considered an inconclusive election, so the regional director would conduct a runoff election between the choices on the ballot that received the highest and the next highest number of votes, i.e., union A and "neither." [264] There can be no runoff of an election in which there are only two choices,[265] so there can be no runoff of a runoff election.[266] A runoff election is held as soon as possible after the original election but not while objections are pending or would still be timely.[267] A timely objection will be considered only insofar as it relates to circumstances subsequent to the original election.[268] Those eligible to vote are those who were eligible at the time of the original election and remained eligible at the time of the runoff.[269]

A rerun election is an exception to the runoff procedure, which is premised upon the emergence of the top two nonmajority choices. On occasion it is not possible to determine which two of

---

261 Rules and Regs. §102.69 (e) .
262 Statements of Procedure §101.19 (a)(4) .
263 Bonwit Teller, Inc. v. NLRB, 197 F 2d 640, 30 LRRM 2305 (CA 2, 1952) .
264 NLRB Field Manual 11350.1.
265 This would include a severance election where there were only two choices on the ballot. NLRB Field Manual 11350.1.
266 NLRB Field Manual 11350.5.
267 NLRB Field Manual 11350.3.
268 Ibid.
269 Thus the list can only change "downward." NLRB Field Manual 11350.5.

the nonmajority choices have received the largest number of votes. This occurs when three or more parties receive an equal number of votes, or where two choices receive an equal number of votes and the third choice receives a higher vote, but still less than a majority. In that event the election is considered a nullity and is rerun.[270] While a runoff may result from a rerun,[271] a second nullity will cause a dismissal of the petition.[272] For rerun purposes, the payroll period determining eligibility is a "recent" one as set by the regional director or the Board.[273] The notice of election may include a paragraph explaining why the original election is being rerun.[274]

A further exception to the runoff procedure occurs where all eligible votes are cast and two or more choices receive an equal number of votes and another choice receives no votes, and there are no challenges; e.g., of 16 valid votes, union A receives none, union B receives eight, and "neither" receives eight.[275] In this situation the election will not be rerun and there will be no certification of representative; the regional director will merely certify the results of the election.

E. Certification

If there are no timely filed objections and the voting is determinative, the regional director issues a certification of the results of the election and, if appropriate, a certification of representative. This certification has the same force and effect as if issued by the Board, and the proceeding is therefore closed.[276] If no union receives more than half the votes, the Board will merely certify the results of the election, showing that the union or unions are not the choice of the majority of the employees.

A union will be certified as the representative of the employees in the unit for purposes of collective bargaining if it receives a majority of the valid votes cast. A union cannot be certified on the basis of a tie vote. The Board may refuse certification if the legal-

---

270 NLRB Field Manual 11350.1.
271 NLRB Field Manual 11456.
272 NLRB Field Manual 11350.1.
273 NLRB Field Manual 11452.
274 NLRB Field Manual 11452.1.
275 NLRB Field Manual 11350.2c.
276 Rules and Regs. §102.69 (b) .

ity of any stage in the representation proceeding is properly called into question.[277]

The Board has consistently held that certifications are subject to reconsideration and that it may police its certifications by amendment, clarification, or even revocation.[278] In *Hughes Tool Co.*,[279] for example, the Board rescinded a certification where the certified unions had executed racially discriminatory contracts and had administered them in a manner that tended to perpetuate racial discrimination in employment.

---

[277] Worthington Pump & Mach. Corp., 99 NLRB 189, 30 LRRM 1052 (1952).
[278] McGuiness, SILVERBERG'S HOW TO TAKE A CASE BEFORE THE NATIONAL LABOR RELATIONS BOARD §10-28 *et seq.* (Washington: BNA Books, 1967); Rules and Regs. §§102.60 (b), 102.61 (d), 102.61 (e).
[279] 147 NLRB 1573, 56 LRRM 1289 (1964). *See* Chapter 27 *infra* at note 109.

Chapter 9

APPROPRIATE BARGAINING UNITS

I. BACKGROUND

The bargaining unit is the formal arena of employee organizational efforts and the framework of mutual bargaining duties at the base of the entire collective bargaining process. The National Labor Relations Act provides as follows:

> Representatives designated or selected for the purpose of collective bargaining by the majority of the employees in *a unit appropriate for such purposes,* shall be the exclusive representative of all the employees in such units. . . .[1]

The boundaries of the bargaining unit often are a subject of dispute between contending unions and between union and employer, since these can determine whether the union is entitled to representative status. A union which may have organized a sufficient number of employees within a small unit, if it is appropriate, may not be able to establish its majority in a larger unit.[2] Similarly, the unit found appropriate may determine which of two contending unions gains representative status.

In the absence of an agreement between the parties,[3] the Board may be called upon to determine what unit of employees is "appropriate" for collective bargaining. In a simple situation the issue may be whether a plant-wide unit or separate units of production and maintenance employees are appropriate. In more complex cases, the Board might face such questions as: (1) Is a single-plant unit appropriate, but not a multi-plant unit? (2) Do

---

[1] Emphasis added.
[2] This chapter does not treat directly the competing short-term interests of the parties involved as such, but focuses primarily upon the problems and policies of the Board in making unit determinations. Among the short-term considerations are those factors which influence a party to seek a unit determination that is most conducive to victory in a representation election.
[3] NLRB v. J. J. Collins' Sons, Inc., 332 F2d 523, 56 LRRM 2375 (CA 7, 1964).

carpenters qualify as a craft for a separate unit? (3) Is a particular department so distinct as to be regarded as an appropriate unit?

In resolving the unit issue, "the Board's primary concern is to group together only employees who have substantial mutual interests in wages, hours, and other conditions of employment." [4] Stated in another fashion, the Board determines whether the employees share a similar *community of interests*. In approaching any unit question, it should be noted at the outset that the statutory language has been construed to mean that Board need not determine "the ultimate unit, or the most appropriate unit; the Act requires only that the unit be 'appropriate.'" [5]

The Board has found the concept of the "appropriate bargaining unit" an elusive one, and has not employed the discretion conferred by the Act to establish hard and fast rules defining it for all cases. Instead, the Board employs a number of tests in resolving the appropriate-unit issue. These determinative factors include (1) extent and type of union organization of the employees; (2) bargaining history in the industry, as well as with respect to the parties before the Board; (3) similarity of duties, skills, interests, and working conditions of the employees; (4) organizational structure of the company; and (5) the desires of the employees.

In the original Wagner Act, Congress imposed on the three-man Board thereby created the duty of determining whether a proposed or existing unit was appropriate as the employees' bargaining unit. [6] Because of the wide differences in forms of employee organizations, the complexities of modern industry, and other variables, it was virtually impossible for Congress to include strict rules and limitations on the Board's actions in making unit

---

4 FIFTEENTH ANNUAL REPORT OF NLRB, 39 (1950).
5 Morand Bros. Beverage Co., 91 NLRB 409, 26 LRRM 1501 (1950), *enforced*, 190 F2d 576, 28 LRRM 2364 (CA 7, 1951); Federal Electric Corp., 157 NLRB 1130, 61 LRRM 1500 (1966); F. W. Woolworth Co., 144 NLRB 307, 54 LRRM 1043 (1963); Capital Bakers, Inc., 168 NLRB 1385, 66 LRRM 1385 (1967).
6 In a case under the Wagner Act, the Supreme Court noted the Board's broad discretion in unit determination as follows:

"Wide variations in the forms of employee self-organization and the complexities of modern industrial organization make difficult the use of inflexible rules as the test of an appropriate unit. Congress was informed of the need for flexibility in shaping the unit to the particular case and accordingly gave the Board wide discretion in the matter."

NLRB v. Hearst Publications, 322 US 111, 134, 14 LRRM 614 (1944).

determinations. Therefore, by the vague term "appropriate" and the broad standard "in order to assure to employees the fullest freedom in exercising the rights guaranteed by this Act," Congress left largely to administrative determination the constitution of the election districts around which organizational efforts would center and on the basis of which bargaining duties would arise. When the National Labor Relations Act was amended in 1947 to set up a five-member Board, Congress re-enacted the same basic language.[7]

The Taft-Hartley amendments of 1947, however, do impose some limitations, as follows:

(1) The Board may not decide that any craft unit is inappropriate on the ground that prior Board determinations established a different unit.[8]

(2) Professional employees may not be included in a unit with other employees unless a majority of such professionals vote for inclusion in that unit.[9]

(3) Guards may not be included in a unit with other employees, and any organization representing guards may not be affiliated with any organization that admits other employees to membership.[10]

(4) The extent of union organization shall not be controlling in determining whether a unit is appropriate.[11]

Notwithstanding these provisions, the discretion remaining for Board judgment is essentially, as practiced by the Board, one of weighing a number of factors under the polestar of fullest freedom in exercise of rights of employees, among which, since 1947, is the right to refrain, with but one exception, from collective action.[12]

The statutory provisions and procedures for determination of bargaining units under the NLRA may be contrasted with those of the Railway Labor Act,[13] under which the National Mediation Board has the duty of deciding in what *class* or *craft* the election and bargaining shall take place.[14] The statute does not define *class* or *craft*, but it has been pointed out that under these pro-

---

[7] *See* §9 (b).
[8] *See* §9 (b) (2).
[9] *See* §9 (b) (1).
[10] *See* §9 (b) (3).
[11] *See* §9 (c) (5).
[12] *See* §7. The exception is contained in the union-shop proviso to §8 (a) (3).
[13] 48 Stat 1188 (1934), 45 USC §151-188 (1964).
[14] *Id.* at §2, ninth.

visions the NMB "does not enjoy that wide latitude of discretion which Congress granted to the National Labor Relations Board."[15] On the other hand, the NMB's authority to determine appropriate classes and crafts is exclusive and not subject to judicial review.[16]

II. CLASSIFICATION OF EMPLOYEES

A. In General

In most instances the Board encounters no difficulty in deciding which persons are "employees" within the meaning of the Act and therefore includable in a bargaining unit. Section 2 (3), which purports to define the term "employee," does so by noting specific exclusions.[17] It may be assumed that a person not in an excluded category is an *employee* within the meaning of the Act if he works for an employer; however, current working status is not always a prerequisite, for the term includes individuals whose work has ceased because of a labor dispute or an unfair labor practice. Because the right to engage in collective bargaining depends on the existence of employee status, persons who do not have that status are excluded from bargaining units which contain those who are defined as employees.

B. Excluded Categories of Employees

The Act has two broad areas of employee exemptions: (1) persons specifically exempted from the definition of employee and the Act's coverage[18] and (2) those persons who work for persons defined by the Act as "non-employers."[19] Personnel excluded from the Act are not prevented from voluntarily organiz-

---

[15] Switchmen's Union of North America v. National Mediation Board, 135 F2d 785, 791 (CA DC, 1943), *reversed for lack of jurisdiction*, 320 US 297, 13 LRRM 616 (1943). *See*: Comment, *Procedures and Judicial Review under Section 2, Ninth of the Railway Labor Act*, 32 J. AIR L. & COMMERCE 249 (1966); A. R. Weber, THE STRUCTURE OF COLLECTIVE BARGAINING 228 (1961).

[16] Switchmen's Union of North America v. National Mediation Board, 320 US 297, 13 LRRM 616 (1943); Brotherhood of Ry. and Steamship Clerks v. Ass'n for the Benefit of Non-Contract Employees, 380 US 650, 59 LRRM 2051 (1965). Judicial review of NLRB unit determinations is discussed in Chapter 32 *infra*. For a comparison of procedures under the RLA and the NLRA, see Morris, *Procedural Reform in Labor Law—A Preliminary Paper*, 35 J. AIR L. & COMMERCE 537 (1969).

[17] For a further discussion of categories excluded from the Act's coverage, see Chapter 28 *infra*.

[18] *See* §2 (3).

[19] *See* §2 (2).

ing and from being voluntarily recognized; and many, if not most, of such personnel are covered by the Railway Labor Act [20] or other state or federal statutes. Also, these excluded persons, though not protected by the Act, may be subject to controls similar to those imposed by it, for example, against restraints of trade, or activities tortious in themselves.

1. Supervisors. One of the most important changes made by the 1947 amendments was the exclusion of supervisors from coverage by the Act. Supervisors are excluded by two provisions, one in Section 2, defining "employee" to exclude supervisors, and the other in Section 14(a), exempting employers from the duty to consider supervisors as employees under any law relating to collective bargaining.

The status of supervisor under the Act is determined by an individual's *duties,* not by his title or job classification.[21] Under the terms of Section 2(11), a supervisor is any person

> having authority in the interest of the employer, to hire, transfer, suspend, lay off, recall, promote, discharge, assign, reward, or discipline other employees, or responsibly to direct them, or to adjust their grievances, or effectively to recommend such action, if . . . such authority is not of a merely routine or clerical nature, but requires the use of independent judgment.

Thus, it is the person's *power* to act as an agent of the employer in relations with other employees, and his exercise of independent judgment of some nature, that establish his status as a "supervisor." Further, the exercise or the authority to exercise any of the above functions may classify one as a supervisor even if most of his time is spent in normal production or maintenance duties.[22]

Prior to 1947, the Board's policy was to exclude supervisory personnel from bargaining units that included employees subject to their supervision. An exception was made in those cases where there was an established history in the industry of including super-

---

20 The Railway Labor Act covers employees of railways and airlines.
21 Annot., 11 ALR2d 250. *See, e.g.,* New Fern Restorium Co., 175 NLRB 142, 71 LRRM 1093 (1969); Food Employees Local 347 v. NLRB, 422 F 2d 685, 71 LRRM 2397 (CA DC, 1969); NLRB v. Bardahl Oil Co., 399 F2d 365, 68 LRRM 3036 (CA 8, 1968). NLRB v. Armstrong Tire & Rubber Co., 228 F2d 159, 37 LRRM 2244 (CA 5, 1955); Red Star Express Lines v. NLRB, 196 F2d 78, 29 LRRM 2705 (CA 2, 1952).
22 NLRB v. Brown & Sharpe Mfg. Co., 169 F2d 331, 22 LRRM 2363 (CA 1, 1948).

visors in such units.[23] The Board did, however, establish units made up entirely of supervisory personnel,[24] and required employers to bargain with the representatives of such units. The Board's position was upheld by the Supreme Court, which held that, even though it was not entirely in agreement, the Board had the power to adopt such a position in the absence of a specific restriction on the term "employee." [25]

The rule was abrogated in the 1947 amendments, and the Board is now without authority either to include supervisors in bargaining units with other employees or to establish units composed entirely of supervisory personnel. Supervisors do organize, however, even though they are not covered by the Act, and employers are not forbidden to engage in voluntary bargaining with organizations that represent them.

2. Agricultural Laborers. The exclusion of "agricultural laborers" from the Section 2 definition of "employee" has given rise to problems of adjudicating whether a particular group of employees falls within the exclusion or not. Although the Act has always excluded agricultural laborers, it contains no definition of the expression. It was in the National Labor Relations Board Appropriation Act of 1947 that Congress adopted the definition of "agricultural laborers" contained in the Fair Labor Standards Act as applicable to the exclusion in the National Labor Relations Act.[26]

The general rule developed before 1947 was that those engaged in the sorting and packing of agricultural items which were *not* grown or produced by the employer were *not* agricultural laborers

---

[23] Packard Motor Car Co., 61 NLRB 4, 16 LRRM 43 (1945).

[24] *Ibid.*

[25] Packard Motor Car Co. v. NLRB, 330 US 485, 19 LRRM 2397 (1947). Confidential employees constitute a related but nonstatutory excluded class. *See* Chrysler Corp., 173 NLRB No. 160, 69 LRRM 1506 (1968); *also* this chapter *infra* at notes 83-88.

[26] National Labor Relations Board Appropriation Act, 60 Stat 698, ch. 672, title IV (1947), referring to the Fair Labor Standards Act §3 (f), 52 Stat 1060, 29 USC §203 (f) (1964), as follows:

"'Agriculture' includes farming in all its branches and among other things includes the cultivation and tillage of the soil, dairying, the production, cultivation, growing, and harvesting of any agricultural or horticultural commodities . . . , the raising of livestock, bees, fur-bearing animals, or poultry, and any practices (including any forestry or lumbering operations) performed by a farmer or on a farm as an incident to or in conjunction with such farming operations, including preparation for market, delivery to storage or to market or to carriers for transportation to market."

within the meaning of the Act.[27] Employees engaged in the same sort of occupations, but who handled products grown by the employer, *were* covered by the exclusion.[28] Even truck drivers were held to be agricultural laborers when hauling farm produce wholly grown by the employer.[29]

Subsequent to the 1947 Appropriations Act, the Board adopted a test which has been generally applied since that time. In *Di Giorgio Fruit Corp.*[30] the Board held that the "ultimate test" would be whether the services in question were performed primarily in connection with an agricultural operation or in connection with a commercial operation.

> If the practice involved is an integral part of ordinary production or farming operations, and is an essential step before the products can be marketed in normal outlets, it retains its agricultural characteristics. However, if the practice . . . is adopted in order to add greater value to the farm products, it acquires the attributes of a commercial venture.[31]

As with other exclusions from the definition of "employee," nothing in the Act prevents agricultural laborers from organizing.

3. Independent Contractors. The amended Act specifically excludes "independent contractors" from the definition of "employee." In introducing the exclusion in 1947, Congress indicated that the Board had exceeded the standards and intent of the original Act by including independent contractors as employees in several cases.[32]

The Board had from time to time used the common-law concept of independent contractor in determining whether an individual or group fell within the employer-employee relationship, placing prime emphasis on the employer's power of control. But in *NLRB v. Hearst Publications* the Board, with the Supreme Court's ap-

---

27 Idaho Potato Growers, Inc. v. NLRB, 144 F2d 295, 14 LRRM 846 (CA 9, 1944), *cert. denied*, 323 US 769, 15 LRRM 972 (1944); North Whittier Heights Citrus Ass'n v. NLRB, 109 F2d 76, 5 LRRM 874 (CA 9, 1940), *cert. denied*, 310 US 632, 6 LRRM 708 (1940).

28 NLRB v. John W. Campbell, Inc., 159 F2d 184, 19 LRRM 2161 (CA 5, 1947).

29 NLRB v. Olaa Sugar Co., 242 F2d 714, 39 LRRM 2560 (CA 9, 1957).

30 Di Giorgio Fruit Corp., 80 NLRB 853, 23 LRRM 1188 (1948).

31 *Id.* at 855. Since 1954 the appropriation rider has contained language expanding the exclusion in the case of certain irrigation employees. *See, e.g.,* Mindoka Irrigation Dist., 175 NLRB No. 143, 71 LRRM 1088 (1969).

32 HOUSE REPORT NO. 245, on H. R. 3020, 80th Cong., 1st Sess., 18 (1947); *see also* LEGISLATIVE HISTORY OF THE LABOR MANAGEMENT RELATIONS ACT 1947 309 (Washington: GPO, 1948).

proval, departed from the conventional definitions of "employer," "employee," and "independent contractor." [33]

The *Hearst* case arose when Los Angeles newspaper publishers refused to bargain with a union representing newsboys who sold papers full time at fixed locations on the city's streets. The publishers contended that because of a lack of supervision and control the newsboys were independent contractors and not employees under common-law standards. The Board, however, found them to be employees and held that the publishers were guilty of unlawfully refusing to bargain. The Ninth Circuit denied enforcement,[34] but the Supreme Court reversed, stating that Congress had intended ". . . a wider field than the narrow technical legal relation of 'master and servant,' as the common law had worked this out in all its variations. . . ."

Part of the House Committee report was directed specifically at the *Hearst* decision:

> An "employee," according to all standard dictionaries, according to the law as the courts have stated it, and according to the understanding of almost everyone, with the exception of members of the National Labor Relations Board, means someone who works for another for hire. But in the [Hearst] case . . . , the Board expanded the definition of the term "employee." . . . "Employees" work for wages or salaries under direct supervision. "Independent contractors" undertake to do a job for a price, decide how the work will be done, usually hire others to do the work, and depend for their income not upon wages, but upon the difference between what they pay for goods . . . and labor and what they receive for the end result, that is, upon profits.[35]

It is clear from the above that Congress intended the Board and the courts to apply the general common-law definition of "independent contractor" in applying the Act.

Since the passage of the Taft-Hartley amendments, the Board has applied the profit test mentioned in the House report as well as the factors of supervision and control in cases involving the independent-contractor question. In *Kansas City Star* [36] the Board held that newspaper employees who received their income from profits rather than wages, had little supervision, and generally set

---

33 NLRB v. Hearst Publications, 322 US 111, 14 LRRM 614 (1944).
34 Hearst Publications, Inc. v. NLRB, 136 F2d 608, 12 LRRM 786 (CA 9, 1943).
35 See note 32, *supra*.
36 76 NLRB 384, 21 LRRM 1185 (1948).

their own working conditions were independent contractors. Degree of supervision is still given great weight. In *National Freight, Inc.*,[37] for example, the Board held that, because of the high degree of supervision, owner-drivers of leased trucks were employees and not independent contractors. The Board there stated that it was applying the

> common law "right of control" test. If the recipient of the services in question has a right to control not only the end to be achieved but also the means to be used in reaching such result, an employer relationship exists as a matter of law; otherwise there exists an independent contractor relationship. The application of this principle is not a mechanical one in any case, but requires a careful balancing of all factors bearing on the relationship.[38]

Although independent contractors are not covered by the Act as employees, it must be emphasized that they are covered as *employers* when they fall within the definition of "employer" contained in Section 2(2).

4. Family Relationships. An employee of a parent or spouse is expressly exempted from the Section 2(3) definition of "employee." The exclusion in the Act is self-explanatory, and the Board has had no real problem in applying it. The Board has extended the statutory exclusion to cover other individuals with close family ties to the employer. Thus, an employee of a corporation who is a close relative of a corporate officer with special management standing has been excluded.[39] Likewise, the son of a major stockholder in a closely held corporation has been excluded.[40]

5. Domestic Servants. Section 2(3) specifically excludes from the definition of "employee" anyone employed ". . . in the domestic service of any family or person at his home. . . ." This exclusion

---

37 146 NLRB 144, 55 LRRM 1259 (1964). *Compare* Frito-Lay, Inc. v. NLRB, 385 F2d 180, 66 LRRM 2542 (CA 7, 1967), denying enforcement on the ground that the Board had made too much of the lack of evidence that any of the owner-drivers (distributors) had themselves employed drivers to work for them.

38 146 NLRB 144, 145-146, 55 LRRM 1259 (1964). *See also* Deaton Truck Lines, Inc., 143 NLRB 1372, 53 LRRM 1497 (1963), *review dismissed*, 337 F2d 697, 57 LRRM 2209 (CA 5, 1964), quoted at note 43, Chapter 28 *infra*; Bowman Transportation Co., 142 NLRB 1093, 53 LRRM 1201 (1963). *See generally* Chapter 28 for discussion of the Act's coverage of employees, as distinguished from independent contractors and other excluded persons.

39 International Metal Products Co., 107 NLRB 65, 33 LRRM 1055 (1953).

40 Foam Rubber City No. 2 of Fla., Inc., 167 NLRB 623, 66 LRRM 1096 (1967). The exclusion also applies to an employee whose parent or spouse is a partner in the employing firm. NLRB v. Hoffman, 147 F2d 679, 15 LRRM 951 (CA 3, 1945).

also is self-explanatory, and apparently has not been the subject of litigation.

6. Employees of "Nonemployers." Section 2 (2) states that the following groups will not be considered employers for the purpose of collective bargaining under the Act, and anyone working for these groups likewise is excluded:

(1) The United States or any wholly owned government corporation.
(2) Federal reserve banks.
(3) States and political subdivisions thereof.
(4) A corporation or association operating a hospital, if no shareholder or individual benefits from net earnings.
(5) Persons subject to the Railway Labor Act.
(6) A labor union, except when acting as an employer.

Employees of states and their political subdivisions and charitable hospitals, though not covered by the Act, are not prevented from organizing as they wish, subject to whatever application state law may have.

When a labor organization is operating as an employer, it is covered by the Act just like any other employer who is defined as such in the Act. The Supreme Court has held that the Board may not refuse to exercise jurisdiction over labor unions as a class when they are operating as employers, though it may refuse jurisdiction in a case where such exercise would not effectuate the policies of the Act.[41]

C. Special Categories of Employees

There are certain types of employees whose bargaining-unit placement poses special problems. These groups are discussed in this section.

1. Driver-Salesman. In *Plaza Provision Co.*[42] the Board recognized that ordinarily a driver-salesman is primarily a salesman and only incidentally a driver. Therefore it directed that such driver-salesmen be excluded from a unit of truck drivers and warehousemen. The Board followed this decision in *Southern Bakeries,*

---

[41] Office Employees Int'l Union, Local 11 v. NLRB, 353 US 313, 40 LRRM 2020 (1957). *See* discussion at note 27, Chapter 28 *infra*.
[42] 139 NLRB 910, 49 LRRM 1295 (1961). *See also* American Bread Co. v. NLRB, 411 F2d 147, 71 LRRM 2243 (CA 6, 1969).

Inc.,[43] where the problem was not one of excluding the driver-salesmen from a unit of truck drivers. The petitioning union had sought to represent only six transport drivers. To this the employer objected, contending that 47 driver-salesmen also should have been included. Overruling the objection, the Board recognized the difference in the interests of the two types of drivers but also noted the fact that no union was seeking to represent both groups in a combined unit.

A special limitation upon the *Plaza Provision* doctrine was evidenced in *Columbine Beverage Co.*[44] This was not an election case, but a complaint case based upon a refusal to bargain with the union representing employees in a unit consisting of both types of drivers. The refusal had occurred prior to the *Plaza Provision* decision. Since the employer had no good-faith doubt as to the appropriate unit when the request to bargain was made, a bargaining order issued even though the unit might no longer have been appropriate.

2. Casual Employees. *Casuals* are those employees who lack a sufficient community of interest with regular employees to be included in the bargaining unit.[45] They must be differentiated from *regular part-time* employees, who are included in the unit. In *NLRB v. George Groh & Sons* [46] it was held that two part-time employees who were attending school and who had requested employment but were not employed on the date the union requested recognition were casuals, and thus properly excluded from the bargaining unit. Likewise, the court of appeals in *NLRB* v. *Greenfield Components Corp.*[47] upheld the Board in excluding an *ad hoc* specialist who did a single job that took from two to six hours a week on a regular and not a sporadic basis. The court said

---

43 139 NLRB 63, 51 LRRM 1252 (1962).
44 138 NLRB 1297, 51 LRRM 1221 (1962). In NLRB v. Food Employees Council, Inc., 399 F2d 501, 69 LRRM 2077 (CA 9, 1968) the court commented on the scope of the Board's discretion in unit determination in a complaint case. The related question of unit placement of truck drivers who are not salesmen was treated in E. H. Koester Bakery Co., Inc., 136 NLRB 1006, 49 LRRM 1925 (1962). *See also* NLRB v. Cumberland Farms, 395 F2d 745, 68 LRRM 2575 (CA 1, 1968).
45Mission Pak Co., 127 NLRB 1097, 46 LRRM 1161 (1960); P. G. Gray, 128 NLRB 1026, 46 LRRM 1442 (1960); J. R. Simplot Food Processing Div., 128 NLRB 1391, 46 LRRM 1484 (1960); Giordano Lumber Co., Inc., 133 NLRB 307, 48 LRRM 1629 (1961).
46 329 F2d 265, 55 LRRM 2729 (CA 10, 1964), *affirming* 141 NLRB 931, 52 LRRM 1424 (1963).
47 317 F2d 85, 53 LRRM 2148 (CA 1, 1963).

that the exact amount of time spent on the job does not control the determination of whether an employee is a casual or a regular part-time employee; it is, however, an important factor to consider in determining whether the employee has a sufficient community of interest with the other employees to be included in the unit. In *Georgia Highway Express, Inc.*,[48] laborers employed as dockmen by an interstate motor freight carrier only during peak periods were regarded as casuals and thus excluded from the unit. The Board there emphasized that, unlike regular employees, the dockmen were hired each day as needed and without clearance from the company's personnel office. Other determining factors were that they received a lower rate of pay than regular employees and were not entitled to the fringe benefits granted other employees.[49]

3. Regular Part-Time Employees. Non-full-time employees who, because of regularity of employment or otherwise, have a substantial community of interest with the unit's full-time employees in wages, hours, and conditions of employment are regarded as *regular part-time* employees and are includable in the bargaining unit.[50] Thus, in *Booth Broadcasting Co.* a radio technician who worked every Saturday and did the same kind of work as the full-time employees in the bargaining unit was held to be a regular part-time employee and was included.[51]

In *Scoa, Inc.*,[52] the actual number of hours worked during each quarter was used to differentiate between *casuals* and part-time employees. The employer operated a department store and employed, from time to time, a great many persons called *floaters*. Some were designated as *regularly scheduled* and others as *on call*. However, some of the on-call personnel actually worked more than

---

48 150 NLRB, 58 LRRM 1319 (1965).
49 *Compare* Tamphon Trading Co., Inc., 88 NLRB 597, 25 LRRM 1371 (1950), where the Board included casual stevedores in the shipping industry in the unit, stating: "There is nothing in the Act that restricts or limits the definition of an employee to one whose tenure of employment must be fixed to a regular day-to-day or week-to-week or month-to-month basis." Similarly, trainees and probationary employees may be so allied in interest as to be included. Leone Industries, 172 NLRB No. 158, 68 LRRM 1529 (1968).
50 Sears, Roebuck & Co., 172 NLRB No. 132, 68 LRRM 1469 (1968); Southern Illinois Sand Co., 137 NLRB 1490, 50 LRRM 1414 (1962); Jat Transportation Corp., 128 NLRB 780, 46 LRRM 1405 (1960); Greenberg Mercantile Corp., 112 NLRB 710, 36 LRRM 1072 (1955); Sears, Roebuck & Co., 112 NLRB 559, 36 LRRM 1060 (1955); Florsheim Retail Boot Shop, 80 NLRB 1312, 23 LRRM 1234 (1948).
51 134 NLRB 817, 49 LRRM 1278 (1961).
52 140 NLRB 1379, 52 LRRM 1244 (1963).

some of the regularly scheduled and received the same wages as full-time employees, but without all of the same fringe benefits. The Board determined that the floaters who worked a minimum of 15 days during the quarter (90-day period) immediately preceding the election should be included in the unit. In *Columbus Plaza Motor Hotel*[53] the Board also considered the actual quantum of work performed in classifying certain non-full-time employees as part-time employees.

In deciding whether non-full-time employees are casuals (and not included in the unit) or part-time employees (and included in the unit), the Board exercises considerable discretion. Therefore some cases that arrive at one conclusion are difficult to differentiate from cases reaching the other. In *NLRB v. Waukesha Lime & Stone Co.*[54] the court upheld the Board's determination that a one-day-a-week worker was a part-time employee. The case is difficult to distinguish from the *Greenfield case*,[55] except as to the nature of the work performed. Some of the important factors are (1) regularity of work, (2) quantum of work, (3) nature of work, and (4) similarity of pay scale. In *Harvey Russell*[56] an agreement between the employer and the union as to who should be in the unit was regarded as controlling.[57]

4. Dual-Function Employees. Prior to 1951, the Board made a distinction between *part-time* employees and *dual-function* employees. The former category consisted of employees who, although working only part time in the bargaining unit, did no other work for the employer. The balance of their time was spent in working for other employers or not working. Not casual, though part-time, the Board included these employees in the

---

53 Management Directors, Inc., dba Columbus Plaza Motor Hotel, 148 NLRB 1053, 57 LRRM 1119 (1964). The Board has in recent times reversed its earlier position as to employees on Social Security who limited their total earnings to remain eligible for such benefits and now includes them in a bargaining unit. Holiday Inns of America, 176 NLRB 124, 71 LRRM 1333 (1969), *following* Indianapolis Glove Co. v. NLRB, 400 F2d 263, 69 LRRM 2261 (CA 6, 1968).

54 343 F2d 504, 58 LRRM 2782 (CA 7, 1965), *affirming* 145 NLRB 983, 55 LRRM 1103 (1964).

55 Note 47 *supra.*

56 145 NLRB 1486, 55 LRRM 1165 (1964).

57 "In order to facilitate collective bargaining or the speedy disposition of questions concerning representation the Board has long accepted the agreement of the parties concerning the contractual or appropriate unit. Parties are given broad latitude in the reaching of such agreements and the Board will not disturb them unless it can be shown that the exclusion or inclusion of certain employees contravenes the Act or established Board policy." 145 NLRB at 1488.

bargaining unit.[58] Dual-function employees were those who spent part of their time working in the bargaining unit and the balance of their time doing other work for the same employer. The Board included them in the unit but did not allow them to vote unless they spent more than 50 percent of their time working in that bargaining unit.[59]

The rule was changed for dual-function employees in *The Ocala Star Banner*.[60] The issue concerned whether a specified employee could vote. He worked about 60 hours a week for the employer, 25 of which were in the bargaining unit in question and 35 on three other jobs. The Board allowed this employee to vote and created a new rule. The distinction between part-time employees and dual-function employees was erased.

In 1961, however, the Board overruled *Ocala Star Banner* in *Denver-Colorado Springs-Pueblo Motor Way*,[61] and reestablished temporarily the *more than 50 percent rule*. But in 1963 the Board decided *Berea Publishing Co.*,[62] overruling *Denver-Colorado Springs-Pueblo Motor Way* and basically reestablishing the rule of *Ocala Star Banner*. The Board decided that employees who spend 40 percent of their time in the bargaining unit and the balance in other parts of the employer's enterprises are properly included. The intended test was whether the part-time or dual-function employees have a sufficient interest in conditions of employment in the bargaining unit to make their inclusion meaningful.[63]

---

[58] *See* preceding section. And with *Harvey Russell, supra* notes 56-57, *compare,* for dual-function employee placement, R.B.P., Inc., 176 NLRB No. 22, 71 LRRM 1195 (1969).

[59] *E.g.,* Coca-Cola Bottling Co. of St. Louis, 94 NLRB 208, 28 LRRM 1048 (1951).

[60] 97 NLRB 384, 29 LRRM 1108 (1951).

[61] 129 NLRB 1184, 47 LRRM 1145 (1961).

[62] 140 NLRB 516, 52 LRRM 1051 (1963).

[63] It might appear that the Board again changed its mind later in 1963, in *Int'l Ladies' Garment Workers' Union*, 142 NLRB 353, 53 LRRM 1032 (1963), but such was not the case. The union, as an employer, was required to bargain with another union representing its business agents. The Board held that six business agents who also did staff duty for the employer-union should not be included in the unit because their function as business agents was so minor that they lacked a true community of interest with the other business agents. Even as thus limited, the Board's decision was set aside by the Second Circuit with directions to include these six in the unit. The court indicated that the Board's limitations of the bargaining unit might have been proper before the election, but that it was improper in connection with a later unfair labor practice charge. 339 F2d 116, 57 LRRM 2540 (CA 2, 1964).

5. Technical Employees. Technical employees, such as drafts-men or electronics specialists, are to be distinguished from professional employees.[64] Because of their distinctive training, experience, and functions, technical employees are viewed as having different interests from other employees, although they do not meet the strict requirements for professionals. Their work does involve the use of independent judgment, however, and requires the use of specialized training.[65]

Prior to 1961 it was regularly held that technicals were excluded from any bargaining unit at the request of either the employer or the union.[66] This policy was changed in *Sheffield Corp.*[67] No longer are they automatically excluded from production and maintenance units, but are governed by many factors with considerable weight accorded the desires of the parties.[68]

6. Employees on Layoff. Whether or not employees who have some historical connection with the employer but are not currently on his payroll (such as employees on layoff) may be included in the bargaining unit depends on whether such employees still have an interest in wages, hours, and other conditions of employment in the bargaining unit.[69] This will depend on whether the laid-off or other temporarily absent employee has a reasonable expectation of returning.[70] In *American Export Lines*[71] it was held that seamen in a *standby* status, awaiting assignment to a ship,

---

64 Professional employees are treated separately under the Act. *See* §9(b) (1) and discussion at IV.A.1. this chapter *infra*.

65 Litton Industries of Md., Inc., 125 NLRB 722, 45 LRRM 1166 (1959).

66 Westinghouse Electric Corporation, 118 NLRB 1043, 40 LRRM 1310 (1957); Litton Industries of Md., note 65 *supra*.

67 134 NLRB 1101, 49 LRRM 1265 (1961).

68 The Board stated that it would "make a pragmatic judgment in each case, based upon an analysis of the following factors, among others: desires of the parties, history of bargaining, similarity of skills and job functions, common supervision, contact and/or interchange with other employees, similarity of working conditions, type of industry, organization of plant, whether the technical employees work in separately situated and separately controlled areas, and whether any union seeks to represent technical employees separately." 134 NLRB at 1103, 1104. *See* Westinghouse Electric Corp., 173 NLRB No. 43, 69 LRRM 1332 (1968) (classification to include systems analysts in clerical and technical unit); Weyerhaeuser Co., 173 NLRB No. 177, 69 LRRM 1553 (1968) (plant clericals denied separate representation).

69 *Ibid.*

70 Sullivan Surplus Sales, Inc., 152 NLRB 132, 59 LRRM 1041 (1965); Westinghouse Air Brake Co., 119 NLRB 1391, 41 LRRM 1307 (1958); Sheffield Corp., 123 NLRB 1454, 44 LRRM 1155 (1956).

71 81 NLRB 1370, 23 LRRM 1499 (1949).

should be included in the bargaining unit. And in *Scobell Chemical Company* [72] employees on temporary layoff were included.

The employee's status as of the time the union requested recognition must be considered. Thus, in *Sportswear Industries,*[73] a shipping clerk who claimed to be sick and thus was absent on the day the union demanded recognition, although he never returned to work, was considered an employee. At the time recognition was demanded there was no reason to believe that he would not return; therefore, he was counted in the bargaining unit for the purpose of determining whether the union had a majority.

7. Fringe or Residual Employees. Employees who are separated from the main body of employees of a particular employer are considered *fringe* or residual employees. They are usually few in number and too indistinct to be classified with any particular group. A question concerning representation of such employees may occur when the bargaining representative of an established unit seeks to include them, or when an outside union seeks to represent a unit which is already represented by another union and an issue is raised as to the inclusion of the fringe group. Board policy has fluctuated as to how to treat these employees. Under the Board's early practice,[74] if a group of fringe employees had been excluded from a unit in which they appropriately could have been included, they would not be placed in the established unit without first having the opportunity to vote [75] on whether they wished to be represented by the incumbent union. That practice was changed in *Waterous Co.,*[76] which held that where the only union seeking to represent the fringe employees was the one seeking a certification in a basic appropriate bargaining unit, a separate self-determination election would not be held. Four years later, in *Zia Co.,*[77] the Board returned to the pre-*Waterous* doctrine. In

---

[72] 121 NLRB 1130, 42 LRRM 1532 (1958), *enforced,* 267 F2d 922, 44 LRRM 2366 (CA 2, 1959). The facts of the case that are pertinent appear in the court of appeals, rather than in the Board, decision.
[73] 147 NLRB 758, 56 LRRM 1307 (1964). But in *Sylvania Electric Products, Inc.,* 122 NLRB 201, 43 LRRM 1087 (1958), the Board held that employees on maternity leave would be permitted to vote only if they are automatically restored to their jobs upon return from leave.
[74] *E.g.,* Petersen & Lytle, 60 NLRB 1070, 16 LRRM 27 (1945).
[75] In a self-determination *Globe* election. Globe Machine and Stamping Co., 3 NLRB 294, 1-A LRRM 122 (1937) ; Armour and Co., 40 NLRB 1333, 10 LRRM 100 (1942). *See* discussion of *Globe* doctrine in III.C. this chapter *infra.*
[76] 92 NLRB 76, 27 LRRM 1050 (1950).
[77] 108 NLRB 1134, 34 LRRM 1133 (1954).

1961, however, the rule was again modified by *D. V. Displays Corp.*[78] to the extent that where

> there is a question of representation in the historical unit and the incumbent union seeks to add a previously unrepresented fringe group whom no other union is seeking to represent on a different basis, [the Board will] . . . direct only one election which will include all the employees in the unit found to be appropriate.[79]

The Board, in a split decision, reasoned that this result was consistent with what the Board would have done had it been called upon to determine the inclusions when the unit was originally established. It stated that the denial of a separate election "is the more democratic approach because it gives all employees in the appropriate unit an equal voice in choosing a bargaining representative." [80]

In *Felix Half & Brothers, Inc.*,[81] two unions were involved. The intervening union already represented office workers but requested the exclusion of a porter-clerk and an inside salesman, who were not in its unit. The petitioning union sought to represent the same office workers and in addition the porter-clerk and the inside salesman. The Board directed that the employees in the existing unit and the two additional employees vote separately. If the two additional employees chose the petitioner, that union would represent them; if a majority of the existing unit chose the intervenor, that union would continue to represent them; if the intervenor did not carry the existing unit, the votes of the two additional employees would be pooled with those of the existing unit to determine whether the new combined unit should be represented by the petitioner.

It is evident that residual or fringe employees may be represented in a separate unit which would not normally be an appropriate unit, if to deny them that right would preclude their opportunity to vote on being represented.[82]

---

78 134 NLRB 568, 49 LRRM 1199 (1961).

79 *Id.* at 571.

80 *Id.* at 571-72.

81 132 NLRB 1523, 48 LRRM 1528 (1961).

82 A single employee, however, cannot constitute a unit. Cutter Laboratories, 116 NLRB 260, 38 LRRM 1241 (1956). *See* Standard Brands, Inc., 175 NLRB No. 122, 71 LRRM 1057 (1969); NLRB v. Howard Johnson Co., 398 F2d 435, 68 LRRM 2895 (CA 3, 1968); Sonoma-Marin Publishing Co., 172 NLRB No. 62, 68 LRRM 1313 (1968).

8. Confidential Employees. Confidential employees are closely related to managerial and supervisory employees. The latter category is specifically excluded by the Act.[83] Although they may have no supervisory functions, employees who participate in the determination of general company policy are also excluded.[84] This is implied by assimilating nonsupervisory policy makers to the status of supervisory employees. Confidential employees likewise are not expressly excluded by the Act, but their implied exclusion has been deemed necessary in order to make the Act function.[85]

It is not all confidential employees that are excluded, only those whose employment involves labor relations. The cases of *Minneapolis-Moline Co.* and *B. F. Goodrich Co.*[86] provide examples of categories of employees excluded as confidential.[87] In these cases, either by agreement or by decision, the following employees were excluded as being confidential: secretary to plant superintendent, factory personnel department employees, secretary to the personnel manager, secretary of the office manager. The following, who might appear to be excludable confidential employees, were held to be properly within the bargaining unit: accounting clerk, production records clerk, payroll clerks, telephone operators, secretaries to the manager of industrial engineering, checkers, timekeepers, clerks in the time-study department, and all employees in the production-control department. It has also been held that an internal auditor is neither a managerial nor a confidential employee.[88]

III. GENERAL FACTORS IN UNIT DETERMINATION

A. Community of Interest Among Employees

In resolving the unit issue, "the Board's primary concern is to group together only employees who have substantial mutual interests in wages, hours, and other conditions of employment." [89] Stated in another fashion, the Board determines whether the employees share a similar community of interest.

---

83 See note 25 *supra.*
84 Ford Motor Co., 66 NLRB 1317, 17 LRRM 394 (1946); Continental Can Co., 74 NLRB 351, 20 LRRM 1156 (1947); Palace Laundry Dry Cleaning Corp., 75 NLRB 320, 21 LRRM 1039 (1947), *see especially* 75 NLRB 323, n. 4.
85 Minneapolis-Moline Co., 85 NLRB 597, 24 LRRM 1443 (1949); B. F. Goodrich Co., 115 NLRB 722, 37 LRRM 1383 (1956).
86 *Ibid.*
87 *See also* Westinghouse Electric Corp., 138 NLRB 778, 51 LRRM 1172 (1962).
88 Horn & Hardart Co., 147 NLRB 654, 56 LRRM 1311 (1964).
89 FIFTEENTH ANNUAL REPORT OF THE NLRB, 39 (1950).

Community of interest is the fundamental factor in cases involving an election in which employees who are included with other employees in a larger unit are granted the option to elect their own representative. In *Kalamazoo Paper Box Corp.*[90] the Board stated that a severance election will be allowed only if the employees in the unit seeking severance have substantially different interests from other employees in the broader unit. The Board enumerated the factors to be considered in determining the community of interest:

> [A] difference in method of wages or compensation; different hours of work; different employment benefits; separate supervision; the degree of dissimilar qualifications, training and skills; differences in job functions and amount of working time spent away from the employment or plant situs . . . ; the infrequency or lack of contact with other employees; lack of integration with the work functions of other employees or interchange with them; and the history of collective bargaining.[91]

While the *Kalamazoo* case dealt specifically with truck drivers seeking severance from a production unit, the principles announced in that case have been given general application. As special and distinct interests of a particular group were weighed against the community of interest shared with other plant employees in that case, so elsewhere.[92]

Many factors bear upon the judgment of community of interest, whether in connection with severance or determination of original units. They include: technology (or integration of functions); physical location; the history of bargaining, from the standpoint of both the industry as a whole and the relationships between the employer in question and the employees of that employer; and the desires of the employees themselves. These factors affect the appropriateness of multi-employer as well as employer, plant-wide as well as multi-plant, and craft as well as departmental units.

The Act itself suggests the possible appropriateness of aggregating employees by "employer unit, craft unit, plant unit, or subdivision thereof."[93] And the Board has asserted the presumptive

---

[90] 136 NLRB 134, 49 LRRM 1715 (1962). *Compare:* Olincraft, Inc., 179 NLRB No. 61, 72 LRRM 1337 (1969) (refusing to sever truck drivers from a production and maintenance unit because of similarity of employee duties and interests).
[91] *Id.* at 137. For application of the principle by way of unit clarification, *see* Kennecott Copper Corp., 176 NLRB No. 13, 71 LRRM 1188 (1969).
[92] *See* NLRB v. Cambell Sons' Corp., 407 F2d 969, 70 LRRM 2886 (CA 4, 1969).
[93] §9 (b).

appropriateness of the single-plant unit.[94] On the other hand, the specific amendments made in 1947 attach special significance to the community of skills among the employees with respect to professionals and craftsmen, and to the security needs of the employer with respect to plant guards.[95]

B. Extent of Union Organization

One of the touchstones of community of interest is like-mindedness with respect to adherence to the union movement. This factor is now treated separately in the Act[96] and is referred to as *extent of organization.*

Prior to 1947, the Board found the extent of organization to be an especially significant factor in determining appropriateness of a unit on the theory that it is often desirable in the determination of an appropriate unit to render collective bargaining for the employees involved a reasonably early possibility, lest prolonged delay expose the organized employees to the temptation of striking to obtain recognition.[97] The weight given this factor by the Board aroused considerable criticism.[98]

The critics of the Board persuaded Congress in 1947 to enact Section 9(c)(5), which provides that

> In determining whether a unit is appropriate . . . the extent to which the employees have organized shall not be controlling.

The Board continues to give some weight to the extent of organization, which it may do provided there are other substantial factors on which to base the unit determination.[99]

> It has not been the Board's policy to compel labor organizations to represent the most comprehensive grouping. It is not the Board's function to compel all employees to be represented or unrepresented at the same time or to require that a labor organization represent

94 Frisch's Big Boy Ill-Mar, Inc., 147 NLRB 551, 56 LRRM 1246 (1964). For an argument challenging the Board's position, *see* Siegel, *Problems and Procedures in the NLRB Election Process,* in LABOR LAW DEVELOPMENTS 1968 (14th Annual Institute on Labor Law, Sw Legal Foundation) 29, 43.
95 *See* §9 (b) (1) - (3) .
96 §9 (c) (5) .
97 TWELFTH ANNUAL REPORT OF THE NLRB, 21 (1947).
98 *See* dissent by Member Reynolds in *Garden State Hosiery Co.,* 74 NLRB 318, 20 LRRM 1149 (1947), claiming that the Board's application of the doctrine permitted "gerrymandering" by the petitioning union so as to establish a unit in which it could win an election.
99 NLRB v. Morganton Full Fashioned Hosiery Co., 241 F2d 913, 39 LRRM 2493 (CA 4, 1957) ; NLRB v. Smythe, 212 F2d 664, 34 LRRM 2108 (CA 5, 1954) .

employees it does not wish to represent unless an appropriate unit does not otherwise exist.[100]

Provided the Board gives less than controlling weight to the extent of organization, its unit determination does not contravene the statute; [101] however, it may be difficult to determine the precise weight which the Board has given to any particular factor.[102]

C. Desires of the Employees—the *Globe* Doctrine

The effectiveness of the collective bargaining process depends in large part on the coherence of the employees in the unit.[103] There is seldom any real problem in determining the employees' desires when there is no dispute among them as to the appropriate unit. When there is a decision to be made between two or more equally appropriate units, however, the desires of the employees become a critical factor.

When such a situation arises, the Board's *Globe* doctrine comes into play, and an election is held to determine the employees' desires on the unit issue. The doctrine is derived from *Globe Machine and Stamping Co.*[104] In the typical *Globe* situation, craft employees

> are afforded the opportunity to indicate that they prefer to be established as a separate bargaining unit, apart from a broader industrial unit in which they would otherwise be included, by voting for the craft union that seeks to represent them separately, as against the industrial union that desires to represent them as part of the broader unit. But in such an election, a majority of the employees in the

---

100 Ballentine Packing Co., Inc., 132 NLRB 923, 925, 48 LRRM 1451 (1961); Waldensian Hosiery Mills, 83 NLRB 742, 24 LRRM 1129 (1949).

101 NLRB v. Metropolitan Life Ins. Co., 380 US 438, 58 LRRM 2721 (1965); NLRB v. Salant and Salant, 171 F2d 292, 23 LRRM 2265 (CA 6, 1948).

102 NLRB v. Metropolitan Life Ins. Co., note 101 supra; *see also* Metropolitan Life Ins. Co. v. NLRB, 330 F2d 62, 55 LRRM 2930 (CA 6, 1964), *vacated and remanded*, 380 US 525, 59 LRRM 2063 (1965). *See* notes 161-164 *infra* and accompanying text. On state-wide units, *see* Local 1327 Retail Clerks v. NLRB, 414 F2d 1194, 71 LRRM 2721 (CA DC, 1969).

103 The idea of the coherence of the employees has been especially important in craft and departmental severance questions, and the *Globe* doctrine has special impact in these areas. *See* IV.B.1 this chapter *infra*. For determining whether separate multiplant units should be merged into a single employer unit, see Libbey-Owens-Ford Glass Co. 169 NLRB No. 2, 67 LRRM 1096 (1968). (*Cf.* McCulloch v. Libbey-Owens-Ford Glass Co., 403 F2d 916, 68 LRRM 2497 (CA DC, 1968), *cert. denied*, 393 US 1016, 70 LRRM 2225 (1969).) On the necessity of a self-determination election to determine a petition for addition of classifications in existence at the time of certification, see National Cash Register Co., 170 NLRB No. 118, 67 LRRM 1541 (1968).

104 3 NLRB 294, 1-A LRRM 122 (1937). The doctrine was upheld in NLRB v. Underwood Machine Co., 179 F2d 118, 25 LRRM 2195 (CA 1, 1949), *enforcing* 79 NLRB 1287, 22 LRRM 1506 (1948).

craft group will sometimes vote for the "no-union" choice, or for an industrial union which fails to win a majority in the balance of the industrial unit for which it desires to bargain.[105]

The *Globe* procedure involves using two or more ballots in the same election (or holding two or more elections simultaneously among the different groups). To illustrate: The employees in the smaller group—ordinarily but not necessarily a craft group—vote separately to indicate whether they desire representation by (1) the union seeking to represent them in the smaller (craft) unit or (2) the union seeking to represent all of the employees in a broader (*e.g.*, production and maintenance) unit. If a majority of the smaller group selects its own representation, its choice of unions will be certified for the smaller unit, and the representation of the remaining employees in the broader "industrial" unit will be dependent upon the "industrial" union's polling a majority in a unit which excludes the smaller group. If the "industrial" union polls a majority among both groups, its certification will cover both groups of employees.

A *Globe*-type election may also be ordered where only one union is seeking representation and the Board finds either (1) a larger all-inclusive unit or (2) a smaller unit of a group within the larger unit to be appropriate for purposes of collective bargaining. That was the situation in *Underwood Machinery Co.*,[106] where the Board found that the decisive factor was the wishes of the smaller group of employees. Accordingly, it ordered separate elections among the two employee groups and awaited the results of the elections before determining the appropriate unit or units. The Board declared that if the unions secured a majority of the votes cast by the larger (production) group only, it would find that that group, excluding the smaller group (erection and maintenance department), constituted the appropriate unit; but if in addition a majority of the smaller group also selected the union, the smaller group would be included in the same bargaining unit.

D. Bargaining History

The success of bargaining patterns may be judged by their history. The Board is loath to disturb existing units, whether estab-

105 FOURTEENTH ANNUAL REPORT OF THE NLRB, 33 (1949) ; *see also* Western Condensing Co., 85 NLRB 981, 24 LRRM 1506 (1949) .
106 Note 104 *supra*.

lished by agreement or by certification, when bargaining in those units has been successful over a period of time. Bargaining history is therefore an important factor in unit determination.[107] Nevertheless, though bargaining history is customarily accorded great weight, it is not given such weight when the history runs counter to well-established Board policy. The Board is also conditionally prohibited from relying upon its own prior determination against a craft unit.[108]

E. Employer's Organizational Structure

As will be illustrated in the discussion of types of units (this Chapter *infra*), such factors as functional and organizational cohesiveness in the proposed unit and the similarity of interests of the employees in the unit are given considerable weight in determining which unit is appropriate for collective bargaining.[109] By the same reasoning, an established unit may subsequently become inappropriate by reason of changes in the employer's business structure and operational methods.[110] Generally speaking, the employer is vitally interested in having the collective bargaining unit coincide with his table of organization. Similarity of working conditions among employees, lines of supervision, and degree of functional integration [111] in the employer's operations are important factors in unit determination.

IV. TYPES OF UNITS

A. Unit Classifications Required by the Act

1. Professionals. Prior to passage of the Taft-Hartley Act, the Board treated professional employees in the same fashion as other

---

107 Int'l Ass'n of Tool Craftsmen v. Leedom, 276 F2d 514, 45 LRRM 2826 (CA DC, 1960), *cert. denied*, 364 US 815, 46 LRRM 3080 (1960); Gulf Oil Corp., 4 NLRB 133, 1-A LRRM 270 (1937). *Compare* NLRB v. Porter County Farm Bureau Co-op Ass'n, Inc., 314 F2d 133, 52 LRRM 2485 (CA 7, 1963), *denying enforcement*, 133 NLRB 1019, 48 LRRM 1760 (1961).
108 §9(b)(2) prohibits the Board from deciding "that any craft unit is inappropriate . . . on the ground that a different unit has been established by a prior Board determination, unless a majority of the employees in the proposed craft unit vote against separate representation. . . ." *See* discussion in IV.B.1. this chapter *infra*.
109 Douglas Aircraft Co., Inc., 49 NLRB 819, 12 LRRM 212 (1943); Central Greyhound Lines, 88 NLRB 13, 25 LRRM 1273 (1950).
110 Mahoning Mining Co., 61 NLRB 792, 16 LRRM 110 (1945); Frito-Lay, Inc., 177 NLRB No. 85, 71 LRRM 1442 (1969).
111 Minnesota Mining & Mfg. Co., 129 NLRB 789, 47 LRRM 1061 (1960); Kaiser Aluminum & Chemical Corp., 177 NLRB No. 67, 71 LRRM 1422 (1969).

employees. Evidencing a concern that the professionals were different from other employees, and that their legitimate interests could be submerged if they were grouped with other employees, Congress provided in Section 9(b)(1) that a unit including both professionals and other employees was inappropriate "unless a majority of such professional employees vote for inclusion in such unit.[112]

The right to a separate election cannot be limited "to a single opportunity in the course of their employment for a particular employer." [113] Professional employees are entitled to a separate election even though they have on prior occasions been afforded an opportunity to vote.

The holding of a separate election is mandatory even when the number of nonprofessionals is insignificant. In *Leedom v. Kyne*,[114] the Supreme Court found that the failure of the Board to afford 233 professionals an opportunity to vote on whether they wished to be included in a unit with nine nonprofessionals violated the plain command of the statute.

The Board has interpreted Section 9(b)(1) as being applicable "only in situations where a representation election is sought in a unit including professional employees among others." [115] Applying this rule, the Board dismissed a petition to decertify a professional segment of a larger unit.[116] Where a union enters into a contract covering a professional and nonprofessional unit without

---

[112] §2 (12), also added by Taft-Hartley, defines "professional" employee as "(a) any employee engaged in work (i) predominantly intellectual and varied in character as opposed to routine, mental, manual, mechanical or physical work; (ii) involving the consistent exercise of discretion and judgment in its performance; (iii) of such a character that the output produced or the result cannot be standardized in relation to a given period of time; (iv) requiring knowledge of an advanced type in a field of science or learning customarily acquired by a prolonged course of specialized intellectual instruction and study in an institution of higher learning or a hospital as distinguishable from an apprenticeship or from training in the performance of routine, mental, manual or physical processes, or (b) any employee who (i) has completed the courses of specialized intellectual instruction and study described in clause (iv) of paragraph (a), and (ii) is performing related work under the supervision of a professional employee as defined in paragraph (a)." *Compare* Ryan Aeronautical Co., 132 NLRB 1160, 48 LRRM 1502 (1961), and Starrett Bros. & Eken, Inc., 77 NLRB 276, 22 LRRM 1003 (1948).
[113] Westinghouse Electric Corp., 116 NLRB 1545, 1547, 39 LRRM 1039 (1956).
[114] 358 US 184, 43 LRRM 2222 (1958); *see* discussion of this case in Chapter 32 *infra*.
[115] Westinghouse Electric Corporation, 115 NLRB 530, 542, 37 LRRM 1341 (1956).
[116] *Ibid.* The proper method to achieve separation is through a representation proceeding, not through decertification.

first having an election, there is no violation of the law.[117] The
Board holds that such a unit is appropriate on an historical basis,
and that an election is mandatory only when the Board establishes
the unit.[118]

2. Guards. Section 9 (b) (3), which was added by the Taft-
Hartley Act, prevents the Board from including in a unit "any
individual employed as a guard to enforce against employees and
other persons rules to protect property of the employer or to
protect the safety of persons on the employer's premises." In
addition, a union may not be certified as the representative of
guards if it "admits to membership or is affiliated directly or indirectly with an organization which admits to membership employees
other than guards."

The intent of Congress in enacting Section 9(b)(3) was to insure
that during strikes or labor unrest an employer would have available loyal plant-protection employees who would enforce rules for
the protection of both persons and property.[119]

In situations where employees perform the duties of guards as
well as other duties, the Board considers whether the guard function is an essential part of their duties. Thus, the Board has held
that firemen are guards where "an essential part of their duties
and responsibilities is the enforcement of the employer's other
plant protection rules and regulations." [120] Employees of outside
firms furnishing guard service, when acting as plant guards, are
treated as guards within the meaning of the Act [121] and may not

---

117 Retail Clerks Union Local No. 324, 144 NLRB 1247, 54 LRRM 1226 (1963).
The Board stated: "We find nothing in Section 9 (b) (1) or in its legislative history
to suggest that Congress intended . . . to invalidate as inappropriate a historically
established contract unit simply because of a joinder of professional and nonprofessional employees."
118 *Ibid.*
119 McDonnell Aircraft Corp., 109 NLRB 967, 34 LRRM 1489 (1954). "See remarks
of Senator Taft at 93 Congressional Record 6444, in which he stated that Section
9 (b) (3) of the Act was inserted because the conferees were impressed with the
reasoning of the Court of Appeals for the Sixth Circuit in NLRB v. Jones and
Laughlin Steel Corp., 154 F2d 932 [17 LRRM 982], deciding that guards could not
be represented by the same union as represented the production and maintenance
employees at their plant because otherwise they would be confronted with conflicting loyalties during periods of industrial unrest and strikes." 109 NLRB at 969,
n. 3.
120 Chance Vought Aircraft Corp., 110 NLRB 1342, 1346, 35 LRRM 1338 (1954).
121 Armored Motor Service Co., 106 NLRB 1139, 32 LRRM 1628 (1953), in which
the Teamsters sought a representation election. The decision overruled Brink's,
Inc., 77 NLRB 1182, 22 LRRM 1133 (1948), and Am. Dist. Telegraph Co., 89 NLRB
1228, 26 LRRM 1097 (1950). See NLRB v. Am. Dist. Telegraph, 205 F2d 86, 32
LRRM 2210 (CA 3, 1943).

be members of a union "which admits to membership employees other than guards." [122]

As with professional employees, an employer and a union may voluntarily establish a unit including guards with other employees, since only units established by the Board fall within the statutory prohibition.[123]

B. Unit Classifications in General

1. Craft and Departmental Units. *a. Craft units.* Massive organizing campaigns in the latter part of the 1930s, which were conducted on an industrial basis, were contemporaneous with judicial validation of the Wagner Act and with a swelling chorus of complaint that its administration was in the hands of enemies of the traditional craft structure of the American Federation of Labor. Mounting congressional concern attended the Board's assessment of claims that were based upon an established pattern of bargaining. The AFofL espoused the position of cohesive groups appealing against submergence in industrial units, pointing to the community of interest represented by fellowship in the same craft.

This was the problem of *craft severance*. It reached a climax in the *American Can* [124] case, in which the Board held that it would not allow a craft unit to be carved out of an established industrial unit, or other broad unit, if the industrial union could show (1) a successful history of bargaining for a unit containing the craft seeking severance and (2) adequate representation of the craft's interests.[125] The effect of this decision was to deny craft severance once the craft was included in a broader industrial unit.

---

122 §9 (b) (3). *See* City of Boston Cab Assn., 177 NLRB No. 11, 71 LRRM 1370 (1969).

123 NLRB v. J. J. Collins' Sons, Inc., 332 F2d 523, 56 LRRM 2375 (CA 7, 1964). The general rule denying a petition for decertification in a unit other than the existing one does not apply if the existing unit is mixed with guards and other employees. Fisher-New Center Co., 170 NLRB No. 104, 67 LRRM 1502 (1968).

124 American Can Co., 13 NLRB 1252, 4 LRRM 392 (1939).

125 *Id.* at 1256. For a discussion of the craft-severance problem, see 8 B.C. IND. & COM. L. REV. 988 (1967).

In later cases, however, the *American Can* doctrine was not rigidly applied,[126] and in *General Electric Co.*[127] the Board modified the doctrine, declaring that severance would be permitted only if (1) the group constituted a true craft, (2) it had maintained its identity while bargaining in the more comprehensive unit, and (3) the group had protested its inclusion in the broader unit, or the broader unit had been established without its knowledge and there had been no previous consideration of the merits of a separate unit.[128]

With the intention of diminishing the apparent restrictive effect of the *American Can* doctrine,[129] Congress included in the Taft-Hartley Act a proviso, Section 9(b)(2), which states:

> The Board shall . . . not decide that any craft unit is inappropriate on the ground that a different unit has been established by a prior Board determination, unless a majority of the employees in the proposed craft unit vote against separate representation.

Passage of the proviso did not have the expected effect on Board policy in craft-unit determinations. The Board retained its policy of severely limiting craft severance, though it reduced its emphasis on extent of organization and history of collective bargaining. In addition, the Board used as the determining factors the degree of integration of industrial with craft operations in the industry involved, and a restrictive definition of what constitutes a true craft.[130] The application of these two factors formed the basis of a series of decisions dating back to 1948, known collec-

---

126 Bendix Aviation Corporation, 39 NLRB 81, 10 LRRM 4 (1942); Aluminum Co. of America, 42 NLRB 772, 10 LRRM 202 (1942); General Electric Co., Lynn River Works and Everett Plant, 58 NLRB 57, 15 LRRM 33 (1944); Remington Rand, Inc., 62 NLRB 1419, 16 LRRM 274 (1945); International Minerals and Chemical Corp., 71 NLRB 878, 19 LRRM 1059 (1946).

127 58 NLRB 57, 15 LRRM 33 (1944), as cited in 8 B.C. IND. & COM. L. REV. 988, 989-990 (1967).

128 *Ibid.*

129 The SENATE REPORT, No. 105 on S. 1126, 80th Cong., 1st Sess. 13 (1947), charged: "Since the decision in the *American Can case* (13 NLRB 1252), where the Board refused to permit craft units to be 'carved out' from a broader bargaining unit already established, the Board, except under unusual circumstances, has virtually compelled skilled artisans to remain parts of a comprehensive plant unit."

130 For a group to be defined as a craft, its members must possess skills requiring a substantial period of training, the group seeking severance must be homogeneous, and its members must have little or no interchange in the employees working at unskilled or semiskilled jobs. Allis-Chalmers Mfg. Co., 77 NLRB 719, 22 LRRM 1085 (1948); Caterpillar Tractor Co., 77 NLRB 457, 22 LRRM 1033 (1948); American Mfg. Co., 76 NLRB 647, 21 LRRM 1232 (1948); Lockheed Aircraft Corp., 57 NLRB 41, 14 LRRM 216 (1944).

tively as the *National Tube* doctrine,[131] in which the Board denied craft severance and initial establishment of craft units in four broad industries.[132] The rationale of each decision was that the industries were so highly integrated that to allow severance, even of a true craft, would upset the stability of labor relations in these industries, contrary to the purpose of the Act.

In 1954, the Board further revised its policy on craft severance in *American Potash & Chemical Corp.*[133] It decided, in effect, that Section 9(b)(2) generally confers freedom to sever if the craftsmen so choose. The Board stated that henceforth it would permit craft severance if (1) the group seeking severance qualifies as a true craft [134] and (2) the union seeking to represent that group is one that traditionally represents that craft.[135]

In subsequent decisions applying the *American Potash* tests, the Board held that the job title or classification is not the controlling factor in defining a craft, but that it would look instead at the full range of skills and duties performed by the employees.[136] As to the test of traditional representation by a union, it said that a union newly organized to represent a craft is as much a craft union as an older, longer established union.[137]

Although *American Potash* revised the tests for craft-unit determinations, the four industries covered by the *National Tube* doctrine were considered exceptions. The Board stated in *American Potash:*

> [A]s we do not deem it wise or feasible to upset a pattern of bargaining already firmly established, we shall continue to decline to entertain petitions for craft or departmental severance in those

---

131 National Tube Co., 76 NLRB 1199, 21 LRRM 1292 (1948); Permanente Metals Co., 89 NLRB 804, 26 LRRM 1039 (1950); Corn Products Refining Co., 80 NLRB 362, 23 LRRM 1090 (1948); Weyerhaeuser Timber Co., 87 NLRB 1076, 25 LRRM 1173 (1949).
132 The four industries were basic steel, basic aluminum, lumbering, and wet milling.
133 107 NLRB 1418, 33 LRRM 1380 (1954).
134 *Id.* at 1422. The Board defined a true craft unit as consisting of "a distinct and homogeneous group of skilled journeymen craftsmen, working as such, together with their apprentices and/or helpers. To be a 'journeyman craftsman,' an individual must have a kind and degree of skill which is normally acquired only by undergoing a substantial period of apprenticeship or comparable training."
135 *Ibid.*
136 Beaunit Mills, Inc., 109 NLRB 651, 34 LRRM 1423 (1954); *see* 8 B.C. IND. & COM. L. REV. 988, 994.
137 Friden Calculating Machine Co., 110 NLRB 1618, 35 LRRM 1261 (1954); *see* 8 B.C. IND. & COM. L. REV. 988, 995.

industries to which the Board has already applied *National Tube* and where plant-wide bargaining prevails.[138]

The Board's policy of denying craft-severance elections in the four "integrated" industries was rejected twice by the Court of Appeals for the Fourth Circuit. The court reasoned that the policy was "arbitrary and discriminatory," and it refused to enforce a Board order directing a flat-glass company to bargain with a craft union that had won a severance election.[139] The Board adhered to its policy, however, and in 1962 the Fourth Circuit again reversed the Board on the same basis.[140]

The *Potash* regime came to an end in 1966 with *Mallinckrodt Chemical Works* [141] and two related cases,[142] in which the Board held that it would consider the following factors relevant in *all* cases involving the issue of craft severance:

> 1. Whether or not the proposed unit consists of a distinct and homogeneous group of skilled journeymen craftsmen performing the functions of their craft on a nonrepetitive basis, or of employees constituting a functionally distinct department, working in trades or occupations for which a tradition of separate representation exists.
> 2. The history of collective bargaining of the employees sought and at the plant involved, and at other plants of the employer, with emphasis on whether the existing patterns of bargaining are productive of stability in labor relations, and whether such stability will be unduly disrupted by the destruction of the existing patterns of representation.
> 3. The extent to which the employees in the proposed unit have established and maintained their separate identity during the period of inclusion in a broader unit, and the extent of their participation or lack of participation in the establishment and maintenance of the existing pattern of representation and the prior opportunities, if any, afforded them to obtain separate representation.
> 4. The history and pattern of collective bargaining in the industry involved.
> 5. The degree of integration of the employer's production processes, including the extent to which the continued normal operation of the production processes is dependent upon the performance of the assigned functions of the employees in the proposed unit.

---

138 107 NLRB at 1422.
139 NLRB v. Pittsburgh Plate Glass Co., 270 F2d 167, 44 LRRM 2855 (CA 4, 1959), *cert. denied*, 361 US 943, 45 LRRM 2456 (1960).
140 Royal McBee Corp. v. NLRB, 302 F2d 330, 50 LRRM 2158 (CA 4, 1962).
141 162 NLRB 387, 64 LRRM 1011 (1966).
142 Holmberg, Inc., 162 NLRB 407, 64 LRRM 1025 (1966); E. I. du Pont de Nemours & Co., 162 NLRB 413, 64 LRRM 1021 (1966).

6. The qualifications of the union seeking to "carve out" a separate unit, including that union's experience in representing employees like those involved in the severance action.[143]

In deciding *Mallinckrodt* the Board stated that

> by confining consideration solely to the interests favoring severance, the American Potash tests preclude the Board from discharging its statutory responsibility to make its unit determinations on the basis of all relevant factors, including those factors which weigh against severance.[144]

In *Mallinckrodt* the union had sought a unit composed of all instrument mechanics, apprentices, and helpers. There were 12 such employees out of a total of 280 production and maintenance employees, all of whom were represented in the existing bargaining unit. In dismissing the petition, the Board based its decision primarily on the facts that (1) the work of the instrument mechanics was intimately related to the production process, (2) they had been represented as part of a production and maintenance unit for the preceding 25 years, and (3) the petitioner had not traditionally represented the craft of instrument mechanic.

The standards employed by the Board, following *Mallinckrodt,* in cases involving the issue of craft severance are applicable not only to organized plants, but also to the initial formation of units in unorganized plants. Thus, in a case where a union sought a unit of 40 electricians in an unorganized plant with a production and maintenance force of 950 employees, the Board applied the *Mallinckrodt* tests and directed an election in a unit of electricians.[145]

Although *Mallinckrodt* and its companions and progeny [146] reject the *American Potash* inflexibility of denial of severance in the four basic industries, they do not retreat to the earlier stress on history of bargaining in the particular industry. The new array of factors specifically plays down, though it does not ignore, the industry involved in favor of the ever-changing impact of technology, the bargaining history with the particular employer, and

143 162 NLRB 387, 64 LRRM 1011, 1016 (1966).

144 64 LRRM at 1016.

145 E. I. du Pont de Nemours & Co., 162 NLRB 413, 64 LRRM 1021 (1966).

146 *Ibid.;* Holmberg, Inc., 162 NLRB 407, 64 LRRM 1025 (1966); Timber Products Co., 164 NLRB 1060, 65 LRRM 1189 (1967).

a careful examination of the characteristics of a true craft, along with the other factors.[147]

b. Departmental units. The *American Potash* case, although concerned primarily with craft severance, also laid down tests for severance of departmental units. The Board noted that the equities of employees in certain other minority groups, though lacking the hallmark of craft skill, may also require that they be treated as severable units.[148] The Board stated that before permitting departmental severance it would require strict proof (1) that the departmental group is functionally distinct and separate and (2) that the petitioner is a union that has traditionally devoted itself to serving the special interests of the employees in question.[149]

In *American Potash* the Board found that the employees of the power division of the engineering department constituted an appropriate departmental unit, despite the fact that they clearly did not qualify as craftsmen. But it found that pump packers of the engineering department, riggers and crane engineers, and toolroom keepers did not constitute a departmental unit. It based its decision on the fact that the work of those employees was of a repetitive and unskilled nature and there was no functional distinction between them and the other employees in the plant.

Decisions in the department-store industry are representative of the Board's policies in the area of departmental severance. These cases show a trend of approval for smaller bargaining units,[150]

---

147 Address by Hon. John H. Fanning, Member, National Labor Relations Board, *The Taft-Hartley Act—Twenty Years After,* before New York University Institute of Labor Relations, Twentieth Annual Conference on Labor, April 17, 1967, LABOR RELATIONS YEARBOOK—1967, 209 (Washington: BNA Books, 1968). *But see* Abodeely, *NLRB Craft Severance Policies: Preeminence of the Bargaining History Factor After Mallinckrodt,* 11 B.C. IND. & COM. L. REV. 411 (1970), where the Board is strongly criticized for relying too heavily on bargaining history in its post-*Mallinckrodt* decisions.
148 107 NLRB 1418, 1424, 33 LRRM 1383 (1954).
149 *Ibid.* Employee desires may, however, be determinative. Lianco Container Corp., 177 NLRB 116, 71 LRRM 1483 (1969). Multi-departmental units are, however, not ordinarily granted. Lyman Printing & Finishing Co., 177 NLRB No. 117, 71 LRRM 1497 (1969). For denial of a unit of maintenance electricians when the production was being done by the computer, see Dundee Cement Co., 170 NLRB No. 66, 67 LRRM 1409 (1968).
150 The cases cited in this section seem to indicate a liberalizing of Board policy toward departmental units, a trend which is consistent with what is happening in craft units—craft and departmental units being so closely related. *See* Arnold Constable Corp., 150 NLRB 788, 58 LRRM 1086 (1965); Lord & Taylor, 150 NLRB 812, 58 LRRM 1881 (1965); Montgomery Ward & Co., 150 NLRB 598, 58 LRRM 1110 (1964).

notwithstanding the fact that the employer has normally requested a larger unit and the Board has indicated that the larger or store-wide unit would not be inappropriate.

In most cases, the separate units approved have been for selling, nonselling, restaurant, or clerical personnel. In *Montgomery Ward & Co.*[151] a separate unit was also approved for automotive-services personnel. In determining whether a department is a functionally distinct unit, the Board usually places emphasis upon several factors, including the following:

(1) differences in skills,
(2) differences in training (whether in classes or on the job),
(3) degree of supervision,
(4) interchange with other employees, and
(5) differences in types of performance ratings.

In *Montgomery Ward & Co.*, the Board also placed emphasis on the fact that the petitioning employees occupied a different area and wore uniforms.

These and other recent cases indicate that, as in craft-severance cases, the Board's trend is toward greater flexibility. Therefore, the narrow test for the separate departmental unit has not been applied as rigidly as first set forth in *American Potash*.

2. Plant and Employer Units. The administrative structure of the employer and considerations of territorial location may argue for a unit larger than the plant-wide unit, especially if more than one plant is under the control of a common employer. In such circumstances, although the multiplant departmental unit is uncommon, there are appropriate multiplant craft units and units of professional employees as well as guard units.[152] For purposes of the present discussion, the term "plant" comprehends its analogous units, such as the store in retail merchandising and the ship in oceanic transport.

---

[151] 150 NLRB 598, 58 LRRM 1110 (1964). In *Lily-Tulip Cup Corp.*, 177 NLRB 3, 71 LRRM 1378 (1969), the Board approved a unit consisting of maintenance employees in three of the plant's departments, against the employer's contention that the only appropriate unit was a plant-wide one including production and maintenance employees. *And see* American Cynamid Co., 131 NLRB 909, 48 LRRM 1152 (1961).

[152] *See* Boeing Co., 164 NLRB 582, 54 LRRM 1077 (1963), denying craft severance to a single plant's maintenance electricians in the face of an existing multiplant unit and a history of multiplant bargaining. *See also* Twenty-Third Annual Report of the NLRB, 34-35 (1958).

A single employer may be organized into geographical parts for convenience of administration. For example, an employer owning and operating one factory may acquire another across the alley, or across the continent, and make no substantial change in the managerial processes within either factory. The drug store chain may operate with only a modicum of authority in the local manager and much interchange of employees among the stores. The chemical installation may consist of a dozen units on the same tract of land, each unit functionally integrated with the others, but with no interchange of employees among the units. The employer may be organized along divisional lines that coincide with state boundaries, or by cities or other territorial subdivisions.

Doctrine evolved by the Board sometimes speaks in terms that transcend the industry involved, but the reference in Section 9(b) to "plant unit" as potentially appropriate has given rise to no system of categories that operates reliably from one type of industry to another. Hence, an effort is here made to present the appropriate unit pattern for a few types of industry, one by one. They are manufacturing, retail merchandising, insurance, public utilities, and oceanic transport.

a. Manufacturing. Manufacturing enterprises were among the first objects of union organization. The success of this effort has resolved most questions of appropriateness of unit by the direct influence of bargaining history (removing extent of organization as an important factor). The Board's early troubles with the question of an appropriate unit at Libbey-Owens-Ford Glass Co. were but the beginning of an era of vacillation, an era that concluded in 1962 with a case in the textile industry.

In the 1939 *Libbey-Owens-Ford* case [153] the unit approved by the Board consisted of employees at all six of the plants, but when the employer supported the dissenting employees at one of the plants, the Board a year later went along with them and sanctioned a truncated multiplant unit that was less than employer-wide. The Supreme Court, however, affirmed the earlier determination of the six-plant unit at about the same time the Board relented.[154] The

---

[153] Libbey-Owens-Ford Glass Co., 10 NLRB 1470, 3 LRRM 551 (1939); 31 NLRB 243, 8 LRRM 135 (1940).

[154] Pittsburgh Plate Glass Co. v. NLRB, 313 US 146, 8 LRRM 425 (1941).

textile-industry case was *Dixie Belle Mills*,[155] approving a single-plant unit on the premise that although the employer was operating other textile-mill installations but 20 miles away, the distinctness of supervision and low degree of interchange of employees between the two mills was such as to make one of them an appropriate unit. The relevant factors for determining whether less than all of an employer's operations may be taken as an appropriate unit are similar to those for determining noncraft departmental units. They are: location, structure of supervision, integration of functions, and interchange of employees.

b. Retail Merchandising. By contrast with the near-vacuum of Board policy in manufacturing, until recently the chain-store position of the Board had been to follow the employer's administrative structure and deny single-store units when the employing unit was larger.[156] The contrasting firmness of this preference in retailing for multiplant units persisted until 1962, in *Sav-on-Drugs*,[157] at which time the Board approved a single-store unit smaller than the employer's administrative division for an area consisting of several stores. It relied upon the existence of substantial discretion vested in the store manager in labor relations matters and the paucity of employee interchange among stores. It remarked that the administrative unit would also be appropriate, taking into account both the absence of bargaining history in any unit and the fact that the only unit sought was the single-store unit. Thus, extent of organization was acknowledged as an operative, albeit nondeterminative, factor toward acceptance of the smaller unit. The dissenting members saw the result as unlawfully giving controlling effect to extent of organization.

---

[155] 139 NLRB 629, 51 LRRM 1344 (1962). *Compare* White Motor Corp., 164 NLRB 295, 65 LRRM 1063 (1967), denying inclusion of office employees by accretion to a plant unit three or four miles distant. For judicial approval of the Board's presumption favoring a single-plant unit, *see* NLRB v. New Enterprise Stone & Lime Co., 413 F2d 117, 71 LRRM 2802 (CA 3, 1969).

[156] Father and Son Shoe Stores, 117 NLRB 1479, 40 LRRM 1032 (1956); Robert Hall Clothes, 118 NLRB 1096, 40 LRRM 1322 (1957); Daw Drug Co., 127 NLRB 1316, 46 LRRM 1218 (1960); and cases cited by dissenting Member Rodgers in Sav-On Drugs, Inc., 138 NLRB 1032, 51 LRRM 1152 (1962), at 1036, n. 5.

[157] 138 NLRB 1032, 51 LRRM 1152. *Followed,* as to restaurants, in Frisch's Big Boy Ill-Mar., Inc., 147 NLRB 551, 56 LRRM 1246 (1964), and as to supermarkets in Primrose Super Mkt. of Salem, Inc., 148 NLRB 610, 57 LRRM 1057 (1964), *enforced,* 353 F2d 675, 58 LRRM 2863 (CA 1, 1964), *cert. denied,* 382 US 830, 60 LRRM 2234 (1965). The Board decision in *Frisch's Big Boy* was repudiated by the Seventh Circuit in *NLRB* v. *Frisch's Big Boy Ill-Mar, Inc.,* 356 F2d 895, 61 LRRM 2362 (CA 7, 1966); the court said that all of the restaurants involved were "like peas in a pod."

The First Circuit approved the Board's new latitude in one supermarket case but withheld its approval in a second.[158] The Fifth Circuit later relied on the second holding in deciding that the Board abused its discretion in finding that two cafeterias of a chain of eight constituted an appropriate bargaining unit. It quoted from the First Circuit opinion that "the independence of the stores amounts to no more than a few miles of physical separation and the consequent division of a few ministerial responsibilities. This is far from enough."[159] The Board, however, has adhered to its view that single-store units are presumptively appropriate in retail merchandising chains.[160]

c. *Insurance.* In 1944, before Taft-Hartley prohibited extent of organization as a controlling factor, the Board held that a unit of insurance agents would not be appropriate if less than statewide.[161] The state-wide rule was based upon extent of organization in the sense that union organization, it was believed, would be facilitated by such units. The ensuing years failed to support this belief, and in 1961 the Board recognized that its earlier presupposition had not been borne out. Therefore, in *Quaker City Life Insurance Co.*,[162] the employees of a single distinct office were approved as a unit appropriate for bargaining.

The new policy was contested all the way to the Supreme Court, with inconclusive results, in *Metropolitan Life Insurance Co. v. NLRB.*[163] The Board had approved a unit consisting of all debit insurance agents in a single city office of the company. The Court rejected arguments of counsel intended to show that the Board

---

158 Primrose Super Mkt. of Salem, Inc., note 157 *supra.* NLRB v. Purity Food Stores, Inc., 376 F2d 497, 65 LRRM 2261 (CA 1, 1967), *cert. denied,* 389 U.S. 959, 66 LRRM 2507 (1967). *See* NLRB v. De Young's Mkt., 406 F2d 17, 70 LRRM 2262 (CA 6, 1969).

159 NLRB v. Davis Cafeteria, Inc., 396 F2d 18, 68 LRRM 2426 (CA 5, 1968).

160 In later decisions the Board has restated its general approach to the question of retail-chain operations, and while reaffirming its original position, it may have redistributed the weight given to various factors. Haag Drug Co., 169 NLRB No. 111, 67 LRRM 1289 (1968) (although the Board adhered to its view that a single-store unit is presumptively appropriate, it indicated that the presumption could be overcome by a showing that the day-to-day interests of the employees have merged with those of employees in other stores); Star Mkt. Co., 172 NLRB No. 130, 68 LRRM 1497 (1968). *See also* May Department Stores, 175 NLRB No. 97, 71 LRRM 1026 (1969); Super Valu Stores, Inc., 177 NLRB No. 63, 71 LRRM 1459 (1969) (violation of §8 (a) (2)) ; Warehouse Mkts., Inc., 174 NLRB No. 70, 71 LRRM 1192 (1969) (unit clarification).

161 Metropolitan Life Insurance Co., 56 NLRB 1635, 14 LRRM 1635 (1944).

162 134 NLRB 960, 49 LRRM 1281 (1961), *affirmed,* 319 F2d 690, 53 LRRM 2519 (CA 4, 1963).

163 380 US 438, 58 LRRM 2721 (1965).

had not allowed extent of organization to control its approval, and instead sent the decision back to the Board for further explanation.[164]

d. *Public Utilities.* Contrasting with the tendency toward approval of units less than employer-wide for single-plant or single-store or single-office units, the opposite tendency exists for public utilities. Here the Board has favored system-wide units and units of intermediate size which build toward system-wide units.

In *New England Telephone and Telegraph Co.*,[165] the Board relied upon the highly integrated and interdependent nature of the operations of public utilities, their centralized labor relations policies, and the public interest as warranting system-wide units. Even though a company and the intervening union had established bargaining in a smaller unit, the Board granted a petition for an election on a system-wide basis in *Pacific Gas and Electric Co.*[166]

e. *Oceanic Transport.* The Board has regularly favored system-wide units—*fleet-wide*—in the shipping industry.[167] However, in *Moore-MacCormack Lines*[168] bargaining history led the Board to make an exception in favor of continuing established ship-wide units. The decision was also influenced by a "no raiding" agreement which was inconsistent with the union's request for a system-wide unit.

f. *Current Policy.* The foregoing industry summaries do not exhaust the issues concerning the appropriate unit in a multiplant operation. The complex of ballistic-missile and space-vehicle tracking stations, for example, has given rise to approval of a less-than-employer-wide multiplant unit over the employer's objection

---

[164] *See,* for the explanation, 156 NLRB 1408, 61 LRRM 1249 (1966); *see also* discussion at notes 101 and 102 *supra. Compare:* State Farm Mutual Ins. Co. v. NLRB, 411 F2d 356, 70 LRRM 3138 (CA 7, 1969); Continental Ins. Co. v. NLRB, 409 F2d 727, 70 LRRM 3406 (CA 2, 1969); NLRB v. Western & Southern Life Ins. Co., 391 F2d 119, 67 LRRM 2666 (CA 3, 1968).

[165] 90 NLRB 639, 26 LRRM 1259 (1950).

[166] 87 NLRB 257, 25 LRRM 1102 (1949); *see also* The Ohio Power Co., 77 NLRB 320, 22 LRRM 1011 (1948). *But see* Michigan-Wisconsin Pipe Line Co., 164 NLRB 359, 65 LRRM 1065 (1967), where a single-station unit was held appropriate. *Compare* application of a substantial-evidence test to reverse a single-station unit determination in *NLRB v. Pioneer Natural Gas Co.,* 397 F2d 573, 68 LRRM 2723 (CA 5, 1968). Also, the Board agrees with the court in favoring a plant-wide unit as against a separate powerhouse unit. Rayonier, Inc., 170 NLRB No. 96, 67 LRRM 1474 (1968).

[167] *E.g.:* Inter-Ocean Steamship Co., 107 NLRB 330, 33 LRRM 1132 (1953); Ocean Tow, Inc., 99 NLRB 480, 30 LRRM 1086 (1952).

[168] 139 NLRB 796, 51 LRRM 1361 (1962).

that the unit should extend to all its stations.[169] Differences in fringe benefits and variations in workmen's compensation that begin to operate at the state line provided the basis for approval of the California stations as a unit.

The current tenor of Board policy is illustrated by the following passages from the *Capital Bakers* case: [170]

> . . . there is more than one way in which employees of a given employer may be grouped for purposes of collective bargaining.
> In recent years the Board has re-examined its unit policies in the insurance and in the retail chain industry and in each instance modified prior rules and found smaller units appropriate. . . .
> Inasmuch as the Employer in the present case is not only a multi-plant organization engaged in the production of certain goods but is also very substantially engaged on a plant or local basis, in the distribution of such goods at both the wholesale and retail level, the principles stated in Sav-on Drugs . . . are particularly appropriate.
> . . . There is no more reason to withhold application of this policy to the employer's operations because formerly we applied a different policy than there was reason to refrain from changing the basic policy to be applied to the retail store industry. We are satisfied that the freedom of choice of this one cohesive group of employees to have or not to have a bargaining representative should not be dependent upon the interest or lack of interest in such representation on the part of other employees in separated, and in somewhat distant, plants and distribution centers serving other markets.

V. MULTI-EMPLOYER BARGAINING UNITS

This section focuses upon the nature of the multi-employer bargaining unit: how it is formed, how the parties may enter it, and how they may withdraw from it. Once the unit is formed, the multi-employer group becomes the employer for purposes of bargaining, with the obligation under Sections 8(a)(5) and 8(d) to bargain collectively with the representative of all the employees in the unit.[171] The bargaining requirements applicable to the "multi-employer" are substantially the same as for any employer. The major differences are noted in this section. See Chapter 11 *infra* for a discussion of the requirements of good-faith bargaining generally, and Chapter 20 *infra*, which covers lockouts, for a discussion of the body of law relating to lockouts affecting multi-employer units.

---

[169] ITT Federal Electric Corp., 167 NLRB 350, 66 LRRM 1046 (1967).
[170] Capital Bakers, Inc., 168 NLRB No. 119, 66 LRRM 1385, 1387 (1967).
[171] *E.g.*, NLRB v. Strong, 393 U.S. 357, 70 LRRM 2100 (1969).

A. Emergence and Character

The institution of multi-employer bargaining, *i.e.*, bargaining between a union or unions and groups of employers, has existed in this country for over 75 years.[172] Employers first grouped together in the 1880's, forming associations of large corporations, not for the purpose of collective bargaining, but in order to achieve a coordinated counterforce to the Knights of Labor.[173] Since the acceptance of the principle of collective bargaining in this country, however, multi-employer bargaining has become, in large part, a device employed by small employers to help offset the bargaining strength of powerful unions.[174] Large corporations may not feel such pressure strongly enough to justify their entering an association for collective bargaining,[175] although some industries, such as basic steel and refractories, have engaged in industry-wide—hence multi-employer—bargaining for many years.

Prior to the passage of Taft-Hartley, a substantial body of opinion viewed multi-employer bargaining as a lever for big unionism, and therefore a real or potential hazard to many employers. In consequence, many proposals to limit multi-employer bargaining were introduced in the course of the debates on Taft-Hartley. Perhaps the most sweeping of these was sponsored by the National Association of Manufacturers, which would have prohibited unions from "representing the workers of two or more employers to take joint wage action or engage in other monopolistic practices." The Hartley bill, passed by the House of Representatives, included severe restrictions upon multi-employer bargaining.[176] However, none survived in the final version of the Taft-Hartley Act.

---

172 *See* Pierson, MULTI-EMPLOYER BARGAINING: NATURE AND SCOPE (1949) ; Sommers, *Pressures on an Association in Collective Bargaining*, 6 IND. & LAB. REL. REV. 557 (1953) .

173 *See* Perlman, A HISTORY OF TRADE UNIONISM IN THE UNITED STATES, 94, 194, 252 (1952) , Note, 66 HARV. L. REV. 886 (1953) .

174 Frieden, THE TAFT-HARTLEY ACT AND MULTI-EMPLOYER BARGAINING, 4-5 (1949) .

175 *See* Backman, MULTI-EMPLOYER BARGAINING, 60-61 (1951) .

176 Section 9 (f) of H.R. 3020, with certain provisos, made unions representing the employees of one employer ineligible to be certified as the representative of the employees of a competing employer employing more than 100 employees and having a plant or facility less than fifty miles distant. LEGISLATIVE HISTORY OF THE LABOR MANAGEMENT RELATIONS ACT 1947, 187-189 (GPO 1948) . *See* MULTI-EMPLOYER ASSOCIATION BARGAINING AND ITS IMPACT ON THE COLLECTIVE BARGAINING PROCESS, REPORT OF THE GENERAL SUBCOMMITTEE ON LABOR, H.R. REPORT, 88th Cong., 2d Sess.

B. Establishment of the Unit

The Wagner Act had not explicitly authorized the Board to find multi-employer units appropriate, although such bargaining was familiar by 1935. The Board reflected this familiarity with multi-employer bargaining in its interpretation of two definitional postulates from Section 2 as it was then framed. Paragraph 1 of that section included as an "employer" any person acting in an employer's interest, and from paragraph 2 it appeared that a person might be an "association." Since Section 9 named the employer unit as appropriate, reasoned the Board, the employer association unit could be appropriate.[177]

The Taft-Hartley amendments of 1947 substituted for "any person acting in the interest of an employer" the phrase "any person acting as an agent of the employer." The Board had little difficulty reading the amendment as detracting nothing from its authority to conduct elections in multi-employer units.[178] A second thought by one member,[179] that the broadest unit is an employer unit, must now be considered unlikely to be followed, the Supreme Court having concluded that Congress meant "that the Board should continue its established administrative practice" with respect to these units.[180]

The procedures referred to as multi-employer bargaining include industry-wide and multi-association bargaining as well as bargaining between a union and several companies associated on the side of the employer. The Board applies the same principles to all these sub-types.[181]

Unlike other bargaining units, the multi-employer unit is *consensual*. Essential to the establishment of such a unit is the unequivocal manifestation by the employer members of the group that all of them intend to be bound in future collective bargaining

---

177 Shipowner's Ass'n of the Pac. Coast, 7 NLRB 1002, 2 LRRM 377 (1938). *See* note 183 *infra*.

178 Associated Shoe Industries of Southeastern Mass., Inc., 81 NLRB 224, 23 LRRM 1320 (1949).

179 The Board member's dissenting opinion is found in Continental Baking Co., 99 NLRB 777, 787, 30 LRRM 1119 (1952).

180 NLRB v. Truck Drivers Local 449, 353 US 87, 96, 39 LRRM 2603, 2607 (1957). '

181 Chester County Beer Distributors Ass'n, 133 NLRB 771, 48 LRRM 1712 (1961); Morgan Linen Service, Inc., 131 NLRB 420, 48 LRRM 1054 (1961); Mutual Rough Hat Co., 86 NLRB 440, 24 LRRM 1641 (1949). *Distinguish* the "joint employer" issue presented in such cases as Greyhound Corp. v. Boire, 205 F Supp 686, 50 LRRM 2485 (SD Fla, 1962), *affirmed*, 309 F2d 397, 51 LRRM 2509 (CA 5, 1962), *reversed*, 376 US 473, 55 LRRM 2694 (1964). *See* Chapter 29 *infra* at notes 46-47.

by group rather than individual action.[182] The formation of the multi-employer unit, moreover, must be entirely voluntary, the assent of the union having representative status being also required. The Board will not sanction the creation of such a unit over the objection of any party, union or employer.[183]

On the employer side, subjective intent alone is not sufficient; it must be objectively manifested, either by express delegation to the association's bargaining arm or by participation in the group bargaining process by the individual member.[184] In the absence of both participation and delegation of authority, the Board will not accept, over the objection of any party, a mere showing of a custom of past adoption of terms of a multi-employer agreement.[185]

One form of objective manifestation of rejection of the multi-employer unit is the filing of a petition on an individual employer basis. Thus, when there has been a history of individual bargaining, followed by a collective agreement on a multi-employer basis, a rival petition filed by an intervening union on a single-employer basis prevails, and is timely notwithstanding the multi-employer

---

[182] York Transfer & Storage Co., 107 NLRB 139, 33 LRRM 1078 (1953).

[183] Steamship Trade Ass'n of Baltimore, Inc., 155 NLRB 232, 60 LRRM 1257 (1965). Early in the Wagner Act period, the Board established a multi-employer unit over objection of the employers in Shipowners' Ass'n of the Pac. Coast, 7 NLRB 1002, 2 LRRM 377 (1938), *review denied*, 103 F2d 933, 4 LRRM 787 (CA DC, 1939), *affirmed*, 308 US 401, 5 LRRM 670 (1940). Unanimity of employer members began to be relied upon in Alston Coal Co., 13 NLRB 683, 4 LRRM 337 (1939).

[184] Kroger Co., 148 NLRB 569, 57 LRRM 1021 (1964), illustrates that a multi-employer unit does not require a formal association of employers, nor does it require execution of a single, master agreement (*see* note 186 *infra*). It is sufficient if members of the group have bargained as a group over a period of time (17 years in this case), and as a result of joint negotiations have executed separate but substantially similar contracts with the union representing their employees. The Board found such a multi-employer unit to exist "even though the employer may not have specifically delegated to an employer group the authority to represent it in collective bargaining or given the employer group the power to execute final and binding agreements on its behalf, or where some of the contracts have not been signed by all members of the group. What is essential is that the employer member has indicated from the outset an intention to be bound in collective bargaining by group rather than by individual action."
See also: A. B. Hirschfeld, Inc., 140 NLRB 212, 51 LRRM 1607 (1962); Houston Automobile Dealers Assn., 132 NLRB 947, 48 LRRM 1463 (1961); Capital Dist. Beer Distributors Ass'n, 109 NLRB 176, 34 LRRM 1313 (1954); Ward Baking Co., 78 NLRB 781, 22 LRRM 1277 (1948). It is not essential that the association be endowed with formal authority to require acceptance of an agreement negotiated by it. Rayonier, Inc., 52 NLRB 1269, 13 LRRM 91 (1943).

[185] NLRB v. E-Z Davies Chevrolet, 395 F2d 191, 68 LRRM 2228 (CA 9, 1968); Colonial Cedar Co., 119 NLRB 1613, 41 LRRM 1353 (1958); West End Brewing Co., 107 NLRB 1542, 33 LRRM 1432 (1954); Pacific Metals Co., Ltd., 91 NLRB 696, 26 LRRM 1558 (1950); Associated Shoe Industries of Southeastern Mass., Inc., 81 NLRB 224, 23 LRRM 1320 (1949).

agreement if it is timely respecting the insulated period of the individual agreement.[186] Individual bargaining on a limited basis, under a mutually recognized privilege to do so concomitant with group bargaining on subjects of general concern, is not, however, recognized as negating manifestation of desire to be bound on a multi-employer basis.[187]

The freedom of choice extended an employer under the foregoing rules is subject to one limitation resulting from the freedom of association accorded employees by the Act. The Board has held that an employer "could not unilaterally and without the express or implied consent of its employees bind them to representation in a multi-employer unit. . . ." [188] The relevant majority at the time the employer seeks to enter the multi-employer unit is that of the employees of the particular employer; however, once the multi-employer bargaining unit is established the relevant majority is the entire unit.[189] Even if a majority of the employees of a single employer in the unit no longer wish to be represented by the union, "that fact would not relieve the . . . [employer] of its obligation to bargain with the Union as to the appropriate multi-employer unit, nor justify an untimely withdrawal from such unit." [190]

The history of collective bargaining, not only in the particular industry but with respect to particular units, is always an important consideration in determining the appropriateness of a unit. In the multi-employer context, the history of bargaining in the unit assumes unique significance. The absence of any history of multi-employer bargaining in a proposed multi-employer unit is

---

[186] U. S. Pillow Corp., 137 NLRB 584, 50 LRRM 1216 (1962), Member Leedom concurring. *See* Chapter 8 *supra* for discussion of the contract-bar doctrine.

[187] Kroger Co., 148 NLRB 569, 57 LRRM 1021 (1964). The resulting multi-employer agreement may be executed in a series of individual-member agreements embodying the terms of joint bargaining as well as the side agreements reached by member bargaining. Detroit News, 119 NLRB 345, 41 LRRM 1085 (1957); Balaban & Katz, 87 NLRB 1071, 25 LRRM 1197 (1949).

[188] Mohawk Business Machines Corp., 116 NLRB 248, 249, 38 LRRM 1239 (1956); Dancker & Sellew, Inc., 140 NLRB 824, 52 LRRM 1120 (1963), *enforced,* 330 F2d 46, 55 LRRM 2902 (CA 2, 1964). *Cf.* Lamson Bros. Co., 59 NLRB 1561, 15 LRRM 209 (1945); Douds v. Anheuser-Busch, Inc., 99 F Supp 474, 28 LRRM 2277, 2519 (D NJ, 1951).

[189] Sheridan Creations, Inc., 148 NLRB 1503, 57 LRRM 1176 (1964), *enforced,* 357 F2d 245, 61 LRRM 2586 (CA 2, 1966), *cert. denied,* 385 US 1005, 64 LRRM 2108 (1967). *Cf.* Grand Rapids Fuel Co., 107 NLRB 1402, 33 LRRM 1404 (1954).

[190] Sheridan Creations, Inc., note 189 *supra,* 148 NLRB at 1506.

usually determinative against it.[191] There are, however, instances of approval of new multi-employer units in industries where such units are characteristic.[192] Bargaining history is considered qualifying even when it has been carried on under successive agreements containing clauses held to violate the Act.[193] But if either the union or an employer manifests an unequivocal intent to pursue an individual course of action, even a substantial history of multi-employer bargaining would not suffice to establish such a unit in the face of the determination to bargain individually.[194]

A history of individual bargaining within what later becomes a unit covered by a multi-employer agreement may have the profound consequence that employees of a member-employer may, by petition of an intervening union, opt out of the multi-employer arrangement, even if the petition is filed during what would be a contract bar, were the agreement not a multi-employer one.[195] Thus the Board has in effect stated that where there is an antecedent history of single-employer bargaining, the Board's premature contract extension principles will prevail over considerations of multi-employer bargaining history. On the other hand, a prior election in the smaller unit does not invoke the statutory one-year election bar to an election in a more inclusive unit.[196]

C. Dissolution, Entire and Partial

A 1950 case, *Morand Bros. Beverage Co.*,[197] established that a union representing employees in an existing multi-employer unit could be compelled to continue its representation on that basis and could not single out a member of the employer association

---

191 Arden Farms, 117 NLRB 318, 39 LRRM 1216 (1957).

192 *E.g.*: Calumet Contractors Assn., 121 NLRB 80, 42 LRRM 1279 (1958); Western Assn. of Engineers, Architects & Surveyors, 101 NLRB 64, 31 LRRM 1010 (1952). And a new unit without multi-employer bargaining history is appropriate if no party is seeking a single-employer unit. Broward County Launderers & Cleaners Assn., 125 NLRB 256, 45 LRRM 1113 (1959).

193 Tom's Monarch Laundry and Cleaning Co., 168 NLRB 39, 66 LRRM 1277 (1967).

194 Donaldson Sales, Inc., 141 NLRB 1303, 1305, 52 LRRM 1500 (1963).

195 U.S. Pillow Corp., 137 NLRB 584, 50 LRRM 1216 (1962).

196 Leslie Metal Arts Co., 167 NLRB 693, 66 LRRM 1134 (1967).

197 91 NLRB 409, 26 LRRM 1501 (1950), *enforced*, 190 F2d 576 (CA 7, 1951).

for individual bargaining without first having bargained to impasse under the existing framework.[198]

On the other hand, it had become established that even in the face of a long history of multi-employer bargaining the employer member could withdraw from its association, and thus at least reduce the size of the unit by its membership on the employers' side and by its employees with respect to the constituents represented by the union.[199] In 1958 the Board took occasion, in the *Retail Associates* case,[200] to announce that thenceforward either the representative of the employees or an individual employer would be limited in withdrawing from a duly established unit by the requirement of written notice of intention to do so given before the date set by the contract for modification or the date agreed upon for the beginning of multi-employer negotiations. Accordingly, in the *Evening News* case in 1965 the union was held to have the same freedom as employers. The Board stated:

> If, as is apparent, the basis of a multi-employer bargaining unit is both original and continuing consent by both parties, the Board cannot logically deny the bargaining representative the same opportunity it allows the employers of withdrawing from the multi-employer unit by withdrawing its consent to such unit.[201]

The *Retail Associates* rules require that notice of withdrawal be both timely and unequivocal. To be unequivocal, "the decision to withdraw must contemplate a sincere abandonment, with relative permanency, of the multi-employer unit and the embracement of a different course of bargaining on an individual-employer

---

[198] To the same effect, *see* Retail Associates, Inc., 120 NLRB 388, 41 LRRM 1502 (1958) ; Stouffer Corp., 101 NLRB 1331, 31 LRRM 1200 (1952) ; Continental Baking Co., 99 NLRB 777, 30 LRRM 1119 (1952). Note the converse constraint expressed in the Act §8(b) (4) (A), making it an unfair labor practice for a union to employ certain pressures to force an employer "to join any labor or employer organization." General Ore, Inc., 126 NLRB 172, 45 LRRM 1296 (1960). It has been held a violation of §8(a) (3) to use the lockout to force adherence of unions to multi-employer units in bargaining. Great Atlantic & Pac. Tea Co., Inc., 145 NLRB 361, 54 LRRM 1384 (1964), *enforced in part*, 340 F2d 690, 58 LRRM 2232 (CA 2, 1965).

[199] Johnson Optical Co., 87 NLRB 539, 25 LRRM 1135 (1949).

[200] Retail Associates, Inc., 120 NLRB 388, 41 LRRM 1502 (1958). *See also* Joseph Busalacchi, dba Union Fish Co., 156 NLRB 187, 61 LRRM 1012 (1965).

[201] Evening News Ass'n, 154 NLRB 1494, 1496-1497, 60 LRRM 1149, 1150 (1965). *Followed* in Adams Furnace Co., 159 NLRB 1792, 62 LRRM 1356 (1966) ; Hearst Consolidated Publications, Inc., 156 NLRB 210, 61 LRRM 1011 (1965) (Member Brown dissenting), *enforced*, 364 F2d 293, 62 LRRM 2722 (CA 2, 1966), *cert. denied*, 385 US 971, 63 LRRM 2527 (1966).

basis." [202] Should timeliness of the notice of withdrawal turn upon the date agreed upon for the beginning of negotiations, the date in question relates to the actual negotiations, not the service of a notice or demand for conference.[203] It is clear that under these rules once group negotiations have begun withdrawal is untimely until an impasse has occurred.[204]

Partial withdrawal, as will be seen below, takes a different form, depending upon whether the party seeking to withdraw is the union representative of the employees or an employer member of the employer group. In the case of the employer, it takes the form of seeking to continue association on a group basis for some of its employees; whereas for the union it is an effort to take all of the employees of one or more, but less than all of the employers out of the negotiations and thereafter bargain for them on an individual employer basis, and if more than one employer is involved, seriatim. In the employer case, the attempted withdrawal will not operate to affect the established multi-employer unit. But the union representative, since *Evening News* in 1965, may timely seek to reduce the number of employers in the unit.[205]

The principle working against partial withdrawal as applied to employers involves scope of the unit, to be discussed in the next section. It has been invoked in cases going back at least as far as 1949.[206] The individual employer, however, as has been noted, may timely withdraw as far as his own employees are concerned. Comparably, the union may elect to withdraw as to the employees

202 Retail Associates, Inc., 120 NLRB 388, 394, 41 LRRM 1502 (1958).

203 Carmichael Floor Covering Co., 155 NLRB 674, 60 LRRM 1364 (1965); Quality Limestone Products, Inc., 153 NLRB 1009, 59 LRRM 1589 (1965); Daelyte Service Co., 126 NLRB 63, 45 LRRM 1275 (1963).

204 Sheridan Creations, Inc., 148 NLRB 1503, 57 LRRM 1176, *enforced*, 357 F2d 245, 61 LRRM 2586 (CA 2, 1966), *cert. denied*, 385 US 1005, 64 LRRM 2108 (1967); NLRB v. Paskesz, 405 F2d 1201, 70 LRRM 2482 (CA 2, 1969). Exceptions for unusual circumstances have been recognized: U.S. Lingerie Corp., 170 NLRB No. 77, 67 LRRM 1482 (1968) (bankruptcy predating withdrawal). Untimely withdrawal and conclusion of a single employer agreement has been held a violation of §8(a) (2). Tower Iron Works, 150 NLRB 298, 58 LRRM 1090 (1964).

205 Pac. Coast Ass'n of Pulp and Paper Mfrs., 163 NLRB No. 129, 64 LRRM 1420 (1967). On timeliness: H. L. Washum, 172 NLRB 40, 68 LRRM 1535 (1968); Reynolds Electrical & Eng. Co., 171 NLRB 176, 68 LRRM 1291 (1968). On craft severance to single-employer unit: United Metal Trades Assn., 172 NLRB 52, 68 LRRM 1328 (1968).

206 Pioneer, Inc., 86 NLRB 1316, 25 LRRM 1068 (1949). *See also* Coeur d'Alene Mines, 77 NLRB 570, 22 LRRM 1069 (1948). Later cases include Jahn-Tyler Printing & Publishing Co., 112 NLRB 167, 35 LRRM 1730 (1955); P & V Atlas Industrial Center, Inc., 100 NLRB 1443, 30 LRRM 1461 (1952); Washington Hardware Co., 95 NLRB 1001, 28 LRRM 1406 (1951); Coca-Cola Bottling Works Co., 91 NLRB 351, 26 LRRM 1488 (1950).

of some employers.[207] The lockout privilege enjoyed by the employers to defend the established unit, as derived from the *Buffalo Linen* case,[208] is discussed in Chapter 20 *infra*.[209]

D. Scope of the Unit

Until 1952 the Board took the position that the appropriateness of a multi-employer unit was controlling as to all categories of employees of the employers in such unit.[210] Thus, once multi-employer bargaining was established with respect to some employees, all subsequent organization involving participating employers had to proceed on a multi-employer basis. The concern of the Board that this requirement would impede organization led to abandonment of the policy in *Joseph E. Seagram & Sons*.[211] Although the *Seagram* rule was enunciated in the case of a single employer concerning a multi-plant unit, it soon found application in multi-employer cases as well.

The new policy led the Board to approve single-employer units of office clericals [212] and of salesmen,[213] for example, although the employer had been bargaining as to other employees in a multi-employer unit. What is essential to the creation of such single-employer units is that they have an "internal homogeneity and cohesiveness" permitting them to stand alone.[214]

If the unrepresented employees do not form a cohesive group, but comprise groups of miscellaneous employees having in common only the fact that they lack representation, the Board has found a unit consisting of such employees appropriate simply as a residual unit. But such a unit is appropriate only if it includes all unrepresented employees.[215] And a residual multi-employer unit cannot be considered the only appropriate unit on the basis of bargaining history when such unit would embrace the main force

---

[207] Recent cases denying such as option include: Allen, Lane & Scott, 137 NLRB 223, 50 LRRM 1140 (1962) ; Printing Industry of Delaware, 131 NLRB 1100, 48 LRRM 1196 (1961).

[208] NLRB v. Truck Drivers Local 449, 353 US 87, 39 LRRM 2603 (1957).

[209] *And see:* Western States Regional Council v. NLRB, 398 F2d 770, 68 LRRM 2506 (CA DC, 1968) ; Detroit Newspaper Publishers Ass'n v. NLRB, 372 F2d 568, 64 LRRM 2403 (CA 6, 1967).

[210] Kenosha Auto Transport Corp., 98 NLRB 482, 29 LRRM 1370 (1952) ; Columbia Pictures Corp., 84 NLRB 647, 24 LRRM 1291 (1949).

[211] 101 NLRB 101, 31 LRRM 1022 (1952).

[212] Continental Baking Co., 109 NLRB 33, 34 LRRM 1298 (1954) ; Sovereign Productions, Inc., 107 NLRB 359, 33 LRRM 1171 (1953).

[213] Lownsbury Chevrolet Co., 101 NLRB 1752, 31 LRRM 1261 (1952).

[214] Los Angeles Hilton Hotel, 129 NLRB 1349, 1351, 47 LRRM 1194 (1961), where such a unit was denied.

[215] Daily Press, Inc., 110 NLRB 573, 35 LRRM 1048 (1954).

of employees, where multi-employer bargaining has been confined to certain craft and special interest groups.[216] Should an employee classification be employed by one or more but less than all the employer members, they may be represented in a unit smaller than the all-employer unit.[217]

Accretions to an existing multi-employer unit consisting of unrepresented classifications may be appropriate notwithstanding the objection of the employers. Thus the Board rejected the contention of the association, in a longshoring multi-employer case, that an unrepresented group of timekeepers should not be added to a unit of checkers and other classifications. As between the limitation of bargaining authority conferred by the members upon the association and the association's duty to bargain in an appropriate unit, the Board emphasized the latter, holding that if the members could deny the association authority to bargain with respect to timekeepers, its own duty under Section 9 would be eroded.[218]

E. Multi-Level Bargaining.

Multi-level bargaining with a multi-employer bargaining unit was recognized by the Board in *Radio Corp. of America*.[219] The employer and the International Brotherhood of Electrical Workers had been parties to national contracts for a period of years. When a local of the IBEW was certified for a new unit, the employer refused to bargain with the local on matters covered by the national contract, and agreed to bargain only as to local issues. Finding no unlawful refusal to bargain, the Board declared that "[M]ulti-plant master or national agreements are not in every case inconsistent with appropriate single-plant bargaining units." [220]

> This combination of national and local bargaining is commonplace, conforms to the Board's prior holding of the appropriateness of the local unit in this case, and accords to the local union . . . the benefits and the corresponding obligations which the employees in the unit chose when they designated a local with a clear, stated affiliation with the IBEW.[221]

---

216 Pac. Drive-In Theatres Corp., 167 NLRB 661, 66 LRRM 1119 (1967).
217 Holiday Hotel, 134 NLRB 113, 49 LRRM 1095 (1961) (Member Leedom dissenting); Desaulniers & Co., 115 NLRB 1025, 37 LRRM 1481 (1956).
218 Steamship Trade Ass'n of Baltimore, 155 NLRB 232, 60 LRRM 1257 (1965).
219 135 NLRB 980, 49 LRRM 1606 (1962).
220 *Id.* at 982.
221 *Id.* at 983. *See also* NLRB v. Miller Brewing Co., 408 F2d 12, 70 LRRM 2907 (CA 9, 1969), holding that local bargaining as to uniquely local matters (plant rules) may be required of an employer member of a multi-employer bargaining unit.

CHAPTER 10

RECOGNITION WITHOUT AN ELECTION

I. HISTORY

The employer's duty under Section 8 (a) (5) of the Act "to bargain collectively with the representatives of his employees, subject to the provisions of section 9(a)," is not always conditioned upon Board certification under 9(c). The duty to recognize the representative "designated or selected for the purposes of collective bargaining by the majority of the employees in a unit appropriate for such purposes . . ." [1] may exist independently of NLRB election procedures. Although Section 9 (c) of the original Wagner Act authorized the Board to certify unions by using secret ballot elections or "any other suitable method," [2] an established principle under the Act has been that an employer's denial of recognition requires more justification than a lack of Board certification of the union seeking recognition. [3] If the employer acts without due care in ascertaining whether the demanding union has majority status,

---

[1] §9 (a).

[2] §9 (c) of the Wagner Act stated: "Whenever a question affecting commerce arises concerning the representation of employees, the Board may investigate such controversy and certify to the parties, in writing, the name or names of the representatives that have been designated or selected. In any such investigation, the Board shall provide for an appropriate hearing upon due notice, either in conjunction with a proceeding under section 10 or otherwise, and may take a secret ballot of employees, or utilize any other suitable method to ascertain such representatives."

[3] This interpretation of the statute is firmly settled in light of the Supreme Court's decision in *NLRB* v. *Gissel Packing Co.*, 395 US 575, 71 LRRM 2481 (1969). United Mine Workers v. Arkansas Oak Flooring Co., 351 US 62, 37 LRRM 2828 (1956); Franks Bros. v. NLRB, 321 US 702, 14 LRRM 591 (1944). The proposal in the Hartley Bill, H.R. 3020, 80th Cong., 1st Sess. 21, 81 (1947), to restrict the employer duty of recognition to unions certified by the Board was rejected in conference. H.R. Conf. Rep. No. 510, 80th Cong., 1st Sess. 41, June 3, 1947, 1 NLRB Legis. Hist. 545.

recognition of a union which is in fact a minority union is unlawful assistance forbidden by Section 8 (a) (2).[4]

There have been several phases of Board policy regarding the "card check," which usually has been the "other suitable method" alternative to the holding of an election.[5] A *card check* is a comparison of union authorization cards with the corresponding employees on the employer's payroll; it is conducted for the purpose of determining whether a majority of the employees in an appropriate unit has selected the union.[6] Within the narrow limits noted in this chapter, a union may obtain a bargaining order without an election provided it possesses a majority of valid authorization cards.

Until 1939, the Board relied extensively upon authorization cards both to determine violations of the former Section 8(5) duty to bargain and to make certifications. In *Cudahy Packing Co.*[7] it largely abandoned the "other suitable method" device and began relying almost exclusively upon elections in representation cases. In 1947, by statutory amendment, the election process became the only basis for certification.[8] Nevertheless, in those Section 8(a)(5) unfair labor practice proceedings where majority status was in issue, the card check continued to hold its prominence until the early 1950s. Although a near-total eclipse of the card check occurred during the decade of the fifties, there was a vigorous resurgence of such cases in the mid-sixties.[9] The latter cases relied primarily on a 1949 Board decision, *NLRB* v. *Joy Silk Mills, Inc.*[10] By the late sixties, however, the Board and various circuit courts

---

[4] International Ladies' Garment Workers v. NLRB, 366 US 731, 48 LRRM 2251 (1961). This chapter does not treat the "sweetheart" contract and its kindred, recognition deemed unlawful under Section 8 (a) (2) ; see Chapter 7 *supra*. Refusal of an employer to recognize a previously established bargaining agent is also treated elsewhere; see Chapter 11 *infra*.

[5] For a discussion of the early history, see Millis and Brown, FROM THE WAGNER ACT TO TAFT-HARTLEY, 133-134 (1950) ; Memorandum from Secretary of Labor Willard Wirtz to Senator Jacob Javits, in *Hearings on S. 256 Before the Subcommittee on Labor of the Senate Committee on Labor and Public Welfare*, 89th Cong., 1st Sess. 19, 20 (1965) ; 2 NLRB ANN. REP. 108 (1937) .

[6] Other devices, such as petition or polls, have also been used to establish majority authorization. In *San Clemente Publishing Corp.*, 167 NLRB 6, 65 LRRM 1726 (1967) , a bargaining order was based on an unofficial poll of employees, which had been agreed upon by the union and the employer, and was conducted by a third person.

[7] 13 NLRB 526, 4 LRRM 321 (1939) .

[8] Thus, since 1947, §9 no longer contains the alternative "any other suitable method."

[9] SHEPARD'S FEDERAL LABOR LAW CITATIONS has only 94 references to *Joy Silk* from 1950 to 1960, but 61 in 1966 alone.

[10] 185 F 2d 732, 27 LRRM 2012 (CA DC, 1950) , *modifying and enforcing* 85 NLRB 1263, 24 LRRM 1548 (1949) , *cert. denied*, 341 US 914, 27 LRRM 2633 (1951) .

of appeals had substantially modified the *Joy Silk* doctrine. And in 1969 the Supreme Court, in *NLRB* v. *Gissel Packing Co.*,[11] settled some of the major questions relating to the availability of a bargaining order in card-majority cases. This chapter will trace the development and modification of the *Joy Silk* doctrine and its eventual replacement by the rules which the Court approved in *Gissel.* However, *Gissel* did not represent a sudden change; rather, it represented Supreme Court ratification of a set of rules which had already been fashioned by the Board.[12]

II. FROM *JOY SILK* TO *GISSEL*

A. The *Joy Silk* Doctrine

The *Joy Silk* doctrine, as it had evolved up to the time of the Supreme Court's decision in *Gissel,* according to concepts which the Board was then using, consisted of the following elements: (1) union representation of a majority of the employees, (2) an appropriate unit, (3) a request for recognition by the union, (4) a denial of the request by the employer without a good-faith doubt as to the union's majority status, and (5) action by the employer to dissipate the union's majority. The burden of proving each of these elements was upon the General Counsel.[13] The court of appeals in *Joy Silk* declared:

> [A]n employer may refuse recognition to a union when motivated by a good-faith doubt as to that union's majority status. . . . When, however, such refusal is due to a desire to gain time and to take action to dissipate the union's majority, the refusal is no longer justifiable and constitutes a violation of the duty to bargain set forth in section 8 (a) (5) of the Act.[14]

---

11 395 US 575, 71 LRRM 2481 (1969).

12 Beeson, *Recognition Without Election,* LABOR LAW DEVELOPMENTS—1970, 16th Annual Institute on Labor Law, Southwestern Legal Foundation, 89 (1970); Sheinkman, *Recognition of Unions Through Authorization Cards,* 3 GA. L. REV. 319 (1969); Browne, *Obligation to Bargain on Basis of Card Majority,* 3 GA. L. REV. 334 (1969); Lewis, *Gissel Packing: Was the Supreme Court Right?,* 56 A.B.A.J. 877 (1970). Gordon, *Union Authorization Cards and the Duty to Bargain,* LABOR RELATIONS YEARBOOK—1968 128 (1969), also in 19 LAB. L.J. 201 (1968); Lesnick, *Establishment of Collective Bargaining Rights Without an Election,* 65 MICH. L. REV. 851 (1967). *See also* note, *NLRB v. Gissel Packing Co.: Bargaining Orders and Employee Free Choice,* 45 N.Y.U. L. REV. 318 (1970), *and* Christensen & Christensen, note 18 *infra.*

13 Jem Mfg., Inc., 156 NLRB 643, 61 LRRM 1074 (1966); Aaron Bros. Co., 158 NLRB 1077, 62 LRRM 1160 (1966); John P. Serpa, Inc., 155 NLRB 99, 60 LRRM 1235 (1965), *order set aside sub nom.,* Retail Clerks Local 1179 v. NLRB, 376 F 2d 186, 64 LRRM 2764 (CA 9, 1967).

14 185 F 2d 732, 741, 27 LRRM 2012 (CA DC, 1950). The Supreme Court recognized the doctrine in United Mine Workers v. Arkansas Oak Flooring Co., 351 US 62, 37 LRRM 2828 (1956). *See also* Franks Bros. v. NLRB, 321 US 702, 14 LRRM 591 (1944).

Conceding that an election would normally be the best way to ascertain the employees' desire for representation, the Board contended that if "an employer engages in unfair labor practices which make impossible the holding of a free election, the Board has no alternative but to look to signed authorization cards as the only available proof of the choice employees would have made absent the employer's unfair labor practices." [15] The Board reasoned in *Aaron Bros.* that the *Joy Silk* rule conformed to the object of utilizing the "most reliable means available" [16] to ascertain the employees' true desires with respect to the selection of a representative. "Where an employer has engaged in unfair labor practices, the results of a Board-conducted election are a less reliable indication of the true desires of employees than authorization cards, whereas, in a situation free of such unlawful interference, the converse is true." [17] Employer bad faith, sufficient to render an election unnecessary, "may also be demonstrated by a course of conduct which does not constitute an unfair labor practice." [18]

B. The *Gissel* Decision

Since *Gissel*, it would appear that "an employer's good faith

---

[15] Bryant Chucking Grinder Co., 160 NLRB 1526, 63 LRRM 1185 (1966). In Aaron Bros. Co., note 13 *supra*, at 1078, the Board defined the policy as follows: "While an employee's right to a Board election is not absolute, it has long been established Board policy that an employer may refuse to bargain and insist upon such an election as proof of a union's majority unless its refusal and insistence were not made with a good-faith doubt of the union's majority. An election by secret ballot is normally a more satisfactory means of determining employees' wishes, although authorization cards signed by a majority may also evidence their desires. Absent an affirmative showing of bad faith, an employer, presented with a majority card showing and a bargaining request, will not be held to have violated his bargaining obligation under the law simply because he refuses to rely upon cards, rather than an election, as the method for determining the union's majority." The Second Circuit, however, held that independent unfair labor practices committed by an employer did not establish that the employer lacked a good-faith doubt as to the union's majority, since the unfair practices were as consistent with a desire to prevent the union from achieving majority status as with a purpose of dissipating a majority already attained. NLRB v. River Togs, Inc., 382 F 2d 198, 65 LRRM 2987 (CA 2, 1967).
[16] 158 NLRB at 1079.
[17] *Ibid.*
[18] *Ibid.*, citing Snow & Sons, 134 NLRB 709, 49 LRRM 1228, *enforced*, 308 F 2d 687, 51 LRRM 2199 (CA 9, 1962); Dixon Ford Shoe Co., Inc., 150 NLRB 861, 58 LRRM 1160 (1965); Kellogg Mills, 147 NLRB 342, 56 LRRM 1223 (1964), *enforced*, 347 F 2d 219, 59 LRRM 2340 (CA 9, 1965); Greyhound Terminal, 137 NLRB 87, 50 LRRM 1088 (1962), *enforced*, 314 F 2d 43, 52 LRRM 2335 (CA 5, 1963); Jem Mfg., Inc., 156 NLRB 643, 61 LRRM 1074 (1966). *See* discussion of *Gissel*, *infra*, indicating that the Board may no longer follow *Snow & Sons*, although the Supreme Court expressed no view on that case, *also see* note 96 *infra*. *But see* Christensen & Christensen, *Gissel Packing and "Good Faith Doubt": The Gestalt of Required Recognition of Unions Under the NLRA*, 37 U. Chi. L. Rev. 411 (1970). *Cf.* Wilder Mfg. Co., 185 NLRB No. 76, 75 LRRM 1023 (1970).

doubt is largely irrelevant, and the key to the issuance of a bargaining order is the commission of serious unfair labor practices that interfere with the election process and tend to preclude the holding of a fair election." [19] This change in approach may have been more apparent than real, for the Supreme Court noted that during the oral argument "the Board announced that it had virtually abandoned the *Joy Silk* doctrine altogether." [20] Thus, even prior to the Court's opinion in *Gissel,* the Board was deciding cases by making *Joy Silk* findings of employer lack of good-faith doubt of majority status based upon evidence of the commission of substantial unfair labor practices; but, viewed in hindsight, it appears that the effect of these unfair labor practices may have been dispositive of the issue, not the lack of good faith.[21]

The major principles relating to the establishment of bargaining rights without an election may now be found in *Gissel.* The Court consolidated four cases for decision: *Gissel Packing Co., Heck's Inc., General Steel Products, Inc.,* and *Sinclair Company*—the first three from the Fourth Circuit and the last from the First Circuit. The facts in each of the Fourth Circuit cases were similar: The union had waged an organizational campaign and had obtained authorization cards from a majority of the employees in an appropriate bargaining unit. Then, on the basis of the cards, it demanded recognition, which was refused in each instance on the ground that authorization cards were inherently unreliable indicators of employee desires. The employers thereafter either embarked on or continued vigorous anti-union campaigns that gave rise to numerous unfair labor practice charges. In *Gissel* and *Heck's* the Board found unfair labor practices, including violations of Section 8(a)(5), and ordered recognition without an election having been held. In *General Steel,* an election had been held and was lost by the union; but the Board set aside the election,

---

19 395 US at 594. In Schrementi Bros., 179 NLRB No. 147, 72 **LRRM** 1481 (1969), decided after the Supreme Court's decision in *Gissel,* the Board noted that the employer's good-faith doubt in refusing to recognize a union is now "largely irrelevant." For a discussion of the open question of how irrelevant is "largely irrelevant," *see* Christensen & Christensen, note 18 *supra.*
20 395 US at 594.
21 *See* Board Member Jenkins' concurring opinion in *Aaron Brothers Co.,* 158 NLRB 1077, 62 LRRM 1160 (1966), in which he said: "In my view, the proper test (and the one in fact applied by my colleagues) in such cases is whether or not the employer's refusal to accept the cards as proof of majority, and to recognize and bargain with the union, was made in bad faith, with the General Counsel having the burden of showing affirmatively the existence of bad faith. . . . [T]he concept of 'good-faith doubt of majority,' . . . has become irrelevant to the decision of cases of this type. . . ."

because of the employer's preelection unfair labor practices, and issued an order requiring the employer to bargain. In each case the Board found that the union had valid authorization cards [22] for a majority of the employees in an appropriate unit and held that the employer's refusal to bargain "was motivated not by a 'good faith' doubt of the union's majority status, but by a desire to gain time to dissipate the status." [23] The Fourth Circuit reversed the Board's findings of refusal to bargain, but affirmed the findings relating to other unfair labor practices.[24]

The facts in *Sinclair* were similar to those in *Gissel* and *Heck's*, except that an additional issue was raised as to whether specific statements made by the employer, and found by the Board to be unfair labor practices, fell outside the protection of the First Amendment to the Constitution and Section 8(c) of the Act.[25] The First Circuit upheld both the Board's findings of unfair labor practices and the Board's order requiring the employer to recognize and bargain with the union.[26]

The Supreme Court divided the questions as follows: "[1] whether the duty to bargain can arise without a Board election under the Act; [2] whether union authorization cards, if obtained from a majority of employees without misrepresentation or coercion, are reliable enough generally to provide a valid, alternate route to majority status: [3] whether a bargaining order is an appropriate and authorized remedy where an employer rejects a card majority while at the same time committing unfair labor practices that tend to undermine the union's majority and make a fair election an unlikely possibility. . . ." [27] The Court answered each question in the affirmative.

In holding, first, that the Act allowed establishment of a bargaining obligation by means other than a Board election, the Court noted that it had consistently accepted this interpretation under

---

[22] In *General Steel*, the validity of the cards and the manner of their solicitation were contested. See discussion *infra*, notes 35-40 and accompanying text.

[23] 395 US at 583.

[24] 398 F 2d 336, 337, 339, 68 LRRM 2636, 2638 (1968).

[25] See Chapter 5 *supra* for a discussion of the Supreme Court's treatment of this issue in *Gissel*.

[26] 397 F 2d 157, 68 LRRM 2720 (1968).

[27] 395 US at 579. A fourth question, relating to free speech and §8 (c) of the Act, is treated in Chapter 5 *supra*.

both the Wagner Act and the Taft-Hartley Act.[28] It emphasized that Congress had rejected a House bill [29] in 1947 which would have required either a Board election or current recognition of a union as a precondition to the finding of a violation of Section 8(a)(5).[30] The Court also saw nothing in Section 9(c)(1)(B), which allows employers to petition for elections, that would suggest that Congress intended to relieve any employer of his bargaining obligation "where, without good faith, he engaged in unfair labor practices disruptive of the Board's election machinery." [31] The Court therefore concluded that an employer's duty to bargain was not restricted to unions holding Board certifications.

In response to the second question, the Court considered whether cards were a reliable indicia of majority status, but it answered this question only as to situations where, because of employer unfair labor practices, "a fair election probably could not have been held, or where an election that was held was in fact set aside." [32] The Court pointed out that it was not deciding whether a union could rely on authorization cards as a "freely interchangeable substitute for elections where there has been no election interference." [33]

Agreeing with the Board, the Court stated that "cards, though admittedly inferior to the election process, can adequately reflect employee sentiment when that process has been impeded. . . ." [34] The Court thus rejected the employer's arguments that the cards were unreliable because of group pressure, that reliance on cards made it impossible for the employees to express an informed choice, and that misrepresentation and coercion are too often employed in soliciting cards. The only case which raised any issue as to the validity of the cards or the manner in which they had been solicited was *General Steel,* where the union had used a single-purpose card, *i.e.,* a card that clearly and unambiguously designates the union as bargaining representative and does not state that it

---

[28] *Citing* NLRB v. Bradford Dyeing Ass'n, 310 US 318, 339-340, 6 LRRM 684 (1940); Franks Bros. Co. v. NLRB, 321 US 702, 14 LRRM 591 (1943); United Mine Workers v. Arkansas Oak Flooring Co., 351 US 62, 37 LRRM 2828 (1956).
[29] §§8 (a) (5) of H.R. 3020, 80th Cong., 1st Sess. (1947).
[30] *See* note 3 *supra.*
[31] 395 US at 600.
[32] *Id.* at 601, footnote 18.
[33] *Ibid.*
[34] 395 US at 603. *See* note 18 *supra.*

might also be used to obtain an election. In each of the four cases before the Court, the cards used were single-purpose cards. Holding that these cards were valid and approving the Board's findings as to the manner of their solicitation in *General Steel*, the Court approved the doctrine which the Board had promulgated in 1963 in *Cumberland Shoe Corp.*:[35]

> [I]f the card is unambiguous (*i.e.* states on its face that the signer authorizes the union to represent the employee for collective bargaining purposes and not to seek an election), it will be counted unless it is proved that the employee was told that the card was to be used *solely* for the purpose of obtaining an election.[36]

In thus resolving a conflict among the Circuits,[37] the Court pointed out that

> employees should be bound by the clear language of what they sign unless that language is deliberately and clearly cancelled by a union adherent with words calculated to direct the signer to disregard and forget the language above his signature.[38]

---

[35] 144 NLRB 1268, 54 LRRM 1233 (1963), *enforced*, 351 F 2d 917, 60 LRRM 2305 (CA 6, 1965).

[36] 395 US at 584.

[37] The Court reviewed the differing views of the Circuits as follows: ". . . even where the cards are unambiguous on their face, both the Second Circuit . . . (NLRB v. S. E. Nichols Co., 380 F 2d 438, 65 LRRM 2655 (CA 2, 1967) and the Fifth Circuit (Engineers & Fabricators, Inc. v. NLRB, 376 F 2d 482, 64 LRRM 2849 (CA 5, 1967)) have joined the Fourth Circuit below in rejecting the Board's rule that the cards will be counted unless the solicitor's statements amounted under the circumstances to an assurance that the cards would be used only for an election. And even those circuits which have adopted the Board's approach have criticized the Board for tending too often to apply the *Cumberland* rule too mechanically, declining occasionally to uphold the Board's application of its own rule in a given case. See, *e.g.*, NLRB v. Southbridge Sheet Metal Works, Inc., 380 F 2d 851, 65 LRRM 2916 (CA 1, 1967); NLRB v. Sandy's Stores, Inc., 398 F 2d 268, 68 LRRM 2800 (CA 1, 1968); NLRB v. Swan Super Cleaners, Inc., 384 F 2d 609, 66 LRRM 2385 (CA 6, 1967); NLRB v. Dan Howard Mfg. Co., 390 F 2d 304, 67 LRRM 2278 (CA 7, 1968); Furrs, Inc. v. NLRB, 381 F 2d 562, 64 LRRM 2422 (CA 10, 1967); UAW v. NLRB, 392 F 2d 801, 66 LRRM 2548 (CA DC, 1967). Among those who reject the *Cumberland* rule, the Fifth Circuit agrees with the Second Circuit (see S. E. Nichols, *supra*), that a card will be vitiated if an employee was left with the impression that he would be able to resolve any lingering doubts and make a final decision in an election, and further requires that the Board probe the subjective intent of each signer, an inquiry expressly avoided by *Cumberland*. See NLRB v. Southland Paint Co., 394 F 2d 717, 728, 730, 68 LRRM 2169 (CA 5, 1968); Engineers & Fabricators, Inc. v. NLRB, *supra*. Where the cards are ambiguous on their face, the Fifth Circuit, joined by the Eighth Circuit (see, *e.g.*, NLRB v. Peterson Bros., 342 F 2d 221, 58 LRRM 2570 (CA 5, 1965), and Bauer Welding & Metal Fabricators, Inc. v. NLRB, 358 F 2d 766, 62 LRRM 2022 (CA 8, 1966), departs still further from the Board rule. And there is a conflict among those courts which otherwise follow the Board as to single-purpose cards (compare NLRB v. Lenz Co., 396 F 2d 905, 908, 68 LRRM 2577 (CA 6, 1968), with NLRB v. C. J. Glasgow Co., 356 F 2d 476, 478, 61 LRRM 2406 (CA 7, 1966))." 395 US at 604-605. (The Court's citations have been conformed to the style of this volume.)

[38] 395 US at 606.

The Court saw nothing inconsistent in an employee's being handed a card which says the signer authorizes the union to represent him, while being told orally that the card would probably be used first to get an election, because elections would continue to be held in the vast majority of cases and Board rules require signatures from at least 30 percent of the employees before the Board will conduct an election on the petition of a union.[39]

The Court also acknowledged the inherent unreliability of any probing of an employee's subjective motivation in signing a card. Single-purpose cards would be invalidated not for what an employee allegedly thought but only for what he was actually told, provided that what he was told amounted to a misrepresentation of the card's purpose. The Court, however, avoided expressing any opinion as to the validity of "ambiguous, dual-purpose cards." [40]

The Court answered the third question, whether a bargaining order is an appropriate and authorized remedy in card-majority cases, by differentiating as to the seriousness of the unfair labor practices in various types of situations. It specifically approved the Board's use of the bargaining order where the employer's practices "have the tendency to undermine majority strength and impede the election process." [41]

C. Elements of the Bargaining Obligation in the Absence of an Election

Gissel changed the rhetoric used to describe an employer's bargaining obligation in the absence of an NLRB election, but the elements needed to establish that obligation appear to differ little from pre-*Gissel* Board practice. This is apparent if one looks only at the employer's conduct rather than at the Board's finding of subjective bad faith as to an employer's alleged doubt of union majority. The form of the authorization card and the means of its solicitation are also essential elements of inquiry in these types of cases.

1. Majority Representation. The initial point of inquiry in each of these cases is whether a majority of the employees has

---

39 See Chapters 8 *supra* and 30 *infra*.
40 395 US at 609. *See* note 49 *infra*.
41 *Id.* at 614. *See:* "Applying the *Gissel* test," *infra*, this Chapter.

signed union authorization cards as of the date of the employer's alleged refusal to bargain. This may be when the employer receives the demand [42] or when the employer sends his reply.[43] The Board accords validity to majority choice by cards even if they are obtained during the one-year period in which the statute interdicts a second election; a union that met the requirements of the *Joy Silk* doctrine was not precluded from insisting on recognition during that period.[44]

a. Form of designation. The card may be a regular union membership card,[45] an application for membership,[46] an authorization for check-off of union dues,[47] or simply a card that explicitly designates the union as the signer's bargaining representative.[48] Dual-purpose cards, carrying both a designation of the union as the signer's exclusive bargaining representative and an expression of desire for an election, are honored by the Board, but without agreement from many of the appellate courts.[49]

b. Name of union. Union designation may be indicated in the most general terms, without identification of a particular local or

---

[42] Allegheny Pepsi-Cola Bottling Co. v. NLRB, 312 F 2d 529, 52 LRRM 2019 (CA 3, 1962).

[43] NLRB v. Burton-Dixie Corp., 210 F 2d 199, 33 LRRM 2483 (CA 10, 1954).

[44] Conren, Inc., 156 NLRB 592, 61 LRRM 1090 (1966), *enforced*, 368 F 2d 173, 63 LRRM 2273 (CA 7, 1966), *cert. denied*, 386 US 974, 64 LRRM 2640 (1967). The Board held that neither the legislative history of the 12-month rule in §9(c)(3), "nor its plain terms, manifest any congressional purpose to preclude a union from obtaining recognition either without an election, or within a year after an election, or within a year after an election which it did not win, if it in fact acquires majority status in an appropriate unit." 156 NLRB at 599.

[45] NLRB v. Federbrush Co., 121 F 2d 954, 8 LRRM 531 (CA 2, 1941).

[46] NLRB v. Dahlstrom Metallic Door Co., 112 F 2d 756, 6 LRRM 746 (CA 2, 1940); NLRB v. Valley Broadcasting Co., 189 F 2d 582, 28 LRRM 2148 (CA 6, 1951).

[47] Lebanon Steel Foundry v. NLRB, 130 F 2d 404, 10 LRRM 760 (CA DC, 1942), *cert. denied*, 317 US 659, 11 LRRM 839 (1942).

[48] NLRB v. Stow Mfg. Co., 217 F 2d 900, 35 LRRM 2210 (CA 2, 1954), *cert. denied*, 348 US 964, 35 LRRM 2612 (1955).

[49] *See* notes 37 and 40 *supra*, and accompanying text; also: Brandenburg Telephone Co., 164 NLRB 825, 65 LRRM 1183 (1967); Lenz Co., 153 NLRB 1399, 59 LRRM 1638 (1965); S.N.C. Mfg. Co., 147 NLRB 809, 56 LRRM 1313 (1964), *enforced*, 352 F 2d 361, 59 LRRM 2232 (CA DC, 1965), *cert. denied*, 382 US 902, 60 LRRM 2353 (1965). *Contra:* Davco Corp. v. NLRB, 382 F 2d 577, 65 LRRM 3093 (CA 6, 1967); NLRB v. S. E. Nichols Co., 380 F 2d 438, 65 LRRM 2655 (CA 2, 1967); NLRB v. Freeport Marble & Tile Co., 367 F 2d 371, 63 LRRM 2289 (CA 1, 1966); NLRB v. Peterson Bros., 342 F 2d 221, 58 LRRM 2570 (CA 5, 1965); NLRB v. Swan Super Cleaners, 384 F 2d 609, 66 LRRM 2385 (CA 6, 1967). However, in a case decided after the Supreme Court's decision in *Gissel*, the Board rejected as ambiguous certain dual-purpose cards where the top half of the card stated that its purpose was to obtain an election, and the bottom half contained a reference to the signer being invited to join the union "should the union be elected" to represent him. John S. Barnes Corp., 180 NLRB No. 139, 73 LRRM 1215 (1970).

even an international. The designation "AFL-CIO" has been held sufficient.[50]

c. Status of solicitor. Any person, so long as he is not a supervisor or other representative of management, may solicit another to sign an organization card. A supervisor-solicited card is invalid and will not be counted toward the union majority.[51] However, the Board has distinguished, as less than solicitation, the mere "passing along" of a card by a supervisor.[52]

d. Time of execution. To be counted in determining a union's majority status, the card must have been executed during the union's current organizing campaign.[53]

e. Authentication. To prove the union's majority status, the employees who have executed cards are generally called as witnesses to identify their signatures. But other competent evidence establishing authenticity also may be used; for example, the testimony of a witness who saw the card executed.[54] The General Counsel has the burden of proving authenticity,[55] and if he fails, the cards will be rejected.[56]

f. Affirmative defenses. Various affirmative defenses are available to the employer. He may take issue with the alleged majority status on the ground that the employees who signed the cards have since revoked the authority; he may concede the fact of author-

---

[50] Southbridge Sheet Metal Works, Inc., 158 NLRB 819, 62 LRRM 1163 (1966), *enforced,* 380 F 2d 851, 65 LRRM 2916 (CA 1, 1967). But if an employee executes similar cards for rival unions, neither card will be counted. International Metal Products Co., 104 NLRB 1076, 32 LRRM 1194 (1953). See Chapter 7 *infra* for a discussion of the *Midwest Piping* doctrine and the requirement of employer neutrality between rival unions.

[51] Leas & McVitty, Inc., 155 NLRB 389, 60 LRRM 1333 (1965); Insular Chemical Corp., 128 NLRB 93, 46 LRRM 1268 (1960); Flint River Mills, Inc., 107 NLRB 472, 33 LRRM 1177 (1953).

[52] Engineers & Fabricators, Inc., 156 NLRB 919, 61 LRRM 1156 (1966), *enforcement denied in part,* 376 F 2d 472, 64 LRRM 2849 (CA 5, 1967).

[53] Grand Union Co., 122 NLRB 589, 43 LRRM 1165 (1958), *enforced,* 279 F 2d 83, 46 LRRM 2492 (CA 2, 1960). In Greenfield Components Corp. v. NLRB, 317 F 2d 85, 53 LRRM 2145 (CA 1, 1963), cards signed nine months before the demand was made were counted, there having been no hiatus in the union's organizational effort. Over *two years* was not too long where there was a delay in proceeding upon a petition for election. Northern Trust Co., 69 NLRB 652, 18 LRRM 1252 (1946).

[54] Colson Corp., 148 NLRB 827, 57 LRRM 1078 (1964), *enforced,* 347 F 2d 128, 59 LRRM 2513 (CA 8, 1965), *cert. denied* 382 US 904, 60 LRRM 2353 (1965); NLRB v. Economy Food Center Inc., 333 F 2d 468, 56 LRRM 2263 (CA 7, 1964).

[55] Southern Cotton Oil Crude Mill, 144 NLRB 959, 54 LRRM 1161 (1963).

[56] Franke's Inc., 142 NLRB 551, 53 LRRM 1086 (1963); Dixie Cup, Div. of American Can Co., 157 NLRB 167, 61 LRRM 1329 (1966); *see also* cases cited in note 13 *supra.*

ization in the first place but show that the employees had been lured by misrepresentation or driven by coercion; he may establish that signatures were forged.

An authorization card revoked prior to the demand for recognition will not be counted [57] unless the revocation is the product of the employer's unfair labor practice.[58]

The Board in 1961, in *Englewood Lumber Co.*,[59] advanced the doctrine that if employees were solicited with the plea that their signatures were needed so that the Board might hold a secret-ballot election, their cards would not be counted. This principle was applied also to cards carrying on their face, in bold type, "I WANT AN NLRB ELECTION," where the employees had been told that the cards were not binding.[60] Then in 1963 the Board reversed itself. In *Cumberland Shoe Corp.*[61] it held that it would thenceforth count cards which clearly designated the union as bargaining representative even though procured through representations that they were to be used to obtain an election. Thus, cards were counted that bore on their face in bold type, "I WANT AN ELECTION NOW." [62] Under the new ruling, the Board refused to count a card if it was obtained by the solictor's blandishment that the card's *only* purpose is to obtain an

---

[57] TMT Trailer Ferry, Inc., 152 NLRB 1495, 59 LRRM 1353 (1965); Reilly Tar & Chemical Corp. v. NLRB, 352 F 2d 913, 60 LRRM 2437 (CA 7, 1965).

[58] Quality Markets, Inc., 160 NLRB 44, 62 LRRM 1582 (1966); Abrasive Salvage Co., 127 NLRB 381, 46 LRRM 1033 (1960).

[59] 130 NLRB 394, 47 LRRM 1304 (1961).

[60] Morris & Associates, Inc., 138 NLRB 1160, 51 LRRM 1183 (1962).

[61] 144 NLRB 1268, 54 LRRM 1233 (1963), *enforced*, 351 F 2d 917, 60 LRRM 2305 (CA 6, 1965). *See* note 35 *supra* and accompanying text.

[62] S.N.C. Mfg. Co., 147 NLRB 809, 56 LRRM 1313 (1964), *enforced*, 352 F 2d 361, 59 LRRM 2232 (CA DC, 1965), *cert. denied*, 382 US 902, 60 LRRM 2353 (1965). In NLRB v. Freeport Marble & Tile Co., 367 F 2d 371, 63 LRRM 2289 (CA 1, 1966), enforcement was denied, the First Circuit holding that applications for membership conditioned upon the holding of an election should not have been counted, that cards bearing the legend "no obligation if no election" were applications for membership so conditioned. *See also* NLRB v. Dan Howard Mfg. Co., 390 F 2d 304, 67 LRRM 2278 (CA 7, 1968); NLRB v. Swan Super Cleaners, 384 F 2d 609, 66 LRRM 2386 (CA 6, 1967); Dayco Corp. v. NLRB, 382 F 2d 577, 65 LRRM 3093 (CA 6, 1967).

election.[63] Similarly, cards stating "For Election Only" will not be counted.[64] As previously noted, the Supreme Court expressly approved the *Cumberland* rule in the *Gissel* opinion.[65]

The question to be determined is not what the employee believed when he signed the card but what he was told, orally or in writing. One appellate court has noted its "dim view of post-event testimony of subjective understanding;" [66] and the Supreme Court accepted the observation that employees are likely "many months after a card drive . . . to give testimony damaging to the union. . . ." [67] Accordingly, employees may have believed that the cards were to be used only to obtain an election, but the Board still will count such cards if the employees were not *solicited* on this basis.[68] A misrepresentation will be disregarded when it is clear that the employee did not rely upon it in executing the

---

[63] Levi Strauss & Co., 172 NLRB No. 57, 68 LRRM 1338 (1968); Winn-Dixie Stores, Inc., 166 NLRB 227, 65 LRRM 1637 (1967); American Cable Systems, 161 NLRB 332, 63 LRRM 1296 (1966), *enforced in part*, 414 F 2d 661, 71 LRRM 2979 (CA 5, 1969), *affirming* 179 NLRB No. 149, 72 LRRM 1524 (1969), *remanding* 427 F 2d 446, 73 LRRM 2913 (CA 5, 1970), *see* note 106 *infra;* Happach v. NLRB, 353 F 2d 629, 60 LRRM 2489 (CA 7, 1965); Aero Corp., 149 NLRB 1283, 57 LRRM 1483 (1964), *enforced*, 363 F 2d 902, 62 LRRM 2361 (CA DC), *cert. denied*, 385 US 973, 63 LRRM 2527 (1966). *Contra:* NLRB v. S. E. Nichols Co., 380 F 2d 438, 65 LRRM 2655 (CA 2, 1967), *denying enforcement in part to* 156 NLRB 1201, 61 LRRM 1234 (1966); Engineers & Fabricators, Inc. v. NLRB, 376 F 2d 482, 64 LRRM 2849 (CA 5, 1967). For cases refusing to follow the *Cumberland* "sole" or "only" purpose rule, *see* note 37 *supra* and cases cited therein.
[64] Bannon Mills, Inc., 146 NLRB 611, 55 LRRM 1370 (1964). But authorizations of employees who concede in response to leading questions, on cross-examinations, that they were told the cards were to be used only for an election are not thereby invalidated. American Cable Systems, *supra*, note 63; General Steel Products, Inc., 157 NLRB 636, 61 LRRM 1417 (1966). *See* discussion of the Supreme Court's review of *General Steel* in the *Gissel* case, notes 35-40 *supra*. According to *Quarterly Report on Case Developments*, NLRB Release No. R-1007, issued by the General Counsel, April 26, 1965, a card will not be counted if it was presented with a handbill describing the card as "only your request" for an election.
[65] NLRB v. Gissel Packing Co., 395 US 575, 71 LRRM 2481 (1969). The Court also specifically approved the Board's own warnings to trial examiners contained in *Levi Strauss*, note 63 *supra*, "that in hearing testimony concerning a card challenge, trial examiners should not neglect their obligation to ensure employee free choice by a too easy mechanical application of the *Cumberland* rule." 395 US at 607.
[66] NLRB v. Freeport Marble and Tile Co., 367 F 2d 371 n. 2, 63 LRRM 2289 (CA 1, 1966). *Cf.* Colson Corp. v. NLRB, 347 F 2d 128, 59 LRRM 2512 (CA 8, 1965), *cert. denied*, 382 US 904, 60 LRRM 2353 (1965); NLRB v. Winn-Dixie Stores, Inc., 341 F 2d 750, 754, 58 LRRM 2475, (CA 6, 1965), *cert. denied*, 382 US 830, 60 LRRM 2234 (1965); Joy Silk Mills v. NLRB, 185 F 2d 732, 27 LRRM 2012 (CA DC, 1950), *cert. denied*, 341 US 914, 27 LRRM 2633 (1951).
[67] 395 US at 608. *Followed in* Marie Phillips, Inc., 178 NLRB No. 53, 72 LRRM 1103 (1969).
[68] Henry I. Siegel, Inc., 165 NLRB 493, 65 LRRM 1505 (1967); Peterson Bros., 144 NLRB 679, 54 LRRM 1113 (1963), *enforced in part*, 342 F 2d 221, 58 LRRM 2570 (CA 5, 1965).

authorization.[69] And if the card unequivocally and unconditionally gives the union authority, then misrepresentation, to invalidate the card, must have indicated that the card would be used only for a different, more limited, purpose than that stated on the card.[70]

Examples of coercion invalidating cards include threats that the union would make it hard for an employee and force her to quit,[71] or that once the union organized the establishment, those who did not sign would lose their jobs.[72]

Cards of employees who testify that their signatures were forged will not be counted.[73]

2. Form of Request and Appropriate Unit. A valid bargaining request, or "demand," must be made before an employer is obligated to recognize the requesting union. It is not necessary that the union state explicitly that it has majority status.[74] But, to be effective, the request must be made when the union in fact possesses signed authorizations from a majority of the employees in an appropriate unit,[75] unless the Board finds the initial demand to have been a continuing one and the deficiency is subsequently overcome by additional cards making up a majority.[76] If the re-

---

69 Engineers and Fabricators, Inc., 156 NLRB 919, 61 LRRM 1156 (1966), *enforcement denied in part*, 376 F 2d 482, 64 LRRM 2849 (CA 5, 1967).

70 NLRB v. Gissel Packing Co., note 65 *supra*. "This must be done on the basis of what the employees were told, not on the basis of their subjective state of mind when they signed the cards." Aero Corp., 149 NLRB 1283, 1290, 57 LRRM 1483 (1964); *cf.* NLRB v. Sehon Stevenson Co., 386 F 2d 551, 66 LRRM 2603 (1967), where the court enforced an NLRB bargaining order where the employer's *own* investigation confirmed the union's claim of majority status.

71 Dixie Cup, Div. of American Can Co., 157 NLRB 167, 61 LRRM 1329 (1966); S. E. Nichols Co., 380 F 2d 438, 65 LRRM 2655 (CA 2, 1967).

72 Heck's Inc., 156 NLRB 760, 61 LRRM 1128 (1966), *enforced in part*, 386 F 2d 317, 66 LRRM 2495, *and see* 398 F 2d 337, 68 LRRM 2638 (1968), *reversed and remanded sub. nom.*, NLRB v. Gissel Packing Co., 395 US 575, 71 LRRM 2481 (1969); I. Posner, Inc., 133 NLRB 1573, 49 LRRM 1062 (1961). NLRB v. James Thompson & Co., 208 F 2d 743, 33 LRRM 2205 (CA 2, 1953). The burden of proof is on the party asserting coercion. Texas Electric Cooperative, Inc., 160 NLRB 440, 62 LRRM 1631 (1966).

73 Imco Container Co., 148 NLRB 312, 56 LRRM 1497 (1964), *enforcement denied*, 346 F 2d 178, 59 LRRM 2255 (CA 4, 1965).

74 Lincoln Mfg. Co., 160 NLRB No. 146, 63 LRRM 1245 (1966), *enforced*, 382 F 2d 411, 65 LRRM 2913 (CA 7, 1967).

75 Decision, Inc., 166 NLRB 464, 65 LRRM 1660 (1967).

76 Ed's Foodland of Springfield, Inc., 159 NLRB 1256, 62 LRRM 1465 (1966). *But see* Filler Products v. NLRB, 376 F 2d 369, 65 LRRM 2029 (CA 4, 1967), denying enforcement of a bargaining order based on authorization cards when the employer had refused to read the letter containing the request and claim of majority status. The court reasoned that the Board should have taken into account its own election regulations, which seem to require a request as a prerequisite to obtaining an election. The evidence also showed that the union never intended to

quest is not couched in terms sufficiently clear, under all the circumstances, to apprise the employer of the contemplated unit, it may be insufficient.[77]

A request is superfluous in a case where the bargaining order is designed to remedy unfair labor practices other than refusal to bargain.[78] The Board has granted such a remedy to unions having majority status, judged by authorization cards, even though no request for recognition had been made, when a bargaining order seemed appropriate to effectuate the policies of the Act. According to the Board, in such cases the employer, whether or not guilty of a refusal to bargain, has by commission of unfair labor practices reduced the bargaining representative from majority to minority status, thereby rendering ineffectual the Board's processes under Section 9.[79]

The fact that the union has filed a petition for election concurrently with its request for recognition does not absolve the employer of the duty to bargain.[80]

---

rely on a card check. See §9(c)(1)(A)(i): "their employer *declines* to recognize their representative. . . ." (Emphasis added)

[77] National Can Co. v. NLRB, 374 F 2d 796, 64 LRRM 2607 (CA 7, 1967); Bryant Chucking Grinder Co., *infra*, note 78. But the Board has held sufficient a claim to represent "the employees." Monahan Ford Corp., 157 NLRB 1034, 1046, 61 LRRM 1483 (1966). *See* notes 85-87 *infra*.

[78] *See* NLRB v. Gissell Packing Co., note 22 *supra* and accompanying text. Contrast the Second Circuit's refusal to enforce a bargaining order in the absence of a request, NLRB v. Flomatic Corp., 347 F 2d 74, 59 LRRM 2535 (CA 2, 1965), with its readiness to grant enforcement when there was a request, Irving Air Chute Co. v. NLRB, 350 F 2d 176, 59 LRRM 3052 (CA 2, 1965). In the latter case, *Flomatic* was distinguished on the ground that the employer's unlawful acts were "only minimal" and there was no demand and refusal. *See* note 110 *infra* and discussion under part III of this chapter. The D. C. Circuit rejected the reasoning of the Second Circuit in *Flomatic*, emphasizing that determining the extent of the employer's interference is within the Board's expertise. Steelworkers v. NLRB (Northwest Engineering Co.), 376 F 2d 770, 64 LRRM 2650, *cert. denied*, 389 US 932, 66 LRRM 2444 (1967). *See also* NLRB v. Gotham Shoe Mfg. Co., 359 F 2d 684, 61 LRRM 2177 (CA 2, 1966).

[79] Steelworkers v. NLRB (Northwest Engineering Co.), note 78 *supra*; Henry I. Siegel, Inc., 165 NLRB 493, 65 LRRM 1505 (1967); Bryant Chucking Grinder Co., 160 NLRB 1526, 63 LRRM 1185 (1966); American Sanitary Products Co. v. NLRB, 382 F 2d 53, 65 LRRM 3122 (CA 10, 1967). In Wausau Steel Corp. v. NLRB, 377 F 2d 369, 65 LRRM 2001 (CA 7, 1967), the court disapproved the Board finding of refusal to bargain but nonetheless enforced the bargaining order because of other violations that destroyed the union's majority. *But see* NLRB v. Li'l General Stores, Inc., 422 F 2d 571, 73 LRRM 2522 (CA 5, 1970) (the Fifth Circuit refused to enforce a bargaining order where there were unfair labor practices described as "extensive if not bordering on the flagrant" because the union had neither claimed a majority nor demanded recognition, and there was no finding that the employer was aware of the union's majority when the petition for an election was filed).

[80] Mink-Dayton, Inc., 166 NLRB 604, 65 LRRM 1642 (1967); Tonkin Corp. of Calif., 165 NLRB 607, 65 LRRM 1521 (1967). *Cf.* Filler Products Co. v. NLRB, 376 F 2d 369, 65 LRRM 2029 (CA 4, 1967).

Evidently the request may be made to almost any upper-level management representative. According to the Board, a management representative's lack of authority to discuss the matter does not relieve the employer of his duty to extend recognition; nor is it a satisfactory response to reply that the matter "is in the hands of an attorney." [81] If the union agent has made an adequate request, he is not required to repeat that request to the employer's attorney. [82]

3. Employer misconduct. Under the *Joy Silk* rule, if the union validly represented a majority in an appropriate unit and a proper request had been made, the employer could not deny recognition unless he had a good-faith doubt as to the union's majority status. [83] If the employer had such a doubt, no duty to bargain would arise. [84] Under the *Gissel* test, however, good faith is largely irrelevant, for the bargaining duty does not arise unless the employer has engaged in unfair labor practices that tend to impede the election process.

Before the meaning of this new test is discussed, significant cases decided under the *Joy Silk* influence will be reviewed to illustrate the development of the law and to provide a framework of factual situations to which the *Joy Silk* rules were originally applied, for these situations might as easily or more easily be accommodated to the *Gissel* rules.

a. The Joy Silk cases. Although a good-faith doubt may have stemmed from uncertainty about the unit—doubt either as to what the union was proposing or as to what was appropriate [85]—unless such uncertainty was relevant to the union's majority status it did not provide a legal justification for insistence upon an election. [86] If the unit requested by the union was found appropriate,

---

81 S. E. Nichols Co., 61 LRRM 1234, 156 NLRB 1201 (1966), *enforcement denied on other grounds,* 380 F 2d 438, 65 LRRM 2655 (CA 2, 1967).
82 *Ibid.*
83 Joy Silk Mills, Inc., *supra,* note 10; Artcraft Hosiery Co., 78 NLRB 333, 22 LRRM 1212 (1948).
84 NLRB v. Bedford-Nugent Corp., 317 F 2d 861, 53 LRRM 2371 (CA 7, 1963); NLRB v. Remington Rand, Inc., 94 F 2d 862, 1-A LRRM 585 (CA 2, 1938), *cert. denied,* 304 US 576, 2 LRRM 623 (1938).
85 NLRB v. Morris Novelty Co., 378 F 2d 1000, 65 LRRM 2577 (CA 8, 1967); Clermont's, Inc., 154 NLRB 1397, 60 LRRM 1141 (1965).
86 NLRB v. Ralph Printing & Lithographing Co., 379 F 2d 687, 65 LRRM 2800 (CA 8, 1967). Good-faith belief that another unit is appropriate, if erroneous, is irrelevant. Benson Wholesale Co., Inc., 164 NLRB 536, 65 LRRM 1278 (1967).

the employer had to bargain, even though he may have preferred a different unit. An employer who refused to bargain solely because of disagreement as to the appropriate unit acted "at its peril and in violation of the Act." [87]

Want of a good-faith doubt as to the union's majority—incumbent upon the General Counsel to prove [88]—was established in various ways. The proof most frequently invoked consisted of evidence of unfair labor practices, which was found to indicate a desire to gain time to undermine the union or a rejection of the principle of collective bargaining.[89] But "[w]hether an employer is acting in good faith or bad faith in questioning the union's majority is a determination which . . . must be made in the light of all the relevant facts of the case, including any unlawful conduct of the employer, the sequence of events, and the time lapse between the refusal and the unlawful conduct." [90] But commission of unfair labor practices which were too insubstantial to warrant an inference of bad faith, or which were not inconsistent with a good-faith doubt of majority status, would not support an order to bargain without an election.[91]

The General Counsel, in seeking to sustain his burden, employed evidence of employer unfair labor practices to show not only that they reduced the union's majority but that they were intended to do so, thus demonstrating the employer's awareness of the majority status of the union and negating a good-faith belief that the cards were inadequate to establish majority status. Such

---

[87] Tom Thumb Stores, Inc., 123 NLRB 833, 835, 44 LRRM 1005 (1959). *See also* Southland Paint Co., 156 NLRB 22, 61 LRRM 1004 (1965) *and* Oklahoma Sheraton Corp., 156 NLRB 681, 61 LRRM 1115 (1965).

[88] Aaron Bros., 158 NLRB 1077, 62 LRRM 1160 (1966). *See* notes 13 and 15 *supra.*

[89] Joy Silk Mills, Inc., *supra,* note 10; Benson Wholesale Co., Inc., 164 NLRB 536, 65 LRRM 1278 (1967) ; Taitel & Son, 119 NLRB 910, 41 LRRM 1230 (1957).

[90] Aaron Bros., *supra* note 88 at 1079; Converters Gravure Service, Inc., 164 NLRB 397, 65 LRRM 1098 (1967). In *NLRB* v. *River Togs, Inc.,* 382 F 2d 198, 65 LRRM 2987 (CA 2, 1967) , the Second Circuit denied enforcement of a bargaining order, pointing out that when the evidence shows a good-faith doubt, the antiunion activities of an employer—including his unfair labor practices—are " 'as consistent with a desire to prevent the acquisition of a majority status as with a purpose to destroy an existing majority,' " quoting Lesnick, *Establishment of Bargaining Rights Without an NLRB Election,* 65 MICH. L. REV. 851, 855, (1967) . *Accord,* Lane Drug Co., Div. A. C. Israel Commodity Corp. v. NLRB, 391 F 2d 812, 67 LRRM 2873 (CA 6, 1968) . *But see* Furr's, Inc. v. NLRB, 381 F 2d 562, 64 LRRM 2422 (CA 10, 1967) , *cert. denied,* 389 US 840, 66 LRRM 2307 (1967) , enforcing a bargaining order and sustaining a finding of bad faith, wherein the court accepted violation of §8 (a) (1) as strong evidence of lack of good-faith doubt.

[91] Hammond & Irving, Inc., 154 NLRB 1071, 60 LRRM 1073 (1965) ; Hercules Packing Corp., 163 NLRB 264, 64 LRRM 1331, *affirmed,* 386 F 2d 790, 66 LRRM 2751 (CA 2, 1967) . *See* Gordon, note 12 *supra* at 131.

proof would entail a showing of the causal relationship between the unfair practice and the loss of a majority of adherents.[92]

Whether employer unfair labor practices would support a refusal-to-bargain finding could not depend upon a mechanical analysis. For example, where there was evidence supporting the employer's doubt of majority status, the unlawful threatening of "a handful of employees in a unit of more than 250" was not sufficient basis to infer a deliberate purpose to gain time to dissipate the majority.[93] What effect unfair labor practices have upon an employer's defense of good faith has often depended on the reviewing court. The Board has been reversed in many of its findings of refusal to bargain based on card majorities.[94]

Absence of a good-faith doubt as to the union's majority status, *i.e.*, the *bad faith* required for a bargaining order, on occasion was demonstrated by employer conduct that in itself was not an unfair labor practice.[95] Examples of such conduct were (1) repudiating a previously agreed-upon card check,[96] (2) withdrawing from negotiations after a card check conducted by a third party had estab-

[92] NLRB v. Clegg, 304 F 2d 168, 50 LRRM 2521 (CA 8, 1962); Manley Transfer Co., 164 NLRB 174, 65 LRRM 1194 (1967). When an employer had engaged in conduct that warranted setting aside two successive elections, the Board's bargaining order was enforced. Borden Cabinet Corp. v. NLRB, 375 F 2d 891, 64 LRRM 2853 (CA 7, 1967). Sponsorship of a rival labor organization by the employer after he had appeared to accord recognition to the union chosen by the majority warranted issuance of a bargaining order. Sturgeon Electric Co., 166 NLRB 210, 65 LRRM 1530 (1967).
[93] Cameo Lingerie, Inc., 148 NLRB 535, 538, 57 LRRM 1044 (1964). *See also* NLRB v. River Togs, Inc., *supra*, note 90. In Hammond & Irving, Inc., 154 NLRB 1071, 1073, 60 LRRM 1073 (1965), the Board noted that "not every act of misconduct necessarily vitiates the respondent's good faith. For, there are some situations in which the violations of the Act are not truly inconsistent with a good-faith doubt that the union represents a majority of the employees. Whether the conduct involved reflects on the good faith of the employer requires an evaluation of the facts of each case."
[94] *E.g.*, NLRB v. River Togs, Inc., note 90 *supra*; Engineers & Fabricators, Inc., *supra*, note 69; Peoples Service Drug Stores, Inc. v. NLRB, 375 F 2d 551, 64 LRRM 2823 (CA 6, 1966); Indiana Rayon Corp. v. NLRB, 355 F 2d 535, 61 LRRM 2311 (CA 7, 1966).
[95] *See* note 18 *supra*.
[96] Snow & Sons, 134 NLRB 709, 49 LRRM 1228, *enforced*, 308 F 2d 687, 51 LRRM 2199 (CA 9, 1962). According to one commentator, later decisions, particularly Strydel, Inc., 156 NLRB 1185, 61 LRRM 1230 (1966), *infra*, note 100, and Furr's Inc., 157 NLRB 387, 61 LRRM 1388 (1966), indicated that the Board was confining *Snow* to its particular facts. Lesnick, note 90 *supra*, at 852-854. *But cf.* Wilder Mfg. Co., 185 NLRB No. 76, 75 LRRM 1023 (1970), where the Board ordered an employer to bargain even though he had not committed other unfair labor practices. The employer had no basis for questioning the union's majority, which was evidenced not only by signed cards but also by the employees' striking and picketing. It was deemed significant that the employer showed no willingness to resolve the question of majority status through an election, and the Board chose to base its order on this narrow ground.

lished the union's majority,[97] (3) insisting upon an election after having participated in negotiations following a card check,[98] (4) questioning the union's majority after examining union membership cards and acknowledging union representation,[99] and (5) rejecting, without reason, a card check that had been conducted by a third party.[100]

b. Applying the Gissel test. The Court in *Gissel* approved what was characterized as the Board's "current practice": [101]

> When confronted by a recognition demand based on possession of cards allegedly signed by a majority of his employees, an employer need not grant recognition immediately, but may, unless he has knowledge independently of the cards that the union has a majority, decline the union's request and insist on an election, either by requesting the union to file an election petition or by filing such a petition himself under §9 (c) (1) (B). If, however, the employer commits independent and substantial unfair labor practices disruptive of election conditions, the Board may withhold the election or set it aside, and issue instead a bargaining order as a remedy for the various violations. A bargaining order will not issue, of course, if the union obtained the cards through misrepresentation or coercion or if the employer's unfair labor practices are unrelated generally to the representation campaign." [102]

The Court differentiated between degrees of employer misconduct in determining whether a bargaining order would be justified. The Fourth Circuit had conceded that a bargaining order without an election would be appropriate in " 'exceptional' cases marked by 'outrageous' and 'pervasive' unfair labor practices." [103] The Supreme Court, however, indicated that the Board could also use the bargaining order in a second category of "less extraordinary cases marked by less pervasive practices which nonetheless still have the tendency to undermine majority strength and impede the election processes." [104] The Court noted two factors which could bear on the determination: (1) "a showing that at one point the

---

97 Kellogg Mills, 147 NLRB 342, 56 LRRM 1223 (1964), *enforced,* 347 F 2d 219, 59 LRRM 2340 (CA 9, 1965).
98 Jem Mfg., Inc., 156 NLRB 643, 61 LRRM 1074 (1966).
99 Greyhound Terminal, 137 NLRB 87, 50 LRRM 1088 (1962), *enforced,* 314 F 2d 43, 52 LRRM 2335 (CA 5, 1963).
100 Dixon Ford Shoe Co., Inc., 150 NLRB 861, 58 LRRM 1160 (1965). However, bad faith was not to be inferred simply from the rejection of a proposal to submit the cards to an impartial determination. Strydel, Inc., note 96 *supra.*
101 395 US at 591.
102 *Ibid.*
103 *Id.* at 613.
104 *Id.* at 614.

union had a majority"; [105] and (2) "the extensiveness of an employer's unfair labor practices in terms of their past effects on election conditions and the likelihood of their recurrence in the future." [106]

Recognizing a third category of cases involving minor or less extensive unfair labor practices, the Court emphasized that the Board's remedial power will not sustain bargaining orders in cases where the unfair practices have only a minimal impact on the election machinery. It noted that under the Board view there is "no *per se* rule that the commission of any unfair labor practice will automatically result in a §8(a)(5) violation and the issuance of an order to bargain." [107]

III. BARGAINING ORDER WITHOUT A FINDING OF REFUSAL TO BARGAIN

An employer who has committed flagrant violations may be required to bargain with a majority union even though he had a good-faith doubt as to the union's majority status. The Board holds that widespread unfair labor practices may warrant issuance of a bargaining order to effectuate the policies of the Act although the refusal to recognize may not itself be a violation of Section

---

[105] *Ibid.*

[106] *Ibid.* For post-*Gissel* cases illustrating the Board's application of these rules, *see* Marie Phillips, Inc., 178 NLRB No. 53, 72 LRRM 1103 (1969); Garland Knitting Mills, 178 NLRB No. 62, 72 LRRM 1112 (1969); Schrementi Bros., 179 NLRB No. 147, 72 LRRM 1481 (1969); West Side Plymouth, Inc., 180 NLRB No. 68, 73 LRRM 1014 (1969); Noll Motors, Inc., 180 NLRB No. 60, 73 LRRM 1036 (1969); Mather Co., 180 NLRB No. 19, 73 LRRM 1037 (1969); Blade-Tribune Publishing Co., 180 NLRB No. 56, 73 LRRM 1041 (1969); C&G Electric, Inc., 180 NLRB No. 52, 73 LRRM 1041 (1969); Lou De Young's Market Basket, Inc., 181 NLRB No. 10, 73 LRRM 1297 (1970), *enforced,* 430 F 2d 912, 75 LRRM 2129 (CA 6, 1970); J. A. Conley Co., 181 NLRB No. 20, 73 LRRM 1301 (1970); in Central Soya of Canton, 180 NLRB No. 86, 73 LRRM 1069 (1970), the Board stressed that relatively minor unfair labor practices were not sufficient indication that a coercion-free rerun election could not be held, therefore a bargaining order was not issued. In *Gibson Products Co.,* 185 NLRB No. 74, 75 LRRM 1055 (1970), the Board held that *Gissel* "contemplated that the propriety of the bargaining order would be judged as of the time of the commission of the unfair labor practices and not in the light of subsequent events"; *see also* American Cable Systems, Inc., 179 NLRB No. 149, 72 LRRM 1524 (1969), where the Board ordered the employer to bargain on account of unfair labor practices which were committed in 1965 (*see* note 63 *supra*), and which "undermined the Union's majority and caused an election to be a less reliable guide . . . than the signed authorization cards. . . ." The Fifth Circuit refused to enforce the order and remanded because of the Board's failure to consider events of the intervening years which could have made a free election possible. NLRB v. American Cable Systems, Inc., 427 F 2d 446, 73 LRRM 2913 (CA 5, 1970). The Board has petitioned the Supreme Court for certiorari. 75 LRR 106.

[107] 395 US at 615. *See* Hammond & Irving, Inc., 154 NLRB 1071, 60 LRRM 1073 (1965). *See* note 91 *supra*.

8(a)(5).[108] The employer also may be ordered to bargain in the absence of a valid bargaining request if the Board finds that the employer has committed unfair labor practices that were designed to destroy the union's majority and thereby disclosed a disposition to evade the duty to bargain.[109] But unlawful practices that fall short of an aggressive or planned campaign to dissipate the union's majority have been held an insufficient foundation, in the absence of a request to bargain, for a bargaining order based on a card majority.[110]

IV. EFFECT OF UNION PARTICIPATION IN AN ELECTION

In 1951 the Board declared that if a union participates in an election and loses, it is not precluded from pursuing the unfair-labor-practice remedy of a bargaining order based upon the employer's unlawful refusal to recognize the union's card majority prior to the election.[111] In 1954, in *Aiello Dairy Farms Co.*,[112] it reversed that position, concluding that when a union, after having suffered a denial of its request for recognition, participates in an election it foregoes the bargaining-order remedy under Section 10 in favor of the election remedy under Section 9, and is therefore confined to the election process to prove majority status. This "waiver" doctrine was followed for 10 years.

---

[108] Kinter Bros., Inc., 167 NLRB 57, 66 LRRM 1004 (1967); Crystal Tire Co., 165 NLRB 563, 65 LRRM 1459 (1967); Better Val-U Stores of Mansfield, Inc., 161 NLRB 762, 63 LRRM 1326 (1966); 77 Operating Co., 160 NLRB 927, 63 LRRM 1057 (1966); Bishop & Malco, Inc., 159 NLRB 1159, 62 LRRM 1498 (1965); NLRB v. Delight Bakery, Inc., 353 F 2d 344, 60 LRRM 2501 (CA 6, 1965). Piasecki Aircraft Corp. v. NLRB, 280 F 2d 575, 46 LRRM 2469 (CA 3, 1960), *cert. denied*, 364 US 933, 47 LRRM 2365 (1961). The Fourth Circuit opinions review by the Supreme Court in *NLRB v. Gissel*, 395 US 575, 71 LRRM 2481, 2484 (1969), conceded that one of the circumstances in which the Board could properly order an employer to bargain without an election was when "the employer's §§8 (a) (1) and (3) unfair labor practices committed during the representation campaign were so extensive and pervasive that a bargaining order was the only available Board remedy irrespective of a card majority."

[109] J. C. Penney Co. v. NLRB, 359 F 2d 983, 66 LRRM 2069 (CA 10, 1967), *enforcing* 160 NLRB 279, 62 LRRM 1597 (1966); Western Aluminum of Oregon, Inc., 144 NLRB 1191, 54 LRRM 1217 (1963).

[110] NLRB v. Flomatic Corp., 347 F 2d 74, 59 LRRM 2535 (CA 2, 1965); *but see* Steelworkers v. NLRB (Northwest Engineering Co.), 376 F 2d 770, 64 LRRM 2650 (CA DC, 1967). *See* notes 78, 79 *supra*.

[111] M. H. Davidson Co., 94 NLRB 142, 28 LRRM 1026 (1951).

[112] 110 NLRB 1365, 35 LRRM 1235 (1954).

In 1964, in *Bernel Foam*,[113] the Board expressly overruled *Aiello* and returned to its earlier position. It reasoned that:

> [T]he so-called "choice" which the union is forced to make under Aiello between going to an election or filing an 8 (a) (5) charge is at best a Hobson's choice. Although an election is a relatively swift and inexpensive way for the union to put the force of law behind its majority status, the procedure is highly uncertain entailing the real possibility that because of conduct by the employer no fair election will be held. . . . Since this difficult and rather dubious "choice" is created by the employer's unlawful conduct, there is no warrant for imposing upon the union which represents the employees an irrevocable option as to the method it will pursue . . . while permitting the offending party to enjoy at the expense of public policy the fruits of such unlawful conduct.[114]

However, the Board has imposed a further requirement for the *Bernel Foam* remedy. An employer will not be ordered to bargain where the union has previously lost an election unless the Board also sets aside the election as a result of meritorious objections filed in the representation case.[115] The election may be set aside upon the basis of objections filed by the employer as well as by the union.[116]

---

[113] Bernel Foam Products Co., 146 NLRB 1277, 56 LRRM 1039 (1964). The doctrine was approved in NLRB v. Southbridge Sheet Metal Works, 380 F 2d 851, 65 LRRM 2916 (CA 1, 1967).

[114] *Id.* at 1280. This doctrine was approved by the Supreme Court in *NLRB v. Gissel Packing Co.,* note 22 *supra. See* text relating to the *General Steel* case. *See also* Colson Corp. v. NLRB, 347 F 2d 128, 59 LRRM 2512 (CA 8, 1965), cert. denied, 382 US 904, 60 LRRM 2553 (1965); IUE v. NLRB (S.N.C. Mfg. Co.), 352 F 2d 361, 59 LRRM 2232 (CA DC, 1965), *cert. denied,* 382 US 902, 60 LRRM 2353 (1965). *Cf.* NLRB v. Flomatic Corp., 347 F 2d 74, 59 LRRM 2535 (CA 2, 1965).

[115] Irving Air Chute Co., 149 NLRB 627, 57 LRRM 1330 (1964), *enforced,* 350 F 2d 176, 50 LRRM 3052 (CA 2, 1965). In Green Bay Aviation, Inc., 165 NLRB 1026, 65 LRRM 1499 (1967), the Board refused to issue a post-election bargaining order where the employer's unfair labor practices occurred prior to the filing of the petition for an election.

[116] Photobell Co., 158 NLRB 738, 62 LRRM 1091 (1966).

PART IV

THE

COLLECTIVE BARGAINING

PROCESS

Chapter 11

THE DUTY TO BARGAIN IN GOOD FAITH

I. INTRODUCTION—HISTORICAL BACKGROUND

There exists in the law generally, and in the field of labor relations particularly, a tendency to rely on catch phrases and key words to describe recurring problems. The shorthand term most frequently used under the National Labor Relations Act refers to the reciprocal duty between the employer and the representative of the majority of its employees to bargain in "good faith." [1] What constitutes "good faith," in terms of the employer's duty to bargain under Section 8(a)(5) or in terms of the union's duty to bargain under Section 8(b)(3), is not readily identifiable, although hundreds of cases and exhaustive commentaries have undertaken the task.[2] The duty to bargain in good faith is an evolving con-

---

[1] §8(d) reads: "For the purposes of this section, to bargain collectively is the performance of the mutual obligation of the employer and the representative of the employees to meet at reasonable times and confer in good faith with respect to wages, hours, and other terms and conditions of employment, or the negotiation of an agreement, or any question arising thereunder, and the execution of a written contract incorporating any agreement reached if requested by either party, but such obligation does not compel either party to agree to a proposal or require the making of a concession. . . ." Under §(a)(5) it is an unfair labor practice for an employer "to refuse to bargain collectively with the representatives of his employees, subject to the provisions of section 9(a)." Under §8(b)(3) it is an unfair labor practice for a labor organization "to refuse to bargain collectively with an employer, provided it is the representative of his employees subject to the provisions of section 9(a)." See note 455 *infra* for the remainder of §8(d).

[2] As one commentator states the problem: "If one were to select the single area of our national labor law which has posed the greatest difficulties for the National Labor Relations Board, that area would be encompassed within the phrase 'the duty to bargain in good faith.'" Cooper, *Boulwarism and The Duty to Bargain in Good Faith*, 20 RUTGERS L. REV. 653, 653 (1966). For other commentaries, *see* the following partial listing: Note, *Boulwarism and Good Faith Collective Bargaining*, 63 MICH. L. REV. 1473 (1965); Fleming, *The Obligation to Bargain in Good Faith*, 16 SW. L.J. 43 (1962); Cox, *The Duty to Bargain in Good Faith*, 71 HARV. L. REV. 1401 (1958); Note, *Good Faith Bargaining and the G.E. Case—The NLRB Views "Boulwarism" and Other Bargaining Practices*, 53 GEO. L.J. 1115 (1965); Duvin, *The Duty to Bargain: Law in Search of Policy*, 64 COLUM. L. REV. 248, 266 (1964); Feinsinger, *The National Labor Relations Act and Collective Bargaining*, 57 MICH. L. REV. 807, 812 (1959); Humphrey, *The Duty to Bargain*, 16 OHIO ST. L.J. 403, 418 (1955); Note, *Duty of a Labor Union to Bargain Collectively in Good Faith*, 25

cept, rooted in statute. The Board has described the test of good faith as a fluctuating one, "dependent in part upon how a reasonable man might be expected to react to the bargaining attitude displayed by those across the table." [3]

A. Origin of Concept of Collective Bargaining

Originally, most case law and legislation in the field of labor relations were concerned with the prevention of open hostility as a result of disputes rather than the prevention of the friction between employers and employees that was the direct cause of the disputes.[4] The United States Strike Commission Report on the Chicago Strike of 1894, the Erdman Act,[5] and *Adair* v. *U.S.*,[6] three of the earliest executive, legislative, and judicial forays into the labor relations area, were concerned primarily with conciliation and arbitration of the disputes. The Clayton Act [7] and the Norris-LaGuardia Act [8] also dealt largely with control of concerted activity and employment disputes rather than prevention of disputes.

However, in 1917, when it became apparent that governmental intervention would be necessary to prevent labor disputes from interfering with war production, the establishment of the War Labor Board gave recognition to the right of workers to organize in trade unions and to bargain collectively through chosen representatives.[9] This granting of governmental protection to collective bargaining was a step toward federal regulation to encourage settlement of conditions of employment at the bargaining table.

FORDHAM L. REV. 319 (1956) ; Sherman, *Employer's Obligation to Produce Data for Collective Bargaining,* 35 MINN. L. REV. 24, 32 (1950) ; Note, *Labor Law—Collective Bargaining—Duty of an Employer to Bargain,* 36 MINN. L. REV. 109 (1951) ; Cox & Dunlop, *The Duty to Bargain Collectively During the Term of An Existing Agreement,* 63 HARV. L. REV. 1097 (1950) ; Note, *Adamant Insistence on a Management Functions Clause as a Refusal to Bargain Collectively,* 52 COLUM. L. REV. 1054 (1952) ; Note, *Employers' Duty to Supply Economic Data for Collective Bargaining,* 57 COLUM. L. REV. 112 (1957) ; Note, *Slowdowns and Work Stoppages Not Evidence of Union's Failure to Bargain in Good Faith,* 69 HARV. L. REV. 1337 (1956) ; Note, *Employer's Duty to Bargain Under the National Labor Relations Act,* 22 NOTRE DAME LAW. 95 (1946) ; Note, *Harassment By Unions as a Refusal to Bargain Under Section 8(b)(3) of the National Labor Relations Act,* 64 YALE L.J. 766 (1955) ; Cox, *Government Regulation of the Negotiation and Terms of Collective Bargaining Agreement,* 101 U. PA. L. REV. 1137 (1953) .
3 Times Publishing Co., 72 NLRB 676, 682-683, 19 LRRM 1199 (1947) .
4 *See* Chapter 1 *supra.*
5 30 Stat 424 (1898) .
6 208 US 161 (1908) .
7 38 Stat 730 (1914) , 15 USC 12 et seq. (1964) .
8 47 Stat 70 (1932) , 29 USC 101 et seq. (1964) .
9 National War Labor Board, Principles and Rules of Procedure 4 (1919) .

The War Labor Board put the principle into effect in *Western Cold Storage* [10] by requiring that the parties "take up the differences that still exist in an earnest endeavor to reach an agreement on all points at issue."

The old National Labor Board, set up under the National Industrial Recovery Act,[11] followed the War Labor Board in announcing that it would follow the "incontestably sound principle that the employer is obligated by the statute to negotiate in good faith with his employees' representatives; to match their proposals, if unacceptable, with counter-proposals; and to make every reasonable effort to reach an agreement." [12] Compromise was an essential part of the statutory obligation under the National Recovery Act, and the National Labor Board decided that the right conferred a duty in employers to bargain, which was more than a bare requirement to meet and confer. The NIRA contemplated that both parties approach negotiations with an open mind and make reasonable efforts to reach a common ground of agreement.[13]

B. The Wagner Act

Section 8(5) of the National Labor Relations Act required that an employer "bargain collectively with the representatives of his employees." Section 9(a) stated that such bargaining should be "in respect to rates of pay, wages, hours of employment, or other conditions of employment." These two brief statements were the only duties of collective bargaining imposed by the original Wagner Act.

Section 8(5) was deleted from the bill in the hearings on S.2926, but was put back in S.1958 at the urging of Lloyd K. Garrison, chairman of the old National Labor Board. While the legislators agreed that Section 8(5) did not compel anyone to make a compact,[14] the opinions among congressmen varied with regard to what Section 8(5) did require. For example, Senator Walsh stated

---

10 War Labor Board, Docket No. 80 (1919).

11 The National Industrial Recovery Act was declared unconstitutional under the Commerce Clause and as an illegal delegation of legislative power in *Schechter Poultry Corp.* v. *United States,* 295 US 495 (1935). See Chapter 1 *supra.*

12 Houde Engineering Corp., 1 NLRB (old) 35 (1934).

13 National Lock Co., 1 NLRB (old) 15 (1934); Hall Baking Co., 1 NLRB (old) 83 (1934); Dresner & Son, 1 NLRB (old) 26 (1934); Edward G. Budd Mfg. Co., 1 NLRB (old) 58 (1933).

14 79 CONG. REC. 7571 (1935). For history of the Wagner Act *see* Chapters 1 and 2 *supra.*

that "[a]ll the bill proposed to do is escort representatives to the bargaining door, not control what goes on behind the door." [15] But Senator Wagner saw a stronger requirement: "The bill requires the parties to match unacceptable proposals and to make every effort to reach agreement." [16]

The Supreme Court sought to clarify the effect of the Act by holding in *Jones & Laughlin* [17] that the Act encourages free opportunity for negotiation to bring about adjustments and agreements. Then in *Pennsylvania Greyhound Lines* [18] the Court, emphasizing the importance of union recognition in securing collective bargaining, found that the legislative intent expressed in the NLRA was an extension of Railway Labor Act principles. Finally, in the 1938 *Consolidated Edison* case [19] the Court stated that the manifest objective of the Act in providing for collective bargaining was the contemplation of the making of contracts with labor organizations.

C. Taft-Hartley Amendments: Present Wording of the Act

The basic shortcomings which Congress sought to remedy in the Taft-Hartley amendments were the lack of a statutory requirement that unions must bargain (reciprocal to that of employers), and the lack of an objective standard by which the courts and the Board could determine whether a party had refused to bargain. The House of Representatives viewed a number of Board decisions [20] as reflecting a tendency by the Board to judge the reasonableness of employers' proposals or counterproposals and the concessions an employer must make.[21] Some court decisions also

---

15 79 CONG. REC. 7660 (1935).

16 *Hearings on H.R. 6288,* 74th Cong., 1st Sess. 16 (1935).

17 NLRB v. Jones & Laughlin Steel Corp., 301 US 1, 1 LRRM 703 (1937).

18 NLRB v. Pennsylvania Greyhound Lines, 303 US 261, 2 LRRM 600 (1938).

19 Consolidated Edison Co. v. NLRB, 305 US 197, 3 LRRM 645 (1938).

20 *See, e.g.,* J. I. Case Co., 71 NLRB 1145, 19 LRRM 1100 (1946) (refusal to consider closed shop); Dallas Cartage Co., 14 NLRB 411, 4 LRRM 445 (1939) (insistence on collective bargaining rather than arbitration provisions); Jasper Blackburn Products Co., 21 NLRB 1240, 6 LRRM 169 (1940) (requiring union to make itself legally responsible for contract violations); Burgie Vinegar Co., 71 NLRB 829, 19 LRRM 1055 (1946) (demand that union agree to reimburse employer for any damages from a strike). The history of the Taft-Hartley Act is treated in Chapter 3 *supra.*

21 Globe Cotton Mills, 6 NLRB 461, 2 LRRM 172 (1938) (refusal to make counterproposals held refusal to bargain); S. L. Allen & Co., 1 NLRB 714, 1 LRRM 29 (1936) (refusal to make concessions with respect to any clause in proposed agreement held to violate duty to bargain). *See* Kuelthau, *The NLRB and the Duty to Make Concessions in Bargaining,* 18 LAB. L.J. 201, 202 (1967).

tended to examine the terms of the proposals rather than the nature of the bargaining that was done.[22] The House proposed a lengthy and detailed objective test for determining what constitutes good faith in collective bargaining.[23]

While the proposed Senate bill, which was subsequently passed almost intact, did not prescribe a purely objective test, it had substantially the same effect since it precluded the Board from determining the merits of the positions of the parties.[24] The Senate's use of the word "concession" as to requirements that might not be made of the employer, rather than the word "counterproposal," was intended to meet the objection of the then-chairman of the National Labor Relations Board that negativing any duty to make counterproposals would remove one of the readiest indicia for Board determinations of good or bad faith.[25] The requirements provided by Congress in Section 8 (d) of the Taft-Hartley amendments, that the parties "confer in good faith," were almost identical to the requirements propounded by the Supreme Court in *NLRB* v. *Jones & Laughlin Steel Corp.*[26]

Both the House and the Senate agreed that Section 8(b)(3) simply promoted equality and responsibility in bargaining by making the duty to bargain mutual.[27] Such mutuality of obligation in the duty to bargain had already been considered by a few courts.[28] The provision was added to the statute as part of the Taft-Hartley amendments.

II. GOOD FAITH—SOME GENERAL DEFINITIONS

The entire concept underlying the statutory requirement that the parties "bargain collectively . . . in good faith" [29] is a difficult

---

[22] "The fair dealing . . . must be exhibited by the parties . . . in their specific treatment of the particular subjects or items for negotiation." NLRB v. George P. Pilling & Son Co., 119 F 2d 32, 37, 8 LRRM 557 (CA 3, 1941). *See also* H. J. Heinz Co. v. NLRB, 311 US 514, 7 LRRM 291 (1941); Texas Foundries v. NLRB, 211 F 2d 791, 33 LRRM 2883 (CA 5, 1954).
[23] H.R. REP. No. 245, 80th Cong., 1st Sess. 19 (1947).
[24] *See House Comm. of Conf. Rep. No. 510*, U.S. CODE CONG. & ADM. NEWS, 80th Cong., 1st Sess. 1140 (1947).
[25] S. REP. No. 105, 80th Cong., 1st Sess. 24 (1947).
[26] 301 US 1, 1 LRRM 703 (1937). *See* Chapter 28 *infra* at notes 1-9.
[27] H.R. REP. No. 245, 80th Cong., 1st Sess. 19 (1947).
[28] Globe Cotton Mills v. NLRB, 103 F 2d 91, 4 LRRM 621 (CA 5, 1939); NLRB v. Sands Mfg. Co., 96 F 2d 721, 2 LRRM 712 (CA 6, 1938).
[29] §8 (d).

one. It is particularly difficult to formulate a precise definition of "good faith" within the meaning of the National Labor Relations Act.

Where an employer had repeatedly declared that it would sign no written agreement, the Fourth Circuit in *NLRB* v. *Highland Park Mfg.*[30] declared that "[t]he act, it is true, does not require that the parties agree; but it does require that they negotiate in good faith *with the view of reaching an agreement if possible;* and mere discussion with the representatives of employees, with a fixed resolve on the part of the employer not to enter into any agreement with them, even as to matters as to which there is no disagreement, does not satisfy its provisions."[31] While various decisions, such as *NLRB* v. *George P. Pilling & Son Co.,*[32] *NLRB* v. *Montgomery Ward,*[33] *NLRB* v. *Reed & Prince Mfg. Co.,*[34] and *NLRB* v. *Boss Mfg. Co.,*[35] have elaborated on the *Highland Park* definition, the basic requirement set forth therein remains the same: that the parties must negotiate with the view of trying to reach an agreement.[36]

The Wagner Act had no explicit requirement that the employer bargain in good faith, only that he bargain. The Board, however, almost immediately included the additional requirement that such bargaining be done in good faith.[37] The Board's concept of this added requirement is clearly illustrated by its statement in the *Atlas Mills* decision:[38]

---

30 110 F 2d 632, 6 LRRM 786 (CA 4, 1940).

31 *Id.* at 637 (emphasis added).

32 119 F 2d 32, 8 LRRM 557 (CA 3, 1941) (requiring that good faith be exhibited in the parties' approach and attitude to negotiations as well as in their specific treatment of particular subjects, plus a common willingness to discuss their claims and demands freely and fully and, when opposed, to justify them on reason).

33 133 F 2d 676, 12 LRRM 508 (CA 9, 1943) (requiring active participation indicating a present intent to find a basis for agreement).

34 118 F 2d 874, 8 LRRM 478 (CA 1, 1941) (allowing the Board to find refusal to bargain from the fact that employer displayed a completely closed mind without any spirit of cooperation and a complete absence of the required good faith).

35 118 F 2d 187, 8 LRRM 729 (CA 7, 1941), *cert. denied*, 313 US 595 (1941) (requiring open and fair mind plus endeavor to overcome existing obstacles and difficulties).

36 Majure Transport Co. v. NLRB, 198 F 2d 735, 30 LRRM 2441 (CA 5, 1952); NLRB v. Southwestern Porcelain Steel Corp., 317 F 2d 527, 53 LRRM 2307 (CA 10, 1963); NLRB v. Herman Sausage Co., 275 F 2d 229, 45 LRRM 2829 (CA 5, 1960); California Girl, 129 NLRB 209, 46 LRRM 1533 (1960).

37 NLRB ANN. REP. 84 (1936).

38 3 NLRB 10, 1 LRRM 60 (1937).

[I]f the obligation of the Act is to produce more than a series of empty discussions, bargaining must mean more than mere negotiation. It must mean negotiation with a *bona fide* intent to reach an agreement if agreement is possible.[39]

When first called upon to enforce Board orders, the federal courts did not adopt the good-faith requirement as such. But they did require an employer to engage in sincere negotiations with an intent to settle differences and arrive at an agreement.[40] Some cases continued to follow this definition of the duty to bargain even after Taft-Hartley specifically added the good-faith requirement.[41] Under the Wagner Act the Supreme Court in *NLRB* v. *Sands Mfg. Co.*[42] upheld a test that did not specify good faith but considered the sincerity of the employer's effort.[43] Two years later, in *National Licorice Co.* v. *NLRB*,[44] the Court used good faith as the standard for an employer's conduct. Cases discussed in this chapter are part of, and add to, the definition of good-faith bargaining.

III. INDICIA OF GOOD AND BAD FAITH

It was recognized by the courts and the Board at an early date that compelling the parties to meet was insufficient, standing alone, to promote the avowed ends of the Act.[45] Early attempts of employers to satisfy the bargaining obligation by merely going through the motions without actually seeking to adjust differences were condemned.[46] The concept of "good faith" was brought into the law of collective bargaining as a solution to the problem of

---

[39] *Id.* at 21.

[40] NLRB v. Biles-Coleman Lumber Co., 98 F 2d 18, 2 LRRM 758 (CA 9, 1938). *Cf.* Jeffrey-DeWitt Insulator Co. v. NLRB, 91 F 2d 134, 1 LRRM 634 (CA 4, 1937), *cert. denied*, 302 US 731 (1937), 2 LRRM 623; Globe Cotton Mills v. NLRB, 103 F 2d 91, 4 LRRM 621 (CA 5, 1939).

[41] NLRB v. Shannon, 208 F 2d 545, 33 LRRM 2270 (CA 9, 1953).

[42] 306 US 332, 4 LRRM 530 (1939), *affirming* 96 F 2d 721, 2 LRRM 712 (CA 6, 1938).

[43] "The sincerity of the employer's effort is to be tested by the length of time involved in the negotiations, their frequency, and the persistence with which the employer offers opportunity for agreement." 96 F 2d 721, 725, 2 LRRM 712 (CA 6, 1938).

[44] 309 US 350, 6 LRRM 674 (1940); *see also* H. J. Heinz Co. v. NLRB, 311 US 514, 7 LRRM 29 (1941).

[45] 1 NLRB ANN. REP. 4-5 (1936): "Collective bargaining is something more than the mere meeting of an employer with the representatives of his employees; the essential thing is rather the serious intent to adjust differences and to reach an acceptable common ground."

[46] NLRB v. Montgomery Ward & Co., 133 F 2d 676, 12 LRRM 508 (CA 9, 1943); Benson Produce Co., 71 NLRB 888, 19 LRRM 1061 (1946).

rgaining without substance.[47] In 1947 the requirement was
xpressly written into Section 8(d).

A. Totality of Conduct

The duty to bargain in good faith is an "obligation . . . to participate actively in the deliberations so as to indicate a present
intention to find a basis for agreement. . . ."[48] This implies both
"an open mind and a sincere desire to reach an agreement"[49] as
well as "a sincere effort . . . to reach a common ground."[50] The
presence or absence of intent "must be discerned from the record."[51] Except in the cases where the conduct fails to meet the
minimum obligation imposed by law or constitutes an outright
refusal to bargain,[52] all the relevant facts of a case are studied in
determining whether the employer or the union is bargaining in
good or bad faith, i.e., the "totality of conduct" is the standard
through which the "quality" of negotiations is tested.[53]

B. Bargaining Techniques in *General Electric*

1. Boulwarism. In 1963 the Board decided a case that provided
background for consideration of the term "Boulwarism."[54] In

---

[47] See Cox, *The Duty to Bargain in Good Faith*, 71 HARV. L. REV. 1401, 1413 (1958).
See e.g.: NLRB v. Montgomery Ward & Co., 133 F 2d 676, 12 LRRM 508 (CA 9,
1943) ; Globe Cotton Mills v. NLRB, 103 F 2d 91, 4 LRRM 621 (CA 5, 1939).
[48] NLRB v. Montgomery Ward & Co., 133 F 2d 676, 686, 12 LRRM 508 (CA 9,
1943).
[49] *Id.* at 686. See NLRB v. Truitt Mfg. Co., 351 US 149, 38 LRRM 2042 (1956)
(separate opinion).
[50] 133 F 2d at 686. See NLRB v. Herman Sausage Co., 275 F 2d 229, 45 LRRM
2829 (CA 5, 1960).
[51] General Electric Co., 150 NLRB 192, 194, 57 LRRM 1491 (1964).
[52] With the important caveat that "intent" may not even be in issue if the outward
conduct amounts to a *de facto* refusal to bargain. See NLRB v. Katz, 369 US 736,
50 LRRM 2177 (1962) ; and *cf.* NLRB v. Cascade Employers Ass'n, 296 F 2d 42, 48,
49 LRRM 2049 (CA 9, 1961) where the court held that the Board had erroneously
applied the *per se* rule rather than looking to the "totality of circumstances surrounding the bargaining."
[53] NLRB v. Stevenson Brick & Block Co., 393 F 2d 234, 68 LRRM 2086 (CA 4, 1968) ;
B. F. Diamond Construction Co., 163 NLRB No. 25, 64 LRRM 1333 (1967) ; General
Electric Co., *supra* note 51; McCulloch Corp., 132 NLRB 201, 48 LRRM 1344
(1961). In *Rhodes-Holland Chevrolet Co.,* 146 NLRB 1304, 1304-1305, 56 LRRM
1058 (1964), the Board stated: "In finding that Respondent violated its obligation
to bargain in good faith, we, like the Trial Examiner, have not relied solely on the
position taken by Respondent on substantive contract terms, a factor which, standing alone, . . . might not have provided sufficient basis for the violation found, but
have considered that factor as simply one item in the totality of circumstances reflecting Respondent's bargaining frame of mind." The "totality of conduct"
doctrine, generally, stems from *NLRB v. Virginia Elec. & Power Co.,* 314 US 469,
9 LRRM 405 (1941).
[54] For a clarification of the term "Boulwarism" *see* note 61 *infra.*

Philip Carey Mfg. Co.[55] the Board found a Section 8(a)(5) violation because of an employer's insistence on a superseniority proposal for nonstrikers. The trial examiner found that the company had, after its eleventh meeting with the union, frozen its position regarding union arguments, so that the subsequent seven meetings accomplished little. The Board disagreed with this aspect of the decision, noting that "the Trial Examiner placed too much stress on finality and not enough on the amount of negotiation that preceded the 'final' offer." [56] The trial examiner had disavowed any intent to pass generally on any technique of bargaining, although he characterized the employer's bargaining as a form of "Boulwarism." [57] The Board, in turn, stated that it, too, was deciding the case on the facts presented and was not passing on a bargaining procedure.[58]

Just over one year later, the Board had occasion to consider the implications of Boulwarism in a case involving the company that developed the concept. In late 1964, the Board rendered its extremely controversial decision in the *General Electric Co.* case.[59] Five years later the Second Circuit enforced the Board's holding.[60]

"Boulwarism" is the name describing the technique utilized by General Electric in its collective bargaining.[61] On the basis of its own research the company formulated a single offer that antic-

---

[55] 140 NLRB 1103, 52 LRRM 1184 (1963), *enforced in part,* 331 F 2d 720, 55 LRRM 2821 (CA 6, 1964), *cert. denied,* 379 US 888, 57 LRRM 2307 (1964).

[56] 140 NLRB at 1104.

[57] *Id.* at 1122.

[58] *Id.* at 1104, n. 2.

[59] 150 NLRB 192, 57 LRRM 1491 (1964).

[60] NLRB v. General Electric Co., 418 F 2d 736, 72 LRRM 2530 (CA 2, 1969), *cert. denied,* 397 US 965, 73 LRRM 2600 (1970).

[61] The term "Boulwarism" is not used by the Board in its opinion, although the trial examiner's report employed the term with reference to General Electric's bargaining practices. *See, e.g.,* 150 NLRB at 207. The technique of "Boulwarism" was named for Lemuel R. Boulware, a vice-president of General Electric who formulated the concept following a bitter and disastrous strike suffered by General Electric in 1946. Briefly, the concept is designed to convince its employees that the company is responsive to their needs and that the union is not needed to force General Electric to grant what it will voluntarily provide. This is accomplished via a massive communications program to employees, a continual research program to discover what is "best" for its employees, and a formulation of a "firm and fair" offer to the union based upon the facts it has gathered. For a full explanation of the history of the 1960 negotiations and the concept of Boulwarism, *see* Cooper, *Boulwarism and the Duty to Bargain in Good Faith,* 20 RUTGERS L. REV. 653 (1966). *See also* Gross, Cullen & Hanslowe, *Good Faith in Labor Negotiations: Tests and Remedies,* 53 CORN. L. REV. 1009 (1968); Note, *Boulwareism: Legality and Effect,* 76 HARV. L. REV. 807 (1963); H.R. Northrup, BOULWARISM (1964).

ipated the union's demands. Some six weeks of meetings (18 sessions) and a massive publicity campaign involving virtually all
media of communication preceded the presentation of the offer on
August 30, 1960. The company characterized its offer as fair and
firm—one which would give no reason for the union to impose a
strike—but it would be open and subject to change if new information showed that the original offer was not "right." [62] However, by September 9 the company had made but four changes
in the offer. A contract eventually was signed on November 10,
1960.

The company was charged with Section 8(a)(1), (3), and (5) violations.[63] The Board found a failure to bargain in good faith in
GE's (a) failure to furnish information requested by the union,[64]
(b) attempt to bargain with locals and thereby undermine the
international's position,[65] (c) presentation of its insurance proposal
on a take-it-or-leave-it basis,[66] (d) overall attitude or approach as
evidenced by the totality of its conduct.[67] In a split decision, the
court of appeals agreed with these rulings and enforced the Board's
order in its entirety.

The importance of the *General Electric* case was underscored
by the Second Circuit's lengthy opinion affirming the Board's
action. The opinion reviewed and analyzed a complex fact situation and arrived at legal conclusions which dramatically reveal
the nature of the collective bargaining process. The *GE* case thus
describes and focuses upon the complex nature of the statutory
duty to "bargain collectively." [68] The duty refers to a *bilateral*
procedure whereby the employer and the bargaining representative *jointly* attempt to set wages and working conditions for the

---

[62] 150 NLRB at 270.

[63] Similar charges had been filed by the union in 1954 and 1958, but had been dismissed. Northrup, BOULWARISM 60 (1964).

[64] 150 NLRB at 193. *See also* Section IV *infra.*

[65] 150 NLRB at 262-266.

[66] *Id.* at 269. Although the trial examiner indicated that this was a separate violation, the Board considered General Electric's position on the insurance proposal
to be indicative of the employer's overall bad faith. 150 NLRB 192, 196.

[67] *Id.* at 193.

[68] §§8(a)(5) and 8(b)(3). The original declaration of policy in the Wagner Act,
reenacted in the Taft-Hartley Act, declared that it is "the policy of the United
States to eliminate the causes of certain substantial obstructions to the free flow
of commerce and to mitigate and eliminate these obstructions when they have
occurred *by encouraging the practice and procedure of collective bargaining. . . .*"
§1. (Emphasis added.)

employees.[69] As this case demonstrates, the bargaining must be conducted in good faith, but more than that, the Act contemplates that a *bargaining process* will occur. The statutory object for which the process was intended was described as follows by the Supreme Court in *H.K. Porter:* [70]

> The object of this Act was . . . to ensure that employers and their employees could work together to establish mutually satisfactory conditions. The basic theme of the Act was that through collective bargaining the passions, agreements, and struggles of prior years would be channeled into constructive, open discussions leading, hopefully, to mutual agreement.

Under the statutory scheme, if wages or working conditions are set unilaterally [71] or in a manner which avoids the bargaining process, such as when the employer bypasses the bargaining representative and deals directly with the employees in the setting of wages and working conditions,[72] collective bargaining has not occurred. Where there is this absence of collective bargaining, good faith may be an irrelevant consideration.[73] The term *per se violation* has generally been used to describe the bypassing of the bargaining process; and *lack of good faith* has often been used to describe refusing to bargain or sham bargaining. But lack of good faith may also refer to a subjective state of mind, evidenced by various types of overt conduct described in this chapter. The *General Electric* case illustrates many of the subtle requirements of this illusive "duty to bargain."

The court majority reviewed in detail the long history of the negotiations. It approved the Board's findings as to specific refusals to bargain: the unilateral promulgation of an accident insurance plan and the employer's refusal to "indicate the cost of union proposals, or how much [GE] was willing to expend. . . ." [74]

---

69 This chapter attempts to define the requirements of that procedure. The subjects about which the parties must bargain, *i.e.,* "the wages, hours, and other terms and conditions of employment" of §8 (d) , are treated in Chapter 15 *infra.*

70 H. K. Porter Co., Inc., 397 US 99, 73 LRRM 2561, 2562 (1970) .

71 NLRB v. Katz, 369 US 736, 743, 50 LRRM 2177 (1962) , where the Supreme Court held "that an employer's unilateral change in conditions of employment under negotiation is . . . a violation of §8(a) (5) , for it is a circumvention of the duty to negotiate. . . ." *See* Part V, *infra,* this chapter.

72 General Electric Co., 150 NLRB 192, 194, 57 LRRM 1491 (1964) , *affirmed,* 418 F 2d 736, 72 LRRM 2530 (CA 2, 1969) , *cert. denied,* 397 US 965, 73 LRRM 2600 (1970) . *See* notes 229-239 *infra.*

73 NLRB v. Katz, note 71 *supra.*

74 418 F 2d at 750.

Relying on *Truitt* [75] and other decisions requiring disclosure of bargaining information, the court stated that

> if the purpose of collective bargaining is to promote the "rational exchange of facts and arguments" that will measurably increase the chance for amicable agreement, then discussions in which unsubstantiated reasons are substituted for genuine arguments should be anathema.[76]

Concerning the employer's conduct in dealing separately with several IUE locals, the court sustained the Board's conclusion that in each instance when the employer "went behind the back of the negotiators and offered separate peace settlements to locals" [77] it committed an unfair labor practice.

In addition to affirming the foregoing three specific unfair labor practices, the court also agreed that the employer was guilty of a refusal to bargain based on a "totality of circumstances." [78] It noted the take-it-or-leave it basis of the insurance proposal, that "General Electric occasionally took untenable and unreasonable positions and then defended them, with no apparent purposes other than to avoid yielding to the Union," [79] and other conduct which was deemed inconsistent with a genuine desire to reach a mutual accommodation. The court observed that General Electric's aim "was to deal with the union through the employees, rather than the employees through the union" [80]—the antithesis of collective bargaining. Underlying the decisions of both the Board and the court of appeals was the view that the employer had locked itself in.[81] GE had put certain benefits in effect, according to its longstanding policy of maintaining uniformity among all its employees, and had taken the public position that there was "nothing more to come." Thus, "having created a view of the bargaining process that admitted no compromise," the court's opinion concluded that GE "was trapped by its own creation." [82] The court summed up what it held as well as what it did not hold:

---

[75] NLRB v. Truitt Mfg. Co., 351 US 149, 38 LRRM 2042 (1956). *See* note 269 *infra*.
[76] 418 F 2d at 750, *citing* Cox, *The Duty to Bargain in Good Faith*, 71 HARV. L. REV. 1401 (1958).
[77] 418 F 2d at 755.
[78] *Id*. at 756.
[79] *Id*. at 758.
[80] *Id*. at 759.
[81] *See* Jaffe, *Major Developments of the Year under the National Labor Relations Act*, NYU EIGHTEENTH ANNUAL CONFERENCE ON LABOR, 61, 67 (1966).
[82] 418 F 2d at 759, 760.

We do not today hold that an employer may not communicate with his employees during negotiations. Nor are we deciding that the "best offer first" bargaining technique is forbidden. Moreover, we do not require an employer to engage in "auction bargaining," or, as the dissent seems to suggest, compel him to make concessions, "minor" or otherwise.[83]

Disagreeing with the majority's reasoning, Judge Friendly, in a concurring and dissenting opinion, warned that the holding constituted a "serious indentation of §§(c) and (d), if not, indeed, of the First Amendment . . . the familiar instance of a hard case producing bad law." [84]

Writing for the majority, Judge Kaufman responded by spelling out the scope of the holding, stating:

Our dissenting brother's peroration conjures up the dark spectre that we have taken a "portentous step" [but] paints over with a broad stroke the care we have taken to spell out the bounds of our opinion. We hold that an employer may not so combine "take-it-or-leave-it" bargaining methods with a widely publicized stance of unbending firmness that he is himself unable to alter a position once taken. It is this specific conduct that GE must avoid in order to comply with the Board's order, and not a carbon copy of every underlying event relied upon by the Board to support its findings. Such conduct, we find, constitutes a refusal to bargain "in fact." . . . It also constitutes, as the facts of this action demonstrate, an absence of subjective good faith, for it implies that the Company can deliberately bargain and communicate as though the Union did not exist, in clear derogation of the Union's status as exclusive representative of its members under section 9 (a) .[85]

The *General Electric* decision contains elements touching upon a wide range of problems in the area covered by this chapter. It therefore serves to introduce the cases which follow.

2. Coalition Bargaining. One important development attributable in some degree to the type of bargaining tactics examined in the *GE* case has been the development of coalition bargaining. Such bargaining offers the participating unions the advantage of a united front in contract negotiations.

---

[83] *Id.* at 762.

[84] *Id.* at 774.

[85] *Id.* at 762-763. *General Electric* was distinguished in *Rangaire Corp.*, 157 NLRB 682, 61 LRRM 1429 (1966). *Cf.* Stark Ceramics, 155 NLRB 1258, 60 LRRM 1487 (1965); Memorial Consultants, Inc., 153 NLRB 1, 59 LRRM 1375 (1965). *See also* Procter & Gamble Mfg. Co., 160 NLRB 334, 62 LRRM 1617 (1966), in which a non-coercive communication campaign did not demonstrate bad faith, especially since the record established the employer's good faith in seeking to reach a common ground for agreement as evidenced by its extensive negotiations, proposals, counterproposals, and concessions.

In 1966 the International Union of Electrical Workers formed a coalition with seven other members of the AFL-CIO Industrial Union Department,[86] with the avowed purpose of evolving national goals and of adopting a "coordinated approach" to the negotiations with GE. Company representatives walked out of a meeting with the coalition committee, contending that representatives of seven other unions were not properly a part of the negotiating committee. Both IUE and the company filed unfair labor practice charges. The General Counsel sustained the union's charge but dismissed the company's Section 8(b)(1)(A) charge that IUE had violated its bargaining duty by insisting that the company deal with the coalition.[87]

The Board found the employer guilty of refusal to bargain because its negotiators had walked out of the meeting with the coordinated bargaining committee and had refused to deal with "outsiders." [88] The Second Circuit upheld the Board's order,[89] finding that the employer violated Section 8(a)(5) by refusing to bargain with the committee; however, it disagreed with the Board regarding the preliminary meeting which the company had refused to attend. The court held that the company could condition its agreement to a preliminary meeting on a requirement that the union negotiating committee be limited to members of the union with which the new contract was to be negotiated.

Addressing itself to the basic issue, "whether a union's inclusion of members of other unions on its bargaining committee justifies an employer's refusal to bargain," the court declared that the

---

[86] A similar coalition was formed prior to the 1960 contract negotiations. *See* Cooper, *supra* note 61, at 666, n. 41.

[87] McLeod v. General Electric Co., 257 F Supp 690, 62 LRRM 2809 (SD NY, 1966), *reversed,* 366 F 2d 847, 63 LRRM 2065 (CA 2, 1966), *remanded,* 385 US 533, 64 LRRM 2129 (1967). The regional director had obtained a temporary injunction from a federal district court under Section 10 (j) restraining the company from refusing to bargain collectively with the IUE negotiating committee. The district court ruled that the company's failure to bargain "could not be justified by the conjectural claim that the IUE team was ineluctably bent on 'multi-union bargaining.'" 257 F Supp at 706. The Second Circuit reversed and vacated the injunction without passing on the merits, holding that "[t]he Board has not demonstrated than an injunction is necessary to preserve the status quo or to prevent any irreparable harm." 366 F 2d at 850. The Supreme Court granted a stay of the Second Circuit's judgment pending certiorari proceedings. On certiorari, however, the Supreme Court in a *per curiam* opinion dissolved the stay of the court of appeals' order and set aside the judgment of the court with directions to remand to the district court, since the employer and IUE had agreed upon a new collective bargaining agreement.

[88] General Electric Co., 173 NLRB No. 46, 69 LRRM 1305 (1968).

[89] 412 F 2d 512, 71 LRRM 2418 (CA 2, 1969).

"right of employees and the corresponding right of employers . . . to choose whomever they wish to represent them in formal labor negotiations is fundamental to the statutory scheme." [90] Although it recognized that the freedom to select representatives was not absolute,[91] it noted that the infrequency of approved exceptions emphasized the importance of the rule. The court therefore held that for the employer to prevail in its objections to the outsider members of the union negotiating committee, it had to sustain the burden of showing a " 'clear and present' danger to the collective bargaining process." [92] Finding no such clear and present danger, the court held that G.E. was not lawfully entitled to refuse to bargain with the multi-union committee so long as the committee sought to bargain solely on behalf of the employees who would be covered under the contract being negotiated.

Employer opposition to coalition bargaining has focused upon the possible obliteration of "unit" determination, under which separately certified unions were selected to represent distinct segments of the company's employees at various locations. Coalition bargaining, it has been argued, might permit a union to act as bargaining agent for a group of employees for which another union has been certified.[93]

Even prior to the *G.E.* case the Board said that an employer could not in good faith refuse to bargain with a union negotiating committee merely because other unions are represented on the committee. In *American Radiator & Standard Sanitary Corp.* the employer was requested by all unions representing employees at its various plant to bargain jointly.[94] The employer, however,

---

90 *Id.* at 516. *See* Prudential Ins. Co. of America v. NLRB, 278 F 2d 181, 46 LRRM 2026 (CA 3, 1960) ; NLRB v. Deena Artware, Inc., 198 F 2d 645, 30 LRRM 2479 (CA 6, 1952) , *cert. denied,* 345 US 906, 31 LRRM 2444 (1953) ; Pueblo Gas & Fuel Co. v. NLRB, 118 F 2d 304, 8 LRRM 902 (CA 10, 1941) ; Oliver Corp., 74 NLRB 483, 20 LRRM 1183 (1947).

91 *Id.* at 517, citing, as exceptions to the general rule: NLRB v. ILGWU, 274 F 2d 376, 45 LRRM 2626 (CA 3, 1960) ("exunion official added to employer committee to 'put one over on the union' ") ; Bausch & Lomb Optical Co., 108 NLRB 1555, 34 LRRM 1222 (1954) ("union established company in direct competition with employer") ; NLRB v. Kentucky Utilities Co., 182 F 2d 810, 26 LRRM 2287 (CA 6, 1950) ("union negotiator had expressed great personal animosity towards employer").

92 412 F 2d at 517.

93 *See:* Benetar, *Coalition Bargaining Under the NLRA,* NEW YORK UNIVERSITY TWENTIETH ANNUAL CONFERENCE ON LABOR 219 (New York: Matthew Bender, 1968) , *and* Abramson, *Coordinated Bargaining By Unions, id.* at 231, where arguments both for and against coalition bargaining are advanced.

94 155 NLRB 736, 60 LRRM 1385 (1965).

declined to meet "with a group not legally certified as collective bargaining representative." [95] As in *General Electric,* the contention was that the unions had coalesced for the purpose of compelling company-wide bargaining. Relying on *Standard Oil Corp.,*[96] the trial examiner, with Board approval, found that the employer was not relieved of the duty to meet with the duly appointed representative, even though other unions had members on the committee, since the composition of the committee was an internal matter over which the company has no control. Furthermore, there was no proof of a conspiracy to force the employer into company-wide bargaining.

The Sixth Circuit's approval of the ruling in *Standard Oil*[97] gave authority to both the *American Radiator* and *General Electric* decisions. *Standard Oil* involved coordinated bargaining by different locals of the same parent union. The court held that the presence on the local's bargaining committee of non-local-union members, designated "temporary representatives," did not justify the company's refusal to bargain:

> Absent any finding of bad faith or ulterior motive on the part of the Unions we conclude that it was the duty of the Company to negotiate with the bargaining committees of the Unions at the respective refinery plants even though the temporary representatives were present.[98]

C. Elements of Good or Bad Faith

In an examination of the conduct of an employer or a union, certain factors are relied upon to ascertain whether the parties have bargained in good or bad faith.[99] Any of these factors, standing alone, is usually insufficient, but their "persuasiveness grows as the number of issues increases." [100]

---

[95] *Id.* at 739.

[96] 137 NLRB 690, 50 LRRM 1238 (1962), *enforced,* 322 F 2d 40, 54 LRRM 2076 (CA 6, 1963).

[97] *Ibid.*

[98] 322 F 2d at 44. *See also,* Independent Drugstore Owners of Santa Clara County, 170 NLRB No. 195, 69 LRRM 1031 (1968); Minnesota Mining & Mfg. Co. v. NLRB, 415 F 2d 174, 72 LRRM 2129 (CA 8, 1969). *But see* discussion of bargaining units as permissive subjects of bargaining in Chapter 16 *infra* at notes 9-16.

[99] "[T]he question of whether an employer is acting in good or bad faith at the time of the refusal is . . . one which . . . must be determined in the light of all relevant facts in the case, including any unlawful conduct of the employer, the sequence of events, and the time lapse between the refusal and the unlawful conduct," *cited in Joy Silk Mills v. NLRB,* 185 F 2d 732, 742, 27 LRRM 2012, 2019 (CA DC, 1950), *cert. denied,* 341 US 914, 27 LRRM 2633 (1951).

[100] Cox, *The Duty to Bargain in Good Faith,* 71 HARV. L. REV. 1401, 1421 (1958).

1. Surface Bargaining. Closely aligned with the concept of viewing the "totality" of the bargaining is the notion of surface bargaining. Although an employer may be willing to meet at length and confer with a union, the Board will find a refusal to bargain in good faith if he is merely going through the "motions" of bargaining.[101] It has been held that when an employer rejects a union's proposal, tenders his own, and does not attempt to reconcile the differences, he is engaged in "surface bargaining." [102] Likewise, the offering of a proposal that cannot be accepted, coupled with an inflexible attitude on major issues and no proposal of reasonable alternatives, has been condemned as violative of the good-faith obligation.[103] In *Irvington Motors* [104] the employer was held to have violated the Act by bargaining without intention of seeking agreement where its offer was to continue only the existing practices and its first written counterproposal was not submitted until 3½ months after it had been requested.[105] An employer's predetermined and inflexible position toward union security and merit increases,[106] dilatory tactics with an apparent

---

[101] Tower Hosiery Mills, 81 NLRB 658, 23 LRRM 1397 (1949), *enforced*, 180 F 2d 701, 25 LRRM 2509 (CA 4, 1950), *cert. denied*, 340 US 811, 26 LRRM 2611 (1950) (employer's insistence on union bond payable in event of breach of no-strike clause, and substitution of a more burdensome requirement after seven months of negotiation without modifying its requirement for open shop, showed "lack of a sincere purpose to reach an agreement"); Texas Coca Cola Bottling Co., 146 NLRB 420, 55 LRRM 1326 (1964) (employer's refusal to accept union's proposed management-rights clause even though it had suggested same clause to union, refusal to agree to arbitration clause after securing union's agreement to no-strike clause, failure to submit counterproposal on dues checkoff, rejection of agreement on workweek, *inter alia*, led to conclusion that employer was merely going through the motions of negotiation without sincere desire to reach agreement); My Store, Inc., 147 NLRB 145, 56 LRRM 1176 (1964), *enforced*, 345 F 2d 494, 58 LRRM 2775 (CA 7, 1965), *cert. denied*, 382 US 927, 60 LRRM 2424 (1965) (furnishing erroneous wage information to union and failure to correct it after discovering error, questioning of union's majority by raising issue covered by consent election, failure to submit counterproposal until four months after certification, and making of minor agreements to give the "appearances of bargaining" considered as "evidence of Respondent's bad faith"). *See also* Collins & Aikman Corp., 165 NLRB 678, 65 LRRM 1484 (1967), *enforced in part*, 395 F 2d 277, 68 LRRM 2320 (CA 4, 1968); Southern Transport, 145 NLRB 615, 55 LRRM 1023 (1963), *enforced*, 343 F 2d 558, 58 LRRM 2822 (CA 8, 1965); Atlanta Broadcasting Co., 90 NLRB 808, 26 LRRM 1287 (1950), *enforced* 193 F 2d 641, 29 LRRM 2327 (CA 5, 1952); Tex Tan Welhausen Co. v. NLRB, 419 F 2d 1265, 72 LRRM 2885 (CA 5, 1970).

[102] A. H. Belo Corp., 170 NLRB No. 175, 69 LRRM 1239 (1968); General Electric Co., 150 NLRB 192, 57 LRRM 1491 (1964), *affirmed*, 418 F 2d 736, 72 LRRM 2530 (CA 2, 1969), *cert. denied*, 397 US 965, 73 LRRM 2600 (1970).

[103] S. Morena & Sons, 163 NLRB 1071, 65 LRRM 1054 (1967); Roy E. Hanson, Jr., Mfg. 137 NLRB 251, 50 LRRM 1134 (1962).

[104] 147 NLRB 565, 56 LRRM 1257 (1964), *enforced*, 343 F 2d 759, 58 LRRM 2816 (CA 3, 1965).

[105] *And see* MacMillan Ring-Free Oil Co., 160 NLRB 877, 63 LRRM 1073 (1966).

[106] Duro Fittings Co., 121 NLRB 377, 42 LRRM 1368 (1958).

intent to reach an impasse,[107] arbitrary scheduling of the day and time of a bargaining meeting,[108] and failure to designate an agent with sufficient authority [109] have been held to be elements which, when coupled with other factors, prove an intention to engage in "surface bargaining" rather than reach a mutually satisfactory basis for agreement.

But the mere tendering by an employer of a counterproposal which is "predictably unacceptable" is not, standing alone, sufficient to justify a finding of lack of good faith if the proposal does not foreclose future discussion. As the Second Circuit stated in *NLRB* v. *Fitzgerald Mills*,[110] "[i]n the realities of the bargaining process, neither party expects its first proposal to be accepted." [111] In *Kohler Co.*[112] the union charged that the company had engaged in "surface bargaining" during prestrike negotiations. The Board, in rejecting this charge, pointed to the company's request to get to the "meat" of the contract, its regular attendance at bargaining sessions, and its exploration of alternatives and the reasonableness of arguments in support of its bargaining positions.[113]

The fact that extensive negotiation fails to produce a contract does not justify an inference that the company is engaged in "surface bargaining," since the Act does not compel the parties to reach an agreement. Where the parties had exchanged contract proposals and had met and discussed them, and the union negotiator had written the company a letter stating he felt that the

---

[107] Wheeling Pacific Co., 151 NLRB 1192, 58 LRRM 1580 (1965); Hilton Mobile Homes, 155 NLRB 873, 60 LRRM 1411 (1965) (by implication). For the effect of an impasse on the bargaining obligation, see Section VII *infra*.

[108] Moore Drop Forging, 144 NLRB 165, 54 LRRM 1024 (1963).

[109] Billups Western Petroleum Co., 169 NLRB No. 147, 67 LRRM 1323 (1968); Bonham Cotton Mills, 121 NLRB 1235, 42 LRRM 1542 (1958), *enforced,* 289 F 2d 903, 48 LRRM 2086 (CA 5, 1961).

[110] 313 F 2d 260, 52 LRRM 2174 (CA 2, 1963), *enforcing* 133 NLRB 877, 48 LRRM 1745 (1961), *cert. denied,* 375 US 834, 54 LRRM 2312 (1963).

[111] 313 F 2d at 265. "Consideration of the negotiations themselves, rather than the proposed contracts within whose framework they were conducted, is a better guide to whether there was good faith bargaining." *Id.* at 266. *See also* note 150 and accompanying text. This view also prevails under the Railway Labor Act. Atlantic Coast Line R.R. v. Brotherhood of Railroad Trainmen, 262 F Supp 177, 185, 64 LRRM 2177 (D DC, 1967), *reversed on other grounds,* 383 F 2d 225, 66 LRRM 2115 (CA DC, 1967).

[112] 128 NLRB 1062, 46 LRRM 1389 (1960), *enforced in part, modified and remanded in part,* 300 F 2d 699, 49 LRRM 2485 (CA DC, 1962).

[113] *Id.* at 1069. The Board did find that Kohler's post-strike conduct in unilaterally increasing the wages of nonstrikers after having previously attached conditions to offer of the same increase to the union, coupled with surveillance and discharge of strikers, constituted a §8(a)(5) violation. *Id.* at 1078. *See also* Star Expansion Indus. Corp., 164 NLRB 563, 65 LRRM 1127 (1967).

parties were "not too far apart on . . . [the] . . . issues," the Board found no bad faith.[114] An employer's adherence to a "package" proposal during contract negotiations has been allowed, in view of the employer's willingness to concede other points.[115] In addition, bargaining without concealing existing "mutual hostility" [116] or negotiating in a "cool atmosphere" [117] will not "dilute a finding of good faith where the totality of the party's conduct conforms to the dictates of the statute." [118]

2. Concessions. "Although . . . state of mind may occasionally be revealed by declarations, ordinarily the proof must come by inference from external conduct." [119] Thus, even though Section 8(d) does not require the making of a concession, the court and Board definitions of good faith [120] suggest that willingness to compromise is an essential ingredient.[121] The granting or withholding of concessions may be of vital importance in defending against charges of refusal to bargain in good faith. The historic language in *Reed & Prince* [122] bears this out:

> [W]hile the Board cannot force an employer to make a "concession" on any specific issue or to adopt any particular position, the employer is obligated to make some reasonable effort in *some* direction to compose his differences with the union, if section 8(a)(5) is to be read as imposing any substantial obligation at all.[123]

In *Herman Sausage Co.*[124] the Board found, as evidence of the employer's bad faith, its unwillingness "to accept or consider any

---

114 Lakeland Cement Co., 130 NLRB 1365, 47 LRRM 1499 (1961). The employer was convicted of independent §8 (a) (1) violations for assisting employees in the processing of withdrawal petitions and interrogating an employee with regard to his union sympathies.
115 Midwestern Instruments, 133 NLRB 1132, 48 LRRM 1793 (1961). But offering a union a contract on a take-it-or-leave-it basis has been consistently held to be a repudiation of collective bargaining. *See, e.g.,* NLRB v. Insurance Agents' Int'l Union, 361 US 477, 487, 45 LRRM 2704 (1960); NLRB v. Truitt Mfg. Co., 351 US 149, 154, 38 LRRM 2042 (1956) (separate opinion.). *See also* discussion of the *General Electric* case notes 59-85, *supra,* and accompanying text.
116 McCulloch Corp., 132 NLRB 201, 48 LRRM 1344 (1961).
117 NLRB v. Almeida Bus Lines, 333 F 2d 729, 731, 56 LRRM 2548 (CA 1, 1964), *setting aside* 142 NLRB 445, 53 LRRM 1055 (1963).
118 333 F 2d at 731.
119 Cox, *The Duty to Bargain in Good Faith,* 71 HARV. L. REV. 1401, 1418 (1958).
120 *See, e.g.,* NLRB v. Highland Park Mfg., 110 F 2d 632, 6 LRRM 786 (CA 4, 1940), and Section II *supra* for general definitions of good faith and cases thereon.
121 Cox, *supra* note 119, at 1414. For this reason, Professor Cox concludes "that the conventional definition of good faith bargaining as a sincere effort to reach an agreement goes beyond the statute." *Id.* at 1416. *See also* Specialty Container Corp., 171 NLRB No. 6, 68 LRRM 1018 (1968).
122 NLRB v. Reed & Prince Mfg. Co., 205 F 2d 131, 32 LRRM 2225 (CA 1, 1953).
123 *Id.* at 134-135.
124 122 NLRB 168, 43 LRRM 1090 (1958), *enforced,* 275 F 2d 229, 45 LRRM 2829 (CA 5, 1960).

contract other than its proposed contract," which, though similar to a contract previously executed by the same union, "constituted such a radical departure from the previous contract in eliminating approximately 26 existing benefits . . . as to be predictably unacceptable to the union." [125]

Pointing to the futility of future negotiations unless the union accepts certain management proposals,[126] insistence that economic items not be discussed until all other terms are agreed upon,[127] failure to offer "concessions of value," [128] and creating the impression that there could be no wage increase in order to assure that negotiations would founder,[129] have all been considered factors [130] pointing to bad-faith bargaining.[131] Moreover, it has been held that "the significant fact is not whether [the employer] was in a

---

[125] 122 NLRB at 170.

[126] Lewin-Mathes Co., 126 NLRB 936, 45 LRRM 1416 (1960), enforcement denied, 285 F 2d 329, 47 LRRM 2288 (CA 7, 1960).

[127] Rhodes-Holland Chevrolet Co., 146 NLRB 1304, 56 LRRM 1058 (1964). See also Vanderbilt Products, Inc., 129 NLRB 1323, 47 LRRM 1182 (1961), enforced, 297 F 2d 833, 49 LRRM 2286 (CA 2, 1961).

[128] Collins & Aikman Corp., 165 NLRB 678, 65 LRRM 1484 (1967), enforced in part, 395 F 2d 277, 68 LRRM 2320 (CA 4, 1968). See also East Texas Steel Castings, 154 NLRB 1080, 60 LRRM 1097 (1965).

[129] Cincinnati Cordage & Paper Co., 141 NLRB 72, 52 LRRM 1277 (1963). "For the Company to refuse at this time [the parties' last meeting and after a strike vote had been taken] to divulge that it would consider a more modest demand than had been theretofore advanced, and for it to state to the union a position which the plant manager later admitted on the witness stand was a falsity—namely, that it could not grant any increase because of competition—establishes that it was not bargaining in good faith." Id. at 77.

[130] In Marden Manufacturing Co., 106 NLRB 1335, 33 LRRM 1025 (1953), enforced 217 F 2d 567, 35 LRRM 2217 (CA 5, 1954), cert. denied, 348 US 981, 35 LRRM 2709 (1955), the Board expressly declined to "adopt a possible implication . . . in . . . the Intermediate Report that the . . . failure to make concessions to the union with respect to wages or financial benefits was per se a refusal to bargain rather than only 'a material factor,' in assessing good faith." 106 NLRB at 1338.

[131] Other "factors" considered include an employer's insistence on a management-prerogatives clause while refusing to negotiate concerning a wage increase and declining to consent to arbitration. "M" System, Inc., 129 NLRB 527, 47 LRRM 1017 (1960). The employer violated §§8(a)(5) and 8(d) by instituting a wage incentive plan and granting individual pay raises without consulting the union while steadfastly refusing to enter any agreement containing a wage increase of any size. Similarly, see Farmers Co-operative Gin Ass'n, 161 NLRB 887, 63 LRRM 1400 (1966), where the employer agreed to payroll deductions not involving the union while refusing a requested checkoff provision. In Fitzgerald Mills, 133 NLRB 877, 48 LRRM 1745 (1961), the employer in contract renewal negotiations submitted a counterproposal that was, in effect, the expiring contract. Thereafter, "the union receded from its original position and made a great many progressively lesser requests but . . . the Respondent at all times maintained an uncompromising attitude, rejecting the union's requests without explanation or discussion. . . . While an employer is not obligated to make any concession, it is required to make a reasonable effort to reach an agreement." Id. at 880. See also Alba-Waldensian, 167 NLRB 695, 66 LRRM 1145 (1967).

position to grant concessions, but rather whether it bargained in good faith on the subject." [132]

Granting of numerous concessions may be considered an indication of good-faith bargaining. Although the decisions purport to look beyond the number of concessions granted or withheld,[133] recognition of "thirty-eight instances where . . . [the employer] adjusted its proposals in striving to induce the union to agree" [134] and a review of bargaining history in order to find "numerous concessions on substantive issues" [135] indicate that consideration is given to the quantity as well as the quality of concessions.

The finding of agreement on many major bargaining subjects may be used as evidence to overcome a refusal-to-bargain charge based on a single specific issue.[136] In *John S. Swift & Co.*[137] the union representing only a portion of the employees at one plant sought to institute its own health and welfare plan. The employer insisted upon retaining its existing company-wide plan, embracing several plants. In finding that the employer had bargained in good faith with respect to the health and welfare plan, the Board noted the company's continued willingness to discuss the issue and the fact that the company and the union had reached agreement "on virtually every major bargaining item excepting health and welfare." [138]

Where an employer would not agree to an arbitration clause but was adamant in insisting upon inclusion of a no-strike clause, the

---

132 Partee Flooring Mill, 107 NLRB 1177, 1178, 33 LRRM 1342 (1954). *But see* NLRB v. Minute Maid Corp., 283 F 2d 705, 47 LRRM 2072 (CA 5, 1960), *denying enforcement to* 124 NLRB 355, 44 LRRM 1376 (1959).
133 *See, e.g.,* Vickers, Inc., 153 NLRB 561, 59 LRRM 1516 (1965).
134 NLRB v. General Tire and Rubber Co., 326 F 2d 832, 833, 55 LRRM 2150 (CA 5, 1964).
135 In *Star Expansion,* 164 NLRB 563, 65 LRRM 1127 (1967) "the company agreed to some 12 or more proposals made by the union. In subsequent negotiations, it made other concessions and offered proposals of its own on wage increases and other matters." In *Dierks Forests, Inc.,* 148 NLRB 923, 57 LRRM 1087 (1964), "the union [initially] presented its proposed contract, consisting of 25 articles, with a total of 61 subsections," and later submitted a wage offer. Employer submitted counterproposals on every issue except no-discrimination clause, checkoff, and insurance. By the end of the negotiations, 54 of the 62 subsections that had been presented were agreed upon. *Id.* at 927-928.
136 *See, e.g.,* Procter & Gamble Mfg. Co., 160 NLRB 334, 62 LRRM 1617 (1966).
137 124 NLRB 394, 44 LRRM 1388 (1959).
138 *Id.* at 395. The company was found guilty of a §8(a)(5) violation in failing to furnish wage data and the cost of its health and welfare plan; the finding was enforced on appeal, 277 F 2d 641, 46 LRRM 2090 (CA 7, 1960), *enforcing in part, denying in part* 124 NLRB 394, 44 LRRM 1388 (1959).

Board found a refusal to bargain in good faith;[139] but the Fifth Circuit denied enforcement,[140] stating that it did "not think that the Supreme Court held, or intended to hold, in *Lincoln Mills,* that a no-strike clause and an arbitration clause were so much one that a persistent demand for the one without acquiescing in the other is a refusal to bargain in good faith."[141]

No single rule is available to measure the significance of specific concessions. Reference must be made to the "totality" of negotiations in order to find good or bad faith. Hard bargaining rather than unlawful bargaining has been inferred from an unyielding position on union security,[142] wage offers,[143] checkoff,[144] and management rights,[145] where a review of the record as a whole showed no dilatory tactics or attempt to stall efforts[146] to reach agreement.[147] Also, the failure of management to retreat from a rigid position has been justified, in part, by the failure of the union to recede from its position or grant concessions "for which it could reasonably expect a *quid pro quo* from the [employer]."[148]

3. Proposals and Demands. The Board will consider the advancement of proposals as a factor in determining overall good faith.[149] The fact that a proposal is "predictably unacceptable" will not justify an inference of bad faith if the proposal does not

---

139 Cummer-Graham Co., 122 NLRB 1044, 43 LRRM 1253 (1959).

140 279 F 2d 757, 46 LRRM 2374 (CA 5, 1960).

141 *Id.* at 759-760. Textile Workers Union v. Lincoln Mills of Alabama, 353 US 448, 40 LRRM 2113 (1957). *See* Chapter 17 *infra* at note 33.

142 McCulloch Corp., 132 NLRB 201, 48 LRRM 1344 (1961).

143 Webster Outdoor Advertising, 170 NLRB No. 144, 67 LRRM 1589 (1968). Midwestern Instruments, 133 NLRB 1132, 48 LRRM 1793 (1961).

144 NLRB v. General Tire & Rubber Co., 326 F 2d 832, 55 LRRM 2150 (CA 5, 1964), *denying enforcement* to 135 NLRB 269, 49 LRRM 1469 (1962); Cone Mills Corp., 169 NLRB No. 59, 67 LRRM 1241 (1968); McLane Co., 166 NLRB 1036, 65 LRRM 1729 (1967); General Asbestos & Rubber Div., Raybestos-Manhattan Inc., 168 NLRB No. 54, 67 LRRM 1012 (1967). *But cf.* Farmers Cooperative Gin Ass'n, 161 NLRB 887, 63 LRRM 1400 (1966). See *H. K. Porter* and discussion of checkoff at notes 163-170 *infra.*

145 Procter & Gamble Mfg. Co., 160 NLRB 334, 62 LRRM 1617 (1966).

146 NLRB v. Wonder State Mfg. Co., 344 F 2d 210, 59 LRRM 2065 (CA 8, 1965), *enforcing in part, denying in part* 147 NLRB 179, 56 LRRM 1181 (1964).

147 "The fact that the respondent did not accede to the union's proposal but endeavored to secure a contract which it regarded would be compatible with its financial condition, does not of itself establish lack of good faith. The Act does not compel either party to agree to a proposal or require the making of a concession." 344 F 2d at 217.

148 NLRB v. Stevenson Brick & Block Co., 393 F 2d 234, 68 LRRM 2086 (CA 4, 1968); Memorial Consultants, Inc., 153 NLRB 1, 15, 59 LRRM 1375 (1965).

149 Reisman Bros. Inc., 165 NLRB 390, 65 LRRM 1409 (1967); Channel Master Corp., 162 NLRB 632, 64 LRRM 1102 (1967). Anderson's, 161 NLRB 358, 63 LRRM 1456 (1966); Procter & Gamble Mfg. Co., 160 NLRB 334, 62 LRRM 1617 (1966).

foreclose future negotiations,[150] unless it is so harsh or patently un-reasonable as to frustrate agreement.[151] However, the withdrawal of a company's solitary proposal which itself embodies only exist-ing conditions [152] and the rejection of proposals that have pre-viously been tentatively accepted have been considered elements of bad faith.[153]

The timing of demands or proposals may also be a factor in ascertaining good faith. The injection of numerous new proposals for the first time after several months of bargaining [154] or the sub-mission of new issues after the parties have reached agreement [155] in order to frustrate or stall contract execution has been found to be an indication of bad faith.[156]

The fact that a proposal merely embodies existing practices, or advances less desirable working conditions, is not, in itself, suffi-

---

[150] NLRB v. Fitzgerald Mills, 313 F 2d 260, 52 LRRM 2174 (CA 2, 1963). *See* Rangaire Corp., 157 NLRB 682, 61 LRRM 1429 (1966). The Ninth Circuit has stated that, "We may also assume arguendo that in certain exceptional cases the extreme or bizarre character of a party's proposals may give rise to a persuasive inference that they were made only as a delaying tactic or that they should be viewed as a facade concealing an intention to avoid reaching any agreement. . . . We believe, however, that such a principle, if accepted at all, must be narrowly restricted. Otherwise, the policy supporting section 8 (d)'s provision that the duty to bargain in good faith does not 'require the making of a concession' would be impermissibly undermined." NLRB v. MacMillan Ring-Free Oil Co., 394 F 2d 26, 29, 68 LRRM 2004 (CA 9, 1968); Taylor Instrument Co., 169 NLRB No. 28, 67 LRRM 1145 (1968).

[151] Architectural Fiberglass Div. of Architectural Pottery, 165 NLRB No. 21, 65 LRRM 1331 (1967). *See also* NLRB v. Tower Hosiery Mills, 180 F 2d 701, 25 LRRM 2509 (CA 4, 1950) (conditioning agreement on union acceptance of proposal re-quiring payment of fines and liquidated damages in event of strike). *Cf.* Arkansas Louisiana Gas Co., 154 NLRB 878, 60 LRRM 1055 (1965) (company proposed changes in no-strike, management rights, arbitration and grievance, insurance and pension provisions not so onerous or unreasonable as to bespeak bad faith); U. S. Gypsum Co., 94 NLRB 112, 28 LRRM 1015 (1951), *amended,* 97 NLRB 889, 29 LRRM 1171 (1951) *enforced in part, denied in part,* 206 F 2d 410, 32 LRRM 2553 (CA 5, 1953), *cert. denied,* 347 US 912, 33 LRRM 2456 (1954).

[152] Berry Kofron Dental Laboratory, 160 NLRB 493, 62 LRRM 1643 (1966).

[153] San Antonio Machine Corp. v. NLRB, 363 F 2d 633, 62 LRRM 2674 (CA 5, 1966); NLRB v. Shannon & Simpson Casket Co., 208 F 2d 545, 33 LRRM 2270 (CA 9, 1953); Satilla Rural Electric Membership Corp., 137 NLRB 387, 50 LRRM 1159 (1962), *enforced,* 332 F 2d 251, 53 LRRM 2841 (CA 5, 1963); but *cf.* Warehouse-men & Mail Order Employees v. NLRB, 302 F 2d 865, 49 LRRM 2466 (CA DC, 1962).

[154] B. F. Diamond Construction Co., 163 NLRB 161, 64 LRRM 1333 (1967); Altex Mfg. Co., 134 NLRB 614, 49 LRRM 1212 (1961), *enforced,* 307 F 2d 872, 51 LRRM 2139 (CA 4, 1962).

[155] Cabinet Mfg. Corp., 144 NLRB 842, 54 LRRM 1144 (1963).

[156] *See* New England Die Casting Co., 116 NLRB 1, 38 LRRM 1175 (1956), *enforced,* 242 F 2d 759, 39 LRRM 2616 (CA 2, 1957); Shovel Supply Co., Inc., 162 NLRB 460, 64 LRRM 1080 (1967).

cient to show bad faith, but is a consideration in evaluating the totality of bargaining conduct.[157]

a. Duration. Proposals for contracts of excessively long or short duration may be indicia of bad faith when judged in the light of attending circumstances.[158] A proposal for a five-year contract has been considered by the Board as evidence of bad faith.[159] Proposals for contracts to be effective for periods of only four months,[160] or very short periods, when obviously keyed to the expiration of the certification year,[161] have been similarly viewed. The bases for such holdings appear to be grounded on the theory that "[w]hile the expiration date of the contract, like its substantive provisions, is a bargainable matter, a contract terminable at the will of a party, or a contract for less than a year to expire at the end of the certification year, is normally not one that will give full force and effect to the Board's certification. Consequently, the Board views insistence upon such contract without good reason . . . as evidencing a lack of good-faith bargaining." [162]

---

157 Existing or less favorable terms embodied in employer's proposal, no violation found: McCulloch Corp., 132 NLRB 201, 48 LRRM 1344 (1961) (more stringent requirements to qualify for holiday pay); Continental Bus System, Inc., 128 NLRB 384, 46 LRRM 1308 (1960), *affirmed*, 294 F 2d 264, 48 LRRM 2579 (CA DC, 1961) (employer proposed renewal of old contract); Marathon-Clark Co-operative v. NLRB, 315 F 2d 269, 52 LRRM 2723 (CA DC, 1963) (across the board reduction in benefits). Violation found: Satilla Rural Electric Membership Corp., 137 NLRB 387, 50 LRRM 1159 (1962), *enforced*, 322 F 2d 251, 53 LRRM 2841 (CA 5, 1963) (withdrawal of proposal of conditions already in effect and failure to make counterproposal); Houston Sheet Metal Contractors Ass'n, 147 NLRB 774, 56 LRRM 1281 (1964) (company's last offer substantially below previous contract and its own earlier offers); Irvington Motors Inc., 147 NLRB 565, 56 LRRM 1257 (1964), *enforced*, 343 F 2d 759, 58 LRRM 2816 (CA 3, 1965) (proposal to continue existing practices conditioned upon union acceptance of new wage plan offered by company); Schnell Tool & Die Corp., 144 NLRB 385, 54 LRRM 1064 (1963); *see* Weinacker Brothers, Inc., 153 NLRB 459, 59 LRRM 1542 (1965).

158 Borg-Warner Controls, 128 NLRB 1035, 46 LRRM 1459 (1960).

159 Vanderbilt Products, Inc., 129 NLRB 1323, 47 LRRM 1182 (1961), *enforced*, 297 F 2d 833, 49 LRRM 2286 (CA 2, 1961); Mooney Aircraft, Inc., 132 NLRB 1194, 48 LRRM 1499 (1961), *enforced*, 310 F 2d 565, 51 LRRM 2615 (CA 5, 1962); Wonder State Mfg. Co., 147 NLRB 179, 56 LRRM 1181 (1964).

160 Solo Cup Co., 142 NLRB 1290, 53 LRRM 1253 (1963), *enforced*, 332 F 2d 447, 56 LRRM 2383 (CA 4, 1964).

161 NLRB v. W. R. Hall Distributors, 341 F 2d 359, 58 LRRM 2378 (CA 10, 1965), *enforcing* 144 NLRB 1285, 54 LRRM 1231 (1963); NLRB v. Henry Heide, Inc., 219 F 2d 46, 35 LRRM 2378 (CA 2, 1955), *enforcing* 107 NLRB 1160, 33 LRRM 1347 (1954).

162 Insulating Fabricators, Inc., 144 NLRB 1325, 1329-1330, 54 LRRM 1246 (1963), *enforced*, 338 F 2d 1002, 57 LRRM 2606 (CA 4, 1964). Similar reasoning has been

b. Checkoff. Refusals to accede to and failure to offer counter-proposals to union demands for checkoff or other forms of union security have been evidence of breach of the duty to confer in good faith. While it has long been the law that the bargaining obligation extends to a proposed checkoff clause,[163] the Board has not condemned an adamant stand against such a clause "where the employer [has shown willingness] to discuss the issue even though such discussions [have] proved fruitless." [164] Nevertheless, if the adamant stand is merely a "device to frustrate agreement" [165] or if it is taken despite a practice of deducting nonunion items from employees' paychecks,[166] the Board will consider such conduct to be demonstrative of bad faith.[167]

---

employed where the employer insisted on a one-year contract. *See, e.g.,* NLRB v. My Store, 345 F 2d 494, 58 LRRM 2775 (CA 7, 1965), *enforcing* 147 NLRB 145, 56 LRRM 1176 (1964), *cert. denied,* 382 US 927, 60 LRRM 2424. *Cf.* Star Expansion Indus. Corp., 164 NLRB 734, 65 LRRM 1127 (1967), where the Board found no bad faith in employer's insistence on contract expiration date coinciding with termination of certification year since contracting union had recently supplanted incumbent union in a close election and employer had reasonable cause to believe that contracting union no longer was supported by majority of employees.

163 U. S. Gypsum Co., 94 NLRB 112, 28 LRRM 1015 (1951); Reed & Prince Mfg. Co., 96 NLRB 850, 28 LRRM 1608 (1951), *enforced,* 205 F 2d 131, 32 LRRM 2225 (CA 1, 1953), *cert. denied,* 346 US 887, 33 LRRM 2133 (1953). *See* Chapter 15 *infra.*

164 Cone Mills Corp., 169 NLRB No. 59, 67 LRRM 1241 (1968); Star Expansion Co., 164 NLRB 563, 65 LRRM 1127 (1967); McLane Co., 166 NLRB No. 127, 65 LRRM 1729 (1967); General Asbestos & Rubber Div., Raybestos-Manhattan Inc., 168 NLRB No. 54, 67 LRRM 1012 (1967); Capital Aviation, Inc. v. NLRB, 355 F 2d 875, 877, 61 LRRM 2307 (CA 7, 1966), *citing* McCulloch Corp., 132 NLRB 201, 211, 48 LRRM 1344 (1961).

165 H. K. Porter Co., 153 NLRB 1370, 1372, 59 LRRM 1462 (1965), *enforced,* 363 F 2d 272, 62 LRRM 2204 (CA DC, 1966), *cert. denied,* 385 US 851, 63 LRRM 2236 (1966) (*see* notes 168-170 *infra* for further history of this case); Roanoke Iron & Bridge Works, Inc., 160 NLRB 175, 62 LRRM 1464 (1966), *enforced,* 390 F 2d 846, 67 LRRM 2450 (CA DC, 1967), *cert. denied,* 391 US 904, 68 LRRM 2097 (1968); Stevenson Brick & Block Co., 160 NLRB 198, 62 LRRM 1605 (1966), *enforcement denied in pertinent part,* 393 F 2d 234, 68 LRRM 2086 (CA 4, 1968); Flowers Baking Co., 161 NLRB 1429, 63 LRRM 1462 (1966). *But see* American Oil Co., 164 NLRB 36, 65 LRRM 1007 (1967) (employer's intransigent position not based on desire to frustrate agreement).

166 Farmers Co-operative Gin Ass'n, 161 NLRB 887, 63 LRRM 1400 (1966); H. K. Porter Co., *supra* note 165.

167 Caroline Farms Div. of Textron Inc., 163 NLRB 854, 64 LRRM 1465 (1967); Alba-Waldensian, 167 NLRB 695, 66 LRRM 1145 (1967); General Tire & Rubber Co., 135 NLRB 269, 49 LRRM 1469 (1962), *enforcement denied,* 326 F 2d 832, 55 LRRM 2150 (CA 5, 1964).

In *H. K. Porter* [168] the employer objected to granting a dues
checkoff solely on the ground that he was not going to give aid
and comfort to the union, for in his view the collection of union
dues was the "Union's business." [169] It was the employer's position
that this was merely "hard bargaining." [170] The Board found, with
the approval of the Court of Appeals for the District of Columbia
Circuit, that the refusal to bargain about checkoff was not done
in good faith, but was done solely to frustrate the making of any
collective bargaining agreement, hence was in violation of Section
8(a)(5).

c. Management Rights. The landmark case on provisions dealing with management rights is the Supreme Court's decision in
NLRB v. *American National Insurance Co.* [171] In that case the
union had submitted a proposed agreement which, in effect, called
for unlimited arbitration. In response the company proposed a

---

[168] H. K. Porter Co., *supra* note 165.   On subsequent motion to clarify the Court's
decree, the case was remanded to the Board for consideration of whether checkoff
should be granted to the union as a remedy for bad-faith bargaining. The court
stated that §8(d) defines the limit of the duty and does not prescribe the remedy for
the breach of that duty. It is within the Board's broad remedial powers, said the
court, to order the employer to grant a checkoff in return for reasonable union concessions or, in the proper case, for no concessions at all. United Steelworkers of
America (H. K. Porter Co.) v. NLRB, 389 F 2d 295, 66 LRRM 2761 (CA DC, 1967).
On remand, the Board directed the employer to grant the checkoff provision. 172
NLRB No. 72, 68 LRRM 1337 (1968). The Supreme Court reversed as to remedy,
397 US 99, 73 LRRM 2561 (1970), holding that the Board had no authority to
compel agreement as to any substantive provision in a collective bargaining contract.
See Chapter 31 *infra* at notes 135-138 for discussion of the remedial aspect of the
case.

The D.C. Circuit also enforced a Board finding of bad faith where the sole issue
was the company's refusal to grant a checkoff. United Steelworkers of America
(Roanoke Iron & Bridge Works) v. NLRB, 390 F 2d 846, 67 LRRM 2450 (CA DC,
1967), *cert. denied*, 391 US 904, 68 LRRM 2097 (1968). The Board found that the
company did not bargain in good faith over checkoff. The company rejected seven
alternative dues collection proposals advanced on the principle that no cooperation
would be given in union dues collection. The company's history of refusing to grant
checkoff in the past was viewed as a stratagem to weaken and destroy the union.
The court found support for this view in the company's disavowal of any business
reason for refusal to grant checkoff. Despite the fact that a contract was ultimately
signed, the court, citing, *NLRB* v. *Katz, supra* note 70, stated that a party may not
assume an intransigent position in bad faith on a mandatory subject "even though
its purpose to frustrate an agreement on that issue coincides with a willingness to
reach some overall agreement." The D.C. Circuit's *Roanoke* decision goes well beyond its earlier *H. K. Porter* decision, in which the Board found the company's
refusal was intended to frustrate any agreement. Though purporting to base its
finding on subjective good faith, the reliance on *Katz* indicated a *per se* approach
reminiscent of *GE* (*supra* note 59, and accompanying text).

[169] 153 NLRB at 1372.

[170] *Id.*

[171] 343 US 395, 30 LRRM 2147 (1952). *See also* discussion of this case in Chapter 14
infra.

management-functions clause in which all matters pertaining to promotions, discipline, and work scheduling were to be within management's exclusive control and not subject to arbitration.[172] The parties deadlocked on the clause but continued bargaining and reached agreement on other matters. Nonetheless the Board found that insistence upon the management-functions clause constituted a *per se* violation of Section 8(a)(5), without regard to considerations of good faith. The Fifth Circuit denied enforcement,[173] and the Supreme Court affirmed, holding that bargaining for such a clause was neither a *per se* violation nor evidence of bad faith.

The Supreme Court reasoned that good faith bargaining is a "two way street," and that the parties' inability to reach an agreement was due not only to the employer's unyielding position but also to the steadfast position of the union in opposing the management-functions clause. The broader significance of the decision lies in its affirmance of the principle that collective bargaining is a method of resolving industrial disputes, while minimizing the role of the Board in policing the substantive character of bargaining proposals.[174]

The Board subsequently has viewed insistence on a "broad" management-prerogative clause, one that would undermine the union's ability to adequately represent the employees,[175] as an element of bad faith. Also, insistence upon the union's waiving

---

172 The clause originally proposed read as follows: "The right to select, hire, to promote, demote, discharge, discipline for cause, to maintain discipline and efficiency of employees, and to determine schedules of work is the sole prerogative of the Company and . . . such matters shall never be the subject of arbitration." *Id.* at 397, n. 2.

173 89 NLRB 185, 25 LRRM 1532 (1950); 187 F 2d 307, 27 LRRM 2405 (CA 5, 1951).

174 "In its general aspect, the decision appears to be an admonition to the Board to moderate its close scrutiny of the play and by-play of collective bargaining negotiations in the application of the 'good faith' standard." From address of Prof. Russell A. Smith, Labor Relations Law Section of American Bar Ass'n., Aug. 24, 1953, *reprinted in part,* 32 LRRM 68, 73-74. *And see* Cox & Dunlop, *Regulation of Collective Bargaining by the National Labor Relations Board,* 63 Harv. L. Rev. 389 (1950): "The growth of strong unions and the spread of collective bargaining have shifted attention from the organization stage of labor relations to the problems of making collective bargaining a more effective institution for the conduct of employment relations."

175 "M" System, Inc., 129 NLRB 527, 47 LRRM 1017 (1960) (employer's proposal preserved job preference, allowed termination of seniority upon discharge for just cause based on management determination, reserved final determination of grievances to management).

most of its rights under the Act,[176] or upon unilateral control of wages, hours, or terms of employment,[177] has been considered by the Board in evaluating motive at the bargaining table.

Insistence upon a management-rights clause reserving the power to assign work and to protect replacements, after a strike has begun, was upheld by the Seventh Circuit in *NLRB* v. *Lewin-Mathes Co.*[178] The court criticized the Board's finding of bad faith which passed judgment ". . . on the reasonableness of the proposals." [179] In *Texas Industries, Inc.*,[180] the Board dismissed a complaint based in part on a management-rights clause which reserved *inter alia* the final decision in the grievance procedure as a management prerogative, where the employer willingly negotiated and explained his proposal. Similarly, no evidence of bad faith was found where the employer insisted upon reserving the right to grant individual merit increases [181] or to subcontract.[182]

4. Dilatory Tactics. The duty to bargain in good faith imposes on the parties the obligation to confer at reasonable times and intervals. Obviously, refusal to meet at all with the union does not satisfy the positive duty imposed on the employer.[183] Less flagrant conduct, such as unreasonable procrastination in executing an agreement [184] or delay in scheduling meetings,[185] has similarly been

---

176 East Texas Steel Castings Co., 154 NLRB 1080, 60 LRRM 1097 (1965) (employer's proposal reserved, *inter alia*, right to allocate work, transfer work from unit, reduce work force, and establish and change plant rules).
177 Dixie Corp., 105 NLRB 390, 32 LRRM 1259 (1953); Heider Mfg. Co., 91 NLRB 1185, 26 LRRM 1641 (1950).
178 285 F 2d 329, 47 LRRM 2288 (CA 7, 1960), *denying enforcement to* 126 NLRB 936, 45 LRRM 1416 (1960).
179 *Id.* at 332.
180 140 NLRB 527, 52 LRRM 1054 (1963).
181 Atlantic Research Corp., 144 NLRB 285, 54 LRRM 1049 (1963).
182 Star Expansion Corp., 164 NLRB 563, 65 LRRM 1127 (1967); Peerless Distributing Co., 144 NLRB 1510, 54 LRRM 1285 (1963).
183 NLRB v. Little Rock Downtowner, 341 F 2d 1020, 58 LRRM 2510 (CA 8, 1965), *enforcing as modified* 145 NLRB 1286, 55 LRRM 1156 (1964).
184 NLRB v. Ogle Protection Service, 375 F 2d 497, 64 LRRM 2792 (CA 6, 1967); NLRB v. Vander Wal, 316 F 2d 631, 52 LRRM 2761 (CA 9, 1963); Lozano Enterprises v. NLRB, 327 F 2d 814, 55 LRRM 2510 (CA 9, 1964), *enforcing* 143 NLRB 1347, 53 LRRM 1502 (1963); Wate, Inc., 132 NLRB 1338, 48 LRRM 1535 (1961), *enforced,* 310 F 2d 700, 51 LRRM 2701 (CA 6, 1962). This duty extends to unions also. *See, e.g.,* Local 717, Ice Cream Drivers (Ice Cream Council, Inc.), 145 NLRB 865, 55 LRRM 1059 (1964); Local 453, UAW (Maremont Automotive Products, Inc.), 134 NLRB 1337, 49 LRRM 1357 (1961).
185 Insulating Fabricators, 144 NLRB 1325, 54 LRRM 1246 (1963), *enforced mem.,* 338 F 2d 1002, 57 LRRM 2606 (CA 4, 1964); NLRB v. Southwestern Porcelain Steel Corp., 317 F 2d 527, 53 LRRM 2307 (CA 10, 1963), *enforcing* 134 NLRB 1733, 49 LRRM 1390 (1961); Solo Cup Co., 142 NLRB 1290, 53 LRRM 1253 (1963), *enforced,* 332 F 2d 447, 56 LRRM 2383 (CA 4, 1964); "M" System, Inc., 129 NLRB 527, 47 LRRM 1017 (1960).

condemned. Wilful avoidance of meetings [186] or delaying and
evasive tactics have been considered evidence [187] of bad faith by
the Board. The duty is a bilateral one. Where it appears that both
parties were equally dilatory [188] or where the union broke off
negotiations and made no further request for bargaining [189] or
wholly failed to request the employer to bargain,[190] the Board has
refused to find bad faith upon the part of the employer.

The employer is under a duty to invest its negotiators with
sufficient authority to carry on meaningful bargaining.[191] Cases
holding the employer guilty of delay in failing to provide a negotiator who is readily available have expanded this duty. Thus non-

---

[186] NLRB v. Exchange Parts Co., 339 F 2d 829, 58 LRRM 2097 (CA 5, 1965),
enforcing 139 NLRB 710, 51 LRRM 1366 (1962).

[187] Dilatory or evasive tactics are considered by the Board in assessing the totality
of an employer's conduct to determine good or bad faith. Standing alone, they
would not be *per se* violations of §8(a)(5). *See, e.g.,* Lloyd A. Fry Roofing Co. v.
NLRB, 216 F 2d 273, 35 LRRM 2009 (CA 9, 1954), *amended,* 220 F 2d 432, 35
LRRM 2662 (CA 9, 1955); Bewley Mills, 111 NLRB 830, 35 LRRM 1578 (1955)
(authority of negotiator considered factor, but not sole factor, in reaching conclusion that employer did not bargain in good faith); Exchange Parts, 139 NLRB 710,
51 LRRM 1366 (1962), *enforced,* 339 F 2d 829, 58 LRRM 2097 (CA 5, 1965),
rehearing denied, 341 F 2d 584, 58 LRRM 2456 (CA 5, 1965) (failure to meet at
reasonable times "occurring as it did in the context of a history of unfair labor
practices committed by Respondents" constituted §8(a)(5) violation); Insulating
Fabricators, Inc., 144 NLRB 1325, 54 LRRM 1246 (1963), *enforced,* 338 F 2d
1002, 57 LRRM 2606 (CA 4, 1964); National Amusements, Inc., 155 NLRB 1200,
60 LRRM 1485 (1965). *In Architectural Fiberglass Div. of Architectural Pottery,*
165 NLRB 238, 65 LRRM 1331 (1967), the employer's insistence on using a tape
recorder throughout the bargaining sessions was held to be evidence of bad faith.
One member took the position that such conduct was a *per se* violation. Borg
Compressed Steel Corp., 165 NLRB 394, 65 LRRM 1474 (1967).

[188] Dunn Packing Co., 143 NLRB 1149, 53 LRRM 1471 (1963); *but cf.* McLean v.
NLRB, 333 F 2d 84, 56 LRRM 2475 (CA 6, 1964), *enforcing* 142 NLRB 235, 53
LRRM 1021 (1963), where the court agreed with the Board's view that the union's
failure to negotiate during an eight-month period was no defense to the employer's
subsequent refusal to meet and negotiate since "it seems to us that it constituted
more of a violation of duty owing to its members than to McLean." 333 F 2d at 88.

[189] NLRB v. Lambert, 250 F 2d 801, 41 LRRM 2345 (CA 5, 1958) (dismissing contempt proceedings against employer for alleged refusal to bargain in compliance
with previous court order).

[190] Lori-Ann of Miami, Inc., 137 NLRB 1099, 50 LRRM 1340 (1962).

[191] NLRB v. Fitzgerald Mills, 313 F 2d 260, 52 LRRM 2174 (CA 2, 1963), *cert.
denied,* 375 US 834, 54 LRRM 2312 (1963); National Amusements Inc., 155 NLRB
1200, 60 LRRM 1485 (1965); Han-Dee Spring & Mfg. Co., 132 NLRB 1542, 48 LRRM
1566 (1961).

availability of the employer's negotiator [192] or its labor counsel [193] has been held to manifest bad faith.[194]

Delay in supplying requested information necessary for negotiations or for administration of the contract may provide the basis for a finding of dilatory tactics.[195] Failure to supply wage information promptly,[196] or delay in furnishing the union a current list of employees, wage rates, and job classifications,[197] or a pension plan,[198] has been considered evidence of bad faith.

No hard and fast rule can be stated with regard to number of meetings between the parties. The Board seemed to suggest in *Insulating Fabricators* [199] that the test, consistent with the other aspects of good-faith conduct, is whether the party's subjective intent shows a willingness to reach an agreement. In *Radiator Specialty Co.*[200] the trial examiner pointed out that "neither the Board nor the courts have evolved, or indeed can evolve, any particular formula by which to test whether any given frequency of meetings or amount of time spent in negotiations, satisfies the statutory requirement to 'meet at reasonable times'. . . ."[201] The

---

[192] Radiator Specialty Co., 143 NLRB 350, 53 LRRM 1319 (1963), *enforced in part,* 336 F 2d 495, 57 LRRM 2097 (CA 4, 1964) (enforcement denied as to failure-to-bargain/unavailability-of-negotiator charges); Solo Cup Co., 142 NLRB 1290, 53 LRRM 1253 (1963), *enforced,* 332 F 2d 447, 56 LRRM 2383 (CA 4, 1964) (company's vice-president and company's counsel); Allis Chalmers Mfg. Co., 106 NLRB 939, 32 LRRM 1585 (1953) (scheduling of negotiating sessions only when they would not interfere with company routine).

[193] *See, e.g.,* Insulating Fabricators Inc., 144 NLRB 1325, 54 LRRM 1246 (1963) (company's labor lawyer resided in Boston, approximately 800 miles from client's plant in Spartanburg, S.C.); Skyland Hosiery Mills, 108 NLRB 1600, 34 LRRM 1254 (1954).

[194] B. F. Diamond Construction Co., 163 NLRB 161, 64 LRRM 1333 (1967); "M" System, Inc., 129 NLRB 527, 549, 47 LRRM 1017 (1960).

[195] Fitzgerald Mills Corp., 133 NLRB 877, 48 LRRM 1745 (1961), *enforced,* 313 F 2d 260, 52 LRRM 2174, *cert. denied,* 375 US 834, 54 LRRM 2312 (1963).

[196] Butcher Boy Refrigerator Door Co., 127 NLRB 1360, 46 LRRM 1192 (1960), *enforced,* 290 F 2d 22, 48 LRRM 2058 (CA 7, 1961); Fitzgerald Mills, *supra* note 195; Rhodes-Holland Chevrolet Co., 146 NLRB 1304, 56 LRRM 1058 (1964).

[197] International Powder Metallurgy Co., 134 NLRB 1605, 49 LRRM 1388 (1961); Gateway Luggage Mfg. Co., 122 NLRB 1584, 43 LRRM 1342 (1959).

[198] Rangaire Corp., 157 NLRB 682, 61 LRRM 1429 (1966).

[199] 144 NLRB 1325, 54 LRRM 1246 (1963).

[200] 143 NLRB 350, 53 LRRM 1319 (1963), *enforced in part,* 336 F 2d 495, 57 LRRM 2097 (CA 4, 1964).

[201] 143 NLRB at 368.

Board has nonetheless relied on the frequency of meetings as evidence of an employer's intent.[202]

5. Imposing Conditions. The duty to bargain under the Act extends to good-faith consideration of all proper subjects for collective bargaining. Attempts to place conditions upon either bargaining or the execution of a contract will be scrutinized closely by the Board to see if the proposed condition is so onerous or unreasonable as to indicate bad faith.[203] For example, in *Fitzgerald Mills*[204] the employer bargained in bad faith by, *inter alia,* demanding a union waiver of grievances pending under the old contract and conditioning further bargaining upon waiver of strikers' reinstatement rights. The Board found the latter to be tantamount to requiring abandonment of the union's unfair labor practice charges pending against the employer, a condition which the Board has frequently condemned.[205] Likewise, refusing to negoti-

---

[202] *See, e.g.,* McCulloch Corp., 132 NLRB 201, 48 LRRM 1344 (1961) (employer, having met 79 times in 11 months and not having caused substantial delay, was not guilty of refusing to meet); Charles E. Honaker, 147 NLRB 1184, 56 LRRM 1371 (1964) (meeting on 11 occasions over five-month period, meetings averaging $3\frac{1}{2}$ to four hours each, was not a failing to meet); Texas Industries, Inc., 140 NLRB 527, 52 LRRM 1054 (1963) (meeting 11 times during four-month period was frequent enough to satisfy Act); Exchange Parts Co., 139 NLRB 710, 51 LRRM 1366 (1962), *enforced,* 339 F 2d 829, 58 LRRM 2097 (CA 5, 1965) (meeting average of eight hours a month over eight-month period was insufficient); Radiator Specialty Co., 143 NLRB 350, 53 LRRM 1319 (1963), *enforced in part,* 336 F 2d 495, 57 LRRM 2097 (CA 4, 1964) ("The parties met 37 times during a 10 month period. Some of these meetings . . . were at close intervals and a few meetings were lengthy. However, the great bulk of the meetings were of short duration, lasting about two hours, and the lags between many were considerable." 143 NLRB at 369. However, Board's finding of bad faith was rejected on ground that evidence did not show bad faith.)

[203] *See, e.g.,* American Flagpole Equip. Co., Case No. 29-CA-1052, 68 LRRM 1384 (1968), where an employer's reopening of negotiations was conditioned upon the union's execution of contracts with the employer's competitors. The fact that the purpose of the condition was to avoid economic disadvantage was held to be no defense to a refusal-to-bargain charge. *See also* Kroger Co., 164 NLRB 362, 65 LRRM 1089 (1967) (agreement to employer's proposal as prerequisite to acceptance of union's proposed plan held unlawful); S & M Mfg. Co., 165 NLRB 663, 65 LRRM 1350 (1967) (submission of contract proposal to union conditioned upon its acceptance on same day held unlawful); Lebanon Oak Flooring Co., 167 NLRB No. 104, 66 LRRM 1172 (1967).

[204] 133 NLRB 877, 48 LRRM 1745 (1961), *enforced,* 313 F 2d 260, 52 LRRM 2174 (CA 2, 1963), *cert. denied,* 575 US 834, 54 LRRM 2312 (1963).

[205] *See, e.g.,* Lion Oil Co. v. NLRB, 245 F 2d 376, 40 LRRM 2193 (CA 8, 1957); Palm Beach Post-Times, 151 NLRB 1030, 58 LRRM 1561 (1965); Kit Mfg. Co., 142 NLRB 957, 53 LRRM 1178 (1963), *enforced in part,* 335 F 2d 166, 56 LRRM 2988 (CA 9, 1964), *cert. denied,* 380 US 910, 58 LRRM 2496 (1965); Butcher Boy Refrigerator Door Co., 127 NLRB 1360, 46 LRRM 1192 (1960), *enforced,* 290 F 2d 22, 48 LRRM 2058 (CA 7, 1961); Taormina Co., 94 NLRB 884, 28 LRRM 1118 (1951), *enforced,* 207 F 2d 251, 32 LRRM 2684 (CA 5, 1953).

ate further unless the union ceases to strike violates the Act, since the obligation to bargain continues during the strike.[206]

Requiring agreement on certain subjects of bargaining as a prerequisite to further negotiation has been viewed as evidence of bad faith. Acceptance by the union of "open shop" and "freedom to discharge" provisions before the company would engage in economic discussion,[207] refusal to negotiate unless the union signed a 120-day moratorium that required, in effect, that the union cease representing the employees for a period of four months,[208] and a company requirement that the union post an indemnity bond as a condition to the signing of a contract [209] all have been evidence of bad faith. Attempting to dictate the composition of the union's negotiating committee,[210] and refusing to bargain with the union unless a former employee on the union committee was removed,[211] have been similarly construed.

6. Unilateral Changes in Conditions. Unilateral action by an employer affecting its employees' compensation during bargaining is a strong indication that it is not bargaining with the required

---

[206] General Electric Co., Battery Products Dept., 163 NLRB 198, 64 LRRM 1312 (1967); Rice Lake Creamery, 131 NLRB 1270, 48 LRRM 1251 (1961), *enforced sub nom.*, General Drivers & Helpers Union Local 662 v. NLRB, 302 F 2d 908, 50 LRRM 2243 (CA DC, 1962), *cert. denied,* 371 US 827, 51 LRRM 2222 (1962).

[207] Vanderbilt Products, 129 NLRB 1323, 47 LRRM 1182 (1961). In *NLRB v. Strong Roofing & Insulating Co.,* 386 F 2d 929, 65 LRRM 3012, (CA 9, 1967), *cert. denied,* 390 US 920, 67 LRRM 2384 (1968), the Ninth Circuit held that the Board was entitled to consider an employer's refusal to sign a contract, which refusal occurred more than six months before the charge was filed, as background evidence of similar refusals occurring within the §10(b) period. See text accompanying note 252, *supra.*

[208] Crusader-Lancer Corp., 144 NLRB 1309, 54 LRRM 1254 (1963). In *Architectural Fiberglass Div. of Architectural Pottery,* 165 NLRB 238, 65 LRRM 1331 (1967), a company's proposal requiring either party to waive its right to bargain during the term of the agreement, as well as the right to information pertaining to wages, hours, or other terms of employment, whether mentioned in the collective bargaining agreement or not, "could not have [been] proposed . . . in the good-faith expectation that such a proposal might afford a basis for the advancement of negotiations . . . as such a provision would require the union to abandon its statutory obligation to bargain collectively as the representative of [employer's] employees. . . ."

[209] F. McKenzie Davison, 136 NLRB 742, 49 LRRM 1831 (1962), *enforced,* 318 F 2d 550, 53 LRRM 2462 (CA 4, 1963). For effect of insistence upon non-mandatory bargaining subjects, *see* Chapters 14 and 16 *infra.*

[210] Cabinet Mfg. Co., 140 NLRB 576, 52 LRRM 1064 (1963).

[211] Fetzer Television, Inc., 131 NLRB 821, 48 LRRM 1165 (1961). *See* General Electric Co., 150 NLRB 192, 57 LRRM 1491 (1964), *affirmed,* 418 F 2d 736, 71 LRRM 2418, *cert. denied,* 397 US 965, 73 LRRM 2600 (1970) and notes 59-85 *supra.*

It considered such action "probative" of prior bad faith in negoti-
[during bargaining] is by far the most important 'unilateral act.' "
good faith.[212] The Second Circuit noted that a "wage increase
ations as a deliberate attempt by the employer to deal directly with
its employees and convince them that benefits come solely from
the employer; if the increase is contemporaneous with a strike,
the "timing is particularly convincing support for the conclusion
that prior negotiations were not conducted in good faith." [213]
Wage increases to employees in excess of any previous offer to the
union are normally violative of Section 8(a)(5),[214] as are increases
in wage-related fringe benefits such as holiday pay,[215] expense
allowances,[216] and incentive programs.[217] Reduction of a wage
benefit,[218] such as discontinuance of a Christmas bonus, may also
be indicative of a refusal to bargain.

There are, however, situations in which an employer may lawfully make unilateral changes, e.g., after the lapse of the certification year if there are reasonable grounds to believe the certified
union has lost majority support.[219] However, justification for

---

212 This section discusses unilateral changes as evidence showing lack of good faith in the bargaining obligation. A unilateral change, however, is usually a *per se* violation and is therefore so treated in Part V, *infra*, this Chapter.

213 NLRB v. Fitzgerald Mills Corp., 313 F 2d 260, 267-268, 52 LRRM 2174 (CA 2, 1963), *cert. denied*, 375 US 834, 54 LRRM 2312 (1963). *See* Trinity Valley Iron & Steel, 127 NLRB 417, 46 LRRM 1030 (1960) (granting wage increases to nonstrikers during economic strike).

214 Aztec Ceramics Co., 138 NLRB 1178, 51 LRRM 1226 (1962); Crater Lake Machinery Co., 131 NLRB 1106, 48 LRRM 1211 (1961); Yale Upholstering Co., 127 NLRB 440, 46 LRRM 1031 (1960); Dinion Coil Co., 110 NLRB 196, 34 LRRM 1623 (1954). *See also* Phil-Modes, Inc., 162 NLRB 1435, 64 LRRM 1303 (1967) (employer's unilateral wage increase constituted illegal change in working conditions despite fact that increases conformed with past practice, but evidence was insufficient to establish discriminatory motive in employer's changing method of wage computation.); Blue Cab Co., 156 NLRB 489, 61 LRRM 1085 (1965), *enforced*, 373 F 2d 661, 64 LRRM 2317 (CA DC, 1967), *cert. denied*, 389 US 836, 66 LRRM 2306 (1967).

215 Mooney Aircraft, Inc., 138 NLRB 1331, 51 LRRM 1230 (1962).

216 Cutter Boats, Inc., 127 NLRB 1576, 46 LRRM 1246 (1960).

217 "M" System, Inc., 129 NLRB 527, 47 LRRM 1017 (1960). Merit increases may not be unilaterally instituted. Berlin Coat Mfg. Co., 162 NLRB 1435, 64 LRRM 1303 (1967).

218 NLRB v. Zelrich Co., 344 F 2d 1011, 59 LRRM 2225 (CA 5, 1965). *See also* Scam Instrument Corp., 163 NLRB No. 39, 64 LRRM 1327 (1967) 394 F 2d 884, 68 LRRM 2280 (CA 7, 1968) (imposing policy rider which reduced benefits to employees who received sums under other insurance policies); NLRB v. Exchange Parts, 339 F 2d 829, 58 LRRM 2097 (CA 5, 1965) (regardless of whether decision to make such reduction was made before or after union certification); *see* Mooney Aircraft, Inc., 138 NLRB 1331, 51 LRRM 1230 (1962) (ceasing to allow employees to make up pay lost in periods of absence).

219 McCulloch Corp., 132 NLRB 201, 48 LRRM 1344 (1961); American Laundry Machine Co., 107 NLRB 1574, 33 LRRM 1457 (1954).

change may require not only that the belief be reasonable but that it be accurate.[220] An employer may grant a rejected wage increase after a bona fide impasse has been reached,[221] but not if the impasse was caused by the employer's lack of good faith.[222] In certain circumstances, however, an increase may be granted even before impasse is reached.[223] Of course, the continuation of traditional payments or implementation of increases already promised to employees is not unlawful.[224] An employer may put wage increases into effect for nonunit employees without incurring an obligation to make the same increase to unit employees absent receipt of any *quid pro quo* from the union.[225] Isolated wage changes for a few employees during negotiations do not necessarily establish bad faith,[226] but are normally vulnerable to such findings.[227]

7. Bypassing the Representative. As early as 1944 the Supreme Court in *J.I. Case* v. *NLRB*[228] upheld the Board's decision that an employer violates its duty to bargain when it refuses to negotiate with the union representative about matters contained in individual contracts of employment, even though such contracts had

---

[220] NLRB v. Superior Fireproof Door & Sash Co., 289 F 2d 713, 47 LRRM 2816 (CA 2, 1961).

[221] American Laundry Machine Co., 107 NLRB 1574, 33 LRRM 1457 (1954). However, a unilateral change as to subject matter which was not included in the negotiations is not permissible even after impasse. Intracoastal Terminal, Inc., 125 NLRB 359, 45 LRRM 1104, *enforced as modified in other respects*, 286 F 2d 954, 47 LRRM 2629 (CA 5, 1961). *But cf.* Laclede Gas Co., 173 NLRB No. 35, 69 LRRM 1316, *remanded*, 421 F 2d 610, 73 LRRM 2364 (CA 8, 1970), discussed in Chapter 20 *infra* at note 66.

[222] NLRB v. Reed & Prince Mfg. Co., 205 F 2d 131, 32 LRRM 2225 (CA 1, 1953).

[223] Fort Smith Chair Co., 143 NLRB 514, 53 LRRM 1313 (1963) (employer ceased bargaining and granted increases when union went on strike in violation of §8(d)(3) time limits); Betty Brooks Co., 99 NLRB 1237, 30 LRRM 1210 (1952) (union had rejected offer which new profit and loss statement showed employer capable of paying).

[224] McCulloch Corp., 132 NLRB 201, 48 LRRM 1344 (1961) (contributions to profit-sharing plan); Cutter Boats, Inc., 127 NLRB 1576, 46 LRRM 1246 (1960) (providing free home insurance arranged before certification, but not immediately conferred due to insurance-brokerage difficulties).

[225] McCulloch Corp., 132 NLRB 201, 48 LRRM 1344 (1961).

[226] White's Uvalde Mines v. NLRB, 255 F 2d 564, 42 LRRM 2001, 2046, 2195 (CA 5, 1958).

[227] "M" Systems, Inc., 129 NLRB 527, 47 LRRM 1017 (1960) (individual wage adjustments in accordance with unilaterally established incentive plan); Insulating Fabricators, Inc., 144 NLRB 1325, 54 LRRM 1246 (1963) (individual merit increases for most of bargaining unit).

[228] 321 US 332, 14 LRRM 501 (1944). The Court defined the collective bargaining contract as follows:

"Contract in labor law is a term the implications of which must be determined from the connection in which it appears. Collective bargaining between employer and the representatives of a unit, usually a union, results in an accord as to terms which will govern hiring and work and pay in that unit."

The Court concluded that:

not been unfairly or unlawfully obtained. The Court's landmark opinion established that the collective bargaining contract superseded the individual employment contract.

In the *Insurance Agents* case the Supreme Court stated that ". . . the duty of management to bargain in good faith is essentially a corollary of its duty to recognize the union."[229] This obligation is said to require "at a minimum recognition that the statutory representative is the one with whom . . . [the employer] . . . must deal in conducting bargaining negotiations, and that it can no longer bargain directly or indirectly with the employees."[230] The statutory obligation thus imposed is to deal with the employees through the union rather than dealing with the union through the employees. Thus, attempts to bypass the representative may be considered evidence of bad faith.

The employer's bargaining obligation is premised upon the majority status of the union. Individual dealings with employees at a time when the union claims, but does not actually represent, a majority may not be used as evidence of bad faith.[231] But a belief that the union has lost its majority is not a ground for refusing to bargain where the majority issue is "raised by the employer in a context of illegal anti-union activities, or other conduct by the employer aimed at causing disaffection from the union" or designed to gain "time in which to undermine the union." [232]

"Individual contracts, no matter what the circumstances that justify their execuion or what their terms, may not be availed of to defeat or delay the procedures prescribed by the National Labor Relations Act looking to collective bargaining, nor to exclude the contracting employee from a duly ascertained bargaining unit; nor may they be used to forestall bargaining or to limit or condition the terms of the collective agreement. 'The Board asserts a public right vested in it as a public body, charged in the public interest with the duty of preventing unfair labor practices.' National Licorice Co. v. National Labor Relations Bd. 309 US 350, 364, [6 LRRM 674]. Wherever private contracts conflict with its functions, they obviously must yield or the Act would be reduced to a futility."

229 NLRB v. Insurance Agents' Int'l Union, 361 US 477, 484-485, 45 LRRM 2705 (1960). *See* note 365 *infra.*

230 General Electric, 150 NLRB 192, 194, 57 LRRM 1491 (1964). *See notes* 59-85 *supra. See also* Medo Photo Supply Corp. v. NLRB, 321 US 678, 14 LRRM 581 (1944); Wings & Wheels, Inc., 139 NLRB 578, 51 LRRM 1341 (1962); Channel Master Corp., 162 NLRB 632, 64 LRRM 1102 (1967); Cal-Pacific Poultry Inc., 163 NLRB 716, 64 LRRM 1463 (1967). In a real sense, bypassing the representative means failing to bargain collectively—a *per se* refusal to bargain; however, the cases generally treat "bypassing" as merely evidence of lack of good faith in the duty to bargain.

231 Insular Chemical Co., 128 NLRB 93, 46 LRRM 1268 (1960).

232 C & C Plywood Corp., 163 NLRB 1022, 64 LRRM 1488 (1967) (for subsequent history of this case, *see* note 406 *infra* and Chapter 17 *infra* at notes 86-92 and 244-46), *quoting from* Celanese Corp. of America, 95 NLRB 664, 673, 28 LRRM 1362 (1951).

The "injury suffered by the union" [233] where unilateral changes in wages or other employment conditions are made without notice or consultation with the union is "not that flowing from a breach of contract [but] to the union's status as a bargaining representative." [234] Flagrant attempts to deal directly with the employees so as to undermine a certified bargaining agent, such as offering the employees a wage raise if they will disavow the union,[235] making speeches or statements to employees demonstrating antiunion animus,[236] or soliciting strikers to return to work,[237] will fall within Board censure. Likewise, granting general wage increases during negotiations without first consulting the union was deemed to be a reflection of the employer's "coercive efforts to curtail the statutory rights of the union. . . ." [238]

Although the employer is required to recognize and deal with the majority union in the handling of employee grievances, he may bypass the union in certain situations where discipline or grievances are not involved. In *Jacobe-Pearson Ford, Inc.*[239] the Board permitted the employer to interview an employee without union representation where the purpose was to investigate a potential disciplinary action. The Board found that union par-

---

[233] C & C Plywood Corp., *supra* note 232. *See* NLRB v. C & C Plywood, 385 US 421, 64 LRRM 2065 (1967).

[234] C & C Plywood Corp., *supra* note 232.

[235] Flowers Baking Co., 161 NLRB 1429, 63 LRRM 1462 (1966); Houston Sheet Metal Contractors Ass'n, 147 NLRB 774, 56 LRRM 1281 (1964); Cincinnati Cordage & Paper Co., 141 NLRB 72, 52 LRRM 1277 (1963); Walsh-Lumpkin Wholesale Drug Co., 129 NLRB 294, 46 LRRM 1535 (1960).

[236] K-D Mfg. Co., 169 NLRB No. 10, 67 LRRM 1140 (1968); Solo Cup Co., 142 NLRB 1290, 53 LRRM 1253 (1963), *enforced*, 332 F 2d 447, 56 LRRM 2383 (CA 4, 1964); Colony Furniture Co., 144 NLRB 1582, 54 LRRM 1308 (1963); Herman Sausage Co., 122 NLRB 168, 43 LRRM 1090 (1958), *enforced*, 275 F 2d 229, 45 LRRM 2829 (CA 5, 1960).

[237] Crater Lake Machinery Co., 131 NLRB 1106, 48 LRRM 1211 (1961); National Furniture Mfg. Co., 130 NLRB 712, 47 LRRM 1414 (1961); Federal Dairy Co., 130 NLRB 1158, 47 LRRM 1465 (1961), *enforced*, 297 F 2d 487, 49 LRRM 2214 (CA 1, 1962); Chanticleer, Inc., 161 NLRB 241, 63 LRRM 1237 (1966).

[238] Flambeau Plastics, 151 NLRB 591, 611, 58 LRRM 1470 (1965); The Crestline Co., 133 NLRB 256, 48 LRRM 1623 (1961). In addition, dealing individually with employees concerning employee placement at a new plant location has been viewed by the Board as in derogation of the union's bargaining rights. Cooper Thermometer Co., 160 NLRB 1902, 63 LRRM 1219 (1966), *enforcement denied on other grounds*, 376 F 2d 684, 65 LRRM 2113 (CA 2, 1967).

[239] 172 NLRB No. 84, 68 LRRM 1305 (1968). The company had informed the union that on the basis of what it knew at that time it was not planning to discharge the man, but that if the man revealed some additional facts it might be necessary to reevaluate its position. This type of investigation was also permitted in a case involving a more imminent potential for discipline, but the "investigation" meeting

ticipation was not warranted because the potential for discipline was remote and the meeting was called essentially for the gathering of information. Had the meeting been for the purpose of adjusting a grievance the union representative would have had a right to be present. The *proviso* to Section 9(a) declares:

That any individual employee or a group of employees shall have the right at any time to present grievances to their employer and to have such grievances adjusted, without the intervention of the bargaining representative, as long as the adjustment is not inconsistent with the terms of a collective-bargaining contract or agreement then in effect: *Provided further,* That the bargaining representative has been given opportunity to be present at such adjustment.

8. Commission of Unfair Labor Practices. The commission of unfair labor practices during negotiations may reflect upon the good faith of the guilty party. Where an employer threatened to close the plant, promoted withdrawal from the union, reduced working hours, and engaged in discriminatory layoffs during bargaining, the Board found Section 8(a)(5) violations.[240] Engaging in other unfair labor practices during the certification year may also be indicative of a course of conduct inconsistent with good faith.[241]

---

was followed by a "discipline" meeting where union representatives were given the right to participate in an attempt to adjust the dispute. Chevron Oil Co., 168 NLRB No. 84, 66 LRRM 1353 (1969). The Board, however, has held that a union representative had the right to attend an interview concerned with the investigation of facts that were already known to management where the probability for punishment was deemed great. Texaco, Inc., 168 NLRB No. 49, 66 LRRM 1296 (1969) (the employee had been seen leaving the premises with company property by his foreman). Although the Board considered the "interview" in *Texaco* to be more than an investigation, the Fifth Circuit disagreed, noting that the employer had not attempted to deal with the *consequences* of the alleged misconduct. Texaco, Inc. v. NLRB, 408 F 2d 142, 144, 70 LRRM 3045 (CA 5, 1970). *Contrast* Braniff Airways, Inc. and Air Carrier Mechanics Assoc., Council 7, 27 LA 892 (1957), a system board proceeding under the Railway Labor Act (45 USC §184) in which it was held that the employee had the right to have union representation at the incipient stage of a potential grievance. In Ingraham Industries, 178 NLRB No. 89, 72 LRRM 1245, 1246 (1969), the NLRB permitted the employer to gather or disseminate information "without any attempt at negotiation or adjusment of grievances." (Employer had refused to permit union representatives to attend sessions conducted by management to explain a profit sharing plan which had been adopted pursuant to a collective bargaining agreement). For treatment of the §9(a) *proviso* in light of a union's duty of fair representation, see *Chapter* 27 *infra* at notes 128-141.
240 Imperial Machine Corp., 121 NLRB 621, 42 LRRM 1406 (1958).
241 Borg-Warner Controls, 128 NLRB 1035, 46 LRRM 1459 (1960); *see also* Evergreen Rambler, Inc., 160 NLRB 864, 63 LRRM 1062 (1966); Berger Polishing, 147 NLRB 21, 56 LRRM 1140 (1964); Coachman's Inn, 147 NLRB 278, 56 LRRM 1206 (1964); Carter Machine & Tool Co., 133 NLRB 247, 48 LRRM 1625 (1961).

An employer's refusal to continue negotiations because of doubt as to the union's continued majority status may violate the Act if the refusal is made in the context of other unlawful employer conduct.[242] A violation will be found, even though other factors may have contributed to the employees' change in attitude, if it cannot be shown with certainty how many of the employees would have withdrawn from the union in the absence of illegal conduct by the employer. This rule is premised upon the proposition that doubts are to be resolved against the party whose conduct created the situation and that the union's continued majority status is to be presumed.[243] Moreover, a good-faith doubt is not one that has been encouraged, prompted, or solicited by the employer.[244] Thus, assisting employees in the preparation of decertification proceedings has been viewed as evidence of bad faith, since the foreseeable purpose of such assistance is to obstruct the bargaining process.[245]

The extent to which prior unfair labor practices may be relied upon as evidence of a present violation has undergone revision by the Board. The old rule, stated in *Larrance Tank Corp.*,[246] was that the Board would not consider conduct antedating a settlement agreement as evidence of a postsettlement unfair labor practice unless the party charged had (1) failed to comply with the terms of the agreement or (2) engaged in independent unfair labor practices since the settlement. In *Larrance* the trial examiner had found that the employer did not bargain in good faith after the settlement agreement and that the employer's "conduct after [the date of settlement] was of the 'same type' as its prior conduct." [247] This evaluation of the employer's postsettlement conduct was colored by the presettlement conduct, which the Board found to be inconsistent with its policy.

The old rule was modified in the 1965 *Hod Carriers* decision.[248] Upon reexamination of *Larrance*, the Board held that presettlement conduct was admissible as "background evidence" to estab-

---

[242] C & C Plywood, 163 NLRB 1022, 64 LRRM 1488 (1967) ; *see* note 232 *supra*. *See also* Chapter 10 *supra*.
[243] Movie Star Inc., 145 NLRB 319, 54 LRRM 1387 (1963). *But see* Part XII, *infra*, this chapter.
[244] Rohlik, Inc., 145 NLRB 1236, 1243, 55 LRRM 1130 (1964).
[245] Wahoo Packing Co., 161 NLRB 174, 63 LRRM 1290 (1966) ; W. R. Hall Distributor, 144 NLRB 1285, 54 LRRM 1231 (1963).
[246] 94 NLRB 352, 28 LRRM 1045 (1951).
[247] *Id.* at 353.
[248] Northern California Dist. Council of Hod Carriers & Common Laborers (Joseph's Landscaping Service), 154 NLRB 1384, 60 LRRM 1156 (1965).

lish the motive or object of a party in its postsettlement activities.[249] The settlement agreement itself may not be used to establish anti-union animus.[250] Even prior to the *Larrance* modification, evidence of conduct preceding a prior finding of an unfair labor practice, as opposed to a settlement, was admitted as a factor to be considered in determining whether subsequent bargaining was in good faith.[251]

A Ninth Circuit opinion in *NLRB* v. *MacMillan Ring-Free Oil Co.*[252] has, in another context, placed some outer limits on the Board's use of "background evidence" in establishing violations. In *MacMillan* the examiner found a refusal to bargain within the Section 10(b) period based on negotiating attitudes substantially unchanged from the period preceding the six-month cutoff date. Denying enforcement of the Section 8(a)(5) portion of the Board's order, the court first rejected the finding that an unfair labor practice had been committed within the six-month period. Turning to consideration of the sufficiency of the background evidence, that is, evidence antedating the cutoff date, the court held that "while evidence of events occurring more than six months before the filing of a charge may be used to 'shed light' upon events taking place within the six month period, the evidence of a violation drawn from within that period must be reasonably substantial in its own right," though not necessarily sufficient within itself to sustain an unfair labor practice finding.[253] Since, in the court's opinion, there was no substantial evidence occurring within the Section 10(b) period, a finding of unlawful conduct would violate the section's clear purpose.

IV. THE DUTY TO FURNISH INFORMATION

A. Nature of the Duty

The Board has long held that, intertwined with the duty to bargain in good faith, is a duty on the part of the employer to

---

249 The *Larrance* exceptions retain their vitality under the *Hod Carriers* case; *see* Bangor Plastics, Inc., 156 NLRB 1165, 61 LRRM 1210 (1965).
250 Metal Assemblies, Inc., 156 NLRB 194, 61 LRRM 1023 (1965).
251 H. K. Porter Co., 153 NLRB 1370, 59 LRRM 1462 (1965), *affirmed sub nom.*, United Steelworkers of America v. NLRB, 363 F 2d 272, 62 LRRM 2204 (CA DC, 1966), *cert. denied*, 385 US 851, 63 LRRM 2236 (1966). *See* note 168 *supra*.
252 394 F 2d 26, 68 LRRM 2004 (CA 9, 1968), *enforcing in part* 160 NLRB 877, 63 LRRM 1073 (1966).
253 394 F 2d at 33. *See* Chapter 30 *infra* at notes 87-88.

supply the union, upon request, with sufficient information to
enable it to understand and intelligently discuss the issues raised
in bargaining.[254] This duty is based upon the belief that without
such information the union would be unable to perform its duties
properly as bargaining agent and therefore no bargaining could
take place.[255] Thus, information must be furnished to the union
for purposes of representing employees in negotiations for future
contracts and policing the administration of an existing contract,[256] and the employer's refusal to supply information is as
much a violation of the duty to bargain as if he had failed to meet
and confer with the union in good faith.[257]

1. Request or Demand. As a prerequisite, the union must make
a request or demand that the information be furnished.[258] While
the request must be made in good faith, this requirement is met
where at least a coordinate purpose of the demand is in good
faith.[259] Findings that a union failed to make a good-faith demand
are usually limited to situations where the union already had

---

[254] S. L. Allen & Co., Inc., 1 NLRB 714 (1936) ("Interchange of ideas, communication of facts peculiarly within the knowledge of either party . . . [are] of the essence
in the bargaining process"). *See also* Industrial Welding Co., 175 NLRB No. 78, 71
LRRM 1076 (1969), Southern Saddlery Co., 90 NLRB 1205, 26 LRRM 1322 (1950);
Oregon Coast Operators Ass'n, 113 NLRB 1338, 36 LRRM 1448 (1955).

[255] Aluminum Ore Co. v. NLRB, 131 F 2d 485, 11 LRRM 693 (CA 7, 1942).

[256] J. I. Case Co. v. NLRB, 253 F 2d 149, 41 LRRM 2679 (CA 7, 1958); B. F. Goodrich Co., 89 NLRB 1151, 26 LRRM 1090 (1950); General Controls Co., 88 NLRB
1341, 25 LRRM 1475 (1950). Weber Veneer & Plywood Co., 161 NLRB 1054, 63
LRRM 1395 (1966).

[257] Curtiss-Wright Corp., Wright Aero. Div. v. NLRB, 347 F 2d 61, 59 LRRM 2433
(CA 3, 1965).

[258] Westinghouse Electric Supply Co. v. NLRB, 196 F 2d 1012, 30 LRRM 2169 (CA
3, 1952) (no violation where union had asked for proof of employer's claim that it
was paying wages above industry level, knowing that employer had survey chart on
industry wages but failing to request it, and employer did not produce chart);
NLRB v. Boston Herald-Traveler Corp., 210 F 2d 134, 33 LRRM 2435 (CA 1, 1954)
(employer compliance with letter but not spirit of union request and Board's order
not a violation); *but see* Boston Herald-Traveler Corp., 110 NLRB 2097, 35 LRRM
1309 (1954).

[259] Utica Observer Dispatch, Inc. v. NLRB, 229 F 2d 575, 37 LRRM 2441 (CA 2,
1956) (union could not demand information solely for purpose of collecting dues,
but desire of wage information also for bargaining purpose justifies demand). *But
see* Snively Groves, Inc., 109 NLRB 1394, 34 LRRM 1568 (1954), where inconsistent
and confusing requests by the union relieved the employer of the obligation to
furnish information.

sufficient information [260] or desired only to harass or humiliate the employer.[261]

2. Relevance. The information demanded must be relevant to the dealings between the employer and the union in its capacity as representative of the employees.[262] However, the Board and the courts have adopted a liberal definition of relevant information, requiring only that it be directly related to the union's function as bargaining representative [263] and that it appear "reasonably necessary" for the performance of this function.[264] Data appropriate for disclosure "should not necessarily be limited to that which would be pertinent to a particular existing controversy." [265]

The Second Circuit has taken the position that, in negotiations on wage scales, information concerning current or immediately past wage rates "must be disclosed unless it plainly appears irrelevant," in accordance with the prevailing rule in discovery procedures under modern codes.[266] According to the Board, wage and

---

[260] Albany Garage, Inc., 126 NLRB 417, 45 LRRM 1329 (1960) (financial statements furnished had been accepted by banks employer dealt with, Internal Revenue Service, employer's shareholders, and union in preceding years). *See* McCulloch Corp., 132 NLRB 201, 48 LRRM 1344 (1961), where the information requested was contained in a publicly distributed handbook; *see also* California Portland Cement Co., 101 NLRB 1436, 31 LRRM 1220 (1952), where the information was posted on a plant bulletin board. *But cf.* B. F. Diamond Construction Co., 163 NLRB 161, 64 LRRM 1333 (1967) (it is no defense to an employer that the information is available from the employees).

[261] NLRB v. Robt. S. Abbot Publishing Co., 331 F 2d 209, 55 LRRM 2994 (CA 7, 1964) (employer offered all financial information he had, but desired to prevent public audit due to company's precarious financial position). In General Electric Co., Battery Products Dept., 163 NLRB 198, 64 LRRM 1312 (1967), the Board held *inter alia* that employer's refusal to furnish information relating to laid-off employees was not violation of §8 (a) (5) since union's request was made during pendency of unfair labor practices complaining of layoff and employer was not obligated to furnish such information while charges were pending.

[262] NLRB v. Item Co., 220 F 2d 956, 35 LRRM 2709 (CA 5, 1955); NLRB v. Jacobs Mfg. Co., 196 F 2d 680, 30 LRRM 2098 (CA 2, 1952); cases, note 308 *infra; but see* McCulloch Corp., *supra* note 259, where an employer's refusal to provide information on nonunit employees was held not violative. *See also* Midwestern Instruments, Inc., 133 NLRB 1132, 48 LRRM 1793 (1961), regarding information on replaced economic strikers; Webster Outdoor Advertising, 170 NLRB 509, 67 LRRM 1589 (1968).

[263] J. I. Case Co. v. NLRB, 253 F 2d 149, 41 LRRM 2679 (CA 7, 1958). Otis Elevator Co., 170 NLRB No. 59, 67 LRRM 1475 (1968). *See also* NLRB v. C&C Plywood Corp., 385 US 421, 64 LRRM 2065 (1967), note 406 *infra,* and its treatment in Chapter 17 *infra* at notes 86-92 and 244-46.

[264] NLRB v. Item Co., 220 F 2d 956, 35 LRRM 2709 (CA 5, 1955).

[265] NLRB v. Whitin Machine Works, 217 F 2d 593, 594, 35 LRRM 2215 (CA 4, 1954).

[266] NLRB v. Yawman & Erbe Mfg. Co., 187 F 2d 947, 27 LRRM 2524 (CA 2, 1951). The court went on to say that "[a]ny less lenient rule in labor disputes would greatly hamper the bargaining process, for it is virtually impossible to tell in advance whether the requested data will be relevant . . ." 187 F 2d at 949.

related information should be made available "without regard to its immediate relationship" to the negotiation or administration of the agreement, or to its "precise relevancy" to particular bargaining issues.[267] Execution of a contract by a union without the information does not render the information irrelevant, since the union may simply have decided that the advantages of a contract in hand would outweigh those which it might enjoy with all the information available to it.[268]

3. Claim of Financial Inability. Financial information is relevant to negotiations in which an employer asserts financial inability to meet a union wage demand. In *NLRB* v. *Truitt Mfg. Co.*[269] the Supreme Court stated that "good faith bargaining necessarily requires that claims made by either bargainer should be honest claims," and that if an inability-to-pay argument "is important enough to present in the give and take of bargaining it is important enough to require some sort of proof of its accuracy."[270] The Court followed a series of Board cases holding that if an employer "does no more than take refuge in the assertion" of poor financial condition, refusing either to prove its statement or permit independent verification, "[t]his is not collective bargaining."[271] Even before the *Truitt* decision, the Second Circuit in *NLRB* v. *Jacobs Mfg. Co.*[272] had somewhat clarified the required degree of necessary substantiation, stating that compliance with the statute does not require that an employer produce proof that its business decision as to what it can afford to do is correct, but only that it

---

[267] Whitin Machine Works, 108 NLRB 1537, 34 LRRM 1251 (1954), *enforced*, 217 F 2d 593, 35 LRRM 2215 (CA 4, 1954). *See* Boston Herald-Traveler Corp. v. NLRB, 223 F 2d 58, 36 LRRM 2220 (CA 1, 1955), where the relevance of wage data was presumed. *See also* NLRB v. Fitzgerald Mills Corp., 313 F 2d 260, 52 LRRM 2174 (CA 2, 1963).

[268] NLRB v. Yawman & Erbe Mfg. Co., 187 F 2d 947, 27 LRRM 2524 (CA 2, 1951); NLRB v. Fitzgerald Mills Corp., 313 F 2d 260, 51 LRRM 2174 (CA 2, 1963). Nor may a waiver be inferred from information prior to the execution of the contract. *See* VIII. A. 2 *infra.*

[269] NLRB v. Truitt Mfg. Co., 351 US 149, 38 LRRM 2024 (1955).

[270] *Id* at 152. For a criticism of the Supreme Court's "honest claims" rule and its reliance on good-faith terminology in the *Truitt* opinion, *see* Duvin, *supra* note 2, at 282.

[271] *Id.* at p. 153. *See also* Pioneer Pearl Button Co., 1 NLRB 837, 1 LRRM 26 (1936); Southern Saddlery Co., 90 NLRB 1205, 26 LRRM 1322 (1950); McLean-Arkansas Lumber Co., 109 NLRB 1022, 34 LRRM 1496 (1954).

[272] 196 F 2d 680, 30 LRRM 2098 (1952); *see also* NLRB v. Southland Cork Co., 342 F 2d 702, 58 LRRM 2555 (CA 4, 1965).

produce whatever relevant information it has "to indicate whether it can or cannot afford" to meet union demands.[273]

Since the honesty of a claim is not in issue until it is actually made, an employer is not obligated to demonstrate that it is unable to raise wages unless it first claims such an inability.[274] But the Board, with judicial support, has broadened the definition of what claims constitute a poverty plea that would, in turn, justify a union's demand for substantiation. In the 1964 case of *Cincinnati Cordage & Paper Co.*[275] the Board held that an employer's resistance to a union's wage demand on the ground that it could not remain competitive with comparable employers in the industry constituted a poverty plea. Notwithstanding the contention that the employer was not pleading "inability to pay" as in *Truitt,* the Board found *Truitt* applicable "because the employer expressed the view that the wage increases would lead to impoverishment. . . ." Thus, the employer's refusal to furnish data to the union showing that it could not stay competitive was unlawful.[276] Similarly, in *Taylor Foundry Co.*[277] the Board equated the employer's contention that it could not increase its labor costs without losing its profit margin and competitive position to a plea of inability to pay. The Board's finding of refusal to bargain was enforced by the Fifth Circuit.[278]

---

[273] 196 F 2d at 684. *See also* William J. Burns Int'l Detective Agency, 137 NLRB 1235, 50 LRRM 1367 (1962); Tennessee Chair Co., 126 NLRB 1357, 45 LRRM 1472 (1960); B. L. Montague Co., 116 NLRB 554, 38 LRRM 1289 (1956) (employer must show contracts on which it claims to have lost money). The *Truitt* case has not been construed so as to limit the findings of violation only where employer's claimed inability to pay relates to wage demand, since other economic benefits may be more coveted than wages. Stanley Bldg. Specialties, Inc., 166 NLRB 984, 65 LRRM 1684 (1967).

[274] Pine Indus. Relations Comm., Inc. 118 NLRB 1055, 40 LRRM 1315 (1957), *enforced,* 263 F 2d 483, 43 LRRM 2462 (CA DC, 1959); *see* Int'l Woodworkers of America v. NLRB 263 F 2d 483, 43 LRRM 2462 (CA DC, 1959).

[275] 141 NLRB 72, 52 LRRM 1277 (1963); For a forerunner of this decision *see* Tennessee Coal & Iron Div., U.S. Steel Corp., 122 NLRB 1519, 43 LRRM 1325 (1959).

[276] But where the employer has voluntarily furnished the union with sufficient information to support a claim of inability to pay, it would be unnecessary for the Board to determine whether "inability" or "inadvisability" to pay was pleaded, since there would be no violation in any event. Albany Garage, Inc., 126 NLRB 417, 45 LRRM 1329 (1960).

[277] 141 NLRB 765, 52 LRRM 1407 (1963).

[278] 338 F 2d 1003, 57 LRRM 2560 (CA 5, 1964). *See also* Stockton District Kidney Bean Growers, 165 NLRB 223, 65 LRRM 1300 (1967) (denying access to books after saying it was in "no mood" to increase costs is tantamount to pleading inability to pay.)

Truitt was extended even further in *NLRB* v. *Western Wire-bound Box Co.*[279] There the employer resisted wage increases because of price competition but declined a request for supporting data, insisting that it was not claiming an inability to pay but simply that price competition dictated its position. Nonetheless, the employer was ordered to supply the data, and the Ninth Circuit specifically stated that *Truitt* is "not confined to cases where the employer's claim is that he is unable to pay the wages demanded by the union."[280] Bargaining, the court reasoned, could be "rendered ineffectual where an employer mechanically repeats his claim but makes no effort to produce substantiating data."[281]

A union is not entitled to financial information for the purpose of arguing with an employer over whether or not its expenditures causing poor financial conditions were justified,[282] or of harassing the employer with the possible result of jeopardizing its financial position further.[283]

4. Prompt Availability of Information. Once a good-faith demand is made for relevant information, it must be made available promptly and in a reasonably useful form. Even though an employer has not expressly refused to furnish the information, his failure to make a diligent effort to obtain or to provide the information "reasonably" promptly may be equated with a flat refusal.[284] A long and unexplained delay in furnishing even partial

---

[279] 356 F 2d 88, 61 LRRM 2218 (CA 9, 1966), *enforcing* 145 NLRB 1539, 55 LRRM 1193 (1964).

[280] *Id.* at 90.

[281] *Id.* at 91. *See also* NLRB v. Celotex Corp., 364 F 2d 552, 62 LRRM 2475 (CA, 5, 1966), where the opinion was cast in terms of whether the information was "plainly irrelevant."

[282] *But see* Metlox Mfg. Co., 153 NLRB 1388 (1965), *enforced,* 378 F 2d 728, 65 LRRM 2637 (CA 9, 1967), *cert. denied,* 389 U.S. 1037, 67 LRRM 2231 (1967), in which an employer's claimed inability to meet a union's pay demands gave the union a right to look at the salaries being paid management officials. The court of appeals upheld the NLRB's determination that the employer violated its bargaining duty by furnishing only profit and loss statements. When the employer asserted that it could not grant the union's request for wage increases or other economic benefits because of its financial plight, the union suggested that the trouble might be due to a deliberate bleeding of the assets by officers and/or controlling stockholders. The employer offered to permit an examination of its books by a certified public accountant at the expense of the union. The CPA, however, could advise the union only as to whether the employer's profit and loss statements were true. The court agreed with the NLRB that the profit and loss statements did not disclose sufficient information for the union to make a fair estimate of the employer's financial inability to pay. An order requiring redress of wrong resulting to employees who struck over the denial of information was enforced by the court.

[283] NLRB v. Robert S. Abbott Publishing Co., 331 F 2d 209, 55 LRRM 2994 (CA 7, 1964).

[284] NLRB v. John S. Swift Co., 277 F 2d 641, 46 LRRM 2090 (CA 7, 1960), where the court stated that the "Company's inaction spoke louder than its words."

information (from September 1958 until at least June 1959) has also supported a conclusion that later bargaining was not in good faith, even though the company had expressly agreed to provide the information.[285] While the Board finds a delay of several months to be inconsistent with good faith,[286] a short delay may be reasonable if justified.[287]

5. Manner and Form. As to the manner and form in which the information must be presented, the Board requires that it be "in a manner not so burdensome or time consuming as to impede the process of bargaining," although not necessarily in the form requested by the union.[288] If the employer claims that compiling the data will be unduly burdensome, it must assert that claim at the time of the request for the information so that an arrangement can be made to lessen the burden.[289] The employer may not simply present the information in any form which it considers adequate but which is, nonetheless, unsuitable for an informed consideration.[290] However, if the employer presents information on its

---

[285] NLRB v. Fitzgerald Mills Corp., 313 F 2d 260, 51 LRRM 2174 (CA 2, 1963) (also, withdrawal by union of earlier unfair labor practice charge based on same refusal of information does not indicate compliance or that union was satisfied, but merely that union felt employer had begun to comply); *see also* NLRB v. My Store, Inc., 345 F 2d 494, 58 LRRM 2775 (CA 7, 1965), *enforcing* 147 NLRB 145, 56 LRRM 1176 (1964) (supplied incorrect information, failed to correct mistake "for months"); NLRB v. Feed & Supply Center, Inc., 294 F 2d 650, 48 LRRM 2993 (CA 9, 1961) (six-month delay); Reed & Prince Mfg. Co., 96 NLRB 850, 28 LRRM 1608 (1951) (two-month delay).

[286] Arkansas Rice Growers Cooperative Ass'n, 165 NLRB 577, 65 LRRM 1567 (1967); International Powder Metallurgy Co., 134 NLRB 1605, 49 LRRM 1388 (1961) (11 months); Peyton Packing Co., 129 NLRB 1358, 47 LRRM 1211 (1961) (three months is too long, even when information is incomplete and the people necessary to compile the information are absent from work).

[287] Partee, 107 NLRB 1177, 33 LRRM 1342 (1954) (15 days not unreasonable).

[288] Old Line Life Insurance Co., 96 NLRB 499, 28 LRRM 1539 (1951) (information being supplied regularly on monthly basis; employer's offer to verify accuracy of union's current list fulfilled statutory obligation); Cincinnati Steel Casting Co., 86 NLRB 592, 24 LRRM 1657 (1949) (oral information held sufficient); B. F. Goodrich Co., 89 NLRB 1151, 26 LRRM 1090 (1950) (wage data identified by employee department number rather than by name not sufficient). *See also* NLRB v. Tex. Tan, Inc., 318 F 2d 472, 53 LRRM 2295 (CA 5, 1963), where the data requested were considered to be too voluminous to compile and thus overly burdensome.

[289] J. I. Case Co. v. NLRB, 253 F 2d 149, 41 LRRM 2679 (CA 7, 1958).

[290] *Id.* at p. 150. (Presenting complicated information orally at single bargaining session in face of demands for copies of records in possession of employer, when union had offered to bear expense of such copies.); NLRB v. Otis Elevator Co., 208 F 2d 176, 33 LRRM 2129 (CA 2, 1953) (contract provision specifying that certain information will be furnished to union does not preclude its getting other information to which it is entitled). General Electric Co., 186 NLRB No. 1, 75 LRRM 1265 (1970) (employer violated §8(a)(5) when it refused the union an opportunity for an in-plant job evaluation and sought to provide a video tape presentation instead.

financial position in a form generally accepted in business, it will
be considered adequate.[291] Also, an employer may attach conditions to the furnishing of such financial information as is
reasonably related to its own business interest.[292] Where it does
allow the union free access to its records and fully cooperates with
the union in answering questions, an employer need not furnish
information in a more organized form than that in which it keeps
its own records.[293]

B. When the Duty Exists

In the 1954 case of *NLRB* v. *Whitin Machine Works* the
Fourth Circuit stated that "[i]t is well settled that it is an unfair
labor practice within the meaning of Section 8(a)(5) of the Act for
an employer to refuse to furnish a bargaining union [such information as] is necessary to the proper discharge of the duties of the
bargaining agent." [294] This duty to furnish to the union relevant
information was given explicit approval by the Supreme Court in
the *Truitt* case.[295]

The duty "does not terminate with the signing of the collective
bargaining contract," but "continues through the life of the agreements so far as it is necessary to enable the parties to administer
the contract and resolve grievances or disputes." [296] Since collective bargaining is a continuing process, and the union not only has
the duty to negotiate collective bargaining agreements but also the
statutory obligation to police and administer existing agree-

---

[291] Albany Garage, Inc., 126 NLRB 417, 45 LRRM 1329 (1960) (a leading case outlining the type of documents that would constitute adequate, voluntary disclosure).
But cf. Metlox Mfg. Co., 378 F 2d 728, 64 LRRM 2350 (CA 9, 1967).
[292] Fruit & Vegetable Packers v. NLRB, 316 F 2d 389, 52 LRRM 2537 (CA DC,
1963).
[293] NLRB v. Tex-Tan, Inc., 318 F 2d 472, 53 LRRM 2295 (CA 5, 1963). *See also*
Fafnir Bearing Co. v. NLRB, 362 F 2d 716, 62 LRRM 2415 (CA 2, 1966) (even
after employer makes time studies and releases results to union, union may demand
access to plan and records to make its own studies to substantiate company information); *but see* NLRB v. Otis Elevator Co., 208 F 2d 176, 33 LRRM 2129 (CA 2,
1953) (opposite).
[294] 217 F 2d 593, 594, 35 LRRM 2215 (CA 4, 1954); Sinclair Refining Co. v. NLRB,
306 F 2d 569, 50 LRRM 2830 (CA 5, 1962); NLRB v. Yawman & Erbe Mfg. Co.,
187 F 2d 947, 27 LRRM 2524 (CA 2, 1951) (employer conceded duty to provide
information to bargaining union as incident of employer's duty to bargain in good
faith); Aluminum Ore Co. v. NLRB, 131 F 2d 485, 487, 11 LRRM 693 (CA 7,
1942) (". . . we do not believe that it was the intent of Congress in this legislation
that, in the collective bargaining prescribed, the union, as representative of the
employees, should be deprived of the pertinent facts. . . .")
[295] 351 US 149, 38 LRRM 2042 (1955). *See* note 269 *supra.*
[296] Sinclair Refining Co. v. NLRB, 306 F 2d 569, 570, 50 LRRM 2830 (CA 5, 1962).

ments,[297] the union's right to information within the sphere of its function as bargaining representative continues after an agreement is signed.[298]

A question that has arisen in this area is whether the right to information useful in processing grievances is limited by the scope of a particular grievance and by the grievance machinery, or whether a broader right exists under the Act so as to justify the exercise of the Board's power in this area.[299] In *Acme Industrial*[300] the Supreme Court upheld the Board's determination that a Section 8(a)(5) violation had occurred where the employer refused to furnish information that would allow the union to determine at the outset whether a breach of the collective bargaining agreement had occurred. The circuit court had refused to enforce the order on the ground that an arbitration clause foreclosed the Board from exercising its statutory power.[301] The Supreme Court reversed and remanded, concluding that the Board was not making a binding construction of the labor contract. "It was only acting upon the probability that the desired information was relevant, and that it would be of use to the union in carrying out its statutory duties and responsibilities." [302]

---

[297] J. I. Case Co. v. NLRB, 253 F 2d 149, 41 LRRM 2679 (CA 7, 1958); Twin City Lines, Inc. 170 NLRB No. 88, 67 LRRM 1553 (1968) (access to files on claims under an arbitration award); Southwestern Bell Telephone Co. 173 NLRB No. 29, 69 LRRM 1251 (1968) (subcontracting cost information to use in processing grievances relating to subcontracting). *See* note 446 *infra*.

[298] Hoerner-Waldorf Paper Products Co., 163 NLRB 772, 64 LRRM 1469 (1967); NLRB v. John S. Swift Co., 277 F 2d 641, 46 LRRM 2090, (CA 7, 1960).

[299] *See* Sinclair Refining Co. v. NLRB, *supra* note 296, where the Fifth Circuit stated that where a determination of the relevancy of requested information requires "determination of the critical substantive issue of the grievance itself," the Board may not adjudicate the grievance dispute "under the guise of determining relevance" any more than a court could determine the merits under the guise of determining arbitrability. The court went on to hold that since the employer sought earnestly to submit the disputed issue—relevance of the data—to the grievance process, the Board was required to stay out of the determination of the intrinsic merits. *Compare* Timken Roller Bearing Co. v. NLRB, 325 F 2d 746, 54 LRRM 2785 (CA 6, 1963), where the Sixth Circuit, in upholding the right to the information, relied more on the value of the information in the general administration of the contract. *Compare also* Curtis Wright Corp., Wright Aero. Div., v. NLRB, 347 F 2d 61, 59 LRRM 2433 (CA 3, 1965), where the Third Circuit attempted to reconcile the differences in the *Sinclair* and *Timken* cases. *See* Puerto Rico Telephone Co. v. NLRB 359 F 2d 983, 62 LRRM 2069 (CA 1, 1966). *See also* American Oil Co., 164 NLRB No. 11, 65 LRRM 1007 (1967) (information requested by union was clearly relevant and might have assisted in disposing of grievances).

[300] NLRB v. Acme Industrial Co., 385 US 432, 64 LRRM 2069 (1967).

[301] Acme Industrial Co. v. NLRB, 351 F 2d 258, 60 LRRM 2220 (CA 7, 1965).

[302] *Supra* note 300 at 437. *See* Chapter 18 generally for discussion of the relation between NLRB action and the arbitration process.

C. Information That Must Be Furnished

A vast majority of the cases concerning a union's right to obtain relevant information involve a refusal of an employer to supply wage information.[303] In accordance with *International Woodworkers of America* v. *NLRB*[304] "it appears that a union's right to such information cannot be seriously challenged." This conclusion was given impetus by *NLRB v. F. W. Woolworth Co.*,[305] in which the Supreme Court reversed, without argument or opinion, the Ninth Circuit's refusal to enforce a Board order requiring production of wage information. This right to information on wages, based on the statutory requirement that collective bargaining take place with respect to "wages, hours, and other terms and conditions of employment," [306] extends to wages paid particular employees, groups of employees, and the methods of computing compensation.[307] The outer limits of a union's right to wage information are difficult to determine because of the presumption of relevance given such information. Disclosure of information regarding compensation of employees outside the bargaining unit has been required with increasing liberality,[308] as well as information on wage rates paid at other plants maintained by the em-

---

[303] Korn Industries v. NLRB, 389 F 2d 117, 67 LRRM 2148 (CA 4, 1967), *clarified*, 67 LRRM 2976 (CA 4, 1968); NLRB v. Fitzgerald Mills Corp., 313 F 2d 260, 52 LRRM 2174 (CA 2, 1963); NLRB v. John S. Swift Co., 277 F 2d 641, 46 LRRM 2090 (CA 7, 1960); Utica Observer-Dispatch, Inc. v. NLRB, 229 F 2d 575, 37 LRRM 2441 (CA 2, 1956); NLRB v. Whitin Machine Works, 217 F 2d 593, 35 LRRM 2215 (CA 4, 1954); NLRB v. Boston Herald-Traveler Corp., 210 F 2d 134, 33 LRRM 2435 (CA 1, 1954); NLRB v. Yawman & Erbe Mfg. Co., 187 F 2d 947, 27 LRRM 2524 (CA 2, 1951); West Side Transfer, 162 NLRB 699, 64 LRRM 1098 (1967).

[304] 263 F 2d 483, 484, 43 LRRM 2462 (CA DC, 1959).

[305] 352 US 938, 39 LRRM 2151 (1956), *reversing* 235 F 2d 319, 38 LRRM 2362 (CA 9, 1956).

[306] 29 USC §158 (d) (1964).

[307] Curtiss-Wright Corp., Wright Aero. Div. v. NLRB, 347 F 2d 61, 59 LRRM 2433 (CA 3, 1965); Puerto Rico Telephone Co. v. NLRB, 359 F 2d 983, 62 LRRM 2069 (CA 1, 1966); Anaconda American Brass Co., 148 NLRB 474, 57 LRRM 1001 (1964); *see* 2 ALR 3d 880, 905, for an exhaustive compilation of the cases involving furnishing of wage information.

[308] Goodyear Aerospace Corp., 388 F 2d 673, 67 LRRM 2447 (CA 6, 1968); Curtiss-Wright Corp., Wright Aero. Div. v. NLRB, 347 F 2d 61, 59 LRRM 2433 (CA 3, 1965); California Portland Cement Co., 103 NLRB 1375, 31 LRRM 1630 (1953); Skyland Hosiery Mills, Inc., 108 NLRB 1600, 34 LRRM 1254 (1954); *but see* NLRB v. Leland-Gifford Co., 200 F 2d 620, 31 LRRM 2196 (CA 1, 1952); Fetzer Television, Inc. v. NLRB, 317 F 2d 420, 53 LRRM 2224 (CA 6, 1963).

ployer.[309] Information in an employer's hands on wage rates paid by his competitors may in some cases have to be divulged.[310]

Items of information related to "hours, and other terms and conditions of employment" have been required to be furnished on the same basis as wage information. Insurance and pension plan information must be furnished.[311] The same treatment has been extended to the employer's cost of an insurance plan, as well as to the employee benefits thereunder, on the theory that the union might desire to forego such insurance plan in favor of increased take-home pay, and therefore the cost of the plan was "necessary to effective negotiations." [312] Likewise, the details of a profit-sharing plan must be furnished.[313] Information on employee job classifications and how they are determined must be furnished on demand,[314] as well as employee status and changes therein.[315] Time-study material and information used in setting wage rates or in-

---

309 Hollywood Brands, Inc., 142 NLRB 304, 53 LRRM 1012 (1963), *enforced*, 324 F 2d 956, 54 LRRM 2780 (CA 5, 1963), *rehearing denied*, 326 F 2d 400, 55 LRRM 2301, *cert. denied*, 377 US 923, 56 LRRM 2095 (1964).

310 General Electric Co., 184 NLRB No. 45, 74 LRRM 1444 (1970); *but see* Westinghouse Electric Supply Co. v. NLRB, 196 F 2d 1012, 30 LRRM 2169 (CA 3, 1952).

311 NLRB v. Feed & Supply Center, Inc., 294 F 2d 650, 48 LRRM 2993 (CA 9, 1961); NLRB v. John S. Swift Co., 277 F 2d 641, 46 LRRM 2090 (CA 7, 1960) (health and welfare plan); Industrial Welding Co., 175 NLRB No. 78, 71 LRRM 1076 (1969); Rangaire Corp., 157 NLRB 682, 61 LRRM 1429 (1966); Skyland Hosiery Mills, Inc., 108 NLRB 1600, 34 LRRM 1254 (1954) (insurance coverage and portions of premiums paid by employer and employees).

312 Sylvania Elec. Products, Inc. v. NLRB, 358 F 2d 591, 61 LRRM 2657 (CA 1, 1966); Cone Mills Corp., 169 NLRB No. 59, 67 LRRM 1241 (1968). *And cf.* Sylvania Electric Products v. NLRB, 291 F 2d 128, 48 LRRM 2313 (CA 1, 1961), *cert. denied*, 368 US 926, 49 LRRM 2173 (1961), in which the First Circuit held that the employer's cost in a noncontributory group insurance program was neither wages nor conditions of employment and refusal to furnish cost information did not constitute a refusal to bargain, since there was no issue of costs arising during negotiations that would bear on the company's willingness to consider any proposal the union might make with respect to changes in the plan. The Board disagreed with the court's distinction between "costs" and benefits in The Electric Furnace Co., 137 NLRB 1077, 50 LRRM 1322 (1962), and General Electric, 150 NLRB 192, 57 LRRM 1491 (1964). In 1965 the Board again found Sylvania had bargained in bad faith in failing to supply the requested information (154 NLRB 1756, 60 LRRM 1178 (1965). However, the First Circuit this time enforced the Board's order. Although holding to its 1961 opinion, the court felt that since the company had proposed changes in the plan, the union had a right to cost information so that it could weigh the company offer against an equivalent increase in take-home pay.

313 NLRB v. Toffenetti Restaurant Co., 311 F 2d 219, 51 LRRM 2601 (CA 2, 1962).

314 Lock Joint Pipe Co., 141 NLRB 943, 52 LRRM 1410 (1963); American Sugar Refining Co., 130 NLRB 634, 47 LRRM 1361 (1961); Stanislaus Implement & Hardware Co., 101 NLRB 394, 31 LRRM 1079 (1952).

315 NLRB v. John S. Swift Co., 277 F 2d 641, 46 LRRM 2090 (CA 7, 1960); NLRB v. New Britain Machine Co., 210 F 2d 61, 33 LRRM 2461 (CA 2, 1954); Keller Industries Inc., dba American Carpet Mills, 170 NLRB No. 197, 69 LRRM 1078 (1968).

centives must be furnished to the union prior to negotiation on such rates.[316]

Other types of information required to be disclosed by the Board have included seniority lists and data,[317] employees' ages,[318] and equipment types and specifications.[319] An employer may attach reasonable conditions to the furnishing financial informations in its own business interest,[320] and need not, for example, furnish financial information on the entire corporate chain controlled by the owners of the unit in question.[321]

Employers are somewhat limited as to the defenses which they may successfully invoke against a charge of refusal to bargain arising from failure to provide information. In *NLRB* v. *Movie Star*,

---

[316] In *Fafnir Bearing Co.*, 146 NLRB 1582, 56 LRRM 1108 (1964), *enforced*, 362 F 2d 716, 62 LRRM 2415 (CA 2, 1966), the employer was held to have violated the act by failing to permit the union to enter the company's production facilities for the purpose of conducting time studies. *See also*: Timken Roller Bearing Co. v. NLRB, 325 F 2d 746, 54 LRRM 2785 (CA 6, 1963); J. I. Case Co. v. NLRB, 253 F 2d 149, 41 LRRM 2679 (CA 7, 1958); NLRB v. Otis Elevator Co., 208 F 2d 176, 33 LRRM 2129 (CA 2, 1953); Johns-Manville Products, 171 NLRB No. 65, 69 LRRM 1068 (1968); Wilson Athletic Goods Mfg. Co., 169 NLRB No. 82, 67 LRRM 1193 (1968); Emeryville Research Center, 174 NLRB No. 23, 70 LRRM 1099 (1969); *but see* General Aniline & Film Corp., 124 NLRB 1217, 44 LRRM 1617 (1959) (such information must have been used in wage rates, not just for employer cost determination purposes, for employer to be required to furnish it). *And see* General Electric Co., note 290 *supra*.

[317] NLRB v. Gulf Atlantic Warehouse Co., 291 F 2d 475, 48 LRRM 2376 (CA 5, 1961); Post Publishing Co., 102 NLRB 648, 31 LRRM 1336 (1953); Oliver Corp., 162 NLRB 813, 64 LRRM 1092 (1967), where a union's request for information about the length of employment and the reasons for the discharge of employees during their probationary period was relevant to future contract negotiations. Finding that an employer had engaged in an unfair labor practice by refusing to furnish the union with this data, the Board ordered that it be provided. The dispute arose when an employee was discharged during his trial period, and the employer refused to tell the union why the man was terminated. The union asked the employer for data on all employees discharged during their probationary period over a two-year span. The employer responded that the information was not relevant or necessary to prepare for bargaining. Disagreeing with its trial examiner, the Board held that to deny the union access to this data would significantly impair its ability to engage in meaningful bargaining concerning the terms and conditions of employment of probationary employees. In *Standard Oil Co. of Calif.* v. *NLRB*, 399 F 2d 639, 69 LRRM 2014 (1968), the employer was required to supply a mailing list of names and home addresses of all employees in the bargaining unit after the employer had mailed literature to the employees in support of its bargaining position. In *Prudential Insurance Co.*, 412 F 2d 77, 71 LRRM 2254 (1969), the employer was required to supply names and addresses of employees in a nationwide bargaining unit which the union contended it needed to communicate regarding contract benefits and policing the agreement.

[318] Reed & Prince Mfg. Co., 96 NLRB 850, 28 LRRM 1608 (1951).

[319] Oregon Coast Operators Ass'n, 113 NLRB 1338, 36 LRRM 1448 (1955).

[320] Fruit & Vegetable Packers & Warehousemen v. NLRB, 316 F 2d 389, 52 LRRM 2537 (1963).

[321] Braswell Motor Freight Lines, Inc., 141 NLRB 1154, 52 LRRM 1467 (1963).

Inc.,[322] an employer was excused from the duty to provide information where its failure to do so was attributable to a breakdown in negotiations not caused by the employer's lack of good faith.[323] However, employer contentions that information is confidential or privileged have been rejected,[324] as have similar contentions that the divulgence of such information violates employees' right of privacy.[325] A few cases have pardoned an employer's refusal to furnish information on the ground that the union had waived its right to information by "clearly and unmistakably" bargaining the right away,[326] but even fewer have inferred a waiver from the union's bargaining conduct.[327] Most cases involving waiver state that since the duty to furnish information arises under the Act, the union's right to such information can be waived only in express terms and such a waiver can never be found by implication.[328] Thus forfeiture of the right must be by "clear and unmistakable" language and not merely by omission from the contract.[329] A general contract provision to the effect that the agreement has settled all issues and all collective bargaining obligations for its term does not normally amount to a waiver.[330]

---

322 361 F 2d 346, 62 LRRM 2234 (CA 5, 1966).

323 Oklahoma Rendering Co., 75 NLRB 1112, 21 LRRM 1115 (1948) (employer need not provide striking union with information as to how many strikers have been replaced, where union is engaged in economic strike and demands that all strikers be reinstated as condition to ending strike).

324 Aluminum Ore Co. v. NLRB 131 F 2d 485, 11 LRRM 693 (CA 7, 1942); Kroger Co., 163 NLRB 441, 64 LRRM 1364 (1967); Boston Herald-Traveler Corp., 110 NLRB 2097, 35 LRRM 1309 (1954).

325 Utica Observer-Dispatch, Inc. v. NLRB, 229 F 2d 575, 37 LRRM 2441 (CA 2, 1956) (employer's notification to employees that it would furnish information if they did not object, and withholding of information only on those who did object, is refusal to bargain); NLRB v. Item Co., 220 F 2d 956, 35 LRRM 2709 (CA 5, 1955); Northwestern Photo Engraving Co., 140 NLRB 24, 51 LRRM 1550 (1962); Industrial Welding Co., *supra* note 254 (violation found despite employer contention that disclosure of wage rates would cause dissension in shop). *But cf.* Webster Outdoor Advertising Co., 160 NLRB 1781, 67 LRRM 1589 (1968), holding that an employer did not violate the Act by refusing to supply wage data for replacements of economic strikers. The fact that the replacements had been subject to harassment and threats justified the employer's request for assurance by the union that the need was for legitimate union purposes and would not be used to facilitate further harassment. Furthermore, the refusal was not categorical.

326 International News Service Div. of Hearst Corp., 113 NLRB 1067, 36 LRRM 1454 (1955); Hughes Tool Co., 100 NLRB 208, 30 LRRM 1265 (1952).

327 Square D. Co. v. NLRB, 332 F 2d 360, 56 LRRM 2147 (CA 9, 1964); Berkline Corp., 123 NLRB 685, 43 LRRM 1513 (1959). *See* further discussion of waiver and duty to furnish information in Chapter 17 *infra.*

328 NLRB v. Perkins Machine Co., 326 F 2d 488, 55 LRRM 2204 (CA 1, 1964); Skyway Luggage Co., 117 NLRB 681, 39 LRRM 1310 (1957).

329 Timken Roller Bearing Co. v. NLRB, 325 F 2d 746, 54 LRRM 2855 (CA 6, 1963); California Portland Cement Co., 103 NLRB 1375, 31 LRRM 1630 (1953).

330 J. I. Case Co. v. NLRB, 253 F 2d 149, 41 LRRM 2679 (CA 7, 1958). *See* further discussion of waiver in Part VIII, *infra,* this Chapter.

D. Categorizing the Failure to Furnish Information

The question arises whether a refusal to supply requested information is a *per se* violation of the duty to bargain, merely evidence of lack of good faith, or a violation of the statute at all. The Supreme Court in *Truitt* [331] stated explicitly that "[w]e do not hold, however, that in every case in which economic inability is raised as an argument against increased wages it automatically follows that the employees are entitled to substantiating evidence. ... The inquiry must always be whether or not under the circumstances ... the statutory obligation to bargain in good faith has been met." [332] According to the dissent, the Board had applied the wrong standard by ruling that the employer's failure to supply information constituted a *per se* refusal to bargain in good faith. The view that *Truitt,* properly interpreted, means that refusal to supply information is only evidence of bad faith was given strong support by *NLRB* v. *Insurance Agents Int'l Union,*[333] in which the Supreme Court stated that the refusal to furnish information was weighty evidence of lack of good faith, but that the judgment of the Board must turn on all facts pertinent to the party's state of mind.[334]

V. *PER SE* VIOLATIONS

In determining whether an unlawful refusal to bargain has occurred, the Board and the courts normally probe the conduct of the parties for evidence of the presence or absence of subjective "good faith." However, certain types of conduct have been viewed as independent, or *per se,* refusals to bargain, without regard to any considerations of good or bad faith.[335]

---

[331] 351 US 149, 38 LRRM 2042 (1955).

[332] 351 US at 153.

[333] 361 US 477; 45 LRRM 2704 (1960).

[334] *See also* Int'l Woodworkers of America v. NLRB, 263 F 2d 483, 43 LRRM 2462 (CA DC 1959) ; J.I. Case Co. v. NLRB, 253 F 2d 149, 41 LRRM 2679 (CA 7, 1958) . *But see* Curtis-Wright Corp., Wright Aero. Div. v. NLRB, 347 F 2d 61, 59 LRRM 2433 (CA 3, 1965) , where the court stated that once it is established that information is relevant, it is a *per se* refusal to bargain for the employer to fail to produce the information on request. The court added that this was consistent with *Truitt* since it was there held that financial information is not always relevant but depends on the circumstances. *See also* Timken Roller Bearing Co. v. NLRB, *supra* note 329; Puerto Rico Telephone Co. v. NLRB, *supra* note 299.

[335] During the period prior to the passage of Taft-Hartley, this same category of cases existed, but the distinction did not begin to become pronounced until the passage of the Taft-Hartley amendments added the good-faith requirement separately from the general duty-to-bargain requirement.

A. Unilateral Changes [336]

Unilateral changes by an employer during the course of a collective bargaining relationship concerning matters which are proper subjects of bargaining are normally regarded as *per se* refusals to bargain.[337] These actions, which have the effect of by-passing the union, also have supported the inference of lack of good faith. While such conduct had been analyzed by the Board and circuit courts both in *per se* terms [338] and in terms of good faith,[339] the Supreme Court did not give express recognition to the *per se* doctrine in this context until the 1962 case of *NLRB* v. *Katz*.[340] In *Katz* the employer's unilateral changes in conditions of employment (change in sick-leave policy, merit-wage-increase policy, and general wage increase) were characterized by the Court in these terms:

> A refusal to negotiate *in fact* as to any subject which is within §8(d) and about which the union seeks to negotiate, violates §8(a)(5) though the employer has every desire to reach agreement with the union upon an over-all collective agreement and earnestly and in all good faith bargains to that end.[341]

Thus, a violation was found despite the possibility of subjective good faith.

The Court in *Katz* referred to its earlier decision in *NLRB* v. *Crompton-Highland Mills*,[342] in which a wage increase greater than that offered to the union was granted immediately after an impasse had developed. While the opinion was not framed in *per se* language, the absence of any other indicia of bad faith placed the

---

336 *See* discussion of unilateral changes, III C. 6, *supra*, this Chapter.
337 NLRB v. Katz, 369 US 736, 50 LRRM 2177 (1962) ; NLRB v. American Mfg. Co. of Tex., 351 F 2d 74, 60 LRRM 2122 (CA 5, 1965) (granting wage increase under pressure of Interstate Commerce Commission) ; NLRB v. Mid-West Towel & Linen Service, Inc., 339 F 2d 958, 57 LRRM 2433 (CA 7, 1964) (all unilateral wage increases) ; NLRB v. Wonder State Mfg. Co., 344 F 2d 210, 59 LRRM 2065 (CA 8, 1965) ; NLRB v. Zelrich, 344 F 2d 1011, 59 LRRM 2225 (CA 5, 1965) ; McLean v. NLRB, 333 F 2d 84, 56 LRRM 2475 (CA 6, 1964) (granting health insurance) ; NLRB v. Citizens Hotel Co., 326 F 2d 501, 55 LRRM 2135 (CA 5, 1964) (stopping Christmas bonus) ; NLRB v. Central Illinois Public Service Co., 324 F 2d 916, 54 LRRM 2586 (CA 7, 1963) (discontinuing employee discount). Exceptions have been made in the case of impasse, necessity, and waiver, *infra* notes 351-353.
338 369 US at 738.
339 *See, e.g.,* NLRB v. F. M. Reeves & Sons, 273 F 2d 710, 713, 45 LRRM 2295 (CA 10, 1959), *enforcing* 121 NLRB 1280, 42 LRRM 1555 (1958), *cert. denied*, 366 US 914, 48 LRRM 2071 (1961) ; NLRB v. Century Cement Mfg. Co., 208 F 2d 84, 33 LRRM 2061 (CA 2, 1953), *enforcing* 100 NLRB 1323, 30 LRRM 1447 (1952).
340 *Supra* note 337.
341 369 US at p. 743.
342 337 US 217, 24 LRRM 2088 (1949).

decision on a *per se* basis, and a number of later cases rested upon this approach,[343] some expanding it [344] and others distinguishing it.[345]

In *Katz* the Court did, however, note that circumstances might justify unilateral employer action,[346] and exceptions dealing with impasse,[347] necessity,[348] and waiver [349] have been developed.

B. Other *Per Se* Violations

Section 8(d) gives specific statutory recognition to certain basic procedural elements of collective bargaining. Failure to comply with these procedural criteria has been deemed a *per se* refusal to bargain.

1. "The execution of a written contract incorporating any agreement reached." The failure to sign a written memorandum of the agreement made has been uniformly regarded as a *per se* refusal to bargain.[350] Even prior to the Taft-Hartley enactment of Sec-

---

[343] Korn Industries v. NLRB, 389 F 2d 117, 67 LRRM 2148 (CA 4, 1967); NLRB v. Almeida Bus Lines, Inc., 333 F 2d 725, 56 LRRM 2545 (CA 1, 1964).

[344] NLRB v. Tom Joyce Floors, Inc., 353 F 2d 768, 60 LRRM 2334 (CA 9, 1965) (increased wages to strike replacements); NLRB v. Erie Resistor Corp., 373 US 221, 53 LRRM 2121 (1963) (superseniority to strike replacements); Taft Broadcasting Co., 185 NLRB No. 68, 75 LRRM 1076 (1970) (unilateral elimination of arbitration procedure).

[345] NLRB v. Southern Coach & Body Co., 336 F 2d 214, 57 LRRM 2102 (CA 5, 1964) (employer may continue "automatic" increases to which it is already committed, since these are not a "change" in working conditions); NLRB v. Tex-Tan, Inc., 318 F 2d 472, 53 LRRM 2298 (CA 5, 1963) (employer may make changes, but only to extent of previous offers to union, after impasse is reached); NLRB v. Superior Fireproof Door & Sash Co., 289 F 2d 713, 45 LRRM 1487 (CA 2, 1961) (employer may make isolated individual wage adjustments); Armstrong Cork Co. v. NLRB, 211 F 2d 843, 33 LRRM 2789 (CA 5, 1954); NLRB v. Dealers Engine Rebuilders, Inc., 199 F 2d 249, 31 LRRM 2007 (CA 8, 1952); NLRB v. Landis Tool Co., 193 F 2d 279, 29 LRRM 2255 (CA 3, 1952) (employer may make wage increase which union has rejected, but only after notice to and consultation with union); NLRB v. Bradley Washfountain Co., 192 F 2d 144, 29 LRRM 2064 (CA 7, 1951).

[346] 369 US at 747-748.

[347] See NLRB v. U. S. Sonics Corp., 312 F 2d 610, 52 LRRM 2360 (CA 1, 1963); see also discussion of impasse in Part VII, *infra,* this chapter.

[348] See Duvin, *supra* note 2, at 278, n. 210.

[349] Where a union is put on notice of an intended change and does not seek to bargain about it, the employer may act unilaterally. U.S. Lingerie Corp., 170 NLRB No. 77, 67 LRRM 1482 (1968). *See* discussion of waiver in Part VIII, *infra,* this chapter.

[350] NLRB v. Big Run Coal & Clay Co., 385 F 2d 788, 66 LRRM 2640 (CA 6, 1967), *enforcing* 152 NLRB 1144, 59 LRRM 1287 (1965); Lozano Enterprises v. NLRB, 327 F 2d 814, 55 LRRM 2510 (CA 9, 1964) (employer signed contract, but refused to return it to union); NLRB v. Wate, Inc., 310 F 2d 700, 51 LRRM 2701 (CA 6, 1962); Int'l Union, Operating Engineers, Local No. 12 (Tri-County Ass'n Civil Engineers), 168 NLRB No. 27, 66 LRRM 1270 (1967); Standard Oil Co., 137 NLRB 690, 50 LRRM 1230 (1962) (union refused to sign agreement). The requirement is

tion 8(d), this conduct had been viewed by the Supreme Court as an independent refusal to bargain in *H. J. Heinz v. NLRB*.[351] While this 1941 decision is not specifically cast in *per se* language, the language does form a basis for the *per se* doctrine.

2. "To meet at reasonable times." Section 8(d) does not define the term "reasonable," but, as an objective standard, it would include a minimal number of meetings.[352] Where an employer insists upon bargaining by mail or insists that the union submit all its proposals in writing despite union requests for personal meetings, an unlawful refusal to bargain will result.[353]

3. "Confer in good faith with respect to wages, hours and other terms and conditions of employment." While the subjective condition of "good faith" is set forth in the Act, the further requirement that the parties "confer" also provides the basis for a *per se* analysis, as indicated in the *Katz* case. A refusal to bargain about a mandatory subject or an insistence to the point of impasse about a permissive subject may constitute a *per se* violation.[354] For example, a demand that a union post a performance bond [355] or that it agree to a "ballot" clause requiring a strike vote on the employer's last offer has been held to be a *per se* violation.[356]

---

also applicable to individual employer members of multi-employer bargaining units. NLRB v. Sheridan Creations, Inc. 384 F 2d 696, 61 LRRM 2586 (1966); Strong Roofing & Insulating Co., 393 US 357, 70 LRRM 2100 (1969). *See* discussion of multi-employer bargaining units in Chapter 9 *supra*.

351 311 US 514, 7 LRRM 291 (1941).

352 *See* Duvin, *supra* note 2, at 264-270. *See* discussion on dilatory tactics *supra*.

353 *See* NLRB v. U.S. Cold Storage Corp., 203 F 2d 924, 32 LRRM 2024 (CA 5, 1953); NLRB v. P. Lorillard Co., 117 F 2d 921, 7 LRRM 475 (CA 6, 1941); *see also* NLRB v. Yutana Barge Lines, 315 F 2d 524, 52 LRRM 2750 (CA 9, 1963) (refusal to bargain with respect to part of bargaining unit); NLRB v. American Aggregate Co., 305 F 2d 559, 50 LRRM 2580 (CA 5, 1962) (ignoring requests for bargaining); Duro Fittings, 121 NLRB 377, 42 LRRM 1368 (1958) (refusal to sit across table and bargain in person).

354 For a critical analysis of the application of *per se* rules to this aspect of bargaining, *see* Duvin, supra note 2, at 271. *See also* Chapter 14 *infra* for a discussion of mandatory and permissive subjects of bargaining.

355 NLRB v. American Compress Warehouse, 350 F 2d 365, 59 LRRM 2739 (CA 5, 1965); Union Mfg. Co., 76 NLRB 322, 21 LRRM 1187 (1948); Jasper Blackburn Products, 21 NLRB 1240, 6 LRRM 169 (1940).

356 NLRB v. Borg-Warner Corp., 356 US 342, 42 LRRM 2034 (1958). *See* discussion of *Borg-Warner* in Chapter 14 *infra*. *See also* Sears Roebuck & Co., 139 NLRB 471, 51 LRRM 1327 (1962) (insistence that bargaining be with representatives from local plant, rather than with international representatives); American Laundry Machinery, 76 NLRB 981, 21 LRRM 1275 (1948) (insistence that union withdraw unfair labor practice charges and abandon strike). *See also* discussion of imposition of conditions on bargaining *supra*. Direct dealings with employees on bargainable matters may also be violative. Medo Photo Supply Corp. v. NLRB, 321 US 678, 14 LRRM 581 (1944); Wings & Wheels, Inc., 139 NLRB 578, 51 LRRM 1341 (1962).

C. Union Conduct

Union insistence upon subjects outside the scope of mandatory bargaining, such as the posting of an employer performance bond, may also constitute a *per se* refusal to bargain.[357] Likewise, a union may not refuse to execute an agreed-upon contract.[358] However, the *Katz* analysis concerning unilateral changes in working conditions by employers is not readily applicable to unions because of their relative inability to effect unilateral changes.[359] Normally some implementation is required by the employer to effect the changes, and thus the matter is on the bargaining table as a demand. Whether a union may actually compel a company to accede to its demand is a matter of economic power, and the possession of such power has been termed "not inconsistent with good faith." [360] However, the Ninth Circuit has viewed a union's unilateral imposition of production quotas, enforced by fines upon member employees, as a refusal to bargain on a mandatory subject and thus a violation of Section 8(b)(3).[361] This represented the first application of the *Fibreboard* [362] doctrine to a union. However, the case has been distinguished on the ground that the union

---

[357] NLRB v. Local 1082, Hod Carriers, 384 F 2d 55, 66 LRRM 2333 (CA 9, 1967), *cert. denied*, 390 US 920, 67 LRRM 2385 (1968); Local 3, Bricklayers, 162 NLRB 476, 64 LRRM 1085 (1966); Painters District Council No. 36, 155 NLRB 1013, 60 LRRM 1431 (1965). *See also* District Council 16, Southern California Pipe Trades, 167 NLRB No. 143, 66 LRRM 1233 (1967), where a number of nonmandatory subjects were insisted upon. Union insistence upon hot-cargo agreements may also, in certain circumstances, be violative. NLRB v. Bricklayers, 381 F 2d 381, 65 LRRM 2563 (CA 6, 1967); Local 26, Sheet Metal Workers, 168 NLRB No. 118, 67 LRRM 1130 (1967). For general treatment of permissive subjects of bargaining *see* Chapter 16 *infra*.

[358] Local 12, Operating Engineers, 168 NLRB No. 27, 66 LRRM 1270 (1967).

[359] In *NLRB v. Insurance Agents Int'l Union*, 361 US 477, 45 LRRM 2704 (1960), the Supreme Court expressly left open the question of whether a union's unilateral imposition of new terms and conditions is subject to the same treatment under §8(b)(3) as an employer's unilateral action. In *Local 802, Musicians (Ben Cutler)*, 164 NLRB 23, 65 LRRM 1048 (1967), *affirmed*, 395 F 2d 287, 68 LRRM 2317 (CA 2, 1968), the Board distinguished the *Katz* case and declined to find a *per se* refusal to bargain where the union amended its bylaws during negotiations to specify a higher wage scale and to establish a new welfare fund. Union members were placed under threat of union discipline for failing to observe the scales. Distinguishing *Katz*, the Second Circuit pointed out that the union could not unilaterally effect changes, but could only demand that the employer make them.

[360] 361 US at 477. *See* Part VI, *infra*, this chapter, for further discussion of *Insurance Agents* and union conduct in bargaining.

[361] Associated Home Builders of Greater East Bay, Inc., 352 F 2d 745, 60 LRRM 2345 (CA 9, 1965). *But compare* Scofield v. NLRB, 393 F 2d 49, 67 LRRM 2673 (CA 7, 1968), *affirmed*, 393 US 995, 70 LRRM 3105 (1969), where a union's enforcement of production quotas was held not to be violative of §8(b)(1). *See* Chapter 5 *supra*.

[362] Fibreboard Paper Products Corp. v. NLRB, 379 US 203, 57 LRRM 2609 (1964). *See* Chapter 15 *infra*.

was modifying an existing collective bargaining agreement without meeting the requirements of Section 8(d).[363] An attempt to modify or terminate a collective bargaining agreement, by means of a strike, without serving the requisite statutory notice upon federal and state mediation agencies, as required by Section 8(d), is a violation of the union's bargaining obligation.[364]

VI. ECONOMIC PRESSURE DURING BARGAINING

The Supreme Court's 1960 decision in *NLRB* v. *Insurance Agents Int'l Union*[365] affirmed the principle that economic power goes hand in hand with "reasoned discussion" in determining the outcome of collective bargaining negotiations. The Court held that the Board cannot find a lack of good-faith bargaining by a party solely because tactics designed to exert economic pressure were employed during bargaining. To exert such pressure during the period of bargaining, union members refused to solicit new business, held half-day walkouts, and refused to perform ordinary reporting duties. The Board found such action to be a *per se* violation of Section 8(b)(3), despite the union's desire to reach an agreement, but the District of Columbia Circuit Court denied enforcement. The Supreme Court, affirming, conceded that such economic activity is unprotected by the Act but held that the use of such pressure is not in and of itself inconsistent with the duty to bargain in good faith. The Court stated that "the truth of the matter is . . . the two factors—necessity for good-faith bargaining between parties, and the availability of economic pressure devices

---

[363] Local 802, Musicians, *supra* note 359.
[364] Mine Workers (McCoy Coal Co.), 165 NLRB 592, 65 LRRM 1450 (1967); Sheet Metal Workers Local 141 (American Sign Co.), 153 NLRB 537, 59 LRRM 1512 (1965). *See* note 455 *infra*.
[365] 361 US 477, 45 LRRM 2704 (1960). The case involved charges against a union for violation of §8(b)(3) based upon its use of harassing tactics while collective bargaining was in progress. The employees (insurance agents) did not engage in conventional strike activities; instead they refused to solicit new business, refused to comply with reporting procedures, reported to work late, engaged in "sit-in-mornings," distributed union leaflets, solicited policyholders' signatures directed to the company, and engaged in other such tactics. The Court agreed that this conduct was not protected concerted activity, *citing* Automobile Workers v. Wisconsin Board (Briggs-Stratton), 336 US 245, 23 LRRM 2361 (1949), *and* NLRB v. Fansteel Metallurgical Corp., 306 US 240, 4 LRRM 515 (1939), but this did not mean that the activity constituted a refusal to bargain. (The dissent maintained that while such economic activity was not a *per se* violation, the Board should have been able to consider it as evidence of bad faith in the totality of the circumstances.) Part V of this volume treats generally various types of economic activity associated with labor-management relations.

to each to make the other party incline to agree on one's terms—exist side by side." [366]

The issue considered by the Supreme Court had confronted the District of Columbia Circuit Court on two occasions in the mid-1950s.[367] Refusing enforcement in both instances, the latter court found no violation of Section 8(b)(3) despite harassing tactics. It took the view that Congress had not specifically limited the use of economic pressure in support of lawful demands.

Economic activity by employers during bargaining has involved primarily the use of a lockout. Prior to 1965 this tactic was permitted only in limited defensive situations.[368] In 1957, for example, the Supreme Court upheld the right of members of a multi-employer bargaining unit to lock out employees in an effort to counter a union's use of a "whipsaw" strike against one of the members of the employer group.[369] However, in 1965 the Supreme Court in *American Ship Building Co. v. NLRB*[370] held that a single employer, after a bargaining impasse has been reached, may temporarily shut down its plant "for the sole purpose of bringing economic pressure to bear in support of [its] legitimate bargaining position." [371] In *NLRB* v. *Brown*,[372] decided the same day as *American Ship Building*,[373] the Court held that members of a multi-employer bargaining unit may operate with temporary replacements during a multi-employer lockout. The Court, however, left open the question of whether a single employer who uses the lockout as an offensive bargaining weapon may utilize

---

[366] *Id.* at 489. The Court stated that "collective bargaining . . . cannot be equated with an academic collective search for truth—or even with what might be thought to be the ideal of one. . . . The presence of economic weapons in reserve, and their actual exercise on occasion by the parties, is part and parcel of the system that the Wagner and Taft-Hartley Acts have recognized." *Id.* at 488-489.

[367] United Mine Workers (Boone County) v. NLRB, 257 F 2d 211, 42 LRRM 2264 (CA DC, 1958) ; Textile Workers (Personal Products) v. NLRB, 227 F 2d 409, 36 LRRM 2778 (CA DC, 1955) .

[368] *See, e.g.,* Betts Cadillac Olds, Inc., 96 NLRB 268, 28 LRRM 1509 (1951) ; International Shoe Co., 93 NLRB 907, 27 LRRM 1504 (1951) ; Duluth Bottling Ass'n, 48 NLRB 1335, 12 LRRM 151 (1943) ; Link-Belt Co., 26 NLRB 227, 6 LRRM 565 (1940) . *See also* Chapter 20 *infra* on lockouts.

[369] NLRB v. Truck Drivers Union, 353 US 87, 39 LRRM 2603 (1957) .

[370] 380 US 300, 58 LRRM 2672 (1965) .

[371] *Id.* at 318.

[372] 380 US 278, 58 LRRM 2663 (1965) . The Court noted in both *Brown* and *American Ship Building* the absence of anti-union animus. *See* discussion in Chapter 5 *infra* on the impact of these cases on the issue of motive as an essential element of a §8(a)(1) violation.

[373] *Supra* note 359.

temporary replacements. Since the *Brown* and *American Ship Building* decisions, the Board and the courts have adopted a more tolerant view of lockouts, so long as they are not motivated by anti-union animus.[374]

Because of the unilateral changes involved in a lockout, a question arises as to whether an impasse in bargaining must be reached as a prerequisite to a lockout by a single employer. Shortly after the *American Ship Building* decision, the Sixth Circuit, in *Detroit Newspaper Publishers Ass'n v. NLRB,*[375] took the position that an impasse was not a prerequisite to a lockout.

In *Darling & Co.*[376] the Board upheld a pre-impasse lockout,[377] and was affirmed by the court of appeals for the District of Columbia Circuit[378] on the basis of the following considerations: (1) the absence of an anti-union motive, (2) the large number of negotiating sessions both before and after the lockout (there was no allegation of bad-faith bargaining), (3) the relative strength of the union, (4) the many concessions which the employer had made during negotiations, (5) the possibility of the union calling a strike at a time of its own choosing, (6) the highly seasonal nature of the employer's business, and (7) the unusual harm which would have resulted from a strike.

---

[374] Newspaper Drivers (Detroit Newspaper Publishers Ass'n) v. NLRB, 404 F 2d 1159, 70 LRRM 2061 (CA 6, 1968) *affirming* 166 NLRB 219, 65 LRRM 1425 (1967), where an employer's lockout to support the bargaining position of a struck employer was permitted on the ground that any concessions on important issues granted by the struck employer could have impact on the nonstruck employer's ability to maintain its own bargaining position. The court distinguished *David Friedland Painting Co.,* 377 F 2d 983, 65 LRRM 2119 (CA 3, 1967), where the economic interest of the employer in the conditions in other bargaining units was more remote. *See* Publishers Ass'n of New York City v. NLRB, 364 F 2d 293, 62 LRRM 2722 (CA 2, 1966) (even where union withdraws from multi-employer unit, lockout can be utilized); Acme Markets, Inc., 156 NLRB 1452, 61 LRRM 1281 (1966) (allowing lockout in stores not in unit); Weyerhaeuser Co., 155 NLRB 921, 60 LRRM 1425 (1965) (employers do not have to be recognized as multi-employer unit by union); *see also* Body & Tank Corp. v. NLRB, 344 F 2d 330, 59 LRRM 2123 (CA 2, 1965); NLRB v. Tonkin Corp. of Cal. 352 F 2d 509, 60 LRRM 2404 (CA 9, 1965), where the courts remanded to the Board in the light of *American Ship Building.* For a more detailed treatment of the subject of lockouts *see* Chapter 20 *infra.*

[375] 346 F 2d 527, 59 LRRM 2401 (CA 6, 1965).

[376] 171 NLRB No. 95, 68 LRRM 1133 (1968).

[377] *But see* Laclede Gas Co., 173 NLRB No. 35, 69 LRRM 1316 (1968), which distinguished *Darling* on the ground that it relied on §§8(a)(1) and (3) considerations, that the impasse had not been challenged on the ground of unilateral action under §8(a)(5).

[378] Lane v. NLRB (Darling & Co.), 48 F 2d 1208, 72 LRRM 2439 (1969).

VII. IMPASSE

The duty to bargain does not require a party "to engage in fruitless marathon discussions at the expense of frank statements and support of his position." [379] Where there are irreconcilable differences in the parties' positions after exhaustive good-faith negotiations, the law recognizes the existence of an impasse.[380] Some difficulty exists in drawing a line between an impasse reached by hard and steadfast bargaining and one resulting from an unlawful refusal to bargain. It may be that in collective bargaining "part of the difficulty arises from the fact that the law recognizes the possibility of the parties reaching an impasse." [381]

Where an impasse is reached, the duty to bargain is not terminated but only suspended.[382] During this suspension the employer may not take action in disparagement of the collective bargaining process or action amounting to a withdrawal of recognition of the union's representative status.[383]

The existence or nonexistence of an impasse is normally put in issue when, after negotiations have been carried on for a period of time, the positions of the parties become fairly well fixed and talks reach the point of stalemate. When this occurs, the employer is free to make unilateral changes in working conditions (i.e., wages, hours, etc.) consistent with his rejected offers to the union.[384] By the very nature of the bargaining process it is not always apparent when an impasse has been reached. Prior to mak-

---

[379] NLRB v. American Nat'l Ins. Co., 343 US 395, 404, 30 LRRM 2147 (1952).

[380] Usually the more meetings, the better the chance of a finding that an impasse had arisen. Fetzer Television v. NLRB, 317 F 2d 420, 53 LRRM 2224 (CA 6, 1963). On the doctrine of impasse generally, see Schatzki, The Employer's Unilateral Act— A Per Se Violation—Sometimes, 44 TEX. L. REV. 470, 495, (1966) ; Comment, Impasse in Collective Bargaining, 44 TEX. L. REV. 769 (1966).

[381] Speech of Board Member Jenkins, 40 LRRM 98, 105-106 (1957).

[382] NLRB v. Tex-Tan, Inc., 318 F 2d 472, 53 LRRM 2298 (CA 5, 1963) ; Philip Carey Mfg. Co., 140 NLRB 1103, 52 LRRM 1184 (1963) ; Boeing Airplane Co., 80 NLRB 477, 25 LRRM 1107 (1948).

[383] Central Metallic Casket Co., 91 NLRB 572, 26 LRRM 1520 (1950).

[384] Almeida Bus Lines, Inc., 333 F 2d 729, 56 LRRM 2548 (CA 1, 1964) ; Eddie's Chop Shop, 165 NLRB 861, 65 LRRM 1408 (1967) ; American Laundry Machinery Co., 107 NLRB 1574, 33 LRRM 1457 (1954). An employer's right to hire replacements for strikers is based on the same rationale. Since the employer would request that he be allowed to hire replacements, and the union would obviously refuse, the employer's right to keep his business operating allows him to hire replacements. NLRB v. MacKay Radio & Telegraph Co., 304 US 333, 2 LRRM 610 (1938). See Chapter 19 infra.

ing unilateral changes,[385] however, an employer must have reasonable cause to believe that an impasse exists.

The transient nature of the suspension of the duty to bargain as a result of an impasse is exemplified by the many exceptions to the suspension. For example, impasse on a single issue does not suspend the obligation to bargain on other unsettled issues.[386] Further, the suspension is inapplicable to a party when the impasse is the result of that party's bad faith or unfair labor practices.[387] Similarly, an employer may not make changes inconsistent with offers made to and rejected by the union during negotiations.[388]

A legal impasse may end easily; almost any changed condition or circumstance will terminate the suspension of the duty to bargain. A strike after an impasse is reached changes the bargaining atmosphere and therefore indicates that bargaining might be resumed,[389] as do changes in the business outlook of the general industry, or of the employer's specific firm,[390] or a substantial change in the bargaining position of one party.[391] Even after the certification year has passed, if changed circumstances end the impasse

---

[385] NLRB v. U. S. Sonics Corp., 312 F 2d 610, 52 LRRM 2360 (CA 1, 1963) ; Cheney California Lumber Co., v. NLRB, 319 F 2d 375, 53 LRRM 2598 (CA 9, 1963) (a belief that talks or negotiations are deadlocked or stalemated is sufficient). *See also* NLRB v. Cambria Clay Products Co., 215 F 2d 48, 34 LRRM 2471 (CA 6, 1954) (presence of federal mediator may indicate an impasse if agreement still cannot be reached after he is called in; since Federal Mediation and Conciliation Service has the duty to use its best efforts to bring the parties to agreement, a mediator's refusal to call any more meetings may indicate there is no chance of agreement).

[386] Chambers Mfg. Co., 124 NLRB 721, 44 LRRM 1477 (1959) ; Pool Mfg. Co., 70 NLRB 540, 18 LRRM 1364 (1946). There is a distinction, however, between exhaustion of the continuing duty to bargain despite an impasse on one issue, as in *Chambers*, and the circumstances under which an impasse is created on a single though crucial issue. *Cf.* American Fed. of Television & Radio Artists v. NLRB, 395 F 2d 622, n. 13, 67 LRRM 3032 (CA DC, 1968) (". . . [a] deadlock is still a deadlock whether produced by one or a number of significant and unresolved differences in position") ; Taft Broadcasting Co., 163 NLRB 55, 64 LRRM 1386 (1967) ; Dallas General Drivers v. NLRB, 355 F 2d 842, 61 LRRM 2065 (CA DC, 1966) ; NLRB v. Intracoastal Terminal, Inc., 286 F 2d 954, 47 LRRM 2629 (CA 5, 1961).

[387] NLRB v. Herman Sausage Co., 275 F 2d 229, 45 LRRM 2829 (CA 5, 1960).

[388] NLRB v. Intracoastal Terminal, Inc., supra note 386.

[389] NLRB v. U.S. Cold Storage Corp., 203 F 2d 924, 32 LRRM 2024 (CA 5, 1953). The occurrence of a strike does not necessarily mean that negotiations prior to the strike have reached an impasse. J. H. Bonck Co., 170 NLRB No. 164, 69 LRRM 1172 (1968).

[390] Kit Mfg. Co., 138 NLRB 1290, 51 LRRM 1224 (1962) (general industry increase in production and sales, union obtaining wider membership and certification in entire industry, and improved financial condition of employer).

[391] NLRB v. Sharon Hats, Inc., 289 F 2d 628, 48 LRRM 2098 (CA 5, 1961) , *enforcing* 127 NLRB 947, 46 LRRM 1128 (1960) (dropping part of benefit-clause requests).

the employer must bargain unless he has reasonable grounds for believing that the union has lost its majority.[392]

VIII. DEFENSE, EXCEPTIONS, AND SUSPENSION

Under certain conditions the duty to bargain in good faith either does not arise or is obviated.

A. Waiver of Bargaining Rights

Among the arguments often raised in defense of unilateral changes is the contention that the charging party has waived its right to bargain about the particular subject matter. Since the obligation to bargain is one which may continue during the term of the agreement,[393] the issue of waiver may be raised either before or after entry into a written agreement.[394] With increasing frequency the waiver issue arises in connection with some form of unilateral employer action, such as subcontracting, where the primary defense is that the subject matter is not a mandatory topic of collective bargaining and the secondary defense is that the union waived whatever right it may have had to bargain.[395]

A waiver may result from action or inaction by the parties. A party may agree to contractual language specifically waiving its right to bargain about a particular matter,[396] or it may relinquish

---

[392] Celanese Corp. of America, 95 NLRB 664, 28 LRRM 1362 (1951). *See* discussion in Section XI *infra*.

[393] NLRB v. Jacobs Mfg. Co., 196 F 2d 680, 30 LRRM 2098 (CA 2, 1952). Under the Wagner Act an employer was under a duty, upon request, to bargain with the union as to terms and conditions of employment whether or not the subject had been discussed and previously embodied in a collective bargaining agreement. *See* NLRB v. Sands, 306 US 332, 4 LRRM 530 (1939). The addition of §8(d) modified this obligation by expressly stating that parties to the agreement are not required "to discuss or agree to any modification of the terms and conditions . . . if such modification is to become effective before such terms and conditions can be reopened under the provisions of the contract." In *Jacobs*, 196 F 2d at 684, the court held that §8(d) does not relieve the employer of the duty to bargain "as to subjects which were neither discussed nor embodied in any of the terms and conditions of the contract." *See also* NLRB v. Niles-Bement-Pond Co., 199 F 2d 713, 31 LRRM 2057 (CA 2, 1952); Proctor Mfg. Corp., 131 NLRB 1166, 48 LRRM 1222 (1961).

[394] The question may arise as to whether the union has waived its right to hold the employer to a binding agreement. In Tanner Motor Livery, 160 NLRB 1669, 63 LRRM 1242 (1966), the issue arose when the company asserted that union conduct evincing an unwillingness to accept its offer constituted a rejection allowing it to withdraw its prior proposal. In rejecting the employer's argument, the Board noted the employer's action subsequent to the purported rejection which indicated that it did not consider the union conduct to be a rejection.

[395] U.S. Lingerie Corp., 170 NLRB No. 77, 67 LRRM 1482 (1968); American Oil Co., 151 NLRB 421, 58 LRRM 1412 (1965); New York Mirror, 151 NLRB 834, 58 LRRM 1465 (1965).

[396] *See, e.g.,* Ador Corp., 150 NLRB 1658, 58 LRRM 1280 (1965).

its right during negotiations for the collective agreement.[397] In these circumstances established past practices of the parties may be persuasive evidence of a waiver.[398] In addition, the failure to protest unilateral action [399] or the failure to request bargaining despite knowledge of a contemplated unilateral change [400] may directly result in a waiver. Nonetheless, the Board and the courts have been reluctant to infer a waiver and have construed the waiver doctrine strictly.[401]

1. Waiver by Express Agreement. A party may contractually waive its right to bargain about a particular mandatory subject.[402] Where such an assertion is raised, the test has been whether the waiver is in "clear and unmistakable" language.[403] In this regard, a waiver is normally construed as applicable only as to the specific item mentioned.[404] Thus, a "zipper clause" specifying that the contract represents the complete expression of the agreement of the parties, does not, standing alone, constitute a sufficiently clear and unmistakable waiver as to a specific item.[405] Conversely, a specific waiver will not embrace a more general grouping. For example, a waiver as to particular compensation afforded an individual employee does not necessarily constitute a waiver with respect to unilateral changes for groups of employees.[406]

---

[397] *See, e.g.,* Speidel Corp., 120 NLRB 733, 42 LRRM 1039 (1958). *See also* discussion of waiver in Chapter 17 *infra.*
[398] *Id.* at 741. New York Mirror, *supra* note 395; American Oil Co. *supra* note 395.
[399] Justenson's Food Stores, Inc., 160 NLRB 687, 63 LRRM 1027 (1966); Motorresearch Co., et. al., 138 NLRB 1490, 51 LRRM 1240 (1962).
[400] U.S. Lingerie Corp., *supra* note 395; NLRB v. Spun-Jee Corp., 385 F 2d 379, 66 LRRM 2485 (as amended, 67 LRRM 2308) (CA 2, 1967), *decision on remand,* 171 NLRB No. 64, 68 LRRM 1121 (1968); Montgomery Ward & Co., 137 NLRB No. 418, 50 LRRM 1162 (1962). *See also* Fruehauf Trailer Co., 162 NLRB 195, 64 LRRM 1037 (1966).
[401] *E.g.,* New York Mirror, *supra* note 395, and cases cited therein.
[402] Ador Corp., *supra* note 396; Druwhit Metal Products Co., 153 NLRB 346, 59 LRRM 1359 (1965) (containing clause identical to that in *Ador*).
[403] NLRB v. Perkins Machine Co., 326 F 2d 488, 55 LRRM 2204 (CA 1, 1964); Timken Roller Bearing Co. v. NLRB, 325 F 2d 746, 751, 54 LRRM 2785 (CA 6, 1963), *cert. denied,* 376 US 971, 55 LRRM 2878 (1964), where the Sixth Circuit, in dealing with the union's right to wage information, drew a distinction between waiver of a statutory right and waiver of a right obtained by contract; Smith Cabinet Manufacturing Co., Inc., 147 NLRB 1506, 56 LRRM 1418 (1964); *see also* NLRB v. Item Co., 220 F 2d 956, 35 LRRM 2709 (CA 5, 1955), *cert. denied,* 350 US 836, 36 LRRM 2716 (1955).
[404] New York Mirror, *supra* note 395.
[405] *Id.* at 840; *see also* Beacon Journal Publishing Co., 164 NLRB 734, 65 LRRM 1126 (1967); Unit Drop Forge Div., Eaton, Yale and Towne, 171 NLRB No. 73, 68 LRRM 1129 (1968).
[406] C & C Plywood Corp., 148 NLRB 414, 57 LRRM 1015 (1964), *enforcement denied,* 351 F 2d 224, 60 LRRM 2137 (CA 9, 1965), *reversed and remanded,* 385 US 421, 64 LRRM 2065 (1967

a. *"Management rights" clause.* When a "management rights" clause is the source of an asserted waiver, it is normally scrutinized by the Board to ascertain whether it affords specific justification for unilateral action. In *Ador Corp.*[407] a discontinuance of a line of products and the consequent layoff of employees without notice to the union was held to be justified by a management-rights clause which gave to the employer the right to take that precise action unilaterally. The Board reasoned that in agreeing to such a clause the "parties had, in effect, bargained about the manner in which such decisions were to be made during the term of the collective bargaining agreement, and had agreed that the 'Company' could take unilateral action in that regard." [408] Similarly, where a management-rights clause afforded the employer the sole right to determine employee qualifications, the Board held that the union had waived its right to bargain over the subject of physical examinations during the term of the collective agreement.[409] On the other hand, the Board refused to find a specific waiver of the right to bargain on a retirement plan despite a management-rights clause reserving exclusive control over the retirement of employees as a management prerogative.[410] Normally, a mere catchall phrase in a management-rights clause to the effect that the "Company retains the responsibility and authority of managing the Company's business," [411] or that "all management rights not given up in the contract are expressly reserved to it," [412] falls short of a "clear and unmistakable" relinquishment.

b. *Board's jurisdiction to construe collective agreements.* The Board and the courts may differ as to whether a particular contractual provision amounts to a waiver of the union's right to bargain.[413] Their interpretation may also differ from that of an arbitrator who may be called upon to determine the effect of, for

---

407 *Supra* note 396.
408 *Ibid. See also* Druwhit Metal Products Co., *supra* note 402; International Shoe Co., 151 NLRB 693, 58 LRRM 1483 (1965); *But see* General Motors Corp., 149 NLRB 396, 57 LRRM 1277 (1964), *remanded*, 60 LRRM 2283 (CA DC, 1966), *on remand*, 158 NLRB 229, 62 LRRM 1009 (1966), *reversed*, 381 F 2d 265, 64 LRRM 2489 (CA DC, 1967), *cert. denied*, 389 US 875, 65 LRRM 2307 (1967) (the District of Columbia Circuit Court took a more restrictive view of the waiver language than did the Board, and reversed the Board's dismissal of the complaint).
409 Leroy Machine Co., 147 NLRB 1431, 56 LRRM 1369 (1964).
410 Tide Water Associated Oil Co., 85 NLRB 1096, 24 LRRM 1518 (1949).
411 Leeds & Northrup v. NLRB, 391 F 2d 874, 67 LRRM 2793 (CA 3, 1968), *enforcing* 162 NLRB 987, 64 LRRM 1110 (1967).
412 *E.g.* Proctor Mfg. Corp., 131 NLRB 1166, 48 LLRM 1222 (1961).
413 *See* General Motors Corp., *supra* note 408. *See also* extensive discussion of NLRB position on waiver of statutory rights, Chapter 17 *infra*.

example, a management-rights clause. In the undertaking of these determinations, a question has arisen as to the extent to which the Board may enter into the area of interpreting collective bargaining agreements. In *NLRB* v. *C & C Plywood* [414] the Supreme Court held that the Board had jurisdiction to interpret collective bargaining agreements to the extent necessary to determine whether the union waived its right to bargain about a specific mandatory subject. The Court explained that the Board had not "construed a labor agreement to determine the extent of contractual rights which were given the union by the employer" but simply whether the union had waived its right to bargain.[415]

2. Waiver by Bargaining History. Where a subject has been discussed in contract negotiations but has not been specifically covered in the resulting contract, a waiver will be found only where the union "consciously yielded" its position.[416] This normally requires that the matter be "fully discussed" and "consciously explored." [417]

The payment of bonuses has been a source of controversy because the collective agreement is often silent on this topic. The effect of an unsuccessful attempt by the union to incorporate this benefit into the agreement directly or by way of a "maintenance of benefits" clause turns on close factual circumstances. Where the demand is withdrawn from negotiations without "full discussion," there is a likelihood that no waiver will result.[418] This is especially true where the employer gives assurances that it has no intention of discontinuing the bonus.[419] However, where the employer specifically explains the reasons for its rejection and the union remains silent, the absence of any contractual provision may

---

414 *Supra* note 406. *See* Chapter 17 *infra* for further discussion of this case.
415 *Id.* at 428. *See also* NLRB v. Huttig Sash & Door Co., 377 F 2d 964, 65 LRRM 2431 (CA 8, 1967); Gravenslund Operating Co., 168 NLRB No. 72, 66 LRRM 1323 (1967) (discussing the effect of the availability of grievance and arbitration machinery in the contract and the desirable procedural priorities).
416 New York Mirror, *supra* note 395; Proctor Mfg. Corp., *supra* note 412; The Press Co., Inc., 121 NLRB 976, 42 LRRM 1493 (1958). *See* Chapter 17 *infra.*
417 *Id.* at 978. Mere silence or inaction is not "conscious exploration," Clifton Precision Products Div., Litton Precision Products, Inc., 156 NLRB 555, 61 LRRM 1096 (1966); J. C. Penney Co., 161 NLRB 69, 63 LRRM 1309 (1966). *But cf.* Berkline Corp., 123 NLRB 685, 43 LRRM 1513 (1959).
418 Beacon Journal Publishing Co., *supra* note 405, where the union's unsuccessful attempt to obtain a Christmas bonus provision in the agreement was not found to be as persuasive by the Board majority as by the dissent.
419 General Telephone Co., 144 NLRB 311, 54 LRRM 1055; *enforced and modified,* 337 F 2d 452, 57 LRRM 2211 (CA 5, 1964).

be deemed to be conscious acquiescence by the union in the position taken by the employer in negotiations.[420]

A waiver does not usually turn on the presence or absence of a single factor. Even clear contract language is not always determinative. In *Kennecott Copper Corp.*,[421] for example, the employer unilaterally subcontracted work, relying upon a broad and inclusive management-rights clause held by the trial examiner to reserve to the employer "the right to take precisely the action it took." [422] Although it dismissed the complaint, the Board did so because of the "particular circumstances" of the case, including the fact that the employees in the appropriate unit suffered "no significant detriment" [423] and that the employer agreed to bargain when the union protested. The theory of lack of "significant detriment" to bargaining-unit employees, relied upon in *Kennecott,* was followed in a series of Board decisions upholding subcontracting without prior notification to the union.[424] However, in distinguishing the *Fibreboard* [425] doctrine (which required such notification regarding certain types of subcontracting), the Board has not relied solely upon the "significant detriment" principle.[426] Rather, the subcontracting has been viewed as consistent with established past practice so that there was no departure from the norm. Furthermore, the failure of the union to obtain a contractual restriction on subcontracting has also been viewed as persuasive.[427] While the Board seemed reluctant to decide in terms of a waiver doctrine,[428] the reasoning and result appear to have been the same.

---

[420] Speidel Corp., *supra* note 397, where the union dropped its demand for a "maintenance of privileges" clause and remained silent in the face of an employer explanation that a provision in the collective agreement would make the unilateral practice contractually binding, and, as such, it would be objectionable to him. *See* Tucker Steel Corp., 134 NLRB 323, 49 LRRM 1164 (1961), where the employer indicated the possibility of unilateral termination of bonuses if the union's vacation demands were met. The union's silence and the absence of a contractual provision created an estoppel.

[421] 148 NLRB 1653, 57 LRRM 1217 (1964).

[422] *Id.* at 1656.

[423] *Id.* at 1654.

[424] Westinghouse Electric Corp. (Mansfield Plant), 150 NLRB 1574, 58 LRRM 1257 (1965); American Oil Co., 151 NLRB 421, 58 LRRM 1412 (1965); Allied Chemical Corp., 151 NLRB 718, 58 LRRM 1480 (1965); Shell Oil Co., 149 NLRB 283, 57 LRRM 1271 (1964); Shell Chemical Co., 149 NLRB 298, 57 LRRM 1275 (1964).

[425] Fibreboard Paper Products Corp., 379 US 203, 57 LRRM 2609 (1964). *See* Chapter 15 *infra* at notes 121-172.

[426] *Supra* note 424.

[427] *E.g.,* American Oil Co., *supra* note 424.

[428] Westinghouse Electric Co., *supra* note 424.

Cases in which union acquiescence in the past practice of an employer constitutes a maintenance of the status quo (*e.g.*, an employer's continued unilateral subcontracting during the term of the agreement) may be distinguished, however, from those in which a change in the status quo is made without consulting the union.[429] In *Leeds & Northrup* [430] the employer had unilaterally instituted a supplementary compensation plan, renewing it annually. In defending its right to alter unilaterally the formula by which benefits were computed, the employer asserted an implied waiver, relying upon the Board's subcontracting decisions. This was rejected by the Board and the Third Circuit on the ground the status quo was represented by the formula which the employer had unilaterally altered, whereas in the subcontracting cases the employer simply continued the norm of subcontracting and thus did not alter the status quo.

3. Waiver by Inaction. In the absence of a *fait accompli*, the duty to bargain arises upon request, and where an opportunity exists to bargain but no request is made, a waiver may result.[431] If a union has been put on notice, for example, that the employer plans removal of its operations and makes no attempt to bring issues relating to plant removal to the bargaining table, it waives its rights in the matter.[432] It is not essential that the union be given formal notice of the intended unilateral change, if the union does, in fact, know of the plans and a formal announcement would be futile.[433]

The interrelationship of doctrines of waiver and futility are aptly illustrated in *U.S. Lingerie Corp.*[434] In that case an employer's demand for union cooperation because of its economic plight was rejected. Despite the clear warning to the union that plant removal would otherwise be necessitated, the union remained intransigent. The subsequent failure of the employer to

---

429 Leeds & Northrup Co. v. NLRB, *supra* note 411.
430 *Ibid.*
431 *Supra* notes 398, 400. A "union cannot charge an employer with refusal to negotiate when it has made no attempt to bring the employer to the bargaining table." NLRB v. Alva Allen Industries, Inc., 369 F 2d 310, 63 LRRM 2515 (CA 8, 1966), citing NLRB v. Columbian Enameling & Stamping Co., 306 US 292, 4 LRRM 524 (1939).
432 U.S. Lingerie Corp., *supra* note 395.
433 *Ibid; cf.* McLoughlin Mfg. Corp., 164 NLRB 140, 65 LRRM 1025 (1967); Southern California Stationers, 162 NLRB 476, 64 LRRM 1227 (1967); Dove Flocking & Screening Co., 145 NLRB 682, 55 LRRM 1013 (1963).
434 *Supra* note 395.

advise the union formally of its decision to remove and to bargain with it was therefore excused on the ground of futility, and the failure to request bargaining over the removal was held to be a waiver.

B. Section 8(f)—Construction Industry Proviso

The Labor-Management Reporting and Disclosure Act of 1959 [435] added Section 8(f) [436] to the National Labor Relations Act. Designed to meet some of the problems presented in the building and construction industry, the section acts as a savings clause, allowing union security agreements under circumstances which would otherwise constitute unfair labor practices. Thus, an employer primarily in the building and construction industry may enter a prehire agreement requiring union membership as a condition of employment, where not prohibited by state law, notwithstanding the undetermined majority status of the union.[437] Since under conventional theory an employer can be guilty of an unfair labor practice in extending recognition to a minority union,[438] with the result that any agreement executed is invalid even though bargained for under the erroneous but good-faith belief that it

---

[435] See Chapter 4 supra and Chapter 26 infra.

[436] §8 (f) provides in part:
"It shall not be an unfair labor practice under subsections (a) and (b) of this section for an employer engaged primarily in the building and construction industry to make an agreement covering employees engaged (or who, upon their employment, will be engaged) in the building and construction industry with a labor organization of which building and construction employees are members (not established, maintained, or assisted by an action defined in section 8(a) of this Act as an unfair labor practice) because (1) the majority status of such labor organization has not been established under the provisions of section 9 of this Act prior to the making of such agreement, or (2) such agreement requires as a condition of employment, membership in such labor organization after the seventh day following the beginning of such employment or the effective date of the agreement, whichever is later, or (3) such agreement requires the employer to notify such labor organization of opportunities for employment with such employer, or gives such labor organization an opportunity to refer qualified applicants for such employment, or (4) such agreement specifies minimum training or experience qualifications for employment or provides for priority in opportunities for such employment based upon length of service with such employer, in the industry or in the particular geographical area: Provided, That nothing in this subsection shall set aside the final proviso to section 8 (a) (3) of this Act: Provided further, That any agreement which would be invalid, but for clause (1) of this subsection, shall not be a bar to a petition filed pursuant to section 9 (c) or 9 (e).

[437] Administrative Ruling SR-813, 46 LRRM 1515 (1960). General Counsel refused to issue complaint where construction industry employer complained that minority union had coerced it into signing contract. Although poll of the employees showed that the majority did not wish to be represented by the union, the Act specifically allows union security agreements within the industry.

[438] ILGWU v. NLRB, 366 US 731, 48 LRRM 2251 (1961). See Chapter 7 supra.

was dealing with a majority union, a limited though significant departure from the traditional bargaining obligation exists.[439] An important qualification diminishes the potential impact of this section, however. Although Section 8(f) does not validate prehire agreements where the union has been established, maintained or assisted by any action of the employer otherwise violative of Section 8(a)(1), a valid prehire agreement is no bar to an election petition subsequently filed to determine the majority representative.[440]

C. Suspension During Illegal Activity

Although the duty to bargain and recognize a union is a continuing one, certain aspects of the employer's duty may be temporarily suspended while the union is engaged in unlawful activity. Accordingly, it was held that an employer was not obligated to continue negotiations during those periods in which the union endorsed illegal strike conduct, including violence and vandalism, and encouraged mass demonstrations at the homes of nonstriking employees.[441]

An employer has been held justified in suspending negotiations when the union called a slowdown [442] or engaged in a strike in violation of a contractual no-strike pledge.[443] However, the obligation to bargain is suspended only so long as the period of the breach or unlawful action continues.[444]

---

[439] It remains an open question, however, as to whether the parties bargaining under a §8(f) sanction must bargain in good faith. In *Bricklayers & Masons Int'l*, 162 NLRB 476, 64 LRRM 1085 (1966), the union contended that bargaining under §8(f) is free of the usual obligations of good-faith bargaining imposed by §8(a)(5) and §8(b)(3). The trial examiner found that bargaining under the construction industry proviso was not free of the obligations imposed by other sections of the Act, but the Board found it unnecessary to pass on that holding since the issues involved in the case grew out of renewal of an existing agreement and §8(f) was intended to apply only where parties are attempting to establish bargaining relationships for the first time.

[440] Bear Creek Construction Co., 135 NLRB 1285, 49 LRRM 1674 (1962). *See* Chapter 8 *supra* at notes 102-104.

[441] Kohler Co., 128 NLRB 1062, 46 LRRM 1389 (1960).

[442] Phelps Dodge Copper Prods. Corp., 101 NLRB 360, 31 LRRM 1072 (1952).

[443] *See* International Shoe Corp., 152 NLRB 699, 59 LRRM 1176 (1965); United Elastic Corp., 84 NLRB 768, 24 LRRM 1294 (1949).

[444] United Elastic Corp., *supra* note 443; Dorsey Trailers, Inc., 80 NLRB 478, 486, 23 LRRM 1112 (1948).

IX. BARGAINING DURING TERM OF EXISTING AGREEMENT [445]

Collective bargaining is not limited to negotiation of an agreement under which the parties will operate. In some instances bargaining can and must be carried on during the term of an existing agreement. In the words of the Supreme Court, "Collective bargaining is a continuing process" [446] involving among other things day-to-day adjustments in the contract and working rules, resolution of problems not covered by existing agreements, and protection of rights already secured by contract. The continuing nature of the duty to bargain, even when a contract exists, was recognized in the early cases of *NLRB* v. *Sands Mfg. Co.*[447] and *NLRB* v. *Highland Park Mfg. Co.*[448] Following the *Highland Park* concept that the bargaining agreement provides the "framework" within which the process of collective bargaining may be carried on, the Sixth Circuit in *Timken Roller Bearing Co.* v. *NLRB*[449] ruled that the employer could insist that grievances be processed in accordance with the contractual terms. Since grievance and arbitration machinery is the contractual method for continuing bargaining, disputes over interpretation of the contract must be resolved through such machinery.

In *NLRB* v. *Jacobs Mfg. Co.*[450] the Second Circuit elaborated on just what matters are open to negotiation during an existing agreement. The court held that the exception to the duty to bar-

---

[445] *See* discussion of waiver *supra* this chapter and in Chapter 17 *infra*.

[446] Conley v. Gibson, 355 US 41, 46, 41 LRRM 2089, (1957). *Accord:* NLRB v. Acme Industrial Co., 385 US 432, 64 LRRM 2069 (1967).

[447] 306 US 332, 4 LRRM 530 (1939) (". . . the Act imposes upon the employer the further obligation to meet and bargain with his employees' representatives respecting proposed changes of an existing contract and also to discuss with them its true interpretation. . . ." *Id.* at 342). The same idea was expressed in regard to bargaining under the Railway Labor Act in *Rutland Ry. Corp.* v. *Locomotive Engineers,* 307 F 2d 21, 50 LRRM 2535 (CA 2, 1962) (". . . clarification through collective bargaining of ambiguous contractual provisions is a most laudable purpose and should be encouraged rather than hampered by the courts." *Id.* at 45 (*dissenting opinion*)).

[448] 110 F 2d 632, 6 LRRM 786 (CA 4, 1940) (". . . the mere fact that the collective bargaining agreement provides a framework within which the process of collective bargaining may be carried on is of incalculable value in removing the causes of industrial strife." *Id.* at 638).

[449] 161 F 2d 949, 20 LRRM 2204 (CA 6, 1947). *Accord:* NLRB v. Knight Morley Corp., 251 F 2d 753, 41 LRRM 2242 (CA 6, 1957). *Cf.* Long Lake Lumber Co., 160 NLRB 1475, 63 LRRM 1160 (1960). *But see* discussion of *C&C Plywood,* notes 414-415 *supra.*

[450] 196 F 2d 680, 30 LRRM 2098 (CA 2, 1952); *see also* NLRB v. Lion Oil Co., 352 US 282, 39 LRRM 2296 (1957).

gain while an agreement is in effect, set up by Section 8(d) of the Act,[451] does not relieve an employer of the duty to bargain "as to subjects which were neither discussed nor embodied in any of the terms and conditions of the contract." [452] The court's reasoning was that since the Section 8(d) exception conflicts with the general purpose of the Act (to encourage peaceful resolution of industrial disputes through collective bargaining), the general purpose should be given effect to the extent that there is no contrary provision. However, the court expressly stated that it did not intend to pass on the effect on the duty to bargain, if any, of mere previous discussion without the inclusion of any terms or provisions on the matter in the contract. Some cases have indicated that such previous discussion forecloses later bargaining on the subject,[453] while others have been hesitant to rule that a union loses a right merely by talking it over with the employer.[454]

Closely related to the *Jacobs Mfg.* decision are two Supreme Court cases which also interpret the modification, notification, and termination provisions of Section 8(d).[455] According to the Court

---

[451] The exception provides that the duty to bargain collectively ". . . shall not be construed as requiring either party to discuss or agree to any modification of the terms and conditions contained in a contract for a fixed period, if such modification is to become effective before such terms and conditions can be reopened under the provisions of the contract."

[452] 196 F 2d at 684.

[453] Timken Roller Bearing Co. v. NLRB, 325 F 2d 746, 54 LRRM 2785 (CA 6, 1963) (if right or benefit for which union desires to bargain during term of existing agreement is one that could be acquired only by virtue of bargaining agreement, and proposal for such benefit was pressed and rejected during bargaining, failure to include right or benefit necessarily results in failure to acquire it); United States Steel Corp. v. Nicholas, 229 F 2d 396, 37 LRRM 2420 (CA 6, 1956) (if existing policy of employer is bargained over in negotiations, and contract is silent on subject because of no agreement, topic was not inadvertently overlooked but was intentionally omitted from contract for its term).

[454] *See* Section VIII *supra.*

[455] (See note 1 *supra*). ". . . *Provided,* That where there is in effect a collective-bargaining contract covering employees in an industry affecting commerce, the duty to bargain collectively shall also mean that no party to such contract shall terminate or modify such contract, unless the party desiring such termination or modification—

" (1) serves a written notice upon the other party to the contract of the proposed termination or modification sixty days prior to the expiration date thereof, or in the event such contract contains no expiration date, sixty days prior to the time it is proposed to make such termination or modification;
" (2) offers to meet and confer with the other party for the purpose of negotiating a new contract or a contract containing the proposed modifications;
" (3) notifies the Federal Mediation and Conciliation Service within thirty days after such notice of the existence of a dispute, and simultaneously therewith notifies any State or Territorial agency established to mediate and conciliate disputes within the State or Territory where the dispute occurred, provided no agreement has been reached by that time; and
" (4) continues in full force and effect, without resorting to strike or lockout,

in *Mastro Plastics Corp.* v. *NLRB*,[456] the Section 8(d) time limits apply only to economic strikes, not to strikes in protest of employer unfair labor practices. Since an unfair labor practice strike is *"not to terminate or modify* the contract, but [is] designed instead to protest"* [457] an employer's activities, the loss-of-status provisions,[458] as well as the Section 8(d)(4) prohibition, are inapplicable.[459] In *NLRB* v. *Lion Oil Co.*[460] the question was whether, under a contract providing for negotiation and modification at an intermediate date during its term, the union might strike in support of modification demands after the 60-day notice period had elapsed but prior to the terminal date of the contract. The Supreme Court, with reasoning similar to that in the *Jacobs Mfg.* case, found that Congress recognized a duty to bargain over modifications "when the contract itself contemplates such bargaining," and that it would be "anomalous" for Congress to recognize such a duty and at the same time deprive the union of the strike or strike threat.[461] The Court also held that Congress meant by "expiration date" to encompass both the final terminal date of the contract and any intermediate dates provided for reopening of terms of the contract.[462]

---

all the terms and conditions of the existing contract for a period of sixty days after such notice is given or until the expiration date of such contract, whichever occurs later:

"The duties imposed upon employers, employees, and labor organizations by paragraphs (2), (3), and (4) shall become inapplicable upon an intervening certification of the Board, under which the labor organization or individual, which is a party to the contract, has been superseded as or ceased to be the representative of the employees subject to the provisions of section 9(a), and the duties so imposed shall not be construed as requiring either party to discuss or agree to any modification of the terms and conditions contained in a contract for a fixed period, if such modification is to become effective before such terms and conditions can be reopened under the provisions of the contract. Any employee who engages in a strike within the sixty-day period specified in this subsection shall lose his status as an employee of the employer engaged in the particular labor dispute, for the purposes of sections 8, 9, and 10 of this Act, as amended, but such loss of status for such employee shall terminate if and when he is reemployed by such employer."
[456] 350 US 270, 37 LRRM 2587 (1956). *See also* discussion in Chapter 17 *infra.*
[457] *Id.* at 286.
[458] 29 USC §158(d): "Any employee who engages in a strike within the sixty-day period specified in this subsection shall lose his status as an employee of the employer engaged in the particular labor dispute, for the purposes of section 8, 9, and 10 of this Act. . . ."
[459] *See* comment of Senator Ball, 93 CONG. REC. 5014 (1947), that the provisions of §8(d) are "aimed primarily at protecting the public, as well as the employees, who have been the victims of 'quickie' strikes. I do not think that is taking away any rights of labor. . . ."
[460] 352 US 282, 39 LRRM 2296 (1957).
[461] *Id.* at 290-291.
[462] Local No. 3, United Packinghouse Workers v. NLRB, 210 F 2d 325, 33 LRRM 2530 (CA 8, 1954), had held otherwise.

Local Union No. 9735, UMW v. *NLRB* [463] and *Cheney California Lumber Co.* v. *NLRB* [464] expand the *Lion Oil* rule along the line of the *Jacobs* rule, *i.e.,* the Section 8(d) time limits and notice provisions do not apply to strikes whose purpose is not to modify the terms of the agreement but to obtain an objective which the agreement has not settled or has expressly left open. *Brotherhood of Locomotive Firemen* v. *NLRB,*[465] holding that notice need not be given to a state agency under Section 8(d)(3) if such agency has no funds for conciliation or mediation, followed the *Lion Oil* and *Mastro Plastics* "dual purpose" rule. This rule, that the Taft-Hartley Act was intended both to substitute collective bargaining for economic warfare and to protect the right of concerted activity of employees, required that Section 8(d)(3) not be given a construction which served neither of these aims. Since a completely powerless state agency could not promote collective bargaining, the right of employees to engage in concerted activities freed the union from the notice requirements of Section 8(d)(3).

X. DUTY OF FAIR REPRESENTATION [466]

When a union is designated as the exclusive bargaining agent of an appropriate unit, it undertakes contract negotiations which are generally unregulated in the sense of following statutory directives. "Inevitably differences arise in the manner and degree to which the terms of . . . [the] . . . agreement affect individual employees. . . ." [467] But "[t]he . . . existence of such differences does not make them invalid. The complete satisfaction of all who are represented is hardly to be expected. A wide range of reasonableness must be allowed a statutory bargaining representative . . ., subject always to complete good faith and honesty of purpose in the exercise of its discretion." [468]

Because the majority's choice is imposed on all members of the unit, the Supreme Court has held that both the Railway Labor Act and the National Labor Relations Act require the union to

---

463 258 F 2d 146, 42 LRRM 2320 (CA DC, 1958).
464 319 F 2d 375, 53 LRRM 2598 (CA 9, 1963).
465 302 F 2d 198, 50 LRRM 2015 (CA 9, 1962). *But cf.* Milk, Ice Cream Drivers & Dairy Employees, Local 783, 147 NLRB 264, 56 LRRM 1194 (1964).
466 *See* Chapter 27 *infra* for detailed treatment.
467 Ford Motor Co. v. Huffman, 345 US 330, 338, 31 LRRM 2548 (1953).
468 *Id.* at 338.

represent everyone in the unit fairly.[469] A breach of this statutory duty of fair representation "occurs only when a union's conduct toward a member of the collective bargaining unit is arbitrary, discriminatory or in bad faith." [470]

Whether the failure to represent employees fairly may itself be the subject of an unfair labor practice charge was a much-debated issue.[471] Not until the *Miranda* [472] case in 1962 did the Board majority decide that a breach of the union's duty of fair representation is an unfair labor practice. Although it denied enforcement of the Board's order,[473] the Second Circuit split three ways with only one judge rejecting the Board's approach. In *Miranda*, Section 8(b)(3) was not used as a basis for decision, but in *Hughes Tool Co.*[474] the Board found that a white local's failure to process a Negro employee's grievance constituted a violation of Section 8(b)(3), as well as Section 8(b)(1) and 8(b) (2), since the processing of grievances is an extension of the bargaining function. Likewise, in *Local 12, United Rubber Workers*,[475] the union was held to have violated its duty of fair representation and was convicted of violating Sections 8(b)(1)(A), 8(b)(2), and 8(b)(3) for refusing, for racial reasons, to process the grievance of a Negro member of the bargaining unit.

The clearest statement of good-faith bargaining including the "fair representation" concept is found in *Local 1367, International Longshoremen's Ass'n:* [476]

---

[469] Steele v. Louisville & Nashville R.R., 323 US 192, 15 LRRM 708 (1944) (Railway Labor Act) ; Syres v. Oil Workers, 350 US 892, 37 LRRM 2068 (1955) (National Labor Relations Act).

[470] Vaca v. Sipes, 386 US 171, 64 LRRM 2369 (1967), *citing* Humphrey v. Moore, 375 US 335, 55 LRRM 2031 (1964).

[471] *See, e.g.* Cox, *The Duty of Fair Representation,* 2 VILL. L. REV. 151 (1967); Sovern, *The National Labor Relations Act and Racial Discrimination,* 62 COLUM. L. REV. 563 (1962); Sherman, *Union's Duty of Fair Representation and the Civil Rights Act of 1964,* 49 MINN. L. REV. 771 (1965).

[472] Miranda Fuel Co. Inc., 140 NLRB 181, 51 LRRM 1584 (1962).

[473] NLRB v. Miranda Fuel Co., 326 F 2d 172, 54 LRRM 2715 (CA 2, 1963).

[474] Independent Metal Workers Union (Hughes Tool Co.), 147 NLRB 1573, 56 LRRM 1289 (1964).

[475] Local 12, United Rubber Workers (Business League of Gadsden), 150 NLRB 312, 57 LRRM 1535 (1964), *enforced,* 368 F 2d 12, 63 LRRM 2395 (CA 5, 1966) *cert. denied,* 389 US 837, 66 LRRM 2306 (1967).

[476] Local 1367, Int'l Longshoremen's Ass'n (Galveston Maritime Ass'n), 148 NLRB 897, 57 LRRM 1083 (1964), *enforced,* 368 F 2d 1010, 63 LRRM 2559 (CA 5, 1966) (local discriminated by a 75-25 percent work distribution between Locals 1367 (white local) and 1368 (Negro local), respectively, based upon race and union membership in successive collective-bargaining agreements with the several employer associations and by "maintaining and enforcing a 'no doubling' arrangement forbidding the assignment of white and Negro gangs to work together in ship hatches . . ."). 148 NLRB at 897.

Because collective-bargaining agreements which discriminate invidiously are not lawful under the Act, the good-faith requirements of Section 8 (d) necessarily protect employees from infringement of their rights; and both unions and employers are enjoined by the Act from entering into contractual terms which offend such rights. . . . Section 8(d) cannot mean that a union can be exercising good faith toward an employer while simultaneously acting in bad faith toward employees in regard to the same matters. . . . We conclude that when a statutory representative negotiates a contract in breach of the duty which it owes to employees to represent all of them fairly and without invidious discrimination, the representative cannot be said to have negotiated the sort of agreement envisioned by Section 8(d) nor to have bargained in good faith as to the employees whom it represents or toward the employer. In summary we find that the Respondents violated Section 8 (b) (3).[477]

Whether a union's violation of its duty of fair representation is a violation of Section 8(b)(3) is unclear because of the lack of a definitive Supreme Court pronouncement.[478] In *Humphrey* v. *Moore* [479] the Court deliberately avoided the question by holding that a union member's action challenging the decision of a joint employer-union committee to dovetail seniority lists (where one company absorbed the business of another) was maintainable as a Section 301 suit for breach of contract rather than one for unfair representation. The Court said:

Although there are differing views on whether a violation of the duty of fair representation is an unfair labor practice under the Labor Management Relations Act, it is not necessary for us to resolve that difference here. Even if it is, or arguably may be, an unfair labor practice, the complaint here alleged that Moore's discharge would violate the contract and was therefore within the cognizance of federal and state courts.[480]

Although the Fifth Circuit Court of Appeals enforced the Board's decisions in both the *Rubber Workers* [481] and *Galveston*

---

477 148 NLRB at 899-900.
478 There is also a lack of any circuit court discussion.
479 375 US 335, 55 LRRM 2031 (1964).
480 *Id.* at 344. *But cf.* Justice Goldberg's concurring opinion: "It is my view rather that Moore's claim must be treated as an individual employee's action for a union's breach of its duty of fair representation . . ." *Id.* at 351. *See* Republic Steel Corp. v. Maddox, 379 US 650, 652, 58 LRRM 2193 (1965), in which the Court held that an employee could not sue an employer directly for an alleged breach of contract without first processing his claim through the contractual grievance procedure. But the Court said that if "the union refuses to press or only perfunctorily presses the individual's claim, differences may arise as to the forms of redress then available." (Citation omitted.)
481 Local 12, Rubber Workers v. NLRB, 368 F 2d 12, 63 LRRM 2395 (CA 5, 1966).

Maritime Workers [482] cases, in each instance the court found as the threshold question that the union had committed a Section 8(b)(1)(A) violation. It was therefore unnecessary for the court to consider whether such conduct was violative of either Section 8(b)(2) or 8(b)(3). [483]

In *Vaca v. Sipes* [484] the Supreme Court upheld the jurisdiction of the state courts to entertain fair-representation suits. The Court acknowledged an individual's right to bring suit in a state court after the union to which he belonged refused to continue processing his grievance to obtain his reinstatement following his alleged wrongful discharge. The union's position was that the state court lacked jurisdiction because the gravamen of the suit was an unfair labor practice within the exclusive jurisdiction of the Board.

The Court rejected this argument, reasoning that one primary justification for the doctrine that the Board has exclusive jurisdiction in unfair labor practice cases is the avoidance of conflicting rules of substantive law and the desirability of leaving the development of such rules to the Board. But the Court concluded that these reasons do not apply to cases involving breaches of the union's duty to provide fair representation for its members. [485]

XI. UNION LOSS OF MAJORITY

The Act requires the employer to recognize and bargain with the representative of the majority of his employees in an appropriate bargaining unit; thus, if a union loses its majority status, under the *literal* language of the statute the employer would not be required to extend recognition or to bargain. An obvious defense to the duty to bargain would therefore be the loss of majority by the incumbent union. However, there are several exceptions to the literal requirement of majority status. These have been

---

[482] NLRB v. Local 1367, ILA, 368 F 2d 1010, 63 LRRM 2559 (CA 5, 1966).

[483] In the *Galveston Maritime Workers* case, Judge Choate's concurring opinion expressly disapproved the "method" of relying on Board action rather than individual suits for the reason that "it puts the court in the position of approving the Board's action in telling a labor union . . . how to perform its functions." *Id.* at 1010.

[484] 386 US 171, 64 LRRM 2369 (1967). *See* Chapter 29 *infra* for general treatment of the doctrine of federal preemption.

[485] In subsequent unfair representation cases the Board has tended to rely on §8(b)(1)(A) alone without reference to the union's duty to bargain under §8(b)(3). *E.g.*, Port Drum Co., 170 NLRB No. 51, 67 LRRM 1506 (1968), *and* Local 485, IUE (Automotive Plating Corp.), 170 NLRB No. 121, 67 LRRM 1609 (1968).

developed by both statutory provision and case law for the purpose of stabilizing industrial relations.[486] For example, a certified union must be recognized for a full year following certification, absent unusual circumstances, even when it has lost its majority.[487] The mandatory bargaining period has also been extended following an order to bargain.[488] Another exception is the presumption of majority status which prevails during the term of a collective bargaining contract. Presumption is applicable in contract bar cases in Section 9 (representation) proceedings.

The latter presumptions may also apply to the duty to bargain. This presumption of majority status applies "to situations where the refusal to bargain is with a Board certified union or with an incumbent union which has theretofore achieved a bargaining status evidenced by a collective bargaining agreement, or, at least, by prior recognition." [489] That presumption, however, is rebuttable.[490] In *United States Gypsum Co.*,[491] the Board found the following factors insufficient to rebut the presumption of majority status: "reliance on nonpayment of dues, the union's failure to hold meetings of the employees until after the certification year had expired, or a growing dissatisfaction with the union." [492] The Board has also applied the majority status presumption, based on expiration of a collective bargaining contract, to the refusal of a *successor employer* to bargain with an incumbent union. It also held in the same case that illegal recognition of the union by the predecessor employer was no defense, for the recognition had occurred four years earlier and therefore was barred by limitations under Section 10(b).[493]

---

486 *See* discussion of one year rules and contract duration in Chapter 8 *supra*.
487 Brooks v. NLRB, 348 US 96, 35 LRRM 2158 (1954).
488 Mar-Jac Poultry Co., 136 NLRB 785, 49 LRRM 1854 (1962).
489 Ramada Inns, Inc., 171 NLRB No. 115, 68 LRRM 1209, 1211 (1968).
490 *Ibid. See also:* Celanese Corp. of America, 95 NLRB 664, 28 LRRM 1362 (1951); Ref-Chem Co. v. NLRB, 418 F 2d 127, 72 LRRM 2733 (CA 5, 1969); NLRB v. Gallaro Bros., 419 F 2d 97, 73 LRRM 2043 (CA 2, 1969).
491 143 NLRB 1122, 53 LRRM 1454 (1963).
492 *Id.* at 1126. *Contra:* NLRB v. Gallaro, note 490 *supra*. The presumption of majority status during the term of a collective bargaining contract is not rebuttable, but is subject to the rules governing the contract-bar doctrine. *See* Chapter 8 *supra*.
493 Tragniew, Inc., 185 NLRB No. 132, 75 LRRM 1226 (1970).

CHAPTER 12

EFFECT OF CHANGE IN BARGAINING REPRESENTATIVE

I. CONTEXT IN WHICH PROBLEM ARISES

This chapter treats the effect of a change of representation of employees in a bargaining unit. If such change occurs when there is not a bargaining agreement in effect, or when the bargaining agreement is "open," the ordinary rules applicable to representation procedures, treated in Chapter 8 *supra,* will prevail.[1] The law discussed in this chapter relates primarily to the effect of a change in union representation upon an existing collective bargaining agreement. The focus of the discussion here is upon the question of whether such agreement binds the superseding union and the employer.

The existence of a collective agreement often constitutes a bar to an election and to the recognition of a new collective bargaining representative. However, there are situations where the contract does not constitute such a bar, and a change in bargaining representatives may occur during the term of an existing agreement. It is in the context of this type of problem that a question concerning the effect of such a change on an existing contract often arises. More particularly, the question arises in cases (1) where the existing contract is not a bar to an election by reason of its duration,[2] (2) where there has been a schism in the bargaining

---

[1] Chapter 8 treats the contract-bar cases in detail; *see e.g.,* Avco Manufacturing Corp., 106 NLRB 1104, 32 LRRM 1618 (1953); General Cable Corp., 139 NLRB 1123, 51 LRRM 1444 (1962). For consideration of the recognitional problems which are encountered when two or more unions are claiming representation in the same bargaining unit, see Chapter 7 *supra* and the discussion therein of the *Midwest Piping* doctrine.

[2] *E.g.,* American Seating Co., 106 NLRB 250, 32 LRRM 1439 (1953). *See* Chapter 8 *supra* at notes 79-86.

representative,[3] (3) where the contracting union has become defunct,[4] or (4) where another union, as a result of evolution or reorganization, inherits the powers, assets, and membership of the contracting union.[5] If a new bargaining representative displaces the prior representative, the Board may be required to determine whether the employer may refuse to bargain with the new union for a new contract to replace the unexpired contract with the prior union.

II. RIGHTS AND OBLIGATIONS OF NEW BARGAINING REPRESENTATIVE AND EMPLOYER UNDER CONTRACT WITH PRIOR REPRESENTATIVE

A. Representation Proceedings

In representation cases, the Board does not pass upon the effect of the certification of a new bargaining representative on an unexpired collective bargaining contract between a prior bargaining representative and the employer, although at one time it would pass on this question in a representation proceeding. In a few early cases [6] where a rival union was seeking an election during the term of a collective bargaining contract, the Board indicated that certification of the new union would have only a limited effect. In one case, the Board stated that "it is not our intention to invalidate the contract or to disturb it in any respect. . . . The election which we shall hereinafter direct is for the purpose of determining the identity of the representative which shall administer the contract." [7] The rationale for such a rule, as later articulated by Board member Reynolds in a dissenting opinion, was that "neither the employer nor the employee should be enabled by virtue of a

---

3 *E.g.,* Purity Baking Co., 124 NLRB 159, 44 LRRM 1314 (1959); Boston Machine Works Co., 89 NLRB 59, 25 LRRM 1508 (1950). *See* Chapter 8 *supra* at notes 123-124.
4 *E.g.,* Hershey Chocolate Corp., 121 NLRB 901, 42 LRRM 1460 (1958). *Cf.* Rocky Mountain Phosphates, Inc., 138 NLRB 292, 51 LRRM 1019 (1962) (defunct union superseded by union which secured recognition with authorization cards from a majority of employees). *See* Chapter 8 *supra* at notes 125-127.
5 *See* Montgomery Ward & Co., Inc., 137 NLRB 346, 50 LRRM 1137 (1962); Gate City Optical Co., 175 NLRB No. 172, 71 LRRM 1118 (1969). *See also* Note, *Change of Status of a Party to a Collective Bargaining Agreement,* 60 YALE L. J. 1026 (1951).
6 New England Transportation Company, 1 NLRB 130, 1 LRRM 97 (1936); Swayne and Hoyt, Ltd., 2 NLRB 282, 1 LRRM 99 (1936); *see* The Register and Tribune Co., 60 NLRB 360, 15 LRRM 233 (1945).
7 The Register and Tribune Company, *supra* note 6, at 362.

proceeding before this Board to discard unilaterally any obligations incurred as a result of their collective bargaining agreement." [8] Generally, however, the Board refrained from ruling in representation cases upon the effect of the certification on the existing agreement.

In *Boston Machine Works* [9] the Board expressly decided that it would not make any determination in a representation case of the effect of the certification of a new representative upon an existing bargaining agreement, and it overruled its earlier contrary decisions. It ordered an election in this case because of a schism in the ranks of the incumbent bargaining representative. The opinion noted, and apparently relied upon, the fact that Congress had failed to include in the Act a provision restricting the functions of a new representative. The Board stated that "we do not believe that this Board should qualify its certification of the employees' bargaining representative by imposing restrictions not to be found in any provision of the Act and, indeed, deliberately omitted therefrom." [10]

B. Section 8(a)(5) Proceedings: *American Seating*

The Board has squarely faced the question of the effect of certification upon the existing contract in several unfair labor practice cases.

The earliest of these was *Pacific Greyhound Lines.* [11] The Board had ordered an election despite the existence of an unexpired contract because the contract had been made with a union which, due to illegal employer action, was not deemed to be a freely chosen representative. [12] Following certification of the new representative, the employer refused to bargain with the new union. In the ensuing unfair labor practice case, the employer contended that its contract with the illegally assisted union "cannot be abro-

---

[8] Boston Machine Works Co., 89 NLRB 59, 64, 25 LRRM 1508, 1510 (1950) (dissenting opinion).

[9] Note 8 *supra.*

[10] *Id.* at 62. *Accord,* Hershey Chocolate Corp., 121 NLRB 901, 42 LRRM 1460 (1958).

[11] 22 NLRB 111, 6 LRRM 189 (1940). *See* Freidin, *The Board, the "Bar," and the Bargain,* 59 COLUM. L. REV. 61, 82-92 (1959); Note, *Effect of Pre-Existing Contract on New Bargaining Agent,* 54 COLUM. L. REV. 132 (1954).

[12] Chapter 7 *supra* discusses this subject of employer assistance and domination of labor organizations under §8(a)(2) of the Act.

gated by employees for whose benefit it was made nor by another representative selected by a majority of the employees of the unit . . . ," a position which the Board rejected. It held that the newly selected representative could, at its option, abrogate the terms of the prior contract.

Board member Edwin S. Smith, in a concurring opinion, expressed a different view as to the effect of a certification upon the existing agreement. He would have allowed abrogation of only those provisions of the contract which provided for recognition of the contracting union, a closed shop, and administration of the contract. He believed that provisions covering wages, hours of service, and other working conditions of the covered employees should continue in force.

The Board's leading decision on this question was rendered in *American Seating Company*.[13] The pertinent facts were as follows: Two years after the execution of a three-year contract between the employer and the United Auto Workers, the Pattern Makers Union petitioned for an election in a craft unit covered by the UAW contract. The NLRB ruled in the representation proceeding that the UAW contract constituted no bar to an election since three-year contracts were not customary in the industry.[14] Thereafter the Pattern Makers Union was certified as the representative of the unit. The employer insisted that the UAW contract remained in effect as to all employees in the plant, although it agreed to bargain with the Pattern Makers Union in certain limited areas. In the subsequent unfair labor practice proceeding, the employer maintained that the Pattern Makers, as bargaining representative of the craft employees, must administer the substantive terms of the existing contract. It contended that the employees, as principals, were bound by the contract executed on their behalf by their agent, and that a mere change in agents could not abrogate the contract. The Pattern Makers took the position that the certification rendered the contract inoperative as to the employees in the unit which it now represented. It urged that the unique functions of a statutory collective

---

[13] 106 NLRB 250, 32 LRRM 1439 (1953).
[14] This case arose before the Board's ruling that three-year contracts could be a bar for the entire term regardless of custom in the industry. General Cable Corp., 139 NLRB 1123, 51 LRRM 1444 (1962). *See* Chapter 8 *supra*.

bargaining representative precluded a blind application of common-law agency principles to the problem.

The Board ruled that unless the collective bargaining representative was to be "emasculated" in the exercise of its functions, it had to be permitted to negotiate the terms and conditions of employment. It refused to "hobble" the newly certified collective bargaining representative with its predecessor's contract. The Board noted: "[T]he rule urged by the [employer] seems hardly calculated to reduce 'industrial strife' by encouraging the 'practice and procedure of collective bargaining,' the declared purpose of the National Labor Relations Act as amended. . . ." [15]

The Board thus adopted the general proposition that if an existing contract constitutes no bar to an election, then it also is no bar to full bargaining by the new representative. In the course of its opinion the Board said that "a great part of the benefit to be derived from the no-bar rule" [16] would be dissipated unless the new bargaining representative had such power.

Following the decision in *American Seating,* the Court of Appeals for the Sixth Circuit cast some doubt upon the validity of the Board's doctrine in that case. In *Modine Manufacturing Co. v. Int'l Association of Machinists,*[17] the court appeared to be of the view that while the union-shop and the check-off provisions became inoperative as soon as a new bargaining representative entered the scene, the other provisions of the contract remained in effect to be administered by the newly certified union. *Modine,* however, involved a Section 301 suit by a decertified union against an employer for breach of contract, and the court's statements concerning the matter of administration of the contract by the newly certified union are dicta. The only holding required was that the superseded union did not have rights under the unexpired contract. The Board subsequently reaffirmed its *American Seating* decision, holding in *Ludlow Typograph Co.*[18] that an employer

---

15 106 NLRB at 255.
16 *Ibid.*
17 216 F 2d 326, 35 LRRM 2003 (CA 6, 1954). The court did not refer to *American Seating.* It did state that it was not ruling on "[w]hether or not the substantive provisions as to wages, hours, etc., were still binding after the certification . . ." of the successor union 216 F2d at 329.
18 113 NLRB 724, 36 LRRM 1364 (1955). The Board expressly rejected any contrary inference that might have been derived from the *Modine* case.

was *required,* not simply *permitted,* to bargain with a new bargaining representative over rates of pay, hours, and other matters covered in the unexpired contract with the superseded union.

C.   *American Seating* Limited

Although the *American Seating* doctrine is founded firmly upon a policy of protecting the statutory rights of a new collective bargaining representative, a rigid application of it would subordinate another important policy also required by the Act. As the Board recognized in *American Seating,* industrial peace requires contractual stability. Such stability ought not to be disturbed by mere formal changes in the bargaining representative. Employees may not abrogate the terms of a contract by merely making a formal change in the structure of their union any more than an employer may do so by mere formal alteration of the structure of its business.[19]

The problem turns upon a determination of the circumstances that will move the Board to view a change in the representative as the kind of change that allows the new representative to bargain for a new contract.

Many changes in the internal structure of the union, or changes caused by transfer of responsibility from one union to another, as by merger, consolidation, or transfer of affiliation, are not the type of changes which should affect the substantive terms of the contract. The rule of *American Seating* is therefore restricted to cases in which the noncontracting union constitutes a new and different representative rather than a mere continuation or successor of the contracting party.

In cases involving mere successorship, as distinguished from a true change in representative, the Board imposes upon the successor all of the obligations of the predecessor. Thus, where by process of evolution or reorganization one union inherits the powers, assets, and membership of the contracting party, the successor union will not be permitted to escape the obligations of the existing contract. By the same token, an employer is obligated to bargain with a "successor" union.

For example, the survivor of several merged or consolidated unions assumes all the obligations of its predecessors. In *Mont-*

---

[19] The Board has adhered to the same doctrine in the case of employer changes. *See* Chapter 13 *infra.*

gomery Ward,[20] Retail Clerks Local 1594, the certified representative of the employees, executed a five-year contract with the employer. Prior to expiration of this contract, Local 1594 merged with three other Clerks locals. No significant change in membership occurred, and the international officers who had administered all the locals prior to the merger continued to administer the survivor, Local 1099. For nine months following the merger the employer checked off dues for Local 1099, and, as the Board noted, there was an "apparent understanding of both the employer and the union that the consolidated group intended to function as a continuation of the constituent unions. . . ."[21] Accordingly, the Board ruled that Local 1099 was the "successor" of Local 1594 and as such inherited the latter's contract and the benefits of its certification. While this was a representation case, there is no reason to believe that the Board would reach a different result in an unfair labor practice case.

Similarly, mere changes in the name of the union will not affect the rights and duties of the parties to the collective bargaining relationship.[22]

The *Hershey Chocolate* case[23] raises a question as to the applicability of *American Seating* in schism situations. Although the Board in *Hershey* held that, because of a schism in the incumbent union the existing contract constituted no bar to an election, it expressly refrained from considering "the effect on the existing

---

[20] Montgomery Ward & Company, Inc., 137 NLRB 346, 50 LRRM 1137 (1962). By similar reasoning, an employer was obligated to bargain with a consolidated union which resulted from the merger of a certified union with another union. The latter union succeeded to the certified union's representative status. Union Carbide & Carbon Co. v. NLRB, 224 F 2d 672, 40 LRRM 2084 (CA 6, 1957), *enforcing* 116 NLRB 488, 38 LRRM 1284 (1956).

[21] *Id.* at 350.

[22] *See* Marshal Maintenance Corp., 154 NLRB 611, 59 LRRM 1784 (1965). In Radio Corp. of America, 135 NLRB 980, 49 LRRM 1606 (1962), the Board distinguished *American Seating*, holding that a national agreement between a parent union and the employer was binding upon a local union affiliate in a newly certified local bargaining unit.

[23] Hershey Chocolate Corp., 121 NLRB 901, 42 LRRM 1460 (1958). The schism resulted from the local union voting to disaffiliate from its parent union. The Board's schism doctrine was used principally during two periods in American labor history: when the CIO expelled certain unions for alleged Communist influence and replaced them with rival unions; and when the AFL-CIO met the problem of alleged corruption and misuse of union funds (the situation involved in the *Hershey* case) by similar action. R. Smith, L. Merrifield, & T. St. Antoine, LABOR RELATIONS LAW, CASES AND MATERIALS, 265 (4th ed. 1968).

contract of the certification of a new bargaining representative." [24] The Board noted that it had considered "whether an election directed on the basis of a schism should be held for the limited purpose of determining which of the organizations directly involved in the schismatic situation should be entitled to administer the existing contract." [25] It then held that "it would be inappropriate to require [in a representation case] the winning union, if any, to assume the existing contract." [26]

The failure of the Board to refer to *American Seating* raises a question as to whether it will treat the *American Seating* rule as coterminous with its no-bar rule. Perhaps the explanation for the Board's failure to refer to *American Seating* in the *Hershey* case is that *Hershey* was a representation case and not an unfair labor practice case.[27] Whatever may be the basis for withholding application of the *American Seating* doctrine to schism cases, the reasoning and language employed by the Board in *American Seating* suggest that the Board may have intended its ruling to be coterminous with its no-bar rules.

In a later unfair labor practice proceeding involving the same parties, the Court of Appeals for the Third Circuit refused to enforce an NLRB decision that held that the new local had violated the Act by attempting to enforce a maintenance-of-membership clause in the contract it took over from the old local. The court said that even applying the schism requirements set forth in the *Hershey* case, there was no schism at Hershey, the new local being the same entity as the old local with no basic intra-union conflict.[28]

D. Right of Superseded Contracting Union

The Board and the courts have made amply clear that no union other than the duly recognized or certified collective bargaining

---

24 *Id*. at 909-10.
25 *Id*. at 910.
26 *Ibid*.
27 *Cf*. Purity Baking Co., 124 NLRB 159, 44 LRRM 1314 (1959), and Great A&P Tea Co., 123 NLRB 1005, 44 LRRM 1045 (1959). These cases, which involved schisms, show that while the Board in a representation case will not compel the employer and new union to enter into a new contract or for that matter to adopt the old contract, neither will it, in the interest of industrial stability, do anything to discourage unions from assuming the contracts of their predecessors.
28 NLRB v. Hershey Chocolate Corp., 297 F 2d 286, 49 LRRM 2173 (CA 3, 1961). *But cf*. National Biscuit Div. v. Leedom, 265 F 2d 101, 43 LRRM 2464 (1959), *cert. denied*, 359 US 1011, 44 LRRM 2194 (1959).

representative retains any rights under a collective bargaining contract.[29] Even a union that is signatory to a contract retains no rights under that contract once it is decertified or otherwise loses its status as collective bargaining representative.[30] This feature of the collective bargaining contract underscores the *sui generis* nature of the collective agreement.[31]

---

[29] NLRB v. Jones and Laughlin Steel Corp., 301 US 1, 44-45, 1 LRRM 703 (1937); National Licorice Co. v. NLRB, 309 US 350, 364-65, 6 LRRM 674 (1940). *Compare* obligations under union contract evolving upon a successor employer, discussed in Chapter 13 *infra*.

[30] Modine Manufacturing Co. v. Association of Machinists, 216 F2d 326, 35 LRRM 2003 (CA 6, 1954) (Section 301 suit by decertified union to enforce collective bargaining agreement). See note 17 *supra*. *But see* discussion of the survival of a union's right to enforce contract provisions upon a successor employer, *e.g., John Wiley & Sons v. Livingston,* 376 US 543, 55 LRRM 2769 (1964), *and Wm. J. Burns Int'l Detective Agency, Inc.,* 182 NLRB No. 50, 74 LRRM 1098 (1970), Chapter 13 *infra*.

[31] See Chapter 17 for a discussion of the nature of the collective agreement and the relation of NLRB action to court action enforcing such agreements.

Chapter 13

EFFECT OF CHANGE IN EMPLOYING UNIT

I. SCOPE OF THE TOPIC

A. Typical Changes

The Board has often been required to assess the impact of various kinds of changes in the employing unit on the rights of parties under the Act.[1] Changes in corporate structure and other business rearrangements are common.

Where there is a sale of a business operation, the new employer may or may not use the same plant. He may use the same or a different work force operating under the same or different working conditions. He may or may not continue to use the same supervisors and the same equipment. He may make the same or a different product. Many variations in the nature of the sale are possible.

Other kinds of changes may involve a merger or consolidation of business operations. Such changes may result in a considerable expansion of the work force of the resulting enterprise. Another type of change involves a transfer of assets or plant removal. Or there may be a change in the nature of the operation at the same location.

The present chapter explores the effect of such changes on the rights of parties under the NLRA.

---

[1] For a comprehensive discussion of the subject matter of this chapter, see Fanning, *The Purchaser and the Labor Contract—An Escalating Theory*, LABOR RELATIONS YEARBOOK—1967, 284 (Washington: BNA Books, 1968). *See also* Goldberg, *The Labor Law Obligations of a Successor Employer*, Nw. U. L. Rev. 735 (1969); Gordon, *Legal Questions of Successorship*, 3 GA. L. REV. 280 (1969); Feller, *The Successor and the Collective Agreement*, LABOR LAW DEVELOPMENTS—1967 (Proceedings of 13th Ann. Inst. on Labor Law, Sw. Legal Foundation) 1.

B. Types of Issues Presented

Following a change in ownership of a business or other change in the business enterprise, various issues may arise. Some of these issues come before the Board in unfair labor practice proceedings, others in representation proceedings. Further issues come before the courts under Section 301.[2]

When a change is made in the employing unit, the bargaining representative for the employees of the predecessor employer may contend that the business has remained essentially unchanged and that the successor employer commits an unfair labor practice by refusing to bargain with the exclusive bargaining representative. The Board thus is required to determine the impact of the change on the bargaining obligations of the parties in an unfair labor practice proceeding. This kind of issue has come before the Board frequently.

Filing a representation petition is another method by which the representative status of the union may be tested after a change in the employing unit. If there is an unexpired collective bargaining agreement in effect, the Board may be required to decide whether the contract is a bar to the processing of the representation petition. If the Board finds that the contract-bar rule applies and that the bargaining agent that is a party to the contract retains its representative status, it logically follows in most cases that the employer must bargain with that union. Thus, as a practical matter, it is possible for the issue with respect to bargaining obligations to be resolved in a representation proceeding. Similar results may be obtained when there has been an expansion or contraction of the bargaining unit as a result of a change in operations and a petition is filed with the Board for clarification of the unit.[3]

After a change by sale, merger, or consolidation, the bargaining agent of the employees of the predecessor employer may seek, through a Section 301 action in federal or state court, to compel the new employer to arbitrate under the contract which the union negotiated with the predecessor employer. Although such suits do not involve Board action, rulings by the Supreme Court in situations of this type have influenced the Board.

---

[2] For a general discussion of the interrelation of Board process and court action under §301, *see* Chapter 17 *infra*.
[3] *See* Chapter 8 *supra*.

Still another issue is whether a successor employer must remedy unfair labor practices committed by the predecessor employer.

These issues are explored in the following sections.

II. IMPACT OF CHANGE ON BARGAINING OBLIGATIONS

A. Historical Development

1. Early Rulings. In 1939, long before the Supreme Court held in *Wiley v. Livingston* [4] that a bargaining agent for employees of a predecessor employer could compel a successor employer to arbitrate under the predecessor's collective bargaining agreement, the Board held that a successor employer was required to bargain with the bargaining agent of the employees following a nominal change in corporate organization which did not materially affect the nature of the business or the employees. [5] The Board continued to hold that the bargaining status of the majority representative remained unchanged where an alteration of business operations did not change the essential attributes of the employment relationship. [6] Moreover, this type of ruling was not limited to situations where one employer was simply the *alter ego* of the predecessor. In several cases, the Board held that a bona fide transferee of the business operation was bound by the certification of the bargaining agent. [7]

In one case where a purchaser of a business continued to produce the same products with the same equipment and work force, the Board, amending the certification to include the purchaser, stated that

> where, as here, no essential attribute of the employment relationship has been changed as a result of the transfer, the certification continues with undiminished vitality to represent the will of the employees with respect to their choice of a bargaining representative, and the consequent obligation to bargain subsists, notwithstanding the change in the legal ownership of the enterprise. [8]

---

4 John Wiley & Sons v. Livingston, 376 US 543, 55 LRRM 2769 (1964).
5 Chas. Cushman Co., 15 NLRB 90, 5 LRRM 113 (1939).
6 Stonewall Cotton Mills, 80 NLRB 325, 23 LRRM 1085 (1948).
7 Simmons Engineering Co., 65 NLRB 1435, 17 LRRM 291 (1946); National Bag Co., 65 NLRB 1078, 17 LRRM 283 (1946), *enforced*, 156 F 2d 679 (CA 8, 1946); Syncro Machine Co., Inc., 62 NLRB 985, 16 LRRM 230 (1945).
8 Stonewall Cotton Mills, 80 NLRB 325, 327. 23 LRRM 1085 (1948).

Likewise, the Board has held more recently that a successor employer is bound by the certification of the bargaining agent where the successor continues to produce the same product at the same location with the same equipment, serves the same customers, and where the employees of the predecessor, constituting a majority of the bargaining unit, are retained by the successor to perform the same functions.[9] The Board took the position that a mere change in ownership did not affect the certification of the bargaining agent in the "employing industry."

Nevertheless, a holding that a successor employer must bargain with the incumbent union did not necessarily mean that the successor employer would be bound by the agreement between the union and the predecessor employer. The distinction between contract rights and the statutory duty to bargain was pointed up by the Board in the *Cruse Motors* case:

> That the Respondent may not have been bound by O'Keefe's contract with the Union—indeed that the contract may be construed as specifically rejecting such an obligation—is not controlling. Whether the Respondent was required by the statute to continue dealing with the Union as the exclusive representative of its employees is a matter of interpretation of the Act and not of the contract. Though the contract may create private rights and duties enforceable under other laws, so far as the statute is concerned, the obligation to bargain is one neither created nor alterable by private agreement.[10]

2. Judicial Reaction. The principles adopted by the Board in these early cases received substantial judicial approval. There are decisions of the First, Fourth, Fifth, and Tenth Circuits in accord with Board rulings.[11] The Fourth Circuit held that a successor employer was obligated to bargain with a union representing employees of the predecessor where no significant change in operations had taken place. The obligation to bargain was found to exist even though the collective bargaining contract with the

---

9 Johnson Ready Mix, 142 NLRB 437, 53 LRRM 1068 (1963).

10 Cruse Motors, Inc., 105 NLRB 242, 248, 32 LRRM 1285 (1953). Contract rights are enforced in court actions under Section 301. In *Rohlik, Inc.*, 145 NLRB 1236, 55 LRRM 1130 (1964), the Board held that a successor employer was not bound by its predecessor's collective bargaining contract which it had not assumed, but the successor did have a duty to bargain with the incumbent union. *Compare* later development of the law. *See* notes 34-37 *infra*.

11 NLRB v. Lunder Shoe Corp., 211 F 2d 284, 33 LRRM 2695 (CA 1, 1954); Overnite Transportation Co., 157 NLRB 1185, 61 LRRM 1520, *enforced*, 372 F 2d 765, 64 LRRM 2359 (CA 4, 1967), *cert. denied*, 389 US 838, 66 LRRM 2307 (1967); NLRB v. Auto Vent-Shade Inc., 276 F 2d 303, 45 LRRM 3010 (CA 5, 1960); NLRB v. McFarland, 306 F 2d 219, 50 LRRM 2707 (CA 10, 1962).

predecessor had expired at the time of the sale and the successor had announced in advance that he did not intend to adhere to the terms established by that contract.[12]

In a few cases the courts refused to enforce Board orders directing successor employers to bargain with the unions representing employees of the predecessor employers. But even in these cases the courts did not reject the "employing industry" concept adopted by the Board.

In *NLRB* v. *Alamo-White Truck Service,* the Fifth Circuit posed the following critical question: "[I]s the employing enterprise substantially the same under Alamo as it was under White?" [13] A branch of a large trucking service had been sold to an independent group, the principals of which were the former manager and principal salesman of the branch. The new enterprise purchased only the physical assets without the accounts receivable; it did not assume any indebtedness or obligation of the predecessor. New bookkeeping and insurance arrangements were instituted. The building used by the branch was put up for sale by the predecessor, although the new enterprise was given a one-year lease with no renewal option. The selling of parts was discontinued, and the parts department of the branch was eliminated. The new business opened with seven mechanics; the predecessor had employed 12 mechanics.

The court noted that the branch, a subsidiary of a nationwide company engaged in manufacturing trucks, had been converted into a small independent service operation of a local nature. Refusing to enforce the Board's order requiring the successor employer to bargain, the court relied on the change in the nature of the business and the change from an employer-employee relationship in a large corporation to a close personal relationship in a small local business.[14]

---

[12] Overnite Transportation Co. v. NLRB, note 11 *supra.*

[13] 273 F 2d 238, 240, 45 LRRM 2330, 2331 (CA 5, 1959). *Compare* the 1970 Fifth Circuit decision in *NLRB* v. *Zayre Corp.,* 424 F 2d 1159, 74 LRRM 2084 (CA 5, 1970) (affirming the Board's finding of successorship notwithstanding changes in the bargaining unit made by the successor employer). *See* note 42 *infra.*

[14] It may be significant that if the Board's order had been enforced, the union representing the employees of the predecessor would have been bargaining for employees not one of whom was a member of the union.

In another case where the successor purchased the assets and hired nine of the drivers of the predecessor, NLRB v. McFarland, 306 F 2d 219, 50 LRRM 2707 (CA 10, 1962), the Tenth Circuit enforced the Board's order to the successor to bargain; the successor was not aware of the fact that the union representing the predecessor's employees had won an election in which 14 of 16 drivers had voted for the union.

Citing *Alamo-White,* the Second Circuit in *Aluminum Tubular* [15] refused to find the continuity in the operation requisite for an order to bargain where one company absorbed a newer and smaller enterprise and continued the operation of the acquired unit for the sole purpose of fulfilling certain contracts which were outstanding when the former employer went out of business. The court also noted that the assimilating business had its own labor contract with another union.[16]

In *Stepp's Friendly Ford,*[17] the Ninth Circuit refused to uphold the Board where there was a "substantial" change of personnel. The case involved the sale of an automobile agency (whose 12 salesmen were represented by a union) located across the street from the purchaser. The purchaser retained three of the employees of the predecessor, used four of his own employees, and hired one additional employee. The court held that the purchaser, not having retained a majority of the predecessor's employees, was not obligated to bargain with the union.

All three of the foregoing cases in which the courts refused to enforce Board orders were decided without the benefit of the developments stemming from *Wiley* v. *Livingston,*[18] which the Supreme Court decided in 1964. The results in those cases, however, may be reconciled with *Wiley.* *Wiley* did not involve unfair labor practice problems as did these three cases. And in *Wiley* there was a "wholesale" transfer of the predecessor's employees to the successor's operation, whereas, in *Alamo,*[19] only a fraction of

---

15 NLRB v. Aluminum Tubular Corp., 299 F 2d 595, 49 LRRM 2682 (CA 2, 1962).
16 *Cf.* Martin Marietta Corp., 159 NLRB 905, 62 LRRM 1316 (1966), where the purchasing employer operated the plant on a temporary basis prior to phasing out the operation entirely. But the Board noted that the same management was supervising the operation of the same equipment by the same employees (though reduced in number) while phasing out the operation. Thus, even though there was a clause in the sales agreement providing for no assumption by the purchaser of the seller's obligations, the Board ordered the purchaser to pay back pay to certain employees because of the successor's failure to observe seniority in the retention of the employees. Board member Zagoria felt that the majority should have imposed the remedy on the seller.
17 NLRB v. Stepp's Friendly Ford, 338 F 2d 833, 57 LRRM 2442 (CA 9, 1964). *But cf.* Wackenhut Corp. v. United Plant Guard Workers, 322 F 2d 954 (CA 9, 1964) and K. B. & J. Young's Supermarket, Inc. v. NLRB, 377 F 2d 463 (CA 9, 1967). *See also* the following post-*Wiley* decisions: Tallakson Ford, Inc. 171 NLRB No. 67, 68 LRRM 1136 (1968); Thomas Cadillac, Inc., 170 NLRB No. 6, 67 LRRM 1504 (1968); Northwest Galvanizing Co., 168 NLRB No. 6, 66 LRRM 1244 (1967); Federal Electric Corp., 167 NLRB 469, 66 LRRM 1089 (1967).
18 376 US 543, 55 LRRM 2769 (1964).
19 NLRB v. Alamo-White Truck Service, 273 F 2d 238, 45 LRRM 2330 (CA 5, 1959).

the predecessor's employees were hired by the new enterprise, which was also the situation in *Stepp's Friendly Ford*.[20] And in *Aluminum Tubular*,[21] the successor already had a labor contract. In *Wiley*, the successor's employees were not represented by a union. Although the results in these three cases may be reconciled with *Wiley*, they should, nevertheless, be evaluated in the light of *Wiley* and subsequent developments.

3. *Wiley* v. *Livingston*.[22] The decision of the Supreme Court in the *Wiley* case could be viewed simply as a logical extension of the Court's reliance upon arbitration as a means of effectuating national labor policy with no implication for Board proceedings. On the other hand, the Board necessarily is influenced by Supreme Court decisions which are related to problems it must consider.

The basic facts of *Wiley* are as follows: In 1961 Interscience, Inc., for valid business reasons, was merged into a much larger publishing company, John Wiley and Sons. At the time of the merger Wiley's employees (about 300) were not organized, but Interscience had a labor agreement with a union representing 40 of its 80 employees. All but a few of the Interscience employees were retained by Wiley. In discussions before and after the merger, the union contended that it continued to represent the Interscience bargaining-unit employees and that, after the merger, Wiley was obligated to recognize certain rights which had "vested" under the Interscience union contract. Wiley offered to retain the Interscience employees or to pay them severance pay in excess of the amount specified in the Interscience contract. Eleven employees accepted the severance pay. On behalf of the other Interscience bargaining-unit employees, the union brought suit against Wiley under Section 301 to compel arbitration under the collective bargaining agreement. The union raised questions as to whether seniority rights had accrued, whether Wiley was obligated to make

---

20 NLRB v. Stepp's Friendly Ford, 338 F 2d 833, 57 LRRM 2442 (CA 9, 1964).
21 NLRB v. Aluminum Tubular Corp., 299 F 2d 595, 49 LRRM 2682 (CA 2, 1962).
22 John Wiley & Sons v. Livingston, 376 US 543, 55 LRRM 2769 (1964). *See*: Note, *The Successor Employer and His Duty To Arbitrate Under the Collective Bargaining Agreement of the Predecessor: The Progeny of John Wiley and Sons v. Livingston*, 29 U. PITT. L. REV. 273 (1967); Note, *Successor Corporation Subject to Labor Arbitration Agreement of Merged Corporation*, 17 SYRACUSE L. REV. 513 (1966); Note, *The Contractual Obligations of a Successor Employer Under the Collective Bargaining Agreement of a Predecessor*, 113 U. PA. L. REV. 914 (1965); Goldberg, *The Labor Law Obligations of a Successor Employer*, 63 NW. U.L. REV. 735 (1969); Feller, *The Successor and the Collective Agreement*, LABOR LAW DEVELOPMENTS 1967 (13th Annual Institute, Sw. Legal Foundation) 1.

payments to the union's pension plan, whether job-security procedures would be continued, and whether Wiley was liable for vacation and severance pay.

The Supreme Court, unanimously affirming the Second Circuit, held that

> the disappearance by merger of a corporate employer which has entered into a collective bargaining agreement with a union does not automatically terminate all rights of the employees covered by the agreement, and that, in appropriate circumstances, present here, the successor employer may be required to arbitrate with the union under the agreement.[23]

Despite the merger, the Court found that there was a "continuity of operation across the change in ownership." [24] The national labor policy which favors arbitration as the substitute for industrial strife "could be overcome only if other considerations compellingly so demanded." [25] A consideration which might overcome the preference for arbitration was a "lack of any substantial continuity of identity in the business enterprise before and after [the] change." [26] The Court concluded that rights accrued under the contract with Interscience (which had expired) could be enforced against Wiley even though Wiley had not agreed to be bound by the terms of the agreement.

Neither the merger agreement nor the labor agreement in *Wiley* contained a clause which would bind the successor to the labor agreement, but the absence of such a provision was deemed immaterial by the Court. Later cases have held that labor-agreement provisions which bind a successor employer are not essential to the survival of the agreement.[27] Nor is a disclaimer of union-contract obligations in a sale or merger agreement controlling.[28]

---

[23] 376 US at 548. Wiley had recognized that some benefits, such as severance pay, could accrue before termination of the contract and be payable at a later date, and that Interscience would have certain obligations under the agreement even though the agreement had expired.

[24] 376 US at 551.

[25] 376 US at 549-550. The Court also held that procedural arbitrability is a matter for the arbitrator to decide.

[26] 376 US at 551.

[27] Owens-Illinois, Inc. v. Retail Store Union, 276 F Supp 740, 66 LRRM 2024 (SD NY, 1967) ; Retail Store Employees Union v. Lane's of Findlay, Inc., 260 F Supp 655, 63 LRRM 2445 (ND Ohio, 1966). *See* Wm. J. Burns Int'l Detective Agency, Inc., 182 NLRB No. 50, 74 LRRM 1098 (1970), notes 34-37 *infra* and accompanying text.

[28] U.S. Gypsum Co. v. United Steelworkers of America, 384 F 2d 38, 66 LRRM 2232 (CA 5, 1967) ; McGuire v. Humble Oil & Refining Co., 355 F 2d 352, 62 LRRM 2339 (CA 2, 1966) ; United Steelworkers of America v. Reliance Universal, Inc., 335 F 2d 891, 56 LRRM 2721 (CA 3, 1964) ; Hotel Employees v. Joden, Inc., 262 F Supp 390 (D Mass, 1966).

4. Impact of *Wiley*. The Court expressly refused "to suggest
any view on the questions surrounding a certified union's claim to
continued representative status following a change in ownership . . ."; [29] it could therefore be argued that *Wiley* and other cases
involving a union's right to arbitrate with a successor under the
union's agreement with the predecessor are irrelevant to Board
proceedings. But the Court in *Wiley* relied essentially on the same
kinds of criteria that the Board considers in an unfair labor practice
proceeding involving a successorship problem. And it is clear that
the Board has been greatly influenced by the *Wiley* decision.

A few of the more important court decisions which have construed *Wiley* should be noted.[30] In *Wackenhut*,[31] the Ninth Circuit held that a purchaser of assets of a predecessor was "bound"
by the collective bargaining agreement of its predecessor, and that
the successor was required to arbitrate under this agreement. The
Third Circuit in *Reliance*,[32] also involving a sale of assets, construed the Ninth Circuit's decision in *Wackenhut* as treating *Wiley*
as authority for making a pre-existing labor contract "unqualifiedly
binding" upon a new proprietor in a similar situation. The Third
Circuit disagreed with this notion and held that an arbitrator could
consider changed circumstances and decide whether a particular
provision in the contract should be binding upon the successor.[33]

---

[29] 376 US at 551.
[30] For further discussion of these cases, *see:* Goldberg, note 1 *supra;* Gordon, note 1
supra; Banta, *Labor Organizations of Successor Employers,* 36 GEO. WASH. L. REV.
215 (1967); Platt, *The NLRB and the Arbitrator in Sale and Merger Situations,*
N.Y.U. NINTH CONF. ON LABOR 375 (1967); Note, *The Successor Employer and His
Duty To Arbitrate Under the Collective Bargaining Agreement of the Predecessor,
The Progeny of John Wiley and Sons v. Livingston,* 29 U. PITT. L. REV. 273 (1967).
[31] Wackenhut Corp. v. United Plant Guard Workers, 332 F 2d 954, 56 LRRM 2466
(CA 9, 1964).
[32] United Steelworkers v. Reliance Universal, Inc., 335 F 2d 891, n. 3, 56 LRRM 2721
(CA 3, 1964).
[33] *See also* the following cases: Piano and Musical Instrument Workers v. Kimball
Co., 379 US 357, 57 LRRM 2628 (1964), did not involve two different employers.
The company moved a plant to a different location during the term of a labor agreement and refused to honor the old contract at the new site. After the agreement
expired, the union sought arbitration to preserve seniority rights which it claimed
had accrued under the old contract. Citing *Wiley* in a *per curiam* decision, the
Supreme Court held that the union was entitled to arbitration.
     McGuire v. Humble Oil and Refining Co., 355 F 2d 352, 61 LRRM 2410 (CA 2,
1966), a Second Circuit decision, is distinguishable from the cases in which only one
union is involved and the problem of conflict between competing unions does not
exist. In *Humble Oil,* the predecessor's employees were transferred to the successor's
plant, which was already organized. The union representing the former employees
of the predecessor sought to arbitrate with the successor employer. In a bargaining-
unit-clarification proceeding instituted by the successor employer, the Board held
that the predecessor's employees had become part of the Humble bargaining unit.

The impact of the *Wiley* case on bargaining obligations under the NLRA came to fruition in 1970 in four cases that are discussed in the following section.

B. The Successor Doctrine as Currently Applied.

1. The Contractual Obligation. In *William J. Burns International Detective Agency, Inc.*,[34] the lead case in a series of four NLRB decisions based on the Supreme Court's *Wiley* doctrine, the Board held that when a business changes hands, absent unusual circumstances, "the national labor policy embodied in the Act requires the successor-employer to take over and honor a collective bargaining agreement negotiated on behalf of the employing enterprise by the predecessor." [35]

In the *Burns* case, plant protection and security services for an aircraft service company had been performed by Wackenhut Corporation. United Plant Guard Workers of America was certified as bargaining agent for the employees performing these services, and a collective bargaining contract of three years' duration was signed by Wackenhut and the union. Shortly thereafter the plant protection service was let out for bids, and all bidders were ap-

---

Humble Oil and Refining Co., 153 NLRB 1361, 59 LRRM 1632 (1965). The Second Circuit refused to compel arbitration because such an order would have required the company to bargain collectively with the representative of a minority of the bargaining unit. The problem of conflict between competing unions was not presented in *Wiley*. For another series of cases involving a merger of two groups of employees—each represented by a different union, see Teamsters v. Red Ball Motor Freight, Inc., 374 F 2d 932, 64 LRRM 2545 (CA 5, 1967), and Truck Drivers, Local 568 v. NLRB (Red Ball Motor Freight, Inc.), 379 F 2d 137, 65 LRRM 2309 (CA DC, 1967). These cases also show how Board and court proceedings may become interrelated.

In the later *Bath Iron Works* case, a company under contract with a union was absorbed by merger with another company that had a contract with the same union. The Court of Appeals for the First Circuit ruled that arbitration of the contract rights of employees of the absorbed company should be governed by the contract of the surviving company. Bath Iron Works Corp. v. Bath Marine Draftsmen's Assn., 393 F 2d 407, 68 LRRM 2010 (CA 1, 1968).

34 182 NLRB No. 50, 74 LRRM 1098 (1970). The companion cases decided with *Burns* were the following: Kota Div. of Dura Corp., 182 NLRB No. 51, 74 LRRM 1104 (1970) (presenting the reverse issue, with the Board holding that the successor employer has a right to insist that the union adhere to the contract which it signed with the predecessor employer; *see* note 37 *infra*); Travelodge Corp., 182 NLRB No. 52, 74 LRRM 1105 (1970) (required degree of continuity in the employing enterprise lacking, therefore no violation found); Hackney Iron & Steel Co., 182 NLRB No. 53, 74 LRRM 1102 (1970) (a case remanded from the District of Columbia Circuit Court of Appeals, 395 F 2d 639, 68 LRRM 2065 (1968)).

35 74 LRRM at 1100. In addition to finding a violation of 8(a)(5), the Board also found that *Burns* violated Section 8(a)(2) by assisting and recognizing another union.

prised of the existence of the collective agreement. William J. Burns International Detective Agency was the successful bidder and was awarded the contract to perform the service which had formerly been performed by Wackenhut. Burns hired 27 former Wackenhut guards and transferred 15 of its own employees from other locations. Thus, a majority of the work force was made up of ex-Wackenhut employees. The Board found that the nature of the business remained the same.

The union made a demand that Burns recognize it and honor the collective bargaining contract that the predecessor employer had signed. Burns declined. Affirming its trial examiner, the Board held that Burns was a successor employer to Wackenhut and therefore in violation of Section 8 (a) (5) when it refused to recognize and bargain with the incumbent union. The Board went further, however, and also held that Burns was bound under its predecessor's collective bargaining agreement.

In reaching this decision, the Board relied on the *Wiley* rationale, noting that the Supreme Court had refused to apply common law contract doctrine to determine the nature of a purchasing employer's obligation to arbitrate matters arising under a collective bargaining contract that it had not signed. Declaring that a finding of successorship involves a judgment that the *employing industry* has remained essentially the same despite a change in ownership, and that there was no reason to believe that employees within the employing industry, *i.e.*, the bargaining unit, would change their attitudes merely because the employer's identity had changed,[36] the Board concluded that the policy considerations which favored maintenance and adherence to existing collective bargaining agreements were not overborne by the fact that Burns had not signed the contract which its predecessor had negotiated.

The Board deduced that the Section 8 (d) command that the obligation to bargain "does not compel either party to agree to a proposal or require the making of a concession" was inapplicable

---

36 74 LRRM at 1100, *citing* NLRB v. Albert Armato, 199 F 2d 800, 31 LRRM 2089 (CA 7, 1952). The Board stressed that "the finding of successorship involves a judgment that the *employing industry* has remained essentially the same despite the change in ownership." (Emphasis added). 74 LRRM at 1100, relying on Cruse Motors, Inc., 105 NLRB 242, 32 LRRM 1285 (1953), and Kiddie Kover Co. v. NLRB, 105 F 2d 179, 4 LRRM 638 (CA 6, 1939).

to the successor employer's situation. Paralleling the reasoning and conclusion of the Supreme Court in *Wiley*, the Board held as follows:

> Indisputedly, there is a contract. That contract covers the employees of the employing industry which Burns took over. . . . That contract is reasonably related to Burns through the takeover of Wackenhut's . . . service functions contract and its hiring of Wackenhut employees. . . . We find, therefore, that Burns is bound to that contract as if it were a signatory thereto. . . .
>
> In the normal case, we perceive no real inequity in requiring a "successor-employer" to take over his predecessor's collective-bargaining agreement, for he stands in the shoes of his predecessor. He can make whatever adjustments the acceptance of such obligation may dictate in his negotiations concerning the takeover of the business. Normally, employees cannot make a comparable adjustment. Their basic security is the collective bargaining agreement negotiated on their behalf. In the instant case this is certainly so. . . . Accordingly, in order to fully protect the employees' exercise of the right to bargain collectively and to promote the maintenance of stable bargaining relationships and concomitantly industrial peace in this industry, we conclude that Respondent Burns must be held bound to its predecessor's contract.[37]

2. The Bargaining Obligation. In deciding whether a change in the organization or ownership of a business has affected bargaining obligations, the Board has evolved a set of criteria to determine whether the "employing industry" remains substantially the same. Board Member John Fanning has grouped the questions asked by the Board as follows:

(1) whether there has been a substantial continuity of the same business operations;

(2) whether the new employer uses the same plant;

(3) whether he has the same or substantially the same work force;

(4) whether the same jobs exist under the same working conditions;

(5) whether he employs the same supervisors;

(6) whether he uses the same machinery, equipment, and methods of production; and

---

[37] 74 LRRM at 1101. Member Jenkins dissented, contending that the parties should be permitted flexibility in working out new arrangements. He stated: "The new employer is not a party to the agreement, and the union did not join in shaping and executing it with his circumstances in mind. Thus, to impose the agreement on the new relation may in many cases prove a source of friction and disruption, rather than the stability for which my colleagues hope." He cited the companion case of *Kota Div. of Dura Corp.*, note 34 *supra*, as an example. (In *Kota*, the Board dismissed §8(a)(5) charges against a successor employer who had refused to negotiate a new contract with the incumbent union, insisting instead on the binding effect of the contract negotiated by its predecessor).

(7) whether he manufactures the same product or offers the same services.[38]

One critical question which has come before the Board in recent years is whether the successor employer can avoid an obligation to bargain by refusing to hire any of his predecessor's employees. In connection with a Section 301 action, a court has noted that

[I]n practically all the decisions following *Wiley*, the determination of similarity of operation and continuity of identity depended, at least in part, upon the employees of the merged corporation remaining in the employ of the successor. . . . Clearly, however, this is not the only factor to be considered in determining continuity of identity, for, if that were the case, *Wiley* could be easily avoided by the successor corporation's refusal to hire the predecessor's employees.[39]

In *Chemrock Corp.*[40] there was a sale of a business in which the seller had some employees in a production and maintenance bargaining unit and some employees in a truck-driver bargaining unit. Each of the units was represented by a different union. The purchaser, who bought the assets of the predecessor, continued to produce the same products on the same machines with the same production and maintenance employees, and he negotiated an agreement with the bargaining agent for this unit. But he advised the drivers that they would be hired only as "free agents," and refused to bargain with their representative. When the drivers insisted on representation by their union, the purchaser hired new drivers in their place. The Board held that the drivers were employees of the purchaser even though they had not been hired by the purchaser, and thus that the purchaser was obligated to bargain with their union. The Board stated that where

the only substantial change wrought by the sale of the business enterprise is the transfer of ownership, the individuals employed by the seller of the enterprise must be regarded as "employees" of the purchaser as that term is used in the Act. Such individuals possess a substantial interest in the continuation of their existing employee

---

38 Fanning, note 1 *supra*, at 286.
39 Monroe Sander Corp. v. Livingston, 262 F Supp 129, 136, 63 LRRM 2273 (SD NY, 1966), *affirmed*, 377 F 2d 6, 65 LRRM 2273 (CA 2, 1967). *Cf.* NLRB v. Alamo-White Truck Service, 273 F 2d 238, 45 LRRM 2330 (CA 5, 1959) and NLRB v. Stepp's Friendly Ford, 338 F. 2d 833, 57 LRRM 2442 (CA 9, 1964), where the successor did not refuse to hire his predecessor's employees but he hired only a fraction of them. *See* discussion of these cases in text accompanying notes 13-17 *supra*. In *Tri-State Maintenance Co. v. NLRB*, 408 F 2d 171, 69 LRRM 2937 (CA DC, 1968), the court upheld a finding of an 8(a)(3) violation based on employer refusal to consider applications of union employees on a nondiscriminatory basis. *See* Chapter 6 generally for treatment of §8(a)(3).
40 151 NLRB 1074, 58 LRRM 1582 (1965).

status, and by virtue of this interest bear a much closer economic relationship to the employing enterprise than, for example, the mere applicant for employment. . . . The particular individuals involved here were unquestionably "employees" of the enterprise at the time of the transfer of plant ownership. The work they had been doing was to be continued without change. Clearly employees in such a situation are entitled to seek through bargaining to protect their economic relationship to the enterprise that employs them.[41]

Because of the purchaser's refusal to bargain, the Board ordered reinstatement of the drivers, overruling a prior decision that former employees who did not report to work for the successor did not become employees of the successor.[42] Although the Board stated that it was not making a decision on the applicability of the *holding* in *Wiley*, it observed that the following language of the Court in *Wiley* was pertinent to the issue in *Chemrock*:

> Employees and the union which represents them, ordinarily do not take part in negotiations leading to a change in corporate ownership. The negotiations will ordinarily not concern the well-being of the employees, whose advantage or disadvantage, potentially great, will inevitably be incidental to the main considerations. The objectives of national labor policy, reflected in established principles of federal law, require that the rightful prerogative of owners independently to rearrange their business and even eliminate themselves as employers be balanced by some protection to the employees from a sudden change in the employment relationship. . . .[43]

Other rulings in recent years indicate that the Board relies on many factors, and not on any one factor, in determining whether a successor employer has an obligation to bargain with a union representing his predecessor's employees. That one factor may tend to suggest that there is no continuity of the business operation does not necessarily lead to the conclusion that the successor has no obligation to bargain. For example, if the new employer substitutes his

---

[41] 151 NLRB at 1078. Member Zagoria dissented, holding that the majority had placed an unnecessary restraint on the free alienation of parts of a business enterprise. In Martin Marietta Corp., 159 NLRB 905, 62 LRRM 1316 (1966), the Board held that a successor employer violated the Act by failing to give notice to the union before phasing out operators; see note 16 *supra*.

[42] The prior decision was Page Aircraft Maintenance Co., 123 NLRB 159, 43 LRRM 1383 (1959). *Cf.* Piasecki Aircraft Corp., 123 NLRB 348, 43 LRRM 1443 (1959), *enforced*, 280 F 2d 575, 46 LRRM 2469 (CA 3, 1960). *See also* Maintenance, Inc., 148 NLRB 1299, 57 LRRM 1129 (1964); Valleydale Packers, Inc., 162 NLRB 1486, 64 LRRM 1212 (1967), *enforced*, 402 F 2d 768, 69 LRRM 2622 (CA 5, 1968); NLRB v. Zayre Corp., 424 F 2d 1159, 74 LRRM 2084 (CA 5, 1970), *see* note 13 *supra*.

[43] Chemrock Corp., 151 NLRB 1074, 1078-1079, 58 LRRM 1582 (1965). The quoted language was used by the Supreme Court in the context of the wholesale transfer of employees in *Wiley*.

own supervisory staff for that of the prior employer or fails to purchase the assets of the prior employer, he may still be required to bargain with the union of the employees of the prior employer where other factors indicate that essentially the same operation has been continued.[44] Moreover, this may be true even if the successor does not assume the obligations of the prior employer and the two employers agree that the successor has no obligation to hire the employees of the prior employer.[45] And if the successor instigates a discriminatory discharge of the predecessor's employees and a complete replacement of personnel, he may nevertheless be required to bargain where he conducts the same business with the same clients at the same location and there is no change in the duties of the jobs involved.[46]

On the other hand, the mere fact that a new employer retained 11 of 37 employees of the predecessor did not mean that there was substantial continuity of the operation, where the plant was shut down before the new employer assumed control, and the new employer was making different products for different customers.[47]

---

44 Maintenance, Inc., 148 NLRB 1299, 57 LRRM 1129 (1964). *See also* Overnight Transportation Co., 157 NLRB 1185, 61 LRRM 1520, *enforced*, 372 F 2d 765, 64 LRRM 2359 (CA 4, 1967), *cert. denied*, 389 US 838, 66 LRRM 2307 (1967).
45 Johnson Ready Mix Co., 142 NLRB 437, 53 LRRM 1068 (1963). An older case shows that the successor may even have an obligation to bargain if he buys only some of the assets of the prior employer, with the existing collective agreement not providing that it binds successors, and with the prior employer, going into business at a new location, also having obligations under the labor contract. Cruse Motors, Inc., 105 NLRB 242, 32 LRRM 1285 (1953). *See* note 10 *supra*.
46 K. B. & J. Young's Supermarket, Inc., 157 NLRB 271, 61 LRRM 355 (1966).
47 Allied Chemical Corp., 153 NLRB 849, 59 LRRM 1410 (1965), *enforced*, 362 F 2d 943, 62 LRRM 2238 (CA DC, 1966). In *Thomas Cadillac, Inc.*, 170 NLRB No. 92, 67 LRRM 1504 (1968), *affirmed*, 414 F 2d 1135, 71 LRRM 2150 (CA DC, 1969), the Board stated that "[a]mong the central factors in a successorship question is the new employer's relationship to the old employer's work force." Finding that the new employer did not take over or succeed to the bargaining unit, the Board held that the employer was under no duty to recognize or bargain with the union that had represented the employees in the former bargaining unit. Writing for the District of Columbia Circuit, which affirmed the Board, Judge Burger declared:
  "To have concluded otherwise would have deprived the new employees . . . —a majority of whom had no prior affiliation with [union] Petitioners—of rights guaranteed them by Section 7 of the Act to be represented by an agent of their own choice.
  "It should be noted that the Board's finding of nonsuccessorship did not turn on the fact that a majority of the new employees were not members of the old bargaining unit; if the composition of the unit was the controlling factor in determining successorship, a purchaser might well seek to avoid application of the successorship principle by refusing to hire the seller's employees. Of course, if the purchaser deliberately sets out to destroy a union when he takes over a going business other consequences of a violation of the Act might well arise."
Accord: Tallakson Ford, 171 NLRB No. 67, 68 LRRM 1136 (1968); Northwest Galvanizing, 168 NLRB No. 6, 66 LRRM 1244 (1967); Federal Electric Corp., 167 NLRB No. 63, 66 LRRM 1089 (1967).

Furthermore, the failure of the new employer to retain the supervisory force of the predecessor is a factor to be considered.[48] It has been held that a purchaser of assets was not a "successor" where he hired new employees under mostly new supervision to conduct a different business, even though the change in business was merely from a "captive" manufacturer of records to a "custom" manufacturer.[49]

III. IMPACT OF CHANGE ON REPRESENTATION PROCEEDINGS

When a petition is filed for a representation election despite the existence of an unexpired collective agreement, the Board may be required to decide whether, under the contract-bar doctrine, the agreement provides a bar to the election.[50] If the Board decides that the unexpired contract of a predecessor employer is a bar to an election and that the union retains its representative status, it logically follows in most instances that the new employer must bargain with the union. But in certain kinds of cases where changes have taken place in the employing unit the Board may not reach the contract-bar question.

In the cases which preceded the Board's current successorship doctrine, it had been held that a successor employer (who was not viewed as identical to his predecessor for contract-bar purposes) was not subject to contract-bar rules unless he had agreed to be bound by his predecessor's collective bargaining agreement. The Board long ago stated that "the assumption of the operations by a purchaser in good faith who had not bound himself to assume the bargaining agreement of the prior owner of the establishment removes the contract as a bar" to an election.[51] And the Board

---

48 Skagg's Drug Centers, 150 NLRB 518, 58 LRRM 1106 (1964).
49 Apex Record Corp., 162 NLRB 333, 64 LRRM 1044 (1966). Even if a purchaser is a successor, he may refuse to bargain with a union on the basis of a good-faith doubt of the union's continuing majority subsequent to the certification year. Mitchell Standard Corp., 140 NLRB 496, 52 LRRM 1049 (1963). See Chapters 10 and 11 supra.
50 For a discussion of the contract bar doctrine generally, see Chapter 8 supra.
51 General Extrusion Company, Inc., 121 NLRB 1165, 1168, 42 LRRM 1508 (1958). Accord, Jolly Giant Lumber Co., 114 NLRB 413, 36 LRRM 1585 (1955), which indicated that the contract of the prior owner would not serve as a bar to an election unless the union also signs the purchaser's assumption of the agreement.

applied the rule that for an assumption of a prior contract by a new employer to be effective as a bar to an election, such assumption had to be express and in writing.[52]

On the other hand, where there has been no significant change in the employing enterprise, the Board has consistently treated the employer in question as substantially "identical" to the one who signed the agreement; the contract between the employer's predecessor and the union bars an election even though the employer did not expressly assume the contract.[53]

Following the new successorship doctrine enunciated in the *Burns* case, the Board now holds that the presumption of union majority status which attaches during the term of an ordinary collective bargaining contract also applies in successorship cases (notwithstanding that the successor is not "identical" to the predecessor employer). The successor employer, regardless of whether he has voluntarily chosen to assume the contract, "may not, during the life of the contract, assert a doubt as to its obligation to bargain with the incumbent union." [54]

Where a sale leads to various changes in operations so that the employing industry is not essentially the same industry, the Board has said that the purchaser is not a successor and that a contract of

---

[52] M. V. Dominator, 162 NLRB 1514, 64 LRRM 1215 (1967). The Board directed an election upon the petition of an *outside union* since the employer had not assumed in writing the contract of his predecessor. *Cf.* U.S. Gypsum, 157 NLRB 652, 61 LRRM 1384 (1966), where the Board held that an *employer* who seeks an election upon a mere change in ownership of a business must show objective evidence of his doubt of the union's lack of a majority.

[53] Grainger Bros. Co., 146 NLRB 609, 55 LRRM 1380 (1964). *Cf.* Montgomery Ward and Co., 137 NLRB 346, 50 LRRM 1137 (1962). For another case involving a change in internal structure, *see* Farrin Lumber Co., 117 NLRB 575, 39 LRRM 1296 (1957).

[54] Ranch-Way, Inc., 183 NLRB No. 116, 74 LRRM 1389, 1391 (1970). The Board held: "The key test in determining whether a change in the employing industry has occurred is whether it may be reasonably assumed that, as a result of transitional changes, the employees' desires concerning unionization have likely changed." If there is no reason to assume that the employees' attitudes have changed, then the presumption of majority status continues despite the change in ownership and the new owner may not assert a doubt as to its obligation to bargain with the union. 74 LRRM at 1391. *But see* Davenport Insulation, 184 NLRB No. 114, 74 LRRM 1726 (1970) where the presumption of majority status did not exist because the contract of the predecessor employer had been entered into pursuant to 8(f). *See* Chapter 8 *supra* at notes 104 and 111-112.

the predecessor employer, not assumed by the purchaser, is no bar to an election.[55]

Cases involving the question of premature extension of an existing agreement present similar issues. In one such case,[56] new management resulting from a change in stock ownership, without any other change in the operation, was deemed to be the same employer for contract-bar purposes. The Board found that execution of a "new contract" by the new management with the union representing the predecessor's employees constituted a premature extension of the old contract; thus, a petition for an election which was timely filed under the old contract was not barred.

A different result was reached where a successor employer purchased a plant during the term of a labor agreement between the seller and its union, and the purchaser entered into an "extension agreement" with the union.[57] Since the purchaser had not been a party to the original agreement and since the purchaser had entered into a different agreement with new obligations and with different starting and expiration dates, the Board held that a petition for a decertification election, filed by employees who contended that the purchaser's new agreement was a premature extension of the old contract, was barred by the contract-bar rule. To be contrasted with this case is the case in which Shop-Rite merged with Food Mart, and only Shop-Rite survived as an entity.[58] The evidence indicated that there had been no substantial change in the employing industry, since the changes effected by the merger in corporate ownership and structure did not change the basic nature of the operation. The Board found that Shop-Rite's assumption of Food Mart's prematurely extended contract did not result in a new contract, hence did not constitute a bar to a timely filed petition for an election.

Other merger and consolidation cases illustrate additional distinctions the Board has deemed significant. Where two companies owned by the same employer were consolidated at the location of

---

55 Triumph Sales, Inc., 154 NLRB 916, 60 LRRM 1058 (1965). *See* discussion of criteria for determining continuity of the "employing industry," note 38 *supra*.
56 Farrin Lumber Co., 117 NLRB 575, 39 LRRM 1296 (1957).
57 Chrysler Corp., 153 NLRB 578, 59 LRRM 1529 (1965).
58 Shop-Rite Foods, Inc., 162 NLRB 1020, 64 LRRM 1123 (1967). All such cases must now be evaluated in light of *Burns* and *Ranch-Way. See* notes 35-37 and 54 *supra*.

the second company, the Board held that the labor contract at the location of the second company served as a bar to an election.[59] But where the merger of two separate employers resulted in a single new unit that intermingled the former employees of both employers, the Board held that a prior labor agreement of one of these employers did not bar an election in the single new unit since the Board viewed the merger as resulting in a new operation.[60] Likewise, the Board held that a prior contract did not bar an election where the combined operation of merged employers brought about a five-fold expansion of the number of employees employed by the predecessor whose labor agreement was in question.[61]

IV. LIABILITY OF SUCCESSOR FOR PREDECESSOR'S UNFAIR LABOR PRACTICES

A. "Alter Ego" of Predecessor

The Board very early took the position, approved by the courts, that a successor employer was liable for the unfair labor practices of his predecessor if the evidence showed that the successor was the *alter ego* of the predecessor.[62] In *Regal Knitwear Co. v. NLRB* [63] the Supreme Court considered the Board's policy of including in its orders the "successors and assigns" of the employer in question. The Court declared in an extensive discussion that a successor could be held liable for the acts of his predecessor where there was an identity of interest between the employers.

Over the years the Board has continued to direct its unfair labor practice orders against a successor who is the *alter ego* of his predecessor.[64] Factors considered by the Board in determining whether a successor is the *alter ego* of his predecessor are whether (1) stockholders and officers, (2) operations, (3) assets, (4) employees, and (5) supervisory force remain the same.[65]

---

59 Builders Emporium, 97 NLRB 1113, 29 LRRM 1213 (1952).
60 Spear, L. B., & Co., 106 NLRB 687, 32 LRRM 1535 (1953).
61 New Jersey Natural Gas Co., 101 NLRB 251, 31 LRRM 1048 (1952). *See also* Panda Terminals, 161 NLRB 1215, 63 LRRM 1419 (1966) (four-fold expansion) and Bowman Dairy Co., 123 NLRB 707, 43 LRRM 1519 (1959) (30% of the employees in the combined unit had been employed under the contract in question).
62 NLRB v. Hopwood Retinning Co., Inc., 104 F 2d 302, 4 LRRM 555 (CA 2, 1939).
63 324 US 9, 15 LRRM 882 (1945).
64 Ozark Hardwood Co., 119 NLRB 1130, 41 LRRM 1243 (1957), *enforced in part*, 282 F 2d 1, 46 LRRM 2823 (CA 8, 1960) ; Oilfield Maintenance Co., Inc., 142 NLRB 1384, 53 LRRM 1235 (1963).
65 Atlanta Paper Co., 121 NLRB 125, 42 LRRM 1309 (1958).

B. Bona Fide Purchaser

The Board's position has fluctuated on the question whether remedies for unfair labor practices of a predecessor may be imposed on a good-faith purchaser.

Following the Supreme Court's decision in *Regal Knitwear*, the Board extended application of its remedial orders for unfair labor practices to cover a bona fide purchaser who had knowledge of the Board's proceedings against the predecessor where the only real change was in the ownership of the business.[66] But this 1948 ruling was overruled in *Symns Grocer* [67] in 1954. A year earlier, the Tenth Circuit had refused to enforce a bargaining order issued against a successor because the relationship of the successor to the predecessor was not close enough to establish liability for conduct of the predecessor.[68] In *Symns Grocer* the Board reexamined its policy and decided that it had no authority to enforce orders against any party other than the party who had actually engaged in the unlawful practice. In 1967, however, in the *Perma Vinyl* case,[69] the Board overruled *Symns Grocer*.

Between 1954 and 1967 several significant developments had taken place. In 1960 the Fifth Circuit enforced a back-pay order against a successor, but not on the basis of the *alter ego* concept.[70] In 1964 the Board criticized the reasoning of the Fifth Circuit and indicated that the court had confused the distinction between duty to bargain and duty to remedy an unfair labor practice.[71] On the other hand, during this period the Board did order a successor to remedy the unfair labor practice of a predecessor where the successor had notice of and participated in the Board proceedings.[72]

---

66 Alexander Milburn Co., 78 NLRB 747, 22 LRRM 1249 (1948).

67 Symns Grocer Co. and Idaho Wholesale Grocery Co., 109 NLRB 346, 34 LRRM 1326 (1954).

68 NLRB v. Birdsall-Stockdale Motor Co., 208 F 2d 234, 33 LRRM 2086 (CA 10, 1953).

69 Perma Vinyl Corp., Dade Plastics Co. and United States Pipe and Foundry Co., 164 NLRB 968, 65 LRRM 1168 (1967), *enforced sub nom.* U.S. Pipe and Foundry Co. v. NLRB, 398 F 2d 544, 68 LRRM 2913 (1968). *Followed in* Webb Tractor & Equipment Co., 181 NLRB No. 39, 74 LRRM 1018 (1970).

70 Tempest Shirt Manufacturing Co., 285 F 2d 1, 47 LRRM 2298 (CA 5, 1960).

71 M. Eskin and Son, 148 NLRB 1022, 57 LRRM 1121 (1964).

72 Liberty Electronics Corp., Inc., 143 NLRB 605, 53 LRRM 1370 (1963). The Board has been sustained in its position that it may conduct inquiry into the pos-

In overruling *Symns Grocer,* the Board held in *Perma Vinyl* that

> one who acquires and operates a business of an employer found guilty of unfair labor practices in basically unchanged form under circumstances which charge him with notice of unfair labor practice charges against his predecessor should be held responsible for remedying his predecessor's unlawful conduct.[73]

The Board had found Perma Vinyl in violation of the Act and ordered it to reinstate and compensate four discharged employees. Perma Vinyl paid them their back pay to the time of the sale to U.S. Pipe, but the issue which remained was whether and to what extent U.S. Pipe was liable for their reinstatement. It was clear that U.S. Pipe was not the *alter ego* of Perma Vinyl; however, it had purchased Perma Vinyl "with knowledge of the unfair labor proceeding against that company." [74]

Recognizing that U.S. Pipe was the only employer with the power to reinstate the unlawfully discharged employees, the Board held that U.S. Pipe had the responsibility for remedying unfair labor practices attached to the business which it had bought and was continuing. The Board relied on the broad reasoning of the Supreme Court in *Wiley* in fashioning this remedy, pointing to the fact that the "employee victims" of unfair labor practices were especially in need of help, for they were "without meaningful remedy when title to the employing business operation changes hands." [75]

The Board stated that it was considering both the interests of the employees and the interests of the purchaser. The substitution of one employer for another, it noted, made no significant change

---

sible derivative liability of a successor after a court has enforced a Board order for back pay against the predecessor. NLRB v. C.C.C. Associates, Inc., 306 F 2d 534, 50 LRRM 2882 (CA 2, 1962). In one case the court enforced a back pay order against a successor even where the Board did not hold a separate hearing on the successorship question, since the court was satisfied with the evidence already developed. Mastro Plastics Corp., 354 F 2d 170, 60 LRRM 2578 (CA 2, 1965), *cert. denied,* 384 US 972, 62 LRRM 2292 (1966).

73 164 NLRB at 969.

74 168 NLRB at 968. *But see* Ramada Inns, Inc., 171 NLRB No. 115, 68 LRRM 1209, 1212 (1968), where the Board held that "where a successor employer has acquired a business with no knowledge of alleged prior unfair labor practices, we do not think he may be fairly held to have assumed that risk."

75 *Ibid.*

from the standpoint of the discharged employees. Their jobs remained, and they were available to fill these jobs. As far as the purchaser was concerned, the Board advised that a new employer could protect himself against the cost of remedying a known unfair labor practice by requiring an indemnity clause in the sales contract or by taking cost of the remedy into account in the price he paid for the business.[76]

---

[76] The Board did not impose a retroactive back-pay order on U.S. Pipe, however, because at the time of its take-over of Perma Vinyl, existing law imposed no obligation on it to remedy its predecessor's unfair labor practices.

CHAPTER 14

SUBJECTS OF BARGAINING: AN INTRODUCTION

I. HISTORICAL BACKGROUND

The original Wagner Act did not directly enumerate or define the subjects of collective bargaining. Section 8 (5) simply established the employer's duty to "bargain collectively" with the employees' representative, "subject to the provisions of Section 9 (a) ." Section 9 (a) provided that the representatives designated or selected by the employees in an appropriate unit shall be the exclusive representative "for the purposes of collective bargaining in respect to *rates of pay, wages, hours of employment, or other conditions of employment. . . .*" These were the crucial words that formed the basis for determining the subjects about which bargaining was compulsory.

In 1947 Congress briefly defined the procedural requirements of collective bargaining.[1] However, no attempt was made to describe the subjects of bargaining, except that the essential phrase in Section 9 (a), "wages, hours, and other [terms and] conditions of employment," (but omitting "rates of pay") was incorporated into the Section 8 (d) definition of bargaining.

The Supreme Court has declared that

the term "bargaining collectively" as used in the [National Labor Relations] Act "has been considered to absorb and give statutory approval to the philosophy of bargaining as worked out in the labor movement in the United States." [2]

---

[1] §8(d), added by the Labor Management Relations Act of 1947 (Taft-Hartley Act) . *See* Chapter 11 *supra* on the requirements of good faith bargaining.

[2] NLRB v. American Nat'l Ins. Co., 343 US 395, 408, 30 LRRM 2147 (1952) , quoting from Order of R.R. Telegraphers v. Ry. Exp. Agency, 321 US 342, 346, 14 LRRM 506 (1944) , in which the Court had also stated that "effective collective bargaining has been generally conceded to include the right of the representatives of the unit to be consulted and to bargain about the exceptional as well as the routine rates, rules, and working conditions." 321 US at 347.

But the Act contains no simple litmus test for determining whether a particular subject is within that recognized "philosophy of bargaining." Therefore, in the absence of a precise statutory definition, the Board, very early, assumed the role of determining what are and what are not compulsory subjects. In 1940, in *Singer Mfg. Co.*,[3] the Board held that

> [p]aid holidays, vacations, and bonuses constitute an integral part of the earnings and working conditions of the employees and . . . are matters which are generally the subject of collective bargaining. . . . [I]nsistence upon treating such matters as gratuities to be granted and withdrawn at will, constitutes a refusal to bargain. . . .[4]

Following the *Singer* case, the Board held that various integral parts of the employment relationship were embraced by Section 9 (a).[5] These included such subjects as discharges,[6] pensions,[7] profit sharing,[8] work loads and work standards,[9] insurance benefits,[10] the closed and union shop,[11] subcontracting,[12] shop rules,[13] work schedules,[14] rest periods,[15] and merit increases.[16]

---

[3] 24 NLRB 444, 6 LRRM 405 (1940), *enforced,* 119 F 2d 131, 8 LRRM 740 (CA 7, 1941).

[4] 24 NLRB at 470.

[5] Cox & Dunlop, *Regulation of Collective Bargaining by the National Labor Relations Board,* 63 HARV. L. REV. 389, 397-401 (1950).

[6] NLRB v. Bachelder, 120 F 2d 574, 8 LRRM 723 (CA 7, 1941).

[7] Inland Steel Co., 77 NLRB 1, 21 LRRM 1310 (1948), *enforced,* 170 F 2d 247, 22 LRRM 2505 (CA 7, 1948), *cert. denied,* 336 US 960, 24 LRRM 2019 (1949).

[8] Union Mfg. Co., 76 NLRB 322, 21 LRRM 1187 (1948), *enforced,* 179 F 2d 511, 25 LRRM 2302 (CA 5, 1950).

[9] Woodside Cotton Mills Co., 21 NLRB 42, 6 LRRM 68 (1940).

[10] W. W. Cross & Co., 77 NLRB 1162, 22 LRRM 1131 (1948), *enforced,* 174 F 2d 875, 24 LRRM 2068 (CA 1, 1949); General Motors Corp., 81 NLRB 779, 23 LRRM 1422 (1949), *enforced,* 179 F 2d 221, 25 LRRM 2281 (CA 2, 1950).

[11] Winona Textile Mills, Inc., 68 NLRB 702, 18 LRRM 1154 (1946), *enforced,* 160 F 2d 201, 19 LRRM 2417 (CA 7, 1947); Andrew Jergens Co., 76 NLRB 363, 21 LRRM 1192 (1948), *enforced,* 175 F 2d 130, 24 LRRM 2096 (CA 9, 1949), *cert. denied,* 338 US 827, 24 LRRM 2561 (1949); Alexander Milburn Co., 62 NLRB 482, 16 LRRM 202 (1945), *supplemented,* 78 NLRB 747, 22 LRRM 1249 (1948).

[12] Timken Roller Bearing Co., 70 NLRB 500, 18 LRRM 1370 (1946), *enforcement denied on other grounds,* 161 F 2d 949, 20 LRRM 2204 (CA 6, 1947); *cf.* Emerson Elec. Mfg. Co., 13 NLRB 448, 4 LRRM 307 (1939).

[13] Timken Roller Bearing Co., *supra.*

[14] Inter-City Advertising Co., 61 NLRB 1377, 1384, 16 LRRM 153 (1945), *enforcement denied on other grounds,* 154 F 2d 244, 17 LRRM 916 (CA 4, 1946); Wilson & Co., 19 NLRB 990, 999, 5 LRRM 560, 115 F 2d 759, 7 LRRM 575 (CA 8, 1940); Woodside Cotton Mills Co., 21 NLRB 42, 54-55, 6 LRRM 68 (1940).

[15] National Grinding Wheel Co., 75 NLRB 905, 21 LRRM 1095 (1948).

[16] Aluminum Ore Co. v. NLRB, 131 F 2d 485, 11 LRRM 693 (CA 7, 1942), *enforcing* 39 NLRB 1286, 10 LRRM 49 (1942); NLRB v. J. H. Allison & Co., 165 F 2d 766, 21 LRRM 2238 (CA 6, 1948), *cert. denied,* 335 US 814, 22 LRRM 2564 (1948), *enforcing* 70 NLRB 377, 18 LRRM 1369 (1946).

All of these determinations were made during the Wagner Act period.

In a statement presented in 1947 to the Senate committee considering amendments to the Wagner Act, NLRB Chairman Paul Herzog asserted that the scope of collective bargaining "depends upon the industry's customs and history, the previously existing employer-employee relationship, technological problems and demands, and other factors," adding that the scope might "vary with changes in industrial structure and practice." He suggested that the job of defining the area of bargaining should be left to the Board, subject only to judicial review.[17]

Although Congress amended the Act extensively in 1947, it provided for no basic change in the legislative framework supporting the Board's definitions of the subjects of bargaining. As previously noted, the phrase "wages, hours of employment, and other conditions of employment," [18] which the Board had construed in the context of Section 9 (a), now became with the addition of "terms" of employment, part of the definition of collective bargaining written into Section 8 (d).

Despite the failure of Congress to define bargaining in the Taft-Hartley amendments, the developing law of collective bargaining [19] has shown a decided pattern of change—but change based more upon general trends in the economy than upon the predicted exercise of flexible administrative direction applied industry by industry. However, Chairman Herzog's suggestion that the task of defining the subjects of bargaining be left exclusively to the Board and to the courts has been adopted. Indeed, Justice Stewart, joined by Justices Douglas and Harlan, concurring in the 1964 *Fibreboard* decision,[20] concluded that

> [t]here was a time when one might have taken the view that the National Labor Relations Act gave the Board and the courts no power to determine the subjects about which the parties must bar-

---

17 *Hearings Before Senate Committee on Labor and Public Welfare on S. 55 and S. J. Res. 22*, 80th Cong., 1st Sess. 1914 (1947). For a discussion of this legislative background and the early judicial history of collective bargaining, *see* Cox and Dunlop, *supra*, note 5 *and* Smith, *The Evolution of the "Duty to Bargain" Concept in American Law*, 39 MICH. L. REV. 1066 (1941).
18 "[R]ates of pay," evidently deemed redundant, was omitted from §8 (d).
19 *See* Chapter 15 *infra*.
20 Fibreboard Paper Prods. Corp. v. NLRB, 379 US 203, 57 LRRM 2609 (1964). *See* Chapter 15 *infra*.

gain. . . . But too much law has been built upon a contrary assumption for this view any longer to prevail, and I question neither the power of the Court to decide this issue nor the propriety of its doing so.[21]

II. *BORG-WARNER:* THE DISTINCTION BETWEEN MANDATORY AND PERMISSIVE SUBJECTS

From the statutory language requiring the parties to "confer in good faith with respect to wages, hours, and other terms and conditions of employment," a distinction has evolved between *mandatory* and *permissive* subjects of bargaining. In 1958 the Supreme Court affirmed and adopted this distinction in *NLRB v. Wooster Division of the Borg-Warner Corp.*[22] Reading Sections 8 (a) (5) and 8 (d) together,[23] the Court declared that

> these provisions establish the obligation of the employer and the representative of its employees to bargain with each other in good faith with respect to "wages, hours, and other terms and conditions of employment. . . ." The duty is limited to those subjects, and within that area neither party is legally obligated to yield. . . . As to other matters, however, each party is free to bargain or not to bargain, and to agree or not to agree.[24]

Lawful subjects of bargaining have thus been divided into two groupings: mandatory subjects and permissive subjects. These are discussed in Chapters 15 and 16, respectively. A third category, illegal subjects of bargaining, refers to subjects that may not lawfully be included in the collective agreement and about which the parties may not lawfully bargain. This category is also treated in Chapter 16.

The proposals at issue in *Borg-Warner* were a "recognition" clause and a "ballot" clause, both of which had been insisted upon

---

[21] 379 US at 219, n. 2. *Contrast* the statement of Senator Walsh, Chairman of the Senate Education and Labor Committee when the Wagner Act was being passed: "The bill indicates the method and manner in which employees may organize, the method and manner of selecting their representatives or spokesmen, and leads them to the office door of their employer with the legal authority to negotiate for their fellow employees. The bill does not go beyond the office door. It leaves the discussion between the employer and the employee, and the agreements which they may or may not make, voluntary and with that sacredness and solemnity to a voluntary agreement with which both parties to an agreement should be enshrouded." 79 Cong. Rec. 7659 (1935). *See* H. K. Porter Co. v. NLRB, 397 U.S. 99, 73 LRRM 2561 (1970).

[22] 356 US 342, 42 LRRM 2034 (1958).

[23] The same reasoning is also applicable to §8 (b) (3).

[24] 356 US at 349, citing NLRB v. American Nat'l Ins. Co., 343 US 395, 30 LRRM 2147 (1952). For an earlier and somewhat analogous categorization, *see* Cox & Dunlop, *supra,* note 5.

by the employer during collective bargaining. The recognition clause disregarded the Board's certification of the local union's parent international as bargaining agent and would have given contractual recognition to the local union only. The ballot clause provided that with respect to nonarbitrable disputes there would be a 30-day negotiation period followed by a secret-ballot vote of all bargaining-unit employees—union as well as nonunion. If the employer's last offer was rejected, the employer would have 72 hours within which to modify its position, followed by a repetition of the voting process. After exhausting these procedures the union would be free to strike. Borg-Warner maintained that both clauses were prerequisites to its reaching an agreement.

The Board found that Borg-Warner had not bargained in bad faith; but the insistence upon inclusion of both clauses in any agreement signed by the company was held to be *per se* violative of Section 8 (a) (5).[25] Agreeing with the Board's approach, the Supreme Court declared that

> good faith does not license the employer to refuse to enter into agreements on the ground that they do not include some proposal which is not a mandatory subject of bargaining. . . . [S]uch conduct is, in substance, a refusal to bargain about the subjects that are within the scope of mandatory bargaining. This does not mean that bargaining is to be confined to the statutory subjects. Each of the two controversial clauses is lawful in itself. Each would be enforceable if agreed to by the unions. But it does not follow that, because the company may propose these clauses, it may lawfully insist upon them as a condition to any agreement.[26]

The Court then affirmed the Board's findings.

The "ballot" clause related only to the procedure to be followed by the employees before the union acted to reject a final offer or to call a strike. Unlike the ordinary no-strike clause, which "regulates the relations between the employer and the employees," [27] the ballot clause "deals only with relations between the employees and their unions. . . . [B]y weakening the independence of the 'representative' chosen by the employees . . . [i]t

25 Wooster Division of Borg-Warner Corp., 113 NLRB 1288, 36 LRRM 1439 (1955), *enforced*, 236 F 2d 898, 38 LRRM 2660 (CA 6, 1956), *reversed in part*, 356 US 342, 42 LRRM 2034 (1958), *remanded*, 260 F 2d 785, 42 LRRM 2116 (CA 6, 1958).
26 356 US at 349.
27 *Id.* at 350.

enables the employer, in effect, to deal with its employees rather than with their statutory representative." [28]

The "recognition" clause also was deemed a nonmandatory subject because it was considered an evasion of the duty to bargain with the certified representative for the employer "to insist that the certified representative not be a party to the collective bargaining contract." [29]

Borg-Warner thus teaches that regardless of a party's good faith in bargaining, he commits an unfair labor practice by insisting to impasse upon incorporation of permissive subject matter in the collective bargaining contract, i.e., subject matter outside the scope of "wages, hours, and other terms and conditions of employment." [30]

The implications of the *Borg-Warner* distinction may be seen in the Court's decision in *NLRB v. American Nat'l Ins. Co.*,[31] a case pre-dating *Borg-Warner*.

The Court held in *American Nat'l* that an employer's insistence upon a management-rights clause covering such items as promotions, discipline, and work scheduling, and excluding these matters from arbitration, was not a *per se* violation of Section 8 (a) (5). In so holding, the Court rejected the Board's position that such insistence by the employer constituted an independent refusal to bargain.[32] The Board had reasoned that some of the matters covered by the proposed management-rights clause were "conditions of employment" and, therefore, appropriate subjects of bargaining. According to the Board, the employer's insistence that it retain responsibility for these conditions of employment for the duration of the agreement undermined the union's right to bargain with respect to such conditions. Rejecting this argument, the Court stated that

---

28 *Ibid.*
29 *Ibid.*
30 The bargaining rules under §§8 (a) (5) and 8 (b) (3) vary depending on whether a given topic is a mandatory, permissive, or illegal subject for collective bargaining. *See* discussion *infra*. *See also* Note, *Subjects Included Within Management's Duty to Bargain Collectively*, 26 LA. L. REV. 630 (1966) ; Goetz, *Employer's Duty to Bargain About Changes in Operations*, DUKE L. J. 1 (1964) ; Note, *Employer's Duty to Bargain About Subcontracting and Other "Management" Decisions*, 64 COLUM. L. REV. 294 (1964) ; Fleming, *The Changing Duty to Bargain*, 14 LAB. L. J. 297 (1963) .
31 343 US 395, 30 LRRM 2147 (1952) . *See also* discussion in Chapter 15 *infra*.
32 American Nat'l Ins. Co., 89 NLRB 185, 25 LRRM 1532 (1950) , *enforced in part*, 185 F 2d 307, 27 LRRM 2405 (CA 5, 1951) , *affirmed*, 343 US 395, 30 LRRM 2147 (1952) .

Congress provided expressly that the Board should not pass upon the desirability of the substantive terms of labor agreements. Whether a contract should contain a clause fixing standards for such matters as work schedules or should provide for more flexible treatment of such matters is an issue for determination across the bargaining table, not by the Board. If the latter approach is agreed upon, the extent of union and management participation in the administration of such matters is itself a condition of employment to be settled by bargaining.[33]

Stated in *Borg-Warner* terms, the Court was holding that insistence by the employer upon a proposal that would limit the bargaining representative's control over conditions of employment was itself insistence upon a condition of employment and, therefore, not *per se* violative of the Act.[34]

The *Borg-Warner* separation of the mandatory from the permissive is applicable to the entire concept of duty to bargain. The duty to bargain required by Sections 8 (a) (5) and 8 (b) (3), treated in detail in Chapter 11, refers to the duty to bargain about mandatory subjects. There is no legal duty to bargain about permissive subjects.

Illustrative of the absolute nature of the bargaining duty for mandatory subjects is *NLRB v. Katz*.[35] The issue was whether an employer violates the duty "to bargain collectively" by instituting changes in matters that are subjects of mandatory bargaining and that are, in fact, under discussion without first consulting the union with which it is carrying on negotiations. The Supreme Court held such conduct to be *per se* violative of Section 8 (a) (5), reasoning that since

[t]he duty "to bargain collectively" . . . is defined by Section 8 (d) as the duty to "meet . . . and confer in good faith, with respect to wages, hours and other terms and conditions of employment." . . . Clearly, the duty thus defined may be violated without a general failure of subjective good faith; for there is no occasion to consider

---

33 343 US at 408-09.
34 *See* Wollett, *The Borg-Warner Case on the Role of the NLRB in the Bargaining Process*, 12 NYU ANNUAL CONF. ON LABOR 39 (1959), for a different conclusion with respect to the relationship between *Borg-Warner* and *American Nat'l Ins. Co.*
35 369 US 736, 50 LRRM 2177 (1962); *see also* NLRB v. Crompton-Highlands Mills, Inc., 337 US 217, 24 LRRM 2088 (1949); May Dept Stores Co. v. NLRB, 326 US 376, 17 LRRM 643 (1945); Quaker State Oil Ref. Co. v. NLRB, 270 F 2d 40, 44 LRRM 2297 (CA 3, 1959), *cert. denied*, 361 US 917, 45 LRRM 2249 (1959); NLRB v. George P. Pilling & Son Co., 119 F 2d 32, 8 LRRM 557 (CA 3, 1941). *See* Chapter 11 *supra* for discussion of *per se* violations of the duty to bargain.

the issue of good faith if a party has refused even to negotiate *in fact*
—"to meet . . . and confer"—about any of the mandatory subjects.
A refusal to negotiate *in fact* as to any subject which is within Section 8 (d) and about which the union seeks to negotiate, violates
Section 8 (a) (5) though the employer has every desire to reach agreement with the union upon an over-all collective agreement and
earnestly and in all good faith bargains to that end.[36]

Therefore, when the employer unilaterally changes wages or conditions of employment as to which the union has either sought
negotiation or is seeking negotiation, he violates Section 8(a)(5),
"for it is a circumvention of the duty to negotiate which frustrates
the objectives of Section 8(a)(5) much as does a flat refusal." [37]

Absent an impasse in negotiations, a unilateral change in a
mandatory subject of bargaining may be treated as a *per se* refusal to bargain. The cases and principles applicable to such
unilateral changes are treated in Chapter 11; however, some
aspects of the bargaining impasse are here noted. For example,
after bargaining to an impasse,[38] an employer may unilaterally put
into effect his proposed changes in mandatory subject matter. But
the impasse must be legally cognizable. It cannot be attributable
to a failure to bargain in good faith by the party claiming the
"impasse." [39] And the fact that an employer's unilateral action
with respect to certain mandatory subjects, such as seniority rights
and grievance procedures, occurs at a time when no collective
bargaining agreement is in effect does not excuse the employer's
conduct.[40]

The addition of a permissive subject of bargaining to a series of
mandatory bargaining subjects may suffice to establish a violation
of Section 8 (a) (5) where the employer has conditioned agreement on the acceptance of all these terms.[41] In order to establish
a violation of Section 8 (a) (5), it is thus not always essential

---

[36] 369 US at 742-743.
[37] *Id.* at 743. *See* Chapter 11 *supra* at notes 336-349.
[38] As generally used in collective bargaining, "impasse" is synonymous with "dead-lock."
[39] Industrial Union of Marine & Shipbuilding Workers v. NLRB, 320 F 2d 615, 53 LRRM 2878 (CA 3, 1963), *cert. denied,* 375 US 984, 55 LRRM 2134 (1964).
[40] 320 F 2d at 620.
[41] *Id.* at 618. *See also* Philip Carey Mfg. Co. v. NLRB, 331 F 2d 720, 55 LRRM 2821 (CA 6, 1964), *cert. denied,* 379 US 888, 57 LRRM 2307 (1964); NLRB v. American Compress Warehouse, 350 F 2d 365, 59 LRRM 2739 (CA 5, 1965).

to show that insistence upon a permissive subject of bargaining is the sole reason for the impasse.[42]

Some principles to be gleaned from *Borg-Warner* and other cases relating to bargaining about mandatory and permissive subjects, applicable to both parties, may be summarized as follows: [43]

(1) A party has a statutory obligation to bargain only with respect to wages, hours, and other terms and conditions of employment. It is mandatory that he bargain about these issues. A refusal to negotiate as to such matters is, even without a finding of "bad faith," violative of the Act. Unilateral action with respect to such matters may be a *per se* violation.

(2) Since Section 8 (d) imposes no duty upon a party either to agree or to make concessions with respect to mandatory subjects, no violation of the Act results from insistence, to the point of deadlock, upon a proposal relating to wages, hours, and other terms and conditions of employment.

(3) Conversely, if the proposed subject matter is a permissive subject—outside the mandatory preserve—a party has no right to insist on bargaining on such matter. The proponent cannot precondition a bargain upon the inclusion of permissive subject matters in the collective agreement. The opponent has the right to be adamant not only in refusing to include permissive bargaining subjects in the contract but also in refusing even to bargain with respect to such subjects.

(4) Insistence upon incorporation of a permissive bargaining subject in the agreement need not be the sole cause for impasse in order to establish a violation of the duty to bargain.

(5) The foregoing restrictions on bargaining notwithstanding,

---

[42] Preliminary to any determination of a §8 (a) (5) violation by insistence upon a permissive subject of bargaining is definition of the term "insistence." The union in *Philip Carey Manufacturing, supra* note 41, urged that advocacy equalled insistence. However, the Sixth Circuit summarily rejected this argument, holding that "insistence" means positing the nonmandatory subject matter as an ultimatum or as a precondition to the negotiation of an agreement. The case involved a proposed superseniority provision. *Cf.* NLRB v. Erie Resistor Corp., 373 US 221, 53 LRRM 2121 (1963).

[43] For a detailed discussion of the requirements of bargaining, see Chapter 11 *supra*. For treatment of collective bargaining in relation to the antitrust laws, *see* Chapter 29 *infra*.

incorporation of permissive subject matter into a collective bargaining contract does not violate the National Labor Relations Act.

III. ILLEGAL SUBJECTS

Illegal subjects of bargaining include collective bargaining proposals or provisions in a collective contract that require some action that is unlawful or inconsistent with the basic policy of the Act.[44] These subjects may not lawfully be included in a bargaining contract, regardless of the parties' intent and regardless of their efforts to waive or acquiesce with respect to such inclusion. It is recognized that "an employer or union cannot insist upon a clause which would be illegal under the Act's provisions." [45]

Examples of illegal subjects are a provision for a closed shop,[46] a provision for a hiring hall that gives preference to union members,[47] a "hot cargo" clause that violates Section 8 (e) ,[48] a contract provision that is inconsistent with a union's duty of fair representation,[49] and contract clauses that discriminate among employees on the basis of race.[50] Illegal subjects of bargaining are treated in detail in Chapter 16.

---

44 In Meat Cutters Union (Great Atlantic & Pac. Tea Co.) , 81 NLRB 1052, 1061, 23 LRRM 1464 (1949) , the Board declared that "[t]he duty to bargain, which rests alike upon the employer and the representative of the employees, involves the obligation to bargain in good faith concerning terms and conditions of employment which are permitted by law. Neither party may require that the other agree to contract provisions which are unlawful. And when . . . one of the parties creates a bargaining impasse by insisting, not in good faith, that the other agree to an unlawful condition of employment, that party has violated its statutory duty to bargain."
45 NLRB v. Wooster Div. of Borg-Warner, 356 US 342, 360, 42 LRRM 2034 (1958) , concurring opinion, Harlan, J.
46 Penello v. United Mine Workers, 88 F Supp 935, 25 LRRM 2368 (D DC, 1950) . *See* Chapter 26 *infra.*
47 NLRB v. Nat'l Maritime Union, 175 F 2d 686, 24 LRRM 2268 (CA 2, 1949) , *cert. denied,* 338 US 954, 25 LRRM 2395 (1950) . *See* Chapter 26 *infra.*
48 Amalgamated Lithographers, Local 17, 130 NLRB 985, 47 LRRM 1374 (1961) . *See* Chapter 24 *infra.*
49 Local 1367, Int'l Longshoremen's Ass'n (Galveston Maritime Ass'n) , 148 NLRB 897, 57 LRRM 1083 (1964) , *enforced,* 368 F 2d 1010, 63 LRRM 2559 (CA 5, 1966) . *See* Chapter 27 *infra.*
50 *Ibid. Cf.* Indep. Metal Workers Union (Hughes Tool Co.) , 147 NLRB 1573, 56 LRRM 1289 (1964) . *See* Chapter 27 *infra.*

CHAPTER 15

MANDATORY SUBJECTS OF BARGAINING

Since the language of the Act compels bargaining [1] with respect to wages, hours, and other terms and conditions of employment,[2] bargaining about such subjects is, of course, mandatory. But the bargaining must be confined to specifying labor standards for employees within the bargaining unit. "[T]here is nothing in the labor policy indicating that the union and the employers in one bargaining unit are free to bargain about the wages, hours and working conditions of other bargaining units or to attempt to settle these matters for the entire industry." [3] Even an agreement that the union "will seek specified labor standards outside the bargaining unit," that is, with other employers, has been condemned by the Supreme Court as violative of antitrust legislation.[4] Where the other bargaining unit is composed of employees of the same employer, no antitrust issue is presented.

The language "rates of pay, wages, hours and other terms and conditions of employment" fixes not only the subjects about which the employer and the union are compelled by law to bargain but also the field in which (1) the employer is barred from unilateral action and (2) the employee is excluded from making his own individual agreement with the employer, unless the union waives in whole or in part its right to preempt all unilateral action or individual bargaining with respect to this subject matter.[5]

The term "wages and hours," in the conventional sense, requires no elucidation. It suffices to note that as to such subjects collective

---

[1] §§8 (a) (5) and 8 (b) (3).
[2] §8(d). §9(a) refers to "rates of pay, wages, hours of employment, or other conditions of employment. . . ."
[3] United Mine Workers v. Pennington, 381 US 657, 666, 59 LRRM 2369 (1964).
[4] 381 US at 668. See Chapter 29 infra.
[5] NLRB v. Katz, 369 US 736, 742-45, 50 LRRM 2177 (1962). See Chapter 11 supra.

bargaining is compulsory. But what and how much are embraced by the phrase "other terms and conditions of employment," and how broadly or how narrowly have the Board and the courts defined "wages" and "hours"? These are the questions to which this chapter is directed.

Many subjects, as for instance paid holidays, paid vacations, and paid sick leave, literally fall within each of the three classifications, wages, hours, and other terms and conditions of employment. No case has been found which turns upon this distinction.

I. WAGES

The categories "rates of pay" and "wages" have been given a broad construction by the Board and the courts to cover every form of compensation for labor performed, whether direct or indirect, as well as every form of agreement to protect standards of compensation.

A. Obvious Examples

Some mandatory subjects falling under the heading of "wages," as that term is used in the Act, are so obvious that little discussion of these items is required. Basic hourly rates of pay [6] clearly constitute wages. And despite some litigation over piece rates and incentive plans,[7] there apparently is no doubt that these items are mandatory subjects. Overtime pay [8] constitutes wages. The same is true of shift differentials.[9] And there is no question that paid holidays,[10] paid vacations [11] and severance pay [12] also qualify as compensation for services performed.

---

[6] Beacon Piece Dyeing & Finishing Co., 121 NLRB 953, 42 LRRM 1489 (1958).

[7] See C & S Indus., Inc., 158 NLRB 454, 62 LRRM 1043 (1966); Honolulu Star Bulletin, Inc., 153 NLRB 763, 59 LRRM 1533 (1965); Staub Cleaners, Inc., 148 NLRB 278, 56 LRRM 1515 (1964); Skyway Luggage Co., 117 NLRB 681, 39 LRRM 1310 (1957); and Central Metallic Casket Co., 91 NLRB 572, 26 LRRM 1520 (1950). Of course, a union may waive a right to compel bargaining over an item of wages, e.g., inauguration of an incentive plan during the term of an agreement. Libby, McNeill & Libby, 65 NLRB 873, 17 LRRM 250 (1946).

[8] See Braswell Motor Freight Lines, Inc., 141 NLRB 1154, 52 LRRM 1467 (1963).

[9] Smith Cabinet Mfg. Co., 147 NLRB 1506, 56 LRRM 1418 (1964).

[10] Singer Mfg. Co., 24 NLRB 444, 6 LRRM 405 (1940), enforced, 119 F 2d 131 (CA 7, 1941).

[11] Ibid.

[12] See NLRB v. Adams Dairy, 322 F 2d 553, 54 LRRM 2171 (CA 8, 1963), vacated, 379 US 644, 58 LRRM 2192 (1965), on remand, 350 F 2d 108, 60 LRRM 2084 (CA 8, (1965), cert. denied, 382 US 1011, 61 LRRM 2192 (1966).

B. Examples Requiring Elaboration

Some topics which may not appear on their face to be wages have been held to constitute wages for purposes of mandatory bargaining. The discussions under the following subheadings cover some of the less obvious examples of such items.

1. Christmas Bonuses. A Christmas bonus may be viewed as a gift or as wages. If the bonus is deemed compensation for services rendered or considered a condition of employment, it is a mandatory subject for bargaining.

The first significant court decision [13] concerning this issue approved the Board's holding that an employer must bargain over changes in a Christmas bonus which is in the nature of compensation. For a period of years the employer had paid a Christmas bonus to employees in the form of a percentage of employees' earnings. When the company installed a retirement plan, it notified the employees that this plan would cost more than the customary bonus and that consequently the amount of the bonus would be changed. The employer refused to bargain with the union concerning the bonus. The Board held that the bonus was a part of "wages" and required bargaining. Affirming the Board, the Second Circuit articulated the difference between bonus as gift and bonus as wages:

> It does, of course, merely beg the question to call . . . [the bonuses] "gifts" and to argue, however persuasively, that gifts *per se* are not a required subject of bargaining. But if these gifts were so tied to the remuneration which employees received for their work that they were in fact a part of it, they were in reality wages and so within the statute. . . . Where, as here, the so-called gifts have been made over a substantial period of time and in amounts that have been based on the respective wages earned by the recipients, the Board was free to treat them as bonuses not economically different from other special kinds of remuneration like pensions, retirement plans, or group insurance, to name but a few, which have been held within the scope of the statutory bargaining requirements.[14]

More recently, the Eighth Circuit concluded that a bonus was a gift on the basis of the following factors: (1) absence of consistency or regularity in the practice of awarding bonuses (which had been awarded during only three of the five years prior to 1962); (2) lack of uniformity in the amount of the bonus; and

---

[13] NLRB v. Niles-Bemont-Pond Co., 199 F 2d 713, 31 LRRM 2057 (CA 2, 1952).
[14] 199 F 2d at 714.

(3) dependence of the payment and the amount of the bonus on the financial condition of the employer.[15]

The foregoing are the types of factors that have generally been determinative in the characterizing of a particular bonus as gift or wages.[16] For example in *NLRB* v. *Citizens Hotel Co.*[17] the Fifth Circuit, finding that a Christmas bonus constituted wages, based its conclusion upon the regularity with which the employer had granted such bonuses (a period of 14 years), the existence of a formalized policy for establishing eligibility, and the employer's pre-employment reference to the bonus as an inducement to employment. A Section 8 (a) (5) violation was found even in the absence of any anti-union bias, although the lack of such bias prompted the court to deny enforcement of that part of the Board's order which found the company's conduct to be violative of Section 8 (a) (3).

The same court, however, required bargaining over Christmas bonuses in *General Tel. of Florida*,[18] rejecting estoppel as a defense. The company had argued that inaction by the union on this matter during the 35 years in which Christmas bonuses had been awarded estopped the union from asserting that discontinuance of bonuses was a mandatory subject of bargaining.[19]

---

[15] NLRB v. Wonder State Mfg. Co., 344 F 2d 210, 59 LRRM 2065 (CA 8, 1965).

[16] *E.g.*, NLRB v. United States Air Conditioning Corp., 336 F 2d 275, 57 LRRM 2068 (CA 6, 1964); NLRB v. Citizens Hotel Co., 326 F 2d 501, 55 LRRM 2135 (CA 5, 1964); NLRB v. Elec. Steam Radiator Corp., 321 F 2d 733, 54 LRRM 2092 (CA 6, 1963); NLRB v. Toffenetti Restaurant Co., 311 F 2d 219, 51 LRRM 2601 (CA 2, 1962); NLRB v. Wheeling Pipe Line, Inc., 229 F 2d 391, 37 LRRM 2403 (CA 8, 1956); NLRB v. Niles-Bemont-Pond Co., 199 F 2d 713, 31 LRRM 2057 (CA 2, 1952); Stark Ceramics, Inc., 155 NLRB 1258, 60 LRRM 1487 (1965); and American Lubricants Co., 136 NLRB 946, 49 LRRM 1888 (1962). *Cf.* K-D Mfg. Co., 169 NLRB No. 10, 67 LRRM 1140 (1968), where the Board found that an employer violated the Act by giving Christmas gifts only to non-bargaining-unit employees.

[17] 326 F 2d 501, 55 LRRM 2135 (CA 5, 1964). *See also* NLRB v. Exchange Parts Co., 339 F 2d 829, 58 LRRM 2097 (CA 5, 1964).

[18] General Tel. Co. of Fla. v. NLRB, 337 F 2d 452, 57 LRRM 2211 (CA 5, 1964).

[19] The court also rejected the employer's argument that deletion of an "existing benefits" clause from the current agreement constituted a waiver of the union's right to bargain over the question. However, the court modified the Board's remedy, since there was no finding of anti-union bias, and only required the employer to bargain over the two bonus checks which had not been paid and over any future discontinuance of such bonuses. In Peyton Packing Co., 129 NLRB 1275, 47 LRRM 1170 (1961), the Board found that the bonuses were withheld to punish employees for selecting the union, and full payment to all employees in the bargaining unit was required. The Board noted that the sizes of the bonuses were substantial and that payments amounted to as much as $1,000 per employee. *Cf.* Peyton Packing Co., 129 NLRB 1358, 47 LRRM 1211 (1961). For treatment of the unilateral discontinuance of a bonus as a violation of §8 (a) (3), *see* NLRB v. Elec. Steam Radiator Corp., 321 F 2d 733, 54 LRRM 2092 (CA 6, 1963); and for further consideration of Christmas bonuses in computation of back pay awards, *see* NLRB v. United States Air Conditioning Corp., 336 F 2d 275, 57 LRRM 2068 (CA 6, 1964).

2. Pension and Other Welfare Plans. *Inland Steel Co.*[20] raised the question of whether pension benefits are either wages or a condition of employment. The company contended that pension benefits are based upon an economic philosophy which holds them to be unrelated to productive effort on the part of employees, and for this reason pensions are not wages within the meaning of the Act. The Board rejected this argument, stating:

> With due regard for the aims and purposes of the Act, and the evils which it sought to correct, we are convinced and find that the term "wages" as used in Section 9 (a) must be construed to include emoluments of value, like pension and insurance benefits, which may accrue to employees out of their employment relationship. There is indeed an inseparable nexus between an employee's current compensation and his future pension benefits. . . . In substance, therefore, the respondent's monetary contribution to the pension plan constitutes an economic enhancement of the employee's money wage. . . . Realistically viewed, this type of wage enhancement or increase, no less than any other, becomes an integral part of the entire wage structure, and the character of the employee representatives interest in it, and the terms of its grant, is no different than in any other case where a change in the wage structure is effected.[21]

The Board also rejected the company's contention that the term "conditions of employment" was limited to the *physical* conditions under which employees work and did not apply to the terms or conditions under which employment status is offered.

The company's acts had spanned a period both before and after the effective date of the Taft-Hartley amendments adding Section 8 (d). The above comments by the Board were directed to language in the original statute. In considering the effect of the Taft-Hartley amendments, the Board found compelling evidence in legislative history that Congress recognized that pension and similar welfare plans fell within the meaning of wages or other conditions of employment as the Act had been written in 1935 and that Congress was willing to allow that conclusion to stand. The Board's order was upheld by the Seventh Circuit.[22]

---

[20] 77 NLRB 1, 21 LRRM 1310, *enforced*, 170 F 2d 247, 22 LRRM 2505 (CA 7, 1948), *cert. denied*, 336 US 960, 24 LRRM 2019 (1949). *See also* Pacific Coast Ass'n of Pulp & Paper Mfrs. v. NLRB, 304 F 2d 761, 50 LRRM 2626 (CA 9, 1962); Note, *Proper Subjects for Collective Bargaining: Ad Hoc v. Predictive Definition*, 58 Yale L. J. 803 (1949); Note, *Pension and Retirement Matters—a Subject of Compulsory Collective Bargaining*, 43 Ill. L. Rev. 713 (1948).
[21] 77 NLRB at 4-5.
[22] Inland Steel Co. v. NLRB, 170 F 2d 247, 22 LRRM 2505 (CA 7, 1948), *cert. denied*, 336 US 960, 24 LRRM 2019 (1949).

The duty to bargain with respect to pension plans may be continuous. Unilateral effectuation of a pension plan during the term of a collective bargaining agreement that has no provision for pensions violates Section 8 (a) (5). In *Allied Mills Inc.*[23] the employer urged that he was relieved from such a duty to bargain by the last paragraph of Section 8 (d), which provides that:

> the duties so imposed shall not be construed as requiring either party to discuss or agree to any modification of the terms and conditions contained in a contract for a fixed period, if such modification is to become effective before such terms and conditions can be reopened under the provision of the contract.

The Board rejected this argument, however, declaring that Section 8 (d) was intended to give stability to terms and conditions which have been embodied in a written contract; it has no reference to wages, hours, and other terms and conditions of employment that have not been so reduced to agreement.

The duty to bargain about benefits for retired employees is uncertain. In *Pittsburgh Plate Glass Co.*[24] the Board held that retirees are "employees" for purposes of bargaining about retirement benefits. It relied on 8(a)(3) cases covering applicants for employment [25] and former employees,[26] and cases under Section 302. The employer was found guilty of violating Section 8(a)(5) for refusing to bargain about a supplementary plan (prompted by enactment of Medicare legislation) and for unilaterally instituting

---

23 82 NLRB 854, 23 LRRM 1632 (1949). *See also* Tidewater Associated Oil Co., 85 NLRB 1097, 24 LRRM 1518 (1949); Jacobs Mfg. Co., 94 NLRB 1214, 28 LRRM 1162 (1951) (Board held employer had duty to bargain over pensions during negotiations conducted under a wage reopener in the agreement because the contract contained no pension provision and the subject matter had not been discussed when the previous contract was negotiated. The opposite result was reached on health and welfare because this subject had been discussed during prior negotiations.) *See* Wollett, *The Duty to Bargain Over the "Unwritten" Terms and Conditions of Employment,* 36 TEX. L. REV. 863 (1958). *Cf.* McMullans v. Kansas, Okla. & G. Ry., 229 F 2d 50, 37 LRRM 2363 (CA 10, 1956), for treatment of retirement plan under the Railway Labor Act.

24 177 NLRB No. 114, 71 LRRM 1433 (1969), *enforcement denied,* 427 F 2d 936, 74 LRRM 2425 (CA 6, 1970).

25 Phelps Dodge Corp. v. NLRB, 313 US 177, 8 LRRM 439 (1941); Local 872 Int'l Longshoremen's Ass'n, 163 NLRB 586, 64 LRRM 1467 (1967). For general treatment of employee coverage, see Chapter 28 *infra.*

26 Goodman Lumber Co., 166 NLRB No. 48, 65 LRRM 1650 (1967); Chemrock Corp., 151 NLRB 1074, 58 LRRM 1582 (1965).

its own plan instead.[27] Disagreeing with the extension of the statutory definition of "employee" to include retirees, the Sixth Circuit denied enforcement. Supreme Court review of the case was sought by the Board in November 1970.

Group health insurance is another mandatory subject of bargaining.[28] In the words of the First Circuit,

> the word "wages" in . . . the Act embraces within its meaning direct and immediate economic benefits flowing from the employment relationship. . . . [s]o construed the word covers a group insurance program for the reason that such a program provides a financial cushion in the event of illness or injury arising outside the scope of employment at less cost than such a cushion could be obtained through contracts of insurance negotiated individually.[29]

3. Profit-Sharing Plans. Profit-sharing plans have been held by both the Board and the courts to constitute a form of compensation to employees and hence to be a mandatory subject for bargaining.[30] In *Dicten & Masch Mfg.*,[31] the Board found a Section 8 (a) (5) violation because of the employer's refusal to discuss the terms and conditions of a profit-sharing plan. The employer's intention to effect such a plan was made known to the union during the course of a collective bargaining session. When a tentative

---

[27] Dissenting Member Zagoria noted some difficult questions raised by the majority ruling:
"For example, where the union currently representing employees in a bargaining unit is not the same one chosen by the retirees when they were actively employed, which union is the appropriate representative of the retirees? In some situations, the retirees may have earned their pension during a period in which the majority of employees rejected collective-bargaining representation. Is the present bargaining agent obligated to represent these retirees? If it does represent them, what is the extent of its duty of fair representation? Do the retirees have access to the Board or courts, if they feel they have been unfairly represented? May the bargaining agent require pensioners to comply with union-security requirements adopted by the active membership?"
For a discussion of this case and the duty to bargain about pensions generally, see Goetz, *Current Problems in Application of Federal Labor Law to Welfare and Pension Plans*, in LABOR LAW DEVELOPMENTS 1970, 107 (1970) (16th Annual Institute on Labor Law, Southwestern Legal Foundation).
[28] W. W. Cross & Co. v. NLRB, 174 F 2d 875, 24 LRRM 2068 (CA 1, 1949); General Motors Corp., 81 NLRB 779, 23 LRRM 1422 (1949). *See also* The Standard Oil Co., 92 NLRB 227, 27 LRRM 1073 (1950) and Sylvania Elec. Prods., Inc., 127 NLRB 924, 46 LRRM 1127 (1960) wherein the Board found the employer's refusal to furnish data as to the premium cost of a welfare plan to be a refusal to furnish wage data. To the same effect, *see* Stowe-Woodward, Inc., 123 NLRB 287, 43 LRRM 1415 (1959).
[29] 174 F 2d at 878.
[30] NLRB v. Black-Clawson Co., 210 F 2d 523, 33 LRRM 2567 (CA 6, 1954); Kroger Co. v. NLRB, 69 LRRM 2425 (CA 6, 1968).
[31] 129 NLRB 112, 46 LRRM 1516 (1960). *See also:* Union Mfg. Co., 76 NLRB 322, 21 LRRM 1187 (1948), *enforced,* 179 F 2d 511, 25 LRRM 2302 (CA 5, 1950); Kroger Co. v. NLRB, 399 F 2d 455, 68 LRRM 2731 (CA 6, 1968).

draft was shown to the union, the union negotiators suggested that it become a subject matter for discussion. The employer refused to discuss the plan, its position being that the program was entirely voluntary. A few days later, while still engaged in negotiations, the employer put the program into operation. Although the employer advised its employees that the plan was voluntary and could be revised or withdrawn at any time, it indicated that its intention was to continue it on a permanent basis. The Board's decision that such a profit-sharing plan is a mandatory subject for bargaining is consistent with its view that "wages" comprehends all emoluments of value accruing to any employee by reason of the employment relationship.

In accord with this view is a Board decision under Section 8(a)(1).[32] During the course of an organizing campaign at its plant, an employer spokesman indicated to the employees that an existing profit sharing plan was solely within the discretion of the employer, that the employer would not negotiate with respect to such a plan, and that the plan would be discontinued if the union won the election. This threat to refuse to bargain as to mandatory subject matter was held to be a clear threat of reprisal.

4. Stock Purchase Plans. *Richfield Oil Corp.*[33] presented the Board with the issue whether a stock purchase plan falls within the area requiring bargaining. Participation in the plan in question was open to all regular employees who had completed one year of service and who were between the ages of 30 and normal retirement age. Participants contributed a fixed sum from monthly earnings to the plan, and the company made contributions on behalf of participants ranging from 50 to 75 percent of an employee's payments into the plan. The monies were used by the plan's trustees to purchase Richfield common stock. Neither stock nor cash credited to an individual's account was distributable to the individual so long as he was a member of the plan. Despite the voluntary nature of the plan, the Board had no difficulty in concluding that this stock purchase plan was a form of wages and other conditions of employment.

---

[32] Cosmo Plastics, Inc., 143 NLRB 155, 53 LRRM 1278 (1963).
[33] 110 NLRB 356, 34 LRRM 1658 (1954), *enforced*, 231 F 2d 717, 37 LRRM 2327 (CA DC), *cert. denied*, 351 US 909, 37 LRRM 2837 (1956). See Note, *Employee Stock Purchase Plan is Within Scope of Compulsory Collective Bargaining*, 69 HARV. L. REV. 1511 (1956); Note, *Employer's Refusal to Bargain Concerning Terms and Conditions of a Stock Purchase Plan Is an Unfair Labor Practice Under Section 8(a)(5) of the Taft-Hartley Act*, 43 GEO. L.J. 309 (1955).

Management had argued without success that it would do violence to the basic policies of the Act to compel bargaining with respect to this subject. It contended that such bargaining (1) would require the employer to bargain about ownership and control of the company and (2) could result in the union obtaining a seat on both sides of the bargaining table. In reply to the first contention the Board stated:

> To the extent that such compulsory bargaining infringes upon the asserted right of an employer to dispose of his property and to run his business as he sees fit, that interference . . . is not decisively distinguishable from such intrusions in management affairs as occur whenever an employer fulfills his statutory obligation to bargain collectively, as, for example, when he bargains with respect to retirement and pension plans, group health and insurance programs, merit wage-increases, and profit sharing plans, all of which, the Board and Courts have held, lie within the statutory scope of collective bargaining.[34]

With respect to the second contention, the Board noted that the bargaining representative was entitled to represent those employees who were stockholders only in their capacity as employees.

5. Merit Wage Increases. The issue of whether an employer has a duty to bargain with respect to merit increases was first presented to the Board in *J. H. Allison & Co.*,[35] a case arising under the Wagner Act. A currently effective collective bargaining agreement contained a scale of minimum rates. When the employer granted a series of individual wage increases, characterized as "merit increases," the union sought details in order that it might intelligently negotiate on the matter. The employer refused to supply the requested information on the ground that the granting of merit increases is an exclusive managerial function and not a proper subject for bargaining. The union's request during the subsequent contract negotiations to incorporate a clause on merit increases into the contract met with a similar response.

---

[34] 110 NLRB at 362.
[35] 70 NLRB 377, 18 LRRM 1369 (1946), *enforced,* 165 F 2d 766, 21 LRRM 2238 (CA 6), *cert. denied,* 355 US 814, 22 LRRM 2564 (1948). *See also* Armstrong Cork Co. v. NLRB, 211 F 2d 843, 33 LRRM 2789 (CA 5, 1954); NLRB v. Dealers Engine Rebuilders, Inc., 199 F 2d 249, 31 LRRM 2007 (CA 8, 1952); Weston & Brooker Co., 154 NLRB 747, 60 LRRM 1015 (1965); Midwestern Instruments, Inc., 132 NLRB 1182, 48 LRRM 1793 (1961); and J. B. Cook Auto Mach. Co., 84 NLRB 688, 24 LRRM 1321 (1949).

The Board held the increases to be an integral part of the wage structure and as such a required subject for bargaining. In a later case [36] it held that this conclusion is not affected by the fact that it may be difficult or perhaps impossible to establish objective standards for awarding merit increases. On the other hand, where the collective agreement itself contained both a maximum and a minimum rate for each classification and a merit rating plan under which each employee was reviewed every four months, it was held that the company had no obligation to bargain with the union before putting individual merit increases into effect.[37]

The rationale for holding merit increases to be a mandatory bargaining subject is spelled out in the following language by the Fourth Circuit in *NLRB* v. *Berkeley Mach. Works*:[38]

> Merit pay where there are a number of employees means more than a gratuity or bonus paid to an occasional employee whom the company wishes to favor on account of his loyalty or efficiency. It means necessarily the formulation and application of standards; and such standards are proper subjects of collective bargaining. Collective bargaining with respect to wages might well be disrupted or become a mere empty form if the control over the wages of individual employees were thus removed from the bargaining area.[39]

In *White* v. *NLRB* [40] a question was raised whether merit increases can be granted if such action is consistent with the past practice of the employer. During the period between union certification and commencement of initial contract negotiations, the employer unilaterally increased the pay of five of the 60 members of the bargaining unit. Each increase was made in terms of the relationship of the particular individual to his job. The Fifth Circuit held that such increases were permissible. The Board moved for rehearing on the ground that the court had erred in its holding that an employer might grant individual merit increases without negotiating with the bargaining representative.[41] The court clarified its holding in a *per curiam* opinion as follows:

---

36 E. W. Scripps & Co., 94 NLRB 227, 28 LRRM 1033 (1951). *See also* Tidewater Associated Oil Co., 85 NLRB 1096, 24 LRRM 1518 (1949).
37 General Controls Co., 88 NLRB 1343, 25 LRRM 1475 (1950). The terms of the agreement were construed to permit this action and the *Allison* case, *supra* note 35, was thus distinguished.
38 189 F 2d 904, 28 LRRM 2176 (CA 4, 1951).
39 189 F 2d at 907.
40 255 F 2d 564, 42 LRRM 2001 (CA 5, 1958).
41 255 F 2d 564, 42 LRRM 2195 (CA 5, 1958).

Lest there be a misunderstanding, we state that we did not intend to and did not "thus hold." We found that these particular increases were in line with company policy to make merit increases, they had all accrued before bargain sessions commenced, and on the record as a whole did not amount to violations of either Section 8 (a) (1) or Section 8 (a) (5) of the Act. We contrasted this situation to that where there were *general* increases in the cases cited. . . .[42]

The Second Circuit reached a like result in another case.[43] It held that an increase of $5.00 per week to five employees plus an additional $5.00 per week to one of the same employees bore no resemblance to the "general increase" in rates of pay applicable to most employees which had been held to be improper in other cases.

It should be noted that these decisions by the Fifth and Second Circuits were rendered prior to the Supreme Court's decision in *NLRB* v. *Katz*,[44] wherein the Court confirmed that merit increases were subject to mandatory bargaining. In *Katz* the merit increases had been granted, without notice to the union, to less than half of the employees in the bargaining unit. Concerning the effect of the employer's long-standing practice of granting merit increases, which were not automatic but involved the exercise of discretion, the Court made the following observations:

This action . . . must be viewed as tantamount to an outright refusal to negotiate. . . . Whatever might be the case as to so-called "merit raises" which are in fact simply automatic increases to which the employer has already committed himself, the raises here in question were in no sense automatic, but were informed by a large measure of discretion. There simply is no way in such case for a union to know whether or not there has been a substantial departure from past practice, and therefore the union may properly insist that the company negotiate as to the procedures and criteria for determining such increases.[45]

6. Company Houses, Meals, Discounts, and Services. Generally, the rental of company-owned housing is a mandatory subject of bargaining.

In one case employees, though not required to live in company houses, lived there because housing in the area was scarce. Com-

---

[42] 255 F 2d at 574.
[43] NLRB v. Superior Fireproof Door & Sash Co., 289 F 2d 713, 47 LRRM 2817 (CA 2, 1961).
[44] 396 US 736, 50 LRRM 2177 (1962). *See* Chapter 11 *supra* at notes 340-349.
[45] 396 US at 746-47.

pany housing had been supplied to a part of the work force for many years at nominal rentals. The Board found that the housing represented an emolument of value in that it effected a saving of transportation expenses and accordingly ordered the employer to bargain about rentals.[46] The Fourth Circuit enforced the Board's order, holding that rental of company housing is a mandatory subject of bargaining if ownership and management of the housing materially affect the conditions of employment.[47] The court expanded upon an earlier decision [48] in which it had held the general subject matter of company houses to be a mandatory bargaining subject if the houses are a necessary part of the employer's enterprise or are rented at such a rate as to constitute a substantial part of an employee's pay.

The Board's established rule is that employer-provided living accommodations fall within "wages" and "conditions of employment" where the accommodations are an integral part of the employment relationship.[49] However, in some situations company housing may be treated as a permissive subject of bargaining. In one such case [50] the Fifth Circuit found that the evidence failed to support a conclusion that the rent charged for company houses was either wages or a condition of employment since the rental arrangement offered no substantial advantage to the employees. The court noted that other adequate housing was available with no transportation problem, that rentals for company housing were comparable to those of the community generally, and that there was no evidence that employees were required to live in the houses.[51]

[46] Lehigh Portland Cement Co., 101 NLRB 1010, 31 LRRM 1097 (1952).
[47] NLRB v. Lehigh Portland Cement Co., 205 F 2d 821, 32 LRRM 2463 (CA 4, 1953).
[48] NLRB v. Hart Cotton Mills, Inc., 190 F 2d 964, 28 LRRM 2434 (CA 4, 1951).
[49] See Elgin Standard Brick Mfg. Co., 90 NLRB 1467, 26 LRRM 1343 (1950); Hart Cotton Mills, Inc., 91 NLRB 728, 26 LRRM 1566 (1950), enforced, 190 F 2d 964, 28 LRRM 2434 (CA 4, 1951). The Board also has a line of cases holding company housing to be a condition of employment within §8(a)(3), which prohibits discrimination in such maters. W. T. Carter & Brother, 90 NLRB 2020, 26 LRRM 1427 (1950); Indianapolis Wire Bound Box Co., 89 NLRB 617, 26 LRRM 1005 (1950); Industrial Cotton Mills Co., 50 NLRB 855, 12 LRRM 241 (1943); Abbott Worsted Mills, Inc., 36 NLRB 545, 9 LRRM 163 (1941), enforced, 127 F 2d 438, 10 LRRM 590 (CA 1, 1942); and Great W. Mushroom Co., 27 NLRB 352, 7 LRRM 72 (1940).
[50] NLRB v. Bemis Bros. Bag Co., 206 F 2d 33, 32 LRRM 2535 (CA 5, 1953).
[51] Cf. NLRB Gen. Counsel Adm. Ruling No. K-209, 37 LRRM 1316 (1956), where the General Counsel refused to issue a complaint on a charge that an employer informed the employees that they must purchase or vacate company houses and that the company refused to discuss the matter with the union.

Nevertheless, "conditions of employment" are not limited to the compulsory aspects of the employer-employee relationship. Predating the housing cases was a case [52] in which the Board found company-provided meals to be both a condition of employment and wages. Although the company did not expressly require that employees eat on the job, they had no realistic alternative. The Board noted that it had consistently construed "wages" broadly enough to include emoluments of value supplementary to actual wage rates that accrue to an employee from his employment relationship.[53]

Although the Board has treated meal prices as a condition of employment, that position was repudiated by the Fourth Circuit in one notable case where the issue was whether an increase of one cent per cup of coffee served in the company cafeteria by an independent contractor was a mandatory subject of bargaining.[54] The court, sitting *en banc,* reversed both its own panel [55] and the Board, stating that it was not the intent of Congress to bring every act by an employer within the ambit of "conditions of employment." It therefore refused to equate "the trifles here involved" [56] with substantial mandatory subjects of bargaining. The Board did not follow the Fourth Circuit's approach, finding the employer in *McCall Corp.* guilty of a refusal to bargain for rejecting a union's request to bargain about price changes on food dispensed in plant vending machines, only to be reversed again by the same court on appeal.[57]

---

[52] Weyerhaeuser Timber Co., 87 NLRB 672, 25 LRRM 1163 (1949). *See also* Herman Sausage Co., 122 NLRB 168, 43 LRRM 1090 (1958), *enforced,* 275 F 2d 229, 45 LRRM 2829 (CA 5, 1960) (unilateral discontinuance of meal allowance held a §8(a)(5) violation).

[53] See Inland Steel Co., 77 NLRB 1, 21 LRRM 1310, *enforced,* 170 F 2d 247, 22 LRRM 2505 (CA 7, 1948), *cert. denied,* 366 US 960, 24 LRRM 2019 (1949).

[54] Westinghouse Elec. Corp., 156 NLRB 1080, 61 LRRM 1165, *enforcement denied,* 387 F 2d 542, 66 LRRM 2634 (CA 4, 1967).

[55] The court's original opinion had noted that independent eating facilities within a reasonable distance of the plant were inadequate, that the employer subsidized the operation by providing space at a rental of a dollar a year, and that the employer controlled the prices charged by the independent contractor. 369 F 2d 891, 64 LRRM 2001 (CA 4, 1966).

[56] 387 F 2d at 550.

[57] 172 NLRB No. 55, 69 LRRM 1187 (1968), *enforcement denied,* 432 F 2d 187, 75 LRRM 2223 (CA 4, 1970).

The Board has also held that an employer that had maintained a free investment service for employees for a number of years could not unilaterally begin charging a fee for this service.[58] Rejecting *de minimus* treatment, the Board reasoned that if the union could be ignored with respect to the investment service, the employer might later take a similar position with respect to other free employee services. The unilateral elimination of a gas discount has likewise been considered a violation of Section 8 (a) (5).[59] The Seventh Circuit regarded the discount as an emolument of value.

7. Truck Rentals and Price Lists. In several antitrust cases the Supreme Court has held that wages as a mandatory subject of bargaining embraced agreements reasonably designed to protect wage scales, although in form the agreements dealt with prices charged by bands for club dates or rental rates for leased trucks. In *Musicians* v. *Carroll* [60] the Court rejected the idea that "the distinction between mandatory and nonmandatory subjects turns on the form of the method taken to protect a wage scale." [61] In *Teamsters* v. *Oliver* [62] the Court based an antitrust exemption upon its determination that the minimum rental to be paid by carriers to their truck drivers with their own vehicles constituted a mandatory subject of bargaining. The object of the minimum rental provision was "to protect the negotiated wage scale against the possible undermining through diminution of the owner's wages for driving which might result from a rental which did not cover his operating costs." [63]

In *Carroll* the antitrust exemption for minimum price lists for orchestra leaders playing club dates was based on the fact that such minimums were deemed essential to protect the musicians' wage rates. The Court viewed the price floors, including established minimums for orchestra leaders, as "simply a means for

---

58 Seattle-First National Bank, 176 NLRB No. 97 (1969).
59 NLRB v. Central Ill. Pub. Serv. Co., 324 F 2d 916, 54 LRRM 2586 (CA 7, 1963). *See also:* Southland Paper Mills, Inc., 161 NLRB 1077, 63 LRRM 1386 (1966) (holding that a company cannot discontinue a hunting privilege, which the employees had previously enjoyed, without bargaining); Weston and Brooker Co., 154 NLRB 747, 60 LRRM 1015 (1965) (discontinuance of a canteen at which employees had been able to charge purchases and substitution of vending machines which made charging of purchases no longer possible was held to constitute a mandatory subject of bargaining).
60 American Federation of Musicians v. Carroll, 391 US 99, 68 LRRM 2230 (1968).
61 *Id.* at 110. *See* Chapter 29 *infra* at notes 151-155.
62 Local 24, Int'l Bhd. of Teamsters v. Oliver, 358 US 283 (1959).
63 *Id.* at 293-4.

coping with the job and wage competition of the leaders to protect the wage scales of musicians who respondents concede are employees on club dates, namely sidemen and subleaders." [64]

II. HOURS

Hours of employment have caused little difficulty in the area of mandatory subjects of bargaining in light of the express terms of Section 8 (d) of the Act. Thus over the years there have been few cases involving this particular topic.

Speaking in the context of an antitrust case, the Supreme Court expressed the bargaining obligation as follows:

> The particular hours of the day and the particular days of the week during which employees may be required to work are subjects well within the realm of wages, hours, and other terms and conditions of employment about which employers and unions must bargain.[65]

Six Justices in the case agreed that this obligation included whether hours were to fall in the daytime, nighttime, or on Sunday.[66]

In the earlier years, after World War II, however, one court, disagreeing with the Board, had held that the rearrangement of employees' working hours made "in the normal course of business" did not require prior consultation with the union.[67]

The Board, however, held to its original position, but in *Massey Gin and Machine Works, Inc.*[68] it found that the failure of the company to notify the union of a contemplated change in working hours was mitigated by an ambiguous contract provision and subsequent negotiation with the union.

---

[64] 391 US at 109. For a general discussion of the relation of the NLRA to the antitrust laws, *see* Chapter 29 *infra*.

[65] Amalgamated Meatcutters v. Jewel Tea Co., 381 US 676, 691, 59 LRRM 2376 (1965).

[66] For a discussion of the relation of mandatory subjects of bargaining to the antitrust laws, as exemplified by this case and United Mine Workers v. Pennington, 380 US 657, 59 LRRM 2369 (1965) (holding that a union's agreement with multi-employers to impose certain standards relating to mandatory subjects for bargaining on employers outside the multi-employers' bargaining unit would fall outside the union's exemption from the antitrust laws), *see* Chapter 29 *infra*.

[67] NLRB v. Inter-City Advertising Co., Inc., 154 F 2d 244, 17 LRRM 916 (CA 4, 1946).

[68] 78 NLRB 189, 22 LRRM 1191, *enforcement denied, per curiam*, 173 F 2d 758, 23 LRRM 2619 (CA 5, 1949), *cert. denied*, 338 US 910, 25 LRRM 2205 (1950).

In later decisions the Board has adhered to its basic position that hours, including work schedules and whether there should be Sunday work,[69] are a mandatory subject of bargaining. In *Weston and Brooker Co.*[70] the Board, relying upon the *Katz* case,[71] held the length of the workday to be a mandatory subject and that an employer's unilateral change constituted a Section 8 (a) (5) violation.

III. OTHER TERMS AND CONDITIONS OF EMPLOYMENT

A. Obvious and Settled Examples

Numerous topics fall within "other terms and conditions of employment" as this phrase is used in the Act. Many are now so clearly recognized to be mandatory subjects for bargaining that no discussion is required. Among these topics are the following: provisions for a grievance procedure [72] and arbitration,[73] layoffs,[74] discharge,[75] workloads,[76] vacations,[77] holidays,[78] sickleave,[79]

---

[69] Timken Roller Bearing Co., 70 NLRB 500, 18 LRRM 1370, (1946), *enforcement denied on other grounds,* 161 F 2d 949, 20 LRRM 2204 (CA 6, 1947). *See also* Camp & McInnes, Inc., 100 NLRB 524, 30 LRRM 1310 (1952); Inter-City Advertising Co., 61 NLRB 1377, 16 LRRM 153 (1945), *enforcement denied on other grounds,* 154 F 2d 244, 17 LRRM 916 (CA 4, 1946); Wilson & Co., 19 NLRB 990, 5 LRRM 560, 115 F 2d 759, 7 LRRM 575 (CA 8, 1940); Woodside Cotton Mills Co., 21 NLRB 42, 6 LRRM 68 (1940).

[70] 154 NLRB 747, 60 LRRM 1015 (1965).

[71] NLRB v. Katz, 396 US 736, 50 LRRM 2177 (1962), note 44 *supra.*

[72] Bethlehem Steel Co., 136 NLRB 1500, 50 LRRM 1013 (1962), *enforcement denied on other grounds,* 320 F 2d 615, 53 LRRM 2878 (CA 3, 1963); Crown Coach Co., 155 NLRB 625, 60 LRRM 1366 (1965); and Cranston Print Works Co., 115 NLRB 537, 37 LRRM 1346 (1956).

[73] NLRB v. Boss Mfg. Co., 118 F 2d 187, 8 LRRM 729 (CA 7, 1941); NLRB v. Montgomery Ward & Co., 133 F 2d 676, 12 LRRM 508 (CA 9, 1943); and U.S. Gypsum Co., 94 NLRB 112, 28 LRRM 1015 (1951).

[74] U. S. Gypsum Co., 94 NLRB 112, 113, 28 LRRM 1015 (1951); Hilton Mobile Homes, 155 NLRB 873, 60 LRRM 1411 (1965). *See also* Lasko Metal Prods., 148 NLRB 976, 57 LRRM 1108 (1964).

[75] *See* National Licorice Co. v. NLRB, 309 US 350, 6 LRRM 674 (1940); NLRB v. Bachelder, 120 F 2d 574, 8 LRRM 723 (CA 7, 1941).

[76] Beacon Piece Dyeing & Finishing Co., 121 NLRB 953, 42 LRRM 1489 (1958); Little Rock Downtowner, Inc., 145 NLRB 1286, 55 LRRM 1156 (1964) where employer ordered employees to stand at their stations at all times except when on breaks or relief, and the Board found a violation of §8 (a) (5) since there was an actual change in the work beyond "routine job directions." Irvington Motors, Inc., 147 NLRB 565, 56 LRRM 1257, *enforced,* 343 F 2d 759, 58 LRRM 2816 (CA 3, 1965), holding that fixing of sales quotas required bargaining; however, unilateral setting of requirement that salesmen make five telephone sales calls each day was not so clearly beyond a normal management function as to require notice to and consultation with the union. *Cf.* Little Rock Downtowner, Inc., 148 NLRB 717,

work rules,[80] use of bulletin boards by unions,[81] change of payment from a salary base to an hourly base,[82] definition of bargaining unit work,[83] and performance of bargaining unit work by supervisors.[84]

The Board also has held that bargaining about employee physical examinations is mandatory.[85] Duration of the collective agreement has likewise been held to be a mandatory subject.[86]

B. Examples Requiring Elaboration

Some topics of bargaining that constitute "other terms and conditions of employment" require more than a mere listing. Seniority, retirement age, and union security are among these mandatory topics, and litigation concerning them justifies a brief review of the cases in these areas; and with respect to management-rights clauses a note of caution is in order. The cases which

57 LRRM 1052 (1964) where motel maids were instructed to wash motel room windows every day; the Board held that an employer does not have an obligation to notify and consult the union with respect to matters that fall "within the normal area of detailed decisions relating to the manner in which work is to be performed."

77 Great Southern Trucking Co. v. NLRB, 127 F 2d 180, 10 LRRM 571 (CA 4, 1942).

78 NLRB v. Sharon Hats, Inc., 289 F 2d 628, 48 LRRM 2098 (CA 5, 1961); Leiter Mfg. Co., 112 NLRB 843, 36 LRRM 1123 (1955); Bradley Washfountain Co. v. NLRB, 192 F 2d 144, 29 LRRM 2064 (CA 7, 1951); and Instrument Div., Rockwell Register Corp., 142 NLRB 634, 53 LRRM 1113 (1963).

79 NLRB v. Katz, 369 US 736, 50 LRRM 2177 (1962).

80 NLRB v. Southern Transp., Inc., 343 F 2d 558, 58 LRRM 2822 (CA 8, 1965); Tower Hosiery Mills, Inc., 81 NLRB 658, 23 LRRM 1397 (1949); and Timken Roller Bearing Co., 70 NLRB 500, 18 LRRM 1370 (1946), enforcement denied on other grounds, 161 F 2d 949, 20 LRRM 2204 (CA 6, 1947).

81 NLRB v. Proof Co., 242 F 2d 560, 39 LRRM 2608 (CA 7), cert. denied, 355 US 831, 40 LRRM 2680 (1957).

82 General Motors Corp., 59 NLRB 1143, 15 LRRM 170 (1944).

83 Almeida Bus Lines, Inc., 142 NLRB 445, 53 LRRM 1055 (1963).

84 Crown Coach Corp., 155 NLRB 625, 60 LRRM 1366 (1965).

85 Le Roy Mach. Co., 147 NLRB 1431, 56 LRRM 1368 (1964), where the Board held that a management prerogatives clause constituted a union waiver of a right to require the employer to bargain about physical examinations during the term of the existing agreement. Cf. Wilburn v. Missouri-Kansas-Texas R. Co., 268 SW 2d 726 (Tex CivApp, 1954) (physical examinations are a subject of bargaining under the Railway Labor Act).

86 NLRB v. Yutana Barge Lines, Inc., 315 F 2d 524, 528, 52 LRRM 2750 (CA 9, 1963); U. S. Pipe & Foundry Co. v. NLRB, 298 F 2d 873, 49 LRRM 2540 (CA 5, 1962). The question of contract retroactivity is also a mandatory subject of bargaining. Bergen Point Iron Wks., 79 NLRB 1073, 22 LRRM 1475 (1948). However, bargaining about the requirement of employee ratification of a contract is not. In NLRB v. Darlington Veneer Co., 236 F 2d 85, 38 LRRM 2574 (CA 4, 1956), the Fourth Circuit found a violation of §8(a)(5) in an employer's insistence upon ratification of the contract by secret vote of the employees. Cf. NLRB v. Wooster Division of Borg-Warner, 356 US 342, 42 LRRM 2034 (1958); North Country Motors, Ltd., 146 NLRB 671, 55 LRRM 1421 (1964). For further discussion of the subject of ratification, see Chapter 16 infra at notes 33-35.

have involved subcontracting and partial closure of a business (with implications for developments in the area of automation[87]) have been highly controversial and require separate treatment. All of these topics are treated under the following subheadings.

1. Seniority, Promotions, and Transfers. Seniority, promotions, and transfers [88] are recognized as mandatory subjects for bargaining. Since seniority is so obviously a condition of employment—and is a condition commonly existing under union contracts,[89] litigation questioning its mandatory status has been minimal. But a few rulings should be noted. Probationary periods and attendant conditions require bargaining,[90] as do promotions within a bargaining unit.[91] An employer may not unilaterally revoke preferential seniority previously granted informally to union officers and negotiators,[92] nor may he abrogate seniority rights upon expiration of a collective agreement establishing these rights. Elimination of such an accrued benefit constitutes a change in a condition of employment.[93] Aptitude testing may not be unilaterally introduced; bargaining about such testing is required.[94]

2. Compulsory Retirement Age. In the *Inland Steel* case,[95] generally known for its holding that pensions are a mandatory subject for bargaining, it was also held by the Board and the Court of Appeals for the Seventh Circuit that the employer must bargain with the union on the subject of a compulsory retirement age. The Seventh Circuit stated:

> We are unable to differentiate between the conceded right of a Union to bargain concerning a discharge, and particularly a nondiscriminatory discharge, of an employee and its right to bargain

---

[87] *See* Renton News Record, 136 NLRB 1294, 49 LRRM 1972 (1962).

[88] U.S. Gypsum Co., 94 NLRB 112, 28 LRRM 1015 (1951).

[89] Ford Motor Co. v. Huffman, 345 US 330, 31 LRRM 2548 (1953).

[90] Oliver Corp., 162 NLRB 813, 64 LRRM 1092 (1967).

[91] Houston Chapter, Associated Gen. Contractors, 143 NLRB 409, 53 LRRM 1299 (1963), *enforced,* 349 F 2d 449, 59 LRRM 3013 (CA 5, 1965), *cert. denied,* 382 US 1026, 61 LRRM 2244 (1966).

[92] NLRB v. Proof Co., 242 F 2d 560, 39 LRRM 2608 (CA 7), *cert. denied,* 355 US 831, 40 LRRM 2680 (1957).

[93] NLRB v. Katz, 369 US 736, 50 LRRM 2177 (1962); Marine & Shipbuilding Workers v. NLRB (Bethlehem Steel Co.), 320 F 2d 615, 53 LRRM 2878 (CA 3, 1963). *See also* U. S. Gypsum Co., 94 NLRB 112, 28 LRRM 1015 (1951).

[94] American Gilsonite Co., 122 NLRB 1006 (1959).

[95] 77 NLRB 1, 21 LRRM 1316, *enforced,* 170 F 2d 247, 22 LRRM 2505 (CA 7, 1948), *cert. denied,* 356 US 960, 24 LRRM 2019 (1949). *See* note 20 *supra.*

concerning the age at which he is compelled to retire. In either case, the employee loses his job at the command of the employer; in either case, the effect upon the "conditions" of the person's employment is that the employment is terminated, and we think, in either case, the affected employee is entitled under the Act to bargain collectively through his duly selected representatives concerning such termination. In one instance, the cessation of employment comes perhaps suddenly and without advance notice or warning, while in the other, his employment ceases as a result of a plan announced in advance by the Company.[96]

A number of suits have been brought under the Railway Labor Act by employees challenging the validity of provisions in collective bargaining agreements where the union and the employer had agreed upon a compulsory retirement age. The courts have uniformly held these provisions valid and binding on the employees because the issues of whether there should be compulsory retirement and if so, at what age, are required subjects for collective bargaining.[97]

3. Union Shop, Checkoff, Agency Shop, and Hiring Hall. The fact that a union-shop clause is embraced by "conditions of employment" was recognized prior to *Borg-Warner*.[98] In 1949 the Ninth Circuit held that union security fell within the area of required bargaining.[99] But since a union shop is a creature of contract, the Third Circuit held that Section 8 (a) (5) was not violated by an employer who unilaterally ceased giving effect to union-shop and checkoff provisions of a contract subsequent to its expira-

---

[96] 170 F 2d at 252.

[97] Goodin v. Clinchfield R. Co., 229 F 2d 578, 37 LRRM 2515 (CA 6, 1956), *cert. denied*, 351 US 953; McMullans v. Kansas, Oklahoma & Gulf R. W. Co., 229 F 2d 50, 35 LRRM 2512 (CA 10, 1956); Lamon v. Georgia Southern & Florida Ry. Co., 212 Ga 63, 90 SE 2d 658, 37 LRRM 2115 (1955); Jones v. Martin, 37 LRRM 2839 (DCSD Fla 1956).

[98] NLRB v. Wooster Div. of Borg-Warner Corp., 356 US 342, 42 LRRM 2034 (1958). *See* Chapter 14 *supra*.

[99] NLRB v. Andrew Jergens Co., 175 F 2d 130, 24 LRRM 2096 (CA 9), *cert. denied*, 338 US 827, 24 LRRM 2561 (1949). For a later case, *see* U. S. Gypsum Co., 94 NLRB 112, 28 LRRM 1015 (1951). *Cf.* Vanderbilt Prods., Inc. v. NLRB, 297 F 2d 833, 49 LRRM 2286 (CA 2, 1961), where the court found that insistence upon an open shop supported a finding of bad-faith bargaining.

tion.[100] However, the court's reasoning, that "[t]he right to require union membership as a condition of employment is dependent upon a contract. . . ." and that a provision for "checkoff is merely a means of implementing union security . . . ," is consistent with the view that such topics are mandatory bargaining subjects.[101]

The status of an agency-shop proposal has been clarified. Under an agency-shop agreement an employee is not required to join the union, but is required to pay to the union an amount equivalent to union dues. Although the Board initially held that an agency shop was not a subject that required bargaining,[102] it later reversed itself.[103] The Sixth Circuit denied enforcement,[104] but the Supreme Court reversed and agreed with the second decision of the Board,[105] reasoning that the agency-shop proposal imposed no burdens not imposed by union membership, which is lawful and is a mandatory subject.[106]

---

[100] Marine & Shipbuilding Workers v. NLRB (Bethlehem Steel Co.), 320 F 2d 615, 53 LRRM 2878 (CA 3, 1963). A union-shop agreement derives its validity from the *proviso* of §8(a)(3). *See* Chapter 26. "Checkoff" refers to a system by which an employer deducts union dues from wages and remits the dues directly to the union. The legality of the checkoff under federal law is governed by §302(c)(4) of the Labor Management Relations Act, 1947 (Taft-Hartley Act), 29 USC §186(c)(4), which allows payments from an employer to a union "with respect to money deducted from the wages of employees in payment of membership dues in a labor organization: *Provided*, That the employer has received from each employee, on whose account such deductions are made, a written assignment which shall not be irrevocable for a period of more than one year, or beyond the termination date of the applicable collective agreement, whichever occurs sooner. . . ."

[101] 320 F 2d at 619. *See also* NLRB v. Herman Sausage Co., 275 F 2d 229, 234, 45 LRRM 2829 (CA 5, 1960); NLRB v. Reed & Prince Mfg. Co., 205 F 2d 131, 32 LRRM 2225 (CA 1), *cert. denied*, 346 US 887, 33 LRRM 2133 (1953); and U. S. Gypsum Co., 94 NLRB 112, 28 LRRM 1015 (1951). *See also* United Steelworkers v. NLRB (H. K. Porter Co.), 363 F 2d 272, 62 LRRM 2204 (CA DC), *cert. denied*, 385 US 851, 63 LRRM 2236 (1966), upholding a finding of §8(a)(5) violation where the company consistently rejected the union's demand for a dues checkoff. For subsequent history of this case *see:* 389 F 2d 295, 66 LRRM 2761 (1967); 172 NLRB No. 72, 68 LRRM 1337, *affirmed* in H. K. Porter Co. v. NLRB, 414 F 2d 1123, 71 LRRM 2207 (1969), *reversed*, 397 US 99, 73 LRRM 2561 (1970). The Supreme Court's opinion and its impact on the Board's remedial power in refusal to bargain cases are treated in Chapters 11 *supra* and 31 *infra*. The Supreme Court opinion was directed at the Board's remedy, not at the basic finding of refusal to bargain about the checkoff. *See* grant of certiorari (73 LRRM at 2562) and concurring opinion of Mr. Justice Harlan (73 LRRM at 2565).

[102] General Motors Corp., 130 NLRB 481, 47 LRRM 1306 (1961).

[103] General Motors Corp., 133 NLRB 451, 48 LRRM 1659 (1961).

[104] General Motors Corp. v. NLRB, 303 F 2d 428, 50 LRRM 2397 (CA 6, 1962).

[105] NLRB v. General Motors Corp., 373 US 734, 53 LRRM 2313 (1963).

[106] The effect of a right-to-work law which outlaws the agency shop was decided in Retail Clerks v. Schermerhorn, 373 US 746, 53 LRRM 2318 (1963). *See* Chapter 26 *infra* for a detailed discussion of right-to-work laws.

A nondiscriminatory hiring hall operated by a union also is a mandatory subject for bargaining.[107] To the argument that a company is required to bargain only about conditions arising *after* the employment relationship is established and not about conditions for obtaining employment, the Board replied that "since 'employment' connotes the initial act of employing as well as the consequent state of being employed the hiring hall relates to the conditions of employment." The Board also noted that the "employees" referred to in Section 8 (d) were "not limited to those individuals already working for the employer" but also included "prospective employees." [108]

4. Management-Rights Clauses. The key case involving insistence upon a broad management-rights clause is *American Nat'l*.[109] Although the relationship of this case to *Borg-Warner* has been discussed in Chapter 14, a brief additional comment is warranted.

Stated freely, *American Nat'l* holds that an employer's insistence upon a broad management-rights clause covering terms and conditions of employment is not a *per se* violation of Section 8 (a) (5), that the Board may not pass judgment upon the desirability of substantive terms of the agreement, and that the Board must decide in each case whether the good-faith requirements of Section 8 (d) have been met. Notwithstanding, a cautionary note is in order. An employer who had insisted on unilateral control of all subjects of bargaining as a condition precedent to agreement, in the context of refusing to supply relevant data to the union and refusing to accept the appropriate bargaining unit, was held in

---

107 Houston Chapter, Associated Gen. Contractors, 143 NLRB 409, 53 LRRM 1299 (1963), *enforced*, 349 F 2d 449, 59 LRRM 3013 (CA 5, 1965), *cert. denied*, 382 US 1026, 61 LRRM 2244 (1966). *Accord* NLRB v. Tom Joyce Floors, Inc., 353 F 2d 768, 60 LRRM 2434 (CA 9, 1965). The legality of such a hiring hall was established in Local 357, Teamsters Union v. NLRB, 365 US 667, 47 LRRM 2903 (1961). *See* discussion in Chapter 26 *infra*. *Cf.* Pacific Am. Shipowners Ass'n, 90 NLRB 1099, 26 LRRM 1316 (1950), where a §8 (b) (3) charge against a union striking for such a clause was dismissed.
108 143 NLRB at 412, citing NLRB v. Wooster Div. of Borg-Warner Corp., 356 US 342, 42 LRRM 2034 (1958); Phelps Dodge Corp. v. NLRB, 313 US 177, 8 LRRM 439 (1941); Briggs Mfg. Co., 75 NLRB 569, 21 LRRM 1056 (1947); and Texas Natural Gasoline Corp., 116 NLRB 405, 38 LRRM 1252 (1956). For a general discussion of union security, *see* Chapter 26 *infra*.
109 NLRB v. American Nat'l Ins. Co., 343 US 395, 30 LRRM 2147 (1952). For earlier cases dealing with management rights clauses, *see* Old Line Life Ins. Co., 96 NLRB 499, 28 LRRM 1539 (1951); Standard Generator Co., 90 NLRB 790, 26 LRRM 1285 (1950); Franklin Hosiery Co., 83 NLRB 276, 24 LRRM 1047 (1949). For a more recent example, *see* Long Lake Lumber Co. 182 NLRB No. 65, 74 LRRM 1116 (1970).

violation of Section 8 (a) (5).[110] And another employer who made such extreme demands concerning terms and conditions of employment that no "self-respecting" union could accept them was likewise found guilty of refusing to bargain.[111] Thus, although a management-rights clause is a mandatory subject for bargaining and although insistence upon such a clause is not *per se* a violation of Section 8 (a) (5), such bargaining may become so interrelated with other factors as to justify a finding of bad-faith bargaining.[112]

5. Plant Rules. The contents of plant rules are mandatory subjects of bargaining.[113]

6. Safety. The contention of employers that safety regulation is a management function not subject to negotiation has been rejected by the Board and the courts. The Fifth Circuit stated it was "inescapable" that "workers, through their chosen representative should have the right to bargain with the Company in reference to safe work practices." [114]

7. No-strike Clause. A "no-strike" clause is deemed a mandatory subject of bargaining; therefore, an employer may bargain for it to the point of impasse.[115] Such a clause, however, is distinguishable from a strike-ballot clause, held to be only a permissive subject of bargaining in the *Borg-Warner* case.[116]

8. Subcontracting. The Board has said that with the evolution of the relationship between employers and employees "new areas may be found which affect 'wages, hours, and other terms and

---

110 Dixie Corp., 105 NLRB 390, 32 LRRM 1259 (1953), distinguishing *American Nat'l.* In *Stuart Radiator Core Mfg. Co.,* 173 NLRB No. 27, 69 LRRM 1243 (1968), an employer who insisted on a detailed management's rights clause which reserved absolute unilateral control of virtually every significant term and condition of employment, coupled with a limitation of grievances and arbitration to the express terms of the contract and a waiver of bargaining, thereby manifested bad faith.
111 Vanderbilt Prods. Co. 129 NLRB 1323, 47 LRRM 1182 (1961), *enforced,* 297 F 2d 833, 49 LRRM 2286 (CA 2, 1961). *See also* Chevron Oil Co., 182 NLRB No. 64, 74 LRRM 1323 (1970).
112 Such other factors are discussed in Chapter 11 *supra.*
113 Miller Brewing Co., 166 NLRB 90, 65 LRRM 1649 (1967); Hilton Mobile Homes, 155 NLRB 873, 60 LRRM 1411 (1965).
114 NLRB v. Gulf Power Co., 384 F 2d 822, 824, 66 LRRM 2501 (CA 5, 1967), *enforcing* 156 NLRB 622, 61 LRRM 1073 (1966). In *Fibreboard Paper Products Corp.* v. *NLRB,* 379 US 203, 222, 57 LRRM 2609 (1964), "safety practices" were mentioned as a condition of employment for purposes of defining the bargaining duty of an employer. *Fibreboard* is discussed *infra* under *subcontracting. Cf.* Chapter 6 *supra* at note 54 and Chapter 19 *infra* at note 31.
115 Shell Oil Co., 77 NLRB 1306, 22 LRRM 1158 (1948).
116 356 US 342, 42 LRRM 2034 (1958). *See also* Justice Harlan's dissent, 356 US at 351. For a full discussion of *Borg-Warner, see* Chapter 14 *supra.*

conditions of employment,' and thus the list of mandatory subjects of bargaining quite properly is enlarged." [117] And the
Supreme Court has observed that "while not determinative, it is
appropriate to look to industrial bargaining practice in appraising
the propriety of including a particular subject within the scope of
mandatory bargaining." [118] These observations on the tendency to
expand the list of subjects for mandatory bargaining are especially
relevant to developments in the field of subcontracting.

For many years the Board followed the view that an employer
has no duty under Section 8 (a) (5) to consult with the bargaining
representative before deciding to subcontract part of his operation.
In 1945 the Board asserted that it had never held that "an employer may not in good faith . . . change his business structure,
[or] sell or contract out a portion of his operation . . . without
first consulting the bargaining representative. . . ." [119] Nevertheless,
the Board developed a rule in subcontracting and related types of
cases that an employer must bargain with the union about the
impact of a decision to subcontract.[120]

As late as 1961 the Board took the position that a decision on
whether to subcontract was not a mandatory subject of bargaining.
In its initial decision in the famous *Fibreboard* [121] case, the Board
reasoned that the determination of whether an employment relationship shall exist does not relate to a condition of employment
but to a pre-condition necessary to the establishment of the relationship from which conditions of employment arise. Thus, the
Board concluded that Congress did not intend "to compel bargain-

---

117 Houston Chapter, Associated Gen. Contractors, 143 NLRB 409, 413 (1963),
enforced, 349 F 2d 449, 59 LRRM 3013 (CA 5, 1965), *cert. denied*, 382 US 1026, 61
LRRM 2244 (1966).

118 Fibreboard Paper Prods. Corp. v. NLRB, 379 US 203, 211, 57 LRRM 2609 (1964).

119 Mahoning Mining Co., 61 NLRB 792, 803, 16 LRRM 110 (1945). *See also* Walter
Holm & Co., 87 NLRB 1169, 25 LRRM 1270 (1949). Unfair labor practice charges
in subcontracting cases often involve allegations of violation of §8 (a) (3) as well as
claims of violation of §8 (a) (5). The present discussion is concerned with the
§8 (a) (5) aspect of the problem.

120 Shamrock Dairy, Inc., 119 NLRB 998, 41 LRRM 1216 (1957), *modified*, 124
NLRB 494, 44 LRRM 1407 (1959), *enforced*, 280 F 2d 665, 46 LRRM 2433 (CA DC,
1960); Brown Truck, 106 NLRB 999, 32 LRRM 1580 (1953); NLRB Gen. Counsel
Admin. Ruling No. 315, 30 LRRM 1102 (1952); Bickford Shoes, Inc., 109 NLRB
1346, 34 LRRM 1570 (1954); Diaper Jean Mfg. Co., 109 NLRB 1045, 34 LRRM 1504
(1954). *But cf.* NLRB v. Rives Co., 288 F 2d 511, 47 LRRM 2766 (CA 5, 1961).

121 Fibreboard Paper Prods. Corp., 130 NLRB 1558, 47 LRRM 1547 (1961).

ing concerning basic management decisions, such as whether and to what extent to risk capital and managerial effort." [122]

In 1962 the Board repudiated this view. In *Town and Country* [123] the Board found that the employer had violated Section 8 (a) (3) because the decision to subcontract had an anti-union motivation, but it also found that the employer had violated Section 8 (a) (5) even if the subcontracting action was taken to avoid violations of ICC regulations or on account of economic considerations. It was the Board's view that

> the elimination of unit jobs albeit for economic reasons, is a matter within the statutory phrase "other terms and conditions of employment" and is a mandatory subject of collective bargaining within the meaning of Section 8 (a) (5) of the Act.[124]

Relying on this reasoning and the Supreme Court's decision in *Order of R.R. Telegraphers* v. *Chicago & N.W.R.R.*,[125] the Board also reconsidered and reversed its original decision in *Fibreboard*.[126] Although the Fifth Circuit enforced this new order in *Town and Country*, it did so on the ground that the company had subcontracted because of anti-union motivation in violation of Section 8 (a) (3).[127] On the other hand, the District of Columbia Circuit agreed with the Board in the second *Fibreboard* decision and confirmed that the company had violated Section 8 (a) (5).[128] The latter case was taken to the Supreme Court.

Stressing the particular facts in *Fibreboard,* the Supreme Court held that the subcontracting therein constituted a mandatory subject for bargaining even in the absence of anti-union motivation.

---

122 130 NLRB at 1561.
123 Town & Country Mfg. Co., 136 NLRB 1022, 49 LRRM 1918 (1962), *enforced,* 316 F 2d 846, 53 LRRM 2054 (CA 5, 1963).
124 136 NLRB at 1027.
125 362 US 330, 45 LRRM 3104 (1960). It should be noted that in *Telegraphers* the Supreme Court was not dealing with the Labor Management Relations Act but rather with the Railway Labor Act. However, the Board felt that the decision of the Supreme Court made it clear that elimination of jobs in the bargaining unit for reasons that were palpably economic was still a "term or condition of employment" over which an employer must first bargain with the union—reasoning which was equally applicable to both statutes.
126 Fibreboard Paper Prods. Corp., 138 NLRB 550, 51 LRRM 1101 (1962), *enforced,* 322 F 2d 411, 53 LRRM 2666 (CA DC, 1963), *aff'd,* 379 US 203, 57 LRRM 2609 (1964).
127 Town & Country Mfg. Co. v. NLRB, 316 F 2d 846, 53 LRRM 2054 (CA 5, 1963).
128 East Bay Union of Machinists v. NLRB (Fibreboard Paper Prods.), 322 F 2d 411, 53 LRRM 2666 (CA DC, 1963), *aff'd,* 379 US 203, 57 LRRM 2609 (1964).

But the limited nature of the holding is indicated by this language in the opinion:

> We are thus not expanding the scope of mandatory bargaining to hold, as we do now, that the type of "contracting out" involved in this case—the replacement of employees in the existing bargaining unit with those of an independent contractor to do the same work under similar conditions of employment—is a statutory subject of collective bargaining under §8 (d). Our decision need not and does not encompass other forms of "contracting out" or "subcontracting" which arise daily in our complex economy.[129]

Thus the Court held that the company was obligated to bargain over the issue of whether to subcontract the plant maintenance work for economic reasons and that for such refusal to bargain the Board was empowered to order resumption of maintenance operations and reinstatement of employees with back pay.

Justice Stewart concurred because in his view the facts simply involved the substitution of one group of workers for another to perform the same work in the same plant under the ultimate control of the same employer. He saw the situation as similar to one in which an employer discharges his employees and replaces them with others willing to work at a lower labor cost to the company. He noted further that the issue was limited to the consideration of an employer's duty to bargain in the absence of a collective bargaining agreement.

His concurring opinion also noted that many decisions by management may affect the job security of employees, such as those involving advertising, product design, financing, sales, investment in labor-saving machinery, and liquidation of assets. It was Justice Stewart's contention that nothing decided in *Fibreboard* should be understood as imposing a duty to bargain collectively concerning these managerial decisions. Referring to the facts of *Fibreboard,* he stated that:

> This kind of subcontracting falls short of such larger entrepreneurial questions as what shall be produced, how capital shall be invested in fixed assets, or what the basic scope of the enterprise shall be. In my

---

[129] Fibreboard Paper Prods. Corp. v. NLRB, 379 US 203, 215, 57 LRRM 2609 (1964). *Cf.* Local 24, Teamsters Union v. Oliver, 358 US 283, 43 LRRM 2374 (1959) (contract provisions imposing conditions upon contracting out and leasing of employer's trucks, which are intended to prevent loss of employees' jobs and undermining of conditions of employment for members of the bargaining unit, are mandatory subjects of bargaining) .

view, the Court's decision in this case has nothing to do with whether any aspects of those larger issues could under any circumstances be considered subjects of compulsory collective bargaining. . . .[130]

Although *Fibreboard* was widely heralded as a case that would resolve broad issues, the actual holding was narrow and limited. It might be said that *Fibreboard* was not so much an end as a beginning. In the meantime, the process of "elucidating litigation" is occurring with respect to what subcontracting situations require mandatory bargaining. It is too early to forecast precisely what the ultimate outcome will be, but certain areas of controversy will be noted.

Westinghouse Elec. Corp.[131] provides the most definitive explanation of how the Board reads the Supreme Court's *Fibreboard* decision. In *Westinghouse* the Board laid down a series of tests to determine whether a particular subcontracting decision necessitates bargaining. Subcontracting of unit work does not require bargaining, said the Board, if (1) the subcontracting is motivated solely by economic reasons; (2) it has been customary for the company to subcontract various kinds of work; (3) no substantial variance is shown in kind or degree from the established past practice of the employer; (4) no significant detriment results to employees in the unit; and (5) the union has had an opportunity to bargain about changes in existing subcontracting practices at general negotiating meetings.

In 1965, following the promulgation of these criteria, the Board dismissed several complaints,[132] but without giving any precise definition of what was meant by a "significant detriment" to employees. Nevertheless, the 1965 dismissals indicated that the fact that most of the work contracted out could have been performed by unit employees,[133] or that some overtime pay was lost,[134] or that

---

[130] 379 US at 225. Justices Douglas and Harlan agreed with this concurring opinion.
[131] 150 NLRB 1574, 58 LRRM 1257 (1965).
[132] American Oil Co., 152 NLRB 56, 59 LRRM 1007 (1965); American Oil Co., 155 NLRB 639, 60 LRRM 1369 (1965); Central Soya Co., 151 NLRB 1691, 58 LRRM 1667 (1965); Superior Coach Corp., 151 NLRB 188, 58 LRRM 1369 (1965); Fafnir Bearing Co., 151 NLRB 332, 58 LRRM 1397 (1965); American Oil Co., 151 NLRB 421, 58 LRRM 1412 (1965). *See* Note, *Subcontracting, Mandatory Collective Bargaining, and the 1965 NLRB Decisions*, 18 STAN. L. REV. 256 (1965), and Note, *Mandatory Subjects of Bargaining, Operational Changes*, 17 U. FLA. L. REV. 109 (1964).
[133] Fafnir Bearing Co., 151 NLRB 332, 58 LRRM 1397 (1965).
[134] General Tube Co., 151 NLRB 850, 58 LRRM 1496 (1965).

unit pay classifications were reduced because of lack of work,[135] or that employees were assigned to work at unskilled jobs,[136] was not sufficient basis for making subcontracting a mandatory subject of bargaining. And the Board has held that an employer has no duty to bargain over subcontracting of work that falls outside the scope of work normally performed by bargaining-unit employees.[137]

Indeed, the Board in its 1965 decisions held that in order for such contracting out to be a mandatory bargaining subject, some employees have to lose overtime, or be laid off, or transferred to lower-paying jobs as a result of the contracting out of the work.[138] In a later *Westinghouse* case [139] the union charged that unilateral subcontracting by the employer had a substantial detrimental effect on the bargaining unit since employees who were already on layoff were not recalled. The union argued that if the subcontracting had not taken place, or had been more limited, certain of the laid-off employees might have returned to gainful employment. The Board rejected this view and found no refusal to bargain.

The Fourth Circuit, while upholding a Board dismissal of a refusal-to-bargain charge where the employer's subcontracting decisions had no substantial adverse effect on employees (even though employees feared future loss of overtime), has adopted a different approach.[140] It has agreed with the Board that full-scale bargaining should not be required under the facts of the case, but suggests that future situations presenting similar facts

---

[135] American Oil Co., 151 NLRB 421, 58 LRRM 1412 (1965).
[136] Superior Coach Corp., 151 NLRB 188, 58 LRRM 1397 (1965).
[137] Central Soya Co., Inc., 151 NLRB 1691, 58 LRRM 1667 (1965).
[138] *See* cases cited notes 131-137 *supra.* However, where a company is unable to operate at all due to matters beyond its control, even a layoff does not make subcontracting a mandatory bargaining subject. Central Rufina, 161 NLRB 696, 63 LRRM 1318 (1966). *See also* Ador Corp., 150 NLRB 1658, 58 LRRM 1280 (1965). The D. C. Circuit may be applying a more stringent test than the Board. *See* United Auto Workers v. NLRB (General Motors Corp.), 381 F 2d 265, 64 LRRM 2489 (CA DC, 1967), where the court reversed the Board's decision that the company had not violated the act and held that a change in operations which caused the elimination of six jobs within the bargaining unit required mandatory bargaining. *See also* Kennecott Copper Corp., 148 NLRB 1653, 57 LRRM 1217 (1964) (pre-*Fibreboard* case holding no violation since unilateral contracting out did not involve any job losses).
[139] Westinghouse Elec. Corp., 153 NLRB 443, 59 LRRM 1355 (1965).
[140] District 50, UMW v. NLRB (Allied Chem. Corp.), 358 F 2d 234, 61 LRRM 2632 (CA 4, 1966). *See also* Puerto Rico Tel. Co. v. NLRB, 359 F 2d 983, 988, 62 LRRM 2069 (CA 1, 1966) (finding no adverse impact and overruling Board determination requiring bargaining).

might require an alternative to full-scale bargaining: simple notification to the union and an opportunity for the exchange of ideas. The court explained that the union should not be permitted to stall the decision by insisting on protracted negotiations, and, after listening to the union's suggestions, the company should be permitted to accept or reject them as its economic judgment dictates. The court thus appears to be redefining the nature of "impasse" to accommodate it to the court's notion of the exigencies of subcontracting decisions. As the court said:

> An employer may be obligated under the compulsion of some circumstances to make subcontracting decisions without delay. Emergencies could arise that require immediate action. The employer's prerogative in this class of cases should be respected without requiring prior bargaining or even notification of the union. However, other contracting decisions may not demand immediate action and respecting these types of decisions there may be no practical obstacle in notification of the union, and to affording it an opportunity to be heard.[141]

In those cases where employees have lost overtime [142] or any employee has lost his job as a result of subcontracting, the Board has held that the employer had a duty to bargain about the subcontracting.[143] In such circumstances the fact that the subcontracting was economically motivated did not excuse the employer from a mandatory duty to notify and bargain with the union.[144]

Adams Dairy [145] is another well-known case in this area. Adams had been engaged in selling milk and dairy products to retail outlets through both driver-salesmen and independent contractors. Subsequently, it eliminated the use of driver-salesmen and changed its entire distribution system to an independent-contractor arrangement. It informed the union of the change and discharged all of its driver-salesmen. The Board ordered reinstatement and back

---

141 358 F 2d at 238. *Cf.* Jersey Farms Milk Serv., Inc., 148 NLRB 1392, 57 LRRM 1166 (1964), where the Board found that unilateral subcontracting of bargaining unit work violated the Act. The Board simply ordered the company to bargain over resumption of operations and any proposed alternatives thereto; it did not order restoration of the status quo.
142 Cities Service Oil Co., 158 NLRB 1204, 62 LRRM 1175 (1966).
143 Weston and Brooker Co., 154 NLRB 747, 60 LRRM 1015 (1965).
144 Brown Transport Corp., 140 NLRB 954, 52 LRRM 1151 (1963), *modified as to remedy only,* 334 F 2d 243, 56 LRRM 2809 (CA 5, 1964).
145 Adams Dairy Co., 137 NLRB 815, 50 LRRM 1281 (1962), distinguished in Hartmann Luggage Co., 145 NLRB 1572, 55 LRRM 1206 (1964) (company discussed subcontracting with the union while the subcontract was executory). *See also* Georgia Pac. Corp., 150 NLRB 885, 58 LRRM 1135 (1965).

pay, but its decision was reversed by the Eighth Circuit.[146] Upon remand from the Supreme Court with instructions to reconsider the case in the light of *Fibreboard*,[147] the Eighth Circuit adhered to its original decision, reasoning as follows: (1) Contrary to the situation in *Fibreboard, Adams Dairy* involved more than just the substitution of one set of employees for another; the company changed its basic operating procedure and liquidated a part of its business. (2) Unlike *Fibreboard, Adams Dairy* involved a change in the capital structure and a recoupment of capital investment. (3) Also contrary to *Fibreboard,* the work done by the independent contractors for Adams Dairy was not performed primarily in the Adams plant for the benefit of the dairy. (4) In *Adams,* unlike *Fibreboard,* the decision to change to distribution by independent contractors was made at a time when the current contract still had two years to run (and no aura of bad faith appeared to have pervaded the employer's bargaining as in *Fibreboard*).[148]

One issue that has been the subject of considerable litigation concerns the question of subcontracting during a strike. The Ninth Circuit, overruling the Board, has held that an employer need not offer to bargain with a union over subcontracting of bargaining-unit work during a strike.[149] Subsequently, the Board held that an employer need not bargain over subcontracting of bargaining-unit work during a strike if the facts indicate that management views the arrangement as a temporary measure adopted to continue business relationships.[150]

---

[146] NLRB v. Adams Dairy, Inc., 322 F 2d 553, 54 LRRM 2171 (CA 8, 1963).

[147] NLRB v. Adams Dairy, Inc., 379 US 644, 58 LRRM 2192 (1965).

[148] NLRB v. Adams Dairy, Inc., 350 F 2d 108, 60 LRRM 2084 (CA 8, 1965), *cert. denied,* 382 US 1011, 61 LRRM 2192 (1966). *But see* United Auto Workers v. NLRB (General Motors Corp.), 381 F 2d 265, 64 LRRM 2489 (CA DC, 1967). The court reversed the Board, which had held the employer had not violated the act, on the ground that a unilateral change in shipping methods which had resulted in the elimination of six jobs in the bargaining unit adversely affected the employees and, therefore, the company must bargain over the change. *See also* NLRB v. American Mfg. Co., 351 F 2d 74, 60 LRRM 2122 (CA 5, 1965), *and* Winn-Dixie Stores, Inc. v. NLRB, 361 F 2d 512, 62 LRRM 2218 (CA 5, 1967), *cert. denied,* 382 US 830, 63 LRRM 2372 (1966).

[149] Hawaii Meat Co. v. NLRB, 321 F 2d 397, 53 LRRM 2872 (CA 9, 1963).

[150] Empire Terminal Warehouse Co., 151 NLRB 1359, 58 LRRM 1589 (1965). Other cases dealing with the right to subcontract during a strike: Shell Oil Co., 149 NLRB 283, 57 LRRM 1271 (1964); Shell Chem. Co., 149 NLRB 298, 57 LRRM 1275 (1964); and Die Sinkers v. Pittsburgh Forgings Co., 255 F Supp 142, 63 LRRM 2152 (WD Pa., 1966), which quotes the Seventh Circuit in NLRB v. Abbott Publishing Co., 331 F 2d 209, 55 LRRM 2994 (CA 7, 1964).

The Board also has permitted subcontracting without bargaining during a hiatus between contracts, so long as the subcontracting is in line with past practice.[151]

9. Partial Closure of Business and Plant Relocation. Several cases involving the question of whether a company has a duty under Section 8 (a) (5) to bargain over partial closure of its business or plant relocation have turned upon an interpretation of the Supreme Court's decision in *Fibreboard.* But the nature of an employer's duty, if any, to bargain on this subject is not yet clear.[152] The views of the Board are in conflict with those of the Eighth, Ninth, and Third Circuits.[153]

As noted in the discussion of *Adams Dairy* in the preceding section, the Eighth Circuit held that an employer has no duty to bargain over whether to close part of his business and subcontract the work in question to independent contractors.[154] And in *Royal Plating & Polishing Co.*[155] the Third Circuit held that a company had no duty to bargain over whether to close one of its two plants. The court found that the decision to close the plant

---

151 Shell Oil Co., 149 NLRB 283, 287, 57 LRRM 1271 (1964). In a later decision involving another Shell plant, *Shell Oil Co.,* 166 NLRB 128, 65 LRRM 1713 (1967), the Board interpreted a clause in a collective bargaining contract to permit unilateral subcontracting of bargaining unit work in accordance with past practice.

152 The Supreme Court has held that an employer may close his *entire* business for any reason he chooses, including an anti-union motivation. But it was recognized that a partial closing, intended "to chill unionism," could result in a violation of §8 (a) (3). Left open was the question of whether an employer must bargain about an economically motivated decision to close part of the business. NLRB v. Darlington Mfg. Co., 380 US 263, 58 LRRM 2657 (1965), *see* discussion in Chapters 5 & 6 *supra.* For the views of the various circuits prior to *Darlington* and *Fibreboard,* see NLRB v. New Madrid Mfg. Co., 215 F 2d 908, 34 LRRM 2844 (CA 8, 1954); NLRB v. New England Web, Inc., 309 F 2d 696, 51 LRRM 2426 (CA 1, 1962); NLRB v. Lassing, 284 F 2d 781, 47 LRRM 2277 (CA 6, 1960); NLRB v. Adkins Transfer Co., 226 F 2d 324, 36 LRRM 2709 (CA 6, 1955); NLRB v. R. C. Mahon Co., 269 F 2d 44, 44 LRRM 2479 (CA 6, 1959); NLRB v. Rapid Bindery, Inc., 293 F 2d 170, 48 LRRM 2658 (CA 2, 1961); and NLRB v. Adams Dairy, Inc., 322 F 2d 553, 54 LRRM 2171 (CA 8, 1963).

153 *Compare* Ozark Trailers, Inc., 161 NLRB 561, 63 LRRM 1264 (1966), *with* NLRB v. Adams Dairy, Inc., 350 F 2d 108, 60 LRRM 2084 (CA 8, 1965), *cert. denied,* 382 US 1011, 61 LRRM 2192 (1966); NLRB v. Royal Plating & Polishing Co., 350 F 2d 191, 60 LRRM 2033 (CA 3, 1965); NLRB v. Transmarine Navigation Corp., 380 F 2d 933, 65 LRRM 2861 (1967) *(see* note 171 *infra)*; NLRB v. Thompson Transport Co., Inc., 165 NLRB No. 96, *enforcement denied,* 406 F 2d 698 (CA 10, 1969) *(see* notes 167 and 172 *infra).*

154 NLRB v. Adams Dairy, Inc., 350 F 2d 108, 60 LRRM 2084 (CA 8, 1965), *cert. denied,* 382 US 1011, 61 LRRM 2192 (1966). *See also* NLRB v. Wm. J. Burns Intl. Detective Agency, 346 F 2d 897, 59 LRRM 2523 (CA 8, 1965) (partial closure but no subcontracting, thus *Fibreboard* distinguished).

155 NLRB v. Royal Plating & Polishing Co., 350 F 2d 191, 60 LRRM 2033 (CA 3 1965).

instead of moving to another location involved a management decision to recommit and reinvest funds in the business. The decision obviously was made for economic reasons and involved a major change in the economic direction of the company. The court therefore concluded that nothing in *Fibreboard* required bargaining about such managerial decisions "which lie at the core of entrepreneurial control" and that the employer's only duty was to bargain over the impact of the decision on such matters as severance pay, pensions, and seniority.

Nevertheless, in *Ozark Trailers, Inc.*,[156] the Board disagreed with the views of the Eighth and Third Circuits. Examining the Supreme Court's reasoning in *Fibreboard,* the Board concluded that it supported the requirement that an employer must bargain about an economically motivated decision to close part of its business. The Board found that three separate corporations constituted one employer since they were an integrated operation. When one of the corporations closed its plant without consulting the union, the Board held that it had violated its bargaining duty not only because there had been no discussion with the union about the effect of the shutdown,[157] but also because it had failed to negotiate with the union about the decision to close the plant. Since the company based its plant closure in part upon its claim of excessive man-hours for production and on defective workmanship, and since these topics are traditional subjects of collective bargaining, the Board felt that they could have been submitted to collective bargaining just as was required of the labor-cost issues involved in *Fibreboard*.[158] The Board said that "whether a par-

---

[156] 161 NLRB 561, 63 LRRM 1264 (1966). *Accord,* Cooper Thermometer Co., 160 NLRB 1902, 63 LRRM 1219 (1966), *enforced in part,* 376 F 2d 684, 65 LRRM 2113 (CA 2, 1967), where the Second Circuit upheld the Board's finding of a duty to bargain about transfer of employees to a new location, but refused to enforce parts of the remedy relating to back pay and reinstatement. *But see* for distinguishable fact situations, Westinghouse Electric Corp., 174 NLRB No. 95, 70 LRRM 1255 (1969), *and* Desilu Productions, Inc., 166 NLRB No. 117, 65 LRRM 1727 (1967). Schnell Tool & Die Corp., 162 NLRB 1313, 64 LRRM 1184 (1967). *See also* Robertshaw Controls Co., 161 NLRB 103, 63 LRRM 1231 (1966) (holding that an employer had a duty to bargain over seniority rights of employees being transferred along with part of the company's operations from a union-organized plant to a new plant).

[157] *See* Die Supply Corp., 160 NLRB 1326, 63 LRRM 1154 (1966); and Young Motor Truck Serv., Inc., 156 NLRB 661, 61 LRRM 1099 (1966).

[158] The Board did not require that the company reopen the closed plant, but it ordered the company to pay back wages to the employees from the date of the decision to close until the date the plant was actually shut down. During this period employees had been laid off on the basis of seniority.

ticular management decision must be bargained about should [not] turn on whether the decision involves the commitment of investment capital, or on whether it may be characterized as involving 'major' or 'basic' change in the nature of the employer's business. . . ." [159] Focusing on the impact which such a decision has on the employees in the bargaining unit, the Board reasoned that:

> [A]n employer's decision to make a "major" change in the nature of his business, such as the termination of a portion thereof, is also of significance for those employees whose jobs will be lost by the termination. For, just as the employer has invested capital in the business, so the employee has invested years of his working life, accumulating seniority, accruing pension rights, and developing skills that may or may not be salable to another employer. And, just as the employer's interest in the protection of his capital investment is entitled to consideration in our interpretation of the Act, so too is the employee's interest in the protection of his livelihood. . . .[160]

The Board accordingly held that under the Supreme Court's opinion in *Fibreboard,*

> bargaining about contracting out might appropriately be required because to do so effectuated one of the primary purposes of the Act— "to promote the peaceful settlement of industrial disputes by subjecting labor-management controversies to the mediatory influence of negotiation. . . ." [161]

The Board also used *Ozark Trailers* to respond to the argument that to compel bargaining about a decision to relocate or terminate part of a business abridges the employer's freedom to manage. The Board replied that "an employer's obligation to bargain does not include the obligation to agree," [162] for, if efforts at bargaining fail, "the employer is wholly free to make and effectuate his decision." [163] The Board did concede that the bargaining obligation, "which precludes unilateral action absent sufficient bargaining,"

---

159 161 NLRB at 566, 63 LRRM 1264 (1966).
160 *Ibid.*
161 161 NLRB 561 at 567.
162 161 NLRB at 568.
163 *Ibid.* Subsequently the Board reaffirmed this position in McLoughlin Mfg. Co.,

may impede "management flexibility in meeting business opportunities and exigencies." However, Congress had already made
the basic policy determination that "the interests of employees are
of sufficient importance that their representatives ought be consulted in matters affecting them." [164] The Board stressed the
"mediating influence of collective bargaining" [165] and observed
that the widespread bargaining about contracting out, which has
long existed, indicates that complex and difficult bargaining problems can be and are resolved. It concluded that there is "no justification for interpreting the statutory bargaining obligation so
narrowly as to exclude plant removal and shutdown from its
scope." [166]

In subsequent cases, the Board has steadfastly held to its position
in *Ozark Trailers*.[167] Meanwhile, however, the Ninth and Tenth
Circuits have joined the Third and Eighth in repudiating the
Board's approach. In *Transmarine Navigation* [168] the Ninth Cir-

---

[164] NLRB 140, 65 LRRM 1025 (1967), in which it stated: "It is well-settled that
before an employer definitively decides to contract out, move, or relocate its business,
it is obligated to bargain not only with respect to the effect of that decision but
also as to the decision itself." (164 NLRB 140, 141.) But the Board there held
that the employer had satisfied its duty to bargain notwithstanding its unilateral
decision to relocate its plant, because it had notified and bargained with the union
over an earlier decision to close the plant and also over the impact of such closing.
In fact, agreement had been reached on separation and vacation pay.

Cf. Pierce Governor Co., 164 NLRB 97, 65 LRRM 1029 (1967), holding that
the employer had engaged in good-faith bargaining over the transfer rights of
present employees to a new plant, including seniority rights at the new plant, *i.e.*,
the effects of the move. Bargaining as to the move itself was apparently not raised
and was not discussed.

[164] 161 NLRB at 568.

[165] *Ibid.*

[166] 161 NLRB at 570.

[167] *E.g.* Thompson Transport Co., Inc., 165 NLRB 96, 65 LRRM 1370 (1967),
enforcement denied, 406 F 2d 698, 70 LRRM 2418 (CA 10, 1969); Drapery Mfg. Co.,
Inc., 170 NLRB 199, 68 LRRM 1027 (1968). In *Morrison Cafeterias Consolidated,
Inc.*, 177 NLRB 113, 71 LRRM 1449 (1969), *reversed in part*, 431, F 2d 254, 74
LRRM 3048 (CA 8, 1970). The Board sustained a §8 (a) (5) charge of refusing to
bargain about the decision to close, but dismissed a §8 (a) (3) charge, relying on the
Supreme Court's decision in *NLRB* v. *Darlington Mfg. Co.*, 308 US 263, 58 LRRM
2657 (1965); the Eighth Circuit reversed as to the requirement of bargaining about
the decision to close. For a discussion of *Darlington* in the light of §§8 (a) (1) and
8 (a) (3) *see* Chapter 6 *supra*.

[168] NLRB v. Transmarine Navigation Corp., 380 F 2d 933, 65 LRRM 2861 (CA 9,
1967). *Cf.* NLRB v. Dixie Ohio Express Co., 409 F 2d 10, 70 LRRM 3336 (1969),

cuit reversed a finding of refusal to bargain where the employer, solely for economic reasons, terminated his business and became a minority partner in a larger firm. The court noted that "a fundamental alteration of the corporate enterprise" [169] had occurred, and "unlike Fibreboard it was not merely a decision to achieve economies by reducing the work force." [170] Although the court recognized no employer obligation to bargain about the basic economic decision, it held that once the employer had made his decision he was obligated to notify the union and afford it "the opportunity to bargain over the rights of the employees whose employment status will be altered by the managerial decision." [171] The Board's ruling in *Thompson Transport* [172] suffered a similar fate in the Tenth Circuit.

Considering the sharp division between the Board and several of the Circuits, clarification of the extent of the duty to bargain about plant closure and related forms of business reorganization must await resolution by the Supreme Court or a change in the Board's own position on the subject.

10. Arrangements for Negotiations. The Board has ruled that the parties must bargain collectively about the preliminary arrangements for negotiations in the same manner as they must bargain about substantive terms or conditions of employment. Preliminary arrangements include such matters as scheduling the time, place, length and agenda of meetings, establishment of committees of the negotiating committee and whether a stenographic report is to be made. The Board has stated that "such preliminary

---

where the Sixth Circuit reversed a Board holding that an employer was obligated to bargain over a decision to reorganize its freight operations to eliminate inefficiencies. Although the Board had conceded a nondiscriminatory motive, it had rejected the company's argument that the action did not exceed the area of normal day to day operations. The court viewed the changes as involving only ordinary operating procedures and therefore outside the ambit of *Fibreboard*.

169 *Id.* at 937.

170 *Ibid.*

171 *Id.* at 939.

172 NLRB v. Thompson Transport Co., Inc., 406 F 2d 698, 70 LRRM 2418 (CA 10, 1969).

matters are just as much a part of the process of collective bargaining as negotiation over wages, hours, etc." [173]

While adamancy in insisting on any particular arrangement usually evidences bad faith, adamancy is not a violation of the duty to bargain if the circumstances establish good faith. Thus, where the history of the relationship between the parties showed that the union acted in good faith in resisting to the point of refusing to attend negotiating sessions so long as a stenographer was present to record bargaining negotiations, the Board found the union did not violate Section 8 (b) (3). The Board said:

> It is wholly consistent with the purposes of the Act that the parties be allowed to arrive at a resolution of their differences on preliminary matters by the same methods of compromise and accommodation as are used in resolving equally difficult differences relating to substantive terms or conditions of employment. In neither case will we presume to pass upon which is the preferable position or to dictate terms of an agreement, but will, rather, concern ourselves only with whether the parties are acting in good faith.[174]

The constituency of the committee representing either the employer or the union is not a bargaining matter, however, because the law guarantees each party the right to choose its own representatives free of any influence from the other.[175]

---

[173] General Electric Co., 173 NLRB No. 46, 69 LRRM 1305, 1310 (1968). The refusal of the employer to attend scheduled meetings to deal with preliminary matters where such refusal was based on an improper objection to the composition of the union's committee constituted a violation of Section 8 (a) (5). On review, however, the Second Circuit held that the employer "had an absolute right to refrain from preliminary meetings before the formal notice of reopening [of the contract] and it could condition its agreement to preliminary discussions. . . ." The court found a distinction between preliminary and formal bargaining sessions. 412 F 2d 512, 521, 71 LRRM 2418 (1969). (In other respects, particularly relating to the employer's objections to the makeup of the union's bargaining committee, the Board decision and order was affirmed.) See Chapter 11 supra for treatment of coalition and coordinated bargaining.

[174] St. Louis Typographical Union (Graphic Arts Association), 149 NLRB 750, 752, 57 LRRM 1370 (1964).

[175] General Electric Co., 173 NLRB No. 46, 69 LRRM 1305 (1968). For general treatment of bargaining conduct required for good faith bargaining, see Chapter 11 supra, also note 173 supra, this chapter.

CHAPTER 16

PERMISSIVE AND ILLEGAL SUBJECTS OF BARGAINING

A brief review of the relationship of permissive, mandatory, and illegal subjects of bargaining is in order at this point. If a given subject falls within the phrase "wages, hours, and other terms and conditions of employment" (as used in Section 8(d) of the Act), it is a mandatory subject of bargaining; if it falls outside this phrase, it is either a permissive subject (about which the parties may, but need not, bargain), or an illegal subject (about which the parties are forbidden to bargain). The law permits, but does not compel, bargaining about permissive subjects. In 1958 the Supreme Court laid down the distinction between mandatory and permissive subjects in the landmark *Borg-Warner* case.[1]

I. PERMISSIVE SUBJECTS

In *Borg-Warner* the Supreme Court made it clear that bargaining need not be confined to statutory subjects. It is lawful for either party to propose, for inclusion in a collective bargaining contract, any clause within the field of permissive subjects for bargaining, to bargain in good faith about that clause, and, if an agreement is reached, to include it in the final contract. But the Court also made it clear that neither party is required to bargain about permissive subjects. If either party refuses to do so, there is no violation of Section 8(a)(5) or 8(b)(3). Adamant refusal to bargain with respect to a permissive subject, or, if there has been voluntary bargaining with respect to a permissive subject, adamant refusal either to include the subject at all or to agree to a particular resolution of a voluntary subject, is not unlawful. Conversely, if, as a condition precedent to entering into any con-

---

[1] NLRB v. Borg-Warner Corp., 356 US 342, 42 LRRM 2034 (1958). *See* Chapter 14 *supra* for detailed discussion of the case.

tract, one party, in the face of a refusal by the other, adamantly insists upon a clause which constitutes a permissive subject, such conduct is *per se,* without regard to subjective good or bad faith, an unfair labor practice within the meaning of Section 8(a)(5) or 8(b)(3) because "such conduct is, in substance, a refusal to bargain about the subjects that are within the scope of mandatory bargaining." [2] However, a party's conduct in regard to a permissive subject may also be evidence of subjective good or bad faith in bargaining.[3]

No waiver of the right to claim later that a subject is a permissive one results from bargaining without reservation about the subject. Either the employer or the union may bargain about the topic as if it were a mandatory subject without losing its right, at any time before agreement is reached, to take an adamant position that the matter shall not be included in a contract between the parties. To sustain a claim of waiver based upon a course of bargaining "would penalize a party to negotiations for endeavoring to reach agreement by consenting to bargaining upon issues as to which the Act does not require him to bargain." [4] No matter how lengthy the bargaining about a permissive subject, it never changes into a mandatory subject. As the Fourth Circuit stated:

> A determination that a subject which is non-mandatory at the outset may become mandatory merely because a party had exercised this freedom [to bargain or not to bargain] by not rejecting the proposal at once, or sufficiently early, might unduly discourage free bargaining on non-mandatory matters. Parties might feel compelled to reject non-mandatory proposals out of hand to avoid risking waiver of the right to reject.[5]

A. Early Cases

Ever since the issue first was raised in the early years of the Wagner Act, the Board has consistently held that there are certain subjects about which the parties are free to bargain even though their nature is such as not to make them mandatory subjects of bargaining.

---

2 356 US at 349.
3 Steere Broadcasting Corp., 158 NLRB 487, 507, 62 LRRM 1083 (1966).
4 Kit Mfg. Co., 150 NLRB 662, 671, 58 LRRM 1140 (1965), *enforced,* 365 F 2d 829, 62 LRRM 2856 (CA 9, 1966).
5 NLRB v. Davidson, 318 F 2d 550, 558, 53 LRRM 2462 (CA 4, 1963).

Among the earliest of these holdings were the cases dealing with the posting of performance bonds, *i.e.,* surety bonds that would indemnify one party to a contract if damages resulted from a breach by the other party. The Board held that as a matter of law an employer could not insist upon the union's posting such a bond as a condition precedent to the execution of an agreement.[6] In 1944 it reached a similar conclusion in the *Eppinger* case,[7] holding that an employer could not compel a union to bargain on the question of the licensing of union agents under state law, even though Florida statutorily required such licensing.[8]

In none of these cases was the term "voluntary" or "permissive" subjects of bargaining expressly employed. However, the reasoning which supported the holdings demonstrated that these concepts were being used, since in each case an employer was found guilty of a refusal to bargain because it insisted that agreement on a subject, itself not illegal, was nevertheless a condition precedent to bargaining.

Since *Borg-Warner* the Board has dealt much more extensively with the matter of permissive subjects of bargaining.

B.　A Catalog of Permissive Subjects of Bargaining

1. Definition of Bargaining Unit. Whenever bargaining takes place without a prior Board definition of unit, the parties must agree upon the unit to be covered by the contract they negotiate. "The parties cannot bargain meaningfully about wages or hours or conditions of employment unless they know the unit of bargaining." [9] And even when the Board has defined a unit the parties may wish to, and by law are free to, agree on a negotiated unit different from the certified or recognized unit. In advanced forms of collective bargaining there may be a number of different bargaining units applicable to the employees in one certified unit, or there may be one unit including more than a single certified

---

[6] Benson Produce Co., 71 NLRB 888, 19 LRRM 1060 (1946); Scripto Mfg. Co., 36 NLRB 411, 9 LRRM 156 (1941); Interstate Steamship Co., 36 NLRB 1307, 9 LRRM 200 (1941); Jasper Blackburn Products Corp., 21 NLRB 1240, 1254-1256, 6 LRRM 169 (1940).

[7] Eppinger & Russel Co., 56 NLRB 1259, 14 LRRM 164 (1944).

[8] *Cf.* Hill v. Florida, 325 US 538, 16 LRRM 734 (1945), discussed in Chapter 29 *infra.*

[9] Douds v. International Longshoremen's Ass'n, 241 F 2d 278, 282, 39 LRRM 2388 (CA 2, 1957).

or recognized unit.[10] In each instance the combination of units must be established by voluntary agreement of the parties.

Because the law encourages voluntary settlement of disputes without government intervention, the Board has gone far in accepting as lawful negotiating units established by consensual agreement of the parties.[11] Similarly, the accepted legal theory that there may be several appropriate units applicable to any group of employees means that the parties may agree upon which such unit their contract will cover.

Despite the extensive amount of bargaining about the negotiating unit that commonly occurs, the scope of the unit is not a mandatory subject of bargaining. The difference between bargaining about mandatory subjects and determining the unit was explained by the Second Circuit as follows:

> The statute imposes on labor and management alike a duty to bargain in good faith with respect to wages, hours and other conditions of employment in the expressed belief that such bargaining is the most effective way to settle differences without disrupting commerce. This duty "does not compel either party to agree to a proposal," as Section 8 (d) states, "or require the making of a concession," and the Board has no power to settle any of those questions. By way of contrast, it not only has power, but is indeed directed, to decide what is the appropriate bargaining unit in each case.[12]

Even where the Board has originally fixed the unit, "it may be altered by agreement of the parties." [13]

The voluntary combination into one multiplant unit of several previously certified individual plant units has received approval.[14]

---

[10] Consensual bargaining patterns may assume many different forms. The actual unit used for negotiations may not coincide with the certified or recognized unit—some issues may be negotiated in local units while other issues may be negotiated in larger units. For example, it is not uncommon for the negotiating unit for pensions to be larger than the negotiating unit for seniority. See Chapter 9 supra at notes 219-221.

[11] Radio Corp. of America, 135 NLRB 980, 983, 49 LRRM 1606 (1962) ; General Motors Corp., 120 NLRB 1215, 1219, 1221, 42 LRRM 1143 (1958) ; Lever Brothers Co., 96 NLRB 448, 450, 28 LRRM 1544 (1951).

[12] Douds v. International Longshoremen's Ass'n, 241 F 2d 278, 282, 39 LRRM 2388 (CA 2, 1957).

[13] Ibid.

[14] General Motors Corp., 120 NLRB 1215, 1220, 42 LRRM 1143 (1958) ; Radio Corp. of America, 135 NLRB 980, 983, 49 LRRM 1606 (1962).

But insistence on such a combination of prior existing units is unlawful.[15] Similarly, insistence by either party that employees included by the Board in a unit be excluded or that additional employees be included constitutes a refusal to bargain.[16]

2. Supervisors and Agricultural Labor. Although the Act is not applicable to supervisors or to agricultural labor, the Board has held that the parties may bargain about such categories of employees. But a party may not insist, to the point of refusing to sign a contract applicable to employees covered by the Act, that the contract cover supervisors [17] or agricultural labor.[18]

3. Parties to Collective Bargaining Agreement. The only required parties to a collective bargaining agreement are, on the employer's side, the legal employer or employers of the employees in the unit or units covered by the agreement or the employer association to which the employer has delegated bargaining; and, on the employees' side, the certified bargaining representative or representatives of the covered employees.[19] It is customary in many industries or unions, however, to have additional parties to the agreement. For example: (1) the international union as well as the local where only the local is certified; (2) the local as well as the international where only the international is certified; (3) the employer as well as the employer association where the unit is employer-association-wide; (4) the employer association as well as

---

15 Int'l Longshoremen's Ass'n, 118 NLRB 1481, 1483, 40 LRRM 1408 (1957), *set aside on other grounds,* 277 F 2d 681, 45 LRRM 2551 (CA DC, 1958); Douds v. International Longshoremen's Ass'n, 241 F 2d 278, 39 LRRM 2388 (CA 2, 1957).

16 Steere Broadcasting Corp., 158 NLRB 487, 488, n. 2, 507, 62 LRRM 1083 (1966); Int'l Typographical Union, 123 NLRB 806, 823, 43 LRRM 1538 (1959), *set aside in this respect,* 278 F 2d 6, 46 LRRM 2132 (CA 1, 1959), *affirmed in part and reversed in part,* 365 US 705, 47 LRRM 2920 (1961), without considering this issue. *See* AFL-CIO Joint Negotiating Committee (Phelps Dodge Corp.), 184 NLRB No. 106, 74 LRRM 1705 (1970), holding unions in violation of §8(b)(3) when they demanded and struck to obtain company-wide bargaining instead of bargaining within the established bargaining units. *See also* discussion of coalition bargaining in Chapter 11 *supra.*

17 NLRB v. Retail Clerks Int'l Ass'n (Safeway Company), 203 F 2d 165, 31 LRRM 2606 (CA 9, 1953), adjudging union in contempt for insisting on bargaining for supervisory employees in violation of a consent decree enforcing 96 NLRB 581, 28 LRRM 1554 (1951), *cert. denied,* 348 US 839 (1954); So. Cal. Pipe Trades Dist. Council 16 (Aero Plumbing Co.), 167 NLRB No. 143, 66 LRRM 1233 (1967).

18 Dist. 50, United Mine Workers (Central Soya Co.), 142 NLRB 930, 939, 53 LRRM 1178 (1963).

19 Or noncertified representative selected by a majority of the employees in an appropriate unit. *See* Chapter 10 *supra.*

the employer, regardless of whether the unit is the employer or the association.

In a surprisingly large number of cases that have come before the Board, employers have insisted, to the point of impasse, on having as a party to the collective agreement a union entity other than the one certified. So long as the employer and the union, whether certified or not, voluntarily agree, the law gives effect to their solution of this problem. But insistence by either party, to the point of not signing an otherwise agreed-upon contract unless a given organization or individual other than a required party is added or a required party is excluded, is *per se* a refusal to bargain irrespective of good or bad faith. The matter of settling on the parties to a collective bargaining agreement is hence a permissive rather than a mandatory subject.

In *Borg-Warner* [20] the employer insisted that the recognition clause should name only the local as the party to the contract. The international was the certified representative and had proffered a recognition clause naming both the international and its local. The resulting impasse over this issue brought unfair labor practice charges, followed by a Board order that was upheld by the Supreme Court. The Court stated that the proposed recognition of only the local would have been lawful if agreed to by the unions, but it did not follow that because the employer could lawfully so propose, it could lawfully so insist as a condition of agreement. The Court said:

> The "recognition" clause likewise does not come within the definition of mandatory bargaining. The statute requires the company to bargain with the certified representative of its employees. It is an evasion of that duty to insist that the certified agent not be a party to the collective-bargaining contract. The Act does not prohibit the voluntary addition of a party, but that does not authorize the employer to exclude the certified representative from the contract.[21]

An employer cannot lawfully insist as a condition of a contract that a labor federation be a party to a contract where a local union affiliated with that federation is the certified representative.[22] Similarly, a union is guilty of a refusal to bargain when it refuses

---

[20] NLRB v. Borg-Warner Corp., 356 US 342, 42 LRRM 2034 (1958).
[21] *Id.* at 350.
[22] NLRB v. Taormina Co., 207 F 2d 251, 254, 32 LRRM 2684 (CA 5, 1953), *enforcing* 94 NLRB 884, 28 LRRM 1118 (1951); Standard Generator Co., 90 NLRB 790, 26 LRRM 1285 (1950).

to include mention of the employer association in the preamble of the contract, where the employer is part of an established multi-employer unit represented by the employer association.[23]

4. Performance Bonds. Just as in pre-Taft-Hartley days, a performance bond is consistently treated as a permissive bargaining subject.[24] Nor does the amount of the bond sought make any difference.[25] In the *Scripto* case [26] the Board would not permit an employer to insist upon an indemnity bond even though the union was immune from suit under a Georgia law that provided that only by registration would such an entity become amenable to an action in the state courts. And an employer may not insist that the union furnish a bond to indemnify the employer should it be picketed by outside unions or have pressure applied to its customers.[27]

Similarly, a union is guilty of a refusal to bargain if it insists that the employer furnish a bond for the payment of employees' wages and benefits,[28] or to secure performance of the contract.[29]

---

23 United Slate, Tile & Composition Roofers, 172 NLRB No. 249, 69 LRRM 1300 (1968). *See* treatment of multi-employer bargaining units in Chapter 9 *supra*.
24 NLRB v. F. M. Reeves and Sons, Inc., 47 LRRM 2480 (CA 10, 1960), *cert. denied*, 366 US 914, 48 LRRM 2071 (1961), adjudicating contempt for violating 273 F 2d 710, 45 LRRM 2295 (CA 10, 1959); Rabowin v. NLRB, 195 F 2d 906 (CA 2, 1952); Newberry Equipment Co., Inc., 135 NLRB 747, 49 LRRM 1571 (1962); Int'l Brotherhood of Teamsters, Local 294 (Conway's Express), 87 NLRB 972, 978, 25 LRRM 1202 (1949), *enforced sub nom.*, 195 F 2d 906, 29 LRRM 2617 (CA 2, 1952); Amory Garment Co., Inc., 80 NLRB 182, 23 LRRM 1081 (1948), *enforced*, 24 LRRM 2274 (CA 5, 1949); Cookeville Shirt Co. and P. M. French, 79 NLRB 667, 22 LRRM 1438 (1948).
25 Brown & Root, Inc., 86 NLRB 520, 24 LRRM 1648 (1949), *modified on other grounds sub nom.*, NLRB v. Ozark Dam Constructors, 190 F 2d 222, 28 LRRM 2246 (CA 8, 1951). *See also* NLRB v. Cosco Products Co., 280 F 2d 905, 46 LRRM 2549 (CA 5, 1960); IBS Mfg. Co., 96 NLRB 1263, 29 LRRM 1027 (1951), *enforcement denied on other grounds*, 210 F 2d 634, 33 LRRM 2583 (CA 5, 1954); Taormina Co., 94 NLRB 884, 28 LRRM 1118 (1951), *enforced*, 207 F 2d 251, 32 LRRM 2684 (CA 5, 1953); Standard Generator Co., 90 NLRB 790, 26 LRRM 1285 (1950), *enforced*, 186 F 2d 606, 27 LRRM 2274 (CA 8, 1951).
26 Scripto Co., 36 NLRB 411, 9 LRRM 156 (1941).
27 Arlington Asphalt Co., 136 NLRB 742, 49 LRRM 1831 (1962), *enforced sub nom.*, NLRB v. Arlington Asphalt Co., 318 F 2d 550, 53 LRRM 2462 (CA 4, 1963).
28 Excello Dry Wall Co., 145 NLRB 663, 668, 55 LRRM 1015 (1963). *See also* NLRB v. American Compress Warehouse, Div. of Frost-Whited Co., Inc., 350 F 2d 365, 59 LRRM 2739 (CA 5, 1965), *cert. denied*, 382 US 982, 61 LRRM 2147 (1966). *Cf.* Bricklayers, Local 3, 162 NLRB 476, 64 LRRM 1085 (1966) (union may not insist on penalty clause calling for reimbursement to union for dues and initiation fees lost as a result of improper subcontracting).
29 Local 164, Brotherhood of Painters v. NLRB, 293 F 2d 133, 48 LRRM 2060 (CA DC, 1961), *cert. denied*, 368 US 824, 48 LRRM 3110 (1961).

5. Legal-Liability Clauses. Although the so-called legal-liability clause can be distinguished from the performance-bond clause, the Board has held that a clause subjecting a union to legal liability for violation of a no-strike clause, including liability for all injury or damage resulting from such violation, is a permissive clause only.[30] But the Fourth Circuit has disagreed, holding such a clause to be entirely different from an indemnity requirement, and one upon which the company may insist to the point of impasse. The court viewed the clause as simply stating what the law provides.[31] On the other hand, it has been held that an employer violates the Act if it insists, as a condition to execution of an agreement, that the union register with a state court in order to make it amenable to any suit which might be brought thereafter by the employer.[32]

6. Internal Union Affairs. Internal union matters are possibly the best examples of permissive bargaining subjects. An employer may request bargaining about them but may not push such bargaining to an impasse. The Supreme Court in *Borg-Warner* pointed out that a mandatory subject of bargaining must deal with relations between the employer and the employees, not between the union and the employees.

Thus, an employer may not insist upon a clause providing that nonunion employees shall have a right to vote upon the provisions of the contract negotiated by the union as bargaining agent.[33] Nor may it insist upon a clause requiring a strike vote among employees before a strike occurs,[34] or upon employee ratification as a condition precedent to execution of a collective bargaining agreement.[35]

Similarly, a clause providing that the contract should become void whenever the percentage of employees paying their dues by

---

[30] Radiator Specialty Co., 143 NLRB 350, 53 LRRM 1319 (1963), *enforced in part,* 336 F 2d 495, 57 LRRM 2097 (CA 4, 1964). *See also* No. Carolina Furniture, Inc., 121 NLRB 41, 42 LRRM 1271 (1958).
[31] Radiator Specialty Co., 336 F 2d 495, 57 LRRM 2097 (CA 4, 1964).
[32] Dalton Telephone Co., 82 NLRB 1001, 24 LRRM 1001 (1949), *enforced,* 187 F 2d 811, 27 LRRM 2503 (CA 5, 1951).
[33] NLRB v. Corsicana Cotton Mills, 178 F 2d 344, 347, 24 LRRM 2494 (CA 5, 1949).
[34] *Ibid. See* the following cases that antedated *Borg-Warner:* Allis-Chalmers Mfg. Co. v. NLRB, 213 F 2d 374, 34 LRRM 2202 (CA 7, 1954); U.S. Gypsum Co., 109 NLRB 1402, 34 LRRM 1595 (1954). *And see* Note, *Strike Vote Clause; Bargainable Matter,* 44 GEO. L.J. 120 (1955).
[35] Houchens Mkt. v. NLRB, 375 F 2d 208, 64 LRRM 2647 (CA 6, 1967), *enforcing* 155 NLRB 729, 60 LRRM 1384 (1965).

checkoff dropped below 50 is a permissive subject of bargaining.[36] Permissive also are proposed clauses that the union must provide withdrawal cards to any employee who might be transferred out of the unit,[37] or that all shop stewards are to be chosen from particular classifications of employees.[38] And the Board has found an employer guilty of a Section 8(a)(5) violation in refusing to bargain unless the certified union qualified to engage in business as a labor union, as required by state law,[39] and submitted an affidavit certifying that none of its officers was affiliated with the Communist Party.[40] However, the Seventh Circuit set aside the Board's finding that an employer had unlawfully refused to bargain by insisting on a contract provision limiting the right of the union to discipline or fine its members for engaging in or refraining from organizational activities. The court held that the clause related to terms and conditions of employment since its object was to permit employees to work during a strike without fear of union reprisal and hence was a mandatory subject.[41]

7. Union Label. The union label is a well-established subject of collective bargaining. Although unions have vigorously contended that the union label is related to wages, hours, and conditions of employment closely enough to be a mandatory subject of bargaining, the Board rejects this view and holds it to be merely permissive. In *Kit Mfg. Co.*[42] the Board noted that whatever economic advantage use of the label may afford an employer, and whatever impact it may have on the salability of its product, "its relation to wages, hours or other terms or conditions of employ-

---

36 NLRB v. Darlington Veneer Co., 236 F 2d 85, 38 LRRM 2574 (CA 4, 1956). *Cf.* Bethlehem Steel, 133 NLRB 1400, 49 LRRM 1018 (1961) (indicating that it would be unlawful for an employer to insist upon a clause requiring individual signatures on grievances).

37 NLRB v. Superior Fireproof Door & Sash Co., 289 F 2d 713, 47 LRRM 2816 (CA 2, 1961).

38 *Ibid.*

39 Herron Yarn Mills, Inc., 160 NLRB 629, 63 LRRM 1022 (1966). *See also* NLRB v. Dalton Telephone Co., 187 F 2d 811, 812, 27 LRRM 2503 (CA 5, 1951), *enforcing* 82 NLRB 1001, 1002-1003, 24 LRRM 1001 (1949), *cert. denied,* 342 US 824, 28 LRRM 2625 (1951).

40 Herron Yarn Mills, Inc., 160 NLRB 629, 63 LRRM 1022 (1966).

41 Allen Bradley Co. v. NLRB, 286 F 2d 442, 47 LRRM 2562 (CA 7, 1961). *But see* NLRB v. Allis-Chalmers Mfg. Co., 388 US 175, 61 LRRM 2498 (1966), discussed in Chapter 5 *supra.*

42 Kit Mfg. Co., 150 NLRB 662, 671, 58 LRRM 1140 (1964), *enforced,* 365 F 2d 829, 62 LRRM 2856 (CA 9, 1966).

ment is at best remote and speculative." [43] Accordingly, the employer was found guilty of a refusal to bargain when he insisted upon a contract provision granting him permission to use the union label without also including a union security clause in the agreement.

8. Industry Promotion Funds. A union's demand that an employer contribute to an industry promotion fund has been held in a series of cases to be a permissive subject of bargaining. A union violates Section 8(b)(3) by insisting on the adoption of such a clause.

In the *Daelyte Service* case [44] a member of a multi-employer bargaining unit refused to sign a contract that had been negotiated by the union and the employer association on the ground that the clause requiring it to contribute to a promotion fund was illegal. Subsequently the employer filed a refusal-to-bargain charge against the union, alleging that the latter's conduct in demanding such a clause was violative of Section 8(b)(3). Dismissing the complaint, the Board held that the union's demand for an employer contribution to the industry fund was not unlawful; thus, the acquiescence of the multi-employer group was not unlawful. Since the parties had mutually agreed to the clause, there was no necessity for the Board to pass on whether the subject itself was mandatory or permissive.

Shortly thereafter, in the *Mill Floor* case,[45] the Board specifically decided this question. The union had demanded a clause providing as follows:

> Each employer agrees to contribute one (1¢) cent per hour for each hour worked by each Employee covered by this Agreement to [a] Promotional Fund. . . . A uniform collection machinery will be established to collect the contributions due under this section.[46]

The Board found such a fund to be a permissive and not a mandatory subject of bargaining; therefore, the union had violated Section 8(b)(3) of the Act when it insisted upon inclusion of this

---

43 *Id.* at 662, n. 1.

44 Detroit Window Cleaners Union Local 139 (Daelyte Service Company) 126 NLRB 63, 45 LRRM 1275 (1960).

45 Detroit Resilient Floor Decorators Local 2265 (Mill Floor Covering, Inc.), 136 NLRB 769, 49 LRRM 1842 (1962), *enforced,* 317 F 2d 269, 53 LRRM 2311 (CA 6, 1963).

46 136 NLRB at 776.

clause to the point of impasse. The Board considered the industry promotion fund "to be outside the employment relationship." It is concerned "rather with the relationship of employers to one another, or, like advertising, with the relationship of an employer to the consuming public." [47] Emphasizing the permissive nature of the subject matter, the Board stated:

> Nothing prevents an employer and a union from joining voluntarily in the mutual effort to attempt to influence their industry's course of development, provided, of course, that other legislative enactments do not prohibit such activities. To hold, however, under this Act, that one party must bargain at the behest of another on any matter which might conceivably enhance the prospects of the industry would transform bargaining over the compensation, hours, and employment conditions of employees into a debate over policy objectives.[48]

If the parties to a collective bargaining contract voluntarily agree on an industry advancement or promotion fund, either party commits a refusal to bargain if it thereafter refuses to execute the contract containing the clause. Thus, a union was held to have violated Section 8(b)(3) when it refused to sign a contract with a promotion-fund clause, since the parties had previously agreed to the clause in negotiations.[49] Conversely, it is not a refusal to bargain on the part of the union if it insists on the inclusion of a provision for such a fund in the written contract once the agreement to include it has been negotiated.[50]

9. Settlement of Charges. Neither party is compelled to negotiate with the other about the settlement of unfair labor practice charges filed with the Board.[51] If a party demands that charges

---

[47] *Id.* at 771.

[48] *Ibid. Accord,* Sheet Metal Workers Local 270 (General Sheet Metal Co.), 144 NLRB 773, 54 LRRM 1130 (1963).

[49] Associated Bldg. Contractors of Evansville, Inc., 143 NLRB 678, 53 LRRM 1395 (1963), *enforced as to this issue,* NLRB v. Painters Union, 334 F 2d 729, 56 LRRM 2648 (CA 7, 1964). The Board, however, stated again that such a clause is permissive, and that the union could have refused to bargain on the issue during negotiations.

[50] General Sheet Metal Co., 144 NLRB 773, 54 LRRM 1130 (1963).

[51] Jefferson Standard Broadcasting Co., 94 NLRB 1507, 28 LRRM 1215 (1951).

against it be withdrawn as a condition to negotiating,[52] or if it seeks to condition wage increases upon the withdrawal of charges against it,[53] it violates the Act.

II. ILLEGAL SUBJECTS

A. Examples of Illegal Subjects

Although there are not many decisions to show precisely what constitute illegal subjects of bargaining, some guides are available.[54] A provision for a closed shop is illegal under the Act,[55] as is a provision for a hiring hall giving preference to union members.[56] A "hot cargo" clause in violation of Section 8(e) is an illegal subject for bargaining.[57] And it has been held that a union breaches its duty to bargain in good faith under Section 8(b)(3)

---

[52] Palm Beach Post Times, Div. of Perry Publications, Inc., 151 NLRB 1030, 58 LRRM 1561 (1965); Ohio Car and Truck Leasing, Inc., 149 NLRB 1423, 58 LRRM 1008 (1964); NLRB v. Kit Mfg. Co., 142 NLRB 957, enforced, 335 F 2d 166, 56 LRRM 2988 (CA 9, 1964), cert. denied, 380 US 910, 58 LRRM 2496 (1965); Silby-Dolcourt Chemical Indus., Inc., 145 NLRB 1348, 55 LRRM 1160 (1964). See also American Stores Packing Co., 142 NLRB 711, 53 LRRM 1137 (1963); Body and Tank Corp., 144 NLRB 1414, 54 LRRM 1268 (1963); American Laundry Mach. Co., 76 NLRB 981, 21 LRRM 1275 (1948), enforced, 174 F 2d 124, 24 LRRM 2033 (CA 6, 1949); Sussex Hats, Inc., 85 NLRB 399, 24 LRRM 1407 (1949); Burns Brick Co., 80 NLRB 389, 23 LRRM 1122 (1948). The same principle applies to a union. Int'l Ass'n of Bridge, Structural and Ornamental Iron Workers, Local 600, 134 NLRB 301, 49 LRRM 1134 (1961).

[53] Butcher Boy Refrigeration Door Co., 127 NLRB 1360, 46 LRRM 1192 (1960), enforced, 290 F 2d 22, 48 LRRM 2058 (CA 7, 1961).

[54] This section is concerned with illegal bargaining subjects. It does not embrace the broader topic of improper insistence upon fulfillment of certain conditions before bargaining can continue. Insistence on withdrawal of charges filed with the Board is covered under Permissive Subjects, supra, this chapter. Other examples of improper conditions include employer insistence that a union relinquish its claim that a prior contract is still in effect or that a union withdraw a wage demand. Bergen Point Iron Works, 79 NLRB 1073, 22 LRRM 1475 (1948); NLRB v. Hoppes Mfg. Co., 170 F 2d 962, 23 LRRM 2129 (CA 6, 1948); Vanette Hosiery Mills, 80 NLRB 1116, 23 LRRM 1198 (1948). Nor may an employer condition negotiations upon termination of a strike. Binder Metal Products, Inc., 154 NLRB 1662, 60 LRRM 1198 (1965); West Coast Luggage Co., 105 NLRB 414, 32 LRRM 1290 (1953). See also Teamsters Local No. 662 v. NLRB, 302 F 2d 908, 50 LRRM 2243 (CA DC, 1962), cert. denied, 371 US 827, 51 LRRM 2222 (1962). The nature of the duty to bargain is treated in Chapter 11 supra.

[55] Penello v. United Mine Workers, 88 F Supp 935, 25 LRRM 2368 (DDC, 1950); Honolulu Star-Bulletin, Ltd., 123 NLRB 395, 43 LRRM 1449 (1959), enforcement denied on other grounds, 274 F 2d 567, 45 LRRM 2184 (CA DC, 1959). See Comment, Subjects Included Within Management's Duty to Bargain Collectively, 26 LA. L. REV. 630, 632 (1966). See Chapter 26 infra.

[56] NLRB v. National Maritime Union, 175 F 2d 686, 24 LRRM 2268 (CA 2, 1949), cert. denied, 338 US 954, 25 LRRM 2395 (1950). See Chapter 26 infra for a discussion of hiring-hall agreements.

[57] Amalgamated Lithographers Local 17, 130 NLRB 985, 47 LRRM 1374 (1961). See also Amalgamated Lithographers Local 78, 130 NLRB 968, 47 LRRM 1380 (1961). And see Chapter 24 infra.

when it demands a contract provision that is inconsistent with the duty of fair representation owed by the union to the employees.[58] The Board views a proposal which requires separation of employees on the basis of race to be an unlawful subject of bargaining.[59]

If a union seeks to have its rules and regulations incorporated in an agreement with an employer, a rule or regulation requiring discrimination in favor of union members must be excluded since it would clash with the Act.[60] But the rule would have to be explicit in calling for illegal conduct to support a finding of violation. "[I]n the absence of provisions calling explicitly for illegal conduct, the contract cannot be held illegal because it failed affirmatively to disclaim all illegal objectives." [61]

Since an employer's insistence that it have a contractual right to discharge employees for "union activity" is a violation of Section 8(a)(5),[62] it may be argued that such a contractual clause is an illegal bargaining topic. And since an employer's grant of a 20-year seniority credit to strikers who return to work during a strike has been held to be inherently discriminatory,[63] it may be argued that such a superseniority plan is an illegal topic for bargaining.[64] As these holdings indicate, such provisions are inconsistent with the underlying policies of the Act.[65]

The cases that have been cited so far in this section involve questions of illegality under the NLRA or inconsistency with the policies of the Act. The federal antitrust statutes [66] may also deter-

---

[58] ILA Local 1367 (Galveston Maritime Ass'n, Inc.), 148 NLRB 897, 57 LRRM 1083 (1964). *See* Chapter 27 *infra.*

[59] Hughes Tool Co., 147 NLRB 1573, 56 LRRM 1289 (1964). *See* Chapter 27 *infra.*

[60] NLRB v. News Syndicate Co., 365 US 695, 47 LRRM 2916 (1961).

[61] *Id.* at 699-700, *citing* NLRB v. News Syndicate Co., 279 F 2d 323, 330, 46 LRRM 2295 (CA 2, 1960).

[62] Gay Paree Undergarment Co., 91 NLRB 1363, 27 LRRM 1006 (1950).

[63] NLRB v. Erie Resistor Corp., 373 US 221, 53 LRRM 2121 (1963).

[64] *See* Great Lakes Carbon Corp. v. NLRB, 360 F 2d 19, 62 LRRM 2088 (CA 4, 1966), holding that a negotiated contract provision giving superseniority to replacements for striking employees was unlawful on its face and must be eliminated from the contract. *But cf.* Philip Carey Mfg. Co. v. NLRB, 331 F 2d 720, 55 LRRM 2821 (CA 6, 1964), *cert. denied,* 379 US 888, 57 LRRM 2307 (1964).

[65] Similarly, other contractual provisions which contravene prohibitions in the statute would be illegal. For example, if an incumbent union sought a contract provision that would give it advantages over an outside union in soliciting or distributing literature in contravention of the underlying policies of the Act, the same reasoning could be employed to make the topic illegal for bargaining. *See* Chapters 5 *supra* and 17 *infra.*

[66] 15 USC §§1-7; 15 USC §§12-27 (1964).

mine the illegality of certain subjects of bargaining. As the Supreme Court declared in *Mineworkers v. Pennington*,[67] "[A]n agreement resulting from union-employer negotiations" is not "automatically exempt from Sherman Act scrutiny simply because the negotiations involve a compulsory subject of bargaining. . . . [T]here are limits to what a union or an employer may offer or extract in the name of wages," so that antitrust laws are violated when a union agrees "with one set of employers to impose a wage scale on other bargaining units." [68]

With respect to state law, the Supreme Court has suggested that the preemption by federal labor law leaves certain state legislation still applicable. In *Teamsters v. Oliver*,[69] in holding the Ohio antitrust act inapplicable because federal law preempted the antitrust field, the Court indicated that a different result might have been reached if it had had before it "a collective bargaining agreement in conflict with a local health or safety regulation." A few states have enacted statutes which outlaw or restrict the use of lie detector tests for determining whether an individual may acquire or retain employment.[70] How should the Board treat an employer proposal that would violate such a state law? One possible approach is for the Board to take state laws into consideration in determining what constitutes an illegal topic for bargaining. On the other hand, if the case is within the jurisdiction of the Board, it might be found that the state law is preempted by the NLRA, and the Board might rely on the fact that the federal statute contains no ban on the use of lie detector tests.

B. Relationship to Duty to Bargain

Neither party may require that the other agree to contract provi-

---

67 United Mine Workers v. Pennington, 381 US 657, 59 LRRM 2369 (1965).

68 *Id.* at 664-665. *See also* Amalgamated Meat Cutters Local 189 v. Jewel Tea Co., 381 US 676, 59 LRRM 2376 (1965). For a detailed discussion of *Pennington* and *Jewel* see Chapter 29 *infra*.

69 Teamsters Local 24 v. Oliver, 358 US 283, 297, 43 LRRM 2374 (1959). *See* Chapter 29 *infra* for discussion of federal preemption and the relation of the NLRA to other laws.

70 ALAS. STAT., ch. 10, § 23.10.037 (Supp. 1964); CAL. LABOR CODE § 432.2 (West 1963); ANN. LAWS OF MASS., ch. 149, § 198 (1963); ORE. REV. STAT., ch. 659, § 659.225 (1963); R. I. GEN. LAWS § 28-6.1-1, (Supp. 1966).

sions which are unlawful under the Act.[71] In 1948 the Board stated:

> [W]hat the Act does not permit is the insistence, as a condition precedent to entering into a collective bargaining agreement, that the other party to the negotiations agree to a provision or take some action which is unlawful or inconsistent with the basic policy of the Act. Compliance with the Act's requirement of collective bargaining cannot be made dependent upon the acceptance of provisions in the agreement which, by their terms or in their effectuation, are repugnant to the Act's specific language or basic policy.[72]

Insistence upon an illegal provision thus violates the duty to bargain. Two prominent types of clauses that violate specific provisions of the Act are *closed shop* clauses (or other illegal union security clauses), prohibited by Sections 8(a)(3) and 8(b)(2), and *hot cargo* clauses, prohibited by Section 8(e). "Neither party may require that the other agree to contract provisions which are unlawful. And when . . . one of the parties creates a bargaining impasse by insisting, not in good faith, that the other agree to an unlawful condition of employment, that party has violated its statutory duty to bargain." [73]

A question to which the answer is not clear is whether the proposal of an illegal subject is in itself an unfair labor practice under Sections 8(a)(5) or 8(b)(3), or whether additional evidence of bad faith is required. Most of the cases involving proposals of illegal subjects for bargaining arise in a context of other indicia of bad faith, especially insistence upon the proposals.

No decision has been found holding that a violation of the Act occurs when an illegal subject is proposed for negotiation. As a practical matter, however, would a party receiving the illegal re-

---

[71] Amalgamated Meat Cutters Union Local 421 (Great Atl. & Pac. Tea Co.), 81 NLRB 1052, 23 LRRM 1464 (1949); Nat'l Maritime Union (Texas Co.), 78 NLRB 971, 22 LRRM 1289 (1948), *enforced*, 175 F 2d 686, 24 LRRM 2268 (CA 2, 1949), *cert. denied*, 338 US 954, 25 LRRM 2395 (1950). *Cf.* concurring opinion of Mr. Justice Harlan in the *Borg-Warner* case, where he said that "[o]f course an employer or union cannot insist upon a clause which would be illegal under the Act's provisions." NLRB v. Borg-Warner Corp., 356 US 342, 360, 42 LRRM 2034 (1958).
[72] Nat'l Maritime Union (Texas Co.), 78 NLRB 971, 981-982, 22 LRRM 1289 (1948).
[73] Amalgamated Meat-Cutters Union (Great Atl. & Pac. Tea Co.), 81 NLRB 1052, 1061, 23 LRRM 1464 (1949), in which the Board found a union's insistence upon an illegal union security clause to be a violation of §8(b)(3) as well as §8(b)(2). *See* Chapter 26 *infra* for discussion of union security caluses. *See* Chapter 24 *infra* for discussion of "hot cargo" and other clauses which contravene §8(e). For the effect of unlawful clauses on the contract bar doctrine in representation proceedings, *see* Chapter 8 *supra*.

quest be likely to file unfair labor practice charges when the other party merely presents the illegal subject and does not press for its inclusion in the contract?

If the proposal of an illegal subject of bargaining only becomes a violation of Sections 8(a)(5) or 8(b)(3) when it is pressed to the point of impasse, the distinction between illegal subjects and permissive subjects loses much of its significance. Nevertheless, although a party may not insist on a permissive subject to the point of impasse, such a subject may, by mutual approval of the parties, be incorporated in the agreement. But an illegal subject cannot properly be included in the agreement.[74]

---

[74] Honolulu Star-Bulletin, Ltd., 123 NLRB 395, 43 LRRM 1449 (1959), *enforcement denied on other grounds,* 274 F 2d 567, 45 LRRM 2184 (CA DC, 1959).

CHAPTER 17

RELATION OF BOARD ACTION TO ENFORCEMENT OF AGREEMENTS UNDER SECTION 301

I. INTRODUCTION

The process of collective bargaining generally results in a contract.[1] This chapter explores the relation of Board action to the enforcement of the contract.[2] The question of accommodating Board action to the arbitration process is reserved for the following chapter;[3] this chapter is concerned only with the Board's practice and jurisdiction in relation to a contract. It presents the

---

[1] "The Act contemplates the making of contracts with labor organizations. That is the manifest objective in providing for collective bargaining." Consolidated Edison Co. v. NLRB, 305 US 197, 236, 3 LRRM 645, 656 (1938).

[2] For bibliographic materials, see the following: Hanley, *The NLRB and the Arbitration Process: Conflict or Accommodation,* in LABOR LAW DEVELOPMENTS 1968, 151 (Sw. Legal Foundation, 14th Labor Law Institute); Jones & Smith, *Impact of the Emerging Federal Law of Grievance Arbitration on Judges, Arbitrators, and Parties,* 52 VA. L. REV. 831 (1966); Kovarsky, *Individual Suits and Arbitration,* 12 How. L.J. 213 (1966); Kovarsky, *Labor Arbitration and Federal Pre-emption: The Overruling of Black v. Cutter Laboratories,* 47 MINN. L. REV. 531 (1963); Kramer, *Arbitration Under the Taft-Hartley Act,* 11 N.Y.U. CONF. LAB. 255 (New York: Matthew Bender & Co., 1963); Lesnick, *Arbitration as a Limit on the Discretion of Management, Union, and NLRB: The Year's Major Developments,* 18 N.Y.U. CONF. LAB. 7 (Washington: BNA Books, 1966); Smith & Jones, *The Supreme Court and Labor Dispute Arbitration: The Emerging Federal Law,* 63 MICH. L. REV. 751 (1965); Sovern, *Section 301 and the Primary Jurisdiction of the NLRB,* 76 HARV. L. REV. 529 (1963); Note, *Labor Relations: Removal Under Section 301(a),* 16 BAYLOR L. REV. 400 (1964); Note, *Jurisdiction of Arbitrators and State Courts Over Conduct Constituting Both a Contract Violation and an Unfair Labor Practice,* 69 HARV. L. REV. 725 (1956); Note, *Collective Bargaining and the No-Strike Clause: The Sinclair Refining Case,* 15 MAINE L. REV. 93 (1963); Note, *Applicability of State Arbitration Statutes To Proceedings Subject To LMRA Section 301,* 27 O.S.U. L.J. 692 (1966); Note, *Concurrent Jurisdiction of Arbitrators and the NLRB,* 38 U. COLO. L. REV. 363 (1966); Note, *Section 301(a) and the Federal Common Law of Labor Agreements,* 75 YALE L.J. 877 (1966).

[3] Contracts usually contain agreements to arbitrate. Hence, many cases in this chapter which bear upon the interpretation of contracts by the Board will also involve arbitration. However, the cases are here treated only insofar as they relate to general contractual problems.

440

statutory source of this jurisdiction, compares this with the jurisdiction of the courts under Section 301,[4] and analyzes the problems faced by the Board in interpreting a contract.

II. SECTION 10(a) POWER OF BOARD

Under Section 10(a) of the LMRA, "the Board is empowered . . . to prevent any person from engaging in any unfair labor practice. . . . This power shall not be affected by any other means of adjustment or prevention that has been or may be established by agreement, law, or otherwise. . . ."

Prior to 1947, the Section read: "This power shall be exclusive, and shall not be affected by any other means of adjustment. . . ." In the amendments made by Taft-Hartley, the exclusive nature of the Board's power to remedy unfair labor practices was modified by striking the words "shall be exclusive, and" and by adding a proviso. The proviso empowers the Board to cede jurisdiction to a state or territorial agency under certain conditions.

This proviso was drafted in response [5] to the decision of the Supreme Court in *Bethlehem Steel Co.* v. *New York Labor Board.*[6] That case had left a "doubt whether a state board could act, either after a formal cession by the National Board or upon a declination of jurisdiction 'for budgetary or other reasons.' "[7] The proviso to Section 10(a) "is the exclusive means whereby States may be enabled to act concerning the matters which Congress has entrusted to the National Labor Relations Board."[8]

Thus, as is shown elsewhere,[9] the NLRB has exclusive and primary jurisdiction over the adjudication of unfair labor practices, except where it cedes jurisdiction as provided in Section 10(a) or declines jurisdiction as provided in Section 14(c).[10] The Board has never concluded a cession agreement with a state agency.

---

4 This chapter does not attempt full coverage of §301. Since this section is not part of the NLRA, it falls outside the scope of the book.
5 *See* S. Rep. No. 105, pt. 2, 80th Cong., 1st Sess. 26 (1947); Amalgamated Ass'n of Street Employees v. Wisconsin Employment Relations Bd., 340 US 383, 397, 27 LRRM 2385 (1951); Algoma Plywood Co. v. Wisconsin Employment Relations Bd., 336 US 301, 313, 23 LRRM 2402 (1949).
6 330 US 767, 19 LRRM 2499 (1947).
7 Guss v. Utah Labor Relations Bd., 353 US 1, 8, 39 LRRM 2567 (1957).
8 *Id.* at 9.
9 For a full development of the doctrine of preemption, *see* Chapter 29.
10 The powers of a state in matters of violence and of "peripheral concern" are treated in Chapter 29; the powers of the courts under §301 are discussed in this chapter *infra;* the powers of the arbitrator are discussed in Chapter 18.

III. SCOPE OF SECTION 301

A. History

1. Background. The greatly increased strength of organized labor, which followed upon the enactment of the Wagner Act, led Congress to reconsider the extent to which labor unions should be required to accept responsibilities as full partners to collective bargaining agreements.[11] The prevailing philosophy of the 1930s had been that labor must have a preferred position in dealing with management in order to offset the employer's great economic power.[12] The Wagner Act did not set standards for union conduct, nor did it provide for a means of enforcing union compliance with the terms of a collective bargaining agreement. In addition, the prevailing theory was that unions were not legal entities; thus, they could not be sued for failure to honor their contractual obligations.[13]

By 1947, unions had prospered and could be considered the bargaining equals of management. Section 301[14] of the Labor Management Relations Act proposed to regulate suits by and against labor organizations and to give the courts power to enforce contractual agreements.

2. Legislative History.[15] Section 301 (a) of the Labor Management Relations Act provides:

> Suits for violation of contracts between an employer and a labor organization representing employees in an industry affecting commerce as defined in this Act, or between any such labor organizations, may be brought in any district court of the United States having jurisdiction of the parties, without respect to the amount in controversy or without regard to the citizenship of the parties.[16]

---

11 Cox, Some Aspects of the Labor-Management Relations Act, 1947, 61 HARV. L. REV. 274, 277 (1947).

12 *Ibid. See* Chapters 1 and 2 *supra.*

13 Pullman Standard Car Mfg. v. Local 2928, USW, 152 F 2d 493, 17 LRRM 624 (CA 7, 1945).

14 61 Stat. 156 (1947), 29 USC §185 (1964).

15 A summary of the legislative history of Section 301 is given in the appendix to the dissenting opinion of Justice Frankfurter in *Textile Workers Union* v. *Lincoln Mills*, 353 US 448, 485, 40 LRRM 2113 (1957). It is also discussed in *Ass'n of Westinghouse Salaried Employees* v. *Westinghouse Electric Corp.*, 348 US 437, 35 LRRM 2643 (1955) (Frankfurter, J.), and in the majority opinion of *Lincoln Mills*, 353 US 448 (1957). In spite of the reliance of courts upon the legislative history, it has been described as "extremely fragmentary." McCarroll v. Los Angeles County Dist. Council of Carpenters, 49 Cal. 2d 45, 58, 315 P 2d 322, 329, 40 LRRM 2709, (1957). *See also* Chapter 3 *supra.*

16 61 Stat. 156 (1947), 29 USC §185 (1964).

As early as 1943, Congress had considered questions of union responsibility under a collective bargaining agreement.[17]   In 1946 Congress passed a provision making voluntary associations suable in the federal courts;[18] this provision was vetoed by the President.[19]   In the 80th Congress, bills were introduced to make collective bargaining contracts mutually enforceable.[20]   In the same Congress, the Labor Management Relations Act was adopted, including Section 301.   This section has raised issues of interpretation, preemption, and jurisdiction—all of which have a bearing upon the NLRB's power to interpret a contract.

One important goal of Congress in enacting Section 301 was that collective bargaining contracts containing no-strike agreements should be enforced.   The Senate report stated that "[s]tatutory recognition of the collective agreement as a valid, binding, and enforceable contract is a logical and necessary step. It will promote a higher degree of responsibility upon the parties to such agreements, and will thereby promote industrial peace."[21]

The Senate bill contained a proposal to make a breach of contract an unfair labor practice. This was deleted in conference on the ground that "[o]nce the parties have made a collective bargaining contract the enforcement of that contract should be left to the law and not to the National Labor Relations Board."[22]

B. Grant of Federal Substantive Law

The first major issue in litigation based on Section 301 was whether this section authorized the application of federal substantive law or whether it was simply procedural. In *Ass'n of Westinghouse Salaried Employees* v. *Westinghouse Electric Corp.*[23] a divided bench refused to permit a union to recover wages owed to an individual employee which were alleged to have been with-

---

17 *E.g.*, H.R. 1781, 78th Cong., 1st Sess. (1943) (federal incorporation); S. 1641, 79th Cong., 1st Sess. (1945) (sanctions for contract violators); S. 1656, 79th Cong., 1st Sess. (1945) (cause of action for strikes in violation of contract); S. 55, 80th Cong., 1st Sess. (1947) (federal jurisdiction); S. 937, 80th Cong., 1st Sess. (1947) (federal labor courts).
18 *See* S. REP. No. 1177, 79th Cong., 2d Sess., pt. 2, at 3-4, 10-14 (1946).
19 H.R. DOC. No. 651, 79th Cong., 2d Sess. (1946).
20 H.R. 3020, 80th Cong., 1st Sess., Section 302 (1947); S. 1126, 80th Cong., 1st Sess., §301 (1947).
21 S. REP. No. 105, 80th Cong., 1st Sess., 17-18 (1947).
22 H.R. CONF. REP. No. 510, 80th Cong., 1st Sess., 42 (1947).
23 348 US 437, 35 LRRM 2643 (1955).

held in violation of a collective bargaining agreement. There was no majority opinion, although six judges in three opinions concurred that the section did not permit a union to enforce what was said to be a personal right of the employee.[24] The opinions discussed several issues which had attended prior litigation over Section 301,[25] but did not resolve them. The opinion of Justice Frankfurter held that the language of the statute and the legislative history indicated that the section was "a mere procedural provision." [26] He interpreted the section as a jurisdictional grant to the federal courts over contracts governed by state substantive law.[27] Noting that this exercise of power was not based on "diversity of citizenship," he found a constitutional difficulty in affirming that cases based on Section 301 involved a "federal question" so as to meet the alternate test of federal jurisdiction. To avoid this constitutional issue and the difficulties in working out a federal common law, he concluded that, whether or not applicable substantive law (federal or state) recognizes a right in the union to vindicate individual causes of action, nevertheless "Congress did not intend to burden the federal courts" with such suits.[28]

The concurring opinion of Chief Justice Warren and Justice Clark rested only on statutory interpretation to the effect that Congress by Section 301 did not intend "to authorize a union to enforce in a federal court the uniquely personal right of an employee." [29] Mr. Justice Reed proposed that at least some federal law was applicable in Section 301 suits, but that a suit for wages arose out of a separate hiring contract and not out of the collective bargaining agreement, as would be required under Section 301.[30]

---

24 See 348 US at 439-461 (Frankfurter, Burton & Minton, J.J.) ; *id.* at 461 (Warren, C.J., Clark, J.) ; *id.* at 464 (Reed, J.). These rights are variously characterized as "peculiar to the individual benefit which is their subject matter," *id.* at 460, "uniquely personal," *id.* at 461, and arising "from separate hiring contracts between the employer and the employee," *id.* at 464.
25 Does §301 give to the federal courts jurisdiction to apply state law? Is such a grant of jurisdiction in conflict with Article III, §2, of the Constitution? Does §301 create a federal substantive law? Or may the federal courts apply state law under a theory of "protective jurisdiction"? For relevant cases, *see* 348 US 452, nn. 25, 26. *See also* Textile Workers Union v. Lincoln Mills, 353 US 448, 450-451, nn. 1, 2.
26 348 US at 449.
27 *Id.* at 459.
28 *Ibid.*
29 *Id.* at 461.
30 *Id.* at 462.

The dissent stated that Congress "created federal sanctions for collective bargaining agreements, made the cases and controversies concerning them justiciable questions for the federal courts, and permitted those courts to fashion from the federal statute, from state law, or from other germane sources, federal rules for the construction and interpretation of those collective bargaining agreements." [31] In addition, it would have held that the union had standing to bring the suit.[32]

The basic constitutional question of *Westinghouse* was settled in *Textile Workers Union* v. *Lincoln Mills*,[33] in which a union brought an action under Section 301 for specific enforcement of an agreement to arbitrate. The Supreme Court, stating that an agreement to arbitrate is a "quid pro quo" for a no-strike agreement, viewed the section as expressing a federal policy that "federal courts should enforce these agreements . . . and that industrial peace can be best obtained only in this way." [34] The Court went on to hold that "the substantive law to apply in suits under §301(a) is federal law, which the courts must fashion from the policy of our national labor laws." [35] It thus rejected theories that Section 301 is not itself a source of substantive law but merely jurisdictional, permitting the federal courts to apply otherwise applicable state or federal laws.

Nevertheless, state law "if compatible with the purpose of §301, may be resorted to in order to find the rule that will best effectuate the federal policy." [36] Such state law, however, is "not . . . an independent source of private rights." [37] Since federal law was at issue, the Court found no constitutional difficulty; a case arising under Section 301 is a case arising under the laws of the United States. "It is not uncommon for federal courts to fashion federal law where federal rights are concerned." [38]

---

31 *Id.* at 465. (Black and Douglas, J.J.) .
32 *Ibid.*
33 353 US 448, 40 LRRM 2113 (1957). Two companion cases were also decided: Goodall-Sanford, Inc. v. United Textile Workers, 353 US 550, 40 LRRM 2118 (1957) ; General Elec. Co. v. Local 205, United Elec. Workers, 353 US 547, 40 LRRM 2119 (1957) .
34 353 US at 455.
35 *Id.* at 456.
36 *Id.* at 457.
37 *Ibid.*
38 *Ibid.*

The concurring opinion of Mr. Justice Burton, in which Mr. Justice Harlan joined, would have espoused the theory of protective jurisdiction, *i.e.*, that the federal courts had jurisdiction to apply state law consistent with federal law since Congress could have passed substantive laws to protect an undoubted federal interest. Hence, lacking an applicable federal statute, state substantive law would be applied, although an appropriate federal remedy could be fashioned.

The dissent of Mr. Justice Frankfurter relied on his earlier analysis in *Westinghouse*: that Section 301 is merely procedural. To this he added the argument that any effort to construct a federal common law was unwise, ineffective, and cumbersome. And he concluded that Section 301 was unconstitutional as a procedural device to permit the federal courts either to apply state law or to exercise "protective jurisdiction."

Although *Lincoln Mills* distinguished *Westinghouse*, it also undermined its rationale.[39] Thus it was no great surprise when in 1962, in *Smith* v. *Evening News Ass'n*,[40] the Supreme Court finally announced the demise of *Westinghouse*. At the same time, it held that under Section 301 an individual employee also has a right to sue for the breach of a collective bargaining agreement.[41]

C. Jurisdiction of the Courts: State and Federal

The jurisdiction of the courts was clarified in *Charles Dowd Box Co.* v. *Courtney*[42] and in *Local 174, Teamsters* v. *Lucas Flour Co.*[43] In the first of these cases the Court held that state courts have concurrent jurisdiction with the federal courts over suits brought under Section 301. In affirming the Supreme Judicial Court of Massachusetts, the Court held that Section 301 does not divest the state courts of jurisdiction, but rather was meant to supplement state jurisdiction. Section 301 provides that suits of the kind described "may" be brought in the federal district

---

39 Even after *Lincoln Mills*, some courts continued to deny unions the right to sue for employee wages. *See, e.g.,* Local 2040, IAM v. Servel, Inc., 268 F 2d 692, 44 LRRM 2340 (CA 7, 1959).
40 371 US 195, 199, 51 LRRM 2646 (1962).
41 *Id.* at 200. The contrary view had been held in *Copra* v. *Suro*, 236 F 2d 107, 38 LRRM 2355 (CA 1, 1956). *Cf.* Republic Steel Corp. v. Maddox, 379 US 650, 58 LRRM 2193 (1965).
42 368 US 502, 49 LRRM 2619 (1962).
43 369 US 95, 49 LRRM 2717 (1962).

courts, not that they must be.[44] The Court noted that "nothing in the concept of our federal system prevents state courts from enforcing rights created by federal law. . . ."[45] This jurisdiction of state courts to enforce federal rights had been established in *Claflin* v. *Houseman*,[46] where it was said that "[I]f exclusive jurisdiction [in the federal courts] be neither express nor implied, the State courts have concurrent jurisdiction whenever, by their own constitution, they are competent to take it."[47]

In *Lucas Flour* the Court made clear that federal law prevails in the substantive interpretation of labor contracts. Where local laws are incompatible with the principles of federal labor law, the former must give way to the latter.[48] In stressing the need for uniform law in cases arising under Section 301, the Court noted that "the existence of possibly conflicting legal concepts might substantially impede the parties' willingness to agree to contract terms for final arbitral or judicial resolution of disputes."[49] The Court concluded that "in enacting Section 301 Congress intended doctrines of federal labor law uniformly to prevail over inconsistent local rules."[50]

D. Jurisdiction of the Courts: Preemption

As we have seen, *Lincoln Mills* established the jurisdiction of the courts to enforce collective bargaining agreements. But Section 301 does not take away the jurisdiction of the Board to deal with unfair labor practice cases which also involve violations of collective bargaining agreements. Under the doctrine of preemption,[51] in matters arguably subject to Section 7 or Section 8 "the states as well as the federal courts must defer to the exclusive competence of the National Labor Relations Board."[52] But a series

---

[44] 368 US at 506.
[45] 368 US at 507.
[46] 93 US 130 (1876).
[47] *Id.* at 136.
[48] 369 US at 104.
[49] *Ibid.*
[50] *Ibid.*
[51] *See* the general discussion in Chapter 29 and the particular discussion therein of §301. *See also* the discussion of preemption in Chapter 27.
[52] San Diego Bldg. Trades Council v. Garmon, 359 US 236, 245, 43 LRRM 2838 (1959).

of cases [53] has securely established that the courts have jurisdiction over suits over collective bargaining contracts brought under Section 301, even though it be urged that the conduct involved is arguably subject to the provisions of the NLRA.[54]

In *Smith* v. *Evening News Ass'n*,[55] the Court expressly held that: "The authority of the Board to deal with an unfair labor practice which also violates a collective bargaining contract is not displaced by §301, but it is not exclusive and does not destroy the jurisdiction of the courts under §301." [56]

E. Conflict or Accommodation?

1. The Courts. Since both state and federal courts have jurisdiction, "[i]t is implicit . . . that 'diversities and conflicts' may occur, no less among the courts of the eleven federal circuits, than among the courts of the several States." [57] It is the function of the Supreme Court "to resolve and accommodate such diversities" [58] under one federal law.

Lucas Flour Co. explicated the preeminence of federal law, a matter which had been considered by only a few of the state courts that assumed jurisdiction in Section 301 suits.[59] In so affirming, the Court reemphasized that "the subject matter of §301(a) 'is peculiarly one that calls for uniform law.' " [60]

"The possibility that individual contract terms might have different meaning under state and federal law would inevitably exert a disruptive influence upon both the negotiation and administra-

---

[53] Smith v. Evening News Ass'n, 371 US 195, 51 LRRM 2646 (1962), Atkinson v. Sinclair Ref. Co., 370 US 238, 50 LRRM 2433 (1962); Local 174, Teamsters v. Lucas Flour Co., 369 US 95, 49 LRRM 2717 (1962), Dowd Box Co. v. Courtney, 368 US 502, 49 LRRM 2619 (1962).
[54] Prior to these decisions, some courts had opted for the exclusive jurisdiction of the NLRB. *See, e.g.,* International Chem. Workers Union v. Olin Mathieson Chem. Corp., 202 F Supp 363, 49 LRRM 2646 (S.D. Ill., 1962); International Union of Doll & Toy Workers v. Metal Polishers Union, 180 F Supp 280, 45 LRRM 2567 (S.D. Cal., 1960).
[55] 371 US 195, 51 LRRM 2646 (1962).
[56] *Id.* at 197. The arguments in favor of the exercise of concurrent jurisdiction by the courts are thoroughly analyzed in Sovern, *Section 301 and the Primary Jurisdiction of the NLRB,* 76 HARV. L. REV. 529 (1963).
[57] 368 US at 514.
[58] *Ibid.*
[59] *See, e.g.,* McCarroll v. Los Angeles County Dist. Council of Carpenters, 49 Cal. 2d 45, 60, 315 P 2d 322, 330, 40 LRRM 2709, 2715 (1957), *cert. denied,* 355 US 932, 41 LRRM 2431 (1958); Local 774, IAM v. Cessna Aircraft Co., 186 Kan. 569, 352 P 2d 420, 46 LRRM 2459 (1960).
[60] 369 US at 103.

tion of collective agreements." [61] The existence of possibly conflicting legal concepts would impede the process of negotiating
collective agreements, would stimulate and prolong disputes, and
would militate against the inclusion of arbitration provisions into
a contract.[62] The area of federal labor policy is so important that
"the need for a single body of federal law [is] particularly compelling." [63]

2. The Board and the Courts. The Court has recognized that
the exercise of concurrent jurisdiction by Board and courts might
raise "serious problems," but it has preferred to face these problems as they occur.[64] It may be noted that the NLRB is on record
as believing that concurrent jurisdiction will promote the purposes of the LMRA.[65] In addition, the Board may decline to
exercise its own jurisdiction where it believes that the federal
labor policy is better served by leaving the parties to other procedures.[66] As pointed out in *Charles Dowd Box,* Congress "deliberately chose to leave the enforcement of collective agreements
'to the usual processes of the law.' " [67] Yet the Court indicated at
the same time that enforcement of a contract by a court does not
affect the jurisdiction of the Board to remedy unfair labor practices.[68] Thus, while the Supreme Court may assure uniformity
of legal principle by reason of final review, it remains possible
for the Board and a court or jury to render contradictory decisions
on the facts.[69] It has been suggested that some inconsistency is the
price to be paid to ensure prompt and efficient enforcement of
contract rights.[70]

---

[61] Local 174, Teamsters Union v. Lucas Flour Co. 369 US 95, 103, 49 LRRM 2717
(1962).
[62] *Ibid.*
[63] 369 US at 104. "The existence of two bodies of law which cannot be accommodated by any conflict-of-laws rule . . . is calculated to aggravate rather than to
alleviate the situation." Wellington, *Labor and the Federal System,* 26 U. CHI. L.
REV. 542, 557 (1959).
[64] Smith v. Evening News Ass'n, 371 US 195, 197-198, 51 LRRM 2646 (1962).
[65] *Id.* at 197, n. 6.
[66] *Ibid.*
[67] 368 US 502, 511, 49 LRRM 2619 (1962).
[68] *Ibid.* See also Dunau, *Contractual Prohibition of Unfair Labor Practices: Jurisdictional Problems,* 57 COL. L. REV. 52 (1957).
[69] *Compare* United Brick and Clay Workers v. Deena Artware, Inc., 198 F 2d 637,
30 LRRM 2485 (CA 6), *cert. denied,* 344 US 897, 31 LRRM 2157 (1952), *with*
NLRB v. Deena Artware, Inc., 198 F 2d 645, 30 LRRM 2479 (CA 6, 1952), *cert.
denied,* 345 US 906, 31 LRRM 2444 (1953). The court's jurisdiction was here based
on §303 and §10 (e) respectively. "Each fact finding agency was entitled to make
its own decision upon the evidence before it." 198 F 2d at 642. *See* Chapter 23 *infra.*
[70] See Sovern, *Section 301 and the Primary Jurisdiction of the NLRB,* 76 HARV. L.
REV. 529, 570-572 (1963).

F. Jurisdiction of the Courts: Application of Norris-LaGuardia

Section 301 cannot be read in isolation from Section 4 of the Norris-LaGuardia Act.[71] This section deprives the federal courts of jurisdiction to issue injunctions that would prohibit certain specified acts. *Lincoln Mills* rejected the argument that Norris-LaGuardia withdrew from the courts jurisdiction to compel arbitration.[72] But in *Sinclair Refining Co.* v. *Atkinson* [73] the Supreme Court held that no-strike clauses in collective bargaining agreements were not specifically enforceable in the federal courts and that Section 301 had in no way diminished the force of the federal anti-injunction legislation. This decision prevailed for eight years.

The *Sinclair Refining* case was made even stronger by another decision of the Supreme Court, which held that a suit brought in a state court under Section 301 to enforce a no-strike clause [74] was removable to the federal courts.[75] But the Court did not resolve the questions of whether a state court could enjoin a strike in violation of contract,[76] or whether a Section 301 suit could be maintained to enforce an arbitrator's award enjoining such a strike.[77]

Suits to enforce arbitration awards granting injunctive relief were brought successfully in both state and lower federal courts.[78] In an early state case, the court confirmed an arbitration award containing an injunction and stated that the state anti-injunction

---

[71] 29 USC §104 (1964). *See* Chapter 1 *supra.*

[72] 353 US at 457-459.

[73] 370 US 195, 50 LRRM 2420 (1962).

[74] *See, e.g.,* McCarroll v. Los Angeles County Dist. Council of Carpenters, 49 Cal. 2d 45, 315 P 2d 322, 40 LRRM 2709 (1957), *cert. denied,* 355 US 932, 41 LRRM 2431 (1958).

[75] Avco Corp. v. Aero Lodge 735, IAM, 390 US 557, 67 LRRM 2881 (1968). But the Court reserved judgment on whether the restrictions of the Norris-LaGuardia Act are applicable in this instance. 390 US at 562 (concurring opinion).

[76] *See* Summers, *Labor Law Decisions of Supreme Court, 1961 Term,* ABA LABOR RELATIONS LAW PROCEEDINGS 51, 63 (1962). A New York court has held that the *Sinclair Refining* rule is limited in its application to the federal courts since it construes only the federal Norris-LaGuardia Act. C. D. Perry & Sons v. Robilotto, 39 Misc. 2d 147, 53 LRRM 2156 (initial application), 240 NYS 2d 331, 53 LRRM 2745 (injunction) (NY Sup Ct, 1963), *affirmed,* 260 NYS 2d 158, 59 LRRM 2445 (NY App Div, 1965). In *Avco Corp.* v. *Aero Lodge 735, IAM,* the Supreme Court reserved decision on whether the remedies in state courts are limited to the remedies under federal law. 390 US 557, 560, n. 2 (1968). The same reservation was made in *Brotherhood of R.R. Trainmen* v. *Jacksonville Terminal Co.,* 394 US 369, 382, n. 18, 70 LRRM 2961 (1969).

[77] The problem is posed in Summers, *supra* note 76, at 63-64.

[78] For a general discussion of these cases see M. Bernstein, PRIVATE DISPUTE SETTLEMENT 601-640 (New York: Free Press, 1968); Note, *Circumventing Norris-LaGuardia with Arbitration Clauses* 44 NOTRE DAME LAW. 431 (1969).

statute was no bar.[79] This position was followed by at least one
federal court in enforcing a suit brought under Section 301,
Norris-LaGuardia notwithstanding.[80]

In *Philadelphia Marine Trade Association v. ILA, Local
1291*,[81] the Third Circuit held that the Norris-LaGuardia Act did
not prohibit the enforcement of an arbitration award since such
enforcement merely called for specific performance. The Supreme
Court reversed on the ground that the order was too vague, without reaching the question of the power of a federal court to enforce an award against work stoppages.

Finally, eight years after *Sinclair*, the Supreme Court, in *Boys
Markets, Inc. v. Retail Clerks, Local 770*,[82] reversed *Sinclair* in a
five-to-two decision.[83] The Court held that a federal district court
can issue an injunction to halt a strike where "a collective bargaining contract contains a mandatory grievance adjustment or arbitration procedure."

IV. JURISDICTION OF BOARD TO INTERPRET CONTRACTS

A contract violation is not of itself an unfair labor practice.[84]
Only when a violation of a union contract is also a violation of a
right under the NLRA is the matter within the jurisdiction of the

---

[79] Ruppert v. Egelhofer, 3 NY 2d 576, 148 NE 2d 129 (1958).

[80] New Orleans S.S. Ass'n v. General Longshore Workers, Local 1418, 389 F 2d 369,
67 LRRM 2430 (CA 5), *cert. denied*, 393 US 828, 69 LRRM 2434 (1968). *Contra*,
Marine Transp. Lines v. Curran, 65 LRRM 2095 (SD NY, 1967); Tanker Serv.
Comm. v. International Organization of Masters, Mates & Pilots, 269 F Supp 551, 65
LRRM 2848 (ED Pa, 1967).

[81] 365 F 2d 295, 62 LRRM 2791 (CA 3, 1966), *reversed on other grounds*, 389 US
64, 66 LRRM 2433 (1967).

[82] 398 US 235, 74 LRRM 2257 (1970). *See* Chapter 29 *infra* at notes 108-109 and
Isaacson, *A Fresh Look at the Labor Injunction*, in LABOR LAW DEVELOPMENTS—
1971 (Sw. LEGAL FOUNDATION, 17TH LABOR LAW INSTITUTE).

[83] Justice Black, joined by Justice White, dissented, observing that nothing had
changed since 1962 except "the membership of the Court and the personal views of
one Justice." Justice Stewart, the Justice to whom he referred, explained in a concurring opinion, quoting the late Justice Frankfurter, that "[w]isdom too often never
comes, and so one ought not to reject it merely because it comes too late."

[84] United Mine Workers v. NLRB, 257 F 2d 211, 214-215, 42 LRRM 2264 (CA DC,
1958); Independent Petroleum Workers v. Esso Standard Oil Co., 235 F 2d 401, 405,
38 LRRM 2307 (CA 3, 1956); NLRB v. Pennwoven, Inc., 194 F 2d 521, 524, 29
LRRM 2307 (CA 3, 1952). *See* Chapter 11 *supra*.
   Congress rejected a bill, S. 1126, 80th Cong., 1st Sess. §§8 (a) (6), 8 (b) (5) (1947),
that would have made it an unfair labor practice for an employer to violate a labor
contract. *See* H.R. CONF. REP. No. 510, 80th Cong., 1st Sess. 42 (1947).

NLRB.[85] When this is considered together with the Section 301 provision for the judicial enforcement of contracts and the interpretations of that section, it is perhaps not surprising that the Board's jurisdiction to construe a contract was challenged in *NLRB* v. *C & C Plywood Corp.*[86]

In that case, the contract authorized the employer "to pay a premium rate over and above the contractual classified wage rate to reward any particular employee for some special fitness, skill, aptitude or the like." [87] Relying on this provision, the employer unilaterally established an incentive pay scale. The NLRB found that the contract did not authorize this action and that the employer violated Section 8(a)(5).[88] The court of appeals refused to enforce the Board's order because the "existence . . . of an unfair labor practice [did] not turn entirely upon the provisions of the Act, but arguably upon a good-faith dispute as to the correct meaning of the provisions of the collective bargaining agreement." [89] In such a situation, as the court held, the construction of the contract is a matter for the courts.[90] Thus, the basic theory of the employer and of the court of appeals was that

> since the contract contained a provision which *might* have allowed the wage plan in question, the Board was powerless to determine whether that provision *did* authorize the respondent's action, because the question was one for a state or federal court under §301 of the Act.[91]

The Supreme Court reversed. It held that the Board did "no more than merely enforce a statutory right" [92] and that the Board's interpretation of the agreement went no further than to see that the union had not agreed to give up the statutory safeguards.[93] The Court said that legislative history, precedent, and the inter-

---

[85] Sbicca, Inc., 30 NLRB 60, 72, 8 LRRM 33 (1941). The Supreme Court decided the same point in *J.I. Case* v. *NLRB*, 321 US 332, 340, 14 LRRM 501 (1944). *See* Dunau, *Contractual Prohibition of Unfair Labor Practices: Jurisdictional Problems*, 57 COL. L. REV. 52, 58, 72-74 (1957).
[86] 385 US 421, 64 LRRM 2065 (1967). *See* note 226 *infra*.
[87] 385 US at 423.
[88] 148 NLRB 414, 57 LRRM 1015 (1964).
[89] 351 F 2d 224, 228, 60 LRRM 2137 (CA 9, 1965).
[90] *Ibid.* Or for the arbitrator, where the contract so provides. 351 F 2d at 227. The court relied on its own decision in *Square D Co.* v. *NLRB*, 332 F 2d 360, 56 LRRM 2147 (CA 9, 1964).
[91] 385 US at 425-426.
[92] 385 US at 428. *See also* Strong Roofing & Insulating Co. v. NLRB, 393 US 357, 70 LRRM 2100 (1969). *See* Chapter 18 *infra* at notes 52-53 and Chapter 31 *infra* at note 143.
[93] *Ibid.*

est of efficient administration[94] all led to the conclusion that the Board does not exceed its jurisdiction in construing a labor agreement where necessary to decide an unfair labor practice case.

The precedent upon which the Court relied is *Mastro Plastics Corp. v. NLRB.*[95] There the employer was charged with violation of Section 8(a)(1), (2) and (3). The Board was forced to construe the scope of a no-strike clause in the contract in deciding the legality of the employer's action. The Supreme Court affirmed the Board's decision and stressed that the case turned upon the proper interpretation of the contract. Although the case did not involve Section 8(a)(5), there is no ground for distinguishing *Mastro Plastics* and *C & C Plywood* insofar as they recognize the Board's right to construe a contract. *C & C Plywood* conclusively shows that the Board's jurisdiction under Section 10(a) is not displaced by the fact that relief may also be available to a party under Section 301[96] or by the fact that the Board must interpret the contract.[97]

But it must not be supposed that *C & C Plywood* gives *carte blanche* to the Board to interpret the provisions of a contract. First, there may be some limit on the Board's contract interpretation powers in the light of Section 301.[98] The case is premised on

---

94 *See id.* at 430.

95 350 US 270, 37 LRRM 2587 (1956). *See also* discussion in Chapter 11 *supra.*

96 385 US at 429-430; NLRB v. Great Dane Trailers, Inc., 388 US 26, 30-31, n. 7, 65 LRRM 2465 (1967). *See also* Smith v. Evening News Ass'n, 371 US 195, 197, 51 LRRM 2646 (1962): "The authority of the Board to deal with an unfair labor practice which also violates a collective bargaining contract is not displaced by §301"; Carey v. Westinghouse Elec. Corp., 375 US 261, 268, 55 LRRM 2042 (1964): "[A] suit either in the federal courts, as provided by §301(a) . . . or before such state tribunals as are authorized to act . . . is proper, even though an alternative remedy before the Board is available, which, if invoked by the employer, will protect him. . . . The superior authority of the Board may be invoked at any time." 375 US at 272. *See also* Local 174, Teamsters Union v. Lucas Flour Co., 369 US 95, 101, n. 9, 49 LRRM 2717 (1962); NLRB v. Strong, 393 US 357, 70 LRRM 2100 (1969).

97 The Board may, "if necessary to adjudicate an unfair labor practice, interpret and give effect to the terms of a collective bargaining contract." NLRB v. Strong, 393 US 357, 361, 70 LRRM 2100 (1969), citing C & C Plywood. "In the face of the legislative history just recited, it would seem that the Board has a heavy burden of persuasion that it does have authority to treat a violation of a term of a collective bargaining contract, even a term providing for the settlement of grievances by arbitration, as an unfair labor practice, and, in effect, decree its specific performance." United Mine Workers (Boone County Coal Corp.) v. NLRB, 257 F 2d 211, 215, 42 LRRM 2264 (CA DC, 1958).

98 *See* NLRB v. Great Dane Trailers, Inc., 388 US 26, 36, 65 LRRM 2465 (1967) (dissenting opinion). In *C & C Plywood,* no judicial proceeding under §301 was pending or decided. "[T]he Board has no plenary authority to administer and enforce collective bargaining contracts." NLRB v. Strong, 393 US 357, 360, 70 LRRM 2100 (1969).

the necessary connection between the contract clause and the legality of the employer's action and cannot be read to give the NLRB an independent power to enforce the contract.[99] Second, the Court emphasized that the contract involved did not contain an arbitration clause [100] and that the "Board's action . . . was in no way inconsistent with its previous recognition of arbitration as 'an instrument of national labor policy for composing contractual differences.' " [101] Thus, it follows that the presence of an arbitration clause may perhaps affect the jurisdiction or decision of the Board.[102]

The preceding discussion has centered on the jurisdiction of the Board in cases where a contract provision is asserted as a defense to an unfair labor practice charge. There are other ways in which issues of contract interpretation can be relevant to the Board's jurisdiction over unfair labor practices. First, a collective bargaining agreement may incorporate a statutory obligation. In these cases, the Board may resolve the question even though the decision about the unfair labor practice is *pro tanto* a resolution of the contract question. Second, the NLRA makes certain contractual arrangements illegal; *e.g.*, Section 8(a)(3) prohibits closed-shop agreements, and Section 8(e) bars hot-cargo clauses. Here the Board must measure the contract by the statutory standard to test its legality.[103]

V. NLRB INTERPRETATION OF THE COLLECTIVE BARGAINING AGREEMENT

A. Interpreting and Invalidating Clauses and Contracts in Representation and Complaint Cases

The purpose of this section is to provide a checklist of Board decisions and policies that relate to the interpretation and invalidation of clauses and contracts. No attempt is made here to

---

99 385 US at 428.
100 *Id.* at 423, 426, 429.
101 *Id.* at 426.
102 The specific question of Board accommodation to arbitration is treated in Chapter 18 *infra*.
103 As to §8 (a) (3) , *see* Great Lakes Carbon Corp. v. NLRB, 360 F 2d 19, 62 LRRM 2088 (CA 4, 1966) ; Red Star Express Lines v. NLRB, 196 F 2d 78, 29 LRRM 2705 (CA 2, 1952) . As to §8 (e) , *see* Meat Drivers Local 710 v. NLRB, 335 F 2d 709, 56 LRRM 2570 (CA DC, 1964) ; Truck Drivers Local 413 v. NLRB, 334 F 2d 539, 55 LRRM 2878 (CA DC) , *cert. denied*, 379 US 916, 57 LRRM 2496 (1964) . *See also* Chapters 16 *supra* and 24 and 26 *infra*.

present an extensive analysis of the issues set forth, since these matters are covered elsewhere in the book. Nevertheless, it is important, in order to understand the role of the Board, to have these issues brought together and identified in one place.

The section is divided into two major parts.[104] The first part provides a catalog of cases in which contract interpretation is an important issue but in which there is no question as to the legality of the contract. The second major part embraces cases where contract interpretation is connected with the issue of the validity of the contract.

1. Interpretation of Lawful Contract Clauses. *a. Types of Cases.* The principal types of Board cases in which issues involving interpretation of lawful contract provisions have arisen are the following:

1. *Section 8(a)(5) cases* in which the employer is accused of refusing to bargain during the term of the contract, either by: (a) making some unilateral change in the wage structure (*e.g.*, installation of merit or incentive plan, withdrawal of bonus) or in some other term or condition of employment,[105] or (b) subcon-

---

104 It should be noted that contract-interpretation questions and related jurisdictional questions concerning work-assignment disputes, as they arise under §§8 (b) (4) (d) and 10 (k), constitute a unique category of cases. Examples are found in *New Orleans Typographical Union No. 17* v. *NLRB*, 368 F 2d 755, 63 LRRM 2467 (CA 5, 1966) and *Millwrights Local 1102 (Don Cartage Co.)*, 160 NLRB 1061, 63 LRRM 1085 (1966). The relationship of Board action to arbitration in this type of case is treated in Chapter 18. Work-assignment disputes are treated primarily in Chapter 25 *infra*.

105 C & C Plywood Corp., 148 NLRB 414, 57 LRRM 1015 (1964), *enforcement denied*, 351 F 2d 224, 60 LRRM 2137 (CA 9, 1965), *reversed*, 385 US 421, 64 LRRM 2065 (1967); C & S Industries, 158 NLRB 454, 62 LRRM 1043 (1966); Crescent Bed Co., 157 NLRB 296, 61 LRRM 1334, *enforced*, 63 LRRM 2480 (CA DC, 1966); Long Lake Lumber Co., 160 NLRB 1475, 63 LRRM 1160 (1966); Litton Precision Products, 156 NLRB 555, 61 LRRM 1096 (1966); Century Papers, 155 NLRB 358, 60 LRRM 1320 (1965); Huttig Sash and Door Co., 154 NLRB 811, 60 LRRM 1035 (1965), *enforced*, 377 F 2d 964, 65 LRRM 2431 (CA 8, 1967); Square D Co., 142 NLRB 332, 53 LRRM 1023 (1963), *enforcement denied*, 332 F 2d 360, 56 LRRM 2147 (CA 9, 1964); Smith Cabinet Mfg. Co., 147 NLRB 1506, 56 LRRM 1418 (1964); LeRoy Machine Co., 147 NLRB 1431, 56 LRRM 1369 (1964); Bemis Brothers Bag Co., 143 NLRB 1311, 53 LRRM 1489 (1963); Speidel Corp., 120 NLRB 733, 42 LRRM 1039 (1958); Beacon Piece Dyeing and Finishing Co., 121 NLRB 953, 42 LRRM 1489 (1958); United Telephone Co. of the West, 112 NLRB 779, 36 LRRM 1097 (1955); Nash-Finch Co., 103 NLRB 1695, 32 LRRM 1026 (1953), *enforcement denied*, 211 F 2d 622, 33 LRRM 2898 (CA 8, 1954); McDonnell Aircraft Corp., 109 NLRB 930, 34 LRRM 1472 (1954); Crown Zellerbach Corp., 95 NLRB 753, 28 LRRM 1357 (1951); Consolidated Aircraft Corp., 47 NLRB 694, 12 LRRM 44 (1943), *enforced as modified*, 141 F 2d 785, 14 LRRM 553 (CA 9, 1944); Tide Water Associated Oil Co., 85 NLRB 1096, 24 LRRM 1518 (1949); Proctor Mfg. Corp., 131 NLRB 1166, 48 LRRM 1222 (1961).

tracting work,[106] or (c) refusing to supply information sought by the union.[107] In these cases the employer may defend in whole or in part by claiming that the contract justifies his action.

2. *Section 8(a)(3) cases* in which the employer discharges or disciplines an employee or takes other action with respect to an employee and defends in whole or in part against the charge of violation of the Act by claiming that the action was justified by the contract.[108] (These cases occur less frequently than the 8(a)(5) cases described in paragraph 1 above. Sometimes these cases include allegations that the union violated 8(b)(1)(A) and

---

[106] International Shoe Co., 151 NLRB 693, 58 LRRM 1483 (1965); Cloverleaf Div. of Adams Dairy Co., 147 NLRB 1410, 56 LRRM 1321 (1964); General Motors Corp., 149 NLRB 396, 57 LRRM 1277 (1964); Puerto Rico Telephone Co., 149 NLRB 950, 57 LRRM 1397 (1964); National Dairy Prods. Corp., 126 NLRB 434, 45 LRRM 1332 (1960); Timken Roller Bearing Co., 70 NLRB 500, 18 LRRM 1370 (1946), *enforcement denied*, 161 F 2d 949, 20 LRRM 2204 (CA 6, 1947). *Cf.* the related situation involving discontinuation of a product. New York Mirror, 151 NLRB 834, 58 LRRM 1465 (1965); Ador Corp., 150 NLRB 1658, 58 LRRM 1280 (1965). The obligation to bargain over subcontracting is discussed in Chapter 15 *supra*.

[107] Acme Industrial Co., 150 NLRB 1463, 58 LRRM 1277, *enforcement denied*, 351 F 2d 258, 60 LRRM 2220 (CA 7, 1965), *reversed*, 385 US 432, 64 LRRM 2069 (1967); Fafnir Bearing Co., 146 NLRB 1582, 56 LRRM 1108 (1964), *enforced*, 362 F 2d 716, 62 LRRM 2415 (CA 2, 1966); General Elec. Co., 160 NLRB 1308, 63 LRRM 1153 (1966); Square D Co., 142 NLRB 332, 53 LRRM 1023 (1963), *enforcement denied*, 332 F 2d 360, 56 LRRM 2147 (CA 9, 1964); Timken Roller Bearing Co., 138 NLRB 15, 50 LRRM 1508 (1962), *enforced*, 325 F 2d 746, 54 LRRM 2785 (CA 6, 1963), *cert. denied*, 376 US 971, 55 LRRM 2878 (1964); Perkins Mach. Co., 141 NLRB 98, 52 LRRM 1276 (1963), *enforced*, 326 F 2d 488, 55 LRRM 2204 (CA 1, 1964); Anaconda American Brass Co., 148 NLRB 474, 57 LRRM 1001 (1964); Sinclair Refining Co., 145 NLRB 732, 55 LRRM 1029 (1963); Hercules Motor Corp., 136 NLRB 1648, 50 LRRM 1021 (1962); Sinclair Refining Co., 132 NLRB 1660, 48 LRRM 1544 (1961), *enforcement denied*, 306 F 2d 569, 50 LRRM 2830 (CA 5, 1962); Berkline Corp., 123 NLRB 685, 43 LRRM 1513 (1959); Item Co., 108 NLRB 1634, 34 LRRM 1255 (1954), *enforced*, 220 F 2d 956, 35 LRRM 2709 (CA 5, 1955); International News Serv. Div. of Hearst Corp., 113 NLRB 1067, 36 LRRM 1454 (1955); Avco Mfg. Corp., 111 NLRB 729, 35 LRRM 1542 (1955); Otis Elevator Co., 102 NLRB 770, 31 LRRM 1334 (1953); Hekman Furniture Co., 101 NLRB 631, 31 LRRM 1116 (1952). *See also* the following cases, in which the employer insisted that the contract limited the union's role in the grievance procedure: Brunswick Corp., 146 NLRB 1474, 56 LRRM 1071 (1964); Sohio Chemical Co., 141 NLRB 810, 52 LRRM 1390 (1963).

[108] Flasco Mfg. Co., 162 NLRB 611, 64 LRRM 1077 (1967); International Harvester Co., 138 NLRB 923, 51 LRRM 1155 (1962), *enforced sub nom.* Ramsey v. NLRB, 327 F 2d 784, 55 LRRM 2441 (CA 7, 1964), *cert. denied*, 377 US 1003, 56 LRRM 2544 (1964); Dubo Mfg. Corp., 142 NLRB 431, 53 LRRM 1070 (1963), 142 NLRB 812, 53 LRRM 1158 (1963), 148 NLRB 1114, 57 LRRM 1111 (1964); Pontiac Motors Div., 132 NLRB 413, 48 LRRM 1368 (1961); Mastro Plastics Corp. v. NLRB, 350 US 270, 37 LRRM 2587 (1956). *See also Anaconda Aluminum Co.*, 160 NLRB 35, 62 LRRM 1370 (1966), in which the Board found the contract did not justify denial of a benefit and held the action constituted a violation of §8(a)(5), and *Morton Salt Co.*, 119 NLRB 1402, 41 LRRM 1312 (1958), where the Board dismissed, without deciding the contract interpretation issue, a complaint charging the employer with a §8(a)(2) violation for failing to honor checkoff revocations which the employer claimed were untimely under the contract.

(2) by participating in the discriminatory action and the union also asserts the contractual defense.)

3. *Representation cases* (election or unit-clarification petitions) in which one or another of the parties urges that an existing contract, properly interpreted, supports his position.[109] (Sometimes these representation cases in which there is a contract interpretation issue are brought to the Board in the context of a refusal-to-bargain case.)[110]

b. Trends. The following discussion assumes the right of the Board to interpret a contract and disregards the particular problems presented by an arbitration clause.[111] It is concerned only with the Board's approach to contract interpretation and its general policies.

In the Section 8(a)(5) cases [112] the Board tends to consider that the contract-interpretation question turns on whether the union contractually waived its rights under the Act: (1) to consultation before the employer institutes changes in conditions not covered by the contract, (2) to have the employer discuss subcontracting before it occurs, or (3) to have the employer provide it with particular information in connection with the administration of the contract.[113] Viewing such cases as waiver [114] cases, the Board has tended to reserve to itself the task of interpreting the contract.

When the Board decides to pass upon the question of contract interpretation, it examines and compares contract provisions, studies negotiations and other history leading up to the contract, and looks at the experience of the parties under the contract. The

---

109 Westinghouse Elec. Corp., 162 NLRB 768, 64 LRRM 1082 (1967); Hotel Employers Ass'n, 159 NLRB 143, 62 LRRM 1215 (1966), Raley's Supermarket, 143 NLRB 256, 53 LRRM 1347 (1963); Insulation & Specialties, Inc., 144 NLRB 1540, 54 LRRM 1306 (1963). *See* Chapter 8 *supra.*
110 Montgomery Ward & Co., 137 NLRB 418, 50 LRRM 1162 (1962).
111 *See* Chapter 18.
112 Specific questions are discussed in this chapter *infra.* Among the §8 (a) (5) Board cases decided after *C & C Plywood* are: Univis, 169 NLRB No. 18, 67 LRRM 1090 (1968); Gravenslund Operating Co., 168 NLRB No. 72, 66 LRRM 1323 (1967); W. P. Ihrie & Sons, 165 NLRB 167, 65 LRRM 1205 (1967) (held not to be a contractual issue); Hoerner-Waldorf Paper Prods. Co., 163 NLRB 772, 64 LRRM 1469 (1967); K & H Specialties, 163 NLRB 644, 64 LRRM 1411 (1967); Adelson, Inc., 163 NLRB 365, 64 LRRM 1346 (1967); Scam Instrument Corp., 163 NLRB 284, 64 LRRM 1327 (1967), *enforced,* 394 F 2d 884, 68 LRRM 2280 (CA 7, 1968), *cert. denied,* 393 US 980, 69 LRRM 2851 (1968).
113 The right-to-information cases are discussed in this chapter *infra* and in Chapter 11 *supra.*
114 This issue is fully discussed in the next section of this chapter.

fact that a contract is silent on a given subject is not held by the Board to be proof that the union has waived its bargaining rights with respect to that subject. But an affirmative provision on a given subject may be interpreted to mean that the union has to some extent waived its right to bargain. Whenever a waiver is found, negotiations usually constitute part of the proof. A management-rights clause may be found to constitute a waiver, particularly in subcontracting cases.

In deciding contractual issues, the Board will test the meaning of a clause by looking to the scope and tradition of statutory rights, to its own experience with labor relations, and to the history of the labor negotiations.[115] A few Board cases involving interpretation of lawful contract clauses have reached the courts.[116] The Board's position has been sustained in most instances.

c. Potential for Expansion of Board's Role. The landmark Supreme Court decision in *Wiley* v. *Livingston*[117] opened up the possibility that the Board would become even more deeply involved in the interpretation of lawful contract clauses. *Wiley* held that when Company A has a contract with Union A, and is sold to or merged with Company B, the employees of Company A who become employees of Company B have the right to compel Company B to arbitrate under Company A's contract with Union A. This decision raises a number of problems. The Third Circuit grappled with some of them in *Reliance Universal*,[118] also a Section 301 suit to compel arbitration. The court recognized that new circumstances arising out of the acquisition of a business by a new owner may require an arbitration award at variance with some of the terms of the collective bargaining agreement negotiated by a different party.

---

[115] *See* NLRB v. C & C Plywood Corp., 385 US at 430-431; brief for the NLRB, C & C Plywood, 385 US 421 (1967), at 5-6, 8, 16-17.
[116] Among recent cases decided after *C & C Plywood* are the following: Leeds & Northrup Co. v. NLRB, 391 F 2d 874, 67 LRRM 2793 (CA 3, 1968), *enforcing* 162 NLRB 987, 64 LRRM 1110 (1967); American Fire Apparatus v. NLRB, 380 F 2d 1005, 65 LRRM 3082 (CA 8, 1967), *enforcing* 160 NLRB 1318, 63 LRRM 1151 (1966); NLRB v. Huttig Sash & Door Co., 377 F 2d 964, 65 LRRM 2431 (CA 8, 1967), *enforcing* 154 NLRB 811, 60 LRRM 1035 (1965); NLRB v. Honolulu Star Bulletin, 372 F 2d 691, 64 LRRM 2342 (CA 9, 1967), *denying enforcement* to 153 NLRB 763, 59 LRRM 1533 (1965).
[117] 376 US 543, 55 LRRM 2769 (1964). This decision is evaluated in Chapter 13.
[118] Steelworkers v. Reliance Universal, Inc., 335 F 2d 891, 56 LRRM 2721 (CA 3, 1964).

These Section 301 cases tended to compromise Board decisions which indicated that a successor employer had no obligation under the old contract.[119] *Wiley* makes it appear, however, that a successor employer has obligations under the old contract. Is a refusal to accept these obligations a violation of Section 8(a)(5)? Carried to its logical end, *Wiley* would bring the Board deeper than ever into the field of contract interpretation, making it labor to determine what the old contract required of the new employer to determine in what respects the employer had refused to bargain. After sidestepping this problem for several years, the Board held in *William J. Burns International Detective Agency, Inc.*[120] that absent unusual circumstances, "the national labor policy embodied in the Act requires the successor-employer to take over and honor a collective bargaining agreement negotiated on behalf of the employing enterprise by the predecessor." It is too early to assess the potential impact of this holding. We can only speculate as to the effect it will have on the Board's role in contract interpretation. The Board likely will have the option to defer to the arbitration process in certain refusal-to-bargain situations resulting from successor-employer inheritance of contract obligations under the *Burns* doctrine. In any event, new problems relating to accommodation of Board action to arbitration will probably arise under this doctrine.

2. Invalidation of Clauses and Contracts. An entire contract may be invalidated by Board action. Where a contract is obtained under the erroneous though good-faith claim of majority representation by a union, the contract is invalid.[121] The "unlawful genesis" of the agreement precludes a finding that it is valid for union members only, since the employer might not have entered into the agreement if it had known that the union was not a majority representative.

---

119 General Extrusion Co., 121 NLRB 1165, 42 LRRM 1508 (1958). See Chapter 13 *supra* for full discussion of successor-employer problems. *See also* Chemrock Corp., 151 NLRB 1074, 58 LRRM 1582 (1965); Overnite Transp. Co., 157 NLRB 1185, 61 LRRM 1520 (1966), *enforced,* 372 F 2d 765, 64 LRRM 2359 (CA 4, 1967), *cert. denied,* 389 US 838, 66 LRRM 2307 (1967); Perma Vinyl Corp., 164 NLRB No. 119, 65 LRRM 1168 (1967), *enforced sub nom.,* United States Pipe & Foundry Co., 398 F 2d 544, 68 LRRM 2913 (CA 5, 1968). These cases do not deal with contractual obligations.

120 Wm. J. Burns Int'l Detective Agency, Inc., 182 NLRB No. 50, 74 LRRM 1098, 1100 (1970). *See* Chapter 13 *supra,* at notes 34-37, for discussion of this and related cases.

121 Int'l Ladies Garment Workers v. NLRB, 366 US 731, 48 LRRM 2251 (1961). *See* Chapter 7 *supra.*

An entire contract with one union may become invalidated as a result of the Board's refusal to permit the existing contract to operate as a bar to recognition of another union.[122] The Board has held that a contract with a defunct union [123] will not operate as a bar to recognition of another union. Nor will a contract of unreasonable duration [124] operate as a bar to recognition of another union, or a contract containing clearly unlawful union security provisions,[125] or a contract with a union involved in a schism,[126] or a contract that discriminates among the employees on racial grounds.[127] When the Board permits another union to obtain bargaining rights in such circumstances, the Board's action often has the practical effect of invalidating the contract which the employer executed with the displaced union.

Moreover, as noted above, the Board may recognize that displacement of one employer by another may have a significant impact on the status of an existing collective bargaining agreement. Part or all of the agreement may become invalidated.

Under the Act the Board may have to interpret and pass upon the validity of certain types of clauses in collective bargaining agreements.[128] The Board determines whether union security clauses comply with the requirements of Section 8(a)(3).[129] The Board is empowered to strike down contract provisions that discriminate in favor of union members over nonunion members or in favor of members of one union over members of another

---

122 *See* discussion of contract-bar doctrine in Chapter 8 *supra.*
123 Container Corp., 61 NLRB 823, 16 LRRM 112 (1945).
124 General Cable Corp., 139 NLRB 1123, 51 LRRM 1444 (1962) extended the two-year contract-bar rule to three years. Earlier contract-bar rules are set forth in *Reed Roller Bit Co.*, 72 NLRB 927, 19 LRRM 1227 (1947), and *General Motors Corp.*, 102 NLRB 1140, 31 LRRM 1344 (1953). Even a contract of unreasonable duration will be a bar during its entire term to a petition for an election by either of the parties to the contract as distinguished from a petition by a rival union. Montgomery Ward & Co., Inc., 137 NLRB 346, 50 LRRM 1137 (1962).
125 Paragon Prods. Corp., 134 NLRB 662, 49 LRRM 1160 (1961), *modifying* Keystone Coat, Apron & Towel Supply Co., 121 NLRB 880, 42 LRRM 1456 (1958).
126 Pittsburgh Plate Glass Co., 80 NLRB 1331, 23 LRRM 1237 (1948); Hershey Chocolate Corp., 121 NLRB 901, 42 LRRM 1460 (1958). *But cf.* Swift & Co., 145 NLRB 756, 55 LRRM 1033 (1963).
127 Pioneer Bus Co., 140 NLRB 54, 51 LRRM 1546 (1962).
128 *See* discussion of illegal subjects of bargaining in Chapter 16.
129 Union security is covered primarily in Chapter 26.
130 NLRB v. Buitoni Foods Corp., 298 F 2d 169, 49 LRRM 2397 (CA 3, 1962). *See also* Great Lakes Carbon Corp. v. NLRB, 360 F 2d 19, 62 LRRM 2088 (CA 4, 1966) (holding that a negotiated contract provision giving superseniority to replacements for striking employees was unlawful on its face and must be eliminated from the contract). The Board also passes on clauses which allegedly encourage union membership in violation of §8 (a) (3). Radio Officers Union v. NLRB, 347 US 17, 33 LRRM 2417 (1954). *See* Chapter 6 *supra.*

union.[130] Hot-cargo clauses that allegedly violate Section 8(e) require the Board to engage in contract interpretation to determine whether such clauses should be invalidated.[131] And the Board sometimes interprets and passes upon the validity of contract clauses in determining whether a union has breached its duty of fair representation.[132]

The Board's current position is that contract clauses that forbid the distribution of literature, including union literature, on the plant premises are valid insofar as they prevent distribution of literature in support of the bargaining agent that executed the contract, but that they are invalid insofar as they prevent distribution of literature in support of rival unions.[133] In other words, says the Board, the bargaining agent can waive the rights of employees to distribute literature in its own behalf, but it cannot waive the rights of employees to distribute literature in opposition to itself. The Board's current position on these clauses is a reversal of its position for many years that such clauses were valid.[134]

The Board's argument is that a clause forbidding the distribution of literature must, as a practical matter, discriminate in favor of the incumbent union. But since the ban applies to all literature and all employees and thus is nondiscriminatory on its face, some circuits that have considered the issue have been unwilling, in the absence of proof of discrimination, to accept the inference drawn by the Board. Other circuits, however, have enforced Board orders condemning such clauses.[135]

---

[131] Orange Belt Dist. Council of Painters No. 48 v. NLRB, 328 F 2d 534, 55 LRRM 2293 (CA DC, 1964), 365 F 2d 540, 62 LRRM 2553 (CA DC, 1966). Hot-cargo clauses are covered primarily in Chapter 24. Despite an illegal hot-cargo clause, the contract may operate as a bar to an election. Food Haulers, Inc., 136 NLRB 394, 49 LRRM 1774 (1962), overruling Pilgrim Furniture Co., 128 NLRB 910, 46 LRRM 1427 (1960).

[132] NLRB v. Miranda Fuel Co., 326 F 2d 172, 54 LRRM 2715 (CA 2, 1963); Hughes Tool Co., 147 NLRB 1573, 56 LRRM 1289 (1964).

[133] Gale Prods., 142 NLRB 1246, 53 LRRM 1242 (1963), enforcement denied, 337 F 2d 390, 57 LRRM 2164 (CA 7, 1964); Armco Steel Corp., 148 NLRB 1179, 57 LRRM 1132 (1964), order set aside, 344 F 2d 621, 59 LRRM 2077 (CA 6, 1965); General Motors Corp., 147 NLRB 509, 56 LRRM 1241 (1964), order set aside, 345 F 2d 516, 59 LRRM 2080 (CA 6, 1965); General Motors Corp., 158 NLRB 1723, 62 LRRM 1210 (1966), enforcement denied, 381 F 2d 265, 65 LRRM 3103 (CA 9, 1967); Mid-States Metal Prods. Inc., 156 NLRB 872, 61 LRRM 1159 (1966), enforced, 403 F 2d 702, 69 LRRM 2656 (CA 5, 1968). See further discussion and cases in Chapter 5 supra at notes 166-168.

[134] May Dep't Store Co., 59 NLRB 976, 15 LRRM 173 (1944); North Am. Aviation, Inc., 56 NLRB 959, 14 LRRM 172 (1944); Clinton Foods, Inc., 112 NLRB 239, 36 LRRM 1006 (1955); Fruitvale Canning Co., 90 NLRB 884, 26 LRRM 1281 (1950).

[135] See note 133 supra. See also Getreu v. Armco Steel Corp., 241 F Supp 376,.56 LRRM 2501 (S D Ohio, 1964).

In 1953, in *NLRB* v. *Rockaway News Supply Co.*,[136] the Supreme Court nullified a Board practice of setting aside an entire contract when it contained an illegal clause. "The total obliteration of this contract," it said, "is not in obedience to any command of the statute. It is contrary to common-law contract doctrine." [137]

B. Special Questions

1. NLRB Position on Waiver of Statutory Rights. *a. In General.* It has long been established that a bargaining representative may waive certain rights guaranteed to employees by the NLRA.[138] The principal use of the waiver doctrine, however, is in relation to the question of what matters are subject to the duty to bargain during the term of a contract,[139] especially as to the right to bargain and the right to receive information. This section assumes the right of the NLRB to interpret a contract and is limited to outlining the NLRB position on waiver.

The Board's policy with respect to waiver was enunciated in *Tide Water Associated Oil Co.*,[140] where the Board stated that "[w]e are reluctant to deprive employees of . . . rights guaranteed them by the Act in the absence of a clear and unmistakable showing of a waiver of such rights." [141] With court approval, the Board

---

[136] 345 US 71, 31 LRRM 2432 (1953).
[137] 345 US at 79.
[138] Shell Oil Co., 77 NLRB 1306, 22 LRRM 1158 (1948) (right to strike); Tide Water Associated Oil Co., 85 NLRB 1096, 24 LRRM 1518 (1949) (right to bargain over pension plan); Shell Oil Co., 93 NLRB 161, 27 LRRM 1330 (1951) (right to handle grievances); E. W. Scripps Co., 94 NLRB 227, 28 LRRM 1033 (1951) (right to bargain over merit increases); International News Serv., Div. of Hearst Corp., 113 NLRB 1067, 36 LRRM 1454 (1955) (right to information). *See also* NLRB v. American Nat'l Ins. Co., 343 US 395, 30 LRRM 2147 (1952) (broad management-rights clause).
  It is, of course, a well-settled principle that the policy of the Act may not be thwarted by contractual agreement. As regards collective bargaining rights, *see* J.I. Case Co. v. NLRB, 321 US 332, 337, 14 LRRM 501, 504 (1944), *affirming* 134 F 2d 70, 12 LRRM 538 (CA 7, 1943), *enforcing* 42 NLRB 85, 10 LRRM 172 (1942); National Licorice Co. v. NLRB, 309 US 350, 6 LRRM 674 (1940), *affirming* 104 F 2d 655, 4 LRRM 559 (CA 2, 1939), *enforcing* 7 NLRB 537, 2 LRRM 306 (1938); NLRB v. Poultrymen's Serv. Corp., 138 F 2d 204, 13 LRRM 543 (CA 3, 1943), *enforcing* 41 NLRB 444, 10 LRRM 117 (1942); NLRB v. Reed & Prince Mfg. Co., 118 F 2d 874, 8 LRRM 478 (CA 1), *cert. denied,* 313 US 595, 8 LRRM 458 (1941), *enforcing* 12 NLRB 944, 4 LRRM 208 (1939); Hartsell Mills Co. v. NLRB, 111 F 2d 291, 6 LRRM 794 (CA 4, 1940), *enforcing as modified* 18 NLRB 268, 5 LRRM 390 (1939); Scripto Mfg. Co., 36 NLRB 411, 9 LRRM 156 (1941); Duffy Silk Co., 19 NLRB 37, 5 LRRM 469 (1940).
[139] *See* discussion in Chapter 11 *supra.*
[140] 85 NLRB 1096, 24 LRRM 1518 (1949).
[141] 85 NLRB at 1098.

has held that a waiver of statutory rights must be clear and unmistakable [142] and that such waiver will not be found merely from the circumstance that the contract omits specific reference to a subject protected by the NLRA, that it contains a general management-prerogatives clause, or that the union failed in contract negotiations to obtain contract protection of its statutory right.[143] This rests on the theory that, since a provision protecting a statutory right "would normally be implied in an agreement by operation of the act itself," [144] that protection can be lost only by express action.

Since a waiver is generally bargained for in negotiations and is included along with other provisions of the contract,[145] neither the employer nor the union, in the absence of fraud or duress, will be permitted to retract a contract waiver. Such a waiver, properly incorporated in a contract, will bind all employees.[146]

b. Evidence of Waiver. (1) Contract language. Specific language in a contract will support a waiver. In *Leroy Machine Co.*[147] the employer was held not to have violated the Act when he refused to bargain over his requirement that employees with bad absentee records submit to physical examination. His action

---

[142] *See, e.g.,* Beacon Journal Pub. Co. v. NLRB, 401 F 2d 366, 367-368, 69 LRRM 2232 (CA 6, 1968), *enforcing in part* 164 NLRB 734, 65 LRRM 1126 (1967); Dura Corp. v. NLRB, 380 F 2d 970, 973, 65 LRRM 3025 (CA 6, 1967), *enforcing* 156 NLRB 285, 61 LRRM 1016 (1965); Fafnir Bearing Co. v. NLRB, 362 F 2d 716, 722, 62 LRRM 2415 (CA 2, 1966), *enforcing* 146 NLRB 1582, 56 LRRM 1108 (1964); NLRB v. Perkins Mach. Co., 326 F 2d 488, 489, 55 LRRM 2204 (CA 1, 1964), *enforcing* 141 NLRB 98, 52 LRRM 1276 (1963); Timken Roller Bearing Co. v. NLRB, 325 F 2d 746, 751, 54 LRRM 2785 (CA 6, 1963), *enforcing* 138 NLRB 15, 50 LRRM 1508 (1962), *cert. denied,* 376 US 971, 55 LRRM 2878 (1964); NLRB v. Item Co., 220 F 2d 956, 958-959, 35 LRRM 2709 (CA 5, 1955), *cert. denied,* 350 US 836, 36 LRRM 2716 (1955), *enforcing* 108 NLRB 1634, 34 LRRM 1255 (1954). [143] In addition to the cases cited in the preceding footnote, see NLRB v. Jacobs Mfg. Co., 196 F 2d 680, 30 LRRM 2098 (CA 2, 1952), *enforcing* 94 NLRB 1214, 28 LRRM 1162 (1951); NLRB v. J. H. Allison & Co., 165 F 2d 766, 768, 21 LRRM 2238 (CA 6, 1948), *cert. denied,* 335 US 814, 22 LRRM 2564 (1948), *enforcing* 70 NLRB 377, 18 LRRM 1369 (1946); New York Mirror, 151 NLRB 834, 839-841, 58 LRRM 1465 (1965); Proctor Mfg. Co., 131 NLRB 1166, 48 LRRM 1222 (1961). [144] NLRB v. Perkins Mach. Co., 326 F 2d 488, 489, 55 LRRM 2204 (CA 1, 1964). *See also* Cloverleaf Div. of Adams Dairy, 147 NLRB 1410, 1413-14, 56 LRRM 1321 (1964). [145] *Cf.* Textile Workers Union v. Lincoln Mills, 353 US 448, 455, 40 LRRM 2113 (1957) (agreement to arbitrate is the *quid pro quo* for no-strike agreement). *But see* Berkline Corp., 123 NLRB 685, 687, 43 LRRM 1513 (1959). [146] *Cf.* Kordewick v. Brotherhood of Ry. Trainmen, 181 F 2d 963, 26 LRRM 2164 (CA 7, 1950) (Railway Labor Act). Of course, the union will be held to its duty of fair representation. See Chapter 27 *infra.* [147] 147 NLRB 1431, 56 LRRM 1369 (1964).

was warranted in the light of a management-prerogatives clause which specified that "[t]he company retains the sole right to . . . determine the qualifications of employees." [148]

In *Hughes Tool Co.*[149] a petitioning union was found to have waived its right to bargain over subcontracting. The contract between the employer and the union's predecessor contained a management clause which, in relevant part, provided that the "Company shall have responsibilities for decision . . . concerning . . . right to subcontract or to have work done by independent contractors." [150] The contract between the petitioning union and the company contained a clause specifying that the company "shall continue to have all of the rights which it had prior to the execution of this agreement except such rights as are relinquished herein." [151]

If the contract specifies the procedures to be followed in administering a plan or system, the union may be deemed to have waived its right to bargain over the administration of the plan or system during the term of the contract. The union waived its right to bargain over merit increases in *General Controls Co.*,[152] where the contract specified minimum and maximum rates in each classification and the parties agreed upon an elaborate merit-rating system.

But a management-rights clause not dealing specifically with a subject will probably not be viewed as a waiver as to that subject. In the *Tide Water* case, the employer acted unilaterally with regard to the company's retirement plan. The contract contained a management-functions clause providing that the hiring, demotion, promotion, transferring, retiring, discharging, and laying off of employees, the establishment or elimination of jobs, the scheduling of work, and the regulation and use of equipment were the exclusive function of management.[153] The Board held that, in view of the vagueness of the management-functions clause and in the absence of a specific waiver of the union's right to bargain

---

148 147 NLRB at 1432.
149 100 NLRB 208, 30 LRRM 1265 (1952).
150 *Ibid.*
151 *Id.* at 209. *See also* Ador Corp., 150 NLRB 1658, 58 LRRM 1280 (1965).
152 88 NLRB 1341, 25 LRRM 1475 (1950).
153 85 NLRB at 1098, n. 4.

on the retirement plan, the employer violated the Act.[154] Similarly, a specific clause will be construed narrowly, even when the clause is not a broad management-rights provision.[155]

(2) Bargaining history. In *Jacobs Manufacturing Co.*[156] the Board held that a union had waived its right to bargain on pensions during the term of a contract because the parties had fully discussed the subject during negotiations. Though the dissenters on this point would have required also that the matter be reduced to writing,[157] it is enough that "the matter has once been discussed in a manner which may warrant an inference that the failure to mention that subject in the contract was part of the bargain."[158] Member Herzog, whose vote was decisive, said that, when matters have been fully discussed, "the other party had every good reason to believe [they] were put to rest for a definite period."[159]

Member Reynolds, on the other hand, would have gone further to hold that the contract should be read so as to stabilize "the rights and obligations of the parties with respect to all bargainable subjects whether the subjects are or are not specifically set forth in the contract."[160]

> The basic terms and conditions of employment existing at the time the collective bargaining agreement is executed, and which are not specifically altered by, or mentioned in, the agreement, are part of the *status quo* which the parties, by implication, consider as being adopted as an essential element of the agreement.[161]

It should be emphasized that Member Reynolds' opinion, which would establish a waiver and thus eliminate any obligation during

---

[154] *Id.* at 1098. *Accord,* Timken Roller Bearing Co., 70 NLRB 500, 18 LRRM 1370 (1946).

[155] *See, e.g.,* California Portland Cement Co., 101 NLRB 1436, 1438-39, 31 LRRM 1220 (1952) (clause specifying disclosure of information). *Cf.* NLRB v. C & C Plywood, 385 US at 430-431. For discussion of the effect of a contract defense to unilateral action by an employer, *see* Chapter 18 *infra.*

[156] 94 NLRB 1214, 28 LRRM 1162 (1951), *enforced,* 196 F 2d 680, 30 LRRM 2098 (CA 2, 1952).

[157] 94 NLRB at 1220-1221. *See also* Tide Water Associated Oil Co., 85 NLRB 1096, 24 LRRM 1518 (1949).

[158] *Id.* at 1221. The court of appeals, 196 F 2d at 683, n. 1, 684, did not pass on whether there is a duty to bargain where the subject is not written into the contract. The court ruled only that there is a duty to bargain where the matter is neither discussed nor embodied in the terms of the contract.

[159] 94 NLRB at 1228.

[160] *Id.* at 1232.

[161] *Ibid.*

the contract period to bargain over new contractual terms,[162] has never been adopted by the Board.

The effect of *Jacobs Manufacturing*, therefore, is to require each party to bargain over matters which were neither discussed nor embodied in the contract.[163] Where a waiver can be proved from the bargaining history, it is a defense to a charge under Section 8(a)(5) or 8(b)(3).[164]

Employers have frequently argued that a union waives its right to bargain by abandoning a bargaining demand during contract negotiations. But the Board will not find a waiver "unless it can be said from an evaluation of the prior negotiations that the matter was 'fully discussed' or 'consciously explored' and the union 'consciously yielded' or clearly and unmistakably waived its interest in the matter." [165]

An unsuccessful attempt by a union to include in a contract a provision requiring management to bargain and to obtain the consent of the union before changing certain working conditions does not constitute a waiver. To hold that a union's failure to obtain such a provision constitutes a waiver would limit good-faith exploration of issues and tend to be disruptive in its effect upon collective bargaining.[166]

In *Press Co., Inc.*,[167] the union requested a contract clause prohibiting a cut in salesmen's commissions. Management contended that commissions were within its sole prerogative. Although the union dropped its bargaining demand, it expressly reserved the right to take legal action should the employer unilaterally alter commission rates. The Board held that the union did not waive its right to bargain, since it at least implicitly challenged the employer's management-prerogative position by continuing to seek the prohibiting clause. The Board reasoned:

---

162 The obligation to bargain over grievances would remain. 94 NLRB at 1233. Contrary to the opinion of the majority, 94 NLRB at 1218, §8 (d) as understood by Member Reynolds would also seem to prohibit economic action to compel bargaining.
163 The employer was required to bargain over an insurance program. The majority opinion, however, did not hold that the union could strike to compel the addition of a new contract provision. 94 NLRB at 1218, n. 10.
164 But this opinion also indicates that, even though a party is not obliged to bargain, the other party may take economic action to compel bargaining. 94 NLRB at 1218.
165 Press Co., Inc., 121 NLRB 976, 978, 42 LRRM 1493 (1958).
166 Cloverleaf Div. of Adams Dairy Co., 147 NLRB 1410, 56 LRRM 1321 (1964).
167 121 NLRB 976, 42 LRRM 1493 (1958).

To hold that, without regard to the nature of pre-contract negotiations, the mere discussion of a subject not specifically covered in the resulting contract removes the matter from the realm of collective bargaining during the contract term would be to place a premium (a) upon the employer's ability to avoid having the subject included in the contract, despite his knowledge of the union's position that it was a bargainable matter and not within his unilateral control; and (b) upon the union's ability to have the subject specifically referred to in the contract by engaging—if necessary—in a strike.[168]

It was the opinion of the Board that such a doctrine would result in increasing industrial discord.

The abandonment of a specific demand is, at best, an implied waiver. An implied waiver does not meet the Board's "clear and unmistakable" test.[169]

Although the abandoning of a bargaining demand does not *per se* constitute a waiver, silence in the face of a management assertion of unilateral control may be a waiver of the right to bargain. In *Speidel Corp.*[170] the union attempted to have included in the contract a "maintenance of privileges" clause. Management rejected the clause, fearing that it might encompass bonuses, which it contended were a management prerogative. Thereafter the union did not press the privilege clause or comment on the company's position, nor did it seek a counterproposal. The Board held that, in view of its complete silence and failure to contradict the employer's position, the union had acquiesced in management's understanding.

On the other hand, where both parties at the bargaining table treat a subject as bargainable and the employer does not take a position that he retains the right to take unilateral action, the abandonment of a union demand is not a waiver of union bargaining rights enabling the employer to take unilateral action.[171]

---

168 121 NLRB at 978.
169 Beacon Piece Dying & Finishing Co., 121 NLRB 953, 42 LRRM 1489 (1958); *accord,* Proctor Mfg. Co., 131 NLRB 1166, 48 LRRM 1222 (1961). *See also* Nash-Finch Co., 103 NLRB 1695, 32 LRRM 1026 (1953), *enforcement denied,* 211 F 2d 622, 33 LRRM 2898 (CA 8, 1954) (the execution of an original contract which does not mention benefits previously granted by the employer does not constitute a waiver of the right to bargain over these benefits during the contract term).
170 120 NLRB 733, 42 LRRM 1039 (1958).
171 Beacon Piece Dyeing and Finishing Co., 121 NLRB 953, 42 LRRM 1489 (1958); Press Co., Inc., 121 NLRB 976, 42 LRRM 1493 (1958). In each of these cases, the Board distinguished *Speidel* on the facts.

In the foregoing cases, the employer's claim of waiver goes beyond *Jacobs Manufacturing*. In that case there was no claim of a right to take unilateral action, only that there was no obligation to discuss changes proposed by the union. But in these cases the employer claimed a right to take action without bargaining. A waiver, of course, may be as broad as the parties wish. But in any case the union must acquiesce in or consciously yield to the specific demand. The cases do not stand for the proposition that a waiver of the right to bargain (by full discussion during negotiation) is the same as a conscious yielding to a claim of unilateral control. In the light of the available cases, therefore, it is possible that a party may waive the right to initiate bargaining over a particular demand during the contract term while reserving the right to demand bargaining over any later unilateral change proposed by the other party.

The following cases are illustrative of waivers by the union that permit unilateral control by the employer. The petitioner in *Tucker Steel Corp.*[172] was found to have waived its right to bargain over the discontinuance of a Christmas bonus. The Board found that: (1) the union had allowed the employer to deal unilaterally with bonuses for 12 years; (2) in the most recent contract negotiations the employer had intimated that the bonus would be discontinued and the union had made no comment; (3) the employer notified all the employees, including shop stewards, of the change, and the union did not comment; (4) the existing contract was signed without mention of the discontinuance, and the employer had good reason to believe the union was aware of this.

In *California Portland Cement Co.*[173] the Board found a waiver by construing the collective bargaining agreement in the light of the parties' bargaining history. The employer was found not to have violated Section 8(a)(5) by unilaterally increasing the salaries of three employees since (1) the contract provided that "[w]ages specified . . . are minimum wages and are not to be considered as preventing the employer from giving . . . additional compensation," [174] (2) negotiations indicated that the term "wages" included

---

172 134 NLRB 323, 49 LRRM 1164 (1961).
173 101 NLRB 1436, 31 LRRM 1220 (1952), *supplemented*, 103 NLRB 1375, 31 LRRM 1630 (1953).
174 101 NLRB at 1437.

salaries, (3) the clause had been retained from previous contracts, and (4) the employer had always acted unilaterally and the union had always acquiesced.

Two brief points can complete this analysis of the use of bargaining history as evidence of waiver. First, the application of fact to principle can, of course, lead to disagreement in individual cases.[175] Second, the parol-evidence rule is not a bar preventing the Board from looking to the negotiations of the parties.[176]

In summary, then, the present state of the law on waiver seems to be this:

1. There is a continuing statutory duty to bargain, even during the term of a contract.[177]

2. The continuing duty to bargain embraces not only grievances [178] but also all mandatory subjects [179] that are not contained in a contract for a fixed period.[180]

3. A party may waive his right to bargain, either by relinquishing a right to bring up a particular subject or by agreeing that the other party may exercise unilateral control over the subject.

4. Such a waiver must be clear and unmistakable and must indicate an acquiescence, agreement, or conscious yielding to a demand.

---

175 See, e.g., Beacon Journal Pub. Co., 164 NLRB 734, 65 LRRM 1126 (1967); LeRoy Mach. Co., 147 NLRB 1431, 56 LRRM 1369 (1964); Berkline Corp., 123 NLRB 685, 43 LRRM 1513 (1959); International News Serv., Div. of Hearst Corp., 113 NLRB 1067, 36 LRRM 1454 (1955).

176 See E. W. Scripps Co., 94 NLRB 227, 229, 28 LRRM 1033 (1951).

177 See general discussion in Chapter 11. See also NLRB v. Acme Indus. Co., 385 US 432, 64 LRRM 2069 (1967); NLRB v. Goodyear Aerospace Corp., 388 F 2d 673, 67 LRRM 2447 (CA 6, 1968); Timken Roller Bearing Co. v. NLRB, 325 F 2d 746, 54 LRRM 2785 (CA 6, 1963), cert. denied, 376 US 971, 55 LRRM 2878 (1964); Curtiss-Wright Corp. v. NLRB, 347 F 2d 61, 59 LRRM 2433 (CA 3, 1965); J.I. Case Co. v. NLRB, 253 F 2d 149, 41 LRRM 2679 (CA 7, 1958).

178 See §8 (d) (duty to confer with respect to any question arising under an agreement).

179 See Chapter 15. Many of the cases cited and discussed in the present chapter are couched in the language of waiver, although the arguments presented (especially in subcontracting cases) also go to the duty to bargain. E.g., in New York Mirror, 151 NLRB 834, 58 LRRM 1465 (1965), the Board held that there was no waiver, but that there was no duty to bargain under the circumstances.

In the area of subcontracting, a distinction should be made between the waiver cases and those like Westinghouse Elec. Co., 150 NLRB 1574, 58 LRRM 1257 (1965). In Westinghouse the Board said: "[I]t is wrong to assume that, in the absence of an existing contractual waiver, it is a per se unfair labor practice in all situations for an employer to let out unit work without consulting the unit bargaining representative." 150 NLRB at 1576. The Board thus laid down special rules to indicate those circumstances which would justify unilateral action.

180 Jacobs Mfg. Co., 94 NLRB 1214, 28 LRRM 1162 (1951).

(3) Zipper clauses. That there have been relatively few cases involving a demand to bargain on a subject not in the contract may be due to the general use of "zipper clauses." In *Jacobs Manufacturing,* the Board suggested:

> [I]f the parties originally desire to avoid later discussion with respect to matters not specifically covered in the terms of an executed contract, they need only so specify in the terms of the contract itself. Nothing in our construction of Section 8(d) precludes such an agreement, entered into in good faith, from foreclosing future discussion of matters not contained in the agreement.[181]

Such clauses generally recite that the parties had full opportunity to bargain, that the contract is complete in itself and sets forth all the terms and conditions of their agreement, and that each waives his right to bargain and agrees that the other is not obligated to bargain on any subject during the term of the agreement.

But a zipper clause seems to limit only the right to require the other party to respond to a bargaining demand and is not recognized as granting a unilateral right to change conditions of employment that are present when the contract is signed. Thus, in *New York Mirror,*[182] the Board said:

> This boilerplate clause, carried over from previous agreements, does no more than indicate that the parties embodied their full bargaining agreement in the written contracts. A wrap-up clause of this nature affords no basis for an inference that the agreement contains an implied undertaking over and beyond those actually written into the agreement.

That a zipper clause does not permit unilateral action is a position to which the Board has consistently adhered.[183] Where unilateral action has been permitted,[184] the Board has not relied on an all-inclusive zipper clause as the basis for the waiver.[185] Even

---

181 94 NLRB at 1220.
182 151 NLRB 834, 840, 58 LRRM 1465 (1965).
183 *See, e.g.,* Unit Drop Forge Div., Eaton Yale & Towne, Inc., 171 NLRB No. 73, 68 LRRM 1129 (1968); Rockwell-Standard Corp., 166 NLRB 124, 65 LRRM 1601 (1967), *enforced,* 410 F 2d 953, 71 LRRM 2328 (CA 6, 1969); Beacon Journal Pub. Co., 164 NLRB 734, 65 LRRM 1126 (1967), *enforced in part,* 401 F 2d 366, 69 LRRM 2232 (CA 6, 1968); C & C Plywood, 148 NLRB 414, 57 LRRM 1015 (1964), *enforced,* 385 US 421, 64 LRRM 2065 (1967), *reversing* 351 F 2d 224, 60 LRRM 2137 (CA 9, 1965).
184 *E.g.,* Borden Co., 110 NLRB 802, 35 LRRM 1133 (1954).
185 *See* New York Mirror, 151 NLRB at 840, n. 14, stating that in *Borden Co.,* 110 NLRB 802, 35 LRRM 1133 (1954), the Board found a waiver on the basis of the parties' positions in negotiations, in the terms of the contract, and in the availability of grievance procedures for the dispute.

an unusually broad waiver of statutory rights, extending to subjects not referred to or covered in the agreement "even though such subject or matter may not have been within the knowledge or contemplation of either or both parties,"[186] does not constitute a waiver of the right to be consulted about a change in working conditions, unless it appears that the particular matter was fully discussed and that the union consciously yielded or unmistakably waived its interest in the change.[187]

Yet, even where a zipper clause states that the parties waive their own right to initiate bargaining,[188] this waiver has not been read so as to prohibit all changes. The cited cases either permit a change to stand (requiring bargaining only over the effects and not the restoration of the *status quo ante*), or merely hold that the employer may not initiate a change without affording the union an opportunity to bargain.

  c. Right to Information.[189] A waiver of the right to bargain over an issue does not necessarily constitute a waiver of the right to receive information.[190] The Board in *Sinclair Refining Co.*[191] found, for example, that the contract indisputably gave management the sole prerogative to discharge for lack of work. Nevertheless, this provision did not constitute a waiver of the right to receive information relevant to lack of work, nor did it foreclose a

---

186 Unit Drop Forge Div., Eaton Yale & Towne, Inc., 171 NLRB No. 73, 68 LRRM 1129 (1968). *See* Chapter 18 *infra* regarding arbitrability of the unilateral change.
187 *Ibid.*
188 *See, e.g.,* Jacobs Mfg. Co., 94 NLRB at 1220, n. 13: Each party "waives the right, and each agrees that the other shall not be obligated, to bargain collectively. . . ." *See also* Unit Drop Forge Div., Eaton Yale & Towne, Inc., 171 NLRB No. 73, 68 LRRM 1129 (1968); Rockwell-Standard Corp., 166 NLRB 124, 65 LRRM 1601 (1967); C & C Plywood, 148 NLRB 414, 57 LRRM 1015 (1964).
189 Insofar as the statutory duty to furnish information is concerned, see the discussion in Chapter 11 *supra*. This question is also discussed in Chapter 18 *infra* in its relation to arbitration. The present section is concerned only with the contract interpretation issue of waiver.
190 "The right to grant merit increases without the consent of a statutory bargaining agent obviously should not imply the right to withhold information thereon, since such a rule might foster discrimination against union adherents in the granting of merit increases, and thereby promote that industrial strife and unrest which the Act seeks to avoid." NLRB v. Item Co., 220 F 2d, 956, 959, 35 LRRM 2709, 2711 (CA 5), *cert. denied,* 350 US 836, 36 LRRM 2716 (1955). *Accord:* Square D Co., 142 NLRB 332, 336, 53 LRRM 1023 (1963) (trial examiner's report); Zenith Radio Corp., 177 NLRB No. 30, 71 LRRM 1555 (1969).
191 132 NLRB 1660, 48 LRRM 1544 (1961), *enforcement denied,* 306 F 2d 569, 50 LRRM 2830 (CA 5, 1962).

grievance over whether there existed a lack of work. It only barred challenge of the company's right to discharge if there was in fact a lack of work.[192]

A waiver of the statutory right to information may, however, be found in the terms of the contract or in the negotiating history.[193] This waiver must be in clear and unmistakable terms [194] and is not to be inferred merely from the existence of a grievance procedure.[195] The union in *Timken Roller Bearing Co.*[196] requested wage data in connection with particular grievances and general wage data for the purpose of administering the contract. It was the contention of the employer that the contract contained a comprehensive grievance procedure and that, therefore, the union had waived its right to obtain the data except through the grievance procedure. In addition, the employer maintained that there was a waiver by virtue of the union's failure to get a contract clause imposing upon the employer a contractual obligation to furnish the information. The Board found that the contract clause was limited to complaints involving the interpretation and application of the agreement and did not, therefore, affect the union's statutory right to information. As for the second contention, an unsuccessful attempt to obtain a contract clause is not a "clear and unequivocal" waiver.[197]

Abandoning a demand for information during contract negotiations does not constitute a waiver. Where an employer had previously furnished wage information for only those employees who signed authorization cards and where the union abandoned its demand for a disclosure-of-information clause, the Board found that the union did not waive its right to relevant wage data.[198]

---

192 132 NLRB at 1661-1662; *accord,* Hekman Furniture Co., 101 NLRB 631, 31 LRRM 1116 (1952), *enforced,* 207 F 2d 561, 32 LRRM 2759 (CA 6, 1953); General Controls Co., 88 NLRB 1341, 25 LRRM 1475 (1950).

193 *E.g.,* International Shoe Co., 151 NLRB 693, 58 LRRM 1483 (1965); International News Serv., Div. of Hearst Corp., 113 NLRB 1067, 36 LRRM 1454 (1955); Hughes Tool Co., 100 NLRB 208, 30 LRRM 1265 (1952).

194 Hekman Furniture Co., 101 NLRB 631, 632, 31 LRRM 1116 (1952).

195 Timken Roller Bearing Co., 138 NLRB 15, 50 LRRM 1508 (1962), *enforced,* 325 F 2d 746, 54 LRRM 2785 (CA 6, 1963), *cert. denied,* 376 US 971, 55 LRRM 2878 (1964); Hekman Furniture Co., 101 NLRB 631, 31 LRRM 1116 (1952).

196 138 NLRB 15, 50 LRRM 1508 (1962), *enforced,* 325 F 2d 746, 54 LRRM 2785 (CA 6, 1963), *cert. denied,* 376 US 971, 55 LRRM 2878 (1964). *See also* discussion in Chapter 18 *infra.*

197 138 NLRB at 16.

198 Westinghouse Air Brake Co., 119 NLRB 1391, 41 LRRM 1252 (1957).

Where a contract contains a provision requiring the employer to furnish information on specified issues and also states that the contract embodies the entire agreement of the parties, the Board has held that the union has not waived its statutory right to receive information on a nonenumerated issue.[199]

The Board, moreover, is hesitant to find a waiver of the right of information.[200] Even where a union has waived its right to information for one purpose (as for administering the contract), it may demand the information for another purpose not covered by the waiver (as, for instance, for future contract negotiations).[201] In the light of the broad holding of *NLRB* v. *Acme Industrial Co.,*[202] it may be expected that the Board rarely will find such waivers.

2. Contract Interpretation and Section 8(d).   Section 8(d) provides that a party to a contract shall not "terminate or modify" it except under certain conditions.   One condition is that he will continue "in full force and effect, without resorting to strike or lockout, all the terms and conditions of the existing contract . . . until the expiration date of such contract." [203]

As indicated in the earlier discussion of *Jacobs Manufacturing,* it is not clear what effect this section has on bargaining over subjects and terms not in the contract. Member Reynolds' dissent held that a request to bargain on such subjects is a request to modify the contract.[204] He said that the addition of a new term to a contract is a modification, as is "any change in the basic terms and conditions of employment existing at the time the collective bargaining instrument was executed." [205] The majority, however, maintained that Section 8(d) "does not mean that the other party is prohibited from taking economic action to compel bargain-

---

[199] California Portland Cement Co., 101 NLRB 1436, 31 LRRM 1220 (1952), *supplemented,* 103 NLRB 1375, 31 LRRM 1630 (1953); Leland Gifford Co., 95 NLRB 1306, 28 LRRM 1443 (1951), *enforced in part,* 200 F 2d 620, 31 LRRM 2196 (CA 1, 1952).

[200] *See* the dissents in Berkline Corp., 123 NLRB 685, 43 LRRM 1513 (1959), and *International News Serv., Div. of Hearst Corp.,* 113 NLRB 1067, 36 LRRM 1454 (1955).

[201] Berkline Corp., *supra* note 200.

[202] 385 US 432, 64 LRRM 2069 (1967). Here it was said that the Board could act "upon the probability that the desired information was relevant, and that it would be of use to the union in carrying out its statutory duties and responsibilities." 385 US at 437. For further discussion of this case, *see* Chapter 18 *infra.*

[203] NLRA §8 (d). *See also* discussion in Chapter 11 *supra.*

[204] 94 NLRB at 1229.

[205] *Id.* at 1233.

ing." [206] But this does not mean that, without complying with the requirements of Section 8(d), "a union may strike to compel bargaining on a modification of a contract which seeks to add a matter not contained in the contract." [207] However, the case does not decide the ambit of Section 8(d) in relation to an actual change or addition,[208] as the holding is limited to requiring bargaining discussions on subjects not contained in the contract.[209]

Subsequent cases [210] lend weight to the theory that, where a matter can or must be bargained over, a change may be effected after bargaining, even though there is no agreement on the matter between the parties. This would, of course, not establish any contractual obligation, but the subsequent imposition of changed conditions of employment would not of itself be a violation of the duty to bargain.

This conclusion is reinforced by cases in which the employer has claimed that he has a right of unilateral control without any obligation to bargain over a mandatory subject. The Board (upon finding no waiver) usually orders that the employer return to the conditions existing prior to the unilateral action and bargain with the union upon request.[211] The regularity of these cases seems almost to create a presumption that an employer can, after bargaining, change conditions. Some cases make it clear that a party need only bargain to impasse [212] before taking the contemplated action. The issues in these cases are dealt with elsewhere.[213]

But a party runs the risk that the Board, in its interpretation of contract terms, may find that the contract governs the matter and that no change can be effectuated without the consent of the union. Since the Board has opted not to include in the contract all existing conditions of employment,[214] a specific decision must be made

---

206 *Id.* at 1218.

207 *Id.* at 1218, n. 10.

208 *See also:* Adams Dairy Co., 137 NLRB 815, 816, 50 LRRM 1281, 1283 (1962); Beacon Piece Dyeing & Finishing Co., 121 NLRB 953, 962, n. 15, 42 LRRM 1489 (1958).

209 94 NLRB at 1219-1220.

210 *See* the discussion on waiver *supra.*

211 *See, e.g.,* Beacon Piece Dyeing & Finishing Co., 121 NLRB 953, 42 LRRM 1489 (1958); C & C Plywood Corp., 148 NLRB 414, 57 LRRM 1015 (1964).

212 *E.g.,* Dixie Ohio Express Co., 167 NLRB No. 72, 66 LRRM 1092 (1967).

213 *See* the discussion on bargaining during the contract term in Chapter 11 *supra,* and subcontracting as a subject of bargaining in Chapter 15 *infra.*

214 Jacobs Mfg. Co., 94 NLRB 1214, 28 LRRM 1162 (1951).

in each case as to whether the contract controls a particular matter. Again, contract terms and bargaining history will be looked to in reaching this determination.

Where a contract fixes an item, a party cannot compel renegotiation during the term of the contract.[215] Thus, the Board has sometimes interpreted a contract and concluded that a subject is so defined that the employer may not institute changes without the consent of the union. An unjustified repudiation or rescission of a contract has been found to be in violation of Section 8(d), and the offending party has been ordered to assume the obligations of the contract.[216] Where a contract called for the payment of wages on a cents-per-hour basis, the employer could not superimpose a wage incentive plan, even though he sought to negotiate with the union.[217] The incentive plan was said to be a "modification of the specific terms of the contract within the meaning of Section 8(d)." [218] Where an employer reduced the wages of his employees without notifying the union, Section 8(d) afforded an independent basis for finding a violation of Section 8(a)(5), since the reductions were held to be modifications of the existing contract.[219]

In *C & S Industries* [220] the employer instituted a wage incentive system during the term of a collective bargaining agreement. Even assuming an adequate offer to bargain,[221] the change constituted a modification of the contract in violation of Section 8(d). The Board rejected the company's contention that Section 8(d) relieves a party of the duty to bargain over changes in an existing contract but imposes no duty to refrain from acting unilaterally when the other party rejects an offer to bargain. Such a reading of the statute, the Board said, would make the provisions of Section 8(d) "meaningless" and "nugatory." [222]

> Of course, the breadth of 8(d) is not such as to make any default in a contract obligation an unfair labor practice, for that section, to the extent relevant here, is in terms confined to the "modification" or "termination" of a contract. But there can be little doubt that

---

215 *See, e.g.,* Milk Drivers, Local 783, 147 NLRB 264, 56 LRRM 1194 (1964); Proctor Mfg. Corp., 131 NLRB 1166, 48 LRRM 1222 (1961).
216 Crescent Bed Co., 157 NLRB 296, 61 LRRM 1334 (1966).
217 John W. Bolton & Sons, Inc., 91 NLRB 989, 26 LRRM 1598 (1950).
218 91 NLRB at 990.
219 Kinard Trucking Co., 152 NLRB 449, 59 LRRM 1104 (1965).
220 158 NLRB 454, 62 LRRM 1043 (1966).
221 The Board so assumed. 158 NLRB at 456.
222 *Id.* at 458.

where an employer unilaterally effects a change which has a continuing impact on a basic term or condition of employment, wages for example, more is involved than just a simple default in a contractual obligation. Such a change manifestly constitutes a "modification" within the meaning of 8(d).[223]

A contractually established wage structure and a provision requiring written union consent to any change in the method of payment for employees made it clear that the institution of the wage incentive plan was a modification in derogation of the obligations under Section 8(d).

In *Huttig Sash & Door Co.*[224] the employer was held to have violated Section 8(a)(5) by unilaterally reducing hourly rates set by the contract without following the procedures set out in Section 8(d) and incorporated in the contract. He was obligated not only to give the 60-day notice and to notify the mediation services, but also "to continue all terms and conditions of the contract in full force and effect as required." [225]

Although *C & C Plywood*[226] is factually similar to *C & S Industries*,[227] the Board in the former case did not reach the issue posed by Section 8(d). Although the Board was there content to rest a violation merely upon the failure to consult and to bargain, it is not clear that, in the future, similar cases will be so decided. Indeed, since its decision in *C & C Plywood*, the Board seems to have given increased attention to contract interpretation under Section 8(d) and to limiting the freedom to engage in unilateral changes of operation, even after bargaining.[228] In *NLRB* v. *Scam Instrument Corp.*[229] the court pointed out that, once an insurance program is incorporated in a contract, it constitutes a part of the terms and conditions of employment and the benefits are frozen for the contract period, "absent mutual consent of the contracting parties to their alteration or qualification, or compliance with the

---

223 *Ibid.*
224 154 NLRB 811, 60 LRRM 1035 (1965), *enforced,* 377 F 2d 964, 65 LRRM 2431 (CA 8, 1967).
225 154 NLRB at 815 (trial examiner's report).
226 148 NLRB 414, 57 LRRM 1015 (1964). *See* note 86 *supra.*
227 *See also* John W. Bolton & Sons, Inc., 91 NLRB 989, 26 LRRM 1598 (1950).
228 *See* Standard Oil Co. of Ohio, 174 NLRB No. 33, 70 LRRM 1115 (1969); W. P. Ihrie & Sons, 165 NLRB 167, 65 LRRM 1205 (1967) (repudiation of dues-checkoff provision); Scam Instrument Corp., 163 NLRB 284, 64 LRRM 1327 (1967), *enforced,* 394 F 2d 884, 68 LRRM 2280 (CA 7), *cert. denied,* 393 US 980, 69 LRRM 2851 (1968); Century Papers, Inc., 155 NLRB 358, 60 LRRM 1320 (1965).
229 394 F 2d 884, 68 LRRM 2280 (CA 7, 1968).

provisions of Section 8(d)." [230] But the Board's approach to this issue also emphasized an obligation to bargain. "Bargaining over the reduction would not necessarily have been a mere formality. . . . The Union might well have acquiesced in the rider, but sought some compensating advantage. . . ." [231]

The foregoing discussion has shown that, where the employer engages in unilateral action, the Board may conclude on the facts: (1) that there is no obligation to bargain; (2) that the union has waived its right to bargain and granted a unilateral right to the employer; (3) that the union has not waived its right and the employer must bargain before taking action; or (4) that the contract regulates the matter and the employer cannot effectuate a change without the consent of the union. A further puzzlement arises in that the Board, in appropriate instances, will defer to arbitration for a resolution of the contract issue.[232] Since the next chapter deals with deference to arbitration, the subject is only mentioned here. But, along with the other complexities of Section 8(d), it goes to show the truth of the comment that Section 8(d) is "convoluted" and mysterious and that when the Supreme Court finally deals with this section and Section 301, "it may be even more puzzled than was Alice in the Queen's croquet game." [233]

3. Management Rights.[234] There seem to be three differing concepts relating to management's freedom of action subsequent to the signing of a collective bargaining contract: (1) management retains full freedom to act except insofar as its functions are limited or surrendered in the agreement (residual rights); [235] (2)

---

230 *Id.* at 887.

231 NLRB Brief in Opposition on Petition for Cert. at 7, n. 3, Scam Instrument Corp., 393 US 980 (1968).

232 See, *e.g.*, Jos. Schlitz Brewing Co., 175 NLRB No. 23, 70 LRRM 1472 (1968); Crescent Bed Co., 157 NLRB 296, 61 LRRM 1334 (1966); National Dairy Prods. Corp., 126 NLRB 434, 45 LRRM 1332 (1960); Morton Salt Co., 119 NLRB 1402, 41 LRRM 1312 (1958); United Tel. Co. of the West, 112 NLRB 779, 36 LRRM 1097 (1955). In this last case, the Board said: "The Respondent's action was in accordance with the contract as they construed it, and was not an attempt to modify or to terminate the contract. The provisions of Section 8 (d) of the Act are therefore inapplicable in this case." 112 NLRB at 781.

233 Summers, *Labor Law Decisions of Supreme Court, 1961 Term,* in ABA Labor Relations Law Proceedings 51, 67 (1962).

234 For fuller discussion, see F. & E. A. Elkouri, How Arbitration Works 284-302 (Washington: BNA Books, 1960); Phelps, *Management's Reserved Rights: An Industry View,* in Management Rights and the Arbitration Process 102 (Washington: BNA Books, 1956); Goldberg, *Management's Reserved Rights: A Labor View,* in Management Rights and the Arbitration Process 118 (Washington: BNA Books, 1956).

235 See Phelps, *supra* note 234.

management cannot make a unilateral change in a major condition
of employment during the term of an existing agreement even
though the contract does not deal with the subject matter; [236] and
(3) management remains free to bargain, and then to act, on all
matters not governed by the contract.[237]

The right of a company to manage its business has in fact been
limited by application of the Act. For instance, the obligation to
bargain, which is central to the statutory purpose, is a basic restriction.[238] And, of course, the employer may surrender additional
rights by contract. The real issue here, however, is in defining management rights after a contract has been signed. In this
regard, the issues of waiver and of past practice have a bearing on
the meaning of a contract. For those who would argue that the
contract embraces all conditions of employment existing at the
time of contractual agreement, past practices are especially relevant. For those who maintain that management reserves all rights
except as specifically provided in the agreement, the inclusion of
a management-rights clause in the contract is meant to spell out
the broad scope of unilateral control. But the Board holds that a
broad management-rights clause in no way relieves management
of its obligation to bargain.[239] Even where a contract contains
language reserving to management the right unilaterally to administer matters not set forth in the contract, the employer may be
required to bargain or to give information with respect to actual
administration of the plan.[240] A vaguely worded management-
rights clause is not to be interpreted as a waiver of the union's
right to bargain, at least where the contract does not specifically
spell out the terms.[241]

Where a management-prerogatives clause gives the employer the
sole right to determine the qualifications of employees, the em-

---

[236] See Cox & Dunlop, *The Duty To Bargain During the Term of an Existing
Agreement*, 63 HARV. L. REV. 1097, 1110-1117, 1125 (1950).

[237] This is the Board's position as developed above in this chapter.

[238] Note, however, that the right to go out of business endures. Textile Workers v.
Darlington Mfg. Co., 380 US 263, 58 LRRM 2657 (1965). *See* Chapter 6 *supra* at
notes 39-42. The obligation to bargain also recognizes management rights. *E.g.*,
Westinghouse Elec. Co., 150 NLRB 1574, 58 LRRM 1257 (1965).

[239] Timken Roller Bearing Co., 70 NLRB 500, 18 LRRM 1370 (1946), *reversed on
other grounds*, 161 F 2d 949, 20 LRRM 2204 (CA 6, 1947). *Accord*, Proctor Mfg.
Corp., 131 NLRB 1166, 48 LRRM 1222 (1961).

[240] *Square D Co.*, 142 NLRB 332, 53 LRRM 1023 (1963), *reversed*, 332 F 2d 360, 56
LRRM 2147 (CA 9, 1964).

[241] Tide Water Associated Oil Co., 85 NLRB 1096, 24 LRRM 1518 (1949).

ployer may without bargaining require employees with bad absentee records to submit to a medical examination.[242] And the
Board will recognize normal management functions and will permit the continuation of longstanding procedures required by
business.[243]

But the Board, both in reading a contract and in defining the
duty to bargain during a contract period, rejects the residual-
rights theory.

> [W]hen an employer . . . claims that his unilateral action is privi-
> leged under the contract, the evaluation of this claim usually
> requires more than the interpretation of a specific contract provision.
> The employer claim is ordinarily based, at least in part, on such
> general circumstances as a management prerogative clause, the fact
> that the contract does not specifically prohibit the action taken, or
> the union's failure to gain a specific prohibition during contract
> negotiations. The Board, under the NLRA, has developed principles
> for evaluating these general circumstances. . . . An arbitrator, on
> the other hand, who is ordinarily merely concerned with whether
> there has been a breach of the agreement, might never consider these
> principles, and, if he did, he might well apply them differently than
> would the Board. Many arbitrators, for example, apply the so-
> called "residual rights" theory when management takes unilateral
> action, holding that it is free to act unless the collective agreement
> expressly provides otherwise. . . . Such a doctrine, which bestows
> upon management all "residual rights," stands on its head the
> established rule that a statutory waiver must be express and clear;
> it flows from an approach wholly inconsistent with decisions such
> as that of . . . [the Supreme Court in *Fiberboard Paper*] holding that
> the NLRB, in certain circumstances, imposes a duty to bargain
> about subcontracting apart from any requirement in the collective
> agreement itself.[244]

The Supreme Court, in upholding the Board's position in *C & C
Plywood* [245] and in rejecting the company's argument [246] in *NLRB
v. Acme Industrial Co.*, has thereby supported the Board rationale
as a proper principle of contract interpretation whenever it is
necessary to interpret the contract to resolve an issue of statutory
rights.

---

[242] LeRoy Mach. Co., 147 NLRB 1431, 56 LRRM 1369 (1964).
[243] Chatham Mfg. Co., 172 NLRB No. 219, 69 LRRM 1228 (1968).
[244] Brief for NLRB at 28-29, n. 20, NLRB v. C & C Plywood Corp., 385 US 421, 64
LRRM 2065 (1967).
[245] 385 US 421 (1967).
[246] Brief for Respondent at 31-38, NLRB v. Acme Indus. Co., 385 US 432, 64 LRRM
2069 (1967).

CHAPTER 18

ACCOMMODATION OF BOARD ACTION TO THE ARBITRATION PROCESS [1]

I. THE ARBITRATION PROCESS AND THE COURTS

The grievance-arbitration procedure has been described as being

> at the very heart of the system of industrial self-government. Arbitration is the means of solving the unforeseeable by molding a system of private law for all the problems which may arise and to provide for their solution in a way which will generally accord with the variant needs and desires of the parties. The processing of disputes through the grievance machinery is actually a vehicle by which meaning and content is given to the collective bargaining agreement.

---

[1] The problem discussed in this chapter is closely identified with the problem of accommodating court action under §301 to Board jurisdiction of unfair labor practices and representation cases treated in Chapter 17 *supra*.

For bibliographical material, see: M. Trotta, Labor Arbitration 109-132 (1961) ; Bloch, *The NLRB and Arbitration: Is the Board's Expanding Jurisdiction Justified?*, 19 Lab. L.J. 640 (1968) ; Brown, *The National Labor Policy, the N.L.R.B. and Arbitration*, in Developments in American and Foreign Arbitration 83 (1968) ; Christensen, *Arbitration, Section 301, and the National Labor Relations Act*, 37 N.Y.U. L. Rev. 411 (1962) ; Clark, *Interplay Between the LMRA and Arbitration: Concurrent Unfair Labor Practices and Grievances*, 16 Lab. L.J. 412 (1965) ; Cummings, *NLRB Jurisdiction and Labor Arbitration: "Uniformity" vs. "Industrial Peace,"* 12 Lab. L.J. 425 (1961); Cushman, *Arbitration and the Duty to Bargain*, 1967 Wis. L.R. 612 (1967) ; Dunau, *Contractual Prohibition of Unfair Labor Practices: Jurisdictional Problems*, 57 Colum. L. Rev. 52 (1967) ; Hanley, *The NLRB and the Arbitration Process: Conflict or Accommodation?*, in Labor Law Developments 1968 (14th Annual Institute on Labor Law, Sw. Legal Foundation) 151 (1968); Harris, *The National Labor Relations Board and Arbitration—The Battle of Concurrent Jurisdiction*, 16 Syracuse L. Rev. 545 (1965) ; Lesnick, *Arbitration as a Limit on the Discretion of Management, Union, and NLRB: The Year's Major Developments*, N.Y.U. Eighteenth Annual Conference on Labor 7 (1966) ; Levitt, *Interrelationships in the Interpretation of Collective Bargaining Agreements*, 10 Lab. L.J. 484 (1959) ; McCulloch, *The Arbitration Issue in NLRB Decisions*, 19 Arb. J. 134 (1964) ; McCulloch, *Arbitration and/or the NLRB*, 18 Arb. J. 3 (1963) ; McDermott, *Arbitrability: The Courts Versus the Arbitrator*, 23 Arb. J. 18 (1968) ; Moss, *Arbitration and the NLRB's Jurisdiction*, N.Y.U. Seventeenth Annual Conference on Labor 65 (1965) ; O'Brien, *Should the NLRB Arbitrate Labor Contract Disputes?*, 6 Washburn L.J. 39 (1966) ; Ordman, *Arbitration and the N.L.R.B.— A Second Look*, in The Arbitrator, the N.L.R.B. and the Courts 47 (1967) ; Rothschild, *Arbitration and the National Labor Relations Board: An Examination of Preferences and Prejudices and Their Relevance*, 28 Ohio S. L.J. 195 (1967) ;

. . . . The grievance procedure is, in other words, a part of the continuous collective bargaining process.[2]

This recognition of the centrality of the arbitral process was long in coming. The federal courts first applied the common-law rule that an executory agreement to arbitrate is not specifically enforceable.[3] Then, after passage of the United States Arbitration Act,[4] it was argued that the courts had the power to enforce arbitration agreements in collective bargaining contracts.[5] The issues of statutory interpretation under the Arbitration Act were soon sidetracked by the breadth of the decision in *Textile Workers Union* v. *Lincoln Mills*,[6] which held that Section 301[7] furnishes a body of federal substantive law for the enforcement of collective bargaining agreements. This case, rejecting an argument that the Norris-LaGuardia Act[8] would bar an injunction, specifically enforced the obligation to arbitrate grievance disputes.

As the role of the courts under Section 301 was being elucidated, the relation of the courts to arbitration was specified by the Su-

---

Peck, *Accommodation and Conflict Among Tribunals: Whatever Happened to Preemption?*, in Labor Law Developments 1969 (15th Annual Institute on Labor Law, Sw. Legal Foundation) 121 (1969) ; Samoff, *Arbitration, Not NLRB Intervention*, 18 Lab. L.J. 602 (1967) ; Samoff, *The NLRB and Arbitration: Conflicting or Compatible Currents*, 9 Lab. L.J. 689 (1958) ; Seitz, *Grievance Arbitration and the National Labor Policy*, N.Y.U. Eighteenth Annual Conference on Labor 201 (1966); Stein, *Arbitration and the NLRA*, 5 Lab. L.J. 163 (1954) ; Summers, *Labor Law Decisions of Supreme Court, 1961 Term*, ABA Labor Relations Law Proceedings 51 (1962) ; Summers & Samoff, *A New Look at the NLRA and Arbitration*, 5 Lab. L.J. 535 (1954) ; Summers & Samoff, *The Labor Board Looks at Arbitration*, 2 Lab. L.J. 477 (1951) ; Wollett, *The Interpretation of Collective Bargaining Agreements: Who Should Have Primary Jurisdiction?*, 10 Lab. L.J. 477 (1959) ; Note, *Employers' Duty To Supply Economic Data for Collective Bargaining*, 57 Colum. L. Rev. 112 (1957) ; Note, *Jurisdiction of Arbitrators and State Courts*, 69 Harv. L. Rev. 725 (1965) ; Note, *Procedural Arbitrability Under Section 301 of the LMRA*, 73 Yale L.J. 1459 (1964) ; Note, *The NLRB and Deference to Arbitration*, 77 Yale L.J. 1191 (1968) .
[2] United Steelworkers v. Warrior & Gulf Navigation Co., 363 US 574, 581, 46 LRRM 2416, 2419 (1960) .
[3] *See, e.g.,* Red Cross Line v. Atlantic Fruit Co., 264 US 109 (1924) .
[4] 9 USC §§1-14.
[5] *Compare* Local 205, United Elec. Workers v. Gen. Elec. Co., 233 F 2d 85, 38 LRRM 2019 (CA 1, 1956) , *and* Hoover Motor Express Co. v. Teamsters Union, 217 F 2d 49, 35 LRRM 2301 (CA 6, 1954) (holding that the Act applies to collective bargaining agreements containing arbitration clauses) , *with* United Elec. Workers v. Miller Metal Prods., Inc., 215 F 2d 221, 34 LRRM 2731 (CA 4, 1954) , *and* Mercury Oil Ref. Co. v. Oil Workers, 187 F 2d 980, 983, 16 LA 129 (CA 10, 1951) (excluding collective bargaining contracts from the coverage of the act) . *See also* Signal-Stat Corp. v. Local 475, United Elec. Workers, 235 F 2d 298, 38 LRRM 2378 (CA 2, 1956) ; Tenney Eng., Inc. v. United Elec. Workers, 207 F 2d 450, 21 LA 260 (CA 3, 1953) .
[6] 353 US 448, 40 LRRM 2113 (1957) .
[7] For a general discussion of §301, see Chapter 17 *supra*.
[8] 29 USC §104 (1964) .

preme Court in the *Steelworkers* Trilogy.[9] These cases established the following propositions: (1) the function of the court is limited "to ascertaining whether the party seeking arbitration is making a claim which on its face is governed by the contract;" [10] (2) doubts as to the coverage of the arbitration clause should be resolved in favor of arbitration; [11] (3) an arbitrator's award, though it must be based on the collective bargaining agreement, must be enforced by the courts even if his interpretation of the contract would differ from the court's or is ambiguous.[12] The Court has found support for this deference to arbitration both in legislative history [13] and in Sections 201 and 203(d) of the LMRA,[14] which provide that final adjustment by an agreed-upon method is the desirable method for settling contract disputes. The end result of these developments has been to resolve most questions of conflict between the arbitrator and the courts in favor of the arbitral process.[15]

Since the issue of substantive arbitrability in a Section 301 case is for the courts, the court must determine both whether the parties agreed to arbitrate and what issues are included in the agreement.[16] Hence, it can be seen that the court will look to see what is embraced in the agreement to arbitrate. The clause may be

---

[9] United Steelworkers v. American Mfg. Co., 363 US 564, 46 LRRM 2414 (1960); United Steelworkers v. Warrior & Gulf Navigation Co., 363 US 574, 46 LRRM 2416 (1960); United Steelworkers v. Enterprise Wheel & Car Corp., 363 US 593, 46 LRRM 2423 (1960).

[10] United Steelworkers v. American Mfg. Co., 363 US 564, 568, 46 LRRM 2414 (1960). In thus rejecting the right of the court to decide the merits under the guise of arbitrability, the Court expressly reprobated *IAM* v. *Cutler-Hammer, Inc.,* 271 App. Div. 917, 67 NYS 2d 317, 19 LRRM 2232, aff'd, 297 NY 519, 74 NE 2d 464, 20 LRRM 2445 (1947).

[11] United Steelworkers v. Warrior & Gulf Navigation Co., 363 US 574, 46 LRRM 2416 (1960).

[12] United Steelworkers v. Enterprise Wheel & Car Corp., 363 US 593, 46 LRRM 2423 (1960).

[13] *See* Textile Workers Union v. Lincoln Mills, 353 US 448, 40 LRRM 2113 (1957).

[14] *See* Carey v. Westinghouse Elec. Corp., 375 US 261, 264-65 n. 4, 55 LRRM 2042 (1964); United Steelworkers v. American Mfg. Co., 363 US 564, 46 LRRM 2414 (1960).

[15] This book does not attempt to develop the case law governing the relation of court and arbitrator or to analyze the enforcement of awards or the problems of arbitrability.

[16] Atkinson v. Sinclair Ref. Co., 370 US 238, 241, 50 LRRM 2433 (1962); *accord,* United Steelworkers v. Warrior & Gulf Navigation Co., 363 US 574, 582, 46 LRRM 2416 (1960); John Wiley & Sons, Inc. v. Livingston, 376 US 543, 55 LRRM 2769 (1964).

narrow or broad,[17] but it is up to the parties to delimit the area of arbitration.[18]

II. JURISDICTION OF THE NLRB

Preliminary to a discussion of Board practice in deferring to arbitration, it will be helpful to set forth the arguments which show that the NLRB has jurisdiction over unfair labor practice cases even where the decision involves the interpretation of contracts that are subject to arbitration. The Board's power is not "affected by any other means of adjustment or prevention that has been or may be established by agreement, law, or otherwise." [19] This statutory grant makes it clear that the Board enforces "public rights" [20] and that private contracts [21] and arbitral awards [22] cannot limit the Board's jurisdiction. The enforcement of a private contract under Section 301 does not deprive the Board of its statutory jurisdiction.[23] Since an agreement to arbitrate is a specific type of private contract, it would seem to follow that an arbitration clause does not limit NLRB jurisdiction although the case may also be before a court or arbitrator. Indeed, on matters properly before the Board the Board's decision prevails over that of the arbitrator. The Supreme Court has said that "[s]hould the

---

17 For a discussion of the construction to be placed upon typical arbitration clauses, see Cox, *Reflections Upon Labor Arbitration,* 72 HARV. L. REV. 1482, 1507-10 (1959).
18 As an example of the difficulty in narrowing the scope of arbitration, see IUE v. General Elec. Co., 407 F 2d 253, 70 LRRM 2082 (CA 2, 1968), *cert. denied,* 395 US 904, 71 LRRM 2254 (1969); IUE v. General Elec. Co., 332 F 2d 485, 56 LRRM 2289 (CA 2), *cert. denied,* 379 US 928, 57 LRRM 2608 (1964).
19 § 10(a).
20 *See:* Amalgamated Utility Workers v. Consolidated Edison Co., 309 US 261, 264-65, 267-69, 6 LRRM 669 (1940); National Licorice Co. v. NLRB, 309 US 350, 365, 6 LRRM 674 (1940).
21 Lodge 743, IAM v. United Aircraft Corp., 337 F 2d 5, 10, 57 LRRM 2245, 2247-48 (CA 2, 1964), *cert. denied,* 380 US 908, 58 LRRM 2496 (1965). NLRB v. Walt Disney Prods., 146 F 2d 44, 48, 15 LRRM 691, (CA 9, 1944), *cert. denied,* 324 US 877, 16 LRRM 918 (1945); Kelly-Springfield Tire Co., 6 NLRB 32, 347-48, 2 LRRM 153 (1938), *enforced,* 97 F 2d 1007, 2 LRRM 679 (CA 4, 1938); Ingram Mfg. Co., 5 NLRB 908, 2 LRRM 79 (1938).
22 Carey v. Westinghouse Elec. Corp., 375 US 261, 272, 55 LRRM 2042 (1964); NLRB v. Hershey Chocolate Corp., 297 F 2d 286, 293, 49 LRRM 2173 (CA 3, 1961); NLRB v. Bell Aircraft Corp., 206 F 2d 235, 237, 32 LRRM 2550 (CA 2, 1953); Zoe Chem. Co., 160 NLRB 1001, 1034, 63 LRRM 1052 (1966) (trial examiner's decision).
23 *See:* Humphrey v. Moore, 375 US 335, 343-44, 55 LRRM 2031 (1964); Carey v. Westinghouse, 375 US 261, 272, 55 LRRM 2042 (1964); Smith v. Evening News Ass'n, 371 US 195, 197-98, 51 LRRM 2646 (1962). *See also* Chapter 17 *supra.*

Board disagree with the arbiter . . . the Board's ruling would, of course, take precedence . . . ." [24]

However, in cases dealing with arbitration,[25] the Supreme Court has exalted the role of arbitration and has limited the authority of the courts. Thus, the question has been asked: has Board jurisdiction likewise been preempted or limited by arbitration? This question must be distinguished from the broader issue of the Board's power to interpret a contract enforceable under Section 301.[26] The issue now is whether the Board may interpret a contract which includes an applicable arbitration clause.

The cases which introduced the problem also dealt with the right to information. In *Sinclair Refining Co. v. NLRB*,[27] the Fifth Circuit refused to require the production of data relevant to a demotion grievance. The employer argued that the demotion was caused by lack of work and that the contract committed to the employer's sole discretion the right to determine lack of work and thus barred the filing of a grievance. The court stated that there must first be arbitration to determine the merits of this contention. Relying on the *Steelworkers* Trilogy, it said that the Board had improperly adjudicated the underlying grievance under the guise of determining the relevance of the data sought.

The Board had, in fact, interpreted the contract and had decided the extent of the management prerogative.[28] It had concluded that the union had not waived its right to dispute the claim of lack of work.[29]

In *Timken Roller Bearing Co. v. NLRB*,[30] the company maintained that the union had waived its right to certain wage data and that the waiver question was itself arbitrable under the contract. The Sixth Circuit, however, relied on the statutory right

---

[24] Carey v. Westinghouse Elec. Corp., 375 US 261, 272, 55 LRRM 2042, 2047 (1964).
[25] *See* John Wiley & Sons, Inc. v. Livingston, 376 US 543, 55 LRRM 2769 (1964). *See* United Steelworkers v. American Mfg., 363 US 564, 46 LRRM 2414 (1960); United Steelworkers v. Warrior & Gulf Navigation Co., 363 US 574, 46 LRRM 2416 (1960); United Steelworkers v. Enterprise Wheel & Car Corp., 363 US 593, 46 LRRM 2423 (1960).
[26] This is discussed in Chapter 17 *supra*.
[27] 306 F 2d 569, 50 LRRM 2830 (CA 5, 1962).
[28] 132 NLRB 1660, 48 LRRM 1544 (1961).
[29] *Id.* at 1662.
[30] 325 F 2d 746, 54 LRRM 2785 (CA 6, 1963), *enforcing* 138 NLRB 15, 50 LRRM 1508 (1962), *cert. denied*, 376 US 971, 55 LRRM 2878 (1964).

of the union to information, since a clear and explicit waiver [31] was lacking. Yet, the court spoke favorably of the decision in *Sinclair.* It said:

> The Court held that the Board proceeding could not be used to secure data for use in a grievance procedure where determination of relevance and pertinency required determination of the critical substantive issue of the grievance itself, which issue was . . . for the arbitrator. This is but another example of the now established law that where a dispute or "difference" is subject to grievance procedure and arbitration . . . that procedure *is exclusive and will be enforced.*[32]

Hence, the significant point in the *Timken* case is that the court found the employer's contention to be not arbitrable.

Square D Co. v. *NLRB* [33] also was a case involving a union claim for data, an employer contention that the union had waived any right to the data, and an argument that the meaning of the contract in regard to the waiver should go to arbitration. Here the NLRB defined the issue as one of statutory obligation to give data rather than of arbitrability.[34] But the Second Circuit, distinguishing *Timken,* refused to follow the Board. Rather, it said:

> The answer to the dispute lies not in the provisions of the Act, for the Act does not purport to control the issue of what matters shall be subject to a contract grievance procedure. The answer lies solely in a construction of the contract—an area in which the parties themselves have agreed that the dispute shall be arbitrated.
>
> Thus we are not faced with a situation in which the issue of a violation of the Act is related to the collective bargaining agreement only in that there may be a similar violation of the latter. Rather, the existence of an unfair labor practice here is *dependent* upon the resolution of a preliminary dispute involving only the interpretation of the contract.[35]

Sinclair and *Square D* both cited the Board case of *Hercules Motor Corp.*[36] There the union demanded information to support a grievance over a matter which the employer claimed was not grievable under the contract. The Board, noting that the agreed-

---

31 *Id.* at 751.
32 *Id.* at 754 (emphasis added).
33 142 NLRB 332, 53 LRRM 1023 (1963), *enforcement denied,* 332 F 2d 360, 56 LRRM 2147 (CA 9, 1964).
34 142 NLRB at 338 (trial examiner's report).
35 332 F 2d at 365-66.
36 136 NLRB 1648, 50 LRRM 1021 (1962).

upon procedure could settle the dispute, refused to require the production of the information. To do otherwise, it said, "would be frustrating the Act's policy of promoting industrial stabilization through collective bargaining agreements." [37] However, it should be noted that the Board decision in *Hercules* was predicated upon its discretionary power and that the NLRB asserted jurisdiction.[38] In addition, the Board has limited its position in *Hercules*.[39]

The miasma surrounding the preceding cases was dispelled by the Supreme Court in *NLRB* v. *Acme Industrial Co.*[40] This case also involved the refusal of an employer to supply requested information on the ground that the information was not relevant under a disputed interpretation of a contract subject to arbitration. The employer contended that, since the contract had not been violated, there was no basis for a grievance and, therefore, no obligation to furnish the information. The court concluded, however, that the employer did have a statutory obligation to furnish the information in question. Thus, *Acme* is a significant step in a process that requires the parties to aid bargaining procedures by furnishing relevant information.[41] The Board was said by the Court not to have made

> a binding construction of the labor contract. It was only acting upon the probability that the desired information was relevant, and that it would be of use to the union in carrying out its statutory duties and responsibilities. This discovery-type standard decided nothing about the merits of the union's contractual claims.[42]

The Court added that the Board's action was in aid of the arbitral process and thus avoided making the union play blind man's buff in making an appraisal of its right to grieve.[43] *Acme* seems to give a new slant to earlier cases on the right to information. First, the right to information may depend on the statute; if so, the right of the Board to interpret the contract is irrelevant and unnecessary. And, second, the statutory right will be enforced regardless of any characterization of the issues as "arbitrable," as in *Sinclair*

---

[37] 136 NLRB at 1652. The Board referred to §201 (a), 29 USC §171 (a) (1964); §203 (d), 29 USC §173 (d) (1964); and to the *Steelworkers* Trilogy.
[38] 136 NLRB at 1652.
[39] *See:* Timken Roller Bearing Co., 138 NLRB 15, 16 n. 4; Metropolitan Life Ins. Co., 150 NLRB 1478, 1479 n. 1, 58 LRRM 1298 (1965).
[40] 385 US 432, 64 LRRM 2069 (1967).
[41] For a discussion of the basic duty to furnish information, *see* Chapter 11 *supra*.
[42] 385 US at 437.
[43] *Id.* US at 438 n. 8, *citing* Fafnir Bearing Co. v. NLRB, 362 F 2d 716, 721, 62 LRRM 2415 (CA 2, 1966).

and *Square D.*[44] In discussing the reasoning of the court below,[45] the Court noted that the Trilogy "dealt with the relationship of courts to arbitrators" and that "[t]he relationship of the Board to the arbitration process is of quite a different order."[46] The Court concluded that "to view the *Steelworkers* decisions as automatically requiring the Board in this case to defer to the primary determination of an arbitrator is to overlook important distinctions between those cases and this one."[47]

But the Supreme Court, while clarifying these right-to-information cases, did not decide in *Acme* whether the Board may, in determining an unfair labor practice, also determine the merits of a contractual claim where one of the parties claims the matter is arbitrable.[48] Still, the care with which the Court pointed out that the Board's relation to the arbitrator is not the same as that of the courts, the recognition of the primacy of a Board decision over an arbitral ruling,[49] and the history of decisions spelling out the relation of Board and courts under Section 301,[50] are factors which indicate that there is no general requirement that in every case the Board must defer to the arbitral process.[51] Indeed, the Su-

---

44 *See* 385 US at 437-38.

45 The court of appeals had said that "[t]he declared statutory policy, and the judicial admonitions addressed to the courts, are equally applicable to the Board." 351 F 2d 258, 261, 60 LRRM 2220 (CA 7, 1965). Likewise, the Fifth Circuit had asserted: "What the Supreme Court says of the relative incapacity of Judges applies with equal force to those comprising the National Labor Relations Board." Sinclair Ref. Co. v. NLRB, 306 F 2d 569, 576, 50 LRRM 2830 (CA 5, 1962).

46 385 US at 436. The courts, it will be recalled, are concerned with enforcing private rights and duties through the arbitration process. The Board, on the other hand, is concerned with protecting "the rights of the public." §1 (b).

47 385 US at 437 (citing *Sinclair*).

48 In *C & C Plywood*, where the contract *was* interpreted by the Board, the Court seems to leave this question open, pointing out that, unlike *Square D*, no arbitration clause was involved. 385 US at 426 n. 9.

49 Carey v. Westinghouse Elec. Corp., 375 US 261, 272, 55 LRRM 2042 (1964).

50 See Chapter 17 *supra*. It should be remembered that arbitration cases are only special problems under a contract.

51 The courts have generally held that the existence of an arbitration remedy under a contract cannot oust the NLRB from jurisdiction. *See, e.g.,* General Truckdrivers, Local 5 v. NLRB, 389 F 2d 757, 67 LRRM 2410 (CA 5, 1968), *enforcing* 161 NLRB 493, 63 LRRM 1338 (1966); NLRB v. Thor Power Tool Co., 351 F 2d 584, 60 LRRM 2237 (CA 7, 1965), *enforcing* 148 NLRB 1379, 57 LRRM 1161 (1964). Nor does the issuance of an arbitration award preclude the Board from later asserting jurisdiction. *See, e.g.,* NLRB v. Wagner Iron Works, 220 F 2d 126, 35 LRRM 2588 (CA 7, 1955), *cert. denied*, 350 US 981, 37 LRRM 2639 (1956); NLRB v. UAW, Local 291, 194 F 2d 698, 29 LRRM 2433 (CA 7, 1952). Later in this chapter attention will be given to the special case where the employer claims a unilateral right under the contract, subject to arbitration, and the Board finds a violation of §8(a)(5). The jurisdiction of the Board was strongly affirmed in *Office & Professional Employees, Local 425* v. *NLRB*, 419 F 2d 314, 70 LRRM 3047 (CA DC, 1969).

preme Court in *NLRB* v. *Strong* [52] required an employer to pay certain fringe benefits, though it was argued that this "inserts the Board into the enforcement of the collective bargaining agreement, contrary to the policy and scheme of the statute." [53] The Board found that a contract negotiated between an employer association and the union was effective at a date prior to the attempt by the company to withdraw from the association. The company refused to sign the contract. As a remedy for the consequent refusal to bargain, the Board ordered the company to sign the contract and to pay the fringe benefits provided for in the contract. The Court made the following observations: 1) Collective bargaining contracts are normally enforced as agreed upon by the parties, ordinarily by grievance and arbitration procedures; arbitrators and courts are the principal sources of contract interpretation. 2) The jurisdiction of the Board is not displaced, and, where necessary to adjudicate an unfair labor practice, the Board may interpret a contract, give effect to its terms, and proscribe conduct which is an unfair labor practice even though it is also a breach of contract remediable through arbitration. Mr. Justice Douglas, dissenting, would have required arbitration, and Mr. Justice Black, though concurring, would have remanded the case to the Board for a determination as to whether arbitration should be required. However, it should be noted that the Court treated the order to pay the benefits as a remedy, ancillary to the refusal to sign, rather than as an interpretation of a contract subject to arbitration.

Thus, the law as applied by the Board and the courts acknowledges the right of the Board, in the exercise of its jurisdiction over unfair labor practices, to interpret a contract issue which is also subject to arbitration.

III. BOARD PRACTICE

A. Discretionary Jurisdiction

The Board need not decide every case over which it may assert statutory jurisdiction. The Supreme Court rather obliquely favored a discretionary power in the Board when it said that the "Board sometimes properly declines to . . . [take jurisdiction of a complaint], stating that the policies of the Act would not be

---

[52] 393 US 357, 70 LRRM 2100 (1969).
[53] *Id.* at 360.

effectuated." [54] The issue of Board discretion was more clearly presented in a later case, and the self-limitation of the Board was sustained in *Haleston Drug Stores v. NLRB*.[55]

The Board's claim of the right to defer to an arbitration award may be found in *International Harvester Co.:* [56]

> [I]t is . . . well established that the Board has considerable discretion to respect an arbitration award and decline to exercise its authority over alleged unfair labor practice if to do so will serve the fundamental aims of the Act.[57]

The following sections will outline Board practices in the exercise of this discretion.

B. Accommodation to Final Award—*Spielberg* Doctrine

Where an award has already been rendered, the Board will now honor the award if it meets certain standards. But in the early days of the Act, the Board was reluctant to accommodate itself to the decision of any other tribunal. Even where an arbitrator had ordered discriminatorily discharged employees to be reinstated, the Board, relying on Section 10(a) of the Act, refused to recognize the award. It independently examined the charged conduct to ascertain whether there had been any violation of the Act.[58]

Occasionally a trial examiner would honor an arbitration award because he felt it would effectuate the policies of the Act,[59] but

---

54 NLRB v. Denver Bldg. Trades Council, 341 US 675, 684, 28 LRRM 2108 (1938).
55 187 F 2d 418, 421, 27 LRRM 2401 (CA 9), *cert. denied*, 342 US 815, 28 LRRM 2625 (1951). For a discussion of the administrative standards utilized by the Board, see Chapter 28 *infra*.
56 138 NLRB 923, 51 LRRM 1155 (1962).
57 *Id.* at 925-26. *Accord*, Raley's Inc., 143 NLRB 256, 258-59, 53 LRRM 1347 (1963); Flintkote Co., 149 NLRB 1561, 57 LRRM 1477 (1964). *But see* Oscherwitz & Sons, 130 NLRB 1078, 1082, 47 LRRM 1415 (1961) (dissenting opinion).
58 Rieke Metal Prods. Corp., 40 NLRB 867, 10 LRRM 82 (1942).
59 Paramount Pictures, Inc., 79 NLRB 557, 576, 22 LRRM 1428 (1948). The trial examiner relied upon *Timken Roller Bearing Co.*, 70 NLRB 500, 501, 18 LRRM 1370 (1946), *enforcement denied*, 161 F 2d 949, 20 LRRM 2204 (CA 6, 1947), in which the Board had dismissed a refusal-to-bargain complaint initiated by a union that had simultaneously invoked the Board's processes and the grievance machinery in its contract, and lost the arbitral decision. The Board said in *Timken*:
"It is evident that the Union has concurrently utilized two forums for the purpose of litigating the matter here in dispute. . . . [I]t would not comport with the sound exercise of our administrative discretion to permit the Union to seek redress under the Act after having initiated arbitration proceedings which, at the Union's request, resulted in a determination upon the merits."
The Board's theory in *Timken* appeared to have been that the union had made an election of remedies, rather than that the arbitrator's opinion was entitled to any weight.

it was not until 1955 in *Spielberg Mfg. Co.*[60] that the Board set forth criteria for deferral to arbitration awards. These standards require that: (1) the proceedings be fair and regular; (2) all parties agree to be bound; and (3) the decision not be repugnant to the purpose and policies of the Act.[61]

The rationale of *Spielberg* was enunciated in *International Harvester Co.*,[62] where the Board said:

> The Act . . . is primarily designed to promote industrial peace and stability by encouraging the practice and procedure of collective bargaining. Experience has demonstrated that collective-bargaining agreements that provide for final and binding arbitration of grievances and disputes arising thereunder, "as a substitute for industrial strife," contribute significantly to the attainment of this statutory objective. . . .
>
> If complete effectuation of the Federal policy is to be achieved, . . . the Board . . . should give hospitable acceptance to the arbitral process as 'part and parcel of the collective bargaining process itself,' and voluntarily withhold its undoubted authority to adjudicate alleged unfair labor practice charges involving the same subject matter, unless it clearly appears that the arbitration proceedings were tainted by fraud, collusion, unfairness or serious procedural irregularities or that the award was clearly repugnant to the purposes and policies of the Act.[63]

In this case the Board relied in part upon Section 203(d) of the LMRA, which provides that "[f]inal adjustment by a method agreed upon by the parties is hereby declared to be the desirable method for settlement of grievance disputes arising over the application or interpretation of an existing collective bargaining agreement."

Since its *Spielberg* decision the Board has added what, for the purposes of analysis, might be considered a fourth criterion. This requirement is that the issue involved in the unfair labor practice case before the Board must have been presented to and considered by the arbitrator.[64]

The following is a discussion of each of the criteria outlined above.

---

[60] 112 NLRB 1080, 36 LRRM 1152 (1955).
[61] *Id.* at 1082.
[62] 138 NLRB 923, 51 LRRM 1155 (1962), *enforced sub nom.* Ramsey v. NLRB, 327 F 2d 784, 55 LRRM 2441 (CA 7, 1964), *cert. denied,* 377 US 1003, 56 LRRM 2544 (1964).
[63] *Id.* at 926-27.
[64] Raytheon Co., 140 NLRB 883, 52 LRRM 1129 (1963), *set aside,* 326 F 2d 471, 55 LRRM 2101 (CA 1, 1964).

1. Fair and Regular Proceedings. The Board's criteria for fairness and regularity are the equivalent of due process. Thus, where evidence is deliberately withheld from the arbitrator,[65] where the grievant is given insufficient time to prepare [66] or is not afforded an opportunity to confront witnesses,[67] or where the arbitrators are, or are likely to have been, predisposed against the grievant,[68] arbitration awards will not be given any weight.

The latter situation has occasionally occurred under those contracts in which the grievance machinery provides for final adjustment by a joint labor-management committee, and one or more of the participants of the committee would have reason to rule against the grievant regardless of the merits of the dispute. In *Roadway Express, Inc.,*[69] for example, the grievant was the leader of the opposition to the incumbent union officials and also was known for his attacks upon the industry in which he was employed. The Board refused to honor an award that had been adverse to him. Likewise, it refused to honor such an award in *Youngstown Cartage Co.,*[70] where the grievant had been a dissident within the union. Here the Board felt that "the entire arbitration panel may have been arrayed in common interest against [the employee]. . . ." [71] On the other hand, where less than an equal vote on such a panel was given to the person who would be predisposed against the grievant, a trial examiner in *Tanner Motor Livery, Ltd.,*[72] indicated the award might be honored. The Board has pointed out that, in accordance with the Act's policy of permitting parties to resolve their disputes in the manner which they

---

[65] Precision Fittings, Inc., 141 NLRB 1034, 52 LRRM 1443 (1963).

[66] Gateway Transp. Co., 137 NLRB 1763, 50 LRRM 1495 (1962) (grievant pressed to arbitration two days after notice). *But see* Raytheon Co. v. NLRB, 326 F 2d 471, 55 LRRM 2101 (CA 1, 1964), *setting aside* 140 NLRB 883, 52 LRRM 1129 (1963), in which the Board refused to honor an award because, among other reasons, the grievant was not granted a requested continuance. The court said: "We cannot think the Board would have expected us to rule it unfair if a trial examiner, rather than an arbitrator, had refused to grant a further continuance on this record." 326 F 2d at 473, 55 LRRM at 2102.

[67] Honolulu Star-Bulletin, 123 NLRB 395, 417, 43 LRRM 1449 (trial examiner's decision), *enforcement denied on other grounds,* 274 F 2d 567, 45 LRRM 2184 (CA DC, 1959).

[68] Youngstown Cartage Co., 146 NLRB 305, 55 LRRM 1301 (1964); Roadway Express, Inc., 145 NLRB 513, 54 LRRM 1419 (1963).

[69] 145 NLRB 513, 54 LRRM 1419 (1963).

[70] 146 NLRB 305, 55 LRRM 1301 (1964).

[71] *Id.* at 308 n. 4, 55 LRRM at 1305.

[72] 148 NLRB 1402, 1413 n. 6, 57 LRRM 1170 (1964), *remanded,* 349 F 2d 1, 59 LRRM 2784 (CA 9, 1965).

find best, it will consider the decisions of such joint committees to be similar to those of other arbitral tribunals [73] regardless of whether a public member participates.[74]

2. Agreement to be Bound. Another requirement of *Spielberg* is that all parties must have agreed to be bound by the award. Both in *Wertheimer Stores Corp.*[75] (pre-*Spielberg*) and *Hershey Chocolate Corp.*,[76] a base for disregarding the arbitrator's award was that the individual employees had not agreed to be bound.

In *Wertheimer Stores Corp.*, an employee was discharged for his activities in urging other employees to vote against an employer's proposal to reschedule working hours. The arbitrator found that the discharge was not discriminatory. The Board's refusal to honor the award was in part based on the fact that the arbitration proceedings were initiated and carried through over the opposition of the employee. The Board stated that "the circumstances connected with [the employee's] involvement in the arbitration proceedings are not such as would warrant the Board in the exercise of its discretion to decline to assert its jurisdiction." [77]

In *Hershey Chocolate Corp.* the arbitration award was not given effect. The Board held that the award was "contrary to law," and none of the employees involved had agreed to be bound by the award.[78]

---

[73] "[F]ailure to adopt the decision of the Joint Committee would imply an obligation to fix standards of formality in procedure on the part of the grievance and arbitration panels which must be met before their awards could receive endorsement. . . . Where . . . the parties have found that the machinery which they have created for the amicable resolution of their disputes has adequately served its purpose, we shall accept such a resolution absent evidence of irregularity, collusion, or inadequate provisions for the taking of testimony." Denver-Chicago Trucking Co., 132 NLRB 1416, 1421, 48 LRRM 1524, 1526 (1961). *Accord,* Terminal Transport Co., 185 NLRB No. 96, 75 LRRM 1130 (1970).

See also Modern Motor Express, Inc., 149 NLRB 1507, 58 LRRM 1005 (1964); Gen. Counsel Ruling No. SR-2614, 52 LRRM 1405 (1963). *But see* Comment, *Concurrent Jurisdiction of Arbitrators and the NLRB,* 38 U. COLO. L. REV. 363, 376 (1966). The Supreme Court has ruled that a final decision of such a committee may be enforced under §301(a). General Drivers Union v. Riss & Co., 372 US 517, 52 LRRM 2623 (1963).

[74] Denver-Chicago Trucking Co., 132 NLRB 1416, 1421 n. 6, 48 LRRM 1524 (1961).

[75] 107 NLRB 1434, 33 LRRM 1398 (1954).

[76] 129 NLRB 1052, 47 LRRM 1130 (1960), *enforcement denied on other grounds,* 297 F 2d 286, 49 LRRM 2173 (CA 3, 1961).

[77] 107 NLRB at 1435.

[78] 129 NLRB at 1053.

It is interesting to note, however, that in *International Harvester Co.*[79] the arbitration award was honored despite the fact that the employee was given no notice and was not present at the arbitration hearing. The Board stressed that the employer adequately championed the employee's interest. In the light of this rationale, it can be argued that the criterion of "agreement to be bound" is merely part of the composition of a fair and regular hearing, and should not be considered a separate and independent standard.[80]

3. Award Not Repugnant to the Purposes and Policies of the Act. In all cases where the Board has found the arbitration proceedings not to be fair and regular, it can be concluded, ipso facto, that the ultimate award is repugnant to the Act. In addition, however, the Board has held that even though the arbitration hearing conformed to the procedural requisites of *Spielberg*, it may nevertheless refuse to honor an award that is contrary to the Act as interpreted by the Board.

In the *Hershey* case [81] the Board's refusal to honor the award was based primarily on a finding that it was repugnant to the Act. There the arbitrator required former members of a superseded union to maintain membership in the new union. Since the separate identity of the two unions had been established by a prior Board schism determination, a contract requiring members of one union to maintain membership in a second union was deemed contrary to law.

The Board refused to honor the award in *Virginia-Carolina Freight Lines, Inc.*[82] There the arbitrator had upheld the discharge of an employee who was found to be disloyal to the company. The finding of disloyalty was based upon the employee's

---

[79] 138 NLRB 923, 51 LRRM 1155 (1962), *enforced sub nom.*, Ramsey v. NLRB, 327 F 2d 784, 55 LRRM 2441 (CA 7), *cert. denied,* 377 US 1003, 56 LRRM 2544 (1964).
[80] *See* Edward Axel Roffman Associates, Inc., 147 NLRB 717, 724, 56 LRRM 1268 (1964) (employer withdrew from arbitration following arbitrator's ruling that matter was arbitrable; the trial examiner ruled: "Despite Respondent's voluntary withdrawal . . . the arbitration proceedings . . . appear to have been fair and regular.").
[81] 129 NLRB 1052, 47 LRRM 1130 (1960), *enforcement denied on other grounds,* 297 F 2d 286, 49 LRRM 2173 (CA 3, 1961). For treatment of the schism involved in the *Hershey* case, *see* Chapters 8 and 12 *supra. See also* Monsanto Chem. Co., 97 NLRB 517, 29 LRRM 1126 (1951), *enforced,* 205 F 2d 763, 32 LRRM 2435 (CA 8, 1953).
[82] 155 NLRB 447, 60 LRRM 1331 (1965).

action in seeking Board assistance in a dispute between himself and his employer.

4. Unfair Labor Practice Issue Considered by the Arbitrator. The Board has held that it will not consider deferring to an award unless the unfair labor practice issue before the Board was both presented to and considered by the arbitrator.[83] This position is exemplified by the Board's holdings in *Ford Motor Co.*[84] and *Monsanto Chemical Co.*[85] In the *Ford* case the Board refused to give weight to an award where the unfair labor practice issue never had been presented to the umpire. The Board found that the umpire had ruled solely on the factual question of whether the employees had participated in or instigated a work stoppage in violation of the existing contract. "He did not have before him, nor did he pass upon the question, now presented to the Board, whether [the employer] had the legal right to suspend [the employees]. . . ." [86]

In *Monsanto Chemical Co.* the Board refused to recognize an award upholding the discharge of an employee. The Board found that although the issue of whether the employee was illegally discharged for union activity had been presented to the arbitrator, this issue was never passed upon. In refusing deference, the Board stated that "[i]t manifestly could not encourage the voluntary settlement of disputes or effectuate the policies and purposes of the Act to give binding effect in an unfair labor practice proceeding to an arbitration award which does not purport to resolve the

---

[83] Hawkins v. NLRB, 358 F 2d 281, 61 LRRM 2622 (CA 7, 1966), *denial of petition to set aside,* Mitchell Transp. Inc., 152 NLRB 122, 59 LRRM 1028 (1965); Dubo Mfg. Corp., 148 NLRB 1114, 57 LRRM 1111 (1964), *enforced,* 353 F 2d 157, 60 LRRM 2373 (CA 6, 1965); Precision Fittings, Inc., 141 NLRB 1034, 52 LRRM 1443 (1963) (trial examiner's report); Raytheon Co., 140 NLRB 883, 52 LRRM 1129 (1963), *set aside,* 326 F 2d 471, 55 LRRM 2101 (CA 1, 1964); Local 340, IBEW (Walsh Constr. Co.), 131 NLRB 260, 48 LRRM 1022 (1961); Ford Motor Co., 131 NLRB 1462, 48 LRRM 1280 (1961); Hamilton-Scheu & Walsh Shoe Co., 80 NLRB 1496, 23 LRRM 1263 (1948). These cases, in which a discriminatory reason for a discharge had been masked behind a lawful reason, are frequently referred to as the "pretext" cases. *See* McCulloch, *The Arbitration Issue in NLRB Decisions,* 19 ARB. J. (n.s.) 134, 137-38 (1964); McCulloch, *Arbitration and/or the NLRB,* 18 ARB. J. (n.s.) 3, 9 (1963); Comment, 38 U. COLO. L. REV. 363, 372-73 (1966).

[84] 131 NLRB 1462, 48 LRRM 1280 (1961).

[85] 130 NLRB 1097, 47 LRRM 1451 (1961). *Accord,* La Prensa, Inc., 131 NLRB 527, 48 NLRB 1076 (1961).

[86] 131 NLRB at 1463.

unfair labor practice issue which was before the arbitrator and which is the very issue the Board is called upon to decide . . . ." [87]

The criteria for deferral outlined above are applicable only where a final award has been rendered. In *Electric Motors & Specialties, Inc.*,[88] grievances were processed through the preliminary steps of the grievance procedure, but arbitration was not requested by the grievants. The employer argued that, since its contract stated that where arbitration was not requested a grievance would be deemed abandoned, the Board's *Spielberg* rule should be as applicable as though the matter had been finally adjudicated. This argument was rejected by the Board.[89]

C. Effect of Failure to Utilize Contractual Grievance Procedure

In other areas of labor law, parties are required to utilize, and sometimes exhaust fully, the internal machinery which they have devised or to which they are bound before being permitted to appeal for outside aid.[90] The Board, however, in the exercise of its jurisdiction finds that the existence of an unused grievance procedure is not a bar to the processing of a charge. First in *Merrimack Mfg. Co.*[91] and then in succeeding cases,[92] the Board has consistently settled the dispute when it involves charges of discrimination. Its position has not been so consistent in cases

---

[87] 130 NLRB at 1099.

[88] 149 NLRB 131, 57 LRRM 1258 (1964).

[89] *Id.* at 137 (trial examiner's decision); *accord:* Pontiac Motors Div., 132 NLRB 413, 48 LRRM 1368 (1961); Dant & Russell, Ltd., 92 NLRB 307, 311-12, 27 LRRM 1088 (1950) (trial examiner's decision), *set aside on other grounds,* 195 F 2d 299, 29 LRRM 2585 (CA 9, 1952), *reversed,* 344 US 375, 31 LRRM 2303 (1953), *enforced,* 207 F 2d 165, 32 LRRM 2740 (CA 9, 1953); *cf.* General Drivers Union v. Riss & Co., 372 US 517, 52 LRRM 2623 (1963).

[90] *See, e.g.,* Republic Steel Corp. v. Maddox, 379 US 650, 58 LRRM 2193 (1965); Drake Bakeries, Inc. v. Local 50, American Bakery Workers, 370 US 254, 50 LRRM 2440 (1962).

[91] 31 NLRB 900, 8 LRRM 170 (1941).

[92] *See, e.g.,* Flasco Mfg. Co., 162 NLRB 611, 64 LRRM 1077 (1967); Woodlawn Farm Dairy Co., 162 NLRB 48, 63 LRRM 1495 (1966); Local 701, Operating Eng'rs (Peter Kiewit Sons' Co.) 152 NLRB 49, 54, 59 LRRM 1009 (1965); Local 409, Plumbers & Pipefitters, 149 NLRB 39, 45, 57 LRRM 1257 (1964); Electric Motors & Specialties, Inc., 149 NLRB 131, 137, 57 LRRM 1258 (1964); Aerodex, Inc., 149 NLRB 192, 199, 57 LRRM 1261 (1964); National Screen Prods. Co., 147 NLRB 746, 747 n. 1, 56 LRRM 1274 (1964); Lummus Co., 142 NLRB 517, 53 LRRM 1072 (1963); Todd Shipyards Corp., 98 NLRB 814, 29 LRRM 1422 (1952); General Elec. X-Ray Corp., 76 NLRB 64, 21 LRRM 1150 (1948); Marlboro Cotton Mills, 53 NLRB 965, 13 LRRM 142 (1943); Walt Disney Prods., 48 NLRB 892, 12 LRRM 146 (1943), *enforced as modified,* 146 F 2d 44, 15 LRRM 691 (CA 9, 1944), *cert. denied,* 324 US 877, 16 LRRM 918 (1945).

involving a refusal to bargain.[93] Board Member Brown, however, would have deferred almost any decision until a grievance had been processed.[94]

D. Effect of Utilizing Grievance Machinery and the Board's Processes Simultaneously

The Board has tried both the approach of going forward, despite the invocation of grievance machinery by a party,[95] and the approach of deferring to that machinery until an award issues, as it did in *Dubo Mfg. Corp.*[96] In the *Dubo* litigation, the union that had filed a charge alleging an 8(a)(3) violation also secured a court order directing the employer to arbitrate the matter. Under these circumstances the Board deferred to the pending arbitration.[97]

In *Kentile v. Local 457, United Rubber Workers,*[98] the court stayed an arbitration pending the Board's decision.[99] The Board rejected the union's request that it await the arbitration and proceeded to rule, notwithstanding the fact that the union had invoked the contract's grievance machinery. The General Counsel has suggested that, as a matter of practice,

> the Regional Offices, when a charge is pending and the grievance-arbitration procedure is being actively pursued, will defer action on the charge pending the completion of the grievance-arbitration procedure and will encourage active resort to the grievance-arbitration procedure if it appears that there is a substantial likelihood that the utilization of the procedure will set the dispute at rest.[100]

---

93 Cases involving a charge of refusal to bargain and a deferral to arbitration will be discussed in this chapter *infra*.
94 *See, e.g.,* Aetna Bearing Co., 152 NLRB 845, 846 n. 1, 59 LRRM 1268 (1965); Flintkote Co., 149 NLRB 1561, 57 LRRM 1477 (1964); Thor Power Tool Co., 148 NLRB 1379, 1382, 57 LRRM 1161 (1964), *enforced,* 351 F 2d 584, 60 LRRM 2237 (CA 7, 1965); Cloverleaf Div. of Adams Dairy Co., 147 NLRB 1410, 56 LRRM 1321 (1964); Lummus Co., 142 NLRB 517, 527, 53 LRRM 1072 (1963); *enforced in part,* 339 F 2d 728, 56 LRRM 2425 (CA DC, 1964).
95 *See* Electric Motors & Specialties, Inc., 149 NLRB 131, 57 LRRM 1258 (1964). This case may be distinguishable on the ground that although a grievance was filed, arbitration was not invoked.
96 142 NLRB 431, 53 LRRM 1070 (1963) (trial examiner's decision had been issued).
97 *Id.* at 433. The resulting award was thereafter disregarded, however, since the arbitration panel did not consider the allegation of discrimination. Dubo Mfg. Corp., 148 NLRB 1114, 57 LRRM 1111 (1964), *enforced,* 353 F 2d 157, 60 LRRM 2373 (CA 6, 1965).
98 228 F Supp 541, 55 LRRM 3011 (ED NY, 1964).
99 Kentile, Inc., 147 NLRB 980, 56 LRRM 1328 (1964).
100 Arnold Ordman, *Arbitration and the NLRB—A Second Look,* THE ARBITRATOR, THE NLRB, AND THE COURTS 47, 56 (1967).

IV. APPLICATION OF CRITERIA

A. Invalid Contracts

The NLRB exercises its jurisdiction so as to determine the validity of contract clauses that are alleged to be invalid under the Act.[101] The existence of an arbitration clause or a grievance procedure in the contract does not affect the Board's power, and the Board is not compelled to defer to arbitration.[102]

B. Discrimination

An employee who feels that he has been the victim of discrimination in violation of Section 8(a)(3) of the Act may file a charge with the Board and seek redress. If his employment is covered by a collective bargaining agreement that also outlaws such discrimination and provides for redress through a grievance procedure, he may decide to seek relief by filing a grievance. In that event an arbitrator may be called upon to decide the same issues presented to the Board. The employee may file a charge and a grievance at the same time, or in sequence. The Board is likely to treat such discrimination cases in accord with the principles and distinctions set forth above.

An example of Board procedure may be found in *Thor Power Tool Co.*[103] In this case a grievance was filed alleging the alteration of a time card; while the grievance was being processed, strong language was used and the grievant was discharged. The Board found that the employee was engaged in protected conduct and that his discharge was not based solely on his use of epithets. The utilization of the grievance machinery by the union and the employee and the abandonment of the grievance was not a ground for deferring action.

---

[101] *See* Chapter 17 *supra.*
[102] *See, e.g.,* Woodlawn Farm Dairy Co., 162 NLRB 48, 63 LRRM 1495 (1966) ; Great Lakes Carbon Corp., 152 NLRB 988, 59 LRRM 1266 (1965), *enforced,* 360 F 2d 19, 62 LRRM 2088 (CA 4, 1966) .
[103] 148 NLRB 1379, 57 LRRM 1161 (1964) , *enforced,* 351 F 2d 584, 60 LRRM 2237 (CA 7, 1965). *Accord,* Flasco Mfg. Co., 162 NLRB 611, 64 LRRM 1077 (1967) . These cases should be distinguished from 8(a)(5) cases involving a discharge under a claim of contractual right. *See, e.g.* Adelson, Inc., 163 NLRB 365, 64 LRRM 1346 (1967) .

Although the Board applies the principles outlined in prior sections, in fact it does not often defer in discrimination cases even when an award has been made.[104]

C. Representation and Work-Assignment Disputes

Under Section 9(c) of the Act, the Board's function is to determine, for purposes of collective bargaining, what constitutes an appropriate unit and which labor organization, if any, is entitled to represent the employees in that unit.[105] A proceeding under Section 10(k), on the other hand, is one in which the Board is directed to determine disputes relating to work assignment. In such a proceeding the Board must decide which group of competing employees is entitled to the disputed work.[106]

Great impetus was given to the arbitration of such cases by the Supreme Court's decision in *Carey* v. *Westinghouse Electric Corp.*[107] Here a dispute was held to be arbitrable whether viewed as a representation or as a work-assignment dispute, notwithstanding the fact that the Board also had jurisdiction over the matter.[108] While the Board's approach to the problem of accommodation in these areas is similar to that set forth above, some special qualifications will be noted in the following sections.

1. Representation Cases. *a. Unit and representative status questions.* The leading case dealing with the Board's deference to arbitral awards in representation cases is *Raley's Inc.*[109] In *Raley's* the issue before the arbitrator was whether certain employees were covered by the contract between the parties to the

---

104 From 1964 to 1968, according to a survey in Note, *The NLRB and Deference to Arbitration,* 77 YALE L.J. 1191, 1208 (1968), the Board deferred only in *Schott's Bakery, Inc.,* 164 NLRB 332, 65 LRRM 1180 (1967), and *Howard Elec. Co.,* 166 NLRB No. 62, 65 LRRM 1577 (1967). Subsequently, the Board has deferred occasionally. *See, e.g.,* W. R. Grace & Co., 179 NLRB No. 81, 72 LRRM 1455 (1969); McLean Trucking Co., 175 NLRB No. 66, 71 LRRM 1051 (1969).

105 *See* Chapters 8 & 9 *supra.*

106 *See* Chapter 25 *infra.*

107 375 US 261, 55 LRRM 2042 (1964).

108 The Court pointed out that if the Board should disagree with the arbitrator, the Board's ruling would take precedence. 375 US at 272.

109 143 NLRB 256, 53 LRRM 1347 (1963); *accord,* Goodyear Tire & Rubber Co., 147 NLRB 1233, 56 LRRM 1401 (1964); Insulation & Specialties, Inc., 144 NLRB 1540, 54 LRRM 1306 (1963). For a view that the Board's jurisdiction in this field should be exclusive, see Cummings, *NLRB Jurisdiction and Labor Arbitration: "Uniformity" vs. "Industrial Peace,"* 12 LAB. L.J. 425, 433 (1961); Feinberg, *The Arbitrator's Responsibility Under the Taft-Hartley Act,* 18 ARB. J. (n.s.) 77, 86 (1963).

arbitration. The arbitrator held that they were. Subsequently, a rival union filed a petition with the Board seeking to represent the employees in question. At the Board hearing, the union that had prevailed in arbitration intervened, contending that its contract with the employer covered the employees sought to be represented by the petitioner, that the petition was not timely filed with respect to the contract, and that, therefore, the contract should act as a bar and the petition should be dismissed.

The Board, agreeing with the intervenor, dismissed the representation petition and held that:

> The same considerations which moved the Board to honor arbitration awards in unfair labor practice cases are equally persuasive to a similar acceptance of the arbitral process in a representation proceeding such as the instant one. Thus, where, as here, a question of contract interpretation is in issue . . . and an award has already been rendered which meets Board requirements applicable to arbitration awards, we think that it would further the underlying objectives of the Act to promote industrial peace and stability to give effect thereto.[110]

Consistent with its ruling in *International Harvester Co.*[111] (a discrimination case), the Board in *Raley's* disposed of the argument that the petitioner had not been represented before the arbitrator. The Board found that "[w]hile the petitioner was not a party to the arbitration . . . its position was vigorously defended by the Employer. . . ."[112]

The Board has placed limits upon the scope of *Raley's*.[113] In *Hotel Employers Ass'n of San Francisco*[114] the Board noted that

---

[110] 143 NLRB at 258-59.

[111] 138 NLRB 923, 928, 51 LRRM 1155 (1962), *enforced sub nom.*, Ramsey v. NLRB, 327 F 2d 784, 55 LRRM 2441 (CA 7), *cert. denied,* 377 US 1003, 56 LRRM 2544 (1964).

[112] 143 NLRB at 260 n. 17. *But see* Hotel Employers Ass'n, 159 NLRB 143, 148 n. 7, 62 LRRM 1215 (1966); Hamilton-Scheu & Walsh Shoe Co., 80 NLRB 1496, 23 LRRM 1263 (1948).

[113] Westinghouse Elec. Corp., 162 NLRB 768, 64 LRRM 1082 (1967); Hotel Employers Ass'n of San Francisco, 159 NLRB 143, 62 LRRM 1215 (1966); Pullman Indus., Inc., 159 NLRB 580, 62 LRRM 1273 (1966); West Va. Pulp & Paper Co., 140 NLRB 1160, 52 LRRM 1196 (1963); General Motors Corp., Case No. 7-RC-2793, 56 LRRM 1332 (1964). *Cf.* NLRB v. Weyerhaeuser Co., 276 F 2d 865, 45 LRRM 3088 (CA 7, 1960), where the court reviewed the NLRB policy concerning the status of the "no raiding" provision of the AFL-CIO constitution. In this case the Board refused to give any weight to the contention that a union had violated the provision by filing a representation petition and it was reluctant to give any weight to the findings of the impartial umpire.

[114] 159 NLRB 143, 62 LRRM 1215 (1966).

in *Raley's* the sole issue before the Board and the arbitrator was whether the contract included a specified group of employees. In *Hotel Employers,* however, the arbitrator was faced with, but did not consider, the claim of a rival union to represent the employees in question. He applied the contract of the inside union and held that it covered the disputed employees if and when the union attained majority status among the employees. The inside union's showing of a majority interest, however, postdated the filing of the outside union's petition with the Board. Since the award relied upon the contract rather than upon the Board's criteria for making unit determinations, the Board did not defer to the award.

As in unfair labor practice cases, so also in representation cases; the Board will normally proceed and not wait for the arbitrator if an award has not already been rendered.[115] An obvious exception to this policy was made by the Board after the decision of the Supreme Court in *Carey* v. *Westinghouse Electric Corp.*[116] The Court in that case required arbitration even though it was not clear whether the case involved a representation dispute or a work-assignment dispute. In addition, the Court's order bound only the employer and one of the two unions involved in the dispute. Nevertheless, since arbitration might resolve the dispute (if it were against the union in the arbitration proceeding), the Court required the parties to abide by the contractual agreement to arbitrate.

---

[115] *See* Libby, McNeill & Libby, 159 NLRB 677, 62 LRRM 1276 (1966) (suit to compel arbitration had been stayed pending Board decision); Humble Oil & Ref. Co., 153 NLRB 1361, 1363, 59 LRRM 1632 (1965) ("[union's] contractual right to arbitrate disputes . . . does not preclude the Board from determining a question concerning the appropriateness of unit"); Standard Register Co., 146 NLRB 1042, 1043, 56 LRRM 1003 (1964); Savage Arms Corp., 144 NLRB 1323, 1324, 54 LRRM 1253 (1963).

In *Humble,* the circuit court subsequently reversed the district court's order compelling arbitration of the same issues involved in the Board case, on the ground that the Board had effectively decided all of the issues. McGuire v. Humble Oil & Ref. Co., 355 F 2d 352, 61 LRRM 2410 (CA 2, 1966), *cert. denied,* 384 US 988, 62 LRRM 2339 (1966). *But see* A. Seltzer & Co. v. Livingston, 253 F Supp 509, 61 LRRM 2581 (SD NY, 1966) (arbitration with one union not stayed, despite company's contract for same unit with another union, and pending representation petition); *cf.* Local 51, IBEW v. Illinois Power Co., 357 F 2d 916, 61 LRRM 2613 (CA 7), *cert. denied,* 385 US 839, 63 LRRM 2235 (1966). Yet, an employer's claim that the NLRB has sole and exclusive jurisdiction over the subject matter of an arbitration proceeding is not grounds for a court to refuse to enforce an award. *See* Teamsters Local 745 v. Braswell Motor Freight Lines, 392 F 2d 1, 68 LRRM 2143 (CA 5), *rehearing denied,* 395 F 2d 655, 68 LRRM 2632 (CA 5, 1968).

[116] 375 US 261, 55 LRRM 2042 (1964).

The Board stayed its hand,[117] since an order would moot the arbitration case and thereby render the Court's order useless. When the case came to arbitration, the arbitrator made it clear that but for the Supreme Court order he would not have proceeded in the absence of the other union.[118] He found the case to be a representation case and made an award, splitting the disputed unit between the two unions.

Subsequently, the Board refused to defer to the arbitration award,[119] concluding that the ultimate issue of representation could not be decided by the arbitrator's interpreting the contract between the employer and one of the unions. Rather, the award must "clearly reflect the use of and be consonant with Board standards." [120] It is the opinion of the General Counsel that the pivotal issue in cases of this kind is less the participation of an interested party than it is the failure to apply established Board criteria.[121]

b. Eligibility questions. Prior to its decision in *Pacific Tile & Porcelain Co.,*[122] the Board's rule was that discharged employees who had not filed an unfair labor practice charge prior to a representation election were presumptively discharged for cause. They were thus ineligible to vote regardless of whether grievances had been filed on their behalf.[123]

This policy was overruled in *Pacific Tile.* The Board will now defer ruling on challenged ballots of discharged employees (if the ballots might affect the outcome of the election) pending a determination of their grievances by an arbitrator. On the other hand, an election will not necessarily be delayed simply because of such pending grievances since these are matters that may be decided by allowing the grievants to cast challenged ballots.[124]

---

117 After the issuance of the Supreme Court's decision, the employer filed two motions with the Board on February 11, 1964, for clarification of certification. On March 9, 1964, he filed a petition for election. Action on these matters was deferred by order of the Board dated April 21, 1964, pending the outcome of the arbitration proceeding. *See* Westinghouse Elec. Corp., 162 NLRB 768, 64 LRRM 1082 (1967).
118 79 AAA 9 (August 9, 1965).
119 Westinghouse Elec. Corp., 162 NLRB 768, 64 LRRM 1082 (1967).
120 *Id.* at 771.
121 Arnold Ordman, *Arbitration and the NLRB—A Second Look,* THE ARBITRATOR, THE NLRB AND THE COURTS 47, 55 (1967).
122 137 NLRB 1358, 1365-67, 50 LRRM 1394 (1962).
123 Dura Steel Prods. Co., 111 NLRB 590, 591-92, 35 LRRM 1522 (1955).
124 Pepsi-Cola Bottling Co., 154 NLRB 490, 59 LRRM 1786 (1965).

2. Work-Assignment Cases. Section 10(k) of the Act is the only section specifically authorizing the Board to stay its hand if the parties can demonstrate that they have agreed upon means of settling their dispute. In relevant part, this section provides:

> Whenever it is charged that any person has engaged in an unfair labor practice within the meaning of paragraph (4)(D) of section 8(b), the Board is empowered and directed to hear and determine the dispute out of which such unfair labor practice shall have arisen, unless . . . the parties to such dispute submit to the Board satisfactory evidence that they have . . . agreed upon methods for the voluntary adjustment of the dispute.

The Board has required under this section that all parties to the dispute agree to be bound [125] and that all are bound by the same agreement. Accordingly, in *News Syndicate Co.*,[126] where two unions were each bound by separate agreements with the same employer and each received a favorable arbitral award under its own agreement, obviously no particular weight was given by the Board to these awards.[127]

In *New Orleans Typographical Union No. 17* v. *NLRB*,[128] the Fifth Circuit held that an NLRB assignment of work to members of one union took precedence over a contrary arbitration award, even though the award had been enforced by a district court prior to the Board's determination. The court consolidated the employer's appeal from the district court's order confirming the arbitrator's award of disputed work to members of the Typographical Union rather than to members of the Lithographers Union (the Lithographers did not participate in the arbitration), and the Typographical Union's petition to set aside a Board order [129] which made a contrary assignment. Relying on *NLRB* v. *Radio Engineers Union (CBS)*,[130] in which the Supreme Court

---

125 *See, e.g.*, Plumbers & Pipefitters, Local 761 (Matt J. Zaich Constr. Co.), 144 NLRB 133, 54 LRRM 1020 (1963). For treatment of jurisdictional disputes generally, *see* Chapter 25 *infra*.
126 141 NLRB 578, 52 LRRM 1339 (1963). *See also* McLeod v. Newspaper Deliverers' Union, 209 F Supp 434, 51 LRRM 2292 (SD NY, 1962).
127 *Cf.* Transportation-Communication Employees Union v. Union Pacific R.R., 385 US 157, 63 LRRM 2481 (1966), in which it was held that under the Railway Labor Act the National Railroad Adjustment Board should not have determined a work-assignment dispute between two unions without taking the contracts of both unions into account.
128 368 F 2d 755, 63 LRRM 2467 (CA 5, 1966).
129 Typographical Union No. 17 (E. P. Rivas, Inc.), 152 NLRB 587, 59 LRRM 1133 (1965).
130 364 US 573, 47 LRRM 2332 (1961).

directed the Board, in resolving jurisdictional disputes, to "do something more than merely look at . . . a collective bargaining contract to determine whether one or another union has a clearly defined statutory or contractual right to have the employees it represents perform certain work tasks," [131] the Fifth Circuit examined the criteria used by the Board in determining the dispute, found substantial evidence in support of the Board's result, and enforced the Board's order while vacating the district court's judgment.

Although a National Joint Board for the Settlement of Jurisdictional Disputes in the Construction Industry existed prior to 1965, the NLRB did not accord significant weight to its decisions in awarding work to competing unions (unless both unions and the employer were bound). The reason given was that not all of the factors relevant to the NLRB's determinations were considered by the National Joint Board. In 1965, however, an agreement was executed reconstituting the Joint Board. The new agreement added "efficiency" and "economy of operation" to the criteria to be considered by the Joint Board. The NLRB indicated that it would be persuaded to a greater degree by such decisions.[132] In fact, in a case that was before the Board on numerous occasions, *Don Cartage Co.*,[133] the Board gave controlling weight to an award rendered by the new National Joint Board, notwithstanding the fact that the unions but not the employer were bound.[134]

D. Employer Refusal to Bargain

It is in the area of Section 8(a)(5) cases that there has been considerable conflict between the Board and the courts over the application of the criteria for deferral.

---

[131] *Id.* at 579.

[132] *See* Local 65, Plasterers & Cement Masons (Twin City Tile & Marble Co.), 152 NLRB 1609, 59 LRRM 1334 (1965). *See* note 113, *supra* for a reference to the AFL-CIO no-raiding agreement.

[133] 160 NLRB 1061, 63 LRRM 1085 (1966) (Member Jenkins dissenting). In its first decision, the Board based its award on a settlement agreement between one of the competing unions and a regional director, although the other union and the employer opposed the settlement, 154 NLRB 513, 59 LRRM 1772 (1965). Pursuant to a remand by the District of Columbia Court of Appeals, the Board took additional evidence but affirmed its earlier decision, 157 NLRB 10, 61 LRRM 1291 (1966), which was set aside and remanded *per curiam* for determination of the jurisdictional dispute *sub nom.* Quinn v. NLRB, 61 LRRM 2690 (CA DC, 1966).

[134] This decision followed the recommendations contained in the Report of the Special Committee on the Building & Construction Industry of the American Bar Association. 1965 Proceedings, ABA Sec. of Lab. Rel. Law 452, 459.

1. Contract Interpretation and Employer's Duty to Furnish Information. The principal discussion of this issue was presented earlier in this chapter in connection with the definition of the jurisdiction of the NLRB. The key to an understanding of the cases seems to be in *NLRB v. Acme Industrial Co.*[135] There it was stated that the Board did not make a binding construction of the contract and thus did not threaten the power of the arbitrator. The right to information is a statutory right that is enforced without regard to the contract right asserted.[136] Consequently, subsequent to Acme, the Board has consistently required the production of information even though the contracts provide for arbitration.[137]

2. Contract Interpretation and Unilateral Action. Several issues should here be distinguished: 1) Does the Board have jurisdiction to interpret a contract where a contract provision is urged as a defense? [138] 2) Does the existence of an arbitration clause

---

[135] 385 US 432, 64 LRRM 2069 (1967). *See* note 40 *supra*.
[136] Prior to *Acme,* the Board consistently enforced the right to information. *See* Lewers & Cooke, Ltd., 153 NLRB 1542, 59 LRRM 1696 (1965); Metropolitan Life Ins. Co., 150 NLRB 1478, 58 LRRM 1298 (1965); Puerto Rico Tel. Co., 149 NLRB 950, 57 LRRM 1397 (1964), *enforced,* 359 F 2d 983, 61 LRRM 2516 (CA 1, 1966); Fafnir Bearing Co., 146 NLRB 1582, 56 LRRM 1108 (1964), *enforced,* 362 F 2d 716, 62 LRRM 2415 (CA 2, 1966); Square D Co., 142 NLRB 332, 53 LRRM 1023 (1963), *set aside,* 332 F 2d 360, 56 LRRM 2147 (CA 9, 1964); Perkins Mach. Co., 141 NLRB 98, 52 LRRM 1276 (1963), *enforced,* 326 F 2d 488, 55 LRRM 2204 (CA 1, 1964); Timken Roller Bearing Co., 138 NLRB 15, 50 LRRM 1508 (1962), *enforced,* 325 F 2d 746, 54 LRRM 2785 (CA 6, 1963), *cert. denied,* 376 US 971, 55 LRRM 2878 (1964). Sinclair Ref. Co., 132 NLRB 1660, 48 LRRM 1544 (1961), *enforcement denied,* 306 F 2d 569, 50 LRRM 2830 (CA 5, 1962); J. I. Case Co., 118 NLRB 520, 40 LRRM 1208 (1957), *enforced as modified,* 253 F 2d 149, 41 LRRM 2679 (CA 7, 1958); Otis Elevator Co., 102 NLRB 770, 31 LRRM 1334 (1953), *enforced as modified,* 208 F 2d 176, 33 LRRM 2129 (CA 2, 1953); Hekman Furniture Co., 101 NLRB 631, 31 LRRM 1116 (1952), *enforced,* 207 F 2d 561, 32 LRRM 2759 (CA 6, 1953).
The only case that varied from the pattern was *Hercules Motor Corp.,* 136 NLRB 1648, 50 LRRM 1021 (1962). This case was discussed earlier in this chapter; *see* note 36 and accompanying text. It has been called a "sport." Harris, *The National Labor Relations Board and Arbitration—The Battle of Concurrent Jurisdictions,* 16 SYRACUSE L. REV. 545, 553-54 (1965). In addition, it has been limited by the Board to its particular facts. *See* NLRB Brief at 28 n. 19, NLRB v. Acme Indus. Co., 385 US 432 (1967).
[137] *See, e.g.,* Zenith Radio Corp., 177 NLRB No. 30, 71 LRRM 1555 (1969); General Elec. Co. (Hickory, N.C.), 173 NLRB No. 22, 69 LRRM 1254 (1968); Scandia Restaurants, Inc., 171 NLRB No. 51, 69 LRRM 1144 (1968); Johns-Manville Prods. Corp., 171 NLRB No. 65, 69 LRRM 1068 (1968); P. R. Mallory & Co., Inc., 171 NLRB No. 68, 68 LRRM 1097 (1968), *enforced,* 411 F 2d 948, 71 LRRM 2412 (CA 7, 1969); Univis, Inc., 169 NLRB No. 18, 67 LRRM 1090 (1968); Hoerner-Waldorf Paper Prods. Co., 163 NLRB 772, 64 LRRM 1469 (1967).
Where the Board does not require information, it is for reasons independent of the existence of an arbitration clause. *See* Chapter 11 *supra.*
[138] This issue is discussed in Chapter 17 *supra.*

automatically bar the NLRB from interpreting a contract in order to decide an alleged unfair labor practice when a grievance concerning the same matter can be filed?[139] 3) Under what circumstances will the Board defer to arbitration? 4) Does an employer violate his obligation to bargain when, upon taking unilateral action, he defends his action by an appeal to the contract and a demand for arbitration?

The following sections are primarily concerned with a specific situation: unilateral actions taken under a claim of contractual right.

   a. Deference. (1) *Cases favoring deference.* In its early decision in *Consolidated Aircraft Corp.*[140] and again in *Crown Zellerbach*,[141] the Board held that it would refrain from deciding any question of contract interpretation which is capable of being resolved under the contract grievance and arbitration procedure. In each case, the union had filed an unfair labor practice charge without utilizing the grievance-arbitration machinery. The Board, stating that it was being asked to interpret the contract, refused to rule on a charge that the employer had refused to bargain when he took unilateral action.[142] The Board relied on the facts that the employer was not trying to undermine the union; that the parties had demonstrated an ability to conduct successful collective bargaining in the past; that the employer was willing to bargain with the union after the union had made its objections known.[143] The Board, however, did find that the unilateral acts of the employer interfered with, restrained, and coerced employees in the exercise of Section 7 rights.[144] In these cases the Board encouraged the use of contract mechanisms even though, in other circumstances, the employer might have been held in violation of his bargaining obligation.

---

[139] This issue is discussed in this chapter *supra*.

[140] Consolidated Aircraft Corp., 47 NLRB 694, 705-06, 12 LRRM 44 (1943), *enforced as modified*, 141 F 2d 785, 14 LRRM 553 (CA 9, 1944).

[141] Crown Zellerbach Corp., 95 NLRB 753, 753-54, 28 LRRM 1357 (1951).

[142] 47 NLRB at 705-06; 95 NLRB at 753-54.

[143] *Ibid.*

[144] Consolidated Aircraft Corp., 47 NLRB at 709. This aspect of the Board's decision has been termed "inexplicable" in that it "seems futile to eschew a refusal-to-bargain adjudication only to make an indistinguishable interference determination." Dunau, *Contractual Prohibition of Unfair Labor Practices: Jurisdictional Problems*, 57 Colum. L. Rev. 52, 60, n. 30 (1957).

Then, in *Timken Roller Bearing Co.*,[145] the NLRB seemed to view the choice between arbitrator and Board as an election of remedies. Inasmuch as the union had first pursued the arbitral course without satisfaction, the Board dismissed an 8(a)(5) charge even though it concluded there had been a violation.[146] The Board also found there had been a violation of the bargaining obligation in regard to issues not submitted to arbitration, and it issued a cease and desist order.[147]

In *McDonnell Aircraft Corp.*,[148] the contract spelled out job specifications, provided for a grievance procedure, and set out a management-rights clause. The employer unilaterally assigned to certain employees clerical work which was being performed by others. The union filed a grievance and the procedure was followed to the third step. Instead of going to the fourth step, which was arbitration, the union filed a charge. The Board stated that the unilateral action "gave rise to a dispute over the interpretation and administration of the agreement," [149] and the company satisfied its obligation to bargain by treating the union's complaint as a grievance and by being willing to process it under the contract procedure. The complaint was, therefore, dismissed.

United Telephone of the West [150] involved the asserted right of the employer under one clause of the contract to establish a 40-hour week as against the claim of the union that another clause prohibited a change except by mutual consent. The employer, having initiated the change, agreed to discuss the matter. When the parties failed to agree, the union requested arbitration as provided in the contract. While discussing the possibility of arbitration, the company filed suit for a declaratory judgment and the union filed an 8(a)(5) charge. Neither party thereafter sought to negotiate. The Board, citing *Consolidated Aircraft* and *Crown Zellerbach*, found no merit in the charge. The Board viewed the

---

[145] 70 NLRB 500, 18 LRRM 1370 (1946), *enforcement denied,* 161 F 2d 949, 20 LRRM 2204 (CA 6, 1947).
[146] *Id.* at 501. This has been criticized as encouraging a union to disregard the contract procedure. Cox & Dunlop, *The Duty To Bargain Collectively During the Term of an Existing Agreement,* 63 HARV. L. REV. 1097, 1102 (1950).
[147] It was this position of the NLRB which the court of appeals refused to enforce. The question of the obligation to bargain has been discussed generally in Chapter 11, *supra;* in relation to subcontracting in Chapter 15, *supra;* and in relation to contract interpretation in Chapter 17, *supra.*
[148] 109 NLRB 930, 34 LRRM 1472 (1954).
[149] 109 NLRB at 934.
[150] 112 NLRB 779, 36 LRRM 1097 (1955).

case as "one arising out of the parties' conflicting contract interpretations."[151] In such cases, the Board said that it does not try to resolve the conflict, since it does not effectuate statutory policy for the Board to police contracts and to resolve disputed contract interpretations.

The Board again dismissed an 8(a)(5) complaint in *National Dairy Products Corp.*[152] The dispute arose when the employer told the union that for reasons of economy the milk-hauling operations would be subcontracted. The employer refused to consider the union's complaint under the grievance procedure on the ground that the agreed-upon procedure did not cover subcontracting. The union took its case to court in a Section 301 suit and also filed a refusal-to-bargain charge before the NLRB. Holding that "the Board is not the proper forum for parties seeking to remedy an alleged breach of contract,"[153] the NLRB found that the employer had not failed to bargain.[154]

The Board spelled out the basis for deference to arbitration in *Jos. Schlitz Brewing Co.*[155] Even where an employer implements a change in working conditions without complying with the notice requirements of Section 8(d), the Board will leave the issue to the grievance-arbitration procedure where: (1) the contract clearly provides for the arbitration procedure; (2) employer's unilateral action is not designed to undermine the union, (3) the employer's claim is not patently erroneous but rather based on a substantial claim of contractual privilege; (4) it appears that the arbitral inter-

---

[151] 112 NLRB at 781. The Board further said: "The Respondents' action was in accordance with the contract as they construed it, and was not an attempt to modify or to terminate the contract. The provisions of Section 8(d) of the Act are therefore inapplicable in this case." *Ibid.*

[152] 126 NLRB 434, 45 LRRM 1332 (1960).

[153] 126 NLRB at 435. *Accord,* The Crescent Bed Co., Inc., 157 NLRB 296, 61 LRRM 1334, *enforced,* 63 LRRM 2480 (CA DC, 1966); Morton Salt Co., 119 NLRB 1402, 41 LRRM 1312 (1958).

[154] It should be noted that this case does not involve deference to arbitration. Rather it seems to hold that a dispute over whether a grievance is arbitrable is a matter of contract interpretation and is to be settled in another forum. This decision must now be reevaluated in light of more recent authority. *Compare* Fibreboard Paper Prods. Corp. v. NLRB, 379 US 203, 57 LRRM 2609 (1964) (bargaining over subcontract); Cloverleaf Div. of Adams Dairy, 147 NLRB 1410, 56 LRRM 1321 (1964) (Board as proper forum even where arbitration is available); NLRB v. C&C Plywood Corp., 385 US 421, 64 LRRM 2065 (1967) (Board power to interpret a contract).

[155] 175 NLRB No. 23, 70 LRRM 1472 (1968). *Accord,* Vickers, Inc., 153 NLRB 561, 59 LRRM 1516 (1965); Flintkote Co., 149 NLRB 1561, 57 LRRM 1477 (1964); Bemis Bros. Bag Co., 143 NLRB 1311, 53 LRRM 1489 (1963); Montgomery Ward & Co., 137 NLRB 418, 50 LRRM 1162 (1962).

pretation will resolve both the unfair-labor-practice issue and the contract-interpretation issue in a manner not inconsistent with the purposes of the NLRA.

In *Schlitz Brewing,* other factors also made deference particularly appropriate. There had been a long-established and successful bargaining relationship; there was no other alleged unlawful conduct by the parties; and the dispute arose out of good faith assertions of contractual rights. The employer urged the union to arbitrate the issue and even offered to discuss the matter before taking action.

The above decisions offer varied reasons for deference to arbitration where the employer is charged with a violation of Section 8(a)(5) by reason of his unilateral acts. They include a simple encouragement of arbitration,[156] an election of remedies,[157] and a hesitancy to resolve contract disputes.[158] A consideration of cases in which the Board now refuses to defer indicates that these reasons are not now persuasive.[159] *Schlitz Brewing* offers perhaps the fullest rationale of Board principle in relation to unilateral acts, the obligation to bargain, and arbitration. Another general statement of value is found in *Cloverleaf Division of Adams Dairy*[160] where the Board indicated it would defer if the existence of an unfair labor practice

> . . . turns primarily on an interpretation of specific contractual provisions, unquestionably encompassed by the contract's arbitration provisions, and coming to [the Board] in a context that makes it reasonably probable that arbitration settlement of the contract dispute would also put at rest the unfair labor practice controversy in a manner sufficient to effectuate the policies of the Act.[161]

---

156 Consolidated Aircraft Corp., 47 NLRB 694 (1943); Crown Zellerbach Corp., 95 NLRB 753 (1951). This encouragement was given even though the employer might be found to have violated Section 8(a)(5).

157 Timken Roller Bearing Co., 70 NLRB 500 (1946).

158 United Tel. of the West, 112 NLRB 779 (1955); *cf.* National Dairy Prods. Corp., 126 NLRB 434 (1960).

159 *See* following section for cases. An indication that the Board considers the earlier cases to be weakened may be found in NLRB Brief at 18 n. 13, *NLRB* v. *C & C Plywood Co.*, 385 US 421 (1967). *See also* Admin. Decision of Gen. Counsel, No. 869, 33 LRRM 1138 (1953).

160 147 NLRB 1410, 56 LRRM 1321 (1964).

161 147 NLRB at 1416.

Under such circumstances, the Board would refrain from determining the merits of an 8(a)(5) charge.[162]

Perhaps the broadest principle for deference is found in *McDonnell Aircraft*, to the effect that an employer fulfills his bargaining duty by utilizing the arbitration procedure to test his right to take unilateral action. This contention will be discussed below. Attention will also be given to the contention of Member Brown that the utilization of arbitration and contract procedures is preferable to Board determination on the merits.[163]

The main issue discussed in this section involves situations in which an arbitrator's award has not issued. Where it has issued, it seems that the Board will apply the *Spielberg* criteria.

(2) Cases refusing deference. Where an arbitrator's award resolving a contract dispute does not meet the *Spielberg* tests, the Board will assert jurisdiction.[164] In cases where the parties do not try to utilize an arbitration procedure, the Board will likewise assert jurisdiction.[165] Again, where a dispute is not arbitrable

---

162 *See, e.g.,* Vickers, Inc., 153 NLRB 561, 59 LRRM 1516 (1965); Bemis Bros. Bag Co., 143 NLRB 1311, 53 LRRM 1489 (1963); Montgomery Ward & Co., 137 NLRB 418, 50 LRRM 1162 (1962).
163 Eaton Drop Forge Div., Eaton Yale & Towne, Inc., 171 NLRB No. 73, 68 LRRM 1129 (1968); Univis, Inc., 169 NLRB No. 18, 67 LRRM 1090 (1968); Thor Power Tool Co., 148 NLRB 1379, 57 LRRM 1161 (1964); LeRoy Mach. Co., 147 NLRB 1431, 56 LRRM 1369 (1964); Cloverleaf Div. of Adams Dairy, 147 NLRB 1410, 56 LRRM 1321 (1964).
In *Eaton Drop Forge, supra,* Members Brown and Zagoria stated that deference should be given where the parties have an established bargaining history, where the dispute involves substantive contract interpretation, where each party asserts a claim in good faith, where there is no evidence of unlawful conduct, and where the Respondent has urged the union to use a contractual grievance procedure to resolve the dispute. *Cloverleaf Div.* gives an extended rationale of Member Brown's position.
It should also be noted that Members Brown and Zagoria were the principal draftsmen of the opinion in *Jos. Schlitz Brewing Co.*
164 *See, e.g.,* the statement of Member Brown, *concurring,* in Cloverleaf Div. of Adams Dairy, 147 NLRB 1410, 1420, 56 LRRM 1321, 1325 (1964).
165 *See, e.g.,* Zenith Radio Corp., 177 NLRB No. 30, 71 LRRM 1555 (1969) (parties agreed the issue was appropriate for Board determination); Morrison-Knudson Co., Inc., 173 NLRB No. 12, 69 LRRM 1232 (1968); Huttig Sash & Door Co., 154 NLRB 811, 60 LRRM 1035 (1965), *enforced,* 377 F 2d 964, 65 LRRM 2431 (CA 8, 1967) (contractual procedure not utilized); LeRoy Mach. Co., Inc., 147 NLRB 1431, 56 LRRM 1369 (1964); Cloverleaf Div. of Adams Dairy, 147 NLRB 1410, 56 LRRM 1321 (1964); Marlboro Cotton Mills, 53 NLRB 965, 966-67, 13 LRRM 142 (1943).
It should be noted the failure or refusal to arbitrate does not of itself constitute a failure to bargain even where the contract provides for the procedure. Sucesion Mario Mercado E. Hijos d/b/a Central Rufina, 161 NLRB 696, 63 LRRM 1318 (1966); National Dairy Prods. Corp., 126 NLRB 434, 435, 45 LRRM 1332 (1960); United Tel. Co. of the West, 112 NLRB 779, 781, 36 LRRM 1097 (1955); Textron Puerto Rico, 107 NLRB 583, 584, 33 LRRM 1194 (1953).

under a contract, the Board will determine the merits, since there is no real issue of accommodation.[166] In passing, we may note that a special issue may arise should a dispute be arbitrable but the time for filing a grievance be expired.[167]

The major reasons offered for refusing deference in a contract dispute involving unilateral acts, even where the contract provides for arbitration, seem to be that the issue raised is not substantial or that the issue involves a matter central to the system of collective bargaining.[168] In these instances, the Board will apply its own principles of interpretation developed under the policies of the Act [169] and thus may reach a conclusion different from that of an arbitrator who looks to contract interpretation alone.[170] The presence of an arbitration clause is then immaterial.

Thus, whenever the contract defense is considered to be unfounded, the NLRB decides the merits of the defense (whether based on a claim of waiver or of management rights) without regard to the breadth of the arbitration clause.[171]

---

[166] See, e.g., Adelson, Inc., 163 NLRB 365, 367, 64 LRRM 1347 (1967) (issue not within the scope of arbitration provision). Scam Instrument Corp., 163 NLRB 284, 64 LRRM 1327 (1967), enforcement granted, 394 F 2d 884, 68 LRRM 2280 (CA 7), cert. denied, 393 US 980, 69 LRRM 2851 (1968) (arbitration not mandatory); American Fire Apparatus Co., 160 NLRB 1318, 1323, 63 LRRM 1151 (1966) (interpretation of arbitration clause).

[167] Cf. Office & Professional Employees, Local 425, v. NLRB, 419 F 2d 314, 318, 70 LRRM 3047 (CA DC 1969); Thor Power Tool Co., 148 NLRB 1379, 57 LRRM 1161 (1964) (Member Brown dissenting).

[168] See NLRB Brief at 18 n. 13, 27 n. 20, NLRB v. C&C Plywood Co., 385 US 421 (1967).

[169] These principles are given in Chapter 17 supra.

[170] Consider, e.g., the issues of "residual rights," "waiver," and "past practice." See NLRB Brief at 27 n. 20, NLRB v. C&C Plywood Co., 385 US 421 (1967). See also Chapters 11 and 17 supra.

[171] See, e.g., Wisconsin S. Gas Co., Inc., 173 NLRB No. 79, 69 LRRM 1374 (1968); Unit Drop Forge Div., Eaton Yale & Towne Inc., 171 NLRB No. 73, 68 LRRM 1129 (1968), enforced as modified, 412 F 2d 108, 71 LRRM 2519 (CA 7, 1969); Gravenslund Operating Co., 168 NLRB No. 72, 66 LRRM 1323 (1967), and 175 NLRB No. 10, 70 LRRM 1470 (1969) (explaining earlier order); W. P. Ihrie & Sons, 165 NLRB 167, 65 LRRM 1205 (1967); K&H Specialties Co., 163 NLRB 644, 645-46, 64 LRRM 1411 (1967), enforcement granted, 407 F 2d 820, 70 LRRM 2880 (CA 6, 1969); Adelson, Inc., 163 NLRB 365, 64 LRRM 1347 (1967); Scam Instrument Corp., 163 NLRB 284, 64 LRRM 1327 (1967), enforcement granted, 394 F 2d 884, 68 LRRM 2280 (CA 7), cert. denied, 393 US 980, 69 LRRM 2851 (1968); C&S Indus., Inc., 158 NLRB 454, 62 LRRM 1043 (1966); Century Papers, Inc., 155 NLRB 358, 361, 60 LRRM 1320 (1965) (contract provisions plain and unambiguous); Huttig Sash & Door Co., 154 NLRB 811, 816-17, 60 LRRM 1035 (1965), enforcement granted, 377 F 2d 964, 65 LRRM 2431 (CA 8, 1967) (plain and unambiguous provisions); Smith Cabinet Mfg. Co., 147 NLRB 1506, 1508, 56 LRRM 1418 (1964) (contractual provisions insufficient to support inference of waiver); LeRoy Mach. Co., Inc., 147 NLRB 1431, 56 LRRM 1369 (1964); Cloverleaf Div. of Adams Dairy, 147 NLRB 1410, 56 LRRM 1321 (1964).

The Board's approach is well illustrated by *Cloverleaf Division of Adams Dairy*.[172] The Board candidly stated it had considered the contractual claim and had rejected it as without merit. "We may assume that this claim gave rise to a difference over the meaning of contractual provisions that might have been submitted for consideration under the contract's arbitration procedures."[173] Emphasizing its power to interpret a contract, the failure of the parties to arbitrate, and a conviction that arbitration would not resolve the dispute over the right to take unilateral action, the NLRB resolved the issue in accord with its usual principles on subcontracting and waiver.

In shunting aside the arbitral clause, the Board said:

> The contract subjects to its arbitration procedures only such disputes as concern "the interpretation or application of the terms of this Agreement." But in the instant case, the precise Union claim . . . does not relate to the meaning of any established term or condition of the contract, or to any asserted misapplication thereof by Respondent. It is directed instead at Respondent's denial to it of a statutory right guaranteed by Section 8(d) of the Act, namely, the right to be notified and consulted in advance, and to be given an opportunity to bargain, about substantial changes in the working conditions of unit employees in respects *not covered by the contract*.[174]

The Board sometimes says that "an interpretation of the contract" is not necessary for the resolution of the statutory duty to bargain.[175] Yet, it is clear that the Board looks to the contract to see if it covers the issue. Other cases specifically note the necessity of analyzing the contractual provisions before concluding, for example, that the union had not surrendered the right claimed by the employer.[176] Of course, in cases wherein the contractual defense is found to be valid, the Board will dismiss the complaint.[177]

---

[172] 147 NLRB 1410, 56 LRRM 1321 (1964).

[173] *Id.* at 1415.

[174] *Ibid.* In almost the same words, the case is resolved by the trial examiner in Smith Cabinet Mfg. Co., 147 NLRB 1506, 1508-09, 56 LRRM 1418 (1964). *Accord,* Adelson, Inc., 163 NLRB 365, 367, 64 LRRM 1347 (1967).

[175] *See, e.g.,* Gravenslund Operating Co., 168 NLRB No. 72, 66 LRRM 1323, 1324 (1967). In this and similar cases, Member Brown dissents on the ground that an interpretation of the contract is required and should be left to the arbitrator.

[176] *E.g.,* Unit Drop Forge Div., Eaton Yale & Towne Inc., 171 NLRB No. 73, 68 LRRM 1129, 1131 (1968).

[177] *E.g.,* Cello-Foil Prods., Inc., 178 NLRB No. 103, 72 LRRM 1196 (1969) (job classification); Union Carbide Corp., 178 NLRB No. 81, 72 LRRM 1150 (1969) (subcontracting); Zenith Radio Corp., 177 NLRB No. 30, 71 LRRM 1555 (1969) (job classification).

The Board's position on deference and its exercise of discretion have been sustained by courts of appeal which have considered the matter subsequent to *Acme* and *C&C Plywood*.[178] In *NLRB* v. *Huttig Sash & Door Co.*, the court listed the reasons in *Acme* and in *C&C Plywood* which it detected as favoring Board action: to expedite cases and avoid the delays of court or arbitral process; to give priority to statutorily declared rights; to regard as secondary any contractual interpretation aspect of any matter which is basically an unfair labor practice; to take a broad approach to the Act; not to close the door to Board expertise.[179] In *Office & Professional Employees, Local 425,* v. *NLRB*,[180] most attention was given to the general question of the jurisdiction of the Board. Affirming jurisdiction, the court went on to say that the court would not interfere where there were a substantial possibility, if not probability, that the matter would not be resolved through arbitration.[181] Therefore, the court was satisfied that "there is at least a likelihood that the Board is following a tolerable approach." [182]

b. Nature of collective bargaining. The question was earlier asked: Does an employer violate his obligation to bargain when, upon taking unilateral action, he defends his action by an appeal to the contract and a demand for arbitration? Professors Cox and Dunlop in 1950 suggested that "[d]uring the term of a collective bargaining agreement an offer to follow the contract grievance procedure satisfies any duty to bargain collectively with respect to a matter to which the contract grievance procedure may apply." [183] This alternative approach is still warmly urged by commentators.[184] It seems to be in harmony with *McDonnell Aircraft*

---

178 Unit Drop Forge Div., Eaton, Yale & Towne, Inc. v. NLRB, 412 F 2d 108, 71 LRRM 2519 (CA 7, 1969); Office & Professional Employees, Local 425 v. NLRB, 419 F 2d 314, 70 LRRM 3047 (CA DC, 1969), *enforcing* 168 NLRB No. 93, 67 LRRM 1029 (1967); NLRB v. Scam Instrument Corp., 394 F 2d 884, 68 LRRM 2280 (CA 7), *cert. denied*, 393 US 980, 69 LRRM 2851 (1968); NLRB v. Huttig Sash & Door Co., 377 F 2d 964, 65 LRRM 2431 (CA 8, 1967).
179 377 F 2d 964, 969-70, 65 LRRM 2431 (CA 8, 1967).
180 419 F 2d 314, 70 LRRM 3047 (CA DC, 1969).
181 419 F 2d at 320.
182 *Id.* at 318. The court's analysis of Board procedure in 8(a)(5) cases is similar to that of the Board in *Jos. Schlitz Brewing Co.*, 175 NLRB No. 23.
183 Cox & Dunlop, *The Duty To Bargain Collectively During the Term of an Existing Agreement*, 63 HARV. L. REV. 1097, 1101 (1950).
184 *See* Hanley, *The NLRB and the Arbitration Process: Conflict or Accommodation?*, in LABOR LAW DEVELOPMENTS 1968 (14th Annual Institute on Labor Law, Sw. Legal Foundation) 151 (1968); Peck, *Accommodation and Conflict Among Tribunals: Whatever Happened to Preemption?*, in LABOR LAW DEVELOPMENTS 1969 (15th Annual Institute on Labor Law, Sw. Legal Foundation) 121 (1969); Note, *The NLRB and Deference to Arbitration*, 77 YALE L.J. 1191, 1210-18 (1968).

Corp.[185] and with the reasoning of the court in *Timken Roller Bearing Co.* v. *NLRB* [186] which said: "Though the duty to bargain is absolute, it may be channeled and directed by contractual agreement." [187]

Under this approach, should an employer appeal to contractual arbitration when protest is made concerning his unilateral acts, the Board would look, not to the whole contract, but to the meaning of the arbitration clause. Its function, like that of the courts, would be to determine "arbitrability." Although the relation of the Board to the arbitral process is different in several important aspects from that of the courts,[188] the Board would recognize that the parties have bargained to go to arbitration and that the arbitral procedure is "continued bargaining." Thus, the Board would not decide the merits, even under the guise of arbitrability. When the Supreme Court in *United Steelworkers* v. *American Mfg. Co.*[189] reprobated *IAM* v. *Cutler-Hammer, Inc.*[190] it rejected the notion that a court can first find that the meaning of the contract is beyond dispute and then conclude that there is nothing to arbitrate.[191]

As is clear from the prior discussion of NLRB case law, the Board does not accept this thesis. Where the merits are clear, the Board will decide the case. Where the Board believes there is a substantial issue of contract interpretation and that arbitration seems likely to settle it, it will defer; if it does not seem likely that arbitration will settle the issue, the Board will resolve it.

Member Brown proposes, it seems, that whenever a real question of contract interpretation is presented and there is an applicable arbitration procedure, the matter should go to arbitration.[192] He would, however, have the Board decide a case when it is clear that the claimed right is not permitted by the contract.[193]

---

185 109 NLRB 930, 34 LRRM 1472 (1954).

186 161 F 2d 949, 20 LRRM 2204 (CA 6, 1947).

187 *Id.* at 955.

188 *See* NLRB v. Acme Indus. Co., 385 US at 436.

189 363 US 564, 46 LRRM 2414 (1960).

190 271 App. Div. 917, 67 NYS 2d 317, 19 LRRM 2232, *aff'd*, 297 NY 519, 74 NE 2d 464, 20 LRRM 2445.

191 363 US at 567. "[T]he agreement is to submit all grievances to arbitration, not merely those that a court may deem to be meritorious."

192 *E.g.*: Univis, Inc., 169 NLRB No. 18, 67 LRRM 1090 (1968); Wisconsin S. Gas. Co., Inc., 173 NLRB No. 79, 69 LRRM 1374 (1968).

193 *E.g.*, Cloverleaf Div. of Adams Dairy, 147 NLRB 1410, 56 LRRM 1321 (1964).

This position brings him closer to the alternative approach, except that he is unwilling for the Board to defer to arbitration where the contractual claim seems frivolous.[194]

---

[194] *Id.* This concern is cautiously shared by Cox, *Reflections Upon Labor Arbitration,* 72 HARV. L. REV. 1482, 1516 (1959), and Peck, *supra* n. 184, at 160.

PART V

ECONOMIC ACTIVITY

CHAPTER 19

THE PRIMARY STRIKE

I. THE RIGHT TO STRIKE

Collective bargaining, which is a keystone of our national labor policy, presupposes the availability to the parties of certain economic weapons. The use of economic pressure in labor disputes "is not a grudging exception to some policy of completely academic discussion enjoined by the [National Labor Relations] Act; it is part and parcel of the process of collective bargaining." [1] Collective bargaining evidently works as a method of fixing terms and conditions of employment only because the risk of loss is so great that compromise is cheaper than economic strife.[2]

Preeminent among the economic weapons in labor's arsenal is the primary strike. But like so many labor expressions, it is difficult to frame a precise legal definition for the term. A strike has been described as "the act of quitting work by a body of workmen for the purpose of coercing their employer to accede to some demand they have made upon him, and which he has refused."[3] The strike is not a concerted resignation of employees having the intent of securing other employment; rather, the object of the striking employees is to resume work upon terms and conditions of employment acceptable to them and agreed upon by their employer.

---

[1] NLRB v. Insurance Agents' Union, 361 US 477, 495, 45 LRRM 2704 (1960).

[2] A. Cox & D. Bok, CASES ON LABOR LAW 905 (6th ed., 1965).

[3] Jeffery-DeWitt Insulator Co. v. NLRB, 91 F 2d 134, 138, 1 LRRM 634 (CA 4, 1937). *See also* American Mfg. Concern, 7 NLRB 753, 2 LRRM 336 (1938). A strike for purposes of the LMRA ". . . includes any strike or other concerted stoppage of work by employees (including a stoppage by reason of the expiration of a collective bargaining agreement) and any concerted slowdown or other concerted interruption of operations by employees." §501 (2) , 61 Stat 161 (1947) , 29 USC §142 (2) (1964). In *The Point Reyes*, 110 F 2d 608, 6 LRRM 1033 (CA 5, 1940), the court stated two "essential ingredients" to any definition of the term "strike." "There must be the relation of employer and employee, and there must be a quitting of work." 110 F 2d at 609-610.

517

A. Constitutional Protection

The right to strike has never been accorded unqualified constitutional protection. The claim that the Thirteenth Amendment, which forbids involuntary servitude, can be interpreted to prevent any curtailment of the right to strike by legislation has been rejected. The courts have reasoned that the Amendment protects the individual employee from being forced to work, whereas a prohibition against the strike only prevents *concerted* activity and does not affect the individual's right to quit.[4] A more important question, and one that has never been clearly answered, is whether strike activity is protected under the "due process" provisions of the Fifth and Fourteenth Amendments. In *Dorchy v. Kansas* the Supreme Court enunciated the principle that "neither the common law, nor the Fourteenth Amendment confers the absolute right to strike."[5] But the Court has never clearly enunciated the degree of constitutional protection, if any, to which the strike is entitled.

The use of picketing in strikes raises further constitutional issues. In *Thornhill v. Alabama* [6] the Supreme Court equated peaceful picketing in general to freedom of speech, and as such it

---

[4] NLRB v. Local 74, Carpenters & Joiners, 181 F 2d 126, 25 LRRM 2612 (CA 6, 1950), *affirmed*, 341 US 947, 28 LRRM 2121 (1951), NLRB v. Nat'l Maritime Union, 175 F 2d 686, 24 LRRM 2268 (CA 2, 1949), *cert. denied*, 338 US 954, 25 LRRM 2395 (1950), *rehearing denied*, 339 US 926 (1950). *Cf.* UAW-AFL, Local 232 v. Wisconsin Employment Relations Bd., 336 US 245, 23 LRRM 2361 (1949); France Packing Co. v. Dailey, 166 F 2d 751, 21 LRRM 2344 (CA 3, 1948); People v. United Mine Workers, 70 Colo 269, 201 Pac 54 (1921). Other cases have held the 14th Amendment inapplicable because it is concerned only with the freedom of an individual. Wisconsin Employment Relations Bd. v. Amalgamated Ass'n of St., etc., Employees, 257 Wis 43, 42 NW 2d 471, 26 LRRM 2145 (1950), *reversed*, 340 US 383, 27 LRRM 2385 (1950); State v. Traffic Telephone Workers' Federation, 2 NJ 335, 66 A 2d 616, 24 LRRM 2071 (1949); Local 170, Transport Workers v. Gadola, 322 Mich 332, 34 NW 2d 71, 22 LRRM 2460 (1948).

[5] 272 US 306, 311 (1926); *cf.* UAW-AFL, Local 232 v. Wisconsin Employment Relations Bd., 250 Wis. 550, 27 NW 2d 875, 20 LRRM 2357 (1947), *affirmed*, 336 US 245, 23 LRRM 2361 (1949), *rehearing denied*, 336 US 970 (1949), which cited the quoted language with approval. For a discussion of the constitutional questions raised by strike, picketing, and boycott activity see Cox, *Strikes, Picketing and the Constitution,* 4 VAND. L. REV. 574 (1951).

[6] 310 US 88, 6 LRRM 697 (1940). The Court held unconstitutional a state statute that had been applied to ban all picketing, with "no exceptions based upon either the number of persons engaged in the proscribed activity, the peaceful character of their demeanor, the nature of their dispute with an employer, or the restrained character and accurateness of the terminology used in notifying the public of the facts of the dispute." 310 US at 99. In a companion case, *Carlson v. California,* 310 US 106, LRRM 705 (1940), the Court struck down a municipal ordinance which banned picketing designed to discourage customers or to induce other persons to cease performing services.

was protected against abridgment under the First and Fourteenth Amendments, though subject to the same legislative restrictions as other forms of speech. These broad pronouncements, however, were modified and limited by a later series of cases in which the Court held that picketing, because it involved not only communication of ideas but also elements of patrolling and signaling, was not immune from all state regulation.[7] Since pickets not only are exercising their right of speech but also are engaging in an exercise of economic power, the Court stated that when such activity is "counter to valid state policy in a domain open to state regulation"[8] it can be restricted, even though it arises in the course of a valid labor controversy.[9]

In 1968 the Supreme Court revitalized the *Thornhill* doctrine in *Amalgamated Food Employees v. Logan Valley Plaza*,[10] a case involving picketing of an employer within a privately owned shopping center. The employer, Weiss Markets, operated a nonunion supermarket in a large suburban shopping-center complex. Although the market building was posted with a sign prohibiting trespassing or soliciting by anyone other than employees on the adjacent porch and parking lot, nonemployee union members (who were in fact employed by competitors of Weis) picketed outside the market with signs stating that the Weis market was nonunion and that its employees were not "receiving union wages or

---

7 "Picketing by an organized group is more than free speech, since it involves patrol of a particular locality and since the very presence of a picket line may induce action of one kind or another, quite irrespective of the nature of the ideas which are being disseminated." Bakery & Pastry Drivers, Local 802 v. Wohl, 315 US 769, 776, 10 LRRM 507 (1942). *See also* Carpenters & Joiners v. Ritter's Cafe, 315 US 722, 10 LRRM 507 (1942); Hughes v. Superior Court, 339 US 460, 26 LRRM 2072 (1950). For a discussion of the definition of "picketing," *see* Chapter 21 *infra*.
8 Teamsters, Local 695 v. Vogt, Inc., 354 US 284, 291, 40 LRRM 2208 (1957). This decision contains an excellent compilation and summation of all of the pertinent earlier cases in this area.
9 Giboney v. Empire Storage & Ice Co., 336 US 490, 23 LRRM 2505 (1949); Hughes v. Superior Court, 339 US 460, 26 LRRM 2072 (1950); Teamsters v. Hanke, 339 US 470, 26 LRRM 2076 (1950); Building Serv. Emp., Local 262 v. Gazzam, 339 US 532, 26 LRRM 2068 (1950); Local 10, Plumbers and Steamfitters v. Graham, 345 US 192, 31 LRRM 2444 (1953); Teamsters, Local 695 v. Vogt Inc., 354 US 284, 40 LRRM 2208 (1957); Cox v. Louisiana, 379 US 559 (1965). It was Mr. Justice Black's view that Section 8(b)(4)(B) of the National Labor Relations Act is an unconstitutional abridgment of free speech and press. Mr. Justice Harlan took a contrary view. NLRB v. Fruit and Vegetable Packers, Local 760, 377 US 58, 55 LRRM 2961 (1964) (concurring and dissenting opinions). The majority in this case, however, did not reach the constitutional issue. *See also* the discussion of this case in Chapter 23 *infra*.
10 Amalgamated Food Employees Local 590 v. Logan Valley Plaza, Inc., 391 US 308, 68 LRRM 2209 (1968).

other benefits."[11] The picketing was carried out in the parcel-pickup area and the adjacent parking lot, all of which was part of the center owned by Logan Valley Plaza, Inc. Picketing was peaceful at all times. Weis and Logan obtained a state court *ex parte* restraining order, later made final,[12] restraining picketing and trespassing by prohibiting picketing within the shopping center and requiring the union to limit its picketing to the berms beside the public roads outside the shopping center.

The Supreme Court did not pass on the question of federal preemption.[13] Instead, it evaluated the union's conduct solely in the light of First Amendment protection. Relying on *Thornhill,* the Court premised its ruling on the proposition "that peaceful picketing carried on in a location open generally to the public is, absent other factors involving the purpose or manner of the picketing, protected by the First Amendment."[14] Writing for the majority, Mr. Justice Marshall noted "that picketing involves elements of both speech and conduct, *i.e.,* patrolling, and . . . because of this intermingling of protected and unprotected elements, picketing can be subjected to controls that would not be constitutionally permissible in the case of pure speech."[15]

The Court found the shopping center picketing constitutionally protected, notwithstanding its occurrence on private property, "because the shopping center serves as the community business block 'and is freely accessible and open to the people in the area and those passing through,' "[16] citing *Marsh* v. *Alabama.*[17] Thus,

> the State may not delegate the power, through the use of its trespass laws, wholly to exclude those members of the public wishing to exercise their First Amendment rights on the premises in a manner

---

[11] *Id.* at 311. *See* Chapters 21 and 22 *infra* for discussion of this type of picketing under the NLRA.

[12] *See* 391 US at 312, n. 5.

[13] The trial court held that the injunction was justified both in order to protect property rights and because the picketing was unlawfully aimed at coercing Weis to compel its employees to join a union. On appeal, the Pennsylvania Supreme Court affirmed the issuance of the injunction on the sole ground that the union's conduct constituted a trespass on private property. Logan Valley Plaza, Inc. v. Amalgamated Food Employees Local 509, 425 Pa. 382, 227 A 2d 874, 64 LRRM 2699 (1967). *See* Chapter 29 *infra* for a general discussion of federal preemption. *See also* Broomfield, *Preemptive Federal Jurisdiction Over Concerted Trespassory Union Activity,* 83 HARV. L. REV. 552 (1970).

[14] 391 US at 313.

[15] *Ibid.*

[16] *Id.* at 319.

[17] 326 US 501, 508 (1946).

and for a purpose generally consonant with the use to which the property is actually put.[18]

B. Statutory Protection and Restriction

Whether or not there is a constitutional right to strike, strike activity has been both protected and regulated by federal statutes. Judicial recognition that strike activity may be lawful preceded many of the statutory provisions that granted the strike legal sanction. Thus, in *American Steel Foundries* v. *Tri-City C. T. Council*, Chief Justice Taft expressed the view that the strike is a "lawful instrument in a lawful economic struggle."[19] The Clayton Act first extended federal protection to strikes by providing that the federal courts may not prohibit "any person or persons, whether singly or in concert, from terminating any relation of employment, or from ceasing to perform any work or labor."[20] Although this provision was primarily designed to limit the issuance of injunctions, its concluding sentence broadly provides that such activities shall not be "considered or held to be violations of any law of the United States."[21] This language in the Clayton Act was strengthened by the declaration in the Norris-LaGuardia Act that federal courts have no "jurisdiction to issue any restraining

---

18 391 US at 319-320. Following the Court's decision in *Logan Valley*, the NLRB decided *Solo Cup Co.*, 172 NLRB No. 110, 68 LRRM 1385 (1968), in which it compared union solicitation by nonemployees in a privately owned industrial park to the public aspect of the shopping center in *Logan Valley*, holding that employer's exclusion of nonemployee union organizers from park premises violated §8(b)-(1)(A). The Board was reversed by the Seventh Circuit, which distinguished *Logan Valley*. "Here, the public was not invited into the District. None of the companies located there held itself out as being open to the public, and the general public had no reason to enter the area." NLRB v. Solo Cup Co., 422 F 2d 1149, 73 LRRM 2789, 2790 (CA 7, 1970). *See also* Central Hardware Co. and Retail Clerks Union, Local 725, 181 NLRB No. 74, 73 LRRM 1422 (1970). *See* NLRB v. Babcock & Wilcox Co., 351 US 105, 38 LRRM 2001 (1956), and further discussion in Chapter 5 *supra* at note 121.

19 257 US 184, 208-209 (1921). "Is interference of a labor organization by persuasion and appeal to induce a strike against low wages under such circumstances without lawful excuse and malicious? We think not. . . . A single employee was helpless in dealing with an employer. He was dependent ordinarily on his daily wage for the maintenance of himself and family. If the employer refused to pay him the wages that he thought fair, he was nevertheless unable to leave the employ and to resist arbitrary and unfair treatment. . . . They united to exert influence upon him and to leave him in a body in order by this inconvenience to induce him to make better terms with them. They were withholding their labor of economic value to make him pay what they thought it was worth. The right to combine for such a lawful purpose has in many years not been denied by any court. The strike became a lawful instrument in a lawful economic struggle or competition between employer and employees as to the share or division between them of the joint product of labor and capital." *Ibid.*

20 38 Stat 738 (1914), 29 USC §52 (1964).

21 *Ibid.*

order or temporary or permanent injunction in a case involving or growing out of a labor dispute." [22]

The most significant protection of the right to strike, however, is contained in the National Labor Relations Act. The Act guarantees to employees the right to engage in concerted activities [23] and specifically protects that right from infringement by an employer (Section 8(a)(1)) or by a union (Section 8(b)(1)(A)). In addition, Section 13 provides that the Act shall not be construed "to interfere with or impede or diminish in any way the right to strike," except as expressly stated therein.[24] Under Section 2(3) a worker who strikes in connection with "any current labor dispute or because of any unfair labor practice" continues to be regarded as an employee and as such is accorded the right to reinstatement under certain conditions.[25] And the proviso to Section 8(b)(4)(B), added in 1959, specifically exempts otherwise

---

[22] 47 Stat 70 (1932), 29 USC §101 (1964). In *United States v. Hutcheson*, 312 US 219, 7 LRRM 267 (1941), the Supreme Court construed §20 of the Clayton Act in the light of Norris-LaGuardia to achieve a broad immunization of trade union activity under the Sherman Anti-Trust Act, 26 Stat 209 (1890), 15 USC §1 *et seq.* (1964). *But see* Mineworkers v. Pennington, 381 US 657, 59 LRRM 2369 (1965), and cases cited therein. For further discussion *see* Chapters 1 *supra* and 29 *infra.* In addition, many states have anti-injunction statutes patterned after the Norris-LaGuardia Act. ARIZ. CODE ANN., §§26-019, 26-110, 26-111 (1956), 12 SLL 257; CONN. GEN. STAT., §§31-112—31-119 (1959), 16 SLL 280; HAWAII REV. LAWS §545 (1963), 21 SLL 269; IDAHO CODE §§701-713 (1947), 22 SLL 265; ILL. REV. STAT. ch. 48, §2 (a) (1963), 23 SLL 265; BURNS' ANN. IND. STAT., §§40-501—40-514 (1933), 24 SLL 171; KAN. GEN. STAT., §§60-1104—60-1107 (1963), 26 SLL 265; LA. REV. CIV. CODE, §§23:841—23:849 (1950), 28 SLL 265; MAINE REV. STAT. ch. 107, §§23,36—37 (1964), 29 SLL 251; MD. CODE Art. 100, §§65-77 (1957), 30 SLL 271; MASS. ANN. LAWS ch. 149, §§20B, 20c and 24, ch. 214, §§1, 9, 9A and 9B, ch. 220, §§13A—13B (1958), 31 SLL 271; MINN. STAT. ANN., §§185.01—185.22 (1946), 33 SLL 265; N. J. REV. STAT. Art. 8, §§2A:15-51—2A:15-58, ch. 15 (1941), 40 SLL 261; NMS 1953 ANN., ch. 57, Art. 2 (1953), 41 SLL 215; N. Y. LABOR LAW §447 (1935), 42 SLL 261 (McKinney 1935); N. D. CENTURY CODE, ch. 34-08 (1959), 44 SLL 255; ORE. LA AS AMENDED, §§662.010—662.130 (1953), 47 SLL 265; PA. STAT. ANN., tit. 43, §§1-18 (1938), 48 SLL 261; PUERTO RICO CIVIL CODE, §§101-109 (1954), 49 SLL 245; R. I. GEN. LAWS 1956, 50 SLL 265; UTAH CODE ANN. 1953, §§34-1-23—34-1-34 (1953), 55 SLL 251; WASH. REV. STAT., §§49.32.010—49.32.100 (1951), 58 SLL 255; WIS. STAT., §§103.51—103.62 (1963), 60 SLL 265; WYO. COMP. STAT. ANN., §§27-239—27-245 (1957), 61 SLL 241.

[23] Section 7 of the Wagner Act provided that "[e]mployees shall have the right to self-organization, to form, join or assist labor organizations, to bargain collectively through representatives of their own choosing, and to engage in other concerted activities for the purpose of collective bargaining or other mutual aid or protection." Since 1947, Section 7 has also accorded employees the right to refrain from taking part in such activities. *See* Chapter 5 *supra.*

[24] *See* NLRB v. Teamsters Local 639 (Curtis Bros.), 362 US 274, 45 LRRM 2975 (1960), Chapter 21 *infra* at notes 4-8.

[25] *See* Laidlaw Corp., 171 NLRB No. 175, 68 LRRM 1252 (1968), *enforced,* 414 F 2d 99, 71 LRRM 3054 (CA 7, 1969), *cert. denied,* 397 US 920, 73 LRRM 2537 (1970). *See* note 47 *infra.*

lawful primary strike activity from that section's ban on secondary boycotts and other coercive activities.[26]

Nevertheless, the right to engage in a primary strike under the Act is not an unqualified right. Although concerted activity by employees in legitimate furtherance of their common interests is generally not proscribed, those rights must be balanced with contract, property, and other rights of other parties. Thus, Section 8(b) clearly prohibits strikes for proscribed objectives. Section 8(b)(4) expressly restricts the right of a labor organization or its agents to induce or engage in a strike for secondary purposes, for recognition of a union as bargaining agent under certain conditions,[27] or for jurisdictional or work-assignment purposes.[28] And Section 303 of Taft-Hartley accords a right to sue in any United States district court for damages for violations of Section 8(b)(4).[29]

A further sanction against use of the strike is contained in Section 8(d), which provides for a "cooling off" period; a party seeking to modify or to terminate an existing bargaining agreement must give 60 days' notice to the other party and continue work during this period without resort to strike or lockout.[30] Strikes that imperil the national health or safety may be enjoined for 80 days under Title II of the Taft-Hartley Act, at the instigation of the President, during which time various mediation and fact-finding services are available to the parties.[31]

---

[26] See also discussion of 8(b)(4) in IV infra and discussion of the distinction between lawful primary activity and proscribed secondary activity in Chapter 23 infra.

[27] The problem of distinguishing primary strike activity from proscribed secondary activity is treated in Chapters 22 and 23 infra. Striking for organization and recognition is treated in Chapter 21 infra.

[28] See Chapter 25 infra.

[29] The injured private party cannot obtain injunctive relief under §303 for alleged violations of §8(b)(4). Street, Elec. Ry. & Motor Coach Employees v. Dixie Motor Coach Corp., 170 F 2d 902, 23 LRRM 2092 (CA 2, 1948). However, under §10(1) the NLRB must seek an injunction for such violations when its processes are invoked. The Norris-LaGuardia Act, which precludes private parties from such a remedy, does not limit the NLRB in seeking injunctions against unfair labor practices. See Chapters 23 and 31 infra.

[30] See notes 88 and 89 infra and Chapter 11 supra.

[31] §§201-210. E.g., United Steelworkers v. U.S., 361 US 39, 45 LRRM 2209 (1959); see generally, Rehmus, The Operation of the National Emergency Provisions of the Labor Management Relations Act, 62 YALE L.J. 1047 (1953). The participation in strikes of individuals employed by the United States or any agency of the government, including wholly owned government corporations, is prohibited by §305 (69 Stat 624 (1959), 5 USC §§118p-118r (1964)), and may be enjoined. U.S. v. United Mine Workers, 330 US 258, 19 LRRM 2346 (1947) (Norris-LaGuardia Act is not applicable to suits brought by the United States against its employees). A walkout by employees because of abnormally dangerous working conditions existing at their place of employment is expressly deemed by §502 of Taft-Hartley not to be a strike (see Chapter 6, note 54 supra). The provisions of the Taft-Hartley Act here noted do not fall within the direct scope of this book.

II. PERMISSIBLE STRIKES

A. The Labor-Dispute Requirement

For a strike to be protected under the NLRA, there must be a labor dispute between the striking employees [32] and their employer.[33] The Act states that a labor dispute includes

> any controversy concerning terms, tenure or conditions of employment, or concerning the association or representation of persons in negotiating, fixing, maintaining, changing, or seeking to arrange terms or conditions of employment, regardless of whether the disputants stand in the proximate relation of employer and employee.[34]

Since a strike is a forceful and compelling action intended to harm another, the courts have attempted to define the permissible limits within which a strike may be utilized to the detriment of an employer's business. The courts have also considered the purpose, as well as the means employed, in determining the legality of a strike.[35] Strikes protected by the Act fall essentially in two categories: economic strikes and unfair labor practice strikes. These are treated in the following section.

B. Economic and Unfair Labor Practice Strikes

Section 2(3) of the Act provides that strikers retain their employee status while on strike. Whether they have an absolute right to reinstatement, however, depends primarily upon whether the stoppage is determined to be an unfair labor practice strike or an economic strike. An *unfair labor practice strike* is activity initiated in whole or in part in response to unfair labor practices committed by the employer.[36] An *economic strike* is one that is neither caused nor prolonged by an unfair labor practice on the part of the employer.[37] Although economic strikes generally are utilized

---

[32] §2 (3).

[33] *See* New York Shipping Ass'n v. Int'l Longshoremen's Ass'n, 154 NYS 2d 360, 378, 36 LRRM 2663 (NY Sup Ct, 1955) (a strike by a union against government officials is not a labor dispute since no employer-employee controversy motivated the strike).

[34] §2 (9).

[35] In Dorchy v. Kansas, 272 US 306, 311 (1926), the Court stated that ". . . a strike may be illegal because of its purpose, however orderly the manner in which it is conducted."

[36] NLRB v. Mackay Radio & Telegraph Co., 304 US 333, 2 LRRM 610 (1938); NLRB v. Pecheur Lozenge Co., Inc., 209 F 2d 393, 33 LRRM 2324 (CA 2, 1953), *cert. denied,* 347 US 953, 34 LRRM 2027 (1954).

[37] NLRB v. Pecheur Lozenge Co., Inc., note 36 *supra;* NLRB v. Thayer Co., 213 F 2d 748, 34 LRRM 2250 (CA 1, 1954), *cert. denied,* 348 US 883, 35 LRRM 2100 (1954).

in an attempt to enforce economic demands upon the employer, this is not an absolute requirement.[38]

1. The Unfair Labor Practice Strike. Strikers who have been engaged in an unfair labor practice strike are entitled to reinstatement to their former jobs even if the employer has hired permanent replacements.[39] An employer cannot avoid his duty to reinstate such strikers by subcontracting, during the course of the strike, work which the strikers had previously performed.[40] However, strikers who have been guilty of strike misconduct or who have been discharged "for cause" under Section 10(c)[41] need not be reinstated, notwithstanding the fact that the work stoppage was an unfair labor practice strike. However, under the *Thayer* doctrine,[42] it is for the Board to "decide whether under the circumstances there was cause for the respondent's refusal to rehire

---

[38] *See, e.g.,* Philanz Oldsmobile, Inc., 137 NLRB 867, 50 LRRM 1262 (1962) (strike designed to persuade employer to agree to consent election deemed economic strike).
[39] NLRB v. Mackay Radio & Telegraph Co., 304 US 333, 2 LRRM 610 (1938); NLRB v. My Store, Inc., 345 F 2d 494, 498, 58 LRRM 2775 (CA 7, 1965), *cert. denied,* 382 US 927, 60 LRRM 2424 (1965); NLRB v. Fotochrome, Inc., 343 F 2d 631, 633, 58 LRRM 2844 (CA 2, 1965), *cert. denied,* 382 US 833, 60 LRRM 2234 (1965); Philip Carey Mfg. Co., Miami Cabinet Div. v. NLRB, 331 F 2d 720, 55 LRRM 2821 (CA 6, 1964), *cert. denied,* 379 US 888, 57 LRRM 2307 (1964); NLRB v. Efco Mfg., Inc., 227 F 2d 675, 37 LRRM 2192 (CA 1, 1955), *cert. denied,* 350 US 1007, 37 LRRM 2790 (1956); Kitty Clover, Inc., 103 NLRB 1665, 32 LRRM 1037, *enforced,* 208 F 2d 212, 33 LRRM 2177 (CA 8, 1953); NLRB v. Greater N. Y. Broadcasting Corp., 147 F 2d 337, 15 LRRM 953 (CA 2, 1945); Remington Rand, Inc., 2 NLRB 626, 1 LRRM 88 (1937), *enforced,* 94 F 2d 862, 1A LRRM 585 (CA 2, 1938); Brown Shoe Co., Inc., 1 NLRB 803, 1 LRRM 78 (1936).
[40] Hawaii Meat Co., Ltd., 139 NLRB 966, 51 LRRM 1430 (1962).
[41] For discussion of "for cause" proviso in connection with strike, *see* NLRB v. Washington Aluminum Co., 370 US 9, 50 LRRM 2235 (1962); NLRB v. Local 1229, Int'l Bhd. of Elec. Workers, 346 US 464, 33 LRRM 2183 (1953).
[42] Thayer Co., note 37 *supra,* 213 F 2d at 757. Judge Magruder distinguished the status of unfair labor practice strikers who have committed strike misconduct from that of economic strikers: "If an economic strike as conducted is not concerted activity within the protection of §7, then the employer is free to discharge the participating employees for the strike activity and the Board is powerless to order their reinstatement. . . . This is so because, if the particular collective action is not a protected §7 activity, the employer commits no unfair labor practice by thus terminating the employment relation. . . .
"On the other hand, where . . . the strike was caused by an unfair labor practice, the power of the Board to order reinstatement is not necessarily dependent upon a determination that the strike activity was a 'concerted activity' within the protection of §7. Even if it was not, the National Labor Relations Board has power under §10(c) to order reinstatement if the discharges were not 'for cause' and if such an order would effectuate the policies of the act." 213 F 2d at 752-753. On remand of *Thayer,* 115 NLRB 1591, 38 LRRM 1142 (1956), the Board indicated its disagreement with Judge Magruder's rationale and stated that it would not follow it in future cases; however, in *Blades Mfg. Corp.,* 144 NLRB 561, 54 LRRM 1087 (1963), *enforcement denied,* 344 F 2d 998, 59 LRRM 2210 (CA 8, 1965), the Board announced that it intended to follow the *Thayer* doctrine. *See also* Local 833, UAW v. NLRB (Kohler Co.), *enforced in part,* 300 F 2d 699, 49 LRRM 2485 (CA DC, 1962), *cert. denied,* 370 US 911, 50 LRRM 2326 (1962).

the particular strikers involved in the non-Section 7 activity, and if not whether reinstatement of these employees would effectuate the policies of the Act." Unfair labor practice strikers are entitled to vote in elections; their temporary replacements are not.[43]

2. The Economic Strike. When an economic strike occurs, the employer is free to hire permanent replacements for the strikers and may lawfully refuse a striker's request for reinstatement if he has been permanently replaced at the time the strike is ended.[44] However, an economic strike is deemed to be protected activity under Section 7, and, therefore, it is an unfair labor practice for an employer to discharge an employee for engaging in an economic strike.[45] If an economic striker's job has not been filled by a permanent replacement, he may apply for reemployment when the strike ends. Upon receipt of an unconditional request for reemployment, the employer is generally under an obligation to reinstate the striker if a vacancy exists. But even where the employer has abolished jobs during a strike, he is obligated to reinstate strikers when their jobs are reestablished, unless the employer can show "legitimate and substantial business justifications" for failing to do so.[46] In the 1968 *Laidlaw* decision, the Board expanded the employer's obligation and defined the status of replaced economic strikers as follows:

---

[43] Tampa Sand & Material Co., 137 NLRB 1549, 50 LRRM 1438 (1962); Times Square Stores Corp., 79 NLRB 361, 22 LRRM 1373 (1948).

[44] NLRB v. Mackay Radio & Telegraph Co., 304 US 333, 345-346, 2 LRRM 610 (1938); Adams Bros. Manifold Printing Co., 17 NLRB 974, 5 LRRM 360 (1939). *See, e.g.,* Hot Shoppes, Inc., 146 NLRB 802, 55 LRRM 1419 (1964); Texas Foundries v. NLRB, 211 F 2d 791, 33 LRRM 2883 (CA 5, 1954); Insurance Employees Local 65 v. NLRB, 200 F 2d 52, 31 LRRM 2118 (CA 7, 1952); NLRB v. Plastilite Corp., 375 F 2d 343, 348, 64 LRRM 2741 (CA 8, 1967). *But see:* Schatzki, *Some Observations & Suggestions Concerning a Misnomer—"Protected" Concerted Activities,* 47 TEX. L. REV., 378, 382-392 (1969); Getman, *The Protection of Economic Pressure by Section 7 of the National Labor Relations Act,* 115 U. PA. L. REV. 1195, 1203-1205 (1967); Note, *Replacement of Workers During Strikes,* 75 YALE L. J. 630 (1966).

[45] *E.g.,* NLRB v. United States Cold Storage Corp., 203 F 2d 924, 32 LRRM 2024 (CA 5, 1953), *cert. denied,* 346 US 818, 32 LRRM 2750 (1953) (employer found to have committed unfair labor practice by discharging economic strikers prior to filling their jobs).

[46] NLRB v. Fleetwood Trailer Co., Inc., 389 US 375, 378, 66 LRRM 2737 (1967), *citing* NLRB v. Great Dane Trailers, 388 US 26, 34, 65 LRRM 2465 (1967). "The burden of proving justifications is on the employer," 389 US at 378. See discussion of *Great Dane Trailers* in Chapter 6 *supra.* "After the termination of a strike . . . an employer may not discriminatorily refuse to reinstate or reemploy the strikers merely because of their union membership or concerted activity." 8 NLRB Ann. Rep. 32 (1943).

[E]conomic strikers who unconditionally apply for reinstatement at a time when their positions are filled by permanent replacements: (1) remain employees; (2) are entitled to full reinstatement upon the departure of replacements unless they have in the meantime acquired regular and substantially equivalent employment, or the employer can sustain his burden of proof that the failure to offer full reinstatement was for legitimate and substantial business reasons.[47]

Endorsing the *Laidlaw* rationale, the Fifth Circuit affirmed a subsequent Board holding that an employer had violated Section 8(a)(3) by failing to fill vacancies following a strike with qualified economic strikers who had indicated their continued availability at the time the strike was terminated. Although the employer had maintained a list of the names, addresses and telephone numbers of all strikers, he failed to inform them of the job openings. The court found no "legitimate and substantial business justification" in the employer's "protestations that the difficulty of seeking out strikers 'several months' or 'five years' after their application for reinstatement, when a replacement leaves, justifies its conduct. . . ." [48] The court recognized, however, that reasonable rules relating to continuing applications for reemployment could be devised, for "[a] reasonable rule would not contravene Fleetwood's assertion that '[t]he right to reinstatement does not depend upon technicalities relating to application.' " [49]

If strikers are guilty of misconduct, the employer is under no duty to reinstate them regardless of whether replacements have

---

[47] Laidlaw Corp., 171 NLRB No. 175, 68 LRRM 1252, 1258 (1968), *enforced*, 414 F 2d 99, 71 LRRM 3054 (CA 7, 1969), *cert. denied*, 397 US 920, 73 LRRM 2537 (1970). (The Board overruled Brown & Root, Inc., 132 NLRB 486, 48 LRRM 1391, *enforced*, 311 F 2d 447, 52 LRRM 2115 (CA 8, 1963), where it had held that replaced economic strikers were not entitled to preferential status in rehiring and that the employer's only obligation to them was not to discriminate when they applied for reemployment.) Consistent with the Supreme Court's rationale in *Fleetwood, supra* note 46, that under §2(3) the individual whose work ceases due to a labor dispute remains an employee, the Board in *Laidlaw* held that the employer's offer of employment to the strikers ". . . as a new employee or as an employee with less than rights accorded by full reinstatement (such as denial of seniority), was wholly unrelated to any of its economic needs, could only penalize [the employee] for engaging in concerted activity, was inherently destructive of employee interests, and thus was unresponsive to the requirements of the statute. . . ." 68 LRRM at 1256, *citing* NLRB v. Erie Resistor Corp., 373 US 221, 53 LRRM 2121 (1963). For application of the "regular and substantially equivalent employment" standard, *see* Little Rock Airmotive, 182 NLRB No. 98, 74 LRRM 1198 (1970). *See also* Chapter 6 *supra.*
[48] American Machinery Corp. v. NLRB, 424 F 2d 1321, 73 LRRM 2977, 2981 (CA 5, 1970), *enforcing* 174 NLRB No. 25, 70 LRRM 1173 (1969).
[49] *Ibid., citing Fleetwood, supra* note 46, at 381.

been hired.[50] Although the employer may permanently replace economic strikers, subject to the restrictions noted above, he may not discriminate between union and nonunion applicants in hiring replacements.[51] He may not hold out inducements so favoring the nonstriker or replacement over the striker as to destroy the power to strike.[52] Absent a legitimate business purpose, he may not deny benefits to qualified strikers while granting such benefits to nonstrikers.[53] Moreover, the employer's refusal to reemploy may not be based upon anti-union animus.[54] His illicit intent need not be shown by direct proof, but may be presumed from conduct inherently destructive of employee rights, even where he acts to further a good-faith business purpose.[55]

Although economic strikers may lose their right to reinstatement, they remain eligible to vote in a representation election held within 12 months of the commencement of the strike.[56] Strikers who have been discharged because of misconduct, however, are denied the right to vote.[57]

An economic strike may be converted into an unfair labor practice strike by acts of the employer, thereby changing the status of the participants to unfair labor practice strikers and entitling them

---

[50] NLRB v. Fansteel Metallurgical Corp., 306 US 240, 4 LRRM 515 (1939); Republic Steel Corp. v. NLRB, 107 F 2d 472, 5 LRRM 740 (CA 3, 1939); NLRB v. Ohio Calcium Co., 133 F 2d 721, 12 LRRM 559 (CA 6, 1943); Local 833, UAW v. NLRB (Kohler Co.), 300 F 2d 699, 49 LRRM 2485 (CA DC, 1962), *cert. denied*, 370 US 911, 50 LRRM 2326 (1962). *See* note 42 *supra*.

[51] §8 (a) (3) (discriminatory hiring by employer prohibited). *See* Chapter 6 *supra*.

[52] In *NLRB v. Erie Resistor Corp.*, 373 US 221, 53 LRRM 2121 (1963), an employer was held to have illegally discriminated against strikers by offering "super seniority" to the strikers who abandoned the strike and to replacements, so that in the event of a layoff the less-senior employees (strikers) would be laid off first. *See* discussion of this case in Chapter 6 *supra*.

[53] NLRB v. Great Dane Trailers, Inc., 388 US 26, 65 LRRM 2465 (1967). Employer who failed to advance a legitimate business purpose for his actions was held to have illegally discriminated against strikers by denying them vacation benefits accrued under the expired contract while granting the same benefits to nonstrikers. *See* Chapter 6 *supra*.

[54] NLRB v. Brown, 380 US 278, 58 LRRM 2663 (1965); *see, e.g.*, Radio Officers' Union v. NLRB, 347 US 17, 43, 33 LRRM 2417 (1954).

[55] 380 US at 287; NLRB v. Erie Resistor Corp., 373 US 221, 53 LRRM 2121 (1963) (Court finding of illegality even in absence of specific illegal intent and notwithstanding employer's claim that his action was necessary to continue operation during strike); *cf.* Teamsters Local 79 v. NLRB (Redwing Carriers, Inc.), 325 F 2d 1011, 54 LRRM 2707 (CA DC, 1963) (in absence of union animus, employer was justified in discharging employees who had failed to cross picket line of another employer, since this action was found necessary to continue business dealings with this second employer). *See also* American Machinery Corp. v. NLRB, 424 F 2d 1321, 73 LRRM 2977 (CA 5, 1970), notes 48-49 *supra*.

[56] §9 (c) (3).

[57] W. Wilton Wood, Inc., 127 NLRB 1675, 1677, 46 LRRM 1240 (1960).

to reinstatement.[58] The existence of a strike, for example, does not suspend the obligation of the employer to bargain in good faith,[59] and where during an economic strike he refuses to bargain with the employee's representative, the strike becomes an unfair labor practice strike.[60]

III. PROHIBITED STRIKES

Strike activity may be declared unlawful if it has an unlawful purpose or object, or if unlawful means are used to accomplish a lawful purpose. Thus, even though a strike may be conducted to achieve legitimate ends, the strike will be prohibited if unlawful means are employed. And a lawfully conducted strike will be prohibited if its objective is proscribed.

A. Unlawful Means

The so-called *sit-down strike,* in which the strikers remain on the employer's premises during the strike, taking possession of the property and excluding others from entry, is a method of striking which the Supreme Court has condemned.[61] Sit-down strikers are deprived of whatever protection the Act might have afforded them, regardless of their objectives. Because of their disregard for his

---

[58] NLRB v. Pecheur Lozenge Co., 209 F 2d 393, 33 LRRM 2324 (CA 2, 1953), *cert. denied,* 347 US 953, 34 LRRM (1954). *Cf.* NLRB v. My Store, Inc., 345 F 2d 494, 58 LRRM 2775 (CA 7, 1965), *cert. denied,* 382 US 927, 60 LRRM 2424 (1965) (union publicity relating to economic demands during strike does not prove conclusively that strike was solely economic); Radiator Specialty Co. v. NLRB, 336 F 2d 495, 500, 57 LRRM 2097 (CA 4, 1964) (employer's unfair labor practices were too slight to justify strike). *See generally* Stewart, *Conversion of Strikes: Economic to Unfair Labor Practice I & II,* 45 U. Va. L. Rev. 1332 (1949); 49 U. Va. L. Rev. 1297 (1963).
[59] NLRB v. Remington Rand, Inc., 130 F 2d 919, 927, 11 LRRM 575 (CA 2, 1942); Black Diamond Steamship Corp. v. NLRB, 94 F 2d 875, 1-A LRRM 597 (CA 2, 1938), *cert. denied,* 304 US 579, 2 LRRM 623 (1938).
[60] NLRB v. Waukesha Lime & Stone Co., Inc., 343 F 2d 504, 508, 58 LRRM 2782 (CA 7, 1965) (employer had no reason to assume striking union did not represent the majority of employees); Hawaii Meat Co., 139 NLRB 966, 51 LRRM 1430 (1962), *enforcement denied,* 321 F 2d 397, 53 LRRM 2872 (CA 9, 1963) (employer unilaterally subcontracted work at beginning of strike; *see* Chapter 15 *supra* at note 149). NLRB v. Pecheur Lozenge Co., note 58 *supra* (employer's insistence upon abandonment of strike as condition for resumption of negotiations with union constituted refusal to bargain).
[61] NLRB v. Fansteel Metallurgical Corp., 306 US 240, 4 LRRM 515 (1939); Apex Hosiery Co. v. Leader, 310 US 469, 6 LRRM 647 (1940); Stewart Die Casting Corp. v. NLRB, 114 F 2d 849, 6 LRRM 907 (CA 7, 1940), *cert. denied,* 312 US 680, 7 LRRM 326 (1940); NLRB v. Clinchfield Coal Corp., 145 F 2d 66, 15 LRRM 597 (CA 4, 1944) (striking employees rightfully denied reinstatement when they prevented the operation of their employer's mine by maintaining locomotive in entranceway, thereby blocking access to mine); NLRB v. Clearfield Cheese Co., Inc., 213 F 2d 70, 34 LRRM 2132 (CA 3, 1954) (physically barring all entrances to employer's plant). *See* discussion of *Thayer* doctrine at footnote 42 *supra.*

property rights, the employer is deemed justified in discharging such strikers or those who assisted them. Their conduct is not considered protected concerted activity under Section 7.

The *minority strike*—conducted by a minority of a bargaining unit without the authorization of the majority—has generally been considered unprotected.[62] The employer may discharge or take disciplinary action against the participants since he has agreed to bargain only with the union, and the employees also have agreed to bargain only through the union. A view enunciated in 1962 by the Board, and approved by two courts of appeals, is that the legality of a strike, notwithstanding its unauthorized character, is dependent not solely upon majority approval but rather upon whether its object is to protect the union's demands and policies.[63]

The Act has never recognized a right to resort to violence to achieve economic objectives.[64] Engaging in aggravated violence unprovoked by unfair labor practices places employees outside the Act's protection, although minor acts of violence incident to a strike may be disregarded.[65] An employer may refuse to reemploy strikers guilty of assaults upon nonstrikers,[66] malicious destruction of property,[67] or humiliation of or disruption of the work of

---

62 Confectionery & Tobacco Drivers & Warehousemen, Local 805 v. NLRB, 312 F 2d 108, 52 LRRM 2163 (CA 2, 1963); Plasti-Line, Inc. and Sign Fabricators v. NLRB, 278 F 2d 482, 46 LRRM 2291 (CA 6, 1960); Copperweld Steel Co., 75 NLRB 188, 21 LRRM 1016 (1947); NLRB v. Draper Corp., 145 F 2d 199, 15 LRRM 580 (CA 4, 1944); Western Cartridge Co. v. NLRB, 139 F 2d 855, 13 LRRM 690 (CA 7, 1943).

63 NLRB v. R. C. Can Co., 328 F 2d 974, 55 LRRM 2642 (CA 5, 1964); Western Contracting Corp. v. NLRB, 322 F 2d 893, 54 LRMM 2216 (CA 10, 1963). Both decisions base legality upon consistency with union aims rather than union authorization to strike. *See* Tanner Motor Livery Ltd., 148 NLRB 1402, 57 LRRM 1170 (1964), *remanded* 349 F 2d 1, 59 LRRM 2784 (CA 9, 1965), *affirmed*, 166 NLRB 551, 65 LRRM 1502 (1967), where striking employees who demanded that black workers be hired were deemed engaged in protected activities consonant with union demands and policies. *See* Chapter 6 *supra* at notes 52-53.

64 *See, e.g.,* NLRB v. Fansteel Metallurgical Corp., 306 US 240, 4 LRRM 515 (1939); NLRB v. Thayer Co., 213 F 2d 748, 757, 34 LRRM 2250 (CA 1, 1954), *cert. denied,* 348 US 883, 35 LRRM 2100 (1954). *Compare,* NLRB v. Insurance Agents' Union, 361 US 477, 498-499, 45 LRRM 2705 (1960).

65 *See, e.g.,* Republic Steel Corp. v. NLRB, 107 F 2d 472, 479-480, 5 LRRM 740 (CA 3, 1939), *modified on other grounds,* 311 US 7, 7 LRRM 287 (1940); NLRB v. Stackpole Carbon Co., 105 F 2d 167, 176, 4 LRRM 571 (CA 3, 1939), *cert. denied,* 308 US 605, 5 LRRM 694 (1939).

66 Tidewater Oil Co., 145 NLRB 1547, 55 LRRM 1213 (1964); American Tool Works, 116 NLRB 1681, 39 LRRM 1072 (1956); NLRB v. Industrial Cotton Mills, 208 F 2d 87, 33 LRRM 2158 (CA 4, 1953).

67 NLRB v. Fansteel Corp., 306 US 240, 3 LRRM 673 (1939); Republic Steel Corp. v. NLRB, 107 F 2d 472, 5 LRRM 740 (CA 3, 1939); NLRB v. Ohio Calcium Co., 133 F 2d 721, 12 LRRM 559 (CA 6, 1943); Local 833, UAW v. NLRB, 300 F 2d 699, 49 LRRM 2485 (CA DC, 1962), *cert. denied,* 370 US 911, 50 LRRM 2326 (1962).

nonstrikers by subjecting them to profane and insulting language.[68] It has been held, however, that the employer must reinstate those strikers whose misconduct he has condoned.[69] Moreover, all strikers are not to be condemned where the destruction is caused by a few; [70] nor do striking employees forfeit their right to reinstatement by failing to disassociate themselves from the violence, unless they have authorized or ratified the conduct of the participants.[71]

A *partial strike* is a concerted attempt by employees, while remaining at work, to bring economic pressure upon their employer to force him to accede to their demands. Employees who refuse to work overtime [72] or to perform certain tasks while accepting others [73] are denied LMRA protection against discharge. Another form of partial strike is a slowdown—a concerted slowing down of production by employees. The courts also have denied this conduct the protection of the Act and have sustained the employer's right to punish it by discharge.[74] A further example of an unprotected partial strike is the intermittent work stoppage. The Supreme Court has held that a sporadic work stoppage is neither protected nor specifically forbidden by the Act; this form of strike is thus within the states' police power to condemn.[75] The Board has found such activity devoid of Section 7 protection regardless of

---

68 NLRB v. Longview Furniture Co., 206 F 2d 274, 32 LRRM 2528 (CA 4, 1953).
69 NLRB v. E. A. Labs, Inc., 188 F 2d 885, 28 LRRM 2043 (CA 2, 1951), *cert. denied,* 342 US 871, 29 LRRM 2022 (1951). *But see* discussion of *Thayer, supra* note 42.
70 NLRB v. Cambria Clay Products Co., 215 F 2d 48, 34 LRRM 2471 (CA 6, 1954); Berkshire Knitting Mills v. NLRB, 139 F 2d 134, 13 LRRM 675 (CA 3, 1943), *cert. denied,* 322 US 747, 14 LRRM 952 (1944).
71 International Ladies' Garment Workers' Union v. NLRB, 237 F 2d 545, 38 LRRM 2062 (CA DC, 1956). *See* Sahm, *Picket-Line Misconduct and Employee Reinstatement,* 56 A.B.A.J. 561 (1970).
72 C. G. Conn, Ltd. v. NLRB, 108 F 2d 390, 5 LRRM 806 (CA 7, 1939); Mt. Clemens Pottery Co., 46 NLRB 714, 11 LRRM 225 (1943), *enforced as modified,* 147 F 2d 262, 16 LRRM 502 (CA 6, 1945); Scott Paper Box Co., 81 NLRB 535, 23 LRRM 1380 (1949); Valley City Furniture Co., 110 NLRB 1589, 35 LRRM 1265 (1954), *enforced,* 230 F 2d 947, 37 LRRM 2740 (CA 6, 1956).
73 Montgomery Ward & Co., 64 NLRB 432, 17 LRRM 111 (1945), *enforcement denied,* 157 F 2d 486, 19 LRRM 2008 (CA 8, 1946).
74 NLRB v. Blades Mfg. Corp., 344 F 2d 998, 59 LRRM 2210 (CA 8, 1965) (employer is free to discharge participants in deliberate slowdown and walkouts of employees to exert bargaining pressure); Phelps Dodge Copper Products Corp., 101 NLRB 360, 31 LRRM 1072 (1952) (employer not only was free to discharge employees but also was under no obligation to bargain with union during concerted slowdown during course of negotiations for a new contract); Elk Lumber Co., 91 NLRB 333, 26 LRRM 1493 (1950).
75 International Union, UAW-AFL v. Wisconsin Employment Relations Bd., 336 US 245, 23 LRRM 2361 (1949). *See* Chapter 29 *infra* at notes 33-34.

the employer's ability to defend against this conduct and however lawful the economic objective may have been.[76]

B. Unlawful Ends

Strike action in pursuit of an illegal objective is prohibited. Generally, where the common purpose of the striking employees is reasonably related to the betterment of working conditions and no law or contract is violated, the courts will affirm the validity of the strike's objectives. A strike whose objective is proscribed by the Act or some other applicable statute is illegal,[77] since employees are not granted the power to compel their employer to choose between economic ruin and violation of a federal law.[78] In addition, strikes within the jurisdiction of state courts may be unlawful if their objects or methods violate state law.[79]

The jurisdictional or work-assignment strike is one whose purpose is to compel an employer to assign particular work or jobs to employees belonging to the striking union. Such a strike is declared to be unlawful by Section 8(b)(4)(D) of the Act.[80] A strike whose aim is "featherbedding" is illegal under Section 8(b)(6).

---

[76] Pacific Tel. & Tel. Co., 107 NLRB 1547, 33 LRRM 1433 (1954). *But cf.* NLRB v. Insurance Agents Union, 361 US 477, 45 LRRM 2704 (1960). The Supreme Court, reversing the Board's finding of a union refusal to bargain in good faith based solely on the fact that concerted work stoppages of a harrassing nature followed a bargaining impasse, held that the Board ought not to rely solely on the form of economic pressure exerted by the union as establishing the absence of good faith in bargaining. *See* Chapter 11 *supra*.

[77] Southern Steamship Co. v. NLRB, 316 US 31, 10 LRRM 544 (1942) (strike in violation of federal mutiny statute); NLRB v. Sands Mfg. Co., 306 US 332, 4 LRRM 530 (1939) (violating provisions of existing contract by compelling employer to accept modifications thereof); H. M. Newman, 85 NLRB 725, 24 LRRM 1463 (1949) (attempt to cause discriminatory discharge); Thompson Products, Inc., 72 NLRB 886, 19 LRRM 1216 (1947) (to compel violation of Board certification); American News Co., Inc., 55 NLRB 1302, 14 LRRM 64 (1944) (violation of wage stabilization statute).

[78] *E.g.*, Los Angeles v. Los Angeles Bldg. & Constr. Trades Council, 94 Cal App 2d 36, 210 P 2d 305, 308-309, 25 LRRM 2008 (1949). *But cf.* Columbia Pictures Corp., 64 NLRB 490, 17 LRRM 103 (1945).

[79] Carnegie-Illinois Steel Corp. v. United Steelworkers, 45 A 2d 857, 17 LRRM 856 (Pa Sup Ct, 1946) (mass picketing); Molders & Foundry Workers' Union v. Texas Foundries, Inc., 241 SW 2d 213, 28 LRRM 2300 (Tex Civ App, 1951) (violence or coercion); New Hampshire v. Dyer, 98 NH 59, 94 A 2d 718 31 LRRM 2419 (1953) (epithet); Bldg. Trades Council of Reno v. Thompson, 68 Nev 384, 234 P 2d 581, 28 LRRM 2505 (1951) (strike to compel payment of a union fine); Colonial Press v. Ellis, 321 Mass. 495, 74 NE 2d 1, 20 LRRM 2370 (1947) (strike for closed shop prohibited by state law). *But see* discussion of federal preemption in Chapter 29 *infra*.

[80] NLRB v. Radio & Television Broadcast Engineers, Local 1212, (Columbia Broadcasting System), 364 US 573, 47 LRRM 2332 (1961).

The jurisdictional strike and the strike to further a featherbedding practice are discussed fully in a subsequent chapter and are mentioned here only as illustrations of prohibited primary strike action.[81]

Provided no other union has been certified, a primary strike for recognition has a lawful purpose.[82] Certification by the Board, however, normally grants the union the right to be recognized as the exclusive bargaining agent for a one-year period from the date of certification,[83] thus insulating the certified union from representation claims or rival unions. A strike by a union for recognition in the face of another union's certification is an unfair labor practice under Section 8(b)(4)(C),[84] even if the other "labor organization" is an individual.[85] A strike during the proscribed period by persons who have renounced membership in the certified union and have joined the uncertified union also is unlawful.[86] An uncertified union's strike for recognition during an existing certification violates the Act even when the certified union no longer represents a majority of the employees.[87]

A union that desires to terminate or modify an existing collective bargaining agreement may not strike for 60 days after giving written notice to the employer of such intent or before the termination date of the agreement, whichever date occurs later. The parties are required to maintain their collective bargaining contracts "in effect" beyond the "expiration date" if necessary for

---

[81] For an extended discussion of jurisdictional disputes and featherbedding, see Chapter 25 infra.

[82] United Mine Workers, Dist. 50 v. Arkansas Oak Flooring Co., 351 US 62, 48 LRRM 2809 (1956). However, for a discussion of picketing for purposes of organization and recognition proscribed by §8(b)(7), see Chapter 21 infra.

[83] If the contract provides for expiration prior to the one-year period or is subject to renewal during this time, rival unions may make claims for representation. Ludlow Typograph Co., 108 NLRB 1463, 34 LRRM 1249 (1954). See Chapters 7 and 8 supra.

[84] See generally Chapter 21 infra.

[85] ILGW Local 66, Bonnaz Hand Embroiderers, 111 NLRB 82, 35 LRRM 1424 (1955), enforcement denied on other grounds, 230 F 2d 47, 37 LRRM 2495 (CA DC, 1956).

[86] Getreu v. UMW, Dist. 50, 30 LRRM 2048 (ED Tenn, 1952)

[87] Brooks v. NLRB, 348 US 96, 35 LRRM 2158 (1954); Parks v. Atlanta Printing Pressmen & Assistants' Union, 243 F 2d 284, 39 LRRM 2669 (CA 5, 1957), cert. denied, 354 US 937, 40 LRRM 2284 (1957). See §8(b)(4)(C) of the Act.

compliance with the 60-day notice provision.[88] Where no
termination date is provided by the contract, however, a strike
is not precluded as long as it occurs more than 60 days after
notice and after the contractual reopening date.[89] Further procedural requirements are contained in Section 8(d) to prevent hasty
strike action and promote settlement of labor disputes. One provision specifies that employees who strike within the 60-day period
lose their rights as employees under the Act and therefore are not
entitled to reinstatement or to vote in any election conducted
during this period.[90] This provision, however, applies only to
strikes designed to terminate or modify existing contracts. If employees strike prior to the end of the 60-day period solely to protest an employer's unfair labor practice, the strikers do not lose
their employee status.[91] The section additionally requires notification of the impending strike to appropriate federal and state
mediation agencies within 30 days of notification to the employer.
Failure to give such notice makes the strike in violation of Section
8(b)(3) even if timely notice was conveyed to the employer.[92]

The right to strike may be further restricted by an express
commitment not to strike.[93] A clause requiring arbitration of all
disputes arising under the contract implies a no-strike clause as
a *quid pro quo;* therefore, a strike is considered a violation of such

---

[88] §8(d). *See* Chapter 11 *supra. See also:* Carpenters District Council of Denver
& Vicinity (Rocky Mountain Prestress), 172 NLRB No. 87, 68 LRRM 1325 (1968).
Upon consideration of §8 (d) of the Act and "the true nature and role of the collective-bargaining agreement in maintaining and sustaining a collective-bargaining
relationship," the Board held that a strike during the 60-day period was a violation
of the duty to bargain in good faith under §8 (b) (3) of the Act. For further treatment of this subject, *see* Chapter 11 *supra,* notes 450-463 and accompanying text.
Note, 70 YALE L.J. 1366 (1961) ; Note, 47 VA. L. REV. 490 (1961).
[89] NLRB v. Lion Oil Co., 352 US 282, 39 LRRM 2296 (1957).
[90] *Ibid.;* UPWA Local 3 v. NLRB, 210 F 2d 325, 33 LRRM 2530 (CA 8, 1954), *cert.
denied,* 348 US 822, 34 LRRM 2898 (1954).
[91] Mastro Plastics Corp. v. NLRB, 214 F 2d 462, 34 LRRM 2489 (CA 2, 1954),
affirmed, 350 US 270, 37 LRRM 2587 (1956). *But see* Chapters 11 and 17 *supra*
for a full discussion of this holding. *Cf.* NLRB v. Knight Morley Corp., 251
F 2d 753, 41 LRRM 2242 (CA 6, 1957), *cert. denied,* 357 US 927, 42 LRRM
2307 (1958) (60-day provision not applicable where strike is in protest of dangerous
working conditions).
[92] United Furniture Workers of America v. NLRB, 336 F 2d 738, 55 LRRM 2990
(CA DC, 1964), *cert. denied,* 379 US 838, 57 LRRM 2239 (1964) ; Retail Clerks
Local 219 v. NLRB, 265 F 2d 814, 43 LRRM 2726 (CA DC, 1959) ; UMW Local
12915, 118 NLRB 220, 40 LRRM 1155 (1957).
[93] Mastro Plastics Corp. v. NLRB, note 91 *supra;* UEW Local 1113 v. NLRB, 223
F 2d 338, 36 LRRM 2175 (CA DC, 1955), *cert. denied,* 350 US 981, 37 LRRM 2639
(1956). *See* NLRB v. Sands Mfg. Co., 306 US 332, 4 LRRM 530 (1939) (employer's
right to discharge striking employees for violating provisions of collective agreement in absence of express no-strike clause) ; NLRB v. Draper Corp., 145 F 2d 199,
204, 15 LRRM 580 (CA 4, 1944). *See* Chapter 6 *supra,* particularly at note 57.

a contract.[94] The Board has held that a strike over a grievable issue without prior exhaustion of the grievance procedure is not a *per se* violation of the duty to bargain.[95] And a walkout in protest of unfair labor practices, notwithstanding the existence of a no-strike clause, will not deprive employees of the status of unfair labor practice strikers,[96] unless the right to engage in such a strike has been expressly waived.[97]

IV. RIGHTS OF EMPLOYEES RESPECTING PICKET LINES

Picket lines, with accompanying requests by the pickets that employees not cross the lines, are a traditional aspect of lawful primary strikes.[98] The proviso to Section 8(b)(4) states that nothing therein "shall be construed to make unlawful a refusal to enter

---

94 Teamsters Local 174 v. Lucas Flour, 369 US 95, 49 LRRM 2717 (1962), an action brought under §301 of the Taft-Hartley Act. Lewis v. Benedict Coal Corp., 259 F 2d 346, 351, 43 LRRM 2237 (CA 6, 1958), *modified*, 361 US 459, 45 LRRM 2719 (1960); Teamsters Local 25 v. W. L. Mead, Inc., 230 F 2d 576, 583, 37 LRRM 2679 (CA 1, 1956), *cert. dismissed per stipulation*, 352 US 802 (1956); United Construction Workers v. Haislip Baking Co., 223 F 2d 872, 876-877, 36 LRRM 2315 (CA 4, 1955), *cert. denied*, 350 US 847, 36 LRRM 2717 (1955). These cases were brought under §301 of the Taft-Hartley Act. *See* Chapter 17 for discussion of the relation of NLRB action to enforcement of agreements under §301. This book does not directly treat §301, *but see* Chapter 17 regarding the relation of NLRB action to enforcement of agreements under §301.
95 Teamsters Local, No. 741, IBT (Los Angeles-Seattle Motor Express), 170 NLRB No. 13, 67 LRRM 1467 (1968) (the Board noted that the strike occurred only after the grievance committees at the first and second levels of the grievance procedure had deadlocked on the issue, and there was reasonable doubt as to whether a further stage of the grievance procedure would consider the issue); Iron Workers Local Union No. 708 (Billings Contractors Council, Inc.), 169 NLRB No. 152, 67 LRRM 1459 (1968). In *Iron Workers*, Chairman McCulloch concurred in the result, but indicated that he might have reached a different result were the union employing the strike "as a substitute for bargaining rather than as a weapon in support of its bargaining position." 67 LRRM at 1460. *See also* Chapter 11, *supra*, notes 365-379 and accompanying text. *Cf.* United Mine Workers (Boone County Coal Corp.), 117 NLRB 1095, 39 LRRM 1368 (1957), *enforcement denied*, 257 F 2d 211, 42 LRRM 2264 (CA DC, 1958).
96 Drake Bakeries, Inc. v. ABCW Local 50, 370 US 254, 50 LRRM 2440 (1962); Mastro Plastics Corp. v. NLRB, 350 US 270, 37 LRRM 2587 (1956); NLRB v. Wagner Iron Works, 220 F 2d 126, 35 LRRM 2588 (CA 7, 1955), *cert. denied*, 350 US 981, 37 LRRM 2639 (1956), *petition to vacate denied*, 243 F 2d 168, 39 LRRM 2727 (CA 7, 1957). *See also* Chapter 11 *supra*, notes 450-463 and accompanying text.
97 Mastro Plastics Corp. v. NLRB, note 91 *supra; accord*, Arlan's Dept. Store of Michigan, Inc., 133 NLRB 802, 803-808, 48 LRRM 1731 (1961). In Mastro Plastics the Court stated, "In the absence of some contractual or statutory provision to the contrary, petitioners' unfair labor practices provide adequate ground for the orderly strike that occurred here. . . . [W]e assume that the employees, by explicit contractual provision, could have waived their right to strike against such unfair labor practices." 350 US at 278-279.
98 *Cf.* International Rice Milling Co., 341 US 665, 28 LRRM 2105 (1951), *and* Electrical Workers, IUE, Local 761 v. NLRB (General Electric), 366, US 667, 48 LRRM 2210 (1961), in Chapter 23 *infra. See also* Chapter 6, *supra*, notes 67-69.

upon the premises of any employer (other than his own employer), if the employees of such employer are engaged in a strike ratified or approved by a representative of such employees whom such employer is required to recognize under this subchapter. . . ." Upon this proviso, the Supreme Court in *Rockaway News* [99] held that a collective bargaining contract may provide either that the employee may or may not be required to cross a picket line. This proviso has also been interpreted as protection for "the right of employees of a secondary employer, in the case of a primary strike, to refuse to cross a primary strike picket line." [100] It appears that even without this legislative history, case law would require a similar conclusion.[101]

In *Redwing Carriers* the Board held "that employees engage in protected concerted activity when they respect a picket line established by other employees." [102] Although the employees have the right to engage in this protected conduct, the employer has a corresponding right to operate his business.[103] Therefore, the

---

[99] NLRB v. Rockaway News Supply Co., 345 US 71, 80, 31 LRRM 2432 (1952), *affirming,* 197 F 2d 111, 30 LRRM 2119 (CA 2, 1952), *denying enforcement,* 95 NLRB 336, 28 LRRM 1314 (1951). *See also* Meier & Pohlmann Furniture Co. v. Gibbons, 233 F 2d 296, 301, 38 LRRM 2533 (CA 8, 1956), *cert. denied,* 352 US 879, 38 LRRM 2780 (1956); Truck Drivers, Local 413 v. NLRB (Brown and Patton), 334 F 2d 539, 543, 55 LRRM 2878 (CA DC, 1964), *enforcing in part,* 140 NLRB 1474, 52 LRRM 1252 (1963), *cert. denied,* 379 US 916, 57 LRRM 2496 (1964).
[100] 334 F 2d at 544.
[101] *Id.* at 545.
[102] Redwing Carriers, Inc., 137 NLRB 1545, 1546, 50 LRRM 1440, *enforced,* 325 F 2d 1011, 54 LRRM 2707 (CA DC, 1963). The Board expressly held in *Rockaway News* that this activity was a protected form of concerted activity. The Court of Appeals for the Second Circuit agreed on this point, but denied enforcement on another theory. The Supreme Court affirmed the Second Circuit's conclusion, in effect on grounds that the activity in question was a breach of the no-strike clause. Rockaway, *supra* note 99. *See also* Canada Dry Corp., 154 NLRB 1763, 1764 n. 2, 60 LRRM 1208 (1965); A. O. Smith Corp., Granite City Plant, 132 NLRB 339, 400-401, 48 LRRM 1340 (1961); Concrete Haulers, Inc., *et al.,* 106 NLRB 690, 693 n. 11, 32 LRRM 1536 (1953), *enforced,* 212 F 2d 477, 34 LRRM 2122 (CA 5, 1954); Texas Foundries, Inc., 101 NLRB 1642, 1683, 31 LRRM 1224 (1952), *enforcement denied on other grounds,* 211 F 2d 791, 33 LRRM 2883 (CA 5, 1954); Montag Brothers, Inc., 51 NLRB 366, 12 LRRM 270 (1943), *enforced,* 140 F 2d 730, 13 LRRM 776 (CA 5, 1944); NLRB v. West Coast Casket Co., Inc., 205 F 2d 902, 908, 32 LRRM 2353 (CA 9, 1953), *enforcing,* 97 NLRB 820, 29 LRRM 1147 (1951). *Contra,* NLRB v. Illinois Bell Telephone Co., 189 F 2d 124, 28 LRRM 2079 (CA 7, 1951), *cert. denied,* 342 US 885, 29 LRRM 2111 (1951).
[103] In *Redwing Carriers, Inc., supra* note 102, at 137 NLRB 1547, the Board stated that
"Although the Act . . . prohibits any reprisal against the eight Redwing drivers for engaging in the protected activity of not crossing the . . . picket line, we also recognize that the [employer] had a corresponding right which must be balanced against the right of the employees. That is, [the employer] had the right to attempt to run [its] business despite the sympathetic activities of the drivers here involved."

Board has held that the employer does not violate the Act by terminating such employees if the employer acts "only to preserve efficient operation of his business, and . . . only so [that he] could immediately or within a short period thereafter replace them with others willing to perform the scheduled work. . . ." [104] The Board has held that to satisfy this test the employer

> . . . must present more than a mere showing that someone else may have to do the work. . . . Clearly, what is required is the balancing of two opposing rights, and it is only when the employer's business need to replace the employees is such as clearly to outweigh the employees' rights to engage in protected activity that an invasion of the statutory right is justified.[105]

In *Overnite* the Board held that the discharge of an employee that refused to cross a picket line was unjustified when the refusal did not disrupt the employer's business in any significant way.[106] The Board reached a different conclusion, however, in a case where the employer had a compelling interest in maintaining a regular route for the driver which would not be interrupted by the driver's refusal to cross a picket line.[107] In a subsequent case, the fact that the employer's principal customer, upon whose premises the work would have been performed except for the picket line, demanded discharge of the employees was held to be immaterial, since it is well settled that an employer has a duty to resist pressure to discharge employees for unlawful reasons.[108]

---

[104] *Ibid.* In *Thurston Motor Lines, Inc.*, 166 NLRB No. 101, 65 LRRM 1674, 1675 (1967), the Board held that [a]lthough an employer may replace employees who are engaging in a protected concerted activity, *e.g.*, a lawful strike, the employer's right to replace is no greater than its proven need to carry on its business. It is not a punitive right." Therefore, the Board concluded, the employer could replace a driver who refused to make a particular delivery, but could not replace a substitute after the delivery had already been made by a supervisor. In a later case, the Board said that "the right which the employer has in this instance is not to *discharge* employees, but to run his business. [Emphasis by Board]" Swain and Morris Constr. Co., 168 NLRB No. 147, 67 LRRM 1039, 1040 (1968) .

Concerning the need for a balancing of interests, an analogy to employer lockouts may be proper. In *NLRB v. Truck Drivers Local 449, Teamsters* (Buffalo Linen) , 353 US 87, 96, 39 LRRM 2603 (1957) , the Supreme Court said that the right to strike "is not so absolute as to deny self-help by employers when legitimate interests of employees and employers collide. . . . The ultimate problem is the balancing of the conflicting legitimate interests."

[105] Overnight Transportation Co., 154 NLRB 1271, 1275, 60 LRRM 1134, *enforced*, 364 F 2d 682, 62 LRRM 2502 (1966) . *Cf.* NLRB v. Great Dane Trailers, Inc., 388 US 26, 65 LRRM 2465 (1967) . Chapter 6 *supra*.

[106] Overnite, *supra* note 105, 154 NLRB at 1275.

[107] Thruston, *supra* note 104.

[108] Swain and Morris Constr. Co., *supra* note 104.

In *L. G. Everist* [109] the Board equated employees who respect a picket line with economic strikers who are entitled to reinstatement upon unconditional application following a strike. But the Eighth Circuit, recognizing the need of the employer to continue deliveries to a prime employer without interruption by strikes, refused to accept the equation and denied enforcement. In a later case,[110] the Fifth Circuit equated the employee respecting the picket line with an economic striker, where the picket line was located at the employee's own place of work. The court held that by refusing to cross a picket line, the employee "joined in [the strikers'] common cause, and has thus become a striker himself." [111]

---

[109] 142 NLRB 193, 53 LRRM 1017 (1963), *enforcement denied,* 334 F 2d 312, 56 LRRM 2866 (CA 8, 1964).
[110] NLRB v. Southern Greyhound Lines, Inc., 426 F 2d 1299, 74 LRRM 2080 (CA 5, 1970), *enforcing,* 169 NLRB No. 148, 67 LRRM 1368 (1969).
[111] 74 LRRM at 20.

CHAPTER 20

THE LOCKOUT

I. BASIC CONCEPTS

"Lockout" is not defined in federal labor legislation. As a result, various meanings have been attributed to the term by the courts and by the National Labor Relations Board.[1] In its simplest sense and one embodying all its uses, a lockout is the withholding of employment by an employer from his employees for the purpose of resisting their demands or gaining a concession from them. Thus, a layoff having a purpose unrelated to labor relations is not a lockout as the term is ordinarily used. For example, a layoff undertaken because of adverse climatic, physical, or economic conditions is not considered a lockout,[2] nor is a shutdown and accompanying layoff required for the installation of new machinery.[3]

At common law, the employer could lock out his employees "at will,"[4] unless he had surrendered the right by agreement.[5] The Wagner Act, enacted in 1935, specifically preserved the employees' right to strike,[6] but made no mention of the employer's common-law right to lock out. The Taft-Hartley Act of 1947, however,

---

[1] See, e.g., Oberer, Lockouts and The Law: The Impact of American Ship Building and Brown Food, 51 CORNELL L. Q. 193, 194 & note 5 (1966); 173 ALR 674.

[2] NLRB v. Goodyear Footwear Corp., 186 F 2d 913, 27 LRRM 2278 (CA 7, 1951).

[3] Trimfit of California, Inc., 101 NLRB 706, 31 LRRM 1127 (1952). There may, of course, be a duty to bargain over such lockouts, shutdowns, or layoffs. See Fibreboard Paper Prod. Corp. v. NLRB, 379 US 203, 57 LRRM 2609 (1964), and discussion in Chapter 15 supra.

[4] Iron Moulders' Union v. Allis-Chalmers Co., 166 F 45 (CA 7, 1908). See also cases cited in 173 ALR 674.

[5] Moran v. Lasette, 223 NYS 283 (App Div, 1927).

[6] §13 provides: "Nothing in this Act, except as specifically provided for herein, shall be construed so as either to interfere with or impede or diminish in any way the right to strike, or to affect the limitations or qualifications on that right." See Chapter 19 supra.

used the term "lockout" in four sections,[7] thus giving "statutory recognition that there are circumstances in which employers may lawfully resort to the lockout as an economic weapon." [8]

Lockouts used as weapons to oppose union organization or demands have been held to violate any or all of Sections 8(a)(1), 8(a)(3), and 8(a)(5). Therefore, the law of lockouts usually has been concerned with these provisions, though, conceivably, a lockout could also be used to interfere with the internal administration of a union or to retaliate for the filing of unfair labor practice charges, thereby entailing violations of Section 8(a)(2) [9] or 8(a)(4). The lawfulness or unlawfulness of a lockout depends primarily on its purpose.

A. Unlawful-Purpose Lockouts

Perhaps the most common lockout for an unlawful purpose is the locking out of employees to prevent union organizational or recognitional activity. For example, in *Flora Construction Co.* the employer admitted that his operation had been shut down because the employees attempted unionization.[10] In another case violations of Sections 8 (a) (1) and 8 (a) (3) were found where a short lockout had occurred on the day the employer learned of organizational activity and a company official had made anti-union comments immediately before the lockout and upon the employees' return.[11]

---

[7] §8 (d) (4) of the Act prohibits lockouts (and strikes) for the purpose of terminating or modifying a collective bargaining contract until the 60-day notice period has run (*See* Bagel Bakers Council of New York, 174 NLRB No. 101, 70 LRRM 1301 (1969)) §203 (c), 61 Stat 140 (1947), 29 USC §173 (c) requires the Director of the Federal Mediation and Conciliation Service to seek settlements of disputes without the parties resorting to "strike, lockout, or other coercion." §206, 61 Stat 155 (1947), 29 USC §176 and §208 (a), 61 Stat 155 (1947), 29 USC §178 (a) grant powers to the President to deal with threatened and actual lockouts and strikes which constitute national emergencies. *See* Chapters 11 and 19 *supra*.

[8] In NLRB v. Truck Drivers Local 449, (Buffalo Linen), 353 US 87, 92-93, 39 LRRM 2603 (1957), the Supreme Court noted the legislative histories of the Wagner and Taft-Hartley Acts, concluding that the lockout *per se* was not made unlawful.

[9] *Cf.* NLRB v. Golden State Bottling Co., 353 F 2d 667, 60 LRRM 2553 (CA 9, 1965). *See* note 66 *infra*.

[10] 132 NLRB 776, 48 LRRM 1417 (1961). Of course, such an admission is not essential to a finding of intent to harass organizational activity. The usual test of "substantial evidence on the record considered as a whole . . ." is applicable, §10 (e). *See* Universal Camera Corp. v. NLRB, 340 US 474, 27 LRRM 2373 (1951); NLRB v. Walton Mfg. Co., 369 US 404, 49 LRRM 2962 (1962).

[11] North Country Motors, Ltd., 133 NLRB 1479, 49 LRRM 1049 (1961).

Threats to close a plant if a union is selected have been held to be unlawful.[12] Threats and lockouts to force the employer's choice of a rival union upon employees are similarly unlawful. In *NLRB v. Jay Co.*[13] an inside union had been formed at the suggestion of the employer to counteract the organizational efforts of other unions. Later, when the employees decided to disband the inside union, the employer locked them out and permitted them to return to work only after they had agreed to reestablishment of the inside union. The Ninth Circuit sustained the Board's finding of 8 (a) (1), 8 (a) (2), and 8 (a) (3) violations.

Lockouts have also been used to interfere with employee freedom to join or not to join a union. Such a case was the closing of a mine to force employees to join a union.[14] Other examples of evidence showing an intent to discriminate against union members have consisted of (1) threats of lockouts and actual lockouts to discourage employees from joining a union, (2) surveillance of union activities, (3) interrogation about union activities preceding lockouts,[15] (4) lockouts coincident in time with the initiation or culmi-

---

[12] Guard Services, Inc., 134 NLRB 1753, 49 LRRM 1408 (1961). *But see* Textile Workers' Union v. Darlington Mfg. Co., 380 US 263, 58 LRRM 2657 (1965), where the Supreme Court recognized that an employer has an absolute right to go out of business *entirely*, even when prompted by an intent proscribed by §8 (a) (1). In such a case the resulting lockout, though motivated by anti-union bias, is not unlawful unless intended to "chill unionism" in the plants controlled by or substantially affiliated with the employer. *Id.* at 275. *See* Board decision on remand, Darlington Mfg. Co., 165 NLRB 1074, 65 LRRM 1391 (1967), *enforced*, 397 F 2d 760, 68 LRRM 2356 (CA 4, 1968). *See also* discussion of *Darlington* in Chapters 5 and 6 *supra*. The "chill" concept was further developed in Motor Repair, Inc., 168 NLRB No. 148, 67 LRRM 1051 (1968). The Board applied the *Darlington* test, holding that the employer did not violate the Act by closing one of its six shops and discharging all employees who worked there. Even though the closing of the employer's Birmingham operation had been motivated by a desire to thwart the unionization of the Birmingham shop, the employer was not "motivated by a desire to chill unionism at its other shops. . . . [T]here is no evidence that contemporaneous union activity existed at Respondent's other shops, or that the Union's organization of the Birmingham shop was a first step, or was believed by Respondent to be a first step, of an effort to organize all of the shops," and there was no evidence that employees of the other five shops were even aware of the union campaign at the Birmingham shop. *Cf.* Morrison Cafeterias, Inc., 177 NLRB No. 113, 71 LRRM 1449 (1969).

[13] 227 F 2d 416, 34 LRRM 2589, *rehearing*, 37 LRRM 2093 (CA 9, 1955), *enforcing as modified*, 103 NLRB 1645, 32 LRRM 1116.

[14] Perry Coal Co., 125 NLRB 1256, *enforced as modified*, 284 F 2d 910 (1961), *cert. denied*, 366 US 949, 48 LRRM 2324 (1961).

[15] Somerset Classics, Inc., 90 NLRB 1676, 26 LRRM 1376 (1950).

nation of union membership drives,[16] (5) discriminatory layoffs, and (6) discriminatory reinstatement.[17]

A lockout may amount to a refusal to bargain under Section 8 (a) (5). But it is important to distinguish between the lockout which is used to avoid bargaining entirely and the lockout which is used as an economic weapon during the bargaining process.

Lockouts which preclude bargaining before it can begin are clearly illegal. In *Scott Manufacturing Co.*[18] the employer, without consulting the union, laid off employees during the term of a valid collective bargaining agreement. At a later date they were reinstated but at a wage rate below the one set by the contract. Finding that this was done in part to deprive the employees of bargained-for gains, the Board held the conduct violative of Section 8 (a) (5). In *NLRB v. Rapid Bindery*[19] a lockout at one plant and a later reopening of operations at another location, without giving notice to the bargaining representative, was also an unlawful refusal to bargain. The illegality of locking out before bargaining—or to avoid bargaining on a mandatory subject— seems well established.

Obviously, a lockout engaged in for purposes of curtailing employees' Section 7 rights is prohibited by the Act. But the extent to which a lockout may be legitimately used as an employer weapon to support lawful goals has been greatly expanded in recent years.

B. Justifiable and Defensive Lockouts

Until recent years, the Board held that a lockout was illegal *per se* under the Act except in two narrow categories: certain "justifiable" single-employer economic lockouts and certain permissible multi-employer lockouts used to defend against whipsaw strikes.

---

16 North Country Motors, Ltd., *supra* note 11.
17 *See, e.g.,* Ralph's Wonder, Inc., 127 NLRB 1280, 46 LRRM 1188 (1960); Eva-Ray Dress Mfg. Co., 88 NLRB 361, 25 LRRM 1328 (1950).
18 133 NLRB 1012, 48 LRRM 1784 (1961). *Cf.* Port Norris Express Co., 174 NLRB No. 106, 70 LRRM 1339 (1969).
19 293 F 2d 170, 48 LRRM 2658 (CA 2, 1961). However, the Second Circuit found no duty to bargain about the decision to move, which was motivated by economic necessity. *But see* discussion of plant closure and relocation in Chapters 5, 6, and 15 *supra*.

1. Justifiable Economic Lockouts. The first category was the single-employer economic lockout, deemed justified by unusual economic losses or operational difficulties that would result from a threatened strike. But it would not be justified by ordinary losses or difficulties which would be attendant upon any strike.[20] The Board thus found lockouts in each of the following circumstances to be justified: (1) to avoid spoilage of syrup which would result from a strike,[21] (2) to avoid economic loss from disruption of work of an entire plant caused by "quickie" strikes in individual departments of an "integrated assembly-line operation," [22] (3) to prevent inconvenience to customer owners of automobiles under repair at the time of a threatened strike,[23] and (4) to prevent seizure of a plant by a sitdown strike.[24]

The Board's rationale in proscribing all other single-employer offensive lockouts was that such lockouts were in retaliation for protected activity and that they were "inconsistent with Section 7 of the Act, with the statutory protection of the strike embodied in Section 13, and with the statutory objective of reducing economic warfare." Such lockouts, whether or not anti-union animus was present, were therefore viewed by the Board as violative of Sections 8 (a) (1), (3), and (5).[25]

2. Defensive Multi-Employer Lockouts. The Board's second category of permissible lockouts was the multi-employer lockout

---

[20] Professor Oberer has summarized the Board's logic in permitting lockouts in these situations as follows: "(1) The law does not require an employer to continue to operate where to do so makes no business sense. (2) A partial strike or threatened strike may, in the particular circumstances, render further operations sufficiently uneconomical to justify a temporary shutdown. (3) A shutdown in such circumstances is not a punishment for the exercise of Section 7 rights and therefore unlawful, but is 'defensive' in nature and therefore privileged." Oberer, *supra* note 1, at 197.

[21] Duluth Bottling Ass'n, 48 NLRB 1335, 12 LRRM 151 (1943).

[22] International Shoe Co., 93 NLRB 907, 27 LRRM 1504 (1951).

[23] Betts Cadillac Olds, Inc., 96 NLRB 268, 28 LRRM 1509 (1951).

[24] Link-Belt Co., 26 NLRB 227, 6 LRRM 565 (1940).

[25] Prior to *American Ship Bldg.*, note 34 *infra*, the circuit courts of appeal were split in opinion on the legality of the bargaining lockout. *Compare* Body & Tank Corp. v. NLRB, 339 F 2d 76, 57 LRRM 2666 (CA 2, 1964); Utah Plumbing & Heating Contractors Ass'n v. NLRB, 294 F 2d 165, 48 LRRM 2985 (CA 10, 1961) upholding the Board's rationale, with NLRB v. Dalton Brick & Tile Corp., 301 F 2d 886, 49 LRRM 3099 (CA 5, 1962); Morand Bros. Beverage Co. v. NLRB, 190 F 2d 576, 28 LRRM 2364 (CA 7, 1951). For a general discussion of the split in the circuits see Ross, *Lockouts: A New Dimension in Collective Bargaining*, 7 B.C. IND. & COM. L. REV. 874, 852-54 (1966). *See also*, Meltzer, *Single-Employer and Multi-Employer Lockouts Under the Taft-Hartley Act*, 28 U. CHI. L. REV. 614, 616 (1961). Professor Meltzer was critical of the Board's rationale in proscribing the offensive lockout.

used as a defense to a union's whipsaw or selective strike tactic. Although initially the Board held such lockouts illegal,[26] it reversed itself after three circuit courts rejected the Board's position.[27]

The reversal of position occurred in *Buffalo Linen*.[28] The union had struck and picketed the plant of one member of a multi-employer association while contract negotiations with the association were in progress. The nonstruck members responded by locking out their employees; negotiations continued and within a week a contract was signed. Rejecting the union's charges of 8 (a) (1) and 8 (a) (3) violations, the Board, citing the Ninth Circuit decision in *Leonard v. NLRB*,[29] reasoned that

> . . . a strike by employees against one employer-member of a multi-employer bargaining unit constitutes a threat of strike action against the other employers, which threat, *per se,* constitutes the type of economic or operative problem at the plants of the nonstruck employers which legally justifies their resort to a temporary lockout of employees.[30]

The Supreme Court sustained [31] this thesis with language couched in terms of the Board's "defensive" and "economic problem" approach. The Court declared that the Act does not prohibit the lockout *per se.* It specifically stated that "a temporary lockout may lawfully be used as a defense to a union strike tactic which threatens the destruction of the employers' interest in bargaining on a group basis." [32] It reasoned that the right to strike "is not so absolute as to deny self-help by employers when legitimate interests of employees and employer collide." [33] According to the Court, the legitimate interest which the employers were protecting was

---

[26] Morand Bros. Beverage Co., 99 NLRB 1448, 30 LRRM 1178 (1952).

[27] Morand Bros. Beverage Co. v. NLRB, 190 F 2d 576, 28 LRRM 2364 (CA 7, 1951), and 204 F 2d 529, 32 LRRM 2192 (CA 7, 1953) *cert. denied,* 345 US 909, 33 LRRM 2204 (1953); Leonard v. NLRB, 205 F 2d 355, 32 LRRM 2305 (CA 9, 1953); NLRB v. Spaulding Avery Lbr. Co., 220 F 2d 673, 35 LRRM 2711 (CA 8, 1955).

[28] Buffalo Linen Supply Co., 109 NLRB 447, 34 LRRM 1355 (1954).

[29] 205 F 2d 355, 32 LRRM 2305 (CA 9, 1953).

[30] 109 NLRB at 448-49.

[31] NLRB v. Truck Drivers Local 449, 353 US 87, 39 LRRM 2603 (1957).

[32] 353 US at 92-93.

[33] *Id.* at 96.

the multi-employer bargaining unit itself, the disintegration of which was threatened by the union's strike action.[34]

This limited concept of the lockout as a legally permissible weapon to be used only in "defensive" situations has been significantly expanded by the 1965 Supreme Court decision in *American Ship Bldg. Co. v. NLRB.*[35] And the companion decision in *Brown Food* [36] provided still another dimension for employer conduct in a defensive multi-employer lockout of the *Buffalo Linen* type.

II. CURRENT DIMENSIONS

In 1965, the Supreme Court introduced a potent new element into the collective bargaining process. *American Ship Bldg.*[37] and *Brown Food,*[38] decided the same day, provided a new potential for use of the lockout. Henceforth, the lockout would no longer be a purely defensive weapon.

A. The Offensive Economic Lockout

A harbinger of the new respectability that lockouts may now command appeared in a Fifth Circuit decision in 1962, *NLRB v. Dalton Brick & Tile Corp.*[39] That court rejected the Board's thesis that lockouts in the context of contract negotiations are presumptively unlawful "absent special circumstances clearly justifying the need for . . . the lockout as a defensive measure." [40]

---

[34] The *Buffalo Linen* rationale was also evident in New York Mailers Union v. NLRB, 327 F 2d 292, 55 LRRM 2287 (CA 2, 1964), which held valid an agreement of newspaper publishers to shut down all their operations in the event of a breach-of-contract strike at any one plant. On the other hand, in Great Atlantic & Pac. Tea Co., 145 NLRB 361, 54 LRRM 1384 (1963), *enforced in part,* 340 F 2d 690, 58 LRRM 2232 (CA 2, 1965), the Board found a §8(a)(5) violation where an employer locked out its employees for the purpose of forcing multi-employer bargaining on the union (*see* Chapter 16 *supra*), distinguishing such a lockout from a defensive lockout designed to preserve an existing bargaining unit. The Second Circuit approved this part of the Board's order, but denied enforcement of §8(a)(3) findings with respect to the consequent layoff of neutral employees, rejecting "the Board's Pavlovian rule that wherever there is a lockout the consequential layoffs of neutral employees violate the Act." 340 F 2d at 696.
[35] 380 US 300, 58 LRRM 2672 (1965). *See* generally the discussion of the case in Shawe, *The Regenerated Status of the Employer's Lockout: A Comment on American Ship Building,* 41 N.Y.U. L. Rev. 1124 (1966).
[36] NLRB v. Brown, dba Brown Food Store, 380 US 278, 58 LRRM 2663 (1965), discussed *infra,* this chapter.
[37] 380 US 300, 58 LRRM 2672 (1965). *See also* discussion in Chapters 5 and 6 *supra.*
[38] 380 US 278, 58 LRRM 2663 (1965).
[39] 301 F 2d 886, 49 LRRM 3099 (CA 5, 1962).
[40] *Id.* at 892, note 7, 126 NLRB 473, 483 (1960).

Judge Brown, writing for a unanimous panel, denied enforcement of an 8 (a) (1), (3), and (5) order that had branded as unlawful a marginal employer's use of a lockout to enhance his bargaining position. The court extracted from *Insurance Agents* [41] and *Local 357, Teamsters* [42] a "necessity that a statutory basis, either expressed or reasonably implied, be found when the Board undertakes to fashion policies which, in its judgment, are desirable in balancing the conflicting interest between management and labor." [43] Judge Brown concluded that "the statutes do not support any . . . 'prima facie' or 'presumptive' invalidity to the lockout when resorted to during bargaining negotiations." [44] Therefore, absent a finding that the employer has violated a specific provision of the statute, "resort to a lockout may not be made a violation simply on the ground that it gives advantage to the employer, or takes advantage away from the employees, or tips the scales one way or the other." [45]

In *American Ship Bldg.* the Supreme Court deliberately faced the issue of whether the offensive or bargaining economic lockout is *per se* illegal. It upheld its legality without resort to the doctrine of economic justification.

The employer in *American Ship Bldg.* operated several shipyards on the Great Lakes. Its primary business, the repair of ships, was "highly seasonal," being concentrated in the winter months when the lakes were frozen. In other months its limited ship repair business required speed of execution to minimize immobilization of the ships. Prior to the collective bargaining involved in the case, five agreements had been executed between the employer and the eight unions representing the employees. Each agreement had been preceded by a strike. On May 1, 1961, the unions notified the employer of their intention to seek modification of the agreement due to expire on August 1. The parties then engaged in extended negotiations without reaching an agreement. The employer rejected union offers to extend the existing agreement pending continued negotiations; on August 8 the unions' membership rejected the employer's contract proposals. The following

---

41 NLRB v. Insurance Agents, 361 US 477, 45 LRRM 2705 (1960).
42 Local 357, Teamsters v. NLRB, 365 US 667, 47 LRRM 2906 (1961).
43 301 F 2d at 894, 49 LRRM 3104. *Cf.* NLRB v. Great Atlantic & Pac. Tea Co., 340 F 2d 690, 58 LRRM 2232 (CA 2, 1965).
44 301 F 2d at 892.
45 *Id.* at 899.

day, the employer made another offer, which the unions refused to submit to their memberships. No counterproposal was presented by the unions. The parties then separated without setting a new date for further negotiations—a bargaining impasse thus existed. On August 11 the employer shut down some of its operations and locked out its employees with the announcement that "[b]ecause of the labor dispute which has been unresolved since August 1, 1961, you are laid off until further notice." [46] The union charged violations of Sections 8 (a) (1), (3), and (5).

The trial examiner found that the lockout was "economically justified" because the employer had a reasonable basis for believing that a strike was imminent and the property of its customers might be tied up if a strike occurred.[47] The Board, splitting three to two, rejected application of this "economic justification" doctrine. It reasoned that the unions had given sufficient assurances that a strike would not take place. In the Board's view, this lockout was an offensive weapon intended to force abandonment of the union's contract demands and acceptance of the employer's.[48] Accordingly, it was illegal and in violation of Sections 8 (a) (1) and (3).[49] The Court of Appeals for the District of Columbia, *per curiam*, affirmed the Board's decision.[50] The Supreme Court reversed.[51]

The issue in *American Ship Bldg.*, phrased by Mr. Justice Stewart for the majority as the "only issue," was whether "the use of a temporary layoff of employees solely as a means to bring economic pressure to bear in support of the employer's bargaining position, after an impasse has been reached," [52] violates Sections 8 (a) (1) or 8 (a) (3). The Court concluded that under the facts presented it does not.

---

[46] American Ship Bldg. Co., 142 NLRB 1362, 1364, 53 LRRM 1245, 1246 (1963).
[47] *Id.* at 1381-1383. This view was ultimately adopted by Chief Justice Warren and Mr. Justice Goldberg. See note 51 *infra*.
[48] 142 NLRB at 1364-65.
[49] The Board made no finding with respect to the §8 (a) (5) charge since a collective bargaining contract had been executed in the interim.
[50] Boilermakers, Local 374 v. NLRB, 331 F 2d 839, 55 LRRM 2913 (CA DC, 1964).
[51] American Ship Bldg. Co. v. NLRB, 380 US 300, 58 LRRM 2672 (1965). The Court was unanimous in its reversal, with Mr. Justice Stewart writing for the majority. Mr. Justice Goldberg, joined by the Chief Justice, and Mr. Justice White concurred in separate opinions.
[52] 380 US at 314.

As to Section 8 (a) (1), the Court rejected the Board's view that an offensive lockout necessarily interferes with protected rights of employees to bargain collectively and to strike. The lockout was "intended to resist the demands made of [the employer] in the negotiations and to secure modification of these demands." [53] Absent any showing of anti-union animus on the part of the employer, of which there "was no evidence and no finding," [54] such an intention on the part of the employer is not "in any way inconsistent with the employees' rights to bargain collectively." [55] Nor, declared the majority, did the lockout interfere with the right to strike, since the right to strike "is the right to cease work—nothing more," [56] and "there is nothing in the statute which would imply that the right to strike 'carries with it' the right exclusively to determine the timing and duration of all work stoppages." [57]

Rejecting the Board's view that an offensive lockout violated Section 8 (a) (3), the Court stated that a finding of such a violation requires a specific showing "that the employer acted for a proscribed purpose." [58] The Court also discarded the Board's narrow doctrine of economic justification, observing that "the Board itself has always recognized that certain 'operative' or 'economic' purposes would justify a lockout. But the Board erred in ruling that only these purposes will remove a lockout from the ambit of section 8 (a) (3), for *that section requires an intention to discourage union membership or otherwise discriminate against the union.*" [59] Mr. Justice Stewart noted that there was not the slightest evidence, and certainly "no finding, that the employer was actuated by a desire to discourage membership in the union as distinguished from a desire to affect the outcome of the particular negotiations. . . ." [60] The Court therefore concluded that where the employer's proven intention in locking out his employees "is

---

53 *Id.* at 309.
54 *Id.* at 308.
55 *Id.* at 309.
56 *Id.* at 310.
57 *Ibid.*
58 *Id.* at 313.
59 *Ibid.* (emphasis added). *See* Southern Beverage Co., Inc., 171 NLRB No. 128, 71 LRRM 1429 (1969), where the Board found that the lockout was motivated by a desire to destroy the union.
60 *Ibid.*

merely to bring about a settlement of a labor dispute on favorable terms, no violation of §8 (a) (3) is shown." [61]

The Court, however, tempered the requirement that there must be a finding of unlawful intent as a condition to the finding of an 8 (a) (3) violation. It recognized that "there are some practices which are inherently so prejudicial to union interests and so devoid of significant economic justification that no specific evidence of intent to discourage union membership or other anti-union animus is required. In some cases . . . the employer's conduct carries with it an inference of unlawful intention . . . ," [62] citing *Radio Officers'* [63] and *Erie Resistor.*[64] But it observed that the lockout in question "does not fall into that category of cases . . . in which the Board may truncate its inquiry into employer motivation." [65] The Court declared that

> . . . use of the lockout does not carry with it any necessary implication that the employer acted to discourage union membership or otherwise discriminate against union members as such. The purpose and effect of the lockout was only to bring pressure upon the union to modify its demands. . . . [I]t does not appear that the natural tendency of the lockout is severely to discourage union membership. . . .[66]

Did the Court's broad exculpation of the lockout mean that an offensive lockout may also be used as an economic weapon in a pre-impasse situation? Mr. Justice Stewart was careful to point out that the only issue before the Court was the use of a *"temporary layoff . . .* to bring economic pressure to bear in support of the employer's bargaining position, *after an impasse* has been

---

61 *Ibid.* In *Bagel Bakers Council,* 174 NLRB No. 101, 70 LRRM 1301 (1969), the Board found a lockout used to support bad-faith bargaining to be unlawful regardless of whether an impasse had occurred. *See also* Port Norris Express Co., 174 NLRB No. 106, 70 LRRM 1339 (1969).

62 *Id.* at 311-312.

63 Radio Officers Union v. NLRB, 347 US 17, 33 LRRM 2417 (1954). For a general discussion of this case, see Chapter 6 *supra.*

64 NLRB v. Erie Resistor Corp., 373 US 221, 53 LRRM 2121 (1963). For a general discussion of this case, see Chapter 19 *supra.*

65 380 US at 312.

66 *Ibid.* Relying upon *American Ship Bldg.,* the Ninth Circuit reversed a Board finding that an employer violated §§8 (a) (1) and 8 (a) (2) by locking out employees following an impasse in bargaining that led to a split in the union ranks. NLRB v. Golden State Bottling Co., 353 F 2d 667, 60 LRRM 2553 (CA 9, 1966). The Court of Appeals reasoned that an otherwise lawful lockout is not made an unfair labor practice merely because it disrupts the orderly internal functioning of the union. Even though the employer had committed other unfair labor practices, the requisite unlawful intent was found lacking. The Board has applied the *American Ship* doctrine in the following cases, holding that the lockout in each was lawful: Union Carbide Corp., 165 NLRB No. 26, 65 LRRM 1282 (1967), *affirmed sub nom.,* 405

reached." [67] Mr. Justice White, however, expressed concern that the majority's reasoning would permit a pre-impasse lockout. On the other hand, Mr. Justice Goldberg was mindful to point out in his concurring opinion that the "Court itself seems to recognize that there is a difference. . . ." [68]

F 2d 1111, 69 LRRM 2838 (CA DC, 1968); Wantagh Auto Sales, Inc., 177 NLRB No. 19, 72 LRRM 1541 (1969); Guardian Glass Co., Inc., 172 NLRB No. 49, 68 LRRM 1323 (1968); U.S. Sugar Corp., 169 NLRB No. 4, 67 LRRM 1106 (1968); Ruberoid Co., 167 NLRB 987, 66 LRRM 1252 (1967); Delhi-Taylor Ref. Div., 167 NLRB 115, 65 LRRM 1744 (1967). In Laclede Gas Co., 173 NLRB No. 35, 69 LRRM 1316, *remanded*, 421 F 2d 610, 73 LRRM 2364 (CA 8, 1970), the Board treated a partial lockout following a bargaining impasse as a unilateral change in working conditions in violation of the employer's duty to bargain under §8(a)(5). (*See* Chapter 11 *supra*.) But the Eighth Circuit reversed and remanded, holding that the partial lockout, even though not in accordance with the prevailing seniority practice, was not an unlawful refusal to bargain. The court remanded the case for NLRB consideration of whether the lockout constituted interference and discrimination under §§8(A)(1) and (3). In *Hess Oil & Chemical Corp.*, 167 NLRB 115, 65 LRRM 1744 (1967), *enforced*, 415 F 2d 440, 72 LRRM 2132 (CA 5, 1969), the Board found a bargaining lockout to be lawful and not a violation of §8(a)(3), notwithstanding that the employer violated §8(a)(5) by insisting that certain employees be excluded from the bargaining unit (*see* Chapter 16 *supra*). See Note, *New Concepts in Interference & Discrimination Under the NLRA—The Legacy of American Ship Building & Great Dane*, 70 COLUM. L. REV. 81 (1970).

[67] 380 at 308 (emphasis added).

[68] 380 US at 337. Subsequent to *American Ship Bldg.*, the Sixth Circuit, in Detroit Newspaper Publishers Ass'n v. NLRB, 346 F 2d 527, 59 LRRM 2401 (CA 6, 1965), indicated its willingness to hold a pre-impasse lockout lawful; the Supreme Court, however, vacated, *per curiam*, and remanded the case to the Board for further consideration "in light of American Ship Building." Local 372, Teamsters v. Detroit Newspaper Publishers Association, 382 US 374, 61 LRRM 2147 (1966). The Board's final determination of the case avoided answering the question relating to pre-impasse lockouts, for it found that "both parties viewed their negotiations as being deadlocked on key issues," therefore, if an impasse had been reached, the *American Ship Bldg.* doctrine obviously controlled. The Board acknowledged that "American Ship . . . has obliterated, as a matter of law, the line previously drawn by the Board between offensive and defensive lockouts." Evening News Ass'n, 166 NLRB No. 6, 65 LRRM 1425 (1967).

In another case involving the same group of employers, Detroit Newspaper Publishers Assn. v. NLRB, 372 F 2d 569, 572, 64 LRRM 2403 (1967), the Sixth Circuit, in dicta, stated that "where the lockout is to support an employer's legitimate bargaining position, he could no more be deprived of its use than the right to strike could be taken away from the employees. . . . While American Ship Building actually involved an impasse in bargaining, the [majority] opinion of the Court . . . was not so limited." For a discussion of this case, see Chapter 9 *supra*. *Cf.* American Stores Packing Co., 142 NLRB 711, 53 LRRM 1137 (1963) in which a pre-impasse lockout was held unlawful. Although originally affirming in NLRB v. American Stores Packing Co., 58 LRRM 2635 (1965), the Tenth Circuit Court of Appeals later vacated its previous decision and remanded the case to the Board for reconsideration in light of *American Ship Bldg.*, 351 F 2d 308, 60 LRRM 2128 (CA 10, 1965). The Board, however, deemed *American Ship Bldg.* inapplicable because the instant case involved a prelockout refusal to bargain by the employer. It therefore reaffirmed without considering the pre-impasse question. 158 NLRB 620, 62 LRRM 1093 (1966).

In *Darling & Co.*[69] the Board did hold that a pre-impasse lock-out occurring during negotiations was not necessarily unlawful. It said that a determination would have to be made on a case-by-case basis, but that in this instance there was no violation because the parties had engaged in extensive good faith bargaining, the union had discussed striking at a time of its own choosing, and the employer's business was of a highly seasonal nature. The Board indicated that absence of impasse was but a single factor to be considered. Finding no antiunion animus in the employer's motive, it declared that the lockout was neither inherently prejudicial to union interests nor devoid of significant economic justification.

The Supreme Court left open the questions of whether replacements may be hired in a bargaining lockout of the *American Ship Bldg.* type and, if so, whether they may be permanent replacements. Mr. Justice Stewart expressly disclaimed intimation of any view on the subject.[70] In *Inland Trucking Co.*[71] the Board held three employers in violation of Section 8(a)(3) when they utilized temporary replacements to perform the work of locked-out employees. The Board determined that there was no substantial business purpose sufficient to justify the action, even though the employers could have hired replacements had the union chosen to strike.

B. The New Defensive Multi-Employer Lockout

Brown Food[72] broadened the concept of the multi-employer lockout substantially beyond the limitations of *Buffalo Linen.*[73] Like *Buffalo Linen*, *Brown Food* involved a whipsaw strike in a multi-employer bargaining unit. The union struck one member of the employer association, and the other members retaliated by locking out their employees. The essential facts of the two cases

[69] 171 NLRB No. 95, 68 LRRM 1133 (1968), *enforced sub nom.*, Lane v. NLRB, 418 F 2d 1208, 72 LRRM 2439 (CA DC, 1969). Charges alleging violation of §§8 (a) (1) and 8 (a) (3) were dismissed (violation of §8 (a) (5) had not been alleged). The case is also discussed in Chapter 11 *supra*.
[70] 380 US at 308 n. 8. His reference to NLRB v. Mackay Radio & Telegraph Co., 304 US 333, 2 LRRM 610 (1938), called attention to the employers' right to make permanent replacements of strikers in order to protect and continue a business during an economic strike. *See* Chapter 19 *supra*.
[71] 179 NLRB No. 56, 72 LRRM 1486 (1969).
[72] NLRB v. Brown, dba Brown Food Store, 380 US 278, 58 LRRM 2663 (1965).
[73] Note 31 *supra*.

differ, however, in that in *Brown Food* the employers continued to carry on their business by using temporary employees.[74]

Both the Board and the court of appeals agreed [75] that the case was governed by *Buffalo Linen,* in which the Supreme Court had characterized the problem as one of "balancing . . . conflicting legitimate interests." [76] But the Board saw a "critical difference" [77] from *Buffalo Linen* in the hiring of temporary employees to replace the locked-out employees. The Board reasoned that by so doing the employers were not acting "to protect the integrity of the employer unit, but for the purpose of inhibiting a lawful strike. In short, the lockout in these circumstances ceases to be 'defensive' and becomes retaliatory." [78] The Tenth Circuit reversed,[79] declaring that "the acts of [the employers] in hiring replacements . . . do not carry such indicia of intent as to warrant an inference of unlawful motive. . . ." [80]

The Supreme Court affirmed the reversal of the Board, holding that the conduct of employers in locking out employees in defense against a whipsaw strike and the hiring of temporary replacements does not constitute a *per se* violation of Section 8 (a) (1) or 8 (a) (3). Having found no conduct on the part of the employers which could be interpreted as evidence of anti-union motivation, the Court equated the hiring of temporary replacements after a lockout to certain other lawful "economic weapons" used by employers. Such weapons may "either interfere in some measure with concerted employee activities, or . . . [be] in some degree discriminatory and discourage union membership," [81] but are not violative of the Act. The majority, through Mr. Justice Brennan, reminded the Board "that the Act does not constitute the Board as an 'arbiter of the sort of economic weapons the parties can use in seeking to gain acceptance of their bargaining demands.' " [82] However, the Court granted that "where the employer conduct is demon-

[74] All of the temporary replacements were informed by the employers that their employment would be discontinued when the whipsaw strike ended.
[75] 380 US at 281.
[76] 353 US at 96.
[77] Brown Food Store, 137 NLRB 73, 77, 50 LRRM 1046 (1962).
[78] *Id.* at 76.
[79] NLRB v. Brown, 319 F 2d 7, 53 LRRM 2534 (CA 10, 1963). The panel split two to one.
[80] *Id.* at 11.
[81] 380 US at 283.
[82] *Ibid.,* citing NLRB v. Insurance Agents, 361 US 477, 497, 45 LRRM 2704 (1960).

strably destructive of employee rights and is not justified by the service of significant or important business ends," [83] no inquiry need be made into the employer's motivation.[84] The Court rejected the Board's conclusion that the hiring of temporary replacements in the circumstances of this case "carried its own indicia of unlawful intent. . . ." [85] It noted that "[e]ven the Board concedes that an employer may legitimately blunt the effectiveness of an anticipated strike by stockpiling inventories, readjusting contract schedules, or transferring work from one plant to another, even if he thereby makes himself 'virtually strikeproof' . . . [and] he may in various circumstances use the lockout as a legitimate economic weapon." [86] The Court, therefore, concluded:

> We do not see how the continued operations of respondents and their use of temporary replacements any more implies hostile motivation, nor how it is inherently more destructive of employee rights, than the lockout itself. Rather, the compelling inference is that this was all part and parcel of respondents' defensive measure to preserve the multi-employer group in the face of the whipsaw strike.[87]

The Court also refused to accept the Board's assertion that hostile motivation could be inferred from the failure of the employers to use their regular employees, who the Board had found were willing to work at the employers' terms.[88] It explained that requiring the employers to use their regular employees in order to continue doing business "would force them into the position of aiding and abetting the success of the whipsaw strike and consequently would render 'largely illusory' . . . the right of lockout recognized by *Buffalo Linen.*" [89]

The Court admitted that "[t]he pressures on the employees are necessarily greater when none of the union employees are working and the stores remain open." [90] But this was attributed to "the

---

83 380 US at 282.
84 *Citing* NLRB v. Erie Resistor Corp., 373 US 221, 53 LRRM 2121 (1963), and NLRB v. Burnup & Sims, Inc., 379 US 21, 57 LRRM 2385 (1964). *See* NLRB v. Great Dane Trailers, Inc., 388 US 26, 65 LRRM 2465 (1967), discussed in Chapter 6 *supra*, for the Court's further analysis of this §8(a)(3) formula.
85 380 US at 282.
86 380 US at 283.
87 *Id.* at 284. For treatment of multi-employer bargaining units generally, *see* Chapter 9 *supra*.
88 137 NLRB at 76.
89 380 US at 285.
90 *Id.* at 286.

Local's inability to make effective use of the whipsaw tactic." [91] The Court said that "any resulting tendency to discourage union membership is comparatively remote, and that this use of temporary personnel constitutes a measure reasonably adapted to the effectuation of a legitimate business end." [92]

The employers in *Brown Food* thus satisfied the rule which Mr. Justice Brennan summarized in these broad terms:

> When the resulting harm to employee rights is . . . comparatively slight and a substantial and legitimate business end is served, the employer's conduct is prima facie lawful. Under these circumstances the finding of an unfair labor practice under §8 (a) (3) requires a showing of improper subjective intent.[93]

On the issue of employee replacement, the Court again [94] avoided discussing whether the decision would have been the same had the employers hired permanent replacements for the locked-out employees.[95] Mr. Justice Goldberg, in his concurring opinion, expressed "grave doubts as to whether locking out and hiring permanent replacements is justified by any legitimate interest of the nonstruck employers." He pointed out that *"Buffalo Linen* makes clear that the test in such a situation is not whether parity is achieved between struck and nonstruck employers, but, rather, whether the nonstruck employer's actions are necessary to counteract the whipsaw effects of the strike and to preserve the employer bargaining unit." [96]

---

91 *Ibid.*

92 *Id.* at 288.

93 *Id.* at 289. For a discussion of the effect of this rule on the requirement of anti-union motivation under §§8 ((a) (1) and (3), see Oberer, *The Scienter Factor in Sections 8(a)(1) and (3) of the Labor Act: of Balancing, Hostile Motive, Dogs and Tails,* 52 CORNELL L. Q. 491, 506-510 (1967).

94 *See* notes 70 and 71 and accompanying text.

95 Mr. Justice Brennan raised but did not answer the question of "whether the case would be the same had the struck employer exercised its prerogative to hire permanent replacements under . . . [the] rule in Labor Board v. Mackay Radio & Telegraph Co., 304 US 333 [2 LRRM 610], and the nonstruck employers had then hired permanent replacements for their locked-out employees." 380 US at 292, n. 6. *See* Chapter 19 *supra.*

96 380 US at 293-294. Oberer, *supra* note 1, at 224-228, considered the permanent replacement situation posed by *American Ship Bldg.* and *Brown Food* and suggested that it falls "within the *Erie Resistor* exception to the requirement of independent evidence of hostile motivation, in the bargaining lockout and, probably also, multi-employer, defensive lockout situations. While the hiring of permanent replacements may arguably serve a justifiable employer purpose, its potential for destruction of Section 7 rights is sufficiently great to be said to carry 'its own indicia of unlawful intent,' as with the granting of superseniority—the more so since the employer's need for replacements is the product of his voluntary act in locking out." *See* Chapter 6 *supra.*

Since *Brown Food,* the Board has had occasion to apply the Court's new rule to lockout situations where different "business ends" have been in issue. In *Acme Markets, Inc.*[97] the union engaged in a whipsaw strike against all the Acme stores within a multi-employer bargaining unit. Acme, however, also owned other stores outside the unit, which were in competition with unit stores owned by other members of the unit. The other members responded by locking out their employees pursuant to a defensive lockout agreement, admittedly lawful under *Buffalo Linen.*[98] In turn, *Acme* shut down its nonunit stores.[99]

The Board found, by analogy to *Brown Food,* that even though the locked-out employees were not in the unit, their lockout "was designed to serve a legitimate business end of preserving the integrity of the multi-employer unit." [100] The Board found no antiunion animus in the action. It pointed to Acme's reimbursement of wages to the employees of the shut-down stores as evidence that the employer's motive was not to coerce these employees in the exercise of their Section 7 rights. The complaint was therefore dismissed.[101]

In *Friedland Painting Co.,*[102] however, the Board indicated a limitation on the concept of legitimate business purpose. Friedland was a painting contractor who was part of a multi-employer bargaining unit within the jurisdiction of Local 1221. He also operated in jurisdictions of other local unions, including Local 144, although he was not a member of any multi-employer bargaining association except the one that bargained with Local 1221. When Local 144 called a strike, the employer was not doing any work in 144's territory, although he was using nine members of Local 144 on a job in 1221's territory. Claiming that he had a legitimate business end to protect because he often worked in 144's territory under the union agreement prevailing in that territory, the employer laid off the nine Local 144 members. The Board found the action violative of Sections 8 (a) (1) and (3), declaring that allowing such a lockout

---

97 156 NLRB 1452, 61 LRRM 1281 (1966).
98 Note 31 *supra.*
99 Acme continued to pay regular compensation to the employees of these stores.
100 156 NLRB at 1457.
101 Member Brown concurred but with the qualification that in his opinion the employer's closing to the public while continuing to pay wages to the displaced employees does not constitute a lockout. *Id.* at 1459.
102 158 NLRB 571, 62 LRRM 1085 (1966).

... would lead to a proliferation of the use of the lockout so as to render it lawful in any situation where the employer making use of it against members of a certain union could arguably be affected economically by the outcome of particular negotiations between that union and another employer. It would be an invitation to industrial chaos rather than to industrial stability which the Act is designed to foster.[103]

The Third Circuit affirmed,[104] holding that specific evidence of intent to discourage union membership or of other anti-union animus was not required, because the employer "had no significant employer interest to protect or advance," [105] citing *American Ship Bldg.* and *Brown Food.* The court thus indicated that specific anti-union motivation, which the Supreme Court had discussed in *Brown Food,*[106] is not a necessary ingredient to a finding that a lockout is unlawful where the employer does not have a legitimate business interest to protect. The *Friedland* case, therefore, suggests indicia of the kind of business reasons for a lockout which the Board may not deem legitimate.

A later decision indicates that where a lockout fails to satisfy all the requirements of a multi-employer defensive lockout, its lawfulness may be sought in the *American Ship Bldg.* doctrine. In *Weyerhaeuser Co.*[107] the Board found a multi-employer unit and a legitimate utilization of a defensive lockout to counter a whipsaw strike. The Board indicated, however, that since *American Ship Bldg.* the validity of the lockout need not depend on a finding that a formal multi-employer unit existed. A bargaining impasse had been reached; therefore, each employer member of the "informal" bargaining group was independently "entitled to lock out its employees in order 'to affect the outcome of the particular negotiations in which it was engaged.' " [108]

---

103 *Ibid.*
104 NLRB v. Friedland Painting Co., 377 F 2d 983, 65 LRRM 2119 (CA 3, 1967).
105 *Ibid.*
106 *See* notes 63 and 93 *supra.*
107 166 NLRB No. 7, 65 LRRM 1428 (1967). The DC Circuit *affirmed, sub nom.,* Western States Regional Council v. NLRB, 398 F 2d 770, 68 LRRM 2506 (CA DC, 1968), because of the existence of a *Buffalo Linen* type multi-employer unit, without passing on the applicability of the *American Ship* rationale. *Cf.* News Union of Baltimore v. Hearst Corp., 278 F Supp 423, 67 LRRM 2303 (DC Md, 1968) (layoff of employees not a violation of provision in collective bargaining agreement prohibiting lockouts where layoff resulted from defensive lockout of other employees in the multi-employer bargaining unit).
108 Weyerhaeuser Co., *supra* note 107.

Chapter 21

PICKETING FOR ORGANIZATION AND RECOGNITION

I. BACKGROUND

Federal policy has undergone distinct changes with respect to the right of a union to picket for recognitional or organizational purposes. Although the original National Labor Relations Act did not address itself to this activity, the Norris-LaGuardia Act provided some protection to picketing for either purpose. However, after 1935 it became apparent that the law "in good conscience" could not protect such activity by a minority union seeking recognition and at the same time compel an employer to bargain with another union as the certified representative.[1]

A. Taft-Hartley Amendments

Following the passage of the Taft-Hartley amendments, it was suggested that picket-line pressure to force employees to join or support a union was outlawed by the combined effect of the altered Section 7 and Section 8(b)(1)(A).[2] Section 7 had been amended to give a statutory basis to the employee's right not to join a labor organization. Section 8(b)(1)(A) had been added making it an unfair labor practice for a union to restrain or coerce employees in the exercise of Section 7 rights. It was argued that the broad proscription on union activity in Section 8(b)(1)(A) encompassed a ban on picketing by minority unions for recognition or

---

[1] A. Cox & D. Bok, Labor Law Cases and Materials 685 (6th ed., 1965).

[2] *Ibid.* §8(b)(1)(A) provides that "It shall be an unfair labor practice for a labor organization or its agents to restrain or coerce employees in the exercise of the rights guaranteed in §7." For a discussion of the amendment to §7 adding the right to refrain from joining or supporting unions see Chapter 5 *supra*.

organization. Nevertheless, for a number of years after 1947 no General Counsel would issue a complaint on this theory.[3]

B. *Curtis Bros.*

In 1957 the Board in *Curtis Bros.*[4] reversed its position and held that recognition, as distinguished from organizational, picketing by a minority union violated Section 8(b)(1)(A) because of its coercive impact upon employees. The District of Columbia Circuit set aside the Board's order,[5] and the Supreme Court affirmed the court of appeals.[6] The Court held that any prohibition upon peaceful picketing would impede the right to strike and could be sustained only if the prohibition was specifically provided for in the Act itself. The Court emphasized the protection accorded the right to strike in Section 13 of the Act, which "cautions against an expansive reading" adversely affecting the right to strike unless "congressional purpose to give it that meaning persuasively appears either from the structure or history of the statute."[7] The Court noted that the legislative history of §8(b)(1)(A) was concerned en-

---

[3] *See* Administrative Rulings of NLRB General Counsel, Case No. 1069, 35 LRRM 1246 (1954); McGuiness, THE NEW FRONTIER NLRB 176 (1963). In *United Mine Workers (Tungsten Mining Corp.),* 106 NLRB 903, 32 LRRM 1576 (1953), a complaint had issued where a §8(b)(1)(A) was charged as a derivative violation of §8(b)(4)(C) but it was dismissed on that ground.

[4] 119 NLRB 232, 41 LRRM 1025 (1957). The Board reasoned that: ". . . [t]he important fact of the situation is that the union seeks to cause economic loss to the business during the period that the employer refuses to comply with the union's demands.

"And the employees who choose to continue working, while the union is applying this economic hurt to the employer, cannot escape a share of the damage caused to the business on which their livelihood depends. Damage to the employer during such picketing is a like damage to his employees. That the pressure thus exerted upon the employees—depriving them of the opportunity to work and be paid—is a form of coercion cannot be gainsaid. . . .

"There can be no more direct deprivation of the employees' freedom of choice than to impose upon them a collective bargaining agent they have not chosen or have expressly rejected." 119 NLRB at 236-237.

[5] Teamsters Local 639 v. NLRB, 274 F 2d 551, 43 LRRM 2156 (CA DC, 1958).

[6] NLRB v. Teamsters Local 639, 362 US 274, 45 LRRM 2975 (1960).

[7] 362 US at 282. This view of §13 was reiterated in *NLRB* v. *Fruit and Vegetable Packers (Tree Fruits),* 377 US 58, 55 LRRM 2961 (1964) and is consistent with the Court's earlier decision in *NLRB* v. *International Rice Milling Co.,* 341 US 665, 28 LRRM 2105 (1951).

tirely with activities "tinged with violence, duress or reprisal" and not with peaceful picketing.[8]

C. Enactment of Section 8(b)(7)

During the period between the circuit court's decision and that of the Supreme Court in *Curtis Bros.*, subsection 7 was added to Section 8(b) by the Landrum-Griffin Act.[9] The 1959 legislation

---

[8] 362 US at 286. ". . . we hold, that Congress in the Taft-Hartley Act authorized the Board to regulate peaceful 'recognitional' picketing only when it is employed to accomplish objectives specified in 8(b)(4); and that 8(b)(1)(A) is a grant of power to the Board limited to proceed against Union tactics involving violence, intimidation, and reprisal or threats thereof—conduct involving more than the general pressures upon persons employed by the affected employers implicit in economic strikes." *Id.* at 290. For general treatment of §8(b)(1)(A), *see* Chapter 5 *supra.*

[9] *See* Chapter 4 *supra* for general discussion of the Landrum-Griffin amendments. Section 8(b)(7) provides:

"It shall be an unfair labor practice for a labor organization or its agents to picket or cause to be picketed, or threaten to picket or cause to be picketed, any employer where an object thereof is forcing or requiring an employer to recognize or bargain with a labor organization as the representative of his employees, or forcing or requiring the employees of an employer to accept or select such labor organization as their collective bargaining representative, unless such labor organization is currently certified as the representative of such employees:

"(A) where the employer has lawfully recognized in accordance with this Act any other labor organization and a question concerning representation may not appropriately be raised under section 9(c) of this Act,

"(B) where within the preceding twelve months a valid election under section 9(c) of this Act has been conducted, or

"(C) where such picketing has been conducted without a petition under section 9(c) being filed within a reasonable period of time not to exceed thirty days from the commencement of such picketing: Provided, That when such a petition has been filed the Board shall forthwith, without regard to the provisions of section 9(c)(1) or the absence of a showing of a substantial interest on the part of the labor organization, direct an election in such unit as the Board finds to be appropriate and shall certify the results thereof: Provided further, That nothing in this subparagraph (C) shall be construed to prohibit any picketing or other publicity for the purpose of truthfully advising the public (including consumers) that an employer does not employ members of, or have a contract with, a labor organization, unless an effect of such picketing is to induce any individual employed by any other person in the course of his employment, not to pick up, deliver or transport any goods or not to perform any services.

"Nothing in this paragraph (7) shall be construed to permit any act which would otherwise be an unfair labor practice under this section 8(b)."

For detailed discussions of §8(b)(7) *see* Meltzer, *Organizational Picketing and the NLRB: Five on a Seesaw*, 30 U. CHI. L. REV. 78 (1962); Dunau, *Some Aspects of the Current Interpretation of Section 8(b)(7)*, 52 GEO. L. J. 220 (1964); Shawe, *Federal Regulation of Recognition Picketing*, 52 GEO. L. J. 248 (1964); Cox, *The Landrum-Griffin Amendments to the National Labor Relations Act*, 44 MINN. L. REV. 257 (1959); Fairweather, *An Evaluation of the Changes in Taft-Hartley*, 54 NW.U. L. REV. 711 (1960); Richards, *Some Comments on the Nature of the 8(b)(7) Prohibition*, LABOR LAW DEVELOPMENTS (14th Annual Institute, Southwestern Legal Foundation) 51 (1968); For a collection of many early articles and congressional views on this topic, *see* Slovenko, ed., SYMPOSIUM ON THE LABOR MANAGEMENT REPORTING AND DISCLOSURE ACT, 12-130, 926-1018 (1961), referred to as "Symposium."

was, in large part, a response to the disclosures of the McClellan Committee concerning certain types of recognition and organizational picketing which were labeled "blackmail" or "extortion" picketing.[10] Abolishing the cumbersome distinctions between organizational and recognitional picketing, Section 8(b)(7) proscribed picketing for either purpose where another union was lawfully recognized by the employer under Section 9,[11] where a valid election had been held within the preceding 12 months, or where no petition for an election had been filed "within a reasonable period of time not to exceed thirty days from the commencement of such picketing."

Section 8(b)(7) emerged as a legislative compromise after "intense conflict between competing interests."[12] Congressional debate centered on conflict between the need to correct abuses of picketing and the resistance to curtailment of labor's traditional weapon for self-advancement. While legislation aimed at correcting abuses was enacted, none of the protagonists fully prevailed. The compromise effect of the legislation is reflected in what was clearly recognized at the time as "inadequacies of . . . draftsmanship."[13] The resulting language has been described as "confusing"[14] and even "murky."[15]

Significantly, the Supreme Court's decision in *Curtis Bros.* relied, in part, upon the 1959 amendments as a general manifestation of congressional intent with respect to Section 8(b)(1)(A). The Court noted that the limited restrictions imposed by the passage of Section 8(b)(7) indicated a legislative intent not to make un-

---

[10] See "Symposium," *supra* note 9, 12-130; LEGISLATIVE HISTORY OF THE LABOR MANAGEMENT REPORTING AND DISCLOSURE ACT OF 1959 (1959). *See also* Hod Carriers Local 840 (C.A. Blinne Const. Co.), 135 NLRB 1153, 49 LRRM 1638 (1962), for detailed analysis by a divided Board as to the structure, legislative history, and intent of §8(b) (7).

[11] See Meltzer, *supra* note 9, 81-83.

[12] NLRB v. Suffolk County District Council of Carpenters, 387 F 2d 170, 174, 67 LRRM 2012 (CA 2, 1967). For a discussion of the legislative history of many aspects of the subsection, see *Dayton Typographical Union No. 57* v. *NLRB*, 326 F 2d 634, 54 LRRM 2535 (CA DC, 1963), and *Blinne*, *supra* note 10.

[13] Cox, *supra* note 9, at 270. *See also* Dunau, *supra* note 9, 220, 221, where the writer states that "the obvious compromise character of Section 8 (b) (7) as well as a certain opacity in its draftsmanship creates difficult interpretive problems."

[14] *Supra* note 12.

[15] Meltzer, *supra* note 9, at 81.

lawful all recognition picketing by a minority union under Section 8(b)(1)(A), but only such picketing that falls within the restrictions contained in Sections 8(b)(7) and 8(b)(4).[16]

II. DEFINITION OF 'PICKETING'

The prohibitions of Section 8(b)(7) apply only to picketing or causing or threatening to picket, but the Act does not attempt to define the terms "picket" and "picketing." The Act did not contain the terms until they appeared in the 1959 amendments in Sections 8(b)(4) and 8(b)(7).[17]

A. Neither Patrolling nor Carrying Placards a Requisite

To constitute picketing for the purposes of Section 8(b)(7), it is not essential that persons march in front of the employer's premises carrying picket signs. Less orthodox methods of picketing may fall within its proscription. For example, the Board has applied

---

[16] §8 (b) (4) reads as follows: "It shall be an unfair labor practice for a labor organization or its agents—

. . .

" (4) (i) to engage in, or to induce or encourage any individual employed by any person engaged in commerce or in an industry affecting commerce to engage in, a strike or a refusal in the course of his employment to use, manufacture, process, transport, or otherwise handle or work on any goods, articles, materials, or commodities or to perform any services; or (ii) to threaten, coerce, or restrain any person engaged in commerce or in an industry affecting commerce, where in either case an object thereof is:

" (A) forcing or requiring any employer or self-employed person to join any labor or employer organization or to enter into any agreement which is prohibited by section 8 (e) ;

" (B) forcing or requiring any person to cease using, selling, handling, transporting, or otherwise dealing in the products of any other producer, processor, or manufacturer, or to cease doing business with any other person, or forcing or requiring any other employer to recognize or bargain with a labor organization as the representative of his employees unless such labor organization has been certified as the representative of such employees under the provisions of section 9: *Provided,* That nothing contained in this clause (B) shall be construed to make unlawful, where not otherwise unlawful, any primary strike or primary picketing;

" (C) forcing or requiring any employer to recognize or bargain with a particular labor organization as the representative of his employees if another labor organization has been certified as the representative of such employees under the provisions of section 9;

" (D) forcing or requiring any employer to assign particular work to employees in a particular labor organization or in a particular trade, craft, or class rather than to employees in another labor organization or in another trade, craft, or class, unless such employer is failing to conform to an order or certification of the Board determining the bargaining representative for employees performing such work. . . ."

See Chapters 23 and 25 *infra.*

[17] *See* Chapters 3 and 4 *supra* for a discussion of the legislative enactment of §8(b)(7) and §8 (b) (4) .

Section 8(b)(7) to persons who placed signs in a snowbank abutting the employer's premises, watched from the warmth of nearby cars, and emerged from the cars to answer questions about the signs or to speak to delivery drivers.[18] In affirming the Board's application, the Second Circuit stated that "[m]ovement is thus not requisite . . ." and that the "activity was none the less picketing because the union chose to bisect it, placing the material elements in snowbanks but protecting the human elements from the rigors of . . . winter . . . until a delivery truck approached. . . ."[19] The Board took the same view of affixing "On Strike" signs to poles and trees in front of the plant while union representatives and strikers remained in their cars a short distance away, ostensibly to see that the signs were not removed. But the Second Circuit remanded this case for consideration of the need for confrontation as an element of picketing since there was insufficient evidence that persons in the cars could be identified as union representatives or that they could even be seen by employees, customers, or suppliers.[20] The court analogized the latter possibility to a situation where union representatives merely post signs and stay out of sight in a nearby house, in which case the Board "could not reasonably characterize the activity as picketing."[21] The test suggested by the court was whether the presence of union representatives in the car "was intended to and did have substantially the same significance for persons entering the employer's premises as if they had remained with the signs, or was only a necessary precaution to safeguard the signs."[22]

In *Stoltze Land and Lumber Co.*[23] the Board applied the following test:

> The important feature of picketing appears to be the posting by a labor organization or by strikers of individuals at the approach to

---

18 Teamsters Local 182 (Woodward Motors, Inc.), 135 NLRB 851, 49 LRRM 1576 (1962), *enforced,* 314 F 2d 53, 52 LRRM 2354 (CA 2, 1963).

19 314 F 2d at 58.

20 United Furniture Workers (Jamestown Sterling Corp.), 146 NLRB 474, 55 LRRM 1344 (1964), *remanded,* 337 F 2d 936, 57 LRRM 2347 (CA 2, 1964).

21 337 F 2d at 940. *Compare* Phillips v. Ladies Garment Workers, 45 LRRM 2363 (MD Tenn, 1959), where the posting of signs similar to the ones used by pickets but without the physical presence of any person carrying signs was held to constitute picketing.

22 *Ibid.*

23 Lumber & Sawmill Workers Local 2797 (Stoltze Land & Lbr. Co.), 156 NLRB 388, 394, 61 LRRM 1046 (1965). *See* United Mine Workers & Dist. 12 (Truax-Traer Coal Co.), 177 NLRB No. 27, 72 LRRM 1634 (1969) (congregation of men at job site without placards deemed picketing).

a place of business to accomplish a purpose which advances the cause of the union, such as keeping employees away from work or keeping customers away from the employer's business.

The *Stoltze* criteria were satisfied in *Kansas Color Press, Inc.*,[24] where an "on strike" sign was placed on a trailer in front of the company premises and strikers gathered to use the facilities of the trailer or to give out handbills to passers-by. Moreover, the presence of large groups of strikers and union representatives in front of the employer's premises may constitute picketing, even in the absence of an identifying sign, if the organizational appeal for action against the employer is conveyed independently of any written message.[25]

B. Handbilling as "Picketing"

The issue of handbilling as picketing has arisen in the context of both Section 8(b)(4) cases and Section 8(b)(7) cases, with contrary results. In *Lohman Sales Co.*[26] truthful handbilling without persons marching and without placards was held to come within the meaning of "publicity other than picketing" in the second proviso to Section 8(b)(4). But in the *Stoltze* case,[27] a Section 8(b)(7) proceeding, the distribution of handbills in front of the employer's premises was held to constitute picketing. In that case, handbilling continued after placard picketing had stopped, and leaflets were distributed to customers, employees, and prospective employees. Moreover, the expulsion of a member who returned to work was found to be consistent only with the maintenance of a strike picket line. Thus, "what the union was doing after April 6, 1965, (handbilling) was just as much picketing as what it was doing when it carried signs."[28] In *Kansas Color Press, Inc.*,[29] a Section 8(b)(7) case, an attempt was made to reconcile the *Lohman* and the *Stoltze* decisions on their facts without regard to the sub-

---

[24] Lawrence Typographical Union, Local 570 (Kansas Color Press, Inc.), 169 NLRB No. 65, 67 LRRM 1166 (1968), *enforced*, 402 F 2d 452, 69 LRRM 2591 (CA 10, 1968). The trial examiner's decision contains an exhaustive discussion of the issue. For a further discussion of the case and its procedural history, *see* note 120 *infra*.
[25] United Mine Workers, District 30 (Terry Elkhorn Mining Co.), 163 NLRB 562, 64 LRRM 1394 (1967). The trial examiner's decision explores the issue in detail.
[26] Teamsters Local 537 (Lohman Sales Co.), 132 NLRB 901, 48 LRRM 1429 (1961). *But see* Schauffler v. Teamsters Local 107, 182 F Supp 556, 45 LRRM 2945 (ED Pa, 1960).
[27] *Supra* note 23.
[28] *Id.* at 394.
[29] *Supra* note 24.

sections involved. *Lohman* was there characterized as involving "mere handbilling." Where, however, handbilling is used as a substitute for conventional picketing in the context of other union conduct it will be regarded as picketing.[30]

III. PICKETING FOR AN ORGANIZATIONAL OR RECOGNITIONAL OBJECTIVE

Section 8(b)(7) places limitations "on picketing for an object of 'recognition' or 'bargaining' . . . or for an object of organization. Picketing for other purposes is not proscribed by this Section."[31] Thus picketing solely for the purpose of obtaining the reinstatement of a discharged employee[32] or solely for the purpose of protesting "area standards"[33] is not proscribed. But if either recognition or organization is found to be "an" object of the picketing, the limitations of Section 8(b)(7) will apply despite other legitimate objectives.[34] Application of the subsection requires only that recognition or organization be *an* object, not that it be the *sole* object.[35] Whether or not an object of picketing is for recognition or organization is a question of fact.[36]

A. Evidence of Proscribed Object

The factual determination confronting the Board is complicated when a union presents the objectives of its picketing as something

---

[30] Stoltze Land & Lbr. Co., *supra* note 23. For separate treatment of handbilling and consumer picketing, *see* Chapter 22 *infra*.
[31] Hod Carriers' Local 840 (C. A. Blinne Const. Co.), 135 NLRB 1153, 1156, 49 LRRM 1638 (1962). The words "recognize or bargain" as used in §8(b)(7) "were not intended to be read as encompassing two separate and unrelated terms. . . . [T]hey were intended to proscribe picketing having as its target forcing or requiring an employer's initial acceptance of a union as the bargaining representative of his employees." Bldg. & Const. Trades of Santa Barbara (Sullivan Electric Co.), 146 NLRB 1086, 1087, 56 LRRM 1010 (1964). The words "forcing or requiring" contained in the prefatory phrase "where an object thereof is forcing or requiring an employer to recognize or bargain . . ." does not require physical force or violence as an element of the violation. Therefore, the peaceful nature of the picketing is not a defense. Teamsters Local 239 (Stan Jay Auto Parts & Accessories Corp.), 127 NLRB 958, 46 LRRM 1123 (1960), *enforced*, 289 F 2d 41, 48 LRRM 2076 (CA 2, 1961), *cert. denied*, 368 US 833, 48 LRRM 3111 (1961); Dayton Typographical Union No. 57 v. NLRB, 326 F 2d 634, 54 LRRM 2535 (CA DC, 1963).
[32] United Automobile Workers Local 259 (Fanelli Ford Sales, Inc.), 133 NLRB 1468, 49 LRRM 1021 (1961).
[33] Houston Bldg. & Const. Trades Council (Claude Everett Const. Co.), 136 NLRB 321, 49 LRRM 1757 (1962).
[34] But picketing for a proscribed object will not violate §8(b)(7) unless the conditions stated in subparagraph (A), (B), or (C) exist. C. A. Blinne, *supra* note 31.
[35] Retail Clerks Local 345 (Gem of Syracuse, Inc.), 145 NLRB 1168, 1172, 55 LRRM 1122 (1964).
[36] NLRB v. Teamsters Local 182, 314 F 2d 53, 52 LRRM 2354 (CA 2, 1963).

other than recognition or organization. If a proscribed objective is masqueraded as "standards" or "informational" picketing,[37] the informational or area-standards "package"[38] of evidence may include appropriately worded signs, a letter to the employer advising it of the purported objective of the picketing (disclaiming a recognitional objective), and written instructions to pickets consistent with the purported object.[39]

Since the evidentiary problem is a recurring one, the Board has adopted guidelines for determining the objective of picketing. Self-serving legends on picket signs are not regarded as "conclusive evidence of the real objective of the picketing."[40] Since an unlawful objective in most instances "is not shown through admission or by direct evidence, . . . the object of the picketing must be ascertained from the [union's] overall conduct,"[41] including "the events which precede as well as those which accompany the picketing."[42] Specifically, if the union by word or deed confronts an employer with a choice of economic harm or recognition of the union, the proscribed objective will be found.[43] Other factors that tend to show a recognitional or organizational objective include

---

[37] Meltzer, *supra* note 9, at 92. Informational picketing presents slightly different problems since its legality is not necessarily tainted by an organizational or recognitional objective; a Board majority has viewed informational picketing as presupposing such objectives. Hotel and Restaurant Employees Local 681 (Crown Cafeteria), 135 NLRB 1183, 49 LRRM 1648 (1962), *affirmed sub nom.*, Smitley v. NLRB, 327 F 2d 351, 55 LRRM 2302 (CA 9, 1964). For a discussion of informational picketing see VII *infra*, this chapter, and Chapter 22 *infra*.

[38] Comment, *Picketing for Area Standards: An Exception to Section 8(b)(7)*, DUKE L. J. 767, 780 (1968).

[39] *See* Teamsters Local 239 (Abbey Auto Parts Corp.), 147 NLRB 8, 56 LRRM 1137 (1964), *enforcement denied*, 340 F 2d 1020, 58 LRRM 2287 (CA 2, 1965), where the union's written disclaimers and its accompanying conduct were such that the Board was forced to rely primarily upon a single remark by a picket to show a recognitional objective. The Second Circuit reversed on the ground that the agency of the picket was not established.

[40] IBEW Local 953 (Erickson Elec. Co.), 154 NLRB 1301, 1305, 60 LRRM 1120 (1965).

[41] Teamsters, Local 5 (Barber Bros. Cont. Co.), 171 NLRB No. 9, 68 LRRM 1011 (1968), *enforced*, 405 F 2d 864, 70 LRRM 2096 (CA 5, 1968). Direct evidence would exist if a picket sign stated that an employer "does not employ members of" a labor organization, clearly implying an object of organization. A picket sign stating that an employer "does not have a contract with" a labor organization would imply an object or recognition or bargaining. Crown Cafeteria, *supra* note 37.

[42] Gem of Syracuse, Inc., *supra* note 35.

[43] Teamsters Local 445 (Colony Liquor Distributors, Inc.), 145 NLRB 263, 54 LRRM 1359 (1963); Retail Clerks, Local 212 (Maxam Buffalo, Inc.), 140 NLRB 1258, 52 LRRM 1215 (1963); Retail Clerks, Local 899 (State-Mart, Inc., dba Giant Food), 166 NLRB No. 92, 65 LRRM 1666 (1967); Employees' Negotiating Committee (Western Boat Operators, Inc.), 177 NLRB No. 110, 71 LRRM 1510 (1969).

(1) picket signs actually directed to employees,[44] (2) leaflets and oral requests to employees to join the union,[45] (3) a demand for recognition immediately preceding the picketing,[46] (4) the tendering by the union of a proposed contract, or contracts secured at other plants,[47] (5) an indication that the pickets will be removed only when recognition is secured,[48] (6) the use of picket signs proclaiming a recognitional objective, even though later changed,[49] (7) an established union practice of picketing until a collective agreement is executed regardless of majority status,[50] (8) picketing for a purpose shown to be pretextual,[51] and (9) union attempts to persuade an employer to hire union help.[52]

B. Picketing to Protest Unfair Labor Practices or Discharges

The "prohibiting provisions of Section 8(b)(7) do not encompass picketing which is solely in protest against unfair labor practices."[53] Nor do they encompass picketing solely to secure the

---

[44] Retail Clerks, Local 635 (J. W. Mays, Inc.), 145 NLRB 1091, 55 LRRM 1107 (1964). Some of the signs stated "Mays Employees. . . . Join Retail Clerks."

[45] Gem of Syracuse, *supra* note 35; Philadelphia Window Cleaners, Local 125 (Atlantic Maintenance Co.), 136 NLRB 1104, 1105, 49 LRRM 1939 (1962).

[46] Gem of Syracuse, *supra* note 35; Maxam Buffalo, *supra* note 43; District 65, Retail, Wholesale & Dep't Store Union (Eastern Camera & Photo Corp.), 141 NLRB 991, 52 LRRM 1426 (1963).

[47] Maxam Buffalo, *supra* note 43, at 1265. *See also* Grain Millers Local 16 (Bartlett & Co.), 141 NLRB 974, 52 LRRM 1441 (1963), where the union's letter to the regional director stated that the pickets would be removed if "there was a certified bargaining representative for the employees" or if the employer "employed union members." The Board's reaction was, "What is this but a thinly disguised bid for recognition to end the picketing?" 141 NLRB at 980. *See also* Bricklayers, Local 5 (I. C. Minium), 174 NLRB No. 185, 70 LRRM 1449 (1969).

[49] Barber Bros, *supra* note 41; Teamsters Local 743 (Aetna Plywood & Veneer Co.), 140 NLRB 707, 52 LRRM 1107 (1963). *But see* Hotel & Restaurant Employees Local 89 (Stork Restaurant, Inc.), 135 NLRB 1173, 49 LRRM 1653 (1962); Waiters & Bartenders' Local 500 (Mission Valley Inn), 140 NLRB 433, 439, 52 LRRM 1023 (1963).

[50] Painters' Local 130 (Joiner, Inc.), 135 NLRB 876, 49 LRRM 1592 (1962).

[51] Bartenders & Culinary Workers (Holiday Inn of Las Vegas), 169 NLRB No. 102, 67 LRRM 1214 (1968), where a union's purported picketing for maintenance of area standards was undertaken without ascertaining from the employer whether its conditions met the area standards; Construction Laborers Local 1207 (Alfred S. Austin Const. Co.), 141 NLRB 283, 52 LRRM 1309 (1963). *See also infra*, note 90. But this will not substitute for the element of affirmative proof of the object. *Cf.* Mission Valley Inn, *supra* note 49.

[52] Alfred S. Austin Const. Co., *supra* note 51.

[53] Mission Valley Inn, *supra* note 49, at 437; *cf.* C. A. Blinne, *supra* note 31, at 1168, n. 29.

separate objective of reinstatement of strikers[54] or discharged employees.[55]

In the context of a Section 8(b)(4)(C) case,[56] in 1956 the Board held that picketing to secure the reinstatement of discharged employees "necessarily" compelled the employer to recognize and bargain with the union on the matter as a means of settling the dispute. However, in a 1961 Section 8(b)(7) case, *Fanelli Ford*,[57] the Board overruled this precedent on the ground that "picketing would have ceased if the Employer, without recognizing or, indeed, exchanging a word"[58] with the union, had reinstated the employee.

In *Fanelli*, the picketing was found to be for the sole object of seeking reinstatement of a discharged employee. Recognizing that picketing "for an employee's reinstatement may in some circumstances be used as a pretext for attaining recognition," the Board nevertheless decided that it would not infer the broader objective absent an affirmative showing of a recognitional objective.[59] Where, of course, there is independent evidence of a recognitional or organizational objective, the ban of Section 8(b)(7) will be applicable.[60] The finding in *Fanelli* of no proscribed object was facilitated by the fact that the picketing originated with the discharge.[61]

Fanelli was significant in that the reinstatement objective was not premised upon the illegality of the discharge. The Board treated it as a reinstatement protest and not as an unfair labor practice protest. Thus, it was not dependent upon an administrative determination as to the existence of meritorious Section 8(a)(1) and (3) charges.[62] If the picketing stemming from the dis-

---

54 Mission Valley Inn, *supra* note 49.
55 United Automobile Workers Local 259 (Fanelli Ford Sales, Inc.), 133 NLRB 1468, 49 LRRM 1021 (1961).
56 Teamsters Local 626 (Lewis Food Co.), 115 NLRB 890, 37 LRRM 1421 (1956).
57 Fanelli Ford Sales, Inc., *supra* note 55.
58 *Id.* at 1469.
59 *Id.* at 1468-1469.
60 Eastern Camera & Photo Corp., *supra* note 46; Aetna Plywood & Veneer Co., *supra* note 49. This case provides the basis for a detailed analysis of this issue; *see* Dunau, *supra* note 9, at 235-247.
61 *See* distinction noted in Aetna Plywood & Veneer Co., *supra* note 49, at 710. It is not essential, however, since the Board may accept the contention that an initial proscribed objective is no longer operative. Mission Valley Inn, *supra* note 49, at 439.
62 For a critical discussion of the role of administrative determinations in this area, *see* Dunau, *supra* note 9, at 225, 235.

charge had been confined to its unfair labor practice aspect, an administrative determination either dismissing or settling the Section 8(a)(1) and (3) charges might have removed the unfair labor practices as a valid objective of the picketing.[63] Where, however, the picketing for reinstatement has been advanced separately, or in addition to, the protest against the unfair labor practice, the former objective may survive an administrative disposal of the unfair labor practice aspect.[64] Administrative determinations by the General Counsel are significant, since a finding of a meritorious unfair labor practice charge may bolster the union's contention that picketing is for such an object.[65] In addition, dual-purpose picketing accompanied by the administrative finding of a meritorious unfair labor practice charge may effectively impede an expedited election under Section 8(b)(7)(C), despite an illicit objective.[66]

Picketing to protest the employer's unlawful refusal to recognize the union as a majority representative in an appropriate unit creates special problems. It is plainly picketing to protest an unfair labor practice, but at the same time it is just as plainly picketing for a recognitional objective. In *Blinne* the Board resolved the issue by conditioning the union's relief from the limitations of Section 8(b)(7)(C) upon the filing of a timely and meritorious Section 8(a)(5) charge.[67]

C. Area-Standards Picketing

Picketing for area standards has been described as "picketing aimed at causing the picketed employer to adopt employment terms at his enterprise commensurate with those prevailing in his

---

[63] *Cf.* Mission Valley Inn, *supra* note 49, at 438; Aetna Plywood & Veneer, *supra* note 49. Where the charges have been settled, the Board has distinguished between a determination, "with the acquiescence of the union" that the employer had remedied the unfair labor practices and one in which the union refused to join in the settlement but continued to protest for further remedial action, *e.g.*, reinstatement of *all* strikers. 140 NLRB at 441, n. 8, distinguishing Hotel & Restaurant Employees, Local 402 (Evans Hotels), 132 NLRB 737, 48 LRRM 1411 (1961). But despite the union's acquiescence in a settlement of charges against the employer, it has nonetheless been permitted to picket subsequently for the purpose of publicizing the settled unfair labor practices. Teamsters General Local 200 (Bachman Furn. Co.), 134 NLRB 670, 49 LRRM 1192 (1961). *See* Meltzer, *supra* note 9, at 85, 86; and Shawe, *supra* note 9, at 258, for critical discussion of the *Bachman* case.
[64] Mission Valley Inn, *supra* note 49; Fanelli Ford, *supra* note 55.
[65] *See supra* notes 63 and 64.
[66] C. A. Blinne, *supra* note 31, 135 NLRB at 1166, 1167.
[67] *Id.* at 1166, n. 24.

locale.''[68] The factual pattern surrounding such picketing may include a union inquiry about an employer's wage scale and notification to the employer that unless he conforms his wage scale to the "area standard," he will be picketed. If the employer disregards this advice, a picket line is erected with signs declaring the union's desire for conformance with area standards and disclaiming a recognitional or organizational objective.[69]

In determining the object of the picketing the central issue is much the same as that posed by picketing for the reinstatement of strikers or discharged employees,[70] namely, will employer accedence to the union's demands necessitate bargaining or recognition? The issue arose in a Section 8(b)(4)(C) case[71] in 1961. In the first *Calumet*[72] decision the Board held that, despite its disclaimer, such picketing had as its ultimate end a recognitional objective. The Board reasoned as follows:

> While, clearly, no express demand for recognition or bargaining was made, it is equally clear that one of the objects of . . . picketing was to force [the employer] . . . to meet the "prevailing rate of pay and conditions" for the area. It is well established that a union's picketing for prevailing rates of pay and conditions of employment constitutes an attempt to obtain conditions and concessions normally resulting from collective bargaining, and constitutes an attempt by the union to force itself on employees as their bargaining agent.

Later that year, *Calumet* was reconsidered and reversed by a differently constituted, divided Board,[73] which held that the picketed union's

> . . . admitted objective to require the [employer] to conform standards of employment to those prevailing in the area, is not tantamount to, nor does it have an objective of, recognition or bargaining. A union may legitimately be concerned that a particular employer is under-

---

68 Dunau, *supra* note 9.
69 Comment, *Picketing for Area Standards: An Exception to Section 8(b)(7)*, DUKE L. J., 767, 776 (1968) , and cases cited therein.
70 *See* Fanelli Ford, *supra* note 55.
71 A forerunner of this case arose in the context of a representation proceeding in 1954 in *Retail Clerk's Ass'n (Petrie's, Div. of Red Robin Stores, Inc.)*, 108 NLRB 1318, 34 LRRM 1188 (1954) . In *Petrie's* the direction of an election, despite a union disclaimer of recognition, was premised on the view that recognition was inherent in standards picketing.
72 Hod Carriers' Local 41 (Calumet Contractors Ass'n) , 130 NLRB 78, 81-82, 47 LRRM 1253 (1961) , *reversed on reconsideration*, 133 NLRB 512, 48 LRRM 1667 (1961) . In *Calumet* the picketing was conducted despite the existence of another currently recognized union.
73 133 NLRB 512, 48 LRRM 1667 (1961) .

mining area standards of employment by maintaining lower standards. It may be willing to forego recognition and bargaining provided subnormal working conditions are eliminated from area considerations.

In *Claude Everett*,[74] the first case arising under Section 8(b)(7), a Board majority adopted the same rationale for permitting area-standards picketing under Section 8(b)(7) as it had under Section 8(b)(4)(C). It refused to equate picketing solely to maintain area wage standards with picketing for an object of bargaining or recognition or with picketing aimed at organization.[75]

In subsequent cases the majority has continued to emphasize that, while a union normally seeks to organize the unorganized and to negotiate collective bargaining agreements, it has a legitimate interest, apart from organization or recognition, in ensuring that employers meet prevailing wage scales; otherwise area standards may be undermined[76] and "substandard" employers gain a competitive advantage.[77] In a related context the majority has conceded that in the "long view" all picketing might have the ultimate economic objective of recognition or organization; but it stressed that "Congress itself has drawn a sharp distinction between recognition and organization picketing and other forms of picketing, thereby recognizing, as we recognize, that a real distinction does exist."[78] On the other hand, the dissenting view has been that the majority position does not conform with "industrial realities,"[79] and that permitting area-standards picketing does not "take into consideration either the extent to which the standards of the . . . Union are applicable to the Company's operations, [or]

---

[74] Houston Bldg. & Const. Trades Council (Claude Everett Const. Co.) , 136 NLRB 321, 49 LRRM 1757 (1962) .

[75] In the *Calumet* case it was not necessary for the Board to rule upon the organization object since the case arose under §8 (b) (4) , which did not regulate organizational picketing but only recognitional picketing.

[76] Plumbers Local 741 (Keith Riggs Plumbing) , 137 NLRB 1125, 50 LRRM 1313 (1962) ; Hod Carriers' Local 107 (Texarkana Const. Co.) , 138 NLRB 102, 50 LRRM 1545 (1962) . It may be significant that a large, if not predominant, number of area-standards cases arise in the construction industry, where the fluidity of employment patterns may have particular relevance.

[77] For a discussion of the various arguments raised concerning this issue *see* Comment, *supra* note 69, at 774-776. It notes, for example, that unions may find their bargaining position with organized employers weakened because of the lower wage rates of competing employers with whom it does not have collective agreements.

[78] Blinne, *supra* note 31, at 1168, n. 29.

[79] *E.g.,* Keith Riggs Plumbing, *supra* note 76, at 1130, citing Claude Everett, *supra* note 74.

the complications [involved] in changing a wage pattern. . . ." [80]
Any attempt by the employer to adjust the wages and working conditions to its circumstances would "necessarily" [81] call for negotiation and bargaining with the union. Otherwise, the minority
argues, the standards demanded by the union "are not negotiable
and must be accepted on a take-it-or-leave-it basis." [82] Hence the
union would achieve what is normally sought in collective bargaining without the statutory requirements of collective bargaining.[83]

The majority view does not extend to all demands for prevailing
standards. When the standards to which the union demands conformity extend beyond clear wage disparities, the Board has been
less inclined to sustain a union contention that bargaining or
recognition is not an object of the picketing. Thus, a request that
an employer agree in writing to match the wages and fringe benefits contained in the union's agreements with other employers may
be considered a demand for recognition, since it would thwart any
collective bargaining efforts by a representative chosen by the
employees.[84] A "contract adoption" theory[85] may apply even in
the absence of a request for a written agreement. A union's mere
presentation of an entire collective bargaining agreement with
other employers as the area standard creates the inference that its
"true objective was to require and maintain the identical employment terms"[86] as defined in other contracts. This requirement
"clearly reflects a purpose to impose a bargaining relationship on

---

[80] Claude Everett, *supra* note 74, at 325.

[81] Keith Riggs Plumbing, *supra* note 76, at 1131.

[82] *Ibid.* The complexities of wage patterns and other benefits may, in some
instances, require bargaining, and the *Keith Riggs* decision, insofar as it involves
benefits other than clear wage disparities, may no longer reflect the Board's position.
See State-Mart, Inc., *supra* note 43, and discussion in Comment, *supra* note 69, at
784. *See also* Ladies' Garment Workers Union (Romay of California), 171 NLRB
No. 110, 68 LRRM 1187 (1968).

[83] *See* Meltzer, *supra* note 9, at 93-95.

[84] Centralia Bldg. and Const. Trades Council (Pacific Sign & Steel Bldg. Co.), 155
NLRB 803, 60 LRRM 1430 (1965), *enforced,* 363 F 2d 699, 62 LRRM 2511 (CA DC,
1966).

[85] State-Mart, *supra* note 43, at n. 1. The trial examiner's opinion, adopted by the
Board, contains a thorough analysis of this issue.

[86] Bartenders & Culinary Workers (Holiday Inn of Las Vegas), 169 NLRB No. 102,
67 LRRM 1214 (1968).

the Employer, contrary to the provisions of Section 8(b)(7) of the Act."[87]

A wage and fringe package may demand more than is needed to maintain area standards. Thus, while a union might picket for equal wages or equal costs (equivalent to those of organized employers), an attempt to "go beyond this and to dictate what benefits are to be granted . . . is attempting to engage in *pro tanto* bargaining."[88]

Area-standards picketing may be proscribed with less difficulty when there is other evidence that "an object" is recognition or organization, apart from the level of the wages demanded. Thus, inconsistent language on picket signs or contemporaneous demands for recognition[89] would belie union disclaimers and invoke the limitations of Section 8(b)(7). Particularly germane to standards picketing is evidence that the picketing commenced prior to any attempt by the union to determine the wage scale of the employer whose standards it is protesting. In such instances the Board may consider the standards objective a pretext.[90]

Area-standards picketing may have variations. Picketing, for example, in a business area for the purpose of persuading consumers not to patronize stores identified with substandard conditions is not picketing for organization or recognition.[91] Standards

---

87 *Ibid.* A portion of the union's letter demanding adherence to area standards relied upon by the Board is as follows:

"In presenting this evidence of prevailing standards it should be clearly understood that *while we expect you to observe the wages, hours, and other benefits set forth in these documents,* we do not expect or seek any collective bargaining relationship with your firm." (Emphasis added.)

88 State-Mart, Inc., *supra* note 43, where the effect of such demands as health and welfare benefits, seniority, and grievance machinery are discussed.

89 *See* Painters Local 130 (Joiner, Inc.), 135 NLRB 876, 49 LRRM 1592 (1962). *See also* Salem Building Trades Council (Lantz Const. Co.), 153 NLRB 531, 59 LRRM 1466 (1965); Building & Const. Trades Council (Fisher Const. Co.), 149 NLRB 1629, 58 LRRM 1001 (1964); Plasterers & Cement Masons, Local 44 (Penny Const. Co.), 144 NLRB 1298, 54 LRRM 1237 (1963); Construction Laborers, Local 1207 (Alfred S. Austin Const. Co.), 141 NLRB 283, 52 LRRM 1309 (1963). Drug & Hosp. Employees (Janel Sales Corp.), 136 NLRB 1564, 50 LRRM 1033 (1962). *See also supra,* notes 37-52.

90 *See* Alfred S. Austin Const. Co., *supra* note 89. *See particularly* Holiday Inn of Las Vegas, *supra* note 86, Romay, *supra* note 82, and State-Mart, Inc., *supra* note 43, for in those three cases the actual proscribed object appears to have been presumed once the alleged objective was found to be a pretext. *But see* Bachman Furn. Co., *supra* note 63, on the necessity of a prior investigation by the union.

91 Alton-Wood River Bldg. & Const. Trades Council, 144 NLRB 526, 54 LRRM 1099 (1963).

picketing is occasionally confused with informational picketing. The basic distinction was drawn in the *Claude Everett* case,[92] where it was held that the effect of standards picketing on deliveries is immaterial since it is not for a proscribed object, whereas informational picketing assumes a recognitional or organizational objective.[93]

D. Members-Only and Prehire Agreements[94]

Picketing for the object of forcing an employer to sign a members-only contract or a prehire agreement has a recognitional object, and thus the restrictions of Section 8(b)(7) apply. In *Sherwood Construction Co.*,[95] an uncertified union picketed an employer for a contract covering only union members currently or subsequently employed. An election petition was not filed within 30 days. The Board held that such an object, which would require recognition of the union as the representative for union members only, was proscribed by Section 8(b)(7) even though the union had not sought exclusive representation of all employees. Section 8(b)(7) prohibited the picketing of an employer, who employed no operating engineers, for a contract recognizing the union as bargaining agent for future or prospective operating engineers, where no timely election petition was filed.[96] The term "his employees" as used in Section 8(b)(7) applies to future as well as present employees.[97] Although employers and unions in the construction industry may enter prehire agreements under Section 8(f),[98] coercive means, such as picketing, may not be used to force such an agreement.[99]

The District of Columbia Circuit has upheld the Board's application of Section 8(b)(7) to picketing for a prehire agreement which might otherwise be lawful under Section 8(e). In *Dallas*

---

92 *Supra* note 74.
93 *See* discussion on informational picketing at VII *infra*.
94 For a discussion of the particular problems arising in the construction industry, *see* Richards, *supra* note 9.
95 Operating Engineers Local 101 (Sherwood Const. Co.), 140 NLRB 1175, 52 LRRM 1198 (1963).
96 Operating Engineers Local 542 (R. S. Noonan, Inc.), 142 NLRB 1132, 53 LRRM 1205 (1963), *enforced*, 331 F 2d 99, 56 LRRM 2028 (CA 3, 1964), *cert. denied*, 379 US 889, 57 LRRM 2307 (1964).
97 142 NLRB at 1134.
98 *See* Chapters 11 *supra* and 26 *infra*.
99 *Cf.* Int'l Ladies' Garment Workers v. NLRB, 366 US 731, 48 LRRM 2251 (1961).

Bldg. & Const. Trades Council v. *NLRB*[100] the Council, which was not the authorized bargaining agent of any employees, picketed general contractors, despite the existence of currently recognized local unions, when the contractors refused to enter into an agreement for subcontracting. A provision stipulated that the contract was subordinated to any present or future agreements with the contractors. The picketing was found to be for a proscribed object and fell directly under the ban of Section 8(b)(7)(A). The court upheld the Board's view that "[i]t simply does not follow from the fact that the agreement would be lawful [under Section 8(e)] if voluntarily adopted that a labor organization can employ illegal means to obtain it."[101]

IV. PICKETING WHEN ANOTHER UNION IS CURRENTLY RECOGNIZED

Subparagraph (A) of Section 8(b)(7) prohibits recognition or organizational picketing by a noncertified union when another union is lawfully recognized and no question concerning representation may be appropriately raised.[102] The phrase "lawfully recognized" has been interpreted to include "all bargaining relationships immune from attack under Sections 8 and 9 of the Act."[103] Thus, a Section 8(b)(7)(A) charge may not be defended on the ground that the employer's recognition of an incumbent union is unlawful where there is no timely Section 8(a)(2) charge and where the incumbent's contract would bar a representation petition.[104]

A. Contract-Bar Limitations on Picketing

Under Section 8(b)(4)(C) of the Taft-Hartley amendments, protection from rival union picketing was provided only for employers who were obligated to bargain with a union that was certified.

---

100 396 F 2d 677, 68 LRRM 2019 (1968).

101 *Id.* at 682. For treatment of §8 (e) generally, *see* Chapter 24 *infra*.

102 In many instances, picketing by rival unions is forbidden by "no raiding" agreements to which the unions may be signatory. See Thatcher, Symposium, *supra* note 9, at 943.

103 Hod Carriers' Local 1298 (Roman Stone Const. Co.), 153 NLRB 659, n. 3, 59 LRRM 1430 (1965). *See also* United Mine Workers (Seagraves Coal Co.), 160 NLRB 1582, 63 LRRM 1172 (1966); Sheet Metal Workers Local 284 (Quality Roofing Co.), 169 NLRB No. 130, 67 LRRM 1311 (1968).

104 Roman Stone, *supra* note 103.

Section 8(b)(7)(A) of the 1959 Amendments extended this protection to employers who entered into contracts with uncertified but lawfully recognized unions, so long as no question concerning representation could be appropriately raised, *i.e.*, so long as contract-bar rules prevented the holding of an election.[105] For example, a contract renewed during the 60-day "insulated" period bars an election and thus serves to preclude rival-union picketing for recognition or organization.[106] Similarly, if there is an accretion to a bargaining unit that does not remove the contract as a bar to an election, the prohibition upon picketing applies.[107] On the other hand, contract-bar cases hold that, to serve as a bar, the contract must encompass the target employees.[108] Thus, if truck drivers are excluded from a multi-employer contract covering other classifications, subparagraph (A) does not bar recognitional picketing for those employees by a rival union.[109] Likewise, picketing to obtain recognition for work its members normally perform is not prohibited if the contract does not on its face, or in its intent, cover the work performed.[110]

B. Section 8(a)(2) Defense

The defense of unlawful recognition to the incumbent may be raised by the picketing union only if the incumbent's representative status can be challenged directly in a proceeding under Section 8 or 9.[111] A direct challenge is not possible under Section 9 since unfair labor practices, such as unlawful recognition, are not litiga-

---

105 *See* Chapter 8 *supra* for a discussion of contract-bar principles.
106 Teamsters, Local 182 (Sitrue, Inc.), 129 NLRB 1459, 1463, 47 LRRM 1219 (1961); *cf.* Seagraves Coal Co., *supra* note 103. Subparagraph (A) does not preclude the additional application of other bar rules whether or not a contract is in existence. *See, e.g.*, Local 3, IBEW (Darby Electric Corp.), 153 NLRB 717, 724, 59 LRRM 1509 (1965), *enforced*, 362 F 2d 233, 236, 62 LRRM 2384 (CA 2, 1966) where no question concerning representation could appropriately be raised, not only because of a contract bar but because the unit sought was inappropriate.
107 Meat Cutters, Local 378 (Waldbaum, Inc.), 153 NLRB 1482, 59 LRRM 1688 (1965), and McLeod v. Meat Cutters, Local 378, 236 F Supp 709, 58 LRRM 2110 (ED NY, 1964). In the context of a successor question, *see* McLeod v. Teamsters, Local 202, 239 F Supp 452, 59 LRRM 2018 (SD NY, 1965).
108 RCA Communications, Inc., 154 NLRB 34, 37, 59 LRRM 1698 (1965).
109 Teamsters, Local 174 (Durell Products, Inc.), 170 NLRB No. 36, n. 2, 67 LRRM 1488 (1968).
110 Carpenters Local 106 (L. G. Barcus & Son, Inc.), 150 NLRB 1488, 58 LRRM 1245 (1965).
111 Roman Stone, *supra* note 103.

ble in a representation case.[112] A direct challenge to the incumbent's representative status under Section 8 is also barred if made more than six months after the contract was executed, in accordance with the statute of limitations provided for in Section 10(b).[113] Moreover, a subsequent loss of majority by the incumbent during the remainder of the contract bar term would not affect the validity of its recognition.[114] By limiting a rival union's use of the defense of unlawful recognition, the Board seeks to prevent the union from accomplishing "by means of picketing what it could not achieve under established Board procedures."[115] This does not mean that an unlawful bargaining relationship will be afforded unlimited sanctuary from rival-union picketing, for the relationship may be directly challenged by a timely Section 8(a)(2) charge.[116] Such a charge would inhibit the seeking of an injunction against the union under Section 10(1) for an alleged violation of any of the subparagraphs of Section 8(b)(7).[117]

C. Inapplicability of Informational Proviso

The fact that picketing is purely informational is not a defense to a Section 8(b)(7)(A) charge. The informational proviso in Section 8(b)(7)(C) appertains only to situations defined in the principal clause of Section 8(b)(7)(C). It does not apply to other subparagraphs of Section 8(b)(7)."[118]

---

[112] Union Mfg. Co., 123 NLRB 1633, 44 LRRM 1188 (1959); *see also* Lawrence Typographical Union v. McCulloch, 349 F 2d 704, 59 LRRM 2161 (CA DC, 1965), involving §8(b)(7)(B). See Chapter 30 *infra*.

[113] Roman Stone, *supra* note 103. *Roman Stone,* however, dealt only with circumstances in which a §8 challenge would have been untimely in terms of §10(b) and avoided any discussion of challenges within the §10(b) period.

[114] *Id.,* citing Shamrock Dairy of Phoenix, Inc., 119 NLRB 998, 1002, 41 LRRM 1216 (1957).

[115] Roman Stone, *supra* note 103.

[116] *See* Chapter 7 *supra; cf.* Roman Stone, *supra* note 103. In *Roman Stone* the Board addressed itself only to the period outside the §10(b) statute of limitations. *See* Cox, *supra* note 9, at 264, 265.

[117] The actual wording of §10(1) refers to this qualification. *See* Cox, *supra* note 9, at 265, n. 36; *cf.* Hod Carriers' Local 840 (C. A. Blinne Const. Co.), 135 NLRB 1153, 1154, 49 LRRM 1638 (1962).

[118] Drug & Hospital Employees, Local 1199 (Janel Sales Corp.), 136 NLRB 1564, 1567, 1568, 50 LRRM 1033 (1962). *See* Chapter 22 *infra*.

V. PICKETING WITHIN 12 MONTHS OF A VALID ELECTION

Subparagraph B of Section 8(b)(7) seeks to preserve the integrity of the Board's election processes under Section 9(c) by prohibiting recognitional or organizational picketing by a noncertified union where a valid election has been conducted under Section 9(c) within the preceding 12 months.[119] The prohibition is applied without regard to whether the picketing union was a participant in the election. Moreover, it extends to recognition or organizational picketing by former incumbent unions that have been defeated in decertification elections.[120]

Section 8(b)(7)(B) must be read in context with Section 8(b)(7)(C). In cases in which the noncertified picketing union has been a participant in the election, its participation may have been the result of an "expedited election" conducted pursuant to Section 8(b)(7)(C).[121] Theoretically, the 30-day statutory period for recognition picketing permitted under Section 8(b)(7)(C) could be shortened by an expedited election held "forthwith" because, if the picketing union lost, Section 8(b)(7)(B) would be "acti-

---

[119] Picketing for purposes other than recognition or organization may, nonetheless, be conducted within the 12-month period. Waiters & Bartenders, Local 500 (Mission Valley Inn), 140 NLRB 433, 52 LRRM 1023 (1963). But if one of the objectives is recognition, the picketing will violate §8(b)(7); NLRB v. Knitgoods Workers Union Local 155, 403 F 2d 388, 390, 69 LRRM 2666 (CA 2, 1968).

[120] Lumber & Sawmill Workers Union (Stoltze Land & Lbr. Co.), 156 NLRB 388, 61 LRRM 1046 (1965); Lawrence Typographical Union No. 570 (Kansas Color Press, Inc.), 158 NLRB 1332, 62 LRRM 1243 (1966), order vacated and remanded on other grounds, 376 F 2d 643, 65 LRRM 2176 (CA 10, 1967), on remand, 169 NLRB No. 65, 67 LRRM 1166 (1968), enforced, 402 F 2d 452, 69 LRRM 2591 (CA 10, 1968). In Kansas Color Press, the Board said that "[t]he purpose of §8(b)(7)(B) was, not to deal with so-called 'blackmail picketing' but, to provide stability for the 12-month period during which §9(c)(3) of the Act barred a second Board election for the same unit by protecting the employer and employees during that period against the pressures of recognitional and organizational picketing in a situation where neither the picketing union nor any other union was selected as the employees' bargaining representative in a valid Board election." 158 NLRB at 1338-1339.

[121] Kansas Color Press, Inc., supra note 120, at 1339. See also Meltzer, supra note 9, at 82. Query: the effect of Conren, Inc., 156 NLRB 592, 61 LRRM 1090 (1966), enforced, 368 F 2d 173, 63 LRRM 2273 (1966), cert. denied, 386 US 974, 64 LRRM 2640 (1967).

vated."[122] The expeditiousness of this procedure, however, may be largely illusory.[123]

A. Validity of the Election

The prohibition of Section 8(b)(7)(B) is premised upon the holding of a valid election. If the regional director erred in directing an election, or if the election as held was invalid for other reasons, the picketing will not violate subparagraph (B).

1. Invalidity of the Direction of Election. The validity of an expedited election may turn upon whether it should have been directed at all. In *Oakland G. R. Kinney*,[124] the Board established the rule that where picketing does not violate Section 8(b)(7)(C), an expedited election held thereunder is not valid for purposes of finding a violation of Section 8(b)(7)(B).[125] The Board held that the picketing conformed to the publicity proviso of Section 8(b)(7)(C); accordingly, an expedited election was not warranted. In these instances the validity of the holding of the election may be challenged in the hearing on the Section 8(b)(7)(B) allegation. It would also appear that the validity of the election could be tested in the injunction action in which a union is charged with violation of subparagraph (B).[126]

2. Other Assertions of Invalidity. If the validity of the election is challenged in the Section 8(b)(7)(B) proceeding on grounds that

---

[122] *Cf.* C. A. Blinne, *supra,* note 117, at 1157. *See* Meltzer *supra* note 9, at 82, 83. For the prerequisites to holding an expedited election and the procedures to be followed, *see* NLRB RULES AND REGULATIONS (Subpart D), and STATEMENTS OF PROCEDURE (Subpart D); NLRB Field Manual, Sec. 10244.4. *See also* Chapter 8 *supra* and Chapter 30 *infra* on election procedures.

[123] *See* Meltzer *supra* note 9, at 83. The expedited election will still be subject to blocking charges (C. A. Blinne, *supra* note 117), which apparently may be part of union defensive strategy. Richards, *supra* note 9, at 59. Since this procedure is also vulnerable to defenses that could be raised under §8(b) (7) (C) (*see* VI *infra*), it is not surprising that only 16 expedited elections were conducted in the fiscal year ending June 30, 1968, despite the fact that 416 charges were filed under §8(b)(7). 1968 NLRB ANN REP., Tables 2 and 11A. *But see, e.g.,* Retail Clerks Local 1439 (Ames IGA Foodliner, Inc., 136 NLRB 778, 49 LRRM 1852 (1962), where an expedited election was conducted within two weeks of the commencement of the picketing. Query: the effect of the *Excelsior* rule, *supra* Chapter 8, which requires that the union be provided with a list of names and addresses at least 10 days prior to the election.

[124] Dep't & Specialty Store Employees, Local 1265 (Oakland C. R. Kinney Co.), 136 NLRB 335, 49 LRRM 1771 (1962).

[125] *Ibid. See also* Retail Clerks Local 57 (Hested Stores Co.), 138 NLRB 498, 51 LRRM 1061 (1962).

[126] Dep't Store Employees v. Brown, 284 F 2d 619, 47 LRRM 2145 (CA 9, 1960).

could have been raised in the representation case, the Board will not permit the questions to be relitigated.[127] Where eligibility issues affecting the outcome of the election are raised before the regional director and a request for review is denied, such issues may not constitute a defense to Section 8(b)(7)(B).[128] The Board has also taken the position that the General Counsel's administrative determination that no unfair labor practices preventing a fair election have been committed may not be tested in defense of the Section 8(b)(7)(B) allegation.[129]

B. Determinative Dates

To constitute a violation of Section 8(b)(7)(B) the picketing must occur within 12 months following a valid election. In *Irvins, Inc.*,[130] the Board answered two basic questions: what the determinative date is for finding a violation, and what the determinative date is for an appropriate remedy.

1. The Violation. The determinative date for deciding whether a "valid election" under Section 8(b)(7)(B) has been held, "and, consequently, whether that section has been *violated,* shall be the date of certification of results of election for certification of representatives,"[131] rather than the date of the balloting.[132]

---

127 United Furniture Workers (Jamestown Sterling Corp.), 146 NLRB 474, 55 LRRM 1344 (1964). Difficulties exist, however, because in order to expedite these special elections, provision has been made for elections to be conducted without the delay of a formal hearing. *Supra* note 122. But if the union has been precluded from litigating "election issues" in the "election case itself," the Board may, in certain instances, permit such challenge in the §8(b)(7)(B) proceeding. Kansas Color Press, Inc., *supra* note 120. See also Teamsters Local 182 (Woodward Motors, Inc.), 135 NLRB 851, 49 LRRM 1576 (1962), *enforced,* 314 F 2d 53, 52 LRRM 2354 (CA 2, 1963). Although it enforced the Board's order, the court took a permissive view of the possibility of a union's defending a §8(b)(7)(B) charge with proof that "unfair labor practices in fact prevented a fair election," despite the refusal of the General Counsel to issue a complaint. However, the court indicated that a union must do more than simply prove that it had filed charges which were dismissed, but must show that the General Counsel erroneously dismissed the charges. Since the union did neither, the court enforced. The Tenth Circuit has expressed its views in *Kansas Color Press, supra* note 120. For a somewhat puzzling decision in which the Board, in a §8(b)(7)(B) proceeding, held that an election was not valid because it was directed in an inappropriate unit, *see* Teamsters Local 327 (American Bread Co.), 170 NLRB No. 19, 67 LRRM 1427 (1968).
128 Jamestown Sterling Corp., *supra* note 127.
129 Woodward Motors, Inc., *supra* note 127. If such unfair labor practices do exist, they must be disposed of before an expedited election can be held. NLRB Field Manual 10244.4; C. A. Blinne, *supra* note 117.
130 Retail Clerks, Local 692 (Irvins, Inc.), 134 NLRB 686, 49 LRRM 1188 (1961).
131 Teamsters, Local 745 (Macatee, Inc.), 135 NLRB 62, 63, 49 LRRM 1418 (1962), citing *Irvins.*
132 Irvins, *supra* note 130.

2. The Remedy. For purposes of its remedial order the Board will require the "cessation of all recognitional and/or organizational post-election picketing for a period of 12 months, which period shall be *computed from the date the labor organization terminates its picketing activities (either voluntarily or involuntarily)*."[133] Where at the time of the Board's decision a year has already elapsed from the termination of the violative picketing, the Board may require the union to cease and desist from the proscribed picketing "for a year following the conduct of any future valid election in which the union is unsuccessful."[134]

VI. PICKETING OF UNREASONABLE DURATION ABSENT A PETITION

If recognition or organizational picketing is not barred by subparagraphs (A) or (B) of Section 8(b)(7), its duration may nevertheless be limited by subparagraph (C) to a reasonable period not to exceed 30 days, unless a representation petition is filed prior to the expiration of that period. Absent a timely petition, picketing beyond a reasonable period or 30 days violates Section 8(b)(7)(C).[135]

A. Reasonable Period of Time

The statute does not define the term "reasonable period of time." Therefore, the Board has determined, in its discretion, when circumstances justify shortening of the 30-day period. Ten days, for example, was held to be unreasonable when the picketing was accompanied by acts of violence and intimidation.[136] Where

---

133 *Id.* at 691.
134 Macatee, Inc., *supra* note 131.
135 C. A. Blinne, *supra* note 117; Typographical Union, Local 285 (Charlton Press, Inc.), 135 NLRB 1178, 49 LRRM 1650 (1962) ; Hotel & Restaurant Employees Union Local 89 (Stork Restaurant), 135 NLRB 1173, 49 LRRM 1653 (1962). However, the second proviso to §8 (b) (7) (C) provides that picketing for the purpose of truthfully advising the public that the employer "does not employ members of, or have a contract with," the union is not proscribed "unless an effect of such picketing is to induce any individual employed by any other person in the course of his employment, not to pick up, deliver or transport any goods or not to perform any services." Hotel & Restaurant Employees Local 681 (Crown Cafeteria), 135 NLRB 1183, 49 LRRM 1648 (1962), *enforced,* 327 F 2d 351, 55 LRRM 2302 (CA 9, 1964). *See* VII *infra.*
136 Cuneo v. United Shoe Workers, 181 F Supp 324, 45 LRRM 2822 (DC NJ, 1960). *See also* District 65, Retail, Wholesale & Dep't Store Union (Eastern Camera & Photo Corp.), 141 NLRB 991, 52 LRRM 1426 (1963).

the employer suffered severe economic damage, 15 days was held to be unreasonable.[137] A critical aspect of these cases is the issuance of a Section 10(1) injunction by a federal district court. Once the "reasonable period" has passed, the picketing is subject to a Section 10(1) injunction even if a petition is thereafter filed within the 30-day period.

The Board has refused to permit intermittent periods of coordinated picketing by two different unions, neither of whose picketing exceeds 30 days but whose combined picketing is in excess of that period, if the unions are not engaged in a joint venture.[138] Similarly, the 30-day computation will not be affected by the withdrawal of the petition after nine days of picketing.[139] For computational purposes, picketing directed against a primary construction employer will include the period during which the primary employer and his employees were absent from the picketed construction site.[140]

B. Effect of Filing or Refraining From Filing a Petition

Section 8(b)(7)(C) establishes two different routes for dealing with proscribed picketing, depending on whether a petition is filed. If a petition is filed, there will be no violation of subparagraph (C) and the picketing may continue during the processing of the petition. If, in addition, a Section 8(b)(7)(C) charge is filed by the employer, the petition may be processed by the expedited election procedure.[141] However, the expedited election procedure may be invoked only by an employer's Section 8(b)(7)(C) charge; otherwise, unions could obtain expedited elections simply by picketing[142] or perhaps by having sympathetic employees file Section 8(b)(7)(C) charges.[143] If an election is directed, the Section 8(b)(7)(C) charge will be dismissed, since this will resolve the

---

137 Elliot v. Sapulpa Typographical Union, 45 LRRM 2400 (ND Okla, 1959).
138 Const. Prod. & Maintenance Laborers, Local 383 (Colson & Stevens Const. Co.), 137 NLRB 1650, 50 LRRM 1444 (1962), *enforced*, 323 F 2d 422, 54 LRRM 2246 (CA 9, 1963); *contra*, Kennedy v. Const., Prod. & Maintenance Laborers, Local 383, 199 F Supp 775, 48 LRRM 2791 (DC Ariz, 1961).
139 Electrical Workers, Local 113 (I.C.G. Electric, Inc.), 142 NLRB 1418, 53 LRRM 1239 (1963).
140 Chicago Printing Pressmen's Union, Local 3 (Moore Laminating, Inc.), 137 NLRB 729, 50 LRRM 1242 (1962).
141 The expedited election procedure is also discussed in connection with §8(b)(7)(B) at V *supra*.
142 C. A. Blinne, *supra* note 117, at 1157, n. 10.
143 *Ibid.*

representation question.[144] If the union is not certified and it continues to picket for a proscribed object, Section 8(b)(7)(B) will be activated.[145] If the union is certified, Section 8(b)(7) ceases to apply.

For various reasons both the union and the employer may decide not to file a petition. The employer, for example, may decide that activating the expedited election procedure by an RM petition and a Section 8(b)(7)(C) charge will not shorten the time in which proscribed picketing is permitted. Rather, upon the expiration of 30 days of proscribed picketing without the filing of a petition, a Section 8(b)(7)(C) charge will proceed solely along the unfair labor practice route; a petition filed thereafter or lingering Section 8(a)(1) or (3) violations will not affect the issue.[146] If the regional director "has reasonable cause to believe such charge is true and that a complaint should issue," he is required to petition a federal district court for an injunction.[147]

The union may be reluctant to file a petition because of its minority status[148] or because the employer's unfair labor practices would make the election route unduly hazardous. If it simply files unfair labor practice charges concerning violations of Sections 8(a)(1) and (3) and the employer also refrains from filing a petition, the union will be vulnerable to a Section 10(l) injunction despite the fact that the charges are meritorious.[149] There is a specific exception in Section 10(l) for a meritorious Section 8(a)(2) charge; in such case the regional director shall "not apply for a temporary restraining order."[150] A main point of controversy in

---

144 *Id.* at 1169.

145 *Id.* at 1157.

146 *Id.* at 1167.

147 §10 (1).

148 Presumably, a minority union that obtained recognition by proscribed picketing would be vulnerable to another union's picketing to the extent indicated in the discussion of §8 (b) (7) (A) at IV *supra*. *See* Vera Ladies Belt & Novelty Corp., 156 NLRB 291, 61 LRRM 1066 (1965), where an individual employee filed a §8 (a) (2) charge following recognition of a picketing minority union. For the problem of employer capitulation prior to an election and without regard to the union's majority status, see Wollenberger, *The Trouble With 8(b)(7)(C)*, 13 LAB. L. J. 284 (1962), cited in Meltzer, *supra* note 9, at 84, n. 28.

149 *Supra* note 146.

150 §10 (1). *See* Dayton Typographical Union v. NLRB, 326 F 2d 634, 54 LRRM 2535 (CA DC, 1963), for a discussion of the application of this section. *See* Chapter 7 *supra* for a discussion of §8 (a) (2).

the *Blinne* case[151] was whether, in the event the union enjoys majority status, the filing of a Section 8(a)(5) charge within the 30-day period excuses the union's failure to file a petition within that time. In other words, does the charge have the same operative effect as a petition in lifting the limitation of Section 8(b)(7)(C)? In *Blinne* the union had filed charges of Sections 8(a)(1), (2), (3), and (5) while picketing for more than 30 days without filing a petition. The regional director dismissed the Sections 8(a)(5) and (2) charges but found merit in the Sections 8(a)(1) and (3) charges. The union filed a petition after the Sections 8(a)(5) and (2) charges were dismissed, though not within the 30-day period.

In the first *Blinne* decision[152] the majority of the Board viewed the legislative rejection of a provision that would have made all violations of Section 8(a) adequate defenses to Section 8(b)(7) as persuasive evidence of legislative intent not to adopt this position. The amendment to Section 10(l) regarding meritorious Section 8(a)(2) charges specifically provided for a defense to Section 8(b)(7) charges; thus, in the majority view, Congress manifested an intent to make Section 8(a)(2) the sole defense to Section 8(b)(7). Moreover, the Board noted that the Section 8(a)(5) charge was dismissed in any event.

Just one year later, a slightly restructured Board panel reconsidered the *Blinne* case.[153] While the ultimate conclusion was the same, the reasoning of the majority in the second *Blinne* decision was quite different. If a meritorious Section 8(a)(5) charge had been filed, the majority said, a petition would not have been required,[154] since a representation petition assumes an unresolved question concerning representation, whereas a Section 8(a)(5) charge assumes that the employer is "wrongfully refusing to recognize or bargain." Thus, "a meritorious 8(a)(5) charge moots the question concerning representation which the petition is designed to resolve."[155] As to legislative intent, the majority stated that

---

151 Hod Carriers, Local 840 (C. A. Blinne Const. Co.), 130 NLRB 587, 47 LRRM 1318 (1961), *supplemental decision,* 135 LRRM 1153, 49 LRRM 1638 (1962). *See also* Dayton Typographical Union, *supra* note 150.
152 *Supra* note 151.
153 *Ibid.*
154 135 NLRB at 1166-1167, n. 24.
155 *Id.* at 1183. Because of this inconsistency, the Board had adhered to a policy of dismissing representation petitions where meritorious §8(a)(5) charges had been filed.

"[c]ongressional acquiescence in the Board's long-standing practice prior to the enactment of Section 8(b)(7)(C) imports . . . congressional approval. . . ."[156] Since a meritorious charge had not
been filed, the failure to file a petition did not preclude a violation
of Section 8(b)(7)(C).

With respect to the meritorious Sections 8(a)(1) and (3) charges,
the Board maintained its position that there is a violation of Section 8(b)(7)(C) unless a petition is filed. But the Board also adhered to its policy of not holding elections in the face of un-
remedied unfair labor practices. Thus, if a petition had been filed,
it would have been blocked until the charges were resolved.[157]

VII. THE INFORMATIONAL PICKETING PROVISO

Subparagraphs (A) and (B) of Section 8(b)(7) outlaw picketing
and threats to picket for specified proscribed objects and contain
no express exceptions to their coverage. Subparagraph (C), however, is subject to the express limitation that

> . . . nothing in this subparagraph (C) shall be construed to prohibit
> any picketing or other publicity for the purpose of truthfully advis-
> ing the public (including consumers) that an employer does not
> employ members of, or have a contract with, a labor organization,
> unless an effect of such picketing is to induce any individual em-
> ployed by any other person in the course of his employment, not
> to pick up, deliver or transport any goods or not to perform any
> services.

If the picketing satisfies the proviso's requirements, it may continue beyond the 30-day time limit, regardless of whether a majority or minority union is involved,[158] and the expedited-election
procedure is inapplicable.[159]

The proviso is another of the compromise features of Section
8(b)(7). Its purpose was, in part, to obviate constitutional ques-

---

156 *Id.* at 1184.
157 *Id.* at 1167.
158 Hotel & Restaurant Employees, Local 89 (Stork Restaurant), 135 NLRB 1173, 49
LRRM 1653 (1962); Hotel & Restaurant Employees, Local 681 (Crown Cafeteria),
135 NLRB 1183, 49 LRRM 1648 (1962), *enforced,* 327 F 2d 351, 55 LRRM 2302
(CA 9, 1964); Retail Clerks, Local 400 (Jumbo Food Stores, Inc.), 136 NLRB 414,
49 LRRM 1798 (1962). *See* Chapter 22 *infra* for additional discussion of the
§8(b)(7)(C) *proviso.*
159 Dep't & Specialty Store Employees Local 1265 (Oakland G. R. Kinney Co.), 136
NLRB 335, 49 LRRM 1771 (1962).

tions arising from a legislative attempt to inhibit appeals to the general public.[160] While permitting a considerable range of picketing, the proviso imposes a limitation upon the information conveyed and the effect of such appeals. Furthermore, the proviso is applicable solely to subparagraph (C).[161]

A. Scope of the Proviso: Dual-Purpose Picketing

In applying the proviso, the Board initially determined whether the proviso protected informational picketing that also had a recognitional or organizational object. In the first *Crown Cafeteria* case[162] a majority of the Board held that the proviso immunized picketing only "where the sole object is dissemination of information divorced from the present object of recognition."[163] The dissent construed the proviso as a broad exception to the ban on recognitional and organizational picketing, thus presupposing that the picketing was aimed at a recognitional or organizational target.[164]

Upon reconsideration, the original dissenting opinion prevailed.[165] A restructured Board rejected its initial decision, again

---

160 As written, it has thus far withstood the few challenges made to its constitutionality. *See* Hotel & Restaurant Employees v. Sperry, 323 F 2d 75, 54 LRRM 2298 (CA 8, 1963); NLRB v. Local 3, IBEW (Jack Picoult), 339 F 2d 600, 58 LRRM 2095 (CA 2, 1964). However, constitutional issues may still arise with respect to the scope of the injunction order. *See* McLeod v. Hotel & Restaurant Employees, Local 89, 280 F 2d 760, 764, 765, 46 LRRM 2577 (CA 2, 1960).

161 *Supra* note 118.

162 Hotel & Restaurant Employees, Local 681 (Crown Cafeteria), *supra* note 158.

163 *Id.* at 573. The majority argued that §8(b)(7) banned picketing where "an object" was for recognition or organization, even though the picketing may have had other objectives as well. In contrast, the proviso language would permit picketing for "the purpose" of advising the public. Since "an object" was found to be for recognition, "the purpose" could not be informational. The majority cited legislative history which spoke of the proviso as applying only to "purely" informational picketing.

164 *Id.* at 574. The dissent viewed scope of the proviso in precisely the opposite way as applying solely to picketing for recognitional or organizational objectives. It cited the court's language in *Getreu* v. *Hotel & Restaurant Employees Local 58*, 181 F Supp 738, 45 LRRM 2496 (ND Ind, 1960), that "[i]t is difficult, if not impossible, to imagine any kind of informational picketing pertaining to an employer's failure or refusal to employ union members or to have a collective bargaining agreement where another object of such picketing would not be ultimate union recognition or bargaining . In most instances certainly the aim of such informational picketing could only be to bring economic pressure upon the employer to recognize and bargain with the labor organization. To adopt petitioner's interpretation of subparagraph (C) would make the second proviso entirely meaningless." 181 F. Supp. at 741.

For a similar observation *see* Smitley d/b/a Crown Cafeteria v. NLRB, 327 F 2d 351, 353, 55 LRRM 2302 (CA 9, 1964), where the Ninth Circuit affirmed the reconsidered *Crown Cafeteria* case.

165 135 NLRB 1183, 49 LRRM 1648 (1962).

by a divided opinion. First, the majority noted that the advice
to the public to which the proviso expressly refers must clearly
imply a recognitional and bargaining object.[166] Second, Section
8(b)(7) prohibits only picketing for recognition or organization,
so that any appeals to the public "divorced" from that object
would not be prohibited in any event, *i.e.,* the proviso would be
superfluous other than to create an entirely new unfair labor practice.[167] The majority opinion was upheld by the Ninth Circuit.[168]

1. Appeal to the Public. Truthful informational picketing dis-
seminating "no contract" or "no members" advice to the public
is lawful unless it induces stoppages of deliveries and services. The
picketing must constitute an appeal to the public. Mere pro
forma communication with the public accompanied by recognitional and organizational appeals to the employer or its "employees
qua employees" [169] will not be shielded by the proviso.[170] Picketing service entrances rather than customer or public entrances
would belie an informational-publicity purpose.[171] Picket signs
addressed not only to the public but also to the employees may
not escape the ban of Section 8(b)(7).[172]

Whether picketing is addressed to the public has been a troublesome issue, particularly because of the nuances of the picket signs
and the acceptance of the signs, in particular cases, for what they
purport to convey. Where the signs are substantially in the words

---

[166] The signs read "[employer] does not employ members of, or have a contract
with. . . ." *Id.* at 1185.

[167] Nonrecognitional and nonorganizational picketing could become an unfair labor
practice. For the implications of the *Crown* decision, *see Stork Restaurant, supra*
note 158. In that case, the majority raised the question of whether purely informational picketing, divorced from proscribed objectives, would be violative even if it
had the effect of inducing stoppages. The majority reaffirmed its view that a recognitional or organizational objective is a precondition for the applicability of the
entire proviso. *But compare* the trial examiner's opinion, affirmed by the Board
in *Hotel & Restaurant Employees Local 89* (Cafe Renaissance), 154 NLRB 192, 198,
59 LRRM 1725 (1965). The trial examiner stated that even if the picketing had
been solely informational, it would not have been protected by §8(b) (7) (C) because of its effect on deliveries.

[168] 327 F 2d 351, 55 LRRM 2302 (CA 9, 1964).

[169] Philadelphia Window Cleaners & Maintenance Workers Union, Local 125 (Atlantic Maintenance Co.), 136 NLRB 1104, 1105, 49 LRRM 1939 (1962); Typographical Union Local 154 (Ypsilanti Press, Inc.), 137 NLRB 1116, 1117, n. 1,
50 LRRM 1312 (1962).

[170] Atlantic Maintenance Co., *supra* note 169; Normandin Bros. Co., 131 NLRB 1225,
48 LRRM 1224 (1961); Teamsters, Local 618 (Charlie's Car Wash & Service), 136
NLRB 934, 49 LRRM 1891 (1962); Hotel & Restaurant Employees, Local 568
(Restaurant Management, Inc.), 147 NLRB 1060, 56 LRRM 1334 (1964).

[171] Normandin Bros., *supra* note 170.

[172] Atlantic Maintenance Co., *supra* note 169.

of the proviso and are displayed only at public entrances to the premises, there is a greater likelihood that the picketing will be protected by the proviso.[173] Picket signs held to conform to the proviso include: "Please Do Not Patronize. . . . [Employer] Does Not Employ Members Of, Or Have A Contract With . . .";[174] "Notice to Members of Organized Labor and their Friends—This Establishment is Non-Union—Please Do Not Patronize."[175] But the language on picket signs is not determinative, even if it follows the proviso, if the evidence demonstrates that the picketing was not for the purpose of advising the public.[176]

Picket signs that do not conform to the proviso will not afford the picketing protection from Section 8(b)(7). For example, the Board does not regard signs protesting against "substandard" working conditions "as being encompassed within the language or purport of the proviso protecting picketing for the purpose of advising the public 'that an employer does not employ members of, or have a contract with, a labor organization.' "[177]

In determining whether purportedly informational picketing (that is, picketing with signs whose literal language falls within the proviso) does in fact have "the purpose" of advising the public, the Second Circuit has drawn a distinction, apparently adhered to by the Board, between permissible *publicity picketing* and unprivileged *signal picketing*.[178] The court would permit appeals to the unorganized public as individuals—"publicity picketing" to effectuate a consumer boycott—so long as the elements of communication predominate. But the court would severely limit "signal picketing"—calls to other unions for concerted economic action against the picketed employer. Signal picketing is pro-

---

173 Hotel & Restaurant Employees, Local 58 (Fowler Hotel, Inc.), 138 NLRB 1315, 51 LRRM 1180 (1962).
174 Jumbo Food Stores, *supra* note 158.
175 Crown Cafeteria, *supra* note 158.
176 *Cf.* Electrical Workers, Local 3 (Jack Picoult), 144 NLRB 5, 53 LRRM 1508 (1963), *enforced,* 339 F 2d 600, 58 LRRM 2095 (CA 2, 1964); Suffolk County Dist. Council of Carpenters (Island Coal & Lbr. Co.), 159 NLRB 895, 899, 900, 62 LRRM 1443 (1966), *enforced,* 387 F 2d 170, 67 LRRM 2012 (CA 2, 1967).
177 Electrical Workers, Local 113 (I.C.G. Electric, Inc.), 142 NLRB 1418, 53 LRRM 1239 (1963). *See* discussion of area-standards picketing *supra,* this chapter.
178 NLRB v. IBEW, Local 3, 317 F 2d 193, 53 LRRM 2116 (CA 2, 1963), *remanding* 137 NLRB 1401, 50 LRRM 1410 (1962), *on remand,* 144 NLRB 5, 53 LRRM 1508 (1963), *enforced,* 339 F 2d 600, 58 LRRM 2095 (CA 2, 1964). *See also* Dayton Typographical Union, *supra* note 150; Restaurant Management, Inc., *supra* note 170, at 1068; Carpenters Local 2133 (Leonard Ryan), 151 NLRB 1378, 1382, 58 LRRM 1617 (1965).

scribed whenever it has a recognitional or organizational object. Publicity picketing, however, is protected as long as it does not actually interfere with deliveries or communicate more than the limited information permitted under the proviso.[179]

2. Truthfully Advising the Public. The second condition of the proviso requires that picket signs be truthful. A divided Board found picket signs stating that an employer was "nonunion" to be truthful despite the fact that nonselling employees were actually represented by another union. The majority considered it "unreasonable to expect that . . . a union involved in a recognitional and bargaining dispute with an employer and concerned with its own problems should be required to assume the burden of informing the public that the employer may or does have a contract or contracts with other unions."[180] Similarly, picket signs stating that the employer did not employ members of the union were found to be truthful even though some employees had signed union authorization cards. The authorization cards were not equated with completed membership.[181]

3. An Impermissible Effect. The proviso contains the qualification that picketing must not have "an effect" of inducing "any individual employed by any other person" to refuse to deliver, pick up, or transport goods or refuse to perform any services. Since the exception carved out by the proviso is grounded upon appeals to the public, a limitation was placed upon picketing whose effect is not confined to this purpose.[182] The language of the proviso does not indicate the test to be used in determining when such an effect occurs, e.g., whether a single stoppage of one delivery is sufficient. Read literally, restrictive terms such as "any individual" and "any service" argue that a single stoppage should divest the picketing of the protection of the proviso. A Board majority, in *Barker Bros.*,[183] however, rejected a literal reading,

---

[179] NLRB v. IBEW, Local 3, *supra* note 178. *See also* Barker Bros. v. NLRB, 328 F 2d 431, 435, 55 LRRM 2544 (CA 9, 1964), *enforcing,* 138 NLRB 478, 51 LRRM 1053 (1962). *See also* discussion of consumer picketing in Chapter 22 *infra.*

[180] Retail Clerks Local 324 (Barker Bros.), 138 NLRB 478, 51 LRRM 1053 (1962), *enforced, supra* note 179.

[181] Jumbo Food Stores, *supra* note 158.

[182] While the proviso does not apply to §8(b)(7)(B) cases, the "effect" of the picketing in such cases may be considered in determining the real purpose of the picketing. NLRB v. Knitgoods Workers Union, Local 155, 403 F 2d 388, 391, 69 LRRM 2666 (CA 2, 1968).

[183] Barker Bros., *supra* note 180.

stating that a "quantitative" test of number of deliveries or services not performed was an "inadequate yardstick" and that the more reasonable test was the actual impact on the picketed business. It held that the interruption or stoppage must actually have "disrupted, interfered with, or curtailed the employer's business"[184] and that the burden is upon the General Counsel to show that it had this effect.

The exact point at which interruptions of deliveries or work stoppages create the requisite impact upon the employer's business has not been made clear. Three delivery stoppages, two work delays, and several delivery delays in the course of 12 weeks of picketing at 18 retail stores were not sufficient to sustain the existence of an "impact" in *Barker Bros.*,[185] and in *Jay Jacobs* [186] three stoppages in five months were not enough.[187] In both cases, the Board majority appeared to consider union announcements of a desire not to interrupt deliveries of considerable consequence. By contrast, picketing was stripped of the protection of the proviso where a restaurant was forced to "modify its method of doing business with suppliers whose products were essential to its daily operations." In that case the total stoppage of liquor deliveries for 2½ months created the requisite impact.[188] Where many suppliers refuse to enter the employer's premises and require the employer to "divert its own personnel and equipment from their usual functions to obtain deliveries by picking up supplies" at distant locations, the picketing may not be protected.[189] The fact that the deliveries may ultimately have been made, either by employees normally assigned elsewhere or by officials of the supplier, does not negate the "effect" of the picketing.[190] A Board majority

---

184 *Ibid.*
185 *Ibid.*
186 Retail Clerks, Local 1404 (Jay Jacobs Downtown, Inc.), 140 NLRB 1344, 52 LRRM 1237 (1963).
187 *See also* Retail Clerks, Local 57 (Hested Stores Co.), 138 NLRB 498, 51 LRRM 1061 (1962); Retail Clerks, Local 428 (Martino's Complete Home Furnishings), 141 NLRB 503, 52 LRRM 1347 (1963).
188 Hotel & Restaurant Employees, Local 500 (Joe Hunt's Restaurant), 138 NLRB 470, 51 LRRM 1063 (1962). For other disruptions having the proviso "effect," *see* Electrical Workers, Local 429 (Sam Melson), 138 NLRB 460, 463, 51 LRRM 1065 (1962), where, in a construction industry case, subcontractors' employees refused to cross a picket line; Leonard Ryan, *supra* note 178, at 1381, n. 10; Meat Cutters Local 627 (Ershowsky Provision Co., Inc.), 163 NLRB 584, 64 LRRM 1374 (1967); Grain Millers Local 16 (Bartlett & Co., Grain), 141 NLRB 974, 52 LRRM 1441 (1963).
189 Island Coal & Lbr. Co., *supra* note 176 at 901.
190 Restaurant Management, Inc., *supra* note 170, at 1068-1069.

has held, however, that the mere fact that picketing interferes with deliveries or services does not, of itself, constitute a violation of Section 8(b)(7)(C) unless the picketing has a recognitional or organizational objective.[191] This is consistent with the majority view in *Crown Cafeteria* [192] that the proviso applies only to recognitional or organizational picketing, "the subject matter with which the whole of Section 8(b)(7) is exclusively concerned." [193] Thus, in the majority view the effect of nonrecognitional or nonorganizational picketing upon deliveries would not be relevant in determining the legality of the picketing.[194]

---

[191] Houston Bldg. & Const. Trades Council (Claude Everett Const. Co.) , 136 NLRB 321, 49 LRRM 1757 (1962) .
[192] *Supra* note 158.
[193] *Supra* note 191.
[194] *Ibid.*

CHAPTER 22

HANDBILLING AND CONSUMER PICKETING

I. GENERALLY PROTECTED NATURE OF HANDBILLING AND PICKETING

Within legal limits, unions may exert economic pressure upon employers by means of handbills and consumer picketing, notwithstanding the fact that such conduct may constitute a secondary boycott. This chapter treats *lawful secondary activity,* as distinguished from the unlawful secondary activity treated in the next chapter. (Since Congress did not draw a clear line between lawful and unlawful secondary activity, however, some of the case law of the two chapters overlaps. Also, Chapter 23 deals with other forms of lawful secondary activity, *e.g.,* the ally doctrine, in their relation to unlawful activity.)

At the outset, it should be noted that handbilling and peaceful picketing have been safeguarded, as well as limited, by both constitutional and statutory provisions. In varying degrees these communication devices have been accorded freedom of expression guarantees of the First and Fourteenth Amendments to the U. S. Constitution. In 1940 the Supreme Court, in *Thornhill* v. *Alabama,*[1] broadly stated that:

> The freedom of speech and press guaranteed by the Constitution embraces at the least the liberty to discuss publicly and truthfully all matters of public concern without previous restraint or fear of subsequent punishment.

In subsequent cases,[2] however, the Court limited the sweeping pronouncements of *Thornhill,* at least as applied to picketing:

---

[1] 310 US 88, 101-102, 6 LRRM 697 (1940). *See* discussion of the constitutional protection of the right to strike in Chapter 19 *supra.*
[2] *E.g.,* Hughes v. Superior Court, 339 US 460, 26 LRRM 2072 (1950); Bakery & Pastry Drivers v. Wohl, 315 US 769, 10 LRRM 507 (1942); Teamsters Local 695 v. Vogt, Inc., 354 US 284, 40 LRRM 2208 (1957). *See also* Chapter 19 *supra* at notes 7-9.

Picketing by an organized group is more than free speech, since it involves patrol of a particular locality and since the very presence of a picket line may induce action of one kind or another, quite irrespective of the nature of the ideas which are being disseminated.[3]

However, in *Amalgamated Food Employees* v. *Logan Valley Plaza, Inc.,*[4] the Court reaffirmed the applicability of the constitutional guarantee, while noting the basis for limiting picketing:

[P]icketing involves elements of both speech and conduct, i.e., patrolling, and . . . because of this intermingling of protected and unprotected elements, picketing can be subjected to controls that would not be constitutionally permissible in the case of pure speech. . . . Nevertheless, no case decided by this court can be found to support the proposition that the non-speech aspects of peaceful picketing are so great as to render the provisions of the First Amendment inapplicable to it altogether.

In contrast to picketing, handbilling has traditionally represented almost a pure form of speech (or press) entitled to the full array of First Amendment protection. But dictum in *Logan Valley* suggests the contrary, for the Court observed that "[h]andbilling, like picketing, involves conduct other than speech, namely the physical presence of the person distributing leaflets. . . ." [5]

Section 7 of the National Labor Relations Act protects the right of employees "to engage in other concerted activities for the purpose of collective bargaining or other mutual aid or protection," and this statutory language has been interpreted to include the right to picket.[6] Section 13 of the Act, preserving the right to strike "except as specifically provided for," is also held to include the right to picket.[7] It is, nonetheless, within the power of Congress to restrict handbilling and picketing, as well as other forms

---

[3] Bakery & Pastry Drivers v. Wohl, note 2 *supra*, 315 US at 776 (concurring opinion).
[4] 391 US 308, 313, 68 LRRM 2209 (1968). *See* Chapter 19 *supra* at notes 10-18.
[5] Note 4 *supra*, 391 US at 315-316. *Compare,* Lovell v. City of Griffin, 303 US 444, 452 (1938): "The liberty of the press is not confined to newspapers and periodicals. It necessarily embraces pamphlets and leaflets. These have been historic weapons in the defense of liberty, as the pamphlets of Thomas Paine and others in our own history abundantly attest."
[6] NLRB v. Thayer Co.. 213 F2d 748, 34 LRRM 2250 (CA 1, 1954), *cert. denied,* 348 US 883, 35 LRRM 2100 (1954). Under §2 (3) of the Act the term "employee" includes "any employee, and shall not be limited to the employees of a particular employer," and under §2 (9) a controversy may be a "labor dispute" "regardless of whether the disputants stand in the proximate relation of employer and employee."
[7] NLRB v. Teamsters, 362 US 274, 45 LRRM 2975 (1960) ; NLRB v. International Rice Milling Co., 341 US 665, 28 LRRM 2105 (1951).

of speech, for purposes deemed inimical to the public interest. In doing so, it deals "explicitly with isolated evils which experience has established flow from such picketing." [8] In the *Tree Fruits* [9] case, the Supreme Court observed that

> . . . Congress has consistently refused to prohibit peaceful picketing except where it is used as a means to achieve specific ends which experience has shown are undesirable. . . . We have recognized this congressional practice and have not ascribed to Congress a purpose to outlaw peaceful picketing unless 'there is the clearest indication in the legislative history' . . . that Congress intended to do so as regards the particular ends of the picketing under review. Both the congressional policy and our adherence to this principle of interpretation reflect concern that a broad ban against peaceful picketing might collide with the guarantees of the First Amendment.

It is in this setting that we view the statutory provisions and cases relating to handbilling and consumer picketing—two forms of secondary boycott which have not been outlawed by the provisions of the NLRA or its amendments.

II. THE PUBLICITY PROVISO

A. Enactment

The amendments made by the Labor-Management Reporting and Disclosure Act of 1959 in the NLRA were designed to plug some "loopholes" [10] in the statutory treatment of secondary activity proscribed by Section 8(b)(4). In attempting to close these

---

[8] NLRB v. Teamsters Local 639, 362 US 274, 284, 45 LRRM 2975 (1960); Int'l Brotherhood of Electrical Workers v. NLRB, 341 US 694, 28 LRRM 2115 (1951). *See* note 5 *supra*.

[9] NLRB v. Fruit and Vegetable Packers, 377 US 58, 62-63, 55 LRRM 2961 (1964), (*see* note 27 *infra*). This chapter does not treat "informational" picketing except where such picketing is directed, or purports to be directed, toward consumers. Other forms of informational picketing are treated in Chapters 21 and 23. *See* distinction between "publicity picketing" and "signal picketing" discussed in Chapter 21 *supra* at notes 177-178. In particular, picketing under the proviso to Section 8(b) (7) (C) is discussed in Chapter 21 *supra*, as are area-standards picketing and other types of picketing deemed exceptions to the limitations which §8(b) (7) places upon recognitional and organizational picketing. Cases which skirt the edge of the fine distinction between primary and secondary picketing will be found in Chapter 23 *infra*, which treats generally the subject of unlawful secondary activity under Section 8(b) (4) (B).

[10] *See* discussion of legislative history in *NLRB* v. *Fruit and Vegetable Packers*, 377 US 58, 55 LRRM 296 (1964). *See also* Chapter 4 *supra*.

loopholes, Congress added a proviso to Section 8(b)(4) [11] that would preserve for the unions certain avenues of communication with the public and thus obviate constitutional questions.[12]

Under the language of the proviso, it would appear that truthful [13] handbills and similar forms of publicity—but not picketing —may be employed to inform consumers generally, and customers of a secondary employer in particular, that "products produced" by a primary employer with whom there is a labor dispute are being distributed by the secondary employer. The publicity may not, however, "have an effect of inducing" an employee, other than an employee of the primary employer, to refuse to perform his duties.

B. Meaning of "Product or Products" and "Produced"

In *Lohman Sales* [14] a wholesale distributor, the primary employer with whom the union had a labor dispute, argued that it did not "produce" a product but merely "handled" a product "produced" by others. The Board rejected the contention, holding that, "*labor* is the prime requisite of one who produces," and that for purposes of the proviso, an employer "need not be the actual manufacturer to add his labor in the form of capital, enterprise, and service to the product he furnishes the retailers." [15]

---

11 Section 8(b) (4) as amended provides: ". . . That for the purposes of this paragraph (4) only, nothing contained in such paragraph shall be construed to prohibit publicity, other than picketing, for the purpose of truthfully advising the public, including consumers and members of a labor organization, that a product or products are produced by an employer with whom the labor organization has a primary dispute and are distributed by another employer, as long as such publicity does not have an effect of inducing any individual employed by any person other than the primary employer in the course of his employment to refuse to pick up, deliver, or transport any goods, or not to perform any services, at the establishment of the employer engaged in such distribution."

See: Aaron, *The Labor-Management Reporting and Disclosure Act of 1959,* 73 HARV. L. REV. 1086, 1114 (1960) ; Ryan, *Recognition, Organizational, Consumer Picketing,* 48 GEO. L. J. 359, 369-70 (1959) ; Previant, *The New Hot-Cargo and Secondary Boycott Sections: A Critical Analysis,* 48 GEO. L. J. 346, 353 (1959).

12 *See* the second proviso to §8(b) (7) (C), discussed in Chapter 21 *supra,* for a similar approach.

13 For examples of "misleading handbills" *see* Honolulu Typographical Union No. 37, 167 NLRB 1030, 66 LRRM 1194 (1967), *enforced in part,* 401 F2d 952, 68 LRRM 3004 (CA DC, 1968). But truthfulness will be found if there was no intent to deceive and no substantial departure from the truth. Teamsters Local 537 (Lohman Sales Co.), 132 NLRB 901, 906, 48 LRRM 1429 (1961). But truthful handbills may be used as evidence to show illegality of the picketing. Los Angeles Typographical Union (White Front Stores), 181 NLRB No. 61, 73 LRRM 1390 (1970).

14 Teamsters Local 537, 132 NLRB 901, 48 LRRM 1429 (1961).

15 132 NLRB at 907.

With the *Lohman Sales* doctrine as its basis, the Board held in
Middle South [16] that a radio station which advertised automobiles
distributed by a secondary employer, with respect to whom handbills had been circulated to potential customers, was one of the
producers of the product because "the primary employer radio
station, by adding its labor in the form of capital, enterprise and
service to the automobiles . . . becomes one of the producers of
the automobiles." [17] And in *Great Western* [18] the same concept
was applied to advertising by a television station.[19] In *Houston
Armored Car*,[20] handbilling of customers whose money was
handled by an armored car service with whom guards were in dispute was protected by the publicity proviso since the service
"produced" by the primary employer was a "product" and therefore it was a "producer."

In 1964 in *Servette*,[21] the Supreme Court settled the dispute as
to whether the proviso to Section 8(b)(4) was limited to manufacturing operations by holding that any employer, including a
distributor, was a "producer." The court of appeals, relying on
its own decision in *Great Western,* had held that Servette, a wholesale distributor of specialty merchandise, was not directly involved
in the physical process of creating the products and thus did not
"produce any products." Rejecting this view, the Supreme Court
held:

> In its decision in *Great Western Broadcasting Corp.* v. *Labor
> Board, supra,* the Court of Appeals reasoned that since a "proces-
> sor" and "manufacturer" are engaged in the physical creation of
> goods, the word "producer" must be read as limited to one who

---

[16] Radio and Television Engineers, 133 NLRB 1698, 49 LRRM 1042 (1961).

[17] 133 NLRB at 1705.

[18] San Francisco Local, American Federation of Television and Radio Artists, 134 NLRB 1617, 47 LRRM 2775 (1961).

[19] On *petition to review* in *Great Western Broadcasting Corp.* v. *NLRB,* 310 F 2d 591, 51 LRRM 2480 (CA 9, 1962), the court set aside the Board's order because, in the court's view, television advertising was not "production" of the advertised products for purposes of the publicity proviso. But this decision was criticized in *NLRB* v. *Servette, Inc.,* note 21 *infra,* and overruled, *sub silentio,* in *Great Western Broadcasting Corp.* v. *NLRB,* 356 F 2d 434, 61 LRRM 2364 (CA 9, 1966), *cert. denied,* 384 US 1002, 62 LRRM 2392 (1966).

[20] United Plant Guard Workers of America, 136 NLRB 110, 49 LRRM 1713 (1962).

[21] NLRB v. Servette, Inc., 377 US 46, 55 LRRM 2957 (1964), *reversing* NLRB v. Servette, Inc., 310 F 2d 659, 51 LRRM 2621 (CA 9, 1962).

performs similar functions. On the contrary, we think that "producer" must be given a broader reach, else it is rendered virtually superfluous.[22]

C. The Right to Handbill

The facts in *Servette* illustrate the manner in which unions have used "publicity, other than picketing," allowed by the Section 8(b)(4) proviso: The union was engaged in a strike against Servette. Union representatives approached various managers of supermarkets and requested that they discontinue handling merchandise supplied by Servette. In most instances, the union representatives also warned that handbills asking the public not to buy named items distributed by Servette would be passed out in front of those stores that refused to cooperate. In a few instances such handbills were in fact distributed. The Supreme Court held that such conduct was lawful. The handbills truthfully advised the public that the products in question had been "produced" by an employer with whom the union had a primary dispute, thus satisfying the requirements of the proviso. The Court also held that the warnings which threatened distribution of handbills in front of noncooperating stores were not prohibited as 'threats' within the meaning of Section 8(b)(4)(ii). The Court reasoned that "[t]he statutory protection for the distribution of handbills would be undermined if a threat to engage in protected conduct were not itself protected." [23]

---

[22] 377 US at 55. However, the Court was concerned in *Servette* only with the question of whether a distributor was a "producer." Classification of advertisers as producers of the advertised products is going considerably farther; the facts of the original *Great Western* decision are distinguishable from those of *Servette*, and *Great Western* might still be followed so far as it applies to advertisers. *See* note 19 *supra*. Such a distinction was made in Honolulu Typographical Union, Local 37, 167 NLRB 1030, 66 LRRM 1194 (1967), *enforced in part*, 401 F 2d 952, 68 LRRM 3004 (CA DC, 1968). *See* notes 36-40 *infra*.

[23] 377 US at 57. *See* Chapter 23 *infra* at notes 56-61 for further discussion of *Servette* and the issues decided therein. In *Sheet Metal Workers* (Sakowitz, Inc.), 174 NLRB No. 60, 70 LRRM 1215, 1217 (1969), a union was permitted to handbill the downtown location of a store which had rented space in a suburban shopping center. At the shopping center a subcontractor was performing services at wages which the union was protesting as "substandard." The Board held that "[n]either the Act nor the legislative history indicate the existence of a geographic limitation on the publicity proviso. To the contrary, the legislative history indicates that it was contemplated that utilization of mass media was protected by the proviso." *See* Engel, *Secondary Consumer Picketing—Following the Struck Product*, 52 Va. L. Rev. 189 (1966); Lewis, *Consumer Picketing and the Court—The Questionable Yield of Tree Fruits*, 49 Minn. L. Rev. 479 (1965); Comment, *Product Picketing—A New Loophole in Section 8(b)(4) of the National Labor Relations Act*, 63 Mich. L. Rev. 682 (1965); Note, *Picketing and Publicity under Section 8(b)(4) of the LMRA*, 73 Yale L. J. 1265 (1964).

III. CONSUMER PICKETING

Before 1959 the Board's view with respect to the nature of picketing as an inducement or invitation to response was that picketing "necessarily invites employees to [make common cause with the strikers and] refrain from working behind it, irrespective of the literal appeal of the legends on the picket signs," [24] so that "the foreseeable consequence, or stated differently, the natural or probable result of picketing at an entrance used in part by [secondary] employees is to induce a strike." [25]

A. The *Tree Fruits* Case

After 1959, the Board initially continued to adhere to its earlier view of consumer picketing.[26] But in *Tree Fruits*,[27] the Board reconsidered this doctrine and decided that "picketing of a secondary employer's premises does not *per se* constitute inducement or encouragement of employees of neutrals . . . nor does it raise an irrebuttable presumption as to the intent or probable consequences of the picketing." [28] Accordingly, the Board held that secondary picketing directed at consumers only, without the

---

[24] Laundry, Linen Supply & Dry Cleaning Drivers (Southern Service Company, Ltd.) 118 NLRB 1435, 1437, 40 LRRM 1395 (1957), *enforced*, 262 F 2d 617, 43 LRRM 2335 (CA 9, 1958).

[25] United Wholesale and Warehouse Employees (Perfection Mattress and Spring Co.), 125 NLRB 520, 45 LRRM 1129, (1959), *set aside*, 282 F 2d 824, 46 LRRM 2554 (CA DC, 1960), because no warrant was found for the conclusion that "the picketing *had as its necessary effect* the inducing and encouraging of employees to engage in a work stoppage." *See* also Chapter 23 *infra* at notes 65-66.

[26] Local 261, United Wholesale and Warehouse Employees (Perfection Mattress & Spring Co.), 129 NLRB 1014, 47 LRRM 1121 (1960): "the foregoing principles and precedents respecting picketing *vis-à-vis* inducement and encouragement have not been altered or modified by the 1959 amendments; they are just as pertinent now as they were before the amendments. . . ." For text of the amended statutory provision, *see* Chapter 23 *infra* at note 49.

[27] Fruit & Vegetable Packers & Warehousemen (Tree Fruits Labor Relations Committee, Inc.), 132 NLRB 1172, 48 LRRM 1496 (1961). The union had called a strike against fruit packing firms that were members of the Tree Fruits Labor Relations Committee (a multi-employer bargaining association). The struck firms sold Washington State apples to the Safeway chain of retail stores. As part of a consumer boycott, the union placed pickets at the customer entrances of 46 Safeway stores in Seattle. The pickets wore placards and distributed handbills appealing to Safeway customers and to the public generally to refrain from buying Washington State apples. Elaborate precautions were taken to limit the appeals to customers only, thus avoiding appeals to store employees or other employees: letters were sent to the store managers, written instructions given to the pickets, and the pickets were forbidden to request that customers not patronize the store. At all times during the picketing the store employees continued working, and no deliveries or pickups were obstructed. The picketing was entirely peaceful. *Tree Fruits* is also discussed in Chapter 23 *infra* at notes 77-88.

[28] 132 NLRB at 1176.

intent or the effect of inducing employees of neutral persons to engage in work stoppages, was not violative of Section 8(b)(4)(i)(B). But this was not dispositive of *Tree Fruits*. Of more significance was that secondary consumer picketing was, nonetheless, held by the Board to threaten, coerce, or restrain such neutral persons (employers) within the meaning of Section 8(b)(4)(ii))B) because:

> The natural and foreseeable result of such picketing, if successful, would be to force or require [the neutral employer] to reduce or discontinue altogether its purchases . . . from the struck employers. It is reasonable to infer, and we do, that Respondents intended this natural and foreseeable result.[29]

The Court of Appeals for the District of Columbia,[30] in remanding, held that a showing that the secondary picketing would "threaten, coerce or restrain" the secondary employer could be satisfied only by affirmative proof that a substantial impact on the secondary employer had occurred, or was likely to occur, as a result of the conduct.

The Supreme Court adopted neither the Board's nor the circuit court's views.[31] It held that a union could picket to persuade consumers approaching a store not to purchase a product produced by an employer with whom the union had a dispute. The Court was confronted with the specific language in the "publicity proviso," which removed prohibitions only on publicity "other than picketing." Thus, consumer picketing presented a much more troublesome problem than did handbilling.[32] The majority's view of the legislative history, however, was that Congress did not intend to prohibit all consumer picketing at secondary sites. In distinguishing between permissible and proscribed consumer picketing the Court focused its inquiry upon the purpose of the picketing union—is it to cut off all trade with the neutral employer or merely to induce customers to refrain from purchasing

---

[29] *Id.* at 1177.
[30] Local 760, Fruit and Vegetable Packers and Warehousemen, 308 F 2d 311, 50 LRRM 2392 (CA DC, 1962).
[31] NLRB v. Fruit and Vegetable Packers, 377 US 58, 55 LRRM 2961 (1964). *See also* Lewis, *supra* note 23.
[32] *See* discussion of handbilling as compared to picketing in *Honolulu Typographical Union, supra* note 22. *See* distinctions drawn between handbilling and picketing in Chapter 21 *supra* at notes 26-30 and in Note, *supra* note 23. *See also* Los Angeles Typographical Union (White Front Stores), *supra* note 13.

the particular struck product at the neutral employer's premises? The essence of *Tree Fruits* was summarized by the Court as follows:

> When consumer picketing is employed only to persuade customers not to buy the struck product, the Union's appeal is closely confined to the primary dispute. The site of the appeal is expanded to include the premises of the secondary employer, but if the appeal succeeds, the secondary employer's purchases from the struck firms are decreased only because the public has diminished its purchases of the struck product. On the other hand, when consumer picketing is employed to persuade customers not to trade at all with the secondary employer, the latter stops buying the struck product, not because of a falling demand, but in response to pressures designed to inflict injury on his business generally. In such case, the Union does more than merely follow the struck product; it creates a separate dispute with the secondary employer.[33]

The Court's view clearly differed from that of the circuit court, which had applied the test of economic loss. The Court explained that a violation of Section 8(b)(4)(ii)(B) would not be established "merely because respondents' picketing was effective to reduce Safeway's sale of Washington State apples," despite the fact that this "led or might lead Safeway to drop the item as a poor seller." [34]

The majority of the Court interpreted Section 8(b)(4) as not proscribing all peaceful consumer picketing and so did not reach the constitutional question.[35] Mr. Justice Black, in a concurring opinion, argued that the legislative history of the 1959 amendments dictated a view that all peaceful consumer picketing at a secondary site was precluded. He then concluded that the statute,

---

[33] 377 US at 72. As a consequence of the Court's opinion in *Tree Fruits*, reconsideration of secondary consumer picketing by the Board resulted in the dismissal of complaints in the following cases: Local 680, Teamsters (Wooley's Dairy), 147 NLRB 506, 56 LRRM 1286 (1964) ; Local 324, Teamsters (Cascade Employers Assn., Inc.) , 147 NLRB 669, 56 LRRM 1288 (1964) ; Local 559, Teamsters (Anapolsky & Son) , 147 NLRB 1128, 56 LRRM 1366 (1964) .

[34] 377 US at 72-73.

[35] The dissent disagreed with the majority view of the legislative history, particularly with respect to interpretation of the phrase "other than picketing." The dissent also posed the question of treatment of picketing that persuaded customers not to buy the *sole product* of the store. "If, for example, an independent gas station owner sells gasoline purchased from a struck gasoline company, one would not suppose he would feel less threatened, coerced, or restrained by picket signs which said 'Do not buy X gasoline' than by signs which said 'Do not patronize this gas station . . .' " 377 US at 83 (Harlan, J., dissenting) . A slight variation of this issue later arose in *Honolulu Typographical Union,* note 36 *infra.*

interpreted to prevent all such peaceful picketing, prevented free
dissemination of information about a labor dispute and so in-
fringed upon free speech in violation of the First Amendment.

B. Aftermath of *Tree Fruits*

The process of "elucidating litigation," to define the practical
dimensions of the *Tree Fruits* doctrine, has not ripened into easily
applied rules. The decisions tend to turn upon a close examination of the economic setting of the individual disputes.

**1. The Economic Setting: Consumer's Inability to Respond in
Sufficiently Limited Manner.** In some instances the consumer is
unable to refrain from purchasing the primary product without
entirely ceasing patronage of the secondary employer. The Board
has interpreted *Tree Fruits* as inapplicable "where the struck
'product' has become an integral part of the retailer's entire offering," so that any "product boycott will of necessity encompass the
entire business of the secondary employer." [36] This distinction is
aptly illustrated in *Teamsters, Local 327 (American Bread Co.)*,[37]
where *Tree Fruits* was held not to immunize picketing of a restaurant where the primary dispute was with the producer of bread
which the restaurant used in the preparation of meals. The restaurant did not sell the bread at retail other than as part of a meal
served for consumption on the premises. As the Board noted, "a
customer is hardly in a position to choose the brand of bread he
will consume, as a customer in a retail store is able to do." [38] The
restaurant customer "either takes the meal as offered or goes elsewhere for a meal." Thus the bread "loses its identity when served,
and becomes a part of the restaurant's product which is offered to
the customers." [39] According to the Board's view, the picketing,
in reality, sought to divert patronage so that the restaurants would
cease buying the bread and was thus violative of Section
8(b)(4)(ii)(B).

---

36 NLRB v. Honolulu Typographical Union, 401 F 2d 952, 955, 68 LRRM 3004
(CA DC, 1968).
37 170 NLRB No. 19, 67 LRRM 1427 (1968), *enforced*, 411 F 2d 147, 71 LRRM
2243 (CA 6, 1969).
38 67 LRRM at 1429-1430.
39 *Id.* at 1430. It may well be that the Board's interpretation will result in broader
immunity from consumer picketing for those secondary sellers who are "retailing"
struck products that become so integral a part of the seller's business as to make
them indistinguishable therefrom, *i.e.*, restaurants as compared to retail department
stores.

Restaurants also provided the economic setting for the Board's decision, affirmed by the District of Columbia Circuit Court, in *Honolulu Typographical Union*.[40] In that case the union, in support of its strike against a newspaper, also picketed the entrance to a shopping center which housed about 50 shops. Six of the shops (five restaurants and one jewelry store) regularly advertised in the struck newspaper. Each picket sign named one of the five restaurants that were targets of the picketing.

The Board found the union's picketing unlawful because it was directed toward a total boycott of the neutral employers in the shopping center. Consumers were urged not to buy products advertised by the restaurants in the struck newspaper. But the advertising simply promoted the restaurants as places to eat. Thus, the only possible form of support which the union could enlist from the customers was a *complete* withholding of their patronage from those places, whereas in *Tree Fruits* the customers were asked not to withhold patronage from a retail store but simply to forego buying a particular brand of apples once they entered the store. In *Tree Fruits* the union merely followed the struck product to the premises of the secondary employer, and its limited appeal was held not to coerce the secondary employer since it was confined to the primary dispute. In *Honolulu Typographical Union*, however, the union was held to have created a separate dispute with the restaurant—the neutral employer. Viewed in this setting, the court stated that the "only realistic meaning of the appeal is the traditional 'do not patronize this establishment.' " [41]

Where there is no way in which the customers of picketed stores can withhold patronage from the primary employer, the Board has concluded that the sole object and effect of the picketing is to injure the neutral secondary employer. Thus, picketing of stores already built by the primary employer, with whom the stores no longer have any business relationships, would fall into this category.[42] While the lack of any existing business relationship might be a basis for arguing that there was no "cease doing busi-

---

[40] Notes 22 and 36 *supra*.

[41] 401 F 2d at 954. *Accord*, Los Angeles Typographical Union (White Front Stores), 181 NLRB No. 61, 73 LRRM 1390 (1970).

[42] Salem Bldg. Trades Council (Cascade Employers Ass'n), 163 NLRB 33, 64 LRRM 1265 (1967). *Cf.* Janesville Typographical Union, 173 NLRB No. 137, 69 LRRM 1457 (1968).

ness" object as required by the statute, the Board has rejected such an argument in this economic setting.

In this connection the Board places significance upon the presence or absence of a tangible struck product or service offered to consumers. Thus, consumer picketing of a sales office and a retail store to advertise the nonunion status of a janitorial contractor who did occasional cleaning on the premises, was held to be outside the ambit of *Tree Fruits*.[43] Neither the store nor the sales office "was purveying to its customers—who might have been inclined to respect a product boycott picket line—any goods or services furnished by the primary employer." [44]

In one janitorial case, involving a bank, the Tenth Circuit, in upholding the Board, noted that, unlike *Tree Fruits,* the activity involved "did not follow a product (or service) so as to contain a primary dispute, but was specifically divorced from the primary employees' activities and thrust directly at the bank's physical properties, its employees and customers, and during banking hours only." [45] The picketing was, therefore, held to have unlawfully extended the dispute to the secondary employer.

2. Timing, Location, and Specificity of Union's Appeal. Board decisions appear to suggest that in order to come within the *Tree Fruits* doctrine, a union must meet criteria reminiscent of those adopted by the Board in common and roving situs-picketing situations concerning the timing and location of the picketing and the specificity of the union's appeal.[46]

Where the picketing is insufficiently identified with the primary employer or the struck product, it will be viewed as picketing aimed at the secondary employer and outside the scope of *Tree Fruits*.[47] In such circumstances its posture as a consumer boycott would be undermined notwithstanding consumer messages on the

---

43 151 NLRB 341, 58 LRRM 1406 (1965).
44 151 NLRB at 347.
45 NLRB v. Building Service Employees Int'l. Union, Local 105, 367 F 2d 227, 229, 63 LRRM 2307 (CA 10, 1966), *enforcing* 151 NLRB 1424, 58 LRRM 1614 (1965).
46 *E.g.,* Local No. 550, Carpenters (Steiner Lumber Co.), 153 NLRB 1285, 59 LRRM 1662 (1965), *enforced,* 367 F 2d 953, 63 LRRM 2328 (CA 9, 1966); Alton-Wood River Building Trades Council (Alton District Independent Contractors), 154 NLRB 932, 60 LRRM 1067 (1965). *See* Chapter 23 *infra.*
47 Bedding Workers, Local 140 (U. S. Mattress Corp.), 164 NLRB 271, 65 LRRM 1514 (1967). The good faith of the union is deemed irrelevant. It cannot shift its burden of product identification to the public. Atlanta Typographical Union (Times-Journal, Inc.), 180 NLRB No. 164, 73 LRRM 1241 (1970).

picket signs.[48] For example, a picket sign requesting the public to refrain from buying furniture unless it bore a union label did not sufficiently identify and specify the primary employer. It was thus held to be directed at the secondary employer generally and violative of Section 8(b)(4).[49]

On the other hand, picketing of retail stores and signs reading "Teamster Local 150 Protests Unfair Labor Practices of Coca-Cola Bottling Company. Please Do Not Patronize" were held to convey sufficiently the message that the dispute was only with Coca-Cola and that the boycott was confined to its products. The argument that the language "do not patronize" was an implied appeal for a total boycott of the stores was rejected.[50]

The place of the picketing may belie a consumer-boycott attempt, particularly where the sites selected are not accessible to potential consumers. In *Teamsters, Local 327* [51] the union picketed the premises of a secondary employer (an industrial plant) who had a concession agreement with a cafeteria that used the primary employer's bread. By placing pickets at gates used by persons who could not use the cafeteria, the union unlawfully brought the dispute to the secondary employer.

Timing is also persuasive. Picketing assertedly directed to consumers only at a common entrance to a home-building site, protesting a dispute with a lumber company making deliveries to the site, was conducted at such times as to negate its consumer orientation. Picketing coincided with the commencement of construction work 2½ hours before the sales office opened. Furthermore, no picketing occurred on the weekends when construction workers were absent and only prospective home purchasers were on the site.[52]

---

[48] *Ibid. See also* Laundry, Cleaning and Dyehouse Workers (Morrison's of San Diego, Inc.), 164 NLRB 1168, 65 LRRM 1193 (1967).
[49] *Supra* note 47.
[50] Teamsters Local 150 (Coca-Cola Bottling Co.), 151 NLRB 734, 58 LRRM 1477 (1965).
[51] *Supra* note 37.
[52] Steiner Lumber Co., *supra* note 46.

CHAPTER 23

UNLAWFUL SECONDARY ACTIVITY

I. DEVELOPMENT OF THE LAW

A. Pre-Taft-Hartley

In the history of the labor movement, the secondary boycott, in its various shapes and forms, has often proved itself to be one of the most effective weapons in labor's economic arsenal. Although the very ambiguity of the term "secondary boycott" may seem to obscure precise definition, the practice has been described as "a combination to influence A by exerting some sort of economic or social pressure against persons who deal with A."[1] In its simplest form the boycott will usually involve at least three of the following parties: the *labor union;* the *primary employer,* the party who actually does something (by refusal or otherwise) not in keeping with the desires of the union; the *secondary employer,* the party who is neutral or at least not actually performing the act or omission which the union is contesting; the *secondary employees,* who are encouraged to respond sympathetically to the union's objectives.

A secondary boycott involves economic coercion and an attempt to implicate another party or neutral in the dispute. The early judicial decisions condemned boycotts under a variety of theories. "Whether the means of pressure upon a third person be a threat of strike against him,[2] a refusal to work on material of non-union manufacture,[3] an unfair list backed by the show of concerted

---

[1] F. Frankfurter & N. Greene, THE LABOR INJUNCTION 43 (1930). *See* St. Antoine, *Secondary Boycotts and Hot Cargo: a Study in Balance of Power,* 40 U. DET. L. J. 189 (1962). For additional historical background, *see* Chapters 1 and 2 *supra.*
[2] Hopkins v. Oxley Stave Co., 83 F 92 (CA 8, 1897); Reynolds v. Davis, 198 Mass 244 (1908).
[3] Bedford Cut Stone Co. v. Journeymen Stone Cutters Ass'n, 274 US 418 (1911); Shine v. Fox Mfg. Co., 156 F 357 (CA 8, 1907).

action and force of numbers,[4] coercion and intimidating measures generally,[5] or merely notice by circularization, banners or publication[6]—the ban of illegality has fallen upon all alike." [7]

The courts in these prestatutory decisions usually relied on the *ends-means test,* under the conspiracy doctrine, in their attacks on secondary boycotts.[8] For example, in the 1923 case of *Pacific Typesetting Co. v. Typographical Union* [9] the plaintiff had performed linotyping for other companies with which the union had its dispute, whereupon the union called a strike of plaintiff's employees to force him to cease dealing with the primary employers. Noting that "courts holding that a secondary boycott is unlawful have done so upon the broad theory that one not a party to industrial strife cannot, against his will, be made an ally of either one of the parties for the purpose of accomplishing the destruction of the other," [10] and that the union's efforts in this case had been to "conscript the noncombatant appellant into their service," [11] the Washington Supreme Court found the strike unlawful. The court also based its decision on the fact that the union was seeking "to coerce appellant to breach its contracts with the printing establishments," [12] reasoning that "a third party is liable in tort for his persuasion of one to break his contract with another." [13]

Secondary boycotts were also outlawed on criminal charges such as rioting or disturbing the peace. In a New York case [14] which was typical of holdings based on criminal violations, the secondary employers had purchased neon signs from a company that was involved in a dispute between two unions as to which should represent the company's employees. After a sign had been erected one union began picketing the store with signs protesting that the use of the sign on the premises was unfair. The New York Court of

4 Gompers v. Buck Stove & Range Co., 221 US 418 (1911); Seattle Brewing & Malting Co. v. Hansen, 144 F 1011 (ND Cal, 1905).
5 Casey v. Cincinnati Typographical Union Local 3, 45 F 135 (SD Ohio, 1891).
6 Rocky Mountain Bell Telephone Co. v. Montana Fed'n of Labor, 156 F 809 (D Mont, 1907).
7 Frankfurter & Greene, note 1 *supra.*
8 Auburn Draying Co. v. Wardell, 124 NE 97, 227 NY 1 (1909). *See also* RESTATEMENT OF TORTS §§799-808.
9 216 P 358, 362, 125 Wash 273 (1923).
10 *Id.* at 563.
11 *Id.* at 561.
12 *Id.* at 562.
13 *Id.* at 561. *See also* New England Cement Co. v. McGivern, 105 NE 885, 218 Mass 198 (1914).
14 People v. Bellows, 22 NE 2d 238, 281 NY 67 (1939).

Appeals held that the pickets could be convicted of disorderly conduct, saying that the storeowners "were merely purchasers of the product in the market and not parties to any labor dispute." [15]

Not all courts blanketly condemned secondary boycotts. [16] In New York the courts allowed pressure which did not "extend beyond a point where . . . the union's . . . direct interests cease." [17] In one such case [18] the Carpenters notified building contractors that their members would not work on woodworks made by non-union manufacturers. In denying an injunction to the owner of an open-shop woodworking mill, the New York court held that the method, a concerted refusal to work, and the objective, the advancement of working conditions in the workers' own industry, were proper. New York also adopted the "unity of interest" doctrine, which was a forerunner of the present-day ally doctrine. [19] In *Goldfinger* v. *Feintuch* [20] the court held that "where a manufacturer pays less than union wages, both it and the retailers who sell its products are in a position to undersell competitors who pay the higher scale, and this may result in unfair reduction of the wages of union members." [21] Thus the unions were privileged to follow the product to the retail store and ask the public not to buy it. There was also some indication that peaceful picketing within the employees' own industry might be considered a constitutionally protected form of free speech, [22] but the protection was later limited to cases in which the picketing was not contrary to valid state or federal policy. [23]

The courts found another vehicle for outlawing secondary boycotts in the state and federal antitrust laws. [24] In the *Danbury Hatters* [25] case, which involved consumer boycotts, the U.S. Su-

---

15 *Id.* at 239.
16 *See, e.g.,* Live Oak Dairy, Inc. v. Teamsters, 8 LRRM 1061 (Cal Super Ct., 1941).
17 Bossert v. Dhuy, 117 NE 582, 221 NY 342, 365 (1917).
18 *Ibid.*
19 Discussed herein *infra.* The doctrine also received some recognition in federal courts. *See, e.g.,* Aeolian Co. v. Fischer, 27 F 2d 560 (SD NY, 1928).
20 11 NE 2d 910, 276 NY 281 (1937).
21 *Id.* at 913.
22 *See, e.g.,* Bakery & Pastry Drivers Local 802 v. Wohl, 315 US 769, 10 LRRM 507 (1942).
23 Electrical Workers Local 501 v. NLRB, 341 US 694, 28 LRRM 2115 (1951); Giboney v. Empire Storage & Ice Co., 336 US 490, 23 LRRM 2505 (1949). *See* Chapters 19 and 22 *supra.*
24 *See* Chapter 29 *infra* for discussion of the relation of the antitrust laws to the NLRA.
25 Loewe v. Lawlor, 208 US 274 (1908). *See* Chapter 1 *supra* for additional discussion of the pre-Wagner Act cases and statutes.

preme Court decided that unions were covered by the Sherman Act [26] and that their concerted activity violated the Act when it obstructed the flow of the employer's goods and products in interstate commerce. With the advent of the Clayton Act, which declared that labor "is not an article of commerce" [27] and listed several activities that were not to be considered or held to be in violation of any law of the United States,[28] it appeared that labor might gain new freedom of action. In *Duplex Printing*,[29] however, the Court held that Section 20 of the Clayton Act applied only to protect "those who are proximately and substantially concerned as parties to an actual dispute respecting the terms or conditions of their own employment, past, present, or prospective," [30] which excluded secondary activity. It was not until 1941, after the enactment of the Norris-LaGuardia Act,[31] that the Supreme Court gave the Clayton Act the interpretation that the unions had originally expected. In *United States* v. *Hutcheson*,[32] the Court read the Sherman Act, Section 20 of the Clayton Act, and the Norris-LaGuardia Act "as a harmonizing text" [33] and determined that "so long as the union acts in its self-interest and does not combine with non-labor groups, the licit and the illicit under Section 20 are not to be determined by any judgment regarding their wisdom or unwisdom, the rightness or wrongness, the selfishness or unselfishness of the end of which the particular union activities are the means." [34]

Not only did the Norris-LaGuardia Act give labor the freedom it had hoped for under the antitrust laws, but it and similar state statutes also signaled the demise of the injunction as an effective weapon against most concerted labor activities. Under Section 13(c) the limitations on issuing injunctions were made applicable "whether or not the disputants stand in the proximate relation of employer and employee." [35]

---

[26] 26 Stat 209 (1890), 15 USC §§1-7 (1964).

[27] 38 Stat 731 (1914), 15 USC §17 (1964).

[28] 38 Stat 738 (1914), 29 USC §52 (1964).

[29] Duplex Printing Co. v. Deering, 254 US 443 (1921).

[30] *Id.* at 472.

[31] 47 Stat 70 (1932), 29 USC §§101-15 (1964).

[32] 312 US 219, 7 LRRM 267 (1941).

[33] *Id.* at 231.

[34] *Id.* at 232. *Cf.* Allen-Bradley Co. v. Electrical Workers Local 3, 325 US 797, 16 LRRM 798 (1948).

[35] 47 Stat 71 (1932), 29 USC §113 (1964).

The pendulum had swung in labor's favor. Under the *Hutcheson* case and the anti-injunction statutes, federal courts would not enjoin secondary activity, regardless of whether the purposes were justifiable or unjustifiable, if it was in the self-interest of the union. State law was also ineffective as a deterrent, since there was little uniformity in the state antiboycott laws and many states had anti-injunction statutes.[36] And the Wagner Act of 1935 affirmatively encouraged union organization and activity, but it did not address itself to the matter of secondary boycotts. The pendulum did not begin to swing the other way until after World War II.

B. The Taft-Hartley Amendments

Following the war, the clamor for revision of the Wagner Act included accounts of perishable foods and milk rotting when unions refused to handle nonunion products, small businessmen and farmers being driven bankrupt by the effects of secondary boycotts,[37] and laborers being denied the right to choose their representatives freely when union leaders imposed jurisdictional strikes enforced by boycotts.[38]

The result was the addition of Section 8(b)(4) to the National Labor Relations Act in the 1947 Taft-Hartley amendments. Section 8(b)(4)(A) was labeled the "secondary boycott provision," although this term nowhere appears in the statutory language. In fact, the scheme of the legislation has been to outlaw only specific types of conduct, not to outlaw all secondary boycotts as such. Many forms of secondary activity remain legal.[39]

The thrust of the Taft-Hartley amendments was expressed in terms of prohibiting union conduct intended to induce strikes or concerted work stoppages by employees in the course of their employment (the prohibited conduct) where an object was to force any employer or person to cease doing business with another employer or person (the prohibited object). The statute also included

---

36 *See* Chapter 19 *infra* at note 23.
37 93 CONG. REC. 3534 (1947) (remarks of Congressman Hartley).
38 93 CONG. REC. 5296 (1947) (remarks of Senator Ball). *See generally* Chapters 2 and 3 *supra*.
39 This is also true of the 1959 amendments. *See* Chapter 22 *supra* for discussion of handbilling and consumer picketing.

two remedial provisions to aid in enforcing the section: Section 10(l),[40] which provides that the investigating officer *must* petition the federal court for an injunction if he has reasonable grounds for believing that a secondary boycott is in effect, and Section 303, which allows the aggrieved party to sue for damages which result from the secondary boycott.[41]

C. The Landrum-Griffin Amendments

Although application and enforcement of Section 8(b)(4)(A) did much to achieve a balance in labor disputes which had not existed under the Clayton, Norris-LaGuardia, and Wagner Acts, in the view of employers and many members of Congress deficiencies or "loopholes" in the boycott provisions of Taft-Hartley remained.[42] Board and court decisions had exposed three major problem areas in applying the statute.[43]

First, it had been held that the term "employees of any employer" was limited to the statutory definition of those terms. Section 2(2) excludes from the definition of "employer" the federal and state governments and their agencies and subdivisions, nonprofit hospitals, and employers subject to the Railway Labor Act.[44] Similarly, Section 2(3) excludes agricultural laborers, supervisors, and employees of an employer subject to the Railway Labor Act from the definition of "employee." [45] Moreover, because Section

---

[40] *E.g.:* Le Baron v. Los Angeles Bldg. & Const. Trades Council, 84 F Supp 629, 635-36, 24 LRRM 2131 (SD Cal, 1949), *affirmed,* 185 F 2d 405, 27 LRRM 2184 (CA 9, 1950); Styles v. Local 760, Electrical Workers, 8 F Supp 119, 122, 22 LRRM 2446 (ED Tenn, 1948). *See* McCulloch, *The Labor Injunction,* 16 Sw. L. J. 82 (1962). *See also* Chapter 31 *infra,* notes 40-48.
[41] *E.g.:* Sheet Metal Workers v. Atlas Sheet Metal Co., 348 F 2d 101, 65 LRRM 3115 (CA 5, 1967); Building Trades Council v. Hoar & Sons, 370 F 2d 746, 64 LRRM 2198 (CA 5, 1967); Old Dutch Farms, Inc. v. Milk Drivers, 281 F Supp 971, 68 LRRM 2077 (ED NY, 1968); Bricklayers Local 2 (Weidman Metal Masters), 166 NLRB 26, 65 LRRM 1433 (1967). *See* discussion of §303 in Part III *infra.*
[42] *See* Chapter 4 *supra.*
[43] Also, a fourth area, the "hot cargo" agreement, then a legalized form of secondary boycott, is treated in Chapter 24 *infra.*
[44] 44 Stat 577 (1926), 45 USC §§161-63 (1964).
[45] Under the statutory definitions of employee, a union could induce work stoppages by minor supervisors and by railroad, agricultural, and public employees. *See, e.g.,* Sheetmetal Workers Local 28 (Ferro-Co Corp.), 102 NLRB 1646, 1660, 31 LRRM 1479, 1482 (1959) (supervisors); Teamsters Local 878 (Arkansas Express, Inc.), 92 NLRB 255, 21 LRRM 1077 (1950) (supervisors); Lumber & Sawmill Workers Local 2409 (Great Northern Ry.), 122 NLRB 1403, 43 LRRM 1324 (1959), *enforcement denied,* 272 F 2d 741, 45 LRRM 2206 (CA 9, 1959), *supplemented,* 126 NLRB 57, 45 LRRM 1268 (1960) (railroad employees); Woodworkers Local S-426 (Smith Lumber Co.), 116 NLRB 1756, 38 LRRM 1280 (1956), *enforcement denied,* 243

8(b)(4) proscribed only the inducement to engage in a strike or concerted refusal to perform services, it had been held that there was no violation unless the inducement was directed at two or more employees.[46] A key employee could be induced to walk off his job, or a number of employees could be induced, one at a time, to refuse to perform services, and no violation would occur. Finally, because Section 8(b)(4)(A) referred only to inducement of employees, it had been held that inducements and even threats made to the secondary employer himself were not prohibited.[47]

In 1959 amendments Congress dealt affirmatively with these deficiencies. In the words of then Senator John F. Kennedy:

> The chief effect of the conference agreement, therefore, will be to plug loopholes in the secondary boycott provisions of the Taft-Hartley Act. There has never been any dispute about the desirability of plugging these artificial loopholes.[48]

The changes were effected by dividing 8(b)(4) into subsections. Subsection (i) substituted the phrase "any individual employed by any person" for the phrase "The employees of any employer," and subsection (ii) was added, making it unlawful "to threaten, coerce or restrain any person" for the proscribed objectives. Subsection (A) was renumbered (B). The relevant portion of the amended section reads as follows:

> (b) It shall be an unfair labor practice for a labor organization or its agents—
>
> (4) (i) to engage in, or to induce or encourage any individual employed by any person engaged in commerce . . . to engage in, a strike or a refusal in the course of his employment to use, . . . or otherwise handle or work on any goods, . . . or to perform any services; or (ii) to threaten, coerce, or restrain any person engaged in commerce . . . , where in either case an object thereof is—
>
> .　　　.　　　.　　　.　　　.　　　.　　　.
>
> (B) forcing or requiring any person to cease using, . . . or otherwise dealing in the products of any other producer, . . . or to cease doing business with any other person . . . : *Provided,* That nothing

---

F 2d 745, 40 LRRM 2018 (CA 5, 1957) (railroad employees); Automobile Workers Local 883 (Paper Makers Importing Co.), 116 NLRB 267, 38 LRRM 1228 (1956) (municipal employees). *Cf.* Teamsters Local 87 (Di Giorgio Wine Co.), 87 NLRB 720, 25 LRRM 1223 (1949), *enforced,* 191 F 2d 642, 28 LRRM 2195 (CA DC, 1951), *cert. denied,* 342 US 869, 29 LRRM 2022 (1951) (agricultural organization). For further discussion, *see* Chapter 28 *supra.*
46 NLRB v. International Rice Milling Co., 341 US 665, 28 LRRM 105 (1951).
47 Rabouin v. NLRB, 195 F 2d 906, 26 LRRM 2617 (CA 2, 1952).
48 105 CONG. REC. 16413 (1959).

contained in this clause (B) shall be construed to make unlawful, where not otherwise unlawful, any primary strike or primary picketing;[49]

II. COVERAGE OF SECTION 8(b)(4)(B)

A. Definition of Terms

The Landrum-Griffin amendments necessitated a reevaluation of some of the substantive law of Section 8(b)(4).[50] By substituting the phrase "any individual employed by any person," Congress eliminated resort to the statutory definition of "employee" for determining whether subsection (i) would prohibit the conduct. Deletion of the word "concerted" made it clear that inducements could be unlawful even if directed at only one individual. These changes, however, according to the Supreme Court, "did not expand the type of conduct which Section 8(b)(4)(A) condemned, that is, union pressures calculated to induce the employees of a secondary employer to withhold their services in order to force their employer to cease dealing with the primary employer." [51]

A new standard for determining prohibited conduct was written into the statute in subsection (ii), which makes it unlawful "to threaten, coerce, or restrain any person" for the proscribed objectives. Thus, while it is only necessary to "induce or encourage any individual employed by any person" to support a violation of subsection (i), appeals to any person under subsection (ii) must "threaten, coerce, or restrain" to be considered a violation. While subsection (i) is normally thought to apply to secondary employees, and subsection (ii) to secondary employers, "person" includes both persons and groups subject to the Act.[52] Although

---

[49] For a discussion of the hot-cargo aspects, subsection (A), see Chapter 24 infra, and of jurisdictional strikes, subsection (D), see Chapter 25 infra.

[50] The Supreme Court had defined the scope of §8 (b)(4)(A) as forbidding "a union to induce employees to strike against or to refuse to handle goods for their employer when an object is to force him or another person to cease doing business with some third person." Carpenters Local 1976 v. NLRB (Sand Door), 357 US 93, 98, 42 LRRM 2243 (1958). See Lesnik, Job Security and Secondary Boycotts: The Reach of NLRA §8(b)(4) and 8(e), 113 PA. L. REV. 1000 (1965).

[51] NLRB v. Servette, Inc., 377 US 46, 52-53, 55 LRRM 2957 (1964). Cf. Int'l Rice Milling Co., 341 US 665, 28 LRRM 2108 (1951); Electrical Workers, Local 761 v. NLRB (General Electric), 366 US 667, 48 LRRM 2210 (1961), discussed infra, this chapter.

[52] For a discussion of the statutory definition of "person," see Chapter 28 infra. Subsection (ii) also applies to employees. Hod Carriers (Gilmore Construction Co.), 127 NLRB 541, 46 LRRM 1043 (1960), modified and enforced, 285 F 2d 397, 47 LRRM 2345 (CA 8, 1960), cert. denied, 366 US 908, 48 LRRM 2033 (1961).

supervisors are not generally considered to be covered by the Act, the legislative history makes it clear that one of the purposes of the amendments was to eliminate appeals to supervisors.[53] Thus it was necessary to determine whether supervisors would be considered individuals or persons under the Act.

Although a literal interpretation of "individual" would include even the top officials of a company, the Board interpreted the statute to restrict the term to personnel who were more closely related to the rank and file. In *Carolina Lumber Co.*[54] the union made an unsuccessful attempt to induce a labor foreman to instruct his crew to refuse to handle lumber which had been delivered by Carolina, the struck company. A few days earlier the project superintendent at another construction site had been successfully induced by the union to refuse to use the lumber. After a review of the legislative history of Section 8(b)(4), the Board found that the term "individual employed by any person" in Section 8(b)(4)(i) referred to supervisors whose interest was "more nearly related to 'rank and file' employees than to management. . . . On the other hand, the term 'person' as used in Section 8(b)(4)(ii) would seem to refer to individuals more nearly related to the managerial level." [55] On this basis, the Board found that Section 8(b)(4)(i) outlawed attempts to induce or encourage employees and *some* supervisors but that similar attempts to induce and encourage others who were more nearly related to the managerial level, for the same objectives, would be lawful. Accordingly, the Board held that the successful attempt to induce the project superintendent was lawful because he was a management supervisor and the union's action fell short of coercion. Conversely, the attempt to induce the job foreman, although unsuccessful, was unlawful because he was essentially a rank-and-file supervisor.

The Board took the same position in *Servette, Inc.*,[56] holding that store managers of a food chain were not "individuals" and could, therefore, be solicited to discontinue handling merchandise distributed by Servette. The Union had sought to support its

---

53 LEG. HIST. OF THE LABOR-MANAGEMENT REPORTING AND DISCLOSURE ACT OF 1959, Vol. II, pp. 1425-1426 (remarks of Senator Morse) ; pp. 1522-1523 (remarks of Congressman Griffin) ; pp. 1706-1707 (report of Senator Kennedy).
54 Teamsters Local 505, 130 NLRB 1438, 47 LRRM 1502 (1961).
55 *Id.* at 1443.
56 Wholesale Delivery Drivers Local 848 (Servette, Inc.), 133 NLRB 1501, 49 LRRM 1028 (1961).

strike against Servette, a wholesale distributor, by asking the managers of supermarkets and food chains to discontinue handling merchandise supplied by Servette. In most instances the union representatives warned that handbills asking the public not to buy products distributed by Servette would be passed out in front of those stores which refused to cooperate, and in a few instances, handbills were in fact passed out.

The Ninth Circuit reversed,[57] holding that the legislative history of the amendments indicated an intent to prohibit the inducement of all supervisors. The Supreme Court disagreed,[58] stating that, although "the Court of Appeals correctly read the term 'individual' in subsection (i) as including supermarket managers," [59] it erred in finding a violation of that subsection. The Court also rejected the Board's concept of a "high level-low level" dichotomy among supervisors in favor of an interpretation deriving from the purpose of Section 8(b)(4):

> If subsection (i), in addition to prohibiting inducement of employees to withhold employment services, also reaches an appeal that the managers exercise their delegated authority by making a business judgment to cease dealing with the primary employer, subsection (ii) would be almost superfluous. Harmony between (i) and (ii) is best achieved by construing subsection (i) to prohibit inducement of the managers to withhold their services from the employer, and subsection (ii) to condemn an attempt to induce the exercise of discretion only if the inducement would "threaten, coerce or restrain" that exercise.[60]

The Court then held that the appeal to the store managers was an appeal to *managerial discretion* because it was within their authority to decide whether or not to continue handling Servette products.

Cases following *Servette* concerning union attempts to secure participation of supervisors in secondary boycotts have turned upon the question of whether the appeal was calculated to induce the supervisor to withhold his services from the employer, a violation of subsection (i), or was directed at the supervisor's discre-

---

[57] Servette, Inc. v. NLRB, 310 F 2d 659, 51 LRRM 2621 (CA 9, 1962).
[58] NLRB v. Servette, Inc., 377 US 46, 55 LRRM 2957 (1964). For a discussion of the handbilling in this case, see Chapter 22 *supra*.
[59] 377 US at 48.
[60] *Id.* at 54. "[T]he question of applicability of subsection (i) turns upon whether the union's appeal is to cease performing employment services, or is an appeal for the exercise of managerial discretion." *Id.* at 50, n. 4.

tionary powers, in which case the inducement would have to be accompanied by threats or coercion in order to amount to a violation of subsection (ii).[61]

The 1959 amendments incorporated other terms into the section that require definition and clarification. Although the words "induce and encourage" were not new to the section, since the adoption of the amendments they have received a second round of judicial scrutiny. Handbilling and picketing [62]—labor's most frequently employed methods for publicizing complaints—have been closely examined to determine their "inducing" effects. Before 1959 the legality of distributing circulars had generally been conceded by both the Board and the courts.[63] But the Board took a much dimmer view of picketing.[64]

Perfection Mattress [65] was a case which arose a year before the passage of the Landrum-Griffin amendments. Union employees had followed the primary employer's trucks to retail stores to which the mattresses were being delivered. When requests to the managers to stop receiving the mattresses failed, the union employees immediately placed pickets at the entrances to the stores to urge customers not to buy the mattresses. The Board noted the signal effect of the picketing that "necessarily invites employees to make common cause with the strikers . . ." [66] and indicated that directing the appeals to customers did not lessen that effect. According to the Board, "the natural or probable result . . . of picketing at an entrance used in part by employees is to induce a strike." [67] The Board also reiterated the settled principle that "the fact that picketing may not be successful in inducing a work stoppage . . ." is not determinative of its legality and does not

---

[61] *See, e.g.,* Carpenters Local 944 (Interstate Employers Ass'n), 159 NLRB 563, 62 LRRM 1335 (1966) ; NLRB v. Painters Dist. Council 48, 144 NLRB 1523, 54 LRRM 1283 (1963), *enforced,* 340 F 2d 107, 58 LRRM 2165 (CA 9, 1965), *cert. denied,* 381 US 914, 59 LRRM 2240 (1965).

[62] *See* Chapter 22 *supra.*

[63] For a discussion of nonpicketing appeals to secondary employees—the illegal phantom picket line—see Grain Elevator Workers v. NLRB, 376 F 2d 186, 64 LRRM 2718 (CA DC, 1967).

[64] *E.g.,* Dallas General Drivers (Associated Wholesale Grocery), 118 NLRB 1251, 40 LRRM 1349 (1957), *affirmed,* 264 F 2d 642, 43 LRRM 2696 (CA 5, 1959).

[65] Wholesale & Warehouse Employees Local 261, 125 NLRB 520, 45 LRRM 1129 (1959), *enforcement denied,* 282 F 2d 824, 46 LRRM 2554 (CA DC, 1960).

[66] 125 NLRB at 524, *citing,* Laundry Workers Local 298 (Southern Service Co., Ltd.), 118 NLRB 1435, 1437, 40 LRRM 1395 (1957), *enforced,* 262 F 2d 617, 43 LRRM 2335 (CA 9, 1958).

[67] 125 NLRB at 520.

negate "the fact that the picketing activity had as its necessary effect the inducing and encouraging of employees to engage in a work stoppage . . . ."[68]

The federal courts may have been more inclined than the Board to look at the actual intent of the picketing.[69] In the *Coors* case[70] the union had a labor dispute with Coors and picketed retail stores that sold Coors beer. The Board found that the picketing had induced the store employees to refuse to handle the product.[71] The Tenth Circuit reversed,[72] finding "nothing more [in the picketing] than legitimate embarrassment of the strike-breaking Coors driver and the advocacy of a consumer boycott of Coors beer."[73] Thus, the legality of such consumer boycotts had received some recognition by the courts at the time of the 1959 amendments.

These amendments added a proviso to Section 8(b)(4) which affirmed the legality of "publicity, *other than picketing,* for the purpose of truthfully advising the public, including consumers and members of a labor organization . . . ."[74] about primary labor disputes. The proviso was construed in the *Servette case.* The Supreme Court recognized that this proviso covered handbilling and that the "statutory protection . . . would be undermined if a threat to engage in protected conduct were not itself protected."[75] On the other hand, the wording of the proviso necessarily raised the question of whether it was intended to outlaw all consumer picketing.[76]

68 *Id.* at 524. *See also* NLRB v. Associated Musicians, 226 F 2d 900, 37 LRRM 2041 (CA 2, 1955).

69 NLRB v. Bakery Workers Local 50 (Arnold Bakers), 245 F 2d 542, 40 LRRM 2107 (CA 2, 1957); NLRB v. Business Machine & Office Appliance Mechanics Local 459 (Royal Typewriter), 228 F 2d 533, 37 LRRM 2219 (CA 2, 1955). *But see* Dallas General Drivers (Associated Wholesale Grocery), 118 NLRB 1251, 40 LRRM 1349 (1957), *affirmed,* 264 F 2d 642, 43 LRRM 2696 (CA 5, 1959).

70 Brewery Workers Local 366, 121 NLRB 271, 42 LRRM 1350 (1958).

71 *Id.* at 273.

72 NLRB v. Brewery Workers Local 366, 272 F 2d 817, 45 LRRM 2277 (CA 10, 1959).

73 *Id.* at 819.

74 Emphasis added.

75 NLRB v. Servette, Inc., 377 US 46, 57, 55 LRRM 2957 (1964). *See* Chapter 22 *supra* at note 23.

76 377 US at 57. *See* Chapter 22 *supra* at note 23.

In answering this question, the *Tree Fruits*[77] decision sheds some light upon the meaning of "threaten, coerce, or restrain."[78] In *Tree Fruits,* the union had a primary dispute with fruit packers who sold Washington State apples to Safeway Stores. The union picketed stores to induce consumers not to buy the apples, and a letter was sent to the store managers advising them that the pickets were posted only for that purpose. The pickets patrolled customer entrances and appeared after the stores opened and before they closed. Reversing its prior stand, the Board stated that "picketing of a secondary employer's premises does not *per se* constitute inducement or encouragement of employees of neutrals,"[79] and accordingly found no 8(b)(4)(i)(B) violation. It did, however, find a violation of 8(b)(4)(ii)(B). The Court of Appeals for the District of Columbia reversed,[80] requiring, for a violation, an affirmative showing of a substantial impact on the secondary employer. The Supreme Court[81] spurned the "substantial impact" approach and expressly rejected the contention that the proviso outlawed consumer picketing. The Court referred to the established practice under the Act, of forbidding peaceful picketing only where there is a clear indication of congressional intent to do so.[82] After reviewing the legislative history, the Court concluded that prohibited consumer picketing was that aimed at the secondary employer. In finding no violation under Section 8(b)(4)(ii)(B), the Court distinguished "peaceful consumer picketing to shut off all trade with the secondary employer,"[83] which would create "a separate dispute with the secondary employer,"[84] from picketing which "only persuades his customers not to buy the struck product"[85] and

---

77 Fruit & Vegetable Packers Local 760, 132 NLRB 1172, 48 LRRM 1496 (1961). This case is also discussed in Chapter 22 *supra* at notes 26-35.

78 *See also:* Building Service Employees Local 29 (Columbus Service), 163 NLRB 128, 65 LRRM 1008 (1967); Teamsters Local 299 (American Motor Lines), 161 NLRB 60, 63 LRRM 1314 (1966); Plumbers Local 469 (McCullogh Plumbing Co.), 159 NLRB 1119, 62 LRRM 1304 (1966).

79 132 NLRB at 1176.

80 Fruit & Vegetable Packers Local 760 v. NLRB, 308 F 2d 311, 50 LRRM 2392 (CA DC, 1962).

81 NLRB v. Fruit & Vegetable Packers Local 760, 377 US 58, 55 LRRM 2961 (1964).

82 The Court also noted that "when Congress meant to bar picketing *per se* it made its meaning clear . . . ," *citing* §8(b)(7) as an example. 377 US at 68. *See* Chapter 22 *supra*, at note 8, and this chapter *infra* at note 98.

83 *Id.* at 70.

84 *Id.* at 72.

85 *Id.* at 70.

is "closely confined to the primary dispute." [86] Recognizing that Section 8(b)(4) is usually interpreted on the basis of the object of the picketing,[87] rather than on its effect, the Court rejected a test dependent on the possibility of economic loss to the secondary employer for determining whether he has been threatened. In his concurring opinion Mr. Justice Black reviewed the legislative history and concluded that the proviso did intend to outlaw all consumer picketing but was therefore unconstitutional as an abridgment of freedom of speech and press under the First Amendment. Dissenting, Justices Harlan and Stewart also concluded that Congress had intended to outlaw all consumer picketing.[88] They did not, however, believe that this interpretation rendered the proviso unconstitutional inasmuch as there are other avenues open for exercising the right of freedom of speech. Four years later, in *Logan Valley Plaza,*[89] the Supreme Court reaffirmed that "peaceful picketing carried on in a location open generally to the public is, absent other factors involving the purpose or manner of the picketing, protected by the first amendment." [90] Thus, in determining whether the union activity has induced or threatened a neutral, the Board and the courts have had to consider the constitutional aspects of the picketing.[91]

B. The Primary-Secondary Distinction—An Overview

Although a literal reading of Section 8(b)(4) might suggest otherwise, not all secondary activity is outlawed by the Act. The section "describes and condemns specific union conduct directed to specific objectives." [92] Union activity which the courts have interpreted as not falling within the congressional ban is commonly termed pri-

---

[86] *Id.* at 68. *See also* NLRB v. Carpenters' Council, 398 F 2d 11, 68 LRRM 2840 (CA 8, 1968) ; Furniture Workers Local 140 v. NLRB, 390 F 2d 495, 67 LRRM 2392 (CA 2, 1968) ; Teamsters Local 327 (American Bread Co.) , 170 NLRB 19, 67 LRRM 1427 (1968) .
[87] *See, e.g.,* NLRB v. Electrical Workers Local 164, 388 F 2d 105, 67 LRRM 2352 (CA 3, 1968) .
[88] They placed special emphasis on the remarks of Senator John Kennedy. 105 CONG. REC. 17720, II Leg. Hist. 1389; 17898-17899, II Leg. Hist. 1432. *E.g.:* ". . . [T]he union can hand out handbills at the shop, can place advertisements in newspapers, can make announcements over the radio, and can carry on all publicity short of having ambulatory picketing in front of a secondary site."
[89] Amalgamated Food Employees Local 590 v. Logan Valley Plaza, Inc., 391 US 308, 68 LRRM 2209 (1968) .
[90] *Id.* at 313. *See* Chapter 19 *supra* at notes 10-18.
[91] *Cf.* Thornhill v. Alabama, 310 US 88, 6 LRRM 697 (1940) . *See* Chapter 22 *infra.*
[92] Carpenters Union Local 1976 v. NLRB (Sand Door) , 357 US 93, 98, 42 LRRM 2243 (1958) .

mary, although it may be secondary in nature. Only secondary
activity with the forbidden objectives is condemned. The task of
drawing "lines more nice than obvious" [93] between primary and
secondary activity has been made more difficult by the need to
balance the "dual Congressional objectives of preserving the right
of labor organizations to bring pressure to bear on offending
employers in primary labor disputes and of shielding unoffending
employers and others from pressures and controversies not their
own." [94] A general appreciation of this problem may best be
gained by examining three major Supreme Court decisions.

In *International Rice Milling*,[95] one of two landmark cases
decided in 1951, the Court considered the lawfulness of secondary
aspects of an essentially primary strike. The union was engaged in
recognitional picketing at a rice mill. At one point during the
picketing, drivers employed by a neutral employer, Kaplan, with
whom the union had no dispute, arrived at the mill to pick up some
of its products. The pickets told them that a strike was taking place
and asked them to leave without making the pickup. The drivers
agreed and started to depart but were accosted by a mill official,
who asked them to return and receive the products. They decided
to return, but on the way in were chased away by rock-throwing
pickets. The Court found that such "inducements or encouragements reaching individual employees of neutral employers only
as they happen to approach the picketed place of business generally
are not aimed at concerted, as distinguished from individual, conduct by such employees." [96] Accordingly, "[t]he picketing was
directed at the Kaplan employees and their employer in a manner
traditional in labor disputes." [97] The Court thus endorsed the
view that Section 8(b)(4) does not outlaw all secondary activity:

> That Congress did not seek, by Section 8(b)(4), to interfere with the
> ordinary strike has been indicated . . . by this Court. . . .
> By Section 13, Congress has made it clear that Section 8(b)(4), and all
> other parts of the Act which otherwise might be read so as to inter-
> fere with, impede or diminish the union's traditional right to
> strike, may be so read only if such interference, impediment or

---

[93] Electrical Workers Local 761 v. NLRB (General Electric), 366 US 667, 674, 48
LRRM 2210 (1961).
[94] NLRB v. Denver Bldg. & Constr. Trades Council, 341 US 675, 692, 28 LRRM 2108
(1951). For general treatment of the primary strike, *see* Chapter 19 *supra*.
[95] NLRB v. International Rice Milling Co., 341 US 665, 28 LRRM 2108 (1951). The
other case is discussed at note 101 *infra*.
[96] *Id.* at 671.
[97] *Ibid.*

diminution is "specifically provided for" in the Act. No such specific provision in Section 8(b)(4) reaches the incident here.[98]

The Court considered it "significant, although not necessarily conclusive," that the complaint was limited "to an incident in the geographically restricted area near the mill." [99] It noted also that substitution of violent coercion for peaceful persuasion did not "itself bring the complained-of conduct into conflict with Section 8(b)(4)." [100] The case thus established that appeals at the primary situs of a labor dispute to replacements and deliverymen not to enter the plant like appeals to other workers to leave the plant, are not violations of Section 8(b)(4).

Decided the same day as *International Rice Milling* was a second case of equal importance to the primary-secondary distinction, *Denver Building Trades*,[101] in which the Supreme Court considered the relationship of a general contractor and subcontractors at a construction site. The general contractor, Doose & Lintner, awarded a subcontract for electrical work on a building project to Gould & Preisner, a firm which for 20 years had employed nonunion workmen. As construction progressed it became apparent that the employees of the electrical contractor were the only nonunion workmen on the project. All other employees were members of unions affiliated with the Denver Building and Construction Trades Council. Notwithstanding the objection of the Council, Gould & Preisner resolved to complete the work unless bodily removed. Subsequently the Council determined to picket the job, labeling it "unfair" and notifying each affiliated union of its decision. This notification was a signal to union workers to leave the job. When the general contractor failed to respond to the unions' reminders that union men would not work with nonunion men, the project was picketed with a sign that announced: "This job unfair to Denver Building & Construction Trades Council." After all building tradesmen had refused to cross the lines, the general contractor terminated Gould & Preisner's subcontract.

As a defense to the 8(b)(4) charge, the unions claimed that they were engaged solely in a primary dispute with the general con-

---

98 *Id.* at 672-673.
99 *Id.* at 671.
100 *Id.* at 672.
101 NLRB v. Denver Building & Constr. Trades Council, *note 94 supra.*

tractor to force him to make the project an all-union job. In effect they argued that since all the work at a construction site is interrelated and the subcontractors are under the supervision of the general contractor, all employers working on the site should be treated as a single employer. The court rejected this reasoning, stating that

> . . . the fact that the contractor and sub-contractor were engaged on the same construction project, and that the contractor had some supervision over the sub-contractor's work, did not eliminate the status of each as an independent contractor or make the employees of one the employees of the other. . . . [T]he relationship between Doose & Lintner and Gould & Preiser was one of "doing business" . . . .[102]

In reviewing the legislative history, the Court again emphasized that Section 8(b)(4) must be read in conjunction with the Section 7 right to engage in concerted activities and the Section 13 right to strike. But, unlike the decision in *International Rice Milling,* the opinion concluded that the union had violated the section. The Court pointed out that the Council could have made the project an all-union job only by forcing the electrical subcontractor off the site, which meant terminating its subcontract. Thus the Council "must have included among its objects that of forcing Doose & Lintner to terminate that sub-contract." [103] It was therefore "not necessary to find that the sole object of the strike was that of forcing the contractor to terminate the sub-contractor's contract." [104] It was sufficient that it was *an* object.[105]

Ten years later, in the *General Electric* reserved-gate decision,[106] the Supreme Court gave limited approval to the contentions the unions had advanced in *Denver Building Trades.* In the interim the Board adhered to a set of standards for measuring the effects of common-situs and ambulatory picketing which it had developed in the *Moore Dry Dock* [107] case. *Moore Dry Dock,* a case that was

---

102 *Id.* at 689-690.
103 *Id.* at 688.
104 *Id.* at 689.
105 Mr. Justice Douglas, joined by Mr. Justice Reed, dissented, pointing out that "the employment of union and non-union men on the same job is a basic protest" and that "the presence of a sub-contractor does not alter one whit the realities of the situation." *Id.* at 692, 693.
106 Electrical Workers Local 761 v. NLRB, 366 US 667, 48 LRRM 2210 (1961).
107 Sailors Union of the Pacific, 92 NLRB 547, 27 LRRM 1108 (1950). Although decided before *International Rice Milling* and *Denver,* its effects were not felt until afterwards.

to have an important bearing on the direction of future decisions, is discussed in a later section, but its *standards* will here be noted because of their impact on the case law which formed the backdrop for the decision in *General Electric*. The Board's *Dry Dock* standards established that picketing at a common situs would be deemed primary if it met the following conditions:

> (a) The picketing is strictly limited to times when the *situs* of dispute is located on the secondary employer's premises; (b) at the time of the picketing the primary employer is engaged in its normal business at the *situs*; (c) the picketing is limited to places reasonably close to the location of the *situs*; and (d) the picketing discloses clearly that the dispute is with the primary employer.[108]

The 1961 *General Electric* decision [109] is perhaps the most important of the Supreme Court's pronouncements on the reach of Section 8(b)(4), and it will undoubtedly serve as a guide in future litigation. General Electric operated a large plant for the manufacture of electrical appliances in Appliance Park, Ky. GE utilized independent contractors to do a variety of work; some did construction work on new buildings, some installed and repaired ventilation and heating equipment, some were engaged in retooling and rearranging operations necessary to the manufacture of new models of appliances, and others did general maintenance work. To insulate GE employees from frequent labor disputes involving outside contractors, GE set aside a separate gate posted with a sign which read as follows:

> Gate 3-A For Employees of Contractors Only—G.E. Employees use other gates.

Although anyone could pass through the gate, the roadway led to a guardhouse where it was necessary to present identification for admittance.

The union representing the manufacturing plant employees called a strike against GE over various outstanding grievances and picketed all entrances to the plant, including the separate gate described above. The signs carried by the pickets at all gates read: "Local 761 on strike, G.E. Unfair." As a result of the picketing, almost all the employees of the independent contractors refused to enter the company's premises. The sole issue before the Supreme

---

108 92 NLRB at 549.
109 366 US 667, 48 LRRM 2210 (1961).

Court was whether the picketing at the gate exclusively set aside for employees of independent contractors was conduct proscribed by Section 8(b)(4).

The Board had held [110] that this picketing was intended to force the individual contractors to cease doing business with G.E. and thus violated Section 8(b)(4)(A) [111] of the Act, and the Court of Appeals for the District of Columbia granted enforcement.[112] The Supreme Court undertook an extensive examination of the history of the provision (discussed in detail in the next section). The Court repeated the view announced by some of the courts of appeals that "almost all picketing . . . hopes to achieve the forbidden objective, whatever other motives there may be and however small the chances of success." [113] But the Court, recognizing the legality of this hope, declared that "picketing which induces secondary employees to respect a picket line is not the equivalent of picketing which has an object of inducing those employees to engage in concerted conduct against their employer in order to force him to refuse to deal with the struck employer." [114] The Court reiterated its stand in *International Rice Milling* that the location of the picketing is not conclusive. "Where the work done by the secondary employees is unrelated to the normal operations of the primary employer, it is difficult to perceive how the pressure of picketing the entire situs is any less on the neutral employer merely because the picketing takes place at property owned by the struck employer." [115]

This concept of *relatedness* was at the heart of the decision. In viewing the picketing at GE, the Court stated that "the key to the problem is found in the type of work that is being performed by those who use the separate gate." [116] The Court approved the Board's practice of barring picketing only "when the independent workers were performing tasks unconnected to the normal operations of the struck employer—usually construction work on his buildings." [117] Thus, if there were a separate gate for regular

---

110 Electrical Workers Local 761, 123 NLRB 1547, 44 LRRM 1173 (1959).

111 Now §8 (b)(4)(B).

112 Electrical Workers Local 761 v. NLRB, 278 F 2d 282, 45 LRRM 3190 (CA DC, 1960).

113 NLRB v. Teamsters Local 294, 284 F 2d 887, 890, 47 LRRM 2085 (CA 2, 1961).

114 366 US at 673-674.

115 *Id.* at 679.

116 *Id.* at 680.

117 *Ibid.*

plant deliveries, "the barring of picketing at that location would make a clear invasion on traditional primary activity of appealing to neutral employees." [118] The Court emphasized that while the 1959 amendments removed the word "concerted" they included a proviso that "nothing contained in this clause (B) shall be construed to make unlawful, where not otherwise unlawful, any primary strike or primary picketing." This proviso thus made it clear that Congress did not intend by the Landrum-Griffin amendments to overrule *International Rice Milling* and related decisions.[119]

Having noted that "[h]owever difficult the drawing of lines more nice than obvious, the statute compels the task," [120] Justice Frankfurter observed that "it is not surprising that the Board has more or less felt its way during the fourteen years in which it has had to apply §8(b)(4)(A), and has modified and reformed its standards on the basis of accumulating experience." [121] Out of that experience came the *Moore Dry Dock* standards, which the Court approved as consistent with the objectives announced in *Denver Building Trades*:

> The application of the Dry Dock tests to limit the picketing effects to the employees of the employer against whom the dispute is directed carries out the "dual congressional objectives of preserving the right of labor organizations to bring pressure to bear on offending employers in primary labor disputes and of shielding unoffending employers and others from pressures in controversies not their own." [122]

The Court then announced its "reserved-gate doctrine," quoting from the *Phelps Dodge* [123] opinion of the Second Circuit:

> "There must be a separate gate, marked and set apart from other gates; the work done by the men who use the gate must be unrelated to the normal operations of the employer, and the work must be of a kind that would not, if done when the plant were engaged in its regular operations, necessitate curtailing those operations." [124]

---

[118] *Id.* at 681.
[119] *See* 105 Cong. Rec. 16589 (1959) (analysis of bill prepared by Senator Kennedy and Representative Thompson). *See* definitions of terms *supra*.
[120] 366 US at 674.
[121] *Ibid.*
[122] *Id.* at 679.
[123] United Steel Workers v. NLRB, 289 F 2d 591, 595, 48 LRRM 2106 (CA 2, 1961).
[124] 366 US at 681.

The Court remanded the case for a determination of whether some of the employees of the individual contractors had been performing conventional maintenance work necessary to normal operations. If this were the case, such mixed use of the reserved gate would not bar picketing rights unless "the instances of these maintenance tasks were so insubstantial as to be treated by the Board as *de minimis.*" [125] On remand the Board stressed the Court's instruction "that reserved-gate picketing was primary *unless* the work of the independent contractors using the gate met *both* of these conditions: (1) the work of the contractors must be unrelated to the normal operations of the employer . . . and (2) the work of the contractors, if done when the plant was engaged in regular operations, would not necessitate curtailing those operations." [126] The Board determined that the installation by independent contractors of certain conveyors that were necessary to GE's annual changeover to production of new appliance models, was "an essential step in resuming the production of finished products." [127] Additionally, it found that the other work done by the contractors was either identical or substantially similar to the work done by GE employees and that these jobs were related to the normal operations of GE. Thus the picketing was lawful primary activity.

International Rice Milling, Denver Building Trades, and *General Electric,* with a bow toward *Moore Dry Dock,* supply the basic distinction between primary and secondary picketing. Attempting to reconcile the broad prohibition of Section 8(b)(4) with the specific protections of strikes and other concerted activity which the Act guarantees, the Supreme Court has focused on the *nature of the work* involved in the primary dispute rather than upon the physical location of the inducement. *Inducement or encouragement to withhold services directed at those who normally deal with the work in dispute is deemed primary. Inducements and encouragements directed at other persons, even when confined to the situs of the dispute, as in the case of picketing at a gate reserved for those whose contacts are not related to the work in dispute, are deemed secondary.* This is the broad principle which emerges. The following section will trace the development and application

---

125 *Id.* at 682.
126 138 NLRB 342, 51 LRRM 1028 (1962).
127 *Id.* at 345.

of this principle in specific cases and situations, and it will be seen that the outlines of the principle are still uncertain in several areas.

C. Common-Situs and Ambulatory Picketing

Situations in which the primary employees work on the same general site as secondary employees, whether because of the nature of the work or because the ambulatory situs of the primary dispute has come to rest at the secondary premises, have presented some of the most difficult problems in making the primary-secondary distinction. A considerable body of litigation has been built up in this area in an attempt to find a solution consistent with the dual objectives of the Act.[128]

1. Early Board Position. In its early decisions the Board seemed less concerned with how and why unions picketed than with where they picketed. In cases in which the primary employer's business was geographically removed from the premises of any other employer and stationary, the Board based its decision on whether the union's activities were geographically confined to the primary premises.[129] Accordingly, if the premises were occupied solely by the secondary employer, picketing was prohibited.[130]

When the Board approached common-situs cases with the same test, the "primary-situs doctrine" resulted.[131] In *Ryan Construction Corp.*[132] Ryan was under a general contract to perform construction services at the Bucyrus plant. Since Bucyrus employees were on strike, a gate was cut through a fence on the Bucyrus premises for the exclusive use of Ryan's construction employees. The Board found that Bucyrus employees could picket the Ryan

---

[128] See generally, Lesnik, Gravamen of the Secondary Boycott, 62 COLUM. L. REV. 1363 (1962); Comment, Common Situs Picketing—The Reserve Gate Doctrine, 20 SWLJ 815 (1966).
[129] Koretz, Federal Regulation of Secondary Strikes and Boycotts—Another Chapter, 59 COLUM. L. REV. 125, 129 (1959). See, e.g., Teamsters Local 87 (Di Giorgio Wine Co.), 87 NLRB 720, 25 LRRM 1223 (1949), affirmed, 191 F 2d 642, 28 LRRM 2195 (CA DC, 1951), cert. denied, 342 US 869, 29 LRRM 2022 (1951); Lumber Workers Local 1407 (Santa Ana Lumber Co.), 87 NLRB 937, 25 LRRM 1229 (1949).
[130] Carpenters (Wadsworth Bldg. Co.), 81 NLRB 802, 23 LRRM 1403 (1949), enforced, 184 F 2d 60, 26 LRRM 2480 (CA 10, 1950), cert. denied, 341 US 947, 28 LRRM 2132 (1951).
[131] Newspapers & Mail Deliverers (Interborough News Co.), 90 NLRB 2135, 26 LRRM 1440 (1950); Teamsters Local 249 (Crump, Inc.), 112 NLRB 311, 36 LRRM 1012 (1955).
[132] Electrical Workers Local 813, 85 NLRB 417, 24 LRRM 1424 (1949).

gate even though an object of the picketing was to enlist the aid of Ryan employees. Announcing its "primary-situs doctrine" the Board stated:

> When picketing is wholly at the premises of the employer with whom the union is engaged in a labor dispute, it cannot be called "secondary" even though, as is virtually always the case, an object of the picketing is to dissuade all persons from entering such premises for business reasons.[133]

Picketing at the premises of the primary employer was deemed lawful *per se,* despite the extenuating circumstances.

In the common-situs or ambulatory-situs situations in which picketing took place at the premises of a secondary employer, the Board placed its primary emphasis on how the picketing was conducted in an effort to determine why. The standards adopted in *Moore Dry Dock* [134] were briefly referred to earlier.[135] The case itself will now be examined. The union picketed at a dry dock at which the primary employer's ship was being converted. At the time, the crew was aboard and training for a future voyage. Since the union could not picket alongside the ship, it picketed at the only available location—the entrance to the secondary employer's premises. The Board found no violation and set forth the oft-quoted standards.[136] If the union's activities met these standards there was a presumption of legality unless there was persuasive evidence of an illegal object, but a failure to measure up to the standards was not considered presumptive of illegality. The application of these tests was accepted and approved by the federal courts.[137]

---

133 *Id.* at 418.
134 Sailors Union of the Pacific, 92 NLRB 547, 27 LRRM 1108 (1950).
135 *See* note 108 *supra* and accompanying text.
136 "When the secondary employer is harboring the *situs* of a dispute between the Union and a primary employer, the right of neither the Union to picket nor the secondary employer to be free from picketing can be absolute. The enmeshing of *premises and situs* qualifies both rights. In the kind of situation that exists in this case, we believe that picketing of the premises of a secondary employer is primary if it meets the following conditions: (a) The picketing is strictly limited to times when the *situs* of dispute is located on the secondary employer's premises: (b) At the time of the picketing the primary employer is engaged in its normal business at the *situs;* (c) The picketing is limited to places reasonably close to the location of the *situs;* and (d) The picketing discloses clearly that the dispute is with the primary employer." 92 NLRB at 549.
137 Piezonke v. NLRB, 219 F 2d 879, 35 LRRM 2545 (CA 4, 1955); NLRB v. Service Trade Chauffeurs Local 145, 191 F 2d 65, 28 LRRM 2450 (CA 2, 1951). *Cf.* Electrical Workers Local 761 v. NLRB, 366 US 667, 48 LRRM 2210 (1961). *See* note 122 *supra* and accompanying text.

It was at about this time that the Supreme Court decided *International Rice Milling*. It will be recalled that the Court found the location of the picketing to be an important consideration but not necessarily conclusive. Reading this dictum as a disapproval of an unqualified primary-situs doctrine, the Board decided that it could best serve the congressional purpose by applying the *Moore Dry Dock* standards to picketing at a primary as well as at a secondary situs. In *PBM* [138] the union had a labor dispute with a company that was building a housing construction project and serving as its own general contractor. When the union picketed the construction site, the union employees of the subcontractors refused to cross the lines. The Board held the picketing unlawful because the signs had failed to disclose that the dispute was with the primary employer. In *Crystal Palace Mkt.*[139] the Board expressly rejected *Ryan* to the extent that it was inconsistent with this new approach. The union had picketed seven of 11 entrances to a large building which contained about 64 shops. The dispute was with the owners of the building, who operated four of the shops. Finding a violation of Section 8(b)(4), the Board indicated that the controlling consideration was "to require that the picketing be so conducted as to minimize its impact on neutral employees in so far as this can be done without substantial impairment of the effectiveness of the picketing in reaching the primary employees." [140]

In time, the Board began to look exclusively at the "how" of the conduct and seemed to apply the *Dry Dock* standards mechanically. Failure to meet even one of the standards became presumptive of illegality,[141] as was any indication of a direct appeal to neutrals.[142] Some of the courts of appeals refused to adhere to

---

138 Carpenters Local 55 (Professional & Business Men's Life Ins. Co.), 108 NLRB 363, 34 LRRM 1010 (1954), *enforced*, 218 F 2d 226, 35 LRRM 2310 (CA 10, 1954).
139 Retail Fruit & Vegetable Clerks Local 1017, 116 NLRB 856, 38 LRRM 1323 (1956), *enforced*, 249 F 2d 591, 41 LRRM 2131 (CA 9, 1954). *Compare* Ryan, note 132 *supra*.
140 116 NLRB at 859.
141 *E.g.*, Machinists Local 889 (Freeman Constr. Co.), 120 NLRB 753, 42 LRRM 1046 (1958); Gardeners Division of Service Employees Local 399 (Roberts & Associates), 119 NLRB 962, 41 LRRM 1228 (1957).
142 Seafarers (Superior Derrick Corp.), 122 NLRB 52, 43 LRRM 1063 (1958) (silence in response to secondary employees' questions about the purpose of picketing); Machinists Local 889 (Freeman Constr. Co.), 120 NLRB 753, 42 LRRM 1046 (1958) (actual work stoppages by secondary employees); Teamsters Local 390 (U & ME Transfer), 119 NLRB 852, 41 LRRM 1196 (1957) (direct appeals to secondary employees); Teamsters Local 400 (Euclid Foods, Inc.), 118 NLRB 130, 40 LRRM 1138 (1957) (statements by union representatives that the picketing is designed to

this rigid application and, as noted in *General Electric*,[143] recognized that the union could legitimately hope, "even if it does not intend, that all persons will honor the picket line." These courts found no violation when the "pressure put upon the neutral employer was not different from that felt by servicers or suppliers under the most ordinary circumstances when a customer of theirs is picketed." [144]

2. The *Washington Coca-Cola* Doctrine, or a "Fifth Rule." During this mechanical or "literal" period of interpretation the Board developed a fifth standard which was more restrictive than the *Moore Dry Dock* tests as they were then being applied. In *Washington Coca-Cola* [145] a Teamsters local, engaged in a strike at the Washington Coca-Cola Bottling Works, followed Coca-Cola trucks making deliveries at various retail outlets. In addition to picketing the trucks, the picketing crews went into the retail outlets and asked customers not to purchase Coca-Cola. The Board distinguished *Schultz Refrigerated Service, Inc.*,[146] and *Moore Dry Dock* because the situs in those cases was ambulatory and there was no permanent place "where the union could publicize the facts concerning its dispute." [147] The Board concluded that the union had violated Section 8(b)(4) because Washington Coca-Cola had a regular place of business at which the local could have picketed.

At first the new standard was applied with a degree of leniency,[148] but it soon developed into a rigid fifth rule which automatically foreclosed application of the four *Moore Dry Dock* tests. All that was required to make the new rule applicable was that the primary employer have a permanent place of business to which the employees report at some time during the day.[149] Several federal

---

induce secondary employees to cease work); Teamsters Local 659 (Ready Mixed Concrete Co.), 117 NLRB 1266, 39 LRRM 1403 (1957) (requests to secondary employees that they cease dealing with primary employers).
143 See notes 113 and 114 *supra* and accompanying text.
144 Seafarers v. NLRB (Salt Dome), 265 F 2d 585, 591, 43 LRRM 2465 (CA DC, 1959).
145 Brewery & Beverage Drivers Local 67, 107 NLRB 299, 33 LRRM 1122 (1953), *enforced*, 220 F 2d 380, 35 LRRM 2576 (CA DC, 1959).
146 Teamsters Local 807 (Shultz Refrigerated Service, Inc.), 87 NLRB 502, 25 LRRM 1122 (1949).
147 33 LRRM at 1124.
148 Painters Local 193 (Pittsburgh Plate Glass Co.), 110 NLRB 455, 35 LRRM 1071, 1658 (1954).
149 NLRB v. Teamsters Local 182, 272 F 2d 85, 45 LRRM 2202 (CA 2, 1959); Albert Evans, Trustee of Teamsters Local 391, 110 NLRB 748, 35 LRRM 1112 (1954).

courts rejected the *Washington Coca-Cola* rule. The Fifth Circuit insisted that the proper statutory test was the object of the picketing. This test, it held, could not be supplanted "merely by Board findings that the real 'situs' of a labor dispute exists at a location other than that determined by the conduct of the parties, at which place alone it may be 'adequately' publicized with impunity under the Act, and thereby inferring from such findings . . . that the unlawful objective exists." [150]

3. Current Board Position. Faced with such criticism and the rejection of a *per se* application of the *Moore Dry Dock* standards in *General Electric*,[151] the Board in 1962 overruled *Washington Coca-Cola* in the *Plauche Electric* case.[152] Plauche maintained an office in an area to which his employees, as a normal requirement, reported in the morning, from which they were dispatched by truck to a job, and to which they reported back in the evening. The Board held that picketing at the construction site to which the trucks reported was not a violation. Although overruling *Washington Coca-Cola*, the Board observed that it would not find that the place of picketing was irrelevant in determining the legality of picketing but would in the future, as in the past, "consider the place of picketing as one circumstance, among others in determining an object of the picketing." [153] The Board also made it clear that the new standard would be applied with common sense. The mere fact that employees might leave for a coffee break or during lunch hour, it said, would not mean that picketing would have to be synchronized with the temporary work interruption.[154] In short, the Board advanced a new proposition that none of the standards, even those of *Moore Dry Dock,* would be applied "on an indiscriminate *'per se'* basis, but would be regarded merely as aids in determining the underlying question of statutory violation." [155]

---

[150] NLRB v. Teamsters Local 968 (Otis Massey), 225 F 2d 205, 209, 36 LRRM 2541 (CA 5, 1955), *cert. denied*, 350 US 914, 37 LRRM 2142 (1955). *See also* Sales Drivers Local 859 v. NLRB (Campbell Coal Co.), 229 F 2d 514, 37 LRRM 2166 (CA DC, 1955), *cert. denied*, 351 US 972, 38 LRRM 2211 (1956).

[151] "As too often the way of law or, at least, of adjudications, soon the Dry Dock tests were mechanically applied . . . ." 366 US at 677.

[152] Electric Workers Local 861, 135 NLRB 250, 49 LRRM 1446 (1962).

[153] *Id.* at 254.

[154] *But see* Plumbers Local 519 (H. L. Robertson & Associates), 171 NLRB 37, 68 LRRM 1070 (1968), *enforced as modified*, 416 F 2d 1120, 70 LRRM 3300 (CA DC, 1969).

[155] 135 NLRB at 255. *See also* Plant Guard Workers (Houston Armored Car Co., Inc.), 136 NLRB 110, 49 LRRM 1713 (1962); Electrical Workers, IBEW (New

With the demise of the *Washington Coca-Cola* rule, it became easier to establish lawful picketing at a common situs, especially in the construction industry.[156] With the advent of the reserved-gate doctrine, however, a new element was injected into common-situs picketing. Reserved-gate picketing is treated in the following section.

D. The Reserved-Gate Doctrine

In recent years it has not been uncommon for employers to set up reserved gates to ensure that any picketing that occurred at such gates would be directed to those using the gates, usually neutral employees. Because the "object" of the picketing seemed so apparent under those conditions, numerous decisions held this type of picketing to be unlawful.[157] The Board declared picketing at gates reserved for secondary employees on secondary premises *a fortiori* unlawful.[158] In *McJunkin Corp.*[159] the Board found that picketing at one of 10 gates, the entrance used by neutral truckers, was unlawful.

Some federal courts expressed dissatisfaction with the Board's approach. In *Phelps Dodge* [160] the Second Circuit gave a preview of the future. Although it upheld the Board's ruling that picketing at a gate reserved for neutrals was unlawful, the court stated that such picketing would have been legal had the neutral employees been engaged in work that required closure of the plant, or if the

---

Power Wire & Electric Co.), 144 NLRB 1089, 54 LRRM 1178 (1963), *enforced in part,* 340 F 2d 71, 58 LRRM 2123 (CA 2, 1965); Brownfield Electric, Inc., 145 NLRB 1163, 55 LRRM 1113 (1964); Myers Plumbing, 146 NLRB 888, 55 LRRM 1424 (1964); Marshal Maint. Corp., 146 NLRB 1058, 56 LRRM 1013, *enforcement denied,* 320 F 2d 641, 53 LRRM 2895 (CA 3, 1963); Teamsters Local 592 [Estes Express Line], 181 NLRB No. 121, 73 LRRM 1497 (1970); IBEW Local 489 (Gulf Coast Bldg. & Supply Co.), 413 F 2d 1085, 70 LRRM 3339 (CA DC, 1969); Plumbers Local 519 v. NLRB, 416 F 2d 1120, 70 LRRM 3300 (CA DC, 1969); Steelworkers Local 6991 [Auburndale Freezer Corp.], 177 NLRB No. 108, 71 LRRM 1503 (1969).
156 Plumbers Local 471 (Wycoff Plumbing), 135 NLRB 329, 49 LRRM 1489 (1962); Electrical Workers Local 59 (Anderson Co. Elec. Services), 135 NLRB 504, 49 LRRM 1527 (1962).
157 *See, e.g.,* Chemical Workers Local 36 (Virginia-Carolina Chemical Corp.), 126 NLRB 907, 45 LRRM 1407 (1960); McLeod v. Steelworkers, 176 F Supp 813, 44 LRRM 2894 (ED NY, 1959).
158 Machinists Local 889 (Freeman Constr. Co.), 120 NLRB 753, 42 LRRM 1046 (1958).
159 Teamsters Local 175 v. NLRB, 128 NLRB 522, 46 LRRM 1340 (1960). The decision seemed to outlaw all picketing, but the court of appeals reversed, holding that the normal incidents of peaceful picketing could not be restricted. Teamsters Local 175 v. NLRB, 294 F 2d 261, 48 LRRM 2598 (CA DC, 1961).
160 Steelworkers v. NLRB, 289 F 2d 591, 48 LRRM 2106 (CA 2, 1961).

secondary employer had been an ally of the struck employer. Indeed, in *General Electric* [161] the Supreme Court quoted *Phelps Dodge* in enunciating the reserved-gate doctrine. Under *General Electric,* picketing of independent contractors at the situs of the primary dispute is permissible unless their work is unrelated to the normal operations of the employer, and, if done during normal operations of the plant, would not necessitate curtailing those operations. A later Supreme Court decision, *Carrier Corp.,*[162] clarified the Court's rationale in *General Electric.*

The plant union in *Carrier,* failing to reach an agreement with the company on a new contract, struck in support of its demands. There were several entrances to the plant, each of which the union picketed. Adjacent to the plant premises was a railroad right of way used by the railroad for deliveries to Carrier and to three other companies in the area. The railroad spur ran across a public thoroughfare, which bounded Carrier's property, and through a gate in a continuous chain-link fence enclosing both the property of Carrier and the railroad right of way. The gate was locked when the spur was not in use and was accessible only to railroad employees. The picketing at this gate was in issue. The specific incident involved a train destined for use by Carrier. As it approached the spur, the pickets on the public thoroughfare adjoining the fence attempted to impede its progress. Their actions included boarding the engine, lying prostrate across the rails, parking a car on the track, and using invective and threats. The train did, however, enter the gate and pick up Carrier products.

The Board found that services of the railroad employees were connected with the normal operations of the struck corporation and, accordingly, upheld the picketing as primary, relying upon *General Electric.* The Second Circuit reversed,[163] holding that, because the railroad gate was located on the premises of the neutral employer, the picketing was secondary. The Supreme Court found this irrelevant, observing that although the activities were literally secondary activities as defined in Section 8(b)(4), they were nonetheless within the protected area of primary picket-

---

[161] *See* notes 106-127 *supra* and accompanying text.
[162] Steelworkers v. NLRB, 376 US 492, 55 LRRM 2698 (1964).
[163] Steelworkers Local 5895, 132 NLRB 127, 48 LRRM 1319 (1962), *enforcement denied sub nom.* Carrier Corp. v. NLRB, 311 F 2d 135, 51 LRRM 2338, 2771 (CA 2, 1962).

ing preserved by Congress in the proviso to subsection (B). The Court recalled that in *General Electric*:

> [T]he location of the picketing, though important, was not deemed of decisive significance; picketing was not to be protected simply because it occurred at the site of the primary employer's plant. The legality of separate gate picketing depended upon the type of work being done by the employees who used that gate; if the duties of those employees were connected with the normal operations of the employer, picketing directed at them was protected primary activity, but if their work was unrelated to the day-to-day operation of the employer's plant, the picketing was an unfair labor practice.[164]

The Court reiterated that picketing was a traditional weapon in a primary strike and that it

> has characteristically been aimed at all those approaching the situs whose mission is selling, delivering or otherwise contributing to the operations which the strike is endeavoring to halt. . . . [W]e think Congress intended to preserve the right to picket during a strike a gate reserved for employees of neutral deliverymen furnishing day-to-day service essential to the plant's regular operations.[165]

Significantly, the Supreme Court in *Carrier* recognized what was implicit in *General Electric—i.e.* that a union may legitimately direct its appeals to neutral employees when their work is related to the primary employer's normal operations. The test is whether the work is of the type necessary to maintain the employer's operation.[166] More than an "ultimate relationship" is required, however, "since all work performed on the primary employer's premises would in some way contribute to the efficiency or profitability of the employer's operation. . . ."[167] Otherwise, the GE standard would be meaningless.

In *Markwell & Hartz, Inc.*,[168] the Board declined to apply the G.E. related-work standard to the construction industry—at least it declined to apply it literally. Markwell & Hartz was a non-union general contractor working on a plant expansion project in New

---

164 376 US at 497-498. Recognizing that §8 (b) (4) was concerned with *object* rather than *means,* the Court emphasized that the same test was to apply whether the picketing was peaceful or violent.
165 *Id.* at 499.
166 Chemical Workers Local 557 (Crest, Inc.), 179 NLRB No. 26, 73 LRRM 1372 (1969); Oil, Chemical and Atomic Workers (Firestone Tire and Rubber Co.), 173 NLRB No. 195, 69 LRRM 1569 (1968). *See* New Power Wire & Electric Corp., note 155 *supra*; Auburndale Freezer Corp., note 155 *supra*.
167 Janesville Typographical Union (Gazette Printing Co.), 173 NLRB No. 137, 69 LRRM 1457, 1458 (1968).
168 Building & Constr. Trades Council, 155 NLRB 319, 60 LRRM 1296 (1965).

Orleans. M&H performed 80 percent of the work on the project with its own employees, but subcontracted the piledriving and electrical work to subcontractors that employed union employees. The Building & Construction Trades Council sought to become the exclusive representative of the M&H employees and in the course of that labor dispute began picketing all the entrances to the project. In an attempt to insulate the employees of the subcontractors from the effects of the picketing, M&H established four gates, one for its own employees and suppliers, and three for the exclusive use of the subcontractors, their employees and suppliers.[169] The union, however, continued to picket all of the gates.

A majority of the Board held that the legality of this picketing should be determined by applying the *Moore Dry Dock* standards. *General Electric* was deemed to be inapplicable because it involved picketing at the premises of a struck manufacturer, and the facts of this case involved the picketing of one of several employers operating on premises owned by a third party. Only this latter situation presented a common-situs problem, the Board reasoned. Since courts have taken a restrictive view of common-situs picketing, it was necessary for the union to attempt to minimize its impact on the neutral employees. *General Electric* was interpreted as representing "an implementation of the concomitant policy that lenient treatment be given to strike action taking place at the separate premises of a struck employer." [170] The Board further stated that the related-work doctrine could not be applied to separate contractors at a common site in the construction industry because this would overrule *Denver Building Trades,* which was expressly approved in *General Electric.*

> [I]t was precisely this claim, that the close working relations of various building construction contractors on a common situs involved them in a common undertaking which destroyed the neutrality and thus the immunity of secondary employers and employees to picket line appeals, that the Supreme Court rejected in *Denver Building Trades.*[171]

In applying the *Moore Dry Dock* standards the Board reasoned that, if it is an offense to fail to indicate clearly that the dispute is

---

169 Earlier, M&H had designated separate gates for use of "subcontractors and persons making deliveries to the project." Such a designation would also have included suppliers of M&H, to whom the union could lawfully appeal with its picketing. 155 NLRB at 321.
170 *Id.* at 326.
171 *Id.* at 327.

with the primary employer, "it is self-evident that picketing a gate used solely by the neutral subcontractors demonstrates the same purpose." [172] The union had violated Section 8(b)(4)(i) and (ii)(B) by failing to meet the "reasonably close" *Dry Dock* standard.

Members Fanning and Jenkins dissented, arguing that the related-work doctrine should apply to the construction industry. They felt that the Supreme Court had equated subcontractors whose tasks aided the general contractor in his everyday operations with suppliers and deliverymen, since the pressures felt by each are the same. The dissent, however, would have distinguished between situations in which the primary dispute is with the general contractor and those in which it is with a subcontractor:

> [T]he work of the employees of the neutral, general contractor and subcontractors, though obviously bearing a close relationship to the work of the primary employees, is nevertheless not work which the primary subcontractor has obligated himself to perform or which lies within his power to control or to assign to whomsoever he sees fit.[173]

Thus the dissent seemed to indicate that the obligation of the general contractor to the owner and his supervision of the subcontractors' work are paramount to a finding that the subcontractors' work is related.

The Court of Appeals for the Fifth Circuit enforced [174] the Board's order. Although it acknowledged that the real issue was whether the work of the subcontractors was related to the normal activities of Markwell & Hartz, the court concluded that "we need not speculate upon the answer to this question. It is answered authoritatively in *Denver* . . . ." [175] The court found no conflict between *Denver* and *General Electric* and refused to limit *Denver* to its precise facts.

In his dissent, Judge Wisdom stressed that *Denver* should not be an obstacle to applying the related-work standard since it has been criticized and numerous bills have been introduced in Congress to overrule its holding. He also quarreled with the Board's interpretation of common situs. He pointed out that the Supreme

---

172 *Id.* at 326.
173 *Id.* at 335, n. 35.
174 Markwell & Hartz, Inc. v. NLRB, 387 F 2d 79, 66 LRRM 2712 (CA 5, 1968).
175 *Id.* at 83.

Court in *General Electric* used the term to refer to any location where both primary and secondary employers were present. Furthermore, the Board had itself taken this stand in *Crystal Palace Market:* "[*Moore Dry Dock*] principles should apply to all common situs picketing, including cases where, as here, the picketed premises are *owned by the primary employer.*" [176] Judge Wisdom would have gone even further than the Board dissent by applying the related-work test in situations in which the dispute is with a subcontractor. He could find no basis in the statute for a distinction and felt that the logic of one compels the acceptance of the other.

The reserved-gate rationale may be applied to some situations where no separate gate is actually established. In one case where there was no separate gate, the subcontractor involved in a labor dispute scheduled his work after normal working hours of the other contractors and on weekends. Agreeing with the Board, the reviewing court could "perceive no real distinction between 'separate gates' and 'separate hours.' " [177] It is still uncertain what other types of arrangements will be deemed comparable to a reserved gate.[178]

E. The Ally Doctrine

The primary-secondary distinction presupposes the existence of a neutral employer. The policy which demands that innocent third parties be protected from labor disputes not of their own making affords no protection to the employer who is so closely identified or allied with the primary employer that he ceases to be neutral.[179] Accordingly, in the area of this recognized exception to the secondary-boycott rules, the unions achieved early success in their attempts to have these employers treated as one. Essentially, ally employers are of two types: (1) those who perform farmed-out

---

176 Crystal Palace Mkt., 116 NLRB 856, 859, 38 LRRM 1323 (1956) (emphasis added).
177 Plumbers, Local 519 v. NLRB, 416 F 2d 1120, 1125, 70 LRRM 330 (CA DC, 1969), *modifying* 171 NLRB No. 37, 68 LRRM 1070 (1968). When a gate is used, the accompanying signs must be clear as to the employees for whom it is intended. IBEW Local 640 (Timber Buildings, Inc.), 176 NLRB No. 17, 71 LRRM 1193 (1969).
178 Teamsters Local 901 v. NLRB (Gonzales Chemical Indus.), 293 F 2d 881, 48 LRRM 2557 (CA DC, 1960) (distinct uniforms and times of stopping and starting work were found to be insufficient); Electrical Workers Local 44 (Jones & Jones, Inc.), 158 NLRB 549, 62 LRRM 1074 (1966). *But see* NLRB v. UAW Local 677, 201 F Supp 637, 49 LRRM 2293 (ED Pa, 1961).
179 93 CONG. REC. 4323 (1947) (remarks of Senator Taft). For other examples of lawful secondary activity, *see* Chapter 22 *supra.*

"struck work" which, "but for" the strike against the primary
employer, would not be sent to them; and (2) those who, because
of common ownership, control, and integration of operations, become so identified with the primary employer that their businesses
are treated as a single enterprise or straight-line operation.

1. Struck work. Senator Taft, one of the co-authors of the Act,
approved an interpretation of the secondary-boycott ban which
would include the former relationship when he said:

> The spirit of the Act is not intended to protect a man who . . . is
> cooperating with a primary employer and taking his work and doing
> the work which he is unable to do because of the strike.[180]

This category may be divided into (1) employers who are already
dealing with the struck employer and thus are participants in
a straight-line operation, but who receive more work because of
the strike, and (2) those who have had no prior dealings with the
primary employer in the type of work in question and take farmed-
out work during the strike.

In the first division, a landmark case involving allies was Judge
Rifkind's *Metropolitan Architects*[181] decision, an injunction
action under Section 10(l). Ebasco, a corporation engaged in the
business of providing engineering services, had a close business
relationship with Project, a firm providing similar services.
Ebasco subcontracted some of its work to Project, supervised the
work of Project's employees, and paid Project on a modified cost-
plus basis. Ebasco's statements to customers made no differentiation between work done by its own employees and Project's
employees. When Ebasco's employees went on strike Ebasco transferred a greater percentage (amounting to 75 percent of Project's
total jobs) of its work to Project, including some jobs that had
already been started by Ebasco employees. The striking union
requested Project to stop doing Ebasco's work and, upon Project's
refusal, picketed Project.

On this set of facts, Judge Rifkind found that Project was not
"doing business" with Ebasco within the meaning of Section
8(b)(4)(A) and that the union had not, therefore, committed an
unfair labor practice. He observed:

180 95 CONG. REC. 8709 (1947). *See* Egan, *Ally or Co-Employer Doctrine*, 14 LOYOLA
L. REV. 109 (1967).
181 Douds v. Metropolitan Federation of Architects Local 231, 75 F Supp 672, 21
LRRM 2256 (SD NY, 1948). *See* Chapters 30 and 31 *infra* for discussion of §10(l)
procedures.

To suggest that Project had no interest in the dispute between Ebasco and its employees is to look at the form and remain blind to substance. . . . The evidence is abundant that Project's employees did work, which, but for the strike of Ebasco's employees would have been done by Ebasco. The economic effect upon Ebasco's employees was precisely that which would flow from Ebasco's hiring strike-breakers to work on its own premises.[182]

Judge Rifkind felt that to hold otherwise "would almost certainly cast grave doubts upon its [Section 8(b)(4)'s] constitutionality." [183] Furthermore, the fact that this type of arrangement was common practice in the industry did not negate the ally relationship but meant only that the industry might be totally composed of allied firms. This case has been considered the genesis of the ally doctrine, and it well illustrates both aspects of the theory—common elements of control and performance of struck work.

If there were no transfer of work already in progress, but only an increase in business contracted out, the reviewing court would then have to look at the entire factual background to determine whether the dealings between the companies came about because of the strike and whether the companies were sufficiently related to make them allies. On the other hand, where separately owned, unrelated business enterprises already have a business relationship, no ally relationship is created by a continuation of business on the same basis during a strike affecting one of the enterprises.[184] Even if an employer continues an existing relationship on a different basis after the commencement of a strike, he does not necessarily lose his neutral status.[185]

The leading case in the second division—the neutral who deals with the primary employer for the first time after the strike has begun—is the *Royal Typewriter* [186] case. Royal contracted to service typewriters sold and leased to its customers. When Royal's servicemen were called out on strike by their union, the company advised its customers to select an independent repair company,

---

[182] *Id.* at 676-677.
[183] *Id.* at 677.
[184] Metal Polishers Union (Climax Mach. Co.), 86 NLRB 1243, 25 LRRM 1052 (1949); Teamsters Local 379 (Catalano Bros., Inc.), 175 NLRB No. 74, 70 LRRM 1601 (1969).
[185] McLeod v. Teamsters Local 810, 182 F Supp 552, 45 LRRM 3082 (ED NY, 1960). *See also* NLRB v. Woodworkers, Western Regional Council 3, 319 F 2d 655, 53 LRRM 2609 (CA 9, 1963), *enforcing* 137 NLRB 352, 50 LRRM 1146 (1962).
[186] NLRB v. Business Machines Local 459, 228 F 2d 553, 37 LRRM 2219 (CA 2, 1955).

have repairs made, and send a receipted invoice to Royal for reimbursement for reasonable repairs within the agreement. In most instances the customer sent Royal the unpaid repair bill, and Royal paid the independent company directly. The Second Circuit noted that the outside companies benefited from the arrangement, for otherwise they would have extricated themselves from the dispute by refusing to do the work. They were not innocent bystanders, because the pickets and receipt of checks from Royal put them on at least constructive notice of the strike. In holding that the repair companies were allied to Royal, the court said:

> Where an employer is attempting to avoid the economic impact of a strike by securing the services of others to do his work, the striking union obviously has a great interest, and we think a proper interest, in preventing those services from being rendered. This interest is more fundamental than the interest in bringing pressure on customers of the primary employer. . . . We therefore hold that an employer is not within the protection of Section 8(b)(4)(A), when he knowingly does work which would otherwise be done by the striking employees of the primary employer and where this work is paid for by the primary employer pursuant to an arrangement devised and originated by him to enable him to meet his contractual obligations. The result may be the same whether or not the primary employer makes any direct arrangement with the employers providing the service.[187]

Since most of these cases turn on specific fact situations, it is well to keep these questions (which are by no means exclusive) in mind when examining cases: (1) Was the work actually farmed-out work?[188] (2) Did the picketed employer receive benefits for himself? (3) Did he have knowledge or constructive knowledge of the existence of the strike?[189] (4) Was there a preexisting agreement?[190] (5) If so, was it motivated by fear of an impending strike?[191]

---

187 *Id.* at 559.
188 NLRB v. Plumbers Local 638, 285 F 2d 642, 45 LRRM 2189, 2534 (CA 2, 1960).
189 Iron Workers Local 501 (Oliver Whyte Co., Inc.), 120 NLRB 856, 42 LRRM 1069 (1958); Die Sinkers Union (General Metals Corp.), 120 NLRB 1227, 42 LRRM 1145 (1958); General Drivers & Dairy Employees Local 563 (Fox Valley Material Suppliers Ass'n), 176 NLRB No. 51, 71 LRRM 1231 (1969).
190 Longshoremen v. Hershey Chocolate Corp., 378 F 2d 1, 65 LRRM 2583 (CA 9, 1967).
191 Brewery Workers Local 8 (Bert D. Williams, Inc.), 148 NLRB 7281, 57 LRRM 1035 (1964).

Once an employer has accepted struck work and is in the ally position, he must notify the union that he is relinquishing the work in order to reestablish his status as a neutral.[192]

2. The straight-line operation. In 1949 the Board held that picketing an employer that transported logs from a struck lumber company was lawful. Since the companies were engaged in one "straight line" operation and were controlled substantially by the same individuals, the Board concluded that the company was not a neutral or wholly unconcerned employer within the meaning of Section 8(b)(4)(A).[193] This Board view was rejected by two courts of appeal. The First Circuit held that mere common ownership and potential common control does not justify picketing where there is "entirely lacking . . . any substantial evidence of actual common control. . . ."[194] Even where the NLRB found actual control, the Eighth Circuit held that dual picketing was unjustified.[195] The Board clarified its position and held, in *Knight Newspapers, Inc.*, that common ownership of two newspapers (one in Michigan and the other in Florida) with the potentiality of common control did not justify picketing of one paper in support of a strike against the other. They were not "allies" since these two metropolitan daily newspapers appeared to have had separate

---

[192] Laundry Workers (Morrison's of San Diego, Inc.), 164 NLRB 426, 65 LRRM 1091 (1967).

[193] Marine Cooks and Stewards [Irwin-Lyons Lumber Co.], 87 NLRB 54, 56, 25 LRRM 1092 (1949). The Board relied on the following statement of Senator Taft during the debates on the Act: "This provision [Section 8 (b) (4)] makes it unlawful to resort to a secondary boycott to injure the business of a third person who is wholly unconcerned in the disagreement between an employer and his employees." 93 CONG. REC. 4323, April 29, 1947. The Senator also said that the secondary-boycott ban "is not intended to apply to a case where the third person, is, in effect, in cahoots with or acting as a part of the primary employer." 95 CONG REC. 8709 (1947). *See* also Madden v. Teamsters Local 743, 43 LRRM 2472 (DC Wis, 1959); Sheet Metal Workers Int'l Ass'n (Atlas Sheet Metal Co. of Jacksonville), 384 F 2d 101, 65 LRRM 3115 (CA 5, 1967).

[194] J. G. Roy & Sons, 251 F 2d 771, 773-774, 41 LRRM 2445 (CA 1, 1958), *denying enforcement*, 118 NLRB 286, 40 LRRM 1171 (1957).

[195] Bachman Machine Co. v. NLRB, 266 F 2d 599, 44 LRRM 2104 (CA 8, 1959), *adopted on remand*, 124 NLRB 743, 44 LRRM 1481 (1959). The Court indicated that its ruling would be different if (1) the two plants were "integrated," or (2) the secondary employer had taken over some work from the struck firm, or (3) the secondary employer had made "common cause" with the struck employer in resisting the union's demands or had interfered with the union in maintaining the strike. *See also* Penello v. TV & Radio Artists, 291 F Supp 409, 69 LRRM 2517 (DC MD, 1968).

and largely unrelated lives of their own, despite their common ownership. The D.C. Circuit agreed.[196]

In a 1970 decision involving the Hearst newspaper chain, the Board extended the rationale of the *Knight* case to include separate corporate subsidiaries where neither the subsidiaries nor the parent corporation exercise actual control over the day-to-day operations, including labor relations, of the other. The Board reasoned that these separate corporations should be treated as separate "persons" under Section 2(1) and accordingly held that picketing of one subsidiary in the course of a dispute with other subsidiaries, under these conditions, violated Section 8(b)(4)(i)-(ii)(B).[197]

III. SECTION 303 DAMAGE SUITS

A. Nature of the Action

In addition to the cease-and-desist remedies available to the Board after a finding of an unfair labor practice under Section 8(b)(4) of the NLRA, Section 303 of the Labor Management Relations Act provides that suit may be maintained in federal district court for damages resulting from "any activity or conduct defined as an unfair labor practice in section 8(b)(4) of the National Labor Relations Act." The language of Section 303(b) creates a right of action in "(w)hoever shall be injured in his business or property" by the unlawful activity and provides that the injured party may "recover damages by him sustained." Therefore, two initial issues which faced the courts were who may bring an action under Section 303 and what damages may be recovered.

In determining who may bring an action under Section 303, the courts have consistently given a broad interpretation to the term "whoever." In *Deena Artware* [198] it was argued that Section 303

---

196 Miami Pressman's Local 46 v. NLRB (Knight Newspapers, Inc.), 322 F 2d 405 (CA DC, 1963), 53 LRRM 2629, *enforcing* 138 NLRB 1346, 51 LRRM 1169 (1962). In a subsequent case, an opinion adopted by the Board held: "Common ownership is not sufficient. There must be in addition such actual or active common control, as distinguished from merely a potential, as to denote an appreciable integration of operations and management policies." Teamsters Local 639, Drivers, Chauffeurs & Helpers (Poole's Warehousing, Inc.), 158 NLRB 1281, 1285-86, 62 LRRM 1197 (1966).

197 Los Angeles Newspaper Guild, Local 69 (Hearst Corp.), 185 NLRB No. 25, 75 LRRM 1014 (1970). *See also* AFTRA, Washington-Baltimore Local (Hearst Corp.), 185 NLRB No. 26, 75 LRRM 1018 (1970).

198 Brick and Clay Workers v. Deena Artware, Inc., 198 F 2d 637, 30 LRRM 2485 (CA 6, 1952), *cert. denied*, 344 US 897, 31 LRRM 2157 (1952). The 1959 amendments to the Act condensed §303 (29 USC §187) by incorporating by reference "conduct defined as an unfair labor practice in Section 8(b) (4) . . ." *See* Note, *Sections 8(b)(4)*

did not confer a right of action on the primary employer in the dispute and that the section was designed to provide a means by which a neutral third-party employer could obtain compensation for injury suffered as a result of unlawful secondary pressure against another employer. In rejecting this reasoning the court held that Congress was aware of the broad literal meaning of the word "whoever" and that because "Congress considered the use of the secondary boycott in a labor dispute as an unfair labor practice and illegal . . . it was entirely consistent with such decision to give a right of action to anyone who was injured in his business by a violation of the law." [199] However, this broad interpretation is subject to the limitation that the employer must be one directly involved in the labor dispute,[200] unless some actual physical damage has occurred.[201]

Once the right of recovery has been established, the common-law rules for the determination of damages may be applied by the court.[202] The courts have firmly established that the damages sought must be a "direct and proximate result of the proscribed conduct," [203] unless the lawful and unlawful activities are so interrelated as to be inseparable, in which case the total damages suffered are recoverable.[204]

Because Section 303 was enacted for the purpose of providing *compensation* to a party injured by unlawful secondary activity, the courts have consistently held that punitive damages may not be awarded in Section 303 suits. In *Morton* the Supreme Court held that "(p)unitive damages for violations of §303 conflict with

---

and 303; *Indepedent Remedies Against Union Practices Under the Taft-Hartley Act,* 61 Yale L. J. 745 (1952).

199 198 F 2d at 644.

200 Osborne Mining Co. v. United Mine Workers, 279 F 2d 716, 46 LRRM 2380 (CA 6, 1960), *cert. denied,* 364 US 881, 47 LRRM 2065 (1960). Here the employer's agent sought to recover damages suffered by reason of the loss of contracts ordinarily available from the primary employer. Such damages were held by the court to be too remote.

201 Gilchrist v. United Mine Workers, 290 F 2d 36, 48 LRRM 2083 (CA 6, 1961), *cert. denied,* 368 US 875, 48 LRRM 3118 (1961).

202 Wells v. International Union of Operating Engineers Local 181, 303 F 2d 73, 50 LRRM 2198 (CA 6, 1962).

203 United Bhd. of Carpenters Local 978 v. Markwell, 305 F 2d 38, 47, 50 LRRM 2742 (CA 8, 1962). *See also* United Mine Workers v. Gibbs, 383 US 715, 61 LRRM 2561 (1966); San Diego Bldg. Trades Council v. Garmon, 359 US 236, 43 LRRM 2838 (1958); United Constr. Workers v. Laburnum, 347 US 656, 34 LRRM 2229 (1954).

204 Osborne Mining Co. v. United Mine Workers, note 200 *supra. Cf.* NLRB v. Denver Bldg. & Trades Council, 341 US 675, 28 LRRM 2108 (1951). *But cf.* United Mine Workers v. Gibbs, note 203 *supra.*

the congressional judgment, reflected both in the language of the statute and in its legislative history, that recovery for an employer's business losses caused by a union's peaceful secondary proscribed by §303 should be limited to actual compensatory damages." [205]

In *Gibbs* the Supreme Court held that the Labor Management Relations Act "expressly provides that for the purposes of the statute, including §303, the responsibility of a union for the acts of its members and officers is to be measured by reference to the ordinary doctrines of agency." [206] And in *Hawaiian Pineapple* the court held that the union is not liable for the acts of individual members unless "some one or more persons in authority were responsible for what transpired, either the union officers named as individual defendants or some officials or agents not parties." [207] While individual members of the union are generally not subject to Section 303 suits, international unions may be liable as well as local units if they participate in the illegal activity [208] or direct, encourage, or assist in the illegal activity." [209]

B. Relation to Section 8(b)(4)

In *Juneau Spruce,* a damage suit under the original Section 303,[210] it was argued that a finding by the Board of an unfair labor practice under Section 8(b)(4) was required before a Section 303 suit could be maintained. The Supreme Court rejected this argument, stating that "the fact that the two sections have an identity of language and yet specify two different remedies is strong confirmation of our conclusion that the remedies provided were to

---

[205] Teamsters Local 20 v. Morton, 377 US 252, 260, 56 LRRM 2225 (1964). *Compare* §301, for the latter provision was held in *Textile Workers Union v. Lincoln Mills,* 353 US 448, 40 LRRM 2113 (1957), to have the purpose of promoting a higher degree of responsibility between parties to a collective agreement. Therefore, punitive damages, being consistent with the deterrent purpose of the section, may be awarded by the courts in §301 suits. *See* Ratner, *The New Look in Damage Suits, in* LABOR LAW DEVELOPMENTS 1967 (Sw. Legal Foundation 13th Ann. Institute on Labor Law) 251 (1967).
[206] United Mine Workers v. Gibbs, note 203 *supra* at 736.
[207] International Longshoremen's & Warehousemen's Union v. Hawaiian Pineapple Co., 226 F 2d 875, 880, 37 LRRM 2056 (CA 9, 1955), *cert. denied,* 351 US 963, 38 LRRM 2211 (1956).
[208] Flame Coal Co. v. United Mine Workers, 303 F 2d 39, 50 LRRM 2272 (CA 6, 1962), *cert. denied,* 371 US 891, 51 LRRM 2380 (1962).
[209] United Mine Workers v. Patton, 211 F 2d 742, 33 LRRM 2814, (CA 4, 1954), *cert. denied,* 348 US 824, 34 LRRM 2898 (1954).
[210] International Longshoremen's & Warehousemen's Union v. Juneau Spruce Corp., 342 US 237, 29 LRRM 2249 (1952). The original text of §303 did not incorporate §8(b)(4) by reference; rather, it repeated those NLRA provisions verbatim. *See* note 198 *supra.*

be independent of each other." [211] Under the 1959 amendments to the Act, conduct which is a basis for a Section 303 action is by definition an unfair labor practice under Section 8(b)(4). In a 1969 decision the Fifth Circuit held that a Board finding that a union had engaged in an unfair labor practice under Section 8(b)(4) of the Act may be treated as *res judicata* in a suit under Section 303.[212] The policy considerations which underlie the doctrine—finality of litigation, prevention of needless litigation, and avoidance of unnecessary burdens of time and expense—were deemed relevant to its use in a judicial proceeding. However, application of the doctrine has generally been denied.[213]

Whether or not the principle of *res judicata* is applicable, a court may adopt by reference the findings of the Board in a parallel unfair labor practice proceeding,[214] or it may weigh the finding of the Board along with other evidence in making its fact determination.[215] However, where a Section 303 suit is based on a violation of Section 8(b)(4)(C), the Board's determination of certification is essential to the maintenance of the suit,[216] and the certification decision may not be altered by the court.[217]

---

[211] *Id.* at 244.

[212] Painters v. Edgewood Contracting Co., 416 F 2d 1081, 72 LRRM 2524 (CA 5, 1969). *Accord,* H. L. Robertson & Associates, Inc. v. Plumbers Local 519, 429 F 2d 520, 74 LRRM 2872 (CA 5, 1970). *But see* Old Dutch Farms, Inc. v. Teamsters Local 584, 281 F Supp 971, 975, 68 LRRM (ED NY, 1968), in which the court stated that "the congressional scheme of parallel enforcement of Section 8(b)(4) violations by the courts and the Board precludes reliance upon *res judicata* or collateral estoppel based upon the findings of either fact finder."

[213] Brick & Clay Workers v. Deena Artware, *supra* note 198; Old Dutch Farms, *supra* note 212 ("a substantial factual issue remains to be tried"); Aircraft & Engine Maint. Employees, Local 290 v. J. E. Schilling Co., 340 F 2d 286, 58 LRRM 2169 (CA 5, 1965), *cert. denied,* 382 US 972, 61 LRRM 2147 (1966); Aircraft & Engine Maint. Employees, Local 290 v. Oolite Concrete Co., 341 F 2d 210, 58 LRRM 2336 (CA 5, 1965), *cert. denied,* 382 US 972, 61 LRRM 2147 (1966); Fibreboard Paper Products Corp. v. East Bay Union of Machinists, 344 F 2d 300, 58 LRRM 2387, 59 LRRM 2127 (CA 9, 1965), *cert. denied,* 382 US 826, 60 LRRM 2233 (1965); Purvis v. Great Falls Bldg. & Const. Trades Council, 266 F Supp 661, 64 LRRM 2839 (D Mont, 1967).

[214] Carpenter's Union Local 131 v. Cisco Construction Co., 266 F 2d 365, 44 LRRM 2004 (CA 9, 1959), *cert. denied,* 361 US 828, 44 LRRM 2983 (1959).

[215] Kipbea Baking Co. v. Strauss, 218 F Supp. 696, 53 LRRM 2636 (ED NY, 1963).

[216] Tungsten Mining Co. v. United Mine Workers, 242 F 2d 84, 39 LRRM 2460 (CA 4, 1957), *cert. denied,* 355 US 821, 40 LRRM 2680 (1957).

[217] The Supreme Court has held that the matter of certification is one solely for the Board. Brooks v. NLRB, 348 US 96, 35 LRRM 2158 (1954).

C. Federal Preemption

In *Garmon* [218] the Supreme Court held that in order to avoid conflict with the national labor policy the states are preempted from exercising jurisdiction in cases arising from peaceful picketing. Only where the activity regulated is "a merely peripheral concern of the Labor Management Relations Act . . . [o]r where the regulated conduct touch[es] interests . . . deeply rooted in local feeling . . ." [219] may the states exercise jurisdiction over conduct regulated by the Act. On the other hand, Section 303 provides a specific right of action for damages resulting from union activity which, although peaceful in nature, violates Section 8(b)(4). Of particular importance, therefore, are those instances in which both violent and unlawful peaceful activity are involved.

Actions for damages from violent activity may be joined in state or federal court with suits arising under Section 303, provided federal law is applied in the adjudication of the Section 303 action. In addition, the federal court may exercise pendent jurisdiction even in cases where diversity of citizenship is not present. [220] The justification for such jurisdiction "lies in considerations of judicial economy, convenience, and fairness to litigants." [221] Even if the Section 303 action is dismissed, the federal court may maintain pendent jurisdiction over the state claim. [222] In that case, however, the damages recoverable are only those which are a proximate result of the *violent* activity.

---

[218] San Diego Bldg. Trades Council v. Garmon, 359 US 236, 243-244, 43 LRRM 2838 (1958). *See* Chapter 29 *infra* at notes 110-115 for detailed treatment of the subject of federal preemption.
[219] *Id.* at 247.
[220] United Mine Workers v. Meadow Creek Coal Co., 263 F 2d 52, 43 LRRM 2445 (CA 6, 1959), *cert. denied*, 359 US 1013, 44 LRRM 2194 (1959); Flame Coal Co. v. United Mine Workers, 303 F 2d 39, 50 LRRM 2272 (CA 6, 1962), *cert. denied*, 371 US 891, 51 LRRM 2380 (1962).
[221] United Mine Workers v. Gibbs, 383 US 715, 726, 61 LRRM 2561 (1966).
[222] *Ibid.*

CHAPTER 24

THE 'HOT CARGO' AGREEMENT

I. THE LAW BEFORE 1959

Prior to the passage of the Landrum-Griffin amendments to the National Labor Relations Act in 1959, the term "hot-cargo agreements" referred to provisions in collective bargaining agreements providing that union members employed by the contracting employers need not handle nonunion or unfair or struck goods of other employers. Cases concerning such provisions arose in the context of what was then Section 8(b)(4)(A) of the Act, a part of the 1947 Taft-Hartley amendments. It provided as follows:

> It shall be an unfair labor practice for a labor organization or its agents— . . .
>
> (4) to engage in, or to induce or encourage the employees of any employer to engage in, a strike or a concerted refusal in the course of their employment to use, manufacture, process, transport, or otherwise handle or work on any goods, articles, materials, or commodities or to perform any services, where an object thereof is: (A) forcing or requiring . . . any employer or other person to cease using, selling, handling, transporting, or otherwise dealing in the products of any other producer, processor, or manufacturer, or to cease to do business with any other person. . . .

In *Conway's Express*,[1] the first hot-cargo case decided after the passage of Section 8(b)(4)(A), two clauses were involved. One reserved to the union the right to refuse to handle struck goods, and the other reserved to the union "the right to refuse to accept the freight from, or to make pickups from or deliveries to establishments where picket lines, strikes, walkouts and lockouts exist." When Conway's was struck, the union induced employees of other, secondary, employers, with whom the union had contracts con-

---

[1] Teamsters Local 294 (Conway's Express), 87 NLRB 972, 25 LRRM 1202 (1949), *affirmed*, 195 F 2d 906, 29 LRRM 2617 (CA 2, 1952).

taining the hot-cargo provisions, to refuse to handle Conway's freight. The secondary employers acquiesced in this refusal. A majority of the Board held that Section 8(b)(4)(A) did not circumscribe employer-union cooperation as reflected in a hot-cargo provision. It stated:

> [T]here is nothing in the express provisions or underlying policy of Section 8(b)(4)(A) which prohibits an employer and a union from voluntarily including "hot cargo" or "struck work" provisions in their collective bargaining contracts, or from honoring these provisions.[2]

Chairman Herzog concurred with the majority's ultimate finding but did not agree that the hot-cargo provision in question constituted a defense, since it merely provided that employees would not be penalized for refusing to handle hot cargo and did not grant the union the right to take action.[3] Member Reynolds dissented on the ground that hot-cargo provisions were "repugnant to the basic public policies of the Act" and not a valid defense.[4]

By 1954, however, the complexion of the Board was changing, and so was its view of the hot-cargo contract. In *McAllister Transfer, Inc.,*[5] a majority of the Board held that the union had violated Section 8(b)(4)(A), notwithstanding the existence of a hot-cargo provision in the union's contracts with the secondary employers. Two members of the Board attacked hot-cargo clauses as contrary to public policy and concluded that the statutory provisions of Section 8(b)(4)(A), enacted for the protection of primary employers, secondary employers, and the public, could not be waived by an employer in collective bargaining. They therefore concluded that a hot-cargo clause was not a defense to the charge of a violation of Section 8(b)(4)(A), and that *Conway's Express,*[6] and *Pittsburgh Plate Glass Co.,*[7] in which the Board had reaffirmed its holding in *Conway's Express,* should be overruled. Chairman Farmer, concurring, rejected the argument that a hot-cargo clause

---

2 87 NLRB at 982.
3 *Id.* at 983, n. 33.
4 *Id.* at 995.
5 Teamsters Local 554 (McAllister Transfer, Inc.), 110 NLRB 1769, 35 LRRM 1281 (1954).
6 Teamsters Local 294, *supra* note 1.
7 Teamsters Local 135 (Pittsburgh Plate Glass Co.), 105 NLRB 740, 32 LRRM 1350 (1953).

was contrary to public policy and did not agree that *Conway's Express* should be overruled, but found that the union had violated Section 8(b)(4)(A) because in *McAllister Transfer,* unlike *Conway's Express,* the secondary employers had expressly requested their employees to continue to handle the "hot cargo," and had not acquiesced in their refusal to do so. The two dissenting members defended the Board's decisions in *Conway's Express* and *Pittsburgh Plate Glass,* concluding that the contract provisions constituted a meritorious defense to the charge of a violation of Section 8(b)(4)(A).[8]

In 1955, a majority of the Board in *Sand Door & Plywood Co.*[9] again found a violation of Section 8(b)(4)(A) notwithstanding the existence of a hot-cargo clause. Two members of the Board held that, regardless of the existence of a hot-cargo clause, the employer could instruct his employees not to handle the goods; but the union could not, and any direct appeal to the employees by the union to engage in a strike or refusal to handle the goods violated Section 8(b)(4)(A). *Conway's Express* and *Pittsburgh Plate Glass Co.* were overruled to the extent they were inconsistent with the decision in *Sand Door.*[10] Member Rodgers, concurring, argued that hot-cargo clauses were contrary to public policy and therefore could not constitute a defense to a charge of a violation of Section 8(b)(4)(A). Two members dissented and found no violation in view of the hot-cargo clause.[11] The Court of Appeals for the Second Circuit, however, rejected the Board's contentions in a 1957 case, adhered to its original affirmance in *Conway's Express,* and held that "consent in advance to honor a hot cargo clause is not the product of the union's forcing or requiring any employer . . . to cease doing business with any other person" within the meaning of Section 8(b)(4)(A).[12]

In 1958, in a consolidated case known as *Sand Door,*[13] the Supreme Court reviewed the circuit court decisions in *Sand Door*[14]

---

[8] Teamsters Local 554, *supra* note 5, at 1790.
[9] Carpenters Local 1976 (Sand Door & Plywood Co.), 113 NLRB 1210, 36 LRRM 1478 (1955).
[10] *Id.* at n. 22.
[11] *See also* Teamsters Local 886 (American Iron & Mach. Works Co.), 115 NLRB 800, 37 LRRM 1395 (1956).
[12] Milk Drivers Local 338 v. NLRB, 245 F 2d 817, 40 LRRM 2279 (CA 2, 1957), *reversed,* 357 US 345, 42 LRRM 2306 (1958).
[13] Carpenters Local 1976 v. NLRB, 357 US 93, 42 LRRM 2243 (1958).
[14] NLRB v. Carpenters Local 1976, 241 F 2d 147, 39 LRRM 2428 (CA 9, 1957).

and *American Iron and Machine Works*[15] and held, in a six-to-three decision, that the existence of a hot-cargo provision did not constitute a defense to a charge of a violation of Section 8(b)(4)(A), and that inducements of employees which were prohibited under Section 8(b)(4)(A) in the absence of a hot-cargo provision were likewise prohibited where there was such a provision.

Justice Frankfurter, speaking for the Court, traced the checkered history of cases dealing with the relationship of a hot-cargo clause to Section 8(b)(4)(A). He noted that there was nothing in the legislative history to show that Congress had directly considered this relationship, but said:

> Nevertheless, it seems most probable that the freedom of choice for the employer contemplated by §8(b)(4)(A) is a freedom of choice at the time the question whether to boycott or not arises in a concrete situation calling for the exercise of judgment on a particular matter of labor and business policy.[16]

The rationale for this conclusion included the "possibility" that the hot-cargo provision might originally have been accepted by the employer because of strikes or coercion which could not have been used lawfully to secure his consent at the later time when a boycott was sought.

Although the Court held in *Sand Door* that a hot-cargo provision was no longer a defense to a charge of violation of Section 8(b)(4)(A), it rejected the suggestion of two members of the Board in *Genuine Parts*[17] that a hot-cargo clause was prima facie evidence of prohibited inducement of employees. An employer could still voluntarily boycott a struck employer, regardless of the existence or nonexistence of a hot-cargo provision in its contract. The Court did not pass on the legality of a hot-cargo clause but suggested that in some different context the provision might have legal "radiations" affecting the relationship between the employer and the union. Finally the Court held, contrary to the position of two Board members in *Genuine Parts,* that the hot-cargo provision was not unlawful merely because the secondary employers were common carriers subject to the Interstate Commerce Act.

---

15 Teamsters Local 886 v. NLRB, 247 F 2d 71, 40 LRRM 2047 (CA DC, 1957).
16 357 US at 105.
17 Teamsters Local 728 (Genuine Parts Co.), 119 NLRB 399, 41 LRRM 1087 (1957), *enforced,* 265 F 2d 439, 43 LRRM 2813 (CA 5, 1959) ; *cert. denied,* 361 US 917, 45 LRRM 2249 (1959).

The prelude to Section 8(e) was the dissent by Justice Douglas in the *Sand Door* case. He insisted that the decision in *Conway's Express* "squares with the Act" and urged the Court not to substitute itself for Congress but to "leave this policy making to Congress" if, in fact, hot-cargo clauses contain evils that should be outlawed.[18]

II. SECTION 8(e)

Section 8(e), the so-called hot-cargo section, was enacted into law as part of the 1959 Landrum-Griffin amendments to the National Labor Relations Act. Section 8(e) provides:

(e) It shall be an unfair labor practice for any labor organization and any employer to enter into any contract or agreement, express or implied, whereby such employer ceases or refrains or agrees to cease or refrain from handling, using, selling, transporting or otherwise dealing in any of the products of any other employer, or to cease doing business with any other person, and any contract or agreement entered into heretofore or hereafter containing such an agreement shall be to such extent unenforcible and void: *Provided,* That nothing in this subsection shall apply to an agreement between a labor organization and an employer in the construction industry relating to the contracting or subcontracting of work to be done at the site of the construction, alteration, painting, or repair of a building, structure, or other work: *Provided further,* That for the purposes of this subsection and subsection (b) of this section the terms "any employer," "any person engaged in commerce or in industry affecting commerce," and "any person" when used in relation to the terms "any other producer, processor, or manufacturer," "any other employer," or "any other person" shall not include persons in the relation of a jobber, manufacturer, contractor, or subcontractor working on the goods or premises of the jobber or manufacturer or performing parts of an integrated process of production in the apparel and clothing industry. *Provided further,* That nothing in this subchapter shall prohibit the enforcement of any agreement which is within the foregoing exception.[19]

---

18 357 US at 113-115.
19 *See:* St. Antoine, *The Rational Regulation of Union Restrictive Practices,* in LABOR LAW DEVELOPMENTS 1968 (Sw. Legal Foundation 14th Ann. Institute on Labor Law) 1, 14-21 (1968) ; Lesnick, *Job Security and Secondary Boycotts: The Reach of NLRA §§8(b)(4) and 8(e),* 113 U. PA. L. REV. 1000 (1965) ; Comment, *Subcontracting Clauses and Section 8(e) of the National Labor Relations Act,* 62 MICH. L. REV. 1176 (1964) ; St. Antoine, *Secondary Boycotts and Hot Cargo: a Study in Balance of Power,* 40 U. DET. L.J. 189 (1962) ; Comment, *Hot Cargo Clauses: The Scope of Section 8(e),* 71 YALE L.J. 158 (1961) ; Previant, *The New Hot-Cargo and Secondary-Boycott Sections: A Critical Analysis,* 48 GEO. L.J. 346 (1959) .

Section 8(e) brought into issue the validity not only of provisions dealing with struck and common goods and work, but also of picket-line and subcontracting clauses. The Board originally construed the law quite broadly in keeping with what it believed to be congressional intent.[20]

A. Constitutionality

The courts have uniformly upheld the constitutionality of Section 8(e). The Lithographers, in a series of cases, attacked the constitutionality of the provisions on the ground that its industry, like the garment industry, has integrated production processes and that to grant an exemption to the garment industry and not to the lithographic industry constituted a violation of due process under the Fifth Amendment. In *Lithographers Local 17*,[21] a district court in California concluded that the garment-industry exemption need not have been based solely upon the integrated nature of the work processes, and that Congress could consider the economic and social conditions peculiar to that industry. The court added that Congress, in acting under the commerce clause, must be extended wide latitude and that a mere lack of uniformity in the exercise of its commerce powers does not constitute a denial of due process. In *Miami Lithographers*[22] the Fifth Circuit held that the congressional exemption for the garment industry was based on "reasonable considerations." In *Brown*[23] and *Patton*[24] the D.C. Circuit said:

> Courts today no longer sit in review of the economic wisdom of the distinctions drawn by legislature, and the failure to grant exemptions from §8(e) to all industries which claim they merit an exemption

---

20 Lithographers Local 78 (Employing Lithographers of Greater Miami), 130 NLRB 968, 976, 47 LRRM 1380 (1961), *enforced as modified*, 301 F 2d 20, 49 LRRM 2869 (CA 5, 1962); Dan McKinney Co., 137 NLRB 649, 652, 50 LRRM 1225 (1962).

21 Brown v. Lithographers Local 17, 180 F Supp 294, 45 LRRM 2577 (1960); *see also* Lithographers Local 17 (Graphic Arts Employers Assn.), 130 NLRB 985, 47 LRRM 1374 (1961); *enforced*, 309 F 2d 31, 51 LRRM 2093 (CA 9, 1962), *cert. denied*, 372 US 943, 52 LRRM 2673 (1963).

22 Employing Lithographers of Greater Miami v. NLRB, 301 F 2d 20, 49 LRRM 2869 (CA 5, 1962).

23 Teamsters Local 728 (Brown Transport Corp.), 140 NLRB 1436, 52 LRRM 1258 (1963), *consolidated and enforced in part and set aside in part*, 334 F 2d 539, 55 LRRM 2878 (CA DC, 1964), *cert. denied*, 379 US 916, 57 LRRM 2496 (1964).

24 Teamsters Local 413 (Patton Warehouse, Inc.), 140 NLRB 1474, 52 LRRM 1252 (1963), *enforced in part*, 334 F 2d 539, 55 LRRM 2878 (CA DC, 1964), *cert. denied*, 379 US 916, 57 LRRM 2496 (1964).

does not void the Act. In this connection, we note that the unions in the trucking industry were the prime target of Congressional concern.[25]

B. "Entering Into"

The Board and courts have held that the maintenance, enforcement, and reaffirmation of a hot-cargo clause constitutes "entering into" such an agreement even though the contract was executed prior to the effective date of the law.[26] The Board has construed the language "to enter into" broadly, and enforcement of the hot-cargo agreement has been held a violation of Section 8(e) even though the contract itself was signed six months before the charge was filed. In such a situation an employer's voluntary enforcement of such a provision is unlawful "whether or not it was sought, assented to, or acquiesced in by the other party to the contract." [27] The Board has also held that the mere execution of a contract containing an unlawful clause is illegal, regardless of implementation by either party.[28]

It should be noted that Board Members Fanning and Brown have not agreed that an attempted unilateral enforcement of an existing clause which contravenes Section 8(e) necessarily constitutes an entering into within the meaning of the section.[29]

In *Los Angeles Mailers* [30] Board Members Fanning and Brown, dissenting, contended that "entering into" was not the same as "enforcing" an agreement. Their position was that a union's unilateral attempt to enforce an existing hot-cargo clause is not a violation of Section 8(e) or Section 8(b)(4)(A), but may be a violation of Section 8(b)(4)(B).

---

[25] 334 F 2d at 549.
[26] Teamsters Local 618 (Greater St. Louis Automotive Trimmers & Upholsterers Ass'n), 134 NLRB 1363, 49 LRRM 1326 (1961). This was a three-to-two decision with Members Fanning and Brown dissenting on the "entering into" issue. *See also* Typographical Union Local 9 (Hillbro Newspaper Printing Co.), 135 NLRB 1132, 49 LRRM 1659 (1962), *enforced,* 311 F 2d 121, 51 LRRM 2359 (CA DC, 1962).
[27] Dan McKinney Co., 137 NLRB 649, 657, 50 LRRM 1225 (1962); Culinary Alliance, Local 402 (Bob's Enterprises, Inc.), 175 NLRB No. 26, 70 LRRM 1508 (1969). *See* discussion of time for filing charges under §10(b) in Chapter 30 *infra.*
[28] Teamsters Local 210 (American Feed Co.), 133 NLRB 214, 48 LRRM 1622 (1961).
[29] Longshoremen's Local 1332 (Philadelphia Marine Trade Ass'n), 151 NLRB 1447, 58 LRRM 1619 (1965).
[30] Typographical Union Local 9 (Hillbro Newspaper Printing Co.), 135 NLRB 1132, 49 LRRM 1659 (1962), *enforced,* 311 F 2d 121, 51 LRRM 2359 (CA DC, 1962).

.lause

, [31] and *Patton* [32] cases the Board considered the
Section 8(e) of contract clauses providing that it
ı violation of the contract and that it would not be
ıarge or disciplinary action if an employee refused to
ıny property involved in a labor dispute or refused
to cross ___ /ork behind any picket line, including picket lines of
the unions which were parties to the agreement and including
picket lines at the places of business of employers who were parties
to the agreement.

The Board held that a clause granting immunity to employees
who refuse to cross a picket line is valid under Section 8(e) only if
it is limited (a) to protected activities engaged in by employees
against their own employer and (b) to activities directed against
another employer who has been struck by his own employees,
where the strike has been ratified or approved by their representative whom the employer is required to recognize under the Act.[33]
The Board found that the clauses in question were not so limited
and that they violated Section 8(e). It reasoned that to the extent
a picket-line clause protects employees who refuse to cross a picket
line at a secondary employer's premises, its effect may be to cause
a cessation of business between the two employers. However, the
Board found that the legislative history of Section 8(e) clearly
established that it was not intended to change the existing rule
that a contractual provision wherein an employer agreed not to
discharge an employee who refused to cross a picket line at another employer's premises was legal, at least to the extent that
such a provision did not go beyond the proviso to Section 8(b)(4)
which states:

> *Provided,* That nothing contained in this subsection (b) shall be
> construed to make unlawful a refusal by any person to enter upon
> the premises of any employer (other than his own employer), if the
> employees of such employer are engaged in a strike ratified or ap-
> proved by a representative of such employees whom such employer
> is required to recognize under this Act. . . .[34]

---

31 Teamsters Local 728, *supra* note 23.
32 Teamsters Local 413, *supra* note 24.
33 140 NLRB at 1481.
34 *See* discussion of rights of employees respecting picket lines, Chapter 19 *infra*.

The Board concluded, therefore, in *Brown* and *Patton,* that although the effect of a "picket line" clause may be to cause the cessation of business between two employers, it is nevertheless valid under Section 8(e) insofar as it is in conformity with the proviso to Section 8(b).[35]

On review of the Board's decisions in *Brown* and *Patton,* the D.C. Circuit agreed with the Board's holding that a clause which provides that employees shall not be subject to discharge or discipline for refusing to cross a picket line is void under Section 8(e) to the extent that it protects refusals to cross picket lines in support of a secondary strike or boycott, but rejected the Board's conclusion that the clause is only valid under Section 8(e) if it is limited to picket lines in conformity with the proviso to Section 8(b).[36] The court reviewed the legislative history of Section 8(e) and, relying on the Supreme Court's decision in *Rockaway News Supply Co.*[37] and subsequent Board and court cases, concluded that the refusal to cross a lawful primary picket line is protected activity regardless of whether the proviso to Section 8(b) is satisfied, and that whenever the refusal to cross a picket line is protected activity, unions and employers may lawfully sign contracts providing that the refusal shall not be grounds for discharge. Accordingly, the court held that a picket-line clause did not violate Section 8(e) if it was limited to lawful primary picket lines at another employer's premises, since a refusal to cross a primary picket line is itself primary activity and Section 8(e) is limited to secondary actions.[38]

The Board has accepted, at least implicitly, the decision of the court of appeals in the *Brown* and *Patton* cases. In *Madison Employers Council*[39] the picket-line clause stated:

> No employee shall be subject to discipline by the Employer for refusal to cross a picket line or enter upon premises of another employer if the employees of such other employer are engaged in an authorized strike.[40]

---

35 140 NLRB at 1481.
36 Teamsters Local 413 v. NLRB, 334 F 2d 539, 55 LRRM 2878 (CA DC, 1964).
37 NLRB v. Rockaway News Supply Co., 345 US 71, 31 LRRM 2432 (1953).
38 334 F 2d at 545. *Compare:* Carpenters Local 1273 v. Hill, 398 F 2d 360, 68 LRRM 2734 (CA 9, 1968) (where a union seeks an agreement which authorizes "any picket line," and the union pickets to obtain such agreement, it violates §(b)(4)(i) and (ii) (A) of the Act since the desired agreement violates §8 (e).
39 Teamsters Local 695 (Madison Employers Council), 152 NLRB 577, 59 LRRM 1131 (1965), *enforced,* 361 F 2d 547, 62 LRRM 2135 (CA DC, 1966).
40 152 NLRB at 579.

The Board stated that "[t]his clause is so unlimited and so broad in scope and application that it would be illegal even under the rule of the court of appeals to the extent that it applies to unlawful, albeit 'authorized,' secondary activity." [41] In *Jones & Jones, Inc.*,[42] the Board found unlawful a picket-line clause which stated that an employee would not be required to cross a picket line or enter premises where there was "a picket line authorized or approved by the councils." The Board said such a clause was prohibited by either the Board's former test in *Patton,* on which its original finding had been predicated, or by "the modification of that test made by the circuit court in *Patton* . . . to which the Board presently adheres. . . ." [43]

D. Struck and Nonunion Goods and Work

The classic struck-work clause provides that an employer will not do business with a nonunion or struck employer, and permits employees to refuse to handle or perform services on nonunion or struck goods. Such clauses may take many forms, known variously as struck-work, chain-shop, trade-shop, refusal-to-handle, right-to-terminate, and right-to-reopen provisions; but the Board has held, generally with court approval, that all types of struck-work and nonunion-work clauses are illegal, except those that merely incorporate the so-called "ally" doctrine or single-employer theory.[44]

Common ownership and common control, especially over labor relations, may sometimes demonstrate that two separate legal entities constitute a single employer. An "ally" is an employer who, pursuant to an arrangement with a struck employer, performs work that, but for the strike, would be performed by the struck employer's employees. If the neutral employer customarily performed the work prior to the strike, it is not an "ally." [45]

---

41 *Id.* at 581.
42 Hod Carriers Local 300 (Jones & Jones, Inc.), 154 NLRB 1744, 60 LRRM 1194 (1965), *supplementing* 145 NLRB 911, 55 LRRM 1070 (1964).
43 *Id.* at 1745, n. 7.
44 Lithographers Local 78 (Employing Lithographers of Greater Miami), 130 NLRB 968, 47 LRRM 1380 (1961), *enforced as modified,* 301 F 2d 20, 49 LRRM 2869 (CA 5, 1962); Lithographers Local 17 (Graphic Arts Employers Ass'n), 130 NLRB 985, 47 LRRM 1374 (1961), *enforced,* 309 F 2d 31, 51 LRRM 2093 (CA 9, 1962), *cert. denied,* 372 US 943, 52 LRRM 2673 (1963).
45 *See generally* the discussion of the ally doctrine in Chapter 23 *supra.*

In the *Miami Lithographers* and *Graphic Arts* cases [46] the Board considered the legality of struck-work, chain-shop, right-to-terminate, trade-shop, and refusal-to-handle clauses. The struck-work clauses contained a general pledge by the employers not to render assistance to any lithographic employer whose employees were on strike or locked out, and an implementation clause. In the *Miami* case this provided that in furtherance of the general purpose employees would "not be required to handle any lithographic work farmed out directly or indirectly by such employer, other than work which the employer herein customarily has performed for the employer involved in such strike or lockout." [47] In the *Graphic Arts* case it provided that employees would "not be requested to handle any lithographic work (other than work actually in process in the plant) customarily produced by such employer." [48] The Board held, with members Rodgers and Jenkins dissenting, that although the general provision standing alone would be unlawful, it should be read together with and in the context of the implementation clause. As so read, the majority found that the *Miami* struck-work clause embodied nothing more than the Board- and court-sanctioned "ally" doctrine and was, therefore, lawful under Section 8(e). The *Graphic Arts* struck-work clause, however, was interpreted by the Board to preclude the employer from doing not only "farmed out" work, but also work which the employer customarily had performed for the struck employer prior to the strike. The Board thus held that the *Graphic Arts* struck-work clause went beyond the "ally" doctrine and was unlawful.

On review of the Board's decision in *Miami Lithographers,* the Fifth Circuit refused to read the implementation clause as completely modifying the general clause, criticized the Board for rewriting the contract for the parties, and held that the struck-work clause went beyond the "ally" doctrine and was unlawful.[49] The Ninth Circuit, however, on review of the *Graphic Arts* decision, disagreed with the Fifth Circuit, denied that it was rewriting the contract, and read the broad language in conjunction with the implementation clause. Moreover, the Ninth Circuit disagreed with the Board's interpretation of the *Graphic Arts* struck-work

---

46 Cases cited *supra* note 44.
47 130 NLRB at 971.
48 130 NLRB at 997.
49 301 F 2d at 28.

clause, construed the clause to be limited to the "ally" doctrine, and held that it was lawful.[50]

The *Miami Lithographers* chain-shop clause provided that employees would not be required to handle any work in the employer's plant covered under the contract if there was a lithographers' strike or if lithographers were locked out at any plant which was wholly owned and controlled or commonly owned and controlled by the employer. A majority of the Board found that this clause embodied the union's right to strike at the plant of the contracting company in sympathy with a strike at another company, when the two companies constituted a single employer within the meaning of the Act, and held the clause lawful.[51] The Fifth Circuit agreed that such a clause would be lawful if expressly limited to the single-employer exception to the secondary-boycott provisions, but held that the clause in question was not so limited and thus was violative of Section 8(e).[52]

The lithographers' trade-shop clauses were found to be unlawful by the Board and both circuit courts.[53] These provided that, if any employee was requested to handle lithographic work made in any shop not under contract with the union and not authorized to use the union label, the union could reopen the contract as to all terms and terminate it if no agreement was reached. The refusal-to-handle clauses, which protected employees from discharge or discipline if they refused to handle nonunion or struck goods, were similarly condemned.

In determining whether various forms of struck-work clauses violate Section 8(e), the Board does not limit itself to the particular words used in the provisions, nor does it consider only whether the employer has agreed not to handle hot cargo. Instead it considers all the circumstances and necessary implications and effects of the provisions. If an agreement realistically constitutes an agreement not to handle hot cargo, by providing, for example, that the union may reopen or terminate the contract if the employer handles struck or nonunion goods or if employees are required to handle struck or nonunion goods, it violates Section 8(e) even though the

---

50 309 F 2d at 36-38.
51 130 NLRB at 975.
52 301 F 2d at 28-29.
53 Cases cited *supra* note 44.

employer has not expressly agreed not to do business with struck or nonunion employers.[54] According to the Board:

> . . . Congress was intent upon outlawing "hot cargo" clauses no matter how disguised. Probably no language can be explicit enough to reach in advance every possible subterfuge of resourceful parties. Nevertheless, we believe that in using the term "implied" in Section 8(e) Congress meant to reach every device which, fairly considered, is tantamount to an agreement that the contracting employer will not handle the products of another employer or cease doing business with another person.[55]

Nor does the fact that the employer expressly agrees not to cease doing business with a struck or nonunion employer necessarily constitute a defense to a charge of a violation of Section 8(e).[56]

Similarly, struck-work and related clauses do not avoid the sanctions of Section 8(e) simply because they are framed in terms of protecting actions of individual employees.[57] In *Dan McKinney Co.*[58] the Board held that:

> The fact that the disputed section is worded in terms of protection of employees against discharge, rather than a direct prohibition against the Respondent's doing business with others, does not alter the effect, and hence the illegality. . . .
>
> We see no real distinction between a contract which prohibits an employer from requiring that his employees do certain work and one prohibiting an employer from discharging his employees for refusing to perform such work.[59]

In *Brown Transport*[60] the parties executed a "hazardous work" agreement which provided that if employees were required to make deliveries to or pickups from or enter a struck employer's premises, the contracting employer would provide the employees with additional benefits and protection, including insurance and

---

[54] 130 NLRB at 976.

[55] *Ibid.*

[56] *Id.* at 975-977; Teamsters Local 413 (Patton Warehouse, Inc.), 140 NLRB 1474, 1483-1485, 52 LRRM 1252 (1963); *enforced in part and set aside in part,* 334 F 2d 539, 546-547, 55 LRRM 2878 (CA DC, 1964), *cert. denied,* 379 US 916, 57 LRRM 2496 (1964).

[57] See cases cited *supra* note 56. *See also* Teamsters Local 728 (Brown Transp. Corp.), 140 NLRB 1436, 1439, 52 LRRM 1258 (1963), *consolidated and enforced in part and set aside in part,* 334 F 2d 539, 55 LRRM 2878 (CA DC, 1964), *cert. denied,* 379 US 916, 57 LRRM 2496 (1964).

[58] Dan McKinney Co., 137 NLRB 649, 50 LRRM 1225 (1962).

[59] *Id.* at 652.

[60] *See* Teamsters Local 728, *supra* note 57.

triple wages, because of the hazards involved. The Board held
that this clause violated Section 8(e) and said:

> It is comparable in its effect [to another provision held to violate
> 8(e)] which requires an employer to continue to do business with
> a struck employer and to handle his hot cargo, but only by the use
> of strange and uneconomic means. An employer who is permitted
> . . . to require his employees to handle hot cargo, should be able to
> do so in his accustomed manner. To saddle him with new obliga-
> tions if he wishes to comply with the law is to penalize him for his
> observance.[61]

E. Subcontracting and Work-Allocation Clauses

1. Early Developments. The Board and the courts agree that
provisions prohibiting all subcontracting are lawful, but that those
whereby an employer expressly or impliedly agrees that he will
subcontract only to union employers violate Section 8(e).[62]

In the early subcontracting cases under Section 8(e) the Board
held that the prohibition of all subcontracting merely protected
unit work and was primary and lawful. But any provision permitting the contracting employer to subcontract work, but delimiting the persons to whom he might subcontract, or regulating the
terms and conditions of employment of the employees of the subcontractors to whom the contracting employer might send the
work, it ruled, was in violation of the Act.[63]

The D.C. Circuit, however, rejected the Board's position. It
drew a distinction between union-signatory clauses, which provide
that the employer will subcontract only to employers who are
signatory to a union contract, and union-standards clauses, which
provide that the employer will subcontract only to employers who
meet the equivalent of union standards of wages, hours, and

---

[61] *Id.* at 1439.

[62] Machinists District 9 (Greater St. Louis Automotive Trimmers & Upholsterers
Ass'n), 134 NLRB 1354, 49 LRRM 1321 (1961); *enforced,* 315 F 2d 33, 51 LRRM
2496 (CA DC, 1962); Bakery Wagon Drivers & Salesmen Local 484 (Sunrise Transportation), 137 NLRB 987, 50 LRRM 1289 (1962), *enforced,* 321 F 2d 353, 53 LRRM
2286 (CA DC, 1963).

[63] Teamsters Local 710 (Wilson & Co.), 143 NLRB 1221, 53 LRRM 1475 (1963), *enforced in part, set aside in part, and remanded in part,* 335 F 2d 709, 56 LRRM 2570
(CA DC, 1964); Teamsters Local 413 (Patton Warehouse, Inc.), 140 NLRB 1474,
52 LRRM 1252 (1963), *enforced in part,* 334 F 2d 539, 55 LRRM 2878 (CA DC,
1964), *cert. denied,* 379 US 916, 57 LRRM 2496 (1964); Ohio Valley Carpenters
District Council (Cardinal Industries, Inc.), 136 NLRB 977, 49 LRRM 1908 (1962).

working conditions. Thus in the *Orange Belt* case [64] the D.C. Circuit said that the key question presented by subcontracting clauses is whether they are primary in nature and directed at protecting the wages and job opportunities of the employees covered by the contract. In answering this question, it added, the test is "whether the clauses are 'germane to the economic integrity of the principal work unit,' and seek 'to protect and preserve the work and standards [the union] has bargained for,' or instead 'extend beyond the [contracting] employer and are aimed really at the union's difference with another employer.' " [65] The court concluded that union-standards clauses were within the union's legitimate primary interests.[66]

In *Patton Warehouse* [67] the D.C. Circuit considered a subcontracting clause which provided that the employer would not use the services of any person who did not observe the wages, hours, and working conditions established by unions having jurisdiction over the type of services performed. Unlike the Board, the court found the clause lawful. It said:

> Union-signatory subcontracting clauses are secondary, and therefore within the scope of §8(e), while union-standards subcontracting clauses are primary as to the contracting employer. . . .
> This clause would be a union-signatory clause if it required subcontractors to have collective bargaining agreements with petitioner unions or their affiliates, or with unions generally. We interpret it, however, as merely requiring that subcontractors observe the equivalent of union wages, hours and the like.[68]

In a companion case to *Orange Belt,* the court agreed with the Board that a provision in a construction contract violated Section 8(e) by requiring that any subcontract contain a requirement that the subcontractor observe the appropriate labor agreement covering the work involved with the appropriate construction trade union.[69] The requirement of observing the terms of the appropriate labor agreement was held to be a union-signatory and not

---

64 Orange Belt District Council of Painters No. 48 v. NLRB, 328 F 2d 534, 55 LRRM 2293 (CA DC, 1964), *remanding* 139 NLRB 383, 51 LRRM 1315 (1962).
65 *Id.* at 538.
66 *Accord,* Retail Clerks Local 770 v. NLRB, 296 F 2d 368, 48 LRRM 2598 (CA DC, 1961).
67 Patton Warehouse, Inc., *supra* note 60.
68 334 F 2d at 548.
69 Building & Const. Trades Council v. NLRB, 328 F 2d 540, 55 LRRM 2297 (CA DC, 1964), *enforcing in part* 139 NLRB 236, 51 LRRM 1294 (1962).

a union-standards provision. In addition to the language of the agreement, the court noted the testimony that a union representative told the contractor that the clause required it to use union subcontractors.

A similar conflict between the Board and the D.C. Circuit arose in *Wilson & Co.*[70] with respect to a work-allocation clause which provided that certain work, which the employer had recently been subcontracting, would be performed by employees covered by the agreement. *Wilson* arose in the context of an expired agreement and negotiations for a new contract between the Teamsters and Chicago meatpacking companies. The Teamsters represented the employer's local drivers, who, prior to the execution of the expired contract, had made most of the Chicago deliveries. During the term of the expired contract, however, the employers had relocated a large part of their operations outside Chicago and had subcontracted much of the delivery work to over-the-road drivers, who delivered the goods from the employers' plants outside the Chicago area to their final destination in Chicago. The unit drivers continued to make deliveries in Chicago from those plants still remaining in the city, but a substantial reduction in the number of unit jobs had occurred during the term of the contract as a result of the plant relocations and subcontracting. The Teamsters proposed and struck to obtain a clause which provided that truck shipments to customers in Chicago be made from Chicago distribution facilities by employees covered by the agreement.

In a three-to-two decision, a majority of the Board found that the work which the union sought had never been customarily performed by the unit employees because, "[w]hile local deliveries of meat products *originating in the Chicago area* to customers in the area have been made by the employer's drivers represented by Local 710, the deliveries of meat products *originating with the employer out of State* to its consignees in the Chicago area always have been performed by the over-the-road drivers. . . ."[71] The majority held that the clause "would necessarily result in the disruption of well-established business relations between the packers and the interstate carriers, as well as the loss of employment for

---

[70] Teamsters Local 710 (Wilson & Co.), *supra* note 63.
[71] 143 NLRB at 1228.

the over-the-road drivers of the interstate carriers . . .," [72] and concluded that it violated Section 8(e).[73] Chairman McCulloch, in a dissent joined by Member Brown, said that the union had the right to negotiate to "retain, reclaim, or obtain work of the type now being performed by unit members. . . . [74]

The D.C. Circuit reversed the Board in *Wilson,* holding that the work-allocation clause was aimed at the *preservation* of jobs within the bargaining unit and the *recapture* of work formerly performed by employees in the bargaining unit. The court added that a union could legally negotiate a work-acquisition clause if the jobs were "fairly claimable" by the bargaining unit. Terming such activity primary, the court admonished the Board not to read the "cease doing business" language of Section 8(e) literally because inherent in all subcontracting clauses is an agreement not to do business with some person. The effect on subcontractors in such a situation, according to the court, is incidental and does not make primary activity unlawful.[75]

Two other provisions, a union-signatory clause and a union-standards clause, were also found unlawful by the Board in *Wilson.* The D.C. Circuit agreed that the union-signatory clause violated Section 8(e), but reiterated its view, expressed in *Retail Clerks Local 770 v. NLRB,*[76] *Orange Belt,*[77] and *Patton Warehouse,*[78] that a union-standards clause is lawful.[79]

In 1966 the Board reversed itself and adopted the rationale expressed by the D.C. Circuit in *Patton, Orange Belt,* and *Wilson.*

---

[72] *Id.* at 1230.
[73] *But c.f.* Teamsters Local 603 (Drive-Thru Dairy, Inc.) , 145 NLRB 445, 54 LRRM 1397 (1963) , where a majority of the Board held that a subcontracting clause which preserves work which traditionally has belonged to employees in the bargaining unit does not violate §8(e).
[74] Teamsters Local 710 (Wilson & Co.) , *supra* note 63, at 1237 (dissent of Chairman McCulloch) .
[75] 335 F 2d at 713. *See also* American Boiler Mfrs. Ass'n v. NLRB, 404 F 2d 547, 69 LRRM 2851 (CA 8, 1968) , *modifying* 167 NLRB No. 79, 66 LRRM 1098 (1967) , where the Eighth Circuit held "that a collective bargaining agreement which seeks to preserve work currently being performed by unit employees and to reacquire that portion lost is not violative of §8(e) ." (*Citing* National Woodwork, note 87 *infra*) . *See also* Canada Dry Corp. v. NLRB, 421 F 2d 907, 73 LRRM 2582 (CA 6, 1970) . But in *Sheetmetal Workers Local 216,* 172 NLRB No. 6, 69 LRRM 1050 (1968) , the Board held that "fairly claimable" work does not include items which have been fabricated in the past "only on occasions when an emergency or other unusual work condition existed." *See* notes 99-101 *infra*.
[76] 296 F 2d 368, 48 LRRM 2598 (CA DC, 1961) .
[77] Orange Belt District Council of Printers No. 48 v. NLRB, *supra* note 64.
[78] Teamsters Local 413 (Patton Warehouse, Inc.) , *supra* note 63.
[79] 335 F 2d at 715.

In *S & E McCormick* [80] the Board reconsidered the identical union-standards subcontracting provision that it had found illegal in *Patton* and agreed with the Circuit Court that the provision was lawful. In addition, the Board held that the union could lawfully negotiate provisions requiring that all unit work be done by unit employees and prohibiting the employers from utilizing hired or leased equipment unless the equipment was operated by such employees, even though the effect of such provisions would be either a cessation of existing, long-established business relationships between the employers and independent contractors, or a requirement that the owner-operators become "employees" while performing work for the employers and be subject to the wages, hours, and working conditions established by the contract, even to becoming and remaining members of the union while engaged in such work.[81]

The Board noted that the contract covered all work performed by the employers, that it was the entirety of that work which constituted the unit in which the union had a primary interest, and that the work performed by the owner-operators was identical to that performed by employees. It said that

> . . . any increase in the amount of work done by owner-operators or other drivers of leased equipment would cause a corresponding decrease in the amount of work available to the unit employees. Any work of this kind done by those outside the unit, i.e., by the 'independent contractors,' is sufficiently comparable in character, and the terms under which it is done sufficiently affect the terms and conditions of the work done in the unit, to cause the Union to have a direct and necessary interest in the work and to make it unit work within the meaning of *Wilson, supra.*[82]

The provisions were designed to protect unit work and standards against erosion from subcontracting and had a legitimate primary object, in the Board's view. Rejecting the contention that the provisions were violative of Section 8(e) because they would necessitate changes in long-established business relationships between the employers and the owner-operators, the Board said:

> If the clauses are otherwise lawful, the mere fact that, as an incident thereto, a cessation in business relationships may flow from their

---

[80] Teamsters Local 107 (S & E McCormick, Inc.), 159 NLRB 84, 62 LRRM 1224 (1966), *vacated and remanded sub nom.*, A. Duie Pyle, Inc. v. NLRB, 383 F 2d 772, 65 LRRM 3107 (CA 3, 1967), *cert. denied*, 390 US 905, 67 LRRM 2308 (1968).
[81] 159 NLRB at 96-101.
[82] *Id.* at 98.

operation is not alone enough to establish an unlawful secondary object within the intent of Section 8(e). To conclude otherwise would mean that unions would be limited to negotiating clauses prohibiting or restricting subcontracting to those situations where the employer is not engaging in any subcontracting at the time of the making of the contract. Under that view, once work has been subcontracted it could never be considered to be unit work because it would disrupt the business relationships to require the employer to cease doing business with its subcontractors. We have been cautioned against such a result by the judicial admonition that the " 'cease doing business' language in Section 8(e) cannot be read literally." [83]

The Board also rejected the argument that the provisions violated Section 8(e) because they had the effect of requiring owner-operators to become and remain members of the union. It stated:

> The legitimacy of the Unions' objective in requiring all drivers performing unit work to be unit 'employees' subject to the applicable collective-bargaining agreements while performing such work is not converted into an unlawful 'cease doing business' one within the intent of Section 8(e) simply because, as an incident to their unit employee status, the drivers are required to comply with all terms and conditions of the bargaining contract, including the union-security requirement.[84]

On review of the Board's decision in *S & E McCormick* the Third Circuit agreed that although the provisions required the employers to "cease doing business" with independent contractors within the meaning of Section 8(e), they also fell within the union's legitimate primary interests in protecting unit work and standards.[85] The court held, however, that the provisions which required owner-operators to become employees and members of the union were secondary and unlawful. The court said:

> Thus, their effect is to make the continuance of the relationship between the employer and an independent contractor depend upon the latter's decision to become a member of the union if he is an owner-operator and to require his employees as well as himself to become members of the union if he is a fleet-owner. The requirement therefore makes the central test of the employer's continuing to do business with such an individual his internal labor policy and not his maintenance of union wage scales or similar conditions which otherwise might adversely affect the unit members. . . .

---

[83] *Id.* at 99.
[84] *Id.* at 101.
[85] 383 F 2d at 776.

The present provisions, to the extent that they require the sub-contractees to become employees and members of the union, therefore must also be declared invalid. As in the case of secondary boycotts generally, a union may not employ a collective bargaining agreement with one employer as a means of effectuating its object to coerce another employer to unionize. Nor may it by this means seek to coerce self-employed persons to become union members.[86]

2. _National Woodwork:_ the Work-Preservation Doctrine. In April 1967 the Supreme Court, in _National Woodwork_,[87] decided its first Section 8(e) case and, in a five-to-four decision, adopted the principle set forth by the D. C. Circuit that where the object of a provision is the protection and preservation of unit work customarily performed by employees in the unit, even though it may fall within the letter of Section 8(e), it is primary in nature and does not violate Section 8(e). _National Woodwork_ involved a provision negotiated by the Carpenters Union under which its members would not handle prefabricated, factory-precut doors. The Board held the provision lawful. Relying on the fact that the clause was not concerned with the nature of the employer with whom the contractor did business nor with the employment conditions of other employers or employees, the Board reasoned that the language of the contract constituted an attempt to protect or preserve for job site employees work customarily performed at the job site.[88] The Seventh Circuit, disagreeing with the Board, distinguished between job site work and factory made products. It quoted the statement of then-Senator John F. Kennedy that the construction " 'proviso does not cover boycott of goods manufactured in an industrial plant for installation at the jobsite.' " [89]

The Supreme Court agreed with the Board that the intent of the union's "will not handle" provision was to protect and preserve work customarily performed by bargaining-unit employees and was not a product boycott. Justice Brennan, writing for the majority, reviewed the legislative history and judicial decisions

---

86 _Id._ at 777.
87 National Woodwork Mfrs. Ass'n v. NLRB, 386 US 612, 64 LRRM 2801 (1967), _affirming in part and reversing in part_ 354 F 2d 594, 60 LRRM 2458 (CA 7, 1965), _setting aside in part and remanding_ 149 NLRB 646, 47 LRRM 1341 (1964). _See:_ Comment, _Hot Cargo Clauses in Construction Industry Labor Contracts,_ 37 FORDHAM L. REV. 99 (1968); Note, _Product Boycott for Work Preservation,_ 36 TENN. L. REV. 62 (1968); Note, _Union Contracts and Work Stoppages Designed to Preserve Job Opportunities,_ 46 TEX. L. REV. 283 (1967).
88 149 NLRB at 657.
89 354 F 2d at 599.

with respect to labor union "primary" and "secondary" pressures. He distinguished *Allen Bradley*,[90] the antitrust case, on the ground that there the employer-union agreement was used as a "sword" to monopolize other jobs for union members, not, as in the instant case, as a "shield" to preserve work and jobs for members of the bargaining unit. The Court said that such activities are "primary" and hence are not proscribed by Section 8(e).[91]

The Court noted, moreover, that the legitimacy of work-preservation clauses like that involved in *National Woodwork* had been implicitly recognized in its decision in *Fibreboard*,[92] where it held that bargaining on the subject of contracting out of work performed by members of the bargaining unit was mandatory under Section 8(a)(5) of the Act.[93] The Court added:

> It would therefore be incongruous to interpret §8(e) to invalidate clauses over which the parties may be mandated to bargain and which have been successfully incorporated through collective bargaining in many of this Nation's major labor agreements.[94]

In considering the legality of a particular clause, the Court concluded that "[t]he touchstone is whether the agreement or its maintenance is addressed to the labor relationships of the contracting employer *vis-a-vis* his own employees." [95]

In a strong dissent, Justice Stewart, joined by Justices Black, Douglas, and Clark, suggested that the majority approached the issue with preconceptions. He concluded that the union was engaged in a product boycott, which the language of Section 8(e) clearly proscribes. The dissent contended that the majority un-

---

90 Allen Bradley Co. v. Electrical Workers Local 3, 325 US 797, 16 LRRM 798 (1945). *See* Chapter 29 *infra* at notes 142-43.
91 386 US at 630-631.
92 Fibreboard Paper Products Corp. v. NLRB, 379 US 203, 57 LRRM 2609 (1964). *See* Chapter 15 *supra* for discussion of subcontracting as a subject of bargaining.
93 386 US at 642-643.
94 *Id.* at 643.
95 *Id.* at 645. *See* NLRB v. Milk Drivers' Union (Associated Milk Dealers, Inc.), 392 F 2d 845, 67 LRRM 2274 (CA 7, 1968), *enforcing* 159 NLRB 1459, 62 LRRM 1482 (1966), (where a violation of §8(e) was found because the object of a contractual provision was to increase union membership at the expense of another union, not to protect or preserve work customarily performed within the bargaining unit). *Cf.* Sheetmetal Workers Local 141 (Cincinnati Sheet Metal & Roofing Co.), 174 NLRB No. 125, 70 LRRM 1324 (1969). *See also* Canada Dry Corp. v. NLRB, 421 F 2d 907, 73 LRRM 2582 (CA 6, 1970) (where a work-preservation clause was upheld), *and* Sheet Metal Workers Local 216 (Associated Pipe and Fitting Mfrs.), 172 NLRB No. 6, 69 LRRM 1050 (1968) where an alleged work-preservation clause was not upheld. *See* note 100 *infra*.

dertook "a protracted review of legislative and decisional history in an effort to show that the clear words of the statute should be disregarded." [96] Justice Stewart characterized the majority's "sword and shield" distinction as being created out of "thin air" for the purpose of "substituting its own concept of desirable labor policy for the scheme enacted by Congress." [97]

In the companion case of *Houston Insulation Contractors Ass'n v. NLRB*,[98] involving Section 8(b)(4), the bargaining agreement provided that the employer would not contract out work relating to the "preparation, distribution and application of piping and boiler coverings." Johns-Manville, a party to the labor agreement, purchased steel bands precut to specification; customarily the pre-cutting was performed by Johns-Manville employees under the terms of the labor agreement. The union, Asbestos Workers Local 22, ordered its members not to install the precut bands. The Supreme Court agreed with the Fifth Circuit that there was sub-stantial evidence to support the Board's holding that the object of the union's conduct was work preservation. Consistent with *National Woodwork*, the Court also affirmed the Board's decision that Local 113, a sister local of Local 22, did not violate the Act when it refused to install precut fittings at a construction project for Armstrong Co. unless the precutting was performed by Local 22 members in accordance with Local 22's bargaining agreement with Armstrong. Both the members of Local 113 and those of Local 22 were employed by Armstrong; Local 113 had jurisdiction at the construction project, and Local 22 had jurisdiction over the shop where the cutting was customarily done. The Court held that the object of Local 113's activity was primary—the preserva-tion of work customarily performed by Armstrong employees rep-resented by Local 22, and that Local 113 was merely engaging in lawful concerted primary activity in support of Local 22.

National Woodwork provides the standard against which all Section 8(e) cases must be measured. Its basic teaching is that if the object of a questionable clause is to benefit union members

---

[96] *Id*. at 650.
[97] *Id*. at 657-658.
[98] 385 US 664, 64 LRRM 2821 (1967), *affirming in part and reversing in part* 357 F 2d 182, 61 LRRM 2529 (CA 5, 1966), *enforcing in part and reversing in part* 148 NLRB 866, 57 LRRM 1065 (1964). In *Asbestos Workers Local 8*, 173 NLRB No. 55, 69 LRRM 1344 (1968), *Houston Insulation* was distinguished, for the Board held that the employer's use of prefabricated materials did not violate the agreement.

generally, as distinguished from employees within the bargaining unit, the object is proscribed and Section 8(e) is violated. But if the object is to preserve the work of the bargaining unit, the clause is not unlawful. Several cases decided since *National Woodwork* furnish additional guidance for the application of the standard in relation to the following questions: (1) How much is encompassed by the work-preservation concept? (2) Is the employer's "right of control" significant? (3) What degree of evidence is required to establish the unlawful secondary objective?

3. Application of the Doctrine. *a. Scope of the work.* Is the work which may be "preserved" confined to work which the employees in the bargaining unit are presently performing? The Board and the Eighth Circuit addressed themselves to this question in the first of two *American Boiler* cases.[99] At issue was a "fabrication" clause in a Pipefitters' agreement with a multi-employer contractors' association in St. Paul, Minn. The clause provided that trim piping on boilers would be fabricated on the job site or in the shop of the employer covered by the contract. Packaged boilers, however, did not require this work, for they could be delivered with these items prefabricated. Packaged boilers had been introduced and used in the area since before 1941. By the mid-forties, 10 percent of the boiler installations in the St. Paul area were of the packaged variety, and by 1963 the number of such installations had risen to a figure of 60 to 85 percent. The court agreed with the Board that the clause did not violate Section 8(e) and thereby rejected a construction of the *National Woodwork* doctrine which would have confined work preservation to work which is currently, continuously, and exclusively performed by unit employees.

The Eighth Circuit stated that the "traditional" work envisioned by *National Woodwork* included work which had been performed in the past and which, though diminished in amount, was still being performed. It held that the disputed clause protected current work and reacquired a portion of the work which had been lost.

---

99 American Boiler Mfrs. Ass'n v. NLRB (United Ass'n, Pipe Fitters Local 455), 404 F 2d 547, 69 LRRM 2851 (CA 8, 1968), *modifying* 167 NLRB 602, 66 LRRM 1098 (1967), *cert. denied*, 398 US 960, 74 LRRM 2420 (1970). *Cf.* earlier decisions: American Boiler Mfrs. Ass'n v. NLRB 366 F 2d 815, 63 LRRM 2236 (CA 8, 1966), *reversing and remanding* 154 NLRB 285, 59 LRRM 1727 (1965). The companion *American Boiler* decision is discussed at note 107 *infra*.

However, the court carefully defined the limits of its holding:

> We express no opinion as to whether a fabrication clause can be enforced if the objective is to acquire work which unit employees had never performed or work which they may have performed in the past but have completely lost before the clause was negotiated. We hold only that the term "traditional work" includes work which unit employees have performed and are still performing at the time they negotiated a work-preservation clause.
>
> It follows from the teachings of National Woodwork that a union can protect this work by concerted activities where the objective is to affect the labor policies of the employer with whom they have a collective bargaining agreement.[100]

The court thus agreed with the Board that the union's objective was to preserve for employees in the bargaining unit work which was traditionally done by them, not to obtain work for members of the union generally.

The court reversed the Board as to another feature of the case. The union had signed a memorandum agreement with 3-M Company (not a party to the association contract) in which the union had stated that it would not install packaged boilers ordered by 3-M prior to its contracting with an association member for their installation; the union had threatened to strike if the boilers were delivered. When the memorandum agreement was signed, the boiler specifications were changed. The court held that the memorandum violated 8(e) because it was not directed at the primary employer, for 3M was not a party to the original agreement and did not employ members of the bargaining unit.[101]

b. Right of control. The Board has held that it is a violation of Section 8(b)(4)(B) for a union to strike or threaten to strike to

---

[100] 404 F 2d at 552. *Cf.* National Woodwork, *supra* note 87, 386 US at 630-31: "We . . . have no occasion today to decide the questions which might arise where the workers carry on a boycott to reach out to monopolize jobs or acquire new job tasks when their own jobs are not threatened by the boycotted product." *Cf. also* concurring opinion of Justice Harlan, 386 US at 648. The Board has ruled in several cases that a work-preservation clause cannot lawfully embrace work which has not been traditionally performed by employees in the bargaining unit. Culinary Alliance, Local 402 (Bob's Enterprises, Inc.), 175 NLRB No. 26, 70 LRRM 1508 (1969); Sheet Metal Wkrs., Local 98 (Cincinnati Sheet Metal and Roofing Co.), 174 NLRB No. 22, 70 LRRM 1119 (1968). *See also* note 95 *supra*.

[101] 404 F 2d at 556. The Board has declined to rule on this issue because there was no specific allegation in the pleadings as to the validity of the memorandum agreement. The Court held that the Board erred because the issue was material and it had been fairly tried by the parties even though it had not been specifically pleaded. The issue raises questions about the "right of control" doctrine discussed in the next section.

enforce a work-preservation clause when the primary employer does not have the legal right to control the disputed work.[102] One commentator describes a typical right-of-control situation as follows: "A union secures from an employer a standard work preservation clause, valid under Section 8(e). Subsequently, the employer contracts to do a job for a third party, and, in violation of its prior agreement with the union, undertakes to install a prefabricated product which eliminates the need for certain operations covered by the work preservation provision. The union strikes the employer in protest against the loss of work." [103] The Board reasons that such conduct is secondary and unlawful because the employer does not have the right to control the work. The Board adhered to this rule in *National Woodwork*,[104] and the Seventh Circuit affirmed the Board's rationale.[105] However, the union did not seek review of this question, and the Supreme Court expressly refrained from deciding it.[106]

Since *National Woodwork*, three courts of appeals have repudiated the Board's right-of-control test.[107] Although the Third and

---

102 *E.g.*, Int'l Longshoremen's Ass'n, 137 NLRB 1178 (1962), 50 LRRM 1333, *enforced*, 331 F 2d 712, 56 LRRM 2200 (CA 3, 1964); Ohio Valley Carpenters Dist. Council (Cardinal Industries), 144 NLRB 91, 54 LRRM 1003 (1963), *enforced*, 339 F 2d 142, 57 LRRM 2509 (CA 6, 1964); Plumbers & Pipefitters, Local 5 (Arthur Venneri Co.), 137 NLRB 828, 50 LRRM 1266 (1962), *enforced*, 321 F 2d 366, 53 LRRM 2424 (CA DC, 1963), *cert. denied*, 375 US 921, 54 LRRM 2576 (1963). For discussion of §8(b)(4)(B) generally, *see* Chapter 23 *supra*.

103 St. Antoine, *The Rational Regulation of Union Restrictive Practices*, in LABOR LAW DEVELOPMENTS 1968 (Sw. Legal Foundation 14th Ann. Inst. on Labor Law) 1, 20 (1968). Professor St. Antoine comments: "Of course, the employer no longer has the power to dispose of the work, but he gave it up knowingly, in breach of his contract, and it hardly seems proper to punish the union for his wrongdoing." *Ibid*.

104 Note 87 *supra*, 149 NLRB at 658-59.

105 National Woodwork Mfrs. Ass'n v. NLRB, 354 F 2d 594, 60 LRRM 2458 (CA 7, 1965).

106 National Woodwork Mfrs. Ass'n v. NLRB, 386 US 612, 615, n. 3, 64 LRRM 2801 (1967). In a post-*National Woodwork* decision, *Pipe Fitters Local 120* (Mechanical Contractors Ass'n of Cleveland), 168 NLRB No. 138, 67 LRRM 1034 (1968), the Board adhered to its right-of-control doctrine. Member Brown dissented, as he had done in previous cases involving this doctrine, pointing out that the doctrine "shields the offending employer from pressure in a controversy he has created" while the Board "helps to undo what has been done at the bargaining table." *See:* Lesnick, *Job Security and Secondary Boycotts: The Reach of NLRB 8(b)(4) and 8(e)*, 113 U. PA. L. REV. 1000, 1036 (1965); Comment, *Secondary Boycotts and Work Preservation*, 77 YALE L.J. 1401, 1415 (1968).

107 NLRB v. IBEW, Local 164, 388 F 2d 105, 67 LRRM 2352 (CA 3, 1968) (the Third Circuit, prior to *National Woodwork*, had sustained the Board's position in NLRB v. Int'l Longshoremen's Ass'n, 331 F 2d 712, 56 LRRM 2200 (CA 3, 1964)); American Boiler Mfrs. Ass'n v. NLRB, 404 F 2d 556 (CA 8, 1968) (in this companion case to *American Boiler Mfrs. Ass'n v. NLRB*, note 99 *supra*, the court disagreed with the Board's finding that the employer had a right of control, but held

Eighth Circuits expressly noted that " 'right of control' is a factor to be considered in deciding whether concerted activity by unit employees has an illegal objective," [108] they stressed that if a union's conduct is addressed to the enforcement of its collective bargaining agreement and related solely to the preservation of traditional tasks of unit employees, Section 8(b)(4)(B) is not violated. The First Circuit also agrees that the right of control in and of itself "is not of decisive significance." [109] It remains to be seen whether the Board's view or that of these three circuits will prevail.

    c. Establishing secondary objective. In *Dixie Mining Co.*[110] the Board gave some indication of the amount and kind of evidence required to establish the existence of a secondary object to invalidate a work-protection clause. The clause in question provided that each employer-party to the United Mine Worker's Bituminous Coal Wage Agreement was required to make double royalty payments to the union's welfare and retirement fund for every ton of coal it acquired from nonsignatory operations. This clause had been held invalid in an earlier decision, but following remand by the District of Columbia Circuit, which said that the clause would not violate Section 8(e) if it were "germane to the economic integrity of the principal work unit;" [111] the Board issued a second decision holding the clause lawful. The majority opinion was that the clause "was adopted by the contracting parties in order to protect and preserve the 'unit work' of employees covered by the contract by precluding the subcontracting of 'unit work' to operators who did not maintain union standards." [112] This construction rejected the view of Chairman McCulloch, dissenting, who concluded that the parties' stipulation of fact constituted prima facie evidence of a violation of Section 8(e). The stipulation stated that "the purchasing of coal by one producer

---

that the absence of a right of control was not dispositive of the issue); Beacon Castle Square Bldg. Corp. v. NLRB, 406 F 2d 188, 70 LRRM 2357 (CA 1, 1969) (dictum, 406 F 2d at 192, n. 10). For treatment of related matter, *see* discussion *infra* of contracts under the construction industry proviso.
[108] 404 F 2d at 561-62.
[109] 406 F 2d at 192, n. 10.
[110] United Mine Workers (Dixie Mining Co.), 179 NLRB No. 80, 72 LRRM 1426 (1969). The Board reversed its prior decision, 144 NLRB 228, 54 LRRM 1037 (1964), following remand by the D.C. Circuit in *Lewis* v. *NLRB*, 350 F 2d 801, 59 LRRM 2946 (CA DC, 1965).
[111] 350 F 2d at 802, *citing* Orange Belt Dist. Council of Painters v. NLRB, 328 F 2d 534, 538-539, 55 LRRM 2293 (CA DC, 1964), note 64 *supra*.
[112] 72 LRRM at 1428.

from another producer is an essential marketing practice within the industry." [113] The majority found (1) the incidence of supplemental coal purchases too insubstantial to establish a secondary objective and (2) the union had "a legitimate interest in restricting outside purchases of non-unit coal in order to promote better mining of existing capacity, and in preventing operators from purchasing 'substitute coal' under the guise of supplemental coal." [114]

F. Construction Industry Proviso

The construction industry proviso to Section 8(e) is as follows:

> *Provided,* That nothing in this subsection shall apply to an agreement between a labor organization and an employer in the construction industry relating to the contracting or subcontracting of work to be done at the site of the construction, alteration, painting, or repair of a building, structure, or other work. . . .

Initially, the Board held in *Colson & Stevens Construction Co.*[115] that although a subcontracting clause limited to site work in the construction industry was legal under the proviso to Section 8(e), a strike to obtain or enforce such an agreement was illegal. Three circuit courts [116] rejected the Board's position, and in 1964, in *Centlivre Village Apartments,*[117] the Board reversed its position and held that under the construction industry proviso a union can strike to obtain a "hot cargo" subcontracting clause limited to site work. However, the Board, with court approval, has adhered to its original position that it is unlawful to strike to *enforce* such a clause for such a strike violates Section 8(b)(4)(B).[118]

---

113 *Id.* at 1429.

114 *Ibid.*

115 Construction, Prod. & Maintenance Laborers Local 383 (Colson & Stevens Const. Co.), 137 NLRB 1650, 50 LRRM 1444 (1962), *reversed,* 323 F 2d 422, 54 LRRM 2246 (CA 9, 1963).

116 Construction, Prod. & Maintenance Laborers Local 383 v. NLRB, 323 F 2d 422, 54 LRRM 2246 (CA 9, 1963); Orange Belt District Council of Painters No. 48 v. NLRB, 328 F 2d 534, 55 LRRM 2293 (CA DC, 1964); Essex Co. and Vicinity District Council of Carpenters v. NLRB, 332 F 2d 636, 56 LRRM 2091 (CA 3, 1964).

117 Building & Construction Trades Council (Centlivre Village Apartments), 148 NLRB 854, 57 LRRM 1081 (1964). The case was remanded with directions to dismiss on another point in 352 F 2d 696, 59 LRRM 2894 (CA DC, 1965).

118 *Ibid.;* Orange Belt, *supra* note 116, at 537; Essex County Carpenters, *supra* note 116, at 641. A union which sought to enforce a construction site clause by recision of the collective bargaining agreement pursuant to a termination clause was held in violation of Sections 8(b)(4)(A), (B) and 8(e). Use of the termination clause was considered to be a means of exerting economic pressure, hence unlawful. NLRB v. IBEW, Local 769 (Ets-Hokin Corp.), 405 F 2d 159, 69 LRRM 2959 (CA 9, 1968), *enforcing* 154 NLRB 839, 60 LRRM 1045 (1965); *cert. denied,* 395 US 921, 71 LRRM 2294 (1969). *Accord:* IBEW, Local 437 (National Electrical Contractors

In a 1962 case, *Cardinal Industries, Inc.,*[119] the Board held that the construction industry proviso applies only to work actually to be done at the construction site where the work is of a kind that has traditionally been done and can be done on the job site. It rejected a union's contention that the proviso covered off-site work which "could be done at the site of construction," or "would be done [at the site] . . . if not contracted out." [120] The Board also ruled that a clause which allowed prefabrication violated Section 8(e) to the extent that it required off-site production, outside the unit, to be done by union employees.[121]

In *Muskegon General Contractors* [122] a craft union sought and struck to obtain a multiemployer contract in the construction industry which contained a provision giving union members the right to refuse to work on any job where any of the work, irrespective of craft, had been, was being, or would be performed by employees enjoying less favorable conditions of employment than those provided in the agreement between the equivalent craft union and its contracting employers. The union claimed the provision was a work-standards clause, but the Board noted that the clause extended beyond protection of the work of employees in the unit represented by the union and was not limited to situations where the signatory employer had a contractual relationship with the alleged substandard employer on the job. It concluded that the provision went beyond the work-standards exception to Section 8(e) and was therefore secondary, rather than primary. The Board also rejected the argument that the provision was lawful under the construction industry proviso, holding that where "a

---

Ass'n), 171 NLRB No. 53, 68 LRRM 1182 (1968). *See also* NLRB v. Construction & Gen. Laborers' Local 270 (Howard J. White, Inc.), 318 F 2d 86, 68 LRRM 2953 (CA 9, 1968), *enforcing* 161 NLRB 1313, 63 LRRM 1451 (1966). A union may enforce a subcontracting clause limited to on-site construction through grievance procedures and court enforcement under §301. Sheet Metal Workers, Local 48 v. Hardy Corp., 332 F 2d 682, 56 LRRM 2462 (CA 5, 1964).

119 Ohio Valley Carpenters District Council (Cardinal Indus., Inc.), 136 NLRB 977, 49 LRRM 1908 (1962).

120 136 NLRB at 988. In *El Paso Bldg. & Construction Trades Council v. El Paso Associated General Contractors,* 376 F 2d 797, 65 LRRM 2415 (CA 5, 1967), the Fifth Circuit held valid a clause requiring prime contractor to apply terms of contract to any work subcontracted.

121 *See also:* Ohio Valley Carpenters District Council (Hankins & Hankins Const. Co.), 144 NLRB 91, 54 LRRM 1003 (1963), *enforced,* 339 F 2d 142, 57 LRRM 2509 (CA 6, 1964); IBEW, Local 1516 (Mercantile Bank), 172 NLRB No. 78, 68 LRRM 1358 (1968).

122 Bricklayers Local 5 (Greater Muskegon General Contractors Ass'n), 152 NLRB 360, 59 LRRM 1081 (1965), *enforced as modified,* 378 F 2d 859, 65 LRRM 2563 (CA 6, 1967).

limitation upon contracting at a construction site [which] is intertwined with a provision permitting such self-help as striking or
otherwise refusing to perform services, *e.g.*, by permitting employees to refrain from working without suffering disciplinary
action, in the event of a breach of the 'hot cargo' clause, the clause
exceeds the prescribed bounds of the first proviso to Section 8(e)
and is therefore unlawful." [123] Member Fanning dissented on the
ground that the clause was protected by the construction industry
proviso. He suggested that the majority held the clause unlawful
merely because of the self-help provision and contended that this
provision did not sanction union inducement but merely gave the
employees the right to refuse to work and therefore did not permit
conduct proscribed by Section 8(b)(4)(B).

The Sixth Circuit, on review of the *Muskegon* case, agreed with
the Board majority that the clause sanctioned and encouraged
strike action to enforce the secondary boycott agreement, and that
it was, therefore, an effort to authorize by contract, action that is
illegal under Section 8(b)(4)(B). The court therefore concluded
that the provision was illegal and that the union, by insisting on
the provision and striking to obtain it, was guilty of refusing to
bargain collectively in violation of Section 8(b)(3). The court enforced the Board's order to the extent that it was founded on the
8(b)(3) violation, deeming that an adequate remedy. It "therefore
reserve[d] the complex question of whether the building trade
proviso nullifies the application of Sec. 8(e) for all purposes in the
construction industry and hence excludes a finding of a Sec.
8(b)(4)(i) & (ii)(A) violation." [124]

The Board has held, with court approval, that the mixing, delivery, and pouring of ready-mix concrete at a construction site is
not on-site construction work, and that the construction industry
proviso to Section 8(e) is not applicable to provisions related to the
contracting and subcontracting of such work.[125] The Board reasoned that the mixing and pouring of the concrete was merely the

[123] 152 NLRB at 366.
[124] 378 F 2d at 865-866.
[125] Teamsters Local 559 (Connecticut Sand & Stone Corp.), 138 NLRB 532, 51
LRRM 1092 (1962); Teamsters Local 294 (Island Dock Lumber, Inc.), 145 NLRB
484, 54 LRRM 1421 (1963), *enforced*, 342 F 2d 18, 58 LRRM 2518 (CA 2, 1965);
Teamsters Local 695 (Madison Employers Council), 152 NLRB 577, 50 LRRM
1131 (1965), *enforced*, 361 F 2d 547, 62 LRRM 2135 (CA DC, 1966); Teamsters
Local 551, 176 NLRB No. 109, 72 LRRM 1095 (1969).

final act of delivery and that, although the mixing might be done at the job site, it could equally well have taken place away from the site. According to the Board, the construction industry proviso does not exempt from Section 8(e) agreements relating to the delivery of supplies and materials to the construction site, and it therefore does not exempt agreements relating to the mixing and pouring of liquid concrete which, by its very nature, cannot be dumped on the ground and is not actually "delivered" until poured.[126]

G. Garment Industry Proviso.

The second proviso to Section 8(e) grants an exemption for parties in the apparel and clothing industry.[127] A stated congressional purpose for this exemption was to accord legal status "to the integrated process of production in those industries. . . ." [128] According to Senator Javits, "The alternative . . . would have been chaos, the opening of new opportunities to sweatshops, racketeering, sweetheart contracts, and many of the various excesses and scandals which [Congress was] seeking to correct." [129]

Inasmuch as the exemption is an absolute one (whereas the construction industry exemption is limited), there is no room for disagreement as to the meaning of the proviso; consequently, no litigation has resulted. There have been administrative decisions of the General Counsel, however, affirming: (1) that a contract clause requiring garment manufacturers to utilize only the services of union subcontractors is lawful under Section 8(e); [130] and (2) that a union can lawfully induce employees of union subcontractors to strike for the purpose of forcing the subcontractors to cease doing business with an employer engaged in manufacturing clothing with whom a union has a dispute.[131]

---

126 Island Dock, *supra* note 125.
127 *See* text of the proviso at note 19 *supra*. The exemption does not render §8 (e) unconstitutional under the due process clause of the Fifth Amendment. NLRB v. Lithographers, Local 17, 309 F 2d 31, 51 LRRM 2093, *cert. denied*, 372 US 943, 52 LRRM 2673 (1963).
128 Remarks of Senator Javits, 2 LEGISLATIVE HISTORY OF THE LABOR-MANAGEMENT REPORTING AND DISCLOSURE ACT OF 1959, 1446 (1959).
129 *Ibid.*
130 Admin. Ruling of NLRB General Counsel, Case No. SR-741, 46 LRRM 1502 (1960). *Cf.* Ladies Garment Workers Union, Locals 234 and 243 v. Beauty Belt Lingerie, Inc., 48 LRRM 2995 (SD NY, 1961).
131 Admin. Ruling of NLRB General Counsel, Case No. SR-633, 46 LRRM 1340 (1960).

CHAPTER 25

JURISDICTIONAL DISPUTES AND 'FEATHERBEDDING'

I. JURISDICTIONAL DISPUTES

A. Scope of Section 8(b)(4)(D)

Frequent sources of friction between unions and employers, and between two or more contending unions, are work assignment or "jurisdictional" disputes. Prior to 1947, jurisdictional disputes were the cause of numerous and often long and damaging work stoppages.[1] The employer was usually caught in the middle, unable to satisfy either of the unions involved. In the early days of the Wagner Act, the Board generally refused to make any determination as to jurisdictional disputes involving unions affiliated with the same parent organization because the Board considered such conflicts to be internal union matters to be settled by proper procedures established by the parent organization.[2] With the advent of the CIO, the Board changed its practice and proceeded to handle representation disputes involving two unions of the same parent organization.[3] But the original Act contained no machinery to stop jurisdictional strikes.

The prevalence of these jurisdictional disputes reached such serious proportions immediately following World War II that President Truman requested legislation to prevent such conflicts from creating work stoppages.[4] The Taft-Hartley amendments of

---

[1] Memorandum of Senator Morse, 93 CONG. REC. 1890 (1947) ; *see also:* LEGISLATIVE HISTORY OF THE LABOR MANAGEMENT RELATIONS ACT, 1947, 951 (1948).
[2] Aluminum Co. of America, 1 NLRB 530, 1 LRRM 416 (1936).
[3] Interlake Iron Corp., 2 NLRB 1036, 1 LRRM 574 (1937).
[4] Harry S. Truman, *Annual Message on the State of the Union,* PUBLIC PAPERS OF THE PRESIDENT OF THE UNITED STATES 4 (1947).

1947 therefore included Sections 8 (b)(4)(D) [5] and (10 (k),[6] designed to prohibit, as unfair labor practices, activities of labor organizations in support of demands that particular work be assigned to members of a particular labor organization, trade, craft, or class. The Board, however, even under these new provisions, refused to make final settlements in jurisdictional dispute cases, determining only whether strikes in specific cases were legal.[7] However, in 1961 the Supreme Court held that the Act required the Board to accept jurisdictional dispute cases and to make final determinations as to which of the contending parties was in fact entitled to the disputed work.[8]

Section 8(b)(4)(D) prohibits strikes, picketing, boycotts, threats, and coercion where an object is

forcing or requiring any employer to assign particular work to employees in a particular labor organization or in a particular trade, craft, or class rather than to employees in another labor organization or in another trade, craft, or class . . .

---

[5] Section 8 (b) (4) (D) provides:
"Sec. 8 (b) It shall be an unfair labor practice for a labor organization or its agents—
. . .
" (4) (i) to engage in, or induce or encourage any individual employed by any person engaged in commerce or in an industry affecting commerce to engage in a strike or a refusal in the course of his employment to use, manufacture, process, transport, or otherwise handle or work on any goods, articles, materials, or commodities or to perform any services; or (ii) to threaten, coerce, or restrain any person engaged in commerce or in an industry affecting commerce, where in either case an object thereof is—
. . .
" (D) forcing or requiring any employer to assign particular work to employees in a particular labor organization or in a particular trade, craft, or class rather than to employees in another labor organization or in another trade, craft, or class, unless such employer is failing to conform to an order or certification of the Board determining the bargaining representative for employees performing such work . . ."
[6] Section 10 (k) provides:
"Whenever it is charged that any person has engaged in an unfair labor practice within the meaning of paragraph (4) (D) of section 8 (b), the Board is empowered and directed to hear and determine the dispute out of which such unfair labor practice shall have arisen, unless, within ten days after notice that such change has been filed, the parties to such dispute submit to the Board satisfactory evidence that they have adjusted, or agreed upon methods for the voluntary adjustment of, the dispute. Upon compliance by the parties to the dispute with the decision of the Board or upon such voluntary adjustment of the dispute, such charge shall be dismissed."
[7] Local 173, Wood, Wire & Metal Lathers' Union (Newark & Essex Plastering Co.), 121 NLRB 1094, 42 LRRM 1519 (1958), discussed at note 43 *infra*.
[8] NLRB v. Radio and Television Broadcast Engineers Union, Local 1212 (Columbia Broadcasting System), 364 US 573, 47 LRRM 2332 (1961).

The traditional jurisdictional dispute, in which two unions have collective bargaining agreements with one employer and each claims the work for its members through activities proscribed by 8 (b) (4) , is clearly condemned.[9] But actions designed to force an employer to make work assignments which conform to a Board order or certification are expressly excepted from the general prohibition.[10] The focus of this chapter is upon disputes which fall between these extremes.

What kind of dispute will give rise to an 8 (b) (4) (D) charge if a labor organization resorts to strikes, picketing, or threats to press its claim? [11]

If all strikes whose object is to have work assigned to one group rather than to another were construed as prohibited by Section 8 (b) (4) (D), all strikes continuing after the replacement of economic strikers would be deemed unlawful, for such strikes would have as one object the assignment of work to strikers rather than to replacements. However, the Board limits the application of 8 (b) (4) (D), holding that "a strike for lawful economic objectives" is not an unlawful jurisdictional strike.[12] Yet, despite this general principle, a strike ostensibly for a legitimate end can be tainted. Picketing solely for the purpose of protesting rates of pay is not a violation of the Act,[13] though evidence of an oral request for the work by the union business agent coupled with picketing to protest rates of pay can give reasonable cause for the belief that the real object of the picketing is the assignment of the work to the

9 Local 27, Int'l Typographical Union (Heiter Starke Printing Co.) , 121 NLRB 1013, 42 LRRM 1501 (1958) ; St. Louis Stereotypers' Union Local 8 (Pulitzer Publishing Co.) , 152 NLRB 1232, 59 LRRM 1292 (1965) ; New Orleans Typographical Union Local 17 v. NLRB, 368 F 2d 755, 63 LRRM 2467 (CA 5, 1966) .
10 See proviso in clause (D) , note 5 supra.
11 For a comprehensive review of the subject, see Johns, Jurisdictional Disputes Under The NLRA, (LABOR LAW DEVELOPMENTS 1967, 13th Annual Institute on Labor Law, Southwestern Legal Foundation) 31 (1967) , where the suggestion is made that an employer does not really have to make this determination. If he "feels pinched" by prohibited conduct which has for its object reassignment of work of any kind, he should file a charge with the Board and let it decide whether there is or is not a jurisdictional dispute within the meaning of the Act. For a well-documented critique of the Board's handling of §10 (k) cases, see Sussman, Section 10(k): Mandate for Change?, 47 B. U. L. REV. 201 (1967) .
12 Sheet Metal Workers Int'l Ass'n, Local 99 (Albers Milling Co.) , 90 NLRB 1015, 26 LRRM 1320 (1950) ; American Wire Weavers Protective Ass'n (Lindsay Wire Weaving Co.) , 120 NLRB 977, 42 LRRM 1090 (1958) .
13 Ship Scaling Contractors' Association, 87 NLRB 92, 25 LRRM 1086 (1949) . For treatment of the related subject of area-standards picketing, see Chapter 21 supra.

members of the picketing union.[14] Such picketing may thus violate 8 (b) (4) (D).

Primary economic activity of a labor organization where the object is negotiation of a collective bargaining agreement is generally protected by the Act. If, however, the only dispute remaining in the negotiation of an agreement is a union demand that certain work currently being performed by others be granted to the demanding union, a strike to enforce such a demand is an unfair labor practice. If the underlying dispute is over a work assignment, the fact that the demand is made under the guise of a contractual demand confers no immunity from a violation of Section 8 (b) (4) (D).[15] If no other group is currently doing the work over which a labor organization seeks contractual jurisdiction, there is no jurisdictional dispute under the Board's interpretation of 8(b)(4)(D). Thus, it was found lawful for a union to strike for an agreement that the employer would assign future work only to contractors having an agreement with the striking union.[16]

If an employer assigns work in violation of a jurisdictional clause in a collective bargaining agreement, the union's remedy is based on the contract: it may be by arbitration if available or by an action in court under Section 301.[17] Engaging in a strike or other activity proscribed by 8(b)(4)(D), though ostensibly to compel the employer to arbitrate, may lead to the conclusion that the strike was to force a change in the work assignment.[18]

The language of Section 8 (b) (4) (D) is directed against union activity designed to force an employer to change work assignments. The provision is silent as to whether there must be an active claim to the work by the group to which it has been assigned in order to give rise to a violation. Since the 1961 Supreme Court decision

---

14 Local 25, Int'l Brotherhood of Electrical Workers (Sarrow-Suburban Electric Co.), 152 NLRB 978, 59 LRRM 1113 (1965); Local 472, International Laborers' Union (Ernest Renda Contracting Co.), 123 NLRB 1776, 44 LRRM 1236 (1959).
15 Int'l Union of Operating Engineers, Local 825, 118 NLRB 978, 40 LRRM 1291 (1957); Int'l Longshoremen and Warehousemen Union, Local 8 (General Ore, Inc.), 124 NLRB 626, 44 LRRM 1445 (1959).
16 District No. 9, Int'l Ass'n of Machinists (Anheuser-Busch), 101 NLRB 346, 31 LRRM 1084 (1952). But see Chapter 24 supra for the "hot cargo" implications, since 1959, of such an agreement under §8 (e).
17 See Chapters 17 and 18 supra generally and, for discussion of the superior jurisdiction of a Board §10(k) award over an arbitration award, see Carey v. Westinghouse Elec. Corp., 375 US 261, 55 LRRM 2042 (1964), (also discussed in Chapter 29 infra at note 104).
18 New Orleans Typographical Union Local 17 (E. P. Rivas, Inc.) v. NLRB, 368 F 2d 755, 63 LRRM 2467 (CA 5, 1966). See Chapter 18 supra at notes 128 and 129.

in the *CBS* case,[19] however, the Board has concluded that there can be no jurisdictional dispute within the meaning of 8 (b) (4) (D) unless there are two competing claims to the particular work, stressing that the purpose of the section is to protect a neutral employer from a dispute between two groups claiming the work, not a means to arbitrate disputes between an employer and a single labor organization.[20] Thus, if two established labor organizations agree to their respective jurisdictions and the only existing dispute is between the employer, who has assigned work to members of the "wrong" union, and the other union, there is no jurisdictional dispute.[21] However, employees can claim this work individually even though their union concedes jurisdiction to the demanding union,[22] for employees who are not represented by a union have standing to claim disputed work.[23]

The Board's requirement that there be two active competing claims to the work before a jurisdictional dispute can arise is contrary to the judicial authority which prevailed prior to the *CBS* case [24] and has been criticized.[25] The Board's view has, however, been judicially supported since *CBS*.[26]

---

19 NLRB v. Radio and Television Broadcast Engineers Union, Local 1212 (Columbia Broadcasting System), 364 US 573, 47 LRRM 2332 (1961), discussed at notes 45 and 46 *infra*.
20 Highway Truckdrivers & Helpers, Local 107 (Safeway Stores, Inc.), 134 NLRB 1320, 49 LRRM 1343 (1961); Sheet Metal Workers, Local 272 (Valley Sheet Metal Co.) 136 NLRB 1402, 50 LRRM 1017 (1962).
21 Brotherhood of Teamsters, Local 70 (Hills Transportation Co.), 136 NLRB 1086, 49 LRRM 1930 (1962); Wood, Wire & Metal Lathers, Local 328 (Acoustics & Specialties, Inc.), 139 NLRB 598, 51 LRRM 1345 (1962).
22 Local 2, Bricklayers, Masons, & Plasterers (Decora Inc.), 152 NLRB 278, 59 LRRM 1065 (1965).
23 Int'l Brotherhood of Electrical Workers (Bendix Radio Div., Bendix Corp.), 138 NLRB 689, 51 LRRM 1127 (1962). In *Sarrow-Suburban*, note 14 *supra*, employees to whom work was assigned were newly organized. In *Bendix, supra*, they were unorganized. In both cases, evidence as to the claim of the assigned employees was slim. Apparently, an 8 (b) (4) (D) charge can arise in these kinds of situations with very little evidence of an *active* competing claim. See also Plumbers, Local 798 (Moon Beam Pipeline Contractors, Inc.), 177 NLRB No. 62, 71 LRRM 1392 (1969) (dispute found between union and group of non-union employees).
24 Int'l Longshoremen's Union v. Juneau Spruce Corp., 342 US 237, 29 LRRM 2249 (1952); Vincent v. Steamfitters, Local 395, 288 F 2d 276, 47 LRRM 2808 (CA 2, 1961).
25 Johns, note 11 *supra*, at 34-35, points out that no judicial review of the Board's requirement of competing claims is likely, for a §10(k) order is not final and is therefore not directly reviewable. Judicial review is available only following a §8 (b) (4) (D) unfair labor practice determination. No case has been found where the Board's determination of the work assignment has ever been reversed by a court of appeals. The court's scope of review is severely limited. *E.g.*, NLRB v. Int'l Longshoremen & Warehousemen's Union, 413 F 2d 30, 71 LRRM 2500 (CA 9, 1969).
26 Penello v. Local 59, Sheet Metal Workers, 195 F Supp 458, 48 LRRM 2495 (DC Del, 1961).

Jurisdictional disputes giving rise to charges of unfair labor practices are not limited to those between competing labor organizations whose members are the employees of the same employer. The classic example is where the charged labor organization has demanded that certain work be assigned to it rather than to another group of employees.[27] Thus, it is a violation of Section 8 (b) (4) (D) to picket to compel the replacement of unorganized employees with others whom the picketing union represents,[28] or to compel the replacement of employees belonging to one union with members of another union who are not employees.[29]

Indirect attempts to obtain particular work are also prohibited by the section. A strike against a general contractor to compel a change in an assignment of work from a subcontractor employing members of one union to a different subcontractor employing members of the striking union is an unfair labor practice.[30] It is also possible to find a jurisdictional dispute in an intra-union struggle, for Section 8 (b) (4) (D) is operative as to competing claims of two different locals of the same national union.[31]

B. Procedure

Whenever any person files a charge involving a violation of Section 8 (b) (4) (D), the NLRB regional director of the office where the charge is filed or referred must promptly notify all parties and begin an investigation.[32] If the charge appears to have merit and the regional director has not received satisfactory evidence that

---

27 ILWU, Local 16 (Juneau Spruce Corp.), 82 NLRB 650, 23 LRRM 1597 (1949); Marine Cooks and Stewards (Irwin-Lyons Lumber Co.), 82 NLRB 916, 23 LRRM 1623 (1949). A suit for damages in a jurisdictional dispute is also possible under Section 303 of the Taft-Hartley Act, 29 USC §187 (b). Plumbers, Local 761 v. Zaich Const. Co., 418 F 2d 1054, 72 LRRM 2979 (CA 9, 1969). For a general discussion of Section 303 in secondary boycott damage suits, see Chapter 23 supra.

28 Teamsters, Local 175 (Biagi Fruit & Produce), 107 NLRB 223, 33 LRRM 1099 (1953); Int'l Brotherhood of Electrical Workers, Local 639 (Bendix Radio Div., Bendix Corp.), 138 NLRB 689, 51 LRRM 1127 (1962). For the implications of such conduct under §§8 (b) (1) (A) and 8 (b) (2), see Chapters 5 and 6 supra.

29 Note 27 supra.

30 Int'l Brotherhood of Electrical Workers, Local 3 (Western Electric Co.), 141 NLRB 888, 52 LRRM 1419 (1963); Local 5, Plumbing & Pipe Fitting (Arthur Venneri Co.), 145 NLRB 1580, 55 LRRM 1196 (1964). It is immaterial whether or not the work is in progress. Operating Engineers, Local 478, 172 NLRB No. 221, 69 LRRM 1091 (1968). But see Int'l Longshoremen, Local 8 (Waterway Terminals Co.) 185 NLRB No. 35, 75 LRRM 1042 (1970) and Franklin Broadcasting Co., 126 NLRB 1212, 45 LRRM 1455 (1960), involving union attempts to retrieve jobs of displaced employees.

31 Local 595, Ornamental Iron Workers (Bechtel Corp.), 108 NLRB 823, 34 LRRM 1087 (1954); Local 2, Bricklayers, Masons & Plasterers (Decora, Inc.), 152 NLRB 278, 59 LRRM 1065 (1965).

32 NLRB Rules and Regulations, §102.89, Statements of Procedure, §§101.31-101.32.

the parties concerned have either adjusted or agreed upon a method for adjusting the jurisdictional dispute, the Board proceeds with its responsibility under Section 10(k) by issuing, through the regional director, a notice of hearing to be held before a hearing officer not less than 10 days after the parties receive notice of the filing of the charge.[33] Reasonable cause to believe that a violation of Section 8 (b) (4) (D) has occurred is a sufficient showing for Section 10 (k) jurisdiction. Proof of the violation is required only for a later Section 8 (b) (4) (D) unfair labor practice Board proceeding.[34]

If the Board has satisfactory evidence that the parties have agreed to a private method of adjusting the underlying work assignment dispute,[35] it will either refrain from issuing a notice of hearing or, if one has already been issued, quash it. However, it is the Board's practice to keep the unfair labor practice charge alive so that if the agreed method of adjustment does not bring about a settlement of the underlying dispute the charge may still be used as basis for a full-scale unfair labor practice proceeding.[36] If there is a Section 10 (k) determination, a complaint on the 8 (b) (4) (D) charge can be issued only after a failure to comply with the 10 (k) order.[37] Originally, the Board followed a practice of dismissing 8 (b) (4) (D) charges whenever it found that the parties involved had agreed upon a method of voluntary adjustment of the underlying dispute, because it interpreted the Act as requiring a Section 10 (k) hearing as a prerequisite to any unfair labor practice proceeding based on 8 (b) (4) (D). In 1958, when this practice was challenged, the Board concluded that its earlier interpretation was in-

---

[33] NLRB Rules and Regulations, §102.90, Statements of Procedure, §§101.33-101.34. A jurisdictional dispute is not moot, despite the completion of work involved, if nothing indicates that the dispute will not arise in the future. Sheet Metal Workers, Local 541 (Kingery Construction Co.), 172 NLRB No. 108, 68 LRRM 1368 (1968).

[34] Lodge 681, District 27, Machinists (P. Lorillard Co.), 135 NLRB 1382, 49 LRRM 1693 (1962); Local 65, Plasterers & Cement Masons (Twin City Tile & Marble Co.), 152 NLRB 1609, 59 LRRM 1334 (1965).

[35] Section 10 (k) provides that when a Section 8 (b) (4) (D) charge is filed the Board must "hear and determine" the underlying dispute unless within 10 days of receiving notice of the charge the parties show they have adjusted or agreed upon a method for voluntarily adjusting the dispute. See, e.g., Seafarers' Union (Delta Steamship Lines, Inc.), 172 NLRB No. 70, 68 LRRM 1431 (1968). Cf. NLRB v. Operating Engineers, Local 825, 71 LRRM 2079, 410 F 2d 5 (CA 3, 1969).

[36] Wood, Wire & Metal Lathers' Int'l Union (Acoustical Contractor Ass'n), 119 NLRB 1345, 41 LRRM 1293 (1958).

[37] Although the unfair labor practice charge is suspended during the 10 (k) determination, injunctive relief under 10 (l) is available if the General Counsel thinks "such relief is appropriate . . ." A 10 (k) hearing is not prerequisite for a 10 (l) petition. Herzog v. Parsons, 181 F 2d 871, 25 LRRM 2413 (CA DC, 1950), cert. denied, 340 US 810, 26 LRRM 2611 (1950). See Chapter 31 infra.

consistent with the statutory scheme and intent and held that where there is an agreed method of voluntary adjustment, but also a strike either in repudiation of such method or against a decision issued pursuant to it, the Board may, without first hearing and determining the underlying dispute in a Section 10 (k) proceeding, find in a complaint proceeding that such strike violates Section 8 (b) (4) (D).[38]

An agreement which constitutes "an agreed method of voluntary adjustment," and thus deprives the Board of 10 (k) jurisdiction to hear and determine the underlying dispute, must be one to which all parties to the dispute, including the employer, are bound. For example, a 10 (k) hearing was held to determine a dispute between the Carpenters' Union and the Lathers' Union over installation of bars used in construction of suspended ceilings. Although both unions and the general contractor had agreed to submit the dispute to the National Joint Board of the construction industry and to be bound by its award, the lathing subcontractor had not agreed to be so bound.[39] Also, an agreement between an employer and one union to submit the issue to arbitration is not a voluntary method of adjustment which will oust the Board of 10 (k) jurisdiction.[40]

The Section 10 (k) hearing is conducted by a hearing officer under procedural rules which are similar to those in representation proceedings.[41] As in representation hearings, the hearing officer gathers and forwards the pertinent facts without making any recommendation. However, unlike present-day representation proceedings, the determination is made by the Board itself and not by the regional director.

C. Factors Determining Jurisdictional Disputes

Prior to the decision of the Supreme Court in the *CBS* case,[42]

---

[38] Wood, Wire & Metal Lathers Int'l Union, note 36 *supra*.

[39] Carpenters Local 1622 (O. R. Karst), 139 NLRB 591, 51 LRRM 1379 (1962).

[40] New York Mailers, Local 6 ITU (New York Times Co.), 137 NLRB 665, 50 LRRM 1231 (1962). *See also* New Orleans Typographical Union No. 17 v. NLRB (E. P. Rivas, Inc.), 368 F 2d 755, 63 LRRM 2467 (CA 5, 1966). *Cf.* Washington Mailers Union, Local 29 (McCall Printing Co.), 178 NLRB No. 28, 72 LRRM 1032 (1969) (where there were conflicting arbitration awards, the Board awarded the work on the basis of past practice).

[41] Marine Cooks and Stewards (Irwin-Lyons Lumber Co.), 82 NLRB 916, 23 LRRM 1623 (1949); NLRB Rules and Regulations, §101.34: "The hearing is nonadversary in character . . . ;" §102.90.

[42] NLRB v. Radio & Television Broadcast Engineers, 364 US 573, 47 LRRM 2332 (1961).

in conducting hearings under Section 10(k) the Board consistently confined itself to determining whether an 8 (b) (4) (D) jurisdictional dispute existed. If so, the employer's assignment of work was accepted as determinative unless it was found to be contrary either to a Board order or to a certification or collective bargaining agreement. The Board construed 8 (b) (4) (D) as congressional recognition of an employer's right to make a work assignment "free of strike pressure, unless the employer is failing to conform to an order or certification of the Board determining the bargaining representative for employees performing such work, or the claimant union has an immediate or derivative right under an existing contract upon which to predicate a lawful claim to the work in dispute." [43] Under this interpretation, if a certification or bargaining agreement did not clearly cover the disputed work, the Board refused to consider either the employer's past practice or the custom in the industry.[44]

In *CBS* the Court rejected the Board's construction and held that Section 10 (k) required the Board to determine the merits of a jurisdictional dispute and make an affirmative award concerning the work assignment in issue, pointing out that

> [t]he language of §10 (k), supplementing §8 (b) (4) (D) as it does, sets up a method adopted by Congress to try to get jurisdictional disputes settled. The words "hear and determine the dispute" convey not only the idea of hearing but also the idea of deciding a controversy. And the clause "the dispute out of which such unfair labor practice shall have arisen" can have no other meaning except a jurisdictional dispute under §8 (b) (4) (D) which is a dispute between two or more groups of employees over which is entitled to do certain work for an employer. To determine or settle the dispute as between them would normally require a decision that one or the other is entitled to do the work in dispute. Any decision short of that would obviously not be conducive to quieting a quarrel between two groups which, here as in most instances, is of so little interest to the employer that he seems prefectly willing to assign work to either if the other will just let him alone.[45]

---

43 Local 173, Wood, Wire & Metal Lathers' Union (Newark & Essex Plastering Co.), 121 NLRB 1094, 1108, 42 LRRM 1519 (1958).

44 *E.g.*, Parkersburg Building & Construction Trades Council, (Howard Price & Co.), 119 NLRB 1384, 41 LRRM 1303 (1958).

45 Note 42 *supra* at 579. For a comparison of the handling of jurisdictional disputes under the Railway Labor Act, *see Transportation-Communication Employees Union* v. *Union Pacific R. Co.*, 385 US 157 (1966), where the Supreme Court ordered the National Railroad Adjustment Board to exercise its jurisdiction to settle the entire work-assignment dispute, dealing with both unions involved.

To the Board's contention that Section 10 (k) provided no standards for determining the merits of a dispute, the Court replied that

> [the Board] has had long experience in hearing and disposing of similar labor problems. With this experience and knowledge of the standards generally used by arbitrators, unions, employers, joint boards and others in wrestling with this problem, we are confident that the Board need not disclaim the power given it for lack of standards. Experience and common sense will supply the grounds for the performance of this job which Congress has assigned the Board.[46]

Following the Supreme Court's construction of Section 10 (k), the Board announced that it would not formulate general rules for making jurisdictional awards, that each case would have to be decided on its own facts. It stated that it would "consider all relevant factors in determining who is entitled to the work in dispute, e.g., the skills and work involved, certifications by the Board, company and industry practice, agreements between unions and between employers and unions, awards of arbitrators, joint boards, and the AFL-CIO, in the same or related cases, the assignment made by the employer, and the efficient operation of the employer's business." [47] This list of factors, however, was not meant to be exclusive, and was only by way of illustration. The Board stated that it could not at that time "establish the weight to be given the various factors. Every decision will have to be an act of judgment based on common sense and experience rather than on precedent." [48] The Board indicated that later, with more experience in concrete cases, it might give a measure of weight to the earlier decisions.[49] In the 1963 *Philadelphia Inquirer* case,[50] the Board appeared to rely upon two additional factors, which a dissenting Board member characterized as "substitution-of-function" and "loss-of-jobs." [51]

The Board's task in that case was to determine a work assign-

---

[46] 364 US at 583. Before the *CBS* case, the Board felt that an affirmative award of the work would require the employer to employ only union members. This would be a discrimination because of membership in a labor organization and would be a violation of 8 (a) (3). The Court in *CBS* dealt with this issue summarily. *See* Johns, note 11 *supra* at 48.

[47] Machinists Lodge No. 1743 (J. A. Jones Construction Co.), 135 NLRB 1402, 1410-11, 49 LRRM 1684 (1962).

[48] *Id.* at 1411.

[49] *Ibid.*

[50] Philadelphia Typographical Union, Local 2 (Philadelphia Inquirer), 142 NLRB 36, 52 LRRM 1504 (1963).

[51] *Id.* at 46.

ment dispute over composing-room work involving a new photo-composition process, which had replaced an earlier "hot metal" process performed by members of the Typographical Union. Since the new process involved developing and printing film on sensitized paper, photographers, represented by the Newspaper Guild, claimed the work under their contract. When the employer assigned the work to the typographers, the Guild processed a grievance over the matter through arbitration. When the arbitrator upheld the grievance, ITU advised the employer that its members would refuse to process the production of the dark-room if the work was not assigned to typographers. In resolving this dispute, the Board majority noted that the usual criteria did not weigh in favor of any of the competing unions and, relying on their "experience and common sense," to which the Court in the *CBS* case had referred, awarded the work to the typographers on grounds that the new process was a substitute for work previously performed by typographers and that a loss of jobs for the typographers would result if the work was assigned to others. However, on substantially the same facts, the Board in a later case ignored these "substitution of function" and "loss of jobs" tests.[52]

In determining jurisdictional disputes since *CBS*, the Board has relied on each of the factors set forth in the *Jones Construction* case,[53] either alone or in conjunction with other factors, to support the result. The relative weight given to each of the enumerated factors and the number of times the Board has relied upon each in making its determinations have been the subject of a number of studies and commentaries.[54] In the vast majority of the cases the

---

[52] New Orleans Typographical Union, Local 17 (E. P. Rivas, Inc.), 147 NLRB 191, 56 LRRM 1169 (1964). *See also* New Orleans Typographical Union, Local 17 (E. P. Rivas, Inc.), 152 NLRB 587, 59 LRRM 1133 (1965), *enforced*, 368 F 2d 755, 63 LRRM 2467 (CA 5, 1966).

[53] Note 47 *supra. E.g.*, Operating Engineers, Local 158 (E. C. Ernst), 172 NLRB No. 192, 69 LRRM 1033 (1968).

[54] *See, generally,* Reports of ABA Section of Labor Relations Law, COMMITTEE ON DEVELOPMENT OF LAW UNDER THE NLRA: 1964, at 231; 1966 at 443; 1968 at 110; 1970 at 104. *See also:* Gitlow, *Technology and NLRB Decisions in Jurisdictional Dispute Cases,* 16 Lab. L.J. 731, 745-8 (1965); Schmidt, *What is the Current Status of Work Assignment Disputes,* 16 Lab. L.J. 270 (1965); Note, *Jurisdictional Disputes Since the CBS Decision,* 39 NYU L. REV. 657 (1964); Atleson, *The NLRB and Jurisdictional Disputes: The Aftermath of CBS,* 53 GEO. L.J. 93, 113-39 (1964). The Board has been severely criticized for failing to award work on a true jurisdictional basis and for simply affirming the employer's assignment in 90 percent of the cases. *See:* Cohen, *The NLRB and Section 10(k): A Study of the Reluctant Dragon,* 14 LAB. L. J. 905 (1963); O'Donoghue, *Jurisdictional Disputes in the Construction Industry Since CBS,* 52 GEO. L.J. 314 (1964); *Supplemental Report of the Special "10(k)" Committee,* SECTION OF LABOR RELATIONS LAW (American Bar Association), 1964 Proceedings, 437; Sussman, *Section 10(k): Mandate for Change?,* 47 B.U.L. REV. 201 (1967).

Board's analysis of the facts and application of the test factors have supported the employer's assignment of the work in dispute. However, the Board has announced that under its interpretation of the *CBS* decision, "an employer's assignment of disputed work cannot be made the touchstone in determining a jurisdictional dispute." [55] Accordingly, the Board has overruled the employer's assignment where it was contrary (1) to the employer's past practice,[56] (2) to an agreement between the international unions concerned in the dispute,[57] (3) to a joint-board award that the employer had voluntarily agreed to follow,[58] or (4) to a joint-board award that the contending unions had agreed to accept but the employer had rejected.[59] In the *Don Cartage* case [60] the Board indicated that, particularly in disputes involving "building trades," it would give great, if not conclusive, weight to decisions of private boards to which the unions had agreed to be bound.

D. Post-Hearing Procedure

At the conclusion of a 10 (k) hearing the Board issues its "decision and determination of dispute." If the parties thereafter submit to the appropriate regional director satisfactory evidence of compliance with the determination, he shall, in accordance with the express provisions of Section 10 (k), dismiss the pending 8 (b) (4) (D) charge.[61] Such evidence of compliance must, at the very least, consist of a good-faith intent to accept and abide by the Board's determination, manifested by performance of substantially the same kinds of acts as are required to demonstrate an intention to abide by a remedial order of the Board. These acts include "a willingness to confer with the regional director regarding imple-

---

[55] Millwrights Local Union No. 1102 (Don Cartage Company), 160 NLRB 1061, 63 LRRM 1085 (1966).

[56] Carpenters Local 690 (The Walter Corp.), 151 NLRB 741, 58 LRRM 1475 (1965); Wood, Wire & Metal Lathers Local Union Local 68 (State Lathing Co., Inc.), 153 NLRB 1189, 59 LRRM 1610 (1965); Plumbers & Pipefitters, Local 412 (Zia Co.), 168 NLRB No. 69, 66 LRRM 1326 (1967) ("work traditionally performed"). But where "the factors of economy and efficiency" outweigh limited past practices, the work has been assigned accordingly. NLRB v. Local 25, IBEW (New York Telephone Co.), 396 F 2d 591, 68 LRRM 2633 (CA 2, 1968), *enforcing* 162 NLRB 703, 64 LRRM 1203 (1967).

[57] Local Union No. 68, Wood, Wire & Metal Lathers (Acoustics & Specialties, Inc.), 142 NLRB 1073, 53 LRRM 1181 (1963).

[58] Sheet Metal Workers Local 162 (Lusterlite Corp.), 151 NLRB 195 (1965).

[59] Don Cartage Co., note 55 *supra*.

[60] *Ibid. But see, e.g.,* Operating Engineers, Local 158 (E. C. Ernst), 172 NLRB No. 192, 69 LRRM 1033 (1968), and critical comment at note 54 *supra*.

[61] NLRB Rules and Regulations, §102.91.

mentation of their avowed intent to accept the Board's determination, furnishing appropriate notices to employees and/or the particular employer, if considered advisable by the regional director, and, giving such additional assurances as the regional director might require to insure adherence to the determination." [62]   A union's failure or refusal to give such assurances constitutes evidence of a refusal to comply with the Board's determination,[63] and requires the regional director to issue a complaint and notice of hearing, charging a violation of Section 8 (b) (4) (D).[64]

E. Precedence of 8(b)(4)(D) Charges Over Other Unfair Labor Practice Charges

Some confusion exists as to the interrelationship of Sections 8 (b) (4) (B) and 8 (b) (4) (D). It is obvious that in many 8 (b) (4) (D) cases no 8 (b) (4) (B) charge can possibly arise, for the jurisdictional dispute subparagraph comes into play even though the union activity is entirely primary.[65] However, if a union involved in a jurisdictional dispute threatens another employer or induces work stoppages among employees of that employer in order to bring pressure to bear on the primary employer, Section 8 (b) (4) (B) may also apply.

In *Local 5, Plumbers v. NLRB* [66] the District of Columbia Circuit was faced with the problem of whether decision in an 8 (b) (4) (D) dispute and processing under Section 10 (k) were prerequisites to a finding of an 8 (b) (4) (B) violation arising from the same conduct. The court noted that processing of an 8 (b) (4) (D) charge had, in the past, preceded consideration of other violations, but said that this should not be the case where a secondary boycott was concerned.

> The secondary boycott provisions of the Act were designed to restrict the field of combat in industrial disputes. Section 8 (b) (4) (B) attempts to isolate labor disputes by declaring "off limits" to union pressure certain employers who are powerless to resolve a dispute between the union and another employer. To that end the Board has correctly concluded that, where the union brings pressure on one

62 Iron Workers Local 595 (Bechtel Corp.), 112 NLRB 812, 815, 36 LRRM 1105 (1955).
63 Plumbers Local 157 (Medives & Homes, Inc.), 160 NLRB No. 27, 62 LRRM 1592 (1966).
64 NLRB Statements of Procedure, §101.36.
65 See the text of §8 (b) (4) (D), note 5 *supra*.
66 321 F 2d 366, 53 LRRM 2424 (CA DC, 1963), *cert. denied,* 375 US 921, 54 LRRM 2576 (1963).

of these "neutral" parties, that activity is proscribed regardless of the jurisdictional question. The union would have to restrict its pressure in such a situation to the employer who can satisfy its demands.[67]

Under this view, even where a union may take primary action against an employer because it is entitled to the work in question, no secondary action may be taken to secure the work.[68] Moreover, the Board would proceed to consider both the 8 (b) (4) (B) and the 8 (b) (4) (D) charges and would not defer consideration of the former until the jurisdictional dispute had been settled. Finally, under Section 10 (l) the General Counsel would be obligated to seek an injunction against the alleged 8 (b) (4) (B) violation, whereas the seeking of an injunction against an 8 (b) (4) (D) violation is within the General Counsel's discretion.[69]

However, whether or not the charges are to be processed separately is open to question. Two other circuits have held that secondary activity with an object of forcing advantageous settlement of the jurisdictional dispute does not constitute an 8 (b) (4) (B) violation.[70] Those courts would permit a separate 8 (b) (4) (B) charge to stand only where the union has the specific objective of forcing a secondary employer to cease doing business with a primary employer. The Board has accepted the view that an 8 (b) (4) (D) charge must be considered under 10 (k) before any other violation arising out of the same facts may be considered.[71] The precedence to be accorded an 8 (b) (4) (D) charge over other unfair labor practice charges is thus unsettled.

II. 'FEATHERBEDDING'

A. Background

"Featherbedding" has been defined as

[p]ractices on the part of some unions to make work for their members through the limitation of production, the amount of work to be

---

[67] 321 F 2d at 367.

[68] Local 5, United Ass'n of Journeymen Plumbers, 137 NLRB 828, 832 (1962) ; *see also* O'Donoghue, *Jurisdictional Disputes in the Construction Industry Since CBS*, 52 GEO. L.J. 314, 334-37 (1964) . *See also:* Carpenters, Local 753 (Blount Bros. Corp.) , 179 NLRB No. 95, 72 LRRM 1473 (1969) ; NLRB v. Longshoremen, ILWU, 413 F 2d 30, 71 LRRM 2500 (CA 9, 1969) .

[69] *See* note 37 *supra.*

[70] NLRB v. United Brotherhood of Carpenters, 261 F 2d 166 (CA 7, 1966) ; *compare* NLRB v. Local 825, Int'l Union of Operating Engineers, 326 F 2d 219, 55 LRRM 2116 (CA 3, 1964) *with* Cuneo v. Local 825, Int'l Union of Operating Engineers, 300 F 2d 832, 49 LRRM 2879 (CA 3, 1962) .

[71] Local 502, Int'l Hod Carriers, 140 NLRB 694, 52 LRRM 1093 (1963) .

performed, or other make-work arrangements. Many of these practices have come about because workers have been displaced by mechanization and the union has sought some method of retaining the employees, even though there may be no work for them to perform, or their services may not be required.[72]

The Wagner Act contained no provisions relating to featherbedding. In 1946 Congress passed the Lea (Anti-Petrillo) Act,[73] which was intended to eliminate certain practices of the American Federation of Musicians that required employers "to hire people who do no work, to pay for people the employers do not hire, and to hire more people than the employers have work for." [74] This was a criminal statute and was applicable only to the broadcasting industry. The following year the House passed the Hartley bill,[75] which expressly condemned, as unlawful concerted activities, union practices which required an employer to employ more employees than would reasonably be required to perform actual services, as well as practices which required an employer to pay for services which are not to be performed.[76] The Taft-Hartley Act as finally passed by Congress, however, left most practices described in the above definition untouched. In substituting the present Section 8 (b) (6) for the provisions of the Hartley bill, Congress limited its condemnation of featherbedding to instances where unions exact pay from employers in return for services which either are not performed or are not to be performed.

Section 8 (b) (6) makes it an unfair labor practice for a labor organization or its agents to

cause or attempt to cause an employer to pay or deliver or agree to pay or deliver any money or other thing of value in the nature of an exaction for services which are not performed or not to be performed.

In the debates preceding passage of the statute, Senator Taft stated that the Conference Committee "felt that it was impractica-

---

[72] Roberts, ROBERTS' DICTIONARY OF INDUSTRIAL RELATIONS, 109 (Washington: BNA Books, 1966). The literature on featherbedding includes the following: Brach, *Legislative Shackles on Featherbedding Practices,* 34 CORNELL L. Q. 255 (1948); Van de Water, *Industrial Productivity and the Law: A Study of Work Restrictions,* 43 VA. L. REV. 155, 159 (1957); Aaron, *Governmental Restraints on Featherbedding,* 5 STAN. L. REV. 680 (1953); P. Jacobs, DEAD HORSE AND THE FEATHERBIRD: A REPORT (1962).
[73] Public Law 344, 79th Cong., 2nd Sess., Title 47 USC §506.
[74] H. R. Rep. No. 245, 80th Cong., 1st Sess. 25 (1947).
[75] H. R. 3020, 80th Cong., 1st Sess. (1947).
[76] *Id.* at §§2 (17) and 12 (a) (3) (B).

ble to give to a board or a court the power to say that so many men are all right, and so many men are too many." [77] He indicated, however, that the conferees had accepted "one provision which makes it an unlawful labor practice for a union to accept money for people who do not work." [78] Notwithstanding such limited intent, later the same day Senator Taft said that it seemed "perfectly clear" to him that the intent of the provision was

> to make it an unfair labor practice for a man to say, "You must have 10 musicians, and if you insist that there is room for only six, you must pay for the other four anyway." That is in the nature of an exaction from the employer for services which he does not want, does not need, and is not even willing to accept.[79]

The Senator was probably more accurate in his first assessment of the statute's limitations, for the Supreme Court later made clear that the proscription in the provision depended on whether the extra employees worked, not on whether they were needed.

B. Judicial Interpretation

The application of Section 8 (b) (6) is limited by two 1953 Supreme Court decisions. In *American Newspaper Publishers Association v. NLRB* [80] the Court dealt with the longstanding practice in the printing industry of setting "bogus" type. As a general rule, the type used in printing is set for each newspaper by typesetters who are members of the International Typographical Union. However, when an advertisement is to appear in a number of different newspapers, it is only necessary to set the type once for that advertisement, for it may be used to form a mold, called a "mat." All other newspapers may then use the mat rather than set their own type. To ameliorate the loss of work resulting from this procedure, the ITU many years ago secured from the industry adoption of the practice of setting "bogus" type. Even though the mats are used in the actual printing operation, typesetters at each newspaper where mats are used nevertheless reset the entire advertisement manually. The "bogus" type is later discarded—it is never put to any productive use.

---

[77] Legislative History of the Labor Management Relations Act, 1947, 1535 (1948) ; 93 Cong. Rec. 6598 (1947).
[78] *Ibid.*
[79] Legislative History of the Labor Management Relations Act, 1947, 1545 (1948) ; 93 Cong. Rec. 6603 (1947).
[80] 345 US 100, 31 LRRM 2422 (1953).

Because "bogus" typesetting involves production of materials never used, the Publishers Association charged that ITU had violated Section 8 (b) (6). The Board, however, found the union's conduct lawful, and the Supreme Court, in *Newspaper Publishers,* affirmed. The Court noted that setting "bogus" was service performed: "Thus where work is done by an employee, with the employer's consent, a labor organization's demand that the employee be compensated for time spent in doing the disputed work does not become an unfair labor practice." [81] That the employer had no use for the services and that the services were a mere artifice to prevent loss of work were not sufficient reasons to render the conduct unlawful. Even though the work performed was valueless, the Court said that "Section 8 (b) (6) leaves to collective bargaining the determination of what, if any, work, including bona fide 'made work,' shall be included as compensable services and what rate of compensation shall be paid for it." [82]

In the companion case of *NLRB v. Gamble Enterprises,*[83] decided the same day, the Court extended the rule to cover those situations in which the employer is unwilling to accept the unneeded work. In *Gamble,* the union sought to protect its local members by securing an agreement from the employer that when traveling musical groups, instead of local members, appeared in the employer's theater, members of the local group would be hired to play during intermissions. When the employer refused to agree to such an arrangement, the union induced the traveling groups not to appear in the employer's theater. Since the union did not seek mere "stand-by" pay, but "suggested various ways in which a local orchestra could earn pay for performing competent work . . . ," [84] its proposals were considered to be "in good faith contemplating the performance of actual services . . . ," [85] and therefore lawful.

Newspaper Publishers and *Gamble* thus make it clear that a union can insist upon and receive work for its members provided some actual work is performed, even though the work may be neither necessary nor desirable to the employer. It is only when the union seeks compensation for members who do no work at all that Section 8 (b) (6) is violated. Likewise, a union demand to hire

---

81 *Id.* at 110.
82 *Id.* at 111.
83 345 US 117, 31 LRRM 2428 (1953).
84 345 US at 123.
85 *Ibid.*

more employees than the employer feels he needs does not violate the featherbedding ban as long as there is an actual performance of services by all of the employees hired. Since *Newspaper Publishers* and *Gamble,* the Board and the courts have found no violations of the Section.

Payments sought by a union for the utilization of labor-saving devices apparently do not violate the Act. And union demands that employees be compensated for reporting for work are not unlawful even though the employees reporting perform no work. "Call-in" pay is, therefore, valid under this Section. Payments for lunch, rest, and waiting periods, coffee breaks, and vacations are similarly lawful. Such practices are incidents of an employee's general employment and are not in the nature of exactions of pay for work not performed within the meaning of the statute.[86]

There is a dearth of cases under this section of the Act. Shortly after the section was passed, a complaint was issued alleging that a union demanded that four men be permitted to work when only two were required, and that it had demanded and received compensation for six men for work actually performed by only two. The case was settled by stipulation between the parties providing for a consent order and decree directing the union to cease and desist and to make whole the employer by repayment of any money exacted for services not performed.[87]

A state statute which required that employees be paid for voting time was held not to conflict with the ban on featherbedding.[88] And a union demand that a motor carrier pay the union an amount equal to the wages of a nonunion driver did not violate Section 8 (b) (6).[89] Nor was it a violation of the provision for a union to strike to induce an employer to reinstate discharged employees who had been replaced.[90]

The NLRB General Counsel has refused to issue complaints in the following situations: where a union proposed a welfare plan

---

86 *See* LEGISLATIVE HISTORY OF THE LABOR MANAGEMENT RELATIONS ACT, 1947, note 77 *supra.*
87 Cement Finishers, Local 627 (R. H. Parr & Son), 22 LRRM 1289 (1948).
88 State of Minnesota v. Int'l Harvester Co., 241 Minn. 367, 67 NW2d 547 (1954). This type of voting-time statute was declared valid under the United States Constitution in Day-Brite Lighting, Inc. v. State of Missouri, 342 US 421 (1955).
89 Conway's Express v. NLRB, 195 F 2d 906, 29 LRRM 2617 (CA 2, 1952). The union demand was found to be based on a claim that the union driver had been wrongfully denied his job under the collective bargaining agreement.
90 Kallaher & Mee, Inc., 87 NLRB 410, 25 LRRM 1137 (1949).

calling for an employer association to pay money to trustees over whom it had no control; [91] where a union struck to enforce payment by the employer of employees' expenses in traveling to and from the job site as an incident of employment; [92] where a union demanded that an employer continue to utilize the services of two employees for performance of certain operations where the demand contemplated actual performance of services; [93] and where a union threatened to blacklist an employer unless it paid a debt incurred by its predecessor.[94]

---

[91] NLRB Gen. Counsel Adm. Rul. No. K-337, 37 LRRM 1471 (1956).
[92] NLRB Gen. Counsel Adm. Rul. No. F-276, 41 LRRM 1445 (1958).
[93] NLRB Gen. Counsel Adm. Rul. No. F-1089, 44 LRRM 1318 (1959).
[94] NLRB Gen. Counsel Adm. Rul. No. SR-1683, 49 LRRM 1372 (1961).

PART VI

RELATIONS BETWEEN

THE EMPLOYEE AND THE UNION

CHAPTER 26

UNION SECURITY

I. HISTORICAL EVOLUTION

A. The Old Days: Union Security Before the Wagner Act

Unions, in the early twentieth century, were not secure. The activities and aims of the emerging labor movement were at odds with the traditional property concepts of *laissez faire* economic freedom, and one serious obstacle to union organization was the translation of this established economic theory into common law: concerted labor activity, viewed as a conspiracy in restraint of trade, was repeatedly held unreasonable and therefore illegal.

Legal barriers to unions were of at least two kinds—the rights of labor were severely restricted, and the rights (and powers) of employers were vast. Although employees generally had the right to form and join unions, there was no duty on employers to recognize unions as the collective bargaining agents of the employees. Collective bargaining contracts, if entered into, were not illegal; but employers were under no duty to bargain. The right to strike was qualified by the purpose or motive underlying the strike. For example, the Supreme Judicial Court of Massachusetts stated that "to make a strike legal, the purpose of the strike must be one which the Court, as a matter of law, decides is a legal purpose of a strike, and the strikers must have acted in good faith in striking for such a purpose." [1] Thus armed with strike-approval power, Massachusetts courts granted judicial imprimatur to strikes for higher wages and shorter hours [2] but condemned most others. In *Plant v. Woods* [3] the Supreme Judicial Court

---

[1] De Minico v. Craig, 207 Mass 593, 598, 94 NE 317, 319 (1911). *See* Chapters 1 and 2 for general treatment of the historical background of the Wagner Act.
[2] *See* Pickett v. Walsh, 192 Mass 572, 580, 78 NE 753 (1906).
[3] 176 Mass 492, 57 NE 1011 (1900).

of Massachusetts held illegal strike threats to secure a closed shop. Holmes, dissenting, stated his opinion that "the threats were as lawful for this preliminary purpose (organization) as for the final one (higher wages) to which strengthening the union was a means." [4] Even after enactment of the Wagner Act, the Massachusetts court enjoined peaceful picketing by nonemployee union members who were seeking a closed shop.[5] The judge found no lawful "labor dispute" between employer and employee. As to methods of conducting a strike, Massachusetts early held all picketing to be illegal.[6] Other states differed from Massachusetts on specific points,[7] but many shared the same tendencies.

While unions were thus restricted, employers' rights remained unrestrained. Employers had the absolute right to hire and fire, and there were no legal restraints on their right to discriminate against union members. The Erdman Act,[8] passed by Congress in 1898 to prevent discrimination on account of union membership in the railroad industry, was declared unconstitutional in *Adair v. U.S.*[9] Nondiscrimination statutes were likewise declared unconstitutional in several states.[10]

Yellow-dog contracts, whereby employees agreed not to join unions, were used by employers and approved by the courts. The Supreme Court struck down a Kansas statute which made the use of yellow-dog contracts a criminal offense,[11] and two years later the Court based a sweeping injunction against the Mine Workers largely on the fact that employees had executed yellow-dog contracts.[12] Employers circulated blacklists of union sympathizers. Finally, employers fought unions by competing with them—forming company-dominated "unions" which were predictably ineffective as bargaining agents.

The most prolific lawmakers in the labor field during this era of emerging problems were the courts, and the judges borrowed

---

[4] 57 NE at 1016.
[5] Simon v. Schwachman, 301 Mass 573, 18 NE 2d 1 (1938).
[6] Vegelahn v. Guntner, 167 Mass 92, 44 NE 1077 (1896).
[7] For example, New York permitted a strike for a closed shop so long as it would not result in a monopoly. Curran v. Galen, 152 NY 33, 46 NE 297 (1897).
[8] Act of June 1, 1898, 30 Stat 424.
[9] 208 US 161 (1908).
[10] See H. Millis & R. Montgomery, ORGANIZED LABOR, 510-11 (1945).
[11] Coppage v. Kansas, 236 US 1 (1915).
[12] Hitchman Coal & Coke Co. v. Mitchell, 245 US 229 (1917).

primarily from the law of contracts and private property. The results were not favorable to unions.

B. The Wagner Act

The Congress in 1935 declared the national labor policy to be the encouragement of collective bargaining. Legal obstacles to organization were removed, and the way was cleared for effective union security devices.

The heart of the new National Labor Relations Act, Section 7, guaranteed employees the freedom to choose their bargaining representative. This section was supported by a series of employer unfair labor practices. Section 8 (1) proscribed interference with Section 7 rights. Section 8 (2) outlawed the company union by making it an unfair labor practice to dominate a union or support it financially. Section 8 (3), the most relevant to union security, made discrimination "to encourage or discourage membership in any labor organization" an unfair labor practice, thereby outlawing the yellow-dog contract and the blacklist. A proviso to Section 8 (3) permitted a closed- or union-shop agreement with a union that legitimately represented the employees (*i.e.,* not a company union). Section 9 provided the machinery for selection of majority bargaining representatives, and employer recognition of such representatives was made mandatory. Section 8 (5) made it an unfair labor practice for the employer to refuse to bargain.

C. The Taft-Hartley Changes

By 1947 both unions and Republicans had gained in strength; the result was the Taft-Hartley Act. Title I of Taft-Hartley amended the National Labor Relations Act, and with additional titles formed the new Labor-Management Relations Act. (The Taft-Hartley changes are treated generally in Chapter 3 *supra.*)

The amendments significantly changed the status of union security. Added to Section 7 (which guarantees freedom of organization) was a guarantee of employees' right to *refrain* from union activity. (This latter right is, however, limited to the extent that certain union security clauses continue to be permitted by the Taft-Hartley Act.) Under Section 8 (a) (3) (formerly 8 (3)) the closed shop was outlawed, and a limited form of union shop was substituted. To be enabled to negotiate a union shop, a majority bargaining representative could request an authorization election pursuant to Section 9 (e) (1). If a majority of the employees in the affected unit approved, the union could then seek to negotiate a union-shop agreement with the employer. In 1951 this requirement of authorization elections was repealed.[13] In practice, 97 percent of the elections had resulted in authorization of the union shop, and 77.5 percent of the voters had endorsed the arrangement.[14] A union shop *de*authorization election was provided for instead, pursuant to which a majority of the employees involved can deprive their representative of the authority to continue a union security arrangement in effect.[15]

In the Taft-Hartley amendments, a new subsection (b) to old Section 8 added union unfair labor practices. Section 8 (b) (2) is the union counterpart to Section 8 (a) (3): discrimination is outlawed. A union is guilty if it seeks to cause an employer to discriminate in violation of Section 8 (a) (3), or discriminates against an employee when membership in the union has been denied or terminated for reasons other than the failure to tender the uniformly required dues and initiation fees. Section 8 (b) (5) limits to a reasonable and nondiscriminatory amount the initiation fee which a union may charge employees required to become members under a union-shop agreement.

Perhaps the most controversial amendment was Section 14 (b). It permits states to prohibit "agreements requiring membership in a labor organization as a condition of employment."

One final provision in the Taft-Hartley Act relevant to union security was Section 302 of the Labor-Management Relations Act. This section contains a general prohibition of payments of money by employers to unions, but a proviso in subsection (c) creates an important exception: the checkoff. Employers may agree with a union to deduct union dues from employees' pay checks and remit directly to the union. Such dues deduction may take place, however, only if authorized in writing by the affected employee; and such authorization cannot, in any event, be irrevocable for a period longer than one year or beyond the termination date of the applicable collective agreement, whichever occurs earlier.

---

[13] Act of Oct. 22, 1951, ch. 534, § 1 (b), 65 Stat 601.
[14] SIXTEENTH ANNUAL REPORT OF NLRB 54 (1952).
[15] § 9 (e) (1), Act of Oct. 22, 1951, § 1 (c), deleted former subdivision (1) and renumbered subdivisions (2) and (3) as (1) and (2).

II. REQUIRED MEMBERSHIP: THE UNION SHOP

Although Sections 8 (a) (3) and 8 (b) (2) sanction an agreement for a union shop, the arrangement is subject to substantial limitation. The provisos to 8 (a) (3) provide that employees must be allowed at least 30 days to join the union, that a majority of the affected employees may vote to discontinue the union shop, and that an employee may not be discharged for failure to join the union if it appears that he was denied membership on a discriminatory basis or for *any* reason other than failure to pay customary dues and initiation fees. (Sections 8(a)(3) and 8(b)(2) are treated generally in Chapter 6 *supra*.)

A. The 30-Day Grace Period

Any union-shop agreement must allow new employees a minimum of 30 days [16] to become members of the union. An agreement which allows nonmembers less than 30 days to join is invalid, and enforcement of it constitutes an unfair labor practice.[17] However, a contract which did not *explicitly* provide for the grace period for present employees,[18] and another which specified that membership must be secured "within 30 days," [19] have been held to satisfy the requirements of Section 8 (a) (3).

If a union-shop agreement allows a period longer than 30 days for nonmembers to join, or if the union, in enforcing the agreement, has established a practice of allowing a longer period, the statutory 30-day period may not be used to justify an earlier discharge for failure to join.[20] The primary purpose of Sections 8 (a) (3) and 8 (b) (2) is to prevent discrimination, and the Board's decisions indicate a concern with consistent application of a uniform policy. The provision for a 30-day grace period is applied strictly. A requirement that a nonmember must state his *intent* to join before 30 days is invalid,[21] as is a retroactive agreement which shortens the statutory period.[22]

---

16 § 8 (a) (3). *But cf.* § 8 (f) allowing only a seven-day grace period for construction employees. *See* section E *infra*.

17 NLRB v. Hribar Trucking, Inc., 337 F2d 414, 57 LRRM 2195 (CA 7, 1964).

18 American Seating Co., 98 NLRB 800, 29 LRRM 1424 (1952).

19 NLRB v. Television & Radio Broadcasting Studio Employees, 315 F2d 398, 52 LRRM 2774 (CA 3, 1963).

20 Busch Kredit Jewelry Co., 108 NLRB 1214, 34 LRRM 1167 (1954); Film Editors, 124 NLRB 842, 44 LRRM 1511 (1959).

21 Argo Steel Construction Co., 122 NLRB 1077, 43 LRRM 1255 (1959).

22 Associated Machines, Inc., 114 NLRB 390, 36 LRRM 1582 (1955), *enforced,* 239 F2d 858, 39 LRRM 2264 (CA 6, 1956). *Cf.* NLRB v. Boilermakers Local Lodge 338, 409 F2d 922, 70 LRRM 2662 (CA 10, 1969).

The 30-day period applies, however, only to persons not members of the union on the date of the execution of the agreement. Employees who already are members may be compelled to retain their membership during the grace period.[23]

B.   The Belated Tender

If an employee fails to join the union within the period allowed in the union-shop agreement, the union may request his discharge. In certain circumstances, however, a late attempt to join may be sufficient. In a much-criticized 1955 opinion [24] the NLRB held that a full and unqualified tender of dues and initiations fees made prior to actual discharge, even if made after a union request for discharge, is valid; and a subsequent discharge based on the union's request is unlawful. In 1961 the Board overruled[25] that policy, stating that it would henceforth look to the record to determine the reasons for a discharge. If a discharge occurs *solely* because of dues delinquency, a tender after a union request for discharge comes too late.[26]

In other cases the Board and the courts have given great weight to the particular facts involved. An employee cannot be discharged for dues delinquency unless he knew or reasonably should have known that union membership was necessary to keep his job.[27] A late tender that was accepted by a union steward has been deemed to have been accepted by the union.[28]

---

23 Krause Milling Co., 97 NLRB 536, 29 LRRM 1120 (1951).

24 Aluminum Workers Int'l Union, 112 NLRB 619, 36 LRRM 1077 (1955), *enforced* (but criticized), 230 F2d 515, 37 LRRM 2640 (CA 7, 1956), also criticized in Machinists v. NLRB, 247 F2d 414, 420, 40 LRRM 2497 (CA 2, 1957), and NLRB v. Technicolor Motion Picture Corp., 248 F2d 348, 40 LRRM 2660 (CA 9, 1957).

25 General Motors Corp., 134 NLRB 1107, 49 LRRM 1283 (1961).

26 *Ibid.*

27 Electric Auto-Lite Co., 92 NLRB 1073, 27 LRRM 1205 (1950), *enforced,* 196 F2d 500, 30 LRRM 2115 (CA 6, 1952), *cert. denied,* 344 US 823, 30 LRRM 2711 (1952); NLRB v. Teamsters Local 182, 401 F2d 509, 69 LRRM 2388 (CA 2, 1968). If the union-shop contract is oral, the union or employer taking action against an employee pursuant to such contract bears a stringent burden of proof in establishing the existence and the precise terms of the contract and that the employees affected have been notified fully and unmistakably of their union-security obligations. Pacific Iron & Metal Co., 175 NLRB No. 114, 71 LRRM 1006 (1969). Cf. Rabouin dba Conway's Express v. NLRB, 195 F2d 906, 29 LRRM 2617 (CA 2, 1952).

28 NLRB v. International Woodworkers, 264 F2d 649, 43 LRRM 2701 (CA 9, 1959), *cert. denied,* 361 US 816, 44 LRRM 2983 (1959).

C. Dues and Fees

An employee in a union shop must, in order to keep his job, tender to the union initiation fees and dues. Section 8 (b) (5) prohibits excessive or discriminatory initiation fees,[29] and there are limits on *what* constitutes dues and on the *amount* of dues that may be required.

Whether a union's initiation fee is excessive depends on a number of factors, including the income of the affected workers,[30] the practices of other unions in the industry,[31] and the motive underlying any increase in dues. Although each case depends on its facts, fees are quite likely to be held excessive where the intent of the union is to monopolize the employment field.[32] Discriminatory initiation fees are those not based upon a reasonable classification of employees. Charging "old" employees who failed to join before the union shop became effective more than new employees is discriminatory; [33] but charging a "reinstatement" fee to a former member greater than the initiation fee is not.[34] Fees may be increased [35] or decreased [36] or waived [37] during an organizational campaign. A reduced fee may be offered as an incentive to authorize the dues checkoff.[38]

---

29 It is an unfair labor practice for a union "to require of employees covered by an agreement authorized under subsection (a) (3) the payment, as a condition precedent to becoming a member of such organization, of a fee in an amount which the Board finds excessive or discriminatory under all the circumstances. In making such a finding, the Board shall consider, among other relevant factors, the practices and customs of labor organizations in the particular industry, and the wages currently paid to the employees affected. . . ."

30 Administrative Decision of General Counsel, Case No. SR-1057, 47 LRRM 1190 (1960). Periodic dues may be based on a percentage of earnings if they are assessed regularly and uniformly. Stage & Motion Picture Employees, Local 409 (Radio Corp. of America), 140 NLRB 759, 52 LRRM 1101 (1963).

31 NLRB v. Television & Radio Broadcasting Studio Employees, 315 F2d 398, 52 LRRM 2774 (CA 3, 1963).

32 Motion Picture Screen Cartoonists, 121 NLRB 1196, 42 LRRM 1540 (1958). *See also* Teamsters Local 611 (St. Louis Bakery Employers Council) 125 NLRB 1392, 45 LRRM 1246 (1959).

33 Ferro Stamping and Mfg. Co., 93 NLRB 1459, 27 LRRM 1593 (1951).

34 Food Mach. & Chem. Corp., 99 NLRB 1430, 30 LRRM 1171 (1952). *See also:* Metal Workers Alliance, Inc., 172 NLRB No. 34, 68 LRRM 1351 (1968); NLRB v. Boilermakers, 409 F2d 922, 70 LRRM 2662 (CA 10, 1969).

35 Ferro Stamping and Mfg. Co., 93 NLRB 1459, 27 LRRM 1593 (1951).

36 J. J. Newberry Co., 100 NLRB 84, 30 LRRM 1234 (1952); Gruen Watch Co., 108 NLRB 610, 34 LRRM 1067 (1954).

37 NLRB v. Economy Food Center, Inc., 333 F2d 468, 56 LRRM 2263 (CA 7, 1964).

38 Administrative Decision of General Counsel, Case No. 1033 (1954). *Cf. Pulp & Paper Workers, Local 171* (Boise Cascade Corp.), note 45 *infra.*

Two provisos to Section 8 (a) (3) [39] specify that no nonmember may be discharged under a union-shop contract (A) if he was discriminated against or (B) if he was denied membership for any reason other than failure to tender the necessary dues and fees. These were interpreted by the Board in *Union Starch and Refining Co.*[40] as follows: Proviso (A) means that union membership must be available on a fair and nondiscriminatory basis. Proviso (B) goes further: any requirement for membership in addition to dues and initiation fee, even if such requirement is fair and nondiscriminatory, may *not* be used as a basis for the nonmember's discharge. Where an employee tendered the requisite money to the union, but refused to attend meetings or take an oath of loyalty, the Board found both the company and the union guilty of unfair labor practices for discharging the employee for nonmembership.[41]

Once an employee joins the union, Section 8 (a) (3) authorizes his discharge for violation of the union-shop agreement only for failure to pay dues. Failure to pay dues for prehire months is not a valid ground for discharge;[42] nor is refusal to "donate" money to a strike-support fund.[43] Fines are not included within "dues"; therefore, refusal to pay a fine, even a fine imposed before the union shop went into effect,[44] is not cause for discharge. However, a union may refund a portion of the monthly dues for members who regularly attend union meetings.[45] And dues

39 "[N]o employer shall justify any discrimination against an employee for nonmembership in a labor organization (A) if he has reasonable grounds for believing that such membership was not available to the employee on the same terms and conditions generally applicable to other members, or (B) if he has reasonable grounds for believing that membership was denied or terminated for reasons other than the failure of the employee to tender the periodic dues and the initiation fees uniformly required as a condition of acquiring or retaining membership." For treatment of the "reasonable grounds for believing" requirement, *see* NLRB v. Zoe Chemical Co., Inc., 406 F2d 574, 70 LRRM 2276 (CA 2, 1969). *See* generally Mayer, *Union Security and the Taft-Hartley Act,* 1961 DUKE L. J. 505 (1961); Pulsipher, *The Union Shop: A Legitimate Form of Coercion in a Free-Market Economy,* 19 IND. & LAB. REL. REV. 529 (1966); Rosenthal, *The National Labor Relations Act and Compulsory Unionism,* 1954 WIS. L. REV. 53 (1954).
40 87 NLRB 779, 25 LRRM 1176 (1949), *enforced,* 186 F2d 1008, 27 LRRM 2342 (CA 7, 1951), *cert. denied,* 342 US 815, 28 LRRM 2625 (1951).
41 *Ibid.*
42 NLRB v. Spector Freight System, Inc., 273 F2d 272, 45 LRRM 2388 (CA 8, 1960).
43 NLRB v. Die & Tool Makers, Lodge 113, 231 F2d 298, 37 LRRM 2673 (CA 7, 1956), *cert. denied,* 352 US 833, 38 LRRM 2717 (1956).
44 Pen and Pencil Workers, 91 NLRB 883, 26 LRRM 1583 (1950).
45 Pulp & Paper Wkrs., Local 171 (Boise Cascade Corp.), 165 NLRB No. 97, 65 LRRM 1382 (1967), *overruling* Leece-Neville Co., 140 NLRB 56, 51 LRRM 1563 (1962), *modified,* 330 F2d 242, 55 LRRM 2926 (CA 9, 1964), *cert. denied,* 379 US 819, 57 LRRM 2238 (1964).

charged to those who attend meetings may not be lower than dues charged to whose who do not attend.[46]

D. The Contract Bar

1. **Representation Elections.** The Board has, in addition to the statutory election bar contained in Section 9 (c) (3) and to its administratively created certification bar, developed contract-bar rules designed to foster stability in labor relations.[47] Difficulty has arisen when a collective bargaining contract asserted as a bar to an election contains an illegal union security clause.

The Board held in 1958[48] that "a contract containing a union security clause which does not on its face conform to the requirements of the Act . . . will not bar an election."[49] In 1961 the Board observed that this strict rule entailed "a presumption of illegality with respect to any contract containing a union security clause which did not expressly reflect the precise language of the statute."[50] The 1958 decision was therefore overruled, and new rules were established for determining whether a contract containing a union security provision would bar an election: "[O]nly those contracts containing a union security provision which is clearly unlawful on its face, or which has been found to be unlawful in an unfair labor practice proceeding, may not bar a representation proceeding."[51] Thus, the burden of proof as to illegality was shifted.

2. **Union-Shop Deauthorization Elections.** Although no election is required to authorize a union and an employer to *enter*

---

[46] Electric Auto-Lite Co., 92 NLRB 1073, 27 LRRM 1205 (1950), *enforced,* 196 F2d 500, 30 LRRM 2115 (CA 6, 1952), *cert. denied,* 344 US 823, 30 LRRM 2711 (1952).
[47] *See* Chapter 8 *supra,* at notes 87-94.
[48] Keystone Coat, Apron & Towel Supply Co., 121 NLRB 880, 42 LRRM 1456 (1958). The decision also contained the following sample union shop clause which the Board deemed valid for contract bar purposes:
"It shall be a condition of employment that all employees of the employer covered by this agreement who are members of the Union in good standing on the effective date of this agreement shall remain members in good standing and those who are not members on the effective date of this agreement shall, on the thirtieth day or such longer period as the parties may specify following the effective date of this agreement, become and remain members in good standing in the Union. It shall also be a condition of employment that all employees covered by this agreement and hired on or after its effective date shall, on the thirtieth day following the beginning of such employment or such longer period as the parties may specify become and remain members in good standing in the Union."
[49] *Id.* at 883.
[50] Paragon Products Corp., 134 NLRB 662, 664, 49 LRRM 1160 (1961).
[51] *Id.* at 666.

into a union security agreement,[52] Section 9 (e) provides that a majority of employees may vote to *rescind* such authority. As with representation elections, a valid deauthorization election may be held only once in any 12-month period. However, the holding of a representation election does not bar the holding of a deauthorization election within the ensuing 12-month period,[53] and such deauthorization elections are not subject to the ordinary contract-bar rules.

The deauthorization election must be initiated by a petition supported by 30 percent of the employees in the affected unit; [54] and any employee in the unit, even one not required by the terms of the union security agreement to join, may petition for deauthorization.[55] An election may be ordered to deauthorize an invalid, as well as a valid, union security provision, although such an invalid clause could also be declared illegal in an unfair labor practice proceeding.[56] The effect of an affirmative deauthorization vote is immediately to relieve employees of the requirements imposed by the union security agreement.[57]

E.   The 8(f) Exception: The Construction Industry

In 1959, Section 8 (f) was added to the NLRA to exempt the construction industry from some of the general requirements of the Act. Under Section 8 (f) a union need not be the certified representative of a majority of the employees, and, more important, even a demonstrably minority union may sometimes enter into a valid union security agreement.[58] However, such a contract does not bar an election either to decertify the union or to deauthorize the union security agreement.[59] Secondly, prehire contracts, entered into before any employees are hired, are valid. Thirdly, the required grace period before an employee must join the union under a union-shop agreement is only seven days (com-

---

[52] *See* discussion of 1951 amendment *supra* at notes 13-15.
[53] Monsanto Chemical Co., 147 NLRB 49, 56 LRRM 1136 (1964).
[54] § 9 (e). *See* Morgan, *The Union Shop Deauthorization Poll,* 12 IND. & LAB. REL. REV. 78 (1958).
[55] F. W. Woolworth & Co., 107 NLRB 671, 33 LRRM 1212 (1953).
[56] Andor Co., 119 NLRB 925, 41 LRRM 1184 (1957).
[57] Monsanto Chemical Co., note 53 *supra.*
[58] Administrative Decision of General Counsel, Case No. SR-813, 46 LRRM 1515 (1960).
[59] § 8 (f), final proviso. *See* Chapter 8 at note 103 *supra. See also* general discussion of §8(f) in Chapters 11 and 24 *supra.*

pared with 30 days for other industries). The full seven days must, however, be allowed.[60] Finally, the agreement may require the employer to give the union an opportunity to refer qualified applicants for job openings, without running afoul of restrictions on hiring halls.[61]

III. MAINTENANCE OF MEMBERSHIP AND THE AGENCY SHOP

A. Maintenance of Membership

Maintenance-of-membership agreements are similar to, but more permissive than, the union shop. Such agreements require all employees who are union members at the time the contract is executed or at a specified time thereafter, and all employees who later become members, to retain membership as a condition of employment. Such compulsion may then run for the duration of the agreement. However, an "escape period" is often provided for the benefit of members who wish to escape the requirements of compulsory unionism, and members who resign during the specified period are not subject to the agreement.[62] Nonmembers have no duty to join.[63] The "membership" requirement is satisfied so long as a worker continues to pay his dues.[64] Such an agreement may not be given retroactive effect—the union may neither require membership prior to the effective date of the contract [65] nor obtain an employee's discharge for dues delinquency prior to the effective date.[66]

B. The Agency Shop

The agency shop is a hybrid form of union security which evolved both as a theoretical alternative to compulsory *membership* under a union-shop agreement and as a practical evasion of state right-to-work laws. Typical agency-shop agreements provide that employees, as a condition of continued employment, must either become members of the union or pay the union a service fee—usually equal in amount to union dues.

---

[60] Harder's Construction Co., 146 NLRB 698, 55 LRRM 1377 (1964).
[61] *See* discussion of hiring halls *infra*.
[62] Addressograph-Multigraph Corp., 110 NLRB 727, 35 LRRM 1109 (1954).
[63] Montgomery Ward & Co., 142 NLRB 650, 53 LRRM 1109 (1963).
[64] Marlin Rockwell Corp., 114 NLRB 555, 36 LRRM 1592 (1955).
[65] Colonie Fibre Co. v. NLRB, 163 F2d 65, 20 LRRM 2399 (CA 2, 1947).
[66] General Motors Corp., 134 NLRB 1107, 49 LRRM 1283 (1961).

Controversial questions arose about such agreements—whether the agency shop was in conflict with Section 8 (a) (3) and whether states had the power under Section 14 (b) to regulate it. Section 8 (a) (3) makes it an unfair labor practice for an employer to discriminate against his employees "to encourage or discourage membership in any labor organization" but the proviso states that a union-shop agreement requiring membership is legal. Since an agency-shop agreement does not require *membership,* it is not literally within the exception. However, the Board decided in 1952 [67] that the agency shop is not a form of discrimination outlawed by Section 8 (a) (3). In *American Seating Co.*[68] a union-shop agreement provided that employees who had religious objections to union membership could retain their employment by paying the union an amount equal to dues. In upholding the provision the Board noted that "Congress intended not to illegalize the practice of obtaining support payments from nonunion members who would otherwise be 'free riders' "; and therefore "the provision for support payments in the instant contract does not exceed the union security agreements authorized by the Act." [69]

The Supreme Court expressly agreed with this conclusion in 1963. In *NLRB v. General Motors Corp.,*[70] one of the two leading cases [71] on this problem, the employer refused to bargain [72] concerning the agency shop, contending that such an agreement would entail discrimination in violation of Section 8 (a) (3). The Supreme Court noted that Congress, in passing the Taft-Hartley Act, did not intend to make the union shop the only valid union security device but rather meant to limit the union's power to obtain discharge for any reason other than failure to pay dues. The agency shop is "the practical equivalent of union 'member-

---

[67] Even earlier the NLRB had held that a support-money clause was valid under § 8 (3) of the original Wagner Act, on the theory that it would be unreasonable to find that the same Congress that approved the closed shop and union shop intended to outlaw less compulsory forms of union security. Public Service Co. of Colorado, 89 NLRB 418, 26 LRRM 1014 (1950).

[68] 98 NLRB 800, 29 LRRM 1424 (1952).

[69] *Id.* at 802.

[70] 373 US 734, 53 LRRM 2313 (1963).

[71] The other is Local 1625, Retail Clerks Int'l Ass'n v. Schermerhorn, 373 US 746, 53 LRRM 2318 (1963), *on reargument,* 375 US 96, 54 LRRM 2612 (1963), discussed *infra.*

[72] *See* Chapter 11 *supra* for a discussion of mandatory subjects of bargaining.

ship' as Congress used that term in the proviso to 8 (a) (3)" [73] and is therefore legal.

The next question was whether the agency shop could be prohibited by the states by right-to-work laws enacted pursuant to Section 14 (b).[74] The *General Motors* case arose in Indiana, where a right-to-work law had been construed by the state supreme court as not prohibiting the agency shop.[75] In the companion case to *General Motors, Retail Clerks v. Schermerhorn*,[76] the situation was the reverse: the Florida Supreme Court had held that Florida's right-to-work constitutional provision did prohibit the agency shop.[77] The union's position in *Schermerhorn*, that states could not prohibit the agency shop under Section 14 (b), was weakened by the fact that the Supreme Court, in *General Motors*, had concluded that the agency shop was a permissible form of union security under Section 8 (a) (3), being virtually identical to the form of union shop permitted by the Taft-Hartley Act. The union sought in *Schermerhorn* to differentiate its case from *General Motors* by contending that, unlike the General Motors situation, money collected from nonmembers paid only for bargaining services rendered by the union as the exclusive bargaining agent. The Supreme Court found this unsupported by the record [78] and, having already decided in *General Motors* that the agency shop is the practical equivalent of compulsory membership, concluded that "the agency shop is within Section 14 (b). At least to that extent did Congress intend 8 (a) (3) and 14 (b) to coincide." [79]

---

73 373 US at 743. *Accord*, Street, Elec. Ry. & Motor Coach Employees, Division 1225 v. Las Vegas-Tonopak-Reno Stage Line, Inc., 202 F Supp 726, 49 LRRM 2732 (D Nev 1961), *affirmed*, 319 F2d 783, 53 LRRM 2720 (CA 9, 1963).

74 Allowing states to ban "agreements requiring membership in a labor organization as a condition of employment." *See* discussion in section IV *infra*.

75 Meade Elec. Co. v. Hagberg, 129 Ind App 631, 159 NE2d 408, 42 LRRM 2312 (1959). Indiana subsequently repealed its right-to-work statute.

76 Local 1625, Retail Clerks Int'l Ass'n v. Schermerhorn, 373 US 746, 53 LRRM 2318 (1963), *on reargument*, 375 US 96, 54 LRRM 2612 (1963). *See* discussion in section IV *infra*.

77 Schermerhorn v. Local 1625, Retail Clerks Int'l Ass'n, 141 So2d 269, 50 LRRM 2055 (1962).

78 The "service fee" charged nonmembers was equal to the dues charged members. If the entire service fee was in fact allocated to collective bargaining costs, it is clear that nonmembers were required to pay more for the same services than members. Whether an agency-shop agreement requiring nonmembers to pay only their pro-rata share of bargaining costs could be prohibited by states under 14 (b) is an open question.

79 373 US at 752. *See generally* Hopfl, *The Agency Shop Question*, 49 Cornell L. Q. 478 (1964); Comment, *The Agency Shop: A Lawful Form of Union Security*, 57 Nw. U.L. Rev. 75 (1962).

Thus the law concerning the agency shop is relatively settled. Such arrangements are not prohibited by Section 8 (a) (3), but agreements calling for service fees equal to dues may be regulated or proscribed by the states under Section 14 (b).

IV. SECTION 14 (b) AND STATE RIGHT-TO-WORK LAWS

In the 1947 Taft-Hartley amendments to the NLRA Congress empowered the states to prohibit the union security devices allowed under Section 8 (a) (3):

> Sec. 14 (b). Nothing in this Act shall be construed as authorizing the execution or application of agreements requiring membership in a labor organization as a condition of employment in any State or Territory in which such execution or application is prohibited by State or Territorial law.

The laws so passed are commonly known as right-to-work laws (though unions object to the term as "loaded"). Twenty states, either by statute [80] or constitutional amendment,[81] have elected to regulate this area of union security more strictly than does the federal law. The United States Supreme Court has explicitly upheld the validity of three of these measures against contentions that they violated the First Amendment (freedom of speech, assembly, and petition), the Fourteenth Amendment (due process and equal protection), and Article I, Section 10 (impairment of contracts) of the Constitution.[82] Whether a local government (city or county) right-to-work ordinance would be valid under Section 14(b) appears to be an open question. The California Supreme Court has struck down two such ordinances—but on the ground that state law to the contrary was controlling.[83]

There is substantial overlap between what may be *prohibited* by a state under Section 14 (b) and what is *permitted* by Section

---

[80] Alabama, Georgia, Iowa, Louisiana (applying to agricultural workers only), Nevada, North Carolina, North Dakota, South Carolina, South Dakota, Tennessee, Texas, Utah, Virginia, Wyoming.
[81] Arizona, Arkansas, Florida, Kansas, Mississippi, Nebraska. See LRX 665 (BNA, 1966) for a cumulative list of right-to-work statutes and constitutional provisions with applicable state court decisions.
[82] Lincoln Federal Labor Union v. Northwestern Iron & Metal Co., 335 US 525, 23 LRRM 2199 (1949) (Nebraska and North Carolina); A. F. of L. v. American Sash & Door Co., 335 US 538, 23 LRRM 2204 (1949) (Arizona).
[83] Chavez v. Sargent, 339 P2d 801, 44 LRRM 2134 (Cal Sup Ct, 1959); Stephenson v. City of Palm Springs, 340 P2d 1009, 44 LRRM 2371 (Cal Sup Ct, 1959).

8 (a) (3) [84]—most prominently the union shop and the agency shop. *All* right-to-work laws prohibit the union shop, and whether or not a particular law prohibits the agency shop is a matter for interpretation by the state.[85] Of the 20 right-to-work laws, 13 [86] by their terms outlaw the agency shop, five [87] have been construed either by a court or the state attorney general to prohibit the agency shop, and one state [88] has indicated that, while such an agreement would not of itself be illegal, enforcement by discharge would be. Hiring-hall arrangements, however, may not be proscribed by the states under Section 14 (b).[89]

An important question was left unanswered in the original *Schermerhorn* opinion: whether states have power to furnish a *remedy* for a violation of right-to-work laws; or whether such a violation, arguably being an unfair labor practice, falls within the exclusive province of the Board. After reargument, the Court held that states have power to enforce prohibitions against agency-shop agreements.[90] In Section 8 (a) (3) "Congress undertook pervasive regulation of union security agreements" and could preempt as much of the field as it chose. But in Section 14 (b) Congress abandoned the idea of federally-imposed uniformity in order to leave states free to legislate. The Court concluded that Congress, in granting the states authority to prohibit certain union security devices, also extended the power to enforce that prohibition.[91] The Court noted, however, that the jurisdiction

---

[84] Local 1625, Retail Clerks Int'l Ass'n v. Schermerhorn, 373 US 746, 53 LRRM 2318 (1963), *on reargument,* 375 US 96, 54 LRRM 2612 (1963).

[85] *Ibid.*

[86] They prohibit exacting fees from nonmembers: Alabama, Arkansas, Georgia, Iowa, Louisiana, Mississippi, Nebraska, North Carolina, South Carolina, Tennessee, Utah, Virginia, Wyoming.

[87] Arizona, Florida, Kansas, Nevada, Texas.

[88] North Dakota.

[89] NLRB v. Tom Joyce Floors, Inc., 353 F2d 768, 60 LRRM 2434 (CA 9, 1965). *See also* NLRB v. Houston Chapter, AGC, 349 F2d 449, 59 LRRM 3013 (CA 5, 1965), note 105 *infra.*

[90] 375 US 96, 54 LRRM 2612 (1963).

[91] The Court noted that the decision in San Diego Building Trade Council v. Garmon, 359 US 236, 43 LRRM 2838 (1959), holding that "when an activity is arguably subject to §7 or §8 of the Act, the States as well as the federal courts must defer to the exclusive competence of the National Labor Relations Board," was not a constitutional principle, but rather a mere rule of law. State enforcement of §14 (b) provisions, the Court concluded in *Schermerhorn,* "is within the ambit of Algoma Plywood" [& Veneer Co. v. Wisconsin ERB], 336 US 301, 23 LRRM 2402 (1949), where a state court was allowed to prevent an employer from giving effect to a maintenance-of-membership agreement which violated a state law on union security. For a full discussion of preemption, *see* Chapter 29 *infra* at notes 116-121.

of the states under Section 14 (b) "begins *only with actual negotiation and execution of the type of agreement described by §14(b),*"
thus distinguishing earlier cases holding that "picketing in order
to get an employer to execute an agreement to hire all union labor
in violation of a state's union-security statute lies exclusively in
the Federal domain." [92]

V. HIRING HALLS

Following the Taft-Hartley Act's outlawing of the closed shop,
hiring-hall agreements between employers and unions became
subject to extensive reevaluation. A union could no longer operate a hiring hall exclusively for its members, nor could it include
in a collective bargaining contract a provision by which an employer would be obligated to the exclusive use of the hiring hall
as the employment agency. Such an arrangement, common before
enactment of the Taft-Hartley Act amendments, required membership in a labor organization as a precondition of employment
and consequently violated the amended Section 8 (a) (3) and the
newly enacted Section 8 (b) (2).

Nevertheless, hiring halls continue to serve as a means "to
eliminate wasteful, time-consuming, and repetitive scouting for
jobs by individual workmen and haphazard uneconomical searches
by employers." [93] In particular, the service provided by hiring-
hall agreements is utilized in the maritime and construction
industries. As the Supreme Court noted, the Taft-Hartley Act was
not intended to eliminate hiring halls, but rather to *regulate* the
nature of hiring-hall arrangements so as to prevent discrimination
against nonunion applicants or members of union minority
groups.[94]

In its landmark *Mountain Pacific* decision,[95] however, the
Board determined that the possibility of abuse inherent in exclusive hiring-hall agreements could be avoided only by requiring
insertion of explicit safeguards in such agreements. The Board
declared that hiring-hall arrangements were *per se* invalid if they
failed, in clear language, to contain the following requirements: (1)

---

92 375 US at 105.
93 Mountain Pacific Chapter, 119 NLRB 883, 896, note 8, 41 LRRM 1460 (1958),
enforcement denied, 270 F2d 425, 44 LRRM 2802 (CA 9, 1959).
94 *See* Teamsters Local 357 v. NLRB, 365 US 667, 47 LRRM 2906 (1961), notes
98-99 *infra.*
95 119 NLRB 883, 41 LRRM 1460 (1958), *enforcement denied,* 270 F2d 425, 44
LRRM 2802 (CA 9, 1959).

selection of applicants for referral was to be on a nondiscriminatory basis, in no way affected by union membership; (2) the
employer was to retain the right to reject any job applicant referred by the union; and (3) the parties to the agreement were
to post notices announcing the open and nondiscriminatory character of the hiring-hall arrangement.[96]

Hiring-hall provisions which did not conform to the Board's
outline were struck down with the following condemnation:

> [T]he very grant of work at all depends solely upon union sponsor-
> ship, and it is reasonable to infer that the arrangement displays
> and enhances the union's power and control over the employment
> status. . . . [A]ll that appears is unilateral union determination
> and subservient employer action . . . , and it is reasonable to infer
> that the Union will be guided in its concession by an eye towards
> winning compliance with a membership obligation or union fealty
> in some other respect. . . . [T]he inference of the encouragement of
> union membership is inescapable.[97]

If the agreement departed from the conditions laid down by
the Board, a violation of the law was automatically found, without
any requirement of a showing of *actual* discrimination on the basis
of union affiliation.

This policy met an abrupt end in the Supreme Court's decision
in *Teamsters Local 357 v. NLRB.*[98] Like the Board, the Court
assumed that the existence of a hiring hall encourages union
membership, but there the Court's agreement with the Board
ended. The Court admonished that "the only encouragement or
discouragement of union membership banned by the Act is that
which is 'accomplished by discrimination.' " [99] Nothing in the
hiring-hall arrangement itself implied that the union could
discriminate against nonunion applicants for referral, and there

---

96 119 NLRB at 897. *Compare Hunkin-Conkey Construction Co.,* 95 NLRB 433, 28
LRRM 1327 (1951), where the Board earlier said that an agreement that employees
be hired only through a particular union's offices does not violate the Act "absent
evidence that the union unlawfully discriminated in supplying the company with
personnel." *Id.* at 435. For a concise commentary on *Mountain Pacific* and the
Board's evolving attitude toward hiring halls, *see* Fenton, *Union Hiring Halls Under
The Taft-Hartley Act,* 9 Lab. L. J. 505 (1958).
97 119 NLRB at 896.
98 365 US 667, 47 LRRM 2906 (1961), *reversing* 275 F2d 646, 45 LRRM 2752 (CA
DC, 1960), *enforcing with modification* 121 NLRB 1629, 43 LRRM 1029 (1958).
See also discussion in Chapter 6 at note 92 *supra.*
99 365 US at 676. *See, e.g.,* Int'l Longshoremen's & Warehousemen's Local 17 (Associated Metals Co.), 173 NLRB No. 95, 69 LRRM 1413 (1968) (Union discriminated
by refusing to refer employee on account of his failure to perform picket duty during
a strike).

was no showing or even an attempt to show that the union had departed from its obligation to refer all qualified persons, *regardless* of union affiliation. To sustain its burden, the Court declared, the Board must be able to point to specific acts of discrimination and may not proscribe hiring-hall arrangements as such, if not discriminatory on their face, merely because they fail to include the precautionary formula established by the Board.

With the status of hiring-hall arrangements thus settled by the Supreme Court, much of the controversy now centers around the type of evidence required to show discrimination or an attempt to discriminate. What may be a typical, though obvious, example of discriminatory conduct is set forth in *Local 1332, International Longshoremen's Ass'n*,[100] where the union, a party to a hiring-hall agreement valid on its face, brazenly attempted to cause the employer to depart from the contract and to accord preferential hiring treatment to longshoremen on the basis of union membership rather than on the basis of seniority on the docks.

Another example of illegal discrimination is the charging of excessive service fees. Whether the fee charged to nonunion members is discriminatory will depend on the facts of the particular case. Thus, the Board has held both that a fee slightly greater than monthly union dues was *not* discriminatory [101] (because union members had to pay dues throughout the year, whereas nonmembers had to pay the fee only while registered with the hiring hall), and that a fee equal to monthly union dues *was* discriminatory [102] (because a portion of the dues was used to support union expenses unrelated to job opportunities of nonmembers, and other union institutional expenses.)

Where the practice under a hiring-hall provision has not been proved discriminatory, unions can lawfully require the employer to discharge employees who have sidestepped the union as the exclusive referral agency and have dealt directly with the company. The practice in the building and construction industry indicates the pervasive effect that a hiring-hall agreement has over the employment relationship. Construction agreements com-

---

100 150 NLRB 1471, 58 LRRM 1308 (1965). *See also* NLRB v. Operating Engineers Local 12, 413 F2d 705, 71 LRRM 3144 (CA 9, 1969); Local 269, IBEW (Mercer County NECA), 149 NLRB 768, 57 LRRM 1372 (1964).
101 Operating Engineers Local 825, 137 NLRB 1043, 50 LRRM 1310 (1962).
102 J. J. Hagerty, Inc., 153 NLRB 1375, 59 LRRM 1637 (1965).

monly provide that the employer shall give the union notice of its need for workmen and may not, within a specified period, hire persons not referred by the union. If the union fails to refer the needed workers within the specified time, the employer has the right to hire persons not referred by the union. In two cases [103] employers, being parties to the type of hiring-hall provision described above, were awarded contracts which required construction work in the area of the union's jurisdiction. The employers already had employees working for them and brought them to the new construction site. The union demanded their discharge because they had not been referred to the employer by the union, and the employer complied. The Board, on charges brought by the discharged employees,[104] dismissed the complaints against the union, reasoning that the purpose of the hiring hall was to provide employment for workers on construction projects in their area, and that if the agreement were construed to except currently employed workers, "employers coming from outside the area could fulfill their employment needs by wholesale transferring of employees from other projects outside the area. Such a practice appears to be contrary to the general practice in the industry and contrary to congressional policy." [105]

Undoubtedly the Board's fear, articulated in *Mountain Pacific Chapter,* continues to be a source of concern, insofar as hiring halls do encourage adherence to unions and do allow them an opportunity to disguise discrimination against nonunion adherents by employing seemingly "objective" criteria such as "seniority in the area." Nevertheless, in the hiring-hall area, discrimination within the meaning of Sections 8 (b) (2) and 8 (a) (3) must be proved rather than presumed.

---

103 Carpenters Local 1849, 161 NLRB 424, 63 LRRM 1279 (1966) ; Local 542, Int'l Union of Operating Engineers (Ralph A. Marino), 151 NLRB 497, 58 LRRM 1440 (1965).

104 In each case, the employees were members of a local union other than the one which operated the hiring hall.

105 Int'l Union of Operating Engineers, Local 542 (Ralph A. Marino), 151 NLRB 497, 500, 58 LRRM 1440 (1965). *Cf.* Int'l Longshoremen's Ass'n (Ryan Stevedoring Co.), 179 NLRB No. 67, 72 LRRM 1369 (1969). Section 8(f)(4) of the Act provides that it shall not be an unfair labor practice when an agreement between an employer and a union of which building and construction employees are members gives priority for employment based upon length of service in the particular geographical area. *Cf. also* Houston Chapter, Associated General Contractors, 143 NLRB 409, 53 LRRM 1299 (1963), *enforced,* 349 F2d 449, 59 LRRM 3013 (CA 5, 1965), where the Board ruled that a hiring-hall arrangement of the type considered in the principal cases was a mandatory subject of bargaining. *See* note 89 *supra.*

VI. THE DUES CHECKOFF

The dues checkoff is a device whereby the employer deducts union dues directly from the employee's pay and remits the amount to the union. Its value to the union is *administrative convenience:* the time and effort which otherwise would have to be spent making individual monthly collections is eliminated. In right-to-work states the checkoff assumes even greater significance, for it is the only lawful union security device available (other than the hiring hall, which has applicability in a limited number of industries). Like other union security devices, the checkoff is a product of collective bargaining; [106] and even if the employer agrees to the checkoff of dues, each affected employee must authorize in writing the deduction from his pay. The practice is permitted by the Labor Management Relations Act.[107]

A. The LMRA

The LMRA both legalizes checkoff agreements and creates criminal penalties for unauthorized employer payments to unions. Enforcement of the criminal sanctions of the statute is within the province of the Justice Department; enforcement of a *valid* checkoff agreement is a matter for the parties.

---

[106] Under the original NLRA, collection of dues had been held not a matter for collective bargaining. Hughes Tool Co. v. NLRB, 147 F2d 69, 15 LRRM 852 (CA 5, 1945). However, after Congress passed the Taft-Hartley Act (part of which amended the NLRA and part of which became the LMRA), the Board indicated a revised view in a footnote: "Congress intended that the bargaining obligation contained in Section 8 (a) (5) should apply to checkoff." U. S. Gypsum Co., 94 NLRB 112, 113, 28 LRRM 1015 (1951), *amended,* 97 NLRB 889, 29 LRRM 1171 (1951), *modified,* 206 F2d 410, 32 LRRM 2553 (CA 5, 1953), *cert. denied,* 347 US 912, 33 LRRM 2456 (1954). *See also* Reed & Prince Mfg. Co., 96 NLRB 850, 28 LRRM 1608 (1951), *enforced,* 205 F2d 131, 32 LRRM 2225 (CA 1, 1953), *cert. denied,* 346 US 887, 33 LRRM 2133 (1953); H. K. Porter, 153 NLRB 1370, 59 LRRM 1462 (1965), *enforced,* 363 F2d 272, 62 LRRM 2204 (CA DC, 1966), *cert. denied,* 385 US 851, 63 LRRM 2236 (1966), *reconsideration,* 389 F2d 295, 66 LRRM 2761 (1967), *reversed and remanded,* 397 US 99, 73 LRRM 2561 (1970), discussed in chapters 11 and 15 *supra* and Chapter 31 *infra.*

[107] LMRA § 302 (a) prohibits, in broad terms, any payments from an employer to a representative of his employees. However, § 302 (c) provides, "The provision of this article shall not be applicable . . . (4) with respect to money deducted from the wages of employees in payment of membership dues in a labor organization: *Provided,* That the employer has received from each employee, on whose account such deductions are made, a written assignment which shall not be irrevocable for a period of more than one year, or beyond the termination date of the applicable collective agreement, whichever occurs sooner. . . ." The LMRA, other than Title I (which embraces the amended NLRA), is generally beyond the scope of this book, but §302 (c) will be treated because of its relation to §8 (a) (5) of the NLRA.

Section 302 (d) of the LMRA provides for penalties of a $10,000 maximum fine or one year maximum imprisonment or both for willfully illegal payments from employer to employee representative. A payment which purports to be a dues checkoff, but which fails to meet the statutory requirements, is illegal; and the questions for purposes of criminal prosecution are whether the deductions were authorized, whether the authorization has been revoked, and whether the deductions were "in payment of membership dues."

Since these matters have been largely settled from the beginning, surprisingly few cases deal with criminal violations involving the dues checkoff. The statute is clear as to what an authorization must include, and an employer must "wilfully violate" the provision of Section 302 to incur criminal liability. Although the checkoff provision states that no authorization may be irrevocable for longer than one year, the Justice Department announced in 1949 that it would not prosecute for an authorization with an automatic-renewal clause, so long as an annual "escape period" is retained.[108] In the same document, the Justice Department also indicated that it would not prosecute for *authorized* deductions for payment of initiation fees and assessments —thus giving a broad interpretation to the statutory term "membership dues."

The parties, of course, are concerned primarily with the construction and performance of a particular agreement. Reported court cases deal mainly with the employer's right or obligation to check off and with the union's rights to funds checked off but retained by the employer.

In general, the courts have followed the Justice Department opinion that fines and assessments, as well as dues, may be checked

---

[108] Opinion Letter of May 13, 1949, 22 LRRM 46. *Followed in:* Brooks v. Continental Can Corp., 59 LRRM 2779 (SD NY, 1965) ; Murtha v. Pet Dairy Prod. Co., 314 SW2d 185, 42 LRRM 2850 (Tenn Ct App, 1957). However, the U. S. Supreme Court in *Felter v. Southern Pac. R. R.*, 359 US 326, 43 LRRM 2876 (1959), struck down a union requirement that revocation be on a form furnished by the union. The holding, decided under the Railway Labor Act, seems to be analogous to the LMRA. *Cf.* W. R. Grace Corp. v. Nat'l Maritime Union, Professional Employees Div., 72 LRRM 2405 (SD Ga, 1969), where a Georgia statute making check-off authorizations revocable at will was preempted by the LMRA provision allowing irrevocability for one year. *See* also Operative Potters, Local 355 v. Tell City Chair Co., 295 F Supp 961, 70 LRRM 3113 (SD Ind, 1968) .

off if the employee consents.[109] Agency-shop service fees may also be deducted.[110] Even a 1½ percent "tax" on orchestra members' salaries was held valid under Section 302 because it was "similar" to dues.[111] The main question is whether questioned deductions have been authorized by the employee.

Occasionally, a dispute arises as to who is entitled to funds checked off but not disbursed. It was determined in 1948 that the union has a prior claim against the employer in a bankruptcy situation.[112] If two or more unions are contesting the right to funds, interpleader [113] is an appropriate remedy for the employer to pursue. One case, however, held that the interpleader action depends on diversity of citizenship and is not a federal-question action under Section 301 of the LMRA.[114]

B. The NLRB

The NLRB is without jurisdiction to enforce Section 302 of the Labor-Management Relations Act. In *Salant & Salant, Inc.*,[115] the Board noted that the LMRA provided for enforcement by criminal sanctions and injunction procedures and that therefore

> Congress did not intend the newly created limitations on check-off in Section 302 to have any impact on the unfair labor practice jurisdiction of this Board under Section 8 [of the NLRA]. . . . [T]he intent of Congress was rather to leave undisturbed the application by the Board to checkoff . . . [of] its pre-existing criteria for determining whether such conduct as is engaged in constitutes a violation of the broad proscriptions of Section 8.[116]

Similarly, the Board held that inclusion of an illegal checkoff clause in a collective bargaining agreement does not *per se* make the agreement ineffective as a bar to a representation election because the *legality* of the clause under Section 302 is irrelevant

---

109 Mine, Mill & Smelter Workers, Local 515 v. American Zinc, Lead & Smelting Co., 311 F2d 656, 52 LRRM 2142 (CA 9, 1963). Previous NLRB definitions of "dues" under other provisions of labor statutes (NLRA §§ 8 (a) (3) and 8 (b) (2)) were held immaterial to this question.
110 Grajczyk v. Douglas Aircraft, Inc., 210 F Supp 702, 51 LRRM 2444 (SD Cal 1962).
111 Schwartz v. Associated Musicians, Local 802, 340 F2d 228, 58 LRRM 2133 (CA 2, 1964).
112 *In re* C. A. Reed Furniture Co., 22 LRRM 2528, 22 LRRM 2528 (SD Cal 1948).
113 28 USC § 1335 (1965).
114 Sun Shipbuilding & Dry-Dock Co. v. Marine & Shipbuilding Workers, 95 F Supp 50, 27 LRRM 2250 (ED Pa 1950).
115 88 NLRB 816, 25 LRRM 1391 (1950).
116 *Id.* at 818.

in a proceeding before the NLRB.[117] Thus the Board established its policy that Section 302 requirements as to checkoff will not affect unfair labor practice findings.[118] Furthermore, it will not police enforcement of checkoff provisions where the only question is one of contract interpretation.[119]

Unfair labor practices involving the checkoff are more common than illegal checkoff agreements. Clearly, the employer has a duty to bargain under Section 8 (a) (5) concerning the dues checkoff.[120] However, too great an eagerness by an employer to enter into such agreement may be evidence of Section 8 (a) (2) domination.[121] Thus, violations have been found when employers have agreed to the checkoff without bargaining [122] or during an organizational campaign between an inside and an outside union.[123]

An employer may be engaged in illegal domination under Section 8 (a) (2), or illegal interference under Section 8 (a) (1), or both, if he encourages his employees to authorize checkoff. To require such authorization as a condition of employment is clearly unlawful.[124] Less severe coercion, such as a request from a supervisor in a private meeting,[125] may be similarly unlawful. Unions too may commit unfair labor practices by overly zealous solicitation of checkoff authorizations. A union would be guilty of restraint within the meaning of Section 8 (b) (1) if it agreed with an employer to *require* checkoff of dues [126] or assessments [127]

---

117 Crown Prod. Co., 99 NLRB 602, 30 LRRM 1098 (1952).

118 Pacific Intermountain Express Co. (Teamsters, Local 41), 107 NLRB 837, 33 LRRM 1252 (1954), *modified and enforced,* 225 F2d 343, 36 LRRM 2632 (CA 8, 1955).

119 Morton Salt Co., 119 NLRB 1402, 41 LRRM 1312 (1958).

120 *See* note 106 *supra.*

121 Clinton Cotton Mills, 1 NLRB 97, 1 LRRM 345 (1935). *See generally* Chapter 7 *supra.*

122 Jack Smith Beverages, Inc., 94 NLRB 401, 28 LRRM 1199 (1951), *enforced,* 202 F2d 100, 31 LRRM 2366 (CA 6, 1953), *cert. denied,* 345 US 995, 32 LRRM 2247 (1953).

123 Guy's Food, Inc., 158 NLRB 936, 62 LRRM 1143 (1966), *enforced,* 379 F2d 160, 65 LRRM 2315 (CA DC, 1967).

124 *E.g.,* Hampton Merchants Ass'n, 151 NLRB 1307, 58 LRRM 1621 (1965); Safeway Stores, Inc., 111 NLRB 968, 35 LRRM 1627 (1955); Sterling Precision Corp., 131 NLRB 1229, 48 LRRM 1242 (1961).

125 *E.g.,* NLRB v. Revere Metal Art Co., 280 F2d 96, 46 LRRM 2121 (CA 2, 1960), *cert. denied,* 364 US 894, 47 LRRM 2095 (1960).

126 Biazevich, dba M. V. Liberator, 136 NLRB 13, 49 LRRM 1700 (1962).

127 NLRB v. Food Fair Stores, Inc., 307 F2d 3, 50 LRRM 2913 (CA 3, 1962).

as a condition of employment. Making the alternative to authorizing checkoff unreasonably burdensome may also be unlawful.[128]

Checkoff is valid only insofar as it is authorized; and a checkoff without an authorization, or beyond its terms, may constitute an unfair labor practice. Thus, an unauthorized deduction of a fine for nonattendance at a union meeting was held to be employer interference with the employee's right to refrain from union activities (*i.e.*, a violation of Section 8(a)(1)).[129] Likewise, although assessments may legally be checked off under LMRA Section 302, it is an unfair labor practice to do so without authorization.[130] The employee's authorization also determines the period during which an employer may check off funds. Section 8 (a) (2) violations have been found where an employer paid initiation fees and dues over to the union in anticipation of authorization,[131] where checkoff was continued *after* the expiration of the collective bargaining agreement,[132] and where timely revocations of the authorizations were ignored.[133] Finally, an employer may be caught by unusual circumstances. In *Penn Cork & Closures, Inc.*,[134] the Board held that irrevocable authorizations were in fact revoked when employees deauthorized their union-shop agreement and several members subsequently resigned. The employer was found to have violated Sections 8 (a) (1) and 8 (a) (2) by continuing to deduct dues.

---

[128] American Screw Co., 122 NLRB 485, 43 LRRM 1153 (1958). An employee in a union shop would have been required either to authorize checkoff or drive to another city to tender his union dues.

[129] NLRB v. Injection Molding Co., 211 F2d 59, 33 LRRM 2699 (CA 8, 1954). *Cf.* Pacific Intermountain Express Co. note 118 *supra*. *And compare* Pulp & Paper Workers, Local 171 (Boise Cascade Corp.), 165 NLRB 971, 65 LRRM 1382 (1965), note 38 *supra*.

[130] NLRB v. Food Fair Stores, Inc., note 127 *supra*.

[131] ABC Mach. & Welding Service, 122 NLRB 944, 43 LRRM 1227 (1959).

[132] Stainless Steel Prod., Inc., 157 NLRB 232, 61 LRRM 1346 (1966). However, employer may lawfully continue to deduct dues after another union has won a representation election until the termination date of the contract with the defeated union. Fender Musical Instruments, 175 NLRB No. 144, 71 LRRM 1083 (1969).

[133] Administrative Decision of NLRB General Counsel, Case No. K-604, 38 LRRM 1276 (1956).

[134] 156 NLRB 411, 61 LRRM 1037 (1956), *enforced*, 376 F2d 52, 64 LRRM 2855 (CA 2, 1967), *cert. denied*, 389 US 843, 66 LRRM 2308 (1967). The remedy in this case, as in many unlawful deduction cases, was reimbursement. Reimbursement in cases where employees were compelled to authorize checkoff to a company dominated union was approved by the U.S. Supreme Court in Virginia Elec. & Pow. Co. v. NLRB, 319 US 533, 12 LRRM 739 (1943).

If a union shop is in effect, execution of a checkoff authorization constitutes a tender of dues required under Section 8 (a) (3).[135] In an early leading decision, the Board held that an employee in a union shop may not be discharged for dues delinquency when funds checked off by the employer were instead applied to union fines without authorization by the employee.[136]

Thus, while the LMRA provisions as to *what* constitutes legal checkoff have been liberally construed, NLRB policy in enforcing NLRA unfair labor practices in checkoff situations has been largely unaffected. To a great extent the employee himself controls the legal consequences through his authorization.

VII. POLITICAL EXPENDITURES

American trade unions have long engaged in political activities designed to foster a favorable environment for themselves and their members. Delicate legal questions arise when such unions, acting pursuant to congressional permission, negotiate union security clauses and use funds from dues, which employees are compelled to pay, for political purposes to which some employees object.

These questions arose in litigation involving the Railway Labor Act, and the Supreme Court of the United States dealt with them in three leading decisions.[137] Since the Railway Labor Act's union security provisions are similar to those contained in the NLRA, there is little doubt that the principles established by the Court are equally applicable to both statutes. The Court noted in the *Hanson* decision that "[the] union shop provision of the Railway Labor Act was written into the law in 1951. Prior to that date the Railway Labor Act prohibited union shop agreements. . . . Those [prohibitions] were enacted in 1934 when the union shop was being used by employers to establish and maintain company unions." [138] This belated congressional authorization of the

---

135 Ferro Stamping & Mfg. Co., 93 NLRB 1459, 27 LRRM 1593 (1951).
136 Electric Auto-Lite Co., 92 NLRB 1073, 27 LRRM 1205 (1950), *enforced,* 196 F2d 500, 30 LRRM 2115 (CA 6, 1952), *cert. denied,* 344 US 823, 30 LRRM 2711 (1952).
137 Railway Employees' Dept. v. Hanson, 351 US 225, 38 LRRM 2099 (1956); Int'l Ass'n of Machinists v. Street, 367 US 740, 48 LRRM 2345 (1961); Bhd. of Railway & Steamship Clerks v. Allen, 373 US 113, 53 LRRM 2128 (1963).
138 351 US at 231.

union shop in the railroad industry inspired constitutional attack by groups of objecting employees. *First,* it was claimed in *Hanson* "that the union shop agreement violates the 'right to work' provision of the Nebraska constitution." [139] This claim was rejected by virtue of an explicit provision in the Railway Labor Act permitting union-shop agreements, notwithstanding state law to the contrary.[140] The Railway Labor Act's approach on this point is thus opposite to that of the NLRA, presumably because of the distinctly interstate character of the industry. The state right-to-work-law approach was not deemed practical for employees working on interstate trains and airplanes.

Second, "[wide-ranged] problems [were] tendered under the First Amendment. It [was] argued that the union shop agreement forces men into ideological and political association which violate their right to freedom of conscience, freedom of association, and freedom of thought protected by the Bill of Rights." [141] These contentions were rejected as being unsupported by the record, the Court holding narrowly "that the requirement for financial support of the collective-bargaining agency by all who receive the benefits of its work is within the powers of Congress under the Commerce clause and does not violate either the First or the Fifth Amendments." [142] Hence, authorization by Congress of compulsory support of a union's collective bargaining activities was declared to be constitutional.

Two subsequent cases required the Court to give further consideration to the problem. Both involved claims by employees that railroad unions, administering congressionally permitted union security clauses, were using funds from dues for political purposes to which the employees objected. In *Int'l Ass'n of Machinists v. Street* [143] the Georgia courts "found that the allegations were fully proved and entered a judgment and decree enjoining the enforcement of the union-shop agreement on the grounds that [the Railway Labor Act] violates the Federal Constitution to the extent that it permits such [political] use . . . of

---

139 *Id.* at 228.
140 64 Stat 1238, 45 USC §152 (1965). In this respect the RLA provision differs from that of the NLRA, which yields to state right-to-work laws in §14(b). *See* section IV *supra.*
141 351 US at 236.
142 *Id.* at 238.
143 367 US 740, 48 LRRM 2345 (1961).

funds exacted from employees." [144] The Supreme Court of the
United States determined that "[the] record in this case is adequate squarely to present the constitutional questions reserved
in *Hanson*." [145] Thereupon, a majority of the Court construed
the union shop provisions of the Railway Labor Act in a manner
which avoided the constitutional problems presented. Concluding that Congress had not intended to authorize the compulsory support of political expenditures to which a member
objected, the Court found in the Railway Labor Act a right on
the part of a dissenting member in effect to "contract out" of
those of the union's political activities of which the member
disapproved.

As to the remedy for that right, it was the Court's view that to
restrain enforcement of the union-shop clause or to prohibit all
union political expenditures would be excessive. Concerning the
latter, the Court made this observation:

> The fact that these expenditures are made for political activities
> is an additional reason for reluctance to impose such an injunction
> remedy. Whatever may be the powers of Congress or the States to
> forbid unions altogether to make various types of political expendi-
> tures, as to which we express no opinion here, many of the ex-
> penditures involved in the present case are made for the purpose
> of disseminating information as to candidates and programs and
> publicizing the positions of the unions on them. As to such ex-
> penditures an injunction would work a restraint on the expression
> of political ideas which might be offensive to the First Amendment.
> For the majority also has an interest in stating its views without
> being silenced by the dissenters.[146]

Instead, the Court proposed the following remedial devices:

> One remedy would be an injunction against expenditures for politi-
> cal causes opposed by each complaining employee of a sum, from
> those moneys to be spent by the union for political purposes, which
> is so much of the moneys exacted from him as is the proportion of
> the union's total expenditures made for such political activities to the
> union's total budget. . . . A second remedy would be restitution to
> each individual employee of that portion of his money which the
> unions expended, despite his notification, for the political purposes
> to which he has advised the union he was opposed.[147]

---

144 *Id*. at 744-745.
145 *Id*. at 749.
146 *Id*. at 773.
147 *Id*. at 775.

The subsequent *Brotherhood of Railway & Steamship Clerks v. Allen* [148] case, while reaffirming the principles announced in *Street,* eased somewhat the burden of the dissenting employee by enabling him to "contract out" of *all* union political expenditures without the need of specifying particular ones as being objectionable. As to remedy, the Court suggested that a decree in such an employee's favor "would order (1) the refund to [the employee] of a portion of the enacted funds in the same proportion that union political expenditures bear to total union expenditures, and (2) a reduction of future such exactions from him by the same proportion." [149]

Of considerable importance to unions is the circumstance that the Court decided that cases of this type could not be treated as class actions. Hence, only employees *actually* objecting to political expenditures are entitled to the afforded remedies. And these remedies, although protecting the *principle* of political dissent, are likely to furnish fairly meager economic rewards, provided political expenditures represent only a small portion of a union's total budget.

In the passage from the *Street* case quoted above,[150] the Court referred to the constitutional problems raised by legislative prohibition altogether of political expenditures by unions, regardless of the existence of a union shop. Congress enacted one such measure in 1947 when, in Section 304 of the NLRA, it amended the Federal Corrupt Practices Act to make it applicable to labor organizations. In consequence, such organizations are prohibited from making "a contribution or expenditure in connection with any election at which Presidential and Vice Presidential electors or a Senator or Representative in, or a Delegate or Resident Commissioner to Congress are to be voted for, or in connection with any primary election or political convention or caucus held to select candidates for any of the foregoing offices." [151]

The constitutionality of that statute has twice been challenged before the Supreme Court, but in both instances the Court declined to reach the question. In *U.S. v. C.I.O.*[152] the federal dis-

---

148 373 US 113, 53 LRRM 2128 (1963).
149 *Id.* at 122.
150 *See* note 146 *supra.*
151 18 USC §610 (1965) (treated here because of its relation to compulsory unionism).
152 335 US 106, 22 LRRM 2194 (1948).

trict court had dismissed an indictment charging use of a union weekly publication to advocate the cause of a candidate for federal office.[153] Although the Supreme Court stated that the First Amendment guarantees of freedom of speech and press protected the union, it affirmed the dismissal of the indictment on the ground that it failed to state an offense under the statute—thus leaving the question of the statute's constitutionality open. In 1957 the Court stopped short of ruling on constitutionality. In *U.S. v. U.A.W.*[154] the Court held that an indictment charging the union with using dues moneys for a television political commercial stated an offense under the statute.[155] On trial of the case following remand, the union was acquitted by a jury.

Lower courts have held that the ban on political expenditures does not apply to television programs supported by voluntary contributions of members,[156] to the salary of an union employee working actively for a candidate,[157] or even to the purchase of advertisements for the purpose of communicating with members where the union published no newspaper.[158] Nor does the statute purport to reach routine lobbying activities.

[153] U. S. v. C.I.O., 21 LRRM 2451 (D DC, 1948).
[154] 352 US 567, 39 LRRM 2568 (1957).
[155] Chief Justice Warren and Justices Black and Douglas would have held the statute unconstitutional.
[156] U.S. v. Anchorage Central Labor Council, 193 F Supp 504, 48 LRRM 2143 (D Alas, 1961).
[157] U.S. v. Construction and General Laborers Local 264, 101 F Supp 869, 29 LRRM 2408 (WD Mo, 1951).
[158] U.S. v. Painters Local 481, 172 F2d 854, 23 LRRM 2331 (CA 2, 1949). The court relied on *U.S. v. C.I.O.*, note 152 *supra*. The later decision of *U. S. v. U.A.W.*, note 154 *supra*, conflicts with the Second Circuit's holding in *Painters Local 481*.

CHAPTER 27

THE DUTY OF FAIR REPRESENTATION

I. SOURCE OF THE DUTY

Although the statute does not explicitly declare such a duty, it has long been recognized that the National Labor Relations Act imposes upon unions a duty to act fairly toward the employees whom they represent. This duty of fair representation [1] was first

---

[1] This subject has been popular among legal writers. *See:* Aaron, *The Union's Duty of Fair Representation Under the Railway Labor and National Labor Relations Acts,* 34 J. AIR L. & COM. 167 (1968); Aaron, *Some Aspects of the Union's Duty of Fair Representation,* 22 OHIO STATE L. J. 39, 63 (1961); Blumrosen, *Duty of Fair Representation,* 15 LAB. L. J. 598 (1964); Blumrosen, *Employee Rights, Collective Bargaining, and Our Future Labor Problem,* 15 LAB. L. J. 15 (1964); Blumrosen, *Legal Protection for Critical Job Interests: Union-Management Authority Versus Employee Autonomy,* 13 RUTGERS L. REV. 631 (1959); Blumrosen, *The Worker and Three Phases of Unionism: Administrative and Judicial Controls of the Worker-Union Relationship,* 61 MICH. L. REV. 1435 (1963); Carter, *The National Labor Relations Board and Racial Discrimination,* 2 L. IN TRANS. Q. 87 (1965); Comment, *Applicability of LMRDA Section 101(a)(5) to Union Interference with Employment Opportunities,* 114 U. PA. L. REV. 700 (1966); Cox, *The Duty of Fair Representation,* 2 VILL. L. R. 151 (1957); Cox, *Rights Under a Labor Agreement,* 69 HARV. L. REV. 601 (1956); Dunau, *Employee Participation in the Grievance Aspect of Collective Bargaining,* 50 COLUM. L. REV. 731 (1950); Ferguson, *Duty of Fair Representation,* 15 LAB. L. J. 596 (1964); Givens, *Federal Protection of Employee Rights Within Unions,* 29 FORDHAM L. REV. 259 (1960); Gould, *Negro Revolution and the Law of Collective Bargaining,* 34 FORDHAM L. REV. 207 (1965); Hanslowe, *The Collective Agreement and the Duty of Fair Representation,* 14 LAB. L. J. 1052 (1963); Hanslows, *Individual Rights in Collective Labor Relations,* 45 CORNELL L. Q. 25 (1959); Herring, *The "Fair Representation" Doctrine: An Effective Weapon Against Union Racial Discrimination?,* 24 MD. L. REV. 113 (1964); Katzman, *Labor Law—Duty of Fair Representation—NLRA Section 8(b)(1)(A),* 45 B. U. L. REV. 141 (1965); Lewis, *Fair Representation in Grievance Administration: Vaca v. Sipes,* SUPREME CT. REV. 81 (1967); Molinar, *National Labor Relations Act and Racial Discrimination,* 7 B. C. IND. & COM. L. REV. 601 (1966); Murphy, *The Duty of Fair Representation Under Taft-Hartley,* 30 MO. L. REV. 373 (1965); Note, *Union's Duty of Fair Representation: Does It Exist and Who Should Enforce It?,* 9 VILL. L. REV. 306 (1964); Note, *Labor Law—National Labor Relations Act—Violation of the Duty of Fair Representation in an Unfair Labor Practice,* 78 HARV. L. REV. 679 (1965); Note, *Labor Law—National Labor Relations Act—Union's Duty of Fair Representation Not Implicit in Section 7—Discrimination Based on Other than Union Membership*

726

established by the Supreme Court in a series of cases arising under the Railway Labor Act.[2] Subsequently, the doctrine was also applied to the NLRA.[3] The leading and earliest case was *Steele v. Louisville & N.R.R.*,[4] which involved a suit by a Negro railroad fireman to set aside a seniority agreement negotiated by his union which discriminated against Negroes. The suit had been brought in the Alabama courts, and the supreme court of that state held that the complaint did not state a cause of action.

The Supreme Court approached the problem by indicating that if the Railway Labor Act conferred exclusive bargaining authority on a union "without any commensurate statutory duty toward its members, constitutional questions arise. For the representative is clothed with power not unlike that of a legislature, which is subject to constitutional limitations. . . ."[5] The Court avoided these constitutional difficulties by holding that the act implicitly "expresses the aim of Congress to impose on the bargaining representative of a craft or class of employees the duty to exercise fairly the power conferred upon it in behalf of all those for whom it acts, without hostile discrimination against them."[6]

Not a Violation of Section 8(a)(3), 18 VAND. L. REV. 268 (1964); Note, *Administrative Enforcement of the Right to Fair Representation: The Miranda Case*, 112 U. PA. L. REV. 711 (1964); Note, *Refusal to Process a Grievance, the NLRB, and the Duty of Fair Representation: Plea for Pre-emption*, 26 U. PITT. L. REV. 593 (1965); Rosen, *Fair Representation, Contract Breach and Fiduciary Obligations: Unions, Union Officials and the Worker in Collective Bargaining*, 15 HASTINGS L. J. 391 (1964); Sherman, *Union's Duty of Fair Representation and the Civil Rights Act of 1964*, 49 MINN. L. REV. 771 (1965); Sovern, *Legal Restraints on Racial Discrimination in Employment*, (Twentieth Century Fund 1966); Sovern, *The National Labor Relations Act and Racial Discrimination*, 62 COLUM. L. REV. 563 (1962); Sovern, *Race Discrimination and the National Labor Relations Act: The Brave New World of Miranda*, N.Y.U. 16TH ANN. CONF. ON LAB. 3 (1963); Sovern, *Section 301 and the Primary Jurisdiction of the NLRB*, 76 HARV. L. REV. 529 (1963); Summers, *Individual Rights in Collective Agreements and Arbitration*, 37 N.Y.U. L. REV. 362 (1962); Wellington, *Union Democracy and Fair Representation: Federal Responsibility in a Federal System*, 67 YALE L. J. 1327 (1958); Wolk, *The Decline of Individual Rights*, 16 LAB. L. J. 266 (1965); Wyle, *Labor Arbitration and the Concept of Exclusive Representation*, 7 B. C. IND. & COM. L. REV. 783 (1966); Yablonski, *Refusal to Process a Grievance, the NLRB and the Duty of Fair Representation: A Plea for Pre-emption*, 26 U. PITT. L. REV. 593 (1965).

2 44 Stat. 577 (1926), as amended by 48 Stat. 1185 (1934), 49 Stat. 1189 (1936), 54 Stat. 785, 786 (1940), 64 Stat. 1238 (1951), 78 Stat. 748 (1964), and 80 Stat. 208 (1966); 45 USC §§151-88.

3 Ford Motor Co. v. Huffman, 345 US 330, 31 LRRM 2548 (1953); Syres v. Oil Workers, Local 23, 350 US 892, 37 LRRM 2068 (1955).

4 323 US 192, 15 LRRM 708 (1944). *See also* Tunstall v. Loco. Firemen, 323 US 210, 15 LRRM 715 (1944); Graham v. Bhd. of Loco. Firemen, 338 US 232, 25 LRRM 2033 (1949); Bhd. of R.R. Trainmen v. Howard, 343 US 768, 30 LRRM 2258 (1952).

5 Steele v. Louisville & N.R.R., 323 US 192, 198, 15 LRRM 708 (1944).

6 *Id.* at 202-03.

The Court acknowledged that "the statutory representative of a craft is [not] barred from making contracts which may have unfavorable effects on some members of the craft represented." [7] But a bargaining representative must not make discriminatory contracts based on irrelevant or invidious considerations such as race, the Court said. When such a violation of the duty of fair representation occurs, an injured employee may "resort to the usual judicial remedies of injunction and award of damages when appropriate. . . ." [8]

Although the duty of fair representation developed mainly in cases arising under the Railway Labor Act, it was not long before the same duty was found to exist under the National Labor Relations Act. Indeed, in a case decided the same day as *Steele*, the Court suggested such a duty, indicating that under the NLRA, bargaining agents are "charged with the responsibility of representing . . . [the employees'] interests fairly and impartially." [9] In 1953, in *Ford Motor Co. v. Huffman*,[10] the Court, in a case arising under the National Labor Relations Act, readily applied the same principles which it had previously developed in Railway Labor Act cases.

One question raised in *Huffman* that was not controlled by the RLA cases has come to the forefront: Is the duty of fair representation under the NLRA enforceable by the courts or by the NLRB? No parallel question arises under the RLA because no corresponding administrative enforcement machinery exists under that act. In *Huffman* the Court acknowledged the existence of this issue and chose to avoid it because it had not been raised below, but also because the Court was able to decide the case in favor of the union on the merits, thus obviating the necessity of resolving the jurisdictional problem.[11]

But the problem remains. And technically it is still unresolved, for in the 1967 *Vaca v. Sipes* case [12] the Supreme Court implied, but declined to state specifically, that a breach of a union's duty of fair representation is an unfair labor practice under Section 8(b)

---

7 *Id.* at 203.
8 *Id.* at 207.
9 Wallace Corp. v. NLRB, 323 US 248, 255, 15 LRRM 697 (1944).
10 345 US 330, 31 LRRM 2548 (1953).
11 345 US at 332, note 4.
12 386 US 171, 64 LRRM 2369 (1967). *See* Feller, *Vaca v. Sipes One Year Later,* N.Y.U. 21ST ANN. CONF. ON LAB. 141 (1969).

of the NLRA. One of the issues in the case was whether a court has jurisdiction over a breach of the duty if such breach is deemed to be an unfair labor practice, or even *arguably* an unfair labor practice. Among the reasons given by the Supreme Court for upholding the jurisdiction of the courts to decide such cases was that it could not assume from the NLRB's "tardy assumption of jurisdiction" [13] in unfair representation cases that Congress "intended to oust the courts of their traditional jurisdiction to curb arbitrary conduct by the individual employee's statutory representative." [14] The Court had reference to the fact that the Board waited until late 1962 before deciding that such a breach of duty constituted an unfair labor practice.[15]

The jurisdictional aspects of the *Vaca* case are discussed below.[16] But the decision is also significant for its exposition of the requirements which the duty of fair representation imposes upon a union in processing an employee's grievance under a collective bargaining contract.

The case involved a suit for damages brought by an employee against his union. The employee had been discharged for reasons of health. The union had processed his grievance through the pre-arbitration steps of the grievance procedure but, in the light of conflicting medical opinion concerning the grievant's capacity to work, declined to take the case to arbitration. The trial court had set aside, on the ground of exclusive NLRB jurisdiction, a jury verdict awarding actual and punitive damages, but the Missouri Supreme Court ordered the verdict reinstated, concluding that the jury could properly have found that the union had arbitrarily failed to represent the plaintiff in the handling of his grievance by refusing to take his case to arbitration.[17] The United States Supreme Court reversed.

---

13 *Id.* at 183.
14 *Ibid.*
15 *See* Miranda Fuel Co., 140 NLRB 181, 51 LRRM 1584 (1962), notes 42-49 *infra.*
16 The case is also treated in this chapter under Remedies *infra.*
17 The action was instituted by Benjamin Owens, Jr., an employee of a packing company, against his union in a class action. The trial resulted in a jury verdict for plaintiff in the amount of $7,000 actual and $3,300 punitive damages. The trial court set aside the judgment on the verdict and entered judgment for the defendants on grounds of federal preemption. Plaintiff appealed to the intermediate court of appeals, which affirmed the judgment (plaintiff died while the appeal was pending, and Sipes, his administrator, was substituted as appellant). The Missouri Supreme Court reversed and ordered reinstatement of the verdict and judgment for plaintiff. Sipes v. Vaca, 397 SW2d 658, 61 LRRM 2054 (Mo Sup Ct, 1965).

After disposing of the jurisdictional issue, the Court turned its attention to the substantive nature of the duty of fair representation. It indicated that the critical focus of inquiry is the good faith of the union in the handling of the grievance. Reiterating that a breach of the statutory duty occurs when the union's conduct in representation is "arbitrary, discriminatory, or in bad faith," [18] it took note of the "considerable debate over the extent of this duty in the context of a union's enforcement of the grievance and arbitration procedures in a collective bargaining agreement. . . ." [19]

> Some have suggested that every individual employee should have the right to have his grievance taken to arbitration. Others have urged that the Union be given substantial discretion (if the collective bargaining agreement so provides) to decide whether a grievance should be taken to arbitration, subject only to the duty to refrain from patently wrongful conduct such as racial discrimination or personal hostility.
>
> Though we accept the proposition that a union may not arbitrarily ignore a meritorious grievance or process it in a perfunctory fashion, *we do not agree that the individual employee has an absolute right to have his grievance taken to arbitration regardless of the provisions of the applicable collective bargaining agreement.*[20]

Finding authority in the Taft-Hartley provisions creating the Federal Mediation and Conciliation Service,[21] the Court declared that

> [i]n providing for a grievance and arbitration procedure which gives the union discretion to supervise the grievance machinery and to invoke arbitration, the employer and the union contemplate that each will endeavor in good faith to settle grievances short of arbitration. Through this settlement process, frivolous grievances are ended prior to the most costly and time-consuming step in the grievance procedures.[22]

The Court pointed out that by allowing the union to negotiate the settlement of grievances within the stated limits, the parties would be assured that similar grievances were treated consistently

---

18 386 US at 207.

19 *Id.* at 190-191.

20 *Ibid.* (Emphasis added.)

21 "Final adjustment by a method agreed upon by the parties themselves is . . . the desirable method of settlement of grievance disputes arising over the application or interpretation of an existing collective bargaining agreement." LMRA §203 (d), 29 USC §173 (d).

22 386 US at 191.

"and major problem areas in the interpretation of the collective bargaining contract can be isolated and perhaps resolved . . . ," thereby enhancing the union's interest as bargaining agent.[23]

Applying these standards to the union's decision that the grievance lacked sufficient merit to justify arbitration,[24] the Court concluded that no breach of fair representation had occurred. For one thing, the Missouri tribunals had focused upon the wrong question by considering the merits of the grievance, *i.e.*, whether the grievant was fit to work, rather than whether the union had acted unfairly.

The governing substantive principle for the case was that *both* union and employer liability depended upon allegations and proof of breach of contract by the employer *and* breach of the duty of fair representation by the union in the handling of the grievance process.

From *Steele* to *Vaca,* the historical development of the doctrine of fair representation, including its substantive components, has depended primarily on court decisions. Only in later years has the Labor Board contributed any cases. To present a total picture, this Chapter traces the evolution of the doctrine through both the courts and the Board.

II. JURISDICTION TO ENFORCE THE DUTY

A. The Court Cases

Consideration of the question of the appropriate forum in which to enforce the duty of fair representation under the National Labor Relations Act has until recently reflected the origin of the duty under the Railway Labor Act. In *Steele,* the Supreme Court declared that "in the absence of any available administrative remedy, the right here asserted . . . is of judicial cognizance." [25] The "judicial cognizance" of which the Court spoke was the con-

---

23 *Ibid.*

24 The union had arranged for a medical examination at union expense, which resulted in an opinion adverse to the grievant.

25 323 US at 207.

current jurisdiction of state and federal courts.[26] As stated by one commentator:

> Since the employees are asserting a federal right arising under a law regulating commerce, the action may be brought in a federal district court without diversity of citizenship, and regardless of the amount in controversy. Alternatively, the employees may sue in a state court of general jurisdiction and take any federal question to the Supreme Court of the United States either by certiorari or in appropriate cases by appeal.[27]

As noted above, the Court in *Huffman* [28] analogized the duty of a bargaining agent under Section 9(a) of the NLRA to that of a representative under Section 2, Fourth, of the Railway Labor Act.[29] Subsequently, in *Syres v. Oil Workers Union*,[30] the Supreme Court reversed, *per curiam*, the Fifth Circuit's holding [31] that a class action brought by employees alleging discriminatory representation should be dismissed for lack of jurisdiction in the absence of diversity of citizenship.

Many actions alleging breach of the duty have been entertained in the courts without reference to the possibility of NLRB jurisdiction.[32] Occasionally the issue was raised, but since the Board did not hold until 1962 that it had jurisdiction to remedy a violation of the duty as an unfair labor practice, the courts tended to assume that enforcement of the duty was not within the Board's authority.[33]

B. The Labor Board Cases

1. Representation Cases. Once the court-imposed obligation of fair representation had been placed upon unions, the NLRB was

---

26 Bhd. of R.R. Trainmen v. Howard, note 4 *supra,* Graham v. Bhd. of Loco. Firemen, note 4 *supra,* and Tunstall v. Loco. Firemen, note 4 *supra,* originated in federal district courts; Steele v. Louisville & N.R.R., note 2 *supra,* in the Alabama Circuit Court.

27 Cox, *The Duty of Fair Representation,* 2 VILL. L. REV. 151, 170 (1957).

28 345 US 330, 31 LRRM 2548 (1953).

29 48 Stat 1187 (1934), 45 USC §152, Fourth.

30 350 US 892, 37 LRRM 2068 (1955).

31 223 F2d 739, 33 LRRM 2290 (CA 5, 1955).

32 *See, e.g.,* Trotter v. Amalgamated Ass'n of St. Ry. Employees, 309 F2d 584, 51 LRRM 2424 (CA 6, 1962), *cert. denied,* 372 US 943, 52 LRRM 2673 (1963); Hardcastle v. W. Greyhound Lines, 303 F2d 182, 50 LRRM 2239 (CA 9, 1962), *cert. denied,* 371 US 920, 51 LRRM 2616 (1962); Stewart v. Day & Zimmermann, Inc., 294 F2d 7, 48 LRRM 2989, (CA 5, 1961); Ostrofsky v. Steelworkers, 171 F Supp 782, 43 LRRM 2744 (D Md 1959), *affirmed per curiam,* 273 F2d 414, 45 LRRM 2486 (CA 4, 1960), *cert. denied,* 363 US 849 (1960).

33 *See, e.g.,* Berman v. Nat'l Maritime Union, 166 F Supp 327 (SD NY, 1958).

confronted with cases in which it was asked to revoke the certifications of unions which had failed to represent all employees fairly. In *Hughes Tool Co.*[34] a Board majority, following the reasoning of *Steele,* held that a union certified under Section 9 assumes

> the basic responsibility to act as a genuine representative of *all* the employees in the bargaining unit. . . . To hold otherwise, in view of the language of Section 9, would be to allow the exclusive position of the representative obtained through the authority of the Act to be used in a manner detrimental to the very employees the statute is designed to protect." [35]

The Board therefore concluded that "the duty of equal representation . . . is inherent in the exclusive representation status accorded by the statute." [36] In consequence, it ordered the certification of the union revoked unless the unfair conduct ceased immediately.[37]

Chairman Herzog and Member Peterson dissented in the *Hughes* case, maintaining that Congress, in the 1947 Taft-Hartley amendments, had only "sought to proscribe certain union behavior which it considered inimical to sound collective bargaining," and that hence the Board had no right "to prohibit other conduct which might appear . . . to interfere with employees' rights." [38]

The majority's assertion of the Board's right to revoke a certification of representation upon a failure of the union to represent all employees in the unit has prevailed.[39] The Board has also held that an otherwise valid contract executed by a union which does not represent all employees fairly will not serve as a bar to an intervening representation petition.[40]

2. Unfair Labor Practice Cases. Although the Board at an early date was called upon to decide in a representation proceeding the consequences of a union's failure to represent employees fairly,[41] it was not until late 1962, in *Miranda Fuel Co., Inc.,*[42] that the

[34] 104 NLRB 318, 32 LRRM 1010, 1232 (1953).
[35] *Id.* at 325.
[36] *Ibid.*
[37] A similar conclusion had been reached in a pre-Taft-Hartley case. *See* Larus & Bro. Co., 62 NLRB 1075, 16 LRRM 242 (1945).
[38] 104 NLRB at 331.
[39] Pittsburgh Plate Glass Co., 111 NLRB 1210, 35 LRRM 1658 (1955); A. O. Smith Corp., 119 NLRB 621, 41 LRRM 1153 (1957).
[40] Pioneer Bus Co., 140 NLRB 54, 51 LRRM 1546 (1962). *See* Chapter 8 *supra.*
[41] Larus & Bro. Co., note 21 *supra;* Hughes Tool Co., note 19 *supra.*
[42] 140 NLRB 181, 51 LRRM 1584 (1962).

Board, by a three-to-two majority, held that similar conduct was an unfair labor practice in violation of Sections 8(b)(1)(A) and 8(b)(2). *Miranda* involved a union's decision to reduce an employee's seniority for reasons which the NLRB found to be arbitrary, though unrelated to the employee's attachment to the union. The majority reasoned that the obligation imposed by Section 9 to represent *all* employees fairly and impartially must be read into the rights which were guaranteed employees by Section 7. According to the majority's reasoning, any default in the performance of the Section 9 duty amounts to an infringement of a Section 7 right, and is therefore a violation of Section 8(b)(1)(A). Moreover, the Board held that when an employer accedes to a union's request which violates the duty of fair representation, the employer thereby violates Section 8(a)(1) as well.[43]

In addition, the Board held that such conduct by the union violates Section 8(b)(2) and by the employer violates Section 8(a)(3).[44] The Board reasoned that any arbitrary union action which adversely affects an employee tends to encourage or discourage union membership, even if "the moving consideration does not involve the specific union membership or activities of the affected employee." [45]

Chairman McCulloch and Member Fanning dissented, arguing that while the Board did have authority, under Section 9, to insure compliance with the duty of fair representation "by withholding or revoking certifications in situations where the duty . . . has been egregiously flouted," [46] no such authority exists in a Section 10 proceeding to remedy unfair labor practices. Moreover, the dissenters noted, "the courts have furnished, and do furnish, a remedy," and "Congress has throughout the years indicated no dissatisfaction with this remedial scheme." [47]

The Second Circuit denied enforcement in *Miranda,* but without any majority position on the question of whether a violation of the duty of fair representation is an unfair labor practice. Judge

---

[43] *See* Chapter 5 *supra* for a general discussion of interference under §§8 (a) (1) and 8 (b) (1) (A).
[44] *See* Chapter 6 *supra* for a general discussion of discrimination under §§8 (a) (3) and 8 (b) (2).
[45] 140 NLRB at 188.
[46] 140 NLRB at 200.
[47] 140 NLRB at 202.

Medina said that the Board's jurisdiction is limited to cases where "the union or the employer . . . [has] committed some act the natural and foreseeable consequence of which is to be beneficial or detrimental to the union," [48] and that other forms of unfair or discriminatory action by a union are remediable only in the courts.[49] Judge Lumbard concurred in the result without reaching the question. Judge Friendly, in dissent, agreed with the Board majority with respect to the Section 8(b)(2) violation, but did so on the basis of an orthodox 8 (b)(2) and 8 (a)(3) analysis rather than in terms of the duty of fair representation.

Subsequently, in *Independent Metal Workers Union (Hughes Tool Co.)*,[50] the Board ruled that a union's failure to process an employee's grievance because of his race was an unfair labor practice under Sections 8 (b) (1) (A), 8 (b) (2), and 8 (b) (3). The Board majority there expressly asserted that the duty was enforced by the courts under the Railway Labor Act solely because, under that Act, there was no administrative enforcement machinery:

> When the Supreme Court enunciated the duty of fair representation in *Steel* and *Tunstall*, . . . which were Railway Labor Act cases, the Court emphasized in each case the lack of an administrative remedy as a reason for holding that Federal courts constitute a forum for relief from breaches of the duty. In this connection, it should be noted that provisions of the Railway Labor Act which are substantially identical to certain unfair labor practice provisions of the National Labor Relations Act are enforceable by the Federal courts, not an administrative agency. . . . After enactment of the Taft-Hartley Act . . . an administrative remedy became available in our view. . . .[51]

The majority added another string to its *Miranda* bow by relying not only upon Sections 8 (b) (1) (A) and 8 (b) (2) but also upon Section 8 (b) (3). The Board thus adopted the theory that a union's statutory duty to bargain in good faith is owed to the employees whom it represents as well as to the employer, and that a breach of the duty of fair representation constitutes bad-faith bargaining.

In subsequent decisions the Board has continued to apply the doctrine that breach of the duty of fair representation is an

---

[48] 326 F2d at 176.
[49] 326 F2d at 175-180.
[50] 147 NLRB 1573, 56 LRRM 1289 (1964). For discussion of the duty of fair representation in relation to a union's duty to bargain, *see* Chapter 11 *supra*.
[51] 147 NLRB at 1575.

unfair labor practice.[52] Two of these cases have been enforced by the Fifth Circuit. In *Local 12, United Rubber Workers v. NLRB*,[53] a unanimous panel of the court adopted the Board's view that a breach of the duty of fair representation violates Section 8 (b) (1) (A) of the Act. The court therefore found it unnecessary to pass on the contention that such conduct also violates Sections 8 (b) (2) and (3). Subsequently, in *NLRB v. Local 1367, Int'l Longshoremen's Ass'n (Galveston Maritime Ass'n)*,[54] a divided panel of the same court followed *Rubber Workers*. In the later case Judge Hutcheson dissented and District Judge Choate concurred, but reluctantly, indicating that he regarded the *Rubber Workers* case as a "dangerous precedent" and that judicial enforcement of the duty of fair representation was the "preferable procedure." The Supreme Court denied review of both the *Rubber Workers* and the *Longshoremen's* cases.[55] The Court thus retains its options regarding the Board's unfair-labor-practice jurisdiction over fair representation cases.

The Court of Appeals for the District of Columbia Circuit has also reviewed the Board's assertion that violation of a union's duty of fair representation constitutes an unfair labor practice under Section 8(b) of the Act. In *Truck Drivers, Local 568 (Red Ball Motor Freight, Inc.)*,[56] it affirmed a Board order finding that a union had violated Section 8(b)(1)(A) by announcing, during an election campaign, that it would adamantly refuse to dovetail seniority lists consisting of members of the two rival organizations involved. The case originated from a representation proceeding

---

52 Cargo Handlers, Inc., 159 NLRB 321, 62 LRRM 1228 (1966); UAW, Local 453 (Maremont Corp.), 149 NLRB 482, 57 LRRM 1298 (1964); Local 12, United Rubber Workers (Goodyear Tire & Rubber Co.), 150 NLRB 312, 57 LRRM 1535 (1964), *enforced*, 368 F2d 12, 63 LRRM 2395 (CA 5, 1966), *cert. denied*, 389 US 837, 66 LRRM 2306 (1967); Local 1367, Int'l Longshoremen's Ass'n (Galveston Maritime Ass'n, 148 NLRB 897, 57 LRRM 1083 (1964), *enforced*, 368 F2d 1010, 63 LRRM 2559 (CA 5, 1966), *cert. denied*, 389 US 837, 66 LRRM 2307 (1967); Red Ball Motor Freight, Inc., 157 NLRB 1237, 61 LRRM 1522 (1966), *enforced sub nom.*, Truck Drivers, Local 568 v. NLRB, 379 F2d 137, 65 LRRM 2309 (CA DC, 1967); Int'l Union of Electrical Workers, Local 485 (Automotive Plating Corp.), 170 NLRB No. 121, 67 LRRM 1609 (1968), *modified*, 183 NLRB No. 131, 74 LRRM 1396 (1970); Houston Maritime Ass'n, Inc., 168 NLRB No. 83, 66 LRRM 1337, *reversed for insufficiency of evidence*, 426 F2d 584, 74 LRRM 2200 (CA 5, 1970); Port Drum Co. (OCAW Local 4-23), 170 NLRB No. 51, 67 LRRM 1506 (1968), *modified*, 180 NLRB No. 90, 73 LRRM 1068 (1970).
53 Note 52 *supra*.
54 *Ibid*.
55 368 F2d 1010; *cert. denied*, 389 US 837, 66 LRRM 2306 (1967); 389 US 837, 66 LRRM 2307 (1967).
56 *See* note 52 *supra*.

which was necessitated by the consolidation of two bargaining units. In reviewing the ensuing unfair labor practice case initiated by the union which had lost the election, the court of appeals concluded (1) that breach of the duty of fair representation is an unfair labor practice, (2) that arbitrarily placing a minority group at the bottom of the seniority list would be a breach of that duty, (3) and that threatening to breach the duty during an organizational campaign for "the purely political motive of winning an election by a promise of preferential representation to the numerically larger number of voters" [57] "inevitably introduced improper influences into the election process tantamount to restraint or coercion contemplated by Section 7." [58] The court therefore affirmed the Board's finding that such threats violated Section 8(b)(1)(A).

C. Preemption—Courts and/or Board

The jurisdictional significance of the Board's position becomes apparent when the *Miranda-Hughes Tool* doctrine is considered in conjunction with the preemption doctrine. The latter doctrine, on the basis of the Supremacy Clause and a finding of legislative intent, declares that the NLRB has exclusive jurisdiction to remedy unfair labor practices, and that "[w]hen an activity is arguably subject to §7 or §8 of the Act, the States as well as the federal courts must defer to the exclusive competence of the National Labor Relations Board if the danger of state interference with national policy is to be averted." [59] Hence, the Board's assertion of jurisdiction, instead of resulting in the creation of an additional forum for the redress of the duty, might conceivably have led to a determination that the Board's jurisdiction is exclusive. A division of authority had developed on this point prior to the Supreme Court's decision in *Vaca v. Sipes.* The Court in *Vaca* assumed, without deciding,[60] that the Board had the power to remedy breaches of the duty of fair representation and upheld the

---

57 379 F2d at 143.
58 *Id.* at 145.
59 San Diego Bldg. Trades Council v. Garmon, 359 US 236, 245, 43 LRRM 2838 (1959). *See* Chapter 29 for a general discussion of the doctrine of federal preemption and its exceptions.
60 According to the D.C. Circuit's reading of *Vaca,* "[a] necessary premise of the Supreme Court majority's statement that Labor Board jurisdiction in such cases does not exclude court relief was its explicit assumption that unfair representation is an unfair labor practice." Truck Drivers Local 568 (Red Ball Motor Freight, Inc.), 379 F2d 137, 142, 65 LRRM 2309 (CA DC, 1967).
See Chapter 29 *infra* for additional discussion of the preemption aspects of *Vaca.*

jurisdiction of the courts to remedy such breaches.[61] This result had been foreshadowed in the Court's decision in *Humphrey v. Moore*.[62] In that case a state court had enjoined the dovetailing of the seniority rosters of two companies dealing with the same local union. An exchange of operating rights between the companies had resulted in the elimination of one of the firms from the local's geographical jurisdiction. Subsequently, the "dovetailing" of seniority had been directed by a joint employer-union committee authorized by a multi-employer contract to decide grievances arising under the agreement.[63] The plaintiffs claimed that their rights under the contract had thereby been violated and that the agreement of the joint committee was void because the union had breached its duty of fair representation when it made the agreement. The Supreme Court dealt with the preemption problem by treating the case as essentially a suit to enforce a collective bargaining agreement:

---

[61] For cases which had upheld the exclusivity of Board jurisdiction, *see, e.g.,* Mendicki v. UAW, 61 LRRM 2142 (D Kan, 1965); Stout v. Constr. & Gen. Laborers Dist. Council, 226 F Supp 673, 55 LRRM 2464 (1963); Knox v. UAW, 223 F Supp 1009, 54 LRRM 2661 (ED Mich, 1963), *affirmed,* 351 F2d 72, 60 LRRM 2253 (CA 6, 1965); Cosmark v. Struthers Wells Corp., 412 Pa 211, 194 A2d 325, 54 LRRM 2333 (1963), *cert. denied,* 376 US 962, 55 LRRM 279 (1964); Webster v. Midland Elec. Corp., 43 Ill App 2d 359, 193 NE 2d 212, 54 LRRM 2616 (1963), *cert. denied,* 377 US 964, 56 LRRM 1416 (1964). Operating Engineers v. Cassida, 376 SW2d 814, 55 LRRM 2383 (Tex Civ App, 1964), *writ of error denied,* 58 LRRM 2448 (Tex Sup Ct, 1964), *cert. denied,* 380 US 955, 58 LRRM 2720 (1965). *Cf.* Green v. Los Angeles Stereotypers, No. 58, 356 F2d 473, 61 LRRM 2419 (CA 9, 1966); Hiller v. Liquor Salesmen Local 2, 338 F2d 778, 57 LRRM 2629 (CA 2, 1965); Wheatley v. Teamsters Union, 15 Utah2d 80, 387 P2d 555, 55 LRRM 2133 (1963).

Some commentators seem to favor concurrent jurisdiction based upon a pragmatic concern with respect to the effectiveness of remedies. One scholar, after enumerating some of the procedural difficulties inherent in court action, observes that "experience has demonstrated a judicial tendency to defer to almost any arrangement to which union and management agree, in the interest of promoting collective bargaining at the expense of the rights of the employees." Blumrosen, *The Worker and Three Phases of Unionism: Administrative and Judicial Control of the Worker-Union Relationship,* 61 MICH. L. REV. 1435, 1517 (1963). Another authority stresses that "private suits are not an effective sanction unless financed by an organized group." (Cox, note 27 *supra* at 173.) Professor Sovern, who earlier had noted that "if the exclusive jurisdiction principle is now extended to suits to enforce the duty of fair representation, it would itself interfere with the policies and administration of federal labor legislation" [Sovern, *The National Labor Relations Act and Racial Discrimination,* 62 COLUM. L. REV. 563, 610 (1962)], has more recently in a post-*Miranda* sequel concluded that "the high cost of suing has effectively sapped the right to be represented fairly of much of its efficacy," Sovern, *Racial Discrimination and the National Labor Relations Act: the Brave New World of Miranda,* 16TH ANN. CONF. ON LAB. 3, 6 (1963). *See also* Feller, *Vaca v. Sipes One Year Later,* N.Y.U. 21ST ANN. CONF. ON LAB. 141 (1969).

[62] 375 US 335, 55 LRRM 2031 (1964).

[63] *See* Gen. Drivers, Local 89 v. Riss & Co., 372 US 517, 52 LRRM 2623 (1963).

Although there are differing views on whether a violation of the duty of fair representation is an unfair labor practice under the Labor Management Relations Act, it is not necessary for us to resolve that difference here. Even if it is, or arguably may be, an unfair labor practice, the complaint here alleged that Moore's discharge would violate the contract and was therefore within the cognizance of federal and state courts, . . . subject, of course, to the applicable federal law.[64]

The Court squarely faced the jurisdictional issue in *Vaca* and upheld the authority of the courts, both state and federal, to entertain fair representation suits. The majority opinion stressed that the duty of fair representation was judicially created and noted the possibly inadequate remedial powers of the Board in cases of this type. In keeping with prior rulings, the Court further held that the employee's suit would have been a Section 301 suit even if the employee had to prove an unfair labor practice by the union.[65] Thus, whatever the authority of the NLRB to enforce the duty of fair representation, it is not exclusive. The Court deemed it desirable that one tribunal—the court which hears such a case—have all the parties and issues before it. It concluded that the applicable law in such cases is federal law.

---

[64] 375 US at 344. *See* Dowd Box Co. v. Courtney, 368 US 502, 49 LRRM 2619 (1962) ; Smith v. Evening News Ass'n, 371 US 195, 51 LRRM 2646 (1962) ; Carey v. Westinghouse Electric Corp., 375 US 261, 55 LRRM 2042 (1964) ; *see also* discussion of the relation of §301 suits for enforcement of collective agreements to the doctrine of federal preemption, Chapter 29 *infra*, and to the enforcement of agreements under §301 generally in Chapter 17 *supra*. It should be noted that the employee's suit in *Vaca* was based on a collective agreement, and that the Supreme Court compared fair representation cases to §301 cases for purposes of demonstrating that the doctrine of federal preemption was inapplicable:

"For the fact is that the question of whether a union has breached its duty of fair representation will in many cases be a critical issue in a suit under L.M.R.A. §301 charging an employer with a breach of contract." 386 US at 183.

But query: Will concurrent jurisdiction between Board and courts also exist where the employee alleges a breach of fair representation outside the context of an executed collective bargaining agreement? The Court in *Vaca* did not limit its holding to §301 situations; *but see* Local 100, United Ass'n v. Borden, 373 US 690, 53 LRRM 2322 (1963) ; Operating Engineers v. Cassida, 376 SW2d 814, 55 LRRM 2383 (Tex Civ App, 1964) , *writ of error denied*, 58 LRRM 2448 (Tex Sup Ct, 1964) , *cert. denied*, 380 US 955, 58 LRRM 2720 (1965) ; *see* Lewis, *Fair Representation in Grievance Administration: Vaca v. Sipes,* SUPREME CT. REV. 81, 99 (1967) :

"[E]ven if all unfair representation claims are within the jurisdiction of the courts, cases like *Borden* can be recognized by inquiring whether conduct alleged to reflect unfair representation constitutes an arguable unfair labor practice even if the judicially created duty of fair representation is ignored. In the absence of a substantial §301 claim, such cases should remain within the exclusive jurisdiction of the Board."

[65] *See* note 64 *supra*.

Another aspect of the preemption problem is posed by the situation in which conduct violative of the duty of fair representation may also be violative of some other legal duty enforceable by the courts. In those situations courts would have pendant jurisdiction. For example, federal courts have jurisdiction under Title I of the Labor-Management Reporting and Disclosure Act [66] to remedy violations of the "bill of rights of members of labor organizations," and in a suit claiming violation of such rights arising in connection with a breach of the duty of fair representation it seems clear that the court would also have jurisdiction to hear the claim of unfair representation.[67]

The enactment of Title VII of the Civil Rights Act,[68] proscribing discriminatory employment practices by unions and employers on the basis of race, religion, national origin, and sex, establishes still another forum for relief from conduct that might also constitute a breach of the duty of fair representation. Title VII authorizes suits to be brought in the federal district courts after exhaustion of the administrative conciliation procedures of the Equal Employment Opportunities Commission. Although dual regulation and overlapping jurisdiction may result, Title VII does not appear to preempt Labor Board and court jurisdiction over the duty of fair representation.[69]

---

[66] 73 Stat 522 (1959), 29 USC §§411-415.

[67] Thus, a suit would lie under Section 101 (a) (1) of the LMRDA on a claim that members of a labor organization had been deprived of their equal rights under the union's constitution to vote on the ratification of a collective bargaining agreement and also that negotiation and enforcement of particular terms of the agreement violate the duty of fair representation.

[68] 78 Stat 253 (1964), 42 USC §§2000 (e) 1-15 (1964). See Gould, *Seniority and the Black Worker: Reflections on Quarles and its Implications*, 47 TEX L. REV. 1039 (1969); Jones, *Racial Discrimination in Employment and in Labor Unions*, LABOR LAW DEVELOPMENTS 1970 (Sw. Legal Foundation 16th Ann. Lab. Law Inst.) 179 (1970).

[69] This view is supported by the legislative history of the statute. A Justice Department memorandum presented to the Senate by Senator Joseph S. Clark during that body's discussion of Title VII stated in part:

"Nothing in title VII or anywhere else in this bill affects rights and obligations under the NLRA and the Railway Labor Act. The procedures set up in title VII are the exclusive means of relief against those practices of discrimination which are forbidden as unlawful employment practices by sections 704 and 705. Of course, title VII is not intended to and does not deny to any individual, rights and remedies which he may pursue under other Federal and State statutes. If a given action should violate both title VII and the National Labor Relations Act, the National Labor Relations Board would not be deprived of jurisdiction. . . . At any rate, title VII would have no effect on the duties of any employer or labor organization under the NLRA or under the Railway Labor Act, and these duties would continue to be enforced as they are now. . . ." 110 CONG. REC. 7207 (1964).

III. NATURE OF THE DUTY

Whatever forum is utilized to enforce the duty of fair representation, the problem of defining the scope and nature of the duty is essentially the same.

In the *Steele* case, the Court said that the union's duty is to "exercise fairly the power conferred upon it, in behalf of all those for whom it acts, without hostile discrimination against them." [70] The Court decreed that the union's power had to be exercised "fairly, impartially, and in good faith" [71] and that "discriminations based on race alone are obviously irrelevant and invidious." [72]

The Court imposed the same duty upon a bargaining agent selected under the NLRA, observing in *The Wallace Corp. v. NLRB* [73] that

[t]he duties of a bargaining agent selected under terms of the Act extend beyond the mere representation of the interests of its own group members. By its selection as bargaining representative, it has become the agent of all the employees, charged with the responsibility of representing their interests fairly and impartially. [74]

Senator Clark added that Title VII "would not affect the present operation of any part of the National Labor Relations Act or rights under existing labor laws." 110 CONG. REC. 7207 (1964).

See also 110 CONG. REC. 13652 (1964), reporting the Senate's rejection of Senator Tower's proposal to make Title VII "the exclusive means whereby any department, agency, or instrumentality in the executive branch of the Government, or any independent agency of the United States, may grant or seek relief from, or pursue any remedy with respect to, any employment practice of any employer, employment agency, labor organization, or joint labor-management committee covered by this title, if such employment practice may be the subject of a charge or complaint filed under this title." *Cf.* Civil Rights Act of 1964, §1103.

The National Labor Relations Board has already concluded in Local 12, United Rubber Workers, 150 NLRB 312, 57 LRRM 1535 (1964), that its "powers and duties are in no way limited by Title VII." 150 NLRB at 321.

See generally, Fuchs and Ellis, *Title VII: Relationship and Effect on the National Labor Relations Board,* 7 B. C. IND. & COM. L. REV. 575 (1966). *See also* Sherman, *Union's Duty of Fair Representation and the Civil Rights Act of 1964,* 49 MINN. L. REV. 771 (1965). It is there concluded that the NLRB's asserted jurisdiction to enforce the duty of fair representation should yield to the extent of overlap with the Civil Rights Act. 49 MINN. L. REV. at 815-820.

70 323 US at 203.

71 *Id.* at 204.

72 *Id.* at 203.

73 323 US 248, 15 LRRM 697 (1944).

74 323 US at 255; *see also* Hughes Tool Company v. NLRB, 147 F2d 69, 15 LRRM 852 (CA 5, 1945).

The Board in *Miranda* [75] adopted the same standard that had been established judicially in *Steele* and *Wallace*. The Board stated that in its opinion "Section 7 thus gives employees the right to be free from unfair or irrelevant or invidious treatment by their exclusive bargaining agent in matters affecting their employment." [76]

Similar language is to be found in *Vaca v. Sipes,* where the Court noted that a "breach of the statutory duty occurs . . . when a union's conduct toward a member of the collective bargaining unit is arbitrary, discriminatory, or in bad faith." [77] At the same time the decision recognized a necessary area of union discretion, subject, of course, to the good-faith requirement, in the processing of employee grievances. The Court stated that "[t]hough we accept the proposition that a union may not arbitrarily ignore a meritorious grievance or process it in perfunctory fashion, we do not agree that the individual employee has an absolute right to have his grievance taken to arbitration. . . ." [78]

Thus the duty imposed by the Board and the courts leaves a significant area of discretion to be exercised by the union. Even in the *Steele* case the Court recognized that the duty of fair representation "does not mean that the statutory representative of a craft is barred from making contracts which may have unfavorable effects on some of the members of the craft represented." [79] The Court observed:

---

[75] 140 NLRB 181, 51 LRRM 1584 (1962). *See* Feller, note 61 *supra* at 167, for a discussion of the Court's use of the term "arbitrary" to describe the union's duty. (". . . [T]he word 'arbitrary' can be as broad as the courts want to make it. My guess is that in the years to come the courts will make 'arbitrary' quite broad indeed, at least in discharge cases which the union refuses to arbitrate." *Ibid.*)

[76] 140 NLRB at 185; *see also* Hughes Tool Company, 104 NLRB 318, 32 LRRM 1010, 1232 (1953), and cases cited in note 52 *supra*.

[77] 386 US at 207.

[78] *Id.* at 191. The Court observed that "[i]f the individual employee could compel arbitration of his grievance regardless of its merit, the settlement machinery provided by the contract would be substantially undermined, . . . [and a] significantly greater number of grievances would proceed to arbitration. This would greatly increase the cost of the grievance machinery and could so overburden the arbitration process as to prevent it from functioning successfully." *Id.* at 191-192.

In *Figueroa v. Trabajadores Packinghouse,* 425 F2d 281, 74 LRRM 2028, 2032 (CA 1, 1970), it was held that an "arbitrary and perfunctory handling by a union of an apparently meritorious grievance is not acceptable under the standard of fair representation."

[79] 323 US at 203.

Variations in the terms of the contract based on differences relevant to the authorized purposes of the contract in conditions to which they are to be applied, such as differences in seniority, the type of work performed, or the competence and skill with which it is performed, are within the scope of the bargaining representation of a craft, all of whose members are not identical in their interest or merit.[80]

The latitude available to the union in the exercise of its statutory duty as exclusive bargaining representative was set forth by the Court in the following guidelines in *Ford Motor Co. v. Huffman:*

Any authority to negotiate derives its principal strength from a delegation to the negotiators of a discretion to make such concessions and accept such advantages as, in the light of all relevant considerations, they believe will best serve the interests of the parties represented. A major responsibility of negotiators is to weigh the relative advantages and disadvantages of differing proposals. . . . Inevitably differences arise in the manner and degree to which the terms of any negotiated agreement affect individual employees and classes of employees. The mere existence of such differences does not make them invalid. The complete satisfaction of all who are represented is hardly to be expected. A wide range of reasonableness must be allowed a statutory bargaining representative in serving the unit it represents, subject always to complete good faith and honesty of purpose in the exercise of its discretion.[81]

The key problem in every fair-representation case is to determine whether the specific factual situation shows "hostile discrimination" based on "irrelevant and invidious" considerations,[82] or falls within the "wide range of reasonableness" [83] granted bargaining agents.

Under the decisions, it is now quite clear that the duty of fair representation applies to all phases of collective bargaining. The duty is applicable both to the negotiation of collective agreements and to the processing of grievances arising under such agreements. In one of the cases arising under the RLA, the Supreme Court spelled out the continuous bargaining process involved in representation by a union:

---

80 *Ibid.*
81 345 US 330, 337-338, 31 LRRM 2548 (1953).
82 Steele v. Louisville & N.R.R., 323 US 192, 203, 15 LRRM 708 (1944).
83 Ford Motor Co. v. Huffman, 345 US 330, 338, 31 LRRM 2548 (1953).

The bargaining representative's duty not to draw "irrelevant and invidious" distinctions among those it represents does not come to an abrupt end . . . with the making of an agreement between union and employer. Collective bargaining is a continuing process. Among other things, it involves day to day adjustments in the contract and other working rules, resolution of new problems not covered by existing agreements, and the protection of employee rights already secured by the contract. The bargaining representative can no more unfairly discriminate in carrying out these functions than it can in negotiating a collective agreement.[84]

In the context of an early Railway Labor Act case, the Supreme Court indicated that the latitude of the union for action with respect to contract administration and processing of grievances pursuant to a contract is not as broad as its authority for negotiation of a labor agreement.[85] However, subsequent decisions of both the Board and the courts have failed to expressly note this distinction. Nor was such a distinction mentioned in *Vaca v. Sipes,* which involved a claim of improper union failure to process a grievance to arbitration.[86] The cases reviewed herein generally uphold similar broad union power in both the administration and the negotiation of contracts. They also indicate that a similar duty of fair representation rests upon the union in both situations. However, a *caveat* should be noted: While the duty may be similar, the scope of the union's discretion will be limited by the nature of the grievance. Grievances involving individual job rights, as opposed to the collective interest involved in contract negotiations and in certain grievances concerning contract interpretation, provide fewer options for the bargaining representative in reaching settlements with the employer.

Although the authority of unions to negotiate and subsequently to enforce contracts is broad, the duty of fair representation, which has evolved in case law since 1944, establishes definite limitations upon that authority.

---

[84] Conley v. Gibson, 355 US 41, 46, 41 LRRM 2089 (1957).

[85] Elgin, Joliet & Eastern Ry. Co. v. Burley, 325 US 711, 16 LRRM 749 (1945). The Court held that statutory status as bargaining agent under the Railway Labor Act, without further authorization from the employee, did not confer upon the union the authority to settle an employee's back-pay grievance before the National Railroad Adjustment Board.

[86] The Court's failure to follow *Burley,* note 85 *supra,* without however citing it, may indicate that *Burley* will be confined to its facts, which involved formal representation of claimants before the NRAB. The Court in *Vaca* declared:
"[W]e do not agree that the individual employee has an absolute right to have his grievance taken to arbitration regardless of the provisions of the applicable collective bargaining agreement." 386 US at 191.

Certainly racial discrimination is a violation of the union's duty.[87] And although no decided cases have involved the issue, without question discrimination because of an employee's religion or national origin, being based on irrelevant considerations, would constitute a similar breach of the duty. It is also clear that a failure to represent fairly occurs where discrimination is motivated by internal union political differences.[88]

Other forms of discrimination present more difficult problems. For example, is discrimination based on age a breach of the duty?[89] Is there a failure to represent fairly when discrimination against an individual employee results from an unpopular political position which he has taken, the effect of which has been to disrupt plant harmony? Or, is there a violation of the duty when a union negligently, but not intentionally, fails to file or appeal a grievance on time? These are but a few of the types of situations that must eventually be resolved by the Board and the courts.

The courts have generally sustained union decisions and actions taken in good faith and without malice. Thus, it was held not to be a violation of the duty (1) to give seniority credit for military service to veterans even though they did not previously work for the employer,[90] (2) to initiate pension plans and other programs of forced retirement even though job rights of older employees built up through years of service were eliminated,[91] (3) to grant union officials seniority preference over longer-service employees

---

[87] Steele v. Louisville & N.R.R., 323 US 192, 15 LRRM 708 (1944); Hughes Tool Company, 104 NLRB 318, 32 LRRM 1010, 1232 (1953); Local 1367, Int'l Longshoremen's Association, 148 NLRB 897, 57 LRRM 1083 (1964); Local 12 United Rubber Workers, 150 NLRB 312, 57 LRRM 1535 (1964); UAW (Maremont Corporation), 149 NLRB 482, 57 LRRM 1298 (1964); Cargo Handlers, Inc., 159 NLRB 321, 62 LRRM 1228 (1966). Houston Maritime Ass'n, Inc., 168 NLRB No. 83, 66 LRRM 1337, *reversed for insufficiency of evidence*, 426 F2d 584, 74 LRRM 2200 (CA 5, 1970). *See* Gould, *Black Power in the Unions: The Impact Upon Collective Bargaining Relationships*, 79 YALE L. J. 46 (1969). *Cf.* Tanner Motor Livery Ltd., 148 NLRB 1402, 57 LRRM 1170 (1964), *remanded*, 349 F2d 1, 59 LRRM 2784 (CA 9, 1965), *affirmed in Supplemental Decision*, 166 NLRB No. 35, 65 LRRM 1502 (1967); *see* Chapter 6, note 53, *supra*.
[88] Int'l Union of Electrical Workers (Automotive Plating Corp.), 170 NLRB No. 121, 67 LRRM 1609 (1968), modified, 183 NLRB No. 131, 74 LRRM 1396 (1970), where the Board found that the real reason for a union's refusal to process an employee's grievance was his outspoken opposition at a union meeting to a policy of the union business manager. *See* notes 105-106 *infra*.
[89] *See* Age Discrimination in Employment Act of 1967, 29 USC 621-634.
[90] Ford Motor Co. v. Huffman, 345 US 330, 31 LRRM 2548 (1953).
[91] Goodin v. Clinchfield R.R., 229 F2d 578, 37 LRRM 2515 (CA 6, 1956), *cert. denied*, 351 US 953, 38 LRRM 2160 (1956).

in layoff situations,[92] or (4) to dovetail seniority lists of two merging companies.[93]

In similar fashion, the Board since its *Miranda* [94] decision has sustained the broad range of authority granted to a union acting as the exclusive representative of all employees in the unit. Thus, neither "the Union's classification of employees on the basis of permanent residence and the Union's insistence on differences in compensation based on distance from home to work" nor the attempt to "police and enforce" these contractual provisions was held to be "arbitrary or invidious." [95]

The Board also concluded that where the purpose of certain contractual provisions was to attempt to give "work of the trade to those who presumably needed it, rather than to those who held full-time positions elsewhere," the classification of an employee as "not at trade" was not "arbitrary and invidious." Instead, such action was held to be based upon "a reasonable classification of employees." [96]

In another case the Board held that a union which incorporates into a collective bargaining agreement a provision which "seeks to restrict the transfer of employees from one category to another" is presumptively within the "wide range of reasonableness" allowed to a statutory bargaining representative. Such conduct by the union was deemed as not "inconsistent with its duty fairly to represent all employees in the bargaining unit." [97]

In still another instance the Board absolved a union of a claimed violation of its duty when the union enforced a bylaw which by practice between the union and the employer had become a rule of employment. Since the bylaw was "justified by non-discriminatory business purposes [and] by non-discriminatory attempts to benefit all the represented employees," the Board determined that its enforcement fell within the area of permissible union action.[98]

---

[92] Aeronautical Lodge 727 v. Campbell, 337 US 521, 24 LRRM 2173 (1949).
[93] Humphrey v. Moore, 375 US 335, 55 LRRM 2031 1964).
[94] 140 NLRB 181, 51 LRRM 1584 (1962).
[95] Millwrights' Local 1102, United Bhd. of Carpenters & Joiners of America, AFL-CIO (Planet Corporation), 144 NLRB 798, 801, 54 LRRM 1136 (1963). *Cf.* Bricklayers Local 28 (Plaza Builders, Inc.), 134 NLRB 751, 49 LRRM 1222 (1961).
[96] N.Y. Typographical Union Local 6, ITU (The New York Times Company), 144 NLRB 1555, 1558, 54 LRRM 1281 (1963). *Cf.* IBEW Local 367 (Easton Branch, NECA), 134 NLRB 132, 49 LRRM 1127 (1961).
[97] Armored Car Chauffeurs Local 820, IBT (U.S. Trucking Co.), 145 NLRB 225, 229, 54 LRRM 1356 (1963).
[98] Houston Typographical Local 87, ITU (Houston Chronicle Publishing Co.), 145 NLRB 1657, 1663 55 LRRM 1190 (1964).

The content of the duty of fair representation lies within these very general guidelines. The cases construe the statute as granting to the union wide authority to act in the collective bargaining process. This very fact makes it difficult to set forth any easily applicable standard by which to determine when latitude given the union has been exceeded. Whether the duty of fair representation has been breached depends upon analysis of each of a large variety of possible fact situations.[99]

IV. REMEDIES

A. The Board

While concern over the inadequacy of judicial remedies may have been responsible in part for the Board's assertion of jurisdiction,[100] the Board in its first judicial test was met with the Second Circuit's conclusion that "the machinery of the Board and the remedies applied in the enforcement of findings of unfair labor practices . . . are not suited to the task of deciding general questions of private wrongs, unrelated to union activities, suffered by employees as a result of tortious conduct by either employers or labor unions." [101] The adequacy of the remedies which can be provided by the Board and the courts, respectively, may thus be a factor in the ultimate determination of the issue of jurisdiction.

1. Unfair Labor Practice Proceedings. The Board has exercised its remedial powers to order unions to cease and desist from breaches of the duty of fair representation.[102] In appropriate cases the Board has also ordered reinstatement of employees with full seniority and back pay.[103] When, however, the violation involves failure to process a grievance, the Board apparently prefers to order that the grievance be processed fairly rather than to adjudi-

---

99 *E.g.*, Trotter v. St. Elec. Ry. and Motor Coach Employees of America, 309 F2d 584, 51 LRRM 2424 (CA 6, 1962) , *cert. denied,* 372 US 943, 52 LRRM 2673 (1963) .
100 "Negroes have gone to court to redress unfair representation on an average of less than once a year since *Steele* was decided." Sovern, *Racial Discrimination and the National Labor Relations Act: the Brave New World of Miranda,* Proceedings of New York University Sixteenth Annual Conference on Labor 3, 5 (1963) .
101 NLRB v. Miranda Fuel Co., 326 F2d 172, 180, 54 LRRM 2715 (CA 2, 1963) .
102 Cargo Handlers, Inc., 159 NLRB 321, 62 LRRM 1228 (1966) ; Local 12, United Rubber Workers (Business League of Gadsden) , 150 NLRB 312, 57 LRRM 1535 (1964) ; Local 1367, Int'l Longshoremen's Ass'n (Galveston Maritime Ass'n) , 148 NLRB 897, 57 LRRM 1085 (1964) ; Independent Metal Workers Union (Hughes Tool Co.) 147 NLRB 1573, 56 LRRM 1289 (1964) .
103 Miranda Fuel Co., 140 NLRB 181, 51 LRRM 1584 (1962) . *See* note 42 *supra.*

cate the claim itself. For example, in *Local 12, United Rubber Workers*,[104] the Board ordered the union to process in good faith grievances concerning back pay and segregation of employee dining, toilet, and recreational facilities. And in *International Union of Electrical Workers, Local 485 (Automotive Plating Corp.)*,[105] the Board, finding a Section 8(b)(1)(A) violation by virtue of an arbitrary union refusal to press an employee's grievance, ordered the union to process the grievance and, if necessary, to take it to arbitration. In an effort to comply with the Board's order, the union requested the employer to arbitrate, but the employer refused. Since the Board had no jurisdiction over the employer, the Board, by supplemental order, required the union to pay back pay from the date of the initial refusal to handle the grievance "until such time as union fulfills its duty of fair representation, or discharged employee obtains substantially equivalent employment, whichever is sooner." [106]

2. Representation Proceedings. The Board has declared that it will not permit its contract-bar rules to be utilized to shield contracts containing provisions violative of the duty of fair representation from the challenge of otherwise-appropriate election petitions.[107] In *Pioneer Bus Co.* it held that

> where the bargaining representative of employees in an appropriate unit executes separate contracts, or even a single contract, discriminating between Negro and white employees on racial lines, the Board will not deem such contracts as a bar to an election.[108]

In *Hughes Tool Co.*[109] the Board went a step further and re-

---

[104] 150 NLRB at 322.
[105] 170 NLRB No. 121, 67 LRRM 1609 (1968), *modified,* 183 NLRB No. 131, 74 LRRM 1396 (1970), note 88 *supra*. The Board contended, on the authority of *NLRB v. C & C Plywood Corp.*, 385 US 421, 64 LRRM 2065 (1967), that it had the authority to construe the provisions of the collective agreement, but declined to do so, deferring, at least initially, to the arbitration process.
[106] The supplemental opinion indicated that a §301 action by the union would fulfill that duty. Chairman McCulloch dissented, asserting that *Vaca v. Sipes* precluded the Board from assessing against the union all of the damages arising from the discharge, especially damages flowing from a breach of contract by the employer. (*See infra* at notes 136-139.) He suggested, however, that the Board could order the union to pay reasonable legal fees for a §301 action by the employee against the employer. These remedial difficulties, attributable to limitations on the Board's jurisdiction, were foreseen and commented upon in Morris, *Procedural Reform in Labor Law—A Preliminary Paper*, 35 J. AIR L. & COM. 537, 558, n. 143 (1969). *See also* Port Drum Co. (OCAW Local 4-23), 170 NLRB No. 51, 67 LRRM 1506 (1968), *modified,* 180 NLRB No. 90, 73 LRRM 1068 (1970), where union was ordered to make employee's estate whole for loss of earnings when union failed to take effective steps to comply with Board's order requiring it to arbitrate employee's grievance.
[107] Pioneer Bus Co., 140 NLRB 54, 55, 51 LRRM 1546 (1962).
[108] *Id.* at 55. *See* Chapter 8 *supra* at note 97.
[109] 147 NLRB 1573, 56 LRRM 1289 (1964).

voked an offending union's certification, reasoning that, having issued the certification, it had the power to police its use and to revoke it in a proper case.[110] This remedy, however, would be effective only in those cases where a certification not only had been issued but also was of some importance to the union. "[E]ven when past violation of the duty of fair representation has made rescission of certification appropriate, the Board has usually not prevented the offending union from immediately participating in a new representation election. . . ." [111]

Although it has been suggested that "the Board should not certify a union likely to represent unfairly," [112] it is doubtful that the Board will adopt this approach in the light of its decision in *Alto Plastics:* [113]

> If the Petitioner herein qualifies as a "Labor organization," then clearly the Board may not refuse to process its petition. For it must be remembered that, initially, the Board merely provides the machinery whereby the desires of the employees may be ascertained, and the employees may select a "good" labor organization, a "bad" labor organization, or no labor organization, it being pre-supposed that employees will intelligently exercise their right to select their bargaining representative.[114]

B. The Courts

The courts will continue to provide a forum for remedying unfair-representation cases.[115]

1. Damages. In enforcing the duty of fair representation, the courts have accorded aggrieved parties the traditional remedies

---

110 Pioneer Bus Co., 140 NLRB 54, 51 LRRM 1546 (1962) (dictum); Alto Plastics Mfg. Corp., 136 NLRB 850, 49 LRRM 1867 (1962); A. O. Smith Corp., 119 NLRB 621, 41 LRRM 1153 (1957); Plant City Welding & Tank Co., 118 NLRB 280, 40 LRRM 1168 (1957); Pittsburgh Plate Glass Co., 111 NLRB 1210, 35 LRRM 1658 (1955); Hughes Tool Co., 104 NLRB 318, 32 LRRM 1010, 1232 (1953); Coleman Co., 101 NLRB 120, 31 LRRM 1020 (1952); Larus & Bro. Co., 62 NLRB 1075, 16 LRRM 242 (1945).

111 Sovern, *supra* note 61, at 596, citing Pittsburgh Plate Glass Co., 111 NLRB 1210, 35 LRRM 1658 (1955); Hughes Tool Co., 104 NLRB 318, 32 LRRM 1010, 1232 (1953); Larus & Bro. Co., 62 NLRB 1075, 16 LRRM 242 (1945).

112 Sovern, note 61 at 597-98 *supra.* "Given the considerable power of unions to represent Negroes unfairly without realistic fear of detection, the Board should not certify unions likely to transgress in this way." *Id.* at 599.

113 136 NLRB 850, 49 LRRM 1867 (1962).

114 Id. at 851.

115 Vaca v. Sipes, 386 US 171, 64 LRRM 2369 (1967). Inasmuch as the focus of this book is on NLRB jurisdiction, this section will not treat exhaustively the volume of fair representation litigation in the state and federal courts. Some representative cases and problems will, however, be noted.

of injunctions and/or compensatory damages.[116] Damages in the nature of back pay have been awarded.[117] Such damages are measured by the difference between what the plaintiff actually earned, or with the exercise of due diligence would have earned, and what he would have earned but for the breach.[118] In *Thompson v. Bhd. of Sleeping Car Porters*,[119] the Fourth Circuit affirmed a judgment awarding an employee damages calculated on the basis of future as well as past earnings where the failure of the union to represent the employee fairly with respect to his seniority resulted in the "phase-out" of his job. The court noted that the employer had not been joined in the suit and that under the applicable collective bargaining agreement employees were not required to retire until reaching the age of 70. Under these circumstances the court concluded that the award of future damages was the only effective remedy.

2. Injunctive and Other Equitable Remedies. The anti-injunction provisions of the Norris-LaGuardia Act [120] have not precluded the issuance of judicial decrees enjoining unfair representation.[121] In cases involving contract clauses which on their face are violative of the duty, both the union and the employer have been joined in a suit for an injunction against the enforcement of the discriminatory provisions.[122]

Alleged violations of the duty of fair representation in the administration of the contract raise more difficult questions as to remedy than do the cases involving discriminatory contract clauses.

---

116 "[T]he statute contemplates resort of the usual judicial remedies of injunction and award of damages when appropriate. . . ." 323 US at 207; Tunstall v. Bhd. of Loco. Firemen, 323 US 210, 15 LRRM 715 (1944); Syres v. Oil Workers Local 23, 223 F2d 739, 36 LRRM 2290 (CA 5, 1955), *reversed per curiam*, 350 US 892, 37 LRRM 2068 (1955); *Cf.* Sipes v. Vaca, 397 SW2d 658, 61 LRRM 2054 (Mo Sup Ct, 1965), *reversed*, 386 US 171, 64 LRRM 2369 (1967).

117 Cent. of Ga. Ry. v. Jones, 229 F2d 648, 37 LRRM 2435 (CA 5, 1956), *cert. denied*, 352 US 848, 38 LRRM 2716 (1956).

118 Thompson v. Bhd. of Sleeping Car Porters, 367 F2d 489, 63 LRRM 2111 (CA 4, 1966), *cert. denied*, 386 US 960, 64 LRRM 2574 (1967).

119 *Ibid.*

120 29 USC §§101-115 (1964).

121 Steele v. Louisville & N.R.R., 323 US 192, 15 LRRM 708 (1944); Tunstall v. Bhd. of Loco. Firemen, 323 US 210, 15 LRRM 715 (1944); Bhd. of R.R. Trainmen v. Howard, 343 US 768, 30 LRRM 2258 (1952); Syres v. Oil Workers Union, 350 US 892, 37 LRRM 2068 (1955); Cent. of Ga. Ry. v. Jones, note 117 *supra*.

122 Bhd. of R.R. Trainmen v. Howard, 343 US 768, 30 LRRM 2258 (1952); Steele v. Louisville & N.R.R., 323 US 192, 15 LRRM 708 (1944); Cent. of Ga. Ry. v. Jones, note 117 *supra*.

Frequently the employer has agreed with the union that grievances are to be processed by the union through an established
procedure subject to specific time limitations. Thus, from the
employer's viewpoint, the failure of the union to resort to the
grievance procedure, regardless of motivation, is urged as a reason
for excusing the employer. In addition, the contract usually provides that unresolved disputes concerning application of the
contract may be submitted to arbitration and the arbitrator's
decision shall be final and binding upon the parties. Hence, in
the typical case in which an employee has sued the union and his
employer, claiming a wrongful refusal on the part of the union
to process his grievance as well as a breach of contract by the employer, the questions of appropriate remedy and against whom
the remedy should be applied have been the subject of much
judicial as well as scholarly concern.[123]

Several positions have been advanced. One position is that if
the employer has not encouraged or participated in the union's
breach of duty the employer should not be held liable in a suit
by an individual employee for breach of contract. Under this
theory the employee is limited to "pursuing any remedy at law
which might be available for breach of fiduciary duty owing by
the union." [124]

Another view was adopted by the Maryland Court of Appeals
in *Jenkins v. Wm. Schluderberg-T. J. Kurdle Co.*[125] Even though
the plaintiff had sued only the employer, the court concluded that

> as a general rule grievance procedures provided by a collective
> bargaining agreement should be a bar to suits by individuals against
> the Employer based upon alleged violation of the agreement, but
> . . . such suits are not barred if the Union acted unfairly towards

---

123 *See* bibliographical note 1 *supra.* This problem closely parallels, and will in
large part ultimately depend upon, resolution of the separate and no less perplexing
issue of the right of the individual employees to enforce collective bargaining agreements *in the absence* of a claimed breach of duty by the union. *See* Republic Steel
Corp. v. Maddox, 379 US 650, 58 LRRM 2193 (1965), note 140 *infra.*
124 Matter of Soto, 180 NYS2d 397 (1958), 165 NE 2d 855 (1960). Prof. Archibald
Cox describes this theory as follows:
"Unless a contrary intention is manifest, the employer's obligations under a collective
bargaining agreement which contains a grievance procedure controlled by the union
shall be deemed to run solely to the union as the bargaining representative, to be
administered by the union in accordance with its fiduciary duties to employees in the
bargaining unit. The representative can enforce the claim. It can make reasonable,
binding compromises. It is liable for breaches of trust in a suit by the employee bene-
ficiaries." Cox, *Rights Under a Labor Agreement,* 69 HARV. L. REV. 600, 619 (1956).
125 217 Md 556, 144 A2d 88, 30 LA 875 (1958).

the employee in refusing to press the employee's claim through to, and including, arbitration under the collective bargaining agreement.[126]

Under this view, if a union has violated the duty by refusing to process an employee's grievance, the employee, at his election, seemingly could bring his action against either the union or the employer or both.

A third position, advanced by a law professor [127] and adopted by the New Jersey Supreme Court in *Donnelly v. United Fruit Co.*,[128] would permit an employee to compel arbitration notwithstanding the union's refusal to process the grievance. In *Donnelly*, a discharged employee sued his union and his employer for damages resulting from loss of employment and improper failure to consider his grievance. Although the court affirmed summary judgment for both defendants, it did so in an elaborate opinion in which it spelled out its view of individual rights under collective agreements and their grievance and arbitration procedures. The court concluded that "an individual employee has a statutorily-vested right [129] to present his grievance to, and to have it determined by, his employer when the union declines to process it in his behalf." [130]

---

[126] 217 Md at 574-575, 144 A2d at 99.

[127] Summers, *Individual Rights in Collective Agreements and Arbitration*, 37 N.Y.U. L. REV. 362 (1962).

[128] 40 NJ 61, 190 A2d 825, 53 LRRM 2271 (1963). *See also* Clark v. Hein-Werner Corp., 8 Wis2d 264, 99 NW2d 132, 43 LRRM 2733 (1959), *rehearing denied*, 100 NW2d 317, 45 LRRM 2659 (1960), *cert. denied*, 362 US 962, 45 LRRM 2137 and 46 LRRM 2033 (1960).

[129] The Court was relying upon the proviso to §9(a) of the NLRA:
"That any individual employee or a group of employees shall have the right at any time to present grievances to their employer and to have such grievances adjusted, without the intervention of the bargaining representative, as long as the adjustment is not inconsistent with the terms of a collective-bargaining contract or agreement then in effect: *Provided further*, That the bargaining representative has been given opportunity to be present at such adjustment."

[130] 190 A2d at 839. Further, the court set forth, in elaborate dicta, the following principles to govern cases of this type:
"[F]or purposes of obtaining reinstatement and back pay or simply back or lost pay where reinstatement is not asked, the individual must pursue or attempt in good faith to pursue the grievance procedure set forth in the collective bargaining contract before seeking a court remedy. . . . If the union refuses to handle the matter for him or if it has a conflicting interest, the employee should request the employer to take up the grievance with him according to the contractually-prescribed mode, but with the employee in control of the procedural steps wherever necessary to achieve a just determination. On refusal, recourse may be had to the courts for specific performance of the agreement to process the dispute through to arbitration or, at the option of the employee, for damages suffered by him because of the employer's conduct (for example, discharge without cause) which gave rise to the grievance.

On the facts of the particular case, the court found that the plaintiff employee had not attempted to process his grievance personally, that the union had not acted unfairly in refusing to proceed to arbitration, and that the employer had at no time refused to entertain the grievance in accordance with the contract. Since the employee had committed his grievance to the union and had failed to prove bad faith, the court declined to upset the resolution of the grievance by union and employer.

The NLRB does not follow the interpretation of the Section 9(a) proviso which the court in *Donnelly* espoused. The Board refuses to permit an individual to process his own grievance to arbitration [131] or to permit a minority union to do so on his behalf.[132] Pursuant to the proviso, the Board requires that the statutory representative be notified and given an opportunity to be present at any grievance adjustment.[133] The Board relies on a pre-Taft-Hartley Fifth Circuit holding that although the grievant may ask "an experienced friend to assist him, he cannot present his grievance through any union except his representative." [134] In a First Circuit case, which has not been followed, Judge Learned Hand disagreed with the Board. He would have permitted a union other than the designated majority union to represent an indi-

---

"During the argument before us, questions were raised as to where the burden of costs would rest when, in order to obtain relief, an employee finds it necessary to 'present' his grievance personally. If the matter is presented to the final stage of arbitration, decision as to expenses may be left to the arbitrator. Obviously, the union should not be saddled with costs of arbitrating worthless or petty claims of disputatious employees. On the other hand, if the employee is successful and the grievance is one which in the judgment of the arbitrator should have been handled by the union, presumably, costs would follow the course fixed in the collective agreement or usually followed by custom or practice. Further, even if the employee is unsuccessful after arbitration, if his cause is colorable and presented in good faith, and in the judgment of the arbitrator refusal of the union to press was unfair and arbitrary, he should be relieved of costs. But if he fails and has no colorable claim of a substantial nature, he must shoulder the costs." *Id.* at 841-42.

[131] Black-Clawson Co. v. Machinists, Lodge 355, 313 F2d 179, 52 LRRM 2038 (CA 2, 1962); Woody v. Sterling Aluminum Products, Inc., 243 F Supp 755, 59 LRRM 2996, *affirmed on other grounds sub nom.*, 365 F2d 448, 63 LRRM 2087 (CA 8, 1966), *cert. denied*, 386 US 957, 64 LRRM 2574 (1967). The United States Supreme Court in *Vaca*, 386 US at 190, n. 13, specifically noted the *Donnelly* decision and declined to follow it. *See* note 20 *supra*.

[132] Hughes Tool Co., 56 NLRB 981, 14 LRRM 165 (1944), *enforced*, 147 F2d 69, 15 LRRM 852 (CA 5, 1945); U.S. Automatic Corp., 57 NLRB 124, 14 LRRM 214 (1944); Federal Telephone and Radio Co., 107 NLRB 649, 33 LRRM 1203 (1953).

[133] *See also* J. I. Case Co. (Racine Plant), 71 NLRB 1145, 19 LRRM 1100 (1946).

[134] 147 F2d at 73. *See* Federal Telephone and Radio Co., note 132 *supra*.

vidual or group in the settlement of any grievances that had not been resolved by the collective bargaining contract.[135]

The Court in *Vaca* discussed various remedies which might be available in fair-representation cases. An order compelling arbitration was one remedy suggested. Other equitable relief may also be appropriate. As to damages, the Court made clear that only the employer, and not the union, is liable for the damages flowing from the employer's breach of contract (even though in a case of this type the employer's liability would be contingent upon a breach of the union's duty of fair representation), and that the union is liable only to the extent that the employee's damages were increased "by the union's refusal to process the grievance. . . ." [136] The Court said:

> The governing principle, then, is to apportion liability between the employer and the union according to the damage caused by the fault of each. Thus, damages attributable solely to the employer's breach of contract should not be charged to the union, but increases if any in those damages caused by the union's refusal to process the grievance should not be charged to the employer.[137]

The Court said that joint liability would be appropriate only where "a union has affirmatively caused the employer to commit the . . . breach of contract." [138]

Justice Fortas, with Chief Justice Warren and Justice Harlan, concurred on the basis of an exclusive NLRB jurisdiction to

---

135 Douds v. Retail Store Union, 173 F2d 764, 23 LRRM 2424 (CA 2, 1949). *Cf.* Olin Industries, 86 NLRB 203, 24 LRRM 1600 (1949), *enforced*, 191 F2d 613, 28 LRRM 2474 (CA 5, 1951), *cert. denied*, 343 US 919, 29 LRRM 2661 (1952); Agar Packing & Provision Corp., 81 NLRB 1262, 23 LRRM 1489 (1949). *See also* Sherman, *The Individual and the Grievance—Whose Grievance Is It?*, 11 PITT. L. REV. 35, 38, 55 (1949); Dunau, *Employee Participation in the Grievance Aspects of Collective Bargaining*, 50 COL. L. REV. 731, 740-44 (1950); *Report of Committee on Improvement of Administration of Union-Management Agreements*, 1954, 50 NW. L. REV. 143, 169-86 (1955); Comment, *Collective Bargaining, Grievance Adjustment, and the Rival Union*, 17 U. CHI. L. REV. 533, 540 (1950). Minority rail unions have been permitted to take employee grievances to adjustment boards in some circumstances. *See:* Locomotive Engineers v. Denver R.R. Co., 411 F2d 1115, 71 LRRM 2690 (CA 10, 1969); McElroy v. Terminal R.R. Ass'n of St. Louis, 392 F2d 966, 67 LRRM 2681 (CA 7, 1968), *cert. denied*, 393 US 813, 70 LRRM 2225 (1969). *Cf.* Elgin, J. & E. Ry. Co. v. Burley, 325 US 711, 16 LRRM 749 (1945), *adhered to on rehearing*, 327 US 661, 17 LRRM 899 (1946).
136 386 US at 198.
137 *Ibid.* "In this case," the Court said, "even if the Union had breached its duty, all or almost all of Owens' damages would still be attributable to his allegedly wrongful discharge by Swift. For these reasons, even if the Union here had properly been found liable for a breach of duty, it is clear that the damage award was improper." *Ibid.*
138 386 US at 197, note 18.

remedy breaches of the duty of fair representation. Therefore, they deemed it unnecessary to resolve the problem, discussed by the Court, of the circumstances under which an employee could sue the *employer* for breach of contract. They did, however, suggest as an alternative to the Court's position that perhaps "all . . . [the employee] would have to show to maintain an action for wrongful discharge against the employer is that he demanded that the union process his claim to exhaustion of available remedies and that it refused to do so." [139]

Justice Black dissented, recalling his disagreement with the Court's decision in *Republic Steel Corp. v. Maddox*[140] to the effect that an individual employee's suit must fail in the absence of the employee's attempt to invoke the grievance procedure. *A fortiori,* he would allow the suit where, as in *Vaca,* the employee had invoked that procedure. And he would not make the employer's liability for a breach of contract depend upon proof of the union's breach of the duty of fair representation. Justice Black pointed out that under the majority's decision the plaintiff "will be no more successful in his pending breach-of-contract action against . . . [the employer] than he is here in his suit against the union." [141]

By not mentioning the proviso to Section 9(a), the Supreme Court impliedly rejected the position of the court in *Donnelly* respecting individual rights to enforce the grievance and arbitration machinery.

3. Statutes of Limitations. An additional factor complicating the remedial problem is the unsettled state of the law of limitations in court cases in contrast to the six-month limitation governing unfair labor practice cases.[142] The limitations problem has been made even more complex by the Supreme Court's decision in *UAW v. Hoosier Cardinal Corp.*[143] This was a suit by a union for damages alleged to result from an employer's denial to his employees of accrued vacation pay. The Court held that "since no federal provision governs, . . . the timeliness of [such] a §301

139 *Id.* at 198-203.
140 379 US 650, 58 LRRM 2193 (1965).
141 386 US at 204.
142 NLRA §10 (b), 49 Stat 453 (1935), 29 USC §160 (b) (1964); *See* Bryan Mfg. Co. v. NLRB, 362 US 411, 45 LRRM 3212 (1960); *see also* Chapter 30 *infra.*
143 383 US 696, 61 LRRM 2545 (1966).

suit . . . is to be determined as a matter of federal law, by reference to the appropriate state statute of limitations." [144]

The First Circuit Court of Appeals, rejecting a six-month period of limitation, has held that "the logic of Hoosier Corp. dictates the adoption of express state statutes of limitation in the absence of an express federal limitation period." [145] That court could see no reason why such private litigation had to be limited by the same period as that used by the NLRB in unfair labor practice cases. The court predicted that "giving individual employees a period longer than the NLRB's six months [would] encourage initial recourse to the Board without precluding a subsequent civil suit if the Board refused to pursue the matter for the individual employee." [146]

---

[144] 383 US at 702.

[145] Figueroa v. Trabajadores Packinghouse, 425 F2d 281, 287 74 LRRM 2028 (CA 1, 1970), cert. denied, sub nom. Puerto Rico Telephone Co. v. Figueroa de Arroyo, —— US ——, 75 LRRM 2455 (1970).

[146] 74 LRRM at 2033. Additionally, the court rejected a theory of a "contractual basis" between the union and its members to support the union's duty of fair representation. The court concluded that "[t]he union's duty seems more akin to, though less rigorous than the duty of due care normally associated with tort actions." Id. at 2032.

PART VII

ADMINISTRATION OF THE ACT

CHAPTER 28

JURISDICTION: COVERAGE OF THE ACT

I. CONSTITUTIONALITY

The constitutionality of the National Labor Relations Act was confirmed by the Supreme Court in 1937 in *NLRB v. Jones & Laughlin Steel Corp.*[1] The Court held that the Commerce Clause of the Constitution gave Congress the power to regulate industrial relations of employers whose activities "affected" interstate commerce.[2] Congress had declared in Section 1 of the Act that the denial of the right of employees to organize and the refusal of some employers to accept collective bargaining led to strikes and industrial unrest and had the effect of burdening and obstructing commerce. Accordingly, in seeking to remedy these ills, Congress had, in the Supreme Court's view, properly legislated concerning matters affecting interstate commerce.[3]

Prior to *Jones & Laughlin* the Supreme Court had held that local production or mining operations could not be considered "commerce."[4] Consequently, there was a substantial body of opinion that the Wagner Act would be held unconstitutional if applied to employers engaged in manufacture and production, as contrasted with employers engaged *directly* in interstate commerce. The NLRB had ordered *Jones & Laughlin* to reinstate employees found to have been discriminatorily discharged because of their

---

[1] 301 US 1, 1 LRRM 703 (1937).
[2] §10 (a) empowers the Board "to prevent any person from engaging in any unfair labor practice (listed in §8) affecting commerce," and §9 extends the jurisdiction to representation cases where commerce would be affected. §§2 (6) and 2 (7) provide statutory definitions of "commerce" and "affecting commerce."
[3] *See* Chapter 2 for historical treatment of the constitutionality of the Act.
[4] Utah Power & Light Co. v. Pfost, 286 US 165 (1932); Chassaniol v. Greenwood, 291 US 584 (1934); Carter v. Carter Coal Co., 298 US 238 (1936).

union activities. The company argued that its operations were intrastate in character and subject solely to regulation by the states, relying on the fact that the discharged employees had been engaged only in the *manufacture* of steel. The Court of Appeals for the Fifth Circuit agreed with the company and denied enforcement of the Board's order.[5]

Reversing the court of appeals and beginning a new chapter in Constitutional history, the Supreme Court, speaking through Chief Justice Hughes, declared that "the Congressional authority to protect interstate commerce from burdens and obstructions is not limited to transactions which can be deemed to be an essential part of 'flow' of interestate or foreign commerce. Burdens and obstructions may be due to injurious action springing from other sources." [6] The Court identified the touchstone of commerce jurisdiction as the "fundamental principle . . . that the power to regulate commerce is the power to enact 'all appropriate legislation' for its 'protection or advancement. . . .' " [7]

The Court held that although such activities as manufacturing may be intrastate in character when separately considered, if they have such a close and substantial relation to interstate commerce that some control of their actions is essential or appropriate to protect this commerce from burdens or obstructions, Congress cannot be denied the power to exercise that control. It was therefore not difficult for the Court to conclude that a work stoppage in steel production "would have a most serious effect on interstate commerce." [8] Hence, the Board's order was enforced, and the constitutionality of the NLRA was established.[9]

On the same day, the Court extended the coverage of its *Jones & Laughlin* decision to employers with a smaller volume of busi-

---

[5] 83 F 2d 998, 1 LRRM 271 (1936).
[6] 301 US at 36.
[7] *Id.* at 36-37.
[8] *Id.* at 41.
[9] The Court also disposed of a due-process argument, in which the company asserted its right to conduct its business in an orderly manner without being subjected to arbitrary restraints, by noting that the "employees have their correlative right to organize for the purpose of securing the redress of grievances and to promote agreements with employers relating to rates of pay and conditions of working" (301 US at 43, 44), citing Texas & New Orleans R.R. Co. v. Railway Clerks, 281 US 548 (1930), and Virginian Ry. Co. v. System Federation, No. 40, 300 US 515 (1937). The Court stressed that "the act does not compel agreements between employers and employees. It does not compel any agreement whatever." 301 US at 45.

ness,[10] and two years later it determined that the relative amount of the volume of commerce affected in any particular case is not a material consideration.[11]

Subsequent decisions, as, for example, the Supreme Court's decision in *NLRB v. Reliance Fuel Oil Corp.*,[12] have reemphasized and even extended the constitutional coverage of the Act over transactions and practices that "affect" interstate commerce. Reliance, a New York fuel oil distributor, purchased within the state from an interstate enterprise oil that was delivered from tanks located in that state. The Court held that Reliance was engaged in a business affecting interstate commerce and reiterated that "Congress intended to and did vest in the Board the fullest jurisdictional breadth constitutionally permissible under the Commerce Clause." [13] It repeated the admonition it had given in *Polish National Alliance v. NLRB*: [14] whether practices "affect interstate commerce is not to be determined by confining judgment to the quantitative effect of the activities immediately before the Board," [15] but consideration also must be given to the many other similar activities throughout the country "the total incidence of which, if left unchecked, may well become far-reaching in its harm to commerce." [16]

II. STATUTORY JURISDICTION

A. General Jurisdiction

As noted in the previous section, the general jurisdiction of the National Labor Relations Board extends to "labor disputes," which include representation questions and unfair labor practices, "affecting" interstate commerce. In the absence of a "labor dispute" the Board may not act.[17]

---

10 NLRB v. Fruehauf Trailer Co., 301 US 49, 1 LRRM 715 (1937); NLRB v. Friedman-Harry Marks Clothing Co., 301 US 58, 1 LRRM 718 (1937).
11 NLRB v. Fainblatt, 306 US 601, 4 LRRM 535 (1939).
12 371 US 224, 52 LRRM 2046 (1963).
13 371 US at 226. In its first Annual Report, the Board asserted that its jurisdiction was coextensive with congressional power to legislate under the Commerce Clause, a position which was upheld in NLRB v. Fainblatt, *supra*, note 11.
14 322 US 643, 14 LRRM 700 (1944).
15 371 US at 226.
16 *Id.* at 226. *See also* Guss v. Utah L.R.B., 353 US 1, 39 LRRM 2567 (1957).
17 NLRB v. International Longshoremen's Association, 332 F 2d 992, 56 LRRM 2244 (CA 4, 1964). The definition of "labor dispute" in the National Labor Relations Act (§2 (9)) is substantially the same as the definition of "labor dispute" in the Norris-LaGuardia Act (§13 (c), 49 Stat. 70, 29 USCA §113 (c)).

The plenary scope of the Board's jurisdiction has never been fully exercised, for the Board properly may decline, subject to limitations hereinafter noted, to take jurisdiction of a case, because "the policies of the Act would not be effectuated by assertion of jurisdiction." [18] As the Supreme Court observed in *Polish National Alliance v. NLRB,* "Congress . . . . left it to the Board to ascertain whether proscribed practices would in particular situations adversely affect commerce. . . ." [19]

When the Taft-Hartley amendments were enacted in 1947, Congress left unchanged the basic language of Section 10 (a), which "empowered" but did not direct the Board to prevent unfair labor practices. The Board and the courts have consistently adhered to the principle, expressed in a dissenting opinion in *Guss v. Utah,* that "[t]he Board is not a court whose jurisdiction over violations of private rights must be exercised. It is an administrative agency whose function is to adjudicate public rights in a manner that will effectuate the policies of the Act." [20] The Taft-Hartley amendments, however, added a proviso to Section 10 (a) that empowered the Board by agreement with an appropriate state or territorial agency to cede jurisdiction of NLRB cases to such agency, unless the applicable state or territorial statute was inconsistent with, or had been construed to be inconsistent with, the NLRA. But this authority has never been exercised because, in the Board's view, no state law has met the statutory requirement.[21]

In *Guss v. Utah,* the Court held the Section 10 (a) proviso to be "the exclusive means whereby States may be enabled to act concerning the matters which Congress has entrusted to the National Labor Relations Board," [22] even as to cases over which the Board declines to assert jurisdiction.[23] The Court thus gave judicial recognition to a "no-man's land" where the states were barred from asserting jurisdiction and where the Board was declining to exercise jurisdiction. This situation lasted until the passage of the Landrum-Griffin amendments in 1959.[24]

---

18 NLRB v. Denver Bldg. Trades Council, 341 US 675, 684, 28 LRRM 2108 (1951).
19 322 US at 648.
20 353 US at 13.
21 NLRB v. Fant Milling Co., 360 US 301, 308, 44 LRRM 2236 (1959).
22 353 US at 9.
23 *See also* Chapter 29 *infra* at notes 52-56.
24 §14(c). *See* discussion *infra.*

This no-man's land resulted from the Board's practice of establishing minimum standards for assertion of jurisdiction. During the early years the Board decided on a case-by-case basis whether to take jurisdiction, a practice it abandoned in 1950 when it announced in *Hollow Tree Lumber Co.*[25] that the time had come to establish standards that would better clarify and define where the line could best be drawn to cover "enterprises whose operations have, or at which labor disputes would have, a pronounced impact upon the flow of interstate commerce." The Board accordingly began the practice, still in existence, of establishing minimum standards for assertion of jurisdiction. These standards are given largely in terms of yearly dollar amounts of inflow and outflow of interstate products or services.[26]

The Board's discretion to decline jurisdiction in certain areas has been limited in recent years both by the Supreme Court and by Congress. Following the Board's refusal to assert jurisdiction over a dispute involving the employees of a labor organization, the Court in *Office Employees Local 11 v. NLRB* held that "an arbitrary blanket exclusion of union employers as a class is beyond the power of the Board," [27] though it noted the recital in the joint congressional committee report on the Taft-Hartley amendments that the activities of nonprofit organizations or their employees were considered within the coverage of the Act only "in exceptional circumstances and in connection with purely commercial activities." [28] In *Hotel Employees Local 255 v. Leedom* the Court again rebuked the Board, this time because of its "long standing policy not to exercise jurisdiction over the hotel industry as a class," [29] whereupon the Board promptly established a yardstick for assertion of jurisdiction over hotels.[30]

Congress took note of these judicial developments when it enacted Section 14 (c) (1) with the passage of the Labor-Management Reporting and Disclosure Act of 1959:

The Board, in its discretion, may, by rule of decision or by published rules adopted pursuant to the Administrative Procedure Act,

---

25 91 NLRB 635, 636, 26 LRRM 1543 (1950).
26 *See* Part III *infra*, this chapter.
27 353 US 313, 318, 40 LRRM 2020 (1957).
28 353 US at 319, citing H.R. REP. No. 510, 80th Cong., 1st Sess. 32 (1947).
29 358 US 99, 43 LRRM 2137 (1958).
30 Floridan Hotel of Tampa, Inc., 124 NLRB 261, 44 LRRM 1345 (1959). *See* note 94 *infra*.

decline to assert jurisdiction over any labor dispute involving any class or category of employers, where, in the opinion of the Board, the effect of such labor dispute on commerce is not sufficiently substantial to warrant the exercise of its jurisdiction: *Provided,* That the Board shall not decline to assert jurisdiction over any labor dispute over which it would assert jurisdiction under the standards prevailing upon August 1, 1959.

Congress thus sanctioned the Board's policy of nonassertion of jurisdiction as to an entire class or category of employers, but prevented the Board from narrowing its jurisdiction by refusing to assert jurisdiction over those employers who were covered under the jurisdictional standards that were in effect on August 1, 1959. The court of appeals that had earlier rebuked the Board in *Hotel Employees v. Leedom* held, following the 1959 amendment, that the Board had properly declined to assert class jurisdiction over proprietary hospitals.[31]

A question raised by Section 14 (c) (1) was whether the Board could decline jurisdiction for a reason other than lack of a substantial effect on commerce. The answer was forthcoming in the Supreme Court's decision in *McCulloch v. Sociedad Nacional de Marineros de Honduras.*[32] The Board had asserted jurisdiction over foreign-flag vessels in several cases because the foreign corporation employer was a wholly owned subsidiary of an American corporation and the two corporations were held to be joint employers. When the foreign-flag operators urged the Board to decline jurisdiction, the Board responded that it was proscribed from declining by the Section 14 (c) (1) proviso, since it would have asserted jurisdiction prior to August 1, 1959. The Court dismissed this contention and held that the Board had no jurisdiction, discretionary or otherwise, over foreign-flag vessels, relying on the absence of specific statutory language clearly expressing an affirmative congressional intent to cover such vessels.[33]

---

[31] Leedom v. Fitch Sanitarium, Inc., 294 F 2d 251, 48 LRRM 2545 (CA DC, 1961). *But see* note 66 *infra* and accompanying text.

[32] 372 US 10, 52 LRRM 2425 (1963).

[33] The Court also relied upon the "rule of international law that the law of the flag state ordinarily governs the internal affairs of a ship"; this rule was deemed especially applicable in view of the "highly charged international circumstances." 372 US at 21. *See also* Incres Steamship Co. v. Int'l Maritime Workers, 372 US 24, 52 LRRM 2431 (1963). *But see* Longshoremen, ILA, Local 1416 v. Ariadne Shipping

amendments also sought the elimination of the no-
the existence of which had been confirmed by the
Guss case. Section 14 (c) (2) was enacted for this

his Act shall be deemed to prevent or bar any agency
of any State or Territory (including the Common-
erto Rico, Guam, and the Virgin Islands), from assum-
ting jurisdiction over labor disputes which the Board
uant to paragraph (1) of this subsection, to assert

On the basis of this provision, state courts and boards have
assumed jurisdiction over disputes in which the NLRB has declined or would decline jurisdiction. Augmenting Section
14 (c) (2), the Board has established a procedure for parties and
state agencies to seek advisory opinions in instances where the
Board has not acted.[34] Such advisory opinions are limited to the
jurisdictional issue and do not discuss the merits of the case. In
addition to advisory opinions, the Board will issue declaratory
orders to the General Counsel on jurisdictional issues when both
unfair labor practice charges and election petitions are pending
concurrently and involve the same parties.[35]

In enacting Section 14 (c) (2), Congress failed to specify whether
federal or state law would be applied in the state forum. The
language of the provision refers only to "assuming and asserting
jurisdiction," which could have reference solely to procedural
jurisdiction, in which case federal substantive law might be applicable. However, the states generally have applied their own

---

Co., Ltd., 397 US 195, 73 LRRM 2625 (1970) (the Court reversed a state court injunction against picketing by the ILA protesting substandard wage conditions in
loading operations, where there was no evidence that the longshoremen were seeking
to affect internal affairs of the ships.) In *Herbert Harvey, Inc.*, 171 NLRB No. 36,
68 LRRM 1053 (1968), *following remand*, 385 F 2d 684, 66 LRRM 2412 (CA DC,
1967), *reversing* 162 NLRB 890, 64 LRRM 1127 (1967), the Board declined to
assert jurisdiction over the World Bank, although it held that janitorial employees
of an independent contractor, performing work for the bank, were within the
Board's jurisdiction. *See also* notes 112-114 *infra* and accompanying text.

[34] NLRB Rules and Regulations, Series 8, Revised Jan. 1, 1965, §§102.98—102.104.
In Cox's Food Center v. Retail Clerks, 420 P 2d 645, 64 LRRM 2042 (1966), the Idaho
Supreme Court directed a lower state court to seek an advisory opinion from the
NLRB under those procedures.
[35] NLRB Rules and Regulations, Series 8, Revised Jan. 1, 1965, §§102.105—102.110.

laws,[36] and the issue as to which law should apply has not been settled.[37]

B. Limitations on Coverage

The statute itself contains specific limitations upon the Board's jurisdiction. Coverage is limited by statutory definition of the parties to whom the Act applies. Thus, the Act covers employers, employees, and labor organizations, but only as those parties or "persons" are defined in Section 2 of the statute.

1. Person. The Act uses "person" as the generic term for persons and groups who are generally subject to the Act. Section 2 (1) defines "person" to include "one or more individuals, labor organizations, partnerships, associations, corporations, legal representatives, trustees, trustees in bankruptcy, or receivers." However, the term "person" is more broadly used in connection with the Act's secondary boycott provisions in Section 8(b)(4).[38]

As originally written, Section 8 (b) (4) referred only to the inducement or encouragement of "employees." A union, therefore, could direct pressure against a secondary employer without violating the Act. No violation would lie inasmuch as no "employees" were contacted by the union.[39] Further, since the prohibition was directed only against inducement of "employees," unions also could threaten supervisors, farm laborers, government employees, railroad employees, and others who did not fall within the Act's definition of "employee" and who were not generally subject to the Act.[40] The 1959 amendments closed these loopholes by mak-

---

36 Pennsylvania Labor Relations Board v. Boat Supply Co., 49 LRRM 1764 (Pa LRB, 1962), where the Pennsylvania Labor Relations Board held that it had jurisdiction over a combined wholesale and retail hardware supply business that failed to meet the NLRB's jurisdictional standards. The State Board then proceeded to find violations of the Pennsylvania Labor Relations Act. *See also* Mr. Snow Man, Inc., 23 NY SLRB 379, 46 LRRM 1375 (1960); New Orleans Opera Guild, Inc. v. Local 174, 127 So 2d 358, 47 LRRM 2681 (La Ct App, 1961).

37 Kempf v. Carpenters, 367 P 2d 436, 49 LRRM 2637 (Oregon Sup Ct, 1961), applied state law. For legislative history indicating that state substantive law was intended, see statements by Senator Kennedy, 105 CONG. REC. 16255 (1959), and Representative Griffin, 105 CONG. REC. 16539 (1959).

38 See Chapter 23 *supra* for a detailed analysis of the statutory definition under the secondary boycott provisions of the Act.

39 Teamsters Union (Texas Industries), 112 NLRB 923, 36 LRRM 1117 (1955), *enforced,* 234 F 2d 296, 38 LRRM 2224 (CA 5, 1956).

40 Automobile Workers (Paper Makers Importing Co.), 116 NLRB 267, 38 LRRM 1228 (1956). *But see* W. T. Smith Lumber Company, 116 NLRB 1756, 39 LRRM 1082 (1956), *reversed,* 246 F 2d 129, 40 LRRM 2276 (CA 5, 1957).
1957).

ing it unlawful for a union to "threaten, coerce, or restrain any *person* engaged in commerce" [41] for any of the proscribed reasons. Thus, it is now unlawful for a union to "threaten, coerce, or restrain" any of the enumerated groups in the statutory definition for prohibited purposes.[42]

2. Employers. Section 2 (2) of the Act defines "employer" as follows:

> The term "employer" includes any person acting as an agent of an employer, directly or indirectly, but shall not include the United States or any wholly owned Government corporation, or any Federal Reserve Bank, or any State or political subdivision thereof, or any corporation or association operating a hospital, if no part of the net earnings inures to the benefit of any private shareholder or individual, or any person subject to the Railway Labor Act, as amended from time to time, or any labor organization (other than when acting as an employer), or anyone acting in the capacity of officer or agent of such labor organization.

The Board has the duty of determining whether the relationship between certain parties constitutes an employer-employee relationship within the meaning of the definitions in the Act.

A number of factors are pertinent to a finding that such a relationship exists. The most important is the degree of control that the alleged employer maintains over the working life of the alleged employee. The Board has stated that an employer-employee relationship exists "where the person for whom the services are performed reserves the right to control not only the end to be achieved but also the means to be used in reaching such end." [43] Another factor that is relevant, but not necessarily determinative, is whether the alleged employer withholds such items as social security and income taxes from the payments made to the alleged employee.[44] Similarly relevant is whether or not the agreement or conditions were arrived at through negotiations or whether they were in fact imposed by the alleged employer.[45]

---

41 Emphasis added.
42 Hod Carriers (Gilmore Construction Co.), 127 NLRB 541, 46 LRRM 1043 (1960), *modified and enforced*, 285 F 2d 397, 47 LRRM 2345 (CA 8, 1960), *cert. denied*, 366 US 908, 48 LRRM 2345 (1961).
43 Deaton Truck Lines, Inc., 143 NLRB 1372, 53 LRRM 1497 (1963), *review dismissed*, 337 F 2d 697, 57 LRRM 2209 (CA 5, 1964); Albert Lea Cooperative Creamery Assn., 119 NLRB 817, 821-22, 41 LRRM 1192 (1957).
44 Frederick O. Glass, et al., dba Miller Road Dairy, 135 NLRB 217, 49 LRRM 1477 (1962), *enforced in part*, 317 F 2d 726, 53 LRRM 2336 (CA 6, 1963).
45 Mohican Trucking Co., 131 NLRB 1174, 48 LRRM 1213 (1961).

The Board also must determine who the "employer" is, for an "employer" may be a composite of a number of employers. For example, where a busy company subcontracted the maintenance work at one of its terminals to a service company, the Board held that, by reason of elements of common control, the bus company and the service company were joint employers of the maintenance workers.[46] Also where a licensee of a department in a store had given substantially all the control over the employment conditions of its employees to the store-licensor, the licensee and licensor were held to be joint employers.[47]

The question frequently arises as to whether two or more companies can be considered a "single employer" under the Act. The "corporate veil" having been pierced with ease over the years by the Board and the courts, the tests generally applied involve only whether there is (a) a present unity of interest,[48] (b) common ownership and control,[49] (c) interdependence of operations,[50] and (d) common direction of labor relations policies.[51] Determination of whether or not the single-employer theory applies may turn upon the particular facts in each case.

Thus, the Board was upheld by the Fourth Circuit in one case where control was exercised by a substantial creditor who took over to protect his investment,[52] but the Sixth Circuit reversed the Board in a case where two corporations were operated in many aspects on an arm's-length basis but with indicia of common ownership and control.[53] Another significant case involved two newspapers, one in Miami, Fla., and the other in Detroit, Mich.[54] The union which had struck the Florida paper also picketed the Detroit paper. Although admittedly there was common ownership, both

---

[46] Greyhound Corp., 153 NLRB 1488, 59 LRRM 1665 (1965), *enforced,* 368 F 2d 778, 63 LRRM 2434 (CA 5, 1966).

[47] S. S. Kresge Co., 161 NLRB 1127, 63 LRRM 1385 (1966).

[48] American District Telegraph Co., 128 NLRB 345, 46 LRRM 1315 (1960).

[49] NLRB v. Winn Dixie Stores, Inc., 341 F 2d 750, 58 LRRM 2475 (CA 6, 1965), *cert. denied,* 382 US 830, 60 LRRM 2234 (1965).

[50] U. S. Mattress Corp., 135 NLRB 1150, 49 LRRM 1668 (1962).

[51] Liebmann Breweries, Inc., of New Jersey, 142 NLRB 121, 52 LRRM 1527 (1963).

[52] NLRB v. Gibralter Industries, Inc., 307 F 2d 428, 51 LRRM 2029 (CA 4, 1962), *enforcing* 133 NLRB 1527, 49 LRRM 1054 (1960), *cert. denied,* 372 US 911, 52 LRRM 2471 (1963).

[53] NLRB v. Deerfield Screw Machine Products Co., 329 F 2d 588, 55 LRRM 2812 (CA 6, 1964). For other circuits that have rejected the Board's inferences of common control on a factual basis, see J. G. Roy and Sons Co. v. NLRB, 251 F 2d 771, 41 LRRM 2445 (CA 1, 1958), *and* Bachman Machine Co. v. NLRB, 261 F 2d 599, 44 LRRM 2104 (CA 8, 1959).

[54] Miami Newspaper Pressmen, Local 46 v. NLRB, 322 F 2d 405, 53 LRRM 2629 (CA DC, 1963).

the Board and the D.C. Circuit found that the two papers were operated independently of each other and therefore rejected the union's single-employer defense to a secondary boycott charge. The union's claim that the Detroit paper was not a "neutral" employer was defeated by a showing that the two newspapers were operated "independently of each other, as separate autonomous newspaper enterprises." [55]

The Act also provides that any person who acts as an agent of the employer is, in effect, the employer for purposes of fixing responsibility in those areas over which the Board has jurisdiction. Under the Wagner Act the definition of "employer" included persons "acting in the interest of an employer." Under this language employers were held liable for acts committed by employees below the level of supervisor [56] and, in rare cases, by third parties not in their employ.[57] In 1947, the definition was amended to substitute the language "acting as an agent of an employer." At the same time, Section 2 (13) was added:

> In determining whether any person is acting as an "agent" of another person so as to make such other person responsible for his acts, the question of whether the specific acts performed were actually authorized or subsequently ratified shall not be controlling.

The stated purpose of these changes was to make both unions and employers subject to "the ordinary common law rules of agency." [58] Thus, an employer is liable for the acts of a supervisor acting under his apparent authority even though the acts are contrary to instructions.[59] The supervisor in such cases is, in effect, the employer.

An employer may still be liable for the acts of third parties not in his employ, as for example where an assistant plant superintendent was present but failed to disavow a local police chief's promise to an employee of financial reward and immunity from arrest if the employee physically attacked a union representative.[60]

---

55 Printing Pressmen's Union, 138 NLRB 1346, 51 LRRM 1169 (1962). Expanding this ruling, the Board has also held that a virtually autonomous division of a corporation will be considered a "person" within the meaning of the Act. Los Angeles Newspaper Guild, 185 NLRB No. 25, 75 LRRM 1014 (1970). See Chapter 23 supra.
56 IAM v. NLRB, 311 US 72, 7 LRRM 282 (1940).
57 Consumers Lumber & Veneer Co., 63 NLRB 17, 16 LRRM 292 (1945).
58 H. R. Rep. No. 510, 80th Cong., 1st Sess. 36 (1947).
59 Aladdin Industries, Inc., 147 NLRB 1392, 56 LRRM 1388 (1964).
60 Dorsey Trailers, Inc., 80 NLRB 478, 23 LRRM 1112 (1948), enforced in part, 179 F 2d 589, 25 LRRM 2333 (CA 5, 1950).

Similarly, employers have been held responsible for the activity of nonemployee persons in the community who have worked to discourage the employer's employees from unionizing,[61] unless their actions are specifically disavowed by the employer.[62] The Act's definition of "agent" is applicable both to unfair labor practice proceedings and to damage suit actions under Section 303.[63]

While a particular company or organization may fulfill all the normal requisites of "employer" status, it may nevertheless be exempt from coverage under the Act if it is of the type specifically excluded under the definition of "employer." Thus the United States government is not an "employer" under the terms of the Act. However, where private enterprise is involved in work with the government, who is the employer, the government or the private enterprise? The chief test is who has the real control over the employees. Where the private enterprise has the control, the Board will hold that the private enterprise, generally a contractor, is the employer and that, therefore, the employees are entitled to coverage under the Act.[64]

Nonprofit hospitals are excluded under the statutory language.[65] Until recently, the Board also refrained from asserting jurisdiction over proprietary hospitals on the ground that they were essentially local in nature and that labor disputes involving these hospitals

---

61 Universal Mfg. Corp., 156 NLRB 1495, 61 LRRM 1258 (1966). In Dean Industries, Inc., 162 NLRB 1078, 64 LRRM 1193 (1967), the Board issued an order that ran against a third party in his personal capacity and not merely as an agent of the employer; the mayor of a city was ordered to refrain from interfering with the rights of an employer's employees in an attempt to discourage their unionization.
62 Claymore Mfg. Co., 146 NLRB 1400, 56 LRRM 1080 (1964).
63 *Compare* the definition in §6 of the Norris-LaGuardia Act, 29 USC §106.
Both definitions may be applicable in the same court proceeding. In Gibbs vs. United Mine Workers, 383 US 715, 61 LRRM 2561 (1966), plaintiff sued the union in federal court for damages under §303 and also under state tort law. Although the §303 claim failed because no secondary action was found, the Supreme Court recognized that the Taft-Hartley definition of agency would have applied. As to the state law claim, the Court held that the stricter Norris-LaGuardia definition was controlling and that, under it, the union was not liable for the violence that had occurred. *See* discussion of §303 in Chapter 23 *supra*.
64 Geronimo Service Co., 129 NLRB 366, 46 LRRM 1553 (1960); Great Southern Chem. Corp., 96 NLRB 1013, 28 LRRM 1626 (1951); Am. Smelting and Ref. Co., 92 NLRB 1451, 27 LRRM 1259 (1951).
65 Where the services provided by a contractor to a nonprofit hospital or other exempt institution are intimately connected with the operation of the institution, the Board generally finds that the contractor also shares the institution's exempt status. However, where the contractor's operations are not intimately related, the Board will assert jurisdiction. Bay Ran Maintenance Corp., 161 NLRB 820, 63 LRRM 1345 (1966); Woods Hole Oceanographic Institution, 143 NLRB 568, 53 LRRM 1296 (1963).

would not substantially affect commerce. However, in 1967 the Board took note of the substantial growth that had occurred in the hospital industry and of the impact of federal programs, such as Medicare, and asserted jurisdiction over private hospitals [66] and private nursing homes.[67]

While the definition of "employer" also specifically excludes "persons" subject to the provisions of the Railway Labor Act, the Supreme Court has held that the secondary boycott sections of the National Labor Relations Act may be utilized to provide relief for such "persons." [68] Similarly, these secondary boycott provisions are applicable where a governmental body becomes enmeshed in such a dispute.[69]

The Board also has held that a union may be an employer within the meaning of the Act when its own employees seek to organize.[70] The fact that the union may be one that regularly represents employees of employers who are excluded from the Act's coverage does not alter the status of the union as a covered employer.[71]

3. Employees. The statutory jurisdiction of the Board is further limited by the definition of the term "employee" found in Section 2 (3) of the Act:

The term "employee" shall include any employee, and shall not be limited to the employees of a particular employer, unless the Act explicitly states otherwise, and shall include any individual whose work has ceased as a consequence of, or in connection with, any current labor dispute or because of any unfair labor practice, and who has not obtained any other regular and substantially equivalent employment, but shall not include any individual employed as an agricultural laborer, or in the domestic service of any family or per-

---

[66] Butte Medical Properties, 168 NLRB No. 52, 66 LRRM 1259 (1967) *overruling* Flatbush General Hospital, 126 NLRB 144, 45 LRRM 1286 (1960). *See* note 103 *infra*. *See also* A.A.A. Air Duct Cleaning Co., 169 NLRB No. 137, 67 LRRM 1460 (1968).

[67] University Nursing Home, Inc., 168 NLRB No. 53, 66 LRRM 1263 (1967). *See* note 104 *infra*.

[68] Teamsters Local 25 v. New York, New Haven & Hartford RR., 350 US 155, 37 LRRM 2271 (1956). *See also* Building Service Employees Union, Local 254 (University Cleaning Co.), 151 NLRB 341, 58 LRRM 1406 (1965), *enforced*, 384 F 2d 904, 61 LRRM 2709 (CA 1, 1966).

[69] Plumbers and Steamfitters Local 298 v. County of Door, 359 US 354, 44 LRRM 2034 (1959).

[70] International Ladies Garment Wkrs. Union, 131 NLRB 111, 47 LRRM 1616 (1961).

[71] Brotherhood of Locomotive Firemen and Enginemen, 145 NLRB 1521, 55 LRRM 1177 (1964); Air Line Pilots Association, 97 NLRB 929, 29 LRRM 1155 (1951).

son at his home, or any individual employed by his parent or spouse, or any individual having the status of an independent contractor, or any individual employed as a supervisor, or any individual employed by an employer subject to the Railway Labor Act, as amended from time to time, or by any other person who is not an employer as herein defined.

Whereas the Wagner Act was silent on the status of independent contractors and supervisors, the amended definition of the term "employee" specifically excludes these groups from direct coverage by the Act. The key questions are whether a particular individual or group enjoys independent contractor or supervisory status.

a. Independent contractors. In a pre-Taft-Hartley case in which street newspaper vendors were held to be employees rather than independent contractors, the Supreme Court found that the publisher dictated buying and selling prices for the vendors, fixed their markets, controlled their supply of papers and hours of work, partially supervised their efforts on the job, and supplied their sales equipment and advertising material. In the absence of any statutory definition of the term "independent contractor" in the Taft-Hartley Act, the Board uses a similar "right of control" test which has had court approval." [72]

Presented with a similar issue more recently, the Supreme Court updated the *Hearst* decision. In *NLRB v. United Insurance Co.,*[73] the Court took note of the 1947 statutory amendment and said that its purpose was to have the Board and the courts apply general agency principles in distinguishing between employees and independent contractors. Then, invoking the common law test of agency, the Court found that the debit agents of an insurance company, whose main function was to collect premiums from policyholders and prevent policies from lapsing, were employees and not independent contractors. Those agents did not operate their own independent businesses, but performed functions which were found to be essential to the company's normal operations. Although "right of control" was not specifically mentioned, the Court did stress that the agents did not exercise any of the initiative or decision-making authority customarily associated with independent contractors.

---

[72] NLRB v. Hearst Publications, Inc., 322 US 111, 14 LRRM 614 (1944); Blue Cab Co. and Village Cab Co., 156 NLRB 489, 61 LRRM 1085 (1965), *enforced,* 373 F 2d 661, 64 LRRM 2317 (CA DC 1967).
[73] 390 US 254, 67 LRRM 2649 (1968).

b. Supervisors. Prior to the 1947 amendments, the Board, with the Supreme Court in agreement, accorded supervisors all employee rights under the statute in the absence of language to the contrary.[74] The Taft-Hartley amendment to Section 2 (3) clearly excludes supervisors as employees, and Congress further spelled out its intent in an explanatory Section 2 (11):

> The term "supervisor" means any individual having authority, in the interest of the employer, to hire, transfer, suspend, lay off, recall, promote, discharge, assign, reward, or discipline other employees, or responsibly to direct them, or to adjust their grievances, or effectively to recommend such action, if in connection with the foregoing the exercise of such authority is not of a merely routine or clerical nature, but requires the use of independent judgment.

The problem of identifying supervisors—the subject of the foregoing statutory definition—is an important and recurring one. Whether or not a person enjoys supervisory status will determine, among other matters, his right to vote in a union election, his entitlement to Section 7 rights, and his ability to bind the employer by his statements and actions.

In order to be classified as a supervisor, a person need not meet all the criteria of Section 2 (11).[75] The criterion which the Board looks to first and most often, however, is the following: the authority of the person in question to hire and fire employees or effectively to recommend (without further investigation by superiors) such hiring and firing.[76] The fact that a person may be only a part-time supervisor does not detract from his supervisory status.[77]

In certain industries, such as printing, maritime, and construction, it is customary for certain levels of supervision to be members of a union, a practice that Congress recognized in Section 14 (a):

> Nothing herein shall prohibit any individual employed as a supervisor from becoming or remaining a member of a labor organization, but no employer subject to this Act shall be compelled to deem

---

[74] Packard Motor Car Co. v. NLRB, 330 US 485, 19 LRRM 2397 (1947).

[75] National Welders Supply Co., 129 NLRB 514, 47 LRRM 1022 (1960); Ohio Power Co. v. NLRB, 176 F 2d 385, 24 LRRM 2350 (CA 6, 1949), *cert. denied,* 338 US 900, 25 LRRM 2129 (1949).

[76] W. Horace Williams Co., 130 NLRB 223, 47 LRRM 1337 (1961).

[77] Swift & Co., 129 NLRB 1391, 47 LRRM 1195 (1961), *supplemented,* 131 NLRB 1143, 48 LRRM 1219 (1961), where a worker who substituted for a foreman 15 percent of his total working time was considered a supervisor. *See also* Sears Roebuck & Co., 127 NLRB 583, 46 LRRM 1055 (1960).

individuals defined herein as supervisors as employees for the purpose of any law, either national or local, relating to collective bargaining.

While supervisors are generally not accorded the protection of the Act, there have been infrequent cases in which the Board has held the discharge of a supervisor to be an 8(a)(1) violation because of its alleged impact on unit employees. For example, supervisors who were discharged for failure to prevent unionization by means of unfair labor practices at the employer's behest were ordered reinstated with back pay.[78]

4. Labor Organizations. Section 2 (5) of the Act defines "labor organization" as follows:

> The term "labor organization" means any organization of any kind, or any agency or employee representation committee or plan, in which employees participate and which exists for the purpose, in whole or in part, of dealing with employers concerning grievances, labor disputes, wages, rates of pay, hours of employment, or conditions of work.

It is thus obvious that a "labor organization" need not necessarily be a union. In *NLRB v. Cabot Carbon Co.*,[79] the Supreme Court held that an employee committee that discusses with management various subjects pertaining to working conditions, wages, or grievances is a labor organization within the meaning of Section 2 (5). The Court ruled that there is no requirement that such a committee must engage in actual bargaining or in the negotiation of contracts. The Board has similarly held that loosely formed committees are "labor organizations" where their purpose is to represent employees' interests in dealing with employers.[80]

Bona fide unions are obviously labor organizations, but councils of unions are also considered labor organizations within the meaning of the Act, even though employees do not hold membership directly in such council.[81]

Organizations or groups that represent persons employed as agricultural or railway laborers, or other excluded employees, are

---

[78] Talladega Cotton Factory, 32 LRRM 1479, 106 NLRB 295 (1953), *enforced,* 213 F 2d 391, 34 LRRM 2196 (CA 5, 1954).
[79] 360 US 203, 44 LRRM 2204 (1959).
[80] Perry Norvell Co., 80 NLRB 225, 23 LRRM 1061 (1948).
[81] NLRB v. Kennametal, Inc., 182 F 2d 817, 26 LRRM 2203 (CA 3, 1950), *affirming* 80 NLRB 1481, 23 LRRM 1265 (1948).

not labor organizations within Section 2(5) because they represent persons who are not "employees" under the Act, regardless of the functions of such organizations or groups on behalf of their members. However, an organization composed both of members who *are not* "employees" within the meaning of the Act and of others who *are* "employees" within such meaning has been held to be a labor organization.[82]

III. ADMINISTRATIVE STANDARDS

Although the Board may have jurisdiction under the statutory test—*i.e.,* the business involved may "affect" interestate commerce—it may nevertheless refuse to act in a particular case because of a failure to meet administrative standards promulgated by the Agency itself. As the Court of Appeals for the Second Circuit noted in *NLRB v. Pease Oil Company*: [83]

> The phrase "jurisdictional standard," though coined by the Board itself, is a misnomer. Early in its history, however, the Board came to the conclusion that if it were to take cognizance of all complaints within its statutory grant of power it would be unable to decide any complaint with the thoroughness and promptitude necessary to achieve the objectives of the Act. Therefore the Board refused to hear certain complaints which clearly were within its statutory power to decide. In determining whether to hear a given complaint, a principal criterion the Board adopted was the volume of interstate commerce engaged in by the employer.

As previously noted, the Board in 1950 declared in *Hollow Tree Lumber Co.*[84] that the time had come for the establishment of "standards which will better clarify and define where the difficult line can best be drawn." Thus in a series of cases in 1951 the Board established nine general jurisdictional standards whereby it would assert jurisdiction over certain categories of enterprises if the enterprise in question met the required annual dollar volume of business. The Board's adoption of these written standards governing future exercise of jurisdiction meant that for the first

---

[82] DiGiorgio Fruit Corp. v. NLRB, 191 F 2d 642, 28 LRRM 2195 (CA DC, 1951), *affirming* 87 NLRB 720, 25 LRRM 1223 (1949). *See also,* Masters, Mates & Pilots (Chicago Calumet Stevedoring Co.), 144 NLRB 1172, 54 LRRM 1209 (1963), *enforced,* 351 F 2d 771, 59 LRRM 2566 (CA DC, 1965), where the Board held that a union constituted a labor organization although only 300 of its 11,000 members were employees within the meaning of the Act.
[83] NLRB v. Pease Oil Co., 279 F 2d 135, 137, 46 LRRM 2286 (CA 2, 1960), *enforcing* 123 NLRB 660, 43 LRRM 1500 (1959).
[84] 91 NLRB 635, 636, 26 LRRM 1543 (1950). *See* note 25 *supra*.

time parties seeking to invoke the processes of the Board could determine for themselves, with a high degree of predictability, when jurisdiction would be asserted.

In 1954 the Board modified its administrative standards by increasing the dollar minima and thus limited further the exercise of jurisdiction.[85]

On October 2, 1958, the Board, by press release, announced the standards that, except for certain additions, are currently effective. The substance of this release was embodied in *Siemons Mailing Service*.[86] The Board stated that

> experience under its 1950 and 1954 jurisdictional standards demonstrated that the utilization of jurisdictional standards, if simply drawn and relatively few in number, significantly reduces the amount of time, energy and funds expended by the Board and its staff in the investigation and resolution of jurisdictional issues, thus enabling the Board to devote a greater portion of its resources to the processing of substantive problems in a greater number of cases. The Board believes that, in the present circumstances, its primary function is to extend the national labor policies embodied in the Act as close to the legal limits of its jurisdiction established by Congress as its resources permit.

Under these standards and several subsequent revisions, the Board now asserts jurisdiction in the following cases:

1. Nonretail Enterprises—where there is a gross outflow or inflow of revenue of at least $50,000, whether such outflow or inflow be regarded as direct or indirect.[87]

2. Retail Establishments—where there is a gross business volume of at least $500,000 per year and substantial purchases from or

---

85 NLRB Press Release, R-449, 34 LRRM 75.
86 122 NLRB 81, 83-84, 43 LRRM 1056 (1958), *supplemented*, 124 NLRB 594, 44 LRRM 1467 (1959).
87 Siemons Mailing Service, 122 NLRB 81, 43 LRRM 1056 (1958); Culligan Soft Water Service, 149 NLRB 2, 57 LRRM 1229 (1964); Southern Dolomite, 129 NLRB 1342, 47 LRRM 1173 (1961); Trettenero Sand & Gravel Co., 129 NLRB 610, 47 LRRM 1013 (1960). Direct outflow refers to goods shipped or services furnished by the employer outside the state. Indirect outflow includes sales within the state to users meeting any standard except solely an indirect inflow or indirect outflow standard. Direct inflow refers to goods or services furnished directly to the employer from outside the state in which the employer is located. Indirect inflow refers to the purchase of goods or services which originated outside the employer's state but which he purchased from a seller within the state. Direct and indirect outflow may be combined, and direct and indirect inflow may also be combined, to meet the $50,000 requirement. However, outflow and inflow may not be combined.

sales to other states on a direct or indirect basis.[88] When an employer's operations are both retail and nonretail, the nonretail jurisdictional standards are applied unless the nonretail portion is *de minimis*.[89]

3. Office Buildings and Shopping Centers—where there is gross revenue of at least $100,000 per year, of which at least $25,000 is derived from organizations whose operations meet any of the Board's jurisdictional standards other than the nonretail standard.[90]

4. Public Utilities—where there is gross business volume of at least $250,000 per year or where there is an outflow or inflow of goods, materials, or services of $50,000 or more per year, whether directly or indirectly, across state lines.[91]

5. Newspapers—where there is gross business volume of at least $200,000 per year and the employer holds membership in or subscribes to interstate news services, publishes nationally syndicated features, or advertises nationally sold products.[92]

6. Radio and Television Stations; Telephone and Telegraph Systems—where there is gross business volume of at least $100,000 per year.[93]

7. Hotels and Motels—where gross annual revenue totals at least $500,000 per year. However, the Board takes jurisdiction over such hotels and motels only if more than 25 percent of the guests are transients who remain less than one month, or more than 25 percent of rental income is derived from such transient guests.[94]

---

[88] Carolina Supplies & Cement Co., 122 NLRB 88, 43 LRRM 1062 (1958); Dominick's Finer Food, Inc., 156 NLRB 14, 60 LRRM 1565 (1965), *enforcement denied on other grounds*, 367 F 2d 781, 63 LRRM 2365 (CA 7, 1966).

[89] Appliance Supply Co., 127 NLRB 319, 46 LRRM 1020 (1960).

[90] Mistletoe Operating Co., 122 NLRB 88, 43 LRRM 1060 (1958); Joe White IGA, 154 NLRB 1, 59 LRRM 1705 (1965); Canal Marais Improvement Corp., 129 NLRB 1332, 47 LRRM 1883 (1961); Carol Management Corp., 133 NLRB 1126, 48 LRRM 1782 (1961). The Board has extended its jurisdiction over apartment house enterprises that meet a gross annual volume yardstick of $500,000.

[91] Sioux Valley Empire Elec. Assn., 122 NLRB 92, 43 LRRM 1061 (1958); Tri-County Electric Membership Corp., 145 NLRB 810, 55 LRRM 1057 (1964), *enforced*, 343 F 2d 60, 58 LRRM 2704 (CA 4, 1965); Kingsbury Electric Cooperative, Inc., 138 NLRB 577, 51 LRRM 1104 (1962), *enforced*, 319 F 2d 387, 53 LRRM 2693 (CA 8, 1963).

[92] Belleville Employing Printers, 122 NLRB 350, 43 LRRM 1125 (1958); Nutley Sun Printing Co., 128 NLRB 58, 46 LRRM 1260 (1960).

[93] Raritan Valley Broadcasting Co., 122 NLRB 90, 43 LRRM 1062 (1958); Perfect T.V., Inc., 134 NLRB 575, 49 LRRM 1304 (1961).

[94] Floridan Hotel of Tampa, Inc., 124 NLRB 261, 44 LRRM 1345 (1959); Spink Arms Hotel Corp., 133 NLRB 1694, 49 LRRM 1081 (1961).

8. National Defense Enterprises—where a substantial impact on the national defense can be shown, irrespective of whether the operations satisfy any other jurisdictional standard.[95]

9. Employer Associations—where any member meets any jurisdictional standard, or if the combined operations of all members meet any such standard.[96]

10. Secondary Employers—in cases involving union conduct with respect to secondary employers, where the primary employer meets any of the jurisdictional standards or if the combined operations of the primary employer and the business of any secondary employers at the location affected by the conduct meet such standards.[97]

11. Single Employer Engaged in Multiple Enterprises—where the employer's overall operations meet any jurisdictional standard.[98]

12. Instrumentalities, Links, and Channels of Interstate Commerce—where gross revenue of at least $50,000 per year is derived from furnishing interstate transportation services or functioning as essential links in such transportation of passengers or commodities, or from performing local transportation for enterprises over which the Board would assert jurisdiction under any of the jurisdictional standards herein other than the indirect outflow or indirect inflow standards.[99]

13. Other Transit Systems—where there is gross volume of at least $250,000 per year.[100] However, taxicab companies are classified as retail enterprises and are tested by that standard.[101]

---

[95] Ready Mixed Concrete & Materials, Inc., 122 NLRB 318, 43 LRRM 1115 (1958); Geronimo Service Co., 129 NLRB 366, 46 LRRM 1553 (1960). *See also* note 64 *supra.*

[96] Seine & Line Fishermen's Union of San Pedro (Fishermen's Cooperative Assn.), 136 NLRB 1, 49 LRRM 1707 (1962).

[97] Local 886, General Drivers, Teamsters (Ada Transit Mix), 130 NLRB 788, 47 LRRM 1409 (1961).

[98] Kinney System, Inc., NLRB Case No. 2-RC-11395, 48 LRRM 1586 (1961); C. L. Morris, Inc., 127 NLRB 761, 46 LRRM 1084 (1960).

[99] HPO Service, Inc., 122 NLRB 394, 43 LRRM 1127 (1958); Greyhound Terminal, 137 NLRB 87, 50 LRRM 1088 (1962), *enforced,* 314 F 2d 43, 52 LRRM 2335 (CA 5, 1963), Mohican Trucking Co., 131 NLRB 1174, 48 LRRM 1213 (1961).

[100] Charleston Transit Company, 123 NLRB 1296, 44 LRRM 1123 (1959). *See also* Air California, 170 NLRB No. 1, 67 LRRM 1385 (1968).

[101] Cab Services, Inc., 123 NLRB 83, 43 LRRM 1392 (1959); Union Taxi Corp., 130 NLRB 814, 47 LRRM 1422 (1961).

14. Restaurants and Country Clubs—where standards for retail establishments are met.[102]

15. Private Hospitals—where there is at least $250,000 gross annual revenue.[103]

16. Private Nursing Homes—where there is at least $100,000 gross annual revenue.[104]

17. Businesses in the Territories and District of Columbia—the foregoing standards apply in the territories the same as in the states;[105] however, plenary jurisdiction is exercised in the District of Columbia.[106]

18. Baseball—In 1969 the Board extended its jurisdiction to cover organized baseball.[107]

19. Nonprofit, Private, Educational Institutions—In 1970, the Board asserted jurisdiction over private universities and colleges having gross annual revenue of at least $1,000,000 for operating expenses.[108]

---

102 Brennan's French Restaurant, 129 NLRB 52, 46 LRRM 1495 (1960).

103 Butte Medical Properties, 168 NLRB No. 52, 66 LRRM 1259 (1967).

104 University Nursing Home, Inc., 168 NLRB No. 53, 66 LRRM 1263 (1967).

105 Caribe Lumber & Trading Corp., 148 NLRB 277, 56 LRRM 1506 (1964).

106 Westchester Corp., 124 NLRB 194, 44 LRRM 1327 (1959).

107 American League, 180 NLRB No. 30, 72 LRRM 1545 (1969). For many years the Board excluded baseball from the coverage of the Act on the basis of a 1922 Supreme Court decision which ruled that baseball was not interstate in character and, thus, beyond the reach of the antitrust laws. Federal Baseball Club of Baltimore v. National League of Professional Baseball Clubs, 259 US 200 (1922). Perceiving that the Court had undermined this early decision by treating professional football (Radovich v. National Football League, 352 US 445 (1957)) and boxing (U.S. v. Int'l Boxing Club of N.Y., Inc., 348 US 236 (1955)) as being within the coverage of the antitrust laws, the Board doubted that "the Court still considers baseball alone to be outside of interstate commerce." 72 LRRM at 1546.

108 Cornell University, 183 NLRB No. 41, 75 LRRM 1269 (1970), *reversing* Trustees of Columbia University, 97 NLRB 424, 29 LRRM 1098 (1951). Recognizing the extensive noncommercial activities of large universities which help to provide operating funds, the increasing federal interest and support in the operation of schools, the inadequacy of state labor legislation applicable to educational institutions, and the increase in union organization and labor disputes at these institutions, the Board has extended its jurisdiction to cover private universities. However, it declined to establish jurisdictional standards in the instant case. Subsequently, using its rule-making authority for the first time since *NLRB* v. *Wyman-Gordon Co.*, 394 US 759, 70 LRRM 3345 (1969), the Board established jurisdiction at the $1,000,000 figure; however, it excluded from the computation any contributions which because of limitations by the grantor are not available for use for operating expenses. NLRB Reg. 29 C.F.R. §103.1 (1970). See Chapter 30 infra at note 122.

The Board had previously asserted jurisdiction over university projects which are intimately connected to the national defense. Massachusetts Institute of Technology, 110 NLRB 1611, 35 LRRM 1297 (1954).

Regardless of the standards enumerated above, there are certain areas where the Board will not assert jurisdiction. For example, the Board considers that labor disputes involving employers in the horse racing industry do not have a sufficiently substantial effect on commerce to warrant assertion of jurisdiction.[109] And the Board does not take jurisdiction over nonprofit institutions when they are engaged in noncommercial activities.[110] Also the Board does not take jurisdiction over the real estate brokerage business, holding that the services performed by brokers are "essentially local and have at best only a remote relationship to interstate commerce." [111]

When disputes involving labor unions are closely related to operations of a foreign government or to foreign policy questions, the tendency has been to avoid assertion of NLRB jurisdiction. Thus the Court of Appeals for the Fourth Circuit, reversing the Board, held that the NLRB lacked jurisdiction over a dispute involving a union's refusal, pursuant to its policy of boycotting ships trading with Cuba, to refer men to a U.S. employer for work in fitting a British ship in a U.S. port. The court held that the dispute involved a political question and was not a labor dispute concerning "terms and conditions of employment." [112] The Board will decline jurisdiction in cases where the employer enjoys a close relationship with a foreign government. For example, the Board deemed it inappropriate to assert jurisdiction over an employer engaged in selling tickets for British Railways and selling vouchers for rooms and meals in British hotels, in connection with rail travel in Britain, "particularly in view of the Employer's close relationship with . . . an agency of the British Government [British Railways], and without reaching the question whether the Board in fact has jurisdiction over the Employer's operations with respect

---

109 Walter A. Kelley, 139 NLRB 744, 51 LRRM 1375 (1962).

110 Young Men's Christian Association of Portland Oregon, 146 NLRB 20, 55 LRRM 1230 (1964) (civic, religious, educational activities); but see note 107 supra. While such institutions may have a substantial impact on interstate commerce, the Board in the past has held that to assert jurisdiction would not effectuate the purposes of the Act and would not conform to the intent of Congress. However, where the nonprofit institution is engaging in a commercial venture, jurisdiction has generally been asserted over the commercial venture. California Institute of Technology, 102 NLRB 1402, 31 LRRM 1435 (1953) (where a nonprofit educational institution operated a wind tunnel project for the benefit of five sponsoring aircraft companies.)

111 Seattle Real Estate Board, 130 NLRB 608, 610, 47 LRRM 1348 (1961).

112 NLRB v. Longshoremen's Association, 332 F 2d 992, 56 LRRM 2244 (CA 4, 1964) reversing, 146 NLRB 723, 55 LRRM 1389 (1964).

to the employees herein involved. . . ." [113] In addition, the Board may not assert jurisdiction over foreign-flag vessels.[114]

As heretofore noted, under Section 14 (c) (1) the Board may decline to assert jurisdiction over any labor dispute involving any class or category of employees where the effect of such dispute on commerce is not substantial, provided it is not the type of dispute that the Board would have heard under the standards in effect on August 1, 1959. However, while the Board may decline to assert jurisdiction in accordance with this provision, it must do so by rule of decision or by published rules adopted pursuant to the Administrative Procedure Act. It may not do so by advisory opinion.[115]

Since these standards are expressed in terms of dollar volume of business, problems over the availability of information and annual records of employers have naturally arisen. Where complete figures are not available, the Board projects the annual figure on the basis of the information at hand.[116] The Board has also adopted a "totality" doctrine where a component part of the employer's business, standing alone, fails to meet the standards. Hence, in *Rayonier, Inc.*,[117] the Board asserted jurisdiction over a research center that did not meet its standards, inasmuch as the center was an integral part of the company's manufacturing operations.

---

[113] British Rail-International, Inc., 163 NLRB 721, 64 LRRM 1432 (1967).

[114] McCulloch v. Sociedad Nacional de Marineros de Honduras, 372 US 10, 52 LRRM 2425 (1963). *See* notes 32 and 33 *supra* and accompanying text.

[115] Hirsch v. McCulloch, 303 F 2d 208, 49 LRRM 2828 (CA DC, 1962). *But see* NLRB v. Wyman-Gordon Co., 394 US 759, 70 LRRM 3345 (1969), and discussion of rule-making and the NLRB in Chapter 30 *infra,* particularly note 122.

[116] Local 57, Roofers (Atlas Roofing Co.), 131 NLRB 1267, 48 LRRM 1248 (1961), *supplemented,* 134 NLRB 367, 49 LRRM 1180 (1961). In this case the Board held that, in projecting commerce data of a newly formed company on the basis of a 12-month period, "commencement of operations" dates from the beginning of sales or of manufacturing and not from the date of incorporation.

[117] NLRB Case No. 22-RC-1103, 48 LRRM 1336 (1961). *See also* note 98 *supra.*

CHAPTER 29

JURISDICTION: FEDERAL PREEMPTION
AND ITS EXCEPTIONS

I. THE JUDICIAL ROLE

The doctrine of federal preemption is anchored to the "supremacy" clause of the Constitution.[1] The doctrine was argued as early as 1824, for in *Gibbons* v. *Ogden*[2] it was contended that the grant of power to Congress to regulate commerce necessarily excluded any concurrent power in the states. Chief Justice Marshall acknowledged that "[t]here is great force in the argument, and the Court is not satisfied that it has been refuted."[3] Subsequently the Court recognized, as it does today,[4] that as to subjects which are judicially determined to require national uniformity of regulation, state power is preempted even though Congress has not affirmatively exercised its power to regulate.

If the mere existence of congressional power may preclude state power over a given subject, the same result obviously will follow when Congress does exercise its power. If a state law is in conflict with the federal law, the state law is invalid under the supremacy clause. But even where there is no direct conflict, the state regulation may still be invalid if it is judicially determined that the

---

1 "This Constitution, and the Laws of the United States which shall be made in Pursuance thereof . . . shall be the supreme Law of the land; and the Judges in every State shall be bound thereby, any Thing in the Constitution or Laws of any State to the Contrary notwithstanding." U. S. Const., art. VI. *See* Nash v. Florida Industrial Commission, 389 US 235, 66 LRRM 2625 (1967), where the Supreme Court specifically invoked the supremacy clause to invalidate application of a Florida law which denied unemployment insurance benefits to an individual who had filed an unfair labor practice charge with the NLRB against her former employer.
2 22 US (9 Wheat) 1 (1824).
3 *Id.* at 16.
4 *E.g.*, Bro. of R.R. Trainmen v. Jacksonville Terminal Co., 394 US 369, 70 LRRM 2961 (1969).

congressional regulation leaves no room for state regulation of the same subject.[5] *Potential* rather than *actual* conflict between state and federal law provides the justification for such a conclusion, and thus the preemption doctrine may be said to go a step beyond the literal mandate of the supremacy clause.[6] The avoidance of potential conflict between state and federal law under the preemption doctrine, where Congress has legislated, is analytically similar to the national uniformity test which may invalidate state law where Congress has not legislated.[7]

The Supreme Court, in applying preemption to invalidate state action where Congress has legislated, has justified the result in terms of congressional intent to preempt, although there may be no congressional intent in any specific sense. This was the Court's consistent approach to preemption under the National Labor Relations Act [8] for over 20 years. During that period the Court's decisions may have been based on a pragmatic analysis of relevant facts and circumstances, but the results were ascribed to the will of Congress. For example, in *Garner* v. *Teamsters Union* [9] Justice Jackson stated that "[t]he National Labor Management Relations Act . . . leaves much to the states, though Congress has refrained from telling us how much. We must spell out from conflicting indications of Congressional will the area in which state action is still permissible." [10] "This penumbral area," declared Justice Frankfurter, "can be rendered progressively clear only by the course of litigation." [11] He later characterized the statutory implications concerning what had been taken from the states and what had been left to them as of a "Delphic nature, to be translated into concreteness by the process of litigation elucidation." [12] However, in a 1966 preemption case the Court modified, if it did

---

5 *See* discussion and cases in Part II *infra*.
6 *See* note 16 *infra* and accompanying text.
7 *E.g.,* Southern Pac. Co. v. Arizona, 325 US 761 (1945).
8 *From* Hill v. Florida, 325 US 538, 16 LRRM 734 (1945), *until* Linn v. United Plant Guard Workers, Local 114, 383 US 53, 61 LRRM 2345 (1966). *Cf.* Allen-Bradley v. Wisconsin Employment Rel. Bd., 325 US 797, 16 LRRM 798 (1945). *See also* Comment, *The Changing Face of Federal Pre-emption in Labor Relations,* 36 Fordham L. Rev. 731 (1968).
9 346 US 485, 33 LRRM 2218 (1953).
10 *Id.* at 488.
11 Weber v. Anheuser-Busch, Inc., 348 US 468, 480-81, 35 LRRM 2637 (1955).
12 Int'l Ass'n of Machinists v. Gonzales, 356 US 617, 619, 42 LRRM 2135 (1958). (The comparison with the procedures at ancient Delphi was pertinent. At Delphi, the "holy ones," or priests, were charged with the responsibility of interpreting the will of Apollo, expressed through the Pythia, his prophetess. Originally, the

not entirely abandon, its Delphic approach to fathoming the will of Congress on the question of delimiting state action permitted in labor relations. In determining the limits of state jurisdiction in a libel case that involved a handbill distributed during an NLRB election campaign, Mr. Justice Clark, in *Linn* v. *Plant Guards*,[13] candidly acknowledged the Court's active role in the process. His opinion said that allowing the state to redress such a libel if it was issued with "knowledge of its falsity, or with reckless disregard of whether it was true or false," [14] would be consistent with "the actual need of *national labor policy*" [15]—a policy which the Court found implicit in the National Labor Relations Act. Emphasizing the Court's discretionary function in interpreting this national labor policy, the Court concluded that "if experience shows that a more complete curtailment, even a total one, should be necessary to prevent impairment of that policy, the Court will be free to reconsider today's holding. We deal here not with a constitutional issue but solely with the degree to which state remedies have been pre-empted by the Act." [16]

The degree to which the Court has found state remedies pre-empted has varied.[17] For a time state law reigned virtually su-

---

Pythia was a virgin, a virgin being "the purer vehicle for divine communication," according to tradition. Farnell, "Oracle," 20 ENCYCLOPEDIA BRITANNICA 142 (11th ed. 1911). Later, however, using possibly the earliest recorded legal fiction, the Greeks changed the rule, and a married woman over 50 years of age *attired as a virgin* was employed as the Pythia. Inspired by mystic vapors, she spoke the will of Apollo. Her utterances may have been only unintelligible murmurs, but they were interpreted into relevance and set in metric or prose sentences by the "holy ones." *Ibid.* According to Plutarch, "[s]o great became the fame and influence of Apollo that all Greece resorted to his instrument and mouthpiece at Delphi for information on cult procedure, politics, law and personal conduct in everyday affairs, from monarchs and tyrants to ordinary individuals, in spite of the fact that the responses were for the most part vague, evasive and ambiguous, especially on critical questions." E. O. James, THE ANCIENT GODS 244 (1960).)

13 Note 8 *supra.*

14 383 US at 65. *See* note 95 *infra* and accompanying text for a discussion of this case.

15 383 US at 67 (emphasis added).

16 *Ibid.* In a 1969 case involving application of a Florida secondary boycott statute to picketing of a railroad terminal in a dispute governed by the Railway Labor Act, the Supreme Court held that "even though the Florida courts may have jurisdiction over this litigation, the application of state law is limited by paramount *federal policies of nationwide import.*" (Emphasis added.) Bro. of RR Trainmen v. Jacksonville Terminal Co., 394 US 369, No. 69, 70 LRRM 2961 (1969). *See also* the Court's reasoning in rejecting exclusive NLRB jurisdiction in fair representation cases. Vaca v. Sipes, 386 US 171, 64 LRRM 2369 (1967), *infra* notes 95-97 and accompanying text.

17 For detailed commentary upon this changing subject *see generally:* Feinsinger, *Federal-State Relations Under the Taft-Hartley Act,* N.Y.U. FIRST ANNUAL CONFERENCE ON LABOR 463 (1948); Smith, *The Taft-Hartley Act and State Jurisdiction over*

preme in the regulation of strike and boycott activity, especially after the passage of the Norris-LaGuardia Act.[18] However, the picture changed dramatically with the evolution of the preemption doctrine, so that today few areas of state substantive law remain applicable to labor disputes in the private sector.[19] Most of the activity of the state courts in the field of labor relations, except in the public sector,[20] is now confined to the enforcement and application of federal law. The process of judicial evolution which effected this transformation is the subject of this chapter.

II. THE BASIC PREEMPTION DOCTRINE

The National Labor Relations Act of 1935 reflected a congressional intent that labor disputes affecting the free flow of interstate commerce were to be regulated under a uniform federal law. This law was to be administered by the National Labor Relations Board having primary jurisdiction. Broadly stated, the public policy expressed in the NLRA was that of preempting the original jurisdiction of state and federal courts and of other tribunals to decide issues involved in a labor dispute in favor of a single federal agency.[21]

Labor Relations, 46 MICH. L. REV. 593 (1948); Cox, *Federalism in the Law of Labor Relations*, 67 HARV. L. REV. 1297 (1954); Hays, *Federalism and Labor Relations in the United States*, 102 U. PA. L. REV. 959 (1954); Hays, *State Courts and Federal Pre-emption*, 23 MO. L. REV. 373 (1958); Meltzer, *The Supreme Court, Congress, and State Jurisdiction over Labor Relations*, 59 COLUM. L. REV. 6, 269 (1959); Wellington, *Labor and the Federal System*, 26 U. CHI. L. REV. 542 (1959); Michelman, *State Power to Govern Concerted Employee Activities*, 74 HARV. L. REV. 641 (1961); Sovern, *Section 301 and the Primary Jurisdiction of the NLRB*, 76 HARV. L. REV. 529 (1963); Currier, *Defamation in Labor Disputes: Preemption and the New Federal Common Law*, 53 VA. L. REV. 1 (1967); Peck, *Accommodation and Conflict Among Tribunals: Whatever Happened to Preemption?*, LABOR LAW DEVELOPMENTS 1969 (15th Ann. Inst., Southwestern Legal Foundation) 121 (1969); Broomfield, *Preemptive Federal Jurisdiction over Concerted Trespassory Union Activity*, 83 HARV. L. REV. 552 (1970).

18 47 Stat. 70, 29 USC §§101-15 (1964). See Aaron, *Labor Injunctions in the State Courts—Part I: A Survey*, 50 VA. L. REV. 951 (1964).

19 Parallel to the development of the preemption doctrine, the Supreme Court decided a line of cases defining the limits on the power of a state to regulate picketing under the First and Fourteenth Amendments to the Constitution. While the Court was narrowing the First Amendment protection accorded picketing, *e.g.* Teamsters, *Local 695* v. *Vogt, Inc.*, 354 US 284, 40 LRRM 2208 (1957), and thus expanding the permissible area of state action, it was simultaneously contracting the area of state regulation under the preemption doctrine. See notes 6 through 18 in Chapter 19 *supra* and accompanying text.

20 See Morris, *Public Policy and the Law Relating to Collective Bargaining in the Public Service*, 22 SW. L. J. 585 (1968).

21 Amalgamated Utility Workers v. Consolidated Edison Co. of NY, 309 US 261, 6 LRRM 669 (1940); Myers v. Bethlehem Shipbldg. Corp., 303 US 41, 1-A LRRM 575 (1938).

The Supreme Court did not begin the task of spelling out the exclusive nature of the Board's jurisdiction in a positive way until 1945 in *Hill* v. *Florida*.[22] It held that the NLRA and certain provisions of a Florida statute could not "move freely within the orbits of their respective purposes without impinging upon one another." [23] The provisions in question required every union "business agent" to obtain an annual license costing one dollar, but the license was to be withheld from anyone who had not been a citizen of the United States for 10 years, had been convicted of a felony, or was not of good moral character. The Court found that such restrictions conflicted with the full freedom of workers to select their own bargaining agents and to pass upon their qualifications. Because the NLRA protected this freedom in selecting union representatives, the state was preempted from enjoining a labor union or its business agent until the restrictions were satisfied.

In *Hill* v. *Florida* the Board had attempted to exercise its control over union representation in spite of the impediment of state action. In 1947 the Supreme Court found a conflict between the Board's authority to permit unionization of foremen, which it had exercised in a "checkered" fashion, and the power of a state labor board to recognize the foremen's unions.[24] The state board had recognized the union at a time when the NLRB, using its discretion, had not entertained the foremen's petitions. The Supreme Court held that the failure of the federal Board affirmatively to exercise its full authority "takes on the character of a ruling that no such regulation is appropriate or approved pursuant to the policy of the statute." [25] Thus, the Court concluded, it was beyond the power of the state board to apply state law to the foremen.

The fact that a privately owned utility or transit company is the focus of state action does not relieve the effect of a conflict between such action and the federal act. Therefore, the preemption doctrine removed jurisdiction from the state courts and labor board

---

22 325 US 538, 16 LRRM 734 (1945). The Court had discussed preemption, however, in *Allen-Bradley Local 1111, United Elec. Workers* v. *Wisconsin Employment Rel. Bd.,* 315 US 740, 10 LRRM 520 (1942).

23 *Id.* at 543, citing Union Brokerage Co. v. Jenson, 322 US 202 (1944). *But cf.* DeVeau v. Braisted, 363 US 144, 46 LRRM 2304 (1960).

24 Bethlehem Steel Co. v. New York Labor Rel. Bd., 330 US 767, 19 LRRM 2499 (1947).

25 *Id.* at 774. The Supreme Court in *Packard Motor Car Co.* v. *NLRB,* 330 US 485, 19 LRRM 2397 (1947), had held that foremen are employees within §2(3) of the Act.

over a strike by public utility employees which was protected activity under Section 7.[26] The Supreme Court reaffirmed the application of the preemption doctrine to state attempts to restrict strike activity by holding "strictly emergency legislation" invalid.[27] The state law had authorized seizure of public transportation facilities and the issuance of injunctions against striking transportation employees.

As a corollary to its holdings that preemption would apply where the Act protected the subject matter involved in a state court action, the Court recognized certain conduct which was neither protected nor prohibited by the Act and which was therefore deemed to be within state power to regulate. For example, prior to the enactment of the Taft-Hartley Act, when there were no union unfair labor practices, the Court in *Allen-Bradley* v. *WERB* [28] upheld the power of the states to deal with union conduct involving threats and violence because "Congress has not made such employee and union conduct . . . subject to regulation by the federal Board." [29] In 1949, after the Taft-Hartley amendments had added union unfair labor practices to the statute, the Court in *Briggs & Stratton* [30] reviewed an order of the Wisconsin state labor board which directed a union to cease and desist from engaging in intermittent work stoppages during working hours. The union had not resorted to a full-fledged strike, but the NLRB had repeatedly held that work stoppages were "partial strikes" and thus were protected as "concerted activities" under Section 7. In these early cases the Court "undertook for itself to determine the status of the disputed activity." [31] Concluding that work stoppages were not regulated by the federal Act, the Court found *Briggs & Stratton* to be within the *Allen-Bradley* rule:

> There is no existing or possible conflict or overlapping between the authority of the federal and state Boards, because the federal Board

---

[26] Street Employees v. Wisconsin Employment Rel. Bd., 340 US 383, 27 LRRM 2385 (1951) (the Wisconsin Public Utility Anti-Strike Law, which made it a misdemeanor for utility employees to engage in a strike causing an interruption of an essential public utility service, held to conflict with the NLRA and to be invalid under the Supremacy Clause).

[27] Division 1287, Street Employees v. Missouri, 374 US 74, 80, 53 LRRM 2394 (1963).

[28] 315 US 740, 10 LRRM 520 (1942).

[29] *Id.* at 749. The power of the states to regulate conduct involving threats and violence continued to be treated as a separate exception to the preemption doctrine even after such conduct was outlawed by the 1947 amendments to the NLRA. *See* Part III *infra.*

[30] 336 US 245, 23 LRRM 2361 (1949).

[31] San Diego Bldg. Trades v. Garmon, 359 US 236, 245, n. 4, 43 LRRM 2838 (1959).

has no authority either to investigate, approve or forbid the union conduct in question. This conduct is governable by the state or it is entirely ungoverned. . . . We think that this recurrent or intermittent unannounced stoppage of work to win unstated ends was neither forbidden by the federal statute nor was it legalized and approved thereby. Such being the case, the state police power was not superseded by Congressional Act. . . .[32]

In later decisions the Court assumed a less active role in determining whether the conduct fell within the regulatory provisions of the Act. And finally, in *San Diego Building Trades Council* v. *Garmon*,[33] the Court noted that the ruling in *Briggs & Stratton*, in which the Court had determined NLRB coverage, was no longer of general application:

If the Board decides . . . that conduct is protected by §7, or prohibited by §8, then the matter is at an end, and the States are ousted of all jurisdiction. Or the Board may decide that an activity is neither protected nor prohibited, and thereby raise the question whether such activity may be regulated by the States. . . . In the absence of the Board's clear determination that an activity is neither protected nor prohibited or of compelling precedent applied to essentially undisputed facts, it is not for this Court to decide whether such activities are subject to state jurisdiction.[34]

In *Garmon* the Court refined the application of the preemption doctrine to situations where the conflict between state and federal laws is indirect, unclear, or only foreseeable. Two cases which preceded *Garmon,* and which probably provoked the most significant exodus of labor disputes from the state courts,[35] were *Garner* v. *Teamsters Union*[36] and *Weber* v. *Anheuser-Busch, Inc.*[37] *Garner* involved the issuance of an injunction against peaceful picketing which the state court had found was for the purpose of coercing employers into compelling or influencing their employees to join the union. This was considered a violation of provisions of the Pennsylvania Labor Relations Act that were similar to unfair labor practice provisions in Taft-Hartley. Writing in

---

[32] 336 US at 254.
[33] *Supra* note 31.
[34] 359 US at 245-46. The Court also noted that "[t]he approach taken in . . . [the *Briggs & Stratton*] case, in which the Court undertook for itself to determine the status of the disputed activity, has not been followed in later decisions, and is no longer of general application." 359 US at 245, n. 4. *See* notes 51-64 and accompanying text *infra*.
[35] *E.g.,* Ex parte Twedell, 309 SW 2d 834, 41 LRRM 2520 (Tex. S. Ct. 1958).
[36] 346 US 485, 33 LRRM 2218 (1953).
[37] 348 US 468, 35 LRRM 2637 (1955).

the language of primary jurisdiction and holding that the state court lacked jurisdiction, the Court said that the "power and duty of primary decision lies with the Board," [38] not with the court. The question was "whether the state, through its courts, may adjudge the same controversy and extend its own form of relief." [39] Answering in the negative, the Court stated:

> Congress did not merely lay down a substantive rule of law to be enforced by any tribunal competent to apply law generally to the parties. It went on to confide primary interpretation and application of its rules to a specific and specially constituted tribunal and prescribed a particular procedure for investigation, complaint and notice, and hearing and decision, including judicial relief pending a final administrative order. Congress evidently considered that centralized administration of specially designed procedures was necessary to obtain uniform application of its substantive rules and to avoid those diversities and conflicts likely to result from a variety of legal procedures and attitudes toward labor controversies. . . . A multiplicity of tribunals and a diversity of procedures are quite as apt to produce incompatible or conflicting adjudications as are different rules of substantive law.[40]

The *Weber* case involved a state court injunction against union conduct which was found to be illegal under the state's antitrust laws. The union had struck to force an employer to assign certain work to machinists rather than carpenters. In an unfair labor practice proceeding the Board had found no violation of Section 8(b)(4)(D) of the NLRA.[41] Thereafter, a Missouri court found a restraint-of-trade violation and issued an injunction.[42] In reversing, the Supreme Court noted that the Board had not passed upon the question of whether the strike violated Sections 8(b)(4)(A) and (B), and that, moreover, even if it did not violate Section 8, it might be protected conduct under Section 7. In attempting to

---

38 346 US at 489. A procedural problem of great practical importance arises when a state court issues an injunction notwithstanding a preemption defense that the court has no jurisdiction. In *Amalgamated Clothing Workers* v. *Richman Bros.,* 348 US 511, 35 LRRM 2682 (1955), the Court held that the federal district courts were prohibited by 28 U.S.C. §2283 from enjoining the enforcement of the state court injunction. The union's recourse in this situation is to appeal the trial court decision up through the state court system and then, if necessary, to the U.S. Supreme Court. *Followed in* Atlantic Coast Line R.R. Co. v. Locomotive Engineers, 398 US 281, 74 LRRM 2321 (1970) (federal district court barred from revoking a state court injunction against picketing by union subject to the Railway Labor Act).

39 *Ibid.*

40 346 US at 490-91.

41 101 NLRB 346, 31 LRRM 1084 (1952).

42 265 SW 2d 325, 33 LRRM 2519, 2754 (Mo. Sup. Ct. 1954).

devise a test for determining whether preemption should apply, the Court observed that

> where the moving party itself alleges unfair labor practices, where the facts reasonably bring the controversy within the sections prohibiting these practices, and where the conduct, if not prohibited by the federal Act, may be reasonably deemed to come within the protection afforded by that Act, the state court must decline jurisdiction in deference to the tribunal which Congress has selected for determining such issues in the first instance.[43]

The Court stressed that the NLRB, not the state court, was empowered to pass upon the substantive issues to which the federal statute might be applicable. And it was immaterial that the state statute in question was not specifically directed at labor relations. The opinion was based upon a reading of congressional intent,[44] in which the possibility of obvious conflict between the state and federal forums provided the rationale:

> By the Taft-Hartley Act, Congress did not exhaust the full sweep of legislative power over industrial relations given by the Commerce Clause. Congress formulated a code whereby it outlawed some aspects of labor activities and left others free for the operation of economic forces. As to both categories, the areas that have been pre-empted by federal authority and thereby withdrawn from state power are not susceptible of delimitation by fixed metes and bounds. Obvious conflict, actual or potential, leads to easy judicial exclusion of state action.[45]

In another case involving conflict with state antitrust laws, *Teamsters v. Oliver*,[46] the Court held that the duty to bargain required of a union and an employer, which is protected under the NLRA, could not be limited by a state statute regulating restraint of trade. A state court had enjoined effectuation of a provision in a collective bargaining contract between a motor carrier and a union which specified the minimum rental and certain other terms of leases between the carrier and owner-operators who drove their vehicles in the carrier's service. According to the state court,

---

43 348 US at 481. The Court thus laid down a procedural rule which required the state court to make its jurisdictional determination based upon allegations in the plaintiff's pleading. Under this rule, an adroit pleader might avoid an initial finding of preemption. The rule was superseded by the "arguably subject" test of the *Garmon* case, note 63 *infra*.
44 *See* note 12 *supra*.
45 348 US at 480.
46 Int'l Bro. of Teamsters, Local 24 v. Oliver, 358 US 283, 43 LRRM 2374 (1959).

this agreement constituted illegal price-fixing and was only a "remote and indirect approach to the subject of wages." [47] The Supreme Court reversed, concluding that the provision was directly related to the maintenance of the basic wage structure of the contract and therefore was a mandatory subject of bargaining under the NLRA.[48] The Court found no room for "state policy limiting the solutions that the parties' agreement can provide to the problems of wages and working conditions." [49]

The prelude to the clarification of the preemption doctrine in *San Diego Building Trades Council* v. *Garmon* occurred when a California court awarded damages and an injunction against peaceful picketing for the purpose of compelling an employer to execute a union-shop contract with a minority union, conduct which the California Supreme Court recognized to be a violation of Section 8(b)(2) of the Act.[50] At the same time the regional director of the NLRB declined jurisdiction over a representation proceeding brought by the employer.

Three issues were settled by the Supreme Court in its two *Garmon* opinions [51] and in two companion cases to the first *Garmon* decision.[52] As the initial issue in the companion cases, the Court determined whether a state had the power to regulate conduct covered by the Act, and otherwise preempted, in a case where the Board had refused to assert its jurisdiction. Since 1950 the Board had published and followed standards, stated in terms of yearly dollar amounts of interstate outflow and inflow, which were self-imposed limitations on the full measure of its jurisdiction. In *Guss* v. *Utah Labor Relations Board* [53] and in *Amalgamated Meat Cutters* v. *Fairlawn Meats, Inc.,*[54] the Court held that the Board's refusal to assert jurisdiction did not invest the states with power over the activity. *Guss* and *Fairlawn* involved equitable relief and controlled *Garmon* "in its major aspects." [55] This trilogy of opin-

---

47 *Id.* at 293.
48 For a discussion of mandatory subjects of bargaining, *see* Chapter 15 *supra.*
49 358 US at 296.
50 Garmon v. San Diego Bldg. Trades Council, 291 P2d 1, 37 LRRM 2233 (1955).
51 353 US 951, 39 LRRM 2574 (1957); 359 US 236, 43 LRRM 2838 (1959).
52 Guss v. Utah Labor Rel. Bd., 353 US 1, 39 LRRM 2567 (1957); Amalgamated Meat Cutters v. Fairlawn Meats, Inc., 353 US 20, 39 LRRM 2571 (1957).
53 *Supra* note 52.
54 *Supra* note 52.
55 353 US at 28.

ions created a "no-man's-land" [56] subject only to congressional or Board correction.

Since the basis of the award of damages in *Garmon* was uncertain, it was remanded to the California Supreme Court. Although violent conduct was not involved, the employers argued that the award should be sustained on the basis of *United Constr. Workers v. Laburnum Constr. Corp.*[57] Violent conduct such as that in *Laburnum* had formed the basis of an exception to the application of the preemption doctrine.[58] When the California Supreme Court sustained the award of damages on the basis of California law,[59] the Supreme Court granted certiorari to consider a second issue: whether the state court had jurisdiction over tortious, but peaceful, labor activity. The award of damages was reversed on grounds which narrowed the *Laburnum* holding to the type of conduct involved therein.[60] The Court stressed that its primary concern was not the nature of the relief but rather the broad scope of the activities regulated by federal law and protected from state actions by the preemption doctrine.

> . . . [J]udicial concern has necessarily focused on the nature of the activities which the States have sought to regulate, rather than on the method of regulation adopted. When the exercise of state power over a particular area of activity threatened interference with the clearly indicated policy of industrial relations, it has been judicially necessary to preclude the States from acting. . . .
>
> Nor is it significant that California asserted its power to give damages rather than to enjoin what the Board may restrain though it could not compensate. Our concern is with delimiting areas of conduct which must be free from state regulation if national policy is to be left unhampered. Such regulation can be as effectively exerted through an award of damages as through some form of preventive relief.[61]

A third and closely related issue was the judicial formula to be used to apply the preemption doctrine to those cases where activity was not clearly regulated by the Act. The Court enunciated a

---

[56] Guss v. Utah Labor Rel. Bd., *supra* note 52 at 11. *See* Chapter 28 *supra*, notes 20-37.

[57] 347 US 656, 34 LRRM 2229 (1954).

[58] See note 69 *infra* and accompanying text.

[59] Garmon v. San Diego Bldg. Trades Council, 320 P2d 473, 41 LRRM 2496 (1958).

[60] *See* notes 73-77 *infra* and accompanying text.

[61] 359 US at 243, 246-47.

broad test for the application of the preemption doctrine based on the primary jurisdiction of the NLRB:

> At times it has not been clear whether the particular activity regulated by the States was governed by §7 or §8 or was, perhaps, outside both these sections. But courts are not primary tribunals to adjudicate such issues. It is essential to the administration of the Act that these determinations be left in the first instance to the National Labor Relations Board. . . .

> When an activity is *arguably subject* to §7 or §8 of the Act, the States as well as the federal courts must defer to the exclusive competence of the National Labor Relations Board if the danger of state interference with national policy is to be averted.[62]

The Court described its role and that of the Board as dictated by national labor policy:

> It follows that the failure of the Board to define the legal significance under the Act of a particular activity does not give the States the power to act. In the absence of the Board's clear determination that an activity is neither protected nor prohibited or of compelling precedent applied to essentially undisputed facts, it is not for this Court to decide whether such activities are subject to state jurisdiction. . . . The governing consideration is that to allow the States to control activities that are *potentially subject* to federal regulation involves too great a danger of conflict with national labor policy. . . .

> Since the National Labor Relations Board has not adjudicated the status of the conduct for which the State of California seeks to give a remedy in damages, and since such activity is arguably within the compass of §7 or §8 of the Act, the State's jurisdiction is displaced.[63]

Another preemption issue which may be developing relates to the law of trespass. To what extent do property rights prevail in the face of labor union activity that is protected either by the NLRA or by the free speech and free press guarantees of the First

---

62 359 US 244-45 (emphasis added). *Compare* the test used in *Weber* v. *Anheuser-Busch, Inc., supra* notes 37 and 43 and accompanying text. *See also* Bro. of R.R. Trainmen v. Jacksonville Terminal Co., 394 US 369, n. 19, 70 LRRM 2961 (1969); the Court distinguished between two bases of federal preemption which "are often not easily separable": (1) federal protection of the conduct in question and (2) the primary jurisdiction of the Board. *Garmon* was cited as an example of the latter basis.

63 *Id.* at 246 (emphasis added). *See* Chapter 28 *supra* generally for treatment of the scope of the statutory jurisdiction embraced by the Act. For discussion of NLRB and state court jurisdiction in labor matters relating to foreign flag vessels *see*: note 33 therein *and* McCulloch v. Sociedad Nacional de Marineros de Honduras, 372 US 10, 52 LRRM 2425 (1963); Incres Steamship Co. v. Int'l Maritime Workers, 371 US 804, 52 LRRM 2431 (1963); Int'l Longshoremen, Local 1416 v. Ariadne Shipping Co., Ltd., 397 US 195, 73 LRRM 2625 (1970).

Amendment? The issue was briefly raised in the Supreme Court in a case which was dismissed for improvident grant of certiorari. The case concerned the granting of a state court temporary injunction against picketing on a private sidewalk owned and maintained by the picketed employer. If it is assumed that there was no physical obstruction and that the sidewalk was used by the public, it would seem that the picketing might be privileged under both *Garmon* and *Logan Valley*.[64]

III. JUDICIAL EXCEPTIONS TO PREEMPTION

A. Matters of "Overriding State Interest"—Violence and Threats of Violence

While the Court was constructing and applying the *Garner-Garmon* doctrine, it was at the same time recognizing situations where preemption did not apply, regardless of the fact that the challenged activity may have been prohibited or protected by the NLRA. In the most notable situations, state action has been allowed when the challenged conduct was marked by violence or threats to the public peace and order. The Court in *Garmon* explained that "[s]tate jurisdiction has prevailed in these situations because the compelling state interest, in the scheme of our federalism, in the maintenance of domestic peace is not overridden in the absence of clearly expressed congressional direction." [65]

Mass picketing which obstructed streets and plant entrances, violence, and threats of violence were held to be subject to an in-

---

[64] The case in which certiorari was dismissed was Taggart v. Weinacker's, Inc., 397 US 223, 73 LRRM 2628 (1970). *See* decision below, 214 So 2d 913, 69 LRRM 2348 (Ala S Ct, 1968). In Amalgamated Food Employees, Local 590 v. Logan Valley Plaza, Inc., 391 US 308, 68 LRRM 2209 (1968), the Court held that peaceful picketing in a privately owned shopping center "in a location open generally to the public is, absent other factors involving the purpose or manner of the picketing, protected by the First Amendment." The Court did not pass on the issue of preemption. *See* Blue Ridge v. Schleininger, 432 SW 2d 610, 70 LRRM 2597 (KC Mo Ct App, 1968). *See also* Chapter 19 *supra* at notes 10-18.

In *Taggart* v. *Weinacker*, Chief Justice Burger used the occasion to record his view that "any contention that the States are preempted in these circumstances is without merit. The protection of private property, whether a home, factory, or store, through trespass laws is historically a concern of state law." Mr. Justice White concurred. Mr. Justice Harlan responded in a separate opinion, that in the absence of further expression from Congress he would stand by *Garmon*, which would "foreclose state action with respect to 'arguably protected activities,' until the Board has acted. . . ." See Broomfield, *Preemptive Federal Jurisdiction Over Concerted Trespassory Union Activity*, 83 HARV. L. REV. 552 (1970).

[65] San Diego Building Trades Council v. Garmon, 359 US 236, 247, 43 LRRM 2838 (1959).

junction by a state labor board in *UAW* v. *WERB* [66] and by a state court in *Youngdahl* v. *Rainfair.*[67] State jurisdiction was unaffected by the fact that the conduct constituted an unfair labor practice under Section 8(b)(1)(A) and thus was within the jurisdiction of the NLRB. It was likewise immaterial that the state court had exercised its power through a state labor board. In either situation the Supreme Court recognized that the state had jurisdiction over violent or potentially violent conduct on the basis of its general police power. However, in *Youngdahl* the injunctive relief granted by the trial court to prohibit the workers from obstructing the streets, threatening or provoking violence, and "all other picketing and patrolling" was too sweeping.[68] While upholding the issuance of the injunction, the Court set aside that portion prohibiting "other picketing" which was peaceful and therefore was within the preempted domain of the NLRB.

Similarly, the Court permitted a state court to award *damages* for tortious conduct involving violence and threats, even though the conduct was prohibited by the NLRA and was within the jurisdiction of the NLRB. In *United Constr. Workers* v. *Laburnum Constr. Corp.*[69] the union by threats had forced a non-union contractor to abandon certain construction projects, conduct which the Court conceded was an unfair labor practice under the NLRA. Sustaining a state damage award of $129,326, the Court distinguished *Garner* and explained that no conflict existed between the state remedy in *Laburnum* and the Board remedy.

> Here Congress has neither provided nor suggested any substitute for the traditional state court procedure for collecting damages for injuries caused by tortious conduct. . . . If Virginia is denied jurisdiction in this case, it will mean that where the federal preventive administrative procedures are impotent or inadequate, the offenders, by coercion of the type found here, may destroy property without liability for the damage done. . . .

> To the extent that Congress prescribed preventive procedure against unfair labor practices, [*Garner*] recognized that the Act excluded conflicting state procedure to the same end. To the extent, however, that Congress has not prescribed procedure for dealing with the consequences of tortious conduct already committed, there is no

---

66 351 US 266, 38 LRRM 2165 (1956).
67 355 US 131, 41 LRRM 2169 (1957).
68 *Id.* at 139. *Cf.* Milk Wagon Drivers Union v. Meadowmoor Dairies, Inc., 312 US 287, 7 LRRM 310 (1941).
69 347 US 656, 34 LRRM 2229 (1954). *See also* note 60 *supra* and accompanying text.

ground for concluding that existing criminal penalties or liabilities for tortious conduct have been eliminated. The care we took in the *Garner* case to demonstrate the existing conflict between state and federal remedies in that case was, itself, a recognition that if no conflict had existed, the state procedure would have survived.[70]

Later, as will be noted, the Court narrowed and clarified the scope of the exception described in *Laburnum*.

The Court followed the *Laburnum* decision in a suit brought by an employee against a union arising from his confrontation with union members during a strike. In *UAW* v. *Russell* [71] a state court jury had concluded that union pickets, by force of numbers and threats of bodily harm, had prevented Russell, a nonunion member, from entering the struck plant, whereupon Russell obtained a $10,000 judgment against the union for the tort of wrongful interference with a lawful occupation. Conceding that the union conduct was an unfair labor practice, the Supreme Court nevertheless sustained the judgment. Again the Court found no conflict in remedies.

> Congress did not establish a general scheme authorizing the Board to award full compensatory damages for injuries caused by wrongful conduct. . . . We conclude that an employee's right to recover, in the state courts, *all* damages caused him by this kind of tortious conduct cannot fairly be said to be pre-empted without a clearer declaration of congressional policy than we find here.[72]

As an important point of clarification, the Court in *Garmon* pointed out that the focus of its decision in *Laburnum* was not "the fact that the state remedy had no federal counterpart." [73] Although the lack of conflict in remedies had given support to the *Laburnum* opinion and to *Russell,* that fact would have been insufficient to prevent federal preemption in either case. The Court emphasized in *Garmon* that the determining factor in these exceptional cases was "the 'type of conduct' involved, i.e., 'intimidation and threats of violence.' " [74] Indeed, in *Laburnum* the Court had "expressly phrased its grant of certiorari to include only the limited question of the State's jurisdiction to award damages '[i]n view of the type of conduct found by the Supreme Court of Ap-

---

[70] *Id*. at 663-65.
[71] 356 US 634, 42 LRRM 2142 (1958).
[72] *Id*. at 643-646.
[73] 359 US at 248-49.
[74] *Id*. at 249.

peals of Virginia.' " [75] Likewise, the decision in *Russell* stressed the violent nature of the activity and was limited to "the kind of tortious conduct" involved therein.[76] Thus the *Laburnum* and *Russell* holdings were limited to the facts in each case. Nevertheless, the Supreme Court at the same time further explained that the states had the power to act in such situations because "the regulated conduct touched interests so deeply rooted in local feeling and responsibility that, in the absence of compelling congressional direction, we could not infer that Congress had deprived the States" of power.[77]

B. Matters of "Peripheral Concern" to the Federal Law

In another group of cases the Court has permitted actions in state courts against conduct that would otherwise fall within the protection or the prohibition of the NLRA because

> . . . due regard for the presuppositions of our embracing federal system, including the principle of diffusion of power not as a matter of doctrinaire localism but as a promoter of democracy, has required us not to find withdrawal from the States of power to regulate where the activity regulated was *a merely peripheral concern* of the Labor Management Relation Act.[78]

The Court in *Garmon* cited *Machinists* v. *Gonzales* as an example of conduct of peripheral concern to the NLRA. In *Gonzales*[79] the Court sustained a state award of reinstatement and damages for breach of contract against a union for conduct which did not involve violence or threats. The union had illegally expelled a member in violation of California law that gave the expelled worker a cause of action for breach of contract and provided for recovery of damages for physical and mental suffering. Conceding that the union conduct might be a violation of Section 8(b)(2) of the NLRA, the Court went on to state that:

> The National Labor Relations Board could not have given respondent the relief that California gave him according to its local law of contracts and damages. Although, if the unions' conduct constituted an unfair labor practice, the Board might possibly have been empowered to award back pay, in no event could it mulct in dam-

---

75 *Id.* at n. 6.
76 356 US at 646.
77 359 US at 244.
78 San Diego Bldg. Trades Council v. Garmon, 359 US 236, 243, 43 LRRM 2838 (1959) (emphasis added).
79 356 US 617, 42 LRRM 2135 (1958).

ages for mental or physical suffering. And the possibility of partial relief from the Board does not, in such a case as is here presented, deprive a party of available state remedies for all damages suffered.[80]

In determining whether the award of damages in *Gonzales* conflicted with a possible award of pack pay by the Board, the Court compared the situation with that in *Laburnum*:

> In either case the potential conflict is too contingent, too remotely related to the public interest expressed in the Taft-Hartley Act, to justify depriving state courts of jurisdiction to vindicate the personal rights of an ousted union member.[81]

Chief Justice Warren, joined by Justice Douglas, dissented in *Gonzales,* finding on the basis of *Garner* a "duplication and conflict of remedies" which justified the invoking of the preemption doctrine.[82] Because the evidence disclosed "the *probability* of a §8(b)(2) unfair labor practice in the union's refusal to dispatch Gonzales from its hiring hall after his expulsion from membership and his inability thereafter to obtain employment, . . . the existence of the same must for pre-emption purposes be assumed." [83] Since part of the recovery represented lost wages, the dissent found a conflict with the power of the Board to award back pay on the basis of the same conduct, and added that the state award for mental suffering would only "aggravate the evil." [84]

In 1963 the Supreme Court narrowed the *Gonzales* precedent by refusing to apply that decision to peaceful tortious conduct involved in *Plumbers Local 100* v. *Borden.*[85] In *Borden* the union local had refused to refer the plaintiff to a certain job. The state court awarded damages of $3,832 for willful, malicious, and discriminatory interference with Borden's right to contract and to pursue a lawful occupation. The Court based its decision on *Garmon* and distinguished *Gonzales.*[86] Since it was "arguable"

---

80 *Id.* at 621.
81 *Ibid. See also* Lockridge v. Motor Coach Employees, 460 P 2d 719, 72 LRRM 2703 (Idaho S Ct, 1969).
82 *Id.* at 628.
83 *Id.* at 626-27 (emphasis added).
84 *Id.* at 628.
85 373 US 690, 53 LRRM 2322 (1963). *See also* Local 207, Bridge Workers v. Perko, 373 US 701, 53 LRRM 2327 (1963) (holding that state court did not have jurisdiction over claim against union for damages arising from discharge of employee and based on common-law tort).
86 Neither *Gonzales* nor *Borden* was brought on the basis of a violation of the union's duty of fair representation. On that ground preemption would not have applied, as the Court was later to decide in *Vaca* v. *Sipes, infra* note 95.

that the union conduct was prohibited by Sections 8(b)(1)(A) or 8(b)(2) and also "arguable" that it was protected by Section 7, the rule of *Garmon* precluded the exercise of jurisdiction by the state court. *Gonzales* was distinguished as having focused on purely internal matters, whereas *Borden* focused on the union's actions with regard to the employee's effort to obtain employment. This being so, the Court said:

> We need not now determine the extent to which the holding in *Garmon* . . . qualified the principles declared in *Gonzales* with respect to jurisdiction to award consequential damages. . . .
>
> [O]ur concern is with delimiting *areas of conduct* which must be free from state regulation. . . .
>
> In the present case the *conduct* on which the suit is centered, whether described in terms of tort or contract, is conduct whose lawfulness could initially be judged only by the federal agency vested with exclusive primary jurisdiction to apply federal standards.[87]

A new matter considered a peripheral concern of the federal law *and* a matter of overriding interest to the states was added to the exceptions to the preemption doctrine in 1966 in *Linn* v. *United Plant Guard Workers, Local 114*.[88] In that decision the Court opened the way for application of state common law to defamatory conduct occurring in the context of labor relations governed by the NLRA. Simultaneously, as seen by one commentator, "the Court devised safeguards intended to reduce the elbow room that state common law affords to vindictive juries in defamation cases, and to eliminate at least some of the grosser enormities that characterize the common law of defamation in its native habitat, the state courts."[89]

Justice Clark, writing for the Court in *Linn,* sustained the jurisdiction of the state court to award damages for defamatory statements made by a union during an organizing campaign. While recognizing that representation campaigns are heated affairs "characterized by bitter and extreme charges, countercharges, unfounded rumors, vituperations, personal accusations, misrepresen-

---

[87] 356 US at 697.
[88] 383 US 53, 61 LRRM 2345 (1966).
[89] Currier, *State Defamation Remedies in Labor Disputes: Preemption And The New Federal Common Law,* in LABOR LAW DEVELOPMENTS 1967 (13th Ann. Inst., Southwestern Legal Foundation) 57, 58. *See generally* Currier, *Defamation Remedies in Labor Disputes: Pre-emption and the New Federal Common Law,* 53 VA. L. REV. 1 (1967).

tations and distortions," [90] the Court observed that "malicious libel enjoys no constitutional protection in any context. After all, the labor movement has grown up and must assume ordinary responsibilities. The malicious utterance of defamatory statements in any form cannot be condoned, and unions should adopt procedures calculated to prevent such abuses." [91] In addition, the Court noted, malicious libel is not an unfair labor practice, and the Board can grant no relief to the defamed individual. The Court therefore concluded that the state had an overriding interest in the control of malicious libel, which was a "merely peripheral concern" of the NLRA.

To prevent the state jurisdiction from intruding upon the free discussion envisioned by the NLRA, the Court held that recovery of damages was permitted only where (1) the defamatory statements were made with knowledge of their falsity or with reckless disregard of their truth or falsity and (2) there was proof of actual damage. In addition, the Court said that if the amount of damages awarded was excessive, it was the duty of the trial judge to require a remittitur or a new trial. It also said that the defamed party must establish that he has suffered compensable harm as a prerequisite to the recovery of additional punitive damages. Notwithstanding all the foregoing limitations, four Justices dissented, charging that the decision "opens a major breach in the wall which has heretofore confined labor disputes to the area and weaponry defined by federal labor law, except where violence or intimidation is involved." [92]

C. Fair Representation

It was not until 1962 that the Board held that a union's breach of its duty of fair representation [93] was an unfair labor practice.[94] Although the courts of appeals were divided on the question, the Supreme Court in 1967 in *Vaca* v. *Sipes* [95] impliedly recognized

---

[90] 383 US at 58.
[91] *Id.* at 63.
[92] *Id.* at 69 (dissenting opinion of Mr. Justice Fortas, joined by Warren, C. J., and Douglas, J. Justice Black dissented in a separate opinion.)
[93] *See* Chapter 27 *supra* for treatment of fair representation generally, *also* for further discussion of preemption and fair representation, *and* for discussion of the relation of the NLRA to Title VII of the Civil Rights Act of 1964 (42 USC §§1971, 2000e-2000e-15) .
[94] Miranda Fuel Co., 140 NLRB 181, 51 LRRM 1584 (1962) , *enforcement denied*, 326 F 2d 172, 54 LRRM 2715 (CA 2, 1963) .
[95] 386 US 171, 180, 64 LRRM 2369 (1967) .

the Board's jurisdiction. The Court did not resolve the question of whether the breach of the duty constituted an unfair labor practice under Section 8(b), but it acknowledged NLRB jurisdiction to an extent when it determined that the preemption doctrine did not deprive the state courts of jurisdiction in damage suits brought by employees against unions based on unfair representation. In *Vaca* a union member had recovered damages in a Missouri court for the union's refusal to take his grievance to arbitration. After analyzing "the nature of the particular interests being asserted and the effect upon the administration of national labor policies of concurrent judicial and administrative remedies," [96] the court in effect carved out another exception to the preemption doctrine.

A number of reasons led the Court to conclude that the preemption policy was not applicable to cases involving a breach of the duty of fair representation. In the first place, the fair-representation doctrine was originally developed by the judiciary, and since the Board had adopted the doctrine as it had been developed in the courts, there were no conflicting rules of substantive law in such cases. Second, since these suits involve internal union disputes, it was doubtful that the Board could bring substantially greater expertise to bear on these problems than do the courts. Third, if the Board were to have exclusive jurisdiction, its discretion in deciding whether to hear unfair labor charges might result in some cases going unheard. A last but important reason for allowing courts to pass on whether there has been a breach of the duty of fair representation was the fact that the breach would "in many cases be a critical issue in a suit under LMRA Section 301. . . ." [97]

IV. STATUTORY EXCEPTIONS TO PREEMPTION

A. Section 301 Suits

Section 301 of the LMRA provides that the federal courts have jurisdiction in "suits for violations of contracts between an employer and a labor organization representing employees in an industry affecting commerce as defined in this Act, or between any

---

[96] *Id.* at 180.
[97] *Id.* at 183.

such labor organizations." [98] In *Textile Workers Union* v. *Lincoln Mills* [99] the Supreme Court held that in Section 301 suits the courts should fashion a body of federal substantive law based upon the policy of the national labor laws, using "judicial inventiveness" if necessary. The Court stated that state law could be resorted to if compatible with the purposes of Section 301, but that any state law applied would become part of the federal labor law. Accordingly, it has been held that in turning to state law as a source of federal policy, the courts might rely not only on the state law of the forum but on the laws of all the states,[100] and that common law principles might be applied by the courts under Section 301 in their interpretation of collective bargaining agreements and, particularly, arbitration clauses contained in those agreements.[101] But state law as such must yield to the paramount rule of the federal law. In *Lucas Flour* [102] the Supreme Court emphasized that

> . . . the subject matter of §301(a) "is particularly one that calls for uniform law". . . . [W]e cannot but conclude that in enacting §301 Congress intended doctrines of federal labor law uniformly to prevail over inconsistent local rules.

In *Lincoln Mills* the employer violated the collective bargaining contract by refusing to arbitrate an employee's grievance. The Court held that the lower court had jurisdiction under Section 301 to compel arbitration. In cases arising under that section the violation of the contract may also involve conduct constituting an unfair labor practice or a representation question within the jurisdiction of the Board. In *Smith* v. *Evening News* [103] the Court held that: "The authority of the Board to deal with an unfair labor practice which also violates a collective-bargaining contract is not displaced by §301." In a subsequent case, *Carey* v. *Westinghouse Electric Corp.*,[104] an employer violated the contract by refusing to arbitrate on the ground that the determination of a disputed unit was within the exclusive jurisdiction of the Board. The Court reasoned that the same policy considerations favoring arbi-

---

[98] *See* Sovern, *Section 301 and the Primary Jurisdiction of the NLRB,* 76 HARV. L. REV. 529 (1963). *See* Chapter 17 *supra.*
[99] 353 US 448, 40 LRRM 2113 (1957).
[100] Refinery Employees v. Continental Oil Co., 160 F Supp 723, 42 LRRM 2586 (WD La 1958), *affirmed* 268 F 2d 447, 44 LRRM 2388 (CA 5, 1959).
[101] *Ibid.*
[102] Teamsters Local 174 v. Lucas Flour Co., 369 US 95, 103, 49 LRRM 2717 (1962).
[103] 371 US 195, 197, 51 LRRM 2646 (1962).
[104] 375 US 261, 55 LRRM 2042 (1964). The Board's jurisdiction would have been based on §§8(b)(4)(D) and 10(k) (for a jurisdictional dispute) or §9 (for a representation dispute). *See* Chapters 25, 8, 17, and 18 *supra.*

tration, which were determinative in *Smith,* were applicable and that preemption doctrine thus did not deprive the court of jurisdiction to compel arbitration in a Section 301 suit involving a representation question.

In 1962 the Supreme Court, in *Sinclair Ref. Co., v. Atkinson,*[105] held that the Norris-LaGuardia Act [106] deprives federal courts of jurisdiction to enjoin peaceful strikes in Section 301 suits and that, therefore, employers may not, by way of injunction, enforce a contractual no-strike clause in federal court suits instituted under Section 301. Many employers, therefore, sought to enforce no-strike clauses in the state courts. In *Avco Corp. v. Aero Lodge No. 735* [107] such a suit to enforce a no-strike clause was removed from state to federal court, and the injunction issued by the state court was dissolved by the federal court after removal. The Supreme Court affirmed on the ground that suits to enforce collective agreements are governed by federal law; the case was thus one arising under the laws of the United States, and the federal district court had removal as well as original jurisdiction.

The *Sinclair* case was overruled by the Court in *Boys Markets, Inc. v. Retail Clerks Local 770.*[108] The union had struck in breach of a no-strike clause in its contract; the union's grievance was subject to arbitration and the employer was ready to proceed with arbitration; also, the employer suffered irreparable injury by reason of the breach of the no-strike obligation. On these facts, the Court held that under Section 301 the federal district court had jurisdiction to enjoin the strike.

The principal reason for the reversal was the Court's conclusion that *Sinclair* had been a significant departure from the Court's consistent emphasis in other cases upon encouragement of the congressional policy to settle labor disputes through arbitration. This policy was recognized as requiring partial modification of the anti-injunction provisions of Norris-LaGuardia.

Boys Markets makes clear that state courts can also enjoin a strike in breach of contract,[109] and, by implication, supports the

---

105 370 US 195, 50 LRRM 2420 (1962).
106 29 US 104.
107 390 US 557, 67 LRRM 2881 (1968).
108 398 US 235, 74 LRRM 2257 (1970). *See also* Ice Cream Drivers v. Borden, Inc., 413 F 2d 41, 75 LRRM 2481 (CA 2, 1970).
109 The Court *cites* Charles Dowd Box Co. v. Courtney, 368 US 502, 49 LRRM 2619 (1962), to the effect that in the NLRA Congress clearly intended not to disturb the

power of a court to enforce an arbitrator's award granting injunctive relief. The decision should guarantee uniformity of remedy and discourage forum shopping.

B. Section 303 Suits

A second statutory exception to the pre-emption doctrine is provided in Section 303 of the Taft-Hartley Act, which states that an owner of a business or property which is injured by secondary activity defined as an unfair labor practice in Section 8(b)(4) [110]

> . . . may sue therefor in any district court of the United States subject to the limitations and provisions of section 301 hereof without respect to the amount in controversy, or in any other court having jurisdiction of the parties, and shall recover the damages by him sustained and the cost of the suit.

Under this exception, punitive damages cannot be awarded.[111] In 1964, in *Teamsters Local 20* v. *Morton*,[112] the Supreme Court reviewed an award of punitive damages against a union for peaceful secondary activities which were unlawful under state law. The lower court had awarded compensatory damages under Section 303 and punitive damages on the basis of state law. The Court reversed the award of *punitive* damages, reasoning that

> . . . even though it may be assumed that at least some of the secondary activity here involved was neither protected nor prohibited, it is still necessary to determine whether by enacting §303, "Congress occupied this field and closed it to state regulation." [113]

The Court concluded that Section 303 indicated the extent to which unions should be liable for secondary activities and thus

---

preexisting jurisdiction of the state courts, *and* McCarroll v. Los Angeles County Dist. Council of Carpenters, 49 Cal 2d 45, 315 P 2d 322, 40 LRRM 2709 (1957), *cert. denied,* 355 US 932, 41 LRRM 2431 (1958), to the effect that neither the Norris-LaGuardia Act nor §301 deprives state courts of the power to give injunctive remedies. *See also* R.R. Trainmen v. Chicago River & Ind. R.R., 353 US 30, 39 LRRM 2578 (1957), which the Court had declined to follow in *Sinclair. See infra,* this chapter, for general historical discussion of the Norris-LaGuardia Act. *See also* Chapter 17 *supra* at notes 71-83. *And see* Gould, *On Labor Injunctions, Unions, and the Judges: The Law of Industrial Peace According to Boys Market,* in 1970 S. CT. REV. (1971); Isaacson, *A Fresh Look at the Labor Injunction,* in LABOR LAW DEVELOPMENTS—1970 (17th Ann. Labor Law Inst., Sw. Legal Foundation) (1970).

110 *See* Chapter 23 *supra.* §302 of the LMRA, like §§301 and 303, is not treated directly in this book. However, the check-off, discussed in Chapters 11, 15, 27, and 31, is provided for by §302 (c) (4) and also figures in the preemption doctrine. *See* Operative Potters v. Tell City Chair Co., 295 F Supp 961, 70 LRRM 3113 (1968).

111 United Mine Workers Dist. 28 v. Patton, 211 F 2d 742, 33 LRRM 2814 (CA 4), *cert. denied,* 348 US 824, 34 LRRM 2898 (1954).

112 377 US 252, 56 LRRM 2225 (1964).

113 Teamsters Local 20 v. Morton, 377 US 252, 258, 56 LRRM 2225 (1964).

preemption of the state claim would prevent the court from awarding additional damages based on state law:

> If the Ohio law of secondary boycott can be applied to proscribe the same type of conduct which Congress focused upon but did not proscribe when it enacted §303, the inevitable result would be to frustrate the Congressional determination to leave this weapon of self-help available, and to upset the balance of power between labor and management expressed in our national labor policy. . . . Accordingly, we hold that . . . state law has been displaced by §303 in private damage actions based on peaceful union secondary activities. . . .[114]

In a subsequent suit, *United Mine Workers* v. *Gibbs*,[115] a pendant state claim and the award of punitive damages based thereon arose out of violent conduct. The opinion of the Supreme Court indicated that the statutory limitation on recovery in a Section 303 suit which preempts a state claim would not apply under circumstances of violence and intimidation. The district court in *Gibbs* had found no violation of the Taft-Hartley Act by the defendant union, but awarded actual and punitive damages on the basis of the pendant state claim. The Supreme Court noted that the state claim was not preempted, because violent conduct was involved and the district court did not abuse its discretion in refusing to dismiss the state claim even though the Section 303 claim had failed. However, although the jurisdiction of the district court was recognized, the Supreme Court reversed the award of damages because the plaintiff had failed to meet the special proof requirements of Section 6 of the Norris-LaGuardia Act.

C. Union Security Agreements

Section 8(a)(3) of the NLRA validates the establishment and enforcement of contractual union-shop clauses.[116] However, Section 14(b) of the Act provides:

> Nothing in this Act shall be construed as authorizing the execution or application of agreements requiring membership in a labor organization as a condition of employment in any State or Territory in which such execution or application is prohibited by State or Territorial law.

The combination of the two sections has produced the rule that, as between state and federal law, the stricter law applicable to

---

114 *Id*. at 259-60.
115 383 US 715, 61 LRRM 2561 (1966). *See* notes 65-77 *supra* and accompanying text.
116 *See* Chapter 26 *supra*.

union security provisions prevails. It is also recognized that a state may regulate union security clauses under Section 14(b) without any special cession agreement between the state agency and the Board.[117]

In *NLRB* v. *General Motors Corp.*[118] the Supreme Court held that the "agency shop" is within the scope of the proviso to Section 8(a)(3). Building upon this decision, the Court held in *Retail Clerks Int'l Ass'n, Local 1625* v. *Schermerhorn*[119] that the agency shop was subject to regulation by the states under Section 14(b). Thus, the states can permit or prohibit the agency shop. If a state does prohibit a union shop or an agency shop, it follows that the state may provide remedies for violation of the prohibition, e.g., reinstatement with back pay of an employee discharged under a forbidden union security clause.

It has been held, however, that hiring-hall arrangements, not being within the scope of the proviso to Section 8(a)(3), are not within state regulatory power under Section 14(b).[120] State power over union security clauses, under the language of Section 14(b), is confined to the "execution or application" of the union security agreement. On the basis of this language, the Court concluded in *Schermerhorn* that "picketing in order to get an employer to execute an agreement to hire all-union labor in violation of a state union-security statute lies exclusively in the federal domain . . . because state power, recognized by 14(b), begins *only with the actual negotiation and execution of the type of agreement described by 14(b)*."[121]

D. State Jurisdiction Under Section 14(c)

Where the Board lacks jurisdiction because of statutory exclusions,[122] preemption under the Act is not involved. Prior to 1959, preemption would apply in situations where the Board had juris-

---

117 Algoma Plywood & Veneer Co. v. Wisconsin Employment Rel. Bd., 336 US 301, 23 LRRM 2402 (1949). *Cf.* Retail Clerks, Local 1625 v. Schermerhorn, 373 US 746, 53 LRRM 2318 (1963), *on reargument*, 375 US 96, 54 LRRM 2612 (1963).
118 373 US 734, 53 LRRM 2313 (1963).
119 Note 117 *supra. See* Chapter 26 *supra* at notes 67-91.
120 Houston Chapter, Associated Gen. Contractors, 143 NLRB 409, 53 LRRM 1299 (1963), *enforced*, 349 F 2d 449, 59 LRRM 3013 (CA 5, 1965). *See* Chapter 26 *supra* at notes 93-105.
121 375 US at 105.
122 §§ 2(2) and (3). *See* discussion of statutory jurisdiction in Chapter 28 *supra. Cf.* Bro. of R.R. Trainmen v. Jacksonville Terminal Co., 374 US 369, No. 69, 70 LRRM 2961 (1969).

diction but chose not to assert it.[123] The Board had established standards relating to the dollar volume of business done, which had to be met before it would assert jurisdiction. Pursuant to Section 14(c) of the Act, added in 1959, the states may now exercise jurisdiction if the jurisdictional standards are not met: [124] "The Board may . . . decline to assert jurisdiction over any labor dispute involving any class or category of employees, where, in the opinion of the Board, the effect of such labor dispute on commerce is not sufficiently substantial to warrant the exercise of its jurisdiction. . . ." The section specifically empowers state and territorial tribunals to assume jurisdiction over labor disputes over which the Board declines to assert jurisdiction.

The Board's regulations provide for the granting of advisory opinions as to its jurisdiction over a given state of facts.[125]

E. Board Cession Under Section 10(a)

A proviso to Section 10(a) of the Act authorizes the Board to relinquish its jurisdiction over any case in any industry (with specified exceptions) to any state or territorial agency, unless the local statute is inconsistent with corresponding provisions of the Act. No such cession agreement has been made to date.[126]

V. ACCOMMODATING THE NLRA AND THE ANTITRUST LAWS

Under the preemption doctrine state antitrust laws may not regulate conduct which is arguably protected or prohibited by the NLRA.[127] Federal antitrust laws, on the other hand, are applicable in certain situations to union activities, notwithstanding the basic proposition that: "The anti-trust laws are not concerned with competition among laborers or with bargains over the price

---

[123] San Diego Bldg. Trades Council v. Garmon, *supra* note 33.
[124] *See* discussion of no-man's land and the passage of §14(c) in 1959, Chapter 28 *supra*. *See also supra* notes 51-56 and accompanying text.
[125] NLRB Rules and Regs., 29 CFR §102.98 (1965). However, the Board is not bound to adhere to the self-imposed standards. NLRB v. National Survey Serv., Inc., 361 F 2d 199, 61 LRRM 2712 (CA 7, 1966); NLRB v. Carpenters Local 2133, 356 F 2d 464, 61 LRRM 2401 (CA 9, 1966).
[126] *See* Chapter 28 *supra* at note 21.
[127] Weber v. Anheuser-Busch, 348 US 468, 35 LRRM 2637 (1955). *See also* Teamsters Local 24 v. Oliver, 358 US 283, 43 LRRM 2374 (1959) (holding that a union wage agreement, sanctioned by federal law, may not be invalidated under a state antitrust law). See *notes* 37 and 46-49 *supra* and accompanying text.

or supply of labor—its compensation or hours of service or the selection and tenure of employees." [128] In those situations federal antitrust statutes must be accommodated with the policies of the NLRA and the Norris-LaGuardia Act.

Supreme Court decisions in this area have moved from broad application of antitrust law to union activities to broad exemption of such activities except in certain limited situations. In 1908, in the famous *Danbury Hatters* case,[129] the Supreme Court upheld an employer's cause of action for conspiracy under the Sherman Act against a nationwide boycott aimed at forcing him to unionize his shops. Subsequently, when Congress enacted Sections 6 and 20 of the Clayton Act,[130] it was thought that labor unions had been exempted from the antitrust laws. In *Duplex Printing Press Co. v. Deering* [131] the Supreme Court held otherwise, reasoning that Section 6 of the Clayton Act only protected the existence and "lawful" activities of union organizations and that Section 20 prevented the application of the antitrust laws only to a labor dispute between employees and their *immediate employer*. Neither section was held to immunize the secondary boycott involved in *Duplex Printing*.[132]

In 1932 Congress passed the Norris-LaGuardia Act [133] and withdrew from the federal courts jurisdiction to issue injunctions against peaceful conduct arising out of labor disputes. Section 4 described the various kinds of nonenjoinable conduct, and Section 13(c) defined a "labor dispute" as including any controversy concerning terms or conditions of employment "regardless of whether or not the disputants stand in the proximate relation of employer and employee." The *Duplex* decision, permitting injunctive relief against a secondary boycott, was thus repudiated. However, regardless of the broader protection of the Norris-LaGuardia Act, the Supreme Court continued to apply the Sherman Act where the union combined with an employer. This distinction for non-

---

128 Cox, *Labor and the Anti-Trust Laws*, 14 PA. L. REV. 252, 255 (1955). *See* notes 106-109 *supra* for discussion of the accommodation of the Norris-LaGuardia Act to the NLRA.
129 Loewe v. Lawlor, 208 US 274 (1908). For general historical background to the passage of the NLRA, *see* Chapters 1 and 2 *supra*.
130 *See* Chapter 1 *supra*.
131 254 US 443 (1921).
132 *See also* Coronado Coal Co. v. United Mine Workers, 268 US 295 (1925) ; United Mine Workers v. Coronado Coal Co., 259 US 344 (1922).
133 *See* Chapter 2 *supra*. *See also* notes 105-109 *supra* and accompanying text for accommodation of Norris-LaGuardia to §301 of the LMRA.

labor coconspirators was made in 1934 in *Teamsters Local 167* v. *United States*.[134] The case involved a conspiracy among poultry market men, Local 167, and the Shochtim Union (slaughterers) to fix prices, divide territories, and refuse to deal with uncooperative dealers. The Supreme Court upheld the issuing of an injunction under Sections 1 and 2 of the Sherman Act on the ground that a combination of workers with businessmen to monopolize commercial activities had little immediate connection with the needs or objectives of the union.

Beginning with the 1940 decision in *Apex Hosiery Co.* v. *Leader*,[135] the Supreme Court began to apply the antitrust laws less stringently to labor unions. In this case the union attempted to enforce its demands for a closed shop by engaging in a sitdown strike and seizing the plant. The Court observed that the antitrust laws were intended to apply to "business combinations" and restraints upon "commercial competition" in the marketing of goods and services where the effect or the intent was to fix prices or to suppress competition. Thus the employee could not recover treble damage, for it had not been shown that the restrictions "operated to restrain commercial competition in some substantial way." [136] Most importantly, the Court stated:

> A combination of employees necessarily restrains competition among themselves in the sale of their services to the employer; yet such a combination was not considered an illegal restraint of trade at common law when the Sherman Act was adopted, either because it was not thought to be unreasonable or because it was not deemed a "restraint of trade." Since the enactment of the declaration in §6 of the Clayton Act that the "labor of a human being is not a commodity or article of commerce . . . nor shall such [labor] organizations, or the members thereof, be held or construed to be illegal combinations or conspiracies in restraint of trade under the antitrust laws," it would seem plain that restraints on the sale of the employee's services to the employer, however much they curtail the competition among employees, are not in themselves combinations or conspiracies in restraint of trade or commerce under the Sherman Act.[137]

A year later union activity was removed from the application of antitrust law, with one important exception which had been

---

[134] 291 US 293 (1934).
[135] 310 US 469, 6 LRRM 647 (1940).
[136] *Id.* at 497.
[137] *Id.* at 502-03.

recognized in 1934. In *United States* v. *Hutcheson* [138] the United Brotherhood of Carpenters and Joiners and its president had been criminally indicted under the Sherman Act for instituting primary and secondary strikes in retaliation for a disputed work assignment. The major premise of the Court's decision was its holding that "whether trade union conduct constitutes a violation of the Sherman Law is to be determined only by reading the Sherman Act and Section 20 of the Clayton Act and the Norris-LaGuardia Act as a harmonizing text of outlawry of labor conduct." [139] Since the union's conduct was nonenjoinable under the Norris-La-Guardia Act and Clayton Act, it was also immune from criminal prosecution under the Sherman Act. The Court discussed Section 20 of the Clayton Act exempting labor activities from antitrust laws by noting only one qualification:

> *So long as a union acts in its self-interest and does not combine with non-labor groups,* the licit and the illicit under Section 20 are not to be distinguished by any judgment regarding the wisdom or unwisdom, the rightness or wrongness, the selfishness or unselfishness of the end of which the particular union activities are the means. There is nothing remotely within the terms of Section 20 that differentiates between trade union conduct directed against an employer because of a controversy arising in the relation between employer and employee, as such, and conduct similarly directed but ultimately due to an internecine struggle between two unions seeking the favor of the same employer.[140]

The government argued that the Norris-LaGuardia Act limited the Court's jurisdiction only as to the issuance of injunctions, that the *Duplex* case still applied in criminal cases, and that therefore Section 20 of the Clayton Act did not exempt a labor dispute between an employer and his immediate employees from criminal prosecution. Rejecting this reasoning, the Court held that the Norris-LaGuardia Act was intended to free the Clayton Act entirely from the restrictive effect of the *Duplex* decision. In effect, the nonenjoinable activities of Norris-LaGuardia were read into Section 20 of the Clayton Act, thus bringing the activities within the protection of the provision in Section 20 which reads: ". . . nor shall any of the acts specified in this paragraph be considered or held to be violations of any law of the United States." Justice

---

[138] 312 US 219, 7 LRRM 267 (1941).
[139] *Id.* at 231.
[140] *Id.* at 232.

Roberts, dissenting, said this was "a process of construction never heretofore indulged by this Court. . . . I venture to say that no court has ever undertaken so radically to legislate where Congress has refused to do so." [141]

In subsequent litigation, attention was focused on the exception noted in *Hutcheson* that if labor groups conspire with nonlabor groups to restrain trade, the conduct is not exempt from the antitrust laws. This exception was applied in *Allen-Bradley* v. *IBEW Local 3*,[142] where Local 3 was found to have entered into a conspiracy with manufacturers and installation contractors in the electric equipment industry. The purpose was to give the employers a monopoly in the industry in the New York area and the union a monopoly of work opportunity. The fact that the conspiracy was reflected in part in collective bargaining agreements did not give the union exemption from the antitrust laws. The Court stated:

> So far as the union might have achieved this result acting alone, it would have been the natural consequence of labor union activities exempted by the Clayton Act from the coverage of the Sherman Act. . . . But when the unions participated with a combination of businessmen who had complete power to eliminate all competition among themselves and to prevent all competition from others, a situation was created not included within the exemption of the Clayton and Norris-LaGuardia Acts. . . . Our holding means that the same labor union activities may or may not be in violation of the Sherman Act, dependent upon whether the union acts alone or in combination with business groups.[143]

Allen-Bradley exemplified the problem of harmonizing the conflicting policies of the Sherman Act (preservation of competition) and the National Labor Relations Act (the right of labor to bargain collectively). The Court's approach was to balance the interests of both policies so that only legitimate collective bargaining objectives would be outside the scope of antitrust laws. *Allen-Bradley* raised the issue of how far a union might go in bargaining over the terms and conditions of employment, (especially in industrywide bargaining where direct product market restraints might result) and not become involved in an illegal combination.

---

141 *Id*. at 245.
142 325 US 797, 16 LRRM 798 (1945).
143 *Id*. at 809. *See* Chapter 24 *supra* at note 90.

In 1965 the problem once again came before the Supreme Court in *United Mine Workers* v. *Pennington* [144] and *Amalgamated Meat Cutters Local 189* v. *Jewel Tea Co.*[145] Both cases involved actions by employers against labor unions under Sections 1 and 2 of the Sherman Act. The *Pennington* case arose out of the National Bituminous Coal Wage Agreement of 1950, entered into by the United Mine Workers and the larger operating companies. Both sides agreed that the basic problems in the industry were the result of overproduction. In return for higher wages and fringe benefits, the complaint alleged that the union agreed not to oppose automation in the industry and that it would impose terms of the agreement on all operators regardless of their ability to pay. The complainant further alleged that the purpose of the agreement was to eliminate small operators from the industry. The union maintained that it was exempt from the antitrust laws, since the agreement dealt with wage standards.

In what was called the opinion of the Court, three Justices (White, Warren, and Brennan) held that a cause of action under the Sherman Act had been stated, based on the following principles:

(1) A union wage agreement with a multi-employer bargaining unit does not *per se* violate the antitrust laws;

(2) However, the mere fact that a union-employer agreement involved a compulsory subject of bargaining does not automatically exempt the agreement from the Sherman Act;

(3) The union may legally seek to obtain the same benefits from all employers it bargains with; however,

---

144 381 US 657, 59 LRRM 2369 (1965).

145 381 US 676, 59 LRRM 2376 (1965). *See* the following commentary: Cox, *Labor and the Antitrust Laws: Pennington and Jewel Tea*, 46 B.U.L. REV. 317 (1966); St. Antoine, *Collective Bargaining and the Antitrust Laws* in IND. REL. RESEARCH ASS'N. PROCEEDINGS (19th Ann. Meeting) 66 (1966); Williams, *Labor and the Antitrust Laws*, LABOR LAW DEVELOPMENTS (Sw. Legal Foundation, 12th Ann. Institute on Labor Law) 5 (1966); Meltzer, *Labor Unions, Collective Bargaining and the Antitrust Laws*, 32 U. CHI. L. REV. 659 (1965); Summers, *Labor Law in the Supreme Court: 1964 Term*, 75 YALE L.J. 59 (1965); Winter, *Collective Bargaining and Competition: The Application of Antitrust Standards to Union Activities*, 73 YALE L.J. 14 (1963); Cox, *Labor and the Antitrust Laws—A Preliminary Analysis*, 104 U. PA. L. REV. 252 (1955); Comment, *Labor's Antitrust Exemption*, 55 CALIF. L. REV. 254 (1967); Comment, *Labor's Antitrust Exemption After Pennington and Jewel Tea*, 66 COLUM. L. REV. 742 (1966); Comment, *Labor Law and Antitrust: "So Deceptive and Opaque Are the Elements of These Problems,"* 1966 DUKE L.J. 191 (1966); Comment, *Union-Employer Agreements and the Antitrust Laws: the Pennington and Jewel Tea Cases*, 114 U.PA. L. REV. 901 (1966).

(4) The union may not agree with one set of employers to impose certain wage scales on other bargaining units because:

> One group of employers may not conspire to eliminate competitors from the industry and the union is liable with the employers if it becomes a party to the conspiracy. This is true even though the union's part in the scheme is an undertaking to secure the same wages, hours or other conditions of employment from the remaining employers in the industry.[146]

Three Justices (Douglas, Black, and Clark) concurred separately and three Justices (Goldberg, Harlan, and Stewart) dissented.

In *Jewel Tea*, it was claimed that the Meat Cutters Union had violated the Sherman Act by negotiating separate agreements with Chicago food stores and Jewel Tea, each agreement setting the hours when meat could be sold in the city. Jewel Tea alleged that these agreements constituted an illegal conspiracy between the Meat Cutters Union and the food stores to prevent night meat-market operations by the large self-service chains like itself. However, as presented to the Supreme Court, the facts in *Jewel Tea* were held distinguishable from *Pennington*. In *Jewel Tea* there was no evidence of a union-employer conspiracy but rather

> ... a situation where the unions, having obtained a marketing-hours agreement from one group of employers, have successfully sought the same terms from a single employer, Jewel, not as a result of a bargain between the unions and some employers directed against other employers, but pursuant to what the unions deemed to be their own labor union interest.[147]

As in *Pennington*, the Justices divided themselves into three groups of three. There was no majority opinion. Justice White, joined by Justices Warren and Brennan, found that the agreements were within the antitrust exemption. Justices Goldberg, Harlan, and Stewart concurred separately. Justices Douglas, Black, and Clark dissented.

According to the opinion of Justice White, the basic issue in *Jewel Tea*, absent evidence of a conspiracy between the union and other employees, was whether the working-hours provision was so intimately related to wages, hours, and other terms and conditions of employment as to be a mandatory subject of bargain-

---

146 381 US 657, 665-66. On remand the district court held that the evidence was not sufficient to prove a conspiracy. Pennington v. United Mine Workers, 257 F Supp 815, 62 LRRM 2604 (ED Tenn, 1966).
147 381 US 676, 688, 59 LRRM 2376 (1965).

ing. The answer was affirmative, because unions have a direct interest in the work they perform and the hours they work. Since it was found as a fact that self-service meat markets could not operate at night without affecting the hours of butchers, the agreement dealt with a legitimate union interest and was not merely an effort by the unions to protect one group of employers from competition by another. Therefore, Justice White concluded, the union's "successful attempt to obtain that provision through bonafide, arm's-length bargaining in pursuit of [its] own labor union policies and not at the behest of or in combination with nonlabor groups, falls within the protection of the national labor policy and is . . . exempt from the Sherman Act." [148]

The opinion by Justice Goldberg for both *Pennington* and *Jewel Tea* examined "a consistent congressional purpose to limit severely judicial intervention in collective bargaining under cover of the wide umbrella of the antitrust laws and, rather, to deal with what Congress deemed to be specific abuses on the part of labor unions by specific proscriptions in the labor statutes." [149] From the long history of legislation attempting to protect unions from antitrust suits he concluded that "the Court should hold that, in order to effectuate congressional intent, collective bargaining activity concerning mandatory subjects of bargaining under the Labor Act is not subject to the antitrust laws." [150]

A secondary issue raised by the union in *Jewel Tea* concerned the applicability of the doctrine of primary jurisdiction as an alternative ground to limit the jurisdiction of the courts. As Justice White explained, the doctrine "applies where a claim is originally cognizable in the courts" and the court is compelled to defer to the administrative agency because of its own lack of experience with issues or the need to protect the integrity of the agency. Justice White assumed the existence of concurrent jurisdiction originally, but found no reason to compel the court to defer to the NLRB. Justice Goldberg agreed that the doctrine of primary jurisdiction was not applicable in *Jewel Tea,* but for a different reason: the court lacked jurisdiction over the claim originally.

---

[148] *Id.* at 692-93.
[149] *Id.* at 709. Justice White's opinion, however, would not have applied an automatic exemption to an agreement solely because it embraced a mandatory subject of bargaining. *Id.* at 689-91. For treatment of mandatory subjects of bargaining generally, *see* Chapters 14 and 15 *supra*.
[150] *Id.* at 710.

To realize the benefit of the broad labor exemption carved from the antitrust laws by the Norris-LaGuardia Act and polished in *Pennington* and *Jewel Tea,* the union must be involved in a "labor dispute" for the purpose of protecting its interests and must not combine with a nonlabor group. Both of these issues were discussed by the Supreme Court in 1968 in *American Federation of Musicians* v. *Carroll.*[151] This case involved the legality of unilaterally adopted union regulations establishing minimum prices to be charged by orchestra "leaders" on "club date" engagements (providing music for a few hours at a social engagement). Although price-fixing is normally a *per se* violation of the antitrust law, in this case the Court held that the labor exemption was applicable. The price floors were found to constitute a means of protecting the wage scales of the musicians who played in the orchestra on the club-date engagements from the substantial effect of the job and wage competition of the orchestra leaders. The Second Circuit had disqualified the "price list" because it concluded that the list was concerned with prices and not wages.[152] Quoting Justice White's opinion in *Jewel Tea,* the Supreme Court again emphasized that "[t]he crucial determinant is not the form of the agreement—*e.g.,* prices or wages—but its relative impact on the product market and the interests of union members."[153] The price list was found to be indistinguishable from the collective bargaining provisions in *Teamsters Union* v. *Oliver* which had "governed not prices but the mandatory subject of wages."[154]

Although the orchestra leaders were deemed to be independent contractors, they were found to constitute a "labor group" which was party to a "labor dispute" within the meaning of the Norris-LaGuardia Act. As Justice Brennan explained in the majority opinion, the existence of "a job or wage competition or some other

---

[151] 391 US 99, 68 LRRM 2230 (1968). *See* Countryman, *The Organized Musicians* (pts. 1 & 2), 16 U. Chi. L. Rev. 56, 239 (1948-49).
[152] 391 US at 107.
[153] 359 US at 283. The Court, in *Carroll,* stated:
"The majority of the Court of Appeals * * * read the opinions of Mr. Justice White and Mr. Justice Goldberg in that case as requiring a holding that ". . . . mandatory subjects of collective bargaining carry with them an exemption . . . ," but that "[o]n matters outside of the mandatory area . . . no such considerations govern . . ." 372 F 2d, at 165. Even if only mandatory subjects of bargaining enjoy the exemption—a question not in this case and upon which we express no view—nothing Mr. Justice White or Mr. Justice Goldberg said remotely suggests that the distinction between mandatory and nonmandatory subjects turns on the form of the method taken to protect a wage scale, here a price floor." 391 at 110-11.
[154] 391 US at 109. *See* notes 46-49 *supra.*

economic interrelationship affecting legitimate union interests between the union members and the independent contractors" was properly used as a criteria to determine that the leaders were a labor group.[155] There being no evidence of conspiracy and the subject being one of legitimate union interest, there was no antitrust violation. Justices Black and White dissented.

VI. ACCOMMODATING THE NLRA AND THE BANKRUPTCY ACT

A statute which often touches matters that are regulated, either directly or indirectly, by the NLRA is the federal Bankruptcy Act.[156] Some of the more important areas of conflict affecting both statutes are noted in this section.

A. Status of Union Welfare Funds in Bankruptcy

Under the federal Bankruptcy Act priority is given to "wages . . . not to exceed $600 to each claimant, which have been earned within three months before the date of the commencement of the [bankruptcy] proceeding, due to workmen. . . ."[157] For a number of years the status of wages for an employer's contributions to a union welfare fund was a subject of judicial dispute.[158] In *United States* v. *Embassy Restaurant* [159] the Supreme Court settled the conflict of opinion by determining that contributions to a welfare fund were not debts owed to the workmen and thus were not within the class of "wages" given priority under the Bankruptcy Act. Relying upon a literal reading of the Act, the Court reasoned that the funds did not fall within the statutory language because the obligation to make contributions, when incurred, was to the trustees which administered each welfare plan under a formal trust agreement. Justice Clark, writing for the Court, distinguished the decision of the Court in *Shropshire Woodliff & Co.* v. *Bush*,[160] which had allowed the priority of a claim for the benefit of an assignee of wages due a workman and assigned by

---

[155] *Id.* at 106.
[156] 11 USC §101 *et seq.* (1964).
[157] 30 Stat. 563, §64 (1903), as *amended,* 11 USC §104(a)(2) (1964).
[158] *E.g.,* United States v. Embassy Restaurant, 254 F 2d 475, 41 LRRM 2836 (CA 3, 1958); *contra,* Local 140 Security Fund v. Hack, 242 F 2d 375, 39 LRRM 2546 (CA 2, 1957), *cert. denied,* 355 US 833, 40 LRRM 2680 (1957).
[159] 359 US 29, 43 LRRM 2631 (1959). The holding was reaffirmed by the Court in *Joint Bd. of Electrical Ind.* v. *U.S.,* 391 US 224, 68 LRRM 2193 (1968).
[160] 204 US 186 (1907).

him. Because the character of the debts was fixed when the employer incurred the obligation, the assignment in *Shropshire* could not change that character.

B. Powers of the Bankruptcy Courts

In straight bankruptcy, arrangement, and reorganization proceedings under the federal Bankruptcy Act, it has been argued that the NLRA preempts the jurisdiction of the referee or trustee to reject a collective bargaining agreement. In such cases the employer-debtor has negotiated and signed a collective bargaining contract with a union and the union opposes the rejection. Federal district courts have consistently affirmed the power of the trustee or referee to set aside bargaining agreements as executory contracts on the basis of their powers under three chapters of the Bankruptcy Act.[161] The language of the provision in each chapter is similar: the trustee is given the power to reject executory contracts.[162] As a federal district court concluded in a straight bankruptcy proceeding, "There is no question that during the life of a collective bargaining agreement it is an 'executory contract' and falls within the literal language of section 70b." [163] The court rejected the union's preemption argument on several grounds. No conflict was found between the labor legislation and the Bankruptcy Act. In addition, the court noted that there was no language excluding collective bargaining contracts generally from section 70b of the Bankruptcy Act. The lack of exclusionary language was significant because Congress expressly had prohibited the bankruptcy courts in reorganization proceedings from inter-

---

161 Carpenters Local 2746 v. Turney Wood Products, Inc., 289 F Supp 143, 69 LRRM 2977 (WD Ark, 1968) (straight bankruptcy); In re Klaber Brothers, Inc., 173 F Supp 83, 44 LRRM 2176 (SD NY, 1959) (arrangement under Chapter XI); *In re* Public Ledger, 63 F Supp 1008, 17 LRRM 655 (ED Pa, 1945) (corporate reorganization under Chapter X), *remanded* and *reversed on other grounds*, 161 F 2d 762, 20 LRRM 2012 (CA 3, 1947). *But see* In re Mamie Conti Gowns, Inc., 12 F Supp 478 (SD NY, 1935).

162 When there is an adjudication of bankruptcy, Section 70b, 11 USC §1106 (1964), provides: "The trustee shall assume or reject any executory contract, . . ., within sixty days after the adjudication. . . ." In a proceeding for corporate reorganization under Chapter X, Section 116, 11 USC §516(1) (1964), authorizes the court to "permit the rejection of executory contracts of the debtor, except contracts in the public authority, upon notice to the parties to such contracts. . . ." Section 313, 11 USC §713(1) (1964), allows the court in an arrangement proceeding under Chapter XI to permit "the rejection of executory contracts of the debtor, upon notice to the parties to such contracts and to such other parties in interest as the court may designate. . . ."

163 Carpenters Local 2746 v. Turney Wood Products, Inc., 289 F Supp 143, 147, 69 LRRM 2977 (WD Ark, 1968).

fering with collective bargaining agreements between carriers and employees subject to the Railway Labor Act.[164]

C. Limitations on the Jurisdiction of the Bankruptcy Courts

The jurisdiction of the courts in bankruptcy proceedings is strictly limited in matters involving the employer-employee relationship, labor disputes, and union representation. The primary jurisdiction of the NLRB over representation questions and unfair labor practices preempts that of the bankruptcy courts. Therefore, a federal district court may not stay the prosecution of a Board proceeding.[165] Furthermore, a receiver appointed in a reorganization proceeding can be guilty of an unfair labor practice and the Board need not obtain consent of the appointing court before filing its complaint.[166]

Another limitation on the power of the courts is the language of the Bankruptcy Act itself.[167] Section 31 gives the bankruptcy

---

[164] §77n, 11 USC §205n (1964). *See* In re Overseas National Airways, Inc., 238 F Supp 359, 58 LRRM 2427 (ED NY, 1965). *Cf.* Burke v. Morphy, 109 F 2d 572, 5 LRRM 906 (1940).

[165] In re American Buslines, 151 F Supp 877, 40 LRRM 2221 (D Neb, 1957) (court in reorganization proceeding refused to stay representation proceeding). *See also* Bakery Sales Drivers Local 33 v. Wagshal, 333 US 437, 21 LRRM 2441 (1948); NLRB v. Coal Creek Coal Co., 204 F 2d 579, 32 LRRM 2089 (CA 10, 1953); Nathanson v. NLRB, 194 F 2d 248, 29 LRRM 2430 (CA 1, 1952), *reversed on other grounds*, 344 US 25, 31 LRRM 2036 (1952); NLRB v. Baldwin Locomotive Works, 128 F 2d 39, 10 LRRM 446, 632 (CA 3, 1942).

[166] NLRB v. Bachelder, 120 F 2d 574, 8 LRRM 723 (CA 7, 1941), *cert. denied*, 314 US 647, 9 LRRM 416 (1941), *decree modified*, 125 F 2d 387, 9 LRRM 573 (CA 7, 1942).

[167] §272 of Chapter X, 11 USC §672 (1964), reads:

> "The right of employees or of persons seeking employment on the property of a debtor under the jurisdiction of the court to join a labor organization of their choice, or to refuse to join or remain members of a company union, shall be free from interference, restraint, or coercion by the court, a debtor, or trustee. It shall be the duty of a debtor or trustee to report to the judge any agreement restricting or interfering with such right, and the judge shall thereupon enter an appropriate order for the termination of such agreement and for notice to the employees that the same is no longer binding upon them. No funds of the estate shall be used by a debtor or a trustee for the purpose of maintaining company unions."

The NLRA will prevail over 11 USC §672 if there is any conflict in an application of the two statutes. §15 of the NLRA reads as follows:

> "Wherever the application of the provisions of section 272 of chapter 10 of the Act entitled 'An Act to establish a uniform system of bankruptcy throughout the United States', approved July 1, 1898, and Acts amendatory thereof and supplementary thereto (U.S.C., title 11, sec. 672), conflicts with the application of the provisions of this Act, this Act shall prevail: *Provided,* That in any situation where the provisions of this Act cannot be validly enforced, the provisions of such other Acts shall remain in full force and effect."

court in an arrangement proceeding "exclusive jurisdiction of the debtor and his property, wherever located." [168] In such a proceeding a bankruptcy court held that it lacked jurisdiction to enjoin a hearing on a labor grievance brought against the temporary management and purported successor of the debtor company because the hearing would not involve the debtor or its property.[169] The Norris-LaGuardia Act will otherwise restrict the extent to which the bankruptcy court may issue an injunction against labor disputes.[170]

---

[168] 11 USC § 711 (1964). *See also* 11 USC §511 (1964) (corporate reorganization).
[169] In re N.Y. & Worcester Express, Inc., 70 LRRM 2233 (SD NY, 1968). *See also* Chapter 13 *supra.*
[170] *See* 6 Collier On Bankruptcy ¶ 3.09, 479 n. 17 (14th ed. 1965).

CHAPTER 30

NLRB PROCEDURES

I. ORGANIZATION OF BOARD AND OFFICE OF GENERAL COUNSEL

A. Background

From 1935 to 1947 the National Labor Relations Board consisted of three members, appointed by the President for five-year terms.[1] The Board was responsible for investigation and prosecution, as well as adjudication,[2] of all cases over which it exerted jurisdiction. Also, all agency personnel were under the Board's direct control.[3] Because of the volume of work included within these responsibilities, many of the Board's functions were eventually delegated to regional directors or to a part of the Board's staff called the Review Section.[4] Public criticism that the Board operated unfairly as prosecutor, judge, and jury, and that the Review Section improperly exercised immense power, caused Congress,[5] in the Taft-Hartley amendments [6] of 1947, to separate the functions in a way unique to federal administrative agencies.[7]

The Board retained its judicial function and its membership was increased to five, any three of whom could act as a panel.[8] The

---

[1] National Labor Relations Act (Wagner Act), ch. 372, §3a, 49 Stat 451 (1935).
[2] §3 (b).
[3] §4 (a).
[4] FOURTH ANNUAL REPORT OF NLRB 11, 12 (GPO, 1940).
[5] H.R. REP. No. 245, 80th Cong., 1st Sess. 25, reported in 1 LEGISLATIVE HISTORY OF THE LABOR MANAGEMENT RELATIONS ACT, 1947, 316 (GPO, 1948).
[6] Labor Management Relations Act, ch. 120, §101 et seq., 61 Stat 136 (1947).
[7] See 2 K. Davis, Administrative Law Treatise §13.04 (1958), for a discussion of the "new solution" embodied in the 1947 Act to achieve separation of functions.
[8] §3 (a).

Board's former investigative and prosecutorial functions, however, were given to a new official, known as the General Counsel, who was to be appointed by the President for a four-year term.[9] The result has been a single enforcement agency with authority divided between two independent units.[10]

B. The Board

The Board's principal function is judicial in character. It determines all unfair labor practice cases brought before it by the General Counsel. Also, it has complete authority over representation matters, although in 1961 it delegated this power to the regional directors, retaining a right to review any of their decisions.[11]

Each Board member has a chief counsel, an assistant chief counsel, and a staff of about 25 attorneys who act as legal assistants.[12] Unfair labor practice cases are assigned to an individual legal assistant, who normally is the only person on the staff to study the entire record.[13] If the case is a simple one, clearly covered by Board precedent, the legal assistant prepares a draft decision for approval by a three-man panel of the Board.[14] If the case raises arguable questions, it may be referred for further consideration to a subpanel of supervisory attorneys from staffs of three different Board members and then to a panel of three Board members. Only the important cases are discussed by the full Board.[15]

---

[9] §3 (d).

[10] For a detailed account of the operation of these functions, see NLRB RULES AND REGULATIONS AND STATEMENTS OF PROCEDURE, SERIES 8, as amended, revised January 1, 1965 (GPO, 1965) (hereinafter referred to as Rules and Regs. and Statements of Procedure); NLRB FIELD MANUAL, issued by the General Counsel of the NLRB (July 1, 1967); McGuiness, SILVERBERG'S HOW TO TAKE A CASE BEFORE THE NATIONAL LABOR RELATIONS BOARD (Washington: BNA Books, 1967); Murphy, *The National Labor Relations Board—An Appraisal*, LABOR LAW DEVELOPMENTS 1968, 113 (1968) (Fourteenth Annual Institute on Labor Law, Southwestern Legal Foundation). For a critical analysis of NLRA procedures generally, *see* Morris, *Procedural Reform in Labor Law—A Preliminary Paper*, 35 J. AIR L. & COM. 537 (1969).

[11] TWENTY-SIXTH ANNUAL REPORT of NLRB 3, 4 (GPO, 1961); notes 27-28 *infra*. *And see* Rules and Regs. §102.67. Although rarely used, the Board has power to promulgate rules incidental to case adjudication pursuant to the notice and hearing rule-making provisions of the Administrative Procedure Act. *See* part IV *infra*, this chapter.

[12] §4 (a).

[13] Statements of Procedure §101.12.

[14] §3 (b).

[15] For a discussion of the handling of unfair labor practices, see Murphy, *The National Labor Relations Board—An Appraisal*, LABOR LAW DEVELOPMENTS 1968, 113, 128-130 (1968) (Fourteenth Annual Institute on Labor Law, Southwestern Legal Foundation).

A special unit of attorneys, drawn from the staffs of the Board members, handles representation matters, which consist principally of requests for review of the action of regional directors. The decision to grant or deny review is made by the Board through a process similar to that used in unfair labor practice cases.[16]

The Board members and their staffs are located in Washington, D.C.[17] There the Board also is served by an Executive Secretary, whose duties in part are similar to those of the clerk of a court.[18] He carries on necessary correspondence with the parties, prepares Board agendas, and handles the issuance of decisions and orders.[19] In addition, he represents the Board in its dealings with committees and members of Congress and with professional organizations. The Board also has a Solicitor, who serves as legal adviser to the Board, and a Director of Information, who represents the Board in its contacts with the communications media.

C. The General Counsel

Section 3 (d) of the Act provides that the General Counsel "shall exercise general supervision over all attorneys employed by the Board (other than trial examiners and legal assistants to Board members) and over the officers and employees in the regional offices." This section also provides that the General Counsel "shall have final authority, on behalf of the Board, in respect of the investigation of charges and issuance of complaints under Section 10, and in respect of the prosecution of such complaints before the Board." It has been consistently held that this vast authority is not reviewable by the courts.[20] Because of statutory ambiguity in the delineation of responsibility between the Board and the General Counsel, the Board has further delegated to the General Counsel supervision over all nonattorney employees in the Washington offices, who are engaged in various administrative duties.[21]

---

16 Rules and Regs. §§102.67-71 (representation); §§102.48-.51 (unfair labor practices).
17 §5.
18 §4 (a).
19 See Rules and Regs. §§102.115-116; Statements of Procedure §101.11.
20 See, e.g., United Electrical Contractors Ass'n v. Ordman, 366 F2d 776, 63 LRRM 2223 (CA 2, 1966), cert. denied 385 US 1026, 64 LRRM 2158 (1967).
21 MEMORANDUM DESCRIBING THE AUTHORITY AND ASSIGNED RESPONSIBILITIES OF THE GENERAL COUNSEL OF THE NLRB, effective April 1, 1955, 20 FED. REG. 2175 (1955), as amended, reported in McGuiness, SILVERBERG'S HOW TO TAKE A CASE BEFORE THE NATIONAL LABOR RELATIONS BOARD (Washington: BNA Books, 1967).

The General Counsel is also responsible for securing compliance with the Board's orders.

The General Counsel and the Board are located in the same building in Washington, D.C., and share common administrative services. The General Counsel's staff is separated into a Division of Operations, headed by an Associate General Counsel and five Assistant General Counsels, and a Division of Litigation, headed by an Associate General Counsel. The former supervises the work of the regional offices, and the latter carries out the duty delegated to the General Counsel by the Board of representing the Board in court. Special branches of the litigation division, each headed by an Assistant General Counsel, handle litigation in the district courts, the courts of appeals, and the Supreme Court.

D. The Trial Examiners

Formal hearings on unfair labor practice complaints issued by the General Counsel are conducted by trial examiners,[22] who are appointed by the Board from a Civil Service roster based on competitive examinations.[23] Although bound by Board precedent in the decision of cases, the trial examiners occupy an independent status in the performance of their duties. Section 4 (a) of the Act provides:

> No trial examiner's report shall be reviewed, either before or after its publication, by any person other than a member of the Board or his legal assistant, and no trial examiner shall advise or consult with the Board with respect to exceptions taken to his findings, rulings, or recommendations.

Trial examiners function much like trial court judges, hearing witnesses, ruling on admissibility of evidence, and making the initial decisions and findings of fact in unfair labor practice cases. Their decisions are final unless excepted to by a party.[24]

Approximately 85 trial examiners are based in Washington and 20 in San Francisco. Hearings, however, are conducted in the locality where the alleged unfair labor practice occurred.[25]

---

[22] Rules and Regs. §102.34.
[23] THIRTY-FIRST ANNUAL REPORT OF NLRB 3 (GPO 1967).
[24] Rules and Regs. §102.48 (a).
[25] Statements of Procedure §101.10 (a).

E. The Regional Offices

All Board cases originate in regional offices through the filing of petitions (representation cases) or charges (unfair labor practice cases). Prior to 1961 questions concerning representation not settled by agreement of the parties were determined by the five-man Board in Washington on the basis of a record made in a hearing in the field.[26] In 1959 Congress, in Section 3(b) of the Act,[27] authorized the Board to delegate its power in such cases to the regional directors, and this delegation was made in 1961.[28] The General Counsel's authority over the issuance of complaints of unfair labor practices has, historically, been broadly delegated to the regional directors. It is to be noted that review of regional action with respect to issuance of complaints is by the General Counsel, while review of regional action in representation cases is by the Board.[29]

There are 31 regional offices and three sub-regional offices located throughout the country, and they operate under the supervision of the General Counsel.[30] Each regional office is under the immediate direction of a regional director, who is assisted by a regional attorney and a staff of attorneys, field examiners, and clericals. These staffs investigate all petitions and charges, hold representation hearings and elections, and prosecute unfair labor practice cases.[31]

F. Personnel and Budget

The Board in its Washington office is directly responsible for approximately 370 employees, 65 percent of whom are attorneys. The General Counsel in Washington has responsibility for approximately 530 employees, a third of whom are attorneys. The

---

[26] ADVISORY PANEL ON LABOR-MANAGEMENT RELATIONS LAW (Cox Panel), REPORT ON ORGANIZATION AND PROCEDURE OF THE NLRB TO THE SEN. COMM. ON LABOR AND PUBLIC WELFARE, S. DOC. NO. 81, 86th Cong., 2d Sess. 7 (1960).

[27] Labor-Management Reporting and Disclosure Act of 1959 (Landrum-Griffin), PUB. L. 86-257, title VII, §701(b), 73 Stat 542 (1959).

[28] See note 11 supra.

[29] See Chapter 32 infra for a discussion of the availability and scope of judicial review of these actions of the regional directors and General Counsel. And see Rules and Regs. §102.67 (review by Board of representation proceedings) and Rules and Regs. §102.19 (review by General Counsel of refusal to issue).

[30] The thirty-first regional office was opened in Los Angeles, California, in 1966. THIRTY-FIRST ANNUAL REPORT OF NLRB 25 (GPO, 1967).

[31] Statements of Procedure §§101.4, 101.10, 101.18.

budget for all operations of the agency is about $32-million. Total agency personnel at all locations is about 2,325.[32]

II. PROCEDURES IN REPRESENTATION CASES

The system under which a group of employees may select or reject a bargaining representative by secret ballot is outlined in Section 9 (c) of the Act. The statutory provisions are amplified by the Board's Rules and Regulations, Sections 102.60 through 102.82, and its Statements of Procedure, Sections 101.17 through 101.25.[33]

A. The Petition

Section 9 (c) procedures are set in motion by the filing of a representation petition with an appropriate regional office of the Board.[34] Under the Wagner Act the Board had complete discretion in investigating representation questions. Its policy was to accept union petitions on a showing of substantial employee interest, employer petitions only where two or more unions were claiming a majority.[35] The Taft-Hartley amendments provide that a petition may be filed: (1) by any individual or labor organization acting on behalf of a substantial number of employees;[36] (2) by an employer upon whom one or more individuals or labor organizations claim recognition as exclusive bargaining representative of the employer's employees;[37] or (3) by an employee or group of employees claiming that a certified or properly recognized bargaining agent no longer represents a majority of the employees in an appropriate bargaining unit.[38]

These amendments led the Board to firm up the requirement that a petition filed by a union or group of employees must be supported by a showing that the employees involved are interested in an election. The showing of interest may be made by cards or petitions signed by more than 30 percent of the employees,[39] by

---

[32] Information obtained directly from the NLRB for fiscal year 1968.
[33] See Chapter 8 supra for a comprehensive discussion of the representation process.
[34] Rules and Regs. §102.60.
[35] H.R. REP. No. 245, 80th Cong., 1st Sess. 35, reported in 1 LEGISLATIVE HISTORY OF THE LABOR MANAGEMENT RELATIONS ACT, 1947, 326 (GPO, 1948).
[36] §9 (c) (1) (A), added by Labor Management Relations Act, ch. 120, title 1, §101, 61 Stat 143 (1947).
[37] §9 (c) (1) (B).
[38] §9 (e) (1).
[39] Statements of Procedure §101.18 (a).

current status as certified or recognized bargaining agent,[40] or by status as a party to an effective or recently expired collective bargaining agreement.[41] A lesser showing of interest is required for intervention.[42]

The Taft-Hartley Act required labor organizations to file copies of their financial reports, constitutions and bylaws, and their officers to file non-Communist affidavits, as a prerequisite to processing a representation petition by the Board.[43] These requirements were eliminated by the 1959 amendments, and the reports which must now be filed under Title II of the Landrum-Griffin Act [44] do not affect the right of a labor organization to file a petition with the National Labor Relations Board.

B. Timeliness of Petitions

There are several important limitations on the timeliness of petitions.[45] Under the Wagner Act, a union which lost an election could file a new petition within a few months if it could show a gain of members.[46] Taft-Hartley restricted the employees in a bargaining unit to one valid election during a 12-month period.[47] A petition is also untimely if it seeks an election in a unit where a Board certification of representatives has issued within the preceding 12 months.[48] A delay in actual certification of the union as bargaining agent or failure to bargain in good faith on the part of the employer has been held to toll the running of this period.[49] The practical result is to forestall an election, except in unusual circumstances, until there have been 12 months of bargaining opportunity.

Another important limitation on the timeliness of petitions is the "contract bar" doctrine. This principle rests on Board reluc-

---

40 Id. at §101.17.

41 This status is a *prima facie* showing of interest.

42 *See* McGuiness, SILVERBERG'S HOW TO TAKE A CASE BEFORE THE NATIONAL LABOR RELATIONS BOARD. Sec. 7-25 (Washington: BNA Books, 1967).

43 Labor Management Relations Act, §9 (f) — (h), ch. 120, title 1, §101, 61 Stat 143 (1947), *repealed by* PUB. L. 86-257, title II, §201(d), 73 Stat 525 (1959).

44 Labor-Management Reporting and Disclosure Act of 1959, PUB. L. 86-257, title II, §201 (a) — (c) (1959), 73 Stat 524, 29 USC §431 (a) — (c) (1965).

45 *See* Chapter 8 *supra* for a detailed discussion of requirements for the timeliness of petitions.

46 Ingalls Shipbuilding Corp., 73 NLRB 1263, 20 LRRM 1085 (1947).

47 §9 (c) (3).

48 Centr-O-Case & Eng. Co., 100 NLRB 1507, 30 LRRM 1478 (1952).

49 Mar-Jac Poultry Co., Inc., 136 NLRB 785, 49 LRRM 1854 (1962).

tance to disturb bargaining relationships, rather than on statutory grounds. The scope of the doctrine has changed from time to time, but, currently, a valid collective bargaining agreement will operate as a bar to a representation petition filed by an outside union for the full term of the contract but not more than three years. A contract with a term longer than three years will bar a petition filed by the employer or the contracting union, if certified, for its full term.[50]

C. Investigation of Petition

Processing the representation petition involves, in essence, an investigation by the regional staff to determine whether the Board has jurisdiction, whether there are statutory or policy reasons precluding an election, and the scope and composition of the bargaining unit. If a petition is dismissed during the preliminary investigation, the petitioner may request the Board to review the regional director's dismissal,[51] but if that request is denied or the director is upheld by the Board, further review is severely limited.[52]

D. Consent Elections

When the investigation shows that at least one labor organization involved has an adequate showing of interest, that the employer's business is such that the Board will assert jurisdiction, that the bargaining unit sought is appropriate, and that no other bar to a representation election exists, the regional staff will attempt to secure agreement to a consent election. Two types of consent agreements are used. The first—a consent-election agreement—provides for an election with final authority over any disputes vested in the regional director. The second—a stipulation for certification—is similar in form except that it provides for final determination of any disputes by the Board itself, with the regional director writing an interim report and recommendations.[53] In both instances the election is conducted by the regional office.

E. Representation Hearings

If the parties refuse to consent, a formal representation hearing is held before a hearing officer designated by the regional direc-

---

50 General Cable Corp., 139 NLRB 1123, 51 LRRM 1444 (1962). *And see* Chapter 8 *supra*.
51 Rules and Regs. §102.71; Statements of Procedures §101.18 (c).
52 *See* Chapter 32 *infra*.
53 Rules and Regs. §102.62 (a) & (b).

tor.[54] This contrasts with Wagner Act procedures, under which the Board was free to use other methods of determining majority status, *e.g.,* a check of authorization cards.[55] Parties may appear in person, by counsel, or by other representation. The hearing may cover any issue pertinent to the determination of questions concerning representation that have arisen under Section 9, *e.g.,* the appropriate bargaining unit, sufficiency of jurisdictional data, etc.; however, unfair labor practices may not be presented or litigated in a representation proceeding,[56] unless it has been consolidated with a complaint case. The hearing is nonadversary in character and is, in effect, a part of the investigation. The parties and the hearing officer may call and examine witnesses and introduce other evidence. Subpoenas may be used. Rules of evidence prevailing in courts of law are not controlling. Oral argument at the close of the hearing is permitted, although in most cases such argument is waived and the parties instead file written briefs. After the close of the hearing, the hearing officer submits a report to the regional director summarizing the issues and the evidence but making no recommendations. The regional director uses this report in making his decision.[57]

F. Representation Decisions

1. By the Regional Director. Since May 15, 1961, when the Board, exercising authority granted by the Landrum-Griffin Act, delegated much of the representation function to the regional directors, the director has determined, on the basis of the record made at the hearing and the briefs of the parties, whether a question concerning representation exists and the appropriate bargaining unit.[58] Previously, the record of the hearing was forwarded to the Board, without recommendation, and the Board itself ruled upon the issues. The delegation has more than halved the time required to process representation cases.[59] The regional director's

---

[54] *Id.* at §102.64. Since the enactment of Landrum-Griffin, special procedures, eliminating the hearing and reducing the time for appeals, are used if a union attempts to achieve bargaining status through picketing. §8 (b) (7) (C) . *See* Chapter 21 *supra.*
[55] Status at majority representative may still be achieved by unions under certain circumstances on the basis of authorization cards. *See* NLRB v. Gissel Packing Co., 395 US 575, 71 LRRM 2481 (1969) , *and* Chapter 10 *supra.*
[56] Lawrence Typographical Union v. McCulloch, 349 F2d 704, 59 LRRM 2161 (CA DC, 1965) .
[57] Rules and Regs. §102.66.
[58] *Id.* at §102.67 (a) .
[59] Thirtieth Annual Report of NLRB 17, Chart 10 (GPO, 1966) .

decision must set forth his findings of fact, his conclusions of law, and a direction of election or order dismissing the petition.[60]

2. By the Board. In certain cases, usually those involving novel issues of law, the director, before ruling, may transfer the proceeding to the Board for action.[61] Also, a request for review of the director's decision, in the nature of a petition for certiorari, may be filed with the Board by any party. Review will be granted only if substantial questions of law or policy are raised, there is clear error on a substantial factual issue, the conduct of the hearing was prejudicial, or compelling reasons exist for reconsideration of an important Board rule or policy. Board rulings on such requests are not subject to court review except in limited instances.[62]

3. Oral Argument. Although the rules provide for oral argument before the regional director prior to his decision or before the Board, such argument has been rarely held because of the large volume of cases. However, in October 1969 the Board announced a new policy that would increase the number of cases in which it would hear oral argument.[63]

G. The Election

1. Date. If the parties consent to an election, the election date is set out in the agreement and is usually within 60 days after the petition is filed. An election directed by the regional director is normally held between 25 and 30 days after the direction issues in order to provide time for processing a request for review.[64] Board directions of election customarily provide that the election will be held on a date set by the director within 30 days of the issuance of the direction.

---

[60] Rules and Regs. §102.67 (b). There is some controversy over whether the Board must make its own findings of fact as to representation issues previously decided by a regional director in a representation case before it can hold the employer guilty of a refusal to bargain in an unfair-labor-practice proceeding. According to the Second Circuit, the Board must make its own findings of fact in such a case. Pepsi-Cola Buffalo Bottling Co. v. NLRB, 409 F2d 676, 70 LRRM 3185 (CA 2, 1969), *cert. denied,* 396 US 904, 72 LRRM 2659 (1969). But the First Circuit holds, in agreement with the Board, that the rule against relitigation in an unfair labor practice proceeding of issues decided in a representation proceeding applies without regard to whether the representation decision was made by the Board or by a regional director. NLRB v. Magnesium Casting Co., 427 F2d 114, 74 LRRM 2234 (CA 1, 1970). The Supreme Court, however, has granted certiorari in the latter case. 75 LRR 135.

[61] *Id.* at §102.67 (h).

[62] *Id.* at §§102.67 (b) — (g). *See* Chapter 32 *infra.*

[63] *See* note 102 *infra.*

[64] Statements of Procedure §101.21 (d).

2. Eligibility of Voters. Employees eligible to vote are those having employee status on the date of the election who were employed in the appropriate bargaining unit at the end of the payroll period immediately preceding the date of direction of the election or a date set out in the consent agreement.[65] Eligibility of economic strikers has been a consistently vexing problem. Under the Wagner Act the Board permitted such strikers to vote even though they had been permanently replaced.[66] Section 9 (c) (3) of the Taft-Hartley Act reversed this rule and denied the vote to economic strikers who had been replaced. The pendulum swung again in Landrum-Griffin, which entitled "[e]mployees engaged in an economic strike who are *not entitled to reinstatement . . .* to vote . . . in any election conducted within 12 months of the commencement of the strike." [67]

The employer must furnish the Board a list of eligible employees with home addresses within one week of the direction of election or the execution of the consent agreement.[68] This list is turned over to the union or unions involved for their use in contacting employees prior to the balloting.

3. Voting Procedure. The election is conducted by a Board agent and is ordinarily held on the employer's premises. The ballot lists each union claiming majority status in the bargaining unit and "no union." Parties are permitted to have observers at the polling places, but neither supervisors nor nonemployee union representatives may be present during the balloting. All elections are by secret ballot. Either the Board agent or authorized observers may, for good cause, challenge the eligibility of any voter. Persons challenged are permitted to vote, but their ballots are impounded by the Board agent and are not considered further unless their number is sufficient to affect the results of the election.[69]

Immediately after the polls are closed, the Board agent counts and tabulates the ballots in the presence of the observers and other representatives of the parties.[70] A tally is prepared and served on

---

65 American Shuffleboard Co., 85 NLRB 51, 24 LRRM 1345 (1949).
66 Columbia Pictures Corp., 61 NLRB 1030, 16 LRRM 128 (1945) ; 64 NLRB 490, 17 LRRM 103 (1945).
67 §9 (c) (3). (Emphasis added.) See Chapter 19 *supra* at notes 44-49.
68 Excelsior Underwear, Inc., 156 NLRB 1236, 61 LRRM 1217 (1966). See NLRB v. Wyman-Gordon, Inc., 394 US 759, 70 LRRM 3345 (1969), note 109 *infra* and Chapter 8 at notes 174-181.
69 Rules and Regs. §102.69.
70 Statements of Procedure §101.19 (3).

each of the parties. A union must receive a majority of the valid votes cast to be certified as bargaining agent.[71]

H. Objections to the Election—Challenged Ballots

The purpose of the election is to provide the employees with the opportunity to exercise a free and uncoerced selection or rejection of a bargaining representative. Therefore conduct occurring at any time after the filing of the representation petition,[72] whether engaged in by the employer, the unions, Board agents, or outsiders, which creates an atmosphere rendering a free choice improbable invalidates the election.[73] Such issues are raised by objections to the conduct of the election. Conduct may be objectionable even though not sufficiently serious to constitute an unfair labor practice.[74]

Challenged ballots, if sufficient in number to affect the election results, and objections are investigated by the regional office. At the close of the investigation the regional director, frequently without a hearing, rules on the objections and challenges in directed- and consent-election cases. Where the election has been directed, appeals are limited to requests for leave to appeal to the Board.[75] The regional director's decision is final under a consent-election agreement.[76] Where the election has been conducted pursuant to a stipulation for certification, the director merely issues a report on objections or challenged ballots and the Board makes the final ruling. If objections are sustained, a new election is held. Otherwise, a certification of representative is issued if a union wins and a certification of result if it does not.[77]

I. Amendment, Clarification, and Revocation

Although for many years the Board has been willing to amend, clarify, and revoke its certifications, formal procedures for doing so were not incorporated in the rules until 1964.[78] Petitions for this purpose may now be filed, and the procedures used in general are those followed in processing representation petitions.

---

[71] Rules and Regs. §102.7 provides for one runoff election.
[72] Ideal Elec. & Mfg. Co., 134 NLRB 1275, 49 LRRM 1316 (1961); Goodyear Tire & Rubber Co., 138 NLRB 453, 51 LRRM 1070 (1962).
[73] See Chapters 5 and 8 supra.
[74] General Shoe Corp., 77 NLRB 124, 21 LRRM 1337 (1948).
[75] Rules and Regs. §102.69 (c).
[76] Id. at §102.62 (a).
[77] Id. at §102.69 (e).
[78] Id. at §§102.60 (b), 102.61 (d), 102.61 (e). See Chapter 8 supra.

J. Deauthorization Elections

Prior to the 1947 amendments, a union could lawfully insist that an employer hire union members only (closed shop) or that new employees join the union as a condition of employment (union shop). The closed shop was outlawed by those amendments, but the union shop, with certain limitations, was permitted if specifically authorized by the employees in a Board-conducted election.[79] In 1951 the statute was again amended;[80] as a result, prior employee approval of a union-shop agreement is no longer required,. but the agreement may be rescinded through a Board-conducted election.[81] Petitions for such elections are processed in the same manner as representation proceedings.

III. PROCEDURES IN UNFAIR LABOR PRACTICE CASES

The statutory method for the investigation and prevention of unfair labor practices listed in Section 8 is set out in Sections 10 and 11 of the Act.[82] These provisions are supplemented by Sections 102.9 through 102.59 of the Board's Rules and Regulations and by Sections 101.2 through 101.16 of its Statements of Procedure.

A. Background

Under the Wagner Act, agents of the Board itself investigated charges, issued complaints, and prosecuted the complaints. Hearings were conducted by trial examiners, but their decisions were frequently reviewed by supervisors prior to issuance and, at the Board level, by a Review Section rather than by attorneys reporting directly to Board members.

To satisfy widespread criticism of this system, the Taft-Hartley amendments, as described previously,[83] established an independent General Counsel with final authority over investigation of charges, issuance of complaints, and prosecution of cases before the Board. In addition, trial examiners were freed from supervisory influence over their decisions and were forbidden to consult with the Board about exceptions to their rulings. The Review Section was abol-

---

[79] §8 (a) (3). *See* Chapter 26 *supra.*
[80] Oct. 22, 1951, ch. 534, §1 (b), 65 Stat 601, 29 USC §158 (a) (3) (1965).
[81] §9 (e) (1).
[82] Under the Wagner Act, the Board had exclusive power to eliminate unfair labor practices. §10 (a) of Taft-Hartley authorized the Board to cede jurisdiction to state agencies but the authority has never been exercised. *See* Chapters 28 and 29 *supra.*
[83] *See* text accompanying notes 2-10 *supra.*

ished, and the functions of analyzing records and briefs and drafting Board decisions were transferred to attorneys on the staffs of individual Board members.

Taft-Hartley also made other important procedural changes. A six-month statute of limitations was added, replacing a Board-adopted laches doctrine.[84] Use of rules of evidence applicable to the federal district courts, insofar as practicable, was imposed, and the basing of Board findings on "the preponderance of the evidence" rather than on "all the testimony" was required.[85]

B. The Unfair Labor Practice Charge

The Board may not act until an unfair labor practice charge is filed with a regional office of the Board alleging a violation of the Act on the part of an employer, a labor organization, or their agents. Any individual or organization may file a charge.[86]

1. Time for Filing. The Board may not rely upon conduct occurring more than six months before filing and service of the charge as the basis for an unfair labor practice finding. However, if the conduct is of a continuing nature and extends into the six-month period it could establish a violation.[87] Also, evidence of earlier misconduct may be received at a hearing as background for the purpose of throwing light on events which fall within the six-month period.[88]

2. Investigation of Charge. The charge is investigated by a Board agent from a regional office, acting on behalf of the General Counsel. While the charging party is expected to cooperate with the Board agent and supply as much information as is available, the burden of investigation is on the General Counsel's representative.[89] Generally, upon completion of the investigation, the regional director will decide whether a formal complaint is warranted,[90] although complex or novel cases are sometimes sent to the General Counsel in Washington to be ruled upon. Parties participate in this decision only to the extent of furnishing facts

---

84 §10 (b).
85 §§10 (b) and 10 (c).
86 Rules and Regs. §102.9.
87 §10 (b). See NLRB v. Anchor Rome Mills, 228 F2d 775, 37 LRRM 2367 (CA 5, 1956).
88 Local Lodge No. 1424, IAM v. NLRB, 362 US 411, 45 LRRM 3212 (1960); NLRB v. Lundy Mfg. Corp., 316 F2d 921, 53 LRRM 2106 (CA 2, 1963).
89 Statements of Procedure §§101.2, 101.4.
90 Rules and Regs. §102.15.

to the regional office staff and informally presenting their theories of applicable law.

3. Disposition of Charge. If, on the basis of the investigation, the regional director determines that the charge is without merit, he formally refuses to issue a complaint. This refusal, or dismissal, may be appealed to the General Counsel, but if the director's action is upheld there is no right to Board or court review. The General Counsel's authority over issuance of the complaint is absolute.[91] Once a complaint issues, however, it has been held that there are limitations on his power to withdraw or settle the case.[92]

If the investigation discloses merit to the charge, an informal settlement may be used to dispose of the matter, either by the parties' adjustment of the dispute and withdrawal of the charge or by an informal settlement approved by the regional director.[93] Formal settlements, by which the respondent agrees to issuance of a Board remedial order, and in some instances a court decree enforcing the order, are also used where appropriate. Failure to comply with an informal settlement results in withdrawal of the settlement and prosecution of the case. Compliance with formal settlements is secured by enforcement procedures applicable to other final Board orders and court decrees.[94]

C. The Unfair Labor Practice Hearing

In meritorious cases which are not settled, a formal complaint is issued and a hearing held before a Board trial examiner.[95] The

---

91 §3 (d) . *See* Rules and Regs. §102.19. *Cf.* So. Calif. Dist. Council of Laborers v. Ordman (Christiana Western Structures, Inc.) , 75 LRRM 2380 (DC S Calif, 1970) . Oral presentation in Washington, D.C., may be requested to support an appeal to the General Counsel for refusal to issue a complaint. If the request is granted, other parties are afforded a like opportunity at another appropriate time. Rules and Regs. §102.19 (b) .

92 Leeds & Northrup Co. v. NLRB, 357 F2d 527, 61 LRRM 2283 (CA 3, 1966) .

93 Statements of Procedure §101.7.

94 *Id.* at §101.9. In *Leeds & Northrup Co.* v. *NLRB,* 357 F2d 527, 61 LRRM 2283 (CA 3, 1966) , the Third Circuit held that once an unfair labor practice complaint has been issued, the charging party is entitled to an evidentiary hearing on its objections to an informal settlement between the regional director and the respondent. *See* Note, *NLRB Settlement Agreements—Right of a Charging Party to an Evidentiary Hearing,* 20 Sw. L. J. 901 (1966) . *See* Farmers Cooperative Gin Ass'n, 168 NLRB No. 64, 66 LRRM 1341 (1967) for a statement of the principles to be followed by the Board in evaluating unilateral settlement agreements. (A *unilateral settlement agreement* is an agreement to which the charging party has not consented.)

95 When all facts are stipulated, the hearing is sometimes waived and the case submitted directly to the Board. Also, motions for summary judgment are now being used in refusal to bargain cases involving tests of the validity of a representation

case is prosecuted by an attorney from the regional office acting on behalf of the General Counsel.[96] Although some effort may be made to secure stipulations of fact which will shorten the hearing, no pretrial discovery procedures are used. At the hearing before the trial examiner the parties, including the charging party, are entitled to appear, call, examine, and cross-examine witnesses, and introduce evidence.[97] Subpoenas are available.[98] Insofar as practicable, rules of evidence applicable in the United States district courts are used.[99] At the close of the hearing, oral argument may be made to the trial examiner, but as a general rule parties prefer to submit written briefs.

D. The Trial Examiner's Decision

Thereafter the trial examiner issues a decision containing a complete statement of the case, findings of fact, conclusions, and a recommended order.[100] Any party may file exceptions to the trial examiner's decision with the Board and a brief in support. Answering briefs and cross-exceptions also are permitted.[101]

E. The Board Decision

Except in the special cases where the Board grants oral argument, its decision is based on the record taken by the trial examiner, the trial examiner's decision, and the exceptions thereto.[102] After issuance of a Board decision any party may, in extraordinary circumstances, request reconsideration, rehearing, or reopening. Such requests are rarely granted.[103]

F. Compliance With Board Orders

Securing compliance with the Board's order is also a responsibility of the General Counsel acting through the regional offices.[104] This consists of preparing and ascertaining that appro-

---

proceeding. The Board, rather than a trial examiner, rules upon the motion without a hearing—e.g., Gray Line Tours, Inc., 183 NLRB No. 22. Since September, 1967, the Board has emphasized the availability of prehearing conferences in unfair labor practice cases. THIRTY-THIRD ANNUAL REPORT OF NLRB 20 (GPO 1969).
[96] Rules and Regs. §102.34.
[97] Id. at §102.38.
[98] Id. at §102.31.
[99] Id. at §102.39; §10 (b) of the Act.
[100] Id. at §102.45.
[101] Id. at §102.46.
[102] See Chapter 31 infra. In October 1970 the Board began a new policy of holding regular hearings the first Monday of each month for selected cases. NLRB Press Release (R-1175) , Oct. 1970.
[103] See Chapter 32 infra. And see Rules and Regs. §102.48 (d) .
[104] Statements of Procedure §101.13.

priate notices of the Board's order are posted, periodically checking compliance with the terms of the order, and determining the amounts of back pay due those who are found to have been discriminated against. Most back-pay problems are negotiated informally, but the rules provide for formal proceedings after service of a back-pay specification, followed by a hearing and determination of back pay by a trial examiner.[105]

IV. THE NLRB AND RULE-MAKING

The National Labor Relations Board is empowered by Section 6 "to make . . . in the manner prescribed by the Administrative Procedure Act, such rules and regulations as may be necessary to carry out the provisions of this Act." The Board, however has preferred to promulgate rules of general applicability and future effect by the process of ad hoc adjudication rather than by rule-making.[106] While concurring in scholarly criticism [107] of the Board's unwillingness to comply with the rule-making procedures of the APA, the courts generally, until 1969, upheld the right to establish such rules in adjudicative proceedings.[108]

---

[105] Rules and Regs. §102.52-59.

[106] See e.g.: American Potash & Chemical Corp., 107 NLRB 1418, 33 LRRM 1380 (1954) ; Peerless Plywood Co., 107 NLRB 427, 429, 33 LRRM 1151 (1953).

[107] See: Peck, Critique of NLRB Performance in Policy Formulation: Adjudication and Rule-Making, 117 PA. L. REV. 254 (1968) ; Shapiro, The Choice of Rule-Making or Adjudication in the Development of Administrative Policy, 78 HARV. L. REV. 921 (1965) ; Peck, The Atrophied Rule-Making Powers of the National Labor Relations Board, 70 YALE L. J. 729 (1961) ; Summers, Politics, Policy-Making, and The NLRB, 6 SYRACUSE L. REV. 93, 105-107 (1955). See also Davis, ADMINISTRATIVE LAW TREATISE §6.13 (1965 Pocket Part). The American Bar Association has also been critical of the Board. In 1964, the House of Delegates adopted a resolution calling upon the NLRB to follow the rule-making provisions of the APA in contract bar and "all other appropriate areas." 89 ABA REPORTS 133 (1964). Earlier, the Labor Relations Law Section of the ABA had criticized the Board for its failure to engage in rule-making. ABA Committee on NLRB Practice and Procedure, PROCEEDINGS 116, 121 (1958). However, in 1969, a Committee of the Labor Relations Law Section called for the NLRB "to continue its long-standing practice of proceeding by adjudication rather than by formal rule-making regulation." Section of Labor Relations Law, 1969 COMMITTEE REPORTS, Report of the Committee on Practice and Procedure Under the National Labor Relations Act 33, 37 (1969). Despite the absence of rule-making by the Board, Judge Friendly of the Second Circuit has pointed to the NLRB as an example of successful policy-making in the sense that its policies are well understood. H. Friendly, THE FEDERAL ADMINISTRATIVE AGENCIES: THE NEED FOR A BETTER DEFINITION OF STANDARDS 36 (1962).

[108] See e.g.: NLRB v. Penn Cork & Closures, Inc., 376 F2d 52, 64 LRRM 2855 (CA 2, 1967), cert. denied sub nom., 389 US 843, 66 LRRM 2308 (1967) in which the circuit court concluded that, on the facts of the case, it could not hold that the choice to proceed by adjudication was beyond the Board's power; NLRB v. Majestic Weaving Co., 355 F2d 854, 61 LRRM 2132 (CA 2, 1966) ; NLRB v. A.P.W. Products Co., 316 F2d 899, 53 LRRM 2055 (CA 2, 1963).

In its 1969 *Wyman-Gordon* [109] decision, the Supreme Court narrowed the Board's discretion, though the precise meaning of that decision is unclear. The case involved application of the rule which the Board had adopted in *Excelsior Underwear, Inc.*[110] During formulation of the rule, the Board had "invited certain interested parties" [111] to participate by filing briefs and presenting oral arguments; when the Board finally promulgated the rule, it did so prospectively to take effect 30 days from the date of the order, and it was not applied to the parties in *Excelsior*.

In *Wyman-Gordon,* the Supreme Court reviewed the Board's application of the *Excelsior* rule. There was no majority opinion as such; however, a majority of the Court agreed that the Board had engaged in rule-making without complying with the requirements of the Administrative Procedure Act.

The opinion of Justice Fortas, in which Chief Justice Warren and Justices Stewart and White joined, noted that the rule-making provisions of the APA "were designed to assure fairness and mature consideration of rules of general application," [112] and that these procedures "may not be avoided by the process of making rules in the course of adjudicatory proceedings." [113] Accordingly, that opinion, which was the prevailing opinion of the Court, held that the rule had resulted from an invalid rule-making procedure.[114] Nevertheless, it upheld the Board's specific direction

---

[109] NLRB v. Wyman-Gordon Co., 394 US 759, 70 LRRM 3345 (1969). *See* Williams, *NLRB and Administrative Rule-Making,* LABOR LAW DEVELOPMENTS 1970 (16th Ann. Labor Law Institute, Sw. Legal Foundation) 209 (1970); Leahy, *Rule-Making and Adjudication in Administrative Policy-Making: NLRB v. Wyman-Gordon Co.,* 11 B. C. IND. & COM. L. REV. 64 (1969); Robinson, *The Making of Administrative Policy: Another Look at Rule-Making and Adjudication and Administrative Procedure Reform,* 118 PA. L. REV. 485, 508 (1970); Michelman, *The Supreme Court —1968 Term,* 83 HARV. L. REV. 7, 220-227 (1969); Bernstein, *The NLRB's Adjudication-Rule Making Dilemma Under the Administrative Procedure Act,* 79 YALE L.J. 571 (1970).

[110] 156 NLRB 1236, 61 LRRM 1217 (1966). The decision announced "a requirement that will be applied in all election cases. That is, within 7 days after the Regional Director has approved a consent-election agreement entered into by the parties . . ., or after the Regional Director or the Board has directed an election . . ., the employer must file with the Regional Director an election eligibility list, containing the names and addresses of all the eligible voters. The Regional Director, in turn, shall make this information available to all parties in the case. Failure to comply with this requirement shall be grounds for setting aside the election whenever proper objections are filed." *Id.* at 1239-1240. *See* note 68 *supra,* this chapter, and discussion at notes 175-181 in Chapter 8 *supra.*

[111] 394 US at 763.

[112] 394 US at 764.

[113] *Ibid.*

[114] The opinion stated that compliance with the APA required that a notice of hearing "general in character" be given in the Federal Register, that "the terms

against the respondent employer (Wyman-Gordon) "[b]ecause the Board in an adjudicatory proceeding directed the respondent . . . itself to furnish the list. . . ." Absent this specific direction, the company "was under no compulsion to furnish the list because no statute and no validly adopted rule required it to do so." [115] The opinion thus enforced the Board's order while holding that the rule upon which the order was based was invalid.

Justices Douglas and Harlan, in separate opinions, agreed that rule-making had occured, but they would have required strict compliance with the rule-making provisions of the APA and would thus have denied enforcement of the Board's order. Justice Black, in a concurring opinion joined by Justices Brennan and Marshall, contended that the choice between proceeding by rule making or by adjudication was discretionary with the Board. That opinion relied on *SEC* v. *Chenery Corp.,* [116] where the Court had held that "the choice made between proceeding by general rule or by individual ad hoc litigation is one that lies primarily in the informed discretion of the administrative agency." [117] Justice Black saw no reason to impose what he deemed to be an inflexible procedure on administrative agencies. Since the NLRB had complied with the APA requirements governing adjudicatory procedures in *Excelsior,* in his view the Board had properly exercised its discretion. His opinion also noted the *Sunburst Oil Refining* case [118] in which the Court had established the proposition that courts, while deciding a particular case, may declare principles for prospective application; once established as precedent, these adjudications have much the same effect as rules formulated through a rule-making procedure.

In the absence of a majority opinion it is uncertain as to the effect which *Wyman-Gordon* will have on future NLRB action.[119] But six members of the Court did find that the Board violated the APA by promulgating the *Excelsior* rule in an adjudicatory

---

or substance of the rule would have to be stated in the notice of hearing, and [that] all interested parties would have an opportunity to participate in the rule making." 394 US at 764-65.

[115] 394 US at 766. *See* Chapter 5 *supra* at note 165 and Chapter 8 *supra* at note 175.

[116] 332 US 194 (1947).

[117] *Id.* at 203.

[118] Great Northern Refining Co. v. Sunburst Oil & Refining Co., 287 US 358 (1932).

[119] Commenting on the effect of *Wyman-Gordon,* the Fifth Circuit, in American Machinery Corp. v. NLRB, 424 F2d 1321, 73 LRRM 2977 (CA 5, 1970), said: "Wyman-Gordon did not hold that the Board is obligated to follow the rule-making

proceeding. Their finding was based primarily on the Board's failure to apply the rule to the parties immediately involved in the *Excelsior* case, for the Board purported to establish a general rule applicable to future cases only. Therefore, at the very least, *Wyman-Gordon* means that the Court was censuring the Board for failing to follow the rule-making requirements of the APA. Although the Court made no attempt to write a universal definition which would distinguish rule-making from adjudication, a majority of the Court had no difficulty in concluding that the *Excelsior* rule was a rule within the meaning of the APA. It is noteworthy that the NLRB had never made use of the formal rule-making power which both the APA and the NLRA authorize.[120]

Inasmuch as the plurality opinion of Mr. Justice Fortas conceded that the Board could in an adjudicatory proceeding require an employer to furnish a list of employees to the union, and since it had so directed the employer in the instant case, that opinion concluded that the order was a valid adjudicatory order. Six members of the Court, a different combination from that of the preceding paragraph, thus recognize that the Board can apply a rule of general application, regardless of how promulgated, provided specific directions as to the application of the rule are made to parties in adjudicatory proceedings.

It remains to be seen how and to what extent *Wyman-Gordon* will alter the Board's method of operation. The Board may choose simply to incorporate its rules into specific orders in particular adjudicated cases and thus continue to avoid the formalities of APA rule-making. However, this could prove clumsy and inefficient in many types of cases, for example, in run-of-the-mill representation cases where a myriad of rules govern preelection conduct.[121] Or the Board may choose to retain its administrative flexibility by utilizing adjudication in situations where the rule of the case can be made applicable to the immediate parties, and

---

procedures of the Administrative Procedures Act whenever it announces new policies." The court declared that it subscribed to Judge Friendly's views, that "when an administrative agency makes law as a legislature would, it must follow the rule making procedure . . . and when it makes law as a court would, it must follow the adjudicative procedure . . . whether to use one method of law making or the other is a question of judgment, not of power." NLRB v. A.P.W. Products Co., 316 F2d 899, 905, 53 LRRM 2055 (CA 2, 1963).

120 *See* dissenting opinion, Douglas, J., 394 US at 779, n. 2.

121 *See* discussion of conduct affecting organizing and elections, Chapter 5 *supra*.

then apply the rule to future cases through ordinary *stare decisis*. In other situations, where the establishment of formal rules seems appropriate, notice and hearing procedures of the APA could be used.

The concurrence of six members of the Court in *Wyman Gordon* on the central issue of compliance with APA procedures can hardly be ignored. Whether the Board will now give serious consideration to the use of APA procedures when developing and promulgating rules of general application remains to be seen. The Court did not attempt to spell out precise conditions requiring compliance with APA procedures. The Board thus may have wide discretion to engage in cautious, even gradual, experimentation with formalized rule-making. Some of the likely areas for such experimentation are the rules relating to assertion of NLRB jurisdiction [122] and rules of conduct governing preelection activity.[123]

Mr. Justice Douglas, in his dissenting opinion, stressed the significant role of formal rule making in these terms:

> The rule-making procedure performs important functions. It gives notice to an entire segment of society of those controls or regimentation that are forthcoming. It gives an opportunity for persons affected to be heard. . . .

> This is a healthy process that helps make a society viable. The multiplication of agencies and their growing power makes them more and more remote from the people affected by what they do and makes more likely the arbitrary exercise of their powers. Public airing of problems through rulemaking makes the bureaucracy more responsive to public needs and is an important brake on the growth of absolutism in the regime that now governs all of us.

> Rulemaking is no cure-all; but it does force important issues into full public display and in that sense makes for more responsible administrative action.[124]

---

[122] *See generally* Chapter 28 *supra*. Indeed, the Board has begun to experiment with rule-making in connection with a jurisdictional standard applicable to private colleges and universities. *See* 35 Fed. Regis. 11270 (July 14, 1970) and 35 Fed. Regis. 12614 (Aug. 7, 1970) in which views were solicited. *See also* 74 LRR 271 (1970) and Chapter 28 *supra* at note 108.
[123] *See* discussion of conduct affecting organizing and elections, Chapter 5 *supra*.
[124] 394 US at 777.

CHAPTER 31

NLRB ORDERS AND REMEDIES

I. ORDERS IN REPRESENTATION CASES (SECTION 9)

In its grant of authority over representation matters to the Board (Section 9), Congress made explicit reference to providing for appropriate hearings, directing elections and certifying the results (Section 9 (c)(1)), to conducting a "runoff" election (Section 9 (c)(3)), to consent elections (Section 9 (c)(4)), to Board orders based upon facts certified following a representation investigation (Section 9(d)), and to conducting union shop deauthorization elections (Section 9 (e)(1)). Implicit in each of these references is Board authority to issue an appropriate order to carry out the statutory purpose.

These orders under Section 9 vary widely in form and content, depending on their purpose and scope.[1] Most are currently issued by regional directors pursuant to the Board's delegation of authority in representation matters.[2] Board decisions in such matters are usually, though not always, published in the Board's volumes of decisions, but regional directors' decisions are unpublished. Orders in representation cases may be issued (1) upon the consent of the parties (but only if the parties' agreement is in conformity with the statute), (2) after a hearing before a hearing officer or trial examiner, or (3) after an administrative investigation.

The variety of orders issued in representation cases precludes discussion of the characteristics of each type, but their most significant common characteristic is their unreviewable finality. This is the result of the strict limitations on the power of the courts

---

1 *See also* the discussion of orders in representation proceedings and elections in Chapters 8 and 30 *supra*.

2 On May 15, 1961, the Board, exercising power granted by the Landrum-Griffin amendments to § 3 (b) of the Act, delegated much of its initial authority over representation matters to the regional directors. *See* Chapter 30 *supra*.

to review such orders, covered in some depth in Chapter 32, Judicial Review and Enforcement. Briefly, direct court review is strictly limited to those instances where the Board acts outside its statutory authority and contrary to a specific provision of the Act.[3] In effect this means that, with rare exceptions, court review must be obtained through subsequent unfair labor practice proceedings, an unwieldly but useable technique for employers, who may invoke the procedures by declining to bargain. But they are of little value to unions or employees. Thus, for example, an employer whose objections to an election are set aside may refuse to bargain. When charged with an unfair labor practice he may defend on the basis of an invalid certification because of the ruling on his objections and thus bring the issue before a court. But a union whose objections are overruled has no direct recourse to the courts through these procedures, for it has no status from which to refuse to bargain.[4]

While dismissal orders in representation matters are final, as are certifications of results when no union wins majority status in a valid election, all certifications of unions as bargaining agents are subject to amendment or clarification at any time warranted by changed circumstances.[5] Otherwise such certifications normally are considered final and binding for one year after date of certification.[6] Thereafter they continue to be treated as valid in the absence of an affirmative showing that the majority status of the bargaining representative has ceased.[7]

II. ORDERS IN COMPLAINT CASES (SECTION 10)

A. General Types of Remedies Available

The Act provides for two basic types of remedies which the Board may itself grant or obtain in the courts, depending on the nature of the case. These are *provisional remedies* under Sections 10 (e), (f), (j), and (l), and *final remedies* under Sections 10 (a), (c), and (d).

---

[3] Leedom v. Kyne, 358 US 184, 43 LRRM 2222 (1958). *But see* Boire v. Greyhound Corp., 376 US 473, 55 LRRM 2694 (1964). *See* Chapter 32 *infra* at notes 89–99.
[4] In most such cases the union has lost the election and is seeking to have it set aside and a new election ordered.
[5] NLRB Rules and Regs., §§ 102.60 (b), 102.63 (b).
[6] Ray Brooks v. NLRB, 348 US 96, 35 LRRM 2158 (1954). *See* Chapter 8 *supra* at note 66.
[7] *Ibid.*, U. S. Gypsum Co., 157 NLRB 652, 61 LRRM 1384 (1966). *See* Chapter 8 *supra* at notes 486-492.

1. Provisional Remedies. The board has authority to seek injunctive relief in a federal district court in an unfair labor practice case before itself disposing of the case.   In connection with most unfair labor practices the exercise of this authority is discretionary under Section 10(j), although in certain types of cases—such as secondary boycotts,[8] hot cargo agreements,[9] recognitional picketing,[10] and jurisdictional disputes [11] when appropriate—the Board must proceed in this manner under Section 10(l). In both situations Section 10 (h) of the Act frees the courts of the strictures of the Norris-LaGuardia Act.[12] These remedies are provisional, however, since only the Board has primary authority to remedy unfair labor practices—the Section 10 (j) and 10 (l) procedures authorize the district courts to grant relief only pending the Board's processing of the charges before it.

Under Section 10 (j), the Board may, upon issuing a complaint, ask a federal district court "for appropriate temporary relief or restraining order." Section 10 (l) requires the Board to seek "appropriate injunctive relief" in the specified types of unfair labor practice cases "pending the final adjudication of the Board." The Section 10 (l) relief terminates upon issuance of the final adjudication or decision of the Board. Whether district court 10 (j) relief can continue during court of appeals enforcement or review proceedings is uncertain.

In any event, the latter question is more or less academic, for in an enforcement or review proceeding under Section 10 (e) or 10 (f) the Board may apply to the court of appeals for "appropriate temporary relief or restraining order," and the court is empowered to grant "such temporary relief or restraining order as it deems just and proper." [13] These provisions permit the Board not only to obtain interim relief from the courts of appeals pending enforcement of the final relief it has fashioned in a prior Section 10 (j) case, but also to seek continuance of court restraint in prior Section 10 (l) cases, if proper, and, in addition, to apply for any other proper interim relief in any type of case.

---

8 *See* Chapter 23 *supra.*
9 *See* Chapter 24 *supra.*
10 *See* Chapter 21 *supra.*
11 *See* Chapter 25 *supra.*
12 47 Stat 70 (1932) , 29 USC §§ 101-115 (1965) .
13 The restraints of a § 10 (j) injunction were continued in effect pending enforcement through this provision of § 10 (e) in NLRB v. Henry Heide, Inc., *unreported,* No. 66, Docket 23078 (CA 2, 1954) . *See* note 38 *infra.*

2. Remedial Powers of the Board. The power to grant final remedies in unfair labor practice cases rests exclusively with the Board. Section 10 (a) of the Act empowers the Board "to prevent any person from engaging in any unfair labor practices (listed in Section 8). . . ." In carrying out this responsibility, the Board, after a hearing and a finding of the commission of such an act or acts, is empowered to issue "an order requiring such person to cease and desist from such unfair labor practice, and to take such affirmative action including reinstatement of employees with or without back pay, as will effectuate the policies of this Act." Section 10(c) provides that the order may also require the violator to make reports "showing the extent to which it has complied with the order."

Within the limits of the Act, both the Board and the courts have broadly interpreted the Board's power to fashion appropriate remedies to effectuate the policies of the Act. A specific remedy will be sustained unless it is believed to be in excess of the Board's authority. However, the Board may not compel the making of a bargaining concession or agreement to a proposal.[14] Primarily, a remedy must be remedial only and not punitive in nature.[15] Moreover, Board orders must be sufficiently clear to inform the respondent of the conduct that is to be performed or is forbidden.[16]

Illustrative of the limited control of the courts over the Board's authority to fashion remedies is *NLRB v. Mine Workers (P.M.W.), Local 403*,[17] wherein the Supreme Court held that the question of remedy was in the Board's discretion and reversed a court of appeals decision directing an election to determine majority status before a bargaining order might issue.

The Board may issue a broad order restraining the commission of unfair labor practices generally where the particular circum-

---

[14] H. K. Porter Co. v. NLRB, 397 US 99, 73 LRRM 2561 (1970). *See* discussion at notes 135-137 *infra*. Williams Motor Co. v. NLRB, 128 F2d 960, 965, 10 LRRM 796 (CA 8, 1942); NLRB v. National Garment Co., 166 F2d 233, 239, 21 LRRM 2215, 2290 (CA 8, 1948); Northeast Coastal, Inc., 124 NLRB 441, 44 LRRM 1399 (1959). *See* also NLRB v. Gissel Packing Co., 395 US 575, 612, 71 LRRM 2481, 2495, n. 2 (1969); Fibreboard Paper Products Corp. v. NLRB, 379 US 203, 216, 57 LRRM 2609 (1964).

[15] Republic Steel Corp. v. NLRB, 311 US 7, 10-11, 7 LRRM 287 (1940); Phelps Dodge Corp. v. NLRB, 313 US 177, 8 LRRM 439 (1941).

[16] NLRB v. National Garment Co., 166 F2d 233, 21 LRRM 2215 (CA 8, 1948).

[17] 375 US 396, 55 LRRM 2084 (1964). *But see* H. K. Porter Co. v. NLRB, 397 US 99, 73 LRRM 2561 (1970), notes 135-137 *infra, and* Carpenters, Local 60 v. NLRB 365 US 651, 47 LRRM 2900 (1961), note 63 *infra*.

stances of the case justify such sweeping relief.[18] However, if a sweeping cease and desist order is not justified on the record, it will not be enforced by the courts.[19]

B. Specific Types of Remedies Available

1. Provisional Remedies—Injunctions. *a. Discretionary Injunctions Under Section 10(j).*

As stated, under Section 10 (j) of the Act the Board may, upon issuance of a complaint in an unfair labor practice case, at its discretion seek appropriate temporary relief or restraining order in a federal district court without any expressed limitation on the nature of the relief. Over the years this procedure has been followed in few cases. However, the trend in recent years has been toward greater use of Section 10 (j). Thus, whereas in fiscal year 1961 only one application for Section 10 (j) relief was filed, in 1962 11 were filed, in 1963 15 were filed, in 1964 18 were filed, in 1965 22 were filed, in 1966 17 were filed, in 1967 22 were filed, and in 1968 16 were filed.[20]

Normally, such cases involve a Board request for restraint of an alleged unfair labor practice. However, in *Johnston v. Darlington Manufacturing Co.,*[21] where the Board petitioned for "just and proper relief" because the company allegedly had voluntarily dissolved its business to avoid bargaining with a certified union, the court enjoined the further distribution of company assets pending final disposition by the Board of the alleged violations of Sections 8 (a) (1), (3), and (5). Upon finding that the company's action had jeopardized its ability to satisfy potential back-pay obligations, the court restrained the distribution to shareholders of monies received from the sale of assets, but not the payment of creditors.

Generally, the cases under 10 (j) involve situations where the violations are clear and flagrant, and where immediate relief

---

18 NLRB f. Cheney California Lumber Co., 327 US 385, 388-389, 17 LRRM 819 (1946).
19 May Department Stores Co. v. NLRB, 326 US 376, 392-393, 17 LRRM 643 (1945).
20 NLRB Annual Reports. *See also* McCulloch, *New Problems in the Administration of the Labor Management Relations Act: The Taft-Hartley Injunction,* 16 Sw. L.J. 82 (1962); McCulloch, *Remedies for Violations of Bargaining Obligations,* Labor Relations Yearbook—1968, 114 (Washington: BNA Books, 1968); Brown, *Problem of Remedies Under Taft-Hartley Act,* Labor Relations Yearbook—1967, 251, 258 (Washington: BNA Books, 1968).
21 Civil Case No. 126-258 (SD NY, 1957), 23 NLRB Ann. Rep. 127 (1958). *See* general discussion of the *Darlington* plant-closing case in Chapter 6 supra at notes 39-42.

seems necessary because a subsequent Board order and decree would be inadequate to remedy the injury. For example, employers have been enjoined from unlawfully interfering with, restraining, or coercing employees in the exercise of their right to organize,[22] from discharging employees for union membership, interrogating employees about union membership, and threatening union members,[23] and also continuing to refuse to bargain with the employees' chosen bargaining representative.[24]

Section 10 (j) is used by the Board primarily against alleged employer violations, since most of the situations where injunctions against unions are necessary are taken care of in Section 10 (l). In cases not covered by 10 (l), however, unions have been enjoined under 10 (j) from threatening nonstrikers, blocking plant ingress and egress, and surveillance of nonstrikers,[25] from continuing picketing methods which include threats of violence,[26] and from using threats or a concerted refusal to work to attain preferential hiring of union men.[27]

The 1966 *General Electric* case arising from the "coordinated" or "coalition" bargaining technique of several unions involved a unique use of Section 10 (j) proceedings.[28] The Board sought and obtained a district court injunction ordering General Electric to bargain with a committee chosen by the International Union of Electrical Workers (IUE) which included spokesmen for unions other than IUE which also represented G.E. employees.[29] Upon appeal by GE, the Second Circuit Court of Appeals set aside the injunction on the ground that the Board should consider the

---

[22] Boire v. Tiffany Tile Corp., 47 CCH Lab. Cas. ¶ 18,235 (MD Fla, 1963).

[23] Johnston v. Wellington Mfg. Div., West Point Mfg. Co., 49 LRRM 2536 (WD SC, 1961).

[24] Kennedy v. Telecomputing Corp., 49 LRRM 2188 (SD Cal, 1961); Little v. Portage Realty Corp., 73 LRRM 2971 (ND Ind, 1970).

[25] Potter v. Cement Workers, 48 LRRM 2965 (ED Tex, 1961).

[26] Douds v. Longshoremen, 224 F2d 455, 36 LRRM 2329 (CA 2, 1955); *cert. denied,* 350 US 873, 36 LRRM 2756 (1955).

[27] Jaffe v. Newspaper and Mail Deliverers' Union, 97 F Supp 443, 27 LRRM 2583 (SD NY, 1951).

[28] McLeod v. General Electric Co., 257 F Supp 690, 62 LRRM 2809 (SD NY, 1966), *reversed,* 366 F2d 847, 63 LRRM 2065 (CA 2, 1966), *reversed and remanded,* 385 US 533, 64 LRRM 2129 (1967). In 1967 the Board sought a 10 (j) injunction in a case arising from a fact situation similar to that involved in *General Electric.* The Eighth Circuit Court of Appeals reversed the district court's issuance of injunctive relief on the basis that the record failed to support the lower court's finding of irreparable harm. Minnesota Mining & Mfg. Co. v. Meter, 273 F Supp 659, 66 LRRM 2203 (D Minn, 1967), *reversed,* 385 F2d 265, 66 LRRM 2444 (CA 8, 1967).

[29] McLeod v. General Electric Co., 257 F Supp 690, 62 LRRM 2809 (SD NY, 1966).

matter on the merits in the first instance and utilize the 10 (j) injunction procedures "only to preserve the status quo while the parties are awaiting the resolution of their basic dispute by the Board."[30] The court, in effect, held that there were no special circumstances for issuing the injunction and that after the Board had decided the case on the merits, the court could review the order under normal procedures.

Thereafter, Justice Harlan, pending certiorari, granted a stay of the appellate court's order on the basis that "the standards governing the application of Section 10(j) [have] not heretofore been passed upon by this Court and [are] of continuing importance in the proper administration of the Labor Act."[31] On January 16, 1967, the Supreme Court granted certiorari, set aside the judgment of the court of appeals and remanded the case to the district court to determine whether the injunction was still necessary in view of the fact that the parties had executed a new contract.[32] The matter has remained dormant since the remand.

b. Mandatory Injunctions Under Section 10(l). Under Section 10 (l) of the Act the Board is required to seek "appropriate injunctive relief" in certain types of union unfair labor practices "pending the final adjudication of the Board."

As would be expected, the mandatory Section 10(l) procedures have been used more frequently than the discretionary injunction procedures under 10 (j). For example, in fiscal year 1966 there were 173 10 (l) proceedings instituted in the federal courts as compared with 17 10 (j) proceedings.[33]

Mandatory injunction proceedings under Section 10 (l) are available only in certain statutory situations which could cause employers the greatest damage in the shortest period of time. Specifically, Section 10 (l) provides that charges filed under Sections 8 (b) (4) (A), (B), or (C), 8 (e), or 8 (b) (7) (secondary-boycott, hot-cargo-agreement, recognition-picketing, etc., charges), shall be given priority over all other cases and that if, after investigation, the regional attorney determines that there is reasonable cause to believe that the charge is true and a complaint should issue,

---

30 McLeod v. General Electric Co., 366 F2d 847, 850, 63 LRRM 2065 (CA 2, 1966).
31 McLeod v. General Electric Co., 87 S Ct 5, 6, 63 LRRM 2140 (1966).
32 McLeod v. General Electric Co., 385 US 533, 64 LRRM 2129 (1967). *See* discussion of coalition bargaining in Chapter 11 *supra.*
33 31 NLRB ANN. REP. 154, 151 (1966).

he is then required on behalf of the Board to petition a district court "for appropriate injunctive relief pending the final adjudication of the Board with respect to such matter." Section 10 (l) provides further that "upon the filing of any such petition the district court shall have jurisdiction to grant such injunctive relief or temporary restraining order as it deems just and proper." In appropriate cases under Section 8 (b)(4)(D) (jurisdictional-dispute cases), the same procedure applies.

An exception in Section 10 (l) specifies that no restraining order shall be applied for in a recognition or organizational picketing case under Section 8 (b) (7) if after preliminary investigation there is reasonable cause to believe that a Section 8 (a)(2) charge filed against the employer is true and that a complaint should issue.

c. Interim Relief Under Sections 10(e) and (f). As stated, Sections 10 (e) and (f), after Board decision, permit the Board in its discretion to seek "temporary relief" deemed "just and proper" in the circuit courts of appeals pending enforcement or review proceedings in any type of case. These court injunctive provisions are used the least of all, probably because, by the time the matter has reached Board decision, interim relief generally has become moot by the passage of time.

Occasionally, however, situations have existed at the time of enforcement or review that were deemed to warrant application for interim relief. For example, proceedings under Section 10(e) or (f) have been initiated to enjoin the dissipation of assets in Section 8 (a) (3) back-pay cases;[34] to prevent an employer from executing a new labor agreement with a union found by the Board to have been dominated;[35] to restrain an employer from renewed Section 8 (a) (1) activities which would have further postponed an election;[36] to enjoin a refusal by a union during current negotiations to meet and bargain with the employer's designated representative, which refusal during prior negotiations the Board had found violated the Act;[37] to continue after Board order the effect of a

---

[34] NLRB v. Burnette Castings Co., 24 LRRM 2354 (CA 6, 1949) (restraining order issued).
[35] NLRB v. Virginia Electric & Power Co., 132 F2d 390, 11 LRRM 722 (CA 4, 1942).
[36] NLRB v. Servel, Inc., 15 LRRM 577 (CA 7, 1944).
[37] NLRB v. International Ladies' Garment Workers' Union, 44 LRRM 2003 (CA 3, 1959). The Board also filed a §10(e) action against the Ex-Cell-O Corp., seeking a temporary §8(a) (5) bargaining order. 75 LRR 163 (1970). *See* notes 145-146 *infra.*

Section 10 (j) injunction by restraining the employer from entering into a bargaining agreement with a union other than the union found by the Board to be the lawful representative;[38] and to restrain a union, under a broad Section 8 (b) (4) (secondary boycott) order, from engaging in secondary-boycott activities in respect to other primary employers.[39]

d. *Legal Standards for the Issuance of Injunctions Under the Act.* Since Section 10 (l) is utilized to bring a halt to unfair labor practices within its coverage, it is generally sufficient to justify such relief for the regional officer to establish "reasonable cause to believe" that the union has committed the violation as charged and that the violation is continuing or reasonably may be expected to be repeated. The Board need not present all its evidence or prove the unfair labor practices alleged.[40] Similarly, it is not necessary to prove the existence of each element of the unfair labor practice, but only to show that there exists reasonable cause to believe that the elements exist.[41]

A preliminary investigation by the regional director of the unfair labor practice charge is a necessary prerequisite to maintaining a mandatory injunction suit under Section 10 (l).[42] The Board must comply with its own procedures and requirements in this regard, or the injunction suit will be dismissed.[43] But a mere failure to allege the preliminary investigation of charges is not ground for dismissal.[44]

---

[38] NLRB v. Henry Heide, Inc., 219 F2d 46, 35 LRRM 2378 (CA 2, 1954).

[39] NLRB v. International Longshoremen's Ass'n, District Council of Puerto Rico, *unreported,* decided March 27, 1953 (CA 1, 1953). This § 10 (e) application was filed after the Puerto Rico district court indicated that it would not entertain a § 10 (1) petition based on new violations in respect to different employers because of the broad Board order against the union (enjoining the instigation of secondary boycotts against any employer) then pending before the court of appeals for enforcement. Although the court of appeals denied § 10 (e) relief, it remanded the matter to the district court with directions to process the § 10 (1) petition.

[40] Douds v. Local 294, Teamsters, 75 F Supp 414, 418, 21 LRRM 2150 (ND NY, 1947).

[41] Styles v. Local 760, Electrical Workers, 80 F Supp 119, 122, 22 LRRM 2446 (ED Tenn, 1948).

[42] Madden v. Machinists, Automobile Mechanics, Lodge 701, 46 LRRM 2572 (ND Ill, 1960).

[43] Madden v. Masters. Mates and Pilots, Local 3, 259 F2d 297, 299-300, 42 LRRM 2792 (CA 7, 1958).

[44] McLeod v. Local 239, Teamsters, 180 F Supp 679, 681, 45 LRRM 2302 (ED NY, 1959).

In *LeBaron v. Los Angeles Building and Construction Trades Council*[45] it was held that, before the regional director may petition for Section 10 (l) injunctive relief, there must be (1) an unfair labor practice charge, (2) a preliminary investigation, and (3) reasonable cause to believe that the charge is true and that the complaint should issue. However, no prior issuance of a complaint in the Board case is required for a preliminary injunction.[46] Nor is a Section 10 (k) hearing required as a prerequisite to injunctive relief in a jurisdictional dispute case.[47]

Sections 10 (l) and 10 (j) both require service of notice on respondent of the application for injunctive relief. However, Section 10 (l) permits issuance of a temporary restraining order without notice where the petition alleges that "substantial and irreparable injury to the charging party will be unavoidable" without it.

There are several significant differences, however, between the provisions of Section 10 (l) and those of Section 10 (j) which should be noted. Whereas a reasonable cause to believe after a preliminary investigation that there is merit to a charge within the coverage of Section 10 (l) justifies application for relief under that section, a complaint must first be issued before relief under Section 10 (j) may be sought. Also, under Section 10 (l), application for injunctive relief is under the control of the General Counsel's office, whereas, under Section 10 (j), injunctive relief is under the control of the Board. In practice, the Board in Washington authorizes in advance each and every application for Section 10 (j) relief filed in court. This does not mean that the Board sees every request made for Section 10 (j) relief; it does mean, however, that no application for 10 (j) relief is filed in court without its approval. This cumbersome statutory procedure for authorizing the filing of Section 10(j) injunction suits contributes to the limited use of that device and, accordingly, to the difficulty with which the remedy is obtainable.

In addition, a comparison of the general statutory standards for relief under Section 10(j), and of the potential scope of relief under

---

45 84 F Supp 629, 635-36, 24 LRRM 2131 (SD Cal, 1949), *affirmed*, 185 F2d 405, 27 LRRM 2184 (CA 9, 1950).
46 Graham v. Carpenters Local 2247, 34 CCH Lab Cas ¶ 71,289 (D Alaska, 1958); Dooley v. Teamsters Local 107, 182 F Supp 297, 304, 45 LRRM 2960 (D Del, 1960).
47 Operating Engineers Local 450 v. Elliott, 256 F2d 630, 634, 42 LRRM 2347 (CA 5, 1958). *See generally* Chapter 25 *supra*.

that section, with the detailed standards and limited scope of relief under Section 10 (l) suggests that in Section 10 (j) cases the courts will place greater emphasis on the traditional equity criteria for injunctive relief applicable in suits between private parties than they do in Section 10 (l) cases.[48]

Under Sections 10 (e) and (f), the filing and service of a petition or cross-petition for enforcement of a Board order empowers the court of appeals to grant interim relief deemed "just and proper." In the few decisions under these provisions, the courts of appeals have not undertaken to establish any broad standards for this relief; each case has been disposed of on the basis of its individual facts. However, it appears that the standards for injunctive relief under Sections 10 (e) and (f) would be substantially the same as those for relief under Section 10 (j).

2. Final Remedies—Board Orders. *a. Usual Types of Remedies Ordered by the Board.* Under Sections 10(a), (c), and (d) of the Act, the Board is invested with the primary authority for the prevention of unfair labor proctices. When it is charged that a person has engaged in an unfair labor practice, the Board has power to investigate the charge and issue a complaint stating the charge and ordering a hearing. If, upon a preponderance of the evidence taken by the Board, it is determined that a person has engaged in such unfair labor practice, "then the Board shall state its findings of fact and shall issue and cause to be served upon such person an order requiring such person to cease and desist from such unfair labor practice, and to take such affirmative action including reinstatement of employees with or without back pay, as will effectuate the policies of this Act" (Section 10 (c)) .

Such orders are not self-enforcing. Under Section 10 (e) , the Board may petition an appropriate court of appeals for enforcement of the order. It may also seek "appropriate temporary relief or restraining order" pending enforcement. Under Section

---

[48] *See* Angle v. Sacks, 382 F2d 655, 66 LRRM 2111 (CA 10, 1967) , holding that Congress did not intend that injunctive relief under Section 10 (j) "should be limited to those emergencies endangering the national welfare, or to situations with 'heavy and meaningful repercussions' "; *Id.* at 659; however, the Board must demonstrate a probability that the purposes of the Act will be frustrated unless temporary injunctive relief is granted. *Accord,* Little v. Portage Realty Corp., 73 LRRM 2971 (ND Ind, 1970) . *See also* McCulloch, *The Labor Injunction,* 16 Sw. L.J. 82 (1962) .

10(f), any person "aggrieved" by the order may file a petition to obtain review in an appropriate court of appeals without waiting for the Board to seek enforcement.

(1) Orders against employers. (a) Section 8(a)(1) violations. Board orders to remedy employer violations of Section 8 (a) (1) (interference with, restraint, or coercion of employees in the exercise of Section 7 rights) normally are cease and desist orders. The employer is ordered to cease and desist from the activities he has engaged in which are violative of the Act. These orders may be broad blanket orders, or narrow orders directed to the acts alleged in the complaint depending on the particular case.

The order includes a requirement to post for 60 days a notice that the employer will not in the future engage in the conduct found violative of the Act and will take the affirmative action directed. Such notices usually are directed to remedy all unfair labor practice findings, but where only an 8 (a) (1) violation is found posting of the notice generally is the primary part of the remedy. In *NLRB v. Express Publishing Co.*[49] the Supreme Court confirmed that an employer found to have violated the Act may be required to post notices of this kind conspicuously in his place of business.

Blanket cease and desist orders may issue in 8 (a) (1) cases if the unlawful interference, restraint, or coercion violates other sections of the Act or is part of a broad pattern of violation.[50] However, isolated acts of interference may not warrant a remedial order if no useful purpose would be served thereby.[51]

Section 8 (a) (1) orders may be simple cease and desist orders or, in appropriate cases, like other orders, may also require affirmative action. An example of the latter is *H. W. Elson Bottling Co.*,[52] where the employer violated Section 8 (a) (1) and was ordered affirmatively to provide the union with facilities in the

---

[49] 312 US 426, 438-439, 8 LRRM 415 (1941).
[50] NLRB v. Mayrath Co., 319 F2d 424, 428, 53 LRRM 2658 (CA 7, 1963).
[51] Becker and Sons, Inc., 145 NLRB 1788, 1789, 55 LRRM 1235 (1964); Lilliston Implement Co., 171 NLRB No. 19, 68 LRRM 1049 (1968). *But* two courts of appeal have held that, having found a violation of the Act, the Board *must* issue a remedy. Auto Workers v. NLRB (Omni Spectra, Inc.), 427 F2d 1330, 74 LRRM 2481 (CA 7, 1970); Int'l. Woodworkers Local 3-10 v. NLRB, 380 F2d 628, 65 LRRM 2633 (CA DC, 1967); United Steelworkers v. NLRB, 386 F2d 981, 66 LRRM 2417 (CA DC, 1967).
[52] 155 NLRB 714, 60 LRRM 138 (1965). *See* note 167 *infra*.

plant to make a one hour speech to assembled employees on company time, to grant the union access to company bulletin boards for three months, and to mail to employees copies of the Board's cease and desist order. Similarly, the Board may order the rescission of an invalid no-solicitation rule which violates Section 8 (a) (1) .[53]

(b) Section 8(a)(2) violations. There are basically two types of orders utilized to remedy Section 8 (a) (2) violations. Where the company has dominated the union, the usual order is one of disestablishment of the union.[54] An employer may be ordered to cease and desist from recognizing the employer-dominated union or any successor in privity with such union.[55] The order may be so broad as to forbid the employer to recognize any labor organization until it has been certified by the Board.[56] When domination of a union is coupled with a checkoff provision, the Board may order reimbursement of dues checked off,[57] as well as initiation fees collected.[58]

Where there is illegal support or assistance found, short of domination, the usual order is to withhold recognition from and cease dealing with the union unless and until it is certified by the Board.[59] Also, the Board may order termination of a collective bargaining agreement between a company and an assisted union.[60] Where an unlawfully assisted union is granted an illegal union security agreement with a checkoff clause, the employer may be ordered to refund the dues that were illegally checked off under some circumstances.[61]

---

[53] Republic Aviation Corp., 51 NLRB 1186, 1189, 12 LRRM 320 (1943), enforced, 142 F2d 193, 14 LRRM 550 (CA 2, 1944), affirmed, 324 US 793, 16 LRRM 620 (1945). See also HLH Products v. NLRB, 396 F2d 270, 68 LRRM 2454 (CA 7, 1968), enforcing an order to bargain on findings of "flagrant" violations of Sections 8 (a) (1) and (3). See Chapter 5 supra.

[54] See Carpenter Steel Co., 76 NLRB 670, 21 LRRM 1232 (1948). See Chapter 7 for general treatment of §8 (a) (2).

[55] Szekely & Associates, Inc., 118 NLRB 1125, 1127, 40 LRRM 1358 (1957), enforced, 259 F2d 652, 42 LRRM 2808 (CA 5, 1958).

[56] Independent Employees Association of Neptune Meter Co. v. NLRB, 158 F2d 448, 456-457, 19 LRRM 2107 (CA 2, 1946).

[57] Virginia Electric & Power Co. v. NLRB, 319 US 533, 12 LRRM 739 (1943).

[58] NLRB v. Cadillac Wire Corp., 290 F2d 261, 48 LRRM 2149 (CA 2, 1961).

[59] Kearney Corp., 81 NLRB 26, 23 LRRM 1295 (1949); Chicago Rawhide Mfg. Co., 105 NLRB 727, 737, 32 LRRM 1344 (1953), enforcement denied on other grounds, 221 F2d 165, 35 LRRM 2665 (CA 7, 1955).

[60] International Ass'n of Machinists, Lodge 35 v. NLRB, 311 US 72, 81, 7 LRRM 282 (1940).

[61] Dixie Bedding Mfg. Co., 121 NLRB 189, 196-197, 42 LRRM 1319 (1958), enforced, 268 F2d 901, 44 LRRM 2414 (CA 5, 1959).

In *Plumbing and Pipefitters' Local 231 (Brown-Olds Plumbing & Heating Corp.)*[62] an unlawful-assistance case in which only the union was respondent, the Board directed the reimbursement of all dues, fees, and other monies collected under an illegal union security agreement (*Brown-Olds* remedy). The Supreme Court later forbade use of this remedy in the absence of evidence that employees had been coerced by the union security agreement, holding that unless there was evidence that the union membership had been induced, obtained, or retained in violation of the Act, the reimbursement was punitive and beyond the power of the Board.[63] When appropriate,[64] a *Brown-Olds* remedy may be ordered against the union alone,[65] the employer alone,[66] or against the union and employer to make them jointly and severally liable to reimburse illegally collected dues.[67]

(c) *Section 8(a)(3) and (4) violations.* Remedies for employer discrimination in violation of Sections 8 (a) (3) and (4) are tailored to the discrimination involved and are as varied as the violative discriminatory acts. In the typical discrimination case where an employee is discharged for union activity or discriminated against because of charges or testimony under the Act, the Board normally orders reinstatement of the employee with back pay, in addition to the posting of a notice in which the employer states that he will not engage in further discriminatory activity and will take the affirmative action ordered.[68] The power to order reinstatement and back pay is specifically set forth in Section 10 (c), but the Board, with court approval, has expanded this remedy by requiring that back pay be computed under the *Woolworth* formula[69] on a

---

[62] 115 NLRB 594, 37 LRRM 1360 (1956).

[63] Carpenters, Local 60 v. NLRB, 365 US 651, 47 LRRM 2900 (1961).

[64] 26 NLRB Ann. Rep. 1005 (1962); 27 NLRB Ann. Rep. 105 (1963).

[65] NLRB v. Carpenters, Local 111, 278 F2d 823, 46 LRRM 2253 (CA 1, 1960).

[66] Lapeer Metal Products Co., 134 NLRB 1518, 49 LRRM 1380 (1961).

[67] NLRB v. Cadillac Wire Corp., 290 F2d 261, 48 LRRM 2149 (CA 2, 1961).

[68] Chase National Bank, 65 NLRB 827, 829, 17 LRRM 255 (1946); cf. Phelps Dodge Corp. v. NLRB, 313 US 177, 8 LRRM 439 (1941). See also in Chapter 19 supra the discussion of Laidlaw Corp., 171 NLRB No. 175, 68 LRRM 1252 (1968), enforced, 414 F2d 99, 71 LRRM 3054 (CA 7, 1969), cert. denied, 397 US 920, 73 LRRM 2537 (1970), wherein the Board enunciated a new policy in regard to the right of economic strikers to reinstatement. See also: Am. Machinery Corp. v. NLRB, 424 F2d 1321, 73 LRRM 2977 (CA 5, 1970); Little Rock Airmotive, 182 NLRB No. 98, 74 LRRM 1199 (1970). For greater treatment of §§ 8(a) (3) and (4) see Chapter 6 supra.

[69] 90 NLRB 289, 291-294, 26 LRRM 1185 (1950).

quarterly basis, and by also requiring the payment of 6-percent interest on the back pay found to be owing.[70]

The make-whole provision of the back-pay order customarily contemplates reimbursement for vacation benefits,[71] bonuses,[72] shares in profit-sharing programs,[73] pension coverage,[74] health and medical coverage,[75] employer-owned housing,[76] employee discounts on purchases,[77] and the like.

(i) Runaway shops. The Board has fashioned specific remedies for Section 8 (a) (3) runaway-shop cases. In *Jacob H. Klotz*[78] the Board, in addition to the usual remedies, ordered a runaway employer to offer the employees either (1) payment of moving expenses to the new location, or (2) payment, biweekly, of transportation costs to and from the new location, at the option of each employee. In another case, the Board ordered the payment of moving expenses to the new location but did not order transportation expenses paid.[79] Where an employer, to avoid bargaining with the union, switched from a manufacturing to a jobbing operation, the Board ordered the employer, if he voluntarily resumed manufacturing, to reinstate discharged production workers with back pay; or if he did not resume manufacturing, to compensate workers for wages lost until the date they secured substantially equivalent employment elsewhere.[80]

In *Garwin Corp.*[81] the Board ordered a runaway employer to bargain with the union at the new location even though it did not represent a majority of the employees there. The District of Columbia Circuit denied enforcement on the grounds that the

---

[70] Isis Plumbing and Heating Co., 138 NLRB 716, 51 LRRM 1122 (1962) *reversed on other grounds,* 322 F2d 913, 54 LRRM 2235 (CA 9, 1963) ; Reserve Supply Corp. v. NLRB, 317 F2d 785, 789, 53 LRRM 2374 (CA 2, 1963) .
[71] Richard W. Kaase Co., 162 NLRB No. 122, 64 LRRM 1181 (1967) ; Kartarik, Inc., 111 NLRB 630, 35 LRRM 1541 (1955) .
[72] United Shoe Machinery Corp., 96 NLRB 1309, 29 LRRM 1024 (1951) .
[73] W. C. Nabors, 134 NLRB 1078, 49 LRRM 1289 (1961) ; International Harvester Co., 169 NLRB No. 105, 67 LRRM 1435 (1968) .
[74] Richard W. Kaase Co., 162 NLRB 1320, 64 LRRM 1181 (1967) .
[75] Knickerbocker Plastics Co., 104 NLRB 514, 32 LRRM 1123 (1953) .
[76] Kohler Co., 128 NLRB 1062, 46 LRRM 1389 (1960) .
[77] Central Illinois Public Service Co., 139 NLRB 1407, 51 LRRM 1508 (1962) .
[78] 13 NLRB 746, 778, 4 LRRM 344 (1939) .
[79] New Madrid Mfg. Co., 104 NLRB 117, 122, 32 LRRM 1059 (1953) .
[80] Bonnie Lass Knitting Mills, Inc., 126 NLRB 1396, 1398-1399, 45 LRRM 1477 (1960) .
[81] 153 NLRB 664, 59 LRRM 1405 (1965) .

order interfered with the freedom of choice of the employees at the new location and was punitive rather than remedial.[82]

(ii) Successor employers. In a reversal of policy, the Board held in 1967 that a successor employer who acquires a business with notice of prior unfair labor practices, or under circumstances that would charge him with such notice, and continues thereafter to operate the business in basically unchanged form may be compelled to remedy predecessor's unfair labor practices, including the reinstatement with appropriate back pay of employees discriminately terminated by the predecessor.[83]

(iii) Tolling of back pay. In 1962, the Board reversed its long-standing policy of excluding from the computation of back pay the time from the date of the trial examiner's decision absolving the respondent of discrimination to the date of the Board's decision finding discrimination. The whole period is now included.[84] A "considerable delay" by the Board in issuing a back-pay specification for employees found to have been improperly denied reinstatement does not warrant a reduction in the back pay awarded

---

[82] Local 57, ILGWU (Garwin Corp.) v. NLRB, 374 F2d 295, 64 LRRM 2159 (CA DC, 1967), *cert. denied*, 395 US 980, 71 LRRM 2605 (1969). *See also* NLRB v. Savoy Laundry, Inc., 327 F2d 370, 55 LRRM 2285 (CA 2, 1964) where court found that part of an NLRB order requiring a laundry to take reasonable and businesslike steps to resume an improperly closed division was not warranted. The court said that since the laundry had not been operated for three years, it would be unduly harsh to require its resumption.

[83] Perma Vinyl Corp., 164 NLRB 968, 65 LRRM 1168 (1967), *enforced sub nom.*, U.S. Pipe and Foundry Co. v. NLRB, 398 F2d 544, 68 LRRM 2913 (CA 5, 1968). *See also* NLRB v. Frontier Guard Patrol, Inc., 399 F2d 716, 69 LRRM 2106 (CA 10, 1968), *enforcing* 161 NLRB 155, 63 LRRM 1315 (1966). In *Wm. J. Burns Int'l Detective Agency, Inc.*, 182 NLRB No. 50, 74 LRRM 1098 (1970), the Board extended the *Perma Vinyl* rule, holding that a successor employer will normally be bound to honor a collective bargaining agreement signed by the predecessor, and the successor was so ordered. *See* Chapter 13 *supra* at notes 34-37.

[84] APW Products Co., 137 NLRB 25, 28-31, 50 LRRM 1042 (1962), *enforced*, 316 F2d 899, 53 LRRM 2055 (CA 2, 1963). However, "[w]here reinstatement of an employee to his job seems a proper remedy for employer conduct, but there is no element of employer intent which so compellingly fixes the equities as in an 8(a)(3) case, the Board will consider any special factors in the case which may prompt the conclusion that a full backpay award would be inappropriate. . . . When the respondent is not an ill-intentioned offender, as he is in an 8(a)(3) case which turns on motive, the balance of equities between respondent and employee draws closer to equilibrium, and the Board will consider more sympathetically any substantial defenses the respondent may proffer against a full backpay remedy." Ferrill-Hicks Chevrolet, Inc., 160 NLRB 1692, 1695, 1697-1698, 63 LRRM 1177 (1966); Darlington Mfg. Co., 397 F2d 760, 68 LRRM 2356, 2365 (CA 4, 1968). Tolling of backpay will occur when the employer offers reinstatement of unfair labor practice strikers to their former jobs but they turn down the offer because fewer than all the strikers are included. The employer's job offer tolls backpay liability as to strikers who turned down the offer. Southwestern Pipe, Inc., 179 NLRB No. 52, 72 LRRM 1377 (1969).

to the employees. In *Rutter-Rex* the Supreme Court ruled that, even if the Board's delay violated the Administrative Procedure Act, a reviewing court may not interfere with the Board's discretion to balance the interests of the employer and the employees.[85]

(d) Section 8(a)(5) violations. The usual remedy for an employer's refusal to bargain in violation of Section 8 (a) (5) is an order (1) to cease and desist from failing to bargain and (2) upon request, to bargain collectively regarding rates of pay, wages, hours, and other conditions of employment.[86] Such an order may be directed against the successor or assignee of a violating employer if the successor or assignee is merely a disguised continuance of the former employer or if he actively participated with the former employer in the illegal refusal to bargain.[87] A bargaining order may also issue against a purchasing successor if the "employing industry" or "enterprise" remains essentially the same and the only change is a legal transfer of ownership.[88]

Although normally the employer vests his negotiating spokesman with sufficient authority to conclude a binding agreement, where this is not the case the Board, under appropriate circumstances, will order the employer to do so.[89] Where an employer has reached agreement with the union but refuses to reduce the agreement to writing, he will be ordered to do so and abide by its terms.[90] However, the Board may not order a party to incorporate in a collective bargaining contract a specific provision to which it has not agreed. In *H. K. Porter*[91] the Supreme Court denied enforcement of an order which would have compelled the employer to agree to a check-off of union dues.

(i) Unilateral changes. A unilateral change in wages, hours, or

---

[85] NLRB v. J. H. Rutter-Rex Mfg. Co., 396 US 258, 72 LRRM 2881, *reversing* 399 F2d 356, 68 LRRM 2916 (CA 5, 1968), *enforcing as modified* 115 NLRB 388, 37 LRRM 1321 (1956). Three Justices dissented on the ground that the role of the Supreme Court was extremely limited in reviewing Board orders, as compared with the greater role of the courts of appeal.
[86] Burgie Vinegar Co., 71 NLRB 829, 19 LRRM 1055 (1946). *See generally* Chapter 11 *supra.*
[87] NLRB v. Lunder Shoe Corp., 211 F2d 284, 289, 33 LRRM 2695 (CA 1, 1954).
[88] Chemrock Corp., 151 NLRB 1074, 58 LRRM 1582 (1965). *See generally* Chapter 13 *supra.*
[89] Silby-Dolcourt Chemical Industries, Inc., 145 NLRB 1348, 1349-1350, 55 LRRM 1160 (1964).
[90] H. J. Heinz Co. v. NLRB, 311 US 514, 523-526, 7 LRRM 291 (1941); Strong Roofing & Insulating Co., 393 US 357, 70 LRRM 2100 (1969).
[91] H. K. Porter Co., 172 NLRB No. 72, 68 LRRM 1337 (1968), *enforced,* 414 F2d 1123, 71 LRRM 2207 (CA DC, 1969), *reversed,* 397 US 99, 73 LRRM 2561 (1970). *See* discussion *infra* at notes 135-137.

other terms or conditions of employment also is a refusal to bargain in certain circumstances. In addition to ordering bargaining on such matters, the Board usually orders that employees be made whole for any benefits, such as Christmas bonuses, unilaterally discontinued by the employer.[92]

(ii) Supplying information. Employers must furnish certain information, upon request, to unions for purposes of collective bargaining prior to the agreement and also during its term. Therefore, the Board will order an employer to furnish particular data to a union where it is deemed relevant and proper.[93] Similarly, an employer may be ordered to produce data to substantiate a claim of financial or competitive inability to pay a wage increase.[94] Moreover, the Supreme Court has held that an employer must furnish to a union information necessary to enable the union to determine whether it should process a grievance.[95]

(e) Section 8(e) violations. Section 8 (e) (hot cargo) proceedings frequently are directed against both the employer and the union. In this event the usual remedy is a cease and desist order restraining the parties from enforcing the hot cargo clause and from entering into future hot cargo agreements.[96] Often, however, the proceeding is against only the union.[97] When the hot cargo clause appears in contracts with other employers as well, the union is likewise enjoined from giving effect to such clause in those agreements.[98] Also, where the hot cargo clause being maintained by the employer and the union affects more than the charging party, its effect on other persons likewise may be enjoined.[99]

---

[92] American Lubricants Co., 136 NLRB 946, 947-948, 49 LRRM 1888 (1962) ; General Telephone Co., 144 NLRB 311, 316, 54 LRRM 1055 (1963), *enforced as modified,* 337 F2d 452, 57 LRRM 2211 (CA 5, 1964) ; Beacon Journal Publishing Co. v. NLRB, 401 F2d 366, 69 LRRM 2232 (CA 6, 1968) and 417 F2d 625, 72 LRRM 2639 (CA 6, 1969). *See* Chapters 14 and 15 *supra* for a discussion of the mandatory subjects of bargaining.

[93] NLRB v. Yawman & Erbe Mfg. Co., 187 F2d 947, 27 LRRM 2524 (CA 2, 1951) ; Oregon Coast Operation Ass'n, 113 NLRB 1338, 1345-1346, 36 LRRM 1448 (1955) ; General Controls Co., 88 NLRB 1341, 1345, 25 LRRM 1478 (1950) ; B. F. Goodrich Co., 89 NLRB 1151, 1156, 26 LRRM 1090 (1950).

[94] NLRB v. Truitt Mfg. Co., 351 US 149, 38 LRRM 2042 (1956) ; NLRB v. Western Wirebound Box Co., 356 F2d 88, 61 LRRM 2218 (CA 9, 1966). *See* Chapter 11 *supra.*

[95] NLRB v. Acme Industrial Co., 385 US 432, 64 LRRM 2069 (1967). *See* Chapters 11, 17, and 18 *supra.*

[96] American Feed Co., 133 NLRB 214, 48 LRRM 1622 (1961). *See* Chapter 24 *supra.*

[97] Local 294, Teamsters (Van Transport Lines, Inc.), 131 NLRB 242, 48 LRRM 1026 (1961).

[98] *Ibid;* Milk Drivers & Dairy Employees, Local Union 537 (Sealtest Foods), 147 NLRB 230, 56 LRRM 1193 (1964).

[99] Retail Clerks Union, Local 770 (Frito Co.), 138 NLRB 244, 249, 51 LRRM 1010 (1962).

(2) Orders against unions. Orders to remedy union violations under Section 8 (b) of the Act, like those directed against employers under Section 8 (a), include both cease and desist orders and orders for affirmative remedial action.

(a) Section 8(b)(1)(A) and (B) violations. Normally, the remedy in Section 8 (b)(1)(A) and (B) cases of union restraint or coercion is a cease and desist order and the posting of a notice by the union. Affirmative action by a union can also be ordered, as where a union coerces employees by failing to sign a collective agreement and thereby withholds negotiated benefits from employees until they have signed membership applications and dues-checkoff authorizations. The Board orders the union to refund the dues checked off during the period of violation.[100]

(b) Section 8(b)(2) violations. The usual Section 8 (b) (2) remedy for a union *attempt* to cause an employer to discriminate against employees in violation of Section 8 (a) (3)—as distinguished from an actual causing of discrimination—is an order to cease and desist and post a notice of compliance.[101] However, even in these situations affirmative orders may be included in the remedy under Section 8 (b) (2).[102]

In cases of actual discrimination, where both the union and the employer are charged, the usual remedy is an order holding the union and the employer jointly and severally liable, awarding reinstatement with back pay, and directing the respondents to cease and desist and post suitable notices.[103] However, the employer is not a necessary party to the complaint, and a back-pay order may issue against the union alone when the employer is not charged.[104] In this situation the union is ordered to notify the employer and the employee that it has no objection to the reinstatement of the employee.[105]

100 Teamsters Local 886, 119 NLRB 222, 223, 41 LRRM 1056 (1957), *enforced,* 264 F2d 21, 43 LRRM 2693 (CA 10, 1959). *See* Chapter 5 *supra.*
101 National Maritime Union, 78 NLRB 971, 991-992, 22 LRRM 1289 (1948), *enforced,* 175 F2d 686, 24 LRRM 2268 (CA 2, 1949). *See* Chapter 6 *supra.*
102 Rubber Workers Local 12, 150 NLRB 312, 323, 57 LRRM 1535 (1964), *enforced,* 368 F2d 12, 63 LRRM 2395 (CA 5, 1966), *cert. denied,* 389 US 837, 66 LRRM 2306 (1967) (union ordered to end practices of racial discrimination and propose specific contract provisions to prohibit such discrimination). *See* Chapter 27 *supra.*
103 Acme Mattress Co., 91 NLRB 1010, 26 LRRM 1611 (1950).
104 Radio Officers' Union v. NLRB, 347 US 17, 52-55, 33 LRRM 2417 (1954). *See* Chapter 6 *supra. Cf.* Electrical Wkrs., IUE, Local 485 (Automotive Plating Corp.), 170 NLRB No. 121, 67 LRRM 1609 (1968), *supplemental order,* 183 NLRB No. 131, 74 LRRM 1396 (1970), Chapter 27 *supra* at notes 105-106.
105 Pen and Pencil Workers Union, 91 NLRB 883, 26 LRRM 1583 (1950).

A union may, however, at any time limit further back-pay liability by notifying the employer in writing,[106] or orally on the record in the hearing before the Board,[107] that it has no objection to the correction of the discrimination by the employer. If the employer fails thereafter to eliminate the discrimination, he alone henceforth may be held liable for back pay.

Where back pay is ordered in 8 (b) (2) cases, the Board also has added 6-percent interest.[108]

The scope of 8 (b) (2) orders may be broadened beyond the facts giving rise to the immediate violation. Thus, the order may require the union to cease and desist from the illegal conduct throughout its territorial jurisdiction.[109] Similarly, an order requiring a union to cease and desist from giving effect to an illegal contract with the employer has been extended to prohibit all similar contracts between the union and other employers subject to Board jurisdiction.[110]

(c) Section 8(b)(3) violations. A union found guilty of refusal to bargain in good faith will, like an employer, be ordered to cease and desist from such unlawful conduct and, affirmatively, to bargain.[111] In addition, the union will be subject to the additional relief directed against employer refusals to bargain, such as signing an agreement reached and embodying any understanding reached in a written agreement.[112]

(d) Section 8(b)(4) violations. Violations of Section 8 (b) (4) usually are temporarily remedied by use of the mandatory-injunction procedures in Section 10 (l) of the Act. The Board's final determination in such cases normally includes a cease and desist order and a requirement to post notices[113] but may include affirmative orders in appropriate cases.[114]

---

106 Pinkerton's National Detective Agency, Inc., 90 NLRB 205, 26 LRRM 1193 (1950).
107 Acme Mattress Co., 91 NLRB 1010, 26 LRRM 1611 (1950).
108 Richard W. Kaase, 141 NLRB 245, 249, 52 LRRM 1306 (1963).
109 Longshoremen's Ass'n, Local 791, 116 NLRB 1652, 1654, 39 LRRM 1067 (1956).
110 Plumbers and Pipefitters Local 231, 115 NLRB 594, 598-599, 37 LRRM 1360 (1956).
111 American Radio Ass'n, 82 NLRB 1344, 1347-1348, 24 LRRM 1006 (1949); Meat Cutters Local 421, 81 NLRB 1052, 1063, 23 LRRM 1464 (1949).
112 Sheet Metal Workers Union, Local 65, 120 NLRB 1678, 42 LRRM 1231 (1958).
113 Teamsters Local 107, 115 NLRB 1184, 1187-1188, 38 LRRM 1027 (1956). *See generally* Chapter 23 *supra.*
114 Teamsters Local 554 v. NLRB, 262 F2d 456, 463-464, 43 LRRM 2197 (CA DC, 1958).

Extremely broad cease and desist orders have been issued in certain types of secondary-boycott cases where the union has engaged in a pattern of general conduct likely to continue without such an order.[115]

Complaint proceedings in jurisdictional-dispute cases, under the scheme of the Act, must be delayed until the respondent union has failed to comply with a Board determination under Section 10(k) as to which union or group is entitled to the work in dispute,[116] or has refused to adhere to the resolution of the dispute under a method for voluntary adjustment.[117] Thereafter, the remedy in the complaint proceeding is usually restricted to a cease and desist and notice-posting order.[118] As in the case of secondary boycotts, the facts sometimes may justify a broad cease and desist order protecting other employers from similar jurisdictional disputes.[119]

(e) Section 8(b)(5) violations. While there has been little litigation under this section, the Board has held that a union that has exacted a discriminatory initiation fee must return the difference between the amount paid and the lesser fees charged other employees.[120] Such reimbursement of excessive initiation fees is proper even though no restraint or coercion is shown.[121]

(f) Section 8(b)(6) violations. Because of the limited scope of this section (exactions or featherbedding) there has been no significant remedial experience under this section worthy of note, especially since the Supreme Court decisions in the *American Newspaper Publisher Ass'n* and *Gamble Enterprises* cases.[122]

---

115 Glass Workers Local 1892, 141 NLRB 106, 107-108, 52 LRRM 1282 (1963).

116 Juneau Spruce Corp., 82 NLRB 650, 655-656, 23 LRRM 1597 (1949). *See* Chapter 25 *supra* for a discussion of jurisdictional disputes.

117 Acoustical Contractors Ass'n, 119 NLRB 1345, 1350-1355, 41 LRRM 1293 (1958).

118 National Publishing Division, McCall Corp., 152 NLRB 1404, 1407-1408, 59 LRRM 1309 (1965).

119 *See* NLRB v. Local 138, Operating Engineers (Cafasso Lathing & Plastering, Inc.), 377 F2d 528, 65 LRRM 2215 (CA 2, 1967), *enforcing* 153 NLRB 1470, 59 LRRM 1676 (1965); NLRB v. Local 25, IBEW (Emmett Electric Co. and Sarrow Suburban Electric Co.), 383 F2d 449, 66 LRRM 2355 (CA 2, 1967), *enforcing* 157 NLRB 44, 61 LRRM 1307 (Emmett 1966), and 157 NLRB 715, 61 LRRM 1452 (Sarrow 1966).

120 UAW, Local 153, 99 NLRB 1419, 1421-1422, 30 LRRM 1169 (1952).

121 NLRB v. Television and Radio Broadcasting Studio Employees, Local 804, 315 F2d 398, 402, 52 LRRM 2774 (CA 3, 1963), *enforcing* 135 NLRB 632, 49 LRRM 1541 (1962). *See* Chapter 26 *supra* at notes 29-38.

122 345 US 100, 31 LRRM 2422; 345 US 117, 31 LRRM 2428 (1953). *See* Chapter 25 *supra*.

(g) Section 8(b)(7) violations. Violations of Section 8 (b) (7) (recognition or organizational picketing) are also handled under the mandatory-injunction provisions of Section 10(1) pending a final determination by the Board. If an 8(b)(7)(A), (B), or (C) charge is substantiated, the Board's order is to cease and desist and post an appropriate notice.[123] Under Section 8(b)(7)(C), however, if a timely representation petition is filed the Board dismisses the 8 (b) (7) (C) charge and conducts an expedited election.[124]

b. Unusual Remedies Ordered by the Board. Generally, the remedies discussed above are the ones which the Board normally uses for the prevention and correction of unfair labor practices. In recent years, however, the Board has fashioned various special remedies for use in cases involving more serious violations of the Act.

(1) Orders against employers. (a) Status quo ante orders. Where an employer refuses, in violation of Section 8(a)(5), to bargain about a change in operations, such as subcontracting or plant closure or removal, he may be ordered to restore the *status quo ante* by reinstituting his terminated operations, reinstating employees with back pay, and bargaining over future changes.[125] In some cases, however, this *status quo ante* remedy has not been ordered, as where the employer has acted in good faith with compelling business and economic reasons[126] or where such an order is not

---

[123] Local 1199, Drug & Hospital Employees Union, 136 NLRB 1564, 1569, 50 LRRM 1033 (1962); Local 182, Teamsters, 135 NLRB 851, 49 LRRM 1576 (1962), *enforced,* 314 F2d 53, 52 LRRM 2354 (CA 2, 1963); NLRB v. Local 239, Teamsters, 289 F2d 41, 45, 48 LRRM 2076 (CA 2, 1961), *enforcing* 127 NLRB 958, 46 LRRM 1123 (1960).

[124] NLRB Gen. Counsel Rul. No. SR-439, 46 LRRM 1109 (1960). *See* Chapter 21 *supra.*

[125] Fibreboard Paper Products Corp., 138 NLRB 550, 555, 51 LRRM 1101 (1962), *enforced,* 322 F2d 411, 53 LRRM 2666 (CA DC, 1963), *affirmed,* 379 US 203, 215-217, 57 LRRM 2609 (1964); Town and Country Mfg. Co., 136 NLRB 1022, 1030, 49 LRRM 1918 (1962), *enforced,* 316 F2d 846, 53 LRRM 2054 (CA 5, 1963); North western Publishing Co., 144 NLRB 1069, 1073, 54 LRRM 1182 (1963), *enforced,* 343 F2d 521, 58 LRRM 2759 (CA 7, 1965); Richland, Inc., 180 NLRB No. 2, 73 LRRM 1017 (1969). McCulloch, *Remedies for Violations of Bargaining Obligation,* LABOR RELATIONS YEARBOOK—1968 114 (Washington: BNA Books, 1968). *See* Chapter 15 *supra.*

[126] Renton News Record, 136 NLRB 1294, 1297-1298, 49 LRRM 1972 (1962); New York Mirror, 151 NLRB 834, 841-842, 58 LRRM 1465 (1965); Brown, *Problems of Remedies Under Taft-Hartley Act,* LABOR RELATIONS YEARBOOK—1967 255-256 (Washington: BNA Books, 1968). *But* two courts of appeal have held that, having found a violation of the Act, the Board *must* issue a remedy. Auto Workers v. NLRB (Omni Spectra, Inc.), 427 F2d 1330, 74 LRRM 2481 (CA 7, 1970); Int'l Woodworkers Local 3-10 v. NLRB, 380 F2d 628, 65 LRRM 2633 (CA DC, 1967); United Steelworkers v. NLRB, 386 F2d 981, 66 LRRM 2417 (CA DC, 1967).

necessary to effectuate the Act and would impose an unwarranted burden on the employer.[127]

(b) Bargaining orders.

(i) Predicated on card check. An employer may be ordered to bargain collectively with a union that does not have majority status at the time of the order if the employer commits serious unfair labor practices that interfere with the election processes or tend to preclude the holding of a fair election.[128] Even absent a refusal-to-bargain finding, the Board may order bargaining to remedy 8(a)(1) violations where an employer has interfered with the employees' right to self-organization and where loss of majority status was due to the employer's conduct.[129] It has been suggested that the Board should issue a bargaining order when flagrant and clear 8(a)(1) and 8(a)(3) violations have prevented the union from achieving majority status.[130]

In 1964, the Board in *Bernel Foam*[131] held that an employer may be ordered, on the basis of a card check, to bargain with a union which has lost an election if it is shown that the employer, at the time he refused a union demand for recognition, had no reasonable basis for doubting the union's majority and thereafter engaged in other unfair labor practices before the election. In 1954, the Board in *Aiello*[132] had held that the union was required to elect between (a) proceeding with an election

---

[127] NLRB v. American Mfg. Co. of Texas, 351 F2d 74, 60 LRRM 2122 (CA 5, 1965), *enforcing as modified*, 139 NLRB 815, 51 LRRM 1392 (1962); Ozark Trailers, Inc., 161 NLRB 561, 63 LRRM 1264, 1269-1270 (1966); Thompson Transport Company, Inc., 165 NLRB 746, 65 LRRM 1370 (1967); Drapery Manufacturing Co. Inc., 170 NLRB No. 199, 68 LRRM 1027 (1968).

[128] NLRB v. Gissel Packing Co., 395 US 575, 591, 71 LRRM 2481 (1969). *See also:* Franks Bros. Co. v. NLRB, 321 US 702, 14 LRRM 591 (1944); Joy Silk Mills v. NLRB, 185 F2d 732, 27 LRRM 2012 (CA DC, 1950), *cert. denied,* 341 US 914, 27 LRRM 2633 (1951). *See* Chapter 10 *supra.*

[129] Delight Bakery, Inc., 145 NLRB 893, 908-909, 55 LRRM 1076 (1964), *enforced,* 353 F2d 344, 60 LRRM 2501 (CA 6, 1965); United Steelworkers of America v. NLRB, 376 F2d 770, 64 LRRM 2650 (CA DC, 1967), *enforcing* 158 NLRB 624, 62 LRRM 1089 (1966); Wausau Steel Corp. v. NLRB, 377 F2d 369, 65 LRRM 2001 (CA 7, 1967), *enforcing* 160 NLRB 635, 62 LRRM 1650 (1966); NLRB v. Priced-Less Foods, Inc., 405 F2d 67, 70 LRRM 2007 (CA 6, 1968).

[130] *See* Bok, *Regulating NLRA Election Tactics,* 78 Harv. L. Rev. 38, 134-139 (1964); Brown, *Problem of Remedies Under Taft-Hartley Act,* Labor Relations Yearbook —1967 251, 254 (Washington: BNA Books, 1968).

[131] Bernel Foam Products Co., 146 NLRB 1277, 56 LRRM 1039 (1964). *See* Chapter 10 *supra* at notes 108-116. *See also* Affeldt, *Bargaining Orders Without An Election: The National Labor Relations Board's "Final Solution,"* 57 Ky. L. J. 151 (1968-69).

[132] Aiello Dairy Farms, 110 NLRB 1365, 35 LRRM 1235 (1954).

with knowledge of the employer's prior unfair labor practices and (b) foregoing the election and proceeding with unfair labor practice charges, thus reversing its contrary holding of several years before in the *Davidson* case.[133] With *Bernel* the pendulum made full swing, from *Aiello* back to *Davidson*. A *Bernel Foam* order is dependent upon the union's filing and the Board's upholding objections to the employer's conduct affecting the outcome of the election.[134]

(ii) Agreement to specific proposals. The Supreme Court in *H. K. Porter* [135] clarified that the Board lacks remedial authority under the Act to require a party to agree to a specific bargaining proposal or to incorporate any substantive provision into a collective contract. The case involved a Board finding under Section 8(a)(5) regarding check-off of union dues. The Board found the employer's refusal to agree to the check-off had not been made in good faith but was done solely to frustrate the collective bargaining negotiations. The Court of Appeals for the District of Columbia granted enforcement of a conventional bargaining order. In subsequent negotiations, the employer proposed alternate arrangements for collecting union dues, but the union insisted that the employer was required to agree to the check-off, whereupon the union requested a clarification of the court's opinion. The court of appeals then declared that in an appropriate case the Board could order the employer to grant a check-off and that "a check-off in return for a reasonable concession by the union may be the only effective remedy." [136] Thereafter, the Board ordered the employer to grant the union's request for a check-off without requiring a "reasonable concession" in return; this was affirmed by the court of appeals.

The Supreme Court reversed. The Court pointed to Section 8(d) of the Act defining the obligation to bargain collectively and providing that "such obligation does not compel either party to agree to a proposal or require the making of a concession." It held that the Board's remedial powers were limited by the same

---

133 M. H. Davidson Co., 94 NLRB 142, 28 LRRM 1026 (1951).
134 Irving Air Chute Co., 149 NLRB 627, 630, 57 LRRM 1330 (1964), *enforced,* 350 F2d 176, 59 LRRM 3052 (CA 2, 1965).
135 H. K. Porter Co. v. NLRB, 397 US 99, 73 LRRM 2561 (1970). *See also* discussion of bargaining obligation in Chapter 11 *supra* at notes 163-170. For early history of the case, *see* Steelworkers v. NLRB, 363 F2d 272, 62 LRRM 2204 (CA DC, 1966). *See also* Tex Tan Welhausen Co. v. NLRB, —— F2d ——, 75 LRRM 2554 (CA 5, 1970), *on remand following H. K. Porter,* 397 US 819, 74 LRRM 2064 (1970), *vacating and remanding* 419 F2d 1265, 72 LRRM 2885 (CA 5, 1969).
136 Steelworkers v. NLRB, 389 F2d 295, 302, 66 LRRM 2761 (CA DC, 1967).

consideration. Justice Black's majority opinion observed that
. . . [i]t is implicit in the entire structure of the Act that the Board
acts to oversee and referee the process of collective bargaining, leaving the results of the contest to the bargaining strength of the parties.
. . . The Board's remedial powers under §10 of the Act are broad,
but they are limited to carrying out the policies of the Act itself. One
of these fundamental policies is freedom of contract. While the
parties' freedom of contract is not absolute under the Act, allowing
the Board to compel agreement when the parties themselves are
unable to do so would violate the fundamental premise on which
the Act is based—private bargaining under governmental supervision of the procedure alone, without any official compulsion over
the actual terms of the contract.[137]

(iii) Retroactive execution of contract. For a number of years
the Board has remedied employer 8(a)(5) refusals to put into
writing an agreement which the parties have agreed to, by
directing the employer, at the election of the union, either to
put the agreement in writing and adhere to its provisions *in the
future* for the term agreed upon or to bargain about a new
agreement.[138] In recent years the Board has substantially
changed this remedy in several respects. Now, it gives the
union the election between employer excution of and adherence to the terms of the agreement reached *retroactive*
to the effective date orally agreed to, and bargaining for a new
contract.[139] In addition, if the union elects to enforce adherence
to the contract orally reached, the Board now directs that the
employer make the employees whole for any losses suffered
by reason of his refusal theretofore to adhere to the agreement,
with the 6-percent interest previously attached in Section
8 (a)(3) and (4) and 8 (b)(2) cases.[140]

The courts have generally endorsed the individual elements
of this extended relief, such as retroactive adherence to agreements orally reached, make-whole orders with 6-percent interest,
and union election between remedies; however, some of the circuits refused to accept the package in toto. Thus, the Second
Circuit, in enforcing the Board's order in *New England Die
Casting*,[141] placed its stamp of approval upon the election

---

137 397 US at 107.
138 New England Die Casting Co., 116 NLRB 1, 5, 38 LRRM 1175 (1956).
139 Huttig Sash & Door Co., 151 NLRB 470, 475, 58 LRRM 1433 (1965). *See* note
90 *supra.*
140 *Ibid. Cf.* Strong, dba Strong Roofing & Insulating Co., 393 US 357, 70 LRRM
2100 (1969).
141 NLRB v. New England Die Casting Co., 242 F2d 759, 39 LRRM 2616 (CA 2,
1957), *enforcing* 116 NLRB 1, 38 LRRM 1175 (1956).

granted the union by insisting upon *future* adherence to the prior agreement or bargaining for a different contract. However, the Fourth Circuit, in *Huttig Sash*,[142] while supporting the Board's authority to compel adherence to the agreement retroactive to the date orally agreed to, and endorsing the order to make whole with 6-percent interest, refused to enforce that portion of the Board's order which permitted the union, instead, to seek bargaining for a different agreement. The Court reasoned that the latter alternative was inconsistent with the violation found by the Board, namely, the employer's refusal to reduce an agreement reached to writing. The Supreme Court affirmed the Board's authority to require retroactive payment of contractual benefits in *Strong Roofing*.[143] The Court upheld an order requiring the employer to execute a contract negotiated on its behalf by a multi-employer bargaining association and to pay the fringe benefits provided for in the contract.

In a 1968 case the Board ventured down a new remedial avenue for Section 8(a)(5) orders. Finding that the employer deliberately frustrated bargaining and made negotiations a "fruitless waste of time," the trial examiner in *M.F.A. Milling Co.*[144] recommended that the Board order the employer to reimburse the employee members of the union negotiating committee not only for wages they had lost because of attendance at past negotiating meetings but also for wages they would lose attending future meetings. The Board, however, adopted the trial examiner's recommendation only insofar as it recommended reimbursement for attendance at past bargaining sessions.

In 1970 the Board decided the long-awaited *Ex-Cell-O* case,[145] which it had held for three years following oral argument. The decision refused to hold that employees should be compensated for wage increases and fringe benefits which arguably they would have obtained through collective bargaining had their

---

[142] NLRB v. Huttig Sash & Door Co., 362 F2d 217, 220, 58 LRRM 1433 (CA 4, 1966). On a motion for rehearing, however, after denying the motion for mootness since the expiration date of the agreed upon contract had passed, the court stated that it would "not deem the decision in this case as precluding" the issuance of the type of order fashioned by the Board and it would "be prepared to consider it on its merits" in future cases. *See* NLRB v. Beverage-Air Co., 402 F2d 411, 69 LRRM 2369 (CA 4, 1968).

[143] NLRB v. Strong Roofing & Insulation Co., 393 US 357, 70 LRRM 2100 (1969). *See* Chapter 18 *supra* at notes 52-53. For a discussion of multi-employer bargaining, *see* Chapter 9 *supra*.

[144] 170 NLRB No. 111, 68 LRRM 1077 (1968).

[145] Ex-Cell-O Corp., 185 NLRB No. 20, 74 LRRM 1740 (1970).

employer not refused to bargain in violation of Section 8(a)(5). Relying on the Supreme Court's decision in *H. K. Porter,* the majority concluded that the Board lacked statutory authority for such a remedy. Two Board members dissented, contending that the order would have accomplished the Act's purpose of encouraging collective bargaining and would also have prevented the employer from profiting from his unlawful refusal to bargain.[146]

(c) Make whole orders. Although not entirely a new remedy, the Board has specifically directed that an employee be reimbursed for wages lost because of discrimination at the rate of a higher-paid job to which the Board found he would have been promoted absent discrimination.[147] Where such an order involves a period of disability for an industrial accident, the Board disallows back pay for all periods of disability regardless of the cause.[148] If workmen's compensation payments were awarded to an employee, the gross pay will be computed on the basis of the Board's decision in *American Manufacturing.*[149] In that case the Board reversed its policy of not deducting workmen's compensation payments from gross back pay to the following extent: to avoid double payment to the employee, that portion of the award which is payment for wages lost and not for physical injury is to be deducted from gross back pay.

(d) Darlington Manufacturing. In *Darlington Manufacturing,*[150] to remedy a shutdown and dismantling of a plant because the union had won an election, the Board in 1962 ordered the employer, a group of commonly owned and controlled companies,

---

146 *See* IUE v. NLRB (Tiidee Products, Inc.), 426 F2d 1243, 73 LRRM 2870 (CA DC, 1970), *rehearing denied,* 431 F2d 1206, 75 LRRM 2350 (1970), *cert. den.,* 75 LRRM 2752 (US SupCt., 1970) in which the Court of Appeals for the District of Columbia Circuit held that the Board has ample authority to issue make-whole orders in such §8 (a) (5) cases, and remanded the case to the Board for consideration of a meaningful remedy for employees unlawfully denied the fruits of collective bargaining during the period of litigation. *See also:* McCulloch, *New Remedies Under Taft-Hartley Act,* 68 LRR 60, 69 (1968); Brown, *Exploring the World of Remedies,* LABOR LAW DEVELOPMENTS 1968 (Sw. Legal Foundation 14th Ann. Institute on Labor Law) 69 (1968); Fanning, *New and Novel Remedies for Unfair Labor Practices,* 3 GA. L. REV. 256 (1968-69); St. Antoine, *A Touchstone for Labor Board Remedies,* 14 WAYNE L. REV. 1039 (1968); McGuiness, *Is the Award of Damages for Refusals to Bargain Consistent with National Labor Policy?,* 14 WAYNE L. REV. 1086 (1968).

147 Mooney Aircraft, Inc., 156 NLRB 326, 61 LRRM 1071 (1965), *enforced,* 375 F2d 402, 64 LRRM 2837 (CA 5, 1967), *cert. denied,* 389 US 859, 66 LRRM 2308 (1967).

148 American Mfg. Co., 167 NLRB 520, 66 LRRM 1122 (1967).

149 *Ibid.*

150 Darlington Mfg. Co., 139 NLRB 241, 254-259, 51 LRRM 1278 (1962).

to offer the terminated employees jobs at its other plants to the extent that such jobs were available without displacing encumbent employees. Terminated employees for whom there were no jobs immediately available were to be placed on a preferential hiring list for employment at the other plants as jobs arose. Travel and moving expenses were to be paid to those who accepted work at the other plants. The terminated employees were to be made whole by payment of back pay until they either obtained equivalent work or were placed on the preferential list. The refusal to bargain was remedied by directing the employer to bargain with the union about the operations of the preferential hiring list and the terms and conditions for employment of the terminated employees at the employer's other mills.

After a trip by the case through the Supreme Court,[151] the Fourth Circuit, sitting *en banc,* sustained the Board's finding that the purpose of the closing of the Darlington plant had been to "chill unionism" at the employer's other plants and enforced the Board's 1962 order.[152]

(2) Orders against unions. (a) Hiring-hall remedies. In a situation involving repeated discrimination by a union in the operation of its hiring hall, the Board directed the union to operate its hiring hall in a nondiscriminatory manner under the supervision of the regional director, to keep permanent records on its operation, and to submit periodic reports on the referrals and employment of the discriminatees.[153] The Second Circuit Court of Appeals disapproved that portion of the remedy which subjected operation of the hiring hall to the regional director's supervision, but enforced the record-keeping and reporting provisions.[154] Since then the Board has utilized the record-keeping provisions in other discriminatory hiring-hall and referral cases.[155]

---

[151] *See* Darlington Mfg. Co. v. NLRB, 325 F2d 682, 54 LRRM 2499 (CA 4, 1963), *denying enforcement,* 139 NLRB 241, 51 LRRM 1278 (1962), 380 US 263, 58 LRRM 2657 (1965), *reversing and remanding,* 165 NLRB 1074, 65 LRRM 1391 (1967). *See* Chapter 6 at notes 39-42.

[152] Darlington Mfg. Co. v. NLRB, 397 F2d 760, 68 LRRM 2356 (CA 4, 1968). *Contra,* A. C. Rochat Co., 163 NLRB 421, 64 LRRM 1321 (1967); Motor Repair, Inc., 168 NLRB No. 148, 67 LRRM 1051 (1968).

[153] J. J. Haggerty, Inc. (Nassau and Suffolk Contractors Ass'n), 139 NLRB 633, 638-639, 51 LRRM 1349 (1962).

[154] Local 138, International Union of Operating Engineers v. NLRB, 321 F2d 130, 53 LRRM 2754 (CA 2, 1963).

[155] *See, e.g.,* Skouras Theaters Corp., 155 NLRB 157, 158 note 2, 60 LRRM 1275, *enforced,* 361 F2d 826, 62 LRRM 2452 (CA 3, 1966); Local 269, IBEW (Arthur J. Hazeltine), 149 NLRB 768, 776, 789, 57 LRRM 1372 (1964); International Ass'n of Bridge, etc., Workers, Local 350 (Atlantic County Building Trades Employers

(b) Make-whole orders. In recent years the Board has extended its make-whole orders to require union repayment of fines imposed upon members for filing unfair labor practice charges or for failing to exhaust internal remedies prior to filing such charges,[156] as well as repayment of fines exacted to induce employees to engage in an unlawful secondary boycott.[157] These monetary remedial orders, like back-pay orders, all provide for payment of interest.

(c) Orders to arbitrate. In two notable cases the Board, finding that refusals by unions to carry employee grievances through the contract grievance procedures to arbitration were based on union activities or the absence of them and therefore violative of Section 8 (b) (1) (A), adopted novel remedies to rectify the violations.

In the first case[158] the Board found that the union had refused to take the employee's discharge grievance to arbitration because the employee was not a member of the union and thereby had violated Section 8 (b) (1) (A). The Board refused, however, to find that the employer had violated Section 8 (a) (1). It therefore issued an order only against the union in which, *inter alia,* it directed the union "promptly to arbitrate" the employee's grievance. It did, however, retain jurisdiction in the case in the event this remedy should prove ineffective and other relief be required.

In the second case[159] the Board found that the union had violated Section 8 (b) (1) (A) by failing to process the employee's discharge grievance in retaliation for the employee's protected concerted activities at a union meeting in opposition to the union's business agent. There being no charge against the employer in this case, and finding doubt as to whether under the contract the employer could be compelled to consider and arbitrate the grievance at so late a date, the trial examiner recommended that the union be ordered (1) to request the employer to reinstate the employee and (2) to make the employee whole

---

Ass'n), 164 NLRB 644, 65 LRRM 1234 (1967). *See* discussion of hiring halls generally in Chapter 26 *supra.*

156 Charles S. Skura, 148 NLRB 679, 684-685, 57 LRRM 1009 (1964); Wellman-Lord Engineering, Inc., 148 NLRB 674, 677, 57 LRRM 1012 (1964), *enforced,* 350 F2d 427, 59 LRRM 2801 (CA DC, 1965). *See* notes 62-67 and accompanying text for discussion of orders requiring reimbursement of union dues and fees.

157 Robert L. Willis, 166 NLRB 117, 65 LRRM 1433 (1967).

158 Port Drum Co., 170 NLRB No. 51, 67 LRRM 1506 (1968), 180 NLRB No. 90, 73 LRRM 1068 (1970). *See* Chapter 27 *supra* at notes 105-106 for subsequent remedial orders in this case.

159 Automotive Plating Corp., 170 NLRB No. 121, 67 LRRM 1609 (1968), *supplemental order,* 183 NLRB No. 131, 74 LRRM 1396 (1970). *See* Chapter 27 *supra* at notes 105-106 for further discussion of the case and remedy.

for all losses he might suffer from the discharge, including future wage losses and the value of seniority and other benefits which he might lose through the employer's unwillingness voluntarily to reinstate him. The Board, however, refused to endorse this remedy, noting that, whatever losses sustained by the employee were in the first instance caused by the action of the employer, the union's sole fault was in not grieving to arbitration. Accordingly, the Board changed the relief to require the union to request the employer to reconsider the employee's discharge as a grievance under the contract in existence at the time of discharge and, if necessary, to take the matter to arbitration. However, the Board retained jurisdiction "to reconsider appropriate, affirmative remedial provisions" should the employer refuse to process the case through the contract grievance and arbitration procedures. The employer did refuse; the union was therefore ordered to pay back pay from the date the union refused to process the grievance until such time as it "fulfills its duty of fair representation, or discharged employee obtains substantially equivalent employment, whichever is sooner."

(3) Methods of conveying remedial orders to employees. In addition to requiring that remedial notices be posted in places where notices to employees or union members are usually displayed, the Board will, in certain cases, direct other means of conveying notices to employees. Employers have been directed to mail notices to each employee,[160] to distribute notices to employees,[161] to read notices to employees,[162] and to publish notices in newspapers of general circulation in areas where the employer's plants were located.[163] Unions too have been directed to publish remedial notices in newspapers and to post at their offices. [164]

The Board has sought to tighten its remedial orders in this area by a combination and expansion of these remedies in aggravated situations. Thus, in the 1966 *J. P. Stevens* case the Board directed the employer to post notices not only at the plant where the unfair labor practice had occurred but at all of its plants; to mail a copy of the notice to each of its employees not only at the plant where

---

[160] Bickford Shoes, Inc., 109 NLRB 1346, 1352, 34 LRRM 1570 (1954).
[161] Sunbeam Electric Mfg. Co., 41 NLRB 469, 490, 10 LRRM 119 (1942); *enforced,* 133 F2d 856, 11 LRRM 820 (CA 7, 1943).
[162] Jackson Tile Mfg. Co., 122 NLRB 764, 767, 43 LRRM 1195 (1958).
[163] Darlington Mfg. Co., 139 NLRB 241, 253, 51 LRRM 1278 (1962).
[164] Carpenters Local 1400 (Clarence A. Dowdall), 115 NLRB 126, 132, 37 LRRM 1255 (1956).

the unfair labor practice had occurred but to each of its employees at all of its plants; to require company officials to read the notice to assembled employees at working-time meetings at all of its plants; and to grant the union, upon request, access to plant bulletin boards for one year.[165] In the first 1967 case, the Board, in addition to the foregoing, ordered J. P. Stevens to furnish the union with the names and addresses of its employees at all plants upon the union's request made within one year.[166]

In *Marlene Industries* the Board added to the *Stevens* remedies the requirement that the employer grant union organizers access to employees on plant approaches and parking lots during non-working time.[167]

Shortly prior to the series of *Stevens* cases, the Board in *Elson Bottling*[168] had added to the posting requirement the requirement that the employer mail copies of the notices to individual employees; make available, upon the union's request, use of bulletin boards for a period of three months; and, upon request, grant the union opportunity to address the employees for an hour on company premises during working time.

As these expanded remedial orders have reached the courts of appeals, the courts have examined them to see if the additional remedies are justified on the records in the individual cases. Thus, on review of the 1966 *Stevens* case the Second Circuit refused to enforce the provision requiring granting of bulletin-board facilities to the union on the ground that the record failed to show justification for the relief. Also, the court modified the notice-reading provision to require reading only at plants where the unfair labor practices had occurred and to afford the employer

---

165 J. P. Stevens & Co., 157 NLRB 869, 878, 881, 61 LRRM 1437 (1966) (the Board later modified its order to permit the reading of the order by an NLRB rather than a company official); *see also:* Scott's, Inc., 159 NLRB 1795, 1808, 62 LRRM 1543 (1966); Love Box Co. v. NLRB, 422 F2d 232, 73 LRRM 2746 (CA 10, 1970).

166 J. P. Stevens & Co., 163 NLRB 217, 64 LRRM 1289 (1967). This requirement was not repeated in the subsequent 1967 cases. *See* J. P. Stevens & Co., 167 NLRB 266, 66 LRRM 1024 (1967), 167 NLRB 258, 66 LRRM 1030 (1967), *enforced as modified*, 406 F2d 1017, 70 LRRM 2104 (CA 4, 1968). *See also* J. P. Stevens & Co., Inc., 171 NLRB No. 163, 69 LRRM 1088 (1968), *enforced*, 417 F2d 533, 72 LRRM 2433 (CA 5, 1969). *But see* NLRB v. Laney & Duke Co., 369 F2d 859, 63 LRRM 2552 (CA 5, 1966), where the court refused to enforce an order requiring the reading of a notice "as unnecessarily embarrassing and humiliating."

167 Marlene Industries Corp., 166 NLRB 703, 65 LRRM 1626 (1967); *see also* S & H Grossinger's Inc., 156 NLRB 233, 61 LRRM 1025 (1965); H. W. Elson Bottling Co., 155 NLRB 714, 715-718, 60 LRRM 1381 (1965), *enforced as modified*, 379 F2d 223, 65 LRRM 2673 (CA 6, 1967).

168 H. W. Elson Bottling Co., note 167 *supra.*

the option of having the notice read by a Board representative.[169] When the first 1967 *Stevens* case reached the Second Circuit, the court adhered to its former action in modifying the notice-reading provision but this time found justification for the bulletin-board-space provision. However, the court failed to find justification for the added requirement in this case that the employer furnish the union with the names and addresses of its employees and denied enforcement of this provision.[170] The District of Columbia Circuit, on the other hand, refused to enforce the notice-reading provision in any respect.[171]

The provision requiring the employer to grant union organizers access to employees on company property has been enforced in appropriate situations;[172] however, the provision requiring the employer to allow the union to address employees on company time has encountered resistance. In *Grossinger's Inc.*[173] the Second Circuit denied enforcement of the provision requiring the employer to afford the union equal time to address employees during working hours, citing the fact that it was enforcing the provision granting union organizers access to employees on company premises. The Sixth Circuit, however, modified and enforced as modified a provision granting the union opportunity to address employees on company time, notwithstanding that it also enforced the bulletin-board provision. In that case, *Elson Bottling*,[174] the Board had directed the employer to make its premises available to the union for one-hour meetings at its two plants on company time. The court modified the order to require only that the employer afford the union equal opportunity to address the employees on company time should the employer make captive-audience speeches to employees during future election campaigns.

---

169 J. P. Stevens & Co. v. NLRB, 380 F2d 292, 65 LRRM 2829 (CA 2, 1967), *cert. denied,* 66 LRRM 2728 (1967). *See also* NLRB v. Laney & Duke Co., note 166 *supra. Compare* NLRB v. Bush Hog, Inc., 405 F2d 755, 70 LRRM 2070 (CA 5, 1968), upholding an order requiring the employer to read a notice stating that he had violated the Act; the court noted that many of the employees were illiterate.
170 J. P. Stevens & Co. v. NLRB, 388 F2d 896, 67 LRRM 2055 (CA 2, 1967). The Board has adhered to its view that flagrant unfair labor practices require strong remedies. The remedies ordered in *Loray Corp.,* 184 NLRB No. 57, 74 LRRM 1513 (1970) are the most stringent yet employed.
171 International Union of Electrical, etc. Workers v. NLRB (Scott's, Inc.), 383 F2d 230, 66 LRRM 2081 (CA DC, 1967), *cert. denied,* 390 US 905, 67 LRRM 2308 (1968).
172 *See, e.g.,* NLRB v. S & H Grossinger's Inc., 372 F2d 26, 64 LRRM 2295 (CA 2, 1967); NLRB v. H. W. Elson Bottling Co., 379 F2d 223, 65 LRRM 2673 (CA 6, 1967).
173 NLRB v. S & H Grossinger's Inc., note 172 *supra.*
174 NLRB v. H. W. Elson Bottling Co., note 172 *supra.*

CHAPTER 32

JUDICIAL REVIEW AND ENFORCEMENT

I. INTRODUCTION

An order issued by the NLRB is not self-executing. Although phrased in the form of a "cease and desist" order,[1] it merely prescribes what action is necessary to redress and remedy conduct found to be unlawful. If the party or parties against whom a Board order has been issued refuse to obey, no authority exists in the Board itself to enforce the order. To secure enforcement, the Board applies to the appropriate United States court of appeals for the order's affirmance pursuant to Section 10(e) and, until the order is affirmed by the appeals court, no penalty is incurred for disobeying it. Section 10(f) confers upon any person aggrieved by a final order of the Board the right to petition the appropriate court of appeals for a review of such order.

Only final orders of the NLRB are subject to review by the courts under Sections 10(e) and (f).[2] Final orders are entered only in unfair labor practice cases under Section 10(c) after the issuance of a complaint, hearing before a trial examiner,[3] and a decision by the Board.[4] Decisions and directions of elections in representation cases under Section 9(c) are not final orders under Sections 10(e) and 10(f), and review of issues in representation proceedings may only be obtained incidental to review of an order entered in an unfair labor practice proceeding.[5]

---

[1] §10(c).
[2] AFL v. NLRB, 308 US 401, 5 LRRM 670 (1940); NLRB v. Falk Corp., 308 US 453, 5 LRRM 677 (1940); NLRB v. IBEW, 308 US 413, 5 LRRM 676 (1940).
[3] NLRB Rules and Regs. §102.34, Series 8, as amended, revised January 1, 1965 (GPO, Washington, 1965). In rare cases the hearing before a trial examiner may be omitted, either by waiver of the parties or by summary judgment procedures.
[4] See Chapter 30 supra.
[5] AFL v. NLRB, 308 US 401, 5 LRRM 670 (1940). Section 9(d) requires that, whenever a petition is filed with a U. S. court of appeals for either enforcement or review of a Board order in a complaint proceeding, the record in the representation proceeding must be included in the entire record on which the court must base its decree.

As a general rule, U. S. district courts are without jurisdiction
to entertain suits to review Board action in representation or unfair labor practice cases. The Supreme Court has, however, recognized and permitted district courts, pursuant to their jurisdiction
under Section 1337 of the Judicial Code,[6] to review representation
cases in limited situations involving "extraordinary circumstances."[7]

Section 10(e) provides for review by the U. S. Supreme Court
of the judgments and decrees of the circuit courts entered under
the NLRA upon writ of certiorari or certification.[8]

II. APPELLATE REVIEW AND ENFORCEMENT

A. Board's Rulings Subject to Review

The only final orders within the meaning of Sections 10(e) or
(f) are those entered by the Board in unfair labor practice cases,
either dismissing a complaint in whole or in part or finding an
unfair labor practice and directing a remedy.[9] Thus, a decision
of the General Counsel not to issue an unfair labor practice complaint,[10] a denial by the Board of a request for a *subpoena duces
tecum* during a preliminary informal investigation of unfair labor
practice charges,[11] and a determination by the General Counsel
to issue an unfair labor practice complaint are not final orders
subject to review under Section 10(f) of the Act, nor are they
subject to immediate judicial review under Section 10(c) of the
Administrative Procedure Act.[12] They are subject to review only
upon review of a final order of the Board. However, once a complaint has been issued, its dismissal under the terms of an informal
settlement between the regional director and one of the parties

---

6 28 USC §1337 (1965).

7 Leedom v. Kyne, 358 US 184, 43 LRRM 2222 (1958); McCulloch v. Sociedad Nacional de Marineros de Honduras, 372 US 10, 52 LRRM 2425 (1963); Boire v. Greyhound Corp., 376 US 473, 55 LRRM 2694 (1964). *See* Section III *infra.*

8 Pursuant to 28 USC §1254 (1965).

9 Local 542, Int'l Union of Operating Engineers v. NLRB, 328 F2d 850, 55 LRRM
2669 (CA 3, 1964).

10 Lincourt v. NLRB, 170 F2d 306, 23 LRRM 2015 (CA 1, 1948); Manhattan Constr.
Co. v. NLRB, 198 F2d 302, 30 LRRM 2464 (CA 10, 1952); Foreman v. NLRB, 50
LRRM 2855 (CA 6, 1962); Contractor's Ass'n v. NLRB, 295 F2d 526, 49 LRRM
2035 (CA 3, 1961); Anthony v. NLRB, 204 F2d 832, 32 LRRM 2247 (CA 6, 1953);
Local 886, Teamsters Union v. NLRB, 179 F2d 492, 25 LRRM 2237 (CA 10, 1950).

11 Laundry Workers Int'l Local Union 221 v. NLRB, 197 F2d 701, 30 LRRM 2270
(CA 5, 1952).

12 Vapor Blast Mfg. Co. v. Madden, 280 F2d 205, 46 LRRM 2559 (CA 7, 1960).

is reviewable.[13] The absence of a formal Board order will not preclude review in such a case, since the action of the regional director, as the agent of the Board, is "no less 'final' than direct action by his principal."[14]

1. Parties Entitled to Enforcement and Review. In *Amalgamated Utility Workers v. Consolidated Edison Co. of New York*[15] the Supreme Court, after finding that the Board alone is exclusively vested under Section 10(e) with the power and duty to enforce the Act, held that a labor union could not petition the circuit court of appeals for an order adjudging an employer in contempt for failing to abide by an order previously issued by the court directing the employer to cease and desist from certain unfair labor practices. The Supreme Court stated:

> [I]t is apparent that Congress has entrusted to the Board exclusively the prosecution of the proceeding by its own complaint, the conduct of the hearing, the adjudication and the granting of appropriate relief. The Board as a public agency acting in the public interest, not any private person or agency, not any employee or group of employees, is chosen as the instrument to assure protection from the described unfair conduct in order to remove obstacles to interstate commerce.[16]

The principle of *Amalgamated Utility Workers* has been consistently applied to proceedings relating to enforcement of the Board's cease and desist orders in unfair labor practice cases.[17]

Although only the Board may take action to enforce its orders, Section 10(f) provides that "any person aggrieved by a final order of the Board, granting or denying, in whole or in part, the relief sought," may petition the appropriate circuit court for an order setting aside the Board order. When the Board enters a final order against the charged party, it is clear that he is a "person aggrieved" and thus entitled to seek immediate review in the appropriate court of appeals. Alternatively, if the Board deter-

---

13 Leeds & Northrup Co. v. NLRB, 357 F2d 527, 61 LRRM 2283 (CA 3, 1966). *See* note, *NLRB Settlement Agreements—Right of a Charging Party to an Evidentiary Hearing*, 20 Sw. L. J. 901 (1966).
14 *Id.* at 534.
15 309 US 261, 6 LRRM 669 (1940).
16 *Id.* at 265.
17 Electrical Workers (IBEW) v. NLRB, 343 F2d 327, 58 LRRM 2369 (CA 2, 1965); Deaton Truck Line, Inc. v. NLRB, 337 F2d 697, 57 LRRM 2209 (CA 5, 1964); Amalgamated Meat Cutters v. NLRB, 267 F2d 169, 44 LRRM 2126 (CA 1, 1959), *cert. denied*, 361 US 863, 44 LRRM 3000 (1959); Stewart Die Casting Corp. v. NLRB, 132 F2d 801, 11 LRRM 739 (CA 7, 1942); NLRB v. Sunshine Mining Co., 125 F2d 757, 9 LRRM 618 (CA 9, 1942).

mines that the complaint should be dismissed, the charging party has a statutory right to seek review as a "person aggrieved." Moreover, a "hybrid situation" occurs if the Board dismisses certain portions of the complaint and issues an order on the others. As to the portion that results in a remedial order against him, the *charged* party is aggrieved; while the *charging* party is aggrieved "with respect to the portion of the decision dismissing the complaint."[18]

Neither disagreement with certain findings and conclusions upon which a Board order is based[19] nor desire on the part of a successful party for enforcement of a Board order is sufficient to make one a person aggrieved.[20] Ordinarily, to be a person aggrieved, one must have been a party to the proceedings before the Board. However, standing to appeal an administrative order as a person aggrieved "arises if there is an adverse effect in fact"; it does not require "an injury cognizable at law or equity."[21]

Standing to seek review by the Supreme Court of a circuit court decision is limited to parties before the court of appeals.[22]

2. Intervention. The Act does not explicitly give a successful charging or charged party before the Board a right to intervene in the court of appeals proceeding brought either by the Board to enforce its order or by an aggrieved party to review an order. As a result, until 1965 courts of appeals considered applications for intervention under their own rules.[23] Although successful

---

18 UAW Local 283 v. Scofield, 382 US 205, 210, 60 LRRM 2479 (1965) ; *see also* Jacobson v. NLRB, 120 F2d 96, 8 LRRM 599 (CA 3, 1941) ; Kovach v. NLRB, 229 F2d 138, 37 LRRM 2345 (CA 7, 1956).
19 Deaton Truck Lines, Inc. v. NLRB, 337 F2d 697, 57 LRRM 2209 (CA 5, 1964).
20 Amalgamated Meat Cutters v. NLRB, 267 F2d 169, 44 LRRM 2126 (CA 1, 1959), *cert. denied* 361 US 863, 44 LRRM 3000 (1959).
21 Local 1059, Retail Clerks Ass'n v. NLRB, 348 F2d 369, 370, 59 LRRM 2618 (CA DC, 1964). *Cf.* Data Processing Service Organizations v. Camp, 397 US 150 (1970).
22 UMW v. Eagle Picher Mining & Smelting Co., 325 US 335, 16 LRRM 689 (1945).
23 The rules of the courts of appeals typically provided: "A person desiring to intervene in a case where the applicable statute does not provide for intervention shall file with the Court and serve upon all parties a motion for leave to intervene" (Second Circuit Rule 13 (f), Seventh Circuit Rule 14 (f). The circuits that provided for intervention had substantially identical rules. Since July 1, 1968, all appellate procedures in the federal circuit courts have been uniform. *See* Rule 15 (d), Federal Rules of Appellate Procedure, concerning intervention in appeals from decisions of administrative bodies.

charging parties[24] were permitted to intervene in some cases, they were denied the right to intervene in many others.[25]

Successful charged parties, on the other hand, faired better as intervenors. The "vast majority" of the circuit courts, in recognizing the right of a successful charged party to intervene, were influenced by the fact that the charged party may incur a liability on account of an order being entered against him. By permitting intervention, moreover, unnecessary duplication of proceedings could be avoided.[26]

In *UAW Local 283 v. Scofield* and *UAW Local 133 v. Fafnir Bearing Co.*[27] the Supreme Court resolved the longstanding question as to the right of intervention of successful charged and charging parties. In *Scofield* the union had been the respondent before the Board. The Board dismissed the complaint.[28] The charging party sought review in the Seventh Circuit, but that court refused to permit the union to intervene, limiting it to an *amicus* role.[29] *Fafnir* was the converse. There, the union was the successful charging party. The employer who was found guilty of violating the Act petitioned for review of the Board order in the Second Circuit. The union sought to intervene and was again limited to an *amicus* role.[30] The Supreme Court, consolidating the two cases, unanimously reversed both circuits and interpreted the Act as conferring intervention rights upon both the successful charged and the successful charging parties.

A by-product of these decisions could be the removal of a con-

---

24 UMW v. Eagle Picher Mining & Smelting Co., 325 US 335, 16 LRRM 689 1945) ; West Texas Utilities Co. v. NLRB, 184 F2d 233, 26 LRRM 2359 (CA DC, 1950), *cert. denied,* 341 US 939, 28 LRRM 2087 (1951) ; Kearney & Trecker Corp. v. NLRB, 210 F2d 852, 33 LRRM 2621 (CA 7, 1954), *cert. denied,* 348 US 824, 34 LRRM 2898 (1954). *Cf.* Sears, Roebuck & Co. v. Carpet Layers, Local 419, 410 F2d 1148, 71 LRRM 2251 (CA 10, 1969), *vacated & remanded for mootness,* 397 US 655, 74 LRRM 2001 (1970) (absence of standing by charging party to appeal from denial of injunction in §10 (l) proceeding).
25 Amalgamated Meat Cutters v. NLRB, 267 F2d 169, 44 LRRM 2126 (CA 1, 1959), *cert. denied, sub nom,* 361 US 863, 44 LRRM 3000 (1959) ; NLRB v. Retail Clerks Ass'n, 243 F2d 777, 38 LRRM 2555 (CA 9, 1956) ; Haleston Drug Stores v. NLRB, 190 F2d 1022, 28 LRRM 2674 (CA 9, 1951) ; Stewart Die Casting Corp. v. NLRB, 132 F2d 801, 11 LRRM 739 (CA 7, 1942) ; Aluminum Ore Co. v. NLRB, 131 F2d 485, 11 LRRM 693 (CA 7, 1942).
26 UAW Local 283 v. Scofield, 382 US 205, 60 LRRM 2479 (1965). *And see* cases cited in note 7 *supra.*
27 The two cases were consolidated by the Supreme Court. 382 US 205, 60 LRRM 2479 (1965).
28 UAW Local 283, 145 NLRB 1097, 55 LRRM 1985 (1964).
29 UAW Local 283 v. NLRB, 57 LRRM 2496 (CA 7, 1964).
30 UAW Local 133, 146 NLRB 1582, 56 LRRM 1108 (1964), *intervention denied,* 339 F2d 801, 58 LRRM 2077 (CA 2, 1964).

siderable part of the Board's (and the Solicitor General's) power to limit the instances in which Supreme Court review is sought of decisions adverse to it in the courts of appeals.

The impact of these cases was highlighted in *Teamsters Local 372 v. Detroit Newspaper Publishers Association*.[31] The Board had requested the Sixth Circuit to remand a lockout case to it for reconsideration in the light of *American Ship*.[32] The circuit court refused and simply denied enforcement of the Board's order.[33] The charging union then filed a petition for certiorari in the Supreme Court. The Court summarily vacated the judgment below and directed the Sixth Circuit to take the action the Board had requested of it.

3. Place for Filing Petition for Enforcement and Review. Petitions for enforcement under 10(e) and petitions for review under 10(f) may be filed in the circuit court within whose jurisdiction the unfair labor practice occurred or the party resides or does business. The person aggrieved may also file the petition for review in the District of Columbia Circuit. Prior to 1958, if a petition for review by an aggrieved person and a petition for enforcement by the Board were filed in different circuits, the Board was required to choose the circuit court in which to file the record of the Board proceeding. Since 1959, however, conflicts in jurisdiction are resolved in accordance with the terms of 28 U.S.C. Section 2112(a) (1959).[34] This section requires the Board to file the record in the circuit in which a "proceeding with respect to such order was first instituted." The courts have found that "Section 2112(a) in its present form represents a change in the law in two significant respects: first, a judgment as to what forum will be most convenient to the parties is to be made by a court and not by the agency whose order is under review; and, second, the court which is to make that decision is determined by a fixed rule

---

31 382 US 374, 61 LRRM 2147 (1966).

32 American Ship Bldg. Co. v. NLRB, 380 US 300, 58 LRRM 2672 (1965).

33 Detroit Newspaper Publishers Ass'n v. NLRB, 346 F2d 527, 59 LRRM 2401 (CA 6, 1965), *denying enforcement of* 145 NLRB 996, 55 LRRM 1091 (1964).

34 The statute provides in part as follows: "If proceedings have been instituted in two or more courts of appeals with respect to the same order the agency, board, commission or officer concerned shall file the record in that one of such courts in which a proceeding with respect to such order was *first instituted*. The other courts in which such proceedings are pending shall thereupon transfer them to the court of appeals in which the record has been filed. For the convenience of the parties in the interest of justice, such court may thereafter transfer all the proceedings with respect to such order to any other court of appeals" (emphasis supplied).

of thumb—it shall be that court in which the petition for review was first filed."[35] This statutory formula of determining the proper forum by "timeclock precision" has created the so-called "race to the court house."[36]

The statute [37] authorizes the circuit that has exclusive jurisdiction to transfer the petitions to another court if the convenience of the parties and the interest of justice require such a transfer. Relying in part on such discretion, two circuit courts granted Board motions to transfer the cases to the circuit in which the unfair labor practices occurred, since the Board could not determine which party had won the race to the court house.[38] In another case[39] the circuit court granted the employer's motion to transfer the union's petition for review to the circuit in which the employer had filed its petition, but then on reconsideration changed its mind and denied the motion to transfer.

4. Procedure. Subdivisions (g), (h), and (i) of Section 10 of the Act set forth the procedure for enforcement and review contained in subdivisions (e) and (f) of this section. Subdivision (g) provides that the commencement of proceedings, whether for enforcement or review, does not operate as a stay of the Board's order unless otherwise specifically directed by the court. Subdivision (h) declares the Norris-LaGuardia Act[40] inapplicable to enforcement or review proceedings. Subdivision (i) provides that "petitions filed under this Section shall be heard expeditiously and, if possible, within 10 days after they have been docketed."

After the NLRB files a petition for enforcement of its order, it must certify and file with the court the record of the Board proceedings. Notice of the Board's action must also be served upon the party or parties against whom the order is entered.[41] In petitions for review, the party aggrieved by the Board's order makes written application to the court of appeals, asking that the order be modified or set aside. A copy of such a petition will be

---

35 Ball v. NLRB, 299 F2d 683, 687, 49 LRRM 2658 (CA 4, 1962).
36 Insurance Workers Int'l Union v. NLRB, 360 F2d 823, 824, 61 LRRM 2415 (CA DC, 1966).
37 28 USC §2112(a) (1965).
38 IUE v. NLRB (General Electric Co.), 343 F2d 327, 58 LRRM 2369 (CA DC, 1965); General Electric Co. v. NLRB, 58 LRRM 2694 (CA 7, 1965); see also Local 2674 Carpenters Union v. NLRB, 47 LRRM 2688 (CA DC, 1960).
39 UAW v. NLRB, 373 F2d 671, 64 LRRM 2225 (CA DC, 1967).
40 47 Stat 70 (1932), 29 USC §101-115 (1965).
41 §10(e).

transmitted to the Board by a clerk of the court. In petitions for review, the Board is also required to certify and file a transcript of the record.[42]

Prior to 1958 a transcript of the entire record, including pleadings, testimony, findings, and order, was required to be filed with the court. However, since this requirement frequently operated to delay court proceedings and involved unnecessary expenditures of money and effort, the Act was amended in 1958 to permit the several courts of appeals to adopt rules permitting the filing of an abbreviated record, except in those instances where the entire record is required for an adequate determination or where the abbreviation of the record would prove more costly than the transmission of the entire record.[43]

The court of appeals acquires jurisdiction of the proceeding immediately upon the filing of a petition; but prior to the filing of the record, the Board, under Section 10(d) of the Act, may modify or set aside its finding or order. However, once the Board files the record or the aggrieved party files a record certified by the Board, the Board's jurisdiction over the case ceases and it may no longer vacate or modify findings of fact or orders based thereon. Courts of appeal will, however, entertain a motion by the Board prior to argument to remand the case for further consideration of its order.[44]

B. Scope of Review

1. Questions of Fact. In the vast majority of appeals from Board orders, attack is made not upon the Board's interpretation of the statute but, rather, upon the Board's findings of fact upon which its conclusions of law were based. Section 10(e) of the Act states that "[t]he findings of the Board with respect to questions of fact, if supported by substantial evidence on the record considered as a whole, shall be conclusive." Whether they are so supported is a question of law for the courts to decide.

The present Section 10(e) is the result of a 1947 amendment and is directly traceable to congressional concern over the manner in

---

[42] §10(f).
[43] See 28 USC §2112(a) (1965).
[44] Ford Motor Co. v. NLRB, 305 US 364, 3 LRRM 663 (1939); UMW v. Eagle Picher Mining and Smelting Co., 325 US 335, 16 LRRM 689 (1945).

which the courts were reviewing NLRB decisions and orders. The Wagner Act provided that "the findings of the Board as to the facts, if supported by evidence, shall be conclusive."[45] Although the Supreme Court interpreted that provision to mean supported by substantial evidence,[46] some courts felt they were required to affirm the Board even if there was only isolated support in the record for the Board's determinations.[47] Because of such an approach by the courts, Congress sought in the Taft-Hartley Act to make the standard for review of Board decisions more definite.[48] The avowed purpose of changing Section 10(e) was to require a closer review of Board decisions by the courts[49] and to "very materially broaden the scope of the court's reviewing power."[50]

In *Universal Camera* the Supreme Court noted: that Congress intended to end the practice of some courts of accepting as substantial evidence any isolated support for a Board determination, by specifying that "substantial evidence" was to be determined on

---

45 29 USC §120(e) (1946).

46 Washington, Virginia, and Maryland Coach Co. v. NLRB, 301 US 142, 1 LRRM 741 (1937); Consolidated Edison Co. v. NLRB, 305 US 197, 3 LRRM 645 (1938).

47 Universal Camera v. NLRB, 340 US 474, 27 LRRM 2373 (1951). By reason of the language of the old Act, the courts had, as one put it, in effect abdicated their power of review to the Board. NLRB v. Standard Oil Co., 138 F2d 885, 13 LRRM 588 (CA 2, 1943). In many instances, deference on the part of the courts to specialized knowledge that is supposedly inherent in an administrative agency has led the courts to acquiesce in decisions of the Board, even when the findings concerned mixed issues of fact and of law (Packard Motor Co. v. NLRB, 330 US 485, 19 LRRM 2397 (1947); NLRB v. Hearst Publications, Inc., 322 US 111, 14 LRRM 614 (1943)), or when they rested only on inferences that were not, in turn, supported by facts in the record. Republic Aviation Corp. v. NLRB, 324 US 793, 16 LRRM 620 (1945). *But see* American Ship Bldg. Co. v. NLRB, 380 US 300, 318, 58 LRRM 2672 (1965) where the Supreme Court warned: "The deference owed to an expert tribunal cannot be allowed to slip into a judicial inertia which results in the unauthorized assumption by an agency of major policy decisions properly made by Congress." *Cf.* NLRB v. Insurance Agents Int'l Union, 361 US 477, 45 LRRM 2705 (1960).

48 The Administrative Procedure Act of 1946, 5 USC §§1009(e) and 1010, like the Taft-Hartley Act, adopted as a test for review of agency action "substantial evidence on the whole record." *See* Universal Camera Corp. v. NLRB, 340 US 474, 27 LRRM 2373 (1951).

49 *See* Universal Camera v. NLRB, 340 US 474, 477-487, 27 LRRM 2373 (1951), where Justice Frankfurter detailed the "congressional mood."

50 H. R. Rep. 510, 80th Cong., 1st Sess. 54-57 (1947). Another section of the Wagner Act permitted the NLRB to rest its orders upon "all the testimony taken," but this was amended to require the Board's decisions to be supported by "the preponderance of the testimony taken" (§10(c)). The intent was that the decisions of the Board would indicate an actual weighing of the evidence to be made only in accordance with the preponderance of the evidence. Prior to 1947 the Act also provided that unfair labor practice proceedings before the Board were not to be governed by the rules of evidence applicable in district courts of the United States and the rules of civil procedure. Congress, in the 1947 amendments, made the rules of evidence applicable to such Board proceedings in order to assure that the Board receives only legal evidence (§10(b)).

the record viewed as a "whole";[51] that the congressional mood at the time of passage indicated to the Court that both the Taft-Hartley and the Administrative Procedure Act required "stricter" and "more uniform practice" from the courts; and that the circuit courts were to treat findings of the Board with respect, but were to assume more responsibility for the reasonableness of the findings.[52]

The Supreme Court laid down the following guidelines for determining whether the Board's findings of fact were supported by substantial evidence. A reviewing court can set aside a Board decision when it cannot conscientiously find that the evidence supporting that decision is substantial when viewed in the light of the record in its entirety, including the body of evidence opposed to the Board's view.[53] But the Court admonished that a reviewing court cannot set aside a Board decision based on a choice between two fairly conflicting views, even though it might justifiably have reached a different conclusion had the case been before it *de novo*.[54] Further, the right of the reviewing court to test Board findings of fact on the basis of the whole record does not empower the court to discount the weight to which Board findings are entitled by reason of the Board's experience in the specialized field of labor-management relations.[55] Finally, the reviewing courts are not bound by the NLRB's rejection of a trial examiner's findings but may consider the examiner's intermediate report. According to the Court, evidence supporting a conclusion may be less than substantial, and the reviewing court must examine the evidence with greater care "when an impartial experienced examiner who has observed the witness and lived with the case has drawn conclusions different from the Board's."[56]

The *Universal Camera* rule was interpreted in greatly differing ways by the circuit courts of appeal. Although all the circuits quoted from the same language in *Universal Camera* in determining the weight to be given to inferences and credibility findings of the Board, they did not reach the same conclusion.

---

[51] 340 US 474, 488, 27 LRRM 2373 (1951). *See* Jaffe, *Judicial Review: "Substantial Evidence on the Whole Record,"* 64 HARV. L. REV. 1233 (1951).
[52] *Id.* at 490.
[53] *Id.* at 488-490.
[54] *Id.* at 488.
[55] *Ibid.*
[56] *Id.* at 496.

For example, one circuit held that the inferences to be drawn from the facts and the credibility of witnesses were for the administrative agency to determine. The court, therefore, refused to upset the findings of an examiner, not because it thought that it would have reached the same conclusion had the witnesses been before it, but because it thought itself "bound to allow for the possible cogency of the evidence that words do not express."[57]

Prior to *Universal Camera,* the Fifth Circuit developed a doctrine that stronger evidence was required to support a Board order requiring reinstatement of discharged employees with back pay than was necessary to support a simple cease and desist order, and it continued to make this distinction after *Universal Camera.*[58] In *NLRB v. Walton Manufacturing Co.*[59] the Supreme Court repudiated the *Tex-O-Kan* doctrine, holding that under *Universal Camera* there was no place for one test of substantiality of evidence in reinstatement cases and another test in other cases.

But even with the Supreme Court's *Walton* decision there will undoubtedly continue to be differences in interpretation among the circuit courts of appeal as to the application of the substantial-evidence test, because that test, as developed in *Universal Camera,* is not a rigid formula or a closely defined standard; rather, it expresses a flexible and general approach to review of administrative determinations. It will necessarily be fitted to some extent to the predilections of the particular court.

2. Questions of Law. The courts may differ as to what is or is not a question of law, especially where a case presents mixed questions of law and fact. However, having once determined that the issue for decision is a question of law, such as an interpretation of a statutory term, the courts are much less restricted in their review than when reviewing findings of fact and inferences drawn from such facts.[60] As to questions of law, courts are free to substitute their judgment for that of the Board if it appears that the

---

57 NLRB v. James Thompson & Co., 208 F2d 743, 746, 33 LRRM 2205, 2206 (CA 2, 1953); NLRB v. Dinion Coil Co., 201 F2d 484, 31 LRRM 2223 (CA 2, 1952).
58 NLRB v. Tex-O-Kan Flour Mills Co., 122 F2d 433, 8 LRRM 675 (CA 5, 1947); NLRB v. Miami Coca-Cola Bottling Co., 222 F2d 341, 36 LRRM 2153 (CA 5, 1955).
59 369 US 404, 49 LRRM 2962 (1962). *See* Chapter 6 *supra* at notes 7-13.
60 United Steelworkers v. NLRB, 243 F2d 593, 39 LRRM 2103 (CA DC, 1956), *reversed in part on other grounds,* 357 US 357, 42 LRRM 2324 (1958); Goodman Mfg. Co. v. NLRB, 227 F2d 465, 37 LRRM 2047, *superseded,* 234 F2d 774, 38 LRRM 2265 (CA 7, 1955), *cert. denied,* 352 US 871, 38 LRRM 2757 (1956).

Board was in error in its interpretation of the statute.[61] But even when questions of statutory construction are presented in reviewing a Board decision, the courts cannot completely ignore the Board's interpretation. Because of the Board's special duty to administer the statute, courts must give appropriate weight to the judgment of the Board as to the proper interpretation.[62]

One area in which considerable weight must be given by the courts of appeals to determinations of the Board is the area of remedies. The Supreme Court has held that because the relation of remedy to policy is peculiarly a matter of administrative competence, courts must keep to the confines of law and not encroach upon the domain of policy.[63] They may not reverse or modify remedies fashioned by the Board to expunge the effect of unfair labor practices "unless it can be shown that the order [remedy] is a patent attempt to achieve ends other than those which can fairly be said to effectuate the policies of the Act."[64] The application of this principle to determinations by the Board that effectuate the policy of the Act can be seen in cases involving a remedy of reinstatement with or without back pay,[65] and the relief to be awarded where it appears that there was an absence of good faith in collective bargaining.[66]

In the event that a court does find that a remedy of the Board is inappropriate and additional findings are necessary, it will remand the case to the Board. The court will not substitute its judgment as to the appropriate remedy for that of the Board because the fashioning of a remedy is the exclusive function of the Board.[67]

---

[61] NLRB v. Denver Bldg. and Constr. Trades Council, 341 US 675, 28 LRRM 2108 (1951); NLRB v. Radio and Television Broadcast Eng'rs Union, IBEW, 264 US 573, 47 LRRM 2332 (1961).

[62] NLRB v. Hearst Publications, 322 US 111, 14 LRRM 614 (1944); Medo Photo Supply Corp. v. NLRB, 321 US 678, 14 LRRM 581 (1944).

[63] NLRB v. Gullett Ginn Co., 340 US 361, 27 LRRM 2330 (1951); Phelps Dodge Corp. v. NLRB, 313 US 177, 8 LRRM 439 (1941); IAM v. NLRB, 311 US 72, 7 LRRM 282 (1940). Cf. NLRB v. Gissel Packing Co., 395 US 575, 71 LRRM 2481 (1969) (Chapter 10 supra), and Love Box Co. v. NLRB, 422 F2d 232, 73 LRRM 2746 (CA 10, 1970).

[64] Virginia Electric & Power Co. v. NLRB, 319 US 533, 540, 12 LRRM 739 (1943). See H. K. Porter Co. v. NLRB, 397 US 99, 73 LRRM 2561 (1970), and discussion of remedies generally in Chapter 31 supra.

[65] UMW v. Eagle Picher Mining and Smelting Co., 325 US 335, 16 LRRM 689 (1945).

[66] NLRB v. Truitt Mfg. Co., 351 US 149, 38 LRRM 2042 (1956).

[67] United Steelworkers v. NLRB, 386 F2d 981, 66 LRRM 2417 (CA DC, 1967). The Board's remedy, however, is limited by the mandate of the statute. H. K. Porter Co. v. NLRB, note 64 supra.

3. Issues That Can Be Raised on Review. The court of appeal considers the case on the record, as certified by the Board, and its review under Section 10(e) is confined to questions raised before the Board.[68]

In enforcement proceedings, parties who fail to contest issues raised before the Board are deemed to have waived them in the reviewing court.[69] Likewise, if no exception is filed to a finding of a trial examiner, the NLRB is not required to decide questions raised before the examiner, and they cannot be raised on judicial review in the absence of extraordinary circumstances.[70] Where a party enters into a consent order with the Board, a reviewing court has no authority to modify the scope of the NLRB order in enforcement proceedings.[71]

4. Disposition of Case by Reviewing Court. A court of appeals having jurisdiction to review an order of the Board under Sections 10(e) or (f) is not limited to granting or denying enforcement in whole or in part of the Board order. It may modify and enforce as modified and, where the case warrants, may order that it be remanded to the Board. The court adjusts its relief to the exigencies of the case in accordance with the equitable principles governing judicial action.[72]

A remand does not dismiss or terminate the administrative proceedings. A remand simply means that the case is returned to the Board in order that it may take further action in accordance with the court's decision as to the applicable law.[73] The Board may

---

68 NLRB v. Carlton Wood Products Co., 201 F2d 863, 31 LRRM 2323 (CA 9, 1953).

69 Thus, where there was no objection raised before the NLRB as to the wording of the notice that was required to be posted, such an objection could not be considered upon review where no exceptional circumstances were shown. NLRB v. Local 476, United Ass'n of Journeymen and Apprentices of the Plumbing and Pipefitting Industry, 368 US 401, 49 LRRM 2370 (1962); NLRB v. District 50, UMW, 355 US 453, 41 LRRM 2449 (1958) (failure to raise objection as to propriety of Board's reaffirmation of certification could not be considered on review); NLRB v. Pappas & Co., 203 F2d 569, 32 LRRM 2062 (CA 9, 1953) (failure to raise issue of agricultural exemption under Act).

70 Local 745 Teamsters Union v. NLRB, 390 F2d 782, 67 LRRM 2370 (CA DC, 1968); NLRB v. Ra-Rich Mfg. Corp., 276 F2d 451, 45 LRRM 3042 (CA 2, 1960); Kovach v. NLRB, 229 F2d 138, 37 LRRM 2345 (CA 7, 1956).

71 NLRB v. Ochoa Fertilizer Corp., 368 US 318, 49 LRRM 2236 (1962); NLRB v. Las Vegas Sand and Gravel Corp., 368 US 400, 49 LRRM 2369 (1962).

72 Ford Motor Co. v. NLRB, 305 US 364, 3 LRRM 663 (1939).

73 Local 761 IUE v. NLRB, 366 US 667, 48 LRRM 2210 (1961); Local 400 Retail Clerks Ass'n v. NLRB, 360 F2d 494, 59 LRRM 2763 (CA DC, 1965); NLRB v. Am. Fed'n of Television and Radio Artists, 285 F2d 902, 47 LRRM 2463 (CA 6, 1961).

or may not order a further hearing, depending on the basis upon which the court ordered the remand.

No time limit is provided in the Act within which the NLRB must apply for enforcement of its orders. The law is also silent as to when petitions for review must be filed. Delay by the Board in seeking enforcement of its order is no defense, because a Board order does not lose its vitality or effectiveness by reason of the passage of time. Thus, enforcement of a Board order has been granted even where the Board waited over two years to seek enforcement.[74]

III. DIRECT REVIEW AND ENFORCEMENT

Apart from circuit court review of final orders in unfair labor practice cases, provided for in Sections 10(e) and (f), the Supreme Court has held that both district and circuit courts are, as a general rule, without jurisdiction to entertain suits to vacate or direct Board action in connection with representation and unfair labor practice cases.[75] As is true of every general rule, however, there are exceptions that have been recognized by the Court.[76]

A. Review of Certification Action

Section 9 of the NLRA authorizes the Board to certify employee units as appropriate for collective bargaining. The Act makes no express provision for judicial review of certification proceedings under Section 9, except for Section 9(d). This subsection provides for review of certifications that are before the court of appeals under Sections 10(e) and (f) in connection with unfair labor practice orders.

In *AFL v. NLRB*,[77] after considering the congressional history of the Wagner Act, the Supreme Court held that a Board certification action was not a "final order" within the meaning of Section 10(f) and that "the conclusion is unavoidable that Congress,

---

[74] NLRB v. Pool Mfg. Co., 339 US 577, 26 LRRM 2127 (1950); Nabors Co. v. NLRB, 323 F2d 686, 54 LRRM 2259 (CA 5, 1963), *cert. denied*, 376 US 911, 55 LRRM 2455 (1964); NLRB v. United Biscuit Co., 208 F2d 52, 33 LRRM 2155 (CA 8, 1953).
[75] AFL v. NLRB, 308 US 401, 5 LRRM 670 (1940); Myers v. Bethlehem Shipbldg. Corp., 303 US 41, 1-A LRRM 575 (1938).
[76] McCulloch v. Sociedad Nacional de Marineros de Honduras, 372 US 10, 52 LRRM 2425 (1963); Leedom v. Kyne, 358 US 184, 43 LRRM 2222 (1958); *see also* Fay v. Douds, 172 F2d 720, 23 LRRM 2356 (CA 2, 1949).
[77] 308 US 401, 5 LRRM 670 (1940).

as the result of a deliberate choice of conflicting policies, has excluded representation certifications of the Board from the review by the federal appellate courts . . . except in the circumstances specified in §9(d)."[78] Under this decision, an employer desiring to contest a certification must refuse to bargain and then assert his position by way of defense in an unfair labor practice proceeding and subsequently on judicial review.

Apart from the limited review provided in Section 9, the Court in *AFL v. NLRB* expressly reserved the question of whether the review provisions of the Act precluded bringing an independent suit to vacate Board action for violation of a statutory provision.[79] The question was presented more directly in *Inland Empire District Council v. Millis,*[80] where an original equity suit was brought alleging unlawful Board action in a representation proceeding. The Court held that the Board was acting within its discretionary authority and, in refusing to rule on the question of availability of review of extra-statutory Board action, stated that the question reserved in *AFL* would have to await "the required showing of unlawful action by the Board and resulting injury . . . whether by way of departure from statutory requirements or from those of due process of law."[81]

This, then, became the standard applied by the lower courts. Relying upon *Inland Empire,* the courts held that a petitioner had standing to seek review of representation proceedings in a federal district court prior to an unfair labor practice order where the petitioner could show (1) harm or threat of harm that could not be adequately remedied by Board review provisions and (2) that the Board acted without constitutional or statutory authority.[82] This dual test also was applied in cases where certification proceedings were not involved.[83] Thus, a district court's authority to exercise jurisdiction was upheld where the Board had exceeded

---

[78] *Id.* at 411.
[79] *Id.* at 413.
[80] Inland Empire District Council, Lumber and Sawmill Workers v. Millis, 325 US 697, 16 LRRM 743 (1945).
[81] *Id.* at 700.,
[82] DePratter v. Farmer, 232 F2d 74, 37 LRRM 2432 (CA DC, 1956); Fay V. Douds, 172 F2d 720, 23 LRRM 2356 (CA 2, 1949).
[83] Farmer v. UE, 211 F2d 36, 33 LRRM 2196 (CA DC, 1953), *cert. denied,* 347 US 943, 33 LRRM 2821 (1954); Farmer v. Int'l Fur & Leather Workers, 221 F2d 862, 35 LRRM 2488 (CA DC, 1955); *see also* Local 255, Hotel and Restaurant Employees Union v. Leedom, 358 US 99, 43 LRRM 2137 (1958).

its authority in cases involving the Taft-Hartley Act's requirements for filing non-communist affidavits.[84] However, the Supreme Court's decision in *Switchmen's Union v. National Mediation Board,* a case under the Railway Labor Act,[85] cast considerable doubt as to whether there might be review of unlawful action of the NLRB by district courts. This case was relied upon to support the proposition that the provisions for judicial review of the Taft-Hartley Act preclude bringing an equity suit in a district court to set aside a Board certification action. The Supreme Court found that Congress, in the Railway Labor Act, had left the determination of appropriate bargaining units to the discretionary authority of the National Mediation Board. No judicial review was authorized, and "the dispute was to reach its last terminal point when the administrative finding was made." [86]

In 1958, however, the Supreme Court provided a direct answer to the question of the equity jurisdiction of district courts. In *Leedom v. Kyne,*[87] suit was brought in a federal district court under Section 1337 of the Judicial Code [88] to have a certification order of the NLRB set aside on the ground that the Board had allegedly exceeded its authority under Section 9(b)(1) by certifying a unit composed of 233 professional and nine nonprofessional employees without affording the professionals a separate election to determine whether they desired to be included in the unit.

The Supreme Court held that the certification was subject to review. The Court stated that the federal district courts could entertain suits to set aside NLRB certification orders when the Board had plainly exceeded its statutory authority and there was no other adequate remedy.[89] The Court emphasized that Congress had specifically created the right in question and that, unless district courts had equity jurisdiction, the right was meaningless.[90]

---

84 Leedom v. Mine, Mill & Smelter Workers, 352 US 145, 39 LRRM 2146 (1956).
85 320 US 297, 13 LRRM 616 (1943).
86 *Id.* at 305. *See also* Bhd. of Ry. & S.S. Clerks v. Ass'n for the Benefit of Non-Contract Employees, 380 US 650, 59 LRRM 2051 (1965), note 91 *infra.*
87 358 US 184, 43 LRRM 2222 (1958).
88 28 USC §1337 (1965).
89 Leedom v. Kyne, 358 US 184, 189, 43 LRRM 2222, 2225 (1958).
90 Another narrow exception to the rule prohibiting direct review of certification proceedings or a collateral attack in the district courts was enunciated by the Supreme Court in McCulloch v. Sociedad Nacional de Marineros de Honduras, 372 US 10, 52 LRRM 2425 (1963). There the Board attempted to exercise its jurisdiction over alien employees who were represented by a foreign union on a foreign ship bearing a foreign flag. Although the Board did not violate a specific provision of

In the *ABNE* case, another decision under the RLA,[91] the Court pointed out the distinction between *Switchmen's Union* and *Leedom v. Kyne*. *Switchmen's Union* involved the exercise of discretionary statutory authority by the National Mediation Board for which no judicial review was provided by Congress. *Kyne*, on the other hand, did not involve "review" of a decision of the Board made within its jurisdiction but, rather, a charge that the NLRB had acted beyond its authority and contrary to a specific prohibition in the Act.[92]

The scope of the *Leedom v. Kyne* and *McCulloch v. Marineros de Honduras* exceptions was considered by the Court in *Boire v. Greyhound Corp.*[93] In this case the Supreme Court held that a district court did not have jurisdiction to enjoin a representation election on the ground that the Board had erroneously determined that two separate enterprises were joint employers. The Court expressly restricted the *Leedom v. Kyne* exception to instances where the error of the Board is a patently incorrect construction of the Act; a finding of fact, though contrary to the weight of the evidence, is not reviewable under the *Kyne* exception.

The Court emphasized the narrow nature of the exceptions in *Leedom v. Kyne* and *McCulloch v. Marineros de Honduras* to its general rule of refusing to allow direct review of certification or collateral attack of representation orders in district courts. These exceptions, the Court stated, were "characterized by extraordinary circumstances." [94]

Generally, the lower courts have taken to heart this admonition and have exhibited great reluctance to find the *Leedom v. Kyne*

---

the Act, the district court had jurisdiction to review the Board's action because, the Court held, its effect on foreign relations presented "a uniquely compelling justification for prompt judicial resolution of the controversy over the Board's power." 372 US at 17. *See* Chapter 28 *supra* at notes 32-33.

91 Bhd. of Ry. and S. S. Clerks v. Ass'n for the Benefit of Non-Contract Employees, 380 US 650, 59 LRRM 2051 (1965).

92 *Id.* at 660, quoting from Leedom v. Kyne, 358 US 184, 188, 43 LRRM 2222, 2224 (1958).

93 376 US 473, 55 LRRM 2694 (1964). *See also* NLRB v. Greyhound Corp., 368 F2d 778, 63 LRRM 2434 (CA 5, 1966).

94 *Id.* at 479. The Court said that "whether Greyhound possessed sufficient indicia of control to be an 'employer' is essentially a factual issue, unlike the question in *Kyne*, which depended solely upon construction of the statute. The *Kyne* exception is a narrow one, not to be extended to permit plenary district court review of Board orders in certification proceedings whenever it can be said that an erroneous assessment of the particular facts before the Board has led it to a conclusion which does not comport with the law." *Id.* at 481.

or *McCulloch v. Marineros* exceptions applicable to any situation in which the Board has not acted patently and manifestly without legality.[95] Thus, allegations that the Board violated its congressional mandate by withdrawing contract-bar protection from agreements existing prior to the enactment of the amendments regarding hot-cargo clauses,[96] or has acted arbitrarily in finding bus dispatchers not supervisors as defined in Section 2(11) of the Act,[97] have been held insufficient to invoke jurisdiction under the *Kyne* exception. Where the Board has clearly violated an express provision of the statute, the courts have granted relief under *Kyne*.[98] Courts have, however, required the showing of a clear violation of a statutory provision and further, following *Boire*, have refused to grant relief where the issues involved the Board's mistaken evaluation of questions of fact. Such mistaken evaluations are not reviewable except pursuant to an unfair labor practice order.[99]

B. Review of Unfair Labor Practice Proceedings

In the landmark case of *Myers v. Bethlehem Shipbuilding Corp.*,[100] the Supreme Court held that a federal district court did not have jurisdiction over an employer suit to enjoin the Board from holding a hearing upon an unfair labor practice complaint against the employer, even though the employer alleged that the Act was not applicable to his relations with his employees and that the holding of a hearing would subject him to irreparable damage. After analyzing the provisions of the Act, the Court found that the district court was without jurisdiction to enjoin the unfair labor practice hearing because Congress had vested the Board with

---

95 Potter v. Castle Constr. Co., 355 F2d 217, 61 LRRM 2119 (CA 5, 1966); McCulloch v. Libbey-Owens-Ford Glass Co., 403 F2d 916, 68 LRRM 2447 (CA DC, 1968), *cert. denied*, 393 US 1016, 70 LRRM 2225 (1969).
96 Local 1545, United Bhd. of Carpenters v. Vincent, 286 F2d 127, 47 LRRM 2304 (CA 2, 1960).
97 Eastern Greyhound Lines v. Fusco. 323 F2d 477, 54 LRRM 2323 (CA 6, 1963).
98 Local 46, Printing Pressmen's Union v. McCulloch, 322 F2d 993, 53 LRRM 2786 (CA DC, 1963). (Board violated §9(c)(1) by refusing to certify results of an election). Navajo Tribe v. NLRB, 288 F2d 162, 47 LRRM 2645 (CA DC, 1961). IUE v. NLRB (Athbro Precision Engineering Corp.), 67 LRRM 2361 (DC DC, 1968).
99 Potter v. Castle Constr. Co., 355 F2d 217, 61 LRRM 2119 (CA 5, 1966); Boire v. Miami Herald Publishing Co., 343 F2d 17, 58 LRRM 2585 (CA 5, 1965); Lawrence Typographical Union v. McCulloch, 349 F2d 704, 59 LRRM 2161 (CA DC, 1965); Local 130, IUE v. McCulloch, 345 F2d 90, 58 LRRM 2699 (CA DC, 1965); Rocks-Hills-Uris, Inc. v. McLeod, 344 F2d 697, 59 LRRM 2064 (CA 2, 1965); Am. Metal Products Co. v. Reynolds, 332 F2d 434, 56 LRRM 2333 (CA 6, 1964).
100 303 US 41, 1-A LRRM 575 (1938).

exclusive jurisdiction to prevent unfair labor practices.[101] Assertion of such district court jurisdiction was "at war with the long settled rule of judicial administration that no one is entitled to judicial relief for a supposed or threatened injury until the prescribed administrative remedy has been exhausted."[102]

The Court construed the procedural provisions of the Act as "affording adequate opportunity to secure judicial protection against arbitrary action in accordance with the well-settled rules applicable to administrative agencies, set up by Congress to aid in the enforcement of valid legislation."[103] According to the Court, the procedure for reviewing Board action mainly through Sections 10(e) and (f) was appropriate and adequate and was the only method for reviewing unfair labor practice proceedings.[104]

Circuit courts have consistently followed the doctrine of *Myers* and have refused to permit collateral review of unfair labor practice proceedings prior to the issuance of a final Board order. They have not considered *Leedom v. Kyne* as modifying *Myers*.[105] In *Chicago Automobile Trade Association*,[106] the Board prevailed in its appeal from a district court decision enjoining it from proceeding *de novo* in an unfair labor practice case, where the trial examiner had recessed the case *sine die* and disqualified himself because of ill health.

In reversing the district court on the ground of lack of jurisdiction of the subject matter, the Seventh Circuit, citing *Myers*[107] and *Vapor Blast*,[108] pointed out that the Board's ultimate decision and order is subject to review before it can be enforced and that Section 10(e) and (f) of the Act afford an exclusive and adequate review procedure, thus precluding the exercise of equitable jurisdiction by the district court at a preliminary stage of the administrative proceeding.

---

101 *See* Chapters 28 and 29 *supra*.
102 303 US 41, 50-51, 1-A LRRM 575, 578 (1938).
103 *Id.* at 49.
104 *Id.* at 50.
105 Chicago Auto. Trade Ass'n v. Madden, 328 F2d 766, 55 LRRM 2514 (CA 7, 1964), *cert. denied*, 377 US 979, 56 LRRM 2480 (1964); Bokat v. Tidewater Equip. Co., 363 F2d 667, 62 LRRM 2581 (CA 5, 1966); Deering-Milliken, Inc. v. Johnson, 295 F2d 856, 48 LRRM 3162 (CA 4, 1961).
106 Chicago Auto. Trade Ass'n v. Madden, 328 F2d 766, 55 LRRM 2514 (CA 7, 1964).
107 Myers v. Bethlehem Shipbldg. Corp., 303 US 41, 1-A LRRM 575 (1938).
108 Vapor Blast Mfg. Co. v. Madden, 280 F2d 205, 46 LRRM 2559 (CA 7, 1960).

In 1966, in *Bokat v. Tidewater Equipment Co.,*[109] the Board again prevailed in its appeal from a district court decision enjoining it from proceeding with an unfair labor practice proceeding. This action had been instituted after the Board had refused to review the chief trial examiner's denial of a motion (1) to sever a part of the complaint relating to the employer attorney's questioning of the employees and (2) to postpone a hearing on the other charges until a final determination of whether the attorney's conduct violated the Act.

In reversing, the Fifth Circuit observed that the district court should have dismissed the case without looking further than the opinion of the Supreme Court in *Myers v. Bethlehem Shipbuilding Corp.* The court added that the principle of administrative finality, specified by the Supreme Court in *Myers* as a prerequisite to judicial review, has special force where, as in the case before it, the interlocutory order sought to be reviewed relates to the agency's case-handling procedures. This conclusion rests upon the dual premise that Congress has prescribed the method and course of judicial review and that this method is adequate to meet constitutional demands. Implicit in any such standard, the court continued, is the possibility that where that review is not substantially adequate, different and more direct judicial intervention might be available. But in the 30-year history of the Act those instances have been rare. Moreover, the exceptions have involved representation cases, where judicial intervention is restricted, and have been characterized by the Supreme Court as involving "extraordinary circumstances." [110] There was nothing in *Bokat,* the court concluded, that would meet this "extraordinary test." [111]

In the *Chicago Automobile Trades Association* and the *Bokat* cases, the circuit courts, in finding that the *Kyne* exceptions were inapplicable, distinguished the Fourth Circuit's *Deering Milliken v. Johnston*[112] decision. There the court had relied in part upon the *Kyne* exception in ruling that a federal district court had jurisdiction to enjoin a regional director of the Board from proceeding with hearings on a second remand by the Board of unfair labor practice charges. The *Deering Milliken* action was grounded upon

---

109 363 F2d 667, 62 LRRM 2581 (CA 5, 1966).
110 Boire v. Greyhound Corp., 376 US 473, 479, 55 LRRM 2694 (1964).
111 *Id.* at 670.
112 295 F2d 856, 48 LRRM 3162 (CA 4, 1961).

the provisions of the Administrative Procedure Act specifying that courts shall compel agency action that is unlawfully withheld or unreasonably delayed.[113]

An unfair labor practice charge does not become moot for purposes of enforcement and review upon the holding of a subsequent election. In the *Raytheon* case,[114] the Supreme Court held that enforcement of a Board order is justified, despite the occurence of a subsequent election, in order to protect the injured party in future elections. The Court held that "[t]he later election and certification here is simply evidence that the company complied with the Board order during the pendency of the election." [115] Once the Board has determined that a party has engaged in illegal activities, the other party is entitled to an exercise of the Board's remedial power.[116] The Court conceded, however, that "[t]here are situations where an enforcement proceeding will become moot, because a party can establish that 'there is no reasonable expectation that the wrong will be repeated.' " [117]

---

113 The Seventh Circuit in *Chicago Trade Ass'n,* in distinguishing *Deering-Milliken,* stated: "[It] is not apposite here. There, the employer brought suit under Section 10 (e) of the Administrative Procedure Act (5 U.S. C.A. §1009 (e)) to 'compel agency action. . . . unreasonably delayed.' The holding is expressly rested on the factor that unreasonable delay by its very nature constitutes 'final' administrative action for which Section 10 (f) of the National Labor Relations Act affords no redress by judicial review. In the instant case, plaintiff's complaint neither charges unreasonable delay nor alleges facts from which an inference of unreasonable delay attributable to the Board can be drawn." 328 F2d 766, 769, 55 LRRM 2514 (CA 7, 1964). *See also* Templeton v. Dixie Color Printing Co., 313 F. Supp 105, 74 LRRM 2206 (ND Ala., 1970). *Cf.* Int'l Ass'n of Machinists v. National Mediation Board, 425 F2d 527, 73 LRRM 2278 (1970).
114 NLRB v. Raytheon Co., 398 US 25, 74 LRRM 2177 (1970).
115 74 LRRM at 2178.
116 *Id., citing* NLRB v. J. H. Rutter-Rex Mfg. Co., 396 US 258, 72 LRRM 2881 (1969).
117 *Ibid., citing* United States v. W. T. Grant Co., 345 US 629, 633 (1953).

TEXT OF
NATIONAL LABOR RELATIONS ACT

49 Stat. 449 (1935), as amended by Pub. L. No. 101,
80th Cong., 1st Sess., 1947, and Pub. L. No. 257
86th Cong., 1st Sess., 1959; 29 U.S.C.
§§ 151-68, F.C.A. 29 §§ 151-68

Findings and Policies

Section 1. The denial by some employers of the right of employees to organize and the refusal by some employers to accept the procedure of collective bargaining lead to strikes and other forms of industrial strife or unrest, which have the intent or the necessary effect of burdening or obstructing commerce by (a) impairing the efficiency, safety, or operation of the instrumentalities of commerce; (b) occurring in the current of commerce; (c) materially affecting, restraining, or controlling the flow of raw materials or manufactured or processed goods from or into the channels of commerce, or the prices of such materials or goods in commerce; or (d) causing diminution of employment and wages in such volume as substantially to impair or disrupt the market for goods flowing from or into the channels of commerce.

The inequality of bargaining power between employees who do not possess full freedom of association or actual liberty of contract, and employers who are organized in the corporate or other forms of ownership association substantially burdens and affects the flow of commerce, and tends to aggravate recurrent business depressions, by depressing wage rates and the purchasing power of wage earners in industry and by preventing the stabilization of competitive wage rates and working conditions within and between industries.

Experience has proved that protection by law of the right of employees to organize and bargain collectively safeguards commerce from injury, impairment, or interruption, and promotes the flow of commerce by removing certain recognized sources of industrial strife and unrest, by encouraging practices fundamental to the friendly adjustment of industrial disputes arising out of differences as to wages, hours, or other working conditions, and by restoring equality of bargaining power between employers and employees.

Experience has further demonstrated that certain practices by some labor organizations, their officers, and members have the intent or the necessary effect of burdening or obstructing commerce by preventing the free flow of goods in such commerce through strikes and other forms of industrial unrest or through concerted activities which impair the interest of the public in the free flow of such commerce. The elimination of such practices is a necessary condition to the assurance of the rights herein guaranteed.

It is hereby declared to be the policy of the United States to eliminate the causes of certain substantial obstructions to the free flow of commerce and to mitigate and eliminate these obstructions when they have occurred by encouraging the practice and procedure of collective bargaining and by protecting the exercise by workers of full freedom of association, self-organization, and designation of representatives of their own choosing, for the purpose of negotiating the terms and conditions of their employment or other mutual aid or protection.

Definitions

Sec. 2. When used in this Act—

(1) The term "person" includes one or more individuals, labor organizations, partnerships, associations, corporations, legal representatives, trustees, trustees in bankruptcy, or receivers.

(2) The term "employer" includes any person acting as an agent of an employer, directly or indirectly, but shall not include the United States or any wholly owned Government corporation, or any Federal Reserve Bank, or any State or political subdivision thereof, or any corporation or association operating a hospital, if no part of the net earnings inures to the benefit of any private shareholder or individual, or any person subject to the Railway Labor Act, as amended from time to time, or any

labor organization (other than when acting as an employer), or anyone acting in the capacity of officer or agent of such labor organization.

(3) The term "employer" shall include any employee, and shall not be limited to the employees of a particular employer, unless the Act explicitly states otherwise, and shall include any individual whose work has ceased as a consequence of, or in connection with, any current labor dispute or because of any unfair labor practice, and who has not obtained any other regular and substantially equivalent employment, but shall not include any individual employed as an agricultural laborer, or in the domestic service of any family or person at his home, or any individual employed by his parent or spouse, or any individual having the status of an independent contractor, or any individual employed as a supervisor, or any individual employed by an employer subject to the Railway Labor Act, as amended from time to time, or by any other person who is not an employer as herein defined.

(4) The term "representatives" includes any individual or labor organization.

(5) The term "labor organization" means any organization of any kind, or any agency or employee representation committee or plan, in which employees participate and which exists for the purpose, in whole or in part, of dealing with employers concerning grievances, labor disputes, wages, rates of pay, hours of employment, or conditions of work.

(6) The term "commerce" means trade, traffic, commerce, transportation, or communication among the several States, or between the District of Columbia or any Territory of the United States and any State or other Territory, or between any foreign country and any State, Territory, or the District of Columbia, or within the District of Columbia or any Territory, or between points in the same State but through any other State or any Territory or the District of Columbia or any foreign country.

(7) The term "affecting commerce" means in commerce, or burdening or obstructing commerce or the free flow of commerce, or having led or tending to lead to a labor dispute burdening or obstructing commerce or the free flow of commerce.

(8) The term "unfair labor practice" means any unfair labor practice listed in section 8.

(9) The term "labor dispute" includes any controversy concerning terms, tenure or conditions of employment, or concerning the association or representation of persons in negotiating, fixing, maintaining, changing, or seeking to arrange terms or conditions of employment, regardless of whether the disputants stand in the proximate relation of employer and employee.

(10) The term "National Labor Relations Board" means the National Labor Relations Board provided for in section 3 of this Act.

(11) The term "supervisor" means any individual having authority, in the interest of the employer, to hire, transfer, suspend, lay off, recall, promote, discharge, assign, reward, or discipline other employees, or responsibly to direct them, or to adjust their grievances, or effectively to recommend such action, if in connection with the foregoing the exercise of such authority is not of a merely routine or clerical nature, but requires the use of independent judgment.

(12) The term "professional employee" means—

(a) any employee engaged in work (i) predominantly intellectual and varied in character as opposed to routine mental, manual, mechanical, or physical work; (ii) involving the consistent exercise of discretion and judgment in its performance; (iii) of such a character that the output produced or the result accomplished cannot be standardized in relation to a given period of time; (iv) requiring knowledge of an advanced type in a field of science or learning customarily acquired by a prolonged course of specialized intellectual instruction and study in an institution of higher learning or a hospital, as distinguished from a general academic education or from an apprenticeship or from training in the performance of routine mental, manual, or physical processes; or

(b) any employee, who (i) has completed the courses of specialized intellectual instruction and study described in clause (iv) of paragraph (a), and (ii) is performing related work under the supervision of a professional person to qualify himself to become a professional employee as defined in paragraph (a).

(13) In determining whether any person is acting as an "agent" of another person so as to make such other person responsible for his acts, the question of whether the specific acts performed were actually authorized or subsequently ratified shall not be controlling.

National Labor Relations Board

Sec. 3. (a) The National Labor Relations Board (hereinafter called the Board) created by this Act prior to its amendment by the Labor Management Relations Act, 1947, is hereby continued as an agency of the United States, except that the Board shall consist of five instead of three members, appointed by the President by and with the advice and consent of the Senate. Of the two additional members so provided for, one shall be appointed for a term of five years and the other for a term of two years. Their successors, and the successors of the other members, shall be appointed for terms of five years each, excepting that any individual chosen to fill a vacancy shall be appointed only for the unexpired term of the member whom he shall succeed. The President shall designate one member to serve as Chairman of the Board. Any member of the Board may be removed by the President, upon notice and hearing, for neglect of duty or malfeasance in office, but for no other cause.

(b) The Board is authorized to delegate to any group of three or more members any or all of the powers which it may itself exercise. The Board is also authorized to delegate to its regional directors its powers under section 9 to determine the unit appropriate for the purpose of collective bargaining, to investigate and provide for hearings, and determine whether a question of representation exists, and to direct an election or take a secret ballot under subsection (c) or (e) of section 9 and certify the results thereof, except that upon the filing of a request therefor with the Board by any interested person, the Board may review any action of a regional director delegated to him under this paragraph, but such a review shall not, unless specifically ordered by the Board, operate as a stay of any action taken by the regional director. A vacancy in the Board shall not impair the right of the remaining members to exercise all of the powers of the Board, and three members of the Board shall, at all times, constitute a quorum of the Board, except that two members shall constitute a quorum of any group designated pursuant to the first sentence hereof. The Board shall have an official seal which shall be judicially noticed.

(c) The Board shall at the close of each fiscal year make a report in writing to Congress and to the President stating in detail the cases it has heard, the decisions it has rendered, the names, salaries, and duties of all employees and officers in the employ or under the supervision of the Board, and an account of all moneys it has disbursed.

(d) There shall be a General Counsel of the Board who shall be appointed by the President, by and with the advice and consent of the Senate, for a term of four years. The General Counsel of the Board shall exercise general supervision over all attorneys employed by the Board (other than trial examiners and legal assistants to Board members) and over the officers and employees in the regional offices. He shall have final authority, on behalf of the Board, in respect of the investigation of charges and issuance of complaints under section 10, and in respect of the prosecution of such complaints before the Board, and shall have such other duties as the Board may prescribe or as may be provided by law. In case of a vacancy in the office of the General Counsel the President is authorized to designate the officer or employee who shall act as General Counsel during such vacancy, but no person or persons so designated shall so act (1) for more than forty days when the Congress is in session unless a nomination to fill such vacancy shall have been submitted to the Senate, or (2) after the adjournment sine die of the session of the Senate in which such nomination was submitted.

Sec. 4. (a) Each member of the Board and the General Counsel of the Board shall receive a salary of $12,000 a year, shall be eligible for reappointment, and shall not engage in any other business, vocation, or employment. The Board shall appoint an executive secretary, and such attorneys, examiners and regional directors, and such other employees as it may from time to time find necessary for the proper performance of its duties. The Board may not employ any attorneys for the purpose of reviewing transcripts of hearings or preparing drafts of opinions except that any attorney employed for assignment as a legal assistant to any Board member may for such Board member review such transcripts and prepare such drafts. No trial examiner's report shall be reviewed, either before or after its publication, by any person other than a member of the Board or his legal assistant, and no trial examiner shall advise or consult with the Board with respect to exceptions taken to his findings, rulings or recommendations. The Board may establish or utilize such regional, local, or other agencies, and utilize such voluntary and uncompensated services, as may from time to time be needed. Attorneys appointed under this section may, at the direction of the Board, appear for and represent the Board in any case in court. Nothing in this Act shall be construed to authorize the Board to appoint individuals for the purpose of conciliation or mediation, or for economic analysis.

(b) All of the expenses of the Board, including all necessary traveling and subsistence expenses outside the District of Columbia incurred by the members or employees of the Board under its orders, shall be allowed and paid on the presentation of itemized vouchers, therefor approved by the Board or by any individual it designates for that purpose.

Sec. 5. The principal office of the Board shall be in the District of Columbia, but it may meet and exercise any or all of its powers at any other place. The Board may, by one or more of its members or by such agents or agencies as it may designate, prosecute any inquiry necessary to its functions in any part of the United States. A member who participates in such an inquiry shall not be disqualified from subsequently participating in a decision of the Board in the same case.

Sec. 6. The Board shall have authority from time to time to make, amend, and rescind, in the manner prescribed by the Administrative Procedure Act, such rules and regulations as may be necessary to carry out the provisions of this Act.

Rights of Employees

Sec. 7. Employees shall have the right to self-organization, to form, join or assist labor organizations, to bargain collectively through representatives of their own choosing, and to engage in other concerted activities for the purpose of collective bargaining or other mutual aid or protection, and shall also have the right to refrain from any or all of such activities except to the extent that such right may be affected by an agreement requiring membership in a labor organization as a condition of employment as authorized in section 8 (a) (3) .

Unfair Labor Practices

Sec. 8. (a) It shall be an unfair labor practice for an employer—

(1) to interfere with, restrain, or coerce employees in the exercise of the rights guaranteed in section 7;

(2) to dominate or interfere with the formation or administration of any labor organization or contribute financial or other support to it: *Provided,* That subject to rules and regulations

made and published by the Board pursuant to section 6, an employer shall not be prohibited from permitting employees to confer with him during working hours without loss of time or pay;

(3) by discrimination in regard to hire or tenure of employment or any term or condition of employment to encourage or discourage membership in any labor organization: *Provided,* That nothing in this Act, or any other statute of the United States, shall preclude an employer from making an agreement with a labor organization (not established, maintained, or assisted by any action defined in section 8 (a) of this Act as an unfair labor practice) to require as a condition of employment membership therein on or after the thirtieth day following the beginning of such employment or the effective date of such agreement, whichever is the later, (i) if such labor organization is the representative of the employees as provided in section 9 (a) , in the appropriate collective-bargaining unit covered by such agreement when made; and (ii) unless following an election held as provided in section 9 (e) within one year preceding the effective date of such agreement the Board shall have certified that at least a majority of the employees eligible to vote in such election have voted to rescind the authority of such labor organization to make such an agreement: *Provided further,* That no employer shall justify any discrimination against an employee for nonmembership in a labor organization (A) if he has reasonable grounds for believing that such membership was not available to the employee on the same terms and conditions generally applicable to other members or (B) if he has reasonable grounds for believing that membership was denied or terminated for reasons other than the failure of the employee to tender the periodic dues and the initiation fees uniformly required as a condition of acquiring or retaining membership;

(4) to discharge or otherwise discriminate against an employee because he has filed charges or given testimony under this Act;

(5) to refuse to bargain collectively with the representatives of his employees, subject to the provisions of section 9 (a) .

(b) It shall be an unfair labor practice for a labor organization or its agents—

(1) to restrain or coerce (A) employees in the exercise of the rights guaranteed in section 7: *Provided,* That this para-

graph shall not impair the right of a labor organization to prescribe its own rules with respect to the acquisition or retention
of membership therein; or (B) an employer in the selection of
his representatives for the purposes of collective bargaining or
the adjustment of grievances;

(2) to cause or attempt to cause an employer to discriminate
against an employee in violation of subsection (a) (3) or to discriminate against an employee with respect to whom membership in such organization has been denied or terminated on some
ground other than his failure to tender the periodic dues and
the initiation fees uniformly required as a condition of acquiring or retaining membership;

(3) to refuse to bargain collectively with an employer, provided it is the representative of his employees subject to the
provisions of section 9 (a) ;

(4) (i) to engage in, or to induce or encourage any individual employed by any person engaged in commerce or in an
industry affecting commerce to engage in, a strike or a refusal
in the course of his employment to use, manufacture, process,
transport or otherwise handle or work on any goods, articles,
materials or commodities or to perform any services; or (ii)
to threaten, coerce, or restrain any person engaged in commerce
or in an industry affecting commerce where in either case an
object thereof is:

(A) forcing or requiring any employer or self-employed
person to join any labor or employer organization or to enter
into any agreement which is prohibited by section 8 (e) ;

(B) forcing or requiring any person to cease using, selling,
handling, transporting, or otherwise dealing in the products of
any other producer, processor, or manufacturer, or to cease doing
business with any other person, or forcing or requiring any other
employer to recognize or bargain with a labor organization as
the representative of his employees unless such labor organization has been certified as the representative of such employees
under the provisions of section 9: *Provided,* That nothing contained in this clause (B) shall be construed to make unlawful,
where not otherwise unlawful, any primary strike or primary
picketing;

(C) forcing or requiring any employer to recognize or bargain with a particular labor organization as the representative
of his employees if another labor organization has been certified

as the representative of such employees under the provisions of section 9;

(D) forcing or requiring any employer to assign particular work to employees in a particular labor organization or in a particular trade, craft, or class rather than to employees in another labor organization or in another trade, craft, or class, unless such employer is failing to conform to an order or certification of the Board determining the bargaining representative for employees performing such work:

Provided, That nothing contained in this subsection (b) shall be construed to make unlawful a refusal by any person to enter upon the premises of any employer (other than his own employer), if the employees of such employer are engaged in a strike ratified or approved by a representative of such employees whom such employer is required to recognize under this Act: *Provided further,* That for the purposes of this paragraph (4) only, nothing contained in such paragraph shall be construed to prohibit publicity, other than picketing, for the purpose of truthfully advising the public, including consumers and members of a labor organization, that a product or products are produced by an employer with whom the labor organization has a primary dispute and are distributed by another employer, as long as such publicity does not have an effect of inducing any individual employed by any person other than the primary employer in the course of his employment to refuse to pick up, deliver, or transport any goods, or not to perform any services, at the establishment of the employer engaged in such distribution.

(5) to require of employees covered by an agreement authorized under subsection (a) (3) the payment, as a condition precedent to becoming a member of such organization, of a fee in an amount which the Board finds excessive or discriminatory under all the circumstances. In making such a finding, the Board shall consider, among other relevant factors, the practices and customs of labor organizations in the particular industry, and the wages currently paid to the employees affected;

(6) to cause or attempt to cause an employer to pay or deliver or agree to pay or deliver any money or other thing of value, in the nature of an exaction, for services which are not performed or not to be performed; and

(7) to picket or cause to be picketed, or threaten to picket or cause to be picketed, any employer where an object thereof is forcing or requiring an employer to recognize or bargain

with a labor organization as the representative of his employees, or forcing or requiring the employees of an employer to accept or select such labor organization as their collective bargaining representative, unless such labor organization is currently certified as the representative of such employees:

(A) where the employer has lawfully recognized in accordance with this Act any other labor organization and a question concerning representation may not appropriately be raised under section 9 (c) of this Act,

(B) where within the preceding twelve months a valid election under section 9 (c) of this Act has been conducted, or

(C) where such picketing has been conducted without a petition under section 9 (c) being filed within a reasonable period of time not to exceed thirty days from the commencement of such picketing: *Provided,* That when such a petition has been filed the Board shall forthwith, without regard to the provisions of section 9 (c) (1) or the absence of a showing of a substantial interest on the part of the labor organization, direct an election in such unit as the Board finds to be appropriate and shall certify the results thereof: *Provided further,* That nothing in this subparagraph (C) shall be construed to prohibit any picketing or other publicity for the purpose of truthfully advising the public (including consumers) that an employer does not employ members of, or have a contract with, a labor organization, unless an effect of such picketing is to induce any individual employed by any other person in the course of his employment, not to pick up, deliver or transport any goods or not to perform any services.

Nothing in this paragraph (7) shall be construed to permit any act which would otherwise be an unfair labor practice under this section (8) (b).

(c) The expressing of any views, argument, or opinion, or the dissemination thereof, whether in written, printed, graphic, or visual form, shall not constitute or be evidence of an unfair labor practice under any of the provisions of this Act, if such expression contains no threat of reprisal or force or promise of benefit.

(d) For the purposes of this section, to bargain collectively is the performance of the mutual obligation of the employer and the representative of the employees to meet at reasonable times and confer in good faith with respect to wages, hours, and other terms and conditions of employment, or the negotiation of an agreement, or any question arising thereunder, and the execution of a written contract incorporating any agreement reached if requested by either party, but such obligation does not compel either party to agree to a proposal or require the making of a concession: *Provided,* That where there is in effect a collective-bargaining contract covering employees in an industry affecting commerce, the duty to bargain collectively shall also mean that no party to such contract shall terminate or modify such contract, unless the party desiring such termination or modification—

(1) serves a written notice upon the other party to the contract of the proposed termination or modification sixty days prior to the expiration date thereof, or in the event such contract contains no expiration date, sixty days prior to the time it is proposed to make such termination or modification;

(2) offers to meet and confer with the other party for the purpose of negotiating a new contract or a contract containing the proposed modifications;

(3) notifies the Federal Mediation and Conciliation Service within thirty days after such notice of the existence of a dispute, and simultaneously therewith notifies any State or Territorial agency established to mediate and conciliate disputes within the State or Territory where the dispute occurred, provided no agreement has been reached by that time; and

(4) continues in full force and effect, without resorting to strike or lock-out, all the terms and conditions of the existing contract for a period of sixty days after such notice is given or until the expiration date of such contract, whichever occurs later:

The duties imposed upon employers, employees and labor organizations by paragraphs (2), (3), and (4) shall become inapplicable upon an intervening certification of the Board, under which the labor organization or individual, which is a party to the contract, has been superseded as or ceased to be the representative of the employees subject to the provisions of section 9 (a), and the duties so imposed shall not be construed as requiring either party to discuss or agree to any modification of the terms and conditions contained in a contract for a fixed period, if such modification is to become effective before such terms and conditions can be reopened under the provisions of the contract. Any employee who engages in a strike within the sixty-day period specified in this subsection shall lose his status as an employee of the employer engaged in the particular labor dispute, for the purposes of sections 8, 9, and 10 of this Act, as amended, but such loss of status for such employee shall terminate if and when he is reemployed by such employer.

(e) It shall be an unfair labor practice for any labor organization and any employer to enter into any contract or agreement, express or implied, whereby such employer ceases or refrains or agrees to cease or refrain from handling, using, selling, transporting or otherwise dealing in any of the products of any other employer, or to cease doing business with any other person, and any contract or agreement entered into heretofore or hereafter containing such an agreement shall be to such extent unenforcible and void: *Provided,* That nothing in this subsection (e) shall apply to an agreement between a labor organization and an employer in the construction industry relating to the contracting or subcontracting of work to be done at the site of the construction, alteration, painting, or repair of a buldiing, structure, or other work: Provided further. That for the purposes of this subsection (e) and section 8 (b) (4) (B) the terms "any employer," "any person engaged in commerce or an industry affecting commerce," and "any person" when used in relation to the terms "any other producer, processor, or manufacturer," "any other employer," or "any other person" shall not include persons in the relation of a jobber, manufacturer, contractor, or subcontractor working on the goods or premises of the jobber or manufacturer or performing parts of an integrated process of production in the apparel and clothing industry: *Provided further,* That nothing in this Act shall prohibit the enforcement of any agreement which is within the foregoing exception.

(f) It shall not be an unfair labor practice under subsections (a) and (b) of this section for an employer engaged primarily in the building and construction industry to make an agreement covering employees engaged (or who, upon their employment, will be engaged) in the building and construction industry with a labor organization of which building and construction employees are members (not established, maintained, or assisted by any action defined in section 8 (a) of this Act as an unfair labor practice) because (1) the majority status of such labor organization has not been established under the provisions of section 9 of this Act prior to the making of such agreement, or (2) such agreement requires as a condition of employment, membership in such labor organization after the seventh day following the beginning of such employment or the effective date of the agreement, whichever is later, or (3) such agreement requires the employer to notify such labor organization of opportunities for employment with such employer, or gives such labor organization an opportunity to refer qualified applicants for such employment, or (4) such agreement specifies minimum training or experience qualifications for employment or provides for priority in opportunities for employment based upon length of service with such employer, in the industry or in the particular geographic area: *Provided,* That nothing in this subsection shall set aside the final proviso to section 8 (a) (3) of this Act: *Provided further,* That any agreement which would be invalid but for clause (1) of this subsection, shall not be a bar to a petition filed pursuant to section 9 (c) (or 9 (e) .

Representatives and Elections

Sec. 9 (a) Representatives designated or selected for the purposes of collective bargaining by the majority of the employees in a unit appropriate for such purposes, shall be the exclusive representatives of all the employees in such unit for the purposes of collective bargaining in respect to rates of pay, wages, hours of employment, or other conditions of employment: *Provided,* That any individual employee or a group of employees shall have the right at any time to present grievances to their employer and to have such grievances adjusted, without the intervention of the bargaining representative, as long as the adjustment is not inconsistent with the terms of a collective-bargaining contract or agreement then in effect: *Provided further,* That the bargaining representative has been given opportunity to be present at such adjustment.

(b) The Board shall decide in each case whether, in order to assure to employees the fullest freedom in exercising the rights guaranteed by this Act, the unit appropriate for the purposes of collective bargaining shall be the employer unit, craft unit, plant unit, or subdivision thereof: *Provided,* That the Board shall not (1) decide that any unit is appropriate for such purposes if such unit includes both professional employees and employees who are not professional employees unless a majority of such professional employees vote for inclusion in such unit; or (2) decide that any craft unit is inappropriate for such purposes on the ground that a different unit has been established by a prior Board determination, unless a majority of the employees in the proposed craft unit vote against separate representation or (3) decide that any unit is appropriate for such purposes if it includes, together with other employees, any individual employed as a guard to enforce against employees and other persons rules to protect property of the employer or to protect the safety of persons on the employer's premises; but no labor organization shall be certified as the representative of employees in a bargaining unit of guards if such organization admits to membership, or is affiliated directly or indirectly with an organization which admits to membership, employees other than guard⸱

(c) (1) Whenever a petition shall have been filed, in accordance with such regulations as may be prescribed by the Board—

(A) by an employee or group of employees or any individual or labor organization acting in their behalf alleging that a substantial number of employees (i) wish to be represented for collective bargaining and that their employer declines to recognize their representative as the representative defined in section 9 (a), or (ii) assert that the individual or labor organization, which has been certified or is being currently recognized by their employer as the bargaining representative, is no longer a representative as defined in section 9 (a) ; or

(B) by an employer, alleging that one or more individuals or labor orgnizations have presented to him a claim to be recognized as the representative defined in section 9 (a) ;

the Board shall investigate such petition and if it has reasonable cause to believe that a question of representation affecting commerce exists shall provide for an appropriate hearing upon due notice. Such hearing may be conducted by an officer or employee of the regional office, who shall not make any recommendations with respect thereto. If the Board finds upon the record of such hearing that such a question of representation exists, it shall direct an election by secret ballot and shall certify the results thereof.

(2) In determining whether or not a question of representation affecting commerce exists, the same regulations and

rules of decision shall apply irrespective of the identity of the persons filing the petition or the kind of relief sought and in no case shall the Board deny a labor organization a place on the ballot by reason of an order with respect to such labor organization or its predecessor not issued in conformity with section 10 (c).

(3) No election shall be directed in any bargaining unit or any subdivision within which, in the preceding twelve-month period, a valid election shall have been held. Employees engaged in an economic strike who are not entitled to reinstatement shall be eligible to vote under such regulations as the Board shall find are consistent with the purposes and provisions of this Act in any election conducted within twelve months after the commencement of the strike. In any election where none of the choices on the ballot receives a majority, a run-off shall be conducted, the ballot providing for a selection between the two choices receiving the largest and second largest number of valid votes cast in the election.

(4) Nothing in this section shall be construed to prohibit the waiving of hearings by stipulation for the purpose of a consent election in conformity with regulations and rules of decision of the Board.

(5) In determining whether a unit is appropriate for the purposes specified in subsection (b) the extent to which the employees have organized shall not be controlling.

(d) Whenever an order of the Board made pursuant to section 10 (c) is based in whole or in part upon facts certified following an investigation pursuant to subsection (c) of this section and there is a petition for the enforcement or review of such order, such certification and the record of such investigation shall be included in the transcript of the entire record required to be filed under section 10 (e) or 10 (f), and thereupon the decree of the court enforcing, modifying, or setting aside in whole or in part the order of the Board shall be made and entered upon the pleadings, testimony, and proceedings set forth in such transcript.

(e) (1) Upon the filing with the Board, by 30 per centum or more of the employees in a bargaining unit covered by an agreement between their employer and a labor organization made pursuant to section 8 (a) (3), of a petition alleging the desire that such authority be rescinded, the Board shall take a secret ballot of the employees in such unit and certify the results thereof to such labor organization and to the employer.

(2) No election shall be conducted pursuant to this subsection in any bargaining unit or any subdivision within which, in the preceding twelve-month period, a valid election shall have been held.

Prevention of Unfair Labor Practices

Sec. 10. (a) The Board is empowered, as hereinafter provided, to prevent any person from engaging in any unfair labor practice (listed in section 8) affecting commerce. This power shall not be affected by any other means of adjustment or prevention that has been or may be established by agreement, law, or otherwise: *Provided,* That the Board is empowered by agreement with any agency of any State or Territory to cede to such agency jurisdiction over any cases in any industry (other than mining, manufacturing, communications, and transportation except where predominantly local in character) even though such cases may involve labor disputes affecting commerce, unless the provision of the State or Territorial statute applicable to the determination of such cases by such agency is inconsistent with the corresponding provision of this Act or has received a construction inconsistent therewith.

(b) Whenever it is charged that any person has engaged in or is engaging in any such unfair labor practice, the Board, or any agent or agency designated by the Board for such purposes, shall have power to issue and cause to be served upon such person a complaint stating the charges in that respect, and containing a notice of hearing before the Board or a member thereof, or before a designated agent or agency, at a place therein fixed, not less than five days after the serving of said complaint: *Provided,* That no complaint shall issue based upon any unfair labor practice occurring more than six months prior to the filing of the charge with the Board and the service of a copy thereof upon the person against whom such charge is made, unless the person aggrieved thereby was prevented from filing such charge by reason of service in the armed forces, in which event the six-month period shall be computed from the day of his discharge. Any such complaint may be amended by the member, agent, or agency conducting the hearing or the Board in its discretion at any time prior to the issuance of an order based thereon. The person so complained of shall have the right to file an answer to the original or amended complaint and to appear in person or otherwise and give testimony at the place and time fixed in the complaint. In the discretion of the member, agent, or agency conducting the hearing or the Board, any other person may be allowed to intervene in the said proceeding and to present testimony. Any such proceeding shall, so far as practicable, be conducted in accordance with the rules of evidence applicable in the district courts of the United States under the rules of civil procedure for the district courts of the United States, adopted by the Supreme Court of the United States pursuant to the Act of June 19, 1934 (U.S.C., title 28, secs. 723-B, 723-C).

(c) The testimony taken by such member, agent, or agency or the Board shall be reduced to writing and filed with the Board. Thereafter, in its discretion, the Board upon notice may take further testimony or hear argument. If upon the preponderance of the testimony taken the Board shall be of the opinion that any person named in the complaint has engaged in or is engaging in any such unfair labor practice, then the Board shall state its findings of fact and shall issue and cause to be served on such person an order requiring such person to cease and desist from such unfair labor practice, and to take such affirmative action including reinstatement of employees with or without back pay, as will effectuate the policies of this Act: *Provided*, That where an order directs reinstatement of an employee, back pay may be required of the employer or labor organization, as the case may be, responsible for the discrimination suffered by him: *And provided further*, That in determining whether a complaint shall issue alleging a violation of section 8 (a) (1) or section 8 (a) (2), and in deciding such cases, the same regulations and rules of decision shall apply irrespective of whether or not the labor organization affected is affiliated with a labor organization national or international in scope. Such order may further require such person to make reports from time to time showing the extent to which it has complied with the order. If upon the preponderance of the testimony taken the Board shall not be of the opinion that the person named in the complaint has engaged in or is engaging in any such unfair labor practice, then the Board shall state its findings of fact and shall issue an order dismissing the said complaint. No order of the Board shall require the reinstatement of any individual as an employee who has been suspended or discharged, or the payment to him of any back pay, if such individual was suspended or discharged for cause. In case the evidence is presented before a member of the Board, or before an examiner or examiners thereof, such member, or such examiner or examiners, as the case may be, shall issue and cause to be served on the parties to the proceedings a proposed report, together with a recommended order, which shall be filed with the Board, and if no exceptions are filed within twenty days after service thereof upon such parties, or within such further period as the Board may authorize, such recommended order shall become the order of the Board and become effective as therein prescribed.

(d) Until the record in a case shall have been filed in a court, as hereinafter provided, the Board may at any time upon reasonable notice and in such manner as it shall deem proper, modify or set aside, in whole or in part, any finding or order made or issued by it.

(e) The Board shall have power to petition any court of appeals of the United States, or if all the courts of appeals to which application may be made are in vacation, any district court of the United States, within any circuit or district, respectively, wherein the unfair labor practice in question occurred or wherein such person resides or transacts business, for the enforcement of such order and for appropriate temporary relief or restraining order, and shall file in the court the record in the proceedings, as provided in section 2112 of title 28, United States Code. Upon the filing of such petition, the court shall cause notice thereof to be served upon such person, and thereupon shall have jurisdiction of the proceeding and of the question determined therein, and shall have power to grant such temporary relief or restraining order as it deems just and proper, and to make and enter a decree enforcing, modifying, and enforcing as so modified, or setting aside in whole or in part the order of the Board. No objection that has not been urged before the Board, its member, agent, or agency, shall be considered by the court, unless the failure or neglect to urge such objection shall be excused because of extraordinary circumstances. The findings of the Board with respect to questions of fact if supported by substantial evidence on the record considered as a whole shall be conclusive. If either party shall apply to the court for leave to adduce additional evidence and shall show to the satisfaction of the court that such additional evidence is material and that there were reasonable grounds for the failure to adduce such evidence in the hearing before the Board, its member, agent, or agency, the court may order such additional evidence to be taken before the Board, its member, agent, or agency, and to be made a part of the record. The Board may modify its findings as to the facts, or make new findings, by reason of additional evidence so taken and filed, and it shall file such modified or new findings, which findings with respect to questions of fact if supported by substantial evidence on the record considered as a whole shall be conclusive, and shall file its recommendations, if any, for the modification or setting aside of its original order. Upon the filing of the record with it the jurisdiction of the court shall be exclusive and its judgment and decree shall be final, except that the same shall be subject to review by the appropriate United States court of appeals if application was made to the district court as hereinabove provided, and by the Supreme Court of the United States upon writ of certiorari or certification as provided in section 1254 of title 28.

(f) Any person aggrieved by a final order of the Board granting or denying in whole or in part the relief sought may obtain a review of such order in any United States court of appeals in the circuit wherein the unfair labor practice in question was alleged to have been engaged in or wherein such person resides or transacts business, or in the United States Court of Appeals for the District of Columbia, by filing in such court a written petition praying that the order of the Board be modified or set aside. A copy of such petition shall be forthwith transmitted by the clerk of the court to the Board, and thereupon the aggrieved party shall file in the court the record in the proceeding, certified by the Board, as provided in section 2112 of title 28, United States Code. Upon the filing of such petition, the court shall proceed in the same manner as in the case of an application by the Board under subsection (e) of this section, and shall have the same jurisdiction to grant to the Board such temporary relief or restraining order as it deems just and proper, and in like manner to make and enter a decree enforcing, modifying, and enforcing as so modified, or setting aside in whole or in part the order of the Board; the findings of the Board with respect to questions of fact if supported by substantial evidence on the record considered as a whole shall in like manner be conclusive.

(g) The commencement of proceedings under subsection (e) or (f) of this section shall not, unless specifically ordered by the court, operate as a stay of the Board's order.

(h) When granting appropriate temporary relief or a restraining order, or making and entering a decree enforcing, modifying, and enforcing as so modified, or setting aside in whole or in part an order of the Board, as provided in this section, the jurisdiction of courts sitting in equity shall not be limited by the Act entitled "An Act to amend the Judicial Code and to define and limit the jurisdiction of courts sitting in equity and for other purposes," approved March 23, 1932 (U.S.C., Supp. VII, title 29, secs. 101-115).

(i) Petitions filed under this Act shall be heard expeditiously, and if possible within ten days after they have been docketed.

(j) The Board shall have power, upon issuance of a complaint as provided in subsection (b) charging that any person has engaged in or is engaging in an unfair labor practice, to petition any United States district court within any district wherein the unfair labor practice in question is alleged to have occurred or wherein such person resides or transacts business, for appropriate temporary relief or restraining order. Upon the filing of any such petition the court shall cause notice thereof to be served upon such person, and thereupon shall have jurisdiction to grant to the Board such temporary relief or restraining order as it deems just and proper.

(k) Whenever it is charged that any person has engaged in an unfair labor practice within the meaning of paragraph (4) (D) of section 8(b), the Board is empowered and directed to hear and determine the dispute out of which such unfair labor practice shall have arisen, unless, within ten days after notice that such charge has been filed, the parties to such dispute submit to the Board satisfactory evidence that they have adjusted, or agreed upon methods for the voluntary adjustment of, the dispute. Upon compliance by the parties to the dispute with the decision of the Board or upon such voluntary adjustment of the dispute, such charge shall be dismissed.

(l) Whenever it is charged that any person has engaged in an unfair labor practice within the meaning of paragraph (4)

(A), (B), or (C) of section 8 (b) or section 8 (e) or section 8 (b) (7), the preliminary investigation of such charge shall be made forthwith and given priority over all other cases except cases of like character in the office where it is filed or to which it is referred. If, after such investigation, the officer or regional attorney to whom the matter may be referred has reasonable cause to believe such charge is true and that a complaint should issue, he shall, on behalf of the Board, petition any United States district court within any district where the unfair labor practice in question has occurred, is alleged to have occurred, or wherein such person resides or transacts business, for appropriate injunctive relief pending the final adjudication of the Board with respect to such matter. Upon the filing of any such petition the district court shall have jurisdiction to grant such injunctive relief or temporary restraining order as it deems just and proper, notwithstanding any other provision of law: *Provided further,* That no temporary restraining order shall be issued without notice unless a petition alleges that substantial and irreparable injury to the charging party will be unavoidable and such temporary restraining order shall be effective for no longer than five days and will become void at the expiration of such period: *Provided further,* that such officer or regional attorney shall not apply for any restraining order under section 8 (b) (7) if a charge against the employer under 8 (a) (2) has been filed and after the preliminary investigation, he has reasonable cause to believe that such charge is true and that a complaint should issue. Upon filing of any such petition, the courts shall cause notice thereof to be served upon any person involved in the charge and such person, including the charging party, shall be given an opportunity to appear by counsel, and present any relevant testimony: *Provided further,* That for the purposes of this subsection district courts shall be deemed to have jurisdiction of a labor organization (1) in the district in which such organization maintains its principal office, or (2) in any district in which its duly authorized officers or agents are engaged in promoting or protecting the interests of employee members. The service of legal process upon such officer or agent shall constitute service upon the labor organization and make such organization a party to the suit. In situations where such relief is appropriate the procedure specified herein shall apply to charges with respect to section 8 (b) (4) (D).

(m) Whenever it is charged that any person has engaged in an unfair labor practice within the meaning of subsection (a) (3) or (b) (2) of section 8, such charge shall be given priority over all other cases except cases of like character in the office where it is filed or to which it is referred and cases given priority under subsection (1).

Investigatory Powers

Sec. 11. For the purpose of all hearings and investigations, which, in the opinion of the Board, are necessary and proper for the exercise of the powers vested in it by section 9 and section 10—

(1) The Board, or its duly authorized agents or agencies, shall at all reasonable times have access to, for the purpose of examination, and the right to copy any evidence of any person being investigated or proceeded against that relates to any matter under investigation or in question. The Board, or any member thereof, shall upon application of any party to such proceedings, forthwith issue to such party subpenas requiring the attendance and testimony of witnesses or the production of any evidence in such proceeding or investigation requested in such application. Within five days after the service of a subpena on any person requiring the production of any evidence in his possession or under his control, such person may petition the Board to revoke, and the Board shall revoke, such subpena if in its opinion the evidence whose production is required does not relate to any matter under investigation, or any matter in question in such proceedings, or if in its opinion such subpena does not describe with sufficient particularity the evidence whose production is required. Any member of the Board, or any agent or agency designated by the Board for such purposes, may administer oaths and affirmations, examine witnesses, and receive evidence. Such attendance of witnesses and the production of such evidence may be required from any place in the United States or any Territory or possession thereof, at any designated place of hearing.

(2) In case of contumacy or refusal to obey a subpena issued to any person, any district court of the United States or the United States courts of any Territory or possession, within the jurisdiction of which the inquiry is carried on or within the jurisdiction of which said person guilty of contumacy or refusal to obey is found or resides or transacts business, upon application by

the Board shall have jurisdiction to issue to such person an order requiring such person to appear before the Board, its member, agent, or agency, there to produce evidence if so ordered, or there to give testimony touching the matter under investigation or in question; and any failure to obey such order of the court may be punished by said court as a contempt thereof.

(3) No person shall be excused from attending and testifying or from producing books, records, correspondence, documents, or other evidence in obedience to the subpena of the Board, on the ground that the testimony or evidence required of him may tend to incriminate him or subject him to a penalty or forfeiture; but no individual shall be prosecuted or subjected to any penalty or forfeiture for or on account of any transaction, matter, or thing concerning which he is compelled, after having claimed his privilege against self-incrimination, to testify or produce evidence, except that such individual so testifying shall not be exempt from prosecution and punishment for perjury committed in so testifying.

(4) Complaints, orders, and other process and papers of the Board, its member, agent, or agency, may be served either personally or by registered mail or by telegraph or by leaving a copy thereof at the principal office or place of business of the person required to be served. The verified return by the individual so serving the same setting forth the manner of such service shall be proof of the same, and the return post office receipt or telegraph receipt therefor when registered and mailed or telegraphed as aforesaid shall be proof of service of the same. Witnesses summoned before the Board, its member, agent, or agency, shall be paid the same fees and mileage that are paid witnesses in the courts of the United States, and witnesses whose depositions are taken and the persons taking the same shall severally be entitled to the same fees as are paid for like services in the courts of the United States.

(5) All process of any court to which application may be made under this Act may be served in the judicial district wherein the defendant or other person required to be served resides or may be found.

(6) The several departments and agencies of the Government, when directed by the President, shall furnish the Board, upon its request, all records, papers, and information in their possession relating to any matter before the Board.

Sec. 12. Any person who shall willfully resist, prevent, impede, or interfere with any member of the Board or any of its agents or agencies in the performance of duties pursuant to this Act shall be punished by a fine of not more than $5,000 or by imprisonment for not more than one year, or both.

Limitations

Sec. 13. Nothing in this Act, except as specifically provided for herein, shall be construed so as either to interfere with or impede or diminish in any way the right to strike, or to affect the limitations or qualifications on that right.

Sec. 14. (a) Nothing herein shall prohibit any individual employed as a supervisor from becoming or remaining a member of a labor organization, but no employer subject to this Act shall be compelled to deem individuals defined herein as supervisors as employees for the purpose of any law, either national or local, relating to collective bargaining.

(b) Nothing in this Act shall be construed as authorizing the execution or application of agreements requiring membership in a labor organization as a condition of employment in any State or Territory in which such execution or application is prohibited by State or Territorial law.

Federal-State Jurisdiction

(c) (1) The Board, in its discretion, may, by rule of decision or by published rules adopted pursuant to the Administrative Procedure Act, decline to assert jurisdiction over any labor dispute involving any class or category of employers, where, in the opinion of the Board, the effect of such labor dispute on commerce is not sufficiently substantial to warrant the exercise of its jurisdiction: *Provided,* That the Board shall not decline to assert jurisdiction over any labor dispute over which it would assert jurisdiction under the standards prevailing upon August 1, 1959.

(2) Nothing in this Act shall be deemed to prevent or bar any agency or the courts of any State or Territory (including the Commonwealth of Puerto Rico, Guam, and the Virgin Islands), from assuming and asserting jurisdiction over labor disputes over which the Board declines, pursuant to paragraph (1) of this subsection, to assert jurisdiction.

Sec. 15. Wherever the application of the provisions of section 272 of chapter 10 of the Act entitled "An Act to establish a uniform system of bankruptcy throughout the United States," approved July 1, 1898, and Acts amendatory thereof and supplementary thereto (U.S.C., title 11, sec. 672), conflicts with the application of the provisions of this Act, this Act shall prevail: *Provided,* That in any situation where the provisions of this Act cannot be validly enforced, the provisions of such other Acts shall remain in full force and effect.

Sec. 16. If any provision of this Act, or the application of such provision to any person or circumstances, shall be held invalid, the remainder of this Act, or the application of such a provision to persons or circumstances other than those as to which it is held invalid, shall not be affected thereby.

Sec. 17. This Act may be cited as the "National Labor Relations Act."

Sec. 18. No petition entertained, no investigation made, no election held, and no certification issued by the National Labor Relations Board, under any of the provisions of section 9 of the National Labor Relations Act, as amended, shall be invalid by reason of the failure of the Congress of Industrial Organizations to have complied with the requirements of section 9 (f), (g), or (h) of the aforesaid Act prior to December 22, 1949, or by reason of the failure of the American Federation of Labor to have complied with the provisions of section 9 (f), (g), or (h) of the aforesaid Act prior to November 7, 1947: *Provided,* That no liability shall be imposed under any provision of this Act upon any person for failure to honor any election or certificate referred to above, prior to the effective date of this amendment; *Provided, however,* That this proviso shall not have the effect of setting aside or in any way affecting judgments or decrees heretofore entered under section 10 (e) or (f) and which have become final.

TEXT OF
LABOR MANAGEMENT RELATIONS ACT

Pub. L. No. 101, 80th Cong., 1st Sess., 1947,
61 Stat. 136, as amended by Pub. L. No. 257,
86th Cong., 1st Sess., 1959; 29 U.S.C. §§ 141-67,
171-97, F.C.A 29 §§ 141-67, 171-97

AN ACT

To amend the National Labor Relations Act, to provide addi-
tional facilities for the mediation of labor disputes affecting
commerce, to equalize legal responsibilities of labor organiza-
tions and employers, and for other purposes.
Be it enacted by the Senate and House of Representatives of the
United States of America in Congress assembled,
Short Title and Declaration of Policy

Section 1. (a) This Act may be cited as the "Labor Management Relations Act, 1947."

(b) Industrial strife which interferes with the normal flow
of commerce and with the full production of articles and commodities for commerce, can be avoided or substantially minimized if employers, employees, and labor organizations each recognize under law one another's legitimate rights in their relations with each other, and above all recognize under law that
neither party has any right in its relations with any other to
engage in acts or practices which jeopardize the public health,
safety, or interest.

It is the purpose and policy of this Act, in order to promote the
full flow of commerce, to prescribe the legitimate rights of both
employees and employers in their relations affecting commerce,
to provide orderly and peaceful procedures for preventing the
interference by either with the legitimate rights of the other, to
protect the rights of individual employees in their relations

with labor organizations whose activities affect commerce, to define and proscribe practices on the part of labor and management which affect commerce and are inimical to the general welfare, and to protect the rights of the public in connection with labor disputes affecting commerce.

Title I

Amendment of National Labor Relations Act

Sec. 101. The National Labor Relations Act is hereby amended to read as follows:

(The text of the National Labor Relations Act as amended appears in Appendix A, *supra*.)

Effective Date of Certain Changes

Sec. 102. No provision of this title shall be deemed to make an unfair labor practice any act which was performed prior to the date of the enactment of this Act which did not constitute an unfair labor practice prior thereto, and the provisions of section 8 (a) (3) and section 8 (b) (2) of the National Labor Relations Act as amended by this title shall not make an unfair labor practice the performance of any obligation under a collective-bargaining agreement entered into prior to the date of the enactment of this Act, or (in the case of an agreement for a period of not more than one year) entered into on or after such date of enactment, but prior to the effective date of this title, if the performance of such obligation would not have constituted an unfair labor practice under section 8 (3) of the National Labor Relations Act prior to the effective date of this title, unless such agreement was renewed or extended subsequent thereto.

Sec. 103. No provisions of this title shall affect any certification of representatives or any determination as to the appropriate collective-bargaining unit, which was made under section 9 of the National Labor Relations Act prior to the effective date of this title until one year after the date of such certification or if, in respect of any such certification, a collective-bargaining contract was entered into prior to the effective date of this title, until the end of the contract period or until one year after such date, whichever first occurs.

Sec. 104. The amendments made by this title shall take effect sixty days after the date of the enactment of this Act except that the authority of the President to appoint certain officers conferred upon him by section 3 of the National Labor Relations Act as amended by this title may be exercised forthwith.

Title II

Conciliation of Labor Disputes in Industries Affecting Commerce; National Emergencies

Sec. 201. It is the policy of the United States that—

(a) sound and stable industrial peace and the advancement of the general welfare, health, and safety of the Nation and of the best interests of employers and employees can most satisfactorily be secured by the settlement of issues between employers and employees through the processes of conference and collective bargaining between employers and the representatives of their employees;

(b) the settlement of issues between employers and employees through collecctive bargaining may be advanced by making available full and adequate governmental facilities for conciliation, mediation, and voluntary arbitration to aid and encourage employers and the representatives of their employees to reach and maintain agreements concerning rates of pay, hours, and working conditions, and to make all reasonable efforts to settle their differences by mutual agreement reached through conferences and collective bargaining or by such methods as may be provided for in any applicable agreement for the settlement of disputes; and

(c) certain controversies which arise between parties to collective-bargaining agreements may be avoided or minimized by making available full and adequate governmental facilities for furnishing assistance to employers and the representatives of their employees in formulating for inclusion within such agreements provision for adequate notice of any proposed changes in the terms of such agreements, for the final adjustment of grievances or questions regarding the application or interpretation of such agreements, and other provisions designed to prevent the subsequent arising of such controversies.

Sec. 202. (a) There is hereby created an independent agency to be known as the Federal Mediation and Conciliation Service (herein referred to as the "Service," except that for sixty days after the date of the enactment of this Act such term shall refer to the Conciliation Service of the Department of Labor).

The Service shall be under the direction of a Federal Mediation and Conciliation Director (hereinafter referred to as the "Director"), who shall be appointed by the President by and with the advice and consent of the Senate. The Director shall receive compensation at the rate of $12,000 per annum. The Director shall not engage in any other business, vocation, or employment.

(b) The Director is authorized, subject to the civil-service laws, to appoint such clerical and other personnel as may be necessary for the execution of the functions of the Service, and shall fix their compensation in accordance with the Classification Act of 1923, as amended, and may, without regard to the provisions of the civil-service laws and the Classification Act of 1923, as amended, appoint and fix the compensation of such conciliators and mediators as may be necessary to carry out the functions of the Service. The Director is authorized to make such expenditures for supplies, facilities, and services as he deems necessary. Such expenditures shall be allowed and paid upon presentation of itemized vouchers therefor approved by the Director or by any employee designated by him for that purpose.

(c) The principal office of the Service shall be in the District of Columbia, but the Director may establish regional offices convenient to localities in which labor controversies are likely to arise. The Director may by order, subject to revocation at any time, delegate any authority and discretion conferred upon him by this Act to any regional director, or other officer or employee of the Service. The Director may establish suitable procedures for cooperation with State and local mediation agencies. The Director shall make an annual report in writing to Congress at the end of the fiscal year.

(d) All mediation and conciliation functions of the Secretary of Labor or the United States Conciliation Service under section 8 of the Act entitled "An Act to create a Department of Labor," approved March 4, 1913 (U.S.C., title 29, sec. 51), and all functions of the United States Conciliation Service under any other law are hereby transferred to the Federal Mediation and Conciliation Service, together with the personnel and records of the United States Conciliation Service. Such transfer shall take effect the sixtieth day after the date of enactment of this Act. Such transfer shall not affect any proceedings pending before the United States Conciliation Service or any certification, order, rule, or regulation theretofore made by it or by the Secretary of Labor. The Director and the Service shall not be subject in any way to the jurisdiction or authority of the Secretary of Labor or any official or division of the Department of Labor.

Functions of the Service

Sec. 203. (a) It shall be the duty of the Service, in order to prevent or minimize interruptions of the free flow of commerce growing out of labor disputes, to assist parties to labor disputes in industries affecting commerce to settle such disputes through conciliation and mediation.

(b) The Service may proffer its services in any labor dispute in any industry affecting commerce, either upon its own motion or upon the request of one or more of the parties to the dispute, whenever in its judgment such dispute threatens to cause a substantial interruption of commerce. The Director and the Service are directed to avoid attempting to mediate disputes which would have only a minor effect on interstate commerce if State or other conciliation services are available to the parties. Whenever the Service does proffer its services in any disputes, it shall be the duty of the Service promptly to put itself in communication with the parties and to use its best efforts, by mediation and conciliation, to bring them to agreement.

(c) If the Director is not able to bring the parties to agreement by conciliation within a reasonable time, he shall seek to induce the parties voluntarily to seek other means of settling the dispute without resort to strike, lock-out, or other coercion, including submission to the employees in the bargaining unit of the employer's last offer of settlement for approval or rejection in a secret ballot. The failure or refusal of either party to agree to any procedure suggested by the Director shall not be deemed a violation of any duty or obligation imposed by this Act.

(d) Final adjustment by a method agreed upon by the parties is hereby declared to be the desirable method for settlement of grievance disputes arising over the application or interpretation of an existing collective-bargaining agreement. The Service is directed to make its conciliation and mediation services available in the settlement of such grievance disputes only as a last resort and in exceptional cases.

Sec. 204. (a) In order to prevent or minimize interruptions of the free flow of commerce growing out of labor disputes, employers and employees and their representatives, in any industry affecting commerce, shall—

(1) exert every reasonable effort to make and maintain agreements concerning rates of pay, hours, and working conditions, including provision for adequate notice of any proposed change in the terms of such agreements;

(2) whenever a dispute arises over the terms or application of a collective-bargaining agreement and a conference is requested by a party or prospective party thereto, arrange promptly for such a conference to be held and endeavor in such conference to settle such dispute expeditiously; and

(3) in case such dispute is not settled by conference, participate fully and promptly in such meetings as may be undertaken by the Service under this Act for the purpose of aiding in a settlement of the dispute.

Sec. 205. (a) There is hereby created a National Labor-Management Panel which shall be composed of twelve members appointed by the President, six of whom shall be selected from among persons outstanding in the field of management and six of whom shall be selected from among persons outstanding in the field of labor. Each member shall hold office for a term of three years, except that any member appointed to fill a vacancy occurring prior to the expiration of the term for which his predecessor was appointed shall be appointed for the remainder of such term, and the terms of office of the members first taking office shall expire, as designated by the President at the time of appointment, four at the end of the first year, four at the end of the second year, and four at the end of the third year after the date of appointment. Members of the panel, when serving on business of the panel, shall be paid compensation at the rate of $25 per day, and shall also be entitled to receive an allowance for actual and necessary travel and subsistence expenses while so serving away from their places of residence.

(b) It shall be the duty of the panel, at the request of the Director, to advise in the avoidance of industrial controversies and the manner in which mediation and voluntary adjustment shall be administered, particularly with reference to controversies affecting the general welfare of the country.

National Emergencies

Sec. 206. Whenever in the opinion of the President of the United States, a threatened or actual strike or lockout affecting an entire industry or a substantial part thereof engaged in trade, commerce, transportation, transmission, or communication among the several States or with foreign nations, or engaged in the production of goods for commerce, will, if permitted to occur or to continue, imperil the national health or safety, he may appoint a board of inquiry to inquire into the issues involved in the dispute and to make a written report to him within such time as he shall prescribe. Such report shall include a statement of the facts with respect to the dispute, including each party's statement of its position but shall not contain any recommendations. The President shall file a copy of such report with the Service and shall make its contents available to the public.

Sec. 207. (a) A board of inquiry shall be composed of a chairman and such other members as the President shall determine, and shall have power to sit and act in any place within the United States and to conduct such hearings either in public or in private, as it may deem necessary or proper, to ascertain the facts with respect to the causes and circumstances of the dispute.

(b) Members of a board of inquiry shall receive compensation at the rate of $50 for each day actually spent by them in the work of the board, together with necessary travel and subsistence expenses.

(c) For the purpose of any hearing or inquiry conducted by any board appointed under this title, the provisions of sections 9 and 10 (relating to the attendance of witnesses and the production of books, papers, and documents) of the Federal Trade Commission Act of September 16, 1914, as amended (U.S.C. 19, title 15, secs. 49 and 50, as amended), are hereby made applicable to the powers and duties of such board.

Sec. 208. (a) Upon receiving a report from a board of inquiry the President may direct the Attorney General to petition any district court of the United States having jurisdiction of the parties to enjoin such strike or lock-out or the continuing thereof, and if the court finds that such threatened or actual strike or lockout—

(i) affects an entire industry or a substantial part thereof engaged in trade, commerce, transportation, transmission, or communication among the several States or with foreign nations, or engaged in the production of goods for commerce; and

(ii) if permitted to occur or to continue, will imperil the national health or safety, it shall have jurisdiction to enjoin any such strike or lock-out, or the continuing thereof, and to make such other orders as may be appropriate.

(b) In any case, the provisions of the Act of March 23, 1932, entitled "An Act to amend the Judicial Code and to define and limit the jurisdiction of courts sitting in equity, and for other purposes," shall not be applicable.

(c) The order or orders of the court shall be subject to review by the appropriate court of appeals and by the Supreme Court upon writ of certiorari or certification as provided in sections 239 and 240 of the Judicial Code, as amended (U.S.C., title 29, secs. 346 and 347).

Sec. 209. (a) Whenever a district court has issued an order under section 208 enjoining acts or practices which imperil or threaten to imperil the national health or safety, it shall be the duty of the parties to the labor dispute giving rise to such order to make every effort to adjust and settle their differences, with the assistance of the Service created by this Act. Neither party shall be under any duty to accept, in whole or in part, any proposal of settlement made by the Service.

(b) Upon the issuance of such order, the President shall reconvene the board of inquiry which has previously reported with respect to the dispute. At the end of a sixty-day period (unless the dispute has been settled by that time), the board of inquiry shall report to the President the current position of the parties and the efforts which have been made for settlement, and shall include a statement by each party of its position and a statement of the employer's last offer of settlement. The President shall make such report available to the public. The National Labor Relations Board, within the succeeding fifteen days, shall take a secret ballot of the employees of each employer involved in the dispute on the question of whether they wish to accept the final offer of settlement made by their employer as stated by him and shall certify the results thereof to the Attorney General within five days thereafter.

Sec. 210. Upon the certification of the results of such ballot or upon a settlement being reached, whichever happens sooner, the Attorney General shall move the court to discharge the injunction, which motion shall then be granted and the injunction discharged. When such motion is granted, the President shall submit to the Congress a full and comprehensive report of the proceedings, including the findings of the board of inquiry and the ballot taken by the National Labor Relations Board, together with such recommendations as he may see fit to make for consideration and appropriate action.

Compilation of Collective Bargaining Agreements, etc.

Sec. 211. (a) For the guidance and information of interested representatives of employers, employees, and the general public, the Bureau of Labor Statistics of the Department of Labor shall maintain a file of copies of all available collective bargaining agreements and other available agreements and actions thereunder settling or adjusting labor disputes. Such file shall be open to inspection under appropriate conditions prescribed by the Secretary of Labor, except that no specific information submitted in confidence shall be disclosed.

(b) The Bureau of Labor Statistics in the Department of Labor is authorized to furnish upon request of the Service, or employers, employees, or their representatives, all available data and factual information which may aid in the settlement of any labor dispute, except that no specific information submitted in confidence shall be disclosed.

Exemption of Railway Labor Act

Sec. 212. The provisions of this title shall not be applicable with respect to any matter which is subject to the provisions of the Railway Labor Act, as amended from time to time.

Title III

Suits by and Against Labor Organizations

Sec. 301. (a) Suits for violation of contracts between an employer and a labor organization representing employees in an industry affecting commerce as defined in this Act, or between any such labor organizations, may be brought in any district court of the United States having jurisdiction of the parties, without respect to the amount in controversy or without regard to the citizenship of the parties.

(b) Any labor organization which represents employees in an industry affecting commerce as defined in this Act and any employer whose activities affect commerce as defined in this Act shall be bound by the acts of its agents. Any such labor organization may sue or be sued as an entity and in behalf of the employees whom it represents in the courts of the United States. Any money judgment against a labor organization in a district court of the United States shall be enforceable only against the organization as an entity and against its assets, and shall not be enforceable against any individual member or his assets.

(c) For the purposes of actions and proceedings by or against labor organizations in the district courts of the United States, district courts shall be deemed to have jurisdiction of a labor organization (1) in the district in which such organization maintains its principal office, or (2) in any district in which its duly authorized officers or agents are engaged in representing or acting for employee members.

(d) The service of summons, subpena, or other legal process of any court of the United States upon an officer or agent of a labor organization, in his capacity as such, shall constitute service upon the labor organization.

(e) For the purposes of this section in determining whether any person is acting as an "agent" of another person so as to make such other person responsible for his acts, the question of whether the specific acts performed were actually authorized or subsequently ratified shall not be controlling.

Restrictions on Payments to Employee Representatives

Sec. 302. (a) It shall be unlawful for any employer or association of employers or any person who acts as a labor relations expert, adviser, or consultant to an employer or who acts in the interest of an employer to pay, lend, or deliver, or agree to pay, lend, or deliver, any money or other thing of value—

(1) to any representative of any of his employees who are employed in an industry affecting commerce; or

(2) to any labor organization or any officer or employee thereof, which represents, seeks to represent, or would admit to membership, any of the employees of such employer who are employed in an industry affecting commerce; or

(3) to any employee or group or committee of employees of such employer employed in an industry affecting commerce

in excess of their normal compensation for the purpose of causing such employee or group or committee directly or indirectly to influence any other employees in the exercise of the right to organize and bargain collectively through representatives of their own choosing; or

(4) to any officer or employee of a labor organization engaged in an industry affecting commerce with intent to influence him in respect to any of his actions, decisions, or duties as a representative of employees or as such officer or employee of such labor organization.

(b) (1) It shall be unlawful for any person to request, demand, receive, or accept, or agree to receive or accept, any payment, loan, or delivery of any money or other thing of value prohibited by subsection (a).

(2) It shall be unlawful for any labor organization, or for any person acting as an officer, agent, representative, or employee of such labor organization to demand or accept from the operator of any motor vehicle (as defined in part II of the Interstate Commerce Act) employed in the transportation of property in commerce, or the employer of any such operator, any money or other thing of value payable to such organization or to an officer, agent, representative or employee thereof as a fee or charge for the unloading, or in connection with the unloading, of the cargo of such vehicle: *Provided,* That nothing in this paragraph shall be construed to make unlawful any payment by an employer to any of his employees as compensation for their services as employees.

(c) The provisions of this section shall not be applicable (1) in respect to any money or other thing of value payable by an employer to any of his employees whose established duties include acting openly for such employer in matters of labor relations or personnel administration or to any representative of his employees, or to any officer or employee of a labor organization, who is also an employee or former employee of such employer, as compensation for, or by reason of, his service as an employee of such employer; (2) with respect to the payment or delivery of any money or other thing of value in satisfaction of a judgment of any court or a decision or award of an arbitrator or impartial chairman or in compromise, adjustment, settlement, or release of any claim, complaint, grievance, or dispute in the absence of fraud or duress; (3) with respect to the sale or purchase of an article or commodity at the prevailing market price in the regular course of business; (4) with respect to money deducted from the wages of employees in payment of membership dues in a labor organization: *Provided,* That the employer has received from each employee, on whose account such deductions are made, a written assignment which shall not be irrevocable for a period of more than one year, or beyond the termination date of the applicable collective agreement, whichever occurs sooner; (5) with respect to money or other thing of value paid to a trust fund established by such representative, for the sole and exclusive benefit of the employees of such employer, and their families and dependents (or of such employees, families, and dependents jointly with the employees of other employers making similar payments, and their families and dependents) : *Provided,* That (A) such payments are held in trust for the purpose of paying, either from principal or income or both, for the benefit of employees, their families and dependents, for medical or hospital care, pensions on retirement or death of employees, compensation for injuries or illness resulting from occupational activity or insurance to provide any of the foregoing, or unemployment benefits or life insurance, disability and sickness insurance, or accident insurance; (B) the detailed basis on which such payments are to be made is specified in a written agreement with the employer, and employees and employers are equally represented in the administration of such fund, together with such neutral persons as the representatives of the employers and the representatives of employees may agree upon and in the event the employer and employee groups deadlock on the administration of such fund and there are no neutral persons empowered to break such deadlock, such agreement provides that the two groups shall agree on an impartial umpire to decide such dispute, or in event of their failure to agree within a reasonable length of time, an impartial umpire to decide such dispute shall, on petition of either group, be appointed by the district court of the United States for the district where the trust fund has its principal office, and shall also contain provisions for an annual audit of the trust fund, a statement of the results of which shall be available for inspection by interested persons at the principal office of the trust fund and at such other places as may be designated in such written agreement; and (C) such payments as are intended to be used for the purpose of providing pensions or annuities for employees are made to a separate trust which provides that the funds held therein cannot be used for any purpose other than paying such pensions or annuities; or (6) with respect to money or other thing of value paid by any employer to a trust fund established by such representative for the purpose of pooled vacation, holiday, severance or similar benefits, or defraying costs of apprenticeship or other training programs: *Provided,* That the requirements of clause (B) of the proviso to clause (5) of this subsection shall apply to such trust funds; or (7) with respect to money or other thing of value paid by any employer to a pooled or individual trust fund established by such representative for the purpose of (A) scholarships for the benefit of employees, their families, and dependents for study at educational institutions or (B) child care centers for preschool and school age dependents of employees: *Provided,* That no labor organization or employer shall be required to bargain on the establishment of any such trust fund, and refusal to do so shall not constitute an unfair labor practice: *Provided further,* That the requirements of clause (B) of the proviso to clause (5) of this subsection shall apply to such trust funds.

(d) Any person who willfully violates any of the provisions of this section shall, upon conviction thereof, be guilty of a misdemeanor and be subject to a fine of not more than $10,000 or to imprisonment for not more than one year, or both.

(e) The district courts of the United States and the United States courts of the Territories and possessions shall have jurisdiction, for cause shown, and subject to the provisions of section 17 (relating to notice to opposite party) of the Act entitled "An Act to supplement existing laws against unlawful restraints and monopolies, and for other purposes," approved October 15, 1914, as amended (U.S.C., title 28, sec. 381), to restrain violations of this section, without regard to the provisions of sections 6 and 20 of such Act of October 15, 1914, as amended (U.S.C., title 15, sec. 17, and title 29, sec. 52), and the provisions of the Act entitled "An Act to amend the Judicial Code and to define and limit the jurisdiction of courts sitting in equity, and for other purposes," approved March 23, 1932 (U.S.C., title 29, secs. 101-115).

(f) This section shall not apply to any contract in force on the date of enactment of this Act, until the expiration of such contract, or until July 1, 1948, whichever first occurs.

(g) Compliance with the restrictions contained in subsection
(c) (5) (B) upon contributions to trust funds, otherwise lawful, shall not be applicable to contributions to such trust funds
established by collective agreement prior to January 1, 1946,
nor shall subsection (c) (5) (A) be construed as prohibiting contributions to such trust funds if prior to January 1, 1947, such
funds contained provisions for pooled vacation benefits.

Boycotts and Other Unlawful Combinations

Sec. 303 (a) It shall be unlawful, for the purpose of this section only, in an industry or activity affecting commerce, for any
labor organization to engage in any activity or conduct defined as an unfair labor practice in section 8 (b) (4) of the National Labor Relations Act, as amended.

(b) Whoever shall be injured in his business or property by
reason of any violation of subsection (a) may sue therefor in
any district court of the United States subject to the limitations
and provisions of section 301 hereof without respect to the
amount in controversy, or in any other court having jurisdiction of the parties, and shall recover the damages by him sustained and the cost of the suit.

Restriction on Political Contributions

Sec. 304. Section 313 of the Federal Corrupt Practices Act,
1925 (U.S.C., 1940 edition, title 2, sec. 251; Supp. V, title 50,
App., sec. 1509) , as amended, is amended to read as follows:
"Sec. 313. It is unlawful for any national bank, or any corporation organized by authority of any law of Congress, to make a
contribution or expenditure in connection with any election to
any political office, or in connection with any primary election or political convention or caucus held to select candidates
for any political office, or for any corporation whatever, or any
labor organization to make a contribution or expenditure in
connection with any election at which Presidential and Vice
Presidential electors or a Senator or Representative in, or a Delegate or Resident Commissioner to Congress are to be voted for,
or in connection with any primary election or political convention or caucus held to select candidates for any of the foregoing
offices, or for any candidates, political committee, or other person to accept or receive any contribution prohibited by this section. Every corporation or labor organization which makes any

contribution or expenditure in violation of this section shall be fined not more than $5,000; and every officer or director of any corporation, or officer of any labor organization, who consents to any contribution or expenditure by the corporation or labor organization, as the case may be, in violation of this section shall be fined not more than $1,000 or imprisoned for not more than one year, or both. For the purposes of this section 'labor organization' means any organization of any kind, or any agency or employee representation committee or plan, in which employees participate and which exists for the purpose, in whole or in part, of dealing with employers concerning grievances, labor disputes, wages, rates of pay, hours of employment, or conditions of work."

Strikes by Government Employees

Sec. 305. [Repealed by Ch. 690, 69 Stat. 624, effective August 9, 1955. Sec. 305 made it unlawful for government employees to strike and made strikers subject to immediate discharge, forfeiture of civil-service status, and three-year blacklisting for federal employment.]

Title IV

Creation of Joint Committee to Study and Report on Basic Problems Affecting Friendly Labor Relations and Productivity

Sec. 401. There is hereby established a joint congressional committee to be known as the Joint Committee on Labor-Management Relations (hereafter referred to as the committee) , and to be composed of seven Members of the Senate Committee on Labor and Public Welfare, to be appointed by the President pro tempore of the Senate, and seven Members of the House of Representatives Committee on Education and Labor, to be appointed by the Speaker of the House of Representatives. A vacancy in membership of the committee, shall not affect the powers of the remaining members to execute the functions of the committee, and shall be filled in the same manner as the original selection. The committee shall select a chairman and a vice chairman from among its members.

Sec. 402. The committee, acting as a whole or by subcommittee shall conduct a thorough study and investigation of the entire field of labor-management relations, including but not limited to—

(1) the means by which permanent friendly cooperation between employers and employees and stability of labor relations may be secured throughout the United States;

(2) the means by which the individual employee may achieve a greater productivity and higher wages, including plans for guaranteed annual wages, incentive profit-sharing and bonus systems;

(3) the internal organization and administration of labor unions, with special attention to the impact on individuals of collective agreements requiring membership in unions as a condition of employment;

(4) the labor relations policies and practices of employers and associations of employers;

(5) the desirability of welfare funds for the benefit of employees and their relation to the social-security system;

(6) the methods and procedures for best carrying out the collective-bargaining processes, with special attention to the effects of industrywide or regional bargaining upon the national economy;

(7) the administration and operation of existing Federal laws relating to labor relations; and

(8) such other problems and subjects in the field of labor-management relations as the committee deems appropriate.

Sec. 403. The committee shall report to the Senate and the House of Representatives not later than March 15, 1948, the results of its study and investigation, together with such recommendations as to necessary legislation and such other recommendations as it may deem advisable, and shall make its final report not later than January 2, 1949,

Sec. 404. The committee shall have the power, without regard to the civil-service laws and the Classification Act of 1923, as amended, to employ and fix the compensation of such officers, experts, and employees as it deems necessary for the performance of its duties, including consultants who shall receive compensation at a rate not to exceed $35 for each day actually spent by them in the work of the committee, together with their necessary travel and subsistence expenses. The committee is further authorized with the consent of the head of the department or agency concerned, to utilize the services, information, facilities, and personnel of all agencies in the executive branch of the Government and may request the governments of the several States, representatives of business, industry, finance, and labor, and such other persons, agencies, organizations, and instrumentalities as it deems appropriate to attend its hearings and to give and present information, advice, and recommendations.

Sec. 405. The committee, or any subcommittee thereof, is authorized to hold such hearings; to sit and act at such times and places during the sessions, recesses, and adjourned periods of the Eightieth Congress; to require by subpena or otherwise the attendance of such witnesses and the production of such books, papers, and documents; to administer oaths; to take such testimony; to have such printing and binding done; and to make such expenditures within the amount appropriated therefor; as it deems advisable. The cost of stenographic services in reporting such hearings shall not be in excess of 25 cents per one hundred words. Subpenas shall be issued under the signature of the chairman or vice chairman of the committee and shall be served by any person designated by them.

Sec. 406. The members of the committee shall be reimbursed for travel, subsistence, and other necessary expenses incurred by them in the performance of the duties vested in the committee, other than expenses in connection with meetings of the committee held in the District of Columbia during such times as the Congress is in session.

Sec. 407. There is hereby authorized to be appropriated the sum of $150,000, or so much thereof as may be necessary, to carry out the provisions of this title, to be disbursed by the Secretary of the Senate on vouchers signed by the chairman.

Title V

Definitions

Sec. 501. When used in this Act—

(1) The term "industry affecting commerce" means any industry or activity in commerce or in which a labor dispute would burden or obstruct commerce or tend to burden or obstruct commerce or the free flow of commerce.

(2) The term "strike" includes any strike or other concerted stoppage of work by employees (including a stoppage by reason of the expiration of a collective-bargaining agreement) and any concerted slowdown or other concerted interruption of operations by employees.

(3) The terms "commerce," "labor disputes," "employer," "employee," "labor organization," "representative," "person,"

and supervisor" shall have the same meaning as when used in the National Labor Relations Act as amended by this Act.

Saving Provision

Sec. 502. Nothing in this Act shall be construed to require an individual employee to render labor or service without his consent, nor shall anything in this Act be construed to make the quitting of his labor by an individual employee an illegal act; nor shall any court issue any process to compel the performance by an individual employee of such labor or service, without his consent; nor shall the quitting of labor by an employee or employees in good faith because of abnormally dangerous conditions for work at the place of employment of such employee or employees be deemed a strike under this Act.

Separability

Sec. 503. If any provision of this Act, or the application of such provision to any person or circumstance, shall be held invalid, the remainder of this Act, or the application of such provision to persons or circumstances other than those as to which it is held invalid, shall not be affected thereby.

TABLE OF CASES

Bradley, Allen, Co. v. Electrical Workers Local 3, 325 US 797, 16 **LRRM** 798 (1945) 665

Bradley Washfountain Co.; NLRB v., 192 F 2d 144, 29 **LRRM** 2064 (CA 7, 1951) 324, 405

Brandenburg Telephone Co., 164 NLRB 825, 65 **LRRM** 1183 (1967) 255

Braniff Airways, Inc., and Air Carrier Mechanics Assn. Council 7, 27 LA 892 (1957) 307

Braswell Motor Freight Lines, Inc., 141 NLRB 1154. 52 **LRRM** 1467 (1963) 320, 390

Brennan's French Restaurant, 129 NLRB 52, 46 **LRRM** 1495 (1960) 779

Brewery & Beverage Drivers
—(see Teamsters)

Brewery Workers
—Local 8 (Bert D. Williams, Inc.), 148 NLRB 7281, 57 **LRRM** 1035 (1964) 638

—Local 67, 107 NLRB 299, 33 **LRRM** 1122 (1953), enf., 220 F 2d 380, 35 **LRRM** 2576 (CA DC, 1959) 628

—Local 366; NLRB v., 272 F 2d 817, 45 **LRRM** 2277 (CA 10, 1959) 615

Brick & Clay Workers
—Deena Artware, Inc.; NLRB v. 198 F 2d 645, 30 **LRRM** 2479 (CA 6, 1952), cert. den., 345 US 906, 31 **LRRM** 2444 (1953) 285, 449

—v. Deena Artware, Inc., 198 F 2d 637, 30 **LRRM** 2485 (CA 6, 1952), cert. den., 344 US 897, 31 **LRRM** 2157 (1952) 449, 640, 643

Bricklayers, Masons & Plasterers
—162 NLRB 476, 64 **LRRM** 1085 (1966) 339

Locals
—Local 2
——(Decora, Inc.), 152 NLRB 278, 59 **LRRM** 1065 (1965) 680
——(Weidman Metal Masters), 166 NLRB 26, 65 **LRRM** 1433 (1967) 609
—Local 3, 162 NLRB 476, 64 **LRRM** 1085 (1966) 326, 430
—Local 5
——(Greater Muskegon General Contractors Assn.), 152 NLRB 360, 59 **LRRM** 1081 (1965), enf. as modifd., 378 F 2d 859, 65 **LRRM** 2563 (CA 6, 1967) 672
——(I. C. Minium), 174 NLRB No. 185, 70 **LRRM** 1449 (1969) 566
—Local 28 (Plaza Builders, Inc.), 134 NLRB 751, 49 **LRRM** 1222 (1961) 746

Bridge, Structural & Ornamental Iron Workers
—(see Iron Workers)

Briggs & Stratton Corp.
—(see Wisconsin Employment Rel. Bd.)

Briggs Mfg. Co., 75 NLRB 569, 21 **LRRM** 1056 (1947) 409

Brink's, Inc., 77 NLRB 1182, 22 **LRRM** 1133 (1948) 224

British Rail-International, Inc., 163 NLRB 721, 64 **LRRM** 1432 (1967) 781

Brockton Wholesale Grocery Co., 78 NLRB 663, 22 **LRRM** 1264 (1948) 161

Brooklyn Spring Corp., 113 NLRB 815, 36 **LRRM** 1372 (1955), enf. 233 F 2d 539, 38 **LRRM** 2134 (CA 2, 1956) 69

Brooks v. Continental Can Corp., 59 **LRRM** 2779 (SD NY, 1965) 717

Brooks, Betty Co., 99 NLRB 1237, 30 **LRRM** 1210 (1952) 304

Brooks v. NLRB, 348 US 96, 35 **LRRM** 2158 (1954) 164, 347, 533, 643, 842

Brotherhood of Railroad Trainmen
—(see Railroad Trainmen)

Broward County Launderers & Cleaners Assn., 125 NLRB 256, 45 **LRRM** 1113 (1959) 241

Brown v.
—(see name of opposing party)

Brown & Patton
—(see Teamsters, Local 413)

Brown & Root, Inc.
—86 NLRB 520, 24 **LRRM** 1648 (1949), modifd. on other grounds sub. nom., NLRB v. Ozark Dam Constructors, 190 F 2d 222, 28 **LRRM** 2246 (CA 8, 1951) 430

—132 NLRB 486, 48 **LRRM** 1391 (1961), enf., 311 F 2d 447, 52 **LRRM** 2115 (CA 8, 1963) 128, 527

Brown & Sharpe Mfg. Co.; NLRB v., 169 F 2d 331, 22 **LRRM** 2363 (CA 1, 1948) 204

Brown, dba Brown Food Store
—137 NLRB 73, 77, 50 **LRRM** 1046 (1962) 552
—NLRB v., 380 US 278, 58 **LRRM** 2663 (1965) 120, 545, 551, 552

Brown Lumber Co., 143 NLRB 174, 53 **LRRM** 1283 (1963) 194

Brown-Olds Plumbing & Heating Corp. (see Plumbers)

Brown Shoe Co., 1 NLRB 803, 1 **LRRM** 78 (1936) 127, 525

Brown Transport Corp., 140 NLRB 954, 52 **LRRM** 1151 (1963), modifd., 334 F 2d 243, 56 **LRRM** 2809 (CA 5, 1964) 416

Brown Truck, 106 NLRB 999, 32 **LRRM** 1580 (1953) 411

Brownfield Electric Inc., 145 NLRB 1163, 55 **LRRM** 1113 (1964) 630

Busch Kredit Jewelry Co., 108 NLRB 1214, 34 LRRM 1167 (1954) 701
Bush Hog Inc.; NLRB v., 405 F 2d 755, 70 LRRM 2070 (CA 5, 1968) 872
Business Machine & Office Appliance Mechanics
—Local 459; NLRB v., (Royal Typewriter), 228 F 2d 553, 37 LRRM 2219 (CA 2, 1955) 615, 637
Butcher Boy Refrigerator Door Co., 127 NLRB 1360, 46 LRRM 1192 (1960), enf., 290 F 2d 22, 48 LRRM 2058 (CA 7, 1961) 300, 301, 435
Butler; U.S. v., 297 US 1 (1936) 30
Butte Medical Properties, 168 NLRB No. 52, 66 LRRM 1259 (1967) 779
Buy Low Supermarkets, Inc., 131 NLRB 23, 47 LRRM 1586 (1961) 175

C

C & C Plywood Corp.
—163 NLRB 1022, 64 LRRM 1488 (1967) 305, 306, 308
—NLRB v., 148 NLRB 414, 57 LRRM 1015 (1964), enf. den., 351 F 2d 224, 60 LRRM 2137 (CA 9, 1965), revsd., 385 US 421, 64 LRRM 2065 (1967) 306, 311, 333, 335, 340, 452, 453, 455, 458, 465, 470, 471, 474, 476, 479, 487, 507, 508, 510, 748
C & G Electric, Inc., 180 NLRB No. 52, 73 LRRM 1041 (1969) 265
C & S Industries, 158 NLRB 454, 62 LRRM 1043 (1966) 390, 455, 475, 510
Cab Services, Inc., 123 NLRB 83, 43 LRRM 1392 (1959) 778
Cabinet Mfg. Co.
—140 NLRB 576, 52 LRRM 1064 (1963) 302
—144 NLRB 842, 54 LRRM 1144 (1963) 293
Cabot Carbon Co.; NLRB v., 360 US 203, 44 LRRM 2204 (1959) 136, 137, 774
Cadillac Overall Supply Co., 148 NLRB 1133, 1136, 57 LRRM 1136 (1964) 99
Cadillac Wire Corp.; NLRB v., 290 F 2d 261, 48 LRRM 2149 (CA 2, 1961) 853, 854
California Girl, 129 NLRB 209, 46 LRRM 1533 (1960) 276
California Institute of Technology, 102 NLRB 1402, 31 LRRM 1435 (1953) 780
California Portland Cement Co.
—101 NLRB 1436, 1438-39, 31 LRRM 1220 (1952), suppld., 103 NLRB 1375, 31 LRRM 1630 (1953) 311, 318, 321, 465, 468, 473

Calorator Mfg. Corp., 129 NLRB 704, 47 LRRM 1109 (1960) 171
Cal-Pacific Poultry Inc., 163 NLRB 716, 64 LRRM 1463 (1967) 305
Calumet Contractors Assn., 121 NLRB 80, 42 LRRM 1279 (1958) 241
Cambell Sons' Corp.; NLRB v., 407 F 2d 969, 70 LRRM 2886 (CA 4, 1969) 218
Cambria Clay Products Co.; NLRB v., 215 F 2d 48, 34 LRRM 2471 (CA 6, 1954) 331, 531
Cameo Lingerie, Inc., 148 NLRB 535, 538, 57 LRRM 1044 (1964) 263
Camp & McInnes, Inc., 100 NLRB 524, 30 LRRM 1310 (1952) 404
Campbell, John W., Inc.; NLRB v., 159 F 2d 184, 19 LRRM 2161 (CA 5, 1947) 206
Campbell Soup Co., 170 NLRB No. 167, 68 LRRM 1036 (1968) 103
Can, R. C. Co.; NLRB v., 328 F 2d 974, 55 LRRM 2642 (CA 5, 1964) 124, 125
Canada Dry Corp.
—154 NLRB 1763, 1764, n. 2, 60 LRRM 1208 (1965) 536
—v. NLRB, 421 F 2d 907, 73 LRRM 2582 (CA 6, 1970) 661, 665
Canal Marais Improvement Corp., 129 NLRB 1332, 47 LRRM 1883 (1961) 777
Cannery Workers' Union, 159 NLRB 843, 62 LRRM 1298 (1966) 71
Cannon Electric Co., 151 NLRB 1465, 58 LRRM 1629 (1965) 100
Canton, 180 NLRB No. 86, 73 LRRM 1069 (1970) 265
Capital Aviation, Inc.; NLRB v., 355 F 2d 875, 877, 61 LRRM 2307 (CA 7, 1966) 295
Capital Bakers, Inc., 168 NLRB No. 119, 66 LRRM 1385, 1387 (1967) 201, 236
Capital Dist. Beer Distributors Assn., 109 NLRB 176, 34 LRRM 1313 (1954) 239
Carey v. Westinghouse Electric Corp., 375 US 261, 55 LRRM 2042 (1964) 453, 483, 484, 487, 498, 500, 678, 739, 802
Carey, Philip, Mfg. Co., Miami Cabinet Div., 140 NLRB 1103, 52 LRRM 1184 (1963), enf., 331 F 2d 720, 55 LRRM 2821 (CA 6, 1964), cert. den., 379 US 888, 57 LRRM 2307 (1964) 279, 330, 386, 436, 525
Cargill, Inc., Nutrena Mills Div., 172 NLRB No. 24, 69 LRRM 1293 (1968) 97
Cargo Handlers, Inc., 159 NLRB 321, 62 LRRM 1228 (1966) 134, 736, 745, 747

——(Cardinal Industries, Inc.), 144 NLRB 91, 54 LRRM 1003 (1963), enf., 339 F 2d 142, 57 LRRM 2509 (CA 6, 1964) 669
——(Hankins & Hankins Const. Co.), 144 NLRB 91, 54 LRRM 1003 (1963), enf., 339 F 2d 142, 57 LRRM 2509 (CA 6, 1964) 672
—v. Ritter's Cafe, 315 US 722, 10 LRRM 507 (US SupCt., 1942) 519
—Suffolk County Dist. Council (Island Coal & Lbr. Co.), 159 NLRB 895, 899, 900, 62 LRRM 1443 (1966), enf., 387 F 2d 170, 67 LRRM 2012 (CA 2, 1967) 560, 587, 589
—(Wadsworth Bldg. Co.), 81 NLRB 802, 23 LRRM 1403 (1949), enf., 184 F 2d 60, 26 LRRM 2480 (CA 10, 1950), cert. den., 341 US 947, 28 LRRM 2132 (US SupCt., 1951) 625
Carpinteria Lemon Assn. v. NLRB, 240 F 2d 554, 35 LRRM 1724 (CA 9, 1957) 177
Carrier Corp. v. NLRB
—(see Steelworkers, Local 5895)
Carter Machine & Tool Co., 133 NLRB 247, 48 LRRM 1625 (1961) 307
Carter v. Carter Coal Co., 298 US 238 (1936) 30, 759
Carter, W. T. & Brother, 90 NLRB 2020, 26 LRRM 1327 (1950) 400
Cascade Employers Assn.; NLRB v., 296 F 2d 42, 48, 49 LRRM 2049 (CA 9, 1961) 278
Case, J. I. Co.
—71 NLRB 1145, 19 LRRM 1100 (1946) 274
—85 NLRB 576, 24 LRRM 1431 (1949) 77
—118 NLRB 520, 40 LRRM 1208 (1957), enf. as modifd., 253 F 2d 149, 41 LRRM 2679 (CA 7, 1958) 504
—NLRB v., 198 F 2d 919, 30 LRRM 2624 (CA 8, 1952) 124
—v. NLRB, 253 F 2d 149, 41 LRRM 2679 (CA 7, 1958) 310, 311, 315, 317, 320, 321, 322, 469
—v. NLRB 321 US 332, 337, 340, 14 LRRM 501, 504 (1944), affg. 134 F 2d 70, 12 LRRM 538 (CA 7, 1943), enf. 42 NLRB 85, 10 LRRM 172 (1942) 304, 452, 462
—(Racine Plant), 71 NLRB 1145, 19 LRRM 1100 (1946) 753
Casey v. Cincinnati Typographical Union Local 3, 45 F 135 (SD Ohio, 1891) 695
Casino Operations, Inc., 169 NLRB No. 43, 67 LRRM 1177 (1968) 106
Caterpillar Tractor Co.
—77 NLRB 457, 22 LRRM 1033 (1948) 226

—v. NLRB, 230 F 2d 357, 37 LRRM 2619 (CA 7, 1956) 87
C.C.C. Associates, Inc.; NLRB v., 306 F 2d 534, 50 LRRM 2882 (CA 2, 1962) 377
Celanese Corp. of America, 95 NLRB 664, 673, 28 LRRM 1362 (1951) 160, 305, 332, 347
Cello-Foil Prods., Inc., 178 NLRB No. 103, 72 LRRM 1196 (1969) 511
Celotex Corp.; NLRB v., 364 F 2d 552, 62 LRRM 2475 (CA 5, 1966) 314
Cement Finishers, Local 627 (R. H. Parr & Son), 22 LRRM 1289 (1948) 692
Center Brass Works, Inc., 10 NLRB 1060, 3 LRRM 497 (1939) 119
Central Greyhound Lines, 88 NLRB 13, 25 LRRM 1273 (1950) 222
Central Hardware Co. and Retail Clerks Local 725, 181 NLRB No. 74, 73 LRRM 1422 (1970) 521
Central Illinois Public Service Co.
—139 NLRB 1407, 51 LRRM 1508 (1962) 855
—NLRB v., 324 F 2d 916, 54 LRRM 2586 (CA 7, 1963) 323, 402
Central Metallic Casket Co., 91 NLRB 572, 26 LRRM 1520 (1950) 330, 390
Central of Georgia Ry. v. Jones, 229 F 2d 648, 37 LRRM 2435 (CA 5, 1956), cert. den. 352 US 848, 38 LRRM 2716 (1956) 750
Central Rigging & Contracting Corp., 129 NLRB 342, 46 LRRM 1548 (1960) 134
Central Rufina, 161 NLRB 696, 63 LRRM 1318 (1966) 415, 509
Central Soya Co., 151 NLRB 1691, 58 LRRM 1667 (1965) 414, 415
Centralia Bldg. & Const. Trades Council (Pacific Sign & Steel Bldg. Co.), 155 NLRB 803, 60 LRRM 1430 (1965), enf., 363 F 2d 699, 62 LRRM 2511 (CA DC, 1966) 571
Centr-O-Case & Eng. Co., 100 NLRB 1507, 30 LRRM 1478 (1952) 826
Century Cement Mfg. Co.; NLRB v., 208 F 2d 84, 33 LRRM 2061 (CA 2, 1953), enf. 100 NLRB 1323, 30 LRRM 1447 (1952) 323
Century Papers, 155 NLRB 358, 60 LRRM 1320 (1965) 455, 476, 510
Chambers Mfg. Co., 124 NLRB 721, 44 LRRM 1477 (1959) 331
Champion Pneumatic Mach. Co., 152 NLRB 300, 306, 59 LRRM 1089 (1965) 97
Chance Vought Aircraft Corp., 110 NLRB 1342, 1346, 35 LRRM 1338 (1954) 224

D

F

G

General Motors Corp.
—NLRB v., 373 US 734, 53 LRRM 2313 (1963)   408, 708, 709, 806
—v. NLRB, 303 F 2d 428, 50 LRRM 2397 (CA 6, 1962)   408
—v. NLRB, 345 F 2d 516, 59 LRRM 2080 (CA 6, 1964), setting aside 147 NLRB 509, 56 LRRM 1241 (1964) 90
—Case No. 7-RC-2793, 56 LRRM 1332 (1964)   499
—59 NLRB 1143, 15 LRRM 170 (1944) 405
—81 NLRB 779, 23 LRRM 1422 (1949), enf., 179 F 2d 221, 25 LRRM 2281 (CA 2, 1950)   380, 395
—102 NLRB 1140, 31 LRRM 1344 (1953) 460
—107 NLRB 1096, 33 LRRM 1318 (1954) 191
—120 NLRB 1215, 1219, 1221, 42 LRRM 1143 (1958)   427, 428
—130 NLRB 481, 47 LRRM 1306 (1961) 408
—133 NLRB 451, 48 LRRM 1659 (1961) 408
—134 NLRB 1107, 49 LRRM 1283 (1961) 702, 707
—147 NLRB 509, 56 LRRM 1241 (1964), order set aside, 345 F 2d 516, 59 LRRM 2080 (CA 6, 1965)   89, 461
—149 NLRB 396, 57 LRRM 1277 (1964), remand, 60 LRRM 2283, (CA DC, 1966), on remand, 158 NLRB 229, 62 LRRM 1009 (1966), revd., 381 F 2d 265, 64 LRRM 2489 (CA DC, 1967), cert. den., 389 US 875, 65 LRRM 2307 (1967)   334, 456
—158 NLRB 1732, 62 LRRM 1210 (1966), enf. den., 381 F 2d 265, 65 LRRM 3103 (CA 9, 1967)   90, 461
General Ore, Inc., 126 NLRB 172, 45 LRRM 1296 (1960)   242
General Paint Corp., 95 NLRB 539, 28 LRRM 1345 (1951)   162
General Sheet Metal Co., 144 NLRB 773, 54 LRRM 1130 (1963)   434
General Shoe Corp., 77 NLRB 124, 21 LRRM 1337 (1948)   77, 78, 195, 831
General Steel Prods., Inc., 157 NLRB 636, 61 LRRM 1417 (1966)   258
General Telephone Co. of Florida, 144 NLRB 311, 316, 54 LRRM 1055, enf. as modifd., 337 F 2d 452, 57 LRRM 2211 (CA 5, 1964)   335, 392, 858
General Tire & Rubber Co.; NLRB v., 326 F 2d 832, 833, 55 LRRM 2150 (CA 5, 1964), enf. den. to 135 NLRB 269, 49 LRRM 1469 (1962)   291, 292, 295

General Truckdrivers
—(see Teamsters)
General Tube Co.; NLRB v.
—331 F 2d 751, 56 LRRM 2161 (CA 6, 1964)   187
—151 NLRB 850, 58 LRRM 1496 (1965) 414
Georgia Craft Co., 120 NLRB 806, 42 LRRM 1066 (1958)   167
Georgia Highway Express, Inc., 150 NLRB, 58 LRRM 1319 (1965)   211
Georgia Kraft Co., 120 NLRB 806, 42 LRRM 1066 (1958)   139
Georgia Pac. Corp., 150 NLRB 885, 58 LRRM 1135 (1965)   416
Geronimo Service Co., 129 NLRB 366, 46 LRRM 1553 (1960)   770, 778
Getreu v. Hotel & Restaurant Employees Local 58, 181 F Supp 738, 45 LRRM 2496 (ND Ind, 1960)   585
Gibbons v. Ogden, 22 US (9 Wheat) 1 (1824)   782
Gibbs Corp., 131 NLRB 955, 48 LRRM 1167 (1961)   134
Gibbs v. Mine Workers
—(see Mine Workers)
Giboney v. Empire Storage & Ice Co., 336 US 490, 23 LRRM 2505 (1949) 519, 606
Gibralter Industries, Inc.; NLRB v., 307 F 2d 428, 51 LRRM 2029 (CA 4, 1962), enf., 133 NLRB 1527, 49 NLRB 1054 (1960), cert. den., 372 US 911, 52 LRRM 2471 (1963)   768
Gibson Products Co., 185 NLRB No. 74, 75 LRRM 1055 (1970)   265
Gibson, William D., Co., 110 NLRB 660, 35 LRRM 1092 (1954)   143
Gilchrist v. Mine Workers, 290 F 2d 36, 48 LRRM 2083 (CA 6, 1961), cert. den., 368 US 875, 48 LRRM 3118 (1961) 641
Gilmore Industries, Inc.; NLRB v., 341 F 2d 240, 242, 58 LRRM 2419 (CA 6, 1965)   99
Gimbel Bros., 147 NLRB 500, 505, 56 LRRM 1287 (1964)   87
Giordano Lumber Co., Inc., 133 NLRB 307, 48 LRRM 1629 (1961)   210
Gissel Packing Co.
—(see Sinclair Refining Co.)
Glasgow, C. J. Co.; NLRB v., 356 F 2d 476, 478, 61 LRRM 2406 (CA 7, 1966) 253
Glass, Frederick O., dba Miller Road Dairy, 135 NLRB 217, 49 LRRM 1477 (1962), enf. in part, 317 F 2d 726, 53 LRRM 2336 (CA 6, 1963)   767
Glass Workers
—Local 1892, 141 NLRB 106, 107–108, 52 LRRM 1282 (1963)   861

H

Kennecott Copper Corp., contd.
—176 NLRB No. 13, 71 LRRM 1188 (1969) 218
Kennedy
—v. Construction, Production & Maintenance Laborers Local 383, 199 F Supp 775, 48 LRRM 2791 (DC Ariz, 1961) 581
—v. Telecomputing Corp., 49 LRRM 2188 (SD Cal, 1961) 846
Kenosha Auto Transport Corp., 98 NLRB 482, 29 LRRM 1370 (1952) 244
Kenrich Petrochemicals, Inc., 149 NLRB 910, 57 LRRM 1395 (1964) 145, 146, 178
Kentile, Inc.
—147 NLRB 980, 56 LRRM 1328 (1964) 496
—v. Local 457 Rubber Workers, 228 F Supp 541, 55 LRRM 3011 (ED NY, 1964) 496
Kentucky Utilities Co.; NLRB v., 182 F 2d 810, 26 LRRM 2287 (CA 6, 1950) 285
Kerrigan Iron Works, 108 NLRB 933, 34 LRRM 1118 (1954) 127
Keystone Coat, Apron & Towel Supply Co.
—(see Paragon Products Corp.)
Kiddie Kover Co. v. NLRB, 105 F 2d 179, 4 LRRM 638 (CA 6, 1939) 367
Kilgore Mfg. Co., 45 NLRB 468, 11 LRRM 139 (1942) 77
Kimbrell v. NLRB, 290 F 2d 799, 48 LRRM 2310 (CA 4, 1961) 140
Kimel Shoe Co., 97 NLRB 127, 29 LRRM 1069 (1951) 159
Kinard Trucking Co., 152 NLRB 449, 59 LRRM 1104 (1965) 475
King, Carl B., Drilling Co., 164 NLRB 557, 65 LRRM 1096 (1967) 186
Kingsbury Electric Cooperative, Inc., 138 NLRB 577, 51 LRRM 1104 (1962), enf., 319 F 2d 387, 53 LRRM 2693 (CA 8, 1963) 777
Kingsport Press, 146 NLRB 260 and 1111, 56 LRRM 1006, 1007 (1964) 166
Kinney System, Inc., NLRB Case No. 2-RC-395, 48 LRRM 1586 (1961) 778
Kinter Bros., Inc., 167 NLRB 57, 66 LRRM 1004 (1967) 266
Kipbea Baking Co. v. Strauss, 218 F Supp 695, 53 LRRM 2636 (ED NY, 1963) 643
Kit Mfg. Co.
—NLRB v., 142 NLRB 957, enf. in part, 335 F 2d 166, 56 LRRM 2988 (CA 9, 1964), cert. den., 380 US 910, 58 LRRM 2496 (1965) 435
—138 NLRB 1290, 51 LRRM 1224 (1962) 331

—150 NLRB 662, 671, 58 LRRM 1140 (1965), enf., 365 F 2d 829, 62 LRRM 2856 (CA 9, 1966) 425, 432
Kitty Clover, Inc., 103 NLRB 1665, 32 LRRM 1037, enf., 208 F 2d 212, 33 LRRM 2177 (CA 8, 1953) 525
Klaber Bros., Inc., in re., 173 F Supp 83, 44 LRRM 2176 (SD NY, 1959) 817
Klion, H. L., Inc., 148 NLRB 652, 57 LRRM 1073 (1964) 172, 180
Klotz, Jacob H., 13 NLRB 746, 778, 4 LRRM 344 (1939) 122, 855
Knickerbocker Plastics Co., 104 NLRB 514, 32 LRRM 1123 (1953) 855
Knight Morley Corp.; NLRB v., 251 F 2d 753, 41 LRRM 2242 (CA 6, 1967), cert. den., 357 US 927, 42 LRRM 2307 (1958) 124, 340, 534
Knitgoods Workers, Local 155
—(Boulevard Corp.), 167 NLRB 109, 66 LRRM 1157 (1967) 162
—NLRB v., 403 F 2d 388, 390, 69 LRRM 2666 (CA 2, 1968) 577
Knox v. UAW, 223 F Supp 1009, 54 LRRM 2661 (ED Mich, 1963), affd., 351 F 2d 72, 60 LRRM 2253 (CA 6, 1965) 738
Knudson v. Benn, 123 F 636 (D Minn, 1903) 9
Koester, E. H., Bakery Co., Inc., 136 NLRB 1006, 49 LRRM 1925 (1962) 210
Kofran, Berry Dental Laboratory, 160 NLRB 493, 62 LRRM 1643 (1966) 293
Kohler Co., 128 NLRB 1062, 46 LRRM 1389 (1960), enf. in part, mod. and remand. in part, 300 F 2d 699, 49 LRRM 2485 (CA DC, 1962) 288, 339, 855
Kohler, Peter Cailler Swiss Chocolates Co.; NLRB v., 130 F 2d 503, 10 LRRM 852 (CA 2, 1942) 65
Konner Chevrolet, Inc.; NLRB v., 338 F 2d 972, 57 LRRM 2583 (CA 2, 1964) 149
Kordewick v. Ry. Trainmen, 181 F 2d 963, 26 LRRM 2164 (CA 7, 1950) 463
Korn Industries v. NLRB, 389 F 2d 117, 67 LRRM 2148 (CA 4, 1967), clarified, 67 LRRM 2976 (CA 4, 1968) 318, 324
Kota Div. of Dura Corp., 182 NLRB No. 51, 74 LRRM 1104 (1970) 174, 366, 373
Kovach v. NLRB, 229 F 2d 138, 37 LRRM 2345 (CA 7, 1956) 876, 885
Krambo Food Stores, Case No. 13-RC-57, Feb. 14, 1958 164
Krause Milling Co., 97 NLRB 536, 29 LRRM 1120 (1951) 702

Laundry, Linen Supply & Dry Cleaning Drivers
—(see also Teamsters)
—(Southern Service Co., Ltd.), 118 NLRB 1435, 1437, 40 LRRM 1395 (1957), enf., 262 F 2d 617, 43 LRRM 2335 (CA 9, 1958)   597
Laura Modes Co., 144 NLRB 1592, 54 LRRM 1299 (1963)   106
Lawrence Leather Co., 108 NLRB 546, 34 LRRM 1022 (1954)   176
Lawrence Typographical Union No. 570
—(see Typographical Union)
Lea, Albert, Cooperative Creamery Assn., 119 NLRB 817, 821–822, 41 LRRM 1192 (1957)   767
Leas & McVitty, Inc., 155 NLRB 389, 60 LRRM 1333 (1965)   256
Lebanon Oak Flooring Co., 167 NLRB No. 104, 66 LRRM 1172 (1967)   301
Lebanon Steel Foundry v. NLRB, 130 F 2d 404, 10 LRRM 760 (CA DC, 1942), cert. den., 317 US 659, 11 LRRM 839 (1942)   255
LeBaron v. Los Angeles Building & Constr. Trades Council, 84 F Supp 629, 635–36, 24 LRRM 2131 (SD Cal, 1949), affd., 185 F 2d 405, 27 LRRM 2184 (CA 9, 1950)   609, 850
Leece-Neville Co., 140 NLRB 56, 51 LRRM 1563 (1962), mod., 330 F 2d 242, 55 LRRM 2926 (CA 9, 1964), cert. den., 379 US 819, 57 LRRM 2238 (1964)   704
Leedom v.
—(see name of opposing party)
Leeds & Northrup Co.
—v. NLRB, 357 F 2d 527, 61 LRRM 2283 (CA 3, 1966)   834, 875
—v. NLRB, 391 F 2d 874, 67 LRRM 2793 (CA 3, 1968), enf., 162 NLRB 987, 64 LRRM 1110 (1967)   334, 458
Lehigh Portland Cement Co.
—101 NLRB 1010, 31 LRRM 1097 (1952)   400
—NLRB v., 205 F 2d 821, 32 LRRM 2463 (CA 4, 1953)   400
Leiter Mfg. Co., 112 NLRB 843, 36 LRRM 1123 (1955)   405
Leland Gifford Co., 95 NLRB 1306, 28 LRRM 1443 (1951), enf. in part, 200 F 2d 620, 31 LRRM 2196 (CA 1, 1952)   318, 473
Lenscraft Optical Corp., 128 NLRB 836, 46 LRRM 1414 (1960)   149
Lenz Co.
—153 NLRB 1399, 59 LRRM 1638 (1965)   255
—NLRB v., 396 F 2d 905, 908, 68 LRRM 2577 (CA 6, 1968)   253

Leonard v. NLRB, 205 F 2d 355, 32 LRRM 2305 (CA 9, 1953)   544
Leonard Wholesale Meats Co., 136 NLRB 1000, 41 LRRM 1901 (1962)   178
Leone Industries, 172 NLRB No. 158, 68 LRRM 1529 (1968)   211
LeRoy Machine Co., 147 NLRB 1431, 56 LRRM 1369 (1964)   334, 405, 455, 463, 469, 479, 509, 510
Leslie Metal Arts Co., 167 NLRB 693, 66 LRRM 1134 (1967)   241
Lever Bros. Co., 96 NLRB 448, 450, 28 LRRM 1544 (1951)   427
Lewers & Cooke, Ltd., 153 NLRB 1542, 29 LRRM 1696 (1965)   504
Lewin-Mathes Co., 126 NLRB 936, 45 LRRM 1416 (1960), enf. den., 285 F 2d 329, 47 LRRM 2288 (CA 7, 1960)   290, 298
Lewis—
—v. Benedict Coal Corp., 259 F 2d 346, 351, 43 LRRM 2237 (CA 6, 1958), modifd., 361 US 459, 45 LRRM 2719 (1960)   535
—v. NLRB, 350 F 2d 801, 59 LRRM 2946 (CA DC, 1965)   670
Lianco Container Corp., 177 NLRB 116, 71 LRRM 1483 (1969)   230
Libbey-Owens-Ford Glass Co.
—10 NLRB 1470, 3 LRRM 551 (1939)   232
—169 NLRB No. 2, 67 LRRM 1096 (1968)   181, 220
—McCulloch v., 403 F 2d 916, 68 LRRM 2497 (CA DC, 1968), cert. den., 393 US 1016, 70 LRRM 2225 (1969)   220, 890
—v. McCulloch, 67 LRRM 2712 (D DC, 1968)   220
Libby, McNeill & Libby
—65 NLRB 873, 17 LRRM 250 (1946)   390
—159 NLRB 677, 62 LRRM 1276 (1966)   500
Liberator
—(see Biazevich)
Liberty Electronics Corp., Inc.
—138 NLRB 1074, 51 LRRM 1194 (1962)   126
—143 NLRB 605, 53 LRRM 1370 (1963)   376
Liebmann Breweries, Inc. of New Jersey, 142 NLRB 121, 52 LRRM 1527 (1963)   768
Li'l General Stores, Inc.; NLRB v., 422 F 2d 571, 73 LRRM 2522 (CA 5, 1970)   260
Lilliston Implement Co., 171 NLRB No. 19, 68 LRRM 1049 (1968)   852
Lilly-Tulip Cup Corp., 177 NLRB 3, 71 LRRM 1378 (1969)   231

N

P

Pacific Am. Shipowners Ass'n, 90 NLRB 1099, 26 LRRM 1316 (1950)   409

Pacific Coast Assn. of Pulp & Paper Mfrs.
—121 NLRB 990, 42 LRRM 1477 (1958) 168, 171
—163 NLRB No. 129, 64 LRRM 1420 (1967)   243
—v. NLRB, 304 F 2d 761, 50 LRRM 2626 (CA 9, 1962)   393

Pacific Drive-In Theatres Corp., 167 NLRB No. 88, 66 LRRM 1119 (1967) 245

Pacific Gas & Electric Co., 87 NLRB 257, 25 LRRM 1102 (1949)   235

Pacific Greyhound Lines, 22 NLRB 111, 6 LRRM 189 (1940)   350

Pacific Intermountain Express Co. (Teamsters, Local 41), 107 NLRB 837, 33 LRRM 1252 (1954), modifd. & enf., 225 F 2d 343, 36 LRRM 2632 (CA 8, 1955)   719, 720

Pacific Iron & Metal Co., 175 NLRB No. 114, 71 LRRM 1006 (1969)   702

Pacific Isle Mining Co., 118 NLRB 740, 40 LRRM 1253 (1957)   173

Pacific Metals Co., Ltd., 91 NLRB 696, 26 LRRM 1558 (1950)   239

Pacific Telephone & Telegraph Co., 107 NLRB 1547, 33 LRRM 1433 (1954) 126, 127, 532

Pacific Tile & Porcelain Co., 137 NLRB 1358, 50 LRRM 1394 (1962)   186, 187, 501

Pacific Typesetting Co. v. Typographical Union, 216 P 358, 362, 125 Wash 273 (1923)   605

Packard Motor Co.
—61 NLRB 4, 16 LRRM 43 (1945)   205
—v. NLRB, 330 US 485, 19 LRRM 2397 (1947)   205, 773, 786, 881

Packinghouse Workers
—(Farmers' Cooperative) v. NLRB, 416 F 2d 1126, 70 LRRM 2489, 2495 (CA DC, 1969)   64
—Local 3 v. NLRB, 210 F 2d 325, 33 LRRM 2530 (CA 8, 1954), cert. den., 348 US 822, 34 LRRM 2898 (1954) 324, 534

Page Aircraft Maintenance Co., 123 NLRB 159, 43 LRRM 1383 (1959) 370

Painters
—v. Edgewood Contracting Co., 416 F 2d 1081, 72 LRRM 2524 (CA 5, 1069) 643
—District Council No. 36, 155 NLRB 1013, 60 LRRM 1431 (1967)   326

—Orange Belt Dist. Council No. 48
——v. NLRB, 328 F 2d 534, 55 LRRM 2293 (CA DC, 1964), remang. 139 NLRB 383, 51 LRRM 1315 (1962), enf., 365 F 2d 540, 62 LRRM 2553 (CA DC, 1966)   461, 659, 661, 670, 671
——NLRB v., 144 NLRB 1523, 54 LRRM 1283 (1963), enf., 340 F 2d 107, 58 LRRM 2165 (CA 9, 1965), cert. den., 381 US 914, 59 LRRM 2240 (1965) 614

Locals
—Local 130 (Joiner, Inc.), 135 NLRB 876, 49 LRRM 1592 (1962)   566, 572
—Local 164 v. NLRB, 293 F 2d 133, 48 LRRM 2060 (CA DC, 1961), cert. den., 368 US 824, 48 LRRM 3110 (1961)   430
—Local 193 (Pittsburgh Plate Glass Co.), 110 NLRB 455, 35 LRRM 1071 (1954) 628
—Local 481; U.S. v., 172 F 2d 854, 23 LRRM 2331 (CA 2, 1949)   725

Palace Knitwear & Co., 93 NLRB 872, 27 LRRM 1481 (1951)   162

Palace Laundry Dry Cleaning Corp., 75 NLRB 320, 21 LRRM 1039 (1947)   217

Palm Beach Post Times, Div. of Perry Publications, Inc., 151 NLRB 1030, 58 LRRM 1561 (1965)   301, 435

Palmer Mfg. Co., 103 NLRB 336, 31 LRRM 1520 (1953)   163

Panda Terminals, Inc., 161 NLRB 1215, 63 LRRM 1419 (1966)   173, 175, 375

P & V Atlas Industrial Center, Inc.
— (See also Atlas Storage Div.)
—100 NLRB 1443, 30 LRRM 1461 (1952) 243

Pappas & Co.; NLRB v., 203 F 2d 569, 32 LRRM 2062 (CA 9, 1953)   885

Paragon Products Corp., 134 NLRB 662, 49 LRRM 1160 (1961), modifg. Keystone Coat, Apron & Towel Supply Co., 121 NLRB 880, 42 LRRM 1456 (1958) 169–170, 171, 460, 705

Paramount Pictures, Inc., 79 NLRB 557, 576, 22 LRRM 1428 (1948)   489

Park Edge Sheridan Meats, Inc.; NLRB v., 323 F 2d 956, 54 LRRM 2411 (CA 2, 1963)   139

Parkersburg Building & Construction Trades Council (Howard Price & Co.), 119 NLRB 1384, 41 LRRM 1303 (1958) 683

Parks v. Atlanta Printing Pressmen & Assistants' Union, 243 F 2d 284, 39 LRRM 2699 (CA 5, 1957), cert. den., 354 US 937, 40 LRRM 2284 (1957)   533

Parkview Drugs, Inc., 138 NLRB 194, 50 LRRM 1564 (1962)   175

Strong, dba Strong Roofing & Insulating Co., contd.
—393 US 357, 70 LRRM 2011 (1969) 253, 324, 452, 453, 488, 857, 865, 866
Struksnes Const. Co., 165 NLRB 1062, 1063, 65 LRRM 1385, 1386 (1967) 100, 101, 102
Strydel, Inc., 156 NLRB 1185, 61 LRRM 1230 (1966) 263
Stuart Radiator Core Mfg. Co., 173 NLRB No. 27, 69 LRRM 1243 (1968) 410
Sturgeon Electric Co., 166 NLRB 210, 65 LRRM 1530 (1967) 263
Styles v. Electrical Workers Local 760, 8 F Supp 119, 122, 22 LRRM 2446 (ED Tenn, 1948) 609, 849
Sullivan Surplus Sales, Inc., 152 NLRB 132, 59 LRRM 1041 (1965) 214
Sun Shipbuilding & Dry-Dock Co. v. Marine & Shipbuilding Workers, 95 F Supp 50, 27 LRRM 2250 (ED Pa, 1950) 718
Sunbeam Electric Mfg. Co., 41 NLRB 469, 490, 10 LRRM 119 (1942), enf., 133 F 2d 856, 11 LRRM (CA 7, 1943) 870
Sunbeam Lighting Co.; NLRB v., 318 F 2d 661, 53 LRRM 2367 (CA 7, 1963) 125
Sunset House, 167 NLRB 870, 66 LRRM 1243 (1967) 175
Sunshine Mining Co.; NLRB v., 125 F 2d 757, 9 LRRM 618 (CA 9, 1942) 875
Super Valu Stores, Inc., 177 NLRB No. 63, 71 LRRM 1459 (1969) 234
Superior Coach Corp., 151 NLRB 188, 58 LRRM 1369 (1965) 414, 415
Superior Door & Sash Co., 289 F 2d 713, 45 LRRM 1487 (CA 2, 1961) 324
Superior Fireproof Door & Sash Co.; NLRB v., 289 F 2d 713, 47 LRRM 2816, 2817 (CA 2, 1961) 304, 399, 432
Supermarket Housewares, Inc., 133 NLRB 1273, 49 LRRM 1025 (1961) 149
Surprenant Mfg. Co.
—144 NLRB 507, 54 LRRM 1097 (1963) 166
—v. NLRB, 341 F 2d 756, 58 LRRM 2484 (CA 6, 1965) 74
Sussex Hats, Inc., 85 NLRB 399, 24 LRRM 1407 (1949) 435
Swain & Morris Constr. Co., 168 NLRB No. 147, 67 LRRM 1039, 1040 (1968) 537
Swan Super Cleaners, Inc.; NLRB v., 384 F 2d 609, 66 LRRM 2385 (CA 6, 1967) 253, 255, 257

Swayne & Hoyt, Ltd., 2 NLRB 282, 1 LRRM 99 (1936) 349
Swift v. Tyson, 41 US 1 (1842) 8
Swift & Co.
—128 NLRB 732, 46 LRRM 1436 (1958) 144
—130 NLRB 1391, 47 LRRM 1195, suppld., 131 NLRB 1143, 48 LRRM 1219 (1961) 773
—145 NLRB 756, 55 LRRM 1033 (1963) 176, 177, 460
—NLRB v., 294 F 2d 285, 48 LRRM 2699 (CA 4, 1961) 144
Swift, John S. & Co., 124 NLRB 394, 44 LRRM 1388 (1959), enf. on appeal, 277 F 2d 641, 46 LRRM 2090 (CA 7, 1960), enf. in part, den. in part, 124 NLRB 394, 44 LRRM 1388 (1959) 291, 315, 317, 318, 319
Switchmen v. National Mediation Board, 135 F 2d 785, 794 (CA DC, 1943), revsd., 320 US 297, 13 LRRM 616 (1943) 203, 888
Sylvania Electric Products, Inc.
—119 NLRB 824, 828 41 LRRM 1188 (1954) 93
—122 NLRB 201, 43 LRRM 1087 (1958) 215
—127 NLRB 924, 46 LRRM 1127 (1960) 395
—v. NLRB, 291 F 2d 128, 48 LRRM 2313 (CA 1, 1961), cert. den., 368 US 926, 49 LRRM 2173 (1961) 319
—v. NLRB, 358 F 2d 591, 61 LRRM 2657 (CA 1, 1966) 319
Symns Grocer Co. and Idaho Wholesale Grocery Co., 109 NLRB 346, 34 LRRM 1326 (1954) 376
Syncro Machine Co., Inc., 62 NLRB 985, 16 LRRM 230 (1945) 359
Syres v. Oil Workers Local 23, 223 F 2d 739, 36 LRRM 2290 (CA 5, 1955), revsd. per curiam, 350 US 892, 37 LRRM 2068 (1955) 344, 727, 732, 750
Szekely & Associates, Inc., 118 NLRB 1125, 1127, 40 LRRM 1358 (1957), enf., 259 F 2d 652, 42 LRRM 2808 (CA 5, 1958) 853

T

Taft Broadcasting Co.
—163 NLRB 55, 64 LRRM 1386 (1967) 331
—185 NLRB No. 68, 75 LRRM 1076 (1970) 324
Taggart v. Weinacker's, Inc., 214 So 2d 913, 69 LRRM 2348 (Ala SupCt., 1968), cert. den., 397 US 223, 73 LRRM 2628 (1970) 794

Teamsters, contd.
——119 NLRB 222, 223, 41 LRRM 1056 (1957), enf., 264 F 2d 21, 43 LRRM 2693 (CA 10, 1959)   859
——v. NLRB, 179 F 2d 492, 25 LRRM 2237 (CA 10, 1950)   874
——v. NLRB, 247 F 2d 71, 40 LRRM 2047 (CA DC, 1957)   647
—Local 901 v. NLRB (Gonzalez Chemical Indus.), 293 F 2d 881, 48 LRRM 2557 (CA DC, 1960)   635
—Local 968; NLRB v., (Otis Massey), 225 F 2d 205, 209, 36 LRRM 2541 (CA 5, 1955), cert. den., 350 US 914, 37 LRRM 2142 (1955)   629
—Local 983 (Symns Grocer Co. and Idaho Wholesale Grocery Co.), 109 NLRB 346, 34 LRRM 1326 (1954)   376
Technicolor Motion Picture Corp., 248 F 2d 348, 40 LRRM 2660 (CA 9, 1957)   702
Telecomputing Corp.; Kennedy v., 49 LRRM 2188 (SD Cal., 1961)   846
Television & Radio Artists
—NLRB v., 285 F 2d 902, 47 LRRM 2463 (CA 6, 1961)   885
—v. NLRB, 395 F 2d 622, n. 13, 67 LRRM 3032 (CA DC, 1968)   331
—Penello v., 291 F Supp 409, 69 LRRM 2517 (DC MD, 1968)   639
—San Francisco Local, 134 NLRB 1617, 49 LRRM 1391 (1961)   595
—Washington-Baltimore Local (Hearst Corp.), 185 NLRB No. 26, 75 LRRM 1018 (1970)   640
Television & Radio Broadcasting Studio Employees
—Local 804; NLRB v., 315 F 2d 398, 402, 52 LRRM 2774 (CA 3, 1963), enf., 135 NLRB 632, 49 LRRM 1541 (1962)   701, 703, 861
Tempest Shirt Manufacturing Co., 285 F 2d 1, 47 LRRM 2298 (CA 5, 1960)   376
Templeton v. Dixie Color Printing Co., 313 F Supp 105, 74 LRRM 2206 (ND Ala. 1970)   893
Tennessee Chair Co., 126 NLRB 1357, 45 LRRM 1472 (1960)   313
Tennessee Coal & Iron Div., U.S. Steel Corp., 122 NLRB 1519, 43 LRRM 1325 (1959)   313
Tenney Eng., Inc. v. Electrical Workers, 207 F 2d 450, 21 LA 260 (CA 3, 1953)   481
Terminal Transport Co., 185 NLRB No. 96, 75 LRRM 1130 (1970)   492
Terry Poultry Co., 109 NLRB 1097, 34 LRRM 1516 (1954)   125
Tex Tan, Inc., 318 F 2d 472, 53 LRRM 2295 (CA 5, 1963)   315, 316, 330

Tex Tan Welhausen Co. v. NLRB 419 F 2d 1265, 72 LRRM 2885 (CA 5, 1970)   287
Texaco, Inc.
—168 NLRB No. 49, 66 LRRM 1296 (1969)   307
—v. NLRB, 408 F 2d 142, 144, 70 LRRM 3045 (CA 5, 1970)   307
Texas & New Orleans R.R. Co. v. Brotherhood of Railway & S.S. Clerks, 281 US 548, 571 (1930)   20, 21, 760
Texas Coca Cola Bottling Co., 146 NLRB 420, 55 LRRM 1326 (1964)   287
Texas Co.
—(see Maritime Union; Texaco, Inc.)
Texas Electric Cooperative, Inc., 160 NLRB 440, 62 LRRM 1631 (1966)   259
Texas Foundries, Inc., 101 NLRB 1642, 1683, 31 LRRM 1224 (1952), enf. den. on other grounds, 211 F 2d 791, 33 LRRM 2883 (CA 5, 1954)   127, 275, 526, 536
Texas Industries, Inc., 140 NLRB 527, 52 LRRM 1054 (1963)   298, 301
Texas Natural Gasoline Corp., 116 NLRB 405, 38 LRRM 1252 (1956)   409
Tex-O-Kan Flour Mill Co.; NLRB v., 122 F 2d 433, 8 LRRM 675 (CA 5, 1947)   114, 883
Tex Tan Welhausen Co. v. NLRB, 75 LRRM 2554 (CA 5, 1970), on remand following H. K. Porter, 397 US 819, 74 LRRM 2064 (1970), vacating & remandg. 419 F 2d 1265, 72 LRRM 2885 (CA 5, 1969)   864
Textile Workers
—Darlington Mfg. Co. (see Darlington Mfg. Co.)
—v. Lincoln Mills, 353 US 448, 40 LRRM 2113 (1957)   292, 442, 444, 445, 463, 481, 482, 642, 802
—(Personal Products) v. NLRB, 227 F 2d 409, 36 LRRM 2778 (CA DC, 1955)   328
Textron Inc., Caroline Farms Div., 163 NLRB 854, 64 LRRM 1465 (1967)   295
Textron Puerto Rico, 107 NLRB 583, 33 LRRM 1194 (1953)   509
T-H Prods. Co., 113 NLRB 1246, 36 LRRM 1471 (1955)   163
Thayer Co.
—115 NLRB 1591, 38 LRRM 1142 (1956)   525
—NLRB v. 213 F 2d 748, 34 LRRM 2250 (CA 1, 1954), cert. den., 348 US 883, 35 LRRM 2100 (1954)   127, 524, 525, 530, 592
Thomas Cadillac, Inc., 170 NLRB No. 92, 67 LRRM 1504 (1968), affd., 414 F 2d 1135, 71 LRRM 2150 (CA DC, 1969)   362, 371

Z

TOPICAL INDEX

(For references to particular sections of the NLRA see head "National Labor Relations Act")

A

Y